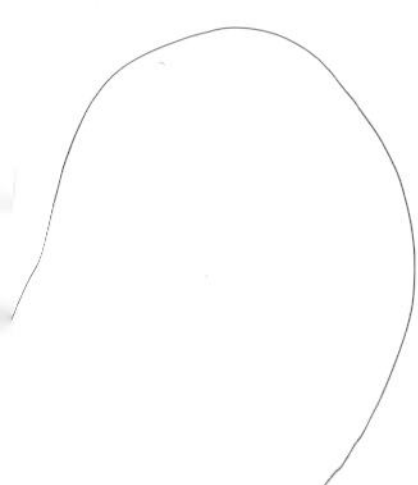

PART 2

The Great Depression and the New Deal to Future Times (1930s—)

Literature and Its Times

Supplement 1

Profiles of Notable Literary Works and the Historical Events That Influenced Them

Joyce Moss

Detroit • New York • San Diego • San Francisco • Cleveland • New Haven, Conn. • Waterville, Maine • London • Munich

Literature and Its Times

Supplement 1
Part 2: The Great Depression and the New Deal to Future Times (1930s—)

JOYCE MOSS

STAFF

Project Editor—David Galens

Editorial—Sara Constantakis, Elizabeth Cranston, Kristen Dorsch, Anne Marie Hacht, Michael L. LaBlanc, Ira Mark Milne, Pamela Revitzer, Kathy Sauer, Tim Sisler, Jennifer Smith, Carol Ullmann, Maikue Vang

Research—Barbara McNeil

Permissions—Kim Davis, Lori Hines

Imaging and Multimedia—Dean Dauphinais, Robert Duncan, Leitha Etheridge-Sims, Mary K. Grimes, Lezlie Light, Dan Newell, David G. Oblender, Christine O'Bryan, Kelly A. Quin, Luke Rademacher

Product Design—Michael Logusz

Manufacturing—Stacy L. Melson

For more information, contact
The Gale Group, Inc.
27500 Drake Rd.
Farmington Hills, MI 48331-3535
Or you can visit our Internet site at
http://www.gale.com

ISBN 0-7876-6552-5

Library of Congress Control Number: 2002152062
Printed in the United States of America

10 9 8 7 6 5 4 3

Contents

General Preface

"Even a great writer can be bound by the prejudices of his time . . . we cannot place Shakespeare in a sealed container. He belonged to his time," notes Alexander Leggatt in his essay "*The Merchant of Venice*: A Modern Perspective" (William Shakespeare, *The Merchant of Venice* [New York: Washington Square Press, 1992], 217). This reasoning, applicable to any work and its author, explains why *Literature and Its Times* fixes a wide range of novels, short stories, biographies, speeches, poems, and plays in the context of their particular historical periods.

In the process, the relationship between fact and fantasy or invention becomes increasingly clear. The function of literature is not necessarily to represent history accurately. Many writers aim rather to spin a satisfying tale or perhaps to convey a certain vision or message. Nevertheless, the images created by a powerful literary work—be it the Greek poem *Iliad*, the Spanish novel *The Adventures of Don Quixote*, or the American play *The Crucible*—leave impressions that are commonly taken to be historical. This is true from works that depict earlier eras to ones that portray more modern occurrences, such as World War II or postwar race relations. The fourteenth-century poem *Inferno* from the *Divine Comedy* by Dante Alighieri is probably the most powerful example. So vividly does *Inferno* describe Hell that for more than two centuries people took its description as fact, going so far as to map Hell according to the details of the poem.

In taking literature as fact, one risks acquiring a mistaken or an unverified notion of history, as the foregoing example suggests. Yet, by the same token, history can be very well informed by literary works. An author may portray events in a way that for the first time aptly captures the fears and challenges of a period, enabling readers to better understand it and their own place in the historical continuum. This is easily illustrated by tracing novels that feature women's issues, from Nathaniel Hawthorne's *The Scarlet Letter* (1640s setting), to Leo Tolstoy's *Anna Karenina* (1870s), to Alice Walker's *The Color Purple* (1920s-40s) and Amy Tan's *The Joy Luck Club* (1940s-80s).

Placing a given work in historical context involves pinpointing conditions in the society in which it was written as well as set. Stephen Crane's *Red Badge of Courage* is set in the early 1860s. Published three decades later, it was written in a different social context and as part of a literary trend in Crane's own era. Only by gaining insight into this later era along with the one in which it takes place can a work be fully appreciated; *Literature and Its Times* therefore addresses the author's time frame too.

The task of reconstructing the historical contexts of a work can be problematic. There are stories—the tales of England's King Arthur, for example—that defy any attempt to fit them neatly into a particular time. Living in a later era, their authors, consciously or not, have mixed together events that belong to two or more different periods. In some cases, this is an innocent mistake by a writer who did not have the benefit of accurate sources. In other cases, fidelity to the actual events of the time is of little concern to the writer; his or her main interest is the fictional world to be portrayed. In still other cases, the mixture of times is intentional. Happily, present-day knowledge makes it possible for this series to begin unweaving the historical mixture in such works.

Literature and Its Times relates history to literature on a case-by-case basis, intending to help readers respond fully to a work and to assist them in distinguishing fact from invention in the work. The series engages in this mission with a warm appreciation for the beauty of literature independent of historical facts, but also in the belief that ultimate regard is shown for a work and its author by positioning it in the context of pertinent events.

Selection of Literary Works

Literature and Its Times includes novels, short stories, plays, poems, biographies, essays, speeches, and documents. The works chosen for inclusion have been carefully selected on the basis of how frequently they are studied and how closely they are tied to pivotal historical events. Reflected in the selection are works written not only by classic and still widely read authors but also by noteworthy ethnic and female authors of the past and present. To finalize the selection, a panel of librarians, secondary teachers, and college professors reviewed the complete list of titles. Please see "Acknowledgments" for a specific listing of these reviewers.

Format and Arrangement of Entries

The five volumes of *Literature and Its Times* and the two volumes of *Literature and Its Times Supplement 1* are arranged chronologically from ancient to future times. The set of entries within each volume is arranged alphabetically by title. As the series progresses, the range of years covered in each successive volume grows narrower due to the increasing number of works published in more recent times.

Each entry is organized according to the following sections.

1. **Introduction**—identifying information in three parts:

   The literary work—describes the genre, the time and place of the work, and the year(s) it was first performed or published;

   Synopsis—summarizes the storyline or contents;

   Introductory paragraph—introduces the literary work in relation to the author's life.
2. **Events in History at the Time the Literary Work Takes Place**—describes social and political events that relate to the plot or contents of the literary work and that occurred during the period the story takes place. Subsections vary depending on the literary work. The section takes a deductive approach, starting with events in history and telescoping inward to events in the literary work.
3. **The Literary Work in Focus**—describes the plot or contents of the work. Following this summary comes a second subsection that focuses on one or more elements in the work to demonstrate how it illuminates real events or attitudes of the period. This subsection takes an inductive approach, starting with the literary work and broadening outward to events in history. It is followed by a third subsection detailing the sources used by the author to create the work. In addition to sources, *Literature and Its Times Supplement 1* discusses the work's literary context, or relation to other works.
4. **Events in History at the Time the Literary Work Was Written**—describes social, political, and/or literary events in the author's lifetime that relate to the plot or contents of the work. When relevant, the section includes events in the author's life. Also discussed in this section are the initial reviews and reception accorded to the literary work.
5. **For More Information**—provides a list of all sources that have been cited in the entry as well as sources for further reading about the different issues or personalities featured in the entry.

If a literary work is set and written in the same time period, sections 2 and 4 of the entry ("Events in History at the Time the Literary Work Takes Place" and "Events in History at the Time the Literary Work Was Written") are combined into a single section, "Events in History at the Time of the Literary Work."

Additional Features

Whenever possible, primary source material is provided through quotations in the text and material in sidebars. There are also sidebars with historical details that amplify issues raised in the main text and with anecdotes that give readers a fuller understanding of the temporal context. Timelines appear in various entries to summarize intricate periods of history. To enrich and further clarify information, historically noteworthy illustrations have been included in the series. Maps as well as photographs provide visual images of potentially unfamiliar settings.

Comments and Suggestions

Your comments on this series and suggestions for future editions are welcome. Please write: Project Editor, *Literature and Its Times*, Gale, 27500 Drake Road, Farmington Hills, Michigan 48331-3535.

Acknowledgments

Literature and Its Times Supplement 1 is a collaborative effort that evolved through several stages of development, each of which was monitored by a team of experts in literature and history. For their incisive participation in selecting the literary works to cover in *Supplement 1,* the editors extend deep appreciation to the following professors, teachers, and librarians:

Robert Aguirre, Wayne State University, Department of English

Roger Beck, Eastern Illinois University, Department of History

Julia Brown, Boston University, Department of English

Barri J. Gold, Muhlenberg College, Department of English

Carol Jago, Santa Monica High School, English Department

Emmanuel Obiechina, Harvard University, Department of Afro-American Studies

Robert Sumpter, Mira Costa High School, History Department

Hilda K. Weisburg, Morristown High School, Library

The following professors, teachers, and librarians carefully reviewed the entries to insure accuracy and completeness of information. Sincere gratitude is extended to these reviewers:

Robert Aguirre, Wayne State University, Department of English

Ehrhard Bahr, University of California at Los Angeles, Department of Germanic Languages

Roger Beck, Eastern Illinois University, Department of History

Michael Bourdaghs, University of California at Los Angeles, Department of Comparative Literature

Matthew Brosamer, Mount St. Mary's College, Los Angeles, Department of English

Julia Brown, Boston University, Department of English

Howard Eiland, Massachusetts Institute of Technology, Department of English

Ana Paula Ferreira, University of California at Irvine, Chair, Department of Spanish and Portuguese

David William Foster, Arizona State University, Department of Languages and Literatures

Eric Gans, University of California at Los Angeles, Department of French and Francophone Studies

Benjamin Hudson, Pennsylvania State University, Department of History

Carol Jago, Santa Monica Public High School, Department of English

Randal Johnson, University of California at Los Angeles, Department of Spanish and Portuguese

Acknowledgments

James Kincaid, University of Southern California, Department of English

Kathryn King, University of California at Los Angeles, Department of Comparative Literature

Efraín Kristal, University of California at Los Angeles, Department of Spanish and Portuguese; Department of Comparative Literature

Kenneth Lincoln, University of California at Los Angeles, Department of English

Eleanor Kay MacDonald, Beverly Hills Public Library

Edwin McCann, University of Southern California, Department of Philosophy

David McCully, St. John's Child and Family Development Center

Michael McGaha, Pomona College, Department of Romance Languages and Literatures, Spanish Section

John McLeod, Leeds University, Department of English

Peter Manning, State University of New York at Stony Brook, Chair, Department of English

Gloria Montebruno, Ph.D. candidate, University of Southern California, Department of East Asian Languages and Cultures

Barbara Moss, Clark Atlanta University, Department of History

Kenneth Moss, Ph.D. candidate, Stanford University, Department of History

Emmanuel Obiechina, Harvard University, Department of Afro-American Studies

Kenneth Orona, University of Colorado, Ethnic Studies

Rafael Pérez-Torres, University of California at Los Angeles, Department of English

Indira Peterson, Mount Holyoke College, Department of Asian Studies

Josna Rege, Dartmouth College, Department of English

Karen Rowe, University of California at Los Angeles, Department of English

Ross Shideler, University of California at Los Angeles, Department of Comparative Literature

Min Song, Boston College, Department of English

Robert Sumpter, Mira Costa High School, Department of History

Hilda K. Weisburg, Morristown High School, Library

Raymond Williams, University of California at Riverside, Department of Hispanic Studies

Olga Yokoyama, University of California at Los Angeles, Slavic Languages and Literature

Steven Young, Pomona College, Department of English

For their painstaking research and composition, the editors thank the writers whose names appear at the close of the entries that they have contributed. A complete listing follows:

Adeleke Adeeko, Associate Professor, University of Colorado, Boulder

Robert Aguirre, Assistant Professor, Wayne State University

Anne Brannen, Associate Professor, Duquesne University

Luke Bresky, Ph.D., University of California at Los Angeles

Lilian P. Carswell, Ph.D. candidate, Columbia University

Francesca Coppa, Assistant Professor, Muhlenberg College

Ruth Feingold, Assistant Professor, St. Mary's College of Maryland

David Frier, Senior Lecturer, University of Leeds

Barri J. Gold, Assistant Professor, Muhlenberg College, Department of English

Martin Griffin, Ph.D. candidate, University of California at Los Angeles

Elisabeth Rose Gruner, Associate Professor, University of Richmond

Ingrid Gunby, Ph.D. candidate, University of Leeds

David K. Herzberger, Professor, Department Head, University of Connecticut

Megan Isaac, Ph.D., University of California at Los Angeles

Lynn Itagaki, Ph.D. candidate, University of California at Los Angeles

Despina Korovessis, Ph.D. candidate, Boston College

Albert Labriola, Professor, Duquesne University

Gail Low, Lecturer, University of Dundee

Pamela S. Loy, Ph.D., University of California at Santa Barbara

Christopher J. Mitchell, Assistant Professor, Eastern Illinois University

Jeff Morris, Assistant Professor, Carroll College

Keidra Morris, Ph.D. candidate, University of California at Los Angeles

Joyce Moss, M.Ed., University Southern California

Christopher M. Mott, Lecturer, University of California at Los Angeles

Danielle Price, Ph.D., University of California at Los Angeles

Diane Renée, B.A., University of California at Los Angeles

Catharine C. Riggs, Ph.D., University of California at Los Angeles

Diane Riggs, Ph.D. candidate, University of California at Los Angeles

Traci Roberts, Ph.D. candidate, University of California at Riverside

David Rosen, Visiting Assistant Professor, Wesleyan University

Susan Staves, Professor, Brandeis University

Erika M. Sutherland, Assistant Professor, Muhlenberg College

Susan Elizabeth Sweeney, Associate Professor, College of the Holy Cross

Erin Templeton, Ph.D. candidate, University of California at Los Angeles

Rachel Trousdale, Assistant Professor, Department of English, Agnes Scott College

Carolyn Turgeon, M.A., University of California at Los Angeles

Amy M. Ware, Ph.D. candidate, University of Texas at Austin

Colin Wells, M.A., Oxford University

Michael Wenthe, Teaching Fellow, Ph.D. candidate, Yale University

Margaret Wong, Assistant Professor, Quinsigamond Community College

Deep appreciation is extended to Michael L. LaBlanc of The Gale Group for his role as production editor. Anne Leach indexed the two volumes of *Literature and Its Times Supplement 1* with great sensitivity to readers and subject matter. Lastly the editors thank Danielle Price for her deft developmental editing, Monica Riordan for her skillful copyediting, and Lisa Blai for her proficient proofreading, word processing, and organizational management.

Introduction

"History repeats itself," or so the adage goes. On February 15, 1894, a terrorist died trying to blow up a landmark scientific edifice, the Greenwich Observatory in London, England, taking, it seems, only himself with him. On September 11, 2001, terrorists died crashing explosive, fuel-laden planes into the World Trade Center and into a landmark military edifice, the Pentagon, in the United States, taking with them close to 3,000 lives. The modus operandi, carnage and destruction, was the same for both sets of terrorists. But the circumstances—time, place, and motivation—diverged radically. So in one sense, history repeated itself; in another, it took on new substance. *The Secret Agent*, a novel by Joseph Conrad, memorializes the first incident, fictionalizing it in ways that document the anarchism of Conrad's generation, along with other currents of late-nineteenth-century human activity. The still-recent second incident will no doubt be memorialized by literary works yet to come, along with other early-twenty-first-century currents of human activity. Understanding the connections between such currents—be they political, social, economic, artistic, or scientific—and the literary works that memorialize them is the central aim of *Literature and Its Times*.

Extending from ancient Greece, through medieval Japan, to Renaissance Europe and revolutionary America, to post-apartheid South Africa, *Literature and Its Times Supplement 1, Parts 1* and *2* continues the foundational *Literature and Its Times* series. Like the original volumes, the *Supplement* covers novels, short stories, essays, drama, and poetry, bringing to the fore nuances of history through works that give voice to perspectives long left out of standard histories. A survey of the works covered shows a resurfacing of issues set forth very early in the *Supplement's* historical span. Sophocles' *Oedipus the King,* for example, struggles with questions of fate, an issue that reappears 23 centuries later in Samuel Beckett's *Waiting for Godot.* Much has changed in the interim. Oedipus is a king who wrestles with fate as foretold through prophecy in a play that was written during an era of religious controversy. Partly a product of Beckett's experience in the French underground during World War II, his play features two hobos who grapple with fate and despair in an era that gave rise to existential philosophy. In the 23 centuries, the focus has shifted from aristocracy to commoners, the intellectual preoccupation from the validity of prophecy to an existential outlook on the human condition as expressed by the ordinary man.

Additional titles reveal other issues that recur across the ages and take on nuances tied to their own times and places:

Justice

Plato's *Apology* (399 B.C.E. Athens); *Crime and Punishment* (1865 Russia); *The Trial* (early 1900s Prague); *The Fixer* (1910s Russia); *A Lesson Before Dying* (late 1940s Louisiana)

Individual's relationship to society
I, Claudius (41 B.C.E. Rome); *Candide* (1700s world); *A Christmas Carol* (1843 England); *The Stranger* (late 1930s Algeria)

Slavery and social class
Great Expectations (early 1800s England); *Kindred* (early 1800s Maryland); *"MASTER HAROLD" . . . and the boys* (1950 South Africa)

Prejudice and racism
The Little Gipsy Girl (early 1600s Spain); "Rothschild's Fiddle" (1890s Russia); *Passing* (1927 New York); "Letter from Birmingham Jail" (1963 Alabama); *The God of Small Things* (late 1900s India)

Minority identity—ethnic and gender experience
Fools Crow (1860s Montana); *Sense and Sensibility* (1790s-1810s England); *Annie John* (1950s-85 Antigua); *Woman Hollering Creek and Other Stories* (1900s Mexico and American Southwest); *Native Speaker* (1990s New York)

Family and generational relations
Twelfth Night (1601 England); *Mill on the Floss* (1800 England); *Fathers and Sons* (1859 Russia); *Dinner at the Homesick Restaurant* (1930-80 Maryland); *Parrot in the Oven: Mi Vida* (1970s California)

Colonial and postcolonial societies
A House for Mr. Biswas (early-to-mid 1900s Trinidad); *Midnight's Children* (1914-77 India); *Anthills of the Savannah* (1960s Nigeria); *Krik? Krak!* (1980s Haiti)

Love and marriage
The Tale of Genji (900s Japan); "My Last Duchess" (1500s Italy); *Emma* (early 1800s England); *The Age of Innocence* (1870s New York); *Blood Wedding* (early 1900s Spain); *The Glass Menagerie* (1930s St. Louis)

Dictatorship, socialism, and the power of the state
The Communist Manifesto (mid-1800s Europe), *Major Barbara* (1906 England); *In the Time of the Butterflies* (1948-60 Dominican Republic); *A Dry White Season* (late 1970s South Africa)

Rise of science, psychology, and the unconscious
On the Origin of Species (mid-1800s England); *Dracula* (1890s Balkans and England); *On Dreams* (1901 Austria); *The Sound and the Fury* (1928 Mississippi)

Ethics and the struggle between good and evil
The Lord of the Rings (a distant time in Middle Earth); *Faust* (1500s Germany); *The Misanthrope* (1600s France); *Blindness* (1900s)

War and power
Richard III (1483-85 England); *The English Patient* (1945 northern Italy); *The Things They Carried* (Vietnam 1969-70; United States 1990); *Martian Chronicles* (near future on Mars)

Of course, new as well as recurring issues emerge with the passage of time, and the new issues also surface in literature. The plight of off-reservation, urban American Indians, a relatively recent subgroup, to take one example, finds expression in novels such as Louise Erdrich's *The Antelope Wife.* Innovation has furthermore affected style as well as content in works of the last hundred years, beginning with stream-of-consciousness writing, related to developments in early-twentieth-century psychology (see, for example, Virginia Woolf's *To the Lighthouse*).

A survey of titles in the original *Literature and Its Times* and in *Literature and Its Times Supplement 1* reveals a dialogue in which later works address much earlier or slightly earlier works in the world literary canon. The interchange joins an even longer-standing dialogue between literature and history. This older, historical-literary dialogue is readily apparent in fiction, poetry, and drama, all of which have invested real-life figures with thoughts and emotions that are mostly unverifiable. William Shakespeare's *Richard III*, about the last king in an English dynasty, is one example. Closer to this day and age, *The Milagro Beanfield War,* about a conflict between Anglos and Hispanics in New Mexico, is another. In such cases, the two parts of *Supplement 1* follow the lead of the earlier volumes in *Literature and Its Times*, laying out the known facts to facilitate distinctions between reality and invention and presenting cutting-edge research that sheds new light on historical periods and peoples (see Bernard Malamud's *The Fixer* or Kyoko Mori's *Shizuko's Daughter*, for example). Going even further, the *Supplement* brings into play another interchange, a type of literary-literary dialogue, which occurs between related works. Featured in this second dialogue are titles that respond to preceding works, which are covered in the original series:

- Anton Chekhov's "The Lady with the Dog" (A response to Leo Tolstoy's *Anna Karenina*)

- Jean Rhys's *Wide Sargasso Sea*
  (A response to Charlotte Brontë's *Jane Eyre*)
- Tom Stoppard's *Rosencrantz and Guildenstern Are Dead*
  (A response to Shakespeare's *Hamlet*)
- John Gardner's *Grendel*
  (A response to the epic *Beowulf*)

Building on and diverging from the originals, writing, in some cases, from the viewpoints of villains and minor characters, the later authors produce works that in effect communicate with the earlier works, as if they were living entities, a characterization well deserved by virtue of the enduring popularity of the earlier works. Certainly the universal qualities of these earlier works have helped them endure, yet they too are a reflection of their times and places, as are the later literary responses to them.

The works in *Literature and Its Times Supplement 1* take on another, more general vitality too, related to their role in promoting self-scrutiny and understanding. This vital attribute is perhaps best illustrated by recent African American literature. From African American drama to fiction, work after late-twentieth-century work features children of the migration North reclaiming their roots in the American South and even in the Caribbean (see Toni Morrison's *Song of Solomon*, Paule Marshall's *Praisesong for the Widow*, and August Wilson's *The Piano Lesson*). In the loftiest tradition of literature, such works both reflect and advance the strivings of their readers to orient themselves in today's world. "The poet's voice," said William Faulkner in his Nobel acceptance speech, "need not merely be the record of man, it can be one of the props, the pillars to help him endure and prevail" (Lewis Copeland, Lawrence W. Lamm, and Stephen J. McKenna, eds., *The World's Great Speeches*, [Mineola, N.Y.: Dover, 1999], 638). From the Greeks to the present day, from the essay to poetry, drama, the short story, and the novel, the works in *Literature and Its Times* and its two-part *Supplement* help people endure and prevail.

Chronology of Relevant Events

CHRONOLOGY OF RELEVANT EVENTS

Note: The following chronology correlates historical events to the literary works covered in *Literature and Its Times Supplement 1* only. For events beside which there is no literary work, please see volume timelines in the original *Literature and Its Times* volumes.

FROM THE RISE OF FASCISM TO WORLD WAR II

The decades between the First and Second World Wars were marked by extremes of prosperity and poverty in the United States. During the 1920s its economy flourished, while in Europe the defeated nations, especially Germany, suffered economic woes and political instability. Even victors like Great Britain experienced soaring unemployment, a condition that would worsen in the following decade. After the United States Stock Market Crash of 1929, unemployment and poverty became pervasive in both Europe and America. In the United States, President Franklin Delano Roosevelt addressed the economic woes with an innovative package of reforms known as the New Deal. Meanwhile, in Europe, the void created by unstable governments was filled by totalitarian regimes; Benito Mussolini's Italy, Adolf Hitler's Germany, and Francisco Franco's Spain became notorious for nationalism, conservatism, and brutally repressive tactics in silencing opposition parties. In the 1930s, Britain and France practiced appeasement towards an increasingly aggressive Germany. Unable to ignore Germany's invasion of Poland, they declared war in September 1939. Initially aloof from the conflict, the United States entered this Second World War after Japan attacked Pearl Harbor, joining the main Allied powers (Great Britain, France, and the Soviet Union) against the Axis powers (Japan, Germany, and Italy). Not until 1945 did the Allies achieve victory, partly because of pivotal wins, partly because of America's decision to use atomic bombs against Japan. Hitler had by this time thoroughly implemented a terrible "Final Solution" against European Jews, transporting millions to death camps where they were exterminated with other Nazi victims.

Date	Historical Events	Related Literary Works (date indicates period in which the work is set)
1919	Worker's Party—the future Nazi (National Socialist German Workers') Party is founded in Germany; in India, Mohandas K. Gandhi emerges as nationalist leader; Home Rule bill divides Ireland into two regions, each with its own parliament; Russian-Polish war; Britain establishes most of Kenya as Crown Colony	
1919–39	Golden Age of Aviation	
1920	League of Nations is founded in Geneva, Switzerland—the U.S. declines to join	
1920s–30s	Anti-British sentiment spreads through colony of Burma; British suppression of Burmese rebellions increases sentiment	1920s "Shooting an Elephant" by George Orwell
1921	Russian Bolsheviks under Vladimir Ilich Lenin defeat "White Russians"	
1922	Gandhi is jailed in India for civil disobedience	
1925	Republic of Ireland is declared; in Germany, Adolf Hitler publishes *Mein Kampf*	
1926	Miners' dispute over wages and salary leads to nine-day general strike in England	
1927	Charles A. Lindbergh flies solo across the Atlantic Ocean from New York to Paris; Sacco and Vanzetti are executed	
1927–49	Chinese Civil War between Guomindang and Communists	
1928	In Great Britain, all women over the age of 21 gain the right to vote	
1928–74	Reign of Portuguese dictator António de Oliveira Salazar whose repressive tactics mirror those of other right-wing totalitarian regimes	(date unspecified) *Blindness* by José Saramago
1929–40s	October 29—"Black Tuesday": Stock market crash on Wall Street in New York leads to worldwide economic depression: businesses close, banks fail, stocks become worthless, and unemployment soars	1930s *The Glass Menagerie* by Tennessee Williams; 1930–80 *Dinner at the Homesick Restaurant* by Anne Tyler; 1936 *Let Us Now Praise Famous Men* by James Agee and Walter Evans
1930s	Fascist movements spread throughout Europe, especially in Italy, Germany, and Spain; reluctant to engage in another war, Britain engages in foreign policy of appeasement with Germany and its allies	(date unspecified) *Lord of the Rings* by J. R. R. Tolkien
1930–61	Rafael Leonidas Trujillo comes to power in the Dominican Republic, implements a brutally repressive regime	1948–60 *In the Time of the Butterflies* by Julia Alvarez
1932	Franklin Delano Roosevelt is elected president of the U.S.; unemployment reaches 25 percent; Amelia Earhart becomes first woman to fly solo across Atlantic Ocean	
1933	Hitler becomes Chancellor of Germany, abolishes all parties but the Nazi party, dissolves parliament, and suspends civil liberties; first concentration camp opens at Dachau; in the U.S., Roosevelt introduces first New Deal relief measures; Twenty-First Amendment repeals Prohibition (the Eighteenth Amendment)	
1934	French Communists and Socialists unite with moderates to form the Popular Front; right-wing riots in Paris leave 15 dead and hundreds injured	1930s *The Stranger* by Albert Camus
1935	Social Security Act in the U.S. guarantees welfare benefits, unemployment insurance, and old-age pension	

Date	Historical Events	Related Literary Works
1936	Italy invades Ethiopia, signs Rome-Berlin axis pact with Hitler; Japan withdraws from League of Nations and begins war against China; Beryl Markham becomes the first pilot to fly across the Atlantic Ocean from England to North America	c. 1905–36 *West with the Night* by Beryl Markham
1936–38	The Great Terror—Russian leader Joseph Stalin has political opponents arrested, tried, and killed in huge numbers	
1936–39	Spanish Civil War pits conservative traditionalists against left-wing radicals; war ends with conservatives, led by General Franco, in power	
1936–39	Under leadership of prime minister Neville Chamberlain, the British government practices policy of appeasement towards Hitler, Grand Chancellor of Germany, whose troops invade European lands	
1938	Germany annexes Austria; in the U.S., Fair Labor Standards Act sets workday hours and minimum wage; Orson Welles presents radio adaptation of novel *The War of the Worlds* that alarms listeners; House of Un-American Activities is established	
1939	Germany invades Poland; World War II erupts; Britain declares intention to establish independent Jewish state in Palestine within 10 years, limits Jewish immigrants to Palestine to 75, 000 for next five years; 9.5 million Americans still out of work	
1939–45	World War II—Britain, Russia, and the Free French, joined in 1941 by the United States, fight Germany, Italy, and Japan	
1940	Japan signs Tripartite Pact with Italy and Germany; Germany invades Denmark, Norway, Holland, Luxembourg, and Belgium; Winston Churchill becomes Prime Minister of England; French capitulate to Germany	
1940–41	Nazis deport Jews to concentration camps throughout Nazi Europe; Hitler implements "Final Solution" to exterminate all European Jews—by war's end, he has killed 6 million; British secret service begins resistance movement against Nazis in France	(date unspecified) *Blindness* by José Saramago; (date unspecified) *Waiting for Godot* by Samuel Beckett
1941	Germany invades Soviet Union; the U.S. enters World War II after the Japanese attack Pearl Harbor, Hawaii	
1941–42	North African campaign concludes with Allied victory after British intelligence cracks German code	1945 *The English Patient* by Michael Ondaatje
1941–43	The United States manufactures arms and other materials to fight the Axis powers, boosting its production to as much as 25 times what it had been in peacetime	1940s *All My Sons* by Arthur Miller
1942	Battle of Midway turns war in the Pacific in Allies' favor; thousands of Americans and Filipinos die on Bataan Death March after surrendering to Japanese	
1943	Italian government signs armistice with Allies; Italy then declares war on Germany; Palestinian Jews protest continuing immigration quotas for European Jews	
1944	Allies liberate Paris from German control	
1945	Allied forces bomb Dresden, Germany; German forces surrender; Hitler commits suicide; the U.S. drops atomic bombs on two Japanese cities—Hiroshima and Nagasaki; Japan surrenders and the Second World War ends; liberation of concentration camps; Holocaust survivors become major force in struggle to establish Jewish state in Palestine	

Date	Historical Events	Related Literary Works

RACE RELATIONS AND RACIAL IDENTITY IN POST-1920S AMERICA

Issues of race and equality that had emerged in the late nineteenth and early twentieth centuries continued to resonate in 1930s America. The migration of African Americans from the rural South to the urban North slowed but continued even during the Great Depression. In the Depression years, African Americans suffered unemployment even more severely than whites. There were gains in the decade too, however. African Americans achieved more access to the federal government than ever before. President Franklin Delano Roosevelt, urged on by Eleanor Roosevelt, established an informal black cabinet in the '30s. Afterward, during the Second World War, African Americans served with distinction in the armed forces, then returned to the United States less willing to tolerate the inequitable status quo. Along with others, the veterans struggled to dismantle discriminatory racial policies in succeeding decades. Their struggle bore fruit, especially with the passage of the Civil Rights Act of 1964 and the Voting Rights Act of 1965. Soon other ethnic minorities—themselves victims of discriminatory policies over the years—began or accelerated their own separate movements for equal rights. More gains followed, but grave inequalities persisted, as did the struggle against them, which continues to this day.

Date	Historical Events	Related Literary Works
1928	Lewis Meriam submits *The Problem of Indian Administration* to federal government; Meriam's report reveals the levels of poverty, disease, infant mortality, and illiteracy on Indian reservations, problems that persist thereafter	
1929–45	During the presidencies of Herbert Hoover and Franklin D. Roosevelt, an Indian New Deal is formulated, which allows Indians more self-governing powers and the right to practice cultural ceremonies and events	
1930s	Black women organize—Southern Women for the Prevention of Lynching sets out to stop mob violence against black Americans	1928, 1910 *The Sound and the Fury* by William Faulkner
1930–60s	After the Great Migration drives 1.5 million African Americans north from 1916–30, the population shift slows but continues, reconfiguring the nation's racial distribution	1936 *The Piano Lesson* by August Wilson; 1930s–60s *Song of Solomon* by Toni Morrison
1931	Scottsboro case begins as nine African American men are tried for the rape of two white women—despite weak evidence, all are convicted by a white jury and ultimately serve long prison terms	
1940	30 known lynchings of African Americans, down from 111 (recorded) in the 1930s; *Hansberry v. Lee*—Supreme Court rules that black Americans cannot be barred from buying homes in white neighborhoods; Selective Training and Service Act initiates America's first peacetime draft	
1940s	About half of the nation's 15 million African Americans continue to suffer discrimination, segregation, and racial violence in the South	1940s *A Lesson before Dying* by Ernest Gaines
1940–60	New York City's Puerto Rican community increases by over half a million, from 70,000 in 1940 to 613,000 in 1960	
1940s–70s	Anglo Americans begin to outnumber long-established Hispanic residents in the state of New Mexico, leading to cultural clashes	c. 1970 *The Milagro Beanfield War* by John Nichols

Date	Historical Events	Related Literary Works
1940s–80s	Black middle class begins to emerge in America, making its mark in such professions as publishing, advertising, banking, and accounting	late 1970s *Praisesong for the Widow* by Paule Marshall
1941	Month-long boycott in New York City results in the hiring of black drivers and mechanics by bus companies; A. Philip Randolph threatens march on Washington to protest racial discrimination in war industries with government contracts; government creates Fair Employment Practices Commission	
1941–45	After the U.S. enters World War II, African American soldiers serve in the armed forces	
1942	An estimated 110,000 Japanese and Japanese Americans on the West Coast are removed to internment camps by Executive Order 9066; race riot in New York City; Sleepy Lagoon murder trial convicts 17 out of 22 Mexican Americans, despite flimsy evidence; white sailors beat Mexican American youths in Zoot Suit Riots	
1943	U.S. Navy promotes first African American officers in February; in July, U.S. Army expands number of black troops and drops all racial barriers to promotion; race riots in Detroit and Harlem	
1944	National Congress of American Indians is founded to preserve Indian cultural values; Mexican American youth is acquitted in Sleepy Lagoon murder trial; in *Smith v. Allwright,* Supreme Court rules that restricting primary elections to white voters only is unconstitutional	
1945	By war's end, more than a million African Americans serve in U.S. Army; black troops fight in segregated units led by white officers	
1946	Two people die in race riot in Columbia, Tennessee	
1947	CORE sends first busload of black and white "freedom riders" on trip through South	
1948	An American Indian, Jessie B. Renick, becomes captain of the U.S. Olympic basketball team	1966–90 *The Lone Ranger and Tonto Fistfight in Heaven* by Sherman Alexie
1950s–70	White officials in the U.S. Bureau of Indian Affairs terminate several Indian reservations to encourage assimilation into mainstream American life; close to 120,000 Indians relocate to big cities	1990s *Grand Avenue* by Greg Sarris
1952	Puerto Rico becomes American commonwealth; Puerto Ricans can travel to and work in the United States	
1954	In *Brown v. Board of Education,* Supreme Court outlaws "separate but equal" policy, mandates desegregation in U.S. schools	
1955	Blacks protest discriminatory seating policy by staging a bus boycott in Montgomery, Alabama	
1957	Martin Luther King Jr. declares goal of black voting rights at Prayer Pilgrimage for Freedom in Washington D.C.; President Dwight Eisenhower mandates integration of high school in Little Rock, Arkansas	
1960	Students stage sit-ins throughout South to protest racial segregation in public places; decade of vigorous movement on behalf of African American civil rights begins	
1960s	Number of Mexican American wives (aged 14–54) in work force grows to 35 percent	early 1900s–80s *Woman Hollering Creek* by Sandra Cisneros
1960s–70s	African American Civil Rights Movement spurs growth of other minority movements, including those of women, Latinos, Asian Americans, and American Indians	1965 *The Way to Rainy Mountain* by Scott Momaday; 1970s *Parrot in the Oven: Mi Vida* by Victor Martinez; c. 1970 *The Milagro Beanfield War* by John Nichols

Date	Historical Events	Related Literary Works
1961	Freedom riders take buses through the South to test compliance with law against segregation in bus terminals and other interstate facilities	
1962	After James Meredith, a black student, enrolls at University of Mississippi, a riot ensues, killing 2 and injuring 375; boxer Sonny Liston becomes world's heavyweight boxing champion	
1963	Reverend Martin Luther King Jr. leads nonviolent demonstration in Birmingham, Alabama; police use hoses, cattle prods, and dogs against demonstrators; 250,000 people march in Washington for civil rights; King delivers "I Have a Dream" speech	1963 "Letter from Birmingham Jail" by Martin Luther King Jr.
1964	Civil Rights Act forbids racial discrimination in public facilities; Martin Luther King Jr. receives Nobel Peace Prize; "Freedom Summer"—over 1,000 activists in Mississippi conduct voter registration drive; activists Andrew Goodman, Michael Schwerner, and James Chaney are murdered; Muhammad Ali wins world's heavyweight boxing championship	
1965	Voting Rights Act forbids the obstruction of registration of black voters; Watts race riots in Los Angeles leave 34 dead and 1,000 injured; the Hart-Cellar Act lifts ban on Asian immigration to the United States	
1965–70	Farm workers mount nationwide strike, led by Cesar Chavez, against grape industry	
1966	African American activist Stokely Carmichael's call for "Black Power" signals new militant wing of civil rights movement; race riots throughout American cities; Robert Weaver becomes first black American to serve in Cabinet	
1967	Thurgood Marshall becomes first African American Supreme Court Justice; riots in 128 American cities, notably Newark and Detroit	
1968	Civil Rights Act prohibits discrimination in sale or rental of housing; Martin Luther King Jr. is assassinated; his widow, Coretta Scott King, leads march of welfare mothers during Poor People's Campaign in Washington D.C.; Robert Kennedy is assassinated; President Lyndon Johnson signs Bilingual Education Act; 10,000 Mexican American students walk out in Los Angeles high school to protest inadequate facilities; American Indian Movement is founded to promote Indian civil rights	
1969	Indians begin "Red Power" movement, seizing control of Alcatraz Island in San Francisco Bay	
1970s–80s	Haitian "boat people" flee Haiti to escape the tyrannical regimes of the Duvaliers; many settle in New York and Florida	1930s–80s *Krik? Krak!* by Edwidge Danticat
1970s–90s	Bolstered by large-scale immigration, the Korean population in America increases elevenfold	1990s *Native Speaker* by Chang-Rae Lee
1971	Supreme Court rules that American schools may be desegregated by busing if necessary	
1972	Red Power activists occupy Bureau of Indian Affairs in Washington D.C.	
1973	Red Power activists occupy the town of Wounded Knee, South Dakota—armed conflict follows	
1974	*Lau v. Nichols*—Supreme Court rules that education on equal terms demands more than the same materials and instructors to all students; case is used to demand more extensive bilingual education provisions	

Date	Historical Events	Related Literary Works
1975	Supreme Court–mandated busing helps desegregate American schools; Agricultural Labor Relations Act gives California farmers the right of collective bargaining; Indian Self-Determination and Education Assistance Act supports tribal independence and Indian management of benefits from U.S. Government	
1976	Alex Haley publishes *Roots*, a fictionalized memoir of his family, which is adapted into a popular television miniseries and sparks interest in African American genealogy	1976, early 1800s *Kindred* by Octavia Butler
1978	Congress amends Bilingual Education Act—languages other than English are to be used only to the extent necessary for child to achieve competence in English; American Indian Religious Freedom Act guarantees the right of Indians to practice traditional religions	
1980s	American Indian tribes take U.S. Government to court over water, resources, and fishing and mineral rights	
1980–88	During Ronald Reagan's presidential administration, funding for education drops 8 percent and spending related to bilingual education drops 46 percent	
1983	American Indians begin to regain status and lands lost during the termination era	
1984	Survey reveals that of 182,000 American Indians living on or near reservations, 33,097 are homeless	
1990	Museums required by Native American Grave Protection and Repatriation Act to return tribal remains and historical artifacts	
1990s	San Francisco's Chinatown has 30,000 living in 24-block area, second densest area in America (after parts of Manhattan)	
1992	Race riots ensue in Los Angeles after four white police officers are acquitted of beating Rodney King, a black motorist	

THE POSTWAR WORLD: DOMESTIC AND FOREIGN POLICY

As in the postwar 1920s, the United States experienced a surge of prosperity in the late 1940s and 1950s, which allowed increasing numbers of Americans to realize the dream of owning their own homes and automobiles. In contrast to the domestic sense of security, however, the period saw troubled international relations. During the Yalta Conference, the United States, Great Britain, and the Soviet Union managed to settle several pressing issues, but a strong sense of rivalry began to brew, especially between the United States and the Soviet Union. The 1950s saw the Cold War intensify, with the two powers growing ever more embroiled in a competition for world leadership, in which the Soviet Union and other East European countries sealed themselves off from contact with the West. For several decades, communist and non-communist factions competed for territory, power, and influence. Back in the United States, anticommunist sentiments led to a series of congressional "red hunts," spearheaded by Senator Joseph McCarthy. Overseas, conflict between communists and non-communists erupted into open warfare in Korea in the 1950s and in Vietnam in the 1960s. Ten years of American involvement in the Vietnam War would claim 58,000 American lives, and to no definitive avail. In the early 1970s the United States withdrew from the war. The failure did not, however, spell defeat in the Cold War. In fact, the next decade saw the United States meet with success in this larger conflict. In 1989 the Berlin Wall was dismantled and Soviet troops withdrew from eastern Europe. The Cold War was over, ending in a loss for the Soviets. But global unrest has continued to flare, much of it centered in the volatile Middle East.

Date	Historical Events	Related Literary Works
1940s	Existential philosophies and writings appear in wartime and postwar France	500s *Grendel* by John Gardner; c. 1601 *Rosencrantz and Guildenstern Are Dead* by Tom Stoppard; (date unspecified) *Waiting for Godot* by Samuel Beckett
late 1940s–50s	The U.S. enjoys an era of postwar prosperity; American families achieve dream of buying suburban home and automobile; vacation trips by car become increasingly popular among Americans	late 1940s *On the Road* by Jack Kerouac; 1950s–60s *Desert Solitaire* by Edward Abbey
1940s–2000s	The U.S. and Soviet Union use German technology from the war to further rocket science and space exploration	(future) *The Martian Chronicles* by Ray Bradbury
1945	Yalta Conference—the U.S. Great Britain, and the Soviet Union meet to settle differences in reaching a World War II Peace Agreement; U.S. and Soviet Union divide Korea into two zones of occupation, dismantle Japanese army; Soviets send 70,000 Japanese to labor camps in Manchuria and Siberia; U.S. begins repatriation of 940,000 Japanese soldiers and citizens living in Korea; 50 countries meet to form United Nations	
1945–70s	Allied occupation forces in Japan implement new constitution and reforms, with lasting impact for the occupied country	1969–76 *Shizuko's Daughter* by Kyoko Mori
1946	Cold War accelerates; U.S. and Soviet Union competition for world leadership prompts greater U.S. involvement in Latin America	1950 *All the Pretty Horses* by Cormac McCarthy
1946–60	National security accounts for 70 percent of U.S. budget; American diplomat George Kennan advises government to contain spread of communism by supporting noncommunist countries	
1947	U.N. committee proposes to divide Palestine into Jewish and Arab states; Truman Doctrine promises U.S. aid to European governments facing communist threats	
1948	Israel is declared an independent Jewish state	
1948–50	Displaced Persons Act allows 40,000 European immigrants—including gypsies, Jews, homosexuals, and others persecuted by the Nazi regime—to become American citizens	1947–52 *Lolita* by Vladimir Nabokov
1948–51	Marshall Plan—U.S. sends $13 billion to help rebuild Europe; Soviet Union blocks western access to West Berlin; U.S. airlifts supplies to city	
1948–58	A dispute between two political parties (the Liberals and the Conservatives) sparks a decade of civil strife, known as La Violencia, in Colombia.	1950s "Tuesday Siesta" and "One of These Days" by Gabriel García Márquez
1949	NATO (North Atlantic Treaty Organization) is founded; Soviets explode their first nuclear device; Chinese civil war ends in communist victory	
1950	In the U.S., Senator Joseph McCarthy heads congressional anticommunist crusade; President Truman approves research into hydrogen bomb	
1950s	Rise of the environmental movement in America, as an increasing number of conservationists protest the use of public parklands for industrial use	1950s–60s *Desert Solitaire* by Edward Abbey
1950–53	Korean War is fought; 1.8 million Americans serve with U.N. forces on side of South Korea against communist North Korea, backed by China and the Soviet Union	
1950–60	U.S. private investment in foreign countries leaps from $19 billion to $49 billion	
1950s–60s	Period of literary innovations in drama, including existentialist and absurdist plays	(date unspecified) *Waiting for Godot* by Samuel Beckett; c. 1601 *Rosencrantz and Guildenstern Are Dead* by Tom Stoppard

Date	Historical Events	Related Literary Works
1950s–70s	Counterculture movement in America leads to exploration of the self	
1953	Death of Joseph Stalin; Americans Ethel and Julius Rosenberg are executed for allegedly passing American nuclear secrets to Soviets	
1954	America's CIA (Central Intelligence Agency) helps overthrow procommunist government in Guatemala; U.S. Senate censures McCarthy after he slanders U.S. Army officials, calling them communists; French forces are defeated at Dien Bien Phu in Vietnam; international conference in Geneva, Switzerland, divides Vietnam into North and South, arranges for cease-fire	
1955	Warsaw Pact, communist counterpart of NATO, is formed	
1957	Soviets launch first earth-orbiting satellite	
1958–64	Administration of Mexican president Adolfo López Mateos who builds social programs and basic services—including water and electrical power—for Mexican people	c. 1960 *Stones for Ibarra* by Harriet Doerr
1959	Fidel Castro takes command of Cuba; U.S. Navy develops radar system to monitor Soviet nuclear tests and rocket launchings	mid-1950s *Aunt Julia and the Scriptwriter* by Mario Vargas Llosa
1960	Assassination of three sisters (the Mirabels) who oppose the Trujillo dictatorship in the Dominican Republican; National Liberation Front (or Vietcong) challenges rule of U.S. supported government of Ngo Dinh Diem	1948–60 *In the Time of the Butterflies* by Julia Alvarez
1960s	Thousands of Cuban refugees flee to Florida	
1961	American "advisers" begin to arrive in Vietnam	
1962	The Sino-Indian War—India and China engage in costly border dispute that results in thousands of deaths and India's humiliating defeat; Russian missiles withdrawn from Cuba after firm stand by U.S. President John F. Kennedy	1969–97 *The God of Small Things* by Arundhati Roy
1963	United States, Russia, and Britain sign nuclear test ban treaty; President Kennedy is assassinated; 16,700 American "advisers" in Vietnam.	
1964	Alleged North Vietnamese attacks on U.S. vessels in Gulf of Tonkin; Congress passes Tonkin Gulf Resolution to authorize President Johnson's retaliatory response; Americans begin bombing North Vietnam	
1964–73	The Vietnam War—U.S. commits troops to fight against communist forces in Vietnam; nearly a decade of war claims an estimated 58,000 American lives.	1969–70 *The Things They Carried* by Tim O'Brien
1966	U.S. steps up bombing of Vietnam; National Organization of Women (NOW), a U.S. women's rights group, is founded by Betty Friedan	
1967	Martin Luther King Jr. leads anti-Vietnam War protest at U.N. building in New York City; Muhammad Ali is stripped of heavyweight boxing title after refusing to be inducted into the U.S. Army	
1968	Half a million American troops in Vietnam	
1969	First American troops are withdrawn from Vietnam; G. I. Movement of soldiers against the war reaches peak; American astronaut Neil Armstrong becomes the first man to walk on the moon.	
1970	Four students are killed by National Guardsmen during antiwar protest at Kent State University	
1973	Paris Accord—U.S. signs peace treaty with North Vietnam	

Date	Historical Events	Related Literary Works
1975	South Vietnam surrenders; war ends	
1976	Vietnam is unified under communist rule	
1977	President Jimmy Carter pardons Vietnam draft evaders	
1979	Soviet Union invades Afghanistan	
1980s	Japanese economy enjoys an unprecedented boom, especially in the automobile, electronics, and banking industries; AIDS epidemic spreads throughout world; United States boycotts 1980 Olympics in Moscow	1986–94 *Japan, the Ambiguous, and Myself* by Kenzaburo Oe
1982	Vietnam War Memorial is erected in Washington, D.C.; Britain defeats Argentina in war over Falkland islands.	
1985–90	Russian general secretary Mikhail Gorbachev implements new policies that contribute to the dissolution of the Soviet Union	
1986	The American space shuttle *Challenger* explodes, killing all seven astronauts aboard	
1989	Berlin Wall is dismantled, marking the fall of Communism and the end of the Cold War.	
1991	The Persian Gulf War—after Iraq invades Kuwait, America deploys troops to the Persian Gulf; Iraq is forced out of Kuwait; one-quarter to one-third of America's homeless are Vietnam veterans	
2001	Terrorists attack World Trade Center in New York and the Pentagon in Washington D.C., killing close to 3,000 people	1894 *Secret Agent* by Joseph Conrad

POSTCOLONIAL SOCIETIES

The aftermath of World War II saw the dissolution of most colonial empires. Exhausted by war, Great Britain, as well as other European countries, gradually relinquished most of their overseas territorial holdings. From the 1940s to the 1960s, colonies in Africa, Asia, and the Caribbean gained independence. In the turmoil associated with the colonial dissolution, many former subjects emigrated, seeking economic opportunities in the home country of the colonial power that had ruled them. In their own countries, new regimes replaced the colonial governments, often not to the benefit of the general population. Postcolonial societies struggled with their own problems of instability, corruption, and repression, while individuals, including writers, strove through art to understand the colonial and postcolonial experience and to further develop their independent literatures.

Date	Historical Events	Related Literary Works
1946	British colonial rule wanes over Trinidad, which is granted universal suffrage	1900s–50s *A House for Mr. Biswas* by V. S. Naipaul
1947	British Empire takes large step in its dissolution—India is granted independence and subcontinent is divided into India (Hindu) and Pakistan (Muslim)	1915–77 *Midnight's Children* by Salman Rushdie
1948–90	Policy of apartheid—segregating black and white races—is implemented in South Africa	1950 *"MASTER HAROLD" . . . and the boys* by Athol Fugard
1950–63	British colonies in Africa gain independence	
1954	French leave Indochina	
1956	Pakistan becomes Islamic republic; Egypt asserts sovereignty, abrogating treaties that made it a virtual colony of Britain	
1957–62	Several British colonies in the Caribbean—including Jamaica,	1950s *Annie John* by Jamaica Kincaid

Date	Historical Events	Related Literary Works
	Trinidad, the Windward and Leeward Islands—form the West Indian Federation as an intermediate step between colonial rule and full independence.	
1957–71	François "Papa Doc" Duvalier is elected president of Haiti; his administration devolves into brutal dictatorship	1980s *Krik? Krak!* by Edwidge Danticat
1958–68	The formerly colonized immigrate to Britain in large numbers, changing its ethnic makeup	
1960s	Sixteen African nations declare independence from European colonial powers	
1960–83	After gaining independence from Britain, Nigeria undergoes decades of war and political turmoil	1960s *Anthills of the Savannah* by Chinua Achebe
1961	South Africa secedes from the British commonwealth	
1971–86	"Baby Doc" Duvalier succeeds his father as president of Haiti, but is deposed in 1986	
1976–77	Confrontations between Africans and police in Soweto and other African townships leave at least 575 dead in South Africa	1970s *A Dry White Season* by André Brink
1984	In anticipation of the 1997 expiration of Britain's lease on Hong Kong, Britain and China agree that Hong Kong's British-established legal, educational, and financial systems will remain in effect until 2047	
1990s	South Africa ends policy of apartheid, begins difficult transition to democracy, coping with implementation of a new constitution and continuing problems of a high crime rate and economic disparity	1995 *The House Gun* by Nadine Gordimer
1991	An estimated 800,000 Irish immigrants are reported to be living in England	1990s *Felicia's Journey* by William Trevor
1997	Possession of Hong Kong reverts to China	
1998	Rough Sleepers' Unit is formed in England to address the problem of homelessness	

Contents by Title

Contents by Title

Contents by Author

Contents by Author

Photo Credits

Miller, Arthur, photograph. The Library of Congress. —Lancaster, Burt, (left) as Chris Keller, Mady Christians as Kate Keller, and Edward G. Robinson as Joe Keller in the 1948 Universal Pictures version of *All My Sons*, photograph. The Kobal Collection/Universal. Reproduced by permission. —Damon, Matt, (left) as John Grady Cole, Lucas Black as Jimmy Blevins, and Henry Thomas as Lacey Rawlins in the 2000 Miramax Films version of *All the Pretty Horses*, photograph. The Kobal Collection/Miramax/Dimension Films/Van Redin. Reproduced by permission. —Kincaid, Jamaica, photograph by Jerry Bauer. © Jerry Bauer. Reproduced by permission. —View of Antigua, photograph by Max Hunn. Archive Photos, Inc. Reproduced by permission. —Erdrich, Louise, photograph. © Jerry Bauer. Reproduced by permission —Two young Native American boys, photograph. National Archives and Records Administration. —Achebe, Chinua, photograph. AP/Wide World Photos. Reproduced by permission. —Federal troops being watched by Biafran villagers, photograph. Corbis. Reproduced by permission. —Vargas, Llosa (Jorge) Mario (Pedro), photograph. AP/Wide World Photos. Reproduced by permission. —Saramago, Jose, photograph. AP/Wide World Photos. Reproduced by permission. —*The Parable of the Blind*, painting by Pieter Brueghel the Elder, 1568. The Art Archive/Museo di Capodimonte Naples/Dagli Orti. Reproduced by permission. —Lorca, Federico Garcia, around age 30, photograph. Getty Images. Reproduced by permission. —Feller, Catherine, (left) and Katina Paxinou in the 1959 BBC television production of *Blood Wedding*, based on the work by Federico Garcia Lorca, photograph. Hulton Archive/Getty Images. Reproduced by permission. —Villa, Francisco "Pancho," and Emiliano Zapata (sitting together, surrounded by large group), Mexico City, Mexico, c. 1916, photograph by Agustin Cassola. Archive Photos. Reproduced by permission. —Rivera, Diego, Mexico, 1936, photograph. AP/Wide World Photos. Reproduced by permission. —Novelist Edward Abbey, a member of Robert Redford's riding party, sitting on a rock in a canyon. Outlaw Trail, Lake Powell, Utah, photograph. © Jonathan Blair/Corbis. Reproduced by permission. —Shiprock mountain rising up out of flat desert plain, New Mexico, c. 1990, photograph. © Jan Butchovsky-Houser/Corbis. Reproduced by permission. —Tyler, Anne, photograph by D. Walker. Gamma Liaison. Reproduced by permission. —Traveling salesman, Paris, Kentucky, November 1940, photograph. © John Vachon/Corbis. Reproduced by permission. —Rioting in Soweto, South Africa, 1976, photograph. Hulton-Deutsch Collection/Corbis. Reproduced by permission. —Brink, André, photograph by Jerry Bauer. © Jerry Bauer. Reproduced by permission. —Ondaatje, Michael, photograph by Thomas Victor. Reproduced by permission of the Estate of Thomas Victor. —Fiennes, Ralph, and Kristin Scott Thomas, photograph by Phil Bray. The Kobal Collection. Reproduced by permission. —Trevor, William, photograph by Kristin Morrison. Mark Gerson Photography. Reproduced by permission. —Hoskins, Bob, (left) as Joseph Ambrose Hilditch, and Elaine Cassidy as Felicia, in the 1999 film version of *Felicia's Journey*, photograph. The Kobal Collection/Artisan Pics/Sophie Baker. Reproduced by permission. —Williams, Tennessee, photograph. The Library of Congress. —From a production still for *The Glass Menagerie* by Tennessee Williams. Archive Photos, Inc. Reproduced by permission. —Roy, Arundhati, author of the Booker Prize-winning novel *The God of Small Things*, photograph, Delhi, India, 1997, photograph. © Karen Kapoor/Corbis. Reproduced by permission. —Sarris, Gregory M., photograph. From the book jacket of *Watermelon Nights*. © Mary Ann Halpin. Reproduced by permission of the author. —Gardner, John, photograph. © Bettmann/Corbis. Reproduced by Corbis Corporation. Reproduced by permission. —Demonstrators confront Illinois National Guardsmen at Grant Park during the 1968 Democratic National Convention in Chicago, photograph. UPI/Corbis-Bettmann. Reproduced by permission. —Naipaul, V. S., photograph. AP/Wide World Photos. Reproduced by permission. —Gordimer, Nadine, photograph. AP/Wide World Photos. Reproduced by permission. —Trujillo Molina, Rafael, photograph. The Library of Congress. —*A Song to Liberty* (Mirabal sisters, mural on an obelisk), Santo Domingo, Dominican Republic, 1997, photograph by John Riley. AP/Wide World Photos. Reproduced by permission. —Kenzaburo Oe, author photo, winner of the Nobel Prize for Literature, speaks during an interview with the Associated Press at his home in Tokyo, Japan, Tuesday, May 25, 1999. Photograph by Itsuo Inouye. AP/Wide World Photos. Reproduced by permission. —Butler, Octavia E., photograph by O.M. Butler. Reproduced by permission of Octavia Butler. —Plantation or farmhouse, white shingles, two-story house with small connected buildings along the right side of house, ladder leaning against house, large tree hung with Spanish moss right foreground, Georgia, 1926, photograph. © E. O. Hoppe/Corbis. Reproduced by permission. —Danticat, Edwidge, photograph by Doug Kanter. AP/Wide World Photos. Reproduced by permission. —Sylvio, Claude, leader of the Opposition Christian Democratic Party of Haiti, addressing supporters at a press conference, a leading opponent of the Duvalier Regime, Port-au-Prince, Haiti, photograph by Lynne Sladky. © Bettmann/Corbis. Reproduced by permission. —Gaines, Ernest J., 1993, photograph by Alex Brandon. AP/Wide World Photos. Reproduced by permission. —"White Only" store in the South prior to Civil Rights legislation, photograph. Archive Photos, Inc. Reproduced by permission. —Agee, James, photograph. The Library of Congress. —Burroughs, Floyd, cotton sharecropper, in Hale County Alabama, photograph. Hulton/Archive Photos. Reproduced by permission. —King, Martin Luther, Jr., photograph. American Stock/Archive Photos, Inc. Reproduced by permission. —King, Martin Luther, Jr., center, is given a welcome home kiss by his wife, Coretta, and is with his children, Yolanda, 5, and Martin Luther III, 3 (right), on his return to Atlanta, Georgia. Photograph by Horace Cort. AP/Wide World. —Nabokov, Vladimir, photograph. AP/Wide World Photos. Reproduced by permission. —Alexie, Sherman, photograph by Rex Rystedt. Reproduced by permission of Rex Rystedt. —Minor, Wendell, illustrator. From a cover of *The Lone Ranger and Tonto Fistfight in Heaven*, by Sherman Alexie. HarperPerennial, 1994. Cover illustration copyright c. 1993 by Wendell Minor. Reproduced by permission of The *Atlantic Monthly* Press. —Tolkien, J.R.R., photograph. The Library of Congress. —Map depicting "Middle Earth" from the 2001 film of *The Lord of the Rings: The Fellowship of the Ring*, based on the novel by J.R.R. Tolkien, directed by Peter Jackson, photograph. The Kobal Collection/New Line/Saul Zaentz/Wing Nut/Pierre Vinet. Reproduced by permission. —Bradbury, Ray, 1991, photograph. Archive Photos, Inc. Reproduced by permission. —Hudson, Rock, and Terence Longdon in a scene from the movie *The Martian Chronicles*, photograph. The Kobal Collection. Reproduced by permission. —Fugard, Athol (seated on couch with Amy Irving), 1988, photograph. AP/Wide World Photos. Reproduced by permission. —From a theatre production of Athol Fugard's *"MASTER HAROLD" . . . and the boys* with Ramolao Makhene as Willie, Duart Sylwain as Hally and John Kani as Sam. Cottesloe Theatre/National Theatre, London, 1983, photograph. Donald Cooper, London. Reproduced by permission. —Rushdie, Salman, photograph. Archive Photos, Inc. Reproduced by permission. —Hundreds of Muslim refugees fleeing India for Pakistan after the end of British rule, 1947, photograph. AP/Wide World Photos. Reproduced by permission. —Nichols, John, holding butterfly specimens, photograph. Reproduced by permission. —Blades, Ruben, as a sheriff in the 1988 film *The Milagro Beanfield War*, based on the book by John

Nichols, directed by Robert Redford, photograph. The Kobal Collection/Universal. Reproduced by permission. —Lee, Chang-Rae, photograph. AP/Wide World Photos. Reproduced by permission. —Kerouac, Jack, photograph. © Jerry Bauer. Reproduced by permission. —Cassady, Neal, San Francisco, California, 1966, photograph by Ted Streshinsky. Corbis/Ted Streshinsky. Reproduced by permission. —Martinez, Victor, photograph by Ruben Guzman. Reproduced by permission of Victor Martinez. —Chavez, Cesar, (left, in leather jacket) and Walter Reuther (center, in suit) leading a group of picketers from the United Farm Workers Union who are trying to gain recognition for the union with the help of the UAW, Delano, California, December 16, 1965. Reporduced by permission. —Wilson, August. AP/Wide World Photo. Reproduced by permission. —The December, 1990, Playbill for August Wilson's *The Piano Lesson*, Directed by Lloyd Richards, with Charles S. Dutton as Boy Willie, at the Walter Kerr Theater, New York City, photograph. PLAYBILL® is a registered trademark of Playbill Incorporated, NYC All rights reserved. Reproduced by permission. —Marshall, Paule, photograph. AP/Wide World Photos. Reproduced by permission. —Carriacou Island with another smaller island, Petit Martinique, in background, Grenada, Caribbean, c. March 1998, photograph. © Bob Krist/Corbis. Reproduced by permission. —Stoppard, Tom, photograph. AP/Wide World Photos. Reproduced by permission. —Oldman, Gary, (left to right), Tim Roth, and Richard Dreyfuss in the 1990 film *Rosencrantz and Guildenstern are Dead*, written and directed by Tom Stoppard, photograph. The Kobal Collection/Odyssey. Reproduced by permission. —Mori, Kyoko, photograph by Katherine McCabe. Reproduced by permission of Kyoko Mori. —*Gladioli*, oil painting on canvas by Claude Monet, photograph. © Francis G. Mayer/Corbis. Reproduced by permission. —Eight Japanese schoolgirls dressed in traditional Japanese kimonos, standing in a double row, Kobe, Japan, c. 1950, photograph. © Michael Maslan Historic Photographs/Corbis. Reproduced by permission. —Morrison, Toni, 1993, photograph. AP/Wide World Photos. Reproduced by permission. —Family tree before and after Civil War, 1880, photograph. CORBIS. Reproduced by permission. —Doerr, Harriet, photograph. Reproduced by permission. —Terraced copper mine, New Mexico, c. 1970-1995, photograph. © Adam Woolfitt/Corbis. Reproduced by permission. —O'Brien, Tim, photograph. © Jerry Bauer. Reproduced by permission. —Soldiers of the 2nd Battalion, 4th Marine Regiment, at Fire Support Base "Russell," opening mail from home during the Vietnam War, northwest of "The Rockpile," South Vietnam, 1969, photograph. Hulton Archive/Getty Images. Reproduced by permission. —Marquez, Gabriel Garcia, photograph. AP/Wide World Photos. Reproduced by permission. —Beckett, Samuel, photograph. Archive Photos, Inc. Reproduced by permission. —A production still of *Waiting for Godot*. Mander & Joe Mitchenson Theatre Collection. Reproduced by permission. —Momaday, N. Scott, photograph. UPI/Corbis-Bettmann. Reproduced by permission. —American Indian Movement (AIM) leaders Russell Means (seated, left) and Dennis Banks (seated, wearing vest) sing an AIM victory song with other AIM members at victory rally after charges were dismissed in the Wounded Knee trial, St. Paul, Minnesota. Used by permission. —Calendar of 37 months, photograph. National Archives and Records Administration. —Markham, Beryl, photograph. © Corbis-Bettmann. Reproduced by permission. —Beryl Markham's monoplane after a crash, near Baleine, Nova Scotia, Canada, September 6, 1936, photograph. © Bettmann/Corbis. Reproduced by permission. —*Virgin of Guadalupe*, painting by Juan de Villegas. Arte Publico Press. Reproduced by permission. —Zapata, Emiliano, photograph. Corbis-Bettmann. Reproduced by permission.

All My Sons

by
Arthur Miller

THE LITERARY WORK

A play set in the mid-1940s in a city in the American Midwest; first performed and published in 1947.

SYNOPSIS

An idealistic son exposes his father, owner of a plant that manufactured airplane engine parts, as having knowingly sent off faulty engine parts that caused the deaths of 21 American pilots in World War II.

Born in 1915 and raised in New York City, Arthur Miller attended college in Michigan during the Great Depression of the 1930s. It was during this time that he grew concerned with how economic and social pressures can warp individual morality, an issue that would dominate his works throughout his long career. Though eventually he would win recognition as one of the preeminent American playwrights of the later twentieth century, Miller had an unsuccessful start with a play called *The Man Who Had All the Luck*, which closed after only four performances in 1944. He spent the next two years writing *All My Sons*, which brought him overnight success when it opened on Broadway in January 1947. While Miller's next play, ***Death of a Salesman*** (1949; also in *Literature and Its Times*), is generally ranked as his foremost achievement, critics continue to rank *All My Sons* as one of the playwright's major works. Like *Death of a Salesman*, *All My Sons* uses the relationship between father and son to explore larger issues, in this case a conflict between family loyalty and social responsibility.

Events in History at the Time of the Play

Arsenal of democracy. The Great Depression that paralyzed the American economy in the 1930s lasted until the United States entered World War II in 1941. From his inauguration in 1933, President Franklin Roosevelt's New Deal legislation set out to help the poor, protect workers, and stimulate the economy, but the New Deal was only partly successful. Nearly 10 million Americans remained unemployed in 1939, the year World War II began. In 1940, when Franklin Roosevelt was reelected to an unprecedented third term as U.S. President, American economic output continued to slump below pre-Depression levels, at approximately $1.5 billion per year. At that time, while sympathetic to Britain (which stood alone against German aggression in Europe), the majority of Americans believed that the war was a European problem and that America should stay out of it. This sentiment, known as isolationism, prevailed until Germany's ally Japan attacked the American naval base at Pearl Harbor, Hawaii, in December 1941. Only then did Americans unite behind the war effort against both Germany and Japan.

Between 1940 and the end of 1943, the economic output of the other major combatants in the war doubled, tripled, or (in Japan's case) even

Arthur Miller

quadrupled. Though these were impressive performances, they paled next to that of the United States. By the end of 1943, only two years after entering the war, the American economy was producing more than *25 times* as much as before 1941. Spurred by massive wartime government spending, production rose from $1.5 billion to a remarkable $37.5 billion. While the stress of war brought its own problems, and many essential materials such as rubber and aluminum were in short supply, Americans soon felt the benefits of full employment and a shared sense of purpose. In *All My Sons* the Keller family's prosperity is established during this period because Joe Keller's small manufacturing plant has been awarded profitable government contracts to produce airplane engine parts.

THE TRUMAN COMMITTEE

A number of genuine production scandals emerged during World War II. Curtiss-Wright, maker of the P-40 "Warhawk" fighter (the plane for which the fictional Joe Keller shipped faulty engine parts) was in reality discovered to have manufactured faulty engines. Investigators responded skeptically to claims by the company that it did not know of the faults. Leading the investigators was Senator (later President) Harry S Truman, whose Senate committee was charged with looking into fraud and waste in war production. Writing to his wife Bess about one aircraft plant, Truman complained, "The managers are all such liars you can't tell anything about the facts."

(Truman in McCullough, p. 264)

America has often been referred to as the arsenal of democracy for its role in supplying arms and materiel for the fight against Nazi Germany and imperial Japan. Under the Lend-Lease Act of 1941, America provided a subsidy for its allies that amounted, by the end of the war, to close to $48 billion in military aid, generally in the form of supplies. For example, most of the Soviet Army's trucks were American-built, 13 million Soviet soldiers wore American boots in the war's bitter Russian winters, and America provided 2,000 locomotives, 11,000 freight cars, and 540,000 tons of rails to keep Russian goods and soldiers moving by train. By 1944 the tide of war had turned in favor of the Allies (mainly Great Britain, France, the Soviet Union, and the United States). Thanks went in large part to U.S. industry, which by this time was equipping nearly a third of Britain's food and arms. American workers (many of them women, since men were needed for the armed services) were producing nearly half the world's new armaments, and completing an average of one ship and nearly 300 airplanes a day. In contrast, the combined Axis powers (mainly Germany, Italy, and Japan) produced altogether about half as much as the United States alone. Military historian John Keegan rates America's industrial capacity as the single most important factor in the Allied victory over the Axis, and calls its aircraft production "the most spectacular of all America's wartime industrial achievements" (Keegan, p. 219).

The war experience. While American industry made a rapid recovery from the ravages of the Great Depression by providing the tools for victory, young soldiers like Joe Keller's two sons, Chris and Larry, were off fighting the war. The U.S. armed forces numbered only about 2 million in 1941, but in that year Congress, at President Roosevelt's urging, instituted the draft and, by the war's end, of the approximately 16 million Americans who served, more than 10 million had been drafted. Relatively few of these, however, experienced the harsh and bloody realities of combat: of the 11 million in the U.S. Army, for example, just 2 million served in its

90 combat divisions, with an estimated 700,000 infantrymen bearing the brunt of the actual fighting. In *All My Sons* Chris Keller has come home after serving as an army infantry captain; Chris's younger brother Larry, a pilot, was killed when his plane crashed off the coast of China, much of which had been occupied by Japan starting in the 1930s. U.S. forces fought in two theaters of war, the European (primarily against Germany) and the Pacific (against Japan). The play does not specify where Chris served in the war. Infantry troops were used in both theaters, but the U.S. Army predominated in the European theater while the U.S. Navy and Marine Corps played a central role in the Pacific campaign.

Like Chris Keller, those who lived through combat were deeply affected by the experience. In the midst of death and carnage, many found that what got them through in the end was not allegiance to a political ideology (like democracy) or even to their country, but simply their bond with their fellow soldiers. As historian William Manchester, himself a U.S. Marine sergeant who was badly wounded fighting the Japanese in the Pacific, observes: "Men do not fight for flag or country, for the Marine Corps or glory or any other abstraction. They fight for one another" (Manchester in Evans, p. 334). The play's Chris Keller uses similar language to describe the selfless behavior of men killed under his command: "they didn't die; they killed themselves for each other. I mean that exactly; a little more selfish and they'd've been here today" (Miller, *All My Sons*, p. 85).

Those who stayed behind had little chance of grasping the horrors that many of their sons, brothers, and husbands were facing on a daily basis. This was true for the United States more than for the other major combatant nations, because geographical isolation protected most Americans from the direct effects of the deadliest war in history.

- Of an estimated 50 million people killed in World War II, some 30 to 35 million were civilians and 15 to 20 million were military personnel.
- The highest price was paid by the Soviet Union, where perhaps 7 to 10 million civilians and about 7.5 million soldiers died as war raged back and forth over its borders and deep into its heartland.
- British battle losses, at 244,000 military personnel killed, compare with those of the United States, which suffered 292,000 killed under arms. By contrast, however, some 65,000 British civilians died from German bombing, while there were no direct American civilian deaths from war.

Postwar prosperity and Cold War anxiety. America's geographical isolation also meant that when the war ended in 1945 the United States emerged with its factories and cities undamaged. Although the Depression would remain a haunting memory for the generation of the play's father, Joe Keller, the economic revival experienced in the war years continued uninterrupted in postwar America. In Europe, on the other hand, massive bombing and shelling had destroyed most major industrial centers and had gutted many of the largest cities. Britain was bankrupt, its people continuing to face the persistent shortages of food and goods they had endured during the war. People in the communist Soviet Union, where millions had starved in the 1930s, still suffered ongoing poverty—although, after repelling Germany's wartime invasion, Soviet

COMING HOME

The real-life reporter who came closest to communicating the experience of war to Americans at home was Ernie Pyle. Pyle's war dispatches, written from the front lines, described in plain language the bonds of comradeship felt by common foot soldiers. Miller met Pyle before the latter's death in 1945, and as he interviewed soldiers for a screenplay about Pyle's life, Miller gathered material he also used in his 1944 book *Situation Normal.* Some of Miller's impressions in *Situation Normal* about these real-life soldiers anticipate feelings the playwright would later embody in Chris Keller, especially a sense of aimlessness that could be felt by those returning to civilian life.

From Situation Normal

No man has ever felt identity with a group more deeply and intimately than a soldier in battle. But . . . the usual veteran returning to his city or town on the usual day finds no common goal at all. . . . Now he must live unto himself, for his own selfish welfare.

(Miller 1944, pp. 156-57)

Chris Keller in All My Sons

Everything was being destroyed, see, but it seemed to me that one new thing was being made. A kind of—responsibility. Man for man. . . . And then I came home and it was incredible. I—there was no meaning in it here. . . . I went to work for Dad, and that rat-race again. I felt . . . ashamed somehow.

(*All My Sons*, p. 85)

armies had marched to the German capital, Berlin, and now they controlled much of the vast territory in between. Especially in defeated Germany the destruction was widespread, and millions of Germans and other Europeans were left homeless (hence the label Displaced Persons). Asia, too was devastated, with civil war raging in China once it had become liberated from Japanese occupation. Japan itself was reeling from defeat and from the destruction caused by American atomic bombs, which had been detonated over the cities of Hiroshima and Nagasaki a few weeks before Japan's surrender officially ended the war in 1945. American prosperity thus stood in stark contrast to the deprivations and hardships that prevailed in much of the rest of the world. While America no longer endured the intense suffering of the Depression years, the specter of such suffering persisted abroad. Moreover, the world, America included, stood at the brink of future global discord.

On March 5, 1946, Britain's wartime leader Winston Churchill put into words the suspicion shared by a growing number of Americans towards their former ally, the Soviet Union. Speaking during a visit to the United States, Churchill warned Americans that "an iron curtain" had fallen over eastern Europe, which was now increasingly under "control from Moscow" (Churchill in Gilbert, p. 866). Eastern Europe would indeed remain under Soviet influence for the next half-century. During that time a tense "Cold War" would be played out around the globe between the two superpowers: the democratic, capitalist United States and the communist, totalitarian Soviet Union. *All My Sons* was written in the immediate aftermath of World War II, as the outlines of this peacetime conflict were just beginning to emerge. The play's often dark atmosphere reflects the postwar bleakness abroad that contrasted so sharply with America's domestic plenty. Early in the play, for example, as Joe Keller sits reading the Sunday paper, he offers to share it with his neighbor, Frank, who responds, "What's the difference? It's all bad news. What's today's calamity?" (*All My Sons*, p. 59).

The Play in Focus

The plot. *All My Sons* is set in "the back yard of the Keller home on the outskirts of an American town" in the Midwest (*All My Sons,* p. 201). Upstage the house and porch are visible, and downstage left stands the freshly broken stump of a slender apple tree, whose trunk and branches lie beside it. Act One takes place on a Sunday morning in August, Act Two that evening, and Act Three at two o'clock the next morning.

As the curtain rises, Joe Keller is idly chatting with his neighbors, Dr. Jim Bayliss and Frank Lubey, as he reads the Sunday paper. From the interchange among the three men, we learn that the apple tree, blown down in a storm the previous night, had been planted in memory of the Kellers' son Larry, a pilot lost three years earlier, during the war. We also learn that Frank, an amateur astrologer, has been working on Larry's horoscope, at the request of Kate Keller, the dead pilot's mother. Larry would have been 27 this month. His body was never recovered, and Kate hopes to establish that the date of Larry's death was astrologically favorable to him and that therefore her son might still be alive.

Keller reveals that Annie Deever, a pretty young woman whose family used to live in the Bayliss house next door, arrived late last night to visit the Kellers. She is asleep inside. The Deevers and the Kellers were more than mere neighbors, for Annie's father was Keller's business partner, and Annie herself was romantically involved with Larry. After his death, Annie moved to New York and never married. Sue Bayliss and Lydia Lubey, the wives of Jim and Frank, enter briefly, and then all four neighbors exit. The Kellers' surviving son Chris enters, and he and Keller discuss the fallen tree. Expressing concern about his mother, Kate, Chris says that they have "made a terrible mistake with Mother" by pretending to share her hope that Larry might still come home (*All My Sons*, p. 66). Kate must accept that Larry is dead.

This is especially important for Chris, who tells his father that he invited Annie to visit because he plans to ask her to marry him. He feels uncomfortable doing so, however, if his mother truly still thinks of Annie as "Larry's girl" (*All My Sons*, p. 68). When Kate enters, her son's fears are confirmed. It becomes clear that she has interpreted Annie's still unmarried state as a sign that she too is waiting for Larry. Chris exits, and Kate claims to Keller that Annie is as "faithful as a rock" and will never marry Chris (*All My Sons*, p. 73). When Chris enters with Annie, Kate presses the younger woman to agree. Annie, however, is clearly surprised, and says firmly that she has not been waiting for Larry at all. She has accepted Larry's death. This, she explains, is one reason why she finds it impossible to forgive her own father, Steve Deever, who is in jail for allowing faulty airplane engine parts to be shipped from the plant that he and Keller operated during the war. After 21 pilots died when their planes crashed, both Keller and Deever were convicted for the crime. However, Keller's conviction was later overturned.

Chris, who now runs the plant with Keller, shares Annie's unforgiving attitude toward her father. They hold him responsible for murdering the pilots, while Kate and Keller insist that the man simply made a mistake and has been unfairly treated. After the elder Kellers exit, Annie accepts Chris's proposal of marriage. As Act One closes, Annie learns that her brother George, a lawyer, has visited their father in prison and now urgently wants to see Annie. He is on his way to the Kellers' house.

Act Two opens at twilight that evening. Chris is clearing the fallen tree from the yard as they wait for George, whom Jim Bayliss has gone to pick up at the train station. His wife Sue jokingly complains to Annie that Jim would do anything for the Kellers, but when the two are alone Sue's jocularity turns to bitterness. Jim, she says, is a successful doctor, but Chris's idealism makes Jim feel as though he has compromised by not giving up his reliable income to engage in the less profitable but more noble pursuit of medical research, which has always been Jim's dream. Chris is hardly one to talk, thinks Sue, who accuses Chris of compromising himself. He works for his father at the plant, she says, when everyone in the neighborhood knows that Joe Keller was as guilty as Annie's father. Shocked, Annie confronts Chris, who assures her of his father's innocence. Joe Keller then proposes that her father return to work at the firm after he gets out of prison. When Chris and Annie object, Keller angrily bursts out that she shouldn't "crucify the man" and that "a father is a father" (*All My Sons*, p. 97).

When George arrives, Jim warns Annie about her brother's mood. George's temper has reached the boiling point; he is itching for a confrontation. He now believes what their father has maintained all along: that their father had discovered the faulty cylinder heads, phoned Keller, and was ordered by Keller to conceal the flaws and send the parts out anyway. Keller's story was that he was sick at home that day and had received no phone call. George and Annie quarrel, and George tells her not to marry Chris. The atmosphere appears to lighten, and George seems to relax as Keller repeats his invitation for George and Annie's father to come work at the plant.

However, the rapprochement is quickly dispelled after George comments on Keller's youthful appearance, and Kate fondly boasts that her husband "hasn't been laid up in fifteen years" (*All My Sons*, p. 111). Except, Keller reminds her awkwardly, "when I was sick during . . . the war" (*All My Sons*, p. 111). Suddenly George's suspicions return more strongly than ever; he accuses Keller of concocting the story of his illness the day the faulty cylinder heads were sent out. Chris orders him to leave, and Kate says that Annie—whom she once more calls "Larry's girl"—should go too (*All My Sons*, p. 113). The bereft mother continues to maintain that Larry is coming home. When Chris tells her to let Larry go, she faces him and says that he must then let his father go. As Chris stands transfixed, she tells him: "Your brother's alive, darling, because if he's dead, your father killed him" (*All My Sons*, p. 114).

Burt Lancaster (left) as Chris Keller, Mady Christians as Kate Keller, and Edward G. Robinson as Joe Keller in the 1948 film version of *All My Sons*.

Chris realizes that his mother's comment can mean only one thing: Keller did indeed know about the faulty parts, and now Chris relentlessly forces him to admit it. "I never thought they'd install them. I swear to God," Keller protests, claiming he did it to protect the business that would one day belong to Chris (*All My Sons*, p. 115). As Act Two closes, the disillusioned Chris rages against his father:

> For me! Where do you live, where have you come from? For me!—I was dying every day and you were killing my boys and you did it

for me? What the hell do you think I was thinking of, the goddamn business? Is that as far as your mind can see, the business? What is that, the world—the business? What the hell do you mean, you did it for me? Don't you have a country? Don't you live in the world? What the hell are you?

(*All My Sons*, p. 115-16)

Act Three opens with mother Kate waiting up for Chris, who has stormed out of the house. Annie has disappeared into Larry's room, where she has been sleeping. When Keller enters, Kate suggests that he acknowledge he "did a terrible thing" (*All My Sons*, p. 119). Maybe then Chris will forgive him. What is there to be forgiven for? Keller demands; supporting his family?

I spoiled the both of you. I should've put him out when he was ten like I was put out, and make him earn his keep. Then he'd know how a buck was made in this world. Forgiven!

(*All My Sons*, p. 120)

And when Kate tells him that for Chris "there's something bigger than the family," Joe responds: "Nothin's bigger than that. . . . I'm his father and he's my son, and if there's something bigger than that I'll put a bullet in my head" (*All My Sons*, p. 120).

Joining them, Annie agrees not to reveal Keller's guilt publicly, but in return insists that Kate finally accept both Larry's death and Annie's union with Chris. Kate refuses, compelling Annie to reveal that she has certain knowledge of Larry's death from a letter Larry wrote to her before he died. Kate reads the letter just as Chris returns. He has decided not to turn in his father, but feels like he has sold out; more exactly, he has renounced his humanity in favor of being "practical" (*All My Sons*, p. 123). Chris reads the letter aloud, revealing that Larry had seen the news of his father's conviction. Unable to face the idea that his father caused the deaths of 21 pilots, Larry intends to crash his own plane. Hearing this, Keller is stunned. He haltingly prepares to turn himself in to the authorities, but Kate objects that even if Chris would let him go to prison, Larry would never want it. "Larry was your son, too, wasn't he?" she demands (*All My Sons*, p. 126). Keller answers, "Sure, he was my son. But I think to him they were all my sons. And I guess they were, I guess they were. I'll be right down" (*All My Sons*, p. 126). Moments later a shot is heard from upstairs. As the curtain falls, Kate sobs, but she comforts Chris, telling him not to blame himself. "Forget now," she urges him tearfully, "Live" (*All My Sons*, p. 127).

"Relatedness." Just before Joe Keller puts a bullet in his head, Chris tells his mother that the only way his parents can redeem themselves is to understand that "there's a universe of people outside and you're responsible to it" (*All My Sons*, p. 126). This idea of larger human responsibility, which Miller has called "relatedness," summarizes the set of values that Chris's war experience has instilled in him (*All My Sons*, p. 18). It contrasts sharply with Keller's conviction that "nothin's bigger" than the well-being of one's family, a belief forged not in the war but in the need to survive the harsh Depression that preceded it. The play thus dramatizes not just a potential conflict between the narrow good of the family and the greater good of humanity, but also one between the differing values of two generations of Americans.

While the isolationism of the 1930s was a complex historical phenomenon with deep roots in the American experience, it also grew out of a perceived necessity to focus on basic needs at home. A generation preoccupied with the struggle to feed, clothe, and house itself was hard-pressed to fight what it saw as other people's battles. While Keller never expresses this sentiment in the play's postwar setting, one can imagine him doing so a decade earlier and his feelings persisting into the next generation. For Keller, a self-made man with little education, his factory, the foundation of his family's financial security, is everything. To him "the world had a forty-foot front, it ended at the building line" (*All My Sons*, p. 121). Outside Keller's own small world, what happens is of little moral consequence to him; thus, he can dismiss the deaths of 21 pilots as merely "a mistake" (*All My Sons,* p. 233). As the text makes clear, if Keller had acknowledged the faulty airplane part at the time, the company would have gone out of business. Against this undesirable outcome is balanced what Miller calls "the full loathesomeness [*sic*] of the anti-social action," action that, in this case, is destructive of human life (*All My Sons*, p. 17).

Only when he learns that the "mistake" meant to benefit his family has instead ruined it—indirectly costing the life of his son Larry—does the shocked Keller expand his small world to take in the wider one. In a reversal of his values, the dead pilots become "all my sons," and thus part of a larger family for which his actual sons have fought.

Chris too achieves some insight into his own uncompromising values. In deciding not to turn his father in, he says, "I know you're no worse than most men but I thought you were better. I never saw you as a man. I saw you as my father" (*All My Sons*, p. 125). In the end, both men must modify their extreme and opposing outlooks. Clearly the extremes further the dramatist's aim of constructing a gripping play. But they also reflect a real-life truism—both outlooks were vital to the war effort. History shows that the victory of democracy over fascism could not have been achieved without the contribution of profit-driven industry or of the selfless men who waged war with its products.

Sources and literary context. As with many of Miller's plays, the basic idea for *All My Sons* came from a real-life incident. As he relates in his introduction to the *Collected Plays*, a visitor from the Midwest told him a story about a family in her neighborhood, in which the daughter had turned in her father for shipping faulty materials to the army during the war. At once, Miller writes, he was captivated by the girl's "absolute response to a moral command" and began toying with the idea (Miller, "Introduction," *Collected Plays*, p. 17). "By the time she had finished the tale," he writes, "I had transformed the daughter into a son and the climax of the second act was full and clear in my mind" (Miller, "Introduction," *Collected Plays*, p. 17). Changing the daughter into a son allowed Miller to combine this incident with material about the lives of soldiers that he had already unearthed while working on *The Story of G.I. Joe*, a screenplay based on the wartime reporting of correspondent Ernie Pyle.

In addition to these real-life models, Miller drew on numerous literary sources. Leading influences include ancient Greek tragedies such as those of Sophocles (fifth century B.C.E.); as well as the more recent plays of the nineteenth-century Norwegian playwright Henrik Ibsen (1828-1906). In Sophocles' play ***Antigone*** (also in *Literature and Its Times*), for example, the title character (a young girl) is forced to choose between her duty to her family and the interests of the state, a dilemma that resembles that of *All My Sons*.

Miller has acknowledged his more overt debt to Ibsen's powerful domestic plays, which include *A Doll's House*, *Ghosts*, and ***Hedda Gabler*** (also in *Literature and Its Times*). Ibsen offered the young Miller motifs and devices with which to construct his own domestic drama. Examples include beginning the story close in time to the climax, so that the relevant details of the past only gradually emerge; a family whose prosperity rests on a guilty secret or deception; and children suffering for the moral transgressions of their parents (a theme that ultimately goes back to Greek tragedy). Later in his career, Miller would adapt Ibsen's play *An Enemy of the People* to a twentieth-century American setting.

Reception. Directed by Elia Kazan, the original production of *All My Sons* opened on Broadway on January 29, 1947, with Ed Begley as Joe Keller and Arthur Kennedy as Chris Keller. Initial theatrical reviews were mixed, as has been subsequent criticism of the play. Many reviewers praised the author but expressed reservations about the play itself. Writing in *The New Yorker*, for example, John Lardner called the playwright "honest" and "ardent" but criticized the work as often sounding "phony" (Lardner, p. 50). The title of Lardner's *New Yorker* review can be seen as aptly summarizing the general response both at first and later: "B for Effort." Critics have particularly singled out the slow, extended opening scene as inviting boredom, and have also complained that the use of coincidence (Larry's letter, Kate Keller's slip of the tongue about her husband's never having been ill) to move the plot forward as heavy-handed and unbelievable.

IN THE TRADITION OF SOPHOCLES

Miller's *All My Sons,* like his other plays, aspires to a universal purpose rather than resting in particulars:

> ***The Crucible*** [also in *Literature and Its Times*] is not any more an attempt to cure witch hunts than *Salesman* is a plea for the improvement of conditions for traveling men, [or] *All My Sons* a plea for better inspection of airplane parts. . . . It is examining . . . the conflict between a man's raw deeds and his conception of himself; the question of whether conscience is in fact an organic part of the human being.
>
> (Miller in Navasky, p. 213)

Yet the day after the play opened, a review appeared that assured the drama of box-office success, and catapulted its young author to instant celebrity. Writing in the highly influential *New York Times*, Brooks Atkinson—the dean of New York theater critics—called *All My Sons* an "honest, forceful drama" containing "a pitiless analysis of character that gathers momentum all evening and concludes with both logic and impact" (Atkinson, p. 21). In subsequent reviews of this and other Miller plays, Atkinson would remain one of the playwright's staunchest defenders. He particularly rejected the charge, made against *All My Sons* as well as against later plays such as *Death of a Salesman*, that Miller uses his characters to preach a social message without endowing them with humanity. Whereas Lardner heard dialogue that sounded "phony" in *All My Sons*, Atkinson by contrast praised its "pithy yet unself-conscious dialogue," going on to say that Miller "has created his characters vividly, picking them out of the run of American society, but presenting them with hearts and minds of their own" (Atkinson, p. 21).

—Colin Wells

For More Information

Atkinson, Brooks. Review of *All My Sons*. *New York Times*, 30 January 1947, 21.

Evans, Harold. *The American Century*. New York: Random House, 1998.

Gilbert, Martin. *Churchill: A Life*. New York: Henry Holt, 1991.

Keegan, John. *The Second World War*. New York: Penguin, 1990.

Lardner, John. "B for Effort." *The New Yorker* 22 (8 February 1947), 22.

McCullough, David. *Truman*. New York: Simon & Schuster, 1992.

Miller, Arthur. *All My Sons*. In *Collected Plays*. Vol. 1. New York: Viking, 1957.

———. *Situation Normal*. New York: Reynal Hitchcock, 1944.

———. *Timebends: A Life*. New York: Grove, 1987.

Navasky, Victor S. *Naming Names*. New York: Viking, 1980.

All the Pretty Horses

by
Cormac McCarthy

Cormac McCarthy was born in Rhode Island in 1933, lived in Tennessee, and moved to El Paso, Texas, 25 years ago. His first novel, *The Orchard Keeper*, was published in 1965. Through a series of books that have appeared since then, McCarthy has pursued his fascination with remote regions of the United States and Mexico, rural communities, and lone individuals who refuse the mediation of the modern world in their struggles with fate or with the forces of nature. *Blood Meridian* (1985) is a Gothic historical novel about outlaws and bounty hunters set in Texas and Mexico at the middle of the nineteenth century. McCarthy's 1992 novel *All the Pretty Horses* became the first novel of his "Border Trilogy," followed by *The Crossing* (1994) and *Cities of the Plain* (1998). With *All the Pretty Horses*, Cormac McCarthy achieved a memorable combination of adventure, psychological intensity, and the violent clash of cultures.

THE LITERARY WORK

A novel, set in West Texas and northern Mexico in 1950; first published in 1992.

SYNOPSIS

John Grady Cole and his friend Lacey Rawlins, two young Texans who love to work with horses, cross into Mexico looking for work as cowboys. While employed on a large ranch in the mountains of Coahuila, John Cole falls in love with the owner's daughter, Alejandra, which leads to a chain of drama and violence as the two Americans try to escape with their lives.

Events in History at the Time the Novel Takes Place

Texas at midcentury. *All the Pretty Horses* opens in the fall of 1949. At the time, the state of Texas was still enjoying the economic boom that the exploitation of large oil reserves had brought with it. From the discovery of the huge Spindletop field, opened in 1901, to the East Texas oil finds of the 1930s, oil had been the driving force that transformed Texas from an agricultural and cattle-raising economy into a major industrial power in the United States. In 1928 Texas became the country's leading oil-producing state with a total annual output of over 250 million barrels. Oil would eventually be discovered in West Texas, so that, in the words of a twentieth-century historian of the region, "one could drive one hundred and fifty miles without ever losing sight of oil derricks" (Frantz, p. 182).

World War II kept Texas oil extraction and processing operating at peak production levels and also brought to the state large military installations where men were trained and weapons tested. Between 1941 and 1945, some 10 percent of all U.S. military personnel received their training in Texas; for the Army Air Force, Texas offered the biggest aviation training region "anywhere in the United States and probably on earth" (Frantz, p. 184). Building on this new economic foundation, the United States Congress—whose key committees were often dominated by Southern Democrats—began in the late 1940s to steer large-scale defense contracts toward the South and Southwest, enabling a gradual integration of what had been the most economically backward part of the nation into the mainstream of the American economy.

COWBOYS AND HORSES

The horse-dominated world of West Texas ranching was on the decline in 1950, when *All the Pretty Horses* is set. Despite the considerable role played by the horse in the improvements in agricultural and the infrastructure improvements in the United States between 1900 and 1940, the heyday of this animal was coming rapidly to a close. In 1940 there were over ten million horses in the U.S., and by 1965 the number had dropped to less than five million. The majority of these five million were no longer on working farms or on ranches, but instead could be found in the wealthy suburbs and on the racetrack. The horse became less a concern of the U.S. Department of Agriculture, which in 1959 stopped collecting statistics on the horse population (Howard, p. 241). Of course, the change had an effect on the nature of ranch employment. As cattle ranching, in the mid-to-late twentieth century, became a business that depended upon the global market, the old order gave way. At midcentury, one study observed that the life of a Texas cowboy has improved. He has gained mechanized transport and other kinds of assistance to make his job easier, and even now "he remains a skilled worker of cattle, changed only by adapting to the technological revolution which eventually reached the range" (Frantz and Choate, p. 60). John Grady Cole, the protagonist of *All the Pretty Horses,* might beg to differ. In his view, the novel suggests, something precious has been lost.

Despite the discovery of oil, however, West Texas remained a comparatively underpopulated and nonindustrialized region. The area from Amarillo in the north to the U.S-Mexico border in the south and west to El Paso, was still marked by the cattle ranches and dirt roads of an earlier era. West Texas had a long tradition of successful cattle ranching ever since a young and adventurous businessman from Illinois, Joseph G. McCoy, had convinced the railroad company in 1867 to build a new cattle-town from scratch at an almost-deserted West Texas crossing called Abilene. Next McCoy convinced Texas ranchers to drive their cattle to this new railhead.

Suddenly the vast herds of cattle on the dusty plains of Texas were being used to meet an ever-increasing demand for beef in northern cities, a very profitable development for Texas. Beyond the economic prosperity, a mix of ingredients—the cattle drives, the wild cattle towns, the tough, hard-riding cowboys who worked the range—gave birth to the most dynamic, enduring myth America has ever produced. The mustang, longhorn, and the cowboy became, as one historian has put it, "the Holy Trinity of Texas . . . They symbolized a freedom which probably never really existed, but which people like to think existed" (Frantz, p. 135). The myth took root, in fact, despite the reality of the cowboy's often bleak lifestyle. The cowboys in the later nineteenth century were mostly rootless, semi-employed drifters, failed outlaws, freed slaves and impoverished dirt farmers. They had frequently cut all family and local ties, and if they spent months on a thousand-mile cattle drive, often there was nobody who would have missed them (Kramer, p. 9).

Still, 80 years later, the romance of the cattle trail fascinates John Grady Cole, the hero of *All the Pretty Horses*. In real life, the lonely freedom of a man on a horse was no longer so easy to find, or experience. Texas at mid-twentieth century was a place of stark and sometimes confusing contrasts: oil and cattle; military installations and nineteenth-century cowboy mythology; economic prosperity and damaged landscapes; the dominance of English, brought in by American settlers of the 1820s and 1830s, and the persistence of Spanish, brought in centuries before by their Mexican predecessors.

Mexico at midcentury. Mexico's history in the first half of the twentieth century was volatile. From revolution and civil conflict (1910-23), to the nationalization of the oil business (1938), to urban development (1940s), the more enlightened Mexican leaders had sought to steer their complex nation into the modern world. The effort to modernize involved some calculated attempts to use oil and mineral revenues to bring basic literacy and a minimum of health care to millions of poverty-stricken rural peasants. The effort also inspired attempts to create a closer, more nationally beneficial relationship with the United States, Mexico's neighbor to the immediate north. By the later 1930s, however, the relationship had reached a point of crisis. As the threat of war grew, the administration of U.S. President Franklin D. Roosevelt became concerned that Nazi German diplomacy in Central and South America was nurturing local resentments against the United States. If America were to become involved in hostilities, Roosevelt believed, good relations with countries to the south would be crucial. He instituted a "Good Neighbor Policy," based on respect for the rights of others. The policy involved the withdrawal of U.S. troops from Nicaragua and Haiti and a commitment to non-intervention in Latin American countries. When the United States entered World War II, the policy paid off. Nearly all the Latin American countries supported the United States during the war.

Manuel Ávila Camacho, Mexico's president at the time, was a committed supporter of the Allies. Under his administration (1940-46), Mexico contributed greatly to the war effort, deploying a squadron of fighter aircraft to the Pacific theater, exporting vast amounts of strategic war materials to the United States, and entering into the *bracero* program to provide America with temporary migrant labor. The program sent 200,000 Mexicans north of the border to fill urgent vacancies in agriculture and industry (Smith, pp. 59-60).

Together Mexico and the United States joined in a struggle against fascism. In fact, the social reforms introduced by President Roosevelt in his New Deal can be seen as an American version of the socialist (or social-democratic) philosophy of Mexican politicians. There was much common ground.

After World War II, however, the relationship between Mexico and the United States became tenser than during the Roosevelt years. As the Cold War, or the competition for world leadership between the United States and the Soviet Union, began to take shape, U.S. leaders came to regard all events in Latin America through the prism of Cold War strategy. Either one was on the side of the United States, or one fell suspect to harboring some affection for Soviet communism. Having adopted this viewpoint, the United States found itself confronted with and involved in a series of crises (in Cuba, Chile, and Nicaragua, for example) over the following decades. In Mexico, the U.S. presence caused some hostility, since the political establishment here was committed to principles of non-intervention, respect for national sovereignty, and their own social revolutionary tradition.

On a national scale, Mexico's economic progress during the 1940s had been considerable. It benefited, on the one hand, from multifaceted cooperation with the United States and, on the other hand, from the tax breaks and surcharges on imports used to protect native industries that had shown signs of growth during the war years. In 1940 Mexico had 13,000 industrial establishments, most of which were involved in food and textile production, but ten years later the country could boast 73,000 plants with chemicals, paper, and steelmaking, which gave the country a much more diverse industrial base (Krauze, p. 543). Yet large regions of Mexico remained untouched by the progress, sometimes due to geographic remoteness, sometimes to customs and values, sometimes to a combination of these elements. Stubborn traces of tradition surface in *All the Pretty Horses* when John Grady Cole journeys through Mexico. Among other experiences, he encounters the aristocratic power of the rich rancher, represented by Don Héctor, and the conservative inflexibility of traditional attitudes to women and foreigners in Mexico. Don Héctor is the owner of a ranch called La Purísima (meaning "purest of women," a reference to the Virgin Mary). In the words of the novel, Don Héctor had distinguished himself as "one of the few hacendados who actually lived on the land he claimed, land which had been in his family for one hundred and seventy years. He was forty-seven years old and he was the first male heir in all that new world lineage to attain such an age" (McCarthy, *Pretty Horses*, p. 97). The description suggests that he hails from an aristocratic family whose members managed to retain their land despite repeated wars and revolutions. Don Héctor is portrayed as an intelli-

A POROUS BORDER

All the Pretty Horses features dialogue that slips from English into untranslated Spanish at various points in the novel. The shift mirrors a real-life facility with the two languages that a large share of the population on both sides of the border had at the time, due in part to how easy it was to cross from one side to the other. The border was a porous one until the early 1950s, when a slowdown in American business and the workers brought in under the *bracero* program prompted a crackdown by the U.S. Border Patrol on illegal crossings.

gent man who interacts with ease in the modern world; he flies his own plane between La Purísima and Mexico City, for example. At the same time, his aristocratic bearing and absolute belief in his own authority mark him as a representative of the Creole elite. His strict concept of honor and his implacable attitude to John Grady's courting of his daughter show that behind the modern rancher is the old Mexican landowning class. The native-born but ethnically Hispanic establishment had been the natural source of leadership after independence was achieved in 1821, a challenge they did not meet successfully. In a country that was, as one historian has expressed it, "centuries behind at birth for its task of creating a regime of civil liberties and economic well-being," the Creole landowning aristocracy had much constitutional theory and nationalist idealism to draw on, but they showed very little sense of practical political structure or economic organization (Krauze, p. 132). The intense poverty in which the greater part of the Mexican peasantry lived would persist well into the next century. In 1953 President Adolfo Ruiz Cortines acknowledged that Mexico remained a generally poor country; there were at the time some 19 million peasants still living in dire poverty.

The Novel in Focus

The plot. *All the Pretty Horses* opens in fall 1949 with the death of John Grady Cole's maternal grandfather, on whose remote West Texas ranch John has grown up. His mother and father have been separated—John Grady's father was missing in action in World War II, but eventually returned. Recently John's parents have divorced. His mother is completely uninterested in the ranch, and spends her time working in a theater company in San Antonio. She wants to sell the ranch. John, who loves working with horses, wants to take over the ranch and keep the ranch going, but his mother dismisses the idea, saying that he is only 16 years old, and has to attend school. The family's attorney confirms to John that the property is his mother's to do with as she wishes.

John and his father go riding together, and his father explains that it was the thought of his wife that got him through the Japanese POW camp alive. He encourages John to develop a better relationship with his mother, but John promises nothing in this regard. His father leaves him with a strange comment that seems to echo the wider world of politics and international affairs at mid-century: "People dont feel safe no more, he said. We're like the Comanches was two hundred years ago. We dont know what's goin to show up here come daylight. We dont even know what color they'll be" (*Pretty Horses*, pp. 25-26).

In March, John Grady decides to go to Mexico, hoping to find a job on a ranch. South of the border, he believes, lies adventure and more freedom than in Texas. Without telling anybody, he and his friend Lacey Rawlins saddle up their horses early one morning and head south. The two boys revel in a feeling of liberation "like thieves newly loosed in that dark electric, like young thieves in a glowing orchard, loosely jacketed against the cold and ten thousand worlds for the choosing" (*Pretty Horses*, p. 30). On their way to the Rio Grande River, John and Rawlins meet an edgy, aggressive boy about 13 years old named Jimmy Blevins. A lone rider, the boy obviously wants to join the other two. Rawlins in particular takes a dislike to Blevins, and feels that he is going to bring them trouble. The two friends suspect that Blevins's horse might be stolen or that he is trying to escape some legal tangle. Loath to just abandon him, John and Rawlins let him ride with them, and they cross the Rio Grande together into Mexico. Blevins reveals that he is armed with a heavy-caliber Colt revolver and is a good shot.

The three travel slowly on horseback through the northern reaches of Coahuila State. A few days after they cross into Mexico they meet a group of nomadic traders and purchase a supply of sotol, a homemade liquor. All of them drink to the point of intoxication, but Blevins ends up seriously deranged from the alcohol. When a storm blows up, Blevins believes he will be struck by lightning, and ends up abandoning his horse, his gun, and most of his clothes. Without the bare essentials, he has to ride with John Grady. They encounter a group of horsemen and join them around a campfire to eat. Blevins looks particularly young and vulnerable in his underwear and borrowed shirt. John, the only one of the three able to speak Spanish, has to negotiate their way out of the camp, as the men have taken a clearly sexual interest in the half-naked Blevins and offer to buy him for cash.

When the three arrive in a pueblo called Encantada, Jimmy Blevins immediately sees a man carrying his Colt pistol, and they discover Blevins's horse tethered in an abandoned house on the edge of the village. Blevins insists that he wants to take the horse back that night, without

Matt Damon (left) as John Grady Cole, Lucas Black as Jimmy Blevins, and Henry Thomas as Lacey Rawlins in the 2000 film version of *All the Pretty Horses*.

discussing the move with anyone, and John Grady and Rawlins agree to wait for him. Unfortunately Blevins causes havoc while retrieving the horse, which leads to the three being chased by armed men. They split up, Blevins taking one path, and John and Rawlins another. Rawlins is still convinced that Blevins means trouble:

> John Grady folded away his knife. Well, he said.
> There's a lot of country out there.
> Yep. Lot of country.
> God knows where he's got to.
> Rawlins nodded. I'll tell you what you told me.
> What's that?
> We aint seen the last of his skinny ass.
> (*Pretty Horses*, p. 89)

Shortly thereafter, John and Rawlins meet a group of vaqueros driving a herd of cattle and inquire about work. The vaqueros bring the two to the ranch, where they are hired.

The ranch, called La Purísima, comprises 11,000 hectares (about 20,000 acres) and is owned by Don Héctor Rocha y Villareal, a rich man who flies his own plane to and from Mexico City, where his wife lives. John Grady comes to the notice of Don Héctor when he breaks a wild horse after four days of struggle—an achievement everyone had considered impossible. During the four days, John sees the owner's daughter, Alejandra, for the first time. Afterward, he is called in for an interview with Don Héctor, who quizzes him about horses:

> Do you know what a criollo is?
> Yessir. That's an Argentine horse.
> Do you know who Sam Jones was?
> I do if you're talkin about a horse.
> Crawford Sykes?
> That's another of Uncle Billy Anson's horses. I heard about that horse all my life.
> (*Pretty Horses*, p. 115)

Don Héctor is impressed with John's enthusiasm and knowledge and promises to let him work with a new horse that he has bought into the United States.

During this time, the attraction between John and Alejandra grows. They begin to meet in secret. Alejandra's great aunt, the dueña Alfonsa, calls John Grady in to see her. She explains that the sight of him and Alejandra together creates a problem: in Mexico, there is no forgiveness whatsoever for a woman who has lost her reputation (*Pretty Horses*, pp. 136-37). After this conversation, John and Alejandra continue to see each other—they meet at a nearby lake at night, swim together, and make love. One evening Don Héctor invites John to play pool with him and during their game talks about a tragic love affair of days past between Alfonsa and Gustavo Madero, a Mexican revolutionary leader. This story of a problematic affection leads into Don Héctor's comment that he intends to send Alejandra to study in Europe.

The following day out on the range, John and Rawlins are captured by a group of armed men. The two are taken back to Encantada and thrown into jail. There, they encounter Jimmy Blevins, who has been locked up for some time. Blevins tells them that he killed one of the *rurales,* the local police, who were pursuing him. The police captain interrogates John Grady and Rawlins and accuses them, along with Blevins, of entering Mexico to steal horses. They protest and reiterate that the horse that Blevins "stole" in Encantada was his own. Back in the cell, John tells Rawlins that Blevins's life is in danger. A few days later, the three Americans are trucked to the city of Saltillo. On the way, the guards stop at a remote wooded area and drag Blevins into the trees. There is the sound of a gunshot, and the guards return alone.

Life in the prison in Saltillo is brutal. In the first few days, both John and Rawlins are attacked and beaten several times. A prisoner named Pérez offers to protect them if they pay him, but the two Americans have no money. The next day, Rawlins is knifed in the stomach, but not fatally. He is taken away for treatment. John prudently buys a knife from another prisoner. Soon he himself is attacked and, though he manages to kill his attacker, his own injuries plunge him into unconsciousness.

Over the next few days, John's wounds are tended, and he is released from the prison and reunited with Rawlins. Rawlins is confused about their good fortune, but John is convinced that Alejandra's aunt has paid for their release. He and Rawlins part company, and John hitches a ride in a truck back to La Purísima. He gains access to the dueña Alfonsa, and she explains that Don Héctor had been aware of the incident with Blevins's horse in Encantada all along and had concluded that John and Rawlins had lied to him about their reasons for coming to Mexico. After the two Americans were arrested, Alfonsa, judging John to be of good character, had defended him to both her brother and Alejandra's mother in Mexico City, but to no effect. She then recounts the story of the doomed Madero brothers, Francisco and Gustavo, and her relationship with Gustavo. At the end of their talk, Alfonsa tells John he must leave and offers him his choice of a horse.

The next day, however, John manages to telephone Alejandra and they arrange to meet in the town of Zacatecas. They stay the night in a hotel and make love. John asks Alejandra to marry him and come to Texas, but she refuses to leave. He brings her to the train station, where they part. Depressed, John returns to Encantada and forces the police captain at gunpoint to return his, Rawlins's, and Blevins's horses. He gets wounded in the ensuing skirmish but escapes with the animals and takes the captain hostage.

That night John realizes that his leg wound is in danger of becoming infected, and he has no possibility of medical treatment. He decides to cauterize the wound himself, and dismantles a

THE MADEROS

Both Don Héctor and Alfonsa allude to the story of the Madero brothers, Francisco and Gustavo. The two brothers came from a well-off landowning family and played key roles in the rebellion against the rule of iron-handed dictator Porfirio Díaz that began in November 1910. Upon the defeat of the Díaz regime, Francisco Madero became the first popularly elected president of Mexico. His mix of political liberalism and economic conservatism, however, displeased many of the revolutionary leaders. His key general, Huerta, conspired against him, along with both Emiliano Zapata (who had supported Madero in the struggle to topple Díaz) and Pancho Villa. Though Gustavo Madero presented his brother Francisco with evidence of betrayal in 1913, Francisco continued to believe in Huerta's loyalty. It was a grave error, for Huerta's forces staged a coup d'état immediately thereafter, and both Gustavo and Francisco were murdered. Huerta assumed the presidency but found himself embroiled in further civil conflict with, among others, his former associates Zapata and Villa. Huerta chose self-exile in 1914.

The reference in *All the Pretty Horses* to the dueña Alfonsa's relationship with Gustavo is McCarthy's fictional embellishment of history. But it serves to highlight her warning to John Grady that Mexico is a society in which different concepts of loyalty and retribution pertain. In Alfonsa's version of the story, the Madero brothers' passionate commitment to the cause of the people's freedom could not save them from betrayal and the murderous anger of the peasant mob. Alfonsa sees a tragic mistake in John's romantic affection for Alejandra, the kind of mistake that Francisco Madero made when he trusted the wrong individual at a moment of crisis.

revolver. He lays the barrel section in the campfire and lets it heat up. When the barrel is white hot, he rams it into the bullet hole in his thigh:

> The captain either did not know what he was going to do or knowing did not believe. . . . John Grady had begun to shout even before the gunmetal hissed in the meat. His shout clapped shut the calls of lesser creatures everywhere about them in the night and the horses all stood swimming up into the darkness beyond the fire and squatting in terror on their great thighs screaming and pawing the stars and he drew breath and howled again and jammed the gunbarrel into the second wound.
>
> (*Pretty Horses*, p. 274)

John survives his emergency treatment and he rides on the next day, still with the rurales captain as his prisoner. Later a mysterious group of armed men seize the captain from him; clearly they do not intend the prisoner any good.

John crosses back into Texas on Thanksgiving Day, 1950. He has been in Mexico for about seven months. Shortly after his arrival, he makes a court appearance because an unknown party claims Blevins's horse. John astonishes the judge and the others in court by describing how he treated his leg wound. The judge dismisses the case, and John rides from town to town trying to trace Blevins's family to inform them about his death and return the horse. He has a strange encounter with a radio preacher called Jimmy Blevins and his wife but cannot establish if the family has any connection with the deceased.

John attends the funeral of Abuela, an elderly Mexican servant who had been like a grandmother to him on his grandfather's ranch. Afterward, he mounts his horse and heads south once more, into an uncertain future. The landscape takes on a surreal quality, as the oil derricks appear "like great primitive birds welded up out of iron by hearsay in a land perhaps where such birds once had been" (*Pretty Horses*, p. 301). The shadow of rider and horse become like the shadow of a single being, a ghost of the desert—"Passed and paled into the darkening land, the world to come" (*Pretty Horses*, p. 302).

Values and gender. Both conversations between John Grady and the dueña Alfonsa, Alejandra's aunt, revolve around the social expectations and the status that define a young woman's life in the Mexico of 1950. Alfonsa admits that she herself was a stubborn and rebellious girl in her youth, and that when she tries to advise Alejandra it is as if she is arguing with a young version of herself. During the first meeting, she tells John Grady that his and Alejandra's behavior is causing gossip:

> In an ideal world the gossip of the idle would be of no consequence. But I have seen the consequences in the real world and they can be very grave indeed. They can be consequences of a gravity not excluding bloodshed. Not excluding death. I saw this in my own family.
>
> (*Pretty Horses*, p. 136)

She comments that a man in Mexico may recover his lost honor, but a woman can never do so.

During their second interview, after John Grady has returned from the prison in Saltillo, Alfonsa says that she is not "a society person" and that societies she has seen have appeared to her to be "largely machines for the suppression of women" (*Pretty Horses*, p. 230). Despite her sympathy for Alejandra and her tolerance for John's feelings, she explains that he cannot just project onto Mexico the easier social relations between the sexes that are found in the United States. There are other powerful traditions at work in Mexico and they must be taken into account. The family, Alfonsa continues, also has had a history of women engaging in unsuitable and tragic love relationships—her sister lost two husbands, both gunned down, before she was 21.

Although romantically committed to his vision of marrying Alejandra, John is defeated by a code of values and behavior entrenched in Mexican society. Alejandra herself soberly resolves to abide by the code. As the writer Octavio Paz expresses it in *The Labyrinth of Solitude*, his pathbreaking study of the psychology of Mexican society, a woman is "the repository of honor" in this society (Paz, p. 38). For Alejandra to leave with John and go to the United States would dishonor her family (by marrying beneath her and without their permission) and her nation (by offering herself to a foreigner). Alejandra shows a stoicism that Paz's study ascribes to Mexican women in the face of her misery. Her words to John after their last night together reflect her resolve to conform to societal expectations: "I cannot do what you ask," she says, "I love you. But I cannot" (*Pretty Horses*, p. 254).

Sources and literary context. Cormac McCarthy has been secretive about the origins and implications of his work. Given the very small number of interviews he has granted, readers and critics are left largely to their own devices when it comes to teasing out the literary influences on his novels. There are, in fact, a few reasonably identifiable sources and contexts for McCarthy's prose. In particular, the laconic conversational dialogue that characterizes *All the Pretty Horses* resembles that of Ernest Hemingway, who in his early fiction from *In Our Time* (1925) to *To Have and Have Not* (1937) pioneered the fine-tuning of American dialogue in a way that revolutionized modern fiction.

JOHN GRADY COLE'S JOURNEY—REAL-LIFE LOCATIONS

Some of McCarthy's locations are fictional, but many exist in reality. After leaving San Angelo, John and Rawlins (and soon Blevins) ride for about 100 miles, then cross the Rio Grande Ride. Traveling along the Sierra la Encantada, via a possibly fictional pueblo of the same name, they find the ranch La Purísima. The nearest city appears to be Cuatro Ciénegas, about 200 miles from the Texas border. After their arrest, John and Rawlins are taken to the state capital, Saltillo, about 150 miles further south. Later Rawlins returns to Texas and John goes back via Cuatro Ciénegas to La Purísima, then travels southwest to Zacatecas to meet Alejandra. They part and he returns via Torreon to La Encantada (about 250 miles), where he kidnaps the police captain and repossesses the horses. His long journey home via Langtry, Texas, is another 200 miles. John Grady's journey, on horseback or motorized, has covered at least 1,200 miles over mostly rugged territory.

The later novels of Texas author Larry McMurtry likewise define the context in which McCarthy writes. McMurtry began with rural, elemental stories such as *Horseman, Pass By* (1961) and *The Last Picture Show* (1966), then moved to the contemporary urban settings in Texas and elsewhere (*Moving On* [1970] and *Terms of Endearment* [1975]). Cormac McCarthy has moved in the other direction, becoming more committed to exploring the isolated consciousness and the violence of the borderlands.

The western myth itself, particularly strong in Texans' imagining of their own past, has influenced a number of writers including McCarthy. As one critic has remarked, "the appeal of the frontier, nearly one hundred years after it ceased to exist, continues to exert a powerful influence on the beliefs and behavior of Texans" (Pilkington and Graham, p. 95). In Texas-related literature, novels, folklore studies, and biographical accounts there are a substantial number of works that take the cowboy, both historically and in the late twentieth century, as the central type around which the narratives are constructed (for example, E. C. Abbott's account of working on cattle drives *We Pointed Them North* [1939] and Elmer Kelton's *The Wolf and the Buffalo* [1980], a western with an African American hero).

Events in History at the Time the Novel Was Written

Looking south, looking north. The years just prior to the publication of *All the Pretty Horses* were marked by some of the most politically significant events of the late twentieth century, related to the collapse of communism in the Soviet Union and the end of the Cold War, which had dominated the world since the late 1940s, just before McCarthy's novel is set.

In Mexico, the discovery of vast new oil fields in the 1970s triggered a program of vigorous public spending by President López Portillo (in office 1976-82). The mistaken belief that the money brought in from oil sales would be infinite led to some unjustified economic decisions that lost Mexico wealth that the newly tapped resources might have otherwise engendered. After the price of oil fell in 1981, the value of the peso plummeted (from 22 to 70 pesos per dollar in a matter of weeks). The crisis forced Mexico to rely on massive borrowing. Soon inflation was destroying the economic security of Mexicans and the stability of the national currency.

> The old nineteenth-century pattern of the creole elite had renewed itself in a minicycle that encompassed the ruin of the country and the ruined reputation of [President] José López Portillo III. In the nineteenth century, led by Santa Anna, they had lost half the territory of the nation. In the eighth decade of the twentieth century, López Portillo and his train of advisors had mortgaged all of Mexico.
>
> (Krauze, p. 760)

The United States played an important role in the negotiations that rescued Mexico from total bankruptcy. Swallowing this somewhat bitter pill reflected a broader attitude in Mexican society toward the United States: for many Mexicans in the 1980s, the large and powerful neighbor to the north remained both a place where dreams of prosperity could be perhaps turned into reality, and also a reminder of Mexico's relative economic weakness and vulnerability.

All the border crossings. In the 1980s, old tensions over migration that had long dominated the

U.S.-Mexico relationship were complicated by a new point of contention: drugs. Whereas the suspected crime in *All the Pretty Horses*, set in 1950, is horse-stealing, by the time the novel was written illegal drug trafficking had become the central issue. The apparently unstoppable growth in the market for illegal drugs in the United States was fueling a substantial drug production and smuggling economy in South and Central America that sought profit from the northern demand. Wanting to be seen as responsive to voters' fears, U.S. congressmen often painted the Americas outside the United States in lurid tones as an undifferentiated landscape of drug crime, corruption, and anti-American hatred—"narco-terrorism" became a buzz word. Mexicans and others countered that Americans should ask themselves why the demand for drugs was so great at home before accusing others of anything:

> During 1990 . . . 8,000 acres of opium poppy fields were destroyed; 1,500 pounds of heroin and a million pounds of marijuana fields were destroyed; 11,000 drug traffickers were arrested, with 5,000 convicted and 6,000 awaiting trial. . . . Mexicans, who themselves do not as yet face a serious drug abuse problem, consider that these efforts merit praise rather than criticism and are outraged by some U.S. sources' disparagement of Mexico's drug efforts.
>
> (Smith, pp. 102-03)

The divergent perceptions of Mexicans and (Anglo-) Americans have continued to overshadow relations between the two nations.

Reception. The prizes collected by *All the Pretty Horses*—the 1992 National Book Award above all—and the weeks it appeared on bestseller lists, both in the United States and abroad, testify to the novel's critical and commercial success. *All the Pretty Horses* became "that most esteemed of literary creations, a popular novel with serious artistic merit" (Owens, p. xiv). Two contemporary reviews point to what have been singled out as strong suits of McCarthy's novel, its visionary intensity and its use of myth and romance. The *New York Times* reviewer spoke of the complex nature of McCarthy's writing, seeing a lofty purpose to it:

> His project is unlike that of any other writer: to make artifacts composed of human language but detached from a human reference point. The sense of evil that seems to suffuse his novels is illusory; it comes from our discomfort in the presence of a system that is not scaled to ourselves. . . . It is an uncomfortable vision, but one that has a strange power to displace all others.
>
> (Bell, p. 11)

The other key response, represented here by a *Newsweek* review, complimented McCarthy's elegant use of classic motifs of the western:

> This hymn to youth and times past is sweet-tempered but never sentimental, accessible without compromise. . . . A modern-day Western full of horses and gunplay and romance. . . . *All the Pretty Horses* is a true American original.
>
> (Jones, p. 68)

Finally critics reacted to the novel's use of untranslated Spanish dialogue in an English-language work. Some saw it as a sympathetic attempt to reflect the bilingual atmosphere of the American Southwest. Viewing this and other features of the novel as pivotal strengths, José Eduardo Limón has argued that *All the Pretty Horses* reconfigures the genre of the western. He applauds McCarthy, identifying him as "the Mexican from Tennessee" (Limón in Wallach, p. 9).

—Martin Griffin

For More Information

Bell, Madison Smartt. "The Man Who Understood Horses." *New York Times Book Review*, 17 May 1992, 9-11.

Frantz, Joe B. *Texas: A History*. New York: W.W. Norton, 1984.

Frantz, Joe B., and Julian Ernest Choate, Jr. *The American Cowboy: The Myth and the Reality*. Norman: University of Oklahoma Press, 1955.

Howard, Robert West. *The Horse in America*. Chicago: Follett, 1965.

Jones, Malcolm Jr. "Literary Lion in the Desert." *Newsweek*, 18 May 1992, 68.

Kramer, Jane. *The Last Cowboy*. New York: Harper and Row, 1977.

Krauze, Enrique. *Mexico: Biography of Power: A History of Modern Mexico, 1810-1996*. Trans. Hank Heifetz. New York: HarperCollins, 1997.

McCarthy, Cormac. *All the Pretty Horses*. New York: Vintage International, 1993.

Owens, Barclay. *Cormac McCarthy's Western Novels*. Tucson: The University of Arizona Press, 2000.

Paz, Octavio, *The Labyrinth of Solitude: Life and Thought in Mexico*. Trans. Lysander Kemp. New York: Grove, 1961.

Pilkington, William T., and Lee Graham, eds. *The Texas Literary Tradition: Fiction, Folklore, History*. Austin: The University of Texas at Austin, 1983.

Smith, Clint E. *The Disappearing Border: Mexico-United States Relations to the 1990s*. Stanford, Calif.: Stanford Alumni Association, 1992.

Wallach, Rick, ed. *Myth, Legend, Dust: Critical Responses to Cormac McCarthy*. New York: St. Martin's Press, 2000.

Annie John

by
Jamaica Kincaid

THE LITERARY WORK

A *bildungsroman* or coming-of-age novel set in Antigua in the 1950s; published in 1985.

SYNOPSIS

A young girl grows up on the Caribbean island of Antigua. In adolescence, she rebels against the model of middle-class femininity foisted on her and, alienated from family and friends, leaves home for England.

Jamaica Kincaid was born Elaine Potter Richardson on May 25, 1949. She lived with her Dominican homemaker mother and Antiguan carpenter stepfather as an only child until the age of nine when her three brothers were born in quick succession. Kincaid was a precocious child and excelled at her studies, attending Antigua girls' school and then Princess Margaret School, government institutions whose curricula were modeled on the British system of education. At the age of 17, Kincaid left for New York to work as an au pair, then studied photography, attended college in New Hampshire, and began a journalistic career writing articles for magazines. In 1973 she changed her name to Jamaica Kincaid and three years later became a staff writer for the *New Yorker* magazine, a position that would last a decade. In 1983 Kincaid published her first collection of short stories, At the Bottom of the River, which includes some tales that had initially appeared in the New Yorker. She would go on to publish the novels *Annie John* (1985), *Lucy* (1990), and *Autobiography of My Mother* (1994). Kincaid has also produced nonfiction works: *A Small Place* (1988), a savage indictment of both the British colonial legacy in Antigua and the complacency of the post-independence generation of politicians; *My Brother* (1997), a biography of her brother who died of AIDS; and *My Garden* (2000), which not only explores the pleasures and pains of cultivating plants but also the historical effect of imperialism and trade on gardens. Many of Kincaid's written works focus on mothers and mother-daughter relationships, though her 2002 novel, *Mr. Potter,* focuses on fatherhood. In *Annie John,* Kincaid explores her childhood and adolescence in Antigua in the poetic, hypnotic, and deceptively simple prose that has characterized her writing.

Events in History at the Time the Novel Takes Place

Antigua—an overview. Antigua is part of the Leeward chain of Caribbean islands of the Lesser Antilles. Its first inhabitants were the Arawak people, replaced in the twelfth century by the fierce Carib peoples, who held sway over most of the region. In 1493, during his second voyage to the Americas, Christopher Columbus landed on the island and christened it "Santa Maria la Antigua." Together, Carib marauders and a lack of fresh water sources prevented the island from

Jamaica Kincaid

being colonized by Europeans until 1632, when a group of Englishmen arrived from overcrowded St. Kitts Island looking for land. They established a British colony, cultivating tobacco and importing African slaves for plantation labor. In 1674 Sir Christopher Codrington set up the first sugar plantation on Antigua, clearing forests to do so. The neighboring island of Barbuda was colonized in 1678, then leased by Codrington from the British Crown to grow produce for his sugar plantations.

It is difficult to overestimate the impact of the plantation economy on the history of the Caribbean region. Plantation slavery totally transformed the economy and the social complexion of the region. From plantation slavery came a rigidly divisive and hierarchical society, separating inhabitants by color and legal status and persisting even after the abolition of slavery in 1834. The remains of the earlier Arawak and Carib cultures, the transplanted colonial European communities, the importation of (predominantly West) African slaves, the later influx of indentured coolie labor from India and China—all these elements contributed to the island's hybrid mixture of cultures. The mixture would provide rich grist for a writer's mill. Residues of old-country religion, beliefs, traditions, folklore, music, and speech survived in the New World, as reflected in African-inspired practice of *obeah* or *vodun* in some Caribbean islands.

From slavery to political independence. Slavery was abolished on Antigua in 1834. Rather than institute a four-year transitional period, Antigua chose immediate and full emancipation, becoming the only island in the Caribbean to do so. The euphoria that greeted emancipation led to the establishment of "free" villages such as Liberta, Freemansville, and Freetown—communities of newly freed ex-slaves. In theory, the conversion of the slave economy into a wage economy offered the former slaves a measure of freedom. In practice, emancipation made little difference; some of the former slaves even found themselves worse off than before. New laws were enacted to prevent free movement of labor. The island also had little land available for farming, since the sugar plantations monopolized so much territory; meanwhile, other occupations, such as peddling, required special licenses. All these factors conspired to shore up the pre-emancipation status quo, giving the freed slaves little choice but to continue working for their former masters. Poverty and dismal working conditions would continue for the remainder of the nineteenth century, beyond the year 1871, when Antigua united under a common council with the rest of the Leeward Islands.

Continuing into the twentieth century, the economic distress on Antigua led to violence in labor relations here. A labor movement, the Antigua Labour Party, formed in the late 1930s under the leadership of Vere C. Bird helped initiate both political reform and a movement for independence from Britain. In 1932 a pan Caribbean Labour Congress met to lay the foundations for a closer union among all the West Indian islands. Talks on constitutional decolonization began in the mid 1940s, but it was felt that some of the smaller colonies would find political, administrative, and economic independence difficult to sustain. All the discussion led to the idea of a West Indian federation of island states, a proposition accepted in principle by the first conference on such a federation (held in 1947). In 1957 Jamaica, Barbados, Trinidad, the Windward Islands, and the Leeward Islands formed a federal union under the control of Britain. The British initiated talks about the federation, whose members would have a degree of independence but without the power of taxation or control external affairs, which would remained in the hands of Britain's colonial government. A type of halfway house between colonial rule and political independence, the federation failed to introduce significant change. It amounted to little other than the distribution of new colonial grants, the administration of a West Indian regiment and support of the newly created University of the West Indies. The federation collapsed in 1962. Antigua assumed the status of a British associated state in 1967—it was self-governing in all except matters of defense and foreign affairs. In 1981 Antigua and Barbuda as a joint territory became politically independent with Vere Bird as its first Prime Minister. Antigua remains a parliamentary democracy and constitutional monarchy within Britain's Commonwealth of Nations; it has a Governor General (appointed by the Prime Minister) who represents the British Crown, Antigua's designated head of state.

Colonial education and Caribbean writing. British colonialism was all-pervasive in Caribbean cultures, especially in education and literature. Colonial educational policies reflected the legacy of Thomas Macaulay's famous speech "Indian Minute on Education" (1835), which sought to impose English language and literature on native cultures so as to "form a class of persons, Indian [or native] in blood and colour, but English in taste, in opinions, in morals, and in intellect" (Macaulay in Young, p. 729). Residues of pre-Christian religions, folk beliefs, words, and song and dances persisted in colonial society but plantation slavery erased much of African cultures. Educational practices sought to impose an English frame of reference. The English language was the sole means of instruction, and English literary texts were the primary fare for reading. Instructors denigrated Creole languages, (dialects based on a European language but specific to the region), dismissing them as pidgin, broken, or substandard English. Students were exhorted to model their speech patterns on proper British English. The use of Cambridge Syndicate Exams, which assessed the knowledge of Antiguan students by British standards, strengthened the educational links between the "mother country" and her colonial "offspring." *Royal Readers*, widely employed in the primary school curriculum, inculcated English frames of reference, presenting students with English botanical examples, English Kings and Queens, English food and celebrations and even a temperate rather than a tropical climate as norms in life. Ending in the 1950s, the decade in which *Annie John* is set, V. S. Naipaul's classic ***A House for Mr. Biswas*** (also in *Literature and Its Times*), about life in Trinidad, would satirize the absurdity of these educational examples being transferred in unmodified ways to the Caribbean context. Even in the early 1970s, when *Nelson's West Indian Readers* would replace the *Royal Readers*, and make some concessions by using local names and products, literary texts still featured mostly English poets novelists such as John Keats, Rudyard Kipling, Jane Austen, John Donne, Charlotte Brontë, Robert Louis Stevenson, and William Wordsworth.

OBEAH

Like the author's mother and grandmother, Annie John's mother and grandmother are practitioners of obeah. Obeah, and the Haitian form of vodun or voodoo, stems from a shamanistic cult that originates in West Africa. Brought to the Caribbean by slaves, obeah was fused with elements of Christianity. In *Annie John,* as in the genuine belief system, the spirits that populate the obeah world can take different forms. For example, Annie's mother is sometimes described as a snake or a crocodile. Instant transmutations are possible. The dead might come back in life and the sore that took a long time healing on Annie's foot might be the result of a spell placed on her by one of her father's jealous former lovers. It follows, given such a world view, that the transformation of Annie's loving mother into a malevolent stranger takes on an almost literal reality for Annie.

The Novel in Focus

The plot. *Annie John* is an impressionistic account of a young girl's life from the age of 10 to 17. The novel describes her initial close relationship with her mother and charts her progressive alienation from family, friends, and the island she loves. Each of its eight short chapters centers around a central motif, event, or figure in the girl's life that offers insights into her developing mind and personality.

"Figures in the Distance" dwells on death and separation and explores various incidents in the ten-year-old's experience, including the death of acquaintances and friends. Her mother's participation in the rituals of cleaning the corpse of a little girl provokes a reaction of extreme horror in Annie, who for the first time associates her mother with death and separation. Fascinated with dying and laying the body to rest, young Annie even participates in the funeral of someone else, a humpback girl she hardly knows, and later has to lie to her mother about why she did not complete her chores. Annie's curiosity about death and burial takes place against the backdrop of obeah, a hybrid version of West African religion based on traditional beliefs and superstitions. Her Antiguan world is not always benign (as shown by the deaths), nor always rational (as reflected in the practice of obeah); in the world of obeah, things are not necessarily what they seem—the dead, for example, may not remain dead.

"The Circling Hand" explores the close bond between mother and daughter in childhood. From the child's perspective, it offers a portrait of Annie's mother as a strong, nurturing figure whose skills and knowledge inspire pride in her offspring. This blissful state is interrupted at the onset of puberty, when Annie's mother starts demanding that her daughter learn to behave like a young lady, a source of tension that ultimately lead to their separation. Annie recalls how disconcerting her mother's behavior was:

> What a new thing this was for me: my mother's back turned on me in disgust. . . . Before this young-lady business I could sit and think of my mother, see her doing one thing or another, and always her face bore a smile for me. Now I often saw her with the corners of her mouth turned down in disapproval of me.
>
> (Kincaid, *Annie John*, p. 28)

The third and fourth chapters of *Annie John* focus on Annie's friendships at school, firstly, her relationship with Gwen, the model of "young ladyness" and then an unnamed Red Girl, a wild and unruly child who represents all that her mother detests. These two friendships occur against the backdrop of Annie's progressive alienation from her mother. Conversations with Gwen make Annie's eyes widen at how much they resemble each other; Annie speaks of falling in love with Gweneth and of being "inseparable" from her (*Annie John*, p. 46). The red girl, on the other hand, is unkempt, her dress dirty and torn, her fingernails full of dirt and she had "such an unbelievable, wonderful smell, as if she had never taken a bath in her whole life" (*Annie John*, p. 57). Annie dreams of spending her life with the red girl on an uninhabited island, feeding on wild pigs and sea grapes. The two chapters also offer glimpses into the delights and horrors with which young girls view their developing bodies: "What perfection we found in each other, sitting on these tombstones of long dead people who had been masters of our ancestors. . . . Sometimes when we looked at each other, it was all we could not do to cry out with happiness." (*Annie John*, p. 50)

In "Columbus in Chains," Annie's upbringing as a girl in an Antiguan household opens out into a consideration of the wider colonial context of her socialization and education. Annie writes a sarcastic caption in her school history book, satirizing the status of Christopher Columbus as a great man. She is punished for her sins by having to copy out sections of the poem **Paradise Lost** by England's John Milton (*also in* Literature and Its Times).

"Somewhere in Belgium" elaborates on Annie's frustration, alienation, and unhappiness and ascribes to her a heroine's assertiveness and self-determination. At this point, she and her mother lead separate lives, only pretending to be mother and daughter for appearances' sake, "but no sooner were we alone, behind the fence, behind the closed door, then everything darkened. . . . I had never loved anyone so or hated anyone so" (*Annie John*, p. 88). "The Long Rain" chronicles Annie's lengthy illness and serves as a prelude to her eventual emergence as a fully independent and self-reliant woman. Introduced is the character of Ma Chess, Annie's grandmother, an obeah woman who lifts Annie out of her depression and illness. Ma Chess becomes a mother substitute: "I would lie on my side, curled up like a little comma, and Ma Chess would lie next to me, curled up like a bigger comma into which I fit" (*Annie John,* p. 120). Annie's separation from her mother, and all that her mother represents, is complete by the end of the book. The circling hand of her mother and her environment that earlier had seemed blissfully protective is now regarded as constrictive. But Annie's anger still rages over what she sees as her mother's betrayal:

> Why, I wonder, didn't I see the hypocrite in my mother when, over the years, she said that she loved me and could hardly live without me, while at the same time proposing and arranging separation after separation, including this one [her departure for England to study nursing], which unbeknownst to her, *I* have arranged to be permanent? So not I, too, have hypocrisy, and breasts (small ones), and hair growing in appropriate places, and sharp eyes, and I have made a vow never to be fooled again.
>
> (*Annie John,* p. 133)

Mothers and daughters. *Annie John* is written in first person from the daughter's point of view. No other voice is offered in the novel. Consequently, readers share all the passion of the young girl's experiences, from her early happy relationship with her mother to her later angry and rebellious responses based on what she reads as her mother's betrayal of her love and trust. Most of the novel is in the past tense. The exception occurs in the final chapter, written in the present tense, as if Annie, on the point of departure, is narrating the tale of her emergence as a young woman.

In the first section of the novel, Annie's mother is portrayed as a figure who fulfils her daughter's every need and desire. The child Annie is valued and protected. Every aspect of her is depicted as special to her mother. Small items of childhood memorabilia are preserved in a trunk and brought out periodically, as part of a ritualized, loving recollection of shared experiences and emotions. Annie feels also included in all aspects of her mother's daily life, from the mundane daily routines of shopping, cooking, and washing to the more esoteric aspects of obeah rituals, such as the special baths they take together to fortify themselves against potentially hostile forces. Annie—who spares no opportunity to dwell on her mother's abilities, beauty, and wisdom—desires nothing less than to be like her mother, often wearing dresses that are an exact copy of her mother's. Even their two names are identical. The portrait is very much that of an intense form of love, with the mother's evident adoration of Annie mirrored by the child's feeling for her mother.

Such a close-knit mother-daughter relationship is in many ways typical of how psychologists spoke of the female child around the time of the novel's publication, describing a daughter's perception of her mother at this stage as either all powerful (the "phallic" mother) or powerless (the "castrated" female). In the former instance, the daughter may find it difficult to separate from her mother, finding her so omnipotent and overwhelming that the daughter has difficulty establishing her own identity. In hindsight, Annie renders an account of her mother that shows how such an encircling arm can feel constrictive and be detrimental to the daughter's development. Psychoanalysts such as Luce Irigary have noted that a mother-daughter relationship can be destructive as well as mutually supportive. Nancy Chodorow has added a cultured understanding by insisting that one should take into account the social context of mothering. When looking after children is culturally sanctioned as primarily a mother's responsibility, and when it becomes the main outlet for expressing a woman's identity, then, argues Chodorow, a woman is likely to invest much more energy in the upbringing of her children

Antigua, Kincaid's birthplace and the setting for the work.

and may look to them exclusively for her own sense of self-worth (Chodorow, pp. 64, 208-9, 212-15). In such a situation, the boundaries between mother and daughter may be more blurred than is beneficial for both; the two may enter into an unhealthy relationship of mutual and child-like dependency and identification.

In Antigua, as elsewhere in Western middle-class society around the time the novel takes place, there was an insistence on the domestic sphere as the proper place for women, which gave Annie's mother and those like her few outlets in life and encouraged their keeping a tight grip on their children. Speaking of her own mother, Kincaid reflects on "the sort of benign, marvellous, innocent moment you have with the great powerful person who, you then realise won't let you go" (Kincaid, *From Antigua to America*, p. 147). Edith Clarke's famous 1957 study of family relations in Jamaican society, *My Mother Who Fathered Me*, lends support to this way of understanding *Annie John*. Clarke describes a pattern of mother-child relationships in the Caribbean that are intense and involving. Clarke's estimation of Caribbean society in the 1950s was that it was by and large patriarchal; men had not only greater roles in public political life, but also enjoyed greater social and sexual freedom. What Clarke discovered was a pattern of woman-centered households in working class Jamaica; the extra-familial and extra-marital relationships of men encouraged their absence from the household. Sexual promiscuity, while seen as a hallmark of virility in men, was frowned upon in women. Meanwhile, child rearing was almost exclusively the responsibility of women so motherhood was of huge significance, with well-brought up children earning women a great deal of praise. The closeness and intensity of the mother-child relationship could be broken by the child's entry into the education system; going to school instituted a rift in what was largely a seamless companionship between mother and child. Annie's development away from her mother begins with her attendance at school and her transfer of affection to girls in her peer group.

Further complications result from Annie's coming of age. Suddenly her mother is a stranger bent on turning her into a young woman who conforms to Antigua's middle-class ideals of femininity and respectability. Annie's manners and behaviors are scrutinized and policed lest she be taken as an unruly child or loose woman. Annie must learn all the social graces of the proper lady. Any departure from this ideal—playing marbles or talking in a free manner with boys—incurs keen displeasure and angry warnings from her mother that her daughter is turning into a "slut" (*Annie John*, p. 102). What is significant about this accusation is that Annie's mother's anxieties about her daughter crystallize around her child's developing sexuality. Another scene in the novel also lends support to such a psychoanalytic reading. Annie's awareness of her parents' sexuality when she stumbles on their love-making is the scene of another quarrel with her beloved mother that leads to mutual antagonism. During her illness, in a bout of fever, Annie wakes up and tries to wash off what seems like dirt on some family photographs. When she finally wakes from her delirium, she finds that her attempts to clean the photographs have resulted not only in her rubbing out of the image of her father and her mother from waist down, but also in the erasure of her own body image. This important scene in the book can be read as indicative of Annie's attempt to avoid confronting her own growing sexual development and to return to a state of infantile sexual ignorance. Annie's desire to erase her sexual knowledge symbolizes an unconscious desire to return to the blissful state of childhood where, in her own mind, mother and daughter relations were perfectly harmonious.

Columbus in chains. If Annie rebels against being a well-behaved girl, her rebellion is also directed at an education and curriculum that is a product of British colonialism. The chapter "Columbus in Chains" dwells on Annie's mother's trust and investment in the school and its colonial curriculum. Annie's socialization as a young girl bears the stamp of a colonizing England whose codes of respectability her mother has adopted. Annie is made to eat big English-style breakfasts because they are deemed good for her. Instinctively the daughter is more aware than her mother of who the daughter is, and who she is being asked to become. Annie proves to be the more canny judge of colonial influence; she prefers new plain exercise books to the older ones adorned with the picture of Queen Victoria, and resists the conventional veneration of Columbus and his heirs by figuring out that their ascendancy has contributed to the slavery of her ancestors. Her observation that the school's dunce cap can sometimes, ironically, seem like a coronet if seen from a certain angle of sunlight suggests that she manages to penetrate the pomp and splendor of empire to reach the colonial subjugation behind it. Finally, her remarks that it was difficult to tell whether one belonged on the side of the colonial masters or slaves from the English lessons to which she was subjected, shows just how damaging colonial education could be to the colonized. Annie's anger is in many ways directed at the betrayal and treachery of her mother *and* a colonial system that pretends to educate the girl for her own good but in reality robs her of her own identity.

Sources and literary context. Kincaid drew on a combination of sources to create *Annie John*, including canonical English works. Not unlike mother-daughter relations, Jamaica Kincaid is aware that the literary legacy of colonialism is an ambivalent one. Annie must copy out Books 1 and 2 of the thoroughly English poem *Paradise Lost* as punishment, but her identification with the rebel figure of Lucifer affords her some understanding of her own state of mind. *Annie John* also uses biblical references to great effect, picturing childhood as a kind of paradise, for example, and comparing her exile from Antigua to the exile from the Garden of Eden. Sometimes her mother is associated with the Garden's serpent, and other times, the innocence of childhood is juxtaposed to serpentlike forces that threaten her (and her mother's) youth. An English novel that has a significant impact on *Annie John* is Charlotte Brontë's ***Jane Eyre*** (also in *Literature and Its Times*). Annie sees her own struggle as not unlike that of Brontë's heroine and even daydreams about Belgium, a place in which Brontë herself spent some time, as a place of refuge. Unsurprisingly, *Jane Eyre* was one of Kincaid's favorite books as a child.

Among Caribbean writings, *Annie John* takes its place as one of a recent stream of works by women from the region. Critic and novelist George Lamming argues that the colonial importation of Englishness had severe consequences for Caribbean writers. First, it threatened to perpetuate colonial structures by grafting English views onto a "native" elite; second, it undermined the growth of a body of independent Caribbean writings by alienating writers from their locale and robbing them of an audience for such writings. Not only did people read the books written by English authors but only they were considered real writers. In this literary and educational climate, the indigenous writer had very little chance to establish himself or herself. The lack of a ready audience, as well as the scarcity of opportunities to publish in the Caribbean, contributed to the self-imposed exile of many Caribbean writers. A collection of prominent writers appeared in Britain, particularly in the post World War II era. The well-known authors of that generation—George Lamming, V. S. Naipaul, Sam Selvon, Wilson Harris, Jan Carew, and Andrew Salkey—met with a warm reception from English publishers and readers, so warm that Caribbean critic Ken Ramchand bemoaned London in the years after World War II as "indisputably the West Indian literary capital" (Ramchand, p. 63).

The stellar success of the postwar male writers has in many ways obscured the presence of female Caribbean writers, such as Una Marson, Sylvia Wynter, Phyllis Shand Allfrey, Gloria Escoffery, Beryl Gilroy, and Jean Rhys (whose ***Wide Sargasso Sea*** is also in *Literature and Its Times*). Until recently works by these writers have suffered critical neglect. Publishers and outlets such as the BBC Caribbean Voices broadcast programme, key in the encouragement of Caribbean writing, tended to veer away from the domestic subjects that was the focus of some women's writing. In her memoirs, Beryl Gilroy, who migrated to London in the 1950s but was published only in the 1980s, observed that the camaraderie of male writers, publishers and their advisers did not easily extend to women like herself, whose writing publishers considered "too psychological, strange, way-out, difficult to categorise" (Gilroy in *Anim-Addo*, pp. 211-13). Not until the 1970s and '80s did Caribbean women command a presence in mainstream publishing.

Annie John can be situated as part of a wave of Caribbean women's writing that entered the mainstream in the 1970s and 1980s. It keeps company with works by Gilroy and others (Merle Hodge, Lorna Goodison, Olive Senior, Grace Nichols, Jean Binta Breeze, Erna Brodber), who share an overriding concern with portraying the distinctiveness of women's experiences. Their works explore how women's identities, sexualities, lives, and experiences have been shaped, not only by colonial history, but also by the predominantly patriarchal biases of Caribbean culture. Many commentators have observed that much of the women's literature of this period is autobiographic and concerned especially with the domestic spaces of women's lives: motherhood, the rituals of child-rearing, storytelling, woman-focused religious practices like obeah, grandmother and motherly ancestral tales, myth and folklore, oral traditions and songs that are passed down by maternal-figures. Noteworthy examples of such bildungsroman include Merle Hodge's ground breaking *Crick Crack Monkey* (1970) and Merle Collin's *Angel* (1987).

Events in History at the Time the Novel Was Written

The personal as political. Some recent readings of *Annie John*, regard Annie's mother as both the agent of colonialism and also of patriarchy, or male-dominated society. There is much evidence to support this understanding in Kincaid's memories about her childhood, and in her account of her own fraught relations with her mother. Kincaid's "On seeing England for the first time" is an angry autobiographic essay on how the veneration of all things English pervaded every aspect of her childhood, from breakfast foods, to the way one held one's fork to eat peas, to the use of language and the biased teaching of history, geography, and literature. The impact of such colonial influence was to make her feel small and powerless because she was not, and could never be English. Asked if her novels are autobiographic, Kincaid has responded by saying that her development as a writer whose fiction touches on broader issues is intimately bound up with her personal psychology:

> It dawned on me that in figuring out the relationship between the girl and her mother, and observing the power of the mother, and eventually her waning authority, that it was leading me to a fictional view of the larger relationship between where I come from and England. I

> must have consciously viewed my personal relationship as a sort of prototype of the larger, social relationship that I had witnessed.
> (Kincaid, "From Antigua to America," p. 144)

All of Kincaid's works have this autobiographic element. An event, incident, or relationship, is to be viewed allegorically—as an expression, for example, of the unequal power structures in contemporary society, whether it be colonial or male-dominated, or both. She herself has acknowledged her particular tendency to focus on "women's things," to "reduce everything to a domestic situation" as a means to understand the world around her (Kincaid in Simmons, p. 19).

A SIMPLE WRITING STYLE?

The house we live in my father built with his own hands. The bed I am laying in my father built with his own hands. . . . The sheets on my bed my mother made with her own hands. The curtain hanging at my window my mother made with her own hands. The nightie I am wearing, with scalloped neck and hem and sleeves, my mother made with her own hands. When I look at things in a certain way, I suppose I should say that the two of them made me with their own hands. . . . Lying in my bed for the last time, I thought, This is what I add up to.

(*Annie John*, pp. 132-33)

Kincaid weaves her tales from clear, precise, simple prose and makes strategic use of repetitions, especially phrases, sentences or incidents that reappear as motifs in a story. Often Kincaid's rhythmic repetitions have a very hypnotic quality and act to draw the reader into the mind of its first-person-narrator. The repetition of "built with his [or her] own hands" in the last chapter of the novel conveys to the reader the all-encompassing and oppressive nature of parental presence and control. Introduced into this repetition and contrasted to it is the assertive use of the personal pronoun, I. Setting the child against the parents, rendering more keenly the girl's single-minded determination to flee them and her island home.

Hence all of Kincaid's novels work on multiple levels. In *Annie John,* her critique of the specific socialization of young girls is also a critique of the larger colonial relationship between Britain and Antigua. Her depiction of motherly betrayal is also that of what she deems the sham idealism of the colonizers, the betrayal of the just and enlightened society that British imperialists pretend to offer the colonized.

The colonial orientation of the 1950s Caribbean educational curriculum largely gave way to a more solidly Caribbean-focused curriculum, beginning in the 1980s. In terms of literary culture, writers from the region are now widely taught in institutions from primary to tertiary levels, reflecting the present stature and importance of Caribbean writers in world literatures. But critics like Tiffin argue that the history of education in the Caribbean is still one of persistent "Anglo-control and Anglo-orientation"; lessons might reflect a greater preoccupation with local matters but entrants to the University of the West Indies in the 1990s were still required to submit a Cambridge "controlled" English exam paper. (Tiffin, p. 47). The situation is similar with respect to language. Educators and linguists now recognize Creole languages as part of a Caribbean language continuum that encompasses both vernacular dialects and Standard English, and Caribbean writers have been employing these variations and nuances of language creatively. Yet Standard English is still the language of formal instruction, and how well one speaks and writes it is used as an effective indicator of class and educational level. The interest in Caribbean women's writing overlapped with the rise of women's movements both in the Caribbean and in the developed Western world in the 1970s. Within the Caribbean, the movement has given rise to women's resource and research centers within institutions of higher learning and to a rich body of sociological and anthropological studies on women, men, and gender relationships. While refusing to be identified as a feminist writer, Kincaid has admitted that a lot of her initial success as a writer is due to the rise of feminism (Kincaid, "Jamaica Kincaid and the Modernist project," p. 401).

Reception. Many of the early reviews of *Annie John* focused exclusively on it as a novel about mothers and daughters rather than one about postcolonial issues (De Abruna in Bloom, p. 26). A critic for the *New York Times Book Review* regarded Kincaid's coming-of-age story as timeless, a "touching and familiar" tale whose lessons about being a daughter can be extended to all cultures and societies (the *New York Times Book Review*, p. 24). Similarly, a *New Statesman* reviewer described *Annie John* as an "evocative idyll of childhood and budding womanhood" that details the "inevitable betrayals" by the mother of the daughter at the onset of puberty (*New Statesman*, p. 30). Many critics write approvingly of the simplicity of Kincaid's writing and find her portrait of Caribbean culture charming. A reviewer for the *Village Voice Literary Supplement* noted the hypnotic quality of Kincaid's writing style, asserting that "her language recalls Henri Rousseau's painting: seemingly natural, but in reality sophisticated and precise" (*Village Voice Literary Supplement*, p. 7). Such observations smack of a certain fascination with exoticism, the exotic mystery and thrill that non-Western societies represent to Western critics. Showing appreciation for the balance her novel strikes, the London *Times* complimented Kincaid's writing style and its "evocative clarity, which make her "universal and well-explored theme" distinctive (*Times Literary Supplement*, p. 1,374).

—Gail Low

For More Information

Anim-Addo, Joan. *Leaves in the Wind: Collected Writings of Beryl Gilroy*. London: Mango, 1998.

Bloom, Harold. ed. *Jamaica Kincaid*. Philadelphia: Chelsea House, 1998.

Chodorow, Nancy J. *The Reproduction of Mothering*. Berkeley, Calif.; London: University of California Press, 1979.

Dyde, Brian. *A History of Antigua*. London: Macmillan Education, 2000.

Kincaid, Jamaica. *Annie John*. London: Vintage, 1997.

———. "Jamaica Kincaid and the Modernist Project." Interview by Selwyn R Cudjoe. *Callaloo* 12 (spring 1989): 396-411.

———. "From Antigua to America: An Interview." In *Frontiers of Caribbean Literature in English*. London: Macmillan Caribbean, 1996.

Lamming, George. *The Pleasures of Exile*. London: Michael Joseph, 1960.

Ramchand, Kenneth. *The West Indian Novel and Its Background*. London: Faber, 1970.

Review of *Annie John*, by Jamaica Kincaid. *New Statesman*, 20 September 1985, 30.

Review of *Annie John*, by Jamaica Kincaid. *New York Times Book Review*, 25 May 1986, 24.

Review of *At the Bottom of the River* and *Annie John*, by Jamaica Kincaid. *Times Literary Supplement*, 29 November 1985.

Review of *Annie John*, by Jamaica Kincaid. *Village Voice Literary Supplement*, April 1985.

Simmons, Diane. *Jamaica Kincaid*. New York: Twayne, 1994.

Tiffin, Helen, "The Institution of Literature." In *A History of Literature in the Caribbean*. Vol. 2. Amsterdam: John Benjamins, 2001.

Young, G. M., ed. *Macaulay Prose and Poetry*. Cambridge, Mass: Harvard University Press, 1957.

The Antelope Wife

by

Louise Erdrich

An enrolled member of the Turtle Mountain Ojibwe, Louise Erdrich was born in Minnesota in 1954 and grew up in North Dakota, where her Ojibwe-French mother and German-American father were teachers at the Wahpeton Indian Boarding School. Before earning a master's degree in writing from Johns Hopkins University, Erdrich became a member of both the first Dartmouth College class to include women and the first group of students recruited to its fledgling American Indian Studies program. She launched her literary career in 1984 with ***Love Medicine*** (also in *Literature and Its Times*), which focuses on two interconnected Ojibwe families with homes on the reservation. An award-winning novel, it became the first in a series of four related works about Indian families on and near the reservation in North Dakota. Her sixth novel, *The Antelope Wife*, moves to urban Minneapolis, where the Indian spirit-world permeates the present and the actions of extended family members hark back to the past.

THE LITERARY WORK

A novel set near the North Dakota-Minnesota border sometime after the Civil War and also set in Minneapolis, Minnesota during the late 1990s; published in 1998.

SYNOPSIS

A U.S. cavalryman adopts a baby he has rescued during a slaughter at an Ojibwe Indian village. His actions, and those of the baby's grief-stricken mother, form a mythical-historical backdrop to family relations in modern-day Minneapolis.

Events in History at the Time of the Novel

The Ojibwe people. Called various names, the Ojibwe are known also as Ojibway, Otchipwe, Chippewa, Chippeway, Anishinaabe, Mississauga and Salteaux. Historically the group called themselves Anishinabe (plural Anishinabeg) after the language they spoke. Having mostly escaped removal to areas further west, the Ojibwe remain in their ancestral lands, which stretch across the northern Great Lakes region of the United States and Canada westward to present-day Montana and Saskatchewan. More than 100,000 Ojibwe lived in the United States in 1990, forming the third largest American Indian people. The group consists of assorted bands, who share the same native language and customary behaviors. Never have the bands united into an organized whole. Originally they were organized into discrete groups of families bound by kinship. Everyone also belonged to a totemic clan, whose members had to marry outside the clan. Society was patrilineal—when a man and woman married, the woman joined her husband's clan. Grandparents and grandchildren had a special relationship, as do Cally and her grandmother Zosie in Erdrich's novel. Ojibwe life involved woodland gathering (of wild rice, maple

Louise Erdrich

and sugar) and hunting (for fish, deer and beaver). During the seventeenth and eighteenth centuries, the woodland Ojibwe became deeply involved in the fur trade with the French and British, who exchanged manufactured goods, such as firearms, metal implements, beads, cloth, and alcohol for furs, mostly beaver. Besides depleting the fur-bearing animals, trading had numerous social repercussions for the Ojibwe, causing extensive intermarriage, especially with the French. Some of the westernmost bands practiced a few different customs. For example, the Turtle Mountain Band in North Dakota and the Little Shell Band of Montana took up buffalo hunting on the Great Plains. Significantly for the novel, antelope ranged with the buffalo on the Plains.

Religion was a daily presence in traditional life. Manitous (spirits) inhabited rocks, trees, animals, and the earth and sky; Kitchi-Manitou, the Great Mystery, presided over all the lesser spirits. While most manitous were benign, malicious ones existed too, including cannibalistic giants called Windigos (associated with winter and starvation). Of special significance in Ojibwe culture, dreams were regularly interpreted for their significance. A namer would be selected for each child soon after birth. Guided by a dream, this person bestowed a sacred name and an associated benefit or power on the child. Later in adolescence, dreams gained a new importance. Teenagers sought to have dream visions, then bring them into reality with the help of a special talent, which would likewise be discovered through a vision. In the novel, young Cally has a pivotal vision that proves vital to her search for identity in 1990s Minneapolis.

Post-Civil War Indian policy. By the end of the Civil War, one of the only areas in the western United States not entirely open to white settlers was Indian Territory (present-day Oklahoma). Continuing native resistance to white incursions prompted debate over the best Indian policy to pursue: should the United States "feed" or "fight" the Indians? The U.S. Indian Service argued for feeding them on the grounds of economy and humaneness, and Congress agreed. It would be cheaper to subdue resistance by negotiating the fulfillment of treaty commitments than by continued warfare. The decision led to the establishment of a peace commission in 1867, charged with convincing Indians to move onto reservations and the mandate to use volunteer troops to force compliance if persuasion failed. This approach to Indian affairs, known as the Peace Policy, drove the remains of tribal nations onto reservations in pursuit of the official goal—assimilating them into mainstream American culture. Intended to create dependence on mainstream modes of existence, the strategy of assimilation entailed the destruction of traditional Indian ways—for example, the age-old Indian custom, practiced by the Ojibwe, of hunting wild game for food. White settlers in the region during the post-Civil War era slaughtered buffalo and antelope, which coincided well with an effort on the part of U.S. authorities to destroy

GLASS BEADWORK

French fur traders brought glass beads to North America in the early seventeenth century, when they established trading posts in Quebec. The glass beads quickly found their way into native American artistry. Initially the beads were thought to have magical properties, which helps explain the name the Ojibwe gave to the item: "the word for beads in the old language is manidominenz, little spirit seed" (Erdrich, *The Antelope Wife*, p. 91). The inspiration for decorative art, the glass beads replaced porcupine quills used in native American quillwork.

the subsistence base of Indian peoples and force them onto reservations: "Sportsmen shot the beasts from train windows. Railroad crews ate the meat. . . . And demand for buffalo bones for fertilizer and hides for robes and shoes encouraged" the slaughter (Nash, p. 588). Depleting the wild game and confining the tribes to reservations made them vulnerable to other forms of coercion too. Attendees of the Lake Mohonk Conference in 1890 plainly discussed starvation as a strategy to compel tribal people to accept white ways:

> *Question:* If the rations were stopped, the people would starve, you say. If they cannot be taught [to farm and raise stock] until they starve, what would you do?
> *Mr. Riggs:* I fear we should practically have to starve them until we got them taught.
> (*Proceedings of the Lake Mohonk Conference* in Wub-e-ke-niew, p. 57)

What emotional effect did the forced removals, erosion of traditional lifeways, and starvation have on the Indians? The policies engendered a desperation that in part accounted for the enormous appeal of the Ghost Dance religion, which took hold among various Indian nations, in a fervor that swept the country during the 1870s and again in the 1890s. Founded by a Paiute Indian named Wodziwob in the late 1860s and revived by Wovoka, another Paiute, two decades later, the Ghost Dance was a religious ceremony centered on circular dancing, with the aim of resurrecting dead ancestors and restoring lost lands and animals. Wovoka's followers included the Dakota Sioux, who took up the Ghost Dance on reservations during a time of widespread hunger. Although U.S. agents had promised to increase rations in exchange for the Indians's consent to a reduction in their landholdings and the creation of six separate reservations, rations were cut precipitously. U.S. officials grew alarmed as thousands left the reservation and took up ghost dancing in hopes of bringing back their loved ones, the buffalo, and the old lifestyle, and of making the whites, who had destroyed this lifestyle, disappear.

In December 1890, a surrendering band of ghost dancers led by a Minneconjou Sioux chief, Big Foot, was massacred by the U.S. Cavalry at Wounded Knee Creek. The massacre led to the deaths of a confirmed 153, but a more likely total of close to 300, mostly Sioux women and children. The opening action of *The Antelope Wife* invokes this era of violence: Scranton Roy's U.S. Cavalry unit attacks an Ojibwe village because they mistake it "for [a] hostile [camp] during the scare over the starving Sioux" (*Antelope Wife*, p. 3).

Allotment. In a discussion of Indian policy that took place in Washington D.C. in 1891, just days after the Wounded Knee massacre, Captain Richard Henry offered his opinion on what should be done to resolve the "Indian question": "every plan should have in view the idea of separating the Indian from his tribe," he said; "The Indian tribes can be and *ought to be made to disappear*" (Pratt in Wub-e-ke-niew, p. 58). Pratt's view both reflected and shaped U.S. Indian policy of the period, which sought tribal submission through a new form of cultural destruction. The General Allotment Act (Dawes Act) of 1887 aimed to ingrain in Indians notions of private rather than collective property and destroy group relationships to the land. The Act broke up shared tribal holdings, then granted 40 to 160 acre parcels to heads of families and other individuals, also conferring U.S. citizenship on them.

To implement the Dawes Act, federal agents had to compile formal membership rolls for each tribal group living on a reservation. Although the act itself did not specify membership criteria, authorities defined tribal membership along racial lines. They disregarded traditionally inclusive tribal methods of determining group membership, which took into account not only heredity but also cultural practices, such as intermarriage and outright adoption. In contrast, federal agents implementing the Dawes Act used biology to identify who was Indian. Generally only those who could prove at least one-quarter-blood—and more often half-blood—ancestry of a particular Indian people were eligible to receive land. Large numbers of mixed-bloods were thereby denied both land and federal recognition of their tribal identities. In the case of the Ojibwe, many had difficulty meeting blood quotas because of heavy intermarriage with the French as a legacy of the fur trade. Not only did such realities inspire resentment against white authorities; the policy also caused resentment within the tribal community as to definition of Indians.

Further divisiveness resulted from a second policy. The authorities issued land deeds outright to those with some measure of white blood but held onto deeds for full-bloods, stipulating that these grants were to be administered by federal agents. Such favoritism toward mixed-bloods led to bitterness against them and, in extreme circumstances, to the attempted expulsion of mixed-bloods from tribal societies.

In the end, allotment created more damage than just reducing tribal land holdings (which it did by 65 percent, with the "surplus" opened to other uses, including homesteading by whites). It also created deep ruptures with formerly inclusive tribal societies.

Boarding schools. To enact the policy of forced acculturation, U.S. officials concentrated on young as well as adult members of Indian tribes. Education became the forum for reaching the young, or more exactly, the Indian boarding school. The same Captain Pratt who wanted to extinguish the existence of tribes came up with a practical means of doing so. He founded the Carlisle Indian School from a former military base in Pennsylvania in 1879, his aim being to "kill the Indian and save the man" in each student. At boarding schools, children were isolated from their families for several years at a time, forced to accept Christianity, and forbidden from speaking their own language or wearing customary dress. *The Antelope Wife* brings to mind these dictates of the missionary-run boarding schools in the naming of twin daughters. Left behind by their mother "to the chances of baptism," they are named Mary, "after the good blue-robed woman [mother of Jesus], and Josephette, for the good husband. Only the Ojibwa tongue made Zosie of the latter name. Zosie. Mary" (*Antelope Wife*, p. 15). The boarding school strategy seemed to U.S. authorities to be a wise one, and, following Pratt's example, they embraced it. By the late 1920s, less than 20 percent of native children were receiving traditional upbringing outside the boarding schools. Dr. Lyman Abbott articulated the rationale for boarding school policy in this keynote address at the Mohonk conference in 1888 "Education for the Indian": "Schools are less expensive than war. It costs less to educate an Indian than it does to shoot him" (Abbott in Wub-e-ke-niew, p. 109).

From reorganization to termination and relocation. By the 1930s, strict assimilation policies had been relaxed in favor of keeping remaining tribal lands in trust for the tribes. In response to the reformist efforts of John Collier, Commissioner of Indian Affairs from 1933-45, the U.S. government reversed itself on many elements of Indian policy and passed the Indian Reorganization Act (IRA) of 1934. Presented positively as native self-government and the "Indian New Deal," the Act nevertheless was criticized by some as having a negative effect on traditional ways. It replaced the remains of existing traditional tribal governments with new tribal constitutions and governments patterned on Euro-American models. Each of these new governments was to become "an agency and instrumentality of the Federal Government" (Collier in Wub-e-ke-niew, pp. 138-39). While each reorganized reservation had to prepare and ratify its new constitution, the process had the effect of codifying the views of those who had been educated at Indian boarding schools in English and Euro-American ideas and values at the expense of the views of traditionalists who spoke only their native language and operated on the basis of native standards and definitions. For example, the constitutions defined tribal membership in terms of blood quotas, transferring to tribal documents the fractional blood requirements that originated in U.S. government documents. Federal policy would change yet again. In 1948 the Hoover Commission declared that assimilation should once more be the goal of federal policy towards Indians. Conservative congressmen pressed for cost-cutting measures such as the termination of federal ties to Indian communities and an end to federal support for tribal governments. At the same time, the "heirship problem" became evident. Individual allotments of land to federally recognized Indians diminished in size, becoming so divided by inheritance that many proved too small to be usable. In *The Antelope Wife*, Cally's twin grandmothers, Mary and Zosie, share such a tract on the "reservation homestead" in northern Minnesota, "the old allotment that belonged to their mother" (*Antelope Wife*, p. 198). Now the authorities faced a new question—how could Indians support themselves on plots that were so small?

In response to renewed support for the policy of assimilation and to the perceived problem of a "surplus" Indian population, the U.S. Congress implemented two new policies—termination and relocation. The Termination Act of 1954 ended the trust relationship between tribal people and the U.S. government. While the Act terminated federal control of more than 100 tribes and bands, it also ended official recognition of and support for these tribes and bands. The federal government meanwhile initiated an intensive effort to relocate people from reservations to urban areas. But there was confusion over which agencies were required to provide social, economic, and educational services for those who relocated and little infrastructure in place to furnish these services. The Bureau of Indian Affairs failed to take responsibility for the needs of relocatees until the U.S. Supreme Court forced the

Bureau to do so a couple of decades later. By this time, U.S. policy had again changed. The newest strategy, still in use, called for the U.S. government to transfer control of Indian services to Indian peoples themselves while continuing to pay for these services.

Urbanization and the Minneapolis Ojibwe. The effect of termination and relocation was to create large urban populations of American Indians. In 1900, 90 percent of federally recognized Indians lived on reservations; by the late 1990s only about 33 percent did. Although the U.S. government chose not to target the Twin Cities of Minneapolis and St. Paul as an official destination for federal relocation efforts (precisely because the area was close to so many reservations), many Ojibwe moved there in the post-World War II years. By the last decade of the century, almost 48,000 Ojibwe were members of the seven Ojibwe reservations in Minnesota (1993). Meanwhile, almost 24,000 Indians of any type lived in the metropolitan area of the Twin Cities, over 12,000 within the city limits of Minneapolis (1990). Indeed, most of these metropolitan-area Indians are Ojibwe. Included are many intermittent residents who travel periodically between the urban centers and the reservations. City life, in the minds and hearts of many of the relocatees, left much to be desired. The first decade of relocation, the 1950s, saw nearly half the migrants return to reservations.

Those who remained in the cities had to face a number of problems: joblessness, extreme poverty, alienation, social ostracism, racism, and physical violence. First the migrants had to adjust to separation from their larger Indian communities (which included not only members of immediate and extended families but animals, plants, and the land). Second they were faced more directly than before with values such as individualism, which conflicted with traditional tribal belief systems. The experience left the Indians disoriented, especially in the 1950s. Outside the reservation environment, many refrained from passing on old customs to their children. Many parents were themselves children of the repressive boarding-school system. Now their foremost aim was to protect their children from inequities that they had suffered; to this end, they did not pass on traditional knowledge.

How their children experienced this silence, according to one researcher who interviewed urban-raised Anishinaabe (Chippewa, Ottawa, and Potawatomi) people living in an undisclosed Great Lakes city, was with "confusion and frustration at their parents' reluctance, unwillingness, or inability to really speak about being Indian" (Jackson, p. 192). When this silence was combined with the fact that urban Indians were often separated from other members of their culture, and thereby denied access to tribal knowledge and traditional practices, members of the urban-raised generation experienced a sense of longing and loss:

> The majority of us [city-raised Indian people] walk around with this hole in our heart. We know we're different, that there's a piece of our life that is missing. And once we can [find out] what's missing, and fill that hole ourselves, then we see a whole person emerge. We start asking questions, and we become these enormous sponges, and we just want to absorb, absorb, absorb. And it fills that hole.
>
> (Duncan in Jackson, p. 195)

The pain of cultural loss has contributed to disproportionately high rates of suicide and alcoholism in American Indian communities, both of the post-World War II generation and later generations. Between the mid-1960s and the late 1980s, American Indian suicide rates almost tripled; urban suicide rates were the highest. A 1996 article reported the involvement of alcohol in an estimated 75 percent of suicides by American Indians; rates of death attributed to alcoholism among Indians ranged from three to thirty-one times as many as those of the general U.S. population (May, pp. 246-47). These alarming rates can ultimately be traced back to the social, cultural, and economic legacy of colonization and more than 200 years of shifting federal Indian policy. As one urban Anishinaabe woman from the Great Lakes region explains, her father's alcoholism was a consequence of his self-denial, and his self-denial stemmed from humiliation at the punishment he received—such as beatings for speaking his native language in Indian boarding school—"for being who he was":

> My father was an alcoholic. A very sad man. Even though he tried not to be. And I understand now that it was because he was denying who he was. He was denying who his children were. And there was a lot of anger he suppressed over the years. And to get rid of that anger, he drank. And my father got in many fights [with co-workers], because they would call him "Chief," or they would make derogatory comments. . . .
>
> (Duncan in Jackson, p. 198)

American Indian children, like the two young boys shown here in boarding-school uniforms, were subjected to forced acculturation as part of U.S. policy after the Civil War.

Efforts to heal these cultural wounds have been underway in Minneapolis since the first half of the twentieth century and have gained momentum since. Aside from giving Indians more control over the programs that benefited them, federal Indian policy after the 1960s increased federal support for Indian services. Cities saw pan-Indian groups gain control over the administration of community programs. In keeping with this trend, American Indians in Minneapolis founded such institutions as the Upper Midwest Indian Center (1954); the American Indian Movement (1968); the Heart of the Earth Survival School and Red School House (founded by Indian parents and the American Indian Movement in 1971); and the Minneapolis American Indian Center (1975). Many actively participate in powwows, which are pan-tribal social events based on group singing and social dancing. The powwow circuit, made up of numerous powwows which are held at various locations and times of the year, continues to provide a bridge between different tribal cultures and between members of reservation and urban communities. The survival schools of contemporary Minneapolis provide an educational forum that encourages urban Indian youth to reclaim and reconstruct their tribal heritage.

The Novel in Focus

The plot. Narrated by several different voices (including that of a clever, irreverent dog), the 1990s part of the novel's plot, which takes place in Minneapolis, is interspersed with comic interludes, tragic events, and multiple stories from the mythical-historical past. Each of the novel's four sections begins with a glimpse of a continuing creation story about a pair of twins' beading the world. One sews with light beads, the other with dark, each sister trying to outpace the other to upset the balance.

The narrative is rooted in past events, which resonate beneath the modern-day happenings. In the post-Civil War era, during a U.S. Cavalry raid on an Ojibwe village, Private Scranton Roy bayonets an old woman, who sacrifices herself to save some village children. Dying, she mysteriously draws him into the moment of his own birth and utters a word, "Daashkikaa"—"cracked apart"—which conjures a vision of his own mother and sets him fleeing west (*Antelope Wife*, p. 4). Scranton Roy soon begins to follow a dog with a baby in a cradle board strapped to its back, evidence of the desperate attempt of a mother (Blue Prairie Woman) to save her baby. Roy rescues the baby, adopts her, and miraculously breast-feeds her.

Blue Prairie Woman is consumed with grief in the following years as she imagines what has happened to her forsaken child. Transformed by her restless searching, Blue Prairie Woman is renamed Other Side of the Earth. She has more children, twins called Mary and Zosie, but abandons them to search for her forsaken daughter. Just when Blue Prairie Woman finds the child, the mother dies of "mottled skin sickness," a possible allusion to smallpox (*Antelope Wife*, p. 17). At the side of her dead mother, the young girl, wearing a necklace of the beautiful blue beads that had once hung from the brow of her cradle board, is approached by a herd of dreamlike antelope, which she begins to follow.

The story resumes several generations later, developing two main plot lines centered on the difficult relationships of the descendants of Scranton Roy and Blue Prairie Woman: the first plot line concerns Klaus Shawano and Sweetheart Calico (the antelope wife of the title); the second plot line concerns Richard and Rozin Whiteheart Beads.

Out on the powwow circuit in Montana, Klaus uses magical antelope medicine to trap a beautiful woman. Separating her from her children and the open plains, he brings her to urban Minneapolis, where her misery drives her to muteness and alcoholism. "I'll do anything for her," he says, "except let her go" (*Antelope Wife*, p. 30). Called Sweetheart Calico (after the piece of cloth Klaus uses to bind her to him), she drives him crazy with her strange, other-than-human power. Klaus becomes a homeless alcoholic, and his brother, Frank Shawano, the owner of a bakery, takes in Sweetheart Calico.

A woman who "alters the shape of things around her and . . . changes the shape of things to come," Sweetheart Calico indirectly sets in motion the tragic events in the Whiteheart Beads family (*Antelope Wife*, p. 106). Fascinated by Sweetheart Calico, a mixed-blood Ojibwe woman named Rozin enters the bakery and meets Frank. This moment marks the beginning of their explosive love. When Frank is diagnosed with cancer (from which he later recovers), Rozin tells her husband, Richard, she is leaving him to be with Frank. In jealousy and despair, Richard, starts to asphyxiate himself. He abandons the attempt but not before inadvertently causing the death of one of his twin daughters, Deanna, who has secretly climbed into the truck in the sealed garage.

Sorrow and guilt over Deanna's death consumes each of her parents. Although she and Richard have not been together since Deanna's death, Rozin refuses for years to see Frank again, believing her infidelity has brought a curse on her children. Her husband continues to self-destruct, first joining Klaus as an alcoholic on the streets, then committing suicide—with a gun in the doorway of Rozin and Frank's room on the night they finally do marry. Life turns out more happily for Klaus. Saved from accidental death by a mysterious dog, he decides to stop drinking and to release Sweetheart Calico, who has been broken and nearly destroyed by his need for her.

Much of the story is told by Deanna's surviving twin sister, Cally, who searches for her identity in the patterns of family stories. One of her twin grandmothers, Zosie, holds the key to Cally's spirit-name, that is, the sacred name given to her by a chosen namer, who dreams the name for a person and bestows it, along with a special power or benefit tied to the name.

The novel concludes with a return to the past, to the family's heritage. Private Scranton Roy, in an effort to appease the spirit of the old woman whom he had bayoneted to death, brings his grandson Augustus to the remains of the village that he had helped destroy. Augustus marries Zosie and then falls victim to the machinations of both twins, becoming, in his mysterious disappearance, the unwitting reparation for the long-past actions of his grandfather.

Cally's vision. *The Antelope Wife* involves an effort to discover and shape a mixed-blood identity by finding and reworking a connection to the past. In its focus on identity, the novel touches on an issue of major importance to contemporary urban mixed-blood youth: how to rediscover a tribal heritage under historical and environmental circumstances that seem to negate it.

TWINS IN THE FAMILY—TIMES THREE

Blue Prairie Woman Matriarch of the mid-to-late nineteenth century; an Ojibwa woman, she bears a set of twins about whom not much is known.

Zosie Showano Roy Granddaughter to Blue Prairie Woman, also a twin.

Rozin Roy Whiteheart Beads Great-granddaughter to Blue Prairie Woman and daughter to Zosie Showano Roy, has a twin sister.

Cally Whiteheart Beads Great-great-granddaughter of Blue Prairie Woman, daughter of Rozin Whiteheart Beads; a twin herself, Cally narrates much of the story.

Cally's search, as an urban Indian, leads her to family stories, her spirit-name, and the land. Her quest is precipitated by an Ojibwe word that recurs in her head, *daashkikaa*. Asking her grandmothers the meaning of the word, Cally learns the story of Zosie's naming dream, which turns out to be the source of Deanna's and her own spirit names. In Ojibwe tradition, children "were given special names, dream names, at birth," which "were sacred and were not revealed to strangers" (Vizenor, p. 13). These names were "like hand-me-downs" that still bore "the marks and puckers" of other owners and their lives (*Antelope Wife*, p. 217).

Cally's spirit-name is a "stubborn and eraseless long-lasting name" that "won't disappear": Blue Prairie Woman (*Antelope Wife*, p. 217). The name connects Cally to her ancestral history and gives her an identity to both take up and alter. Because the name is handed down through the stories and dreams of her ancestors, it also links her to a sense of her tribal heritage that, as an urban child in contemporary Minneapolis, she has lost. Cally longs for something she misplaced in childhood—her birth holder, a turtle-shaped beaded buckskin "*indis*" her mother made from a few raw materials (her birth cord, sage, and sweetgrass). Her longing reveals her sense of a rupture between the past and future.

Cally's discovery of her spirit-name leads her to another revelation related to her search for identity: an understanding of the continuity between past and future as it is embodied in the land. This revelation comes, indirectly, through Sweetheart Calico. Hearing Zosie's naming dream, Cally learns that her own spirit name goes with the extraordinary "northwest trader blue" beads that, as it turns out, Sweetheart Calico has held in her mouth, under her tongue, for all her years of silence as a captive of Klaus Shawano. Pulling the beads out of her mouth, Sweetheart Calico trades them for her liberation; her first spoken words to Cally are "let me go" (*Antelope Wife*, p. 218). Though Klaus is the one who must finally liberate Sweetheart Calico, she and Cally roam the city all night, ending up in community gardens at its edge, where immigrant Chinese grandmothers are cultivating their plots. It is in these gardens that Cally feels renewed longing for her birth holder. The object represents her connection to tradition—to her mother, grandmothers, and the past, and ultimately to the land. "Once we no longer live beneath our mother's heart," says Erdrich, "it is the earth with which we form the same dependent relationship, relying completely on its cycles and elements, helpless without its protective embrace" (Erdrich, "Where I Ought to Be," p. 50).

The land provides a connection between past and future. The smell of soil rising in the warmth leads to Cally's epiphany—it is the "same even in the city, that dirt smell" (*Antelope Wife*, p. 219). Also it enables Cally to suddenly make sense of her mother's adolescent dream vision, a vision that her mother had wondered about all her life. Cally recognizes her own special power—"I see this: I was sent here to understand and to report"—at the moment she interprets her mother's vision: "What she saw was the shape of the world itself. . . . Gakahbekong. [The old-time Ojibwe name for] the city. Where we are scattered like beads off a necklace and put back together in new patterns, new strings" (*Antelope Wife*, p. 220). Though the city has obscured the land, in the gardens Cally realizes that what lies beneath it is the same land that was once a trading village, the same land that was once infused with the stories of a people.

The land is a locus of identity in the Ojibwe worldview. "In a tribal view of the world," says Erdrich, "where one place has been inhabited for generations, the landscape becomes enlivened by a sense of group and family history. . . . People and place are inseparable" (Erdrich, "Where I Ought to Be," p. 50). The urban environment, constantly changing and obliterating natural features, seems to provide little potential for such a tribal conception of identity. Nevertheless, Cally is able to reclaim a sense of the storied environment by recognizing the impermanence of the city on the land: "There are times, like now," Cally says, "I get this sense of the temporary. It could all blow off. And yet the sheer land would be left underneath. Sand, rock, the Indian black seashell-bearing earth" (*Antelope Wife*, p. 125).

Cally's vision restores her sense of cultural continuity, becoming an antidote to her sense of a family, culture, and life-world "cracked apart" by recurring patterns of violence. Although people are no longer connected in the same patterns, in the city they are put back together, like beads, in new designs. Through her vision, Cally reclaims a heritage and identity being created in her own time.

Sources. Erdrich has said in interviews that her writing is inspired by the storytelling practices of her Ojibwe-French mother and German-American father. Her complicated plots derive, she quips, from "a mixture of the Ojibwe storyteller and the German system-maker" (Erdrich in Sprenger). Erdrich's own bicultural background provides a potential model for the psychological predicaments of her characters, many of whom have divided identities. In her earlier novels, Erdrich explores divided cultural, religious, and gender identities; in *The Antelope Wife* she goes even further, introducing characters who are part human and part animal/spirit.

Erdrich's novels have been influenced as well by the traditional stories of the Ojibwe, but she makes no claim to be retelling those particular stories. "The Ojibwe have been telling stories through and in spite of immense hardship," she says, "[b]ut these are the narratives Ojibwe people tell among themselves, in Ojibwemowin" (Erdrich in Bacon).

The urban mixed-blood characters of *The Antelope Wife* are no doubt at least partly inspired by Erdrich's own urban experience. After college, Erdrich became editor of a Boston Indian Council newspaper, the *Circle*. According to Erdrich,

> Settling into that job and becoming comfortable with an urban community—which is very different from a reservation community—gave me another reference point. There were lots of people with mixed blood, lots of people who had their own confusions . . . it was something I *wanted* to write about.
>
> (Erdrich in "Louise Erdrich")

A more haunting similarity between Erdrich's own life and that of her characters occurs in the relationship between Rozin and Richard Whiteheart Beads. In the story, Richard attempts suicide after his wife tries to leave him and succeeds only after accidentally causing the death of their child. In Erdrich's own life, her long-time collaborator and husband Michael Dorris, writer and former Chair of the Native American Studies program at Dartmouth College, committed suicide in 1997 amidst their divorce proceedings (see Dorris's ***A Yellow Raft in Blue Waters,*** also in *Literature and Its Times*). They had lost their oldest adopted child in 1991, the trauma of which Erdrich later identified as the beginning of their marital troubles. Although *The Antelope Wife* was published a year after Dorris's suicide, it was, according to a prefatory note in the book, completed before his death. In a 1998 interview, Erdrich explained: "It was written by a writer who was afraid of what was about to happen and didn't know how to stop it"; "it was written out of dread" (Erdrich in Stone, p. 69).

Reception. Most reviewers praised *The Antelope Wife* for its lyrical language and powerful intermingling of myth and realism. Several critics lauded Erdrich's return to the non-linear, magical style of her first novels.

One reader suggested that, with its emphasis on contemporary, urban, and non-traditional characters, *The Antelope Wife* would go a long way toward answering objections leveled at Erdrich in the past. One such objection was to her earlier work's portrayal of full-blood reservation Indians by someone who is of mixed-blood, East-coast educated, and urban.

Whereas reviews of Erdrich's earlier novels often focused on their political aspects, despite Erdrich's insistence that she did not write political-issue books, many reviews of *The Antelope Wife* touched on the personal, registering the eerie similarities between tragic incidents in the novel and events in Erdrich's own life. "But there is light as well as darkness in this fictional universe," asserted one reviewer; "encountering it offers pain and exhilaration in equal measure" (Postlethwaite, p. 6).

—Lilian Carswell

For More Information

Bacon, Katie. "An Emissary of the Between-World." Interview. *The Atlantic Online*. 17 January 2001. http://www.theatlantic.com/unbound/interviews/int2001-01-17.htm (2 February 2002).

Erdrich, Louise. *The Antelope Wife*. 1998. New York: Perennial-HarperCollins, 1999.

———. "Where I Ought to Be: A Writer's Sense of Place." In *Louise Erdrich's Love Medicine: A Casebook*. Ed. Hertha D. Sweet Wong. New York: Oxford University Press, 2000.

Jackson, Deborah Davis. "This Hole in Our Heart: The Urban-Raised Generation and the Legacy of Silence." In *American Indians and the Urban Experience*. Ed. Susan Lobo and Kurt Peters. Walnut Creek, California: Altamira Press, 2001.

Johnston, Basil. *The Manitous: The Spiritual World of the Ojibway*. New York: HarperCollins, 1995.

"Louise Erdrich." *Contemporary Authors Online*. Reproduced in *Biography Resource Center*. 18 November 2001. http://www.galenet.com/servlet/BioRC (20 Jan. 2002).

May, Philip A. "Overview of Alcohol Abuse Epidemiology for American Indian Populations." In *Changing Numbers, Changing Needs: American Indian Demography and Public Health*. Ed. Gary D. Sandefur, Ronald R. Rindfuss, and Barney Cohen. Washington, D.C.: National Academy Press, 1996.

Nash, Gary B., et al. *The American People: Creating a Nation and a Society*. New York: Harper & Row, 1990.

Postlethwaite, Diana. "A Web of Beadwork." *New York Times Book Review* 103, no. 15 (April 1998): 6.

Stone, Brad. "Scenes from a Marriage: Louise Erdrich's New Novel—and Her Life." *Newsweek* 131, no. 12 (March 1998): 69.

Sprenger, Polly. "More Love Medicine." *The Minnesota Daily*. 11 April 1996. http://www.daily.umn.edu/ae/Print/ISSUE25/cover.html (2 February 2002).

Vizenor, Gerald. *The People Named the Chippewa*. Minneapolis: University of Minnesota Press, 1984.

Wub-e-ke-niew. *We Have the Right to Exist: A Translation of Aboriginal Indigenous Thought, The First Book Ever Published from an Ahnishinabaeo Jibway Perspective*. New York: Black Thistle Press, 1995.

Anthills of the Savannah

by
Chinua Achebe

Born in 1930, in Ogidi in the state of Anambra, Nigeria, Chinua Achebe is the best known Anglophone African writer. Achebe attended an elite secondary school, Government College, Umuahia, during his high-school years. At 18, he joined the first set of students admitted to Nigeria's premier university, then called University College, Ibadan. After college, he taught high school for a short while, then joined the Nigerian Broadcasting Company, where he became the executive in charge of foreign services. Since leaving broadcasting, Achebe has been teaching at universities in Nigeria and the United States. He is the founding general editor of the African Writers Series (Heinemann and Greenwood Press) under which, since 1962, the most significant African writing in English and English translation has been published. In 1971, Achebe founded *Okike*, which has remained a front line African literary journal to the present day. In his own novels, Achebe has portrayed slices of African life, from colonial (*Things Fall Apart* [1958] and *Arrow of God* [1964]) to postcolonial times (*No Longer at Ease* [1960] and A *Man of the People* [1966]). In the 1970s, he produced short stories (*Girls at War and Other Stories* [1972]), poetry (*Christmas in Biafra and Other Poems* [1973]), and essays (*Morning Yet on Creation Day* [1975]). Achebe returned to the novel with *Anthills of the Savannah*. A mature work published two decades after his prior novel, *Anthills* deals with the internal turmoil of an African country after throwing off colonial rule.

THE LITERARY WORK

A novel set in the fictional African nation of Kangan in the late twentieth century, soon after independence from colonialism, published in 1987.

SYNOPSIS

The story details the internal stresses that lead to the fall of an African military dictatorship led by His Excellency and the fates of two of his initially close friends.

Events in History at the Time the Novel Takes Place

Nigerian political history, 1960-1985. *Anthills of the Savannah* is set in the fictional country of Kangan, and its events are not precisely dated. It is therefore possible to argue that Kangan may stand for any African nation in the first two decades after independence. However, narrative elements, such as the names of characters and their use of language, link this fictitious nation more closely to real-life Nigeria than any other country.

Nigeria regained its independence in October 1960 after about a century of British colonial rule. A crucial part of the decolonization process included the general election held in 1959 to configure the government that would take over from the British. The Northern Peoples' Congress (NPC), based largely in the country's Northern

Chinua Achebe

Region, in alliance with the National Council of Nigerian Citizens (NCNC), a party that had widespread acceptance in the Eastern and Western Regions, formed the first independent Nigerian government. The third main political party, the Action Group (AG), based mainly in the Western Region, became the official opposition party. The strongholds of each of these parties corresponded with the homelands of Nigeria's three largest ethnic groups: the Hausa-Fulani people in the North (NPC), the Igbo in the East (NCNC), and the Yoruba in the West (AG). Also peopling each region are hundreds of minority ethnic groups.

Late in 1965, the Action Group, still in control of the Western regional government, underwent a severe internal crisis that reached its peak when its government leader broke away from the party that elected him and joined another political group— the United Progressive Grand Alliance (UPGA). Manipulating the results, the new group declared itself winners of the 1965 Western regional general elections. Citizens sympathetic to the Action Group, who believed that the polls had been rigged, carried out violent protests against the new government of the UPGA. Its opponents set fire to public buildings all over the region and hunted down and killed members of the alliance suspected of having committed the electoral fraud. Nigeria's central government, to which the Action Group had become the official opposition, imposed emergency regulations in the West. But the mayhem continued nonetheless.

The social breakdown in the Western region is one of the justifications given by officers of the Nigerian Army for the January 15, 1966, violent coup d'état that brought General J. T. U. Aguiyi-Ironsi to power as head of state. (It is worth noting, if only in passing, that Achebe's *A Man of the People* was released around this time and that many readers still view the similarity between its fictional ending in a military takeover of government and Nigeria's historical coup as a sign of the novelist's ability to envision the general direction of African political history.) The Aguiyi-Ironsi regime quickly restored peace to the West and, in its most notable decision, issued the decree that dissolved the country's federal structure and took away most of the regional governments' sovereign powers. Aguiyi-Ironsi's military regime was short-lived, however. It collapsed abruptly in July 1966 when army officers who hailed from the Northern region, to their thinking, avenged the wrongs of the January coup by killing the head of state along with the military governor of the Western region. They installed as new head of state Lieutenant Colonel (later General) Yakubu Gowon, an officer trained at the British Sandhurst military academy, who brings to mind the military dictator in *Anthills of the Savannah*. The Northern officers said that the January coup, which had been spearheaded by young officers predominantly from the Eastern region, killed too many Northern military and political leaders and allowed equally corrupt leaders of the Eastern region to escape harm. In short, the July conspirators accused leaders of the January coup of an ethnic vendetta. There followed massive mutinies in the barracks by Northern soldiers against their Eastern colleagues. Within months of the new government coming into office, the Nigerian army was almost completely purged of officers from the Eastern region.

Outside the armed forces, a well-planned ethnic pogrom was launched in the Northern region against persons of Eastern extraction, in other words, against Igbo people. At several conferences, held to stop the ongoing bloodshed and reconcile the factions, the Eastern military governor, Colonel Odumegwu Ojukwu, demanded that the country be ruled by a system of truly federated regions to guarantee the safety of all the country's ethnic groups and stakeholders. Anything short of that, he insisted, would be unacceptable to the Easterners, who at the time were being massacred in the North. Agreements were made to govern under such a representative system, but Ojukwu's demands remained unfulfilled despite the agreements. So in May 1967 the Eastern region seceded from Nigeria and declared itself the Republic of Biafra. A gruesome 30-month-war erupted between the Gowon-led government of Nigeria and the Republic of Biafra. The war ended in defeat for Biafra in January 1970, and Gowon ruled for another five years.

In the postwar years, Nigeria was transformed economically. Instead of an agricultural country it became a rich exporter of crude petroleum. Income from the oil windfall went partly into ambitious reconstruction and development projects, such as roads, dams, the expansion of universities, and a nationwide free primary education project. Meanwhile, under Gowon, the postwar oil boom era saw the growth of new intractable social problems—such as rampant armed robbery and uncontrollable urban sprawl. In January 1970, to deal with the armed robbery menace, the Gowon regime set up the first Armed Robbery and Firearms Tribunal, which tried and sentenced armed robbers to public execution by a firing squad.

Under pressure from politicians, Gowon promised to produce a new constitution, hold elections, and transfer power to a civilian government in 1976. But then Gowon reneged on his promise, declaring that 1976 was unrealistic. Meanwhile, allegations of official corruption and high-handedness by military personnel littered the daily newspapers. Gowon's government was brought down by a bloodless coup on July 29, 1975, the nine-year anniversary of his coming to power. His replacement, General Murtala Muhammed, was killed in a failed but bloody countercoup in February 1976, after which General Olusegun Obasanjo came to power. In October 1979, the Obasanjo government handed control over to a civilian, elected government, headed by Alhaji Shehu Shagari, but it too would be short-lived. This civilian government was toppled in December 1983 by General Muhammadu Buhari. Like His Excellency in *Anthills*, General Buhari had an enemy in his own camp, his Chief of Army Staff, General Ibrahim Babangida. In August 1985, 20 months after coming into office, Buhari was removed by Babangida.

Between 1960 and 1985, Nigeria fell under the rule of five military dictators for 16 years and two democratically elected governments for nine years. Every time a dictator came into office, he would accuse the previous administration of massive corruption and arrest a slew of public officials, some of whom were tried and jailed for lengthy periods. As a rule, it took the new regime, be it a military or an elected one, very little time to settle into its own corrupt ways, at which point many of the jailed officers of the previous administration would be released or their prison terms shortened. Sometimes the reduced jail terms or release from prison redressed a clear miscarriage of justice. But usually the move was calculated to "buy" the support of the influential individual concerned. There were new administrations that did not even reach this stage before being pushed out. In such a case, which occurred under Babangida, the imprisoned officials would be released as a gesture of "good will," to correct the alleged repression of the previous government.

Each government has contended with Nigeria's ethnic mix anew. Its officials have had to confront the problem of allocating resources equitably among the country's ethnic groups. The officials have always to consider whether or not their policies are perceived as favouring one group over the other. One arena of contention in ethnic balancing has been that of appointments into federal offices. Political appointments at the federal level must reflect the balance of ethnic powers in the states. Consequently, the most qualified candidate for an office often does not get appointed to it or is skipped over when promotions are due.

Public opinion and military rule. Important to understanding *Anthills of the Savannah* is the history of social activism among Nigerian college students and labor unions. Since the time of anticolonial agitation, the National Union of Nigerian Students (made up of delegates from the student councils of all the Nigerian colleges) has taken radical positions on national controversies. The students have almost always supported the actions of labor unions against multinational or local corporations, and have repeatedly protested the excesses and unjust policies of both colonial and native governments. At every important stage in the country's political history, the opinion of the students' union has been taken seriously by those in power. Its opinion has carried weight since its beginning days, when the union consisted of the future postcolonial leaders of Nigeria. In 1962, when the newly independent government of Nigeria signed a defense pact with its former colonial ruler, Great Britain, the students' union mounted mass-media campaigns that portrayed the pact as damaging to Nigeria.

As they saw it, the pact would re-establish the old colonial relationship. After much agitation, the students' outcry was heeded and the pact was abrogated, but not every controversy has resolved itself to their satisfaction. In 1977, students staged mass protests against the government's reducing the food-and-board subsidy it provided to them. The police, under orders from the regime, shot at protesting students, killing many of them. That same year the Nigerian government outlawed the students' union, detained many of its leaders without trial, and then expelled them from the universities.

A REAL-LIFE PARALLEL

In 1986, Dele Giwa, the editor of *Newswatch*, a popular news weekly, was killed by a letter bomb. It had been delivered to his home by unknown individuals thought to have been government security agents. Since its debut in January 1985, *Newswatch* has remained one of Nigeria's foremost news magazines, renowned for research-based opinions on pressing sociopolitical issues. In 1989, three years after Giwa's assassination, the magazine would be shut down for six months by the Babangida regime. The murdered news editor in *Anthills of the Savannah*—Ikem Osodi—resembles *Newswatch*'s Giwa. Like him, after studying and working abroad, the fictional Ikem returns to his African home to join in "nation-building" (Achebe, *Anthills* p. 83).

Labor unions became a target of Nigerian governments as well. Here, as elsewhere, labor unions agitated for better working conditions. However, this was the Cold War era, the era of a worldwide competition between communism, which championed workers, and democratic capitalism. In light of this competition, politicians suspected the true motives of labor unions during protests, and Nigeria was no exception. Nigerian governments frequently accused the unions of being unpatriotic stooges for communist governments. The accusation, often made with the intention of turning the larger population against the labor unions, would intensify when the unions went on strike. Also, like student leaders, labor union activists have been harassed and imprisoned by the military governments. Yet the activists have continued to stage strikes and protests. Their labor unions, along with the union of college students, have been virtually the only civil groups able to protest repression with a pronounced measure of credibility. As such, they have been distrusted by those in power.

Meanwhile, newspapers became the only public medium in which opposition to the excesses of the military governments could be aired. Editorials, news reports, and cartoons were published about corruption in high offices, promulgation of decrees that severely curtail civil freedoms, the high-handedness of public officials, and most importantly, the suffering of the general population because of inadequate government policies. A 1970s cartoon, for example, concerned J. S. Tarka, who allegedly embezzled funds, an accusation made by the man who was his supposed accomplice in the affair, Godwin Daboh, but then betrayed him. The cartoon caption—"If you Tarka me, I will Daboh You"—became a countrywide joke.

Oftentimes the military governments would respond by suppressing the publication of unflattering news and opinions. Defiant editors would be arrested and detained without trial, while independent publishing houses were closed down by soldiers. When newspapers and magazines published stories that security agencies considered inflammatory or seditious, armed forces would comb through town confiscating the offensive publications. The importance attached to controlling the mass media is revealed in some of the actions taken by the regimes of the late 1970s. In June 1978, the Obasanjo administration wrote a special decree to proscribe Dr. Obarogie Ohonbamu's *Newbreed* magazine because of its critical views of government policies and because it published an interview with the then-exiled leader of the Biafra secession attempt, former Lieutenant Colonel Odumegwu Ojukwu. The decree called for all printed copies of the offensive magazine to be seized and destroyed. As soon as the Muhammed-Obasanjo government came into office in 1976, it purchased, by force, controlling interests in Nigeria's most prominent newspapers: *Daily Times*, the only truly national daily (the *National Gazette* in Achebe's novel brings this paper to mind), and *New Nigerian*, a daily in the northern states. Meanwhile, the military governments established newspapers of their own. Electronic media, like television and radio, remained under government ownership until the early 1990s.

An allegory for good reason—dictatorship in Africa. Followers of African history know that the pattern of Nigerian history summarized above could apply, with minor variations, to almost all of the newly independent countries of the same era. Except in a few areas (Kenya, Senegal, and Malawi), democratically elected governments are regularly toppled in Africa. Places with no history of military government tend to have dictatorships. Dr. Kamuzu Banda of Malawi, for example, made himself president for life. By the end of 1987 (the year *Anthills of the Savannah* was published), "if South Africa and the remoter island states are excluded," a majority of African states (29 out of 47) had experienced at least one military takeover since independence (Fage, p. 510). As historian J. D. Fage explains, many of the regimes fell "because there was such a paucity of resources that it was extremely difficult for any government to provide the people with any rewards from independence" (Fage, p. 514). We should note, however, that the military men who forced elected governments out of power always failed to improve the situation.

Whether elected or military, all African dictatorships, like totalitarian regimes everywhere, maintain secret forces. In mid-1960s to mid-1970s Nigeria, these included an arm of the Nigerian police called "special branch," as well as intelligence wings of the national army, navy, and air force. The surveillance duties of such forces are often redefined by successive governments. Nigeria's special branch—renamed several times as the Nigerian Secret Organization (NSO), State Security Services (SSS), and Special Task Force—serves as a case in point. Its continuing existence shows how crucial the various dictatorships consider this repressive arm of government to their successful tenure.

The problem of ethnic balancing occurs elsewhere in Africa too. When it gets out of hand and the leaders of a particular group feel, rightly or wrongly, that they are being excluded from power, it is not uncommon for ethnic conflicts to flare into a full-scale civil war. From the 1960s, the major decade of independence, to the present, such ethnically related wars have flared in the Democratic Republic of Congo, Uganda, Sierra Leone, Sudan, and Somalia.

Another feature of post-independence Africa relevant to *Anthills of the Savannah,* especially to the development of its dictator character, is the Organization of African Unity (OAU). This real-world forum was established in 1963 for leaders of newly independent countries. The intent was to provide a platform for the articulation of Africa's collective interests in a way that would have stronger impact on the world than if individual countries acted alone. The OAU, which aims to promote the unity and solidarity of African states, operates through various organs, such as the General Secretariat, the Pan-African News Agency, and the Pan-African Postal Union. Most important among OAU groups has been the annual heads-of-government summit at which yearly agendas are determined and announced. (It is at one such meeting that the dictator in *Anthills of the Savannah* meets other dictators whom he resolves to emulate.) Since its beginnings, the OAU has supported decolonization movements around the continent. In countries like Zimbabwe, South Africa, and Angola, where the freedom struggle took violent forms, the OAU has generally been the first to lend diplomatic prestige to the guerrilla movements. In the year 2002 the Organization would evolve into the African Union.

The Novel in Focus

The plot. The narrative includes two main interwoven threads. One thread provides current information on the final days of His Excellency's government and the deaths of His Excellency and his two bosom friends, Chris Oriko and Ikem Osodi. The other thread provides background information on the personal and national events that culminate in the unhappy fate of these three men.

His Excellency becomes the President of Kangan in a military coup d'état that the populace welcomes. The coup topples elected officials who appear to have "finally got what they had coming to them and landed unloved and unmourned on the rubbish heap" (*Anthills*, p. 11). The forced change of government is carried out by junior officers, and they invite His Excellency to assume the reins of the presidency. Normally easygoing and very amiable, the new President has spent all his life as a career soldier. He has "few ideas about what to do" when he first assumes power (*Anthills*, p. 11). So to fashion a political program, he enlists two high-school friends: Chris Oriko, who edits the *National Gazette* and Ikem Osodi, who is a poet and writes a well-respected column for this same newspaper. His Excellency—at this point they still call him Sam—appoints Chris his Commissioner (Minister) of Information and elevates Ikem to editor of the *National Gazette*.

After attending his first summit of African heads of government in the Organization for African Unity, His Excellency adopts a new goal. He resolves to become Kangan's president-for-life,

Achebe's involvement with Nigeria's political struggle, a struggle marked by coups and war, is echoed in *Anthills of the Savannah.* In this picture, villagers watch Nigerian federal troops in an eastern Nigerian town.

exactly like the despots he has met at the conference. Among them was an especially ruthless and impassive emperor of an unnamed country, "who never smiled nor changed his expression no matter what was going on around him" (*Anthills*, p. 48). This emperor especially makes an unforgettable impression on His Excellency, who afterward says, "I wish I could look like him" (*Anthills*, p. 48). From President Ngongo, of another unnamed country, His Excellency adopts the exclamation "Kabisa!"—the word for an emphatic "no" or "finished" in Ngongo's native language.

Besides cultivating an imperial aloofness both in his personal comportment and official policies, His Excellency takes concrete steps to realize his ambition of remaining president for life. To this end, he sets the government machinery towards organizing a national referendum in which the people will vote either "Yes" or "No" on this issue. (There is no sign that he will not remain in office by force, anyway.) His Excellency becomes increasingly suspicious of his close confidantes, who, he is convinced, are dubious about the wisdom of a life presidency. The plebiscite fails. During the referendum, his friend Ikem Osodi takes his annual leave from the editorship of the *National Gazette*, and the people of Osodi's home region vote a resounding "No" on the life presidency, two developments that, in the eyes of His Excellency, confirm his friend's seemingly lukewarm loyalty.

In spite of the unfavorable vote, His Excellency carries on like a typical African dictator. He makes no plan to set a time limit for his presidency after the referendum fails. Every segment of Kangan society, even high-ranking ministers of state, lives in fear of him. His underlings are especially wary of his perpetually bad nerves. So as not to provoke his displeasure, his cabinet officers either tell him only what he wants to hear or say nothing at all. In the words of Chris Oriko, the Commissioner for Education "is by far the most frightened of the lot. As soon as he had sniffed peril in the air he had begun to disappear into his hole, as some animals and insects do, backwards" (*Anthills*, p. 3).

More than any other government department, His Excellency pays special attention to security services such as the police, the army, and the secret police (named, in this case, the State Research Council). These agencies work as if they have the mandate to track down and eliminate all perceived enemies of the state, the usual suspects being labor unions, students' associations, and critical editors and news reporters. The regular police target His Excellency's old friend, the *National Gazette* editor Ikem Osodi. They trail and harass Ikem as soon as His Excellency begins to doubt his old friend's loyalty. Ikem has written editorials critical of the state, and His Excellency's minions file them as evidence of his treason. Another bit of evidence is reported by the secret police—the "disloyal" Ikem visits with a delegation from his home province, Abazon, who has come to plead for His Excellency's attention to ecological and social perils ravaging the province. Later His Excellency refers to the so-called intelligence report of this visit as the "incontrovertible evidence" he needs to make Chris Oriko, the Information Commissioner, fire Ikem Osodi from the editorship of the *National Gazette* (*Anthills*, p. 132). Chris is incredulous. At his shock when faced with the report of Ikem's treason, His Excellency sneers, "Well, you seem to be in a skeptical mood . . . Good, isn't it, to know that some organs of government [the police] still perform effectively in this country" (*Anthills*, p. 132).

His Excellency's paranoia after the failed referendum fosters a countrywide atmosphere of mistrust. To survive, officials lie to one another and flatter their superiors, the President especially. The attorney general tells the President, "The people have spoken. Their desire is manifest. You are condemned to serve them for life," after the referendum has failed (*Anthills*, p. 5). He lets the President believe that jealousy prevents his closest friends from supporting the referendum wholeheartedly and vows shamelessly that "a man of my background has no problem whatsoever worshiping a man like you" (*Anthills*, p. 22). Deliberately or not, such senseless flattery only nurtures His Excellency's insecurity. Meanwhile, His Excellency is not immune to megalomania. He personalizes the state and elevates himself to a national symbol. When the Central Bank of Kangan floats the idea of embossing his image on the national currency, he does not stop the plan.

His Excellency's government gives marching orders to the larger society in the form of draconian decrees. The problem of violent robberies is addressed with special quasi-judicial tribunals set up to try the accused. Armed robbers found guilty by these panels are sentenced to a firing-squad execution, carried out in a public square, in front of eager spectators. Television cameras relay the macabre spectacle on prime-time news. At one such spectacle, the executioners stick a "bull's eye on the chest of the victim" as if at target practice (*Anthills*, p. 37).

The armed forces terrorize both the general population and the officials into a wretched state of powerlessness. An army truck, for example, drives recklessly through a marketplace, startling a street hawker whose wares are flung all over the place. Instead of apologizing, the truck driver, a soldier, swaggers over to the young trader, and says, "If I kill you, I kill [a] dog," inferring that the nearly killed trader is no more than a stray dog in the soldier's eyes (*Anthills*, p. 44). The trader, who knows full well the soldier's contemptuous meaning, protects his own psyche by interpreting the soldier's comment to mean, "after he kill me he will go home and kill his dog" (*Anthills*, p. 44). With the help of this self-deception, the poor trader swallows the contempt, laughs at himself, and actually wishes the soldier well later that day.

The ill effects of His Excellency's arbitrary ways take on deadly dimensions toward the end of the regime's term in office. After his suspension from the *National Gazette*, Ikem vows not to be silenced. At a university lecture held by the students' union, Ikem relates the allegorical tale of a tortoise and the leopard that wants to kill it. The cornered tortoise makes a request that he be left alone for a few moments before being killed. To the leopard's consternation, the tortoise begins to scratch the ground and throw dust all over. The puzzled leopard asks the tortoise to explain the meaning of his antics. "Even after I am dead," replies the tortoise, "I would want anyone passing by this spot to say, yes, a fellow and his match struggled here" (*Anthills*, p. 117). The import of the tale is not lost on the students: one ought to resist even in a hopeless situation. During the question-and-answer period, Ikem condemns social inertia, acknowledges the sorry state of Kangan society, and reminds his receptive audience that cynicism is ruining the country. He chastises the students for their exclusion of truly downtrodden groups—peasants, the self-employed poor, and women—from their attempts to mobilize society. In this regard, they are no better than other progressive social movements staged by leftist intellectuals and labor unions. The exclusion, asserts Ikem, amounts to elitism. He blames elite pressure groups for "spouting clichés from other people's histories and struggles" while they conveniently forget that "in the real context of Africa today they [the elite] are not the party of the oppressed but of the oppressor" (*Anthills*, pp. 146-47).

Ikem urges the students to "develop the habit of skepticism, not swallow every piece of [ideological] superstition you are told by witch doctors and professors"; then "your potentiality of assisting and directing this nation will be quadrupled" (*Anthills*, p. 148). During the discussion, the idea of putting the President's picture on the currency comes up. Ikem says,

> Yes I heard of it like everybody else. Whether there is such a plan or not I don't know. All I can say is I hope the rumour is unfounded. My position is quite straightforward especially now that I don't have to worry about being Editor of the *National Gazette*. My view is that any serving President foolish enough to lay his head on a coin should know he is inciting the people to take it off; the head I mean.
>
> (*Anthills*, p. 149)

Within the very nervous dictatorship that Kangan has become, Ikem's play on words is an invitation to trouble. *National Gazette*'s interim editor twists Ikem's words into "EX-EDITOR ADVOCATES REGICIDE!" (*Anthills*, p. 149). Shortly thereafter, Ikem is arrested and killed in the middle of the night.

Chris Oriko refuses to accept the official lie that Ikem fought his arrest and was "fatally wounded by gunshot" (*Anthills*, p. 156). He abandons his post and goes into hiding, after contacting alternative news outlets to broadcast the true story of Ikem's murder. All over the capital city, students demonstrate to protest the lies published in the *National Gazette* about Ikem's lecture and his subsequent assassination. The government promptly shuts down the school and declares the president of the students' union a wanted man. Chris escapes the capital with the help of a sympathetic security officer and poor taxi drivers, who house Chris and help him leave town in disguise. Emmanuel, the wanted students' union president, joins Chris on the fateful journey.

On their way to Abazon, news of the fall of His Excellency's government reaches the fugitives. His Excellency has been killed. The new administration, headed by the army's Chief of Staff, broadcasts the untruth that the President has been abducted from the palace by unknown persons. A drunken police sergeant serving at the Abazon regional boundary shows colorful disbelief in the official lie: "This our country na waa! I never hear the likeness before. A whole President de miss! This Africa na waa [is incredible]" (*Anthills*, p. 197). Even in remote parts of the country, as Chris discovers in Abazon, citizens celebrate the fall of His Excellency's tyranny, as they did his predecessor's years earlier. Making inquiries about the coup, Chris spies a policeman trying to rape a nursing student and attempts to stop him. The policeman threatens to shoot Chris if he is not left alone. When Chris persists, the policeman executes him in front of everyone and runs off into the savannah. The country has a new leader, but things, as Chris's killing shows, have not changed for the better.

The nation's story, which is also the story of the three deceased friends, continues in the relationships they leave behind. Little is known of His Excellency's intimate life beyond his sexual misadventures in England. But Chris and Ikem leave behind two women—Beatrice Okoh and Elewa—to mourn their loss. Beatrice, Chris's lover, is a brilliant, high-ranking official in the Kangan civil service. Elewa, Ikem's fiancée, is a barely literate, low-level salesperson at a department store.

Ikem, the story's foremost intellectual, thinks little of women before he is suspended from the *National Gazette*. As Beatrice puts it, "he has no clear role for women in his political thinking" (*Anthills*, p. 83). He neglects them despite writing a full-length novel and a play about the Women's War of 1929 (a protest mounted by thousands of Nigerian women when it was rumored that the British were planning to tax African females). But after his clash with His Excellency, Ikem seems to have had an epiphany for he admits to Beatrice that she is right about his neglecting to make a place for women in his writing. This shift in his thought toward popular inclusiveness surfaces also in his recommendation to Bassa University students to ally themselves with peasants and genuine members of the working class. The wisdom of Ikem's change is apparent in the kind of people who later help Chris escape the government's security traps. The help rendered him by poor taxi drivers, Ikem's old acquaintances, and Emmanuel, the student leader, leads Chris to ponder "Why did we not cultivate such young men before now? Why, we did not even know they existed if the truth must be told!" (*Anthills*, p. 176).

The Ikem-Elewa sexual alliance assumes a more clearly political role after the death of the three main male characters. Beatrice, Chris's girlfriend, takes Elewa into her home, caring for her until she gives birth to a baby girl. Beatrice practically becomes Elewa's husband and the child's father. In her home, Beatrice holds a naming ceremony for the little girl, at which Beatrice presides with authority, notwithstanding the presence of men (the student leader Emmanuel; the security officer who refused to arrest Chris, and a taxi driver who sheltered Chris; and

Elewa's uncle). A jolly old man to whom belongs the traditional right of naming the baby girl, Elewa's uncle, who shows up late, concedes that Beatrice and the others have done well not to wait for him: "If anybody thinks that I will start a fight because somebody has done the work I should do that person does not know me. . . . Rather I will say thank you" (*Anthills,* p. 210).

The story ends on an optimistic note at the naming party where men and women of all classes and from diverse regions of Kangan share a genuine fellowship. Significantly, the name Beatrice gives the young girl, Amaechina, or "May the Path Never Close," portends high expectations for recovery and renewal (*Anthills,* p. 206). People at the ceremony actually interpret the name, which is customarily used for boys, somewhat differently, to mean "the Path of Ikem" and "The Shining Path of Ikem" (*Anthills,* p. 206).

Nwayibuife—"A female is also something." Beatrice's middle name, Nwayibuife, is full of implications, as is the newborn's at the close of the novel. At her naming ceremony, the baby receives the name Amaechina, which is normally reserved for boys in Igbo society. What this says about the role envisioned for women in the future is debatable. At the very least, it points to an activist, leadership role on par with that of men. The two names—Nwayibuife and Amaechina—both point to the importance of including a formerly neglected group—women—who like the poor can prove invaluable to the cause. Beyond participation on an equal footing, the novel can also be seen as envisioning women's leading men. In Achebe's own words,

> I think we must . . . find a way in which the modern woman in Africa . . . brings her . . . special gifts to the running of affairs. This is one of the things that I was tentatively exploring in *Anthills*. . . . It's not enough for men to work out what women should do. . . . Women should . . . not just from a copying of European fashions . . . but out of our own traditions . . . work out a new role for themselves.
>
> (Achebe in Lindfors, p. 150)

In the novel, Beatrice can be seen as forging a path for women out of her own traditions for she is associated with the age-old cult of Idemili, who, according to legend, is the daughter of God. "The role of women," said Achebe when interviewed, "has not yet been fully worked out"; however, "situations can arise in which women are not the underdogs but can take over the affairs of society" (Achebe in Lindfors, p. 150). Such a situation presents itself to Beatrice, who then rises to the occasion. Her character, points out the scholar Emmanuel Obiechina:

> is not looking over her shoulders for any approaching masculine figure to determine the course of the nation's destiny. It has fallen to her lot to provide leadership and she accepts this role without fuss or effusiveness. . . . Her style is that of a true democrat. She listens, discusses, summarizes the consensual views of her compatriots. Tolerance is the key to the new style, in contrast to the despotism of the authoritarians (Obiechina, letter, p. 1).

The two symbolic women's names address not only a political issue but also a literary one. Critical consensus was already forming in the late 1980s that traditional African ideologies and classic novels such as Achebe's ***Things Fall Apart*** (also in *Literature and Its Times*) exclude women's concerns. Choosing a very revealing title, Florence Stratton heads the first chapter of her book on African feminist writing with the question, "How Could Things Fall Apart For Whom They Were Not Together?" an obvious reference to Achebe's famous novel. Along with other leading African writers, Achebe became the object of feminist criticism that works by male writers substituted African men's history and culture for general African history and culture. Stratton argues that in stories "while women are excluded from the male domain of community power, men are permitted to intrude into domestic domain" (*Anthills,* p. 26). Meanwhile, institutions "associated with female industriousness, assertiveness, and prosperity" are either ignored or subordinated to male control (*Anthills,* p. 26).

Some of these issues are echoed in the critical exchanges that Beatrice Okoh has with Ikem Osodi and Chris Oriko. When Ikem acknowledges that Beatrice is correct in her critique of his treatment of women in his writing, *Anthills* seems to be agreeing with women's arguments about how women are treated in literature. Ikem, the writer, thanks Beatrice for her critiques shortly before he is killed: "Thank you BB. . . . I can't tell you what the new role for Woman will be. I don't know. I should never have presumed to know. *You* have to tell us. We never asked you before. And perhaps because you've never been asked you may not have thought about it; you may not have the answer handy" (*Anthills,* p. 90).

Sources and literary context. In the early 1970s, after about a decade of independence, the sociopolitical health of African states looked grim. Writers who had heralded decolonization with optimism began to re-evaluate the state of their unions and to create stories that depicted gloom and doom. They produced novels of "post-independence disillusionment" (Obiechina, *Language and Themes*, p. 121). Examples of such stories are Ayi Kwei Armah's *The Beautyful Ones Are Not Yet Born* (1968) and Yambo Ouologuem's *Bound to Violence* (1968). Achebe condemned their pessimism in his essay "Colonialist Criticism" (1975). The only novels countering these dark tales of post-independence malaise were stories with Marxist solutions, such as Sembène Ousmane's *God's Bits of Wood* (1960).

Anthills of the Savannah forges a path between these two "extremes." The story is not in any way as gloomy as the disillusionment narratives, although it describes similar conditions. At the same time, it shows distrust for the Marxist alternative when it portrays how ambivalent Ikem Osodi feels about Marxism and other trendy radicalisms of the students' and labor unions. Against both the pessimism and the Marxist solution, *Anthills of the Savannah* evokes a measured optimism that comes from the mixing of the intellectuals and the workers at the naming ceremony of Ikem and Elewa's child. The ceremony signifies a gathering together of stakeholders—highly educated citizens, urban working classes, and government officials—to herald the possibility of a better African future. In contrast to other novels of its kind, *Anthills of the Savannah* depicts a path to progress that acknowledges the enormity of the problems without being unduly pessimistic. The novel, and its title, point to the resilience of African societies. In the landscapes (or savannahs) of these societies are anthills that do not succumb to scorching drought but endure for a long time. These long-standing anthills are secure in the certainty that new grass will grow. The hope in that new grass, symbolized by the gathering at Beatrice's apartment, is what the novel wants us to remember most.

Events in History at the Time the Novel Was Written

The trouble with Nigeria. In 1983, close to the end of the first term of the country's Shehu Shagari government, Achebe published a little book entitled *The Trouble With Nigeria*. The book ascribes the unrelenting misrule in Nigeria to a lack of imaginative and selfless leadership. The first sentence squarely declares that "The trouble with Nigeria is simply and squarely a failure of leadership" (Achebe, *The Trouble With Nigeria*, p. 1). Achebe denounces popular politicians who had been in the national limelight since the anticolonial 1950s and were still struggling to rule the country. He condemns Chief Obafemi Awolowo and Dr. Nnamdi Azikiwe for being tunnel-visioned, money-grabbing tribalists. The book also castigates as narrow-minded and opportunistic promoters of these two leaders, who betray their clear mission in the country "to inaugurate a new philosophy and a new practice of politics" (Achebe, *The Trouble With Nigeria*, p. 80). Achebe recommends that "enlightened citizens" chase these self-styled leaders out of office because "if this conscious effort is not made, good leaders, like bad money, will be driven out by bad" (Achebe, *The Trouble With Nigeria*, p. 2).

The starkly partisan nature of his language in the book disagrees with his characteristic even-handedness on other vexing questions. But Achebe is not a completely independent observer here. The book is his contribution to efforts by the Nigerian intelligentsia to participate in righting the teetering ship of state as they saw it at the time. After the death of Alhaji Aminu Kano in 1983, Achebe was elected a national vice-chairman of the left-leaning People's Redemption Party (P.R.P.), whose membership included a very high percentage of intellectuals. *The Trouble With Nigeria* amounts to something like a campaign document for the party, especially the essay's conclusions, in which Achebe declares, "I can see no rational answer to the chaotic jumble of tragic and tragic-comical problems we have unleashed on ourselves in the past twenty-five years, but the example of Aminu Kano—a selfless commitment to the common people of our land" (Achebe, *The Trouble With Nigeria*, p. 84). That same year, 1983, Nigerian dramatist Wole Soyinka, released a record composed in the popular Nigerian pidgin English. Entitled "Unlimited Liability Company," it criticized the elected government and called on voters not to re-elect but to reject President Shagari and his political party at the polls. These efforts of Nigeria's leading intelligentsia to directly participate in partisan politics was unprecedented.

On December 31, 1983, the writers' criticisms were addressed in a way they had not anticipated: another military dictatorship removed from office President Shagari, who three months earlier had been declared the winner of a flawed general election. That coup launched yet another cycle of dictatorships that would last to the time in which Achebe's novel was published.

Reviews. *Anthills* was welcomed with great enthusiasm. Virtually every reviewer remarks its having been eagerly awaited for two decades, since the publication of Achebe's *A Man of the People* in 1966. Neal Ascherson, in the *New York Review of Books*, praises *Anthills of the Savannah* for its honest analysis of the problems of rulership in post-independence African states. Ascherson commends the novel's departure from the conventional lambasting of Europe and America for all of Africa's woes: "It is the courage of this complex novel to cast Africans, even in this wretched decade, always as subject and never as the objects of external forces. It is a tale about responsibility" (Ascherson, p. 4). Fiona Sparrow, writing for *World Literature Written in English*, commends Achebe's profound interest in women's concerns in postcolonial Africa. She calls Beatrice Okoh "the most important female character that Achebe has created" (Sparrow, p. 58). In *West Africa*, the award-winning Somali novelist, Nuruddin Farah, heaps adulation on the story, describing it as an "engaging and a hugely successful novel. There is a great deal of poetry in it, and the quality of writing is charged with informedness, an awareness of high things and high thoughts" (Farah, p. 1,831). Farah compares His Excellency's maltreatment of Abazon, the region that does not endorse his dream of a president for life, to General Siyad Barre's practices in Somalia, for example: "In Somalia, we know what happens when a given province challenges Siyad Barre's authority: the life-line to the region is severed, no bore-holes are dug, no development projects are financed, no teachers are any longer transferred to this area, etc., precisely the very measures described in *Anthills*" (Farah, p. 1,830).

—Adeleke Adeeko

For More Information

Achebe, Chinua. *Anthills of the Savannah*. New York: Anchor Books, 1987.

———. *The Trouble With Nigeria*. Enugu: Fourth Dimension, 1983.

Ascherson, Neal. "Betrayal." *New York Review of Books*, 3 March 1988, 3-4, 6.

Fage, J. D. *A History of Africa*. London, Routledge, 1995.

Falola, Toyin. *The History of Nigeria*. Westport, Conn.: Greenwood Press, 1999.

Farah, Nuruddin. "A Tale of Tyranny." *West Africa*, 21 September 1987, 1,828-31.

Lindfors, Bernth, ed. *Conversations with Chinua Achebe*. Jackson: University Press of Mississippi, 1997.

Obiechina, Emmanuel. *Language and Theme: Essays on African Literature*. Washington, D.C.: Howard University Press, 1990.

———. Emmanuel Obiechina to Joyce Moss, letter, 18 September 2002, Harvard University, Cambridge, Mass.

Sparrow, Fiona. "Reviews." *World Literature Written in English* 28, no. 1 (spring 1988): 58-61.

Stratton, Florence. *Contemporary African Literature and the Politics of Gender*. London: Routledge, 1994.

Aunt Julia and the Scriptwriter

by
Mario Vargas Llosa

> **THE LITERARY WORK**
>
> A novel set in Lima, Peru, in the mid 1950s with an epilogue set roughly ten years later; published in Spanish (as *La tía Julia y el escribidor)* in 1977, in English in 1982.
>
> **SYNOPSIS**
>
> During his struggle to define himself as a serious writer, Varguitas has two transformative experiences: his encounter with Pedro Camacho, an eccentric but successful writer of radio serials, and his own love affair with his Aunt Julia.

Mario Vargas Llosa was born into Peru's small but privileged middle class in 1936. From his birthplace in Arequipa, he moved with his mother and her parents to Cochabamba, Ecuador, where Vargas Llosa's grandfather would direct first a cotton farm and then the Peruvian consulate. The move offered respite from the shame of divorce: the future writer's father, an operator with the Panagra radio chain, had abandoned the family even before Mario was born and did not reappear for a decade. When Vargas Llosa met his father for the first time, it was in the northern city of Piura, Peru, where the grandfather was serving as prefect. The unexpected discovery of his father, followed by his parents' reunion and move to the capital Lima, marked the end of young Vargas Llosa's idyllic, even coddled, childhood. His father was stern and disapproved of the budding literary vocation, sending Vargas Llosa to the Leoncio Prado Military Academy to instill in him more masculine qualities. The writer's experiences as a student there include some of his first close-up encounters with Peru's diverse and often conflictive society, and he weaves them into his earliest fiction (see ***The Time of the Hero*** [1963, also in *Literature and Its Times*]). Later experiences at Lima's San Marcos University, a hotbed of political debate and activism, awakened his interest in the Peruvian politics that would form a backdrop for some of his subsequent novels (*Conversation in the Cathedral* [1969]). The mysteries of daily life in Peru form the backdrop for other novels (*Captain Pantoja and the Special Service* [1973]). Vargas Llosa sets a couple of his works outside Peru (*The War of the End of the World* [1981, Brazil]; *The Feast of the Goat* [2000, The Dominican Republic]). He also explores the nature and form of narrative in various novels (*The Storyteller* [1987] and *The Notebooks of Don Rigoberto* [1997]). In *Aunt Julia and the Scriptwriter*, his exploration exposes the power and perils of a preoccupation with radio melodramas in mid-twentieth-century Peru.

Events in History at the Time the Novel Takes Place

1950s Peru—the political context. In the post-World War II years, economic and other needs drove many nations towards one or the other of

Mario Vargas Llosa

the two global superpowers—the United States or the Soviet Union. The Soviet Union, a communist regime, stood in stark contrast to the United States, a bastion of democratic capitalism, and the two engaged in a struggle for world leadership that forced other nations to choose sides. This so-called Cold War took on special importance in the Americas, where the United States had long taken an active role in the economies and politics of many countries.

In Peru two leaders were in power around the time *Aunt Julia and the Scriptwriter* takes place. The first one, military dictator Manuel Arturo Odría (1948-56), maintained close ties with the United States. His was a bourgeois dictatorship based on an export-oriented plan for growth—foreign trade and investment were encouraged and actively pursued. In the midst of its campaign to combat the spread of international communism, the U.S. Government, particularly its military, became Peru's active business partner. The Odría dictatorship adjusted itself slightly to accommodate the relationship, loosening its controls on business but maintaining a tight grip on the press, civil rights, and political activity.

Already supported by the business community and the military, Odría sought to expand his appeal by courting the coastal working class. This did not sit well with the nation's elite who feared losing their solid financial, professional, and social position to the middle class. Less than ten percent of the population controlled the nation's businesses at the time, while 75 percent lived in poverty or extreme poverty. Yet the elite chafed at what they perceived to be the government's arbitrary policies, unequal distribution of benefits, and constant repression. They attempted in 1954 to unseat Odría in a coup that proved unsuccessful, but nevertheless paved the way for free elections in 1956, again around the time *Aunt Julia and the Scriptwriter* takes place. The following government, under Manuel Prado (1956-62), eliminated some of the harsh excesses of the Odría regime, expanding civil rights, legalizing trade unions, and easing restrictions on the Communist Party (which Odría had outlawed in a nod to the United States and its Cold War interests). In other ways, Prado's government maintained the same stance the earlier government had followed. Prado continued Odría's export and foreign enterprise-friendly policies. Years of aggressive support of businesses began to reveal the hollowness of plans for agrarian reform and social development in the mountain regions, so his term was full of internal divisiveness. Despite impressive growth in exports, economic hardships (unemployment accompanied by inflation and labor unrest) fostered the rise of ever more extreme movements in the politics of the country.

Communism and capitalism in Latin America. Outside Peru, revolution was brewing in Cuba. Here, too, the era opened under a military dictator—Fulgencio Batista. In 1952 Batista seized control in a coup d'état that suspended the 1940 constitution. His military regime won U.S. recognition within weeks, and by the end of the decade was receiving significant U.S. military aid. American businesses owned massive shares of Cuba's mining, utilities, railway, and sugar industries at the time. Foreign-owned companies, who were supported by the island's elite and accounted for 80 percent of the island's sugar production, paid little heed to the needs of the Cuban masses. With planting and harvesting tailored to maximize profits, people were left to go hungry while rich farmlands lay fallow or yielded products that were exported along with the profits. Discontent with this state of affairs—and the government that allowed it to persist—rippled through Cuba. A small but dedicated group of revolutionaries under Fidel Castro (1927-), Raúl Castro (1932-), Camilo Cienfuegos (1932-60), and Ernesto "Che" Guevara (1928-67) took direct aim at Batista's military dictatorship. On July 26, 1953, they staged a military assault on the Moncada barracks, seeking to reinstate the liberal constitution of 1940 and to restore popular rule. The attack on Moncada failed, but Castro's subsequent trial and jail term allowed him to present his views to a wide audience. His defense, later published as *History Will Absolve Me*, yielded him a 15-year-sentence of which he served only two years, thanks to a nationwide amnesty campaign organized on behalf of the young rebels. Afterward the Movement of July 26, as the rebel group was called, continued to agitate for the cause, launching guerrilla attacks from high in the Sierra Maestra mountains from 1956-59. Popular support for the rebels swelled as Batista's troops took increasingly severe measures to crush them, including torture and massacre. The rebels persisted. On the night of January 1, 1959, Che Guevara and Camilo Cienfuegos led them into Havana and Batista fled the island with his family and associates.

Was the Cuban revolution a mere alignment of the island nation with the Soviet Union? By this time the Soviets' still recent experience of severe repression under the leadership of Joseph Stalin had cast a serious pall on communist idealism. Cuba seemed receptive to the Soviet Union, though it had to some degree been forced in this regard. The rebels took some bold measures early in their regime, nationalizing oil refineries and other business interests. In response, the United States cut off relations with Cuba, suspending its commitment to purchase Cuban sugar and severing diplomatic relations. Cuba necessarily turned to the Soviet Union to fill the gap. Some worried that Castro's Cuba would adopt Stalin's tactics; others felt certain that Cuba would not commit these errors. Cuba, promised Che Guevara, seeks "something new which will permit a perfect identification between the government and the community as a whole" with "the ultimate and most important revolutionary aspiration: to see man freed from alienation" (Guevara in Thomas, p. 1423). A nation reborn, it aimed culturally to achieve what many, including Vargas Llosa, saw as a "political ideal—a Communist revolution respectful of artistic freedom" (Kristal, p. 6). This was the revolution being waged when *Aunt Julia and the Scriptwriter* takes place, and it greatly affected the region, inspiring intellectuals in the various closed societies of Latin America. In Peru too, artists like Vargas Llosa looked to Cuba as a new model of hope and tolerance.

1950s Peru—the social context. The communist factions in various countries shared a common ideal that a nation's government should serve all of its people. In countries like Peru and Cuba, where most citizens were not of European descent, this implied the inclusion of those groups that made up the formerly excluded masses—native peoples, mestizos (part European, part native), Africans, mulattos (part European, part African), and sambos (part African, part native). The needs of these long-excluded groups ought to matter as much as those of the white European elite if one lived by this ideal. In Cuba, in keeping with the ideal, Castro's supporters "gathered in their ranks men and women of all colors. When the Rebel Army entered Havana, it swept before it not only the government and army of the dictatorship, but the social conventions, hierarchical structures, and racial practices that had supported dictatorial rule" (Cannon, p. 113). Castro rejected discrimination from the very start, declaring soon after his victory, "We are a mixed race from Africa and Spain. No one should consider themselves a pure race, much less a superior race" (Castro in Cannon, p. 113).

Peru's situation was somewhat different. Like many other Latin American countries, it included a full range of ethnicities—in 1955 its population was 60 percent native (mainly Quechua Indian), 30 percent mestizo, and only 10 percent white European and other ethnicities. But in addition to its ethnic diversity, Peru stretches across an area of enormous geographic diversity including dry colonial cities on the coast, remote Andean villages to the east, and tropical forests on the inland slope of the Andes. The radically different economies and lifestyles dictated by the different climates have divided Peru's population into various social groups from the land's earliest days. It is perhaps this factor that has made Peru one of Latin America's most hierarchical countries, with a class structure as rigid as it is unbalanced. The wealthiest 15 percent of the population forms an elite of European, predominantly Spanish, extraction that controls the vast majority of Peru's political and economic resources from the coastal cities and farms. Meanwhile, the indigenous peoples remain in poor, remote mountain and jungle villages or join other groups in the huge shantytowns around Lima. Combined with little-to-no social mobility, the physical barriers have resulted in only the most minimal and passing interaction between social classes. In the 1950s, as is largely the case now, there was little sense of unity. In the words of one historian, Peru was a nation of "10 million inhabitants but very few Peruvians" (Bethell, p. 457). Earlier in the century some thinkers had tried to address this "problem," noting that Peru was not served by its disunity. They began a movement to incorporate the native or indigenous peoples into the life and progress of the nation. Arguing that "the revolution that would regenerate Peru must come from the sierra, from the Andean Indians, who would destroy the age-old systems of oppression and unify Peru again, restoring the grandeur that had been the Inca empire," Manuel González Prada (1848-1918) inspired what came to be known as the *indigenista* movement (Keen, pp. 388-91). Later *indigenista* thinkers would take González Prada's faith in the Andean spirit several steps further, holding up the communal farms and socialistic structure of the pre-conquest (and therefore more authentic) Peru as models for social revolution. The idea that Peru's indigenous population deserved the same rights and privileges as other Peruvians coincided with migrations of native peasants from the mountain regions to Lima and the growth of an urban working class. From the shared concerns of these peasants and workers, José Carlos Mariátegui (1895-1930) drew inspiration for his *Seven Interpretive Essays on Peruvian Reality* (1928); a year later, these concerns moved him to found the Peruvian Communist party. Although the Communist party itself had been outlawed when *Aunt Julia and the Scriptwriter* takes place, its social ideas could be seen in the powerful APRA (Popular Revolutionary Alliance of America) party and in the increasing visibility of Peru's indigenous peoples on the streets of Lima and on the airwaves. Social classes could meet through radio stations like Lima's Radio Central, which brought indigenous music to the upper classes, and people of all classes could follow the twists and turns of the radio soap operas.

RADIONOVELAS WITH A REAL-WORLD EDGE TO THEM

Already in the early 1940s, before Goar Mestre inaugurated his series of racy radio soaps in Cuba, the CMQ network produced fictional drama with a real-life edge to it. For 15 minutes a day, the network broadcast "The Poor People of Guantanamo," a radionovela-type program that depended on stories from the daily news for its scripts. Writers would cull through the newspapers, swoop down on real-life articles about dramatic incidents, such as the murder of a woman in a lovers' spat, then adapt the news bit into a proper program script.

Broadcasting in Peru. Mentioned in *Aunt Julia and the Scriptwriter* is Cuba's CMQ radio network. CMQ began broadcasting in Cuba in 1933. In the early 1940s three brothers—Goar, Abel, and Luis Augusto Mestre—became half owners of the network. Goar Mestre initiated a series of popular daytime radionovelas (soap operas) that touched on racy subjects. They include, noted Mestre, plenty of adultery. Mestre would become a powerful network presence. He is said to have encouraged Latin American broadcasters to take a united regionwide approach when dealing with dictators. Already by the early 1950s, they had the forum to do so—a broadcast media organization called the Inter-American Association of Broadcasters, which counted 3,800 members and met annually. Within a short while, by the middle of this same decade, Goar Mestre had banded together with an elite group of major Latin American broadcasters, including Genaro Delgado Parker of Peru.

Dictators in the different areas introduced censorship, restricting especially what political commentators could say over the airwaves. Cuba's radio commentators freely criticized Batista at first, until he put a stop to their public criticism. By the mid 1950s his censorship had grown so strict that Abel Mestre, then president of the Cuban Federation of Radio Broadcasters, protested in public, to little avail. The censorship did not ease. Rather, after the onset of the rebel's 1956 guerilla attacks against him, it grew more severe. Batista cracked down on anyone in the media who criticized him; by 1957 the crackdown had grown so fierce "that the media could no longer even mention that their reports were censored" (Salwen, p. 103). Again political commentators bore the brunt of the repression. At least one radionovela escaped it, building on Cuba's already long tradition of indirect political commentary by slyly sneaking such commentary into fictional works. Airing not over the CMQ radio network but over the CNC network beginning late in 1957, the program *The Dictator of the Blue Valley* starred a rebel leader (like Castro) who in each episode would wander through the valley with like-minded men, aiding people in their struggle against an evil dictator (like Batista).

Meanwhile, back in Peru, Genaro ran his radio enterprise. Like Goar Mestre, he "saw broadcasting as a regionwide venture that transcended national borders" (Salwen, p. 115). But Peru had its own set of particular national realities to contend with, many of them divisive. Despite divisions along geographical, racial, and class lines, one component of Peruvian life brought the divided society together: the radio. From its first days, radio here was mainly geared to the interests of the ruling elite, "economic growth and political stability, and a docile commercial broadcasting system satisfied both" (Fox, p. 29). Under Odría the government relaxed official restrictions on commercial broadcasters. But the dictator continued to maintain tight, unofficial control over broadcasts both directly (in the novel, the radio director becomes very agitated about possible repercussions when a visiting economist "violently attack[s] military dictatorships" in an interview) and indirectly (the news that the radio broadcasts is culled from newspapers receiving revenue and bribes "to attack certain individuals and defend others") (Vargas Llosa, *Aunt Julia and the Scriptwriter*, pp. 225, 366). Given these constraints, it is little wonder that the fictional radio melodramas gained favor among radio directors and audiences alike.

Throughout the 1930s and 1940s, radio serials from Cuba, Mexico, and Argentina dominated the Peruvian airwaves, often adapted for local audiences. The Cuban Revolution interfered with Peru's access to plays coming regularly from Cuba, forcing Peru to depend on others or practice self-reliance. In *Aunt Julia and the Scriptwriter*, loss of this access prompts Peru's Radio Central to seek out new scripts from a Bolivian writer, a logical recourse given the sharing of programs among countries. The writer, Pedro Camacho, is brought to work exclusively for Radio Central as an in-house writer, another logical move in view of the increasing unavailability of Cuban scripts due to the revolution. By the end of 1950s the switch to television had begun, and radio melodramas were fast becoming objects of nostalgia. Soon after inaugurating the first government-run television station in 1958, four private stations, including Panamericana Televisión, successor to Peru's Radio Panamericana and a business partner with Cuba's Goar Mestre, began operations (Fox, p. 81).

The Novel in Focus

The plot. *Aunt Julia and the Scriptwriter* is in many ways two novels in one, with chapters alternating between the life of the young writer Mario Vargas and summaries of the radio serials of Pedro Camacho. When the novel opens, Mario Vargas, often identified by his nickname Marito or Varguitas, is in law school and working as news editor for Radio Panamericana. On one extraordinary day he learns that Pedro Camacho has been hired to write, direct, and perform in radio dramas, and he meets his recently divorced Aunt Julia. His initial impression of each is unfavorable, but he soon comes to be fascinated by both of them.

Camacho proves to be a veritable machine. He churns out first four, then ten soap episodes a day, increasing Radio Central's listening share by 20 percent and becoming an object of devotion for hundreds of fans. His episodes, summarized in the novel's even-numbered chapters, are classic melodramas full of hopeless loves, shocking violence, and incest. Invariably they end with breathy questions to set up the next episode. In one such episode, the honorable Sergeant Lituma, "a man in the prime of life, his fifties, whom the entire Civil Guard respected" encounters a scarred, naked, and starving African in the port city of Callao (*Aunt Julia*, p. 60). A painful dilemma arises when Lituma is ordered by his lieutenant to kill the unfortunate man. As the episode ends, the listener is left guessing about what the noble officer will do:

> [T]wo, three, several seconds went by and he didn't shoot. Would he do so? Would he obey? Would the shot ring out? Would the dead body of the mysterious immigrant roll over onto the heap of unidentifiable, rotting garbage? Or would his life be spared, would he flee, blindly, wildly, along the beaches beyond the city, as an irreproachable sergeant stood there, amid the putrid stench and the surge of the waves, confused and sad at heart at having failed to do his duty? How would this tragedy of El Callao end?
> (*Aunt Julia*, p. 83)

Other cliffhanger endings leave listeners wondering how a newlywed will share with her husband the news that she is pregnant with her brother's child, how an obsessed rodent exterminator and tyrannical father can survive the violent rebellion of his family, and whether a ghetto priest will save his community of prostitutes and thieves from censure within the Catholic Church and competition from Protestant orders through reform or extermination.

Camacho eventually finds it impossible to churn out stories at such a maddening pace. As the "machine" breaks down from overuse, he confesses that he is losing control of his characters:

> I'm not the one who's mixing them up; they're getting mixed up all by themselves. And when I realize what's going on, it's too late. I have to perform a juggling act to get them back in their

proper places, to invent all sorts of clever reasons to account for all the shifting ground. A compass that can't tell the north from the south can lead to grave, grave consequences.

(*Aunt Julia*, p. 241)

Camacho attempts to retain a command over his stories by creating a series of disasters contrived to kill off the characters who have slipped from one melodrama and into another. But he fails, and must be sent to a mental hospital. In a panic at the loss of their star scriptwriter, the radio station's owner scrambles to find a replacement, musing over how to remedy the problem:

> CMQ, taking advantage of his situation, of the emergency, had quadrupled the price it was asking for its serials. . . . And to top everything off, it was going to be three weeks to a month before the new serials arrived, because Cuba was in a mess, what with the terrorism and the guerrillas, CMQ had been turned topsy-turvy, with people arrested and all kinds of troubles. But leaving Radio Central listeners without any serials at all for a month was unthinkable, the station would lose its audience, Radio la Crónica or Radio Colonial would lure them all away, they'd already begun to be tough competition because they were broadcasting cheap, vulgar Argentine soap operas.
>
> (*Aunt Julia*, pp. 342-43)

Though listenership plummets with the change, the station is sufficiently desperate to have Varguitas, their young news director, step in to patch together more episodes. In his own writing, the intellectual Varguitas has so far been incapable of winning an audience. Though he has one short story published in *El Comercio*, most of his efforts wind up in the trash. Only when he leaves Peru for graduate study and work in Europe will his writing shift from a stop-gap means of income to a serious career.

As Varguitas moves towards realizing his dream of being a writer, his life takes on the appearance of a novel. His relationship with Julia is, in her words, a "love affair of a baby and an old lady who's also more or less your aunt. . . . A perfect subject for one of Pedro Camacho's serials" (*Aunt Julia*, p. 90). Visiting Lima from her native Bolivia, Julia is surprised to find her ex-husband's young nephew a grown man, and even more surprised when he kisses her:

> "Listen, Marito," I heard her murmur disconcertedly, but I interrupted her by whispering in her ear: "I forbid you to call me Marito ever again—I'm not a little kid any more." She drew her face away to look at me and tried to force herself to smile, and at that point, almost automatically, I leaned over and kissed her on the mouth.
>
> (*Aunt Julia*, p. 58)

The two develop an odd sort of romance, full of clandestine meetings, kisses, and talk of Pedro Camacho but without more intimate contact or a sense of future.

Inevitably, others discover the relationship, first Varguitas's best friend Javier, then his cousin Nancy, then, alarmingly, his aunts and uncles, and more alarming still, his parents in the United States. With the relationship's stakes suddenly raised, Varguitas decides to propose to Julia. He sets off to find a "kindhearted idiot of a mayor" who will marry them despite his young age—at 18 he still needs his parents' approval—and despite Julia's older age (she is 32), divorced status, and Bolivian citizenship (*Aunt Julia*, p. 278). When the family is informed of the wedding, Varguitas's next task is to calm them down, especially his father, and prove that he is old enough to be married. At this point, the story takes a leap, recounting in one short paragraph the transformation of Varguitas into a serious writer during his eight-year marriage to Julia.

The novel ends some years after the marriage does, when Varguitas—remarried now to a blood relative, "a cousin of mine this time (the daughter of Aunt Olga and Uncle Lucho, by some odd coincidence)"—returns to Lima and encounters his old radio station colleagues (*Aunt Julia*, p. 358). Though most have prospered, Pedro Camacho has by this time been reduced to a pathetic shell of a man. The one-time radio star collects crime reports from Lima's police precincts for a scandal sheet and lives with his wife, "[a]n Argentine years past middle age, fat as a sow" who "sings tangos half-naked . . . at the Mezzanine, that nightclub for penniless wretches on the skids" (*Aunt Julia*, p. 371).

A closed circle. As nearly all of Lima tunes in to follow Pedro Camacho's radio serials, they elicit a type of unity that crosses cultural and class lines. It is an illusory unity, though. The divisions resurface in the dramas themselves, as we see in the powerless and anonymous African awaiting his fate at the hands of Sergeant Lituma. Camacho creates his characters with broad strokes and a heavy reliance on stereotypes. One of his first tasks upon arrival in Lima is to map out the neighborhoods where his dramas will be set. The divisions are clear: "Ancient Ancestry, Affluent Aristocracy" for one neighborhood, "Bums Fairies Hoodlums Hetaerae" for another, and "Sailors Fishermen Sambos" for another still (*Aunt Julia*, pp. 48-49). He holds a special antipathy for Argentina, made public through an endless flow of verbal slurs. The Argentine ambassador calls them "'slanderous, perverse, and psychotic' references" to what Camacho sees as the homosexual tendencies and utter cultural and moral poverty of the Argentines (*Aunt Julia*, p. 127). Though his hatred of Argentina may be ascribed to his promiscuous and estranged Argentine wife, his generalized use of broad racial and socioeconomic strokes has everything to do with his vision of the writer's craft:

> I'm a man who can't abide halftones, murky waters, weak coffee. I like a straightforward yes or no, masculine men and feminine women, night or day. In my works there are always blue bloods or the hoi polloi, prostitutes or madonnas. The bourgeoisie doesn't inspire me or interest me—or my public, either.
>
> (*Aunt Julia*, pp. 49-50)

The world of Lima's bourgeoisie, Varguitas's world, is also tightly defined. He snickers at the uneducated. The unusual image of a woman with a llama on her head, a symbol of the motherland, is held up as proof of Peruvian ignorance:

> The foundry workers had not understood the sculptor's instructions to crown her with a votive flame—a *llama votiva*—and instead had topped the statue off with the animal of the same name.
>
> (*Aunt Julia*, p. 193)

On another occasion Varguitas gleefully takes to task a young man for not knowing that the French novelist Honoré de Balzac had been dead for more than a century. The minimal direct contact Varguitas has with Peru's masses is marked by passing and often mocking references to both the class and race of those he encounters. For example, the general assistant at the radio station, Big Pablito, is described as a clumsy and illiterate mestizo whose utter lack of class is reflected in the epilogue by dyed hair slathered with huge quantities of brilliantine "like an Argentine of the 1940's," flashy clothes, and "a gold ring with an Inca design" that advertises his newfound wealth (*Aunt Julia*, p. 362). When Varguitas's friend Javier marvels at "[t]he intelligence of the proletariat" on hearing the mayor of Grocio Prado's suggestion that Varguitas's birth certificate be altered to make him appear to be of age to marry, Varguitas admits that "[i]t never crossed our minds that that was the solution, and this—man of the people, with his brilliant common sense, saw it in a flash" (*Aunt Julia*, p. 314). Nonetheless, he can't resist noting how slowly and painstakingly the mestizo mayor enters the marriage into the log: "I calculated that . . . it had no doubt taken him more than an hour to make the entry" (*Aunt Julia*, p. 315).

When Marito leaves to pursue his dream of being a writer in Europe, the Peru he knows has already begun to change. The hints of diversity found on the radio have become inescapable on the streets of Lima by the time he returns a decade later. Varguitas explores his now unfamiliar city as a spectator would, "going to little popular clubs and to theaters to see indigenous folk dances, wandering about the tenements of slum districts, strolling through sections of town that I was not very familiar with or didn't know at all" (*Aunt Julia*, p. 360).

> Jampacked now and possessed of a distinct Andean flavor, a street on which it was not rare to hear Quechua spoken amid the strong odor of fried food and pungent seasonings, it in no way resembled the broad, austere avenue frequented by white-collar workers . . . ten years before. . . . There in those blocks one could see, and touch, in a nutshell, the problem of the migration from the countryside to the capital, which in that decade had doubled the population of Lima and caused to spring up like mushrooms, on the hillsides, the dunes, the garbage dumps, that ring of slums where thousands and thousands of people ended up, rural folk who had left the provinces because of the drought, the backbreaking working conditions, the lack of prospects for a better future, hunger.
>
> (*Aunt Julia*, p. 361)

This late show of interest in the plight of Peru's masses notwithstanding, Varguitas and his circle of friends and relatives are most at ease operating among their own. The intimacy shared within this circle, where individuals are identified by nicknames (Marito, Varguitas) or family connections (Aunt Julia, Uncle Lucho) but never by race, stands in contrast to the formal use of titles (Don Mario) and consistent ethnic labeling of those outside the family circle. Varguitas's life revolves around his family, with daily meals and conversations with some 18 aunts, uncles, and cousins along with other more distant relatives. Perhaps it is only natural, then, that he fall in love with Julia; who is, albeit by marriage, his aunt. The marriage points to Varguitas's discomfort with the variety of classes and races of his world. The concept of a closed set of relationships reappears in its most radical form— incest—in one of Camacho's radio dramas. Outside the world of *Aunt Julia and the Scriptwriter*, it will reappear later in Vargas Llosa's 1988 foray into the erotic novel, *In Praise of the Stepmother*, and in its 1997 continuation, *The Notebooks of Don Rigoberto*. That the relationship between Varguitas and his aunt Julia borders on the incestuous appears to be of little concern to the family—they are more concerned about the couple's ages and Julia's marital status, and arrange a hasty dispensation to allow Marito's later marriage to his cousin. Beyond the family, the reaction is not so blasé: on hearing that Varguitas and Julia want him, a "mestizo farmer" to perform their marriage, one mayor reacts with indignation, shouting "No, not a chance, there's something fishy going on if a white couple come to get married in this godforsaken village" (*Aunt Julia*, p. 311).

Sources and literary context. In an interview done as he was putting the finishing touches on *Aunt Julia and the Scriptwriter*, Vargas Llosa observed that "it took shape, like almost everything I've written, from my old memories" (Vargas Llosa in Oviedo, p. 155). Culled from his experiences while writing for Radio Panamericana en Lima, the author based his character Pedro Camacho on his recollection of a "literary caricature, the writer of the Bolivian soap operas, Raúl Salmón" (Oviedo, p. 155). Other facts are likewise drawn from actual experience: Cuba's Radio CMQ was indeed run by Goar Mestre and it did in fact sell radio serials to Radio Panamericana, which was run by the Genaro family. From these details to the twists and turns of his own romance with Julia Urquidi, many nuances are transcribed directly from real life. At the outset Vargas Llosa intended "to alternate a chapter totally, or almost totally imagined, with a chapter of personal history, authentic, documented"; however, he found that despite this intention, "memory is tricky and gets contaminated with fantasy, and . . . imagination seeps in, takes hold and inevitably becomes part of what one is writing" (Vargas Llosa in Oviedo, p. 159). Among the fictional elements that creep into this novel is a flexible use of time, with the years of his actual courtship with Julia (1953-54) moved forward to blend more closely with the years of the Cuban revolution (1958-59) (Kristal, p. 92).

Vargas Llosa's real-life models have pointed out other discrepancies. Raúl Salmón, the inspiration for Pedro Camacho, expressed irritation at his presence in the novel. Evidently unimpressed by Vargas Llosa's assertion that he included faithful representations of autobiographical details, Salmón noted that if he ever knew the young Vargas Llosa it was only in passing (Moore). He began his career as a playwright and founder of Bolivia's social theater movement, worked briefly as a radio scriptwriter, then returned to Bolivia to continue writing for the theater and to get elected as mayor of La Paz, a fate far less melodramatic than that of the novel's Camacho. Julia Urquidi Illanes, the inspiration for Aunt Julia, likewise takes issue with the novel's "autobiographical" parts. Although the two parted amicably after their eight-year marriage, the bad feelings and public gossip that arose from the novel changed this. Her bitter 1983 memoir *Lo que Varguitas no dijo* (*My Life with Vargas Llosa* [1988]) was written as a response.

Events in History at the Time the Novel Was Written

The communist star dims. In *Aunt Julia and the Scriptwriter*, there is excitement followed by disappointment in both branches of the novel. Pedro Camacho creates radio serial worlds with massive appeal but eventually they disintegrate, and Varguitas passionately courts Julia but their marriage ultimately fails. Both storylines can be read as a metaphor for the illusions raised and then dashed by the Cuban revolution (Kristal, p. 98). Although the Cuban revolution was widely supported by intellectuals and sympathizers around the world, several events helped dim its glow. As noted, when Castro nationalized several key industries in 1960, the already suspicious United States pulled back from relations with Cuba, breaking off diplomatic ties in 1961. Castro found himself depending more on the Soviet Union for trade and military support and imposed increased Soviet-style restrictions on Cuban society.

Over the course of the 1960s, as Castro's government settled in, some of the original enthusiasm for absolute artistic liberty began to wane. The formation of a Writers' Union in 1961 signaled an early step towards restricting intellectual and artistic freedom. Arts organizations such as the Casa de las Américas were subject to increasing regulation, often self-imposed by directors wanting to support the revolution however they could. Though Cuba never embraced socialist realism, in which real-life stories demonstrate the need for socialism, the argument that "no artist could remain non-political since that in itself implied a political stand" was made on repeated occasions (Thomas, p. 1,466).

The 1971 *caso Padilla* caused many, including Vargas Llosa, to openly break with the Castro regime. The incident began when Cuban poet Heberto Padilla, jailed for his critical stance against Castro's regime, was released and publicly renounced his counter-revolutionary ideas. This gesture was widely seen as one that the regime had forced Padilla to make. Vargas Llosa himself drafted a letter to Castro "affirming the unequivocal allegiance to Cuban socialism by the signatories but also communicating their anger regarding Padilla's confession as an unnecessary and deplorable Stalinist practice on the part of the Cuban government" (Kristal, p. 72). Many leading intellectuals signed the letter, but Vargas Llosa was the first one to be singled out for vilification in the international press, then shunned by editors and colleagues.

Afterward Vargas Llosa grew disenchanted with socialism and gravitated toward capitalism. The successive governments of Fernando Belaúnde (1963-68) and General Juan Velasco (1968-75) had shown that Peru's old economic order was no longer viable. Belaúnde devised but never implemented policies of land reform, placating the coastal landowners but arousing the anger of Andean peasants. Velasco's military government broke with the existing order. He nationalized the oil and other industries, proposed a massive restructuring of the economy, and decreed massive land reforms, but ultimately they were abandoned. Neither Belaúnde nor Velasco was able to stem the growing anxieties of both the upper and the lower classes. As civil crisis loomed, Vargas Llosa became increasingly convinced that communism, with its emphasis on government-led reforms and control of business, was not the solution for Peru. He would eventually propose what he saw as a better solution—free enterprise and international trade—to resolve the nation's social and economic disarray. But this proposal would not be made until years after the release of *Aunt Julia and the Scriptwriter*. This novel instead emerges out of Vargas Llosa's growing disenchantment with leftist ideology, a nostalgic look at reality, and the very real need for fantasy.

The shift to telenovela. By the end of the 1950s, radio serials were giving way to television. When Cuba's serial writers fled the island for other parts of Latin America after the 1959 revolution, they completed the switch to television scriptwriting. Goar Mestre, the former head of Cuba's Radio CMQ, settled in Argentina, where he founded and successfully ran channel 13 until the government nationalized the media in 1974. Despite the emergence of a more political cinema in the 1960s and 1970s, television soap operas have captured the minds and imagination of the continent. Beyond their broad cultural reach, the *telenovelas*, or television soap operas, represent a major source of income for the top-producing nations of Mexico, Venezuela, Argentina, and Brazil. From these countries, the tapes are sold throughout the world for dubbing or adaptation.

VARGAS LLOSA FOR PRESIDENT

As Aunt Julia reminds Varguitas, he "was the hope of the tribe" and his dalliance with writing and his aunt represented a threat to the family's future. After all, as Varguitas admits, "that cancerous family of mine had every expectation that I'd be a millionaire someday, or at the very least President of the Republic" (*Aunt Julia*, p. 169). In the novel these goals are abandoned to the pursuit of literature, but a curious real-life parallel would appear a decade after the book's publication that developed differently. The 51-year old Vargas Llosa would indeed run for president of Peru. During the summer of 1987, Vargas Llosa felt moved to respond to a speech given by the populist president Alan García with an article opposing García's proposed nationalizations of banks and other companies (Vargas Llosa, "A Fish," p. 23). To his surprise, Peru rejected the official plan and embraced Vargas Llosa's resistance, pulling him towards what would become the creation of the conservative Movimiento Libertad (Freedom Movement) and his bid for the 1990 presidential elections. Though widely favored to win, the author lost to another political newcomer, Alberto Fujimori. Frustrated by popular acceptance of what he perceived to be a lack of substance in Fujimori's campaign, Vargas Llosa left Peru and returned to his adoptive home of Europe. In rejecting Fujimori's victory as the mere product of "impressionistic images and metaphors, ham acting, fancy turns of phrase and defiant remarks," the writer echoes the frustration Varguitas feels in the novel, at both the enormous success of Pedro Camacho's dramas and the failure of his own early short stories (Vargas Llosa, "A Fish," pp. 70-71).

Radio serials have continued to broadcast melodramas through the writing of Llosa's novel to the present day. Cuba's Radio Agramonte still offers several radio serials for $70 per 20-minute episode. But today's airwaves are dominated by televised soap operas. Panamericana Televisión of Peru presents nationally and internationally produced series based on historical, contemporary, and even youth-oriented themes. *Simplemente María* [*Simply María*], a drama originally produced for radio, went on to become the most popular telenovela ever. A "simple human tale of a woman who, like so many others, leaves her home and family to move to the city in search of new horizons," *Simplemente María* includes many of the elements seen in Pedro Camacho's dramas (Campo, p. 23; trans. E. Sutherland). The characters are stock. María is poor but hard-working and brave, and she believes in love. Alberto is wealthy but frivolous, selfish, and concerned about social class. From the middle class, Esteban is an idealistic but timid man, who expresses his love for María through his unwavering support. María falls for Alberto's charm and good looks, but when she tells him she's pregnant and suggests they marry, his reply is immediate: "You're crazy! Don't you understand that until I finish school I'll never make enough money to support a family?" (Campo, p. 25; trans. E. Sutherland). Although she will wait for Alberto, María is on her own: "'I alone will fight for my son.' Later, cradling her son, María promises that the child will never experience the misery, hunger, and poverty that she has had to bear" (Campo, p. 25; trans. E. Sutherland). When Alberto finishes school, it becomes clear that class, not money, is what keeps him from marrying María:

> "Your world isn't mine and it never will be! You're just a maid!"
> "I'm the mother of your son, Alberto, the mother of your son!"
> (Campo, p. 31; trans. E Sutherland)

Heartbroken, María buries herself in work, learning first to read, then becoming a seamstress, and eventually opening a series of successful boutiques.

Audiences were mesmerized by María's plight, following the story through its radio, television, film, and even magazine versions. Though an early television version aired in Argentina in 1967, it was the second, Peruvian version that would spawn worldwide imitations. Against this real-life backdrop, the novel's seemingly insatiable audience in Lima for the radio serials of Pedro Camacho is entirely believable. In fact, Peru stands out as Latin America's major consumer of soap operas, with 30 soaps being shown daily on Lima's five television stations.

Reception. *Aunt Julia and the Scriptwriter* was generally recognized as a novel of transition, marking a shift from Vargas Llosa's earlier, more socialist period into later more conservative ideas. Reactions to the novel vary widely: some critics evaluated the work on its literary merit. Others considered it in terms of the writer's politics, and many acknowledged both facets of the work. In her review, Kathleen Leverich praised the "entertainment, wit, imagination, and high style of the novel," while adding that "[a]s with soap operas, the book is best when you're in the thick of things. Beneath the frenetic surface, there's no real exploration of three-dimensional questions" (Leverich in Mooney, p.1,382). In a review for *The New York Times*, William Kennedy deemed the novel "a satire of myriad social types and classes, and . . . a work that celebrates story: story that gives pleasure to a large number of people, story also as a pleasure principle for the writer" (Kennedy in Mooney, p. 1,383). More strident critics condemn *Aunt Julia* for its lack of a clear social message, questioning Vargas Llosa's position "that political advocacy be divorced from the stuff of literature" (Alonso, p. 57). Acknowledging that it is "at first glance, an apolitical novel," Efraín Kristal concludes with an illuminating second glance:

> In fact, the novel makes a subtle political point akin to Vargas Llosa's disenchantment with the Cuban Revolution. . . . With *Aunt Julia and the Scriptwriter* the fifties is no longer, as in Vargas Llosa's previous narrative, a period of hopeless corruption. The fifties in Peru becomes a period that evokes nostalgia because its problems seem innocent and unimportant in comparison to those that the Cuban Revolution would bring.
> (Kristal, pp. 97, 98)

—Erika M. Sutherland

For More Information

Alonso, Carlos J. "*La tía Julia y el escribidor*: The Writing Subject's Fantasy of Empowerment." *PMLA* 106 (1991): 46-59.

Bethell, Leslie, ed. *The Cambridge History of Latin America: Latin America since 1930, Spanish South America*. Vol. 8. New York: Cambridge University Press, 1984.

Campo, Manuel J. *Simplemente María y su repercusión entre las clases trabajadoras*. Barcelona: Avance, 1975.

Cannon, Terrence. *Revolutionary Cuba*. New York: Thomas Y. Crowell, 1981.

Fox, Elizabeth. *Latin American Broadcasting: From Tango to Telenovela*. Luton: University of Luton Press, 1997.

Keen, Benjamin. *A History of Latin America*. Boston: Houghton Mifflin, 1992.

Kristal, Efraín. *Temptation of the Word. The Novels of Mario Vargas Llosa*. Nashville: Vanderbilt University Press, 1998.

Mooney, Martha T., ed. *Book Review Digest*. Vol. 78. New York: H. W. Wilson, 1982.

Moore, Don. "Aunt Julia and a Visit with a Bolivian Scriptwriter." 1994. http://www.swl.met/patepluma/south/bolivia/tiajulia.html (19 July 2002).

Oviedo, José Miguel. "A Conversation with Mario Vargas Llosa about *La tía Julia y el escribidor*." Trans. Marcela Loiseau de Rossman. *Mario Vargas Llosa. A Collection of Critical Essays*. Ed. Charles Rossman and Allan Warren Friedman. Austin: University of Texas Press, 1978.

Salwen, Michael B. *Radio and Television in Cuba: The Pre-Castro Era*. Ames: Iowa State University Press, 1994.

Thomas, Hugh. *Cuba or The Pursuit of Freedom*. New York: Da Capo Press, 1998.

Vargas Llosa, Mario. "A Fish out of Water." Trans. Helen Lane. *Granta* 36 (1991): 17-75.

———. *Aunt Julia and the Scriptwriter*. Trans. Helen Lane. New York: Penguin, 1995.

Blindness

by
José Saramago

José Saramago (1922-) was born in Azinhaga, in the inland Ribatejo region of Portugal, but his family moved to the seaside capital of Lisbon when he was still a child. His parents were not wealthy, so he acquired a secondary education in a vocational school, training to become a mechanic. Saramago nonetheless found time to read widely and worked only briefly as a mechanic before progressing through various newspaper jobs—from clerical worker, to production assistant, proofreader, and newspaper columnist. After the democratic revolution of 1974 deposed Portugal's right-wing dictatorship, Saramago became adjunct editor of the major Lisbon newspaper *Diário de Notícias* (Daily News). Meanwhile, his literary career began unspectacularly, including one novel, two collections of verse, and four volumes of journalistic writing, none of which attracted much attention. It was only after being dismissed from his job at the *Diário de Notícias* in 1975, in the wake of a counter-revolutionary coup, that he took up his writing career in earnest. He produced a collection of short stories and a second novel before writing a third, critically acclaimed, novel, *Levantado do Chão* (1980; untranslated, Raised from the Ground). Similar acclaim and greater commercial success followed for subsequent novels, including *Memorial do Convento* (1982; *Baltasar and Blimunda*, 1987), the work that launched him on a series of critical and commercial triumphs. Saramago's well-publicized loyalty to the Portuguese Communist Party and his outspoken views relating to politics and current affairs (both in Portugal and internationally) have led many to view him as a controversial

THE LITERARY WORK

A novel set in an unnamed city in an unspecified year; published in Portuguese (as *Ensaio sobre a Cegueira*) in 1995, in English in 1997.

SYNOPSIS

A sudden and inexplicable epidemic of blindness devastates a city, and all normal patterns of life break down as its inhabitants slip into barbarism and squalor before some of the blind regain their sight.

figure. His rewriting of the gospel story in *O Evangelho Segundo Jesus Cristo* (1991; *The Gospel According to Jesus Christ*, 1993) provoked heated debate in which government ministers condemned his work. Their reaction contributed to his subsequent emigration to Spain. Meanwhile, worldwide acclaim for Saramago's writing continued, culminating in his being awarded the Nobel Prize for Literature in 1998. Achieving his typical mix of fantasy and awareness of the real world, *Blindness*, influenced by events in Saramago's lifetime, stands as a powerful indictment of man's inhumanity to man in any era.

Events in History at the Time of the Novel

Current events—a global survey. *Blindness* is set in an unspecified present, with references to some of the convenient accessories of contem-

José Saramago

porary living (such as automobiles) being the only specific indicators of this general period. These references, however, are rare and largely incidental to the development of character and plot, allowing essential features of human nature and human society to come into the spotlight. Nonetheless, the novel is clearly influenced by some major world events at the time of the writing, in the early 1990s, as well as by events the writer had witnessed earlier in his life.

Major humanitarian disasters have plagued the world during Saramago's lifetime, among them, the:

- Atrocities of the Spanish Civil War (1936-39)
- Gassing and execution in cold blood of 6 million Jews as well as other victims during World War II (1939-45)
- Dropping of atomic bombs on Hiroshima and Nagasaki in this war (1945), killing several hundred thousand Japanese
- *Gulags*, or labor camps and prisons, in which millions of political dissidents in the Soviet Union perished (1920s-50s)
- Pulverization of Vokovar and other cities in Croatia (1991-92) because of tensions among Serbs, Croats, and Bosnian Muslims
- Genocide of 500,000 to one million Tutsi and moderate Hutus by militant Hutus in Rwanda, east-central Africa (1994)

It is this lifelong experience that led Saramago in an interview given to a Portuguese newspaper at the time of the publication of *Blindness* to use the term "final solution" (with its clear echoes of the Nazi era, when this phrase was a euphemism for Hitler's ambition to totally annihilate the Jewish population of Europe). In the interview, Saramago employs this same phrase in relation to his novel when describing both the incarceration of the blind in an asylum and other events that overtake them there, thus suggesting that he was, indeed, thinking of some of the most horrific events of recent times when he wrote the text (Nunes, p. 16). These events certainly did not stop with the Holocaust, Hitler's final solution. From this mid-twentieth century abyss to the mid-to-late and then the late twentieth century, injustices raged.

Injustice and inhumanity was rife in the author's own home country. Portugal experienced a lengthy dictatorship from 1928 to 1974, mainly under the leadership of a conservative former professor of economics at the University of Coimbra, António de Oliveira Salazar. Salazar, whose dictatorship owed much to the models set by Mussolini's Italy and Hitler's Germany, resorted to brutal tactics to impose his will upon his people. His prisons resembled concentration camps. Among them were the prisons of Aljube, Caxias, and Peniche in Portugal. Caxias and Peniche sat near bodies of water; as the tide rose, the water filled the cells daily, leaving behind household rubbish and human excrement washed in from sewer outlets. But most notorious was the camp at Tarrafal in the Cape Verde Islands, where Salazar officials might jail, often under brutal conditions, anyone (from Portugal or its colonies) suspected of being an enemy of the regime. According to the Portuguese dissident António de Figueiredo, in the post-World War II era, such repression became more rather than less severe: "After 1945, as soon as the regime felt sure of its survival and new alliances, it passed from arbitrary but casual repression to a scientific system" of repression, whose brutality was worthy of the worst excesses of centuries past (Figueiredo, pp. 115-16). One prisoner reported that the camp at Tarrafal lacked the most basic elements of hygiene and that the only doctor on duty (a loyal Salazar supporter) caused many inmates to die of neglect. Prisoners who committed an offense in captivity were placed inside solid concrete blocks with few air ducts and relentless exposure to the baking African sun; coining a sardonic name for them, inmates called the blocks "frying pans" (Figueiredo, p. 113). Even after completing their jail sentences, many Tarrafal prisoners were never freed.

The international credibility of Salazar's fascistic regime was waning by the early 1970s. In July 1973, the Portuguese prime minister, Marcelo Caetano, visited Britain. Overshadowing his visit were revelations in the London *Times* newspaper of the massacre of 400 to 500 unarmed civilians by Portuguese troops at Wiriyamu in Portugal's colony of Mozambique (Hastings, p. 76). The following year Salazar's regime would be overthrown, but mass killings would continue elsewhere in the world.

Two decades later, in the year of the novel's release, huge massacres of rival ethnic groups (the Tutsis and the Hutu) took place in Rwanda. In addition to the immediate loss of human life caused by this conflict, millions were displaced into makeshift refugee camps in neighboring Zaire. Soon the camps were unable to cope with the massive demands placed on them; reports outlined horrific conditions. From September 1994 to September 1995, about a thousand people died in the camp at Gitarama (which was designed for 400 inmates but at one point held over 7,000). Each person had been forced to occupy less than half a square metre of space, many of them having to stand in mud and water constantly (*Keesing's Record of World Events*, p. 40634).

Depths of depravity. "Fighting," says a character in Saramago's novel, "has always been, more or less, a form of blindness" (Saramago, *Blindness*, p. 133). In other words, focusing on what is near at hand has allowed people to ignore their own degradation, as witnessed in the humanitarian disasters outlined above. Certainly the perpetrators of Hitler's final solution sank to these depths, as shown by records related to the annihilation and treatment of prisoners. How did Hitler's gas chambers, where most victims perished, work? In a way that allowed the executioners to avert their eyes, to become blind to the deed.

> The pellets of hydrogen cynanide, Zyklon-B, were supplied in metal canisters that were carried to the crematoria in a Red Cross ambulance. These pellets were poured into the gas chambers in the basement through the looped course of hollow metal shafts and were thrown out through evenly spaced openings. As soon as Zyklon-B came into contact with the air in the chamber it became gas. It worked in an upward direction, so that the first to die were the children and the last were the young and the strong who struggled to climb upward on the piles of corpses. [When] all was quiet . . . the members of the Kommando [forced laborers, mostly Jews] removed the corpses and transferred them to an elevator that carried them to the cremation room.
>
> (Yahil, p. 366)

More blindness followed on the part of the rest of the world. Among enemy targets bombed by the Allied powers (Britain, the United States, the Soviet Union) were German factories—the Buna Works plant, for example, which manufactured oil and rubber for the war effort and stood just outside the main final-solution death camp, Auschwitz. The question haunting the pages of humanitarian history is, Why did the Allies not bomb the gas chambers there? "Research has shown that the refusal of the American and British air force to bomb these installations stemmed from their disinclination to be involved with rescue actions per se" (Yahil, p. 639). The blindness, in this case, was therefore self-inflicted, an intentional averting of the eyes. The death and work camp inmates who escaped execution were put to hard labor for the Germans under abysmal conditions that made dirt, hunger, and brutality the norm. At Auschwitz, "Even the inadequate rations did not reach the prisoners intact: much of the bread and other items of food had been seized by the SS men [Hitler's Special Services force] and rerouted to their own kitchen," which brings to mind the commandeering of food rations by the thugs in *Blindness* (Yahil, p. 371). At one of the most infamous work camps, the Flughafenlager in Poland, was a particularly brutal sergeant by the name of Max Dietrich, who became infamous for his cruelty. On one occasion Albert Fischer, a colleague of Dietrich's and a German work leader himself, bore witness to a particularly savage beating.

> I saw that Dietrich beat the Jew so long until he lay unconscious on the ground. Then Dietrich ordered other Jews fully to undress the unconscious Jew and to pour water on him. When the Jew regained consciousness, Dietrich grabbed the hands of the Jew, who had defecated all over himself, dunked them in the excrement and forced him to eat the excrement. I walked away, as the spectacle sickened me.
>
> (Fischer in Goldhagen, p. 303)

That evening, Fischer found out, the Jewish worker, forced to feed on his own excrement, died. Less savage beatings occurred daily, something Fischer found no fault with at the time. "It was only in the later years that I gradually came to recognize that much was rotten" (Fischer in Goldhagen, p. 303). Here the blindness was genuine, not self-inflicted, the kind it would take another more sighted person to remedy by enlightening Fischer about the error of his colleagues' ways. That such sighted people existed, even in the Nazi Party, is confirmed by the actions of, Georg Duckwitz, an attaché in the German embassy in Copenhagen, Denmark, who alerted the Danes to Hitler's intention to deport their Jews in time for the threatened population to be evacuated to safety in Sweden (see Fralon, p. 79).

Righteous heroes, or the "farsighted." Individuals are for the most part half indifference, half malice, observes *Blindness*, yet at the same time, it is extraordinary "how selfless some people can be" (*Blindness*, p. 29). Aside from its depravities, the twentieth century provided examples of heroic fortitude and self-sacrifice in desperate circumstances. In Saramago's home country, in Portugal, such a hero presented himself in the person of Aristides de Sousa Mendes. The Portuguese Consul in Bordeaux, France, during World War II, Sousa Mendes defied the instructions of his own government by issuing false Portuguese identity papers to 10,000-20,000 Jews to allow them safe passage out of Nazi-occupied France. Circular 14, issued by the Portuguese Ministry of Foreign Affairs in November 1939, expressly forbade Portuguese consuls overseas from granting passports or visas to Jews expelled from their countries or to stateless persons in general. A man approaching the age of 55, who had never before disobeyed the Portuguese authorities, decided from May to July 1940 to rush visas to as many supplicants as possible so they could escape the Nazi grasp via Lisbon. Ignoring nationality, race, and religion, he refused to blindly follow unethical dictates:

> I cannot allow all you people to die. Many of you are Jews, and our constitution clearly states that neither the religion nor the political beliefs of foreigners can be used as a pretext for refusing to allow them to stay in Portugal. I've decided to be faithful to that principle. . . . The only way I can respect my faith as a Christian is to act in accordance with the dictates of my conscience.
>
> (Sousa Mendes in Fralon, p. 60)

After leading one of the most monumental rescue operations during the Nazi attempt to enforce the final solution, Sousa Mendes retired to Portugal, where, shunned by Salazar, he died in poverty in 1954. Certainly there were other such heroes, however rare. Raoul Wallenberg, a Swedish diplomat, facilitated the escape of some 30,000 Hungarian Jews. In Lithuania, for four feverish weeks, another consul, Chiune Sugihara, distributed 6,000 visas that carried Jews to Kobe, Japan, a country soon to be allied with Nazi Germany, and most of them lived out the duration of the war in Japan. As more recent events have shown, not all heroes need to be officials or prominent citizens either. Commoners also qualify: a simple student (reportedly called Wang Weilin) momentarily held up the procession of tanks in Tiananmen Square in Beijing, China, before the army brutally suppressed a pro-democracy student demonstration there in June 1989 (see Iyer). The righteous deeds of such heroes stand in stark contrast to the dastardly ones of the perpetrators of the humanitarian disasters described above. It is this contrast between the conflicting human impulses to good and evil that lies at the heart of *Blindness*.

The Novel in Focus

The plot. *Blindness* opens in the center of a busy modern city. The reader's attention is riveted on the immobility of one car, whose driver has been inexplicably struck blind while waiting at a traffic signal. Another motorist offers to drive him home, but then steals the car from his vulnerable victim. Soon, however, the thief too is struck blind. In short order, one character after another loses his or her sight, each initially linked by some degree of contact with the early victims of the outbreak. Among these early victims is the wife of an ophthalmologist, himself struck blind in this mysterious outbreak. Unique among the victims, she is not blind but chooses, for the love of her husband, to be treated as such. When he is taken away in an ambulance, she lies her way into accompanying him by saying she too has been struck blind. "The doctor's wife," as she is called, becomes the one character to retain her sight throughout the novel.

The government of this unnamed country chooses to protect the rest of the population from what seems to be an epidemic by isolating the blind in an abandoned asylum, where their living conditions are stark and minimal. It is made clear to the inmates that the government will show no concern for any illness or injury suffered by them; food supplies are delivered to the entrance hall of the asylum, then left there for the inmates to retrieve. It is their responsibility to dole out the rations fairly or unfairly, as they so choose. All hygiene and order quickly break down as the asylum becomes overcrowded with a constant influx of new residents—some 300 will end up quarantined here. Before long, in a desperate appeal for help, one inmate (who has suffered an injury) crawls towards the fence at the edge of the compound; he is shot dead by a soldier (*Blindness*, p. 76).

Conditions within the asylum continue to deteriorate as one group of male inmates imposes its own selfish interests on the rest of the population by commandeering all of the food supplies. First the group demands all of the valuables possessed by the others, then it insists that the female inmates provide sexual services in return for provisions. Under the leadership of the doctor's wife, who makes a conscious moral decision to kill the ringleader of the thugs as they rape the women of her ward, the previously victimized inmates rebel and set the asylum ablaze (*Blindness*, pp. 212-13).

When the inmates emerge from quarantine, they discover that those outside have also been stricken by blindness and that all order in the city has broken down. Groups of blind people shuffle around the streets in aimless fashion, desperately searching for whatever scraps of food can be found. The still-sighted doctor's wife has in tow six blind charges from the asylum—her doctor-husband, a girl with dark glasses, an old man with an eyepatch, the first blind man (who opened the novel) and his wife, and a boy with a squint, all of whom remain nameless throughout the novel. The doctor's wife makes use of her no-longer-secret powers of sight to help her charges reorient themselves to daily life. As they roam the city, they have chance encounters with individuals who have refused to give up all hope: a miserable old woman who has remained alive by eating raw chicken and whatever scraps of vegetables she can derive from her garden; a writer, who has continued to commit his experiences to paper even while being totally incapable of reading his own manuscript; and, as in other novels by Saramago (*The Stone Raft* and *History of the Siege of Lisbon*), a dog, the so-called "dog of tears," who watchfully consoles the doctor's wife in her darkest hours.

Eventually some of the characters recover their eyesight, and two—the girl with dark glasses, a former prostitute, and the old man with the eyepatch—declare their love for each other. The novel closes in the very earliest stages of what may prove to be a period of recovery for the city, but, as also happens in other novels by the author, the fate of the characters remains uncertain. There is no definitive happy ending here.

"Born to see this horror." The outstanding figure in *Blindness* is the doctor's wife. Willing to risk her own welfare for the sake of others, she ensures that some grasp is maintained on redeeming values in civilization, even as it threatens to fall apart. Her strength of character is demonstrated at the outset by her false claim to be blind in order to stay with her husband when the ambulance takes him away to the asylum (*Blindness*, p. 36).

STARING EVIL IN THE FACE—THE ALLEGORY CONTINUES

> Then he said, I seem to recognise your voice, And I recognise your face, You're blind and cannot see me, No, I cannot see you, Then why do you say that you recognise my face, Because that voice can only have one face [the face of evil].
>
> (*Blindness*, p. 180)

The two participants in this scene are the doctor's wife and the leader of the gang of thugs. The doctor's wife, who has been attempting to keep secret her ability to see, nearly lets that fact slip as she expresses her disgust at the unscrupulous blackmail inflicted upon her and the other women by these men who demand sexual access to them in return for food. Quickly she retracts her admission that she can see and instead transforms her slip into a deeper truth: the recognition that this man has become a representative of evil. Her consequent decision to kill him is based on moral principle, and the results are positive. It leads to the liberation of the inmates from their physical and emotional incarceration.

This capacity for self-sacrifice in the doctor's wife resurfaces again and again in the novel. She puts herself in her comrades' place, on two occasions quite literally by adopting blindness for limited periods on their behalf. First, she descends into the underworld of a supermarket storeroom in total darkness to find food (*Blindness*, pp. 228-31); second, she gropes through her own house—plunged into darkness in the absence of electric lighting—to fetch water for the boy with a squint. Immediately before this she has taken some trouble to explain to the boy the functioning of a paraffin lamp, promising him "One day you will see and on that day I'll give you the lamp as a present" (*Blindness*, p. 276).

THERE ARE NONE SO BLIND AS THOSE WHO WILL NOT SEE

Why did we become blind, I don't know, perhaps one day we'll find out, Do you want me to tell you what I think, Yes, do, I don't think we did go blind, I think we are blind, Blind but seeing, Blind people who can see, but do not see.

(*Blindness*, p. 326)

This brief conversation (between the doctor and his wife, who has the final word here) takes place on the very last page of the novel. Here the doctor's wife attempts to explain a factor that the novel deliberately leaves unexplained: what caused the epidemic of blindness in the first place? The early stages of the story tease the reader with various explanations, from simple contagion (almost all the early victims have either visited the doctor's surgery or been in contact with the first blind man), to moralistic explanations (the second blind man is a thief; the girl with dark glasses, a prostitute). The explanation above, given by the doctor's wife, becomes clearer when considering the epigraph to the novel's English translation: "If you can see, look. If you can look, observe." This saying (attributed by Saramago to the *Book of Exhortations*, an invented source of wisdom designed to sound as if it had the authority of the Old Testament) conceals a double-meaning: the Portuguese verb *reparar* (equivalent to the English "to notice") can also have the same meaning as the English "to repair," that is, to put right what is wrong. From the novel's earliest pages, almost all of the characters concern themselves primarily with attending to their own needs and fail to take heed of the requirements of others. Gradually they learn from the example set by the doctor's wife. Only after incidents such as the one in which the girl with dark glasses helps the old man with the eyepatch to bathe do the main characters begin to recover their sight.

What her speech indicates is a refusal to accept as inevitable and irreversible the steady decline in societal norms and civilized behaviour that she has witnessed, both inside and outside the asylum. Her speech also displays faith that humanity will recover its vision by recognizing the importance of the other person as an individual. "Let's hold hands and get on with life," says a character in the novel, implying that salvation lies in people's readiness to put themselves on the line for each other, as heroes of humanitarian catastrophes are often wont to do (*Blindness*, p. 304). Illustrating this in the novel, for the good of the community as a whole, a woman in the asylum dies in the act of setting fire to the barrier that blocks the door leading to the hoodlums' ward (*Blindness*, pp. 212-13).

If the doctor's wife knows when to be compassionate and self-sacrificing, she also knows when to make unpleasant moral choices. The incident that demonstrates this above all others is her killing of the leader of the gang of hoodlums who have taken control of the food supplies in the asylum, allowing the others access to them only in return for sexual services from the female inmates. In this instance of degradation, the doctor's wife takes advantage of her powers of sight for the good of the community as a whole; she ultimately kills the leader of the hoodlums while he is trying to take sexual advantage of another woman (*Blindness*, pp. 188-89).

The relationship between the doctor's wife and the hoodlum demonstrates the two opposing sides of human nature. On the one hand, she kills a man out of a sense of moral responsibility to the others, particularly the women, since she knows that he must be murdered if they are to retain their worth as human beings and that she is the only one able to commit the deed. On the other hand, the hoodlum's power is based on his possession of a gun. Emboldened by the assumption that no one can identify him (since they are living in a land of the blind), he exercises this power in an immoral fashion.

The Parable of the Blind, 1568 painting by Pieter Brueghel, also known as Pieter the Elder. Saramago's *Blindness* conjures comparable images.

How reflective of historical reality is his readiness to commit rape (as well as other brutalities) and the willingness of the doctor's wife to commit murder? Documents testify to the practice of both of these behaviors in real-life humanitarian catastrophes. During Hitler's final solution, rape was rare in the six death camps, though rumors and fears of it abounded. In labor camps like Skarzysko in Poland, however, survivors have reported brutal rape by German commanders even though they were not supposed to defile themselves by such shameful conduct with beings they regarded as inferior. One eyewitness told of a mass rape of young Jewish women, who were afterwards buried alive by the rapists in graves the women themselves dug (Ofer and Weitzman, p. 336). They had no savior, no doctor's wife, to rescue them. On other occasions, there were noble if ill-fated attempts to fight the evil, as she does in the novel. "When is it necessary to kill," wonders the doctor's wife, who, deliberating over the morality of her decision to commit murder, concludes that the act is justified "When what is still alive is already dead" (*Blindness,* p. 193). In real life, at Auschwitz, Rosa Robata may have asked herself the same question. With select inmates, she worked in a factory that handled explosives, some of which she smuggled to the crematoria workers, who blew up one of the crematoria on October 6, 1944, killing Nazi SS men in the process. Caught, the rebels were executed; one let slip Rosa's name, which led to her being tortured and executed by hanging.

Sources and literary context. *Blindness* may be related to at least three distinct literary traditions. The first is dystopian-style fiction, which features an imaginary place whose people lead dehumanized, or increasingly dehumanized, often fear-driven lives, as in William Golding's ***Lord of the Flies*** (1954; also in *Literature and Its Times*). Next comes the exploitation of the motif of blindness to depict shortcomings in human awareness of the wider world or of moral imperatives (see, for example, the short story by H. G. Wells "In the Country of the Blind" [1904], or the play *El concierto de San Ovidio* [1962; St. Ovid's Concert] by the Spanish dramatist Antonio Buero Vallejo). The third literary tradition involves the so-called question of "killing the Mandarin." The French expression *tuer le mandarin* ("to kill the Mandarin"), which refers to the notion that people will commit any act if they think they can remain undetected, was exploited by the nineteenth-century Portuguese novelist Eça de Queiroz in his *O Mandarim* (1880; in English, *The Mandarin*, 1993). Probably this notion that human beings lack a sense of responsibility for

THE CITY OF GHOSTS

In the novel, the inmates emerge from quarantine only to be confronted by the appalling realization that the world they knew has been destroyed during their incarceration. The people whom they see (through the eyes of the doctor's wife) on the streets of the city are reduced mostly to scavenging animals. On two occasions in the novel, the doctor's wife and her friends pass groups of blind people haranguing others regarding possible solutions to their crisis (*Blindness*, p. 298 and pp. 310-11). While the first of these passages is dominated by references to futile superstition and religious dogma thus prompting the doctor and his wife to ignore them and move on, the second one concerns different systems of government and social organization ("They were extolling the virtues of the fundamental principles of the great organised systems, private property, a free currency market"—*Blindness*, p. 310). There is in the sequence of the two incidents a gradual progression from the total destruction of the human spirit, through primitive beliefs, to a recognition that the recovery of civilization will be a long and gradual process, and, implicitly, one that will continue beyond the time scale of the novel (in an interview in the Portuguese cultural newspaper *Jornal de Letras* Saramago declared that we can only know if humanity resolves its problems on p. 311 of the novel, when the Portuguese edition of the novel has precisely 310 pages; see Nunes, p. 17). In this way, by deliberately not tying up all the loose ends (in the last few pages of the text, some but, significantly, not all the characters have recovered their sight, and normal life remains far from restored), Saramago effectively invites his readers to reconsider what they can do to improve their coexistence with others.

others influenced Saramago in his writing of this text. In an interview published at the time of the launch of the novel, the author himself remarked that "Our blindness is getting increasingly severe, because we want to see less with each passing day. What this book sets out to say, fundamentally, is precisely that all of us are blind to reason" (Nunes, p. 16).

Blindness, along with Saramago's subsequent two novels, *Todos os Nomes* (1997; *All the Names*, 1999) and *A Caverna* (2000; The Cave, untranslated), constitutes a trilogy of allegorical, apocalyptic novels. This trilogy is distinct from the earlier works that established Saramago as a major figure in Portuguese and world literature. These earlier novels (such as *Baltasar and Blimunda* [1982], or *The Year of the Death of Ricardo Reis* [1984, English 1991]) had a firm base in specific circumstances of Portuguese history, even if, in a number of respects, they reflected on wider issues than those explicitly described. What all of Saramago's novels have in common, however, is a profoundly ethical concern with the best and worst aspects of human nature.

Reception. *Blindness* was enthusiastically received, both in Portuguese and in its English translation. By 1995 Saramago was undoubtedly the pre-eminent literary figure in Portugal, and the allegorical style adopted in this novel, combined with the serious moral issues raised by it, ensured that it would receive extensive attention in his native country. Leading newspapers such as the weekly *Expresso* (The Express) and the cultural journal *Jornal de Letras, Artes e Ideias* (Journal of Literature, Art and Ideas) ran lengthy, in-depth interviews with the author, in the course of which he expanded on some of the principal issues raised by the novel. One of the country's leading literary critics, Maria Alzira Seixo, reviewed the novel prior to its publication and she compared the figure of the doctor's wife to the heroine of an earlier novel by Saramago—Blimunda, in *Baltasar and Blimunda*. This heroine too possesses exceptional and inspirational powers of vision.

In his review of the English edition of the work (in the *Times Literary Supplement*), Michael Kerrigan recognized the novelist's powers of insight into human nature, even in a text where no characters are named, declaring that they "live, thanks to Saramago's gravity-defying gift for creating compelling individuals, without anything in the way of human detail to earth them" (Kerrigan, p. 20). Luís de Sousa Rebelo had earlier written in the same journal of the novel's universal qualities: "There are no characters, only voices who inhabit a mythical space" (Rebelo, p. 40).

Andrew Miller (writing for the *New York Times Book Review*) focused on both the author's individual linguistic style and the overall relevance of the work to our times:

> The unencumbered language hurries us forward at such a pace it is difficult to do justice to the subtlety and occasional beauty of the architecture, as if we were driving headlong through a great city at night. . . . There is no cynicism and there are no conclusions, just a clear-eyed and compassionate acknowledgement of things as they are, a quality that can only honestly be termed wisdom.
>
> (Miller, p. 8)

—David Frier

For More Information

Figueiredo, António de. *Portugal: Fifty Years of Dictatorship.* New York: Holmes and Meier, 1976.

Fralon, José-Alain. *A Good Man in Evil Times: The Story of Aristides de Sousa Mendes—The Man Who Saved the Lives of Countless Refugees in World War II.* Trans. Peter Graham. New York: Carroll and Graf, 1998.

Frier, David G. "Righting Wrongs, Re-Writing Meaning and Reclaiming the City in Saramago's *Blindness* and *All the Names.*" *Portuguese Literary and Cultural Studies* 6 (spring 2001): 97-122.

Goldhagen, Daniel Jonah. *Hitler's Willing Executioners: Ordinary Germans and the Holocaust.* New York: Vintage, 1996.

Hastings, Adrian. *Wiriyamu.* London: Search Press, 1974.

Iyer, Pico. "The Unknown Rebel." *Time Magazine,* 13 April 1998. http://www.time.com/time/time100/leaders/profile/rebel2.html (24 June 2002).

Keesing's Record of World Events 41, nos. 7-8 (25 September 1995): 40634.

Kerrigan, Michael. "The I of Saramago." *Times Literary Supplement,* 19 December 1997, 20.

Miller, Andrew. "Zero Visibility." *New York Times Book Review,* 4 October 1998, 8.

Nunes, Maria Leonor. "José Saramago: O Escritor Vidente". *Jornal de Letras, Artes e Ideias,* 25 October 1995, 15-17.

Ofer, Dalia, and Leonore J. Weitzman, eds. *Women in the Holocaust.* New Haven: Yale University Press, 1998.

Rebelo, Luís de Sousa. "By his readers shall ye know him." *Times Literary Supplement,* 17 October 1997, 40.

Saramago, José. *Blindness.* Trans. Giovanni Pontiero. San Diego: Harcourt, 1997.

Seixo, Maria Alzira. "Crónica sobre um livro anunciado: *Ensaio sobre a Cegueira" Jornal de Letras, Artes e Ideias.* 11 October 1995, 22-23.

Yahil, Leni. *The Holocaust: The Fate of European Jewry.* Trans. Ina Friedman and Haya Galai. New York: Oxford University Press, 1990.

Blood Wedding

by
Federico García Lorca

> **THE LITERARY WORK**
>
> A play set in Andalusia, Spain, in the early 1900s; premiered in Spanish (as *Bodas de sangre*) in 1933; in English (as *Bitter Oleander*) in 1935.
>
> **SYNOPSIS**
>
> A bride abandons her new husband and runs away with her ex-lover on the day of her wedding. Her scorned husband seeks to avenge his honor, which leads to the death of the two men.

Federico García Lorca (1898-1936) was born in the Andalusian town of Fuente Vaqueros, but spent much of his youth in the nearby city of Granada. Many years later he would be executed by a firing squad in Granada during the early weeks of the Spanish Civil War. Lorca studied law at the University of Granada, but in 1919 he moved to Madrid to pursue his passion for art and literature. Lorca published both drama and poetry in the early 1920s. It was not, however, until he released his collection of poems *Gypsy Ballads* (1928), in which he linked Spanish folklore to the new, surreal imagery of his day, that Lorca earned national recognition. His theater during the 1920s alternated between comedy and avant-garde experimentation in works such as *The Shoemaker's Prodigious Wife* (1926) and *Once Five Years Pass* (written in 1929 and 1930). In the 1930s, Lorca began to focus more intensely on tragedy and wrote his three most important dramatic works, all of them about the oppressive society of rural Spain: *Blood Wedding* (1933), *Yerma* (1934), and *The House of Bernarda Alba* (1936). *Blood Wedding*, the most stylized of the three, portrays an unfulfilled passion through an extraordinary blend of lyricism, surrealism, and realistic detail that characterizes the author's artistic and social concerns from the early 1930s until his death in 1936.

Events in History at the Time of the Play

The rise of two Spains. In 1898, the year of Lorca's birth, the United States and Spain went to war. At first glance, this brief conflict between the two countries would appear to offer only a minor rupture within the flow of Spanish history. After all, the war lasted only a few months and the death toll was small on both sides. Yet the symbolic drama of Spain's defeat weighed heavily upon the national community. Although many factors came to a head in 1898 to bring about the Spanish loss—for example, Cuba's desire for independence from Spain, the U.S. government's growing confidence in its own imperial power, and economic and political turmoil in Spain—the moment became a national disgrace that shook Spanish pride to its very core. No longer able to sustain even the appearance of a world power, Spain seemed bereft of historical will. For much of the nineteenth century, it had drifted in and out of political chaos. Liberal and conservative factions formed the center of

Federico García Lorca

ongoing tensions. On the one hand, tradition-bound supporters of the church, military, and monarchy promoted the status quo; on the other hand, liberal and progressive forces pushed for democracy, working-class power, and secularization (the removal from Church control of civic and other matters). With the stark defeat of its forces by the United States at the dawning of a new century, and with no agreement at home on what path to follow in the future, Spain seemed trapped without hope, its society divisive and defeated.

Unfortunately for Spain, circumstances were not about to improve. King Alfonso XIII ruled under a constitutional monarchy from 1902 to 1923, but his government managed to lead the nation only deeper into turmoil. His inability to control conflicts within the central government in Madrid, strife with workers in the emergent labor unions, and prolonged fighting by the Spanish army in wars in Morocco led to Alfonso's fall from influence and then power. In 1923, with the support of the military and conservative factions within government, General Miguel Primo de Rivera proclaimed himself head of state. His rule would last seven years and prove in the end to be as ineffective as King Alfonso's.

Discontent among the liberal and professional classes in Spain undermined Primo de Rivera's government from the beginning, and its troubles worsened as the decade progressed until economic turmoil and the financial crisis of 1929 led to his downfall. When the general resigned his office in January of 1930, Spanish politics again plunged into chaos, with no national consensus or respected political leader to inspire hope that the nation could be unified. Supporters of democracy had, however, won their long fight for change, even if their victory seemed perilously fragile. In April of 1931, when national elections were held for the first time in several decades, the second Spanish Republic was born. Spain was now governed by an elected president and legislative body with the constitutional authority to write laws that could change the face of the nation.

Yet once again matters took a turn for the worse. With wide swings in the outcome of elections in 1931, 1933, and 1936 (which pitted conservative, right-wing against liberal, left-wing political parties), the Republic proved unable to provide economic stability or national unity. Individual liberties, supposedly guaranteed now that Spain was a democratic republic, fell victim to the powerful agendas of political factions. Liberal dominance in the elections of 1931 and 1936, interrupted by a conservative victory in 1933, dashed all hopes of continuity. As each new government proposed radical policy changes to appease its assortment of supporters, the country grew increasingly polarized. An old concept resurfaced, the notion of "two Spains," a nation sharply divided between traditionalists and progressives, with large political factions in each camp. A heightened sense of anxiety plagued a nation in which the notion of two Spains loomed as an unresolvable dilemma. By 1936 conservative forces (supporters of the church, monarchy, and military) stood firmly aligned against progressive forces (the trade unionists, anarchists, and social democrats). Peaceful reconciliation seemed distant and improbable. On July 18 of that year, the conservative General Francisco Franco Bahamonde led a military uprising against the Republican government. Civil war had begun.

Lorca and his times—politics and society. Lorca came of age during these years of turmoil in Spain, and their influence on his personal, artistic, and political views is substantial. It would be inaccurate to claim for Lorca the role of political activist. Throughout his life he refused to join a political party, despite intense pressure from his leftist friends, and he generally avoided election campaigns and endorsements of political candidates. Nonetheless, he often attended rallies and offered broad support for progressive causes, and Lorca embraced the liberal policies of the Republican government elected in 1931. He signed documents promulgated by the Communist Party in support of Spanish workers, and he often spoke on the important role of art in bringing about social justice. In the later years of his life, Lorca even joined with other writers to honor the Communist poet Rafael Alberti, and he paid homage to the controversial writer Ramón del Valle Inclán, a long-time champion of Republican politics. In short, over the course of his adult life, and in particular during the Republican period of the 1930s, Lorca lent visible support to the liberal factions of the "two Spains." As noted, he had by this time achieved national acclaim for his writing. Lorca drew on this celebrity to endorse policies and concepts that clashed with the traditional, orthodox factions set on preserving Spanish ways of the past. In *Blood Wedding* the clash emerges with tragic consequences. The Bride agrees to an arranged marriage for the sake of her family's honor and out of respect for tradition, but then her passion compels her to flee with Leonardo, the man whom she desires but has been prevented from marrying because of their unequal social standing. (Except for Leonardo, all the play's characters bear the generic name of the group they represent in rural Spain.) Lorca's challenge to social tradition could hardly be stronger. Faced with the behavioral codes of a conservative, Catholic Spain that prescribes both custom and convention, his characters choose desire over reason. They opt to transgress, not to conform.

Lorca remained committed to liberal politics in Spain throughout his life. Yet what inspired deeper and more personal passion in the writer transcended the local and peculiarly Spanish. The brutality of fighting in World War I had forever tainted the myths of heroism and the nobility of warfare. Like many writers of the time, Lorca condemned what he perceived as inhuman destruction carried out in the name of nationalism. These antiwar sentiments continued to shape his view of violence later in life. Even as Spain spiraled toward civil conflict in 1935, and Lorca continued to embrace Republican causes, he refused to endorse violence to achieve political goals. As he noted in an interview with the newspaper *El Sol* in 1935, "I am a brother to everyone, and I loathe the man who sacrifices himself for an abstract nationalist ideal (Lorca in Stainton, p. 435).

Lorca thus showed a commitment to human dignity and freedom in the broadest sense. His exposure to other cultures in New York and South America in the late 1920s and early 1930s intensified his awareness of the often harsh obstacles to personal freedom faced by others outside his homeland. In New York especially, Lorca witnessed at close range both the anguish and pride of African Americans long repressed by white society. His collection of poems *Poet in New York* (published individually in 1931) vividly portrays African-American culture; some of Lorca's most difficult poetry, it also underscores his commitment to social justice.

THE "TWO SPAINS"

The idea of a Spain that was divided into two nations—not geographically, but politically and culturally—began to emerge in the late eighteenth century. One Spain was progressive and secular, with an increasing interest in liberal democratic principles. The other Spain was conservative, Catholic, and traditionalist. This second Spain linked the uniqueness of Spanish culture to an imperial time when the Church, the military, and the monarchy gave firm shape to the political and cultural concept of the nation. The conflict between the two Spains persisted throughout the nineteenth and early twentieth centuries, causing political turmoil and economic instability, finally exploding into Spain's early-twentieth-century civil war (1936-39). The roots of the civil war, won by the conservatives, are thus deeply entrenched in Spanish society, which helps explain the violence and bitterness of the conflict that brought Francisco Franco to power.

Lorca's stay in New York proved to be a liberating experience for him personally, above all because it helped bolster his willingness to live more openly as a homosexual. When he returned to Spain in 1930, his concerns turned more inward, to his own alienation in a culture that often seemed to deny him the possibility of personal fulfillment. In the plays that would follow, including *Blood Wedding*, Lorca portrays the repressive elements of Spanish society that made life disconcerting and even perilous for him as a homosexual and a Republican sympathizer: a rigid family structure, class stratification, an honor code rife with hypocrisy, sexual oppression (most strikingly for women), and a moral and social order rooted in Catholic dogma and aristocratic tradition.

Lorca and his times—art and the avant-garde. Early in his career, Lorca was often referred to as the poet of Andalusia (the region in southern Spain) or the poet of the gypsy spirit (he began to write his gypsy ballads in 1924 and published them in book form in 1928). As he matured and grew more secure in his writing through the 1920s, however, Lorca became fully immersed in the movements of the most avant-garde European artists. Of course, he did not stand alone in his interest in exploring innovative and experimental forms of writing, particularly in poetry. Other Spanish authors (for example, Rafael Alberti, Pedro Salinas, Gerardo Diego, and Vicente Aleixandre) shared with Lorca a desire to experiment with the language of poetry. Most importantly, they focused on the creation of new metaphors as they sought to perfect poetic images that would enable language to detach itself from reference to the real world. The goal was to lift poetry above the world and allow it to stand alone. Not only did Lorca and his friends embrace such a purpose; they viewed it as essential for the development of new forms of writing.

Lorca also sought to incorporate innovative techniques into his theater. He developed a keen interest in the dreamlike imagery of surrealism, the early 1900s artistic movement that set out to reunite the conscious and the unconscious, to join the everyday world to that of dreams and fantasy in order to create an absolute reality, or surreality. Lorca praised the experimental drama of his time—from the grotesque plays by Ramón del Valle Inclán in Spain to the inversions of fiction and reality by the playwright Luigi Pirandello in Italy. In works such as *Once Five Years Pass* (1931) and *The Audience* (left incomplete in manuscript form in 1931), Lorca himself experimented by fragmenting time and space and distorting traditional character to such an extreme that he knew even as he wrote these plays that the Spanish public was not prepared for them. He in fact viewed the two works, and later his unfinished *The Dream of Life* (1935), as unperformable.

Yet Lorca remained an independent thinker, and in important ways he stood apart from his avant-garde friends. What distinguished him above all was not only that he had become an accomplished dramatist, but also that he seemed unable to embrace fully a way of writing that isolated itself from social engagement. In other words, while he was drawn to the experimental artistic movements of his era (surrealism, ultraism, cubism), they seemed insufficient for defining the role that literature could play in the larger scheme of life and community. As Lorca recognized, even his most experimental works of drama were tied to social and psychological issues of his time. His drama struck a depth that in fact revealed obsessions of his life as well as his writing: failed love, fear of death, repressed desire and sexuality, and social injustice—the very issues that surface in *Blood Wedding*.

Lorca attached great social value to theater. He believed that it could transform the cultural spirit of Spain and, more specifically, that it could serve as a medium for representing inequality and social oppression. The depth of Lorca's commitment to the potency of theater moved to the fore in the 1930s in two important and somewhat diverse ways. First, impressed by the power of drama to ennoble the spirit and deepen the sensibility of humanity, Lorca brought theater to the people of Spain. In 1931, when the new Republican government set out to reduce the nation's high rate of illiteracy, Lorca not only vigorously supported government programs to educate Spanish youth about literature and art, but volunteered to participate as a music teacher. In the end, however, he took on a much more ambitious project: the formation of a traveling theater company called La Barraca, which was to be funded by the government and directed by Lorca. The company's goal was to rescue Spanish theater from the public's growing indifference, to place it firmly at the center of the cultural consciousness across the nation. Lorca himself was motivated by his belief that the public performance of dramatic works not only brought a shared heritage into the cultural spotlight, but also helped to forge national identity through connections with the classical works of Spanish drama. Under Lorca's directorship (1931-34), La Barraca barnstormed the nation and offered almost 200 free performances of classical Spanish plays over four years. These four years were for Lorca among the most satisfying in his life, for they allowed him to indulge his passion for directing and performing while nurturing his growing sense of social commitment to the Spanish masses.

The second way in which Lorca's commitment to theater moved to the fore in the 1930s was through his writing rather than his directing. During the years of his association with La Barraca, Lorca began to envision more concretely how to represent social despair through tragedy. His insistence on the lyrical and poetic essence of drama meant that his plays had to offer more than a narrow reflection of everyday life. Yet he clearly viewed drama as a medium for challenging deeply entrenched injustices of Spanish society. Lorca declared on many occasions during the 1930s his belief that writers should embrace social causes precisely because they have a unique relationship with the public. As he observed in an interview in 1935, the writer "must set aside his bouquet of white lilies and sink to his waist in the mud" (Lorca in Stainton, p. 435). In other words, writers must expose the ills of culture through their art and inspire the public to seek change. Importantly, this change must occur not only through the implied call to action whenever injustice diminishes a society's well-being, but also through a heightening of public tolerance for difference and individual freedom. It is precisely this concern with individual freedom and desire, frequently constrained by societal tradition and dogma in Spain, that lies at the heart of Lorca's tragic dramas and that gives compelling resonance to *Blood Wedding*.

The Play in Focus

The plot. Lorca's choice of *Blood Wedding* as the title of his play points to a paradox in the movement of the plot, which shuttles back and forth between celebration and tragedy. Indeed, the tension embedded in the juxtaposition of the terms *blood* and *wedding* creates conflict from the very beginning of the play and foretells the tragic outcome: the harmony and joy of marriage (the most traditional of rituals meant to strengthen social order and continuity) will be replaced by its association with blood and the implication of violence and death.

Act 1 introduces the Groom and his Mother, who frets over her son as he leaves home one morning to work in the family vineyard. The Mother's husband and older son had been murdered by the neighboring Félix clan many years before, and the Mother fears that her only remaining son will meet the same fate. When she later learns from a neighbor that her son's bride-to-be was once rumored to have been in love with Leonardo, a member of the rival clan, she grows both angry and afraid. Her mixed emotions portend the spilling of blood, but her desire to have grandchildren and sustain the family name overpowers her fear. She thus agrees to her son's request to marry the Bride, but remains haunted by the specter of the Félix family and the tragedy they have brought to her life.

Following closely the traditions of rural Spanish society, the marriage of the Bride and Groom has been arranged with parental blessing but with little opportunity for the two young people to become acquainted with each other. It is important for them to marry "properly." Their union must represent a linking of wealth between families of equal standing in the community; in this case, the couple's future children will assure the passing of both families' bloodlines to a new generation of landowners and sustain the social status quo. When the Mother and the Groom visit the Bride's house to meet her Father and plan the wedding, the plans are finalized. While the Mother worries about the Bride's commitment to her son and her one-time ties to the Félix clan, the Bride declares her willingness to proceed with the marriage. In particular she embraces the traditional role of women in Andalusian society as explained to her by the Mother: "Do you know what it is to be married, child? . . . A man, some children, and a wall two yards thick for everything else" (García Lorca, *Blood Wedding*, p. 51). The Bride dutifully responds, "I'll know how to keep my word" (*Wedding*, p. 52).

But Lorca knew well that giving one's word and keeping it when desire and passion strain against what it prohibits, were ideal ingredients for a conflict that would lead to tragedy. Hence he created the only character in *Blood Wedding* to bear a name, Leonardo, as the forbidden object of the Bride's passion. Through Leonardo, Lorca sets into motion the series of events that will lead to the wedding of blood. Leonardo's lower social and economic standing precluded any hope of marriage to the Bride a few years earlier, but he has since wedded another (the Wife), and she has borne him a son. Nonetheless, Leonardo gallops his horse each night past the Bride's house hoping to re-ignite their passion. With the Bride herself scarcely able to harness her true feelings, Lorca establishes by the end of Act 1 the social and personal tensions that drive his rural tragedy: the passion of Leonardo and the Bride, at once checked and aroused by the impending wedding; the history of hatred between the Mother and the Félix family; and the practice of arranged marriage for the accumulation of land and wealth.

Lorca uses Act 2 of *Blooding Wedding* to stage a traditional Andalusian wedding, with song, dance, and dialogue that underscore the festive celebration. It is a happy occasion, and the guests enhance the mood with jokes and sly comments about the couple's wedding night. At the same time, however, Lorca uses Act 2 to undermine

Catherine Feller (left) and Katina Paxinou in the 1959 BBC television version of *Blood Wedding.*

the celebration and deepen the force of passion between Leonardo and the Bride. Leonardo is the first to arrive at the Bride's house on the day of the wedding, outpacing his Wife as he sets his horse at full gallop. He and the Bride face one another for perhaps the last time as the sound of voices signals the arrival of other guests. Only the presence of the Bride's Servant seems able to keep the two apart as Leonardo professes his love:

> To burn with desire and keep quiet about it is the greatest punishment we can bring on ourselves. . . . You think that time heals and walls hide things, but it isn't true, it isn't true! When things get that deep inside you there isn't anybody can change them.
>
> (*Wedding*, p. 60)

Leonardo's dramatic declaration that no one can change what is deep inside him foreshadows the climax. It hints that desire may well undo the authority of social custom, represented by both the wedding itself and the Bride's earlier promise to the Groom's Mother to honor her word. Indeed, as the wedding grows closer, its ability to insure proper behavior in the former lovers diminishes.

At the wedding reception, the celebration of the marriage follows the festive rhythms of singing and dancing. Yet the theatergoers know, if the wedding guests do not, that a competing passion is about to erupt. As the celebration reaches a frenzy, the Groom seeks out the Bride for a dance. When she cannot be found, Leonardo's Wife dramatically announces the inevitable turn in the plot: "They've run away! They've run away! She and Leonardo. On the horse. With their arms around each other, they rode off like a shooting star!" (*Wedding*, p. 77). It is the Groom's Mother, however, who embraces the social pact of family honor and personal vengeance and thus compels the tragic outcome. As Act 2 draws to a close, she casts aside her fear of losing another family member to the Félix clan and admonishes her son to act: "Go! After them! . . . No, Don't go. Those people kill quickly and well . . . but yes, run, and I'll follow! . . . The hour of blood has come again" (*Wedding*, pp. 77-78).

The third act of *Blood Wedding* stands among the most discussed of Lorca's theater. Not content with the mix of lyricism and realism that marks the first two acts, Lorca moves the play into the surreal. The third act begins in a forest, where three woodcutters discuss the turn of events at the wedding. Functioning like the chorus of a Greek tragedy, the woodcutters predict the confrontation between Leonardo and the Groom: "The bridegroom will find them with or without the moon. I saw him set out. Like a raging star. His face the color of ashes. He looked the fate of all his clan" (*Wedding*, p. 80). Here the woodcutters not only link the fate of the Groom to that of his brother and father at the hands of a member of the Félix family, but also draw attention to the Moon, which will soon emerge as an important figure.

In short order, the woodcutters' conversation is interrupted by the arrival of a fourth woodcutter with his face painted white and playing the role of the Moon. It is he who will seek out Leonardo and the Bride, shine his light upon them, and compel the tragic destiny that awaits them. Speaking in verse, and calling forth with lyrical force the cosmic and natural images of Andalusia, the Moon covets his role in the violent outcome that awaits:

> But this night there will be
> red blood for my cheeks,
> and for the reeds that cluster
> at the wide feet of the wind. . . .
> O let me enter a breast
> where I may get warm!
> A heart for me!
> Warm! That will spurt
> over the mountains of my chest;
> let me come in, oh let me!
>
> (*Wedding*, p. 82)

As the scene grows increasingly lyrical and symbolic, Death appears in the guise of an old beggar woman dressed in green cloth. She announces that the end is near ("It has to be here, and soon. I'm worn out" [*Wedding*, p. 82]). The Moon and Death now work together—he to light the way and she to claim her victims. The Bridegroom rides by on her horse, and the Beggar Woman shows him the way to Leonardo and to death.

But the play has not yet fully prepared the way for death. Not only is it unclear who must die (the Groom? the Bride? Leonardo?) but the passion of Leonardo and the Bride has so far only been staged at a distance, or more furtively in the presence of others. In one of the most dramatic scenes of the play, the two lovers savor the intensity of their passion but recognize the urgency of their plight. As the couple rides through the forest on Leonardo's horse, they move into the moonlight. Having already placed themselves both literally and figuratively outside of society when they fled the wedding, they foresee their destiny but resist its imposing finality. The Bride pleads for Leonardo to go on without her ("I love you! I love you! But leave me"), but her love and his desire are too strong (*Wedding*, p. 87). Both understand the nature of their transgression; both know the Groom must seek revenge. It is this social imperative of honor and family reputation that will determine the outcome.

Yet as the play underscores this social imperative, it also implies that the transgression is coupled with something else. A more cosmic and perhaps mysterious force shapes the couple's circumstances. Leonardo refuses to abandon the Bride amid an intensely lyrical profession of his love; he senses that his fate lies beyond the rational, beyond his ability to control it:

> And when I saw you in the distance
> I threw sand in my eyes.
> But I was riding a horse
> and the horse went straight to your door.
> . . . Oh, it isn't my fault—
> the fault is the earth's—
> and this fragrance that you exhale
> from your breasts and your braids.
> (*Wedding*, p. 87)

The play thus calls forth the erotic allure of the Bride, linked to the mysterious earth of Andalusia, and suggests that Leonardo will be vanquished by a power that, at least in part, he cannot comprehend. Coupled with the two lovers' flight and explicit rejection of the social order, this power provides the final impetus for the inevitable turn of the plot. Indeed, the hour of death has come. Leonardo and the Bride embrace and leave the stage, two violins are heard, ear-splitting shrieks break the harmony, and abruptly the violins grow quiet. The old Beggar Woman appears on stage without a sound as the scene comes to an end.

THE ROLE OF HONOR

The concept of honor in Spain has long shaped social behavior. While not reducible to a simple, fixed set of rules, the Spanish idea of honor can be viewed within two broad categories: as human virtue and dignity in the eyes of God (intrinsic honor); as reputation and standing in the eyes of society (extrinsic honor). In classical Spanish theater, these dual concepts of honor often helped determine the plot and prescribe the outcome of a play. Restoring one's honor was essential to the resolution of a conflict and to the eventual achievement of social justice. In *Blood Wedding,* Lorca portrays the demands of the honor code as impetus for violence and tragedy. According to this code, the affront to the Groom's good name—the flight of the Bride with her lover Leonardo—must be avenged, not just condemned. Only in this way can the Groom's reputation and social standing be maintained. So strong is the devotion to honor that even the Bride attempts to claim what little remains to her. In the end she desperately declares her virginity intact, but the other women make clear that they will continue to shun her. In both instances the devotion to honor in rural Andalusia begets tragedy. Leonardo and the Groom suffer a violent death; the Bride will forever live isolated within her community.

The final scene of the play clarifies the plot (both Leonardo and the Groom are dead). Three young girls gossiping outside the Mother's house now assume the role of chorus. The Bride, the Mother, and the Wife also enter to lament the loss of their loved ones. The Mother angrily strikes the Bride, who offers no resistance. Instead, she seeks to reclaim her honor, for she and Leonardo have not consummated their affair. Leonardo's Wife can only listen in grief. Each of the women is now condemned to loneliness wrought by a passion that could not be constrained. Moreover, theirs is not a shared loneliness; each will live isolated in her anguish. The women now come to embody the tragic vision of Spanish society, which demands the subjugation of desire to social order.

The social culture of *Blood Wedding*. At first glance, *Blood Wedding* can be seen as a condemnation of passion when it diminishes social order and community well-being. After all, desire seems to blind the two lovers to moral, social, and even economic conventions that make possible the solidity of society and guarantee its continuity. Yet, in the context of Lorca's own beliefs, and his support for liberal Republican ideas of his day, *Blood Wedding* emerges as a cry of protest against traditional Spanish society.

By the early 1930s Lorca understood more clearly than ever that his influence as a dramatist lay in his challenging of social conventions that restrict both individual and collective freedom. While still embracing experimentation in the form and language of his work, he argued that theater must move "along with the rhythms of its time, focusing the emotions, the suffering, the struggles, the dramas of those times. . . . The theater must focus on the total drama of contemporary life" (Lorca in Anderson, p. 34). The rhythms he sought to pursue in his trilogy were personal and political. In particular, they had to do with social impositions on individual desire.

Spanish Republicanism of the 1930s firmly embraced principles that showed higher regard for individual freedom than institutional coercion. Idealistic, perhaps even utopian, the idea of individual freedom—not only freedom to develop as an individual, but freedom from the imposition of rigid moral codes and traditions—gained Lorca's enthusiastic support. In 1931, for example, he attended the legislative debate in Parliament on the role of religion in Spanish life, a debate that produced some of the early and most controversial Republican laws separating state and church. One year later, as he composed *Blood Wedding*, Lorca purposefully set out to lay bare the oppressive underpinnings of the tradition-bound society of rural Spain. He thus builds *Blood Wedding* around the sacrosanct ritual of the wedding, which represents both Catholic morality and conservative social convention. The shared economic status of the Bride and Groom's families that brings them together to begin with, the unequal economic standing of the Bride and Leonardo that keeps them apart, and the overarching social restrictions of arranged marriage all coalesce in *Blood Wedding* to make the natural force of passion the inevitable agent of tragedy.

The tragedy of *Blood Wedding* extends to all those whom the wedding was intended to appease. This group includes all the main characters. The Mother accepts the wedding even though she fears that the Bride's previous relation with Leonardo may have sullied the young woman's purity as well as her son's honor. The Bride agrees to marry the Groom and to accept the role of traditional wife though she does not love him. The Groom readily perceives the benefit of joining his lands with those of the Bride and hopes that love will follow. The Father believes that one day the Bride and Groom will be able to buy additional lands and increase the family wealth. With the Bride married to another, Leonardo's Wife believes that her own family and life with Leonardo may finally be secure. Only Leonardo—the sole named character of the play—stands consistently outside the implied order of the wedding and allows his passion full reign. His pursuit of the Bride thus sets into motion the breakdown of social harmony that the wedding had promised, and a wave of disaster engulfs all those involved.

The question arises, of course, does the play warn against the excess of passion or against the excess of societal control? On the one hand, if Leonardo and the Bride could have restrained their passion and embraced the will of their families, such a sacrifice would clearly benefit the larger social order. On the other hand, if this social order were not dictated by conservative tradition, class distinction, and Catholic morality, Leonardo and the Bride would not have found themselves bereft of a way to fulfill their desire as individuals. The play clearly takes a position. Reflecting Lorca's long-held political and social beliefs, it favors the privilege of individual freedom over the compelled conformity of social restriction. Hence the tragedy of *Blood Wedding* emerges not simply as an instance of thwarted passion but as an illustration of social tyranny.

For Lorca, the consequences of this tyranny far outweigh its potential for establishing social order. Indeed, when the Mother follows social tradition and beseeches her son to avenge the family honor as well as his own, the wedding that seems to mark social harmony spins swiftly out of control and comes instead to mark societal oppression. The Bride who had once embraced the ritual of proper marriage in the end yields to desire, in spite of the shroud of dishonor that the community will wrap around her. As the final curtain falls, Leonardo's wife enters to complete the portrait of these women who, like the men, are victims of narrow, crushing forces of tradition. It should be noted, however, that the play never condemns marriage per se. Indeed, it revels in the gaiety and celebration of ritual, taking advantage of the opportunity to display the music and dance of Andalusia. However, when the stability and order represented by the wedding are imposed at the cost of individual freedom, Lorca is quick to condemn social orthodoxy as an empty pursuit without redemption.

Sources and literary context. When Lorca read in the newspaper in July of 1928 that a bride had fled with her ex-lover on the day of her wedding, and that the lover was later found dead, he knew immediately that he had found the plot of tragedy. The Spanish press gave extensive coverage to the incident, which had taken place in Almería province in southern Spain. One newspaper used the headline "Tragic Conclusion to a Wedding," and soon a ballad about the affair became popular throughout the region. As the drama took shape in Lorca's imagination over the next four years, he changed several details of the real-life story and invented characters and incidents absent from newspaper accounts (for example, in Lorca's play, the Groom and Leonardo die after an offstage fight; in real life the groom's brother murdered the ex-lover of the bride, and the groom himself remained alive). The story appealed to Lorca not just because of its sensational stir in the Spanish press, but also because it echoed the central concerns of much of his writing: passion, oppression, revenge, love, and death. With the elements of a tragic plot provided by the newspapers, he would imagine his own version of the story. He conceived a setting and characters bound by the customs of his native Andalusia, and he thickened the plot to create a rural tragedy with both national and universal dimensions.

Lorca wrote *Blood Wedding* as the first work of a trilogy in which he explores social injustice in rural Spain. *Yerma* (1934), the second work of the trilogy, reveals the tension between desire and social repression when Yerma, a lonely housewife trapped in a loveless marriage, is unable to conceive a child with her husband. Eventually Yerma strangles him, thus forever denying herself the opportunity to bear children. The final work of the series, *The House of Bernarda Alba* (1936), tells the story of a tyrannical mother who compels her five daughters to live confined within their house during the period of mourning for their deceased father. Repressed passions produce rebellion and suicide in the household, which in the end remains bound to the firm authority of Bernarda Alba. Each of the plays features women trapped by social tradition in roles that allow them scant freedom to fulfill their desires or escape the imposed conventions of their everyday lives.

In each of the three plays of his trilogy—*Blood Wedding, Yerma,* and *The House of Bernarda Alba*—Lorca explores the conflict between the overflow of passion and the rigid norms of social custom. It is in *Blood Wedding*, however, that passion most disrupts the social order with tragic consequences. Weighed against the rite of the wedding, the straightforward but powerful desire of the Bride and Leonardo threatens the continuity of the social order as they know it. In contrast, the title character in *Yerma* brings tragedy only to herself by killing her husband. In *The House of Bernarda Alba*, the suicide of Bernarda Alba's youngest daughter brings tragedy to the enclosed space of Bernarda's house. The tragedy of *Blood Wedding*, on the other hand, extends to all those whom the wedding was intended to appease.

Reception. On September 17, 1932, four years after first learning about the bride and her lover, Lorca gave a private reading of *Blood Wedding* to friends. In characteristic fashion, Lorca had mulled over the story for nearly four years without putting pen to paper, then, over a period of two weeks of frenetic writing he completed the entire piece. By all accounts, his friends were transfixed, and the premiere was soon planned for spring 1933.

Blood Wedding premiered in Madrid on March 8, 1933, to enthusiastic reviews. Lorca himself believed that the play would win him the large audiences and critical support that had eluded him in his recent experimental theater. His intuitions were correct. One critic linked the play to *Gypsy Ballads*, Lorca's earlier book of poems, and praised the work as a "stupendous rural tragedy" (Klein, p. 15). The reviewer for *ABC*, one of Spain's most conservative newspapers of the time, also found much to like about the play, although he expressed reservations about the lyrical symbolism of Act 3. On the whole, however, he praised the dramatist's ability to draw out the passion of his characters and compared the play to the Greek tragedies of Sophocles.

Two years later *Blood Wedding* premiered in New York City, this time to disparaging reviews. Critics considered it one of the worst plays of the season. Translated as *Bitter Oleander*, the English was stilted and the work dismissed as confusing, distant, and overstylized. One critic even condemned the use of Andalusian floral imagery in the dialogue as the language for a seed catalog rather than a play (Klein, p. 16). Subsequent productions in the United States, with new translations and more skilled direction, led to largely favorable reviews over the following decades. When *Blood Wedding* returned to New York in 1958 (in a production directed by Patricia Newhall), it received praise for its grace, poetry, and what one critic termed its "terrible beauty" (Klein, p. 17).

Since its first appearance in 1933, *Blood Wedding* has become the most performed of Lorca's theater, both within and outside Spain. Yet it is also generally viewed as the most difficult to produce. The mixture of poetry, prose, song, and dance with the deep sense of drama and tragedy, challenges actors to create authentic voices amid the changing tone and texture of the real and the surreal. Lorca himself co-directed the first run of *Blood Wedding* in 1933 because he understood the fine line in his play between well-staged tragedy and the potential for melodrama. As most critics have since realized, however, when performed as Lorca conceived the play, with both elegance of language and severity of passion, *Blood Wedding* is one of the most important Spanish dramas of the twentieth century.

—David K. Herzberger

For More Information

Anderson, Reed. *Federico García Lorca*. New York: Grove Press, 1984.

Carr, Raymond. *Modern Spain: 1875-1980*. Oxford: Oxford University Press, 1980.

Edwards, Gwynne. *Lorca: The Theatre Beneath the Sand*. London: Marion Boyars, 1980.

García Lorca, Federico. "Blood Wedding" in *Three Tragedies*. Trans. James Graham-Luján and Richard L. O'Connell. New York: New Directions, 1955.

Gibson, Ian. *Federico García Lorca: A Life*. London: Faber, 1989.

Gilmour, John. "The Cross of Pain and Death: Religion in the Rural Tragedies." In *Essays in Honour of J. M. Aguirre*. Ed. Robert Havard. New York: St. Martin's Press, 1992.

Klein, Dennis. *Blood Wedding, Yerma, and The House of Bernarda Alba: García Lorca's Tragic Trilogy*. Boston: Twayne, 1991.

Lima, Robert. *The Theatre of García Lorca*. New York: Las Americas, 1963.

Newton, Candelas. *Understanding Federico García Lorca*. Columbia: University Press of South Carolina, 1995.

Piasecki, Andy, ed. *File on Lorca*. London: Methuen, 1991.

Soufas, C. Christopher. *Audience and Authority in the Modernist Theater of Federico García Lorca*. Tuscaloosa: University Press of Alabama, 1996.

Stainton, Leslie. *Lorca: A Dream of Life*. New York: Farrar, Straus, Giroux, 1999.

The Death of Artemio Cruz

by
Carlos Fuentes

Born in Mexico City in 1928 to a diplomat father, Carlos Fuentes grew up primarily in Mexico and the United States. He was living in Mexico in the 1950s, when his first two novels were published (*Where the Air is Clear* [1958] and *The Good Conscience* [1959]). His third novel, *The Death of Artemio Cruz,* established him as an author of world renown. Fuentes began writing it in 1960 in Cuba, after Fidel Castro's revolution there. At the time "almost the entire intellectual world of Latin America shared a fervor—or at least a sympathy—for the Cuban Revolution" (Krauze, p. 653). It especially touched Mexicans in Fuentes's generation, who had been struggling to define their national essence and were disturbed by the course onto which their own revolution had veered.

THE LITERARY WORK

A novel set in Mexico from 1889 to 1959; published in Spanish as *La Muerte de Artemio Cruz* in 1962, in English in 1964.

SYNOPSIS

On his deathbed, a millionaire tycoon reviews twelve momentous days of his life.

Events in History at the Time the Novel Takes Place

Dual legacy. Fuentes's novel begins during the reign of President Porfirio Díaz, first a fighter for reform but then a dictator who monopolized power for his own sake. In the 1870s Díaz seized control of the government from the legitimate president, going on to "win" reelection seven times. He governed for 34 years (1876-80 and 1884-1911) of painful poverty but also blessed peace. Before Díaz, Mexico had endured a century of armed disputes—the War of Independence (1821), the War of the North American Invasion (otherwise known as the Mexican American War [1848]), and the War of the French Intervention (1862). In collusion with conservative Mexicans, France had seized control briefly, but then internal tensions exploded into more armed conflict: led by Benito Juárez, liberal Mexicans wrested power from the conservatives and threw out the French in the War of the Reform (1867).

Díaz fought under Juárez. By the time Díaz himself was in power, two contrary traditions had emerged—a spirit of reform and a tenacious spirit of dictatorship. The 1800s had been dominated by military strongmen, or *caudillos*, which boded well for dictatorship. Preeminent among the strongmen was Antonio López de Santa Anna, who was president eleven times between 1833 and 1855. Owner of a vast *hacienda* (landed estate) in Veracruz, Santa Anna grew so enamored with power during his decades of rule that he had his minions call him "His Most Serene Highness."

In 1857 the spirit of reform took over, and the liberals drafted a new constitution, a vain at-

A meeting of Pancho Villa and Emiliano Zapata in the Presidential Palace, Mexico City, around 1916.

tempt to break the hold that a small minority of hacienda owners, army leaders, and the Catholic Church had over the nation's wealth. At the time the Church controlled close to one half of all the land, and earned enormous income from rents and loans to its allies, the hacienda owners. The liberals tried but failed to loosen the Church's grip. They auctioned off only a fifth of Church lands, and to little effect. The upper class grew slightly, enlarged by the few Mexicans who, like Artemio's father-in-law, old Gamaliel Bernal, in *The Death of Artemio Cruz,* had the cash to buy the auctioned parcels.

Not at all happy about the 1857 reforms, which infringed on their monopoly of the country's riches, the conservatives attacked the liberals, and Mexico descended into nearly 20 years of civil war. Meanwhile and afterward, the bulk of the nation remained impoverished. In fact, people grew poorer during Díaz's reign, many of them losing their lands because of legal maneuvering, cause enough for revolution. Of 11 million rural dwellers, fewer than 3 percent of them owned any land by 1910. Hacienda owners let vast areas lie fallow year after year, while peasants went hungry and their lives were made even more miserable by *rurales* (rural police), who charged them "for living, for the hens, for the pigs" (García in Krauze, p. 284). In cities and in the countryside, illiteracy was rampant: 75 percent of the Mexican population could neither read nor write.

Again the spirit of reform reared its stubborn head, or, in this case, hand. The spark that lit the Mexican Revolution came not from a rifle or a torch but from a book by a member of the educated elite—*The Presidential Succession of 1910* by Francisco I. Madero. Madero declared Mexico's problem to be the concentration of power in one man, and he prescribed a solution—a return to the Constitution of 1857, along with the principle of "Valid Voting, No Reelection." A president, counseled Madero, should serve as head of the nation for only one term.

Díaz thought Madero's ideas outrageous and proceeded to engineer an eighth reelection for himself and his deputies. Madero mounted an antireelection campaign against Díaz that attracted thousands of supporters, so in 1910 Díaz's government decided to arrest Madero. From prison, Madero wrote the *Plan de San Luis,* calling for revolution: "Fellow citizens, do not hesitate, even for a moment! Take up arms, throw the usurpers out of power, recover your rights as free men!" (Madero in Krauze, p. 255). Released from prison, Madero took up arms. Díaz started his eighth term, but scattered uprisings and Madero's capture of Ciudad Juárez convinced him to resign. Afterward, Madero became temporary president, demobilizing his own troops, and leaving Díaz's federal army and congress in place. The strife had hardly begun.

The Mexican Revolution—an overview. Mexico's was the first of the momentous revolutions of the twentieth century. Lasting more than a decade (1910–24), the Revolution led to subsequent Mexican upheavals, from civil conflicts in the 1920s to radical economic changes in the 1930s. During the war years, the number of men-in-arms at any one time was never great. In 1915, the most factious year, fewer than 100,000 soldiers fought in a nation of over 15 million. Still, the overall human and economic costs of the Revolution were astronomical—240,000 dead in combat and 750,000 dead from related diseases, plus destruction to mines, factories, haciendas, and railroads. And there was also an untabulated cost—the dissolution and betrayal of burgeoning democratic ideals, as reflected in the novel by Artemio and his fellow army officers.

Madero served as president for less than a year. Within months of his victory, federal soldiers, under Victoriano Huerta, staged a counterrevolution that included Madero's assassination (February 22, 1912). Huerta became president until pro-Madero rebels and trouble with the United States drove him into exile in 1914. Three caudillos emerged among the pro-Madero rebels—Francisco "Pancho" Villa, General Álvaro Obregón, and Governor Venustiano Carranza. In the south, a fourth caudillo, Emiliano Zapata, promoted his *Plan de Ayala*, calling for restitution of land to its rightful, deed-carrying owners. These four caudillos took on distinct personae: Zapata became champion of the landless; Villa, though not concerned with land, won renown as a Robin Hood-style fighter out to ravage the rich for the benefit of the poor; Carranza was the landowner-reformer; Obregón was the military genius.

Villa, Obregón, and Carranza met at the Convention of Aguascalientes to hammer out a future government for Mexico, but there was an ominous break between Carranza and Villa. Remaining uncommitted for the moment, Obregón finally sided with Carranza. It was a politically astute choice, since Governor Carranza operated under an aura of legitimacy, in contrast to the renegade Villa.

Exercising his military prowess, Obregón went on to defeat Villa. The great battles of 1915 were fought in the Bajío, the fertile central basin north of Mexico City. A fierce warrior and an expert horseman, Villa's fame spread all the way to the movie capital of the world—Hollywood. Needing the $25,000 that was offered him, Villa allowed the Mutual Film Corporation to film his División del Norte (Northern Division) in action. For the sake of the camera, he fought during the daytime and postponed executions from 5 a.m. to 7 a.m. Villa was clearly preoccupied with fighting, but there were idealists in his camp, too—men like Felipe Ángeles, who promoted the spread of education and democracy.

The 1915 campaign in the Bajío proved fatal to Villa's forces. Against Ángeles's advice, Villa insisted on frontal cavalry charges. He sent one cavalry charge after another against Obregón's soldiers, who had entrenched themselves in ditches surrounding the battleground. In a fateful battle, Obregón's troops fought a defensive war from the trenches, then faked a retreat, after which their reserve forces rushed at the enemy in an offensive attack. The statistics speak for themselves. Obregón's losses totaled 200 dead, wounded, or captured; Villa's totaled 10,000, and his men began deserting in droves. Villa continued fighting, but with a shrunken force of 3000. Wiping out Villa's strongholds in the state of Sonora at the end of 1915, Obregón's troops reduced Villa to guerrilla warfare thereafter. Villa's forces continued to plague the north for years (during which time Carranza served as president). In 1920 the renegade Villa finally surrendered—only to be assassinated in 1923, along with a car full of unfortunate bysitters.

AN ELECTORAL SHOWDOWN

The contest was the 1928 election, not a military campaign, but guns still figured into the equation. An attempt was made on General Álvaro Obregón's life in 1927. President earlier in the decade (1920–24), Obregón ran for reelection in 1928. This not only threatened the right of the sitting president (Plutarco Elias Calles) to designate his own successor, but it also violated the Revolution's commitment to "Valid Voting, No Reelection." As the contest approached, the number of murders escalated, including 25 generals and 150 others. Obregón was elected, only to be assassinated a few months later (July 17, 1928). Subsequently Calles met with Mexico's 30 most notable generals to request their support, a gathering that is mirrored in *The Death of Artemio Cruz* by the meeting of Artemio's war cronies at a whorehouse. Artemio persuades them to switch loyalties to the new man in power, after which they appear at the new man's offices to profess loyalty to him.

Villa's 1915 defeat spelled disaster for Zapata in the south, whose own movement dwindled. He himself retained a religious zeal for his cause—the return of Mexican land to its rightful owners—but the federal army killed 508 of his followers in 1915 and 1916, and finally tricked Zapata into a 1919 meeting that resulted in his murder. Zapata's movement has been described as an independent rebellion, a cause apart from the others, though he briefly joined with Villa. Yet Zapata was bent on justice for his whole village and other pueblos like it. In contrast, after the first assassination—the killing of Madero—most of the Revolution's strongmen seemed out for themselves. In *The Death of Artemio Cruz,* the protagonist winds up in jail with Gonzalo Bernal. Bernal warns him that one day he will have to choose between Carranza and Obregón, foreseeing that their alliance will not last. Artemio makes it clear that Obregón is his man. A few years later, as the 1928 election approaches, a police officer threatens Artemio's life unless he switches his allegiance from General Obregón. Now a congressman, Artemio recalls the oath of loyalty he swore to the general in years past but then dismisses it and behaves like the opportunist he has become, a man loyal, above all, to himself. He agrees to switch allegiances, aligning himself, as always, with the strongest scoundrel, siding with "the emerging leader against the fading leader" (Fuentes, *The Death of Artemio Cruz,* p. 129).

Civil strife in the 1920s. In 1917 the civilian caudillo Carranza oversaw the drafting of a new constitution, a document that turned out to be far more radical than he himself anticipated. There was widespread hostility toward the Church, whose property had been desecrated in the 1910s by Obregón's troops. Soldiers "drank out of chalices, paraded wearing priestly vestments, built fires in confessionals, shot up sacred images, converted churches into barracks, carried out mock executions of the statues of the saints" (Krauze, p. 356). The hostility found its way into the new Constitution. Article 130 required all priests to register with the government, authorized each state to limit its number of priests, and prohibited clerics from criticizing the law of Mexico.

But the movement to punish the Church was far from universal. In 1926, when President Calles set out to apply Article 130, a portion of the population rose up in defense of the priests. The conflict escalated, breaking out into a savage three-year war between the federal army and Church defenders, known as the *Cristeros.* "*Viva Cristo Rey*!" (Long Live Christ the King!) they shouted in the *Cristiada* (War for Christ; also referred to as the "Cristero rebellion" [1926–29]), which spread to 13 states and claimed more than 70,000 lives. Cristeros were hanged, villages burned, and priests killed. In the novel an official informs Artemio, "Tomorrow they shoot the priests" (*Artemio Cruz,* p. 122). Altogether 90 priests were executed during the Cristiada. The Cristeros, in turn, burned government buildings, blew up trains, and brutally killed teachers and other government workers.

Another internal conflict of the 1920s involved the Yaqui Indians. In the novel, Villa's troops capture a daring Yaqui along with Artemio. Tobias, the Yaqui, demonstrates a courage that reflects the real-life reputation of these Indians, who fought for Obregón with such bravery that, according to some historians, they enabled him to defeat Villa. The Yaquis expected afterward to be rewarded with restitution of their land in Sonora, as promised. Instead, a decade after the Yaquis helped him defeat Villa, Obregón led 15,000 soldiers in a campaign against these

Indians (October 1926–April 1927), betraying his revolutionary debt to them.

Radical economic change and war abroad. President Calles (1924–28) became less of a reformer and more of a dictator over the years.

> Hundreds of his enemies were jailed . . . and a large number were reported to have "committed suicide." Moreover, he and his close associates became . . . millionaires. Their lavish estates in the Lomas district of the capital [where Catalina lives in the novel] were referred to as "palaces of Ali Baba and the Forty Thieves."
>
> (Miller, p. 314)

The spirit of reform resurfaced in the 1930s during the presidency of Lázaro Cárdenas (under whom Fuentes's own father was a diplomat). As president, Cárdenas distributed 44 million acres to Mexican peasants, mostly to *ejidos*—communal landholding units—which was not always to the liking of the peasants themselves, as Cárdenas later admitted. Still he distributed far more land than his predecessors had, destroying the oppressive class of *hacendados* (hacienda owners) in Mexico. Article 27 of the new Constitution identified the nation, not private property holders, as the owner of all minerals and oil beneath Mexico's lands. In 1938 Cárdenas invoked this article to appropriate the subsurface oil that foreign, mostly United States, companies had been exploiting.

Wild with enthusiasm, Mexicans banded together to help the government compensate the oil companies for their losses. Of course, not all Mexicans welcomed such change. From 1914 to 1920 General Manuel Peláez had profited from the old laws, charging foreign oil companies a combined 15,000 dollars a month to protect them from the central government. Peláez's kind would soon find their way around new laws. A mineral edict of 1934 declared that concessions would go to applicants with the most economic and technical resources, provided that the applicants were Mexican; this anti-foreigner emphasis continued in 1935, when terms for concessions to foreigners became so stiff that, to set up operations, they needed front men who were Mexican. In the novel Artemio serves as such a front man for a pair of U.S. sulfur miners and, in the tradition of the real-life oil-mogul Peláez, charges them $2,000 just to arrange the concession.

Global affairs exploded during Cárdenas's presidency, beginning with the Spanish Civil War (1936–39). There was a leftist government in power in Spain at the time (the Second Spanish Republic), and some right-wing officers set out to topple it. Mexico backed not the army officers but the legitimate government, as did Spain's liberal citizens. Thousands of Spanish intellectuals sought refuge from the war in Mexico. Traveling in the other direction, 330 Mexicans enlisted to fight on the side of the Spanish Republic. Only 59 would survive the war, so the chances of someone like Artemio's son, Lorenzo, coming out alive were slim. The volunteers sailed to Spain from Veracruz, as Lorenzo does in the novel, on freighters called *Magallanes, Motomar,* and *Mar Cantábrico.*

FROM A FOLK SONG CELEBRATING CÁRDENAS'S AUDACITY

On the eighteenth of March, the day of the great sensation!
He nationalized the oil then! The Chief of our Nation!
(Krauze, p. 475)

In winter 1939 the Spanish Republic was losing the war to the army insurgents under Francisco Franco, who seized the city of Barcelona in January. Madrid fell to them in March, ending the civil war. In the novel Lorenzo leaves for Spain in February, when the fighting is nearly over. Germany, supporting Franco, has been using Spain as a kind of testing ground for World War II, trying out night and bad-weather bombing. It is a gray, dismal day when Lorenzo confronts a barely visible German bomber, and, in one of the novel's most gripping scenes, goes down fighting like a "real macho," while his Spanish companion Miguel rants about the craziness of Lorenzo's courage.

There is sense to Lorenzo's action, however, in light of how the Mexican male regards death. "*La vida no vale nada!*" (Life is worth nothing!) is a familiar cry before mortal combat, meaning that the way one dies is worth everything. The idea is to *hombrearse con la muerte* (face death like a man), which is what Lorenzo has done, and also what Artemio does in the novel by reviewing his whole life—even the painful memories that until now he has repressed—at the moment of his death.

Official betrayal—1940–1950s. Much has been made of the fact that a democratic revolution that was begun to overthrow Díaz's dictatorship ended up creating an equally autocratic government. The president became all-powerful in post-Revolutionary Mexico, handling public property as if it were his own, doling out funds and favors as he chose. Meanwhile, senators and deputies like Artemio Cruz rubber-stamped his decisions, failing to represent their districts yet invoking revolutionary rhetoric. Public officials tried to disguise selfish motivations as benevolent gestures for the good of the people. But no one was fooled. The peasants, an aide informs Artemio in the novel, "realize that you gave them land only good for dry-farming and kept the watered land for yourself. That you go on charging interest on the loans you made them, just like . . . before" the Revolution, but they do not complain because "as bad as things are, these people are better off now" (*Artemio Cruz,* p. 90).

Murals by two Mexicans—Diego Rivera and José Clemente Orozco—depicted the promise and betrayal of the Revolution. Rivera's murals portrayed the promise; Orozco's, the reality of sacrifice and betrayal. Businessmen and politicians invoked Rivera's images, using them as a flimsy cover for the abuse of power that raged through society, especially during the presidency of Miguel Alemán Valdés (1946–52). Alemán managed to protect private property from being redistributed to peasants, amending legislation that had been passed by Cárdenas. Committed to industrializing the nation, Alemán also adopted a policy of replacing imported with Mexican goods. The upper and middle classes grew wealthier as a result; meanwhile, "the scale of corruption attained by [the president's own circle of friends] was something that had never been seen before" (Krauze, p. 556). After becoming public officials, businessmen sold their goods to the government at prices they themselves deemed fit. They learned of upcoming construction projects and purchased nearby land, whose value was sure to rise. And everyone bribed government workers. Life in Mexico seemed splendid at first glance. The newly rich "raised mansions like Hollywood film sets, held bacchanalian parties, poured out rivers of money," but Alemán failed to put anything over on the poor who, like the painter Orozco, perceived the grim reality of ongoing inequity in society (Krauze, p. 556). A post-Alemán poem by Jorge Hernández Campos captures this reality: "I'm the most excellent Mr. President Don So and So of Something / and when . . . I shout Viva Mexico! / what I really mean is Viva me!" (Krauze, p. 564). The industrialization had not brought general progress, but a limited variety, of benefit to a few small pockets of the population.

The Novel in Focus

Plot summary. The novel opens on April 10, 1959, the day of Artemio Cruz's death. Prostrate in bed, the ailing multimillionaire has visitors—his estranged wife, Catalina; his embittered daughter, Teresa; his son-in-law, Gerardo; and his devoted secretary, Padilla. A priest enters, and Artemio's granddaughter, Gloria, appears. Doctors come and go.

Meanwhile, Artemio muses about 12 pivotal days in his life, out of chronological order. His story emerges slowly, like a jigsaw puzzle, whose pieces are laid out in the following sequence:

July 6, 1941: Cruz negotiates a partnership in Mexican sulfur mining with some U.S. investors.

May 20, 1919: A veteran soldier, Artemio insinuates himself into the family of a dead wartime acquaintance, Gonzalo Bernal.

December 4, 1913: Artemio's first love, Regina, is hanged by enemy soldiers.

June 3, 1924: Artemio and his wife, Catalina, an uncommunicative couple, have a pivotal argument; he takes a young mistress, Lilia.

November 23, 1927: Artemio, now a congressman, switches allegiance from his wartime superior to the new powerholder.

September 11, 1947: A middle-aged Artemio brings his mistress, Lilia, to the honeymoon spot of the '40s—Acapulco; she cheats on him with a fellow vacationer, but Artemio takes her back.

October 22, 1915: Villa's retreating troops capture Captain Artemio Cruz and his fellow-in-arms, a Yaquis Indian; after meeting a third prisoner, Gonzalo Bernal, Artemio parleys with the enemy in a way that allows him to save himself from a firing-squad fate.

August 12, 1934: Artemio's lover, Laura, gives him an ultimatum that he turns down, opting to stay in his unfulfilling marriage.

February 3, 1939: Artemio's beloved son, Lorenzo, perishes in the Spanish Civil War.

December 31, 1955: The aged Artemio throws a lavish New Year's Eve party at his home in Coyoacán, where he lives with Lilia.

January 18, 1903: A neighboring landowner threatens to separate 13-year-old Artemio from his guardian/uncle, Lunero; Artemio murders a man to prevent the separation.

April 9, 1889: Artemio is born to a peasant mother who has been raped by the hacendado Atanasio Menchaca.

Diego Rivera at work on one of his murals, 1936.

The novel alternates among three voices and tenses, with Artemio employing the first-person *I* and present tense for thoughts about his physical deterioration on his deathbed; the second-person *you* and future tense to judge his past actions and entertain alternate choices he could have made; and the third person *he* and past tense to narrate the course of his life events. His own voice is interrupted occasionally by his wife's thoughts and by a chapter on his son's experiences in Spain.

BEHIND THE FRONTLINES

Without a commissary or medical corps, the armies of the Mexican Revolution depended on women to forage for their food, wash their clothes, and nurse their wounds. Loosely speaking, a *soldadera* was any woman who followed her man when he left home and joined an army. Soldaderas anticipated the troops' movements, waiting for their arrival at the next campsite with refreshments at the ready. "In the abandoned battlefield they carr[ied] water to their wounded masters and despoil[ed] the dead of their clothing" (Macías, p. 41). They did not, as a rule, wage war themselves. Nonetheless, all the movement often put them in harm's way. Rape followed by murder was commonplace.

Born in Veracruz in 1889 on a hacienda called Cocuya, Artemio is the child of a wealthy hacendado who raped Artemio's mulatta mother and, after the birth, ran her off the estate. Rescuing the infant, her mulatto brother, Lunero, raises the green-eyed boy until he is 13. The uncle and nephew remain in their shed on the decaying hacienda, crafting and selling candles and canoes. Artemio's father, the hacendado Atanasio Menchaca, has been killed and the surviving Menchacas have fallen on hard times. They lead listless, unproductive lives in the main house.

One day a neighboring tobacco grower threatens to take Lunero away. To prevent this, 13-year-old Artemio kills a man. Before he and his uncle can rendezvous to escape, Lunero is shot dead. The boy flees northward utterly alone, then enters into another emotionally important relationship with Sebastián, who teaches the unschooled Artemio how to read, write, and count. Sebastián inspires Artemio, at age 21, to join the Mexican Revolution. He fights in Sonora and Sinaloa, where Artemio one day rapes an unwary young woman, as he and fellow soldiers have done so many times before. This time the lustful encounter grows into love. The young woman, Regina, weaves a fiction about how they met to spare Artemio the shame of it and he plays along with her, in one of the many deceptions that will riddle his lifetime. For seven months, Regina is Artemio's soldadera, anticipating the movements of his troops, meeting him in this town or that, so that the two of them can grasp a few precious moments together.

In 1913 Artemio is fighting Huerta's federal soldiers. He abandons an unknown wounded mate on the battlefield to save himself for Regina's love, then finds that she and nine others have been hanged by Huerta's *federales* as punishment for a town's having supported the rebels.

Two years later the rebels are fighting among themselves. Artemio has been promoted to captain under General Obregón. Pursuing the retreating troops of Pancho Villa, Captain Artemio Cruz and a fellow soldier, a Yaqui Indian named Tobias, are caught. The Yaqui daringly helps Artemio try to effect an escape, but to no avail. Both end up in prison, alongside a young lawyer, Gonzalo Bernal, who feels that the Revolution has been lost no matter who wins because the rebels, the supposed "good guys," have sold out to their own self-interests. Bernal reveals a few details about his life—he has a sister, Catalina, and a father, Don Gamaliel, who inhabit a hacienda of their own in Puebla. Outside the jail cells, the enemy offers Artemio a deal; he can escape the firing squad if he reveals his troops' plans. Opting to relay some bogus plans and save his skin, after trying in vain to save his fellow soldier Tobias, Artemio watches as Bernal and Tobias are executed.

In 1919 the army discharges Artemio who, now a colonel, finds his way to the home of Gonzalo Bernal. On the flimsy strength of having shared Gonzalo's final moments, he latches onto the father's dwindling fortune. The Bernal hacienda has lost control of its workers and is in decline. Employing shrewd, if ruthless, business tactics, Artemio loans money to the workers at low interest and collects debts owed to old Bernal for a share of the take. He marries Catalina, with whom he has fallen in love. Pushed into the marriage, a vengeful Catalina reciprocates his love but does not allow herself the luxury of showing it to a man she believes deserves her wrath, a man she suspects is somehow involved in the death of her brother and whom she blames for the ruin of her father. Artemio shrewdly convinces old Don Gamaliel that it would be to their advantage in revolutionary Mexico to turn over some of his unfertile plots to the peasants on his hacienda. Thereafter, Artemio is regarded as a hero of Mexico's agrarian-reform program.

Five years later Don Gamaliel has died and left his estate to Catalina and Artemio. She reflects on their passion by night and their lack of communication by day, still refusing to reveal her affection for him. Artemio is elected to congress, largely on the strength of his supposed "contribution" to agrarian reform. There is a rift in the marriage when Catalina fails to stick by his side during the election, and Artemio takes a mistress, a young Indian girl, Lilia. Yet Catalina remains with Artemio, because, he thinks, of his money. He and Catalina have two children—a daughter, Teresa, and a beloved son named Lorenzo.

Teresa grows up away at school and later by her mother's side, far from Artemio. At age 12 Lorenzo, to whom Catalina is devoted, is taken from her by Artemio. He rebuilds for his son the hacienda in Veracruz where he himself was born. The boy grows up with a passion for horses and an enjoyment of the countryside. At 19 he ships out for Spain's Civil War, invoking his father's originally pure ideals at the outset of the earlier Mexican Revolution. This touches Artemio deeply and also becomes one of his most haunting memories, as demonstrated by a refrain that crops up repeatedly throughout the novel: "That morning I waited for him with pleasure. We crossed the river on horseback" (*Artemio Cruz*, p. 82).

In Spain, after a defeat, Lorenzo and a fellow soldier named Miguel encounter some young women also fleeing the area. Lorenzo and the young woman Lola dare to lead their small group across a possibly mined bridge. Thankfully, they survive and share a night of passion before joining a long line of France-bound refugees. Lorenzo and his companions fall in step with women carrying mattresses, men hauling mirrors, and carts lumbering toward the border. They are trudging along when a Nazi bomber suddenly fires on them. Instead of putting his own survival first, Lorenzo tries to shoot his rickety old rifle at the menacing bomber. But the worn-out weapon fails to fire, and Lorenzo is killed.

Back in Mexico, Artemio, blocking out his feelings as best he can, goes on to increase his fortune through various means, which include sulfur domes, logging concessions, interest on railroad loans, his take as a front man on behalf of U.S. miners, a daily newspaper of his own, and assorted real-estate investments. He owns some vacant lots, his reward for switching allegiance from Obregón to the current power brokers in government, and he also has a cool $15 million stashed away in U.S. and European banks.

NEWSPAPERS AND LABOR UNIONS

In the novel Artemio owns a Mexico City newspaper and has a vested interest in the nation's railroads, to which he has made loans. He therefore orders his employees to make sure not a single line about police repression gets into his paper during a 1959 railroad strike. There actually was strife in Mexico's railroad industry in 1959. Labor leader Demetrio Vallejo inspired work stoppages to press for higher wages and new union elections to replace corrupt officers. The unrest led to a 16.66 percent pay increase for all but two companies, whose workers proceeded to go on strike. It was Easter week, a time of increased travel, and the government quickly quashed the strike, arresting its leaders and firing 13,000 workers. A few days later all Mexican railroads went on a sympathy strike, and 10,000 more workers were arrested. When a leading rebel, Román Guerra Montamayor, died at the scene of a protest, authorities painted his lips and nails red to brand him a communist, then threw his corpse across a railroad track.

Revolution was very much on everyone's mind, since Fidel Castro had just staged a successful one in Cuba (January 1, 1959). Information about it filtered into Mexico, with people relying on word-of-mouth rather than newspapers. It was generally known that paper owners slanted the news to suit their purposes. They were more concerned with not offending the current strongmen than with reporting facts. So readers could find trustworthy details about parties, bullfights, religious gatherings, and crimes of the heart, but not about hard news. A paper's "news" was affected also by business interests. Mexico City papers grew into rich enterprises, and their owners into tycoons because of advertising, not the number of papers sold. All the large businesses "had to pay up in one way or another or else they might read 'Coca-Cola is bad for your health'" (Revel in Krauze, p. 598).

Artemio's marriage has become meaningless—he and his wife live in separate residences.

Five years before Lorenzo's death, while traveling abroad, Artemio began an affair with Laura, a woman of refined taste who cared little for his money. Their affair continued in Mexico, but one day Laura gave him an ultimatum—Artemio must choose his wife (and current life) or her. Artemio forgoes Laura's love, returning to his mistress, Lilia, and pursuing an empty but convenient relationship with her. The by-now aging congressman takes Lilia on a trip to Acapulco, where she has a brief affair with a younger man. Artemio notices but ignores the betrayal. She is with him in 1955 when he throws a New Year's Eve party at his mansion in Coyoacán, a remodeled convent furnished in the finest of taste. The "Mummy of Coyoacán," they call Artemio, a fact of which he is well aware as he sits regally at the party without letting any of his guests get too close. Surrounding the "mummy" are his hard-won possessions—"my paintings, my wines, my comforts, which I control the same way I control all of you" (*Artemio Cruz,* p. 259).

LAS LOMAS VS. COYOACÁN

In the novel Artemio complains that he is dying at the "wrong" house, the one in Las Lomas, where his wife lives, not at his own house in Coyoacán. Mexican social history recounts the flight of upper-class residents from downtown Mexico City in the 1920s and '30s to suburban *colonias* (communities) like Las Lomas. Distinctly modern, these colonias contrasted sharply with old Spanish-built towns like Coyoacán, which was located farther outside the city in the Valley of Mexico.

Four years later, physically ill, his insides exploding, Artemio lies on his deathbed, reviewing the course of his life, justifying and blaming himself, reflecting on his marriage, recognizing in these final feeble moments that Catalina does love him after all, mourning his son, and ignoring his daughter but mentally thanking her for bringing his granddaughter to his deathbed. He acknowledges his all-consuming quest for power and takes responsibility for having disregarded his effect on others. The multimillionaire Mummy of Coyoacán tells himself that he is who he is because he knew how to violate other people before they could violate him. In retrospect, he realizes that over the years this approach to life has made him betray significant relationships and cheat himself of love. It is too much for a body to take, and Artemio dies, ostensibly, according to the doctors, of mesentery infarct.

National search for an elusive identity. "Is there a single Mexican who believes in me?" wonders Artemio as he negotiates with U.S. sulfur miners. "If the gringos were the only ones willing to finance the explorations, what was he supposed to do?" (*Artemio Cruz,* p. 20). A shrewd businessman, a capitalist through and through, he cements his partnership with the U.S. investors, telling himself,

> You turned your eyes northward and lived with the regret that a geographical error kept you from being part of them in everything. You admire their efficiency, their comforts, their hygiene, their power, and you look around you and the incompetence, the misery, the filth, the languor, the nakedness of this poor country that has nothing, all seem intolerable to you.
> (*Artemio Cruz,* pp. 26–27)

Artemio, however, is not to be taken at his word. His actions and feelings speak louder. He chooses to live not in modern Las Lomas but in Coyoacán, a Spanish-built town from Mexico's colonial past. He represses feelings of indebtedness to Sebastián (the teacher who inspired him with revolutionary ideals), of shame at abandoning a wounded soldier in 1913, and of guilt for not facing the firing squad with his fellow prisoners in 1915. Artemio kills their murderer, but this does not, in his own eyes, atone for his failure. In hindsight, he admits wronging other Mexicans, building his fortune on their decline, facilitating the exploitation of Mexico's resources by Americans, and having his newspaper defend brutal dictators like the Dominican Republic's General Rafael Trujillo. Yet Artemio is not a clear-cut villain. Though merciless and cruel, he is also "endearing, admirable, [and] pitiable"; the man "cheats, but catches himself at it" (Harss and Dohmann, p. 300). A product of complex circumstances and fateful choices, he suffers remorse on his deathbed, spending his last moments in desperate search of himself, a task in which the reader must also engage. "I am not going to say everything I have to say," warns Fuentes. "I am going to leave a door open, so that the reader can complete and collaborate with me in the creation of the novel" (Fuentes in Gazarian Gautier, p. 104).

The flitting between three voices—the *I,* the *you,* and the *he*—underscores Artemio's struggle to find himself. In fact, his (and the novel's) concern for self-definition reflects a real-life preoccupation of intellectuals in mid-twentieth-century Mexico. In 1950 Octavio Paz published *The Labyrinth of Solitude*, a landmark essay positing that the average Mexican man disguises the person he really is. He remains distant from everyone, including himself. This proposition had been tendered before. Paz's essay, however, took it a step further, arguing that the Mexican man prefers not even to acknowledge the existence of the person behind the mask, the reality that he disguises.

At the root of this reality is the conquest of Mexico by Hernán Cortés, the Spaniard who received as a gift from the Indians one of their own, a princess named Malintzin, alias Marina (her Christian name), alias La Malinche (her legendary title). She became Cortés's mistress, gaining folkloric stature over the centuries, growing into a symbol of violation and betrayal because she is said to have gone into Cortés's arms willingly. In 1522 Malintzin and Cortés had a son, Martín. Regarded as the first mestizo, Martín would become the symbolic ancestor of contemporary Mexico. People thought of him as a child of violation and betrayal. Preferring to have no legacy rather than this one, argues Paz, the Mexican male denies his past and breaks with tradition. He is left adrift in this broken state, a fragmented being, as reflected in the novel by the three-way split of Artemio Cruz. Paz speaks also of a word derived from La Malinche, *malinchista,* used in modern Mexico to denounce anyone corrupted by foreign influences, the way Artemio is.

Blocking out the past, the average mid-twentieth-century Mexican male aspired to a masculine ideal. Society steered him into becoming the *macho,* the strongman who retreated into himself and remained a private being. The ideal encouraged him not to share his true feelings with his wife or anyone else. Women too negated their true selves to play a role prescribed for them by society, acting stoical, denying their own desires to fulfill the feminine ideal—absolute service to the needs of everyone else in the family. Even mothers showed disappointment at the birth of a daughter, prompted by the widespread belief that a baby girl was worth less and would surely grow up to suffer more than a boy.

In the novel both parents fawn over their son, Lorenzo, and even Catalina ignores their daughter, Teresa, until she matures. This mother-daughter dynamic is consistent with a real-life syndrome of the time: "As the girl grows older," explains one social historian, "she is drawn into a conscious and highly verbal complicity with her mother against her father" (Barber, p. 27). So hostile are Teresa's outbursts against the dying Artemio that they drive even her mother to distraction.

Living up to the male and female ideals made genuine communication between a man and woman difficult, if not impossible. The ideals militated against a mutually satisfying love relationship, so that Artemio and Catalina were not as atypical as a reader might assume. The result was loneliness for the woman, who took refuge in her children, and for the man, who gravitated to extramarital relationships. Since his macho behavior continued, these relationships often failed too. The man who divulged his true feelings opened himself up to possible scorn, too great a risk in a society whose highest value was manliness—the ability to impose one's will on others. "To the Mexican," says Paz, "there are only two possibilities in life: either he inflicts the actions implied by *chingar* [to violate] on others, or else he suffers them at the hands of others" (Paz in Barber, p. 64). Artemio, who has lived by this principle, dies a powerful but lonely man, having attained the Mexican ideal.

Sources and literary context. Fuentes's novel centers on the betrayal of the initially high values of Artemio and of the Mexican Revolution itself. In the long line of stories that have been written about the Revolution, his novel is not the first to speak of betrayal. Most prior sagas, however, combined fiction with reportorial-style narrative, producing chronicles of local warfare and its combatants. In contrast, Fuentes's novel belongs to a new wave of Latin American fiction that transcends this regional focus. *The Death of Artemio Cruz* also reaches beyond the earlier novels by extending into mid-twentieth-century Mexico, exploring the Revolution's aftereffects and their impact on the Mexican character. In doing so, *Artemio Cruz* coincides with the attempts of other mid-century works, like Paz's essay cited above, to sift out and define the essence of being Mexican. The novel, furthermore, follows the lead of stories such as Leo Tolstoy's *The Death of Ivan Ilich* by placing its protagonist at the end of his life, a vantage point from which he reviews and weighs the value of his days. Among other influences on *The Death of Artemio Cruz* is Orson Welles's *Citizen Kane,* a film in fragmentary style about the death of a newspaper tycoon who became a symbol of his nation.

Events in History at the Time the Novel Was Written

Return to the goals of the Revolution. Fidel Castro's 1959 Cuban Revolution inspired self-reflection in Mexico, especially among intellectuals. Many believed that even though the democratic intentions of their own revolution had been extinquished, they could be reignited. In 1962, when *The Death of Artemio Cruz* was published, Fuentes wrote an article for *Siempre!* Much to the chagrin of Mexico's government (which pulled its advertising from the magazine), the article described the recent murder of Rubén Jaramillo, a peasant who, like the war hero Zapata, had pressed for redistribution of land to the thousands of Mexicans with legal claims to it. The killers, as Fuentes's report shows, murdered not only Jaramillo but also his wife and sons, "certainly with the agreement of the President" (Krauze, p. 642).

> They pushed him down. Jaramillo . . . threw himself at the party of murderers; he was defending his wife and his children, and especially the unborn child; they brought him down with their rifle butts, they knocked out an eye. . . . [A son] cursed at them. . . . While he was still alive, they opened his mouth . . . and laughing filled it with earth. After that . . . the submachine guns spat on the five fallen bodies. The squad waited for them to stop breathing. But they went on living. They put their pistols to the foreheads of the woman and the four men. They fired the finishing shots.
>
> (Fuentes in Krauze, p. 642)

Intellectuals of mid-twentieth-century Mexico spoke out against this and other outrages. They decided that it was time to get back on an ethical track, to call attention to betrayals of their ideals and to resume the genuine revolution, with the help of works like *Artemio Cruz.*

Reviews. *The Death of Artemio Cruz* was favored by critics in Mexico and abroad, though not without some reservations. Various reviewers complimented the rounded portrait of Artemio. There is something "irresistibly heroic" about this "complex, witty, divided" man, declared one such critic (Eberstadt, p. 158). Others applauded the effect achieved by the shifting points of view and use of past, present, and future tenses, although the novel's fragmented style troubled at least two scholars: "Fuentes is at his best in 'straight' narration. The most effective passages in *Artemio Cruz* are linear" (Harss and Dohmann, p. 301).

These and other critics nevertheless deemed *The Death of Artemio Cruz* to be a novel that approaches masterpiece status. Reviewing it for Mexico's *Siempre!* Fernando Benitez would at times have liked to see some themes more fully developed ("*a veces . . . no desarrolla los temas*"), but he praised the rhythmic prose and profound force of a novel described as courageous and exceptionally beautiful (Benitez, p. II). The consensus is perhaps best reflected by the conclusion of one of England's reviewers—"This is a difficult book, but an enormously powerful and rich one, well worth the reading" (Bradbury, p. 359).

—Joyce Moss

For More Information

Barber, Janet. "Mexican Machismo in Novels by Lawrence, Sender, and Fuentes." Ph.D. diss., University of Southern California, 1972.

Benitez, Fernando. Review of *The Death of Artemio Cruz, in Siempre!* no. 465 (May 23, 1962): II.

Bradbury. Malcolm. Review of *The Death of Artemio Cruz, in Punch* (September 1964): 359

Eberstadt, Fernanda. *Montezuma's Literary Revenge. Commentary* 81, no. 5 (May 9, 1986): 35–40.

Fuentes, Carlos. *The Death of Artemio Cruz.* Trans. Alfred MacAdam. New York: Noonday, 1991.

Gazarian Gautier, Marie Lise. *Interviews with Latin American Writers.* Elmwood Park, Ill.: Dalkey Archive Press, 1989.

Harss, Luis, and Barbara Dohmann. *Into the Mainstream: Conversations with Latin American Writers.* New York: Harper and Row, 1967.

Krauze, Enrique. *Mexico: Biography of Power.* Trans. Hank Heifetz. New York: HarperCollins, 1997.

Macías, Anna. *Against All Odds: The Feminist Movement in Mexico to 1940.* Westport, Conn.: Greenwood, 1982.

Miller, Robert Ryal. *Mexico: A History.* Norman: University of Oklahoma Press, 1985.

Powell, T. G. *Mexico and the Spanish Civil War.* Albuquerque: University of New Mexico Press, 1981.

Desert Solitaire: A Season in the Wilderness

by
Edward Abbey

Born and raised in rural Appalachian Pennsylvania, Edward Abbey (1927-89) began his lifelong love affair with the Southwest as an undergraduate at the University of New Mexico in Albuquerque, where after graduation he went on to earn a master's degree in philosophy. He began his writing career as a novelist in the 1950s, scoring a modest success with *The Brave Cowboy* (1958). The story of a traditional cowboy confronted and ultimately crushed by the forces of modernity in the new West, *The Brave Cowboy* was made into the critically acclaimed film *Lonely Are the Brave* (1962), starring Kirk Douglas. Abbey worked at a series of part-time jobs while he wrote, becoming a road inspector for the U.S. Forest Service and a ranger for the U.S. Park Service. Even after the success of *Desert Solitaire* made it no longer financially necessary, Abbey would go on taking seasonal work as a ranger. He also continued to espouse *Desert Solitaire*'s environmental themes later in life, in works such as *The Monkey Wrench Gang* (1975). This widely read novel is often called the Bible of the Earth First! movement, which took up the novel's idea of sabotaging or "monkeywrenching" environmental offenders such as dams, lumber operations, or polluting factories. However, it was *Desert Solitaire*'s angry denunciation of human interference with desert wilderness that first propelled Abbey to the forefront of the emerging environmental movement of the 1960s.

THE LITERARY WORK

An essay set in the American Southwest in the late 1950s and 1960s; published in New York City in 1968.

SYNOPSIS

Drawing on journals written during seasonal work as a National Park Service ranger, Edward Abbey meditates on the solitary life in the desert and protests against human encroachment on its fragile environments.

Events in History at the Time of the Essay

The national park system in the postwar years. In the mid-1950s, when Edward Abbey first worked as a National Park Service ranger, both the service and the national parks themselves were facing an acute crisis. After the Great Depression of the 1930s and the national emergency of World War II (1939-45), a postwar economic boom brought many Americans newfound prosperity and the leisure time in which to enjoy it. Encouraged by low gasoline prices and by a vast automotive industry accustomed to high, wartime levels of production, Americans in large numbers first began vacation trips by car after the war. America's national parks, which together comprised the country's most impressive and beautiful wilderness locations, led the ranks of favored destinations. In the first postwar decade,

Edward Abbey

the numbers of visitors to the parks each year more than quadrupled, from less than 12 million in 1945 to nearly 50 million in 1954.

Yet funding to the National Park Service, which had been drastically cut during the war, remained at or near the low wartime levels. Consequently the parks and the Park Service rangers who cared for them were poorly prepared to handle the new flood of visitors. In October 1953 the well-known writer and historian Bernard DeVoto exposed the park system's problems in a widely read article in *Harper's Magazine*. Entitled "Let's Close the National Parks," the article castigated Congress, which funds government agencies, for treating the parks like an "impoverished stepchild" (DeVoto in Sellars, p. 182). DeVoto noted that roads, camping areas, service buildings, ranger housing, and other facilities had been allowed to deteriorate to the point that "true slum districts" existed in some of the more popular parks such as Yellowstone and Yosemite (DeVoto in Sellars, p. 182). In a rhetorical attempt to arouse public indignation at the chaotic situation, DeVoto suggested closing some of the favorite parks because of the lack of funding.

DeVoto, who served on the park system's advisory board, likely wrote the article with the tacit support of the Park Service's director, Conrad Wirth. A savvy politician who strongly supported tourist development in the parks, Wirth had taken office in 1951 and would serve until 1969. When DeVoto's article failed to stir Congress, Wirth conceived a plan that he could present to Congress that would update the park system on a grand scale. Called Mission 66, Wirth's plan called for millions of dollars to be spent on park development over the coming decade, with completion to coincide with the park system's 50-year anniversary in 1966. In 1956 Wirth successfully shepherded Mission 66 through Congress.

Mission 66 amounted to a massive construction campaign that ultimately cost around one billion dollars. New and renovated physical facilities in the parks included:

- Approximately 1,200 miles of new roads within the parks
- More than 1,500 miles of renovated roads
- Nearly 1,000 miles of new or renovated trails
- More than 1,500 new parking areas and 330 renovated parking areas
- More than 500 new campgrounds, water systems, and sewer systems
- More than 400 new administrative and utility buildings, and more than 200 new power systems
- More than 1,200 new employee housing units
- More than 450 renovated historic buildings
- 114 new visitor centers

(Adapted from Sellars, p. 184)

The program was highly publicized in such periodicals as *National Geographic Magazine*. Meanwhile, during the decade in which Mission 66

MILESTONES IN THE HISTORY OF AMERICA'S NATIONAL PARKS

1872 Yellowstone becomes the first national park.
1890 Yosemite and Sequoia National Parks are established.
1916 The National Parks Act set up the National Park Service to administer parks. Its purpose is "to conserve the scenery and the natural and historic objects and the wild life therein and to provide for the enjoyment of same in such manner . . . as will leave them unimpaired for the enjoyment of future generations" (Sellars, p. 38). *Desert Solitaire* refers to this statement when it argues against allowing automobiles in the parks.
1919 Grand Canyon National Park is established.
1964 Wilderness Act establishes wilderness preserves within certain parks, imposing strict limits on human intrusion.

THE COLORADO RIVER

The Colorado River enters Utah from Colorado and flows diagonally southwest to Utah's southeastern corner through a series of national parks and national monuments:

- Arches National Park (called Arches National Monument when Abbey first worked there in 1956 and 1957; it was upgraded to national park status in 1971)
- Canyonlands National Park (containing the Maze, a geographical feature explored by Abbey and described in *Desert Solitaire*)
- Natural Bridges National Monument
- Glen Canyon National Recreation Area—essentially Lake Powell and associated features, such as Rainbow Bridge National Monument

Below Glen Canyon on the Colorado River, just over the Utah-Arizona border, lies Marble Canyon, the site of a contested and ultimately defeated dam proposal in the 1960s. Below Marble Canyon is Grand Canyon National Park and then Lake Mead National Recreation Area, after which the Colorado turns south, running along Arizona's western border with Nevada and California. From Arches National Park north of Moab, Utah, to the Grand Canyon in Arizona, these locations—clustered along the winding Colorado River—make up the geographical settings most prominent in *Desert Solitaire.*

As many had observed, the Colorado River is especially well suited for damming. Flowing from the western flanks of the Rocky Mountains in Colorado, the river has cut a 1,000-mile-long series of deep canyons (including the Grand Canyon) into the high mesas through which it runs. Many of the narrow canyons can be easily dammed, so that their walls form the sides of a man-made lake. Furthermore, because it begins at nearly 10,000 feet above sea level, the Colorado unleashes immense amounts of energy as it flows downhill to the Gulf of California. Its sharp losses in elevation make the Colorado especially attractive to those wishing to build hydroelectric dams. While some 20 dams now interrupt its flow, most famous is Hoover Dam, completed in 1936, which forms Lake Mead on the Colorado below the Grand Canyon. The Colorado's dams—especially the controversial dam at Glen Canyon—are a major focus of Abbey's criticism in *Desert Solitaire.*

was put into effect, visitor numbers in the parks continued to mushroom. They were bolstered by a new Interstate Highway System, which entailed the simultaneous construction of nearly 40,000 miles of interstate highways throughout the nation. By 1966 annual park visits had climbed to over 133 million; by 1972 they would exceed 211 million.

In promoting Mission 66 to the public, the Park Service emphasized the idea of "accessible wilderness," a scheme that would allow the parks' millions of visitors to "see, sense, and react to wilderness, often without leaving the roadside" (Sellars, p. 187). Wirth and other Park Service officials believed that by encouraging more people to visit the parks, they were helping to protect park wilderness lands from the political pressures of commercial development. Powerful logging, mining, hydroelectric, and other interests were continually lobbying for the right to develop national park lands and other government owned lands for their own profit. Only strong public involvement with the parks would give the Park Service the political clout to resist such efforts, the thinking went. Yet despite what the service touted as Mission 66's success in protecting, refurbishing, and promoting the national parks, by the 1960s a growing number of Americans had begun to question the basic approach that Mission 66 and other like-minded programs exemplified. In *Desert Solitaire* Edward Abbey calls this approach "industrial tourism" and singles it out for his particular wrath. Indeed, he devotes an entire chapter (aptly titled "*Polemic:*

Industrial Tourism and the National Parks [italics original]") to denouncing it.

The rise of the environmental movement. While the tradition of wilderness preservation has roots as far back as the influential American author Henry David Thoreau (1817-62; see **Walden**, also in *Literature and Its Times*), the modern environmental movement first arose in response to the commercial expansion and population pressures of the postwar era. In the arid states of the Southwest, such pressures focused on the question of water, especially on the region's major river, the Colorado. At the urging of real-estate developers, utility companies, and others, in the late 1940s and early 1950s, the U.S. Bureau of Reclamation proposed a number of canyons along the Colorado River as dam sites. The major ones lay within land administered by the National Park Service, which, under Conrad Wirth, deferred to the powerful Bureau of Reclamation. But in the ensuing years these parks would be at the center of a series of highly publicized controversies. The environmental movement can be said to have begun in the early 1950s with the first of these struggles. At that time several conservation organizations took the then revolutionary step of rallying public opposition to a large hydroelectric dam planned at Echo Park, a part of Dinosaur National Monument on the Green River, which is a major tributary of the Colorado. Encouraged by the Sierra Club, the Wilderness Society, and other groups, thousands of Americans wrote letters to Congress expressing their opposition to the proposed Echo Park dam. In 1956, owing to the public outcry, the Bureau of Reclamation agreed to abandon its plans for the dam. The Echo Park campaign has thus been seen as the fledgling environmental movement's first major victory.

However, for many activists victory at Echo Park came at a high price, because as part of their bargain with the Bureau of Reclamation, the Sierra Club and other organizations agreed not to oppose another dam planned farther south on the Colorado, at Glen Canyon. Construction on the Glen Canyon Dam began in 1959, and the dam began operation in 1963. Its impounded waters today form Lake Powell, named (in Abbey's view) "supposedly to honor but actually to dishonor the memory" of John Wesley Powell, the explorer whose journals lovingly describe the canyon as he saw it by raft in 1869 (Abbey, *Desert Solitaire*, p. 188). Because Glen Canyon was a place of rare beauty, its flooding generated the most enduring controversy of all the Colorado River dam projects, with recriminations lasting long after the waters had risen. Abbey himself rafted down Glen Canyon in June 1959 with his friend Ralph Newcomb; his account of that trip comprises *Desert Solitaire*'s longest chapter. A strong opponent of the "goddamned dam," Abbey heaps scorn on "the coalition of persons and avarice" responsible and warns the reader that they are "preparing a like fate for parts of the Grand Canyon" (*Desert Solitaire*, pp. 188, 189). Also hotly contested, the attempts to dam parts of the Grand Canyon would meet with defeat in 1966.

Mormons, prospectors, cowboys, and Indians. While Abbey's main focus is the natural beauty of Utah's Colorado River canyon country, he also devotes attention to the kinds of people he encounters there and to their various cultural histories. Utah was settled in the nineteenth century by pioneers belonging to the Church of Jesus Christ of Latter-Day Saints, commonly called the Mormons. Abbey sprinkles his text with brief references to the Mormons' exploration and settlement of Utah's most inhospitable lands. Mormons in Utah are still noted for the spirit of communal, cooperative living that helped those early settlements prosper. While the hard-drinking, secular Abbey has little sympathy with the Mormons' abstemious, highly religious lifestyle (he complains about the weak beer served in Utah), he does praise this communal spirit.

Mormons make up the majority of Utah's population, but also non-Mormon cattlemen and sheep ranchers settled here, as elsewhere in the West. By the 1950s and 1960s, however, small ranchers throughout the West were being pushed

THE SIERRA CLUB

Founded in 1892 by California naturalist John Muir, its activist leader David Brower made the Sierra Club into the leading environmental group in the United States in the years after World War II. Drawing on lessons learned in the campaign against the proposed dam at Echo Park, the Sierra Club became a highly effective political action group. In the 1960s the organization was instrumental in influencing the National Park Service to give more weight to ecology, biology, and wilderness preservation in its stewardship of the land, and less to accessibility and recreation. This shift in emphasis would reshape Park Service practices starting in the 1970s.

out of business by modern corporate operations, which raise livestock on a large scale and can thus undersell the small rancher. One summer Abbey worked briefly for a crusty old rancher called Roy Scobie in *Desert Solitaire*. While decrying the harmful environmental impact of cattle and sheep, Abbey expresses sadness at the passing of the small, independent ranchers. By the late 1950s, similar competition with large corporations drove off the independent uranium prospectors who had flocked to Utah and other Western states a decade earlier, as nuclear energy came into use. Abbey devotes a brief digression to prospectors in a short chapter called "Rocks."

Finally, Abbey laments the poverty and hardship experienced by the region's original inhabitants, the various Native American peoples who lived along the Colorado before the whites' arrival. Abbey discusses the largest Native American tribe, the Navajos, at some length in *Desert Solitaire*. As he observes, the Navajos have fared better than many other native peoples, partly because they control a vast reservation containing rich natural resources. An aspect of history that Abbey does not mention is the way the Park Service took unilateral possession of native lands in the West during the early to mid-twentieth century. Though some lands were later returned to tribal control and the Park Service changed its policy, a recent study notes that the Navajos often felt "under siege" by the Park Service (Kellar and Turek, p. 186). Yet the Navajos managed to retain control of their communal lands, which occupy parts of Colorado, Utah, New Mexico, and Arizona, and are virtually surrounded by national parks. One measure Navajos took in response to the Park Service threat was to create a number of protected tribal parks within their reservation, such as Monument Valley Tribal Park in Arizona, established in 1958. Such actions ensured that the "continued vitality of the Navajo language, survival of traditional culture, and rich legends" were backed by "a sense of place" in strengthening the Navajos' tribal identity (Kellar and Turek, p. 186).

The Essay in Focus

The contents. In a brief "Author's Introduction" to *Desert Solitaire*, dated April 1967, Abbey writes that "about ten years ago I took a job as a seasonal park ranger" at Arches National Monument, and that "what I found there is the subject of this book" (*Desert Solitaire*, p. ix). He went back for a second season, and would have continued returning "but unfortunately for me the Arches, a primitive place when I first went there, was developed and improved so well I had to leave" (*Desert Solitaire*, p. ix). Yet while he warns the reader that he has "some harsh words" for his employer, the National Park Service, overall he thinks the Service has "done its work rather well" (*Desert Solitaire*, p. xi). Abbey gives credit for this success not to the Park Service's bureaucratic administrators, but to its rangers. Warning readers, he concedes that:

> much of the book will seem coarse, rude, bad-tempered, violently prejudiced, unconstructive—even frankly antisocial in its point of view. Serious critics, serious librarians, serious associate professors of English will if they read this work dislike it intensely; at least I hope so.
> (*Desert Solitaire*, p. x)

A chapter titled "The First Morning" describes Abbey's arrival at Arches at the beginning of April. Pulling in after dark in his pickup truck, he meets the park's two permanent employees, the superintendent and the chief ranger. They give him directions to the small, spartan house trailer, 20 rugged miles into the park's interior, where he will live and work essentially alone for the next six months. The next morning he rises early, thaws his boots over the trailer's gas stove, and goes out to watch the magnificent sunrise over weather-sculpted "windows in stone" that give the region its name (*Desert Solitaire*, p. 6). The "monstrous and inhuman spectacle of rock and cloud and sky and space" evokes in him a desire to "confront . . . the bare bones of existence," to see nature as it really is, "devoid of all humanly ascribed qualities" (*Desert Solitaire*, pp. 6, 7). Brewing coffee and frying some bacon, the new ranger tries to get warm as the rising sun quickly melts the night's thin snowfall. The next chapter, "Solitaire," continues with Abbey's first day on the job, as he tours the park with the superintendent, whom he calls Merle McRae, and the chief ranger, whom he calls Floyd Bence. Leaving a Park Service pickup with Abbey, the two men depart that evening, and beside a fire of fragrant juniper wood Abbey exults in his solitude.

In the next two chapters Abbey describes some of the plants and animals with which he shares the desert. They include snakes, deer, lizards, birds, wildflowers, sage, and juniper and pinyon pine trees. Impulsively he throws a rock at a rabbit, killing it. Examining himself for feelings of guilt, he finds none—instead he feels more connected to the desert's diversity, and its

Desert in New Mexico.

endless tug-of-war between predator and prey, hunter and hunted.

Next is the digression titled "*Polemic*: Industrial Tourism and the National Parks." Looking back in the mid-1960s on the wilderness that was Arches in the late 1950s, Abbey laments the changes—especially the invasive paved roads—that have occurred here as part of the push to develop the parks:

> As I type these words . . . Arches National Monument has been developed. The Master Plan has been fulfilled. Where once a few adventurous people came on weekends to camp for a night or two and enjoy a taste of the primitive and remote, you will now find serpentine streams of baroque automobiles pouring in and out, all through the spring and summer, in numbers that would have seemed fantastic when I worked there: from 3,000 to 30,000 to 300,000 per year. . . . The little campgrounds . . . have now been consolidated into one master campground that looks, during the busy season, like a suburban village: elaborate housetrailers of quilted aluminum crowd upon gigantic camper-trucks of Fiberglass and molded plastic; through their windows you will see the blue glow of television and hear the studio laughter of Los Angeles . . . Progress has come to the Arches after a million years of neglect. Industrial Tourism has arrived.
>
> (*Desert Solitaire*, pp. 55-56)

Ironically calling the park "Arches Natural Money-mint," Abbey writes that what happened there "is of course an old story in the Park Service" (*Desert Solitaire*, p. 56). He lists other parks in which similar development has taken place, including the newly established Canyonlands National Park and Grand Canyon National Park. Instead of serving naturalists such as hikers who are willing to leave their cars behind, the parks are now geared towards "the indolent millions born on wheels and suckled on gasoline, who expect and demand paved highways to lead them in comfort, ease and safety into every nook and corner" of the national parks (*Desert Solitaire*, p. 61). This expectation has been created and encouraged by those politically powerful interests that stand to make money from it: oil companies, road builders, heavy equipment makers, and above all the auto industry. Abbey calls for banning cars from the national parks. Only then will the park system truly live up to its slogan, "Parks are for people," which Abbey says has been intended as meaning "parks are for people-in-automobiles" (*Desert Solitaire*, p. 63).

Over the next three chapters Abbey shifts his focus temporarily from parks to people. In "Rocks" he offers some geological information about the region, then retells an anecdote of an ill-fated love triangle involving prospectors. In "Cowboys and Indians" he recounts his adventures working with a soon-to-be-bankrupt independent cattleman named Roy Scobie, and in "Cowboys and Indians II" he describes the circumstances in which the Navajos have struggled to maintain their cultural identity. The next chapter, "Water," returns to earlier themes. In it, Abbey moves from a lyrical description of water (including flash floods) and its role in the desert to protest schemes to develop the West by hatching plans to fix a supposed water shortage. "There is no lack of water here," Abbey writes, "unless you try to establish a city where no city should be" (*Desert Solitaire*, p. 159). Abbey challenges the modern ideal of growth: "growth for the sake of growth is a cancerous madness. . . . Albuquerque and Phoenix will not be better cities when their populations are doubled and doubled again" (*Desert Solitaire*, pp. 159-60). Despite its lyrical title the next chapter, "The Heat of Noon: Rock and Tree and Cloud" continues in this polemical vein: Abbey argues that wilderness preservation is essential to liberty. In "The Moon-Eyed Horse," he digresses to narrate an encounter with a runaway horse in a remote canyon.

"Down the River" focuses on Glen Canyon, combining protests against the dam with an elegiac narrative of Abbey's 1959 raft trip through the canyon with his friend Ralph Newcomb. Abbey rages against the dam and against what he sees as the hypocrisy of naming the resulting lake after John Wesley Powell, the canyon's nineteenth-century explorer:

> Where he and his brave men once lined the rapids and glided through the silent canyons two thousand feet deep the motorboats now smoke and whine, scumming the water with cigarette butts, beer cans and oil, dragging the water skiers on their endless rounds. . . . To grasp the nature of the crime that was committed imagine the Taj Mahal or Chartres Cathedral buried in mud until only the spires remained visible.
>
> (*Desert Solitaire*, pp. 188-89)

A series of Abbey's experiences follows. In "Havasu" he describes becoming briefly stranded in a side canyon of the Grand Canyon, and in "The Dead Man at Grandview Point" he relates the hunt for the body of a missing hiker. "Tukuhnikivats, the Island in the Desert" reports Abbey's climb up a mountain he selected because he liked the name, which means "where the sun lingers" in the language of the Ute Indians. This reflection spurs a page-and-a-half long list of some of Abbey's favorite place names in the West. In "Episodes and Visions" Abbey writes about his interactions as a ranger with the tourists at Arches. He pokes gentle fun at their sedentariness and their questions ("Where's the Coke machine?"), and he imagines exhorting them to "crawl out of that shiny hunk of GM junk and take a walk" (*Desert Solitaire*, p. 291). He reflects on his attraction to the desert: "There are mountain men, there are men of the sea, and there are desert rats. I am a desert rat (*Desert Solitaire*, p. 298). Unlike the mountains and sea, Abbey suggests, "The desert is different. Not so hostile as the snowy peaks, nor so broad and bland as the ocean's surface, it lies open—given adequate preparation—to leisurely exploration, to extended periods of habitation" (*Desert Solitaire*, p. 302). In "Terra Incognita: Into the Maze" Abbey describes his descent with a friend, Bob Waterman, into the impressive and complex geological feature called the Maze in Canyonlands National Park.

Finally, in "Bedrock and Paradox" Abbey closes his telescoped, composite "season in the wilderness" as the tourists leave and he too prepares to return to civilization. Yet he is not entirely unwilling. "After twenty-six weeks of sunlight and stars, wind and sky and golden sand, I want to hear once more the crackle of clamshells on the floor of the bar in the Clam Broth House in Hoboken" (*Desert Solitaire*, p. 331). He takes a final tour of the park in his pickup, then cleans out the house trailer and accepts a lift from another ranger to Thompson, Utah, where he will catch a train east. "The desert," he writes, "will still be here in the spring" (*Desert Solitaire*, p. 337).

Changing attitudes to land use. In proposing a ban on cars in the national parks, Abbey offers an example of how such a ban might be handled even at popular destinations such as Yosemite and the Grand Canyon. He suggests building large parking lots well away from the parks' scenic hearts, and using a combination of horses, bicycles, and shuttle buses to transport people to their interiors. When Abbey wrote *Desert Solitaire*, this idea was ignored. More than three decades later, however, the Park Service is implementing essentially similar plans at both parks. Abbey also predicted that if "people are liberated from the confines of automobiles there will be a greatly increased interest in hiking, exploring, and back-country packtrips" (*Desert Solitaire*, p. 68). Many tourists still cling to their cars, but since the publication of *Desert Solitaire* hiking, camping, mountain biking, river rafting, kayaking, and other outdoor activities have indeed exploded in popularity. Today, hiking and other wilderness activities have become so popular that in most national park wilderness areas rangers have been forced to issue limited numbers of permits, with enthusiasts often waiting in line overnight in order to obtain one.

During the public debate over Glen Canyon, one argument used by those supporting the dam was that while few would enjoy the river by rafting, many would benefit from motorboating on the resulting lake. Even as similar debates were going on over damming parts of the Grand Canyon, however, greater numbers of people began discovering the pleasures of rafting through the canyon, and today about 26,000 people make this trip every year. Indeed, river-running (rafting) itself has become a nationally popular sport. Ironically, rafting in the Grand Canyon was adversely affected by Glen Canyon Dam upriver, because the dam caused the Colorado to recede during peak power usage. By the early 1990s, however, rafting the canyon was so popular that laws were passed requiring the dam's periodic release of water to approximate that of the natural cycle.

Such changes reflect not just decades of traffic jams in national parks, but also a greatly increased concern for and appreciation of the environment on the part of the American public. Historians have pointed to the first Earth Day, April 22, 1970, as marking a turning point in raising public awareness, and they credit it with bringing the words *environment* and *environmentalism* into their current widespread use. Like the rejection of the dams on the Grand Canyon in 1966, the first Earth Day's overwhelming popularity suggests that even as Abbey was writing *Desert Solitaire* a shift in public attitudes had already begun.

Sources and literary context. Abbey's most important sources for *Desert Solitaire* were the desert itself, and the journals he kept during his seasons as a park ranger there. As he writes in the Introduction, "most of the substance of this book is drawn, sometimes direct and unchanged" from those journals (*Desert Solitaire*, pp. ix-x). Indeed, an early title for the book was *Desert Journal*. The journals also reflect incipient versions of some central ideas Abbey elaborated in the final book. For example, as early as 1957, during Abbey's second season at Arches and well before the development he later objected to, an entry for April 8 (one week after his arrival) records the idea of banning cars from the parks: "DICTUM: NO AUTOMOBILES IN NATIONAL PARKS. . . . God Bless America. Let's save some of it" (Abbey, *Confessions*, p. 141). Selections from Abbey's journals were published in 1994, five years after his death, under the title *Confessions of a Barbarian*.

Many real people from Abbey's life appear in *Desert Solitaire*, some under their own names and some under fictitious ones. For example, Ralph Newcomb and Bob Waterman were the actual names of two friends with whom Abbey enjoyed the adventures recounted in the book, while "Merle McRae" and "Floyd Bence" were names that Abbey made up for Bates Wilson and Lloyd Pierson, the real-life superintendent and chief ranger at Arches. In his original introduction to the book, Abbey praised Bates Wilson, "who might justly be considered the founder of Canyonlands National Park," as "responsible for much of what understanding I have of a country we both love" (*Desert Solitaire*, p. xii). Abbey would have this passage removed from later editions because he came to blame Wilson for the roads and other development that took place during Wilson's tenure as superintendent at Arches.

As a boy growing up in Pennsylvania, Abbey devoured the cowboy books of Western writers such as Zane Grey (1875-1939), an early visitor to Glen Canyon and other sites mentioned in *Desert Solitaire*. He was later profoundly influenced by the writings of Henry David Thoreau, whose seminal book *Walden* (1854) originated American nature writing. Like Thoreau in *Walden*, Abbey compresses more than one season of wilderness living into a single, composite season for literary purposes. Abbey frequently either refers to Thoreau or quotes him directly in *Desert Solitaire*. Another valuable source for Abbey was explorer John Wesley Powell's published journals, which he quotes several times in "Down the River." In addition to passing references to well-known writers from Shakespeare to T. S. Eliot, Abbey refers to previous authors and books celebrating desert environments, including C. M. Doughty's *Travels in Arabia Deserta* (English; 1888) and Joseph Wood Krutch's *The Voice of the Desert* (American; 1955). Krutch (1893-1970) was an eminent author and naturalist whom Abbey met around the time *Desert Solitaire* was published. While both shared a love of nature, Krutch belonged to an older, more conservative generation. Abbey, while not exactly a hippie, shared the irreverent and anarchistic outlook of the emerging 1960s counterculture movement. He and Krutch disagreed over the Vietnam War, which Abbey strongly opposed.

Reception and impact. *Desert Solitaire* received positive reviews on its publication in January 1968, with critics praising Abbey's passion and his forceful style as well as his defense of the environment. "To the 'builders' and 'developers' among park administrators," wrote Edwin Way Teale in the *New York Times Book Review*, *Desert Solitaire:*

> may seem like a ride on a bucking bronco. It is rough, tough and combative. The author is a rebel, an eloquent loner. . . . His is a passionately felt, deeply poetic book . . . set down in lean, racing prose, in a close knit style of power and beauty. Rather than a balanced book . . . it is a forceful presentation of one side. And that side needs presenting. . . . There will always be others to voice the other side, the side of pressure and power and profit.
>
> (Teale, p. 7)

Freeman Tilden in *National Parks Magazine* likened Abbey's chiding of the Park Service to "a love-tap," writing that Abbey has "the yowl of a coyote: but be patient. He has the grace of that animal, too" (Tilden, p. 23).

Sales were modest in a year dominated by tumultuous political events, and Abbey complained that *Desert Solitaire* amounted to "another book dropped down the bottomless well" (Abbey in Cahalan, p. 113). Yet by the fall of 1968 *Desert Solitaire* was being avidly read by, for example, Wallace Stegner, the novelist and chronicler of life in the West, who loaned it to his friend, the poet and essayist Wendell Berry. In this way the book made an early impact among writers and others concerned with environmental issues. Dave Foreman, who later founded the radical environmental group Earth First!, called it "the first book I'd ever read that I totally agreed with" (Foreman in Cahalan, p. 114).

Desert Solitaire has often been compared with Rachel Carson's ***Silent Spring*** (1962; also in *Literature and Its Times*), which first awoke the public to the environmental dangers of pesticide use. But only after environmental issues rose to the forefront of public consciousness with the success of Earth Day in 1970 was Abbey's book published in a mass market paperback edition (the following year). Another author, Russell Martin, in his book about Glen Canyon, compared *Desert Solitaire* to an edgier work than Carson's, J. D. Salinger's classic cult novel of the disaffected: "Slowly at first, then ever more insistently, the book became word-of-mouth required reading, a kind of *Catcher in the Rye* for the coming-of-age environmental movement" (Martin, p. 287).

—Colin Wells

For More Information

Abbey, Edward. *Confessions of a Barbarian: Selections from the Journals of Edward Abbey, 1951-1989*. Ed. David Peterson. Boston: Little, Brown, 1994.

———. *Desert Solitaire: A Season in the Wilderness*. New York: Ballantine, 1971.

Cahalan, James M. *Edward Abbey: A Life*. Tucson: University of Arizona Press, 2001.

Keller, Robert H., and Michael R. Turek. *American Indians & National Parks*. Tucson: University of Arizona Press, 1998.

McClintock, James I. *Nature's Kindred Spirits: Aldo Leopold, Joseph Wood Krutch, Edward Abbey, Annie Dillard, and Gary Snyder*. Madison: University of Wisconsin Press, 1994.

Martin, Russell. *A Story That Stands Like a Dam: Glen Canyon and the Struggle for the Soul of the West*. New York: Holt, 1989.

Sellars, Richard West. *Preserving Nature in the National Parks: A History*. New Haven: Yale University Press, 1997.

Teale, Edwin Way. "Making the Wild Scene." *New York Times Book Review*, 28 January 1968, 7.

Tilden, Freeman. Review of *Desert Solitaire*. *National Parks Magazine* 42, no. 245 (February 1968): 22-23.

Dinner at the Homesick Restaurant

by
Anne Tyler

Anne Tyler (1941-) was born in the northern United States, in Minneapolis, Minnesota, but was raised in the South, in various Quaker communities in North Carolina. She earned her B.A. degree at the age of 19 from Duke University and published her first novel, *If Morning Ever Comes*, in 1964. Her fiction, which focuses on family relationships, tends to include quirky, often profoundly dysfunctional characters who seem disconnected from their immediate settings. Tyler's ninth novel, *Dinner at the Homesick Restaurant* established her reputation as an American writer of note. *The Accidental Tourist* (1985) would be adapted into film and *Breathing Lessons* (1988) would win Tyler the Pulitzer Prize, but *Dinner at the Homesick Restaurant* remains one of her best-loved works. The novel follows the evolution of an American family as the twentieth century progresses.

THE LITERARY WORK

A novel set in Baltimore, Maryland, from around 1930 to 1980; published in 1982.

SYNOPSIS

After being deserted by her husband Beck Tull, a traveling salesman, Pearl Tull singlehandedly raises her three children, Cody, Ezra, and Jenny. The novel follows the Tull family from Beck's and Pearl's marriage through Pearl's death and wake.

Events in History at the Time of the Novel

The twentieth-century American family. Over the first three decades of the twentieth century, both the makeup of the American family and the mythology connected to it changed drastically. Americans entered the century with a newborn discrepancy between the popular model of the family—based on domestic harmony and clear gender roles—and the degree of contentment with that model. A so-called "new woman" had begun to show dissatisfaction with the idea of women as passive nurturers relegated to the private sphere. In 1920 women won the right to vote in America and on the heels of this victory came a new image—that of the flapper—"independent, assertive, pleasure-hungry" (Mintz and Kellogg, p. 111). Again the image hardly represented the reality for most women: "In the 1920s women acquired some sexual freedom and a limited amount of opportunity outside the home, but the . . . hopes that accomplished the suffrage amendment remained unfulfilled" (Nash, p. 802). Most women continued in the role of homemaker and nurturer, feeling driven to these socially acceptable roles, though the seed had been planted for alternative options. In any case, Pearl, the novel's protagonist, who comes of age during the 1920s, maintains attitudes that place her in the mainstream, rather than the groundbreaking avant-garde. As a young woman, she focuses on her inability to catch a husband and throughout she subscribes to an unchanging

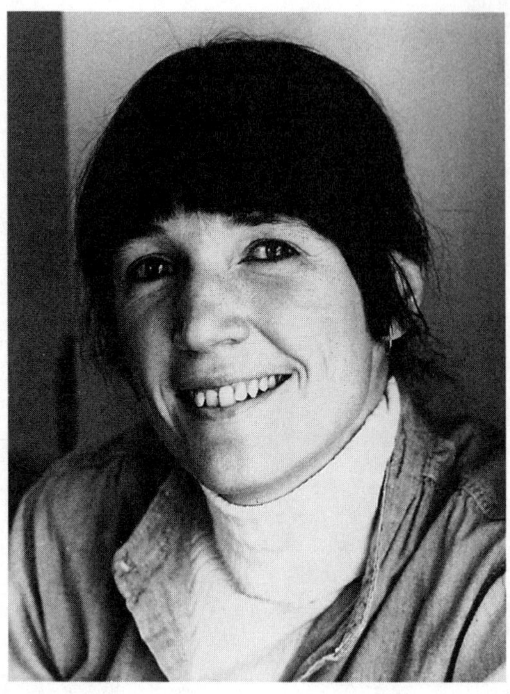

Anne Tyler

ideal of the American family, though she is unable to create it. The ideal, held by the population at large, consisted of a husband who supported the family financially and a wife who ran the household and provided emotional sustenance.

In reality, the American family underwent marked changes as the role of women evolved with the passing decades, from a more public presence in the 1930s and wartime 1940s, back to homemaker-nurturer in the 1950s, and then to self-actualized individual from the 1960s onward. For Tyler's novel, the 1930s appears to be the formative decade for the family it features. It was one in which the Great Depression wreaked havoc on families in general. The self-esteem of many men plummeted because of their inability to earn enough to support their families, which helps explain the soaring number who deserted their households during this decade. In 1940, America counted more than 1.5 million women living apart from their husbands (Mintz and Kellogg, p. 136). The Depression made survival the major preoccupation of American life, undermining gender differentiation, at least as it applied to economic roles. The decade found many men unemployed, women and children more likely to locate work, but the women generally occupied low-paid jobs, often in domestic service. Thus, though the female played a more public role, she did not achieve greater authority. The model family still conferred authority on the father, whose sphere of action was outside the home, not on the mother, whose sphere of action was ideally a domestic one.

During World War II, more than 6 million American women entered the work force for the first time, and the number of families headed by a woman continued to rise as well, hardly surprising since so many men went off to war (Sealander in Hawes and Nybakken, p. 158). The novel's Tull family, though fatherless, does not exactly fall into this category. Beck, the father, is seldom home not because he has gone off to war but because he travels throughout the country, selling farm and garden equipment. The cause differs, but the family structure itself resembles others in the country at the time. Pearl, the mother, however, differs from others in her position. When, in 1944, with the war still going on, her husband leaves the family entirely, she is not a wife singlehandedly keeping her brood together for the war effort but an abandoned woman who tries to raise a family that, as much as possible, resembles the ideal.

Even for more typical families, the ideal of the two-parent household in which the father brings home the livelihood did not change. The wages women contributed to the family were seen as a temporary necessity. Yes, the father of the household was often absent during the war, but the intact family still remained the most typical sort in 1940s America; the war provided a temporary disruption of the normal structure, not a recreation of it. Indeed the wartime media and government stressed the need for women to "keep the home fires burning," to put effort into helping with the war effort, but also into making sure that the America the soldiers would come home to was an essentially unchanged one.

The postwar period was one of growth in America. By 1960 more than 65 percent of American families had a standard of living that was middle class, in contrast to 30 percent in 1929. This middle-class standard sent women back into the home with gusto. The women themselves, initially torn after the war between the desires to work and stay home, learned to readjust, suppress contrary thoughts, and step back into their age-old role. Articles like *Life* magazine's "Busy Wife's Achievements" (1956) made the 1950s a decade that reaffirmed with renewed fervor the ideal family of breadwinner father and homemaker mother. And in fact, American reality coincided more with the ideal in this decade than it had in the past, but even in the prosperous 1950s, the real differed from the ideal. A middle-class existence often depended on two incomes in a family. In the 20 years after the war, the number of married women working outside the home jumped more than 300 percent. *Dinner at the Homesick Restaurant* portrays Pearl Tull as a woman who has continued to work outside the home since 1944. In the 1950s, her family, which so distresses her because of its failure to conform to the ideal, is no longer so atypical. It has grown to resemble a significant minority of American families, or perhaps more accurately, these families have grown to resemble it.

The children born in the 1950s, the "baby boomers," (so-called because of the surge in birth rate, which produced an unprecedented 29 million newborns by the close of the decade) would grow up to form predominantly two-income households. By the late 1970s, just before the novel ends, only 7 percent of America's families would conform to the ideal of provider father and homemaker mother, with *two* children, the number touted by the baby boomers. The traditional family structure lost its monopoly on household life, making room, in light of the rising divorce rate, for the single-parent household and the "blended" family of remarried spouses (Mintz in Hawes and Nybakken, p. 184). Between 1960 and the late 1980s there would be a sharp rise in female-headed households, in particular, with their number doubling. Thus, by the end of *Dinner at the Homesick Restaurant*, Pearl Tull's family is finally "normal." Now including the families of her, by this time, adult children, it has come to represent a variety of acceptable models for the era. Pearl's son Cody has married and lives with his wife and child in a semblance of the old family ideal. Ezra, who has never married, lives with his elderly mother. Jenny, who has been divorced and is now the matriarch of a blended family, not only works outside the home, but has a career as a doctor.

Americans eat. It is not a coincidence that frozen food became popular from the late 1950s on; as more and more women entered the workforce, quicker-cooking, more convenient foods were required for the American kitchen. But in the same way that the ideal family structure contained clearly divided roles for the father and the mother, the ideal dinner continued to remain the laboriously cooked home meal, prepared by the woman of the household. Cookbooks from the 1950s reflect the tension of the decade, often providing recipes for dishes made out of a combination of "convenience" and homemade products. A recipe for Tuna Supreme, for instance, might contain canned tuna and store-bought crackers, but require three cups of a homemade white sauce (*Betty Crocker's Picture Cookbook*, p. 282). Another trend of the time was an interest in both "gourmet" cooking and "exotic" cooking, both departures, in concept at least, from the standard American cooking that had been popular until after the war, characterized by pot roasts, boiled potatoes, and fruit pies. Actually, most of the newly popular dishes, whether served in homes or restaurants, would have been unrecognizable to their originators. The dish spaghetti-and-meatballs, a newly popular favorite, never existed in Italy; chop suey,

THE TRAVELING SALESMAN

According to one source, by the time the novel's Beck Tull took up his trade, the "glory days" of the American traveling salesman were over. After the Civil War, the traveling salesman, "a highly visible figure on the increasingly busy thoroughfares joining urban centers to small towns," seemed an icon of cultural change. By 1900, he had been largely supplanted by mail-order houses and national chains buying directly from suppliers (Spears, p. 1). He nevertheless continued to introduce various items to the American public, selling people on the usefulness of these items. The 1920s saw the first refrigerators sold door-to-door; other items promoted in this way included air conditioners, vacuum cleaners, telephones, and cash registers. Meanwhile, the salesman endured in the American imagination too, his image sometimes evoking "gentle nostalgia and stoic loneliness," sometimes evoking untrustworthiness and cheap commercialism (Spears, p. 3). He featured in American literature for decades, in works such as Sherwood Anderson's *Winesburg, Ohio* (1919), Sinclair Lewis's *Main Street* (1920), Eugene O'Neill's *The Iceman Cometh* (1939), Arthur Miller's *Death of a Salesman* (1949), and Eudora Welty's "Death of a Traveling Salesman" (1936). In *Dinner at the Homesick Restaurant,* Beck Tull evokes a range of stereotypic traits ascribed to the traveling salesman: an excellent salesman, he woos Pearl brilliantly. Untrustworthy in the extreme, he abandons her and his three children. Deeply lonely, he spends the next 35 years wandering the country, writing occasional letters to a wife he never sees again, updating her on his successes and failures.

The typical traveling salesman of the 1950s.

another new passion, never existed in China. "Main Dishes are as American as apple pie or chocolate cake," the introduction to the "Main Dishes" section of the 1956 version of the *Betty Crocker's Picture Cookbook* states, going on to provide recipes that seem at first glance to represent the cuisines of the world (*Betty Crocker's,* p. 274). The following pages include directions for "Chili con Carne" made with canned tomato soup, "Chicken Chow Mein," to be served over crispy noodles, instead of either rice or plain noodles, "Shrimp Supreme" prepared with store-bought mayonnaise, and "Welsh Rarebit" made with American cheese.

Several factors helped effect this change in American eating habits. Food was more plentiful after the stringent rationing of wartime. Also, new dishes emerged because the rationing itself had required cooks to break patterns and be inventive; before the war, to take one example, eggplant was generally served only in Greek and Italian neighborhoods, but during the war, other families began to eat it. Another motivating factor was the demand. The returning soldiers had tasted "new" foods overseas, foods they enjoyed and wished to eat again, and there was money enough to indulge these new tastes. By the 1960s, cookbooks that focused on exotic tastes were common on the American kitchen shelf (Julia Child's popular *Mastering the Art of French Cooking*, for instance, appeared in 1961), and restaurants serving dishes from other countries proliferated.

The trend would not progress unchecked. By the 1970s there was a backlash against both mass-produced processed foods and the exotic or "gourmet" cooking of the 1950s and 1960s. The poor quality and tastelessness of processed cuisine had become infamous, but it was not the only culprit. In the search for new tastes, and in the desire to recreate foreign foods, many cooks, both at home and in restaurants, sacrificed good taste and quality. Indeed, the two seemingly different trends coincided in alarming ways: the use of frozen foods in gourmet restaurants became ubiquitous. At the same time, fast-food franchises sprang up, in large part because of the proliferation of highways. Americans seemed, on the whole, to have lost the ability to discern good food from mediocre food. Paradoxically concerned with exoticism, but desiring standardized fare, and relying more and more on processed foods, they found themselves eating less well.

Then came the counterculture of the late 1960s and the early 1970s, that is, the mostly young Americans who embraced values and lifestyles in opposition to the mainstream. With their movement came a change in American dining, both inside the home and out. Spurred by various concerns—a growing distrust of multinational corporations, such as those that ran the fast food franchises; a growing awareness of environmental issues; a growing interest in the cultures from which exotic foreign foods came; and a growing concern with health issues—more Americans began to turn to whole foods, organically grown; to Asian foods, and to rediscovered, often time-consuming, cooking methods. There was, for instance, a revival of baking bread in the home. Across America, small counterculture restaurants opened, serving vegetarian menus, or ethnic menus, or otherwise unusual menus, menus concerned with individuality. Most of these went in and out of existence quickly, but some survived and thrived, a prime example of which would be the Moosewood Restaurant, in Ithaca, New York, which served (and still serves) vegetarian food, with an ever-changing menu. Due in large part to a series of cookbooks associated with the restaurant, it gained international fame.

ALICE EXPLAINS HOW TO COOK

In 1969, after Arlo Guthrie's song "Alice's Restaurant" had become popular, Alice Brock published *Alice's Restaurant Cookbook,* which contains more general advice than it does actual recipes, in accordance with a culinary philosophy that requires a great deal of flexibility on the part of a cook.

> How you prepare a dish really has to depend on your mood, the season, how much money you have in your pocket, and who's going to eat it. You may never do the same thing twice—or correctly—but don't ever be afraid to do it. There is no ingredient you can't leave out or substitute. There is no tool so perfect that no other will do the job. Don't be afraid to cook something you've never heard of. If you can learn to substitute and fake it—and still make it—you may discover all kinds of new things.
>
> (Brock, p. 6)

Her recipes reflect this philosophy. The recipe for Marinated Vegetables, for instance, reads,

> These can be mushrooms, eggplant, cauliflower, string beans, beets, or anything you choose. Those that need to be peeled, peel. The large vegetables should be cut into cubes or slices. A basic marinade is 2/3 oil, and 1/3 vinegar, lemon or wine. Seasonings can vary, but they should include minced garlic or grated onion, salt, and pepper or peppercorns. You may add a bay leaf or whatever else you feel like throwing in. I would suggest oregano, basil and thyme. There is also something called pickling spice which might be good. . . . Put your vegetables in the marinade and simmer for 15 minutes—or just let them sit in the marinade for a few hours (or days, for that matter).
>
> (Brock p. 93)

For an example of the more usual counterculture restaurant, which had only a brief period of glory, one would be hard pressed to find one better than the Back Room Rest, opened in 1969, in Stockbridge, Massachusetts, by Alice Brock, which stayed open for just a year. Though it did not yet exist in 1967, at the time of the Thanksgiving feast referred to in Arlo Guthrie's popular folk song "Alice's Restaurant," Brock was dreaming of opening her own restaurant at the time, and so it came to be regarded as the original Alice's Restaurant. Its short life was due to Brock's desire to move on, not to a lack of quality in what was served; it was very popular, says a patron of the restaurant: "There wasn't any better food anywhere. The way she cooked was the way you cook today. It wasn't the way people cooked in 1969" (Lee, p. 98). Brock focused on originality, creativity, fresh ingredients, making a restaurant that depended not on a set menu but upon a chef's ability to live and create fully in the moment, a philosophy shared by Ezra Tull, in his creation of the Homesick Restaurant in Tyler's novel.

The Novel in Focus

The plot. Though *Dinner at the Homesick Restaurant* opens and closes with Pearl Tull's dying and the aftermath of her death with scenes from her final days interspersed throughout the novel, the bulk of it concerns the 50 years before her death, starting in 1930. That year, when she was an old maid already, in her early thirties, Pearl married Beck Tull. A traveling salesman, Beck would desert his wife and three children—Cody, Ezra, and Jenny—in 1944, when they were 14, 11, and 9, after a family outing in which a tussle between the boys caused Pearl to be accidentally shot in the shoulder with an arrow.

Pearl supports her children with a job checking out groceries and never discusses their father's absence with the children. His unexplained absence, and their mother's uncontrollable rages, mold the children, who all grow up to find intimacy difficult.

Cody, who becomes a management consultant, feels jealous of his mother's preference for Ezra, whom he torments throughout their childhood. Jenny, who becomes a pediatrician, has a disastrous first marriage to an emotionless college classmate, and a happier second marriage to a man who has children from his own first marriage; Jenny and he go on to have their own child together. Ezra, who works in a high-class eating establishment, dreams of opening his own restaurant, where "people come just like to a family dinner," where he'll "cook one thing special each day and dish it out on their plates and everything will be solid and wholesome, really homelike" (Tyler, *Dinner at the Homesick Restaurant*, p. 75).

In 1958, Ezra takes over the restaurant he works in, and renames it "The Homesick Restaurant." In 1960 he falls in love with one of his cooks and becomes engaged to her. Cody, his older brother, steals her away, mostly because he can, and marries her himself; though strained, their marriage survives. In a fit of rage, Cody reveals to his wife Ruth and his teenaged son, Luke, that he believes Ezra to be Luke's father (a complete fantasy on his part), whereupon Luke runs away to Baltimore, to Ezra's restaurant, from whence Cody fetches him back.

Throughout the years, Ezra plans elaborate dinners for the family at his restaurant, which they attend with poor grace, and which they never manage to complete. Long before dessert, at least one of them gets up angrily from the table and leaves in a huff. When Pearl dies, Ezra plans yet another dinner—a wake for Pearl—and invites his father. None of the children have seen him since the day he left in 1944, but he has continued to write to Pearl occasionally, and his address is in her book. Ezra sets out to fulfill Pearl's last request—to invite everyone in the book to her funeral. Of all the people listed, Beck is the only one still alive. To everyone's surprise but Ezra's, Beck does indeed arrive. Cody insults him, and he leaves; yet another family dinner at the Homesick Restaurant seems to be a failure. But this time the entire family, including Cody, runs out the door to retrieve the lost family member. Cody is the one who finds him. In the process of bringing Beck back, Cody sees his entire family running towards him. The sight dredges up the memory of that fateful family outing on which the archery accident occurred, an outing that in retrospect seems peaceful, at least. As is usual in an Anne Tyler novel, nothing has been fixed: the family is still both discordant and loving, at odds and connected. But in seeing them running towards him, Cody is granted a new vision of his family, one free from pain and actually beautiful. It is a healing vision because it is a re-visioning, the balm a different perspective.

The Homesick Restaurant and the Tull family. That Pearl Tull would raise a chef as proficient as Ezra is astounding; she herself manages to feed her children, but without much flair; in fact, as Cody remembers it, she "whimpered when she burned things. She burned things you would not imagine it possible to burn and served others half-raw, adding jarring extras of her own design such as crushed pineapple in the smashed potatoes" (*Homesick Restaurant*, p. 160). She was also given to interrupting dinners, exploding in a rage, and throwing the food on the floor. Yet Ezra grows up to be someone who likes to cook for people and does so very well. He serves his apprenticeship under Mrs. Scarlatti at Scarlatti's restaurant; one of Ezra's several unsuccessful family dinners is meant to commemorate his purchase, in 1957 (for one dollar), of a partnership in the restaurant.

At that point, the restaurant is not his yet, but in 1958 Mrs. Scarlatti falls seriously ill, so ill that it does not appear that she will ever recover. Unable to stop himself, Ezra begins to take over the restaurant even before she dies, before it is truly his. He begins by serving gizzard soup, a lower-class Italian dish, and hires the restaurant's first waitress (previously only waiters had been hired) to announce that the soup exists (since it's not on the menu), and that it's "really hot and garlicky and it's made with love" (*Homesick Restaurant,* p. 119). Ezra buys a blackboard on which to write the specials he invents. Then he replaces all the waiters with waitresses, and throws out the menus. Also, he has the wall between the dining room and the kitchen torn down, so that the patrons can see the staff at work.

Mrs. Scarlatti, however, recovers unexpectedly and returns to the restaurant—"You might at least have waited till I died," she says, when she sees the change Ezra has made (*Homesick Restaurant,* p. 129). But though Ezra is pained by Mrs. Scarlatti's disapproval, he nevertheless continues his frenzied recreation of the restaurant. The gilt sconces disappear, as do the silhouettes on the restroom doors. Mrs. Scarlatti's last words to her nurse are to tell Ezra to change the name of the restaurant.

None of this makes any sense to Cody. From his point of view, the restaurant has been systematically wrecked. It doesn't even act like a restaurant anymore. Nothing is dependable. Not only does the menu change every day; customers can't assume they'll get what they order. What Ezra serves up depends on the dish he thinks they really need at the moment. Even the prices can't be relied on; elderly customers are charged less.

But the Homesick Restaurant (as it is now called) does survive. Many of Scarlatti's regular customers leave, but some stay on, and many new customers are drawn not only to the good food but also to how fluid the restaurant is. Ezra has manifested his vision of a nurturing, healthy home, one where a customer will be given the exact food that he or she needs at that moment. His family never appreciates this—it seems to them to be a haphazard, sloppy establishment. (Pearl herself never recovers from learning that Ezra never planned to become a professor, one of her most cherished fantasies.) Every time they come to the Homesick Restaurant for one of Ezra's attempts at family solidarity, they recreate the home they have lived in, with the refusals to eat, the resentments, the fights, the inevitable moment of someone's storming out. Over and over again, someone always leaves.

Ezra has entirely invented this restaurant. It represents the home he longs for, not because he came from such a place, but rather because he wishes he did. He wants a home where one is safe and comfortable, a home where one is nourished and understood, a pleasant, ideal home, as ideal as the family after which Pearl quests all her life. Ezra's "home" is also changeable, constantly recreating itself, never the same from one day to the next. It represents both solidity and fluidity. He has broken away from the disorder and rage of Pearl's household, but he has also broken away from Mrs. Scarlatti's conventions. Neither woman has been the cook that he becomes.

Ezra is, of course, ahead of his time. When he takes over the restaurant, in 1958, he is in no way connected to what would become the counterculture from which restaurants like Alice Brock's "Back Door Rest" would spring. Nevertheless, he creates a restaurant that is very much like Brock's. His restaurant is founded not on his political or cultural convictions—as far as we know, he hasn't got any—but on his drive to create a stable family and his dogged belief that this can happen. Twenty years later, after his mother's funeral, when his far-flung family gathers again at the restaurant, his method of feeding people has not changed; he serves them eggplant soup, invented by one of his chefs who "cooked by astrology," the secret ingredient of which is, improbably, bananas.

From the point of view of the inherited ideal family, the family gathered around the table seems just as improbable as the banana soup. How can Beck appear out of nowhere, to sit at the table as a grandfather? How can Cody and Ezra possibly get along? How can Ezra's odd restaurant survive? How have the Tull children managed to grow up to function as well as they do? Why are any of these people sitting together at the same table? The only piece of the family that approximates the American ideal is Cody's, and his is a desperately unhappy marriage.

But the extended family is gathered together nonetheless, and when Beck disappears this time, the family goes after him. They have come to represent not just the fluid form of the American family at the end of the twentieth century, but the continuing American commitment to the family itself, and to the idea of family, even as multiple structures evolve.

Sources and literary context. Tyler is considered a southern writer, and the eccentricity manifested by nearly all her characters connects her firmly to other twentieth-century southern writers, including Flannery O'Connor, William Faulkner, and Eudora Welty. Anne Tyler says that Welty has been the most influential on her writing and the admiration is mutual, as shown by Welty's comment about this novel: "If I could have written the last sentence in *Dinner at the Homesick Restaurant* I'd have been happy for the rest of my life" (Welty in Salwak, p. 11). Welty's influence can be seen most clearly in Tyler's humor, her sense of place, her eccentric characters, her use of language, and her lyrical descriptions.

As mentioned above, Welty has also written a short story concerning a traveling salesman, and it would be tempting to assume this work to be a source for *Dinner at the Homesick Restaurant*. But the only clearly known source is a children's book, *The Little House* by Virginia Lee Burton. A book Tyler loved as a child, it appears in *Dinner at the Homesick Restaurant* as a book beloved by daughter Jenny, who remembers asking her mother to read it over and over. The book concerns a humble country house that becomes a house in the city, as its surroundings change over time, until it is moved out to the country again.

From *The Little House*

Pretty soon there was an elevated train going back and forth above the Little House. The air was filled with dust and smoke, and the noise was so loud that it shook the Little House. Now

she couldn't tell when Spring came, or Summer or Fall, or Winter. It all seemed about the same.
(Burton, p. 24)

Tyler, in "Why I Still Treasure 'The Little House,'" has written of her early experience with the book and what it taught her about time: "It seemed I'd been presented with a snapshot that showed me how the world worked: how the years flowed by and people altered and nothing could ever stay the same" (Tyler in Salwak, p. 98). The sorrow of that understanding of the inevitability of change and loss pervades *Dinner at the Homesick Restaurant.* But in the children's book, and also in Tyler's novel, is the notion of redemption—the idea that the new generations can indeed recreate the past, though in an altered state.

Tyler's relationship to southern literature has been more comfortable than her relationship to women's literature, especially to literature informed by feminist views. Concerning "novels by liberated women," she has in fact, said, "I hate 'em all," a remark made in 1972 and never retracted (Tyler in Salwak, p. 33). Tyler's focus on family relationships and domestic issues has never been unusual for her time; nor is her focus on dysfunctional families. But her method of presenting her material is entirely her own. Her novels contain horrific scenes. Pearl, for instance, is, as Cody puts it, a "raving, shrieking, unpredictable witch" (*Homesick Restaurant,* p. 294).

She slammed up against the wall and called us scum and vipers, and she wished us dead, shook us till our teeth rattled, screamed in our faces. We never knew from one day to the next, was she all right? Was she not? The tiniest thing could set her off. "I'm going to throw you through that window," she used to tell me. "I'll look out that window and laugh at your brains splashed all over the pavement."
(*Homesick Restaurant,* p. 294)

Such a scene is not uncommon in late-twentieth-century American fiction; what is uncommon is Tyler's narrative method of distancing the events. The narrator presents them in a controlled fashion, giving a balanced view, and thereby keeping them from becoming overwhelmingly horrific. And there is constant optimism in her work—here exemplified by Ezra, and fulfilled finally, at the end of the novel, by Cody's new vision of his family. Probably more than any other element, it is Tyler's optimism—her presentation of the possibility of redemption—that sets her work apart from that of other writers who focus on domestic dysfunction. Her characters are maimed, but they not only survive, but often flourish. Her families appear to be dreadful, but they endure, no matter how oddly structured. In the final analysis, everyone always seems on the verge of becoming normal.

Reviews. When *Dinner at the Homesick Restaurant* was published, critics were watching Tyler's work closely. In 1976 novelist John Updike had given a favorable review to Tyler's sixth novel, *Searching for Caleb*, and from then on her novels received careful attention. *Dinner at the Homesick Restaurant* would be the one that catapulted her to fame. It has not, however, been universally admired. In the view of some critics, Tyler's fiction is essentially shallow, the work of a popular, rather than a serious, author. Writing for *The Village Voice*, Vivian Gormick described *Dinner at the Homesick Restaurant* as escapist; for her, the eccentricity of Tyler's characters is "whimsey," the distancing provided by the narrator a "fear of experience" (Gormick, p. 41). Others thought quite differently. Updike himself praised the novel in *The New Yorker,* observing that the work moved its author into new territory, adding a much needed "darkening" to her fiction (Updike, p. 110). But probably most important to the novel's success was scholar Benjamin DeMott's *New York Times* book review;

"Dinner at the Homesick Restaurant" is a book to be settled into fully, tomorrow be damned. Funny, heart-hammering, wise, it edges deep into truth that's simultaneously (and interdependently) psychological, moral and formal—deeper than many living novelists of serious reputation have penetrated, deeper than Miss Tyler herself has gone before. It is a border crossing.
(DeMott, p. 1)

—Anne Brannen

For More Information

Betty Crocker's Picture Cookbook. New York: McGraw-Hill, 1956.

Brock, Alice May. *Alice's Restaurant Cookbook.* New York: Random House, 1969.

Burton, Virgina Lee. *The Little House.* Boston: Houghton Mifflin, 1942.

DeMott, Benjamin. "Funny, Wise and True." *New York Times Book Review,* 15 March 1982, 1, 14.

Gormick, Vivian. "Anne Tyler's Arrested Development." *Village Voice,* 30 March 1982, 40-41.

Hawes, Joseph M., and Elizabeth I. Nybakken, Eds. *American Families: A Research Guide and Historical Handbook.* New York: Greenwood, 1991.

Hess, John L., and Karen Hess. *The Taste of America.* New York: Grossman, 1977.

Lee, Laura. *Arlo, Alice, and Anglicans: The Lives of a New England Church.* Lee, Massachusetts: Berkshire Books, 2000.

Mintz, Steven, and Susan Kellogg. *Domestic Revolutions: A Social History of American Family Life.* New York: The Free Press, 1988.

Nash, Gary B., et al. *The American People: Creating a Nation and a Society.* Vol. 2. New York: Harper and Row, 1990.

Salwak, Dale, Ed. *Anne Tyler as Novelist.* Iowa City: University of Iowa Press, 1994.

Spears, Timothy. *100 Years on the Road: The Traveling Salesman in American Culture.* New Haven: Yale University Press, 1995.

Tyler, Anne. *Dinner at the Homesick Restaurant.* New York: Ballantine Books, 1996.

Updike, John. "More Substance Complexities of Family Relationships—Buried Horrors of Family Life." *New Yorker,* 5 April 1892, 193-97.

A Dry White Season

by
André Brink

Born in Vrede, South Africa, in 1935, André Brink was one of the first Afrikaner writers to produce anti-apartheid, politically charged literature in South Africa. (*Afrikaner*—the former term was *Boer*—refers to whites who descend mainly from the early Dutch but also from the early German and French settlers in the region.) Brink has since become a writer of international renown, publishing regularly in both Afrikaans and English. In the 1950s he earned masters of arts degrees in both English and Afrikaans literature, and then, from 1959 until 1961, engaged in postgraduate study at the Sorbonne in Paris. Brink later became part of the experimental Afrikaner "Sestiger" movement ("Writers of the Sixties"), and in 1968 planned to settle in Paris along with the exiled poet and fellow Sestiger writer, Breyten Breytenbach. However, the Parisian student revolt that year inspired Brink to return to South Africa to "accept full responsibility" for whatever he wrote (Brink in Ross, p. 55). Brink's initial novel to emerge from this new commitment, *Kennis van die aand* (1973), became the first Afrikaans book to be banned by South African censors. His own English translation of this novel, *Looking on Darkness,* was published the following year, and became successful internationally. Since then Brink has written regularly in both Afrikaans and English—often composing each novel twice to make it available in both languages. Written in the wake of the 1976 Soweto Revolt, *A Dry White Season* helped increase anti-apartheid sentiment throughout the world. With this novel, said Brink, "I have tried to accept that responsibility one owes to one's society and one's time" (Brink in Jolly, p. 18).

THE LITERARY WORK

A novel set in Johannesburg and Soweto, South Africa, in the late 1970s; published in Afrikaans (as *'n Droe wit seisoen*) in 1979, in English in 1979.

SYNOPSIS

The novel traces the last year in the life of Ben Du Toit, an Afrikaner schoolteacher who trusts fully in the state until a black friend dies in prison under suspicious circumstances.

Events in History at the Time of the Novel

Apartheid. Like many other South African novels of the 1970s and 1980s, *A Dry White Season* is set against the backdrop of *apartheid,* or the system of legalized racial segregation enforced in South Africa from 1948 until 1990. The system rested on the Afrikaner notion that society in South Africa consisted not of one but of various nations that ought to live in their own distinct homelands or reserves; those from black homelands should, according to this system, be allowed to enter the white homeland only temporarily as workers. In fact, South Africa had a long history of segregationist and racist policies before the 1948 victory of the Nationalist Party, which would institute many of the policies of apartheid. The 1948 election was, in fact, a victory for the Afrikaner nationalists who had themselves been oppressed and condescended to by South Africa's British population. The Boer War (1899 to 1902) had essentially been an attempt on the Afrikaners' part to preserve the independence of their settler states in the face of the British desire for complete dominance in South Africa; after the Afrikaners' crushing loss in this war, a fierce and zealous nationalist movement arose that tried to maintain an Afrikaner identity and culture in the British-dominated colony.

ETHNIC POPULATION OF SOUTH AFRICA IN 1980 (IN MILLIONS)

African	20.8 (72 percent)
Coloured	2.6 (9 percent)
Indian	0.8 (3 percent)
White*	4.5 (16 percent)

* Of the white population, approximately 60 percent were Afrikaner.

(Adapted from Thompson, p. 243)

Though the two groups merged in 1910 to form the Union of South Africa, the Afrikaners always played a subordinate role to the British. While the two groups together created an entire system of power based on the oppression and exclusion of blacks (including Africans, Indians, and "Coloureds," or people of mixed racial descent), the Afrikaner nationalist movement created an entire ideology around the idea that the Afrikaners were a "chosen people" favored by God and destined to rule South Africa. Furthermore, as the country became more urbanized and industrialized and as many poor Afrikaners were forced into competition for jobs with black workers, fear of the "black peril"—the idea that Afrikaners were in danger of being overwhelmed by the black majority—added momentum to the nationalist movement already focused on ethnic separation. When the British-led government brought South Africa into World War II—Britain's war, as many Afrikaners saw it—strident Afrikaners lost patience and finally voted the fascist-influenced National Party into power in 1948.

Almost immediately after assuming power the Nationalists began constructing "an apparatus of laws, regulations and bureaucracies" that would develop into "the most elaborate racial edifice the world had ever witnessed" (Meredith, p. 54). Inter-racial marriages and sexual relationships were banned; different racial groups were compelled by law to use separate restaurants, post offices, theaters, buses, and so on, or to use separate entrances and seats in public buildings; as residential areas for each racial group were demarcated, whole communities were uprooted. Though apartheid rhetoric had spoken of separation but equality, the areas demarcated for nonwhite South Africans represented only a small percentage of the country's total land mass; as a result, many nonwhite people were left no alternative but to build makeshift shantytowns on the outskirts of white-populated cities. Such overwhelming inequality characterized apartheid legislation. Between 1948 and 1971, 151 racial laws were enacted, affecting every aspect of daily life—three times the number of racial laws enacted in the four decades preceding the National Party's reign.

South Africa in the 1970s. While the initial impetus behind apartheid was a desire to maintain Afrikaner culture and restore Afrikaner glory, by the 1970s it was clear that Afrikaners no longer had to fight for power and recognition. Once composed mainly of poor rural farmers, the now predominantly white-collar Afrikaner population had become urbanized and had taken over the economic lead formerly enjoyed by the British. And, now that the Afrikaners controlled the economy, apartheid came under critique as an impractical economic policy that left the labor force mostly unskilled. With the expansion of industry and the demand for skilled labor outweighing the supply, some Afrikaners began to see that the regulations intended to keep nonwhites powerless were preventing national economic advancement. Indeed, South Africa had become a country with a "first-world infrastructure and a third-world labour force" (Le May, p. 241).

The 1970s also saw a major philosophical shift among the black population with the advent of the militant Black Consciousness Movement (BCM), whose spokesman and founder, Steven Biko, rejected white involvement in the anti-apartheid struggle and sought to empower blacks on their own terms. In the two previous decades African revolutionaries had been defiant but muted, and had usually worked alongside white liberals and communists. But, as Biko contended,

> The biggest mistake the black world ever made was to assume that whoever opposed apartheid was an ally. For a long time the black world has been looking only at the governing party and not so much at the whole power structure as the object of their rage.
>
> (Biko in Meredith, p. 139)

Biko believed that blacks, accustomed to oppression and feelings of inferiority, could acquire strength only by distancing themselves from whites. BCM was to dominate black political activity throughout the 1970s. It found outlets in "poetry, literature, drama, music, theology and in local community projects promoting education, health and welfare" (Meredith, p. 140).

Police reaction to black dissent was harsh, once the power of the BCM was acknowledged. In March 1973 eight leaders of the movement, including Biko, were banned; the Minister of Justice, P. C. Pelser, claimed they had advocated "arson, rape and bloody revolution" (Pelser in Harsch, p. 271). Banning, for Biko, meant that he was "restricted to King William's Town, forbidden to speak in public or to write for publication or to be quoted or to be present with more than one person at a time" (Meredith, p. 141). That year more than 100 other black militants were banned or placed under house arrest. In early 1974 O. R. Tiro, another BCM leader, was killed in his home by a bomb; the Bureau of State Security was believed to be behind the murder. As a result of a crackdown during this period, the official leadership of all major BCM groups was effectively wiped out. Determined and resilient, however, other leaders continued to work behind the scenes and new leaders emerged to fill in the gaps. Such commitment was reinforced not only by widespread militant sentiment—a general unwillingness to be cowed by an oppressive system—but also by news of the gains of various liberation movements throughout Africa. The victory of FRELIMO (Front for the Liberation of Mozambique) in Mozambique, where white Portugese rule collapsed, was especially encouraging news to South African revolutionaries, and "Viva FRELIMO" rallies were held throughout the country. In South Africa, the police detained and arrested another 50 prominent BCM activists, most of whom were sentenced to five or six years in prison after an extended trial. The trial succeeded only in stimulating the BCM, whose leaders used it as a platform for revolutionary ideas, and regularly entered the courtroom singing freedom songs and shouting *Amandla* (Zulu for "power").

This new, fierce energy on the part of black militants, as well as old resentments over low wages, police harassment, and, indeed, the entire system of racial subjugation effected by apartheid, would lead inevitably to the bloody, devastating 16 months of riots known as the Soweto Revolt.

Johannesburg and Soweto. *A Dry White Season* takes place mainly in Johannesburg, where the Afrikaner protagonist Ben du Toit lives, and Soweto, where all of the black characters live. Though it may seem surprising that du Toit could live for 50 years as a South African and have had so little direct experience with blacks that he would not be aware of the vast inequalities facing them, the fact is that nonwhite servants tended to the needs of Johannesburg whites and so entered their community, but no white people would ever visit Soweto. Soweto is an acronym for the southwestern townships (SOuth-WEstern TOwnships) of Johannesburg, where in 1984 more than 1.25 million nonwhite Africans lived. Their segregation into this area resulted, in part, from the 1950 Group Areas Act, which required nonwhites and whites to live in previously designated, racially zoned areas. Indeed, a white South African from Johannesburg may well have never even set foot in Soweto. A historian during the apartheid period noted:

> Familiar social barriers to communication between upper and lower classes are reinforced in South Africa, both by racial distinctions and by regulations which discourage the entry of Whites into Black townships. Many leading local Whites who are familiar with London, Paris and New York have never set foot in Soweto.
>
> (Mandy, p. xix)

Around the time of the novel, mine dumps and tall buildings made up the Johannesburg skyline, identifying the city as South Africa's industrial center. Both to the east and the west of the mine dumps were many industrial townships and the homes of low-income whites. North of the mine dumps were the urban center and, further to the north, the rich white suburbs where a character like Ben du Toit would have lived. To the southwest of the mine dumps sat the "drab houses of sprawling Black Soweto and the segregated areas where the Coloureds and Indians [were] required to live" (Mandy, p. xv). Though Soweto was too large to be considered a town, it was "not yet a city because it lack[ed] cohesion

White police and soldiers in Soweto attack blacks protesting a government order to use the Afrikaans language for teaching in secondary schools.

and the normal range of urban anemities" (Mandy, p. 173). It had few paved roads at the time of the novel, and no pharmacies, bakeries, modern shopping centers, or office blocks. Some 75 percent of the groceries purchased by Sowetans were bought in Johannesburg. This arrangement forced Sowetans to remain dependent on the white sections of Johannesburg.

In the early 1970s conditions in the black townships deteriorated. In an attempt to relegate more blacks to their separate homelands, the government restricted urban development, which resulted in severe housing shortages. A survey of ten cities, accounting for half of South Africa's urban black population, showed that from 1970 to 1975 the amount of housing had increased by only 15 percent when, in the same areas, the African population had grown by more than 50 percent. In 1970 an average of 13 people lived in each house; by 1975 the average rose to 17 (Meredith, p. 142). From a new system of township administration—in which local administration boards would no longer receive subsidies from, in Soweto's case, Johannesburg—came harsh consequences in Soweto. Rents rose and services for roads, garbage removal, and sewer systems all declined. A 1976 survey showed that 43 percent of Soweto households were living under the poverty line (Meredith, p. 143).

The Soweto Revolt. The spark that set off the Soweto Revolt was the government's decision to enforce an outdated and impractical 1958 law, which ruled that the Afrikaans language had to be used regularly by secondary school teachers. Despite the fact that many teachers did not even know Afrikaans—the amalgamation of Dutch and African languages used by the Afrikaners—in 1974 the government ordered that the language be used for all practical subjects and for all courses in the general sciences. Parents, teachers, school boards, and administrators protested throughout the country to no avail. In Soweto black students began boycotting classes taught in Afrikaans, which they saw as the language of the oppressor. On June 16, 1976, a large group of students marched through Soweto singing freedom songs and chanting slogans. The students gathered peacefully in front of the Orlando West junior secondary school to protest, and planned to continue the march from there.

The police arrived, and a white policeman threw a tear-gas canister into the crowd. Another white policemen opened fire into the crowd, killing a 13-year-old black boy, Hector Peterson. The students fought back with bricks and stones, and when news of Hector Peterson's death spread, students rioted, attacking government buildings and turning over and burning cars and buses. The riots lasted for days, with riot police driving through the streets of Soweto in armored convoys, firing into the crowds. "Instructions have been given to maintain law and order at all costs," said Prime Minister B. J. Vorster two days after the revolt began (Vorster in Cawthra, p. 19). According to the government, the death toll after the first ten days was 176, with 1,000 wounded; black organizations claimed the figures were much higher.

The government's July 1st withdrawal of the Afrikaans ruling was not enough, by this point, to placate those suffering under apartheid. All over the country students called for the toppling of the entire oppressive education system—or even, in some cases, for the overthrow of the government itself. Black workers and parents joined the protests, and a series of strikes, marches, and battles ensued. Hundreds of activists were arrested and detained, and many died in police custody. By September 1977 the violence had lessened; many black workers no longer participated in strikes, which they came to see as useless, and students focused their attention on school boycotts. Some 600 teachers had resigned, and 250,000 students were on strike.

Then on September 12 news came of Steven Biko's death in detention. Police claims that Biko had died from a self-imposed hunger strike were patently ridiculous. Though suspicious deaths in detention were by no means uncommon, Biko's international fame and importance drew worldwide attention to the travesties of justice in South Africa. Within the country, violence flared up once more, and this time the government responded by outlawing every black consciousness organization in the country. Though a period of relative quiet followed, the Soweto Revolt and the death of Steven Biko marked a great shift in the way that black youth were prepared to fight apartheid. Never again would the government be able to quash black political activism as thouroughly as it had managed to in the past.

The Novel in Focus

Plot summary. *A Dry White Season* opens with the unspectacular death of Ben Du Toit, a 53-year-old white Afrikaner man knocked down on the road by a hit-and-run driver—a death reported in only a few lines on the fourth page of the evening newspaper. As the narrator puts it, the report of Ben's death is "barely enough for a shake of the head" (Brink, *A Dry White Season*, p. 9). The narrator, however, had been an old friend of Ben's from college, and had only recently encountered him again, two weeks before the accident, when, harried and suspicious, Ben had called upon him and asked him to hold on to a pile of "papers and stuff" (*Dry White Season*, p. 13). On these papers he had "written it all down," he had told the narrator; "they've taken it all from me. Nearly everything. Not much left. But they won't get that. You hear me? If they get that there would have been no sense at all" (*Dry White Season*, p. 13). The narrator, confused and slightly irritated by Ben's seemingly paranoid behavior, had agreed to this request while assuring Ben that everything was fine, that all he needed was a "good holiday" (*Dry White Season*, p. 14). Two weeks later Ben turns up dead and the narrator is left with a mess of notebooks and papers and photographs. From these materials the narrator—a middle-aged romance novelist ready to tackle a grander project—slowly, painfully reconstructs Ben's story.

Ben Du Toit is an Afrikaner schoolteacher living comfortably in Johannesburg with his wife and teenage son; he has two grown daughters as well, who live close by. Ben's life is relatively uneventful and his marriage without passion. He keeps to a steady schedule of exercise, work, and, for relaxation when he returns home in the late afternoon, carpentry. A generous man and devoted teacher, Ben inspires trust in his students and helps others when he can. He becomes especially involved in the life of Gordon Ngubene, the black man who cleans the school where Ben teaches. As a young man Gordon had showed scholarly promise, but his father's death forced him to leave school and take work as a domestic servant. Now middle-aged, Gordon hopes to nurture the promise shown by his own son, Jonathan, an intelligent child whom Ben agrees to put through school as long as the boy's grades remain high. Things go well at first, but, as he grows older, Jonathan becomes more and more sullen and angry, especially after being arrested and flogged by the police for a crime he did not commit. Once the Soweto Revolt begins, Jonathan only rarely returns home during the first month, and then one day disappears for good. Some children report that they saw Jonathan "in the crowd surrounded and stormed by the police" but the family is unable to find out any facts or specifics, neither from the police nor the hospitals (*Dry White Season*, p. 41). Gordon comes to Ben for help, and Ben hires an attorney to look into the matter, but during the subsequent investigation the authorities either deny having heard of Jonathan, or fail to respond at all. They assume this attitude despite personal accounts from a nurse and a cleaning man at the prison—the first reports seeing Jonathan in a hospital, his head swathed in bandages; the second claims to have cleaned blood from a prison cell in which Jonathan had been held. Finally the security police telephones the attorney with the news that Jonathan Ngubene died "of natural causes" the previous night (*Dry White Season,* p. 46).

Attempts to claim the body prove even more difficult, as Gordon and his wife, Emily, find themselves shuttled from one bureaucratic office to another, none of which can provide them with answers. At each dead end the couple returns to Ben, who, having utter faith in his country's government and legal system, remains confident that justice will be done and Jonathan's body properly buried. At last the attorney threatens to go public with the situation, and in this way finally elicits a response from the security police: Jonathan had never been imprisoned, but was shot during the riots, his body buried at that time. A request for the medical report elicits only a statement that the report is "unavailable" (*Dry White Season,* p. 47). For Ben the matter seems to end here; when Gordon, still determined to find out the fate of his son, appears at his door, Ben asks, "what good can it do [to keep looking], Gordon?" Gordon responds: "It can do nothing, Baas. But a man must know about his children. . . . I cannot stop before I know what happened to him and where they buried him. His body belongs to me. It's my son's body" (*Dry White Season,* p. 49).

Slowly Gordon begins to track down witnesses, many of them too frightened to sign statements. He pieces together the story of his son's detention, torture, and death. At one point, after much coaxing, an ex-prisoner who had been detained along with Jonathan agrees to sign an affidavit stating, among other things, that both of them were kept naked throughout their detention; that he heard Jonathan being beaten from the next room; that one day they were taken outside the city and forced to crawl through barbed wire fences; and that another day they were interrogated together, standing "on blocks about a yard apart, with half-bricks tied to their sexual organs" (*Dry White Season,* p. 50). Gordon persuades the nurse as well to sign a statement, and, by this point, has begun to believe that he will be able, someday, to find the body of his son and bury it. The day after Gordon obtains the two signed affidavits, however, "he [is] taken away by the Special Branch [security police]. And with him, the affidavits [disappear] without a trace" (*Dry White Season,* p. 51).

It is at this point that Ben begins to suspect that things are not what they seem to be—or, at least, not as he has imagined them to be—in his country. Would Gordon, too, be tortured and killed in prison? Anxious to uncover the truth, however painful it might be, Ben slowly finds himself immersed in Gordon's case and spends almost the entire remainder of the novel going through the same motions, and running up against the same obstacles, as Gordon had before his own detention—and with nearly the same results. Ben visits the police, works continually with a lawyer, visits Gordon's family in Soweto, and spends a great deal of time writing letters and shuffling between various bureaucratic offices—most of this with a black cab driver named Stanley, who describes himself at one point as old-fashioned enough to believe that blacks and whites can fight for change together. Just as in Jonathan's case, the police refuse to be forthcoming, and all the while they deny, even in the face of clear evidence, that Gordon is being tortured and abused, or even that anything is amiss. The injustice of what happened to Jonathan and what is happening to Gordon begins to haunt Ben until he feels he has no choice but to pursue this case until the end. His Afrikaner friends, colleagues, and family do not agree, however, and numerous tensions begin to disrupt Ben's life. His wife, Susan, is especially intolerant of Ben's activity, even more so when this activity begins to threaten the family's safety. Police show up at the house with some regularity—to question the Du Toits, to search the house, and ultimately to threaten them. In this process the marriage dissolves.

Ben thinks of Gordon continually, and one night cannot shake the image of the broken teeth Gordon's wife has found in one of Gordon's pockets, in the clothing the police finally released to her at her request:

> [A]fter the light had been turned out he couldn't sleep, however exhausted he felt. He was remembering too much. The dirty bundle in the newspaper they'd brought him. The stained trousers. The broken teeth. It made him nauseous. He moved into another position but every time he closed his eyes the images returned. . . . Dark and soundless the night lay around him, limitless, endless; the night with

A DRY WHITE SEASON—METAPHOR FOR APARTHEID

The title *A Dry White Season* comes from the Mangone Wally Serote poem that is used as the book's epigraph:

> it is a dry white season
> dark leaves don't last, their brief lives dry out
> and with a broken heart they dive down gently headed for the earth
> not even bleeding.
> it is a dry white season brother,
> only the trees know the pain as they still stand erect
> dry like steel, their branches dry like wire,
> indeed, it is a dry white season
> but seasons come to pass.
>
> (*Dry White Season,* epigraph)

Like Serote's poem, Brink's book uses the image of the dry white season to refer metaphorically to apartheid and the conditions created by it. In the book the image is rooted in a specific event. When the novel's protagonist, Ben du Toit, was nine or ten years old, the Great Drought of 1933 forced his father to trek with all of the sheep from their farm to another district in the Free State, where, it was rumored, some grazing ground still remained. Ben and his father made the journey alone, but before they were able to reach their destination the drought closed in on them, forcing them to slaughter the starving lambs and sheep, and the ewes with no milk left. As Ben tells it, "in the end even the shrubs disappear . . . and day after day there's the sun burning away whatever remains" (*Dry White Season,* p. 30).

At the moment when Ben comes fully into awareness of what apartheid means for most of his country's population, and when he finds that something has changed irrevocably for him because of this awareness, he says:

> The single memory that has been with me all day . . . is [of] that distant summer when Pa and I were left with the sheep. The drought that took everything from us, leaving us alone and scorched among the white skeletons.
>
> What happened before that drought has never been particularly vivid or significant to me: that was where I first discovered myself and the world. And it seems to me I'm finding myself on the edge of yet another dry white season, perhaps worse than the one I knew as a child.
>
> What now?
>
> (*Dry White Season,* p. 163)

> all its multitudes of rooms, some dark, some dusky, some blindingly light, with men standing astride on bricks, weights tied to their balls.
>
> (*Dry White Season,* p. 75)

Gordon eventually dies in prison. An inquest is held, and despite all evidence to the contrary, his death is ruled to have been suicide. Throughout the course of Ben's efforts, possible witnesses are detained or deported, shots are fired into Ben's living room, the police become more and more of a hostile presence in his life, and almost everyone he knows turns against him. By the end of his life, he is able to find solace only with the black cab driver Stanley, and with Melanie, a young British South African journalist also dedicated to the plight of nonwhite South Africa. Ben and Melanie fall in love, but after Melanie visits

England she is denied entrance back into South Africa.

The last portion of the novel documents the crumbling of Ben's world. In one of the last days of his life, Ben finds that his own daughter has betrayed him by revealing the location of the papers he has kept to document the entire affair. Before handing them to the narrator, Ben moves the papers to a new location. A few days later his home is burglarized and the former hiding spot methodically ripped apart.

The novel ends with an epilogue by the narrator, who has taken it upon himself to assemble Ben's detailed but scattered notes, documents, and letters, and to tell the story. The narrator recounts again his last meeting with Ben, Ben's paranoid state, and his insistence that the narrator take his writings so that the story will not die with him. He speculates on Ben's last hours, the hours after Ben's discovery of the burglary and before the "accident" in which he is killed. And finally, having put the entire story together and presented it in the best, most truthful way he could, the narrator asks:

> why do I go ahead by writing it all down here? . . . Prodded, possibly, by some dull, guilty feeling of responsibility towards something Ben might have believed in: something man is capable of being but which he isn't very often allowed to be?
>
> I don't know.
>
> Perhaps all one can really hope for, all I am entitled to, is no more than this: to write it down. To report what I know. So that it will not be possible for any man ever to say again: I know nothing about it.
>
> (*Dry White Season,* p. 316)

Afrikaans literature and white activism in South Africa. The problem of how to contribute to the anti-apartheid struggle vexed politically committed white South Africans, especially after the rise of the Black Consciousness Movement in the 1970s, which disdained any political activity of white "do-gooders" (Biko in Ranuga, p. 93). As Ben du Toit realizes after being attacked by a group of black youths on the streets of Soweto in *A Dry White Season*:

> Whether I like it or not . . . I am white. This is the small, final, terrifying truth of my broken world. I am white. And because I'm white I am born into a state of privilege. Even if I fight the system that has reduced us to this I remain white, and favoured by the very circumstances I abhor. . . . [Yet] what can I do but what I have done? I cannot choose not to intervene: that would be a denial and a mockery not only of everything I believe in, but of the hope that compassion may survive among men.
>
> (*Dry White Season,* p. 304)

Like Ben du Toit, Afrikaner activists were in especially difficult positions, often disdained on all sides of the struggle. Even as the policies of apartheid became less and less attractive for economic reasons in the 1970s, apartheid was still widely seen as aligned with the will of the Afrikaner people, and prominent anti-apartheid activists, such as Bram Fischer, were disowned by Afrikaners the way that Ben is in the novel. In the novel, Ben du Toit is eventually ostracized by every Afrikaner he knows, finding solace only among his black and his white British friends.

For Afrikaner writers the problem was just as acute. Brink, an anti-apartheid white Afrikaner writer, stands out as one of the few internationally famous South African writers who is not only Afrikaner, but who also writes regularly in Afrikaans for an obviously Afrikaner audience. Like many of Brink's other books, *A Dry White Season* was written in two languages. As Brink explains,

> I write regularly in both Afrikaans and English, usually preparing a first draft in Afrikaans, followed by a complete rewriting of the novel in English, and a final translation back into Afrikaans. I regard this laborious process as an essential part of exploring the material, using English as an aid to see more clearly and to evaluate more objectively.
>
> (Brink in Ross, p. 55)

Brink's habit of translating each text into English was prompted by the banning in South Africa of his first politically committed novel, *Kennis van die aand*—the first Afrikaans novel ever to be banned in the country. To write in English was necessary in order to have an audience at all. While several Afrikaner writers prefer to write only in English—J. M. Coetzee, for instance, finds Afrikaans "frankly dull" (Coetzee in Gallagher, p. 48)—Brink sees Afrikaans as a language rich and full of possibility:

> [T]here is a certain virility, a certain earthy, youthful quality about Afrikaans because it is such a young language, and because, although derived from an old European language like Dutch, it has found completely new roots in Africa and become totally Africanized in the process. One writer said . . . that Afrikaans at this stage seems to resemble the English

language in the time of Shakespeare. It is not very firmly and finally organized yet. One can do almost anything with it. If you haven't got a word for something you want to express, you simply make a word or pluck a word from another language and shape it to fit yours.

(Brink in Ross, p. 104)

Afrikaans developed in the late 1800s and was first presented as a literary language in 1876, when a small Afrikaner nationalist group, the Association of True Afrikaners, turned out the newspaper *Die Afrikaanse Patriot.* In the following years many other Afrikaans texts—almost all of them fervently nationalist in sentiment—would appear, including alternative, revisionist histories told from the Afrikaner perspective. This early literature tended to glorify the Afrikaners and to commemorate the bravery and suffering of these "chosen" people, who had first settled in South Africa in the seventeenth century. In these years the existence of the Afrikaner people as a unified and distinct group was very much at risk, as the ruling power of the time, the British empire, sought to establish complete dominance over the region it had partially occupied since the late eighteenth century. When the British won the Boer War (1899-1902), after destroying about 30,000 Afrikaner farmsteads and placing thousands of Afrikaners in concentration camps, the Afrikaner people seemed "destined for decline and oblivion" (Meredith, p. 11). (Also called the South African War, the Boer War—so named by the British—erupted because the British wanted to reestablish dominance over the two independence-minded republics, the Transvaal and the Orange Free State. The two republics were joined with the Cape Colony and Natal to form the Union of South Africa in 1910.)

Resilient under British attempts to quash them, the Afrikaners rallied around the cause of ethnic unity. Their development of a unique, specifically Afrikaner language and literature coincided with the birth of Afrikaner nationalism, with much of the developing literature aligning itself fiercely with the nationalist cause. This ethnic fervor culminated in the victory of the Nationalist Party in 1948. Throughout these struggles Afrikaans literature continued to stress nationalist themes, and also began looking back nostalgically at the farm life that Afrikaners had traditionally led in South Africa; this emphasis on "the land" served to strengthen the idea that the soil of South Africa was somehow divinely connected to the Afrikaners. Where did this leave the blacks who inhabited the region before the arrival of the Afrikaners? As J. M. Coetzee points out, "this proprietorial attitude has made of the black man a temporary sojourner, a displaced person, not only in the white man's laws but in the white man's imaginary life" (Coetzee in Gallagher, p. 42). Playing its part in the development of this attitude, Afrikaans literature was crucial to the nationalist cause that was realized in the 42-year system of apartheid in South Africa.

André Brink

Only in the 1960s did a young group of Afrikaner writers, "the Sestigers," challenge the models on which the whole of early Afrikaans literature was based. Influenced by modern European literature, writers like André Brink, Breyten Breytenbach, Jan Rabie, and others dramatically renewed Afrikaans literature by "destroying all the existing taboos pertaining to sex, ethics, religion, and politics governing [it]" (Brink in Ross, p. 54). Despite the rebelliousness and daring of these writers, however, "they could not distance themselves from the white, oppressive, bourgeois culture" (Coetzee, p. 346). Not until the next two decades, during which *A Dry White Season* was written, did a small group of Afrikaner writers break away from white burgeois culture and create, for the first time, a politically motivated and revolutionary Afrikaans literature. Many of the texts produced by these writers elicited powerful responses in their readers: seeming to have betrayed their own culture, these writers were often seen as either traitors or as revolutionaries; from another perspective they appeared to be complicit, no matter their views, with a system that granted them enormous and disparate privilege. As Brink himself points out, "through history, culture and the colour of his skin [the Afrikaner writer] is linked, like it or not, to the power Establishment" (Brink in Gallagher, p. 43). Another poet admits that "the (white) Afrikaans writers of today . . . have to live with the cultural feeling of guilt, that the language in which they write is not 'innocent of the horrors' of apartheid" (Small in Gallagher, p. 43).

Sources and literary context. *A Dry White Season* was one of many texts written in the wake of the Soweto Revolt, the unprecedented, widespread, and extremely violent rioting that shook South Africa in 1976. Writers were quick to respond to the devastation, and to the undeniable fact that the country had entered into a state of crisis. As the epigraph (from Antonio Gramsci) of Nadine Gordimer's 1978 novel, *July's People*, reads, "the crisis consists precisely in the fact that the old is dying and the new cannot be born . . ." (Gramsci in Coetzee, p. 356).

Brink's idea for the novel was more specifically triggered by "a detainee who had allegedly hung himself near King William's Town—Mohapi. The Mduli case in Durban also contributed to it, but it was mainly the Mohapi one which triggered it" (Brink in Jolly, pp. 21-22). When the famous and charismatic black leader Steven Biko died mysteriously in detention in 1977, Brink stopped working on the novel for a year, but eventually he "realised that it was also a matter of making sure the people knew about it, and were forced never to allow themselves to forget it" (Brink in Jolly, p. 23).

Reviews. *A Dry White Season* was initially banned by South African censors when it came out in 1979. By the end of that year the ban had been lifted, along with the ban on Nadine Gordimer's novel *Burger's Daughter*. Brink points out the apparent liberalization of the censorship system at this time, but also criticizes the fact that "the books which were unbanned were books very obviously chosen from the works of authors with some kind of international reputation, and they were all books by white authors" (Brink in Ross, p. 56). Regardless, the novel had great international success and in 1980 won both the Martin Luther King Memorial Prize and the Prix Medicis Étranger, France's most prestigious prize for fiction in translation. In 1989 an American film version of Brink's novel was released.

—Carolyn Turgeon

For More Information

Brink, André. *A Dry White Season.* New York: William Morrow, 1980.

Cawthra, Gavin. *Policing South Africa: The SAP and the Transition from Apartheid.* London: Zed Press, 1993.

Coetzee, Ampie. "Literature and Crisis: One Hundred Years of Afrikaans Literature and Afrikaner Nationalism." In *Rendering Things Visible: Essays on South African Literary Culture.* Ed. Martin Trump. Johannesburg: Ravan Press, 1990.

Gallagher, Susan VanZanten. *A Story of South Africa: J. M. Coetzee's Fiction in Context.* Cambridge, Mass.: Harvard University Press, 1991.

Harsch, Ernest. *South Africa: White Rule, Black Revolt.* New York: Monad Press, 1980.

Jolly, Rosemary Jane. *Colonization, Violence, and Narration in White South African Writing: André Brink, Breyten Breytenbach, and J. M. Coetzee.* Athens: Ohio University Press, 1996.

Le May, G. H. L. *The Afrikaners: An Historical Interpretation.* Cambridge, Mass.: Blackwell Publishers, 1995.

Mandy, Nigel. *A City Divided: Johannesburg and Soweto.* New York: St. Martin's Press, 1984.

Meredith, Martin. *In the Name of Apartheid: South Africa in the Postwar Period.* London: Hamish Hamilton, 1988.

Ranuga, Thomas K. *The New South Africa and the Socialist Vision: Positions and Perspectives Toward a Post-Apartheid Society.* Atlantic Highlands, N.J.: Humanities Press, 1996.

Ross, Jean W. "Andre Philippus Brink." In *Contemporary Authors.* Vol. 104. Detroit: Gale Research, 1982.

Thompson, Leonard. *A History of South Africa.* New Haven, Conn.: Yale University Press, 1990.

The English Patient

by
Michael Ondaatje

> **THE LITERARY WORK**
>
> A novel set in northern Italy from April to August 1945; published in 1992.
>
> **SYNOPSIS**
>
> A burned man and his three companions search for the secrets to each other's identities during the final months of World War II.

Michael Ondaatje was born in Ceylon, now Sri Lanka, in 1943. Educated in Sri Lanka and England, he immigrated to Canada in 1962. A poet and novelist, Ondaatje has become one of Canada's foremost writers, the center of a literary circle based in Toronto. Ondaatje's major works fuse history with a poet's imagination. *The Collected Works of Billy the Kid: Left-handed Poems* (1970) mixes various literary forms to evoke an outlaw of the American West. *Running in the Family* (1982) is a fictionalized memoir of Ondaatje's own family. *In the Skin of a Lion* (1987) was inspired by the architecture of Toronto and the immigrants who helped build it. *Anil's Ghost* (2000) looks at the civil war in Sri Lanka through the eyes of a young anthropologist. Ondaatje's most praised novel, The *English Patient*, studies the interior lives of four characters swept up in World War II, one of whom is loosely modeled on a Hungarian explorer turned spy for the Germans.

Events in History at the Time the Novel Takes Place

North-African desert exploration in the 1930s. The Libyan Desert, a great sea of sand stretching from Libya to Egypt and south into Sudan, was the site of several geographical expeditions in the 1930s. Since the end of the nineteenth century, European powers had controlled almost all of Africa. Great Britain dominated Egypt and controlled the Suez Canal from 1882 on, while Italy ruled Libya from 1911 forward. These European powers supported exploration, and used the information gathered to map terrain and increase territory. The explorers who came to this part of the Sahara Desert formed a motley group of Europeans, Arabs, and Africans. In 1932 and 1933, several expeditions were made by groups including Sir Robert Clayton-East-Clayton and Lady Clayton-East-Clayton (English), Lázló Almásy (Hungarian), H. W. G. J. Penderel (Scottish), Dr. Kádár (University of Budapest), Dr. Bermann (Austrian), and Major Ralph A. Bagnold (English). These explorers wanted to map the Gilf Kebir, a triangular plateau in the southwest corner of Egypt, and explore the Gebel 'Uweinat ("gebel" or "jebel" is a hill or mountain). Fascinated by the desert and the difficulties it presented, curious about its connection to ancient history, these individuals traversed an area that even today is dangerously isolated.

Lázló Almásy. One of these explorers was Lázló Almásy, born in Hungary in 1895. His biogra-

Michael Ondaatje

phy is contentious, but certain facts are beyond dispute. Almásy was a fighter pilot for the Austro-Hungarian Empire in World War I. Afterwards, keenly interested in the Libyan Desert, he desired to find the ancient oasis of Zerzura. Mentioned in history, in legend, and in travelers' accounts, the oasis of Zerzura, Almásy came to believe, must be located in the Gilf Kebir. Traveling by plane and car in 1932 and 1933, Almásy and his companions first photographed and then visited the *wadis* (valleys or dried riverbeds) that they believed comprised the ancient Zerzura. In the group's travels to the 'Uweinat, Almásy discovered prehistoric cave paintings. He built on his discoveries in subsequent trips during the decade. In 1936, his book about these as well as other discoveries—*Récentes Explorations dans le Désert Libyque* (1932-36)—was published by the Egyptian Geographic Society.

North Africa and World War II. Shortly thereafter, the rumblings of World War II made themselves felt in northern Africa. North Africa would be of key strategic importance to Great Britain and its allies, on the one side, and Germany and Italy on the other. Military commanders knew that control of North Africa would mean control of the Suez Canal, giving their side a clear route to the Persian Gulf countries (and on to Russia). Thus, British Intelligence had been tracking Almásy's steps all through the decade, just as Italian forces were monitoring the predominantly British geographical expeditions. Most of the British explorers were members of the armed forces, and the information they gathered helped Great Britain when war came to North Africa. Working for the other side, Almásy himself used his formidable knowledge of the desert to aid the German Army, in particular, its Afrika Korps, led by General Erwin Rommel (called the "Desert Fox"). As the historian John W. Gordon states, no one else but Almásy could have performed this role (Gordon, p. 99).

Operation Salaam. Almásy's mission, called Operation Salaam, was to lead German agents through the desert into Cairo, Egypt. In 1941, the Italian and German forces had cracked the communication code used by the American military attaché in Cairo. But Rommel, concerned that his information supply might dry up, wanted to plant his own men in Egypt and establish contact with anti-British Egyptians. So in the spring of 1942, Almásy, accompanied by seven others, began his covert trip across the desert from Gialo in Libya to the Nile River. He successfully delivered the two German agents to a town south of Cairo, and then went back into the desert. He reached the German base and was promoted by Rommel. Unbeknownst to Almásy, though, British intelligence had picked up his radio reports and tracked his progress through the desert. The two German agents were caught in Cairo. British intelligence learned that its own security had been compromised, and that the German spies had been using the novel *Rebecca* by Daphne du Maurier to send messages. The British thus began to feed numerous false reports to the Germans, a strategy that contributed to the decisive British victory in November, 1942 at Alamein, Egypt.

The Italian Campaign of 1943-45. With the war in northern Africa concluded in favor of the Allies (Great Britain and the British Commonwealth, the Soviet Union, the United States, France, and China) by the spring of 1943, the British wanted to concentrate on what they felt was the weak chink in the German armor: Italy. Accordingly, British, Canadian, and American forces attacked Sicily in July 1943, in the largest sea-to-land (amphibious) invasion of World War II. Although Italy surrendered in September 1943, the Allies fought the Germans northward in Italy until May 2, 1945, in a campaign that caused 320,955 Allied casualties, and 658,339 German and Italian casualties.

The First Canadian Infantry Division, training in England, was ordered to Italy for the July 1943 invasion of Sicily. Nurses from the First Canadian General Hospital, who had been working in English war hospitals for the previous three years, landed in Sicily and went to work in tent hospitals. Part of the medical corps, the nurses followed the advancing army north into Italy, using abandoned buildings as makeshift hospitals. Always they ran the risk of being hit by enemy fire. After the Allies took the city of Rome in June 1944, the period of heavy casualties ended, and the nurses tended to injured Canadian and German soldiers. Some nurses would eventually be posted to northwest Europe, the focus of military attention after D-Day—the Allied attack on German forces, in Normandy, France, on June 6, 1944.

The Novel in Focus

The plot. *The English Patient* only gradually reveals the identities and motivations of its four primary characters. Part detective novel, part spy story, part romance, it withholds information from both its characters and readers. The novel opens in April 1945 in its main locale—the northern Italian villa of San Girolamo, formerly an Allied hospital, now occupied by only two people, one a 20-year old Canadian nurse named Hana, the other her severely burned patient. He barely survived a plane crash into the North African desert, where he was rescued by a Bedouin tribe and eventually brought to a hospital in Pisa, and then to the villa's makeshift hospital. Now, his face burnt away, he does not know who he is, though he thinks he is English. Scant disjointed memories and his notebook are all that remains from his former life. Hana, shell-shocked by her frequent contact with the dead, in mourning for her father killed in the war, refused to leave the hospital when the rest of the staff did; she insisted on remaining to care for the "English patient."

Hana and the English patient are joined at the villa by David Caravaggio and Kirpal Singh. A thief turned spy for the Allies, Caravaggio has arrived at the villa seeking Hana, whose family he knew in Toronto, and the English patient, whose identity he is trying to ascertain. Caravaggio's hands are bandaged. Caught trying to retrieve incriminating photographs, he was tortured by the Italians, his thumbs brutally razored off. Now he staves off the pain with injections of morphine. Kirpal Singh, a Sikh sapper (mine-clearer), camps in the villa's garden, and ventures from there with his second-in-command, Hardy, on the dangerous job of defusing bombs and mines.

As the four characters interact and converse with each other, details about their pasts gradually emerge. One afternoon, Hana tells Caravaggio that her love affair with a soldier led to her pregnancy, a pregnancy that she terminated after the soldier's death. Then she retreated into a shell: "I courted one man and he died and the child died. I mean, the child didn't just die, I was the one who destroyed it. After that I stepped so far back no one could get near me. . . . Then I met him, the man burned black" (*The English Patient*, p. 85). Caravaggio admits to Kirpal Singh (nicknamed "Kip") that he knew Hana before the war. Kip and the English patient have detailed conversations about the circuitry of bombs. Hana reads snippets of the English patient's notebook. After a bomb kills his second-in-command, Kip and Hana become lovers. As Caravaggio notes about the four characters, "here they are shedding skins. They could imitate nothing but what they were. There was no defence but to look for the truth in others" (*The English Patient*, p. 117).

In the central part of the novel, the English patient talks, mostly to Hana, about his life and love in the previous 15 years. Never identifying himself by name, he describes his membership in a group of desert explorers including Madox, Almásy, Bell, and Bagnold, men who devoted

HERODOTUS, HISTORIAN OF THE DESERT

The English patient uses his copy of Herodotus's *The Histories* as a notebook, or more properly a "commonplace book"—a book in which to record his own thoughts, to make notes on his desert expeditions, and to paste keepsakes from other books. Herodotus (484-430 B.C.E.), often referred to as the "Father of History," was a Greek historian who chronicled the Greek and Persian Wars (499-479 B.C.E.). Filled with desert lore, Herodotus's history spurs the English patient to discover the ancient oasis of Zerzura, while Herodotus's story of King Candaules's wife, which Katharine Clifton reads aloud one evening, causes the English patient to fall in love with her. The English patient describes Herodotus as "one of those spare men of the desert who travel from oasis to oasis, trading legends . . . consuming everything without suspicion, piecing together a mirage" (Ondaatje, *The English Patient*, pp. 119-20).

themselves to mapping the Libyan desert's Gilf Kebir Plateau in the search for the lost oasis of Zerzura. In 1936 Geoffrey Clifton and his wife Katharine joined the desert explorers, setting off a volatile love affair between Katharine Clifton and the English patient. Their adulterous affair, carried out in Cairo, which the explorers used as a base, was torrid, possessive, violent, guilty, and all-encompassing. Katharine, who could not bear the deception, brought it to an end.

CARAVAGGIO (c. 1571-1610)

Caravaggio was the hometown of the renown Italian painter Caravaggio, otherwise known as Michelangelo Merisi, and it provided the artist with his name. Famous for developing the painting technique called "tenebrism" (from the Latin for "shadow"), which depended on stark contrasts between light and dark, Caravaggio had a great effect on European painting. Unconventional in life as well as art, Caravaggio associated with outcasts and killed a man in a fit of temper. *The English Patient*'s Caravaggio likewise led a shady life—as a thief in Toronto and then a spy for the Allies. In the novel, he is often described against a background of light and dark (as in his attempts to retrieve an incriminating role of film). The English patient makes specific reference to the work of Caravaggio the painter, bringing the characters of the villa together in the following description of Caravaggio's *David with the Head of Goliath*: "In it, the young warrior holds at the end of his outstretched hand the head of Goliath, ravaged and old. . . . It is assumed that the face of David is a portrait of the youthful Caravaggio and the head of Goliath is a portrait of him as an older man. . . . Youth judging age at the end of its outstretched hand. The judging of one's own mortality. I think when I see him at the foot of my bed that Kip [Kirpal] is my David" (*The English Patient,* p. 116).

During the English patient's revelations, Caravaggio informs Hana of his own theory about the burned man's identity:

> There was a Hungarian named Almásy, who worked for the Germans during the war. He flew a bit with the Afrika Korps, but he was more valuable than that. In the 1930s he had been one of the great desert explorers. . . . Between the two wars he was always on expeditions out of Cairo. One was to search for Zerzura—the lost oasis. Then when war broke out he joined the Germans. In 1941 he became a guide for spies, taking them across the desert into Cairo. What I want to tell you is, I think the English patient is not English.
>
> (*The English Patient*, p. 163)

Hana responds to Caravaggio's accusation with indifference: "I think we should leave him be. It doesn't matter what side he was on, does it?" (*The English Patient*, p. 165). But Caravaggio, who wants to know if the English patient is his enemy, gives the patient a heady dose of morphine and alcohol, and questions him about the plane crash.

In his drugged state, the English patient recalls that in 1942, he went to the Gilf Kebir to collect the body of Katharine Clifton. Three years before, in 1939, after his affair with Katharine had ended, he had been packing up the desert base camp. Geoffrey Clifton, who was supposed to fly in and pick him up, aimed his plane, with Katharine in it, straight at the ground, expecting to kill himself and Katherine on impact, and the English patient by stranding him in the desert. But only Clifton himself died immediately. Katharine, badly injured, was placed by the English patient in a cave, the Cave of Swimmers, where the two revealed to each other their misery since the end of their affair. Three years later, the English patient returned with fuel, unearthed a buried old plane, and carried Katharine's body into it. When the fuel leaked into the flying plane, he caught fire.

The novel then switches to Kip's past. As a 21-year-old at the beginning of World War II, he joined a Sikh regiment in India and was sent to England. There he was picked for an elite bomb defusal unit, headed by an eccentric country gentleman, Lord Suffolk, and his secretary, Miss Morden. These two English people embraced Kip and introduced him not only to the intricacies of defusing bombs but to English culture. One night, when Kip is alone with Hana, he tells her what propelled him from England to Italy: Lord Suffolk was blown up as he attempted to defuse a bomb. Killed with him were Miss Morden and four sappers in-training. Immediately, Kip had to defuse a second, similar bomb, and then provide instructions to the other defusers. Several months later, Kip was in Italy, trying to escape the burden of memory, and bonding with Hardy, who himself would die: "Only Hardy, he realized, keeps me human now" (*The English Patient*, p. 216).

Over several months, as the four characters become close, the English patient continues to

Ralph Fiennes (left) as Laszlo de Almásy and Kristin Scott Thomas as Katharine Clifton in the 1996 film version of *The English Patient.*

reveal the secrets of his past, often as a result of sharing morphine with Caravaggio. The patient describes how, one night, he fell in love with Katharine Clifton as she read to the explorers, across a desert campfire, a story of betrayal and love from Herodotus. Almost a year later, they became lovers. When their affair ended, the patient became half-mad, disgracing himself in public situations.

As the English patient continues to describe his past, he refers to Almásy in the third person: "Almásy was drunk and his dancing seemed to the others a brutal series of movements. . . . Almásy [was] like a planet out of control" (*The English Patient*, p. 244). Caravaggio must finally ask the patient the lingering question: "Who was talking back then?" and, as if quoting someone, the patient responds, "*Death means you are in the third person*" (*The English Patient*, p. 247). At this point, Caravaggio, the reader, and even the English patient himself, are sure of the patient's identity: he is "Almásy" and this is how he is referred to in these pages of the novel. Almásy now provides more details about the events leading to Katharine's death. He left her in the Cave of Swimmers to find fuel for the plane. When he walked 70 miles through the desert to an English military camp, no one would come to Katharine's aid. Instead, the English saw Almásy as a possible spy and imprisoned him. At this point, Caravaggio comes to his own realization about Almásy: "It no longer matters which side he was on during the war" (*The English Patient*, p. 251). Not until 1942, when Almásy volunteered to take the Germans across the desert, could he return to Katharine's body. Caravaggio informs Almásy that British intelligence, of which Geoffrey Clifton had been a member, knew of Almásy's affair, Clifton's death, and even Almásy's trek with the Germans through the desert. But then, Almásy had seemingly vanished, when he had returned for Katharine's body. Almásy, who believes that "everything [he] has loved or valued has been taken away from [him]," reminisces about the wounded and dead Katharine until he is emptied of memory (*The English Patient*, p. 257).

Caravaggio does not bother to correct Hana and Kip, who still believe the patient is English. It no longer seems to matter. Rather, at the beginning of August 1945, Caravaggio, Kip, and Hana celebrate Hana's twenty-first birthday. But the bombing of Hiroshima and Nagasaki destroys the villa's harmony. Kip rages when he hears the news, and turns against and then away from his former companions. Why is he fighting this war, he wonders:

He feels all the winds of the world have been sucked into Asia. He steps away from the many small bombs of his career towards a bomb the size, it seems, of a city, so vast it lets the living witness the death of the population around them. He knew nothing about the weapon. Whether it was a sudden assault of metal and explosion or if boiling air scoured itself towards and through anything human. . . . His name is Kirpal Singh and he does not know what he is doing here.

(*The English Patient*, p. 287)

As Kip rides off on his motorbike, Hana writes a letter to her stepmother. In this letter, the reader learns that Hana's father had also been severely burned, then left by his unit to die: *"He was a burned man and I was a nurse and I could have nursed him,"* writes Hana. *"I am sick of Europe"* (*The English Patient*, p. 298).

The novel's brief conclusion propels the reader forward 23 years. Kip is a doctor, living in India, married with two children. Something, one evening, reminds him of Hana. Hana, the narrator says, "is a woman I don't know well enough to hold in my wing, if writers have wings, to harbour for the rest of my life" (*The English Patient*, p. 301). The novel's final words suggest a lasting connection between Kip and Hana, though they do not meet again, as Hana, presumably in Toronto, dislodges a drinking glass, and Kip, eating dinner with his family in India, catches the fork that his daughter has dropped.

Identity and nationalism. The English patient says of his fellow desert explorers: "We were German, English, Hungarian, African . . . Gradually we became nationless."; He tells Hana that he wanted to erase his national identity, and "to walk upon such an earth that had no maps" (*The English Patient*, pp. 138, 139, 261).

Regardless of the political and national affinities of the actual desert explorers who criss-crossed the Libyan Desert, *The English Patient* criticizes nationalism, the idea that personal identity is bound up with a particular nation, and that the best form of political organization is the nation state. Instead, the English patient praises the desert because it "could not be claimed or owned" (*The English Patient*, p. 138). Indeed, the English patient states, "I came to hate nations. We are deformed by nation-states" (*The English Patient*, p. 138). By the time of World War II, the English patient claims, "after ten years in the desert, it was easy for me to slip across borders, not to belong to anyone, to any nation" (*The English Patient*, p. 139).

Certainly rampant nationalism was one of the causes of World War II. Adolf Hitler (1889-1945) wanted to expand Germany's territory, creating a "Greater Germany" and purging the nation of "foreign elements,"—Jews, Communists, gypsies, homosexuals—any group not considered properly German. Hitler moved first to possess neighboring German-populated areas of other countries by uniting with Austria in 1938, then in the same year taking over Czechoslovakia's Sudetenland.

In *The English Patient*, Almásy portrays himself as an idealist who does not care about nations, and who aids the Germans only as a means of returning to Katharine's body. He describes both warring sides as "Barbarians," who "would come through the desert with no sense of what it was" (*The English Patient*, p. 257). Madox, Almásy's fellow explorer and dear companion, dies "because of nations," says Almásy (*The English Patient*, p. 242). In 1939 Madox returned to his native home in Somerset, England. Sitting in a church, listening to a priest's pro-war sermon, Madox "pulled out the desert pistol, bent over and shot himself in the heart" (*The English Patient*, p. 242).

Sources and literary context. In writing *The English Patient*, Michael Ondaatje was inspired by a dream image featuring a plane that crashed in the desert and its survivor. In fleshing out the

THE BLITZ

For the British, World War II was not fought only on foreign soil, but endured at home. The Germans, in an attempt to demoralize the British populace, used their aircraft to bomb London and other major British cities. Beginning with the bombing of London in September of 1940, the Blitz ("blitzkrieg" means "lightning war") showered bombs over densely populated civilian areas. Altogether, the Germans sent 71,000 tons of bombs to Great Britain, causing 146,000 civilian deaths. *The English Patient's* Kip describes the Blitz from the perspective of the sapper, the soldier charged with laying and defusing explosive mines: "in one month there were suddenly 2,500 unexploded bombs to be dealt with. Roads were closed, factories deserted. By September the number of live bombs had reached 3,700. One hundred new bomb squads were set up, but there was still no understanding of how the bombs worked. Life expectancy in these units was ten weeks" (*The English Patient,* p. 183).

complex story of this survivor, Ondaatje examined articles by desert explorers from the 1930s that reviewed Almásy's work, and researched techniques for defusing bombs. He read histories of the Canadian forces in the Italian campaign. A short visit to Italy in 1990 influenced his description of *The English Patient*'s Tuscan villa. His own earlier work inspired him as well; two of *The English Patient*'s main characters—Caravaggio and Hana—appear in *In the Skin of a Lion* (1987), a story of the building of Toronto.

Ondaatje's treatment of Lázló Almásy has proved somewhat controversial. Working from scant information, Ondaatje created Almásy as his own character. When the novel was made into a film in 1996, a few critics accused him of romanticizing a villain. Ondaatje responded to this criticism in a letter to Canada's national newspaper:

> From Homer to *Richard III* to the present, literature has based its imaginative stories on historical event. We read those epics and literary works to discover, not the facts of the Trojan War, but the human emotions discovered in the story. . . . I wrote about an enigmatic desert explorer whose role when World War II broke out was to be a betrayer. . . . *The English Patient* is not a history lesson but an interpretation of human emotions—love, desire, betrayals in war and betrayals in peace—in a historical time.
>
> (Ondaatje in Tötösy de Zepetnek, pp. 8-9)

Events in History at the Time the Novel Was Written

North Africa: Egypt and Libya after World War II. Italy's defeat in World War II put Libya in the hands of the British and French until 1951, when the United Nations granted Libya its independence under a Libyan Sanusi king. Meanwhile, Great Britain and the United States, recognizing Libya's strategic importance, maintained military bases there. The discovery of oil in 1959 brought American and British oil companies to the region too. This neocolonialism (economic dominance) would end, however, in 1969, with Muammar Gaddafi's coup. Setting himself up as the head of the armed forces and the state, Gaddafi (1942-) embraced Islamic fundamentalism, expelled foreigners, and closed foreign bases. Relations between Libya and the west have been troubled ever since.

The British continued, informally, to control Egypt after World War II, until Egyptian nationalism, burgeoning since the 1930s, resulted in the overthrow of King Farouk in 1952 and the rise to power of Gamal Abdel Nasser (1918-70). Nasser's plan to nationalize the Suez Canal led to an invasion by Britain, France, and Israel in 1956, which dissolved in the face of world opinion. Nasser's union with Syria between 1958 and 1961 was just one sign of his attempts to bring the Arab world together. With its neighboring Arab countries, Egypt has had a violent relationship with Israel, which led to outright war in 1967 and 1973. Nevertheless, the West sees Egypt as a moderate state attempting to mediate between the West and other Arab countries, as well as between its own democratic ideals and internal Islamic fundamentalism.

MULTICULTURAL TORONTO IN THE 1990s: A WRITING COMMUNITY

Toronto, Canada, is a city of immigrants. After World War II and in the 1950s, European immigrants came here in droves, to be followed in the 1960s by immigrants from Asia and the Caribbean. Toronto now stands as the North American city with the most residents who are foreign-born—42 percent; it has been hailed by the United Nations as the most ethnically diverse city in the world. This influx of people has produced a great deal of creative energy, and a literary circle of which Ondaatje is only the most famous member. Other members of this writing community include Rohinton Mistry (from India), Shyam Selvaduari (from Sri Lanka), and M.G. Vassanji (born in Kenya of East Indian descent). Ondaatje himself says of Toronto, "There is a writing community here. Canada and Toronto are where I learned to write. I remade myself in Toronto" (Ondaatje in Slopen, p. 49).

Indian independence. The main action of *The English Patient* occurs while India is a British colony. Kip joins a Sikh regiment and is sent to England. His older brother, however, will not help the English; indeed, he tells Kip that he is "a fool for trusting the English. As Kip reports, "'One day you will open your eyes,' my brother keeps saying" (*The English Patient*, p. 217). Kips' eyes are opened by the bombings of Hiroshima and Nagasaki; suddenly seeing "the brown races" as sacrificial pawns at the mercy of colonial superpowers, he turns against the West (*The English Patient,* p. 286). To Almásy, whom Kip believes is English, he says, "You and then the Americans converted us. With your missionary rules. And Indian soldiers wasted their lives as heroes so they could be *pukkah* [genuine]. You had wars like cricket. How did you fool us into this?" (*The English Patient*, p. 283).

Two years after World War II, on August 15, 1947, India became independent. Its first prime minister, Jawaharlal Nehru, proclaimed that "at the stroke of the midnight hour, when the world sleeps, India will wake to life and freedom" (Nehru in Lloyd, p. 325). But India's independence was preceded by violence between Hindus and Muslims, who had separate visions of India's future. The solution, the division of the area into a mostly Hindu India and a mostly Muslim Pakistan, both members of the British Commonwealth of Nations, did not and has not dissipated the animosity. Contested territory remains, and tensions remain high between religious majorities and minorities in both countries. The dangers of nationalism and religious fervor have replaced those of colonialism.

Reception. *The English Patient* is Ondaatje's most praised novel. It was co-winner of the British 1992 Booker Prize (open to writers from the British Commonwealth), as well as winning Canada's most prestigious literary honor, the Governor General's Award. Critics were most impressed by Ondaatje's poetic use of language, describing him as a creator of indelible images. These images, put on screen in the movie of *The English Patient* (Ondaatje collaborated on the screenplay), won the 1996 Oscar for best picture. If some critics have thought Ondaatje's language self-indulgent, others see a writer who charts his own way: "He pleases himself, then us" (Balliett, p. 162). In his amalgam of history and fiction, Ondaatje strives above all to give words to human passions, to hold up love and friendship over the terror of war.

—Danielle E. Price

For More Information

Balliett, Whitney. "Michael Ondaatje's Fire." *The New Yorker*, 7 December 1992, 161-62.

Chandler, David G. *Battles and Battlescenes of World War Two*. New York: Macmillan, 1989.

Dancocks, Daniel G. *The D-Day Dodgers: The Canadians in Italy, 1943-1945*. Toronto: McClelland and Stewart, 1991.

Gordon, John W. *The Other Desert War: British Special Forces in North Africa, 1940-1943*. New York: Greenwood, 1987.

Lande, D. A. *Rommel in North Africa*. Osceola, Wis.: MBI, 1999.

Lloyd, T. O. *The British Empire 1559-1995*. 2nd ed. Oxford: Oxford University Press, 1996.

Murray, Jocelyn, ed. *Cultural Atlas of Africa*. Rev. ed. New York: Checkmark, 1998.

Ondaatje, Michael. *The English Patient*. New York: Vintage, 1992.

Slopen, Beverly. "An Interview in *Publishers Weekly*." *Publishers Weekly* 239, no. 44 (5 October 1992): 48-49.

Tötösy de Zepetnek, Steven. "Michael Ondaatje's *The English Patient*, 'History,' and the Other." 1999. http://clcwebjournal.lib.purdue.edu/clcweb99-4/totsy99-2.html (19 May 2002).

Felicia's Journey

by
William Trevor

Born William Trevor Cox in 1928 in County Cork, Ireland, to Irish Protestant parents, William Trevor spent his childhood in Ireland, where he was educated at Trinity College, Dublin. He has lived in Devon, England, however, since the early 1950s. Although many of his works are set in England, he belongs to the Irish Academy of Letters and considers himself an Irish author, a point on which he stands firm. That he has lived all his life on the margins of the dominant culture—a Protestant in Catholic Ireland, an Irish writer in England—is something Trevor considers a source of his artistic strength: "I was fortunate that my accident of birth actually placed me on the edge of things. I was born into a minority that all my life has seemed in danger of withering away" (Trevor, *Memoirs*, p. xiii). The artistic value, feels Trevor, lies in the perspective gained from observing a culture from a distance, which helps explain his early focus on English subjects and his later focus on Irish subjects, now that he has lived so long away from his homeland. Trevor is most widely known for his short stories, but his novels have also won high acclaim. From the early 1960s, Trevor published a stream of novels that tend to center on the thoughts, feelings, and experiences of eccentric or outcast members of society, both of whom appear in *Felicia's Journey*.

THE LITERARY WORK

Set in the English Midlands in the early 1990s; published in 1994.

SYNOPSIS

Felicia, an out-of-work young Irishwoman, is wandering through a town in England's industrial midlands. In search of the young man who got her pregnant, she falls into the clutches of another man, the dangerous Mr. Hilditch, who has at least six young women buried in his back garden.

Events in History at the Time of the Novel

Irish immigration to England. Though most of Ireland won its freedom from England in 1922, becoming the Republic of Ireland, the strong connections between the two countries were not severed. Six Irish counties, generally referred to as Northern Ireland, chose a separate path from the Republic and remained part of Britain. Moreover, both Irelands share cultural ties with England, born of centuries of English governance. Despite a concerted effort early in the century to expand the use of the Irish language, for instance, English remains the first language of nearly the entire Irish population. Family ties to England have also remained strong. Popular imagination connects Irish immigration to places such as Australia, Canada, and—especially—America. But the highest rate of Irish immigration has actually been to England, a reasonable development since it is relatively easy to reach and return from. The difference in numbers is actually staggering. In 1999, while there were 220,000 Irish in the

William Trevor

United States, there were more than 800,000 in England ("Irish Abroad"). They had in fact exceeded this number already at the beginning of the decade in 1991. Comprising 1.5 percent of the English population, the Irish formed the largest migrant minority in Western Europe at the time, a fact not often discussed. Especially since the middle of the nineteenth century (when the Irish Potato Famine struck), England has harbored a large population with close ties to Ireland, with the comparatively short distance between the two lands giving rise to much fluidity and mobility. Irish immigrants often return home for visits (in *Felicia's Journey*, for instance, Johnny Lysaght is back from England when Felicia falls in love with him).

How has the large Irish minority fared in England? Its members have been both ignored and vilified, a pattern that has persisted since the nineteenth century. The Irish were difficult for the English to classify, being neither fully black nor fully white according to nineteenth-century theories of anthropology. These theories assumed the "Teutonic" people (such as the English) to be at the top of human evolution, black peoples to be at the bottom, and peoples such as the Irish and the Jews to be somewhere in the middle. Over time these theories would lose their credibility, but to some degree the old prejudices would remain stubbornly intact.

Researchers point, for example, to psychiatric studies that discount the Irish, ignoring the group as worthy of study: "[It] has been known for over twenty years that the Irish in Britain have the highest rates of psychiatric hospital admission of any immigrant group, yet discussion of the Irish has been extremely limited in the British texts of transcultural psychiatry and completely absent in some" (Bracken, p. 44). No doubt, the cause for the omission has to do with not thinking of the Irish as a full-fledged immigrant group. A paradoxical attitude exists towards Irish immigrants—that, essentially, they are both "English" and "non-English." Thus, while other immigrant groups—such as the Haitian, Jamaican, Indian, Pakistani, and Chinese, are often treated separately in government and other studies, Irish immigrants are often not treated as a group at all.

At the same time, the Irish do not merge unnoticeably into the general British population. Irish immigrants are immediately recognizable by their accents, for one thing. This has often caused grief among Northern Irish citizens, who consider themselves British rather than Irish, but find themselves identified as Irish when they are in England. Once identified as such, the Irish are often dismissed as inconsequential. The novel's Mr. Hilditch dismisses Felicia, whom he thinks of not by her name, as he thinks of his previous victims, but rather as "the Irish girl." For him, the bulk of her attraction lies in the fact that she is wandering unattached, with no one to look for her, which makes her like all the girls who have been Mr. Hilditch's "special friends." On the other hand, he lets her into more facets of his life than any of the others, speaking to her outside his workplace and taking her into his house.

> Mr Hilditch wonders if the breaking of his meticulously kept rule is in some way related to the fact that the Irish girl comes from so far away, a foreigner you might say, the first time there has been that.
>
> (Trevor, *Felicia's Journey*, p. 52)

"A foreigner you might say" is telling, for it reveals Felicia's status as a quasi-foreigner. She is "simple as a bird," he also thinks, "which you'd expect her to be of course, coming from where she does" (*Felicia's Journey*, p. 127). He assumes the Irish are less sophisticated than the English, a prejudice based on his sense of English superiority, and his appraisal of Ireland as a backward country. The fictional Mr. Hilditch gives voice to what the social historian Ken Livingstone has called "crude anti-Irish prejudice," a public as well as a private phenomenon in English society: "[Just] as in previous centuries, the Irish [today] are regularly depicted in the press and on television as stupid, drunken, and backward" (Livingstone, p. 79).

Rough sleeping in England. The English have had a long history of wrestling with the issue of homelessness, having been concerned with the problem for centuries; it first became widespread enough to cause legislation after the Black Death (1348-49), a plague that killed off one-third of the population and drove up wages, since there were not enough workers left. Laws were passed aimed at keeping wages low, fixing them at what they had been before the plague struck. In response, many laborers became vagrants, looking for places where the wages were higher than in their native counties, or where the laws were ignored.

Vagrants were, as they are now, problematic for the government. Indeed society considered them bothersome, for they caused disorder—or at the least looked disorderly — and often committed crimes, a predictable outcome of having no means to support themselves. Meanwhile, they were, as they are now, vulnerable members of the society, vulnerable to the criminal elements of society, to the orderly elements of society (when it decided to punish them), and to disease, weather, and starvation.

In 1388, a law was passed making each county responsible for its own poor citizens, the beginning of governmental involvement in trying to help the homeless, rather than simply punish them. This was followed by three centuries of laws specifying punishments for vagrancy, however, which varied from whipping, to imprisonment, to branding, to temporary slavery. Then in 1601, the "Acte For the Reliefe of the Poore" was passed, an act now referred to as the "Old Poor Law." Under this act, "each parish was obliged to relieve the aged and the helpless, to bring up unprotected children in habits of industry, and to provide work for those capable of it but who were lacking their usual trade" (Higginbottom). Each parish, therefore, was not only responsible for feeding and sheltering its poor, but for finding them work, a task that was not always easy. Previously, the indigent poor—often the elderly or the mentally ill, who had no families to care for them, or illegitimate children and their mothers—had been parceled out to various parish households, their upkeep paid for by parish funds. Now many parishes began to establish so-called "bridewells" (after St. Bride's Well in London, where one of these shelters was founded), known later as "workhouses." These were notoriously dreadful shelters; "at best they were spartan places with meagre food and sparse furnishings—at worst they were unsanitary and uncaring places" (St. Mungo's Charities).

When an amendment was passed in 1723 allowing parishes to consolidate and join together in creating expanded workhouses, which served larger communities, conditions became worse, especially since the workhouses were specifically intended to be places of last resort—they were to be places that no one would wish to go to, in an effort to keep the number of their inhabitants down. Decades of these conditions led, by the Victorian age, to the horrendous circumstances detailed by Charles Dickens in such works as *Oliver Twist*, and to national scandals that, by the close of the nineteenth century, had led to some reforms. By the end of World War I, the workhouse was abolished as a government institution in England, though some of the old workhouses continued to exist, on a much smaller scale. Run by local committees, they were called "hospitals," a situation that would continue until the 1960s.

It was then that the problem of homelessness, which had abated somewhat in the previous decades, became once again of great concern. In 1949, for instance, only six people were sleeping rough in London—the term "rough sleepers" in England, means officially "those who sleep on the streets from very late at night to the early hours, i.e. from midnight to 5 or 6 A.M." ("Rough Sleepers: Government Strategy"). But by the 1980s "around 20,000 single homeless people were living in accommodation for homeless people in London . . . the numbers on the streets of London . . . had risen to more than 1,000" (St. Mungo's Charities). The burgeoning number of not just the homeless in general, but specifically those sleeping rough, would lead to the creation, in 1998, of the Rough Sleepers Unit, a government agency devoted to the problem.

Felicia, the novel's main character, becomes a rough sleeper just before the establishment of that Rough Sleepers Unit, which aimed to cut the number of homeless people in England by two-thirds before 2002. She lives on the streets when the long-standing problem hit its twentieth-century peak. (The Rough Sleepers Unit would have remarkable success. In Birmingham, the city through which Felicia wanders in the novel, the unit would exceed the two-thirds target and ahead of schedule, reducing the homeless from 56 in 1998 to 15 in 2000 ["Press Notice"].)

Serial murderers in the late twentieth century. The phenomenon of serial murder is not new; several serial murders are famous in history—those committed by Caligula, Vlad the Impaler, and Giles de Rais, for instance. Though the term "serial killer" did not come into common use until the 1980s, Jack the Ripper, who terrorized London's East End in 1888, is generally considered the first "modern" serial killer. Serial murders are alarming, but relatively rare. Apparently there has been a rise in the number of serial killers since the 1960s, though the extent of this rise is under debate (Norris, p. 19). Under debate also are the questions of what defines and characterizes a serial killer. Key to *Felicia's Journey,* however, is not scientific debate about serial killers, but rather the popular notion of them. In the late-twentieth-century popular imagination, the serial killer is not instantly recognizable as such. He appears to be a normal male but is in fact a sexual predator, preying especially on the vulnerable (runaways, prostitutes, the homeless), outcasts with whom he has no connection in his everyday life. As a child, the predator was a victim himself, most likely of sexual and/or other physical abuse. Such is the popular profile of a serial killer; the novel's Mr. Hilditch fits this profile exactly.

According to the popular conception, the serial killer is difficult to catch precisely because he is not connected to his victims. Finding them more or less at random, he goes through several phases before, during, and after each murder. The first phase, the "aura phase," during which the killer is somewhat disconnected from reality, can be momentary or it can last for weeks. In the second "trolling" phase, the killer searches for his next victim. Third comes the "wooing phase," in which the killer lures in his victim. The fourth phase, which again can be extremely short or prolonged, is the "capture phase"; in the fifth, the killer actually commits the murder. The sixth is the "totem phase," in which the killer takes some sort of souvenir of the experience, and in the final "depression phase," the killer discovers, to his grief, that the murder has not actually solved his problems. The novel's Mr. Hilditch does not follow this pattern exactly—even in reality, of course, serial killers often don't—but he exhibits enough of these behaviours to have clearly been constructed from the same general conception. His experience with Felicia, for example, leads to his remembering things done to him by his mother in his childhood, which carries him into Norris's last phase, in his case, a suicidal depression.

IRISHMEN AND THE ENGLISH ARMY

In the novel, Felicia's lover, Johnny Lysaght is a soldier in the English army. The British Army will have offered him a pretty good deal—less than $16,000 per year in the early 1990s in United States dollars, but in addition to room and board and with opportunities for advancement. (An equivalent position in the United States Army would have brought in just over $12,000, plus bonuses.) Though Ireland proper is no longer part of Britain, citizens of the Irish Republic join the British Army as easily as do British citizens of English, Scottish, Welsh, or, Northern Irish descent. That Johnny is welcome in the British Army at the same status as British citizens is in itself indicative of the odd position of the Irish in England—the Irish were once part of the English empire, and still have an unstable relationship to the country, neither fully citizens nor fully aliens. Ironically the English Army makes it clear in its recruiting materials that it will provide for the families of its recruits, which means Johnny does not abandon Felicia for economic reasons alone. As Mr. Hilditch infers but Felicia cannot believe, Johnny is simply a cad.

The Novel in Focus

The plot. Pregnant and unmarried, Felicia arrives in England in search of her future baby's father, Johnny Lysaght. At the same time, Mr. Hilditch, the obese manager of a factory canteen in the English Industrial Midlands, just north of the city of Birmingham, is anticipating the turkey pie that will be on the menu at lunch, food being one of his major obsessions. They first meet when Mr. Hilditch encounters Felicia, looking lost and confused, searching for the nonexistent lawn-mower factory in which Johnny has told her he works. Mr. Hilditch sends her off to try a nearby industrial park, which could possibly have a lawn-mower factory. Felicia, who is low on funds, walks for miles through the city and around it, looking vainly for the factory, unable to understand much of what she hears, since it is spoken in an English dialect so different from her own. We learn, while Felicia wanders, of her history: her family has proud ties to the Irish Revolution, which led to the creation of the Irish Republic. Other, more immediate details come to light too. Felicia lost her job at the local meat packers; she met Johnny Lysaght at a wedding. Back home, she has been sharing a room with her very old great-grandmother, the widow of an Irish Revolution hero. The family's entire self-concept has been centered on that fallen hero, and their connection to the Irish Republic.

Felicia continues to wander around the town and its environs for some days, observed by Mr. Hilditch. He takes an interest in her; she reminds him of other young women he has known, waifs also down on their luck, to whom he was helpful. Mr. Hilditch approaches Felicia, offering to aid her in her search. He lies, saying he has a sick wife in the hospital (he has never been married) in order to appear harmless. We learn that Johnny has probably joined the British Army, a high crime in Felicia's father's mind. He ordered Felicia not to see Johnny, but then discovered that she has become pregnant by him. Felicia, who believes that Johnny loves her, refuses to accept that he would do such a terrible thing as join the army of the oppressors. However, while still in Ireland, she tried to obtain information about how to have an abortion, causing the reader to wonder if at some level she doesn't distrust Johnny's sincerity. Felicia's father learns that she is pregnant by Johnny, a member of the "occupying forces," her father's term for the British Army, given its presence in Northern Ireland. Enraged, he calls her a whore, or "hooer" as he pronounces it (*Felicia's Journey*, pp. 58-59). Desperate, Felicia stole the money hidden under her great-grandmother's mattress, broke into Johnny Lysaght's mother's home for Johnny's address (which she failed to find), then took the bus to Dublin and the ferry to England.

Back in the present, Mr. Hilditch drives Felicia to watch for Johnny as workers leave the local factories. Hilditch elaborates on the fiction about the dying wife. While Felicia is out of the car, making inquiries, he rifles through her bags, finds her stash of money, and steals it.

Felicia is next taken up by Miss Calligary, a member of a religious group that goes door-to-door spreading the Message of the Church of the Gatherers. Mr. Hilditch, meanwhile, is busy discovering Johnny's true whereabouts—he is indeed a private in the British Army, stationed nearby, information Hilditch will not pass on to Felicia. Felicia goes to stay in the Gathering House, where she at least does not have to spend any more of her small funds. She stays there for some days, continuing her search for Johnny. Discovering that her money is missing, she accuses the Gatherers of stealing it, whereupon she is promptly thrown out of the Gathering House.

Without money and homeless, Felicia meets up with some of the rough sleepers of the city, who show her where to find shelter in an abandoned house and where to find food. Unwilling to descend to this level yet, she ends up at Mr. Hilditch's door, asking for help—exactly what he has been wanting her to do. He pretends to aid her in her continued search for Johnny, stopping by cafés and relishing the thought that everyone around considers them lovers. He talks Felicia into having an abortion, takes her to the appointment, and makes sure everyone in the clinic thinks the baby is his. Back at Mr. Hilditch's house, Felicia, ill and depressed, asks only to bor-

STATELY HOMES

One of Mr. Hilditch's favorite weekend pastimes is to visit stately homes, of which there are many in England. The fortunes of the nobility have declined over the last century, prompting private stately homes to open themselves up to the public during posted times. Sporting in some cases cafés, such homes provide tours of the house and grounds. The family may still live in the manor, in carefully roped-off sections of the house, or it may have sold the ancestral home to a firm that runs it for a profit. Warwick Castle, close enough to Birmingham for a day trip, is one of the finest medieval castles in England. Owned by a firm in the early 1990s, it charged the equivalent of $11.60 for a tour, which consisted of a visit to its "armory, dungeon, torture chamber, ghost tower, [and] clock tower," as well as the "private apartments" of the former owners (Porter, p. 505). According to *Frommer's Comprehensive Travel Guide*, another part of the state home was a must-see: "Don't miss the Victorian rose garden, a re-creation of an original design from 1868 by Robert Marnock. . . . The romantic castle is host to various colorful pageants" (Porter, p. 505). As indicated in the guide, the castle evokes the past through an amusing combination of historical accuracy—the Victorian rose garden—and historical fluff—the pageants. Such gardens are important to the novel; concerned as it is with innocence and evil, they hark back to the original garden of Eden. Interestingly, while Hilditch enjoys the splendid gardens of the stately home he visits, his garden lies untended at home, showing several patches of overturned earth.

Bob Hoskins (left) as Joseph Ambrose Hilditch and Elaine Cassidy as Felicia in the 1999 film version of *Felicia's Journey*.

row enough money from Mr. Hilditch to make her way back home to Ireland. This is upsetting to Mr. Hilditch, who suddenly remembers that all the girls he has helped have eventually, as he remembers it, left him. When he wakes Felicia in the night, talking about the other girls, she intuitively understands what has happened to them.

> She knows the girls are dead. There is something that states it in the room, in the hoarse breathing, in the sweat that for a moment touches the side of her face, in the way he talks. The dark is oppressive with their deaths, cloying, threatening to turn odorous.
>
> (*Felicia's Journey*, p. 155)

Mr. Hilditch tells her to come down and get into the car, so that he can drive her on the first leg of her journey home. She agrees, but knows better than to climb into the car. While he sits waiting, she runs away.

Things are beginning to fall apart for Mr. Hilditch, so he goes off on one of his frequent visits to a stately home, where he enjoys the beautiful gardens and the luxury of the house itself. The events seem disconnected at first, but apparently whenever one of his "friends" disappears, Mr. Hilditch, who doesn't remember exactly what happened, conducts little rituals to bring his life back into balance, one of which is visiting stately homes, icons of order and beauty. For some weeks after Felicia's disappearance, he continues on with his life. The Gatherers locate him. Miss Calligary discovers that Mr. Hilditch knows Felicia and assumes that she tricked him the way she seems to have tricked the Gatherers. Even though Miss Calligary assumes him to be Felicia's victim, the fact that someone knows of his connection to Felicia disturbs Mr. Hilditch greatly. He becomes increasingly reclusive, abandons work, and begins to recall more of what he does not want to remember, including his mother's sexual abuse of him when he was young. Miss Calligary attempts to "Gather" in or convert Mr. Hilditch. Eventually he confesses that he stole Felicia's money, and she sees how badly the Gatherers have misjudged Felicia. Mr. Hilditch falls completely apart and hangs himself.

Felicia, on the other hand, is well, and even safe, though not by society's standards. She has sold off the last of her possessions and become one of the rough sleepers. Though young to be on the streets, she is careful, and unlike many other girls on the street, does not resort to prostitution. Felicia knows when and where to beg, and when and where not to. She has friends among the other rough sleepers and continually gets help from storekeepers and doctors. Miss Calligary finally finds Felicia and tries to gather her back in, but Felicia refuses. She may not have found Johnny, but she has found serenity and peace.

Felicia drops out. The end of Felicia's journey is a fitting culmination to a trip that takes her through various forms of homelessness. Though she seems to start out from a place of great security—a home, a duty, an identity, an honorable place in the history of Ireland—clearly her family has not provided a true home for her. Their identity with the cause of Irish Republicanism is so complete, that it makes no room for a daughter pregnant by a soldier in the British Army. This is especially ironic, given the changing circumstances in Ireland at the time—historically, Ireland has been an extremely uncomfortable place for unwed mothers, but by the early 1990s, conditions were shifting, as reflected in the changing rate of illegitimate births: "[In] Ireland, the increase in single parenthood and the fall in births inside marriage has been very striking. In 1980 births outside marriage made up 5% of all births, whereas by 1996 they made up one in four of all births" (O' Connor,

p. 8). Felicia's family, however, has not kept up with the times. Locked in the past of the Irish Revolution, they lag behind in other respects as well. Her father's response to Felicia's pregnancy is worthy of earlier in the twentieth century. And if her nuclear home seems to have little room for her in an emotional sense, her national home has little room in an economic one; in her family's economically depressed area of Ireland, Felicia is unlikely to find work.

In England, though Felicia has money and a perceived destination, she is also homeless, cut off from her Irish birthland, seeking a person who does not want to be found. Even when taken in by the Gatherers, Felicia is essentially homeless. Her place there is dependent entirely on their good will, which she quickly loses, and Mr. Hilditch certainly offers her no safe haven—quite the opposite. It's only when Felicia takes to rough sleeping, that she finds peace and comfort, as revealed by her musings at the end of the novel, on a park bench in the sun. The homeless Felicia spends her days in contemplation, considering not the evil done her, nor the evil she has done, but grace: "She looks out now from where she is, and does not brood: what's done is done. She does not focus on her one-time lover's treachery. She walked away from a man who murdered girls. She was allowed to walk away: that is what she dwells upon" (*Felicia's Journey*, p. 209). Her view of mercy and grace extends even to Mr. Hilditch, whom she learns has committed suicide. Felicia does not reveal his secret; in fact she now sees him from an almost inhumanly merciful perspective: "Lost within a man who murdered, there was a soul like any other soul, purity itself it surely once had been" (*Felicia's Journey*, p. 212).

Trevor, who is so interested in the margins of cultures, and the ways in which they collide, takes Felicia from one boundary to another until she assumes a completely marginalized life, yet one that seems curiously resonant and full. The novel turns the usual perception of homelessness on its head: "There will be charity and shelter and mercy and disdain; and always, and everywhere, the chance that separates the living from the dead" (*Felicia's Journey*, p. 213). We are led by her extraordinary serenity and her apparent happiness to contemplate the extent to which our considerations of the state of the homeless resemble Mr. Hilditch's disparaging view of the state of Ireland.

Sources and literary context. William Trevor has not stated any real-life inspiration for the story of Felicia, a fact that is not surprising, since he regularly refuses to pinpoint sources for his stories. "People always ask me how stories begin," he says, "They expect me to say, well, they begin by sitting in a place such as this, because I'm known as quite an eavesdropper. But it's not as neat as that. It's an untidy, rather dirty business" (Trevor in Caldwell, p. 47). Felicia's story seems to have evolved from Trevor's personal concerns, from his growing use of Irish characters, from his interest in questions of innocence and guilt, and from his interest in the intersections of cultures. Of his Irish characters, Trevor says, "Leaving Ireland enabled me to see Ireland through the wrong end of the telescope. You've got to write about the parochial in the most universal way you know how. That's part of distancing, and judgement: to find what is recognizable outside of, say, a small township in Ireland" (Trevor in Caldwell, p. 44). Felicia herself, supremely parochial, becomes, at the end of the novel, so universal as to be completely untethered, a citizen of the world, not of any particular country.

A GLOSSARY OF SOME ENGLISH AND IRISH EXPRESSIONS *IN FELICIA'S JOURNEY*

- "Mr Hilditch weighs nineteen and a half stone."
  A "stone" is 14 pounds—he weighs 273 pounds.
- "Nineteen and six in the pound."
  There were 20 shillings in a pound, and 12 pence in a shilling; the term means that someone isn't "all there," is slightly daft.
- "I have a cheek coming here."
  I've got some nerve coming here.
- "Lay-by."
  A place at the side of a highway where cars can pull off the road.
- "Looking for a kip, dear?"
  "Do you need a place to stay?"
- "The Black and Tans should have sorted that island out."
  The reinforcements for British police action in Ireland in the early 1920s should have completely suppressed the Irish.
- "Is maith liom. . . ."
  Irish for "I like. . . ."

(*Felicia's Journey*, pp. 6, 15, 57, 76, 103, 149, 152)

Reviews. The twenty-first of his published works, a list that includes both novels and short-story collections, *Felicia's Journey* was well received, winning the prestigious Whitbread Book of the Year Award and the Sunday Express Book of the Year Award. Francine Prose, reviewing the novel for *Book World*, considered the book to be not merely extremely well written—she mentions "the depth, the bravery, the felicities of language, style, narrative economy and psychological insight" in it—but also important to read when considering "the misfits and the poor, the underground man and woman" (Prose, p. 10). Hilary Mantel, in the *New York Review of Books*, compliments the novel for having "the elegant tensions of a high-class thriller" in seamless style: "It is rare to find a book which is so gripping as *Felicia's Journey*, yet so subtle. There is no straining for effect, and hardly a false note in it" (Mantel, pp. 4, 6). A later review, by Bruce Allen, praises the "brilliantly worked-out suspense thriller" for its "dual character study whose skilfully calibrated juxtapositions are interesting in themselves" (Allen, pp. 329-30). The novel has since sustained its regard as one of Trevor's finest fictions thus far.

—Anne Brannen

For More Information

Allen, Bruce. "Souls Like Any Other Souls." *Sewanee Review* 106, no. 2 (spring 1998): 329-33.

Bracken, Patrick J., and Patrick O'Sullivan. "The Invisibility of Irish Migrants in British Health Research." *Irish Studies Review* 9, no. 1 (April 2001): 41-51.

Caldwell, Gail. "A Gentleman of Substance." *The Boston Globe*, 30 May 1990, 37, 44.

Higginbotham, Peter. "Poor Laws." *The Workhouse*. http://users.ox.ac.uk/~peter/workhouse/index.html. (August 2002).

"Irish Abroad." *Irish Centre for Migration Studies*. 1999. http://migration.ucc.ie/. (July 2002).

Livingstone, Ken. *Nothing But the Same Old Story: The Roots of Anti-Irish Racism*. London: London Against Racism, 1986.

Mantel, Hilary. "The Mystery of Innocence." *The New York Review of Books* 42, no. 9 (25 May 1995): 4-6.

Norris, Joel. *Serial Killers*. New York: Anchor Books, 1988.

O'Connor, Pat. "Ireland: A Country for Women?" *Jouvert: A Journal of Postcolonial Studies* 4, no. 1 (1999 Fall). 1999. Online: North Carolina State University. http://social.chass.ncsu.edu/jouvert/v4:1/con41.htm. (July 2002).

Porter, Darwin. *Frommer's Comprehensive Travel Guide: England '95*. New York: Macmillan Travel, 1995.

"Press Notice." *Office of the Deputy Prime Minister: Rough Sleepers Unit*. 1999. http://www.housing.odpm.gov.uk. (July 2002).

Prose, Francine. "Mr. Hilditch's Curious Hobby." *Book World* 25, no. 4 (22 January 1995): 1, 10.

"Rough Sleepers: Government Strategy." *Office of the Deputy Prime Minister: Rough Sleepers Unit*. 1999. http://www.housing.odpm.gov.uk (July 2002).

St. Mungo's Charities. "History of Homelessness." 2002. http://www.mungos.org/facts/history.shtml (August 2002).

Trevor, William. *Excursions in the Real World: Memoirs*. New York: Alfred A. Knopf, 1994.

———. *Felicia's Journey*. New York: Penguin, 1994.

The Glass Menagerie

by
Tennessee Williams

> **THE LITERARY WORK**
>
> A play set in the mind and memories of Tom Wingfield, who recalls his escape from St. Louis in the late 1930s; first performed in 1944.
>
> **SYNOPSIS**
>
> Tom Wingfield is haunted by memories of the mother and sister he abandoned.

Tennessee Williams was born Thomas Lanier Williams in Columbus, Mississippi, on March 26, 1911, to Cornelius Coffin, a traveling shoe salesman, and Edwina Dakin Williams, the well-bred daughter of a southern minister. When Williams was seven, the family moved north to St. Louis due to a decline in the family's fortunes. The young Williams wanted to be a writer, but his father forced the would-be-writer to work in a shoe factory, a job he hated and that eventually caused him to suffer a nervous breakdown. Williams attended college at the University of Missouri and Washington University, where he first began writing plays and gained the nickname "Tennessee" because of his southern accent. The Depression interrupted his education for two years; in 1938 he earned a B.A. degree at the University of Iowa, where he had gone to study dramatic writing. After graduating, Williams traveled from city to city working at menial jobs. A course in playwriting in New York City and the prize he took in a writing contest resulted in a job offer to be a screenwriter in Hollywood. It was at this point that Williams began writing what would later become *The Glass Menagerie*, drawing on his early days in St. Louis to portray a declassed Southern family. He wrote the tale into a short story, "Portrait of a Girl in Glass," as well as a screenplay, *The Gentleman Caller,* but it was as a play that the tale would finally find success. With the performance of *The Glass Menagerie*, Williams became famous overnight, though he regarded his success as a "catastrophe" and tried to hide from it (Williams, *The Glass Menagerie*, p. 11). Still drifting from city to city, mostly living in hotels, Williams went on to write such plays as ***A Streetcar Named Desire*** (1947; also in *Literature and Its Times*), *Cat on a Hot Tin Roof* (1955), *Suddenly Last Summer* (1958), *Sweet Bird Of Youth* (1959), and *Night of the Iguana* (1961). Both *A Streetcar Named Desire* and *Cat on a Hot Tin Roof* won Pulitzer prizes, and Williams is now considered one of the three greatest U.S. dramatists, along with Arthur Miller and Eugene O'Neill. Like these two writers, Williams transformed his personal experience into drama that captured the frustrated emotions of his age.

Events In History at the Time the Play Takes Place

The Great Depression. The Great Depression spanned the years from 1929 when the stock market crashed, through 1940 when the American economy began seriously gearing up for the

Tennessee Williams

Second World War. In the intervening years, stocks became worthless, businesses closed, banks failed, agriculture (its setbacks compounded by drought) was in near-complete collapse, and unemployment soared. Many people lost absolutely everything they had. By 1932 a full quarter of the American workforce was unemployed and largely without any resources for coping with their dire financial straits. Government provisions like welfare and unemployment insurance did not yet exist. Families took to living on the streets, and desperate men hawked apples on street corners. Not until Franklin Delano Roosevelt became president in 1933 would conditions begin to improve. Roosevelt started to institute his "New Deal," introducing a host of innovative policies to support the banks, raise farm prices, employ people in federal works projects, and create a welfare system to help the needy. A veritable alphabet soup of programs and institutions emerged: the AAA (Agricultural Adjustment Act), CCC (Civilian Conservation Corps), NRA (National Recovery Administration), WPA (Works Progress Administration), and TVA (Tennessee Valley Authority), to name a few. Some of these programs were successful, but in the end, it would take World War II to lift America out of the Great Depression.

In fact, in the late 1930s when *The Glass Menagerie* takes place, there was an economic downturn within the Depression. Economic recovery had ensued from 1933 through the spring of 1937, peaking in May. Then the economy faltered anew, unemployment climbing back up by the spring of 1938 to more than 19 percent. Sometimes called a depression within the Depression, the crisis was addressed with fresh measures from the president, but with only limited effectiveness. The U.S. economy would not begin to fully recover until 1940, when wartime spending brought unemployment and the Depression to an end. In *The Glass Menagerie*, Amanda believes it worthwhile to send her daughter Laura to a business college where she can learn shorthand and typing, skills that would serve her well when the economy rebounded in 1940, if not earlier. Tom, Amanda's son, is gainfully employed in a shoe warehouse during the late Depression but restless to join the U.S. Merchant Marine, which would in fact be a timely move. The Merchant Marine proved vital to the war effort early in the conflict, when the United States was still neutral. In late 1940 Britain, experiencing grave sea losses, asked Roosevelt for help from U.S. merchant ships to deliver war goods to Britain. Roosevelt obliged, going so far as to request that Congress empower him to arm U.S. merchant vessels and let them enter combat zones. In late 1941, before the bombing of Pearl Harbor, Congress complied.

The Spanish Civil War "In Spain there was a revolution" Tom explains to the audience in *The Glass Menagerie* (*Glass Menagerie*, p. 23). The Spanish Civil War (1936-39) has often been thought of as a dress rehearsal for World War II. The Spanish Nationalists, ultimately led by the fascist General Francisco Franco, were supported by Germany and Italy. The Spanish Republicans were aided by the Soviet Union and a group of foreigners called the International Brigade. Many of these foreigners were liberal or pro-communist British, French, and Americans, although technically Britain, France, and the United States remained neutral in the war. Tom describes American youth at this time as "caught in the folds of Chamberlain's umbrella" (*Glass Menagerie*, p. 57). Famous for his trademark black umbrella, Britain's Prime Minister Neville Chamberlain had gained a reputation for appeasement that became symbolized by the umbrella. Several times *The Glass Menagerie* alludes to the Spanish Civil War. Tom reads a newspaper with the huge headline "Franco Triumphs!" and twice makes reference to Guernica, a Spanish town horribly bombed by the Nationalists (supported by Hitler's air force) on

April 26, 1937 (*The Glass Menagerie*, p. 56). One of the bloodiest conflicts of the twentieth century, recent estimates place the total number killed in this civil war at close to 500,000. Shortly thereafter many of the foes would face each other once again, but on a global rather than a national scale. World War II saw the Germans and Italians pitted against the British, French, and Americans as declared enemies. This time Spain would officially remain neutral.

The dominance of radio. During the 1920s, radio was a flourishing business. The rise of the electronics industry and the growing popularity of the radio were the basis for much of America's economic success in the roaring 1920s, beginning with the first broadcasted commercial blaring from Detroit in 1920. RCA, The Radio Corporation of America, had just been established in 1919; it would be followed in 1926 by the founding of NBC (the National Broadcasting Corporation), then CBS (the Columbia Broadcasting System) in 1927-28. By 1929, ten million American homes had radios; by 1939 the number had reached 27.5 million.

Radio (often called the "wireless" in these years) continued to be popular throughout the Depression, mainly because it was free. It also filled the need for a reliable source of information, providing President Franklin Delano Roosevelt with a medium through which he communicated frequently with the nation, both in official addresses and in a series of so-called "fireside chats." Exploiting radio for how close it could bring him to the American people, he spoke to them in their own living rooms in a confidence-inspiring voice. Listeners tuned in for not only news but also entertainment: plays, comedies, serial dramas, variety shows, quiz shows, game shows, and soap operas found a listening audience. During the era in which *The Glass Menagerie* takes place, this audience heard one of the most famous radio broadcasts ever: the 1938 dramatization of the novel ***The War Of The Worlds*** (also in *Literature and Its Times*), in which narrator Orson Welles unintentionally convinced millions of Americans, who mistook the science-fiction broadcast for a real news show, that New Jersey was under attack by Martians. In the field of entertainment, radio provided a window on the world for people who, like the Wingfields in *The Glass Menagerie*, otherwise had little spare money to spend on leisure-time activities. Tom's coworker in the play, Jim O'Connor, is taking a course in radio engineering, which he hopes will prepare him for a job in the up-and-coming medium of television. "I believe in the future of television!" he tells Laura. "I wish to be ready to go up right along with it. Therefore I'm planning to get in on the ground floor . . . all that remains is for the industry itself to get under way!" (*The Glass Menagerie*, p. 100). The ambition earmarks Jim as a man at the forefront of his generation. In the late 1930s, television was still an experimental technology.

The Golden Age of Hollywood. Between 60 and 90 million people—including Tom Wingfield—went to the movies at least once a week in the 1930s. Hollywood was in its Golden Age. Shaken by the events of the Great Depression, people flocked to the movies to escape the hardships of everyday life, to lose themselves in a world of glamour, mystery, or adventure. It has been said that the United States, a country without an aristocracy, carved out its own variety of kings and queens in Hollywood. Film spawned the closest institution America had to royalty, and the 1930s became the era of great screen stars, including actresses (Bette Davis, Greta Garbo, Marlene Dietrich, Joan Crawford, and Ginger Rogers) and actors (Clark Gable, Gary Cooper, Jimmy Stewart, James Cagney and Humphrey Bogart). A filmgoer could watch gangster movies featuring James Cagney and Humphrey Bogart, or watch Fred Astaire and Ginger Rogers dance the night away. Comedians and child stars flourished too. Filmgoers could be cheered up by the charm of little Shirley Temple, or lose themselves in the antics of comedians like the Marx Brothers and W. C. Fields, or escape into make-believe dramas that gave them relief from their own harsh lives. They could even spend 80 some minutes in an animated fantasyland; *Snow White and the Seven Dwarfs*, Disney's first feature-length cartoon, was produced in 1937.

Unlike today when one goes to see a specific film for roughly two hours, moviegoing was an all-day event in the 1930s. There might be an "A" feature and a "B" feature, plus newsreels and cartoons, so a person might buy a ticket and make a day (or a night) of it. Moviegoing was so popular that some people, like Amanda Wingfield, worried that the movies were having a bad effect on popular morality. In 1934 a production code was put into place to ensure that movies would not "lower the standards" of those who saw them. On-screen flashes of profanity, sex, and violence were thereafter subject to censorship. Still people went to the movies. Apparently moviegoing achieved the purpose that

Tom ascribes to it in *The Glass Menagerie*: "Hollywood characters are supposed to have all the adventures for everybody in America, while everybody in America sits in a dark room and watches them have them!" (*Glass Menagerie*, p. 79).

THE DAUGHTERS OF THE AMERICAN REVOLUTION

The Glass Menagerie's Amanda Wingfield is a member of the D.A.R., the Daughters of the American Revolution. Founded in 1890, the D.A.R. has three goals: to perpetuate the memory and spirit of the men and women who fought the Revolutionary War, to promote institutions that encourage enlightened public opinion, and to foster American patriotism. Membership is restricted to direct descendants of people who fought for American independence during the Revolution, either in a military or a civilian capacity. At one time First Lady Eleanor Roosevelt was a member; she resigned, however, in 1939 when the D.A.R. refused to allow the black singer Marian Anderson to perform in Constitution Hall in Washington D.C. because of her race (instead, at the invitation of the U.S. Government, Anderson sang on the steps of the Lincoln Memorial). That the play's Amanda is a member of the D.A.R. means her family must have had a fairly long and distinguished history in the country. Obsessed by her own past, Amanda seeks to perpetuate the memory and spirit of a bygone age, though her present circumstances show that her family has come down considerably in the world.

Labor unrest and the strengthening of unions. While trade unions certainly existed before the 1930s, they were often disregarded or attacked by employees. During the Great Depression, however, the public began to be more supportive of unions. Because of massive unemployment, it was easy to exploit workers—many employers tried to get the most work out of employees for the least amount of money possible. But in 1935, the National Labor Relations Act (also known as the Wagner Act) was passed as part of Franklin Delano Roosevelt's New Deal. This act explicitly gave workers the right to unionize without interference from an employer. It entitled them to organize, bargain collectively, and go on strike.

Unions took advantage of the moment and began both to create new unions and to build membership in already existing unions. A new group of dedicated, defiant labor leaders emerged to organize workers whose area of business had not yet been unionized, making great progress in mass-production industries such as automobile manufacturing, steel production, textiles, and coal mining. Literally millions of workers were unionized in the 1930s, including for the first time, black workers. Union membership soared from 2.7 million in 1933 to more than 8.5 million by the end of the 1930s.

Of course, many employers were less than happy about this increase in union membership. General Motors, for instance, refused to recognize the United Automobile Workers of America, established in 1935. In 1936 in Flint, Michigan (near Detroit), workers decided to hold a sit-down strike until General Motors recognized the union. Historians have described this strike as the most important in American labor history. By sitting down in the factories rather than leaving, they stopped General Motors from replacing them with other workers. Group singing captured the spirit of defiance: "When the boss won't talk, don't take a walk. / Sit down! Sit down!" (Kennedy, p. 312). Roosevelt took behind-the-scenes action, urging General Motors to recognize the union as the workers' representative, and after a 44-day strike, General Motors did. The company allowed the United Auto Workers union to meet in the lunchroom, and promised to negotiate with it about pay, minimum weekly hours, and various benefits.

Other strikes did not end so peacefully; in May 1937, police in South Chicago, Illinois, opened fire on striking workers, killing ten. That same month and year, United Auto Workers leader Walter Reuther and three of his colleagues were beaten so badly in River Rouge, Michigan, by Ford Motor Company's security police that they had to be hospitalized. Reuther would later survive two assassination attempts. Other companies worked more stealthily, hiring spies and paying them to stir up trouble within unions, or to stop workers from organizing at all in various places. Capturing this moment in labor history, Tom Wingfield, who is himself a worker in a shoe warehouse, notes, "[T]here were disturbances of labor, sometimes pretty violent, in otherwise peaceful cities such as Chicago, Cleveland, Saint Louis . . . " (*The Glass Menagerie*, p. 23).

The Play in Focus

A note on editions. There are two editions of *The Glass Menagerie*: the Acting Edition and the Reading Edition. The Acting Edition, the more

PLUEROSIS, BEING "CRIPPLED" AND ATTITUDES TOWARD DISABILITY

In *The Glass Menagerie,* Jim calls Laura "Blue Roses" because she once had an attack of pleurosis. Pleurosis or pleurisy, is a disease that affects the membranes or air sacs lining the lungs. Characteristic symptoms include pain in the chest or side, fever, and loss of appetite. It is often a complication of other diseases such as scarlet fever or rheumatic fever. Laura also suffers great embarrassment because she wears a brace on her leg; she tells Jim how her brace "clumped so loud! . . . to me it sounded like thunder! . . . I had to go clumping up the aisle with everyone watching!" (*The Glass Menagerie,* p. 93). Jim insists she shouldn't be self-conscious, but the attitude of most people toward disability was not as positive as his during this era, despite the fact that the President of the United States at this time, Franklin Delano Roosevelt, had been paralyzed by polio and governed the country through two of its biggest crises—the Depression and the Second World War—from a wheelchair. On one hand, the fact that Roosevelt was electable to the highest office in the land showed that being disabled wasn't necessarily the end of one's life and career; on the other hand, even Roosevelt attempted to hide his disability, preferring to be photographed standing behind a podium or seated in an armchair with his wheelchair nowhere in sight. So popular was he with the press that its members cooperated, never picturing him in a wheelchair. In the play Laura's mother echoes this same concern. Amanda clearly worries about how people will perceive her daughter's disability; when Laura describes herself as "crippled," her mother snaps, "I've told you never, never to use that word. Why, you're not crippled, you just have a little defect—hardly noticeable, even!" (*The Glass Menagerie,* p. 35)

"realistic" of the two, is commonly used as the basis for productions. The Reading Edition, the one Williams himself preferred, is the version published and anthologized. The Reading Edition features stage directions that include a number of symbolic devices to help tell the story, including the projection of words and images on a background screen, specific themes of music to be played at particular times, and a particular lighting scheme. Despite the clearly theatrical nature of these devices, most producers choose not to use them on stage.

The plot—Scene 1. Tom Wingfield, our narrator, begins the play by speaking directly to the audience. He first informs us that "the play is memory" and is therefore not realistic (*Glass Menagerie*, p. 23). We are about to see the past only as he remembers it, not as it really was. Tom also provides the audience with an overview of the play's social background, sketching the historical context in which his largely personal memories are set. The time, Tom tells us, is the 1930s during the Great Depression; there is a revolution in Spain and labor violence in major American cities. Tom then introduces the play's characters—himself, his mother Amanda, his sister Laura, and the gentleman caller who "appears in the final scenes" (*Glass Menagerie*, p. 23). He explains that the play has a fifth character who never appears—his father, who abandoned the family long ago and whose photograph dominates the back wall. It is at this juncture that the memory part of the play begins.

Over dinner with her son and daughter in their shabby apartment, Amanda reminisces about her carefree youth and all the gentleman callers she had when she was a girl back in Blue Mountain, Mississippi. She asks her shy and crippled daughter Laura how many gentleman callers she thinks they'll be entertaining this evening. But Laura doesn't think she will ever have any gentleman callers. She confides to her brother that "Mother's afraid I'm going to be an old maid" (*Glass Menagerie*, p. 28).

Scene 2. Laura is polishing her collection of glass animals when Amanda comes home, looking shocked; Laura has not been attending her business classes. Laura explains that going to school

Kirk Douglas (left) as Jim O'Connor and Jane Wyman as Laura Wingfield in the 1950 film version of *The Glass Menagerie.*

made her physically ill; she was simply too shy and strange to continue on with her course. Amanda worries about the future; how will Laura support herself if she has neither skills nor the courage to face people long enough to earn a living? "Of course," Amanda muses, "some girls do marry" (*Glass Menagerie*, p. 34). Amanda asks Laura if she has ever liked a boy, and Laura confesses that she had a crush on a boy named Jim back in high school. Jim used to call her "Blue Roses" because Laura got sick with pleurosis, and Jim misheard the name of the disease. Amanda tells Laura that "Girls that aren't cut out for business careers usually wind up married to some nice man" (*Glass Menagerie*, p. 35). Laura protests that she's crippled, but Amanda tells her never to use that word.

Scene 3. Tom tells us that Amanda became obsessed with finding a husband for Laura. He then steps back into the play to argue with his mother, who thinks he's selfish for spending too many nights out at the movies. Tom protests that he's the one supporting the family with his job at the shoe warehouse, a job that he hates. He screams at his mother, calls her a witch, and flings his coat at her across the room, breaking some of Laura's glass animals by accident. Amanda, near tears, says that she won't speak to him again until he apologizes.

Scene 4. Tom comes home drunk but tells his sister he's been out all night at the movies. Laura begs him to apologize to their mother, who still won't talk to him. Tom apologizes to Amanda over breakfast, and she breaks into tears. She is worried that Tom is going to abandon them as her husband has; she is worried that Tom is going to become a drunk; and most of all, she is worried about what is going to happen to Laura. Amanda asks Tom to bring home a nice boy from the shoe warehouse to introduce to Laura, and Tom agrees to do so.

Scene 5. Amanda tries to comb her son's hair, and he escapes outside onto the fire escape to smoke. There, Tom tells the audience that young people that year were looking for adventure, which lurked just around the corner, since the Second World War was about to start. Amanda comes out on the fire escape to talk to Tom, whereupon Tom informs her that they are going to have a gentleman caller; he has invited his friend Jim to come to dinner the following night. Excited, Amanda exclaims that he should have told her sooner—there are so many preparations to make! Tom warns her not to get her hopes up, but in Amanda's mind, Laura is as good as engaged. Frustrated, Tom goes out "to the movies," while Amanda grabs Laura and tells her to make a wish on the moon.

Scene 6. Tom tells the audience about Jim, a highly confident person who is Tom's only friend at the warehouse. Meanwhile, Amanda works furiously to transform the apartment and get Laura prettied up. While Amanda is fixing Laura's dress, she mentions that their caller's name is Jim O'Connor. Laura realizes that this is the same boy she liked in high school. Tom arrives with Jim, but Laura is terrified to open the door and soon escapes into the other room. Tom, left to entertain Jim, confides that he's planning to run away to join the Merchant Seamen, a group of sailors who ship goods during peacetime and become a naval auxiliary during wartime to deliver troops and war materiel. Amanda appears, all dressed up in a gown from her youth, and tries to charm Jim. When called to dinner, Laura nearly faints with terror and has to lie down while the other characters eat.

Scene 7. The lights go out after dinner because Tom has used the electric bill money to join the Union of Merchant Seamen. Amanda lights candles and sends Jim to talk to Laura while she and Tom do the dishes. Jim finds Laura and tries to be nice to her; at first she avoids him, but eventually he coaxes her into conversation. She ad-

WOMEN AND WORK DURING THE GREAT DEPRESSION

While Laura Wingfield's own fears prevent her from attending business school, she would have in any case faced difficulties as a working woman in the late 1930s. With so many people out of work, competition for jobs was fierce. There was pressure to hire men first, because men were considered "breadwinners" while women's incomes were treated as secondary and supplementary. Professional women in previously male-dominated fields (medicine, science) had a particularly hard time staying employed, but women encountered difficulties even in female-dominated areas like social work, clerical work, and teaching. Many women who had the kind of clerical skills that Laura was learning in *The Glass Menagerie* were forced to take less skilled, less well paid work as maids or cleaning women. Guidance counselors of the time warned women that there were fewer and fewer jobs for private secretaries. Secretaries in general were at a disadvantage, not only because of the Depression, but also because of new technological developments like the Dictaphone (a recorder to which businessmen could dictate letters), which made large secretarial pools obsolete. With so many women competing for fewer jobs, a woman's looks and social skills became especially important; the men doing most of the hiring preferred young, pretty, and charming women. So even if Laura Wingfield had finished business college, she would have had a difficult time competing in the late 1930s job market. It is worth noting, however, that the decade gave rise to some new clerical positions and the position of switchboard operator, jobs deemed particularly suitable for women, so that when employment finally improved, women tended to re-enter the work force more rapidly than men.

mits that she knows who he is and reminds him that he used to call her "Blue Roses." Flattered, Jim asks her why she didn't say hello right away, and Laura explains that she's painfully embarrassed about being crippled. But Jim tells her not to be and tries to encourage her to be more confident about herself. He tells her that she's pretty, takes an interest in her glass collection, and finally coaxes her into dancing with him. As they dance, they knock over Laura's favorite glass animal, a glass unicorn, breaking the horn off. Laura takes the mishap in stride, saying that she'll "just imagine that he had an operation. The horn was removed to make him feel less—freakish!" (*Glass Menagerie*, p. 104). Jim tells Laura that she's different and special and kisses her, literally knocking her off her feet. At this point, Jim guiltily admits that while he likes her a lot, he can't see her again because he's going steady with another girl. He doesn't want her to misunderstand; he doesn't want to hurt her feelings. Laura is devastated by this news: "You—won't—call again?" (*Glass Menagerie*, p. 107). Jim tells her he can't, and Laura gives him her broken glass unicorn as a souvenir. When Amanda returns, bringing fruit punch, Jim makes a quick escape, explaining that he has to pick his fiancée up at the train station. Amanda is stunned that Jim is already engaged, and when he leaves, she whirls upon Tom furiously—how could he have brought home a boy who already had a girl?! Tom, who had no idea that Jim was engaged, flees the apartment: "The more you shout about my selfishness to me the quicker I'll go—and I won't go to the movies!" (*Glass Menagerie*, p. 114).

Stepping back into the role of narrator, Tom informs the audience that he left St. Louis soon after that, abandoning his mother and sister. It's been years since he fled, but he is still haunted by guilt, particularly by the memory of his sister's face. Behind him, Laura blows out the candles in the apartment, ending the play.

Fading glory—the American South. *The Glass Menagerie* is a play haunted by memories—not only Tom's memories of a particular set of family events in Saint Louis, but by his mother Amanda's memories (or romantic delusions) of her carefree girlhood in the American South. "She loves to tell it," Laura whispers to Tom, and indeed, Amanda takes every opportunity to reminisce about a past full of cotillions and balls, dances and picnics (*Glass Menagerie*, p. 25). Amanda claims to have been courted by "some of the most prominent young planters of the Mississippi Delta" (*Glass Menagerie*, p. 26). In fact, to hear Amanda talk, one would think that the Old South was a paradise of sorts.

A careful reading of the play tells another story. The South of Amanda's childhood is a deeply racist place; Amanda speaks of having to "send the nigger over to bring in folding chairs" when she had too many gentleman callers in one afternoon (*Glass Menagerie*, p. 26). At another point, she offers to fetch the pudding by telling Laura, "You be the lady this time and I'll be the darky" (*Glass Menagerie*, p. 25). Old-fashioned Southern gentility was dependent on old-fashioned servitude. The planters who courted Amanda were enriched by plantations that depended on slave labor before the Civil War, making the South far from a paradise for a good many of its inhabitants. Underscoring this not immediately obvious fact in the play is the information that at least some of Amanda's gentleman callers met with unhappy fates: one was "drowned in Moon Lake," another was shot "on the floor of Moon Lake Casino" (*Glass Menagerie*, p. 27).

Yet looking back, Amanda's genteel pretensions allow her to idealize the era—"Gone, gone, gone! All vestige of gracious living! Gone completely!" (*Glass Menagerie*, p. 82). In her romantic imagination, the genteel South of her past is as much an escape from current hardships as Tom's trips to the movies. Both escapes dovetail in Amanda's sales pitch for her magazine subscriptions. The new serial novel that will be published, she promises, is as exciting as *Gone with the Wind*, the famous Civil War novel published in 1936 and turned into an epic movie adventure in 1939.

> AMANDA: You remember how *Gone with the Wind* took everybody by storm? You simply couldn't go out if you hadn't read it. All everybody *talked* was Scarlett O'Hara. Well, this is a book that critics already compare to *Gone with the Wind*. It's the *Gone with the Wind* of the post-World War generation!
>
> (*Glass Menagerie*, p. 38)

Gone with the Wind won eight Academy Awards including Best Picture, so the story of a determined Southern woman in a crumbling world was very much in the air as Williams was writing *The Glass Menagerie*. Indeed, Williams himself was perhaps the one to really write "the *Gone with the Wind* of the post-World War generation"—his own story of a determined Southern woman in a crumbling world, *The Glass Menagerie*.

Sources and literary context. *The Glass Menagerie* is Williams's most patently biographical play. Tom Wingfield is an obvious Williams stand-in; he gave the character his first name, his initials, his hated job at the shoe warehouse, his desire to be a writer, his weakness for drink and the movies, and his own restless nature. Williams's mother, Edwina, like Amanda, was a culture-shocked Southern belle, and while his father Cornelius never abandoned the family, he did travel a lot when Williams was young, and became a drunk and an abusive presence once they moved north.

Most importantly, Williams's sister, Rose, like the fictional Laura Wingfield, was a weak and damaged creature. Rose's background, like Laura's, suggested that Rose ought to be a debutante, and in late 1927 she was, in fact, sent south to her aunt in Knoxville to make her debut in a swirl of parties and lunches. But Rose, like Laura, did not find a gentleman caller, and she became increasingly depressed. After the economy collapsed in 1929, the family tried to send Rose out to work, but they had to come get her after only one day; terrified, Rose had hidden herself in the bathroom. After this, Rose became increasingly depressed and erratic, and had several nervous breakdowns. In 1937, around the time in which *The Glass Menagerie* is set, Rose was diagnosed as schizophrenic and paranoid delusional and was committed to the State Hospital in Farmington, where she received insulin shock and Metrazol therapy. Unresponsive to the treatment, in 1943 she was given a bilateral prefrontal lobotomy, which was supposed to cure her depression. Instead it damaged her mind beyond repair, and she spent the rest of her life in an institution. Williams was obviously thinking of his sister Rose when he gave his fictional character Laura the nickname "Blue Roses." Rose's fate haunted her brother for the rest of his life. In fact, one of the reasons that Williams could never enjoy his own success as a writer was because he was keenly aware of how much luckier he had been than the women of his family.

Events in History at the Time the Play Was Written

The Second World War. "Adventure and change were imminent in this year. . . . All the world was waiting for bombardments!" says the play's narrator (*Glass Menagerie*, p. 57). The bombardments of the Second World War began in earnest in 1939, after Hitler invaded Poland. France and Great Britain declared war on Germany on September 3, 1939. Within a year, France would be invaded and forced to surrender to the Germans, and Britain would suffer a series of intense German bombings of its major cities. The bombardments the world was waiting for would indeed come!

The United States did not enter the war until its naval base at Pearl Harbor, Hawaii was attacked by the Japanese on December 7, 1941. But it had been sending planes, tanks, guns, and other goods to England throughout the war, even when Britain didn't have the money to pay for them, and as noted, had used U.S. merchant ships on Britain's behalf. Today people often talk about the Second World War as an obviously "good" war, one that was honest and worth fighting. They tend to forget that before Pearl Harbor, there was a huge and violent controversy in the United States over the question of whether the country should enter the war at all.

There is perhaps more than a little wartime feeling in Williams's play when Jim O'Connor describes his former girlfriend, Emily Meisenbach, as a "kraut-head" (*Glass Menagerie*, p. 97). Anti-German sentiments had reached a feverish pitch during the First World War (1914-18). So vehement were Americans in their antipathy that they renamed sauerkraut "liberty cabbage" and redubbed the German measles "liberty measles." The anti-German feelings subsided in the interwar period—after all, Jim did date Emily in high school. But by the writing of the play, the United States and Germany had been deadly enemies for more than two years and a degree of virulent anti-German feeling had resurfaced.

The rise of television. Jim O'Connor's interest in television, then only an experimental medium, illustrates how forward-thinking he is. In 1937 there were only 18 experimental television stations in the entire United States. Television was publicly demonstrated at the New York World's Fair in 1939, but the Second World War stopped the emerging industry in its tracks as scientists and engineers refocused their attention on technological developments that had more obvious military applications. Electronics factories were needed for the war effort more than the television industry. So for the next few years production centered on the war.

Thus, in 1944, when *The Glass Menagerie* was written, television was poised to explode across the American landscape. Commercial production of television was still banned, so that it wouldn't interfere with the war effort, but many people eagerly anticipated the spread of the new technology. In 1946 the government removed its restrictions on broadcasting; at this point there were about 10,000 television sets in the U.S. The fact that the industry was about to burgeon can be seen in the exponentially increasing numbers of sets shortly after the writing of *The Glass Menagerie*; by 1949, there would be one million; 10 million by 1951; 50 million by 1959. By the 1950s, television was rapidly replacing radio as America's number one medium for communication and entertainment. Certainly for some Americans, the excitement was already in the air during the writing of the play. Williams was obviously paying attention to this medium in the midst of its emergence in the 1940s, since his play links television to Jim O'Connor's confidence and ambition. Like television, the character seems destined for success. He comes across as a man with his eye on the future, in sharp contrast to the Wingfields, a family held down by the weight of their collective past.

THE USE AND ABUSE OF LOBOTOMY

A lobotomy is an operation in which parts of the brain are severed from each other; it is, literally, the intentional infliction of brain damage. The operation was introduced in 1935 by two Portuguese neurophysicians, António Egas Moniz and Almeida Lima, and was soon adopted as a "miracle cure" for mental illness. In practice, what this meant was that a brain-damaged person was more manageable and docile than someone who had a mental illness. A device like an icepick was inserted through the back of the eye and into the frontal lobes of the brain, severing the nerves and causing irreparable damage. Lobotomies were performed widely throughout the 1940s and into the 1950s along with other brutal "treatments" like electroshock therapy. Today, depression, paranoia, and schizophrenia are treated with various kinds of medications, and lobotomies are performed very rarely. Williams's sister Rose, the model for Laura Wingfield, was given a prefrontal lobotomy in 1943, a year before *The Glass Menagerie* was written.

Reviews. When *The Glass Menagerie* first opened in Chicago in 1944, not many people were interested in seeing a first play by an unknown playwright. But critics loved the play and helped it find its audience. *Chicago Tribune* drama critic Claudia Cassidy published a wildly enthusiastic review on December 27, 1944, and continued to go to the play night after night as she exhorted her readers to see the play. Cassidy was convinced that Williams had vast insight into human nature and insisted to her readers that they would find the play spellbinding. Cassidy eventually won an ally in fellow drama critic Ashton Stevens of the *Chicago Herald American,* and thanks largely to their perseverance, *The Glass Menagerie* was soon playing to packed houses. The casting of Laurette Taylor, a beloved stage actress who had gone into semi-retirement after the death of her husband, did much to catapult it to popular success too. Taylor's performance as Amanda has become such a famous theatrical landmark that every Amanda since has been unfavorably compared to her. Three months later, in March, 1945, the play opened on Broadway. The cast received an amazing 25 curtain calls, and the play later went on to win the prestigious New York Critics' Circle Award.

—Francesca Coppa

For More Information

Bigsby, Christopher. "Tennessee's Lost Sister: Obituary: Rose Williams." *The Guardian* (London), 20 September 1996, 19.

Cardullo, Bert. "Williams' *The Glass Menagerie.*" *Explicator* 55, no. 3 (1997):161-64.

Gounaridou, Kiki. "The Quest for Identity in Tennessee Williams' *The Glass Menagerie.*" *Text & Presentation: The Journal of the Comparative Drama Conference* 19 (1998): 33-40.

Gussow, Mel. "Rose Williams, 86, Sister And the Muse of Playwright." *New York Times*, 7 September 1996, 13.

Hoare, Philip. "Obituary: Rose Williams." *The Independent* (London), 12 September 1996, 18.

Kennedy, David M. *Freedom From Fear: The American People in Depression and War, 1929-1945.* New York: Oxford University Press, 1999.

Levy, Eric P. "'Through Soundproof Glass': The Prison of Self-Consciousness in *The Glass Menagerie.*" *Modern Drama* 36, no. 7 (1993): 529-537.

Parker, R. B., ed. *The Glass Menagerie: A Collection of Critical Essays.* Engelwood Cliffs, N.J.: Prentice-Hall, 1983.

Reynolds, James. "The Failure of Technology in *The Glass Menagerie.*" *Modern Drama* 34, no. 4 (December 1991): 522-27.

Roudane, Matthew C., ed. *The Cambridge Companion to Tennessee Williams.* Cambridge, England: Cambridge University Press, 1997.

Tynan, Kenneth. "Tennessee Williams." in *Profiles.* London: Nick Hern, 1990.

Williams, Tennessee. *The Glass Menagerie.* New York: New Classics, 1949.

The God of Small Things

by
Arundhati Roy

Arundhati Roy was born in Shillong, India, in 1960 to a Syrian Christian mother and a Hindu father. The marriage did not last. When Roy was a toddler, her mother, Mary Roy, obtained a divorce and returned to her ancestral home in Kerala, India, where she started a school and raised her two young children. Arundhati Roy was a student in her mother's school until age 11, after which she attended a boarding school. At the age of 16, she ran away from home to study at the Delhi School of Architecture. She eventually left architecture and teamed up with film director Pradip Kishen to write the screenplay for and star in a mildly successful parody of Indian college life called, *In Which Annie Gives It Those Ones* (1988). On the strength of *Annie*, Roy was hired to write the screenplays for the television series *Electric Moon* (1992). When the series ran out of money, she turned to novel writing. For four-and-a-half years, she wrote five hours a day to produce *The God of Small Things*, her only novel to date. Roy has since written for social causes, producing work that displays the political savvy so apparent in *The God of Small Things*.

THE LITERARY WORK

A novel set in 1969 and in present-day Kerala, India; published in 1997.

SYNOPSIS

After being separated from her twin brother Estha for 23 years because of a drowning and a murder, Rahel returns from America to India for a reunion with him.

Events in History at the Time the Novel Takes Place

The 1962 Sino-Indian War. India is a country that was, as Roy's novel explains, "poised forever between the terror of war and the horror of peace" (Roy, *The God of Small Things*, p. 20). Although India has fought many wars since it gained its independence from the British (1948), the one Roy calls specific attention to in her novel is the Sino-Indian War, in the midst of which her main characters, Rahel and Estha, are born. The Sino-Indian war is arguably the most wasteful and ill-advised war India has fought since independence. While the fighting lasted only one month, it involved a half million troops, took 7,000 lives, humiliated India, and left its prime minister, Pandit Jaharwalal Nehru, a broken man. The conflict began as a border dispute with China over Aksai Chin, "a high and desolate plateau, 17,000 feet above sea level, where nothing grows and no one lives, lying between the towering ranges of Karakoram and the Kuen Lun" (Maxwell, p. 13).

In the early 1950s, after driving out the Dalai Lama, the traditional ruler and high priest, and announcing the "peaceful liberation" of Tibet, China decided to consolidate its power in that region by developing the region's infrastructure. Along the India-China border, the Chinese engaged in massive road building, 112 miles of which took place in the remote Aksai Chin region, located in India's Ladakh district. Situated in a rocky and hostile region, which contained no land routes from India, the road was not discovered by India until October of 1958. The Indian government took the Chinese presence in Aksai Chin as an act of "illegal and clandestine seizure," and in response, implemented what was called the "forward policy," establishing a series of fortified and unfortified forward posts (posts that were placed well within the disputed territory) to police India's northern border (Maxwell, p. 177).

By 1962 it was clear to Prime Minister Nehru and his colleagues that the Chinese had no intention of voluntarily evacuating from Indian territory. India slowly began to build up its forces along the border, but was nowhere near a state of readiness to fight a border war with China, when, on September 8, Chinese troops crossed over the Thagla Ridge and surrounded India's Dhola post. The Indian government immediately sent in reinforcement troops, but these were woefully unprepared to fight a war in so remote a region. Outfitted with summer clothing, given three days' worth of food rations, and armed with 50 rounds of ammunition, soldiers of the Indian forces were sent in to achieve the impossible objective of driving the Chinese out of what India considered its territory. When the war began in earnest on October 20, the Indian forces were easily overwhelmed.

In the West, the Chinese forces fought for Aksai Chin. Along their eastern border, they targeted the state of Assam. The posts fell one by one. On October 22, Tsang Dar fell, on October 23 Bum la, and on October 24, Tawang, the headquarters of the Seventh Infantry Brigade. The Chinese offered to negotiate on October 24, but India immediately rejected the offer, so the attack on Assam continued. By November 18, the Chinese had managed to get as far as Tezpur, Assam, nearly 50 miles south of the disputed border protected by the Assam-North-East Frontier Agency. American Ambassador John Kenneth Galbraith, noted, on November 20, that there was "ultimate panic in Delhi, the first time [he] had ever witnessed the disintegration of public morale" (Galbraith in Maxwell, p. 438). Rumors were rampant about an imminent Chinese occupation of Tezpur, about the landing of paratroopers in the capital, and about the capture of General Hridya Nath Kaul, the Chief of General Staff. On November 21, however, much to everyone's surprise, the Chinese stopped their advance and declared a unilateral cease-fire. Defeated and humiliated, India was forced to abandon all of its forward posts along China's claim line and to relinquish the land rights to the 38,000 square kilometer Aksai Chin region of its Ladakh district.

After defeating India, China boldly introduced Maoist communist ideas and propaganda into Assam. Interestingly, no state accepted the spread of communism as readily as the state of Kerala. Assam, located on India's northeastern border, is far from Kerala, located on India's southwestern seacoast, yet similar forces plagued the two states. Maoist communism, unlike Marxist or Marxist-Leninist communism, tended to emphasize armed conflict. Hence the turmoil in northeastern India, into which Rahel and Estha were born, continues to plague them even when their mother, Ammu, takes them and returns to her ancestral homeland in Kerala.

Caste and communism in Kerala. The caste system in Kerala, where much of *The God of Small Things* is set, dates back to 800 B.C.E. It would develop into one of the most oppressive caste systems in India. Members of the untouchable laborer castes (Paravan, Pelayas, and Pulayas) were not allowed to use the public highways, walk on the access path to temples, or wear shoes. Arundhati Roy describes the wretched conditions of the Paravans earlier in the twentieth century:

> Paravans were expected to crawl backward with a broom, sweeping away their footprints so that Brahmins or Syrian Christians would not defile themselves accidentally stepping into a Paravan's footprint. . . . Paravans, like other Untouchables, were not allowed to walk on public roads, not allowed to cover their upper bodies, not allowed to carry umbrellas. They had to put their hands over the mouths when they spoke, to divert their polluted breath away from those whom they addressed.
>
> (*The God of Small Things*, p. 71)

Individuals from these "outcaste" groups were expected to take on tasks considered too polluting for "caste" members, such as: cleaning up human and animal waste, tanning leather, and dealing with the bodies of dead animals or unclaimed humans. Sitting in judgement of them were Brahmans, members of the highest, priestly caste. Though they exempted themselves from the death penalty, Brahmans could put to death a member of the lower castes for theft or for slaughtering a cow, an animal considered sacred in Hindu tradition.

Yet in present-day India, where a legacy of prejudice endures, Kerala prides itself as being among the least caste-conscious of all regions. This turn-around coincides with its taking up the egalitarian principles of Marxism and electing to power a communist government in 1957. Kerala's inflexible espousal of caste traditions in the past and its equally adamant support for communism by the late 1950s and early 1960s are not separate accidents of history. The communists offered a language and framework to analyze the inequities of the caste system. Addressing a 1936 peasant meeting, communist leader Vishnu Bharateeyan told the crowd, "There are only two castes, two religions and two classes—the haves and the have nots" (Bharateeyan in Jha, p. 134). But the communist movement also manipulated local caste and religious identities in the interest of gaining a foothold in the region. In *The God of Small Things*, the relationship and interaction between Chacko, Comrade Pillai, and Velutha, all members of the communist party, offer an illustration of how communism operated in Kerala. Pillai is Hindu, while both Chacko and Velutha are Christians. However, Chacko is an upper caste Syrian Christian, while Velutha, the grandson of an Anglican Church convert, is considered an untouchable. To swell their ranks and gain a majority in Kerala, communist leaders stressed the religious differences between Hinduism and Christianity to attract both the "Chackos" and "Veluthas." At the same time, these leaders would highlight caste distinctions that made allies of upper-caste individuals like Pillai and Chacko, persuading them to ignore their religious differences. In this way, the party could, even within it own ranks, stress similarities of religion or highlight differences in caste to play one group against another to suit its interests. *The God of Small Things* describes communism's attraction:

> The real secret was that Communism crept into Kerala insidiously. As a reformist movement that never overtly questioned the traditional values of a caste-ridden, extremely traditional community. The Marxists worked from within the communal divides, never challenging them, never appearing not to. They offered a cocktail of revolution. A heady mix of Eastern Marxism and orthodox Hinduism, spiked with a shot of democracy.
>
> (*The God of Small Things*, p. 64)

In other words, the type of communism introduced in Kerala was one that not only allowed for, but thrived on, the continued existence of the ancient, traditional caste divides.

The Naxalbari uprising. In 1967, in Naxalbari, located in the Darjeeling district of West Bengal, the beating of a sharecropper escalated into a full-scale, armed peasant uprising. At first the peasants used lathis (clubs of iron and bamboo), spears, and bows and arrows to seize lands and confiscate food grains, killing those who tried to stop them. Eventually, as they took firearms and ammunition from the landlord's houses they raided, the struggle intensified. On May 25 the police in Naxalbari killed nine women and children, escalating the conflict beyond the local authorities' ability to maintain control. Paramilitary troops were brought into the region on July 19. The troops ruthlessly crushed the rebellion, killing dozens of peasants, beating hundreds of them, and arresting thousands.

Although the uprising was suppressed, the struggle continued with the formation of the *Naxalbari Peasants Struggle Aid Committee*, which raised to the status of martyr those who had perished in the uprising. The Naxalites, as the supporters of Naxalbari came to be known, made armed struggle the cornerstone of their politics and rejected the path of "peaceful transition" put forth by both factions of India's Communist Party, the CPI (Communist Party of India), and the CPI(M) (Communist Party of India [Marxist]). Instead the Naxalites supported the concept of a protracted people's war, with guerilla field tactics as the preferred method of engagement. Ideologically, the Naxalites desired an immediate establishment of a people's democratic dictatorship to guide the transition toward socialism and ultimately to communism. Refusing to abide by the practices of a parliamentary government, they called for a boycott of elections.

As stated in *The God of Small Things*, the growing Naxalite movement "struck terror in every bourgeois heart" (*The God of Small Things*, p. 66). Its spread was primarily the work of students, particularly those in the universities in Calcutta, which came to serve as the center for Chinese communist politics in India. In the latter part of the 1960s and early 1970s, hundreds of students left their studies to join the peasants' struggle. The CPI(ML) (Marxist-Leninist), which split off from the CPI(M), provides an account of the first three decades at Naxalbari. In the account, it catalogs the ideals that contributed to the students' taking up the Naxalite cause:

> Youth, with ideals, at last found a meaning to their lives after total disgust with the deceit, corruption, greed and unprincipled opportunism that pervaded parliamentary politics. Naxalbari

symbolised to this youth a new future of justice, truth, equality, humanity and a self-respect for the downtrodden which the present society could never give. Fired with this missionary-like zeal they set out to exterminate the perpetrators of injustice, inhumanity, to eradicate the demons and ghosts who run this oppressive system, to remove the sting of the scorpions, snakes and other vile creatures who roam the corridors of power . . . to execute the executioners. They sought to create a paradise on earth.

(CPI[ML])

The Novel in Focus

The plot. *The God of Small Things* opens with Rahel's return to the Kerala town of Ayemenem from America to reunite with her twin brother, Estha, who has been living with their father in northeastern India. The events of the novel occupy the space of exactly one day, during which Rahel and Estha, now 30 years old, relearn how to relate to each other. Everything else is memory, most of it focusing on the events and circumstances that led to their separation.

NARRATIVE TECHNIQUE IN *THE GOD OF SMALL THINGS*

The most notable feature of *The God of Small Things* is Roy's writing style. As Rahel encounters people and things from her Ayemenem past, the events that occurred 23 years prior reveal themselves in patterns resembling memory; that is, governed by no specific structure, and out of chronological and natural order. Sophie Mol, for instance, the twins' nine-year-old cousin, is presented to readers dead and laid out in a coffin long before they get a glimpse of her alive. Also Velutha, their friend, is shown as a broken, bleeding, dying man, before readers are given a glimpse of his life. Readers are told what has happened before they are aware of what is happening. Thus the idea of fate is driven home. Knowing what will happen to Sophie Mol and Velutha, the reader is encouraged to pay more attention to fatal errors and actions that contribute to their deaths. The novel's last chapter engages in an ultimate revolt against chronological order. When the novel opens, Velutha and Ammu (Rahel's and Estha's mother) have both been dead for decades; when the novel closes, they are vibrantly alive, full of hopeful vitality, and innocently confident about tomorrow.

In chronological order, the remembered past occurs as follows: At age 18, Ammu, the mother of Estha and Rahel, travels to Calcutta, ostensibly to visit a distant aunt. In reality she is searching for a means to escape her abusive father, who, in an episode when she was 13, had cut to shreds her gum (rubber) boots and then had beaten her for having tried to retrieve them in the first place. Her long-suffering mother, Mammachi, who uncomplainingly accepted her husband's daily beatings, is incapable of offering any assistance to her daughter. Thus, in Calcutta, when the 25-year-old assistant-manager of a tea estate from Assam proposes marriage to her, Ammu "just weighed the odds and accepted" (*The God of Small Things*, p. 39). The marriage is rocky from the beginning as the husband "turned out to be not just a heavy drinker but a full-blown alcoholic" (*The God of Small Things*, p. 40). One month into the 1962 Sino-Indian war, with all of Assam beset with fears about India's imminent defeat and Chinese occupation, Ammu gives birth to her twins, Estha and Rahel, while her drunken husband sleeps.

By the time the children are two years old, his drinking has placed Ammu's husband in danger of losing his job. However, Mr. Horlick, his English manager, is willing to grant him a reprieve in exchange for sexual access to Ammu. Ammu is told about this proposal and reacts with stunned silence, whereupon her husband hits her but passes out in a drunken stupor before he can do much damage. Thus begins the pattern of "drunken violence followed by postdrunken badgering" (*The God of Small Things*, p. 42). When the violence starts to involve the children, Ammu divorces her husband and returns, unwelcome, with her twins, to her father's house.

In the Ayemenem house, although Ammu feels keenly the sting of her family's disapproval of her, Estha and Rahel thrive. They are ignorant of the family's abusive past and its politics. In innocence, they befriend Velutha, a Pulaya. A laborer and an untouchable, Velutha is a gifted carpenter and handyman, upon whose skills the running of the family's pickle factory depends. When the twins are seven years old, their Uncle Chacko invites his English ex-wife, Margaret Kochamma, and his daughter, Sophie Mol, to Ayemenem for Christmas. The great excitement of the Ayemenem household over the imminent arrival of their cousin causes Estha and Rahel to question how much Ammu and the others love them.

Because the nearest airport is several hours away in Cochin, the family decides to go to the airport the day before and stay overnight in a hotel. To make the most of the trip, they will also take in a movie. On the way to Cochin, the car is stopped at a railway crossing and while the busy traffic is stalled, a march of workers, organized by the Communist Party, passes through, calling upon the people to unite and to overthrow the landowning classes. Rahel spots Velutha among the marchers and waves to him, but because he knows the family would consider his participation in the march a betrayal of their generosity towards him, Velutha quickly disappears into the crowd without acknowledging her, leaving the others wondering whether it was him after all. Rahel fails to lock her door after hailing Velutha, and one of the marchers pushes his way into the car and forces the terrified Baby Kochamma (Rahel and Estha's grand aunt) to wave a little red flag and chant, "Inquilab Zindabad!" ("Long Live the Revolution!"). The encounter passes quickly, but Baby Kochamma feels humiliated. Linking Velutha to the protesters, she comes to hate him as if he were the one who forced her to wave the flag.

Eventually the family does reach their destination—the Abhilash Talkies, which is showing *The Sound of Music*, whose songs the precocious twins have learned by heart. Because Estha is unable to stop himself from singing out loud, Ammu permits him to go out into the lobby where he can sing without disturbing the other members of the audience. In the lobby, his singing wakens the man who runs the refreshment counter. Taking advantage of Estha's innocence, the Orangedrink Lemondrink man tricks Estha into masturbating him, then frightens Estha into silence with threats that he knows where Estha lives. The encounter leaves Estha terribly shaken and literally ill, forcing the family to walk out on the movie before it is over. In the lobby, Ammu, having no idea that he has just abused her son, is flirtatiously friendly with the Orangedrink Lemondrink Man. Estha worries that his mother will invite the molester into their home if he shows up in Ayemenem. Rahel meanwhile, through her special connection to Estha, senses what the Orangedrink Lemondrink Man has done to her twin, and when Ammu continues to sing the man's praise, she petulantly asks her mother "So why don't you marry him then?" (*The God of Small Things*, p. 106). This is a sore point with Ammu because of her failed marriage, so she retorts with a cutting remark of her own: "D'you know what happens when you hurt people? . . . When you hurt people, they begin to love you less" (*The God of Small Things*, p. 107).

With Rahel frightened and traumatized by the casual ease with which a mother's love could lessen, and Estha frightened and traumatized by memories of the Orangedrink Lemondrink Man, the family arrives at the Cochin airport the next morning to welcome their uncle's ex-wife and their English cousin. Insecure about their futures, uncertain of their mother's affection, and envious of the adoring attention paid to their cousin, Estha and Rahel publicly disobey their mother. Their disobedience causes Baby Kochamma, who is always looking for opportunities to remind Ammu of her failures, to remark that Ammu has lost control of her children.

THE SOUND OF MUSIC AND INDIAN POPULAR CINEMA IN THE 1960s

In the 1950s, Indian films achieved international acclaim through the work of Satyajit Ray, whose classic *Pather Panchali* (a starkly realistic film about a family's tragedy and a father's failed dreams) won the Cannes Film Festival award for the "best human document" in 1955. In the 1960s, however, films that dealt seriously with social concerns of the day were not what people in India flocked to see. India's wars with China and Pakistan, the peasant uprisings, and the bloody reprisals presented the public with enough reality. Instead Indian filmgoers went to the so-called "talkies" to escape their struggle-filled lives. The filmgoers wanted song and romance, and the music-filled Hindi films of the 1960s did not disappoint them. Given this predeliction, the introduction of Rodgers and Hammerstein's *The Sound of Music* to India in 1965 was a case of perfect timing. An escapist fantasy, in which the issues of war (World War II) are black and white and fears are eased with a song, the film provided conflict-torn India with just the type of entertainment for which it yearned.

(*The God of Small Things*, pp. 100-101)

When the group returns to the Ayemenem house—to a cake with all the trimmings prepared to celebrate the arrival of Sophie Mol—Rahel leaves the festivities to play with Velutha, feeling that his love for her is something on which she can more reliably count. Estha, meanwhile, goes to the family pickle factory to mull over how best

Arundhati Roy

to prepare for the possible arrival of the Orangedrink Lemondrink Man, aware that his mother, who might invite this man in for drinks, is in no position to protect him. He plans to store provisions in the abandoned house across the river should he need to leave quickly. He and Rahel find an old boat, which they refurbish with the help of Velutha. When the boat is seaworthy, they begin to cross the river regularly to the "History House," to build up their store of provisions. Sophie Mol, the daughter of their Uncle Chacko and his English wife, soon joins them in their endeavors.

In the meantime, Ammu, who feels even more unwanted in the Ayemenem household after Margaret Kochamma arrives, begins an affair with Velutha, crossing the river at night in the refurbished boat to join him in the abandoned house. Her affair is no secret to the people in the area, and word of it eventually spreads to Velutha's father, Vellya Paapen. Filled with shame at what his son has done, he informs Ammu's mother, Mammachi about the affair, offering to kill his son. Outraged, Mammachi fires Velutha and locks Ammu in her room. When Estha and Rahel try to talk to their mother through the locked door, she yells at them, accusing them of being the millstone around her neck that prevents her happiness. Frightened and angry at her words, Estha and Rahel decide to run away. Sophie Mol convinces them to take her with them. When they are almost across the river, the boat capsizes. Rahel and Estha manage to get to the hideout on the other side, but Sophie Mol, who cannot swim, drowns.

Meanwhile, worried about the scandal of Ammu's affair, Baby Kochamma, bent on also punishing Velutha for the flag-waving incident, goes to the police to accuse him of raping Ammu. Baby Kochamma goes so far as to suggest that he may be a Naxalite. Although Inspector Thomas Mathew is eager to preserve tradition and prevent the intermixing of touchables and untouchables, Velutha's membership in the Communist Party worries him because the party has a powerful voice in Kerala politics, and he does not want to antagonize it. He decides to ask Comrade Pillai, the local party leader, if the Communist Party will object to any action he takes against Velutha. Pillai assures him that he will not interfere with Inspector Mathew's work.

In truth, though, Pillai is a communist, he himself wants to preserve the separation of touchable and untouchable, and he does not harbor these feelings alone. Many in the pickle factory have already complained about working with an untouchable. Inspector Mathew's actions, he reasons, will remove the Velutha problem. At this point, Velutha, having been fired by Mammachi, is worried about the repercussions. He asks Comrade Pillai for advice, but Pillai refuses assistance on the pretext that Velutha's problems are his own and do not involve the Communist Party. Tired and sleepy, Velutha retreats to the History House and falls asleep, unaware of the sleeping forms of Estha and Rahel.

Early the next morning, upon discovering that the children are missing, Baby Kochamma tells the police to add kidnapping and possible murder to the charges against Velutha. The police find Velutha at the History House, and viciously beat him, inflicting upon him what will prove to be fatal injuries before hauling him off to jail. They also locate the children at the History House and discover evidence that they had not been kidnapped but were runaways. It furthermore becomes apparent that Sophie Mol's death was an accident. The police call Baby Kochamma into the station for filing a false report, but she persuades Estha, on pain of destroying Ammu, to give false testimony: he confirms that Velutha is a kidnapper. When Ammu discovers that Velutha has been charged with raping her, she attempts to set the record straight. But Inspector Mathew, interested primarily in maintaining the separation of touchable and untouchables, rejects her suit, openly calling her a *veshya* (prostitute). Eventually Pillai uses Baby Kochamma's report as the pretext to lay a "Communist Party siege" on the family's pickle factory. He sides with Velutha and blames the family for victimizing him. As "Ayemenem's own Crusader for Justice and Spokesman of the Oppressed," Pillai, "claimed that the Management had implicated the Paravan [Velutha] in a false police case because he was an active member of the Communist Party" (*The God of Small Things*, pp. 286-87).

After Sophie Mol's funeral, her father Chacko's anger is directed at his sister, Ammu, thanks to Baby Kochamma. She persuades him to demand that Ammu leave the house. Unable to support both her children, Ammu must send Estha to his father for the time being. But before she can reunite her children, she contracts tuberculosis, and, at the age of 31, dies. Rahel grows up wild and alone, marries an American, and moves to the United States, where she remains after their divorce. Estha stops talking and starts performing servile tasks in his father's house. When his father decides to emigrate to Australia, Estha is returned to Ayemenem; Rahel, who hears news of this, also returns. Reunited, the two stay up the entire night to watch the kathakali dancers. (The classical dance drama of Kerala, kathakali dates back to the seventeenth century and is rooted in Hindu mythology.) In one another's arms, overcome by horrifying memories and "hideous grief," they make love. Like their mother, who slept with an untouchable, "once again they broke the Love Laws" that dictated "who should be loved. And how. And how much" (*The God of Small Things*, p. 311).

The novel's final chapter depicts the last night Velutha and Ammu spend together, before Velutha's father learns about the nature of their relationship and sets the fateful events into motion. The last word in the novel is "Tomorrow," a word filled with promise, but from the point-of-view of the readers, who know what awaits the lovers, it is also one filled with loss.

Caste and power. When Mammachi discovers the relationship between Ammu and Velutha, the normally courteous and judicious matriarch "who wore crisp ironed saris and played the *Nutcracker Suite* on the violin in the evenings" becomes a crass, out-of-control bully, spewing blind venom and insufferable insults (*The God of Small Things*, pp. 268-69). Traditionally, because contact with an untouchable is considered polluting, a woman who has sex with a man from the untouchable caste would become an "outcaste"—expelled from her caste and likely turned out from her home and community as well. A sanctified union, like marriage, between an upper-caste woman and a lower caste man, would be out of the question. Mammachi's fury at her daughter's relationship with an untouchable reveals how entrenched caste prejudices are in India in general and in Kerala in particular. From an outsider's point of view, Mammachi, a Christian, should possess little or none of the traditional Hindu-based caste prejudices. She had had an English-language education derived largely from western models; she plays the music of Stravinski, Brahms, and Tchaikovski on her violin, and she reads primarily British authors. Also her father-in-law set up a school to educate the untouchables, much to

BEHIND THE TITLE: VELUTHA AS "THE GOD OF SMALL THINGS"

Arundhati Roy makes a powerful statement against caste consciousness when she designates Velutha as "The God of Small Things." In the person of Velutha, the God of Small Things is he whom others seek to destroy because he stands to reveal the emptiness of their lives and their gestures. Velutha, for all his lack of power as a member of an abysmally oppressed class, is able to find dignity in every gesture, however small. All who come in contact with him receive the benefit of his effortless grace, his sudden smiles, and his kind actions.

Having wasted her chance for happiness by marrying badly, Ammu knows that the most she can expect from life are small things—a moment of contentment or a kernel of hope. She understands that the God of Small Things governs her life now and that there are strict limitations to how much happiness he could give her: "He could do only one thing at a time. / *If he touched her, he couldn't talk to her, if he loved her he couldn't leave; if he spoke he couldn't listen, if he fought he couldn't win*" (*The God of Small Things*, p. 312). But she is willing to accept what small amount of happiness is left to her. Ammu embraces the God of Small Things in the person of Velutha because, no matter how limited he may be in wealth and power, he knows how to love.

the chagrin of her Brahmin neighbors. But most importantly, it was she who "first noticed Velutha's remarkable facility with his hands," decided to educate him, and then to make him chief facilities manager of her pickle factory (*The God of Small Things*, p. 71). Still, she slips into outrage at her daughter's affair with an untouchable. In the end, the historical baggage of a long-ingrained caste system far outweighs the usual sentiments of a well-meaning, highly-educated, Christian woman. It is important to note that Mammachi's brand of Christianity is not Roman Catholic, the variety introduced to Kerala by the Portuguese in the sixteenth and seventeenth centuries. Nor is it Anglican, the form introduced to Kerala by the British in the eighteenth and nineteenth centuries, which did not wipe away Hindu caste divisions:

> When the British came to Malabar, a number of Paravan, Pelayas, and Pulayas (among them Velutha's grandfather, Kelan) converted to Christianity and joined the Anglican Church to escape the scourge of Untouchability. . . . They were known as Rice Christians. It didn't take them long to realize that they had jumped from the frying pan into the fire. They were made to have separate churches, with separate services and separate priests. As a special favor they were even given their own separate Pariah Bishop.
>
> (*The God of Small Things*, p. 71)

Mammachi is Syrian Christian, purportedly a direct descendent of one of the original Brahmin families whom St. Thomas converted to Christianity in 52 C.E. Unlike later converts to Roman Catholicism and Anglicanism, Syrian Christians are decidedly upper caste. Thus Kochu Maria, Mammachi's cook, allowed "her earlobes [to become] distended into weighted loops that swung around her neck" by the kunukku earrings, thick and gold, she constantly wore: "Kochu Maria couldn't stop wearing her kunnukku because if she did, how would people know that despite her lowly cook's job (seventy-five ruppees a month) she was a Syrian Christian, Mar Tomite? Not a Pelaya, or a Pulaya, or a Paravan. But a Touchable, upper-caste Christian" (*The God of Small Things*, p. 162).

The portrayals of Mammachi and Kochu Maria suggest that the caste system remains strong in part because it offers a lowly cook, who earns 75 rupees a month (about $10.00), and a helpless wife, beaten daily by an ill-tempered husband, some semblance of power. Weak as they are, they at least have power over the untouchables. This misguided sense of empowerment offers insight into why the democratizing principles of communism failed to truly work against the long held caste-based inequities and injustices in Kerala. Many of the party leaders did not really seek equity and justice. They merely desired personal power through the exploitation of the powerless, and among whom the most powerless were the untouchables. Comrade Pillai does not see Velutha the way the principle of communism would have taught him to view this hard-working laborer—as a skilled, intelligent individual oppressed by the forces of a market-driven society. Instead, Velutha is for Pillai merely a means to his goal of empowering himself and his family, and perhaps, as an added bonus, of outclassing the powerful, landowning, Oxford-educated Chacko. In the end, Velutha, intelligent, skillful, loving, a Paravan, an untouchable, is sacrificed to help the novel's "touchables"—Mammachi, Kochu Maria, Inspector Thomas Mathew, Baby Kochamma, Comrade Pillai, the arresting officers—maintain their delusions of power.

Sources and literary context. There are clear similarities between some details of Roy's life and the lives of her novel's characters. Like Rahel, Roy was born in northeastern India in the early 1960s, grew up in Ayamanam, Kerala, (Ayemenem in the novel), and studied architecture. She also has an uncle who owns a pickle factory, promoted by the slogan used in the novel: "Emperor in the realm of taste" (*The God of Small Things*, p. 46). Similarities exist as well

MARY ROY V. STATE OF KERALA

In 1984 Mary Roy brought a lawsuit against the state of Kerala for its inequitable inheritance laws that discriminated against Christian women. According to the 1916 Travancore-Cochin Christian Succession Act, daughters were entitled to inherit only one quarter of a son's share or Rs 5,000 (about $380), whichever was less. By 1986, Roy's case had gone all the way to India's highest court. Roy herself argued the case before the Supreme Court and ultimately won. But Mary Roy's struggle against this unfair law was not without cost. She suffered the penalties of severe social ostracism in Kerala and a permanent break with her brother. However, she has earned the full respect of her daughter, Arundhati, as evidenced by Roy's loving dedication to her mother in *The God of Small Things*: "For Mary Roy who grew me up" (*The God of Small Things*, p. v).

between Mary Roy and Ammu. Like Ammu, Mary Roy divorced her Bengali husband, taking her toddler-aged son and daughter back to her ancestral home in Kerala with the intent of raising them alone by opening a school.

Yet more intriguing are the deeper parallels. When asked in an interview whether the novel is the story of her family, Mary Roy replied, "Some incidents were true. But everything that happens in the novel actually did not happen in real life" (Roy in Ipye). And when asked, "Was the drowning of Sophie Mol in the Minachal river a real incident?" Mary Roy's answer was invitingly ambiguous: "No comment. I am not prepared to talk about it now. Find out for yourself" (Roy in Ipye). George Isaac, Mary Roy's brother and Arundhati's uncle, on whom the character Chacko is based, has also commented on the truths behind the fiction in the novel:

> Mary Roy [the author's mother] marries a Bengali which falls outside the traditional framework of Christian marriages. That marriage collapses and she returns to her family house with her two children in a disturbed state of mind. . . . The only male in the house is me. I have to be father to the children and, in a sense, husband to my sister.
>
> (Venu Menon)

Publication and reception. *The God of Small Things*'s entry into the world's literary scene is the material of legend. In 1996 a reading of Roy's manuscript en route to Delhi from Dehra Dun so excited Pankaj Mishra, a representative of Harper Collins, that he immediately got off the train to contact David Godwin, a well-known British literary agent, about his discovery. Godwin, after a single reading of the manuscript, was so taken with Roy's prose, he immediately flew to Delhi to sign her on and subsequently secured for her a $1.6 million advance. The novel went on to début in 16 countries and 19 languages.

In India, *The God of Small Things* met with criticisms from the left and the right. "Marxists," according to Donald Eichert, "were angered by Roy's disdainful portrait of the former chief minister E. M. S. Namboodiripad" (Eichert). Namboodiripad himself criticized the inter-faith/inter-caste relationship between the fictional Ammu and Velutha as sexual deviance, an example of bourgeois decadence. Also reacting to the Ammu-Velutha affair, Sabu Thomas, a Kerala lawyer, filed formal charges against Roy for obscenity. Roy largely ignored Namboodripad's concerns, and although she tried numerous times to get the courts to dismiss Thomas's charges, as of this writing, the case is still pending. However, the criticism in no way has driven Roy to engage in self-censorship; she remains as committed as ever to illuminating society's inequities and injustices.

Outside India, literary critics were stunned by the beauty of the novel's language. Hailed as the literary sensation of the year, it won England's highest literary award, the Booker Prize, and remained on the *New York Times Best Sellers List* for 49 weeks. Alice Truax wrote in her *New York Times Book Review*:

> The quality of Ms. Roy's narration is so extraordinary—at once so morally strenuous and so imaginatively supple—that the reader remains enthralled all the way through to its agonizing finish.
>
> (Truax, p. 5)

James Wood in his *New Republic* review echoed these sentiments: "The great pleasure of *The God of Small Things* flows from its language" (Wood, p. 32). Comparing the writing to the golfing of champion Tiger Woods, John Updike's review in the *New Yorker* offered perhaps the most telling assessment: "This is a first novel, and it's a Tiger Woodsian début—the author hits the long, socio-cosmic ball but is also exquisite in her short game" (Updike, p. 159).

—Margaret Wong

E. M. S. NAMBOODIRIPAD

E. M. S. (Elankulam Manakkal Sankaran) Namboodiripad the much-beloved leader of the Communist Party of India, died in March 1998, less than a year after *The God of Small Things* was published. The homage to Namboodiripad in *Frontline* (India's most widely circulated national magazine) gives an indication of the extent to which he was loved: "No tribute can do justice to the glorious and multi-faceted life led by EMS—anti-imperialist, social reformer, literary critic, Marxist thinker, theoretician and historian, and above all a person loved and held in esteem by millions of people" (Krishnakumar). Namboodiripad's influence in shaping Kerala's political and social landscape was immense. His writings and analytical commentary helped produce the calculated mixture of Hindu caste tradition and Marxist doctrine that Roy has denounced as hypocritical but that his supporters have praised as being well suited to Indian conditions.

For More Information

Banerjee, Sumanta. *India's Simmering Revolution: The Naxalite Uprising*. London: Zed, 1984.

CPI (ML). "30 Years of Naxalbari: 1967-1997." 1997. http://www.cpiml.org/pgs/30yrs/hist30.htm (9 Jan. 2002).

Eichert, Donald. "To the Booker Born." *The Week*. 1997. http://www.the-week.com/97oct26/cover.htm (9 Jan. 2002).

Ipye, George. "Ammu is Not Mary Roy." *Rediff on the Net*. 1997. http://www.rediff.com/news/sep/18arun.htm (10 Jan. 2002).

Jha, Gulab. *Caste and the Communist Movement*. New Delhi, India: Commonwealth, 1990.

Krishnakumar, R. "A Great Life: E. M. S. Namboodiripad, 1909-1998." *Frontline: India's National Magazine*. 4-17 Apr. 1998. http://www.flonnet.com/fl1507/15070080.htm (28 Jan. 2002).

Maxwell, Neville. *India's China War*. Garden City, N.Y.: Anchor, 1972.

Menon, Venu. "Who's Ammu?" *Rediff On The Net*. 19-20 Oct. 1997. http://www.rediff.com/news/oct/18booker.htm (10 Jan. 2002).

Roy, Arundhati. *The God of Small Things*. New York: HarperCollins, 1997.

Truax, Alice. "A Silver Thimble in Her Fist." Review of *The God of Small Things*. *New York Times Book Review*. 25 May 1997, 5.

Updike, John. "Mother Tongues: Subduing the Language of the Colonizer." Review of *The God of Small Things*. *New Yorker*. 23, 30 June 1997, 156-61.

Wood, James. Review of *The God of Small Things*. *The New Republic* 217 (29 December 1997): 32-37.

Grand Avenue

by
Greg Sarris

THE LITERARY WORK

A novel consisting of 10 linked short stories set in and around Santa Rosa, California, in the mid-1990s; published in New York in 1994.

SYNOPSIS

A clan of indigenous Pomo Indians struggles with the challenges of poverty in multiethnic northern California.

Greg Sarris was born in Santa Rosa, California, in 1952 and educated at the University of California at Los Angeles (UCLA) and at Stanford University, where he earned a Ph.D. He returned to UCLA to teach American Indian and other literatures before becoming a professor at Loyola Marymount University in Los Angeles. In his teaching and writing, Sarris explores a multicultural world that reflects his own ancestry and upbringing. His father descends from Miwok, Pomo, and Filipino ancestors; his mother from Irish and Jewish ancestors. Adopted at birth, Sarris left his foster home as a young boy, then lived with a succession of families, some of whom he found out later were his relatives. By his junior-high and high-school years, he was spending time with Indian and Mexican gangsters on Santa Rosa's streets. At 16 Sarris was informally adopted by Mabel McKay (1907-93), a leading Pomo medicine woman and traditional basketmaker (her baskets are on display at the Smithsonian Institution in Washington, D.C.). McKay helped Sarris turn his life around. Later she would become a key subject in his writings. Sarris's first book, *Keeping Slug Woman Alive: A Holistic Approach to American Indian Texts* (1993), collects a number of his academic articles on Native American and crosscultural issues. Focusing on his adopted aunt, his second book, *Mabel McKay: Weaving the Dream* (1994), combines biography with reflections on the complete history and culture of Pomo, Miwok, and other California Indian peoples. Published the same year as *Grand Avenue*, it provides a nonfiction counterpart to the novel's portrait of contemporary Pomo life. In the same decade that he produced both of these works, Sarris was four times elected to the position of tribal chair of the Coastal Miwok Indians. He also sponsored a bill that would achieve recognition of the Coastal Miwok as a tribe under federal jurisdiction once again. In the midst of this activism, Sarris has continued to teach and write, producing new works that portray struggles common to present-day Indians such as those featured in *Grand Avenue.*

Events in History at the Time of the Novel

California Indians and the arrival of whites. Scholars estimate that about 300,000 or more American Indians occupied California when the first white settlers—Spanish missionaries and

Greg Sarris

colonists—began arriving in the late eighteenth century. Then as now, California offered unusual blessings to its inhabitants. The coast teemed with fish, shellfish, seals, otters, and other sea life; in spring and early summer the rivers abounded with spawning salmon; deer, elk and other large-prey animals abounded on the plains and hills of the great interior valleys. In the marshes and river valleys north of San Francisco Bay, the various peoples who would later be called the Pomos fished, hunted, and gathered berries, acorns, and other wild plant foods. Like their neighbors, they did not practice agriculture, owing in large part to the region's natural bounty. Yet even without practicing agriculture (which usually allows greater population density than hunting and gathering), California Indians comprised what some scholars believe may have been the densest and most culturally diverse collection of native peoples in North America.

As elsewhere in the Americas, however, contact with Europeans brought catastrophe for California's native populations. During the Spanish and Mexican periods—from the 1770s to 1845—disease, enslavement, and outright murder reduced the collective Indian population by about one-half, to an estimated 150,000. Sweeping epidemics did worse damage than they otherwise would have because of the Spanish drive to concentrate Indians in settlements around Catholic missions to convert them to Catholicism. The hope was that such settlements would induce the Indians to adopt sedentary farming, monogamous marriage, and other ways of life thought to be in step with civilization and Christian ideals. Meanwhile the settlements conveniently provided the Spanish missionaries with a ready pool of slave laborers. So the strategy had devastating consequences for the Indians, promoting disease among them, facilitating their enslavement, and disrupting their own traditional culture, deeply demoralizing those who survived these consequences. Impacted most severely were Indian peoples in southern California. For a time, Pomos and other northern peoples remained less accessible, but in 1817 the Spanish established a mission at San Rafael on Coastal Miwok lands, just south of Pomo lands. The Pomos' southern neighbors, Coastal Miwoks, occupied the area between Pomo territory and San Francisco Bay — their days of liberty numbered. With the help of soldiers, Spanish priests forced Miwoks and southern Pomos into the mission settlement.

Mexico achieved independence from Spain in 1821, and under Mexico's new Spanish-descended rulers, white incursions into California accelerated, as did the enslavement of Indians. Most of the slaves worked on large farming and livestock ranches such as those around Santa Rosa, which was founded in 1833 and soon became a regional distribution center for agricultural produce. Mexican immigrants seized the best lands, including the fertile areas along the banks of Santa Rosa Creek, where the ancestors of the fictional clan in *Grand Avenue* are described as once having lived. Many Pomos and other enslaved Indians were also sent south to work out the remainder of their lives away from California on large ranches in Mexico. At about the same time, the subgroups of Kashaya Pomos to the north became one of the peoples to suffer the depredations of Russian traders, who had gradually extended their fur-trapping empire south from Alaska. From the 1820s to the 1840s, the Russians raided middle and northern Pomo villages for slave labor.

Mexican rule in California lasted only until the arrival of Anglo-American squatters in the 1840s and the transfer of California to the United States under the Treaty of Guadalupe Hidalgo in 1848. Just days before the treaty's signing, gold was discovered at Sutter's Mill—in former Miwok lands to the east of the Pomos—and the California Gold Rush began. More than 100,000 Americans flooded into the region within a short few years, leading to California's becoming the 31st state in 1850. All this turmoil resulted in a new rash of devastating consequences for native groups. The rush of migrants, on top of the transfer to U.S. control, led to frequent and bloody confrontations between Indians and the U.S. Army or local militias. It became common as well for lawless whites to shoot Indians for sport with impunity. By 1860 a combination of disease, starvation, and homicide had further devastated California's Indian population, leaving only an estimated 35,000 of the 150,000 who survived in the 1840s. The numbers would continue to dwindle, to some 30,000 by 1900—about 10 percent of the population that had existed when the whites arrived just over a century earlier.

While other works by Sarris deal with these historical events, they form the backdrop for *Grand Avenue* but play little overt role in this novel. Instead, its stories focus on the ways in which the cultural disruption that resulted from the Pomos' history has continued to inform their contemporary existence. Only near the end of the last story, "The Water Place," does Nellie Copaz, the elderly medicine woman and Pomo basketmaker who features in several of the stories, put into words what has loomed over the preceding pages. As she passes her traditional skills on to her young relative Alice, Nellie tells the girl, "Look at what the Spanish did, then the Mexicans, then the Americans. All of them, they took our land, locked us up. Then look at what we go and do to one another" (Sarris, *Grand Avenue*, p. 222). Nellie's lament refers to the violent past as recounted in the stories of the extended family to which she and Alice belong, the suggestion being that the feuding and infighting hark back to the cultural disruptions the clan has suffered as Pomos.

The Pomos in the twentieth century. The stories in *Grand Avenue* are set in the mid-1990s, but by incorporating the memories of older characters such as Nellie Copaz, they effectively span the entire twentieth century. Indeed, the oldest character, Sam Toms (Nellie's uncle by marriage), celebrates his 100th birthday in the story "Sam Toms's Last Song," indicating that he was born sometime in the mid-1890s. At that point perhaps 1,000 Pomos survived; slowly the population would recover. By the 1990s those identifying themselves as Pomos were approaching pre-contact numbers, at nearly 5,000. Like Sarris, the vast majority of these—probably close to 90 percent—were of mixed ancestry, reflecting several generations of intermarriage both with other Indians (such as neighboring Miwoks) and among modern California's numerous ethnic groups. Aside from the economically dominant whites, large numbers of blacks moved to California from the rural South starting in the 1920s. Also, Mexicans, Filipinos, and Portuguese migrants joined the diverse peoples drawn to the Santa Rosa area to harvest agricultural products for the wealthy, mostly white farm owners. Each of these groups is represented in *Grand Avenue*, whose stories reflect both the area's contemporary diversity and the labor that spurred it. Characters of mixed ancestry find work picking or processing prunes, grapes, apples, and other fruits the area has historically produced in abundance.

THE POMOS AND THEIR NEIGHBORS

The Pomos' pre-contact population is estimated to have been between 5,000 and 8,000, or approximately 5 percent of the total number of Indians living in California before the whites' arrival. A collection of subgroups, the population did not consider itself to be a cultural unit; the name Pomo, of uncertain origin, reflected white observers' grouping of them based on shared cultural traits. Pomos spoke seven related but mutually unintelligible languages of the Hokan language family, of which three survive today. A scattered population, the subgroups lived among some 100 villages on the coast, inland valleys, and foothills north of San Francisco Bay. Ethnologists have divided these villages into northern, central, and southern tiers, noting also the distinct role played by the Pomo in their immediate vicinity. The Pomo shared a sophisticated coinage system based on money made from clamshells and magnesite, which have been called their silver and gold respectively. Their elaborate coinage gave the Pomos a role as the bankers for their neighbors, who included the Coastal Miwok to the south, the Wappo, Lake Miwok, Wintun, and Patwin to the east, and the Yuki to the north.

In the early twentieth century, the U.S. Government established a number of small reservations for the Pomos—amounting to a fraction of their ancestral lands—in northern California's Lake, Mendocino, and Sonoma counties. Starting in the 1950s, however, the Pomos were affected by a change in federal policy regarding Indian reservations. Concerned about the persistent poverty and isolation of reservation life, white officials on the U.S. Bureau of Indian Affairs decided that it would be best for Indians to assimilate into mainstream American life. With the proclaimed goal of promoting "complete political equality" for Indians, the federal government enacted a series of so-called "termination" laws, which laid out procedures for abolishing Indian reservations (Trigger and Washburn, p. 241). The Pomos were among native tribes in California and other states (for example, Utah, Oregon, Wisconsin, Nebraska, and Texas) with whom the Bureau of Indian Affairs "negotiated" over the effective loss of their communal lands. In reality white officials informed Indian leaders that their peoples had little choice in the matter (Trigger and Washburn, p. 241).

THE BLOODY ISLAND MASSACRE

Storytelling plays an important role in Pomo culture, and oral history has provided a valuable way to pass on information to future generations. In *Keeping Slug Woman Alive: A Holistic Approach to American Indian Texts* (1993), Greg Sarris writes that some stories are still told about the brutal events following the discovery of gold in 1848, when white Americans—many of them violent, greedy, and unscrupulous—began flooding into California. Some of those stories recall the Bloody Island Massacre, in which the U.S. Army virtually wiped out an island village of Pomos in 1850. The army was taking revenge for the murder of two whites, whom the Pomos had killed. The two whites had enslaved the Indians, murdering many and subjecting others to torture and sexual abuse, and the Pomos had risen in revolt. "Of course," writes Sarris in a passage that illuminates *Grand Avenue*, "for the Pomo the wars continue today . . . the wars of the dispossessed taken away from their ancient lands, cut off from many of their traditions, and relegated to the margins of society where their struggles against invisibility are undermined by poverty, disease, and inadequate education" (Sarris, *Keeping Slug Woman Alive*, p. 55).

The termination period lasted from the 1950s until President Richard Nixon abandoned the policy in 1970. Despite its eventual abandonment, termination had a long-term impact. As intended, termination accelerated an urbanizing trend that had already begun in the 1940s, contributing greatly to the movement of 122,000 Indians into America's large cities between 1940 and 1960. Although from a national standpoint only a small proportion of reservations were terminated, those of the Pomos and other California Indians were among them.

Termination is not mentioned specifically in *Grand Avenue*, but the stories clearly depict its results. Historically, the policy played a large part in the migration of Pomos from area reservations into nearby cities such as Santa Rosa. Many of the characters in the stories share the same squalid, run-down neighborhood on Grand Avenue, the Santa Rosa street that gives the collection its title. The stories' depiction of the poverty in which its characters live reflects the unfortunate reality for many of the urban poor—both Pomos and others—in cities such as Santa Rosa in the 1990s. These "others" include many different Indian peoples. The Grand Avenue of the stories "is far from grand"; rather it is "an Indian ghetto, and Indian people would easily be able to substitute other such street names for similar neighborhoods in any city or town in America with a significant Indian population" (Miller in Lobo and Peters, p. 42).

> Like most of those other neighborhoods, Grand Avenue is a racial mix—Indians, African Americans, Mexicans—of those on the lowest rungs of the economic ladder. One feature of the neighborhood is a park frequented mutually by old people, children, and gangs; another is a slaughterhouse whose owner uses it at night as a place of assignation for the neighborhood girls he recruits into prostitution. Work for most of those who live on Grand Avenue is seasonal, low paying, and punishing—picking fruit in the apple fields or packaging in the local cannery. Indian families form and reform as economic needs demand in overcrowded 'apartments' that are actually refurbished army barracks separated by mud tracks.
>
> (Miller in Lobo and Peters, p. 42)

Activism and the Native American Renaissance. While termination drove Indians to the cities with some disastrous consequences, it also had a second, more positive effect. Termination led to greater unity and more effective activism for Indians, encouraging their banding together into a single, formidable political group. Many members of this group viewed the policy of termination as well intended but misguided. As Indian leaders went to the courts in the fight to retain the reservations' federally protected status, a number of national organizations emerged. The earliest and most influential of the major ones was the National Congress of American Indians. Founded in

1944 "to preserve Indian cultural values," the NCAI led the fight against termination through the 1960s: "Reservations do not imprison us," the NCAI's "Declaration of Indian Rights" stated, "they are our ancestral homelands, retained by us for our perpetual use and enjoyment" (Trigger and Washburn, p. 252). Ultimately the struggle against termination helped give rise to relatively radical groups and incidents in the 1960s. In California, in 1968-69, Indians from a mix of tribes seized control of Alcatraz Island, site of an abandoned federal prison in San Francisco Bay. Holding the island for 19 months, the Indians protested how ineffectively the U.S. Bureau of Indian Affairs dealt with Indian problems and won national attention to the plight of their peoples. In 1973 the group known as the American Indian Movement (AIM) seized the town Wounded Knee, South Dakota, for 10 weeks to protest broken government treaties and dire conditions on the surrounding reservation. One Indian was killed and another wounded in the incident.

Out of this activist atmosphere, in turn, arose a broader cultural and political movement that historians have termed the Native American Renaissance. Beginning in the 1960s, the movement features Indians who have sought not only to reclaim and revive their traditional cultures, but also to reinterpret those cultures within a variety of contemporary contexts, from the law and politics to scholarship and literature. Much in the daily life of these traditional cultures carried an artistic dimension:

> Art is not on the decorative edges of Indian cultures, but alive at the functional heart: in blankets that warm bodies, potteries that store food, songs that gather power, stories that bound peoples, ceremonies that heal. . . .
>
> (Lincoln, p. 12)

As a university professor and author concerned with the place of traditional Indian cultures in a multicultural society, Greg Sarris is himself a leading example of this renaissance. His stories achieve an "extraordinary fusion of cultural inheritance and imaginative innovation" ascribed to Indian writers who propel the renaissance (Ramsey in Lincoln, p. 10). Sarris also portrays the movement in its larger-than-literary sense in *Grand Avenue*, through characters such as Steven Pen, narrator of the story "Secret Letters." An urban Pomo married to an Apache woman, Steven tells his children stories about their ancestors and demands that they draw lessons from the tales to apply in their present-day lives.

The Novel in Focus

The plots. With one exception, "Sam Toms's Last Song," the ten stories that make up *Grand Avenue* are narrated in the first person. All the stories are set in urban Santa Rosa, though reference is made to events that occurred on and off Pomo reservations nearby. The narrators range widely in background and age, but they belong either by birth or by marriage to the same large extended family and include children, teenagers, adults, and the elderly. The stories themselves contain only scattered clues about who's who in the extended family, but Sarris prefaces the work with a family tree that includes all the narrators and other major characters.

POMO RESERVATIONS IN THE 1990s

By the 1990s some two-thirds of the Pomos lived off-reservation, in cities like Santa Rosa or in smaller towns nearby. Yet nearly all could count friends and family members among the remaining one-third, and the reservations, which the Pomos called "rancherias," remain a potent symbol even for those living elsewhere. Their reservations are all the more significant to the group because they represent a victory, fought over many years and won in 1983, to restore the federal status that had been undone in the termination era of the 1950s. In many cases, however, the land had since been sold; thus Pomo communities struggled to repurchase land for reservations that existed only in law. In the 1990s the Pomos held some 17 rancherias, varying in size from several hundred acres (such as the large Kashaya Pomo reservation at Stewart's Point), to a few with no land at all.

"The Magic Pony"—narrated by Jasmine, the teenage daughter of Frances. With her cousin Ruby, her mother, her aunts, her grandmother Zelda, and assorted other relatives, Jasmine lives in the Hole, "a no-color brown refurbished army barracks at the end of Grand Avenue" in Santa Rosa (*Grand Avenue*, p. 5). The story follows two parallel lines: an unsuccessful love affair between Ruby's mother Faye and a shabby, degenerate white man, Jerry; and Ruby's obsession with a pony that she and her cousin Jasmine discover. Earmarked for slaughter, the pony awaits its fate along with other horses at a nearby slaughterhouse. After Jerry leaves her, Faye becomes emotionally unbalanced, and Ruby burns down a barn at the slaughterhouse in order to free the horse.

"The Progress of This Disease"—narrated by Anna, the wife of Albert Silva and the mother of Jeanne, Frankie, and six others. Anna struggles to deal with her young daughter Jeanne's cancer:

> I took myself to the library, read books, learned so much about the disease I came to speak its language, which is a hollow tongue of numbers and strange words. That's why Dr. Kriesel goes on with me about counts and cells. But I moved beyond her. I read about Laetrile, coffee enemas, diets of brown rice and sprouts, support groups—none of which I had time or money for. Visualization seemed the ticket. It's free for the effort. Picture the body healthy. See flowers and things.
>
> (*Grand Avenue*, p. 41)

As Anna tries to help her daughter, she recollects moments from her own childhood. Anna recalls, among other memories, her aunt Sipie's death, which is referred to from various points of view in some of the other stories that follow. Dewey, Anna's uncle, is commonly held to have poisoned his sister Sipie by witchcraft; the family believes the "poison" to have traveled through the generations to Jeanne, causing her cancer.

"Slaughterhouse"—narrated by Anna's son Frankie, a boy of 13 or 14, who has a crush on his second cousin Ruby. Frankie and his friends draw straws to see who will enter the slaughterhouse barn at night, when a local pimp uses the building as a brothel. Frankie is chosen, and accordingly he sneaks inside. Yet he cannot bring himself to report back what he has seen: his young cousin Ruby, dancing drunkenly with two prostitutes. Ruby is wearing lipstick and a "tight red dress that would never let me see the color red again in peace" (*Grand Avenue*, p. 71). Frankie sneaks out numbly as the pimp summons her to his Cadillac.

"Waiting for the Green Frog"—narrated by Nellie Copaz, an elderly medicine woman and traditional basketmaker. Nellie, who appeared briefly in the previous story, describes the songs that accompany her visions and healing powers, and that also dictate the designs for her baskets. The songs are associated with a magical green frog, which visits her from its home in the riverside wetlands where her Pomo ancestors once lived.

"Joy Ride"—narrated by Albert Silva, a Portuguese American married to Anna, the father of Frankie and Jeanne. On his way home one evening Albert picks up a sexy and provocative young hitchhiker, a girl who turns out to be only 16. As he realizes that she is related to him through his wife, he struggles with himself, disturbed and tempted by her seductive suggestion that they "go somewhere" (*Grand Avenue*, p. 93).

"How I Got to be Queen"—narrated by Alice, daughter of Anna's cousin Mollie and sister of Justine (whom the reader now understands is the unnamed girl of the previous story). Alice looks after their younger brothers while Justine, the "queen," parties with her friends (*Grand Avenue*, p. 130). After Justine begins seeing a black boy named Ducker Peoples, Alice watches her sister knock down a much smaller girl, perhaps Ducker's sister, who has come to call Ducker home. When the girl's older sisters show up spoiling for a fight, it is Alice, not Justine, who scatters them by firing a shotgun into the air.

"Sam Toms's Last Song"—the collection's only third-person narrative follows the events of Sam Toms's 100th birthday. Toms lives with his great-granddaughter Linda in a unit in the Hole, turning over his monthly Social Security check to her in exchange for her caring for him. Told by a white doctor that he is going die soon, Toms makes a plan: he will move in down the street with Nellie Copaz, who will look after him better than the inattentive Linda. Nellie, however, despises Toms, who has wronged her in the past. She tricks him into giving up his powerful songs, which he has used to poison rather than to heal. Knowing she can use them to heal, she catches them in a basket, and sends him home in defeat.

"The Indian Maid"—narrated by Stella, the youngest daughter of Zelda. Stella recalls her mother's stories about working as a maid for Mrs. Benedict, the elderly invalid mother of a wealthy white grower known for mistreating Indians. Like the death of Sipie, the Benedict subplot is alluded to in several of the stories; see below, "The Water Place".

"Secret Letters"—narrated by Steven Pen. A Pomo, Steven is married to Reyna, an Apache woman. They have two children, Shawn and Raymond. Steven at first seems unrelated to the clan at the stories' center, but he is harboring a long-held secret. As a teenager he fathered a child with Pauline, one of Zelda's daughters, who lived nearby. Over the years, from a distance, he has kept track of the boy, whose name is Tony. Now Tony is a successful high-school athlete, and—in hopes of offering him guidance—Steven has begun writing him anonymous letters. In the course of the story, Steven's family learns of his secret son and of his anonymous letter writing, but as that happens Steven reveals a deeper secret to the reader.

"The Water Place"—narrated by Nellie Copaz. Alice, the narrator of "How I Got to be Queen," approaches Nellie and begins to learn traditional basketmaking from her, along with the songs and other medicine techniques that are associated with Nellie's craft. Alice's apprenticeship spurs Nellie to recall events that played central roles in the clan's past: their troubled history with the Benedicts, the wealthy growers on whose land near Santa Rosa Creek the clan once lived; and the death of Sipie, Alice's grandmother and Nellie's cousin. Family history and basketmaking intertwine themselves to form a bond between generations:

> I told her where the best willows grew. After that I showed her how to strip the willow branches and how to trim and split sedge roots. Then I explained the different designs. . . . It took about a week for me to explain the basics. I talked. She listened. She never said a word, never asked questions until I was finished talking; then it was always the same thing. She would say, "Tell me about when you saw Sipie. Can you start with the part when you got to the house?" I would tell the story. . . . Then, and only then, would she ask something about baskets.
>
> (*Grand Avenue*, pp. 218-19)

To start her own basket, Alice ties a perfect knot on her first try, something that normally takes weeks for a beginner to accomplish. The story concludes on a note of optimism as Nellie sees a vision of "this girl named Alice singing sure as tomorrow" (*Grand Avenue*, p. 229).

Basketmaking and survival. From a literary standpoint, baskets function in *Grand Avenue* as metaphoric repositories of the Pomos' traditional culture. The metaphor is most clearly suggested when Nellie catches Sam Toms's powerful healing songs in her basket. Also basketmaking represents the weaving of a cultural fabric that can be passed on through the generations. Nellie repeatedly likens it to the telling of stories from the family's past, which she interweaves with her lessons to Alice. Basketmaking furthermore connects Nellie to the land where her clan once lived, the sacred "water place" on Santa Rosa Creek where sedge and willow—the basketmaker's materials—grow. The water place is where her animal helper, the green frog, dwells. From there it seeks Nellie out with the songs that she uses both in healing and in creating her basket designs.

Baskets and basketmaking have had a historical significance that corresponds to the literary prominence Sarris gives them in *Grand Avenue*. Before contact with the whites, Pomos, like other California Indians, used baskets for carrying, cooking, storage, processing plants into goods or food, trapping fish, and many other purposes. Yet the baskets' technical sophistication rose far above the level necessary for the people's mere material survival. Basketmaking was the major art form in Pomo culture, and more than one observer has ranked the Pomos' traditional baskets as the finest in the world. Pomos were the only native people in California who both coiled and twined their baskets, using a twining method (called lattice twining) that was itself unique among their neighbors. Pomo baskets ranged from the size of a pencil eraser to several feet in diameter and length. The most sophisticated baskets were made by women; men restricted themselves to simpler, more strictly functional patterns.

The role of this advanced art form did not end with the whites' arrival. Instead it was extended in new directions. Dispossessed of their lands and facing a flood of white settlers in the late nineteenth century, Pomos realized that their beautiful baskets were highly prized by white traders, who sold them to art collectors and museums. Baskets thus became the Pomos' most important resource for raising cash, with which some Pomo communities were able to purchase small pockets of land from the white settlers. Others traded baskets for food, as Sarris's adoptive aunt Mabel McKay remembers her own family members did to avoid starvation one particularly harsh winter. In the late nineteenth century some Pomo men learned the women's more sophisticated techniques so that they, too, could weave baskets to sell to white traders.

The traditional skills languished in the assimilationist atmosphere of the 1950s, and during the 1960s young Pomo activists tended to focus on political action more than cultural preservation. By the 1980s, however, the preservation of traditional culture had been embraced in the activists' agenda as part of the Native American Renaissance. Among the Pomos, a new generation of young weavers arose under the tutelage of Mabel McKay and others. This younger generation included women such as Susan Billy, who (recalling Alice's apprenticeship in *Grand Avenue*) learned the art from her great aunt, acclaimed basketmaker Elsie Allen (1899-1990). The Pomo women basketmakers had organized themselves politically by this time, waging campaigns to preserve the wetlands where their traditional materials of sedge and willow grow. In the 1990s a basketry revival was underway; Susan Billy and her generation, in turn, began teaching their own students. Pomo baskets fetched good prices not only from collectors but also from tourists, who flocked to northern California's popular wine country nearby. In retrospect, throughout the Pomos' history, the resilient art form of basketmaking has persevered as a primary means of material and cultural survival.

Sources and literary context. Sarris's own personal experience of Santa Rosa and its Pomo community constitutes the major source for *Grand Avenue*. Included in that experience, however, are memories that others, and especially Mabel McKay, have shared with him. Sarris's adoptive aunt clearly provided the inspiration for much of the character of Nellie Copaz, the only one of *Grand Avenue*'s narrators whose voice the reader hears in two stories. In *Mabel McKay: Weaving the Dream*, Sarris describes Mabel McKay in terms that have much in common with the fictional Nellie. Just as Nellie tells Alice stories about their family, so did Mabel McKay frequently tell the teenaged Sarris "stories about places and people she knew" (Sarris, *Mabel McKay*, p. 49). Sarris emphasizes how instrumental the stories were in giving him a sense of family and of being cared for—the same reassuring feelings that Nellie's stories offer Alice. Like Nellie, Mabel McKay was thought to possess supernatural healing powers that she linked to her basketmaking, much as Nellie does in the stories. Sarris describes both women as being sought out by others as healers.

A further detail concerning both Mabel McKay and her own mentor, a well known basketmaker and medicine woman named Essie Parrish, also found its way into *Grand Avenue*. Before Essie Parrish died in 1979, Sarris recounts, she predicted that rain, thunder, and lightning would occur on the day of her death. Although she died on a clear July day—when such weather is unusual in northern California—the sky darkened and the phenomena did indeed happen as foretold. According to a note at the end of *Mabel McKay*, rain and thunder also attended Mabel McKay's death in 1994. In the story "Secret Letters," the tale that Steven Pen tells his children concerns his great-grandmother, a powerful medicine woman whose death brought rain, thunder, and lightning.

By incorporating supernatural phenomena into his fiction, Sarris observes a tradition established by other contemporary Native American novelists such as James Welch and Scott Momaday, both considered founding authors of the Native American Renaissance's literary dimension. For example, in Welch's ***Fools Crow*** (1986; also in *Literature and Its Times*), the hero, a young Blackfeet warrior, encounters talking animals and experiences visions of the future. In Momaday's *The Ancient Child* (1989) the hero turns into a bear at the end of the novel. Critics have seen such departures from conventional realism, to which these and other native authors otherwise generally adhere, as reflecting a perception of reality in keeping with that of their ancestral traditions.

Reception. Two of the stories in *Grand Avenue* were previously published in anthologies, "How I Got to be Queen" in *Talking Leaves* (a 1991 collection of American Indian writing) and "Slaughterhouse" in *Best of the West Short Fiction* (1993). "Slaughterhouse" has proven especially popular among anthologists, and has since been included in at least three other collections.

Grand Avenue in its entirety was strongly acclaimed upon publication, with critics praising its closely observed detail, its unsentimental yet moving portrayals, and its persuasive evocation of a range of authentic narrative voices. Michael Dorris, at the time a leading American Indian writer himself, reviewed *Grand Avenue* together with *Mabel McKay* for the *Los Angeles Times Book Review*, calling them "a dazzling pair of books" that "vault Sarris's subjects—and the author himself—into brilliant, enduring relief" (Dorris, p. 2). Dorris praised *Grand Avenue*'s "vivid blend of street-smart toughness and traditional spirituality" as illuminating "the ways that poverty disrupts relationships, does violence to every social institution, [and] forges an anger that, unchecked, can erode even the impulse of human kindness" (Dorris, p. 2). Calling *Grand Avenue* "a gritty, power-filled book, unsparing and unapologetic," he wondered how Sarris is able to capture his disparate characters' voices so perfectly; the answer, he suggests, is that Sarris is "a master listener" (Dorris, p. 2).

—Colin Wells

For More Information

Cook, Sherburne F. *The Conflict Between the California Indian and White Civilization*. Berkeley: University of California Press, 1976.

———. *The Population of the California Indians 1769-1970*. Berkeley: University of California Press, 1974.

Dorris, Michael. "An Insider's Ear: Greg Sarris Captures the Complexity of Both His Fictional and Nonfictional Characters." *The Los Angeles Times Book Review*, 4 September 1994, p 2.

Heizer, Robert F., ed. *Handbook of the North American Indians*. Vol. 8. Washington, D.C.: Smithsonian, 1978.

Heizer, R. F., and M. A. Whipple. *The California Indians: A Sourcebook*. Berkeley: University of California Press, 1970.

Lincoln, Kenneth. *Native American Renaissance*. Berkeley: University of California Press, 1983.

Lobo, Susan, and Kurt Peters, eds. *American Indians and the Urban Experience*. Walnut Creek, Calif.: Altamira Press, 2001.

Sarris, Greg. *Grand Avenue*. New York: Penguin, 1995.

———. *Keeping Slug Woman Alive: A Holistic Approach to American Indian Texts*. Berkeley: University of California Press, 1993.

———. *Mabel McKay: Weaving the Dream*. Berkeley: University of California Press, 1994.

Trigger, Bruce G., and Wilcomb E. Washburn. *The Cambridge History of the Native Peoples of the Americas*. Vol. 1. Cambridge: Cambridge University Press, 2001.

Grendel

by
John Gardner

Born in Batavia, New York, in 1933, John Gardner suffered lifelong guilt over a fatal tractor accident that killed his younger brother in 1945; the 11-year-old John was at the wheel of the vehicle when his brother, riding in back, fell under its cultipacker, a heavy device designed to crush earth. As an adult, Gardner maintained that "art begins in a wound," and before he himself died in a motorcycle accident in 1982, he published a number of works that sought to heal or at least ease the "wound inherent in the nature of life itself" (Gardner, *On Moral Fiction*, p. 181). Gardner firmly believed in art's ability to shape human experience, for good or ill. In his essay *On Moral Fiction,* Gardner scolds his contemporary novelists for abdicating their responsibility to produce moral art. Though a poet and a critic as well, Gardner became known mainly for his novels, of which *Grendel* was the third (after *The Resurrection*, 1966 and *The Wreckage of Agathon*, 1970). He would go on to produce more novels, but *Grendel,* which addresses some of the searching philosophical questions of Gardner's age, would remain his most enduring. In effect, the novel lets life's inherent wound speak for itself in the brutally cynical voice of a murderous monster, a fiend borrowed from an epic poem who distrusts and fears poetry's power to comfort and create.

THE LITERARY WORK

A novel set in sixth-century Denmark; published in 1971.

SYNOPSIS

The monster Grendel tells the story of his life, focusing on his alienation from his mother, his war against King Hrothgar's Danes, his conversation with an existentialist dragon, and his fatal fight with the Scandinavian hero Beowulf.

Events in History at the Time of the Novel

The Dark Ages. Gardner based the main characters and some of the incidents in *Grendel* on material from the Old English epic ***Beowulf*** (also in *Literature and Its Times*). The monster Grendel, the novel's protagonist and narrator, is a man-eating humanoid who preys on the followers of Hrothgar, the sixth-century king of a Danish tribe known as the Scyldings. The hero-savior Beowulf, a Geat from what is now southern Sweden, comes to Denmark to rid the Danes of the menace, and succeeds. Grendel becomes the first of three monsters that Beowulf slays by the end of the poem.

The exact date of *Beowulf*'s composition is uncertain, with estimates ranging from the late seventh century to around 1000 C.E., around the time the sole surviving manuscript copy of the poem was written. Whatever the precise date, *Beowulf* was composed in the early Middle Ages, a period popularly known as the Dark Ages. The latter term describes the relatively impoverished state of our knowledge about the Dark Ages; the term also offers a value judgment about the

John Gardner

period, seen to have lost or squandered many of the achievements of prior antiquity.

Convention holds that the Dark Ages began with the fall of Christian Rome to Germanic invaders in the late fifth century. In the years that followed, the European classical civilization inherited from the ancient Roman Empire suffered lasting setbacks. Several former Roman colonies, including Celtic Britain and Gaul, were abandoned to Germanic invaders, many of whom—including the Angles and Saxons who immigrated to England in the fifth century—were pagans. By the time *Beowulf* was written down, the Anglo-Saxons had converted to Christianity and learned how to read and write using the Roman alphabet. For many regions of the former Roman Empire, however, the Dark Ages was a period in which literacy and learning went into a serious decline, urban populations dwindled, and the Mediterranean-based economy entered a long period of struggle and slow recovery.

Germanic society. While the place and date of *Beowulf*'s composition remain uncertain, historical references within the poem date its events to mainland Europe in the sixth century C.E. At that time, the Germanic immigrants to England, where *Beowulf* was written down, still retained the pagan beliefs of their continental cousins. They also shared much more than beliefs with the pagan Scandinavians—Hrothgar's Danes and Beowulf's Geats—who are the focus of the poem. Besides speaking related languages, the pagan English and the Scandinavians shared a heroic culture in which societal loyalty centered on the *comitatus*, a band of warrior-retainers (known in England as thanes) who pledged to serve their chieftain or king in return for generous gifts. As described in the poem, the elite, militaristic, and masculine world of the *comitatus* prizes honor, rewards courage, and demands loyalty. When not engaged in battle, warriors gather to drink in large wooden halls where they listen to poetic tales about warlike exploits and make boastful pledges of their future deeds of valor.

The Anglo-Saxons and the Vikings. The shared origins of the insular English and the continental Scandinavians may account for the puzzling fact that the greatest poem of the Christian Anglo-Saxons describes the deeds of pagan Scandinavians. In the late eighth century, those Scandinavians began to attack and raid the English seacoasts, in the process earning a new name: the Vikings. Eventually, some of these Viking raiders settled in England, establishing a permanent presence in the northeast of the country and very nearly conquering all of the English tribal kingdoms. If *Beowulf* was written down in the Viking Age, the poem's interest in continental Scandinavians may reflect the arrival of Scandinavian settlers within England itself. In any case, the Old English epic, like Gardner's novel, directs its attention backward in time, scrutinizing the fantastic events of a pagan past for an understanding of its contemporary world.

The Novel in Focus

The plot. *Grendel* takes place during the last year of the monster's life, during which Grendel reflects on important episodes from his past (some of these are adapted from *Beowulf*, but most are Gardner's invention). With the coming of spring, Grendel feels the return of his anger toward the human race. Grendel claims that his own feelings are as mechanical as all the natural processes he observes, from the budding of plants to the mindless progression of the sun and other stars. Standing at the edge of a cliff, Grendel says, "once again I am aware of my potential: I could die" (Gardner, *Grendel*, p. 5). He screams at the abyss to seize him, knowing full well that the inanimate chasm cannot claim him unless he elects to jump. He chooses to go on living.

Depressed, Grendel heads down a forest path to Hart Hall, where he has for 12 years killed the thanes of the Danish king Hrothgar. On the way, Grendel thinks of his mother, an ancient hag who has lost the power of speech and who could never answer the young Grendel's existential question, "Why are we here?" Grendel then mentions "the old dragon, calm as winter" who later "unveiled the truth" to him, but he does not yet discuss the dragon's truth (*Grendel*, p. 6). Instead, Grendel once more assaults Hrothgar's thanes, killing many before leaving to eat them in peace. Lurking where he can see and hear the survivors, Grendel scoffs at their religious rites and their "theories," yet the solace they take in these rites and theories infuriates him. His scorn turns to rage when the human community finds comfort in the cremation ritual. A large group of men and women sing in unison, "as if by some lunatic theory they had won," and the solitary, angry monster retreats to his den, clawing at himself (*Grendel*, p. 9).

Grendel then recalls an episode from his childhood, when he first emerged from his underground den through a pool of firesnakes to explore the surface world of moonlight, forest animals, and human beings. Then still a child, Grendel clung to the belief that he and his mother were one thing, a part of each other, but an accident during one of his night forays into the woods shattered this childish belief in connectedness. While following the scent of a newborn calf, the young Grendel caught his foot in the space between two tree trunks. Dangling in air, wracked with pain, he cried in vain for his mother, without whom (he thought) the world lacked order. With the coming of sunrise, the unfamiliar light of morning hurt the nocturnal Grendel's eyes, and the monster's daytime vulnerability exposed him to the assaults of a bull that sallied forth to protect the calf. The bull attacked Grendel repeatedly, instinctively, prompting Grendel to laugh at the mechanical stupidity of an animal that acts so mindlessly: "I understood that the world was nothing: a mechanical chaos of casual, brute enmity on which we stupidly impose our hopes and fears. I understood that, finally and absolutely, I alone exist" (*Grendel*, p. 16).

Eventually, the bull left and Grendel fell asleep. When he woke that night, he saw men for the first time. The Danish king Hrothgar and a few of his thanes stood before Grendel, trying to figure out what he was. Grendel understood their speech as a version of his own language, but when he tried to speak to the Danes, it frightened them into violence. Just in time, Grendel's mother arrived to rescue him from what he recognized to be "thinking creatures, pattern makers, the most dangerous things [he had] ever met" (*Grendel*, p. 21). Despite her well-timed rescue, Grendel's childhood faith in his connection with his mother was shattered by his mishaps with the bull and the men. The bull's instinctive attacks had introduced Grendel to the mindless violence of the universe. The Danes, though thinking beings, had connected ideas in a way that produced mistaken conclusions about him, which had taught him the limits of reason to explain reality. Back in his underground den, Grendel tried to express his disillusionment to his mother, but she failed to understand him. This failure confirmed the young Grendel's sense of his separation from his mother. His continued speculations led to the despairing realization that his life was empty and devoid of meaningful connections to the universe he observed.

In the present again, the adult Grendel begins to explain how he came to wage his "war" against Hrothgar, now in its twelfth year. He describes earlier fights between rival bands of Danes; the construction of halls and larger settlements; and thanes' exaggerated boasts threatening violence against their foes. The younger Grendel at first doubted that these threats were serious, but he then came upon a gruesome scene of carnage: a wrecked hall in which the people had been burned to death, animals had been killed in their pens, and nothing had been eaten, though all the gold had vanished. The younger Grendel later overheard heroic verses sung by a court poet or "Scop" (pronounced shope, meaning a "maker" or poet), but where the human audience listened to "the glorious deeds of dead kings," Grendel heard chronicles of violence and plunder (*Grendel*, p. 29).

Sickened by the thought that he is related to these wastefully warlike people, Grendel observed their battles for years until Hrothgar developed a theory of warfare. Thereafter, Hrothgar sought not to destroy his nearest neighbors but to make them allies, and he organized a group of tribes into a powerful coalition that thrived on tribute. Hrothgar soon became the most powerful Danish leader, his power bringing about the wasteful destruction of wildlife as well as the murder of people. Then a blind Scop arrived at Hrothgar's hall and began to sing a heroic poem—in fact, the opening lines of *Beowulf*. He offered, for a price, to sing more heroic poems, about Hrothgar. To Grendel's amazement, the Scop's poetry somehow made even Hrothgar's cruelty "seem true and very fine" (*Grendel*, p. 36). Shocked, Grendel realized that the Shaper had changed the world with his lies, because those "who knew the truth, remembered it his way," preferring the falsehoods of poetry to the truth of their own experience (*Grendel*, p. 36). The stars that had previously seemed "mindless" to Grendel were now "alive with the promise of Hrothgar's vast power, his universal peace" (*Grendel*, p. 37). Grendel ran away from the hall then, a "ridiculous hairy creature torn apart by poetry," and he shrieked wordlessly before fleeing on all fours (*Grendel*, pp. 37-38).

Returning to the present again, Grendel considers the old Scop, 12 years after that first meeting with Hrothgar. The Scop's vision of a grand hall has come true in Hrothgar's construction of Hart, a hall whose glory has given way to the horror of Grendel's attacks. Grendel remembers his earliest reflections on the Shaper's art, an art that seemed to make the best of bad situations, to present "the projected possible," a vision of beauty (*Grendel*, p. 42). Once while approaching the human dwellings, Grendel found the corpse of a murder victim, which he hugged close to himself as he listened to the Shaper's song of creation (closely modeled on a passage from *Beowulf*).

> [The Scop said] that the Almighty created the earth,
> a bright and shining plain, by seas embraced,
> and set, triumphantly, the sun and moon
> to light their beams for those who dwell on land,
> adorned the distant corners of the world
> with leaves and branches, and made life also,
> all manner of creatures that live and move.
>
> (*Beowulf*, lines 92-98)

> [The Scop] said that the greatest of gods made the world, every wonder-bright plain and the turning seas, and set out as signs of his victory the sun and moon, great lamps for light to land-dwellers, kingdom torches, and adorned the fields with all colors and shapes, made limbs and leaves and gave life to the every creature that moves on land.
>
> (*Grendel*, p. 43)

As the Scop continued to perform, Grendel was surprised to learn that, according to the song, he and his mother stemmed from an accursed race, the evil twin of humanity. Still clutching the corpse, his proof that both races are cursed, Grendel stumbled into the human crowd to beg for mercy and peace, crying out "Friend! Friend!" But the terrified people tried to kill him, and an enraged Grendel lashed out murderously (*Grendel*, p. 44). He retreated to his cave, bothered by the thought that poetry might actually create seeming truths out of half-truths and falsehood, but he was also disturbed by his encroaching sense of an older, darker intelligence, one that insisted even more than he did on the "mindless, mechanical bruteness of things" (*Grendel*, p. 46). Clearing his mind, Grendel felt himself falling, sinking mysteriously "like a stone through earth and sea" toward this threatening presence (*Grendel*, p. 48). The dark intelligence he encountered was that of a dragon who quotes the French existentialist philosopher Jean Paul Sartre and who might be nothing more than a figment of Grendel's imagination (Howell, pp. 68-69). Figment or no, the dragon and his bleak logic will continue to grip Grendel until his final days.

The dragon is an ancient cynic lounging on his treasure hoard, who claims to know everything throughout all time. In this, he resembles the wizard Merlin, Arthur's adviser, in another updated medieval tale, T. H. White's ***The Once and Future King*** (1958; also in *Literature and Its Times*), but the dragon lacks Merlin's benevolence. He bullies Grendel with a philosophical harangue that aims to show Grendel the folly of human thought, which struggles to form connections between isolated, paltry facts. To the dragon, human beings live by nonsense, and the Shaper's inspiring vision merely "[p]rovides an illusion of reality . . . with a gluey whine of connectedness" (*Grendel*, p. 55). The dragon insists that the universe is governed by chance, "accident on accident," but Grendel still seeks a reason for his own actions, in particular for his continuing to terrify human beings (*Grendel*, p. 60). The dragon scoffs at any sense of purpose. However, he does acknowledge that Grendel's attacks on people "drive them to poetry, science, religion, all that makes them what they are for as long as they last"; Grendel is "the brute existent by which they learn to define themselves," though Grendel is by no means unique as a brute being (*Grendel*, p. 62). Both humanity and Grendel remain irrelevant, and the dragon's final advice before Grendel departs is "to seek out gold and sit on it" (*Grendel*, p. 63). The dragon even admits to the inconsequence of this goal when he describes his own treasure of rubies, emeralds, gold, and silver as "boobies, hemorrhoids, boils, slaver" (*Grendel*, pp. 50, 60).

After his encounter with the dragon, the younger Grendel feels a lingering aura of futility.

To compound his frustration, he finds himself invulnerable to weapons, apparently owing to a charm put on him by the dragon. He discovers his invulnerability when one of Hrothgar's guards attacks him outside Hart Hall, and that guard becomes the first victim in Grendel's so-called war on Hrothgar. Briefly, Grendel finds purpose in his new role as "Ruiner of Meadhalls, Wrecker of Kings," but he is also more alone than ever, and in the middle of one bloody raid he suddenly feels his ravages to be as meaningless and mechanical as everything else in the universe (*Grendel*, p. 69).

Early on in Grendel's war, Hrothgar's thane Unferth challenges the monster with proud, warlike boasts. Grendel wickedly pummels him with both apples and insults before leaving the hapless Dane to his indignity. To Grendel's great surprise, Unferth tracks Grendel to his lair, where the thane is determined to defeat Grendel or die trying. To his chagrin, neither happens: Unferth is too exhausted from his journey to be a threat, and Grendel refuses to grant him the heroic satisfaction of being another victim. Grendel returns to Hart Hall carrying the spent but living Unferth, then makes sure to kill two guards lest he be "misunderstood" (*Grendel*, p. 78). For the next 12 years of his war on Hrothgar, Grendel continues to spare Unferth among many other doomed Danes, and Unferth's bitter shame acts as Grendel's retort to "the alternative visions of blind old poets and dragons" that the human struggle with adversity can create heroes and make meaning (*Grendel*, p. 78).

Momentarily interrupting his memories to return to the novel's present, Grendel reflects that he has "not committed the ultimate act of nihilism" (a philosophy that holds there is no value or meaning to human life). This ultimate act would be the murder of Hrothgar's queen, Wealtheow, and it is still on his mind (*Grendel*, p. 81). The monster thinks back once more to the second year of his war, when Wealtheow became Hrothgar's queen. She joined Hrothgar as the gift of her brother Hygmod, lord of the Helmings, a rival chieftain who surrendered her rather than face destruction by an army of Scyldings and their allies. Grendel could hardly bear to witness the innocent beauty, Wealtheow, handed over to old Hrothgar, but he did not intervene in the exchange.

Later, seeing Queen Wealtheow receive her brother and a Helming band as guests at Hart Hall, Grendel was again tormented by the possibility that meaning, even so tenuous a meaning as "quality of life," could be based on an absurdity, in this case "the idea of a queen" (*Grendel*, pp. 93-94); in his rage, Grendel very nearly killed Wealtheow in order to disprove the idea and its illusory meaning. Grendel ultimately spared her because "[i]t would be meaningless, killing her. As meaningless as letting her live" (*Grendel*, p. 95). Human beings may still believe in their theories and patterns, but henceforth Grendel has no illusions.

Grendel next relates the arrival at Hart Hall of Hrothgar's nephew Hrothulf, then recently orphaned, who accepted the hospitality of his uncle even while plotting to rebel against him (a plot alluded to, but never directly discussed, in *Beowulf*). Grendel shadows Hrothulf as the young man takes counsel with the aged peasant Red Horse, who urges violent revolution to topple the government because he believes that all systems, including all governments, are evil—"*Monstrously* evil" (*Grendel*, p. 104). Hrothulf argues that he would use violence only to promote greater freedom, but Red Horse considers universal justice a laughable idea. Grendel muses on the numerous dangers that threaten Hrothgar, including the promise of Hrothulf's eventual treachery, but he feels no pity for the old king and is determined to continue his war on the Scyldings. Convinced that his own raids have made Hrothgar noble, Grendel invokes a god's privilege to ask, "Have I not a right to test my own creation?" (*Grendel*, p. 107). Grendel is painfully aware of his own indignity as a mechanical being, but he cannot shake the feeling that "[s]omething is bound to come of all this. I cannot believe such monstrous energy of grief can lead to nothing!" (*Grendel*, p. 107).

The next human system to face Grendel's scorn is religion. Grendel shares Red Horse's view that "Religion is sick," and late one December night he sits musing within the circle of idols, carved in stone and wood, that serve the Scyldings as gods. An old, blind priest named Ork arrives unexpectedly, and Grendel impishly pretends to be one of the Scylding's gods, the Destroyer they beseech for protection against Grendel. Grendel asks Ork what he knows about the King of the Gods, and Ork gives a complicated account of both the King of the Gods and the nature of evil. Before Grendel can puzzle out Ork's speeches, a trio of other priests approach. Grendel hides before they spot him, and he listens to the four priests argue about whether Ork had a vision and what it would mean if he did. A fifth priest, younger and exuberant, shows up and celebrates the granting of a fantastic vision to the rationalist Ork. Put off by their priestly prattle, Grendel retreats. Restlessly he awaits the end of winter.

The days lengthen, the Shaper falls deathly ill, and Grendel hears some news: an old Scylding woman mentions "a giant across the sea who has the strength of thirty thanes" (*Grendel*, p. 124). Grendel dismisses her talk as lies told to children, but the giant she describes is none other than the man Beowulf (unnamed in the novel), who will soon arrive to face the monster. Back in his lair, Grendel's mother mutters incoherent warnings—"Warovvish"—and tries to keep her son at home, but Grendel ignores her and exits to watch the Scop's funeral (*Grendel*, p. 127). Afterwards, Grendel returns to the tedium of his life in winter, a tedium interrupted only by the sense of "restless expectation" that dogs him (*Grendel*, p. 130). He hears a groan "far out at sea" and understands his mother's warning: "*Beware the fish*" (*Grendel*, p. 130). But he does not connect this warning with the coming of the giant man from across the sea.

Then, despite the icebergs that still choke the water, ships arrive on the Danish coast, bearing a company of Geatish warriors. Grendel watches as the men disembark, and he is impressed by the sheer size of them, particularly of their leader, the unnamed Beowulf. Beowulf tells Hrothgar's coast guard that he has come to give the king advice about his enemy, and the enemy, Grendel, knows that Beowulf's "advice" is battle. Grendel cannot decide whether he fears this imposing Geat, but he decides to attack Hart Hall as usual. First, though, Grendel spies on the hall as the Danes, sitting sullen with wounded pride, join the Geats in drink. When Unferth chooses to insult Beowulf, Beowulf calmly answers the offense by humiliating Unferth as the murderer of his own brothers. Hereafter no Danes challenge the Geats. Grendel grows more afraid of the Geatish visitor, yet strangely eager to face him in combat, if only to relieve the winter's tedium.

Once the Danes and Geats have gone to sleep, Grendel bursts in on the hall. He swiftly kills and eats one sleeping fighter, but the second man he targets fights back, catching his arm in a ferocious grip. Shocked by the pain, Grendel faces his attacker, Beowulf, and has a vision of the man as a dragon with flickering eyes and "terrible fiery wings" (*Grendel*, p. 148). Grendel clears his head of this illusion, but he cannot block out the steady stream of words that Beowulf mutters at his ear; to Grendel's hearing, they repeat the dragon's words on the meaningless formation of matter and complexity. Beowulf tells Grendel: "You make the world by whispers, second by second," then he smashes Grendel's head into a wall and forces him to "sing of walls!" that is, to transform his brute experience through art (*Grendel*, p. 150). Beowulf insists on the mind's power to shape reality; Grendel thinks he is crazy, but must sing as he is told. Then, without warning, Beowulf rips Grendel's arm out of its socket; Grendel manages to escape the hall, but he can feel death's approach. He tries to concentrate on what he believes is the accidental nature of his defeat, on the mechanical operation of a universe that follows the "logic of chance." He once more teeters before an abyss, surrounded this time by animals that have come to watch him die, and he wonders: "*Is it joy I feel?*" He whispers a final message to the beasts around him: "Poor Gren-

A MATTER OF PERSPECTIVE

Written from the point-of-view of man, not monster, the poem *Beowulf* describes the end of the Danes' happiness in Heorot at the onset of Grendel's attacks:

—Thus this lordly people lived in joy,
blessedly, until one began
to work his foul crimes—a fiend from hell.
This grim spirit was called Grendel,
mighty stalker of the marches, who held
the moors and fens; this miserable man
lived for a time in the land of giants,
after the Creator had condemned him
among Cain's race

(*Beowulf*, lines 99-107a)

Here the poem describes Grendel's final attack on Heorot:

Then from the moor, in a blanket of mist,
Grendel came stalking—he bore God's anger;
the evil marauder meant to ensnare
some of human-kind in that high hall.
. . .
[H]e seized at once at his first pass
a sleeping man, slit him open suddenly,
bit into his joints, drank the blood from his veins,
gobbled his flesh in gobbets, and soon
had completely devoured that dead man,
feet and fingertips.

(*Beowulf*, lines 740-45; lines 710-13)

A young protestor confronts the National Guard during a 1968 demonstration in Chicago.

del's had an accident. *So may you all*" (*Grendel*, p. 152).

Monstrous society. In Hrothulf's conversation with Red Horse about revolution, Gardner goes further than usual in inventing material not found in his sources. In addition to expanding the role of a secondary character (here Hrothgar's nephew Hrothulf), Gardner has created a new character in the old, rebellious peasant. Their dialogue has no counterpart whatsoever in *Beowulf*, and this conversation between human beings is one of the few such scenes that Grendel overhears. What he hears is notable indeed, for the human-hating monster hears a human being describe all systems and governments as "evil. Not just a trifle evil. *Monstrously* evil" (*Grendel*, p. 104).

In his unflinching opposition to all governments, Red Horse is happy to support Hrothulf's wishes to oust Hrothgar, but he has no enthusiasm for the establishment of a new regime. Indeed, Red Horse rejects the idea that any state could offer real freedom to its citizens, and his rejection of all systems goes so far as to deny the existence of what he laughingly calls "Universal Justice" (*Grendel*, p. 104). Red Horse plays the role of the dragon to Hrothulf, who can likewise be seen as a naïve young Grendel, still hopeful that actions can make a difference in the world. That the monster is a silent onlooker to this conversation suggests how ready human society is to adopt the poisonous views of a monstrous leader who threatens a violent end to society. As narrator, Grendel reports this conversation to the reader with almost none of his usual, editorializing commentary; this suggests that he tacitly endorses the destructive violence of Red Horse's beliefs.

As indicated by Red Horse's dialogue, *Grendel* is a largely philosophical novel. Taking place many centuries ago, the novel explores contemporary ideas even more than it reflects contemporary events, though Gardner playfully includes some deliberate anachronisms that encourage us to identify sixth-century Scandinavia with late-twentieth-century America. Early in the novel, Grendel describes his nighttime forays: "I move through the darkness, burning with murderous lust, my brains raging at the sickness I can observe in myself as objectively as might a mind ten centuries away" (*Grendel,* pp. 5-6). "Ten centuries away" effectively bridges the gap between the composition of *Beowulf* and the modern era. Later, the dragon refers to Grendel as "a creature of the Dark Ages" but then qualifies his statement: "Not that one age is darker than another. Technical jargon from another dark age" (*Grendel,* p. 58). Gardner thereby highlights his method of using material from the past Dark Ages to address the darkness of his own era. Even so, *Grendel* is no simple allegory, and the novel's correspondences between past and present are more suggestive than straightforward.

Red Horse opposes all government as a matter of principle. Opposition to the policies of the United States government was pronounced and vocal during the late 1960s and early 1970s, especially as the war in Vietnam dragged on, and some of Red Horse's anti-establishment sentiments found echoes in the voices of Gardner's contemporaries. Nevertheless, few of the protestors and radicals of Gardner's day would have subscribed to the destructive nihilism of Red Horse. Though militant groups such as the Black Panthers and the Weathermen may have advocated and even resorted to violent confrontation with authority figures, these groups also had political platforms to promote and ideological agendas to pursue. Red Horse's extreme anarchism thus distances him from most political movements that advocated violence in Gardner's day (though Red Horse's name is suggestive of communism, given the fact that communists were pejoratively known as "Reds"). Instead, Red Horse's distrust of all systems brings to mind a variety of so-called counterculture groups that challenged both "the establishment"—those wielding power, especially the government and its perceived allies in the business world—and society's conventions. In both eras, disillusionment with the established authority gives rise to a desire to foment violence, though for Red Horse violence is its own end with no pretense for real political or social betterment. If, by contrast, violence occasionally marked the civil rights and antiwar movements that were part of the counterculture in Gardner's America, this violence occurred within a broader pursuit of justice.

The Scandinavians in Gardner's novel live in a monocultural and largely homosocial society that has little place for the struggles that gripped Gardner's own diverse America, which was experiencing protests, riots, and political battles over civil rights for African Americans, justice for American Indians, and equal rights for women. At the same time, Red Horse's poverty, explicitly noted by Grendel himself, draws attention to the inequity that can be found within even the most homogeneous of societies. Red Horse's depressed socioeconomic status and his criticism of the government that cannot (or will not) support him recall the difficulties and the frustrations faced by the disenfranchised of other times and other places, even if his violent wishes offer little hope of real political change or social justice.

Literary sources. *Grendel*'s most important literary context is the medieval poem *Beowulf*. The influence of *Beowulf*'s Old English verse partly accounts for the poetic effects of Gardner's prose.

His novel presumes some familiarity with *Beowulf* yet nowhere mentions Beowulf's name. Gardner's updated treatment of a medieval poem followed the extremely popular second edition of J. R. R. Tolkien's fantasy trilogy, *The Lord of the Rings* (also in the *Literature and Its Times*). Tolkien's novels drew heavily on his background as a professor of medieval European literature, and Gardner used his own training as a medievalist both to offer a revisionist interpretation of a medieval classic and to comment obliquely on his own time.

Perhaps the best contemporary context for Gardner's sympathetic treatment of Grendel is provided by other works that turned their attention to neglected or secondary figures from literary history. Jean Rhys's novel ***Wide Sargasso Sea*** (also in *Literature and Its Times*), published in 1966, provided a history and a voice for Rochester's mad Creole wife in Charlotte Brontë's *Jane Eyre*. Published this same year, Tom Stoppard's play ***Rosencrantz and Guildenstern Are Dead*** (also in *Literature and Its Times*) explored the relationship and reflections of Hamlet's two doomed schoolmates from Shakespeare's tragedy. Compared with these minor characters, the

ANGLO-SAXON POETRY

From time to time, Gardner imitates the language of his source, the Old English epic *Beowulf.* Old English poetry is highly formalized, using alliteration to link stressed words in each line of verse. It also employs a specialized poetic vocabulary that delights in using synonymous phrases. When Grendel identifies himself as a "shadow-shooter, earth-rim-roamer, walker of the world's weird wall," he uses the modern English of Gardner's day to speak a prose variety of Old English phrases (*Grendel*, pp. 2-3). Several of the Scop's songs are direct translations from passages in *Beowulf,* and even the pathetic Unferth manages an alliterative boast: For many months, unsightly monster, you've murdered men as you pleased in Hrothgar's hall. Unless you can murder me as you've murdered lesser men, I give you my word those days are done forever! (*Grendel,* p. 72).

monster Grendel plays a prominent role in *Beowulf*, but in each case the writer presents an alternative point of view, speaking to the relative open-mindedness of the era in which all three works were written. Gardner's novel allows Grendel to evaluate humanity, showing the solitary monster to be a thoughtful and articulate critic of the human society of his victims.

Grendel's first-person narration includes wild shifts in register and deliberate anachronisms, frequently comments on itself (a technique known as metafiction or metanarrative), and at times veers into the third person to incorporate such diverse genres as poetry and drama. These departures from straightforward narrative techniques also place *Grendel* alongside other experimental works of fiction by such contemporaries as John Barth (*Lost in the Funhouse*, 1968) and William Gass (e.g., *Willie Masters' Lonesome Wife*, 1968).

Events in History at the Time the Novel Was Written

Philosophy: Sartre vs. Whitehead. Gardner liked to describe himself as a philosophical novelist, though not a philosopher; he preferred to set conflicting ideas against each other in the dramatic contests of characters within a narrative. Taking philosophy very seriously, the novelist deliberately fashioned his own art as a corrective to what he considered to be mistaken or dangerous beliefs. In Gardner's view, one symptom of his age's darkness was the continued popularity of existentialism, a philosophy that insisted on the absurdity of an existence that has no innate meaning or order. Existentialism had developed chiefly in France during and after World War II; one of its chief theorizers was the philosopher and author Jean Paul Sartre (1905-80), who argued that, in the absence of universal values, every person shapes his or her own values and creates individual meaning. Coming of age after World War II, Gardner at first found himself attracted to existentialism, particularly as developed by Sartre in works that Gardner admired for their literary qualities. In time, however, Gardner came to reject the nihilistic tendencies of Sartre's philosophy, preferring to endorse the power of art and human "connectedness" to create positive meaning in life.

Gardner borrowed the idea of "organic connectedness" from Alfred North Whitehead (1861-1947), a British philosopher whom Gardner championed against Sartre. Though best known for his early mathematical work, notably the *Principia Mathematica* (1910, written in collaboration with Bertrand Russell), Whitehead later developed a metaphysics that he called "the philosophy of organism." Whereas Sartre's existentialism starts from an isolated individual and looks outward, Whitehead's philosophy of organism starts with an integrated universe and locates the individual through its relations with the larger universe. Though Gardner cleverly stacks Whitehead's philosophy of organism against Sartre's existentialism, Whitehead himself reacted not so much against existentialism (whose popularity flowered after Whitehead's death) as against other materialistic trends current in early twentieth-century science and philosophy. Whitehead rejected the stark materialist view of the universe as a conglomeration of meaningless matter subject to external forces; instead, he insisted on the essential relatedness of all things, a relatedness that conveyed a purpose to be realized not in brute matter but in unfolding events, in processes of becoming that could be compared with artistic creation.

In *Grendel,* Gardner quotes or paraphrases both Sartre and Whitehead, attributing their views and their very words to the dragon and the Scop, respectively. In large measure, the novel describes the development and hardening of Grendel's own affiliation with Sartre's attitudes, beginning with his realization that he and his mother are not connected and continuing with his acceptance of the dragon's assertion that facts only exist in isolation. Against the example of the solitary monster, whose steady soliloquies attest to his friendlessness, the novel holds out the promise of the human capacity to forge meaningful connections not just between persons but between facts, so as to accrue knowledge, guide society, and create art. Gardner is not naïve about the dangers of certain kinds of connection between persons or ideas, and his novel depicts many examples of human cruelty and stupidity. Nevertheless, he endorses the principle that art and connectedness can work to create meaning, be it virtuous or vicious, as opposed to the isolation of existentialism.

The Cold War and Vietnam. While relatively few of Gardner's contemporaries debated the philosophies of Sartre and Whitehead with his enthusiasm, the entire world focused on the political struggle between the United States and the Soviet Union. The finer points of the ideological conflict between the American and Soviet political and economic systems have no direct counterparts in *Grendel*, but the novel's interest in political conflicts and military alliances echoes the alignment of other nations, after World War II, with either the United States or the Soviet Union, as both sides sought to extend their own spheres of influence while containing their opponent. Grendel observes a similar phenomenon as he watches the frequent battles between rival bands of Scandinavian warriors. Only after Hrothgar has organized various tribes into a confederation of allies does an uneasy peace emerge, better described as a stalemate between Hrothgar's tribe and its erstwhile foes. The cessation of armed conflict does not mean the advent of peaceful relations based on trust, however, and the threatening truce between Hrothgar and his brother-in-law Hygmod recalls the tense peace of the Cold War.

Although the Americans and Soviets avoided direct military action against each other, the American effort to counter the spread of communism in southeast Asia did lead to the deadliest American conflict since the Civil War, the undeclared war in Vietnam. Since the 1950s, American presidents had dispatched United States military "advisers" (used as a euphemism for troops, such as helicopter pilots) to South Vietnam to combat the communist Viet Cong forces loyal to the North Vietnamese leader Ho Chi Minh. The American military presence in Vietnam escalated as the conflict persisted, contributing to brutal fighting that resulted in high casualties (more than 58,000 U.S. dead; more than 937,000 communists dead). Among other wartime atrocities, American forces massacred civilians in the village of My Lai in March 1968. Thanks to the extensive coverage of the war in the news media, many in the United States could see for themselves horrific scenes of wartime violence. While *Grendel* nowhere makes a direct, anachronistic reference to Vietnam, it is hard not to hear echoes of the conflict that raged as the novel was being written. Its own descriptions of the cruelty and violence of the raids inflicted by various Danish tribes on each other reverberate through the centuries to those between the Vietnamese factions and their separate allies, with both conflicts involving equally gruesome brutality. Even the monster Grendel recoils in horror and disbelief at the evidence of human destructiveness in war (*Grendel,* p. 30). Some of Grendel's distaste for war may in fact reflect the pacifist wishes of contemporary peaceniks, though the novel's criticisms of war and governments are too broad to provide an endorsement of the specific ideological positions of any one group opposed to America's involvement in Vietnam.

Environmentalism. In another respect, Grendel's opposition to warfare better reflects contemporary environmental movements. Grendel mainly objects to human warfare for its sheer wastefulness, both of human lives and of natural resources. Contemporary environmental activists and conservationists focused on human responsibility for environmental problems; accordingly all the images of ecological harm in *Grendel* stem from human actions. Though Grendel himself chronicles a number of destructive practices related to the expansion of human settlements, the most shocking images of environmental calamity come in the prophetic speeches of the dragon. He conjures up images of eventual apocalypse, describing "[a] sea of black oil and dead things" amidst a "silent universe"—a universe silenced "accidentally" by human beings (*Grendel,* p. 61). These bleak landscapes invoke both the grim forecasts of nuclear destruction and actual environmental disasters.

The nuclear threat had come frighteningly near to reality during the 1962 American-Soviet standoff known as the Cuban missile crisis. Though that crisis was averted, lingering concerns over nuclear warfare helped lead to the Treaty on the Non-proliferation of Nuclear Weapons, signed on July 1, 1968, by three nuclear powers—the United States, the Soviet Union, and the United Kingdom—and 59 other states. In January of the next year, an environmental crisis struck when an accident involving an oil rig off the Santa Barbara coast caused a massive oil spill. The resulting oil slick spread for hundreds of square miles in the ocean, clotted tens of miles of coastline, and killed thousands of birds along with much other sea and shore life. This real "sea of black oil and dead things" was less drastic than the dragon's vision of the future extinction of all life on earth, but its consequences were no less final for the animals that perished. Gardner's dragon goes on to consider the death not only of individual animals but of entire species. Foretelling his own death at Beowulf's hands, the dragon remarks: "A terrible pity—loss of a remarkable form of life. Conservationists will howl" (*Grendel,* p. 60). The existentialist dragon pooh-poohs his own extinction as "meaningless," but American conservationists had won political support in 1966 with the passage of the Endangered Species Act. The first celebration of Earth Day took place 15 months after the Santa Barbara oil spill, in April 1970; in that same year, Congress created the Environmental Protection Agency, and the Nuclear Non-Proliferation Treaty took effect.

The space race. The rivalry between the Soviet Union and the United States extended beyond military actions that threatened life on earth to cultural and scientific contests with a scope beyond the earth. Surely the most dramatic and well publicized of American-Soviet contests was the space race. The Soviets early on led in the development of satellites and spacecraft, launching the first artificial satellite, Sputnik, in 1957 and the first manned orbiter in 1961. But only the American space program successfully sent astronauts to the moon and back, beginning with the Apollo 11 lunar mission of July 1969 and continuing through the early 1970's. Gardner's dragon belittles such extravagant accomplishments when he disparages technology and derides human theories, with their "here-to-the-moon-and-back lists of paltry facts" (*Grendel,* p. 55). Though this phrase recalls medieval conceptions of the so-called sublunary region, the area of existence from the earth to the moon that was subject to change, the importance of the 1969 moonshot and subsequent lunar missions also registers in the dragon's words, showing just how much the dragon disdains human achievement.

Reception. Though not a bestseller, *Grendel* was widely reviewed, earning Gardner his first major critical success as a novelist. Even those critics who found fault with the novel tended to praise Gardner's "disturbing talent" (Bateson, p. 17). Both *Time* and *Newsweek* named *Grendel* one of the best books of fiction of 1971. *Newsweek*'s reviewer asserted that "'Grendel' is not just the kind of facile revisionism in which 'Little Red Riding Hood' is told from the wolf's point of view; it is instead a celebration and conservation of what we most need in one of the greatest poetic myths we have." He further hailed *Grendel* as "witty, intelligent, delightful, so totally a work of the imagination that it creates its own world while touching upon our memories of myth and verse" (Prescott, p. 102). Another reviewer described its world as "marvelous and horrible," concluding that *Grendel* "is a subtle and comic exploration of what evil is, told by its unwilling embodiment. It is fiercely ugly and inventive, and very good" (Dinnage, p. 793).

—Michael Wenthe

For More Information

Bateson, F. W. Review of *Grendel, New York Review of Books* 17, no. 16 (30 December 1971): 16-17.

Beowulf. Trans. R. M. Liuzza. Peterborough, Ontario: Broadview Press, 2000.

Butts, Leonard. *The Novels of John Gardner: Making Life Art as a Moral Process.* Baton Rouge: Lousiana State University Press, 1988.

Chavkin, Allan, ed. *Conversations with John Gardner.* Jackson: University Press of Mississippi, 1990.

Cowart, David. *Arches and Light: The Fiction of John Gardner.* Carbondale: Southern Illinois University Press, 1983.

Dinnage, Rosemary. Review of *Grendel. Times Literary Supplement,* 14 July 1972, 793.

Gardner, John. *Grendel.* New York: Vintage, 1985.

———. *On Moral Fiction.* New York: Basic Books, 1978.

Henderson, Jeff, ed. *Thor's Hammer: Essays on John Gardner.* Conway: University of Central Arkansas Press, 1985.

Howell, John M. *Understanding John Gardner.* Columbia: University of South Carolina Press, 1993.

Prescott, Peter S. Review of *Grendel, Newsweek* 78 (13 September 1971): 102b.

A House for Mr. Biswas

by
V. S. Naipaul

THE LITERARY WORK

A tragicomic novel set in Trinidad at the turn of the century through the 1950s; published in 1961.

SYNOPSIS

An East Indian searches for meaning, identity, and a sense of place in colonial Trinidad.

The descendent of East Indian indentured servants, Vidiadhar Surajprasad Naipaul was born August 17, 1932, in Chaguanas, Trinidad. His father, Seepersad Naipaul (1906-53), was a journalist and an aspiring writer whose literary ambitions spread to his sons Vidiadhar and Shiva. A bright student, Vidiadhar Naipaul gained admission to Queen's Royal College—one of just four secondary schools on the island—and in 1948 won a coveted government-sponsored scholarship to study abroad. He entered University College at Oxford in England as a literature student in 1950, graduated in 1953, and began working for the British Broadcasting Corporation, hosting the program *Caribbean Voices*. He also wrote for the *New Statesman* literary journal and published his first novel, *The Mystic Masseur*, in 1957. Two novels followed, earning him a reputation as a formidable new novelist, but it was with the publication of *A House for Mr. Biswas* in 1961 that Naipaul's work achieved masterpiece status. Not part of the colonial ruling establishment, nor of the native culture, the protagonist is an East Indian in Trinidad, an ethnic outsider searching for a sense of self and place. Through this protagonist, the novel focuses on a displaced people reinventing themselves in a foreign and often inhospitable land.

Events in History at the Time of The Novel

From indentured servant to twentieth-century minority. Trinidad's cultural and ethnic melange stems from its 500-year history of conquest and foreign occupation. Originally the home of Amerindian peoples, the island was sighted in 1498 by Admiral Christopher Columbus, who claimed it for Spain. With the Spanish came thousands of European settlers and African slaves to develop the colony, driving out native peoples and dramatically transforming the landscape. By the 1790s the immigrant population, mainly French Catholics settlers and African slaves, had wholly displaced the indigenous peoples, outnumbering them by a factor of 16 to 1.

By this time sugar had become "king," and plantations dominated the island and economy. Lured by the lucrative trade, the British seized control of the West Indian colony in 1797. A wave of British settlers followed the Spanish and French, while African slaves continued to comprise the bulk of the workforce. In 1834, slaves in the British Empire were emancipated, and indentured servants from another of Britain's colonies, India, were brought to Trinidad as re-

V. S. Naipaul

placements. From 1838 to 1917 some 144,000 East Indians moved to Trinidad under a policy of unrestricted immigration to support the sugar industry. Typically indentured for five years, East Indians received land grants at the expiration of their contracts or after ten years of residence—often in place of return passage to India—in the interest of keeping a low-wage workforce on the island. Approximately one-third of the servants returned to India, while the majority stayed and established shops, opened businesses, and farmed sugar on their newly acquired land.

Because of its colonial heritage and legacy of slavery and indentured servitude, twentieth-century Trinidad lacked a unified national cultural identity. White Europeans dominated the government and upper classes, yet people of African or East Indian descent comprised 80 percent of the population. Racism and discrimination were rampant in society, with the inhabitants strictly divided along economic and color lines.

> Whites in the Caribbean did not fully accept the changing reality of the new post-slavery conditions . . . [and] as long as sugar remained "king," all social goals were subordinated to boosting production. Little positive incentive was given to develop the arts, to inculcate a sense of national identity that was faithful to the plurality of the peoples.
>
> (Knight, p. 188)

What emerged in place of a national identity were two strong "minority" communities who shared only their rejection of European culture and who openly clashed with each other. While white elites remained at the top of society, East Indians and the descendants of African slaves were forced to compete for the same meager allotments of land and opportunities. Put in this competitive position, they showed a general distrust for each other and segregated themselves socially. The two communities adapted differently: while the descendants of African slaves, whose ancestors had come from diverse regions, created their own new culture in Trinidad, East Indians held firmly to old Asian traditions, showing a steadfast refusal to assimilate or change cultural patterns that impressed many of the African descendants as arrogance. Tensions festered and at times flared. The sight of East Indians cheering India's cricket team over that of the West Indies was enough to nearly start a "war" (Saft, p. 77).

The sense of displacement and lack of a national community in Trinidad are key concerns in *A House for Mr. Biswas,* as they were for Naipaul personally. Both Mr. Biswas and Naipaul seek identity—a "home"—a sense of place and self that did not readily exist for East Indians in Trinidad at the time. In the novel Mr. Biswas marvels that Pastor, an African who makes his living filling out forms for illiterates outside the county courthouse, has discovered and assumed his role in society. "Even Pastor, for all his grumbling, had found his place," Mr. Biswas notes. Upon this revelation, Mr. Biswas "perceived that the starts of apprehension he felt at the sight of every person in the street did not come from fear at all; only from regret, envy, despair" (Naipaul, *A House for Mr. Biswas,* p. 318). As an East Indian colonial in a British colony, Mr. Biswas is physically in one place and culturally in another, and so struggles to find his identity.

Exile off Main Street. As a consequence of immigrating as servants, East Indians were "at the bottom of the social scale" in Trinidad (Rodman, p. 19). Their dark skin, comparable to that of the African slave, only intensified their lowly status. According to Trinidad's first black prime minister, Eric Williams (1956-81), West Indians' "concern with colour and lightness of skin was almost an obsession" during the first part of the twentieth century (Williams in Rodman, p. 20).

The legacy of slavery and servitude had long-term effects on living conditions and social interaction in Trinidad. Division existed not only between Europeans and their Asian and African counterparts, but also within Trinidad's Asian and African communities, of which no segment was more removed or outcast than the East Indians. Physically they were separated because they lived in rural Trinidad. East Indians made up just 4 percent of the population of Trinidad's chief town, the Port of Spain, before 1917, although they comprised approximately 40 percent of the total population. Socially they were barred because of their distinct cultural and low-status farm labor.

The living and working conditions of East Indians in Trinidad further isolated them. The 25-cent wage of indenture was tantamount to slavery (a full 43 cents below the recommended minimum wage in 1919). Poverty was widespread, with nearly 20 percent of the population filing for poor relief in 1911 and their numbers surging annually. Through the 1940s, malnutrition soared—80 percent of the rural, mostly East Indian population in 1920 was infested with hookworms. Meanwhile, wages, instead of rising with inflation, dropped annually through 1935.

Compounding the poverty, housing was scarce. Just 48,000 houses existed on the island in 1911, which together with an additional 45,000 barrack rooms (former slave quarters) had to provide shelter for the bulk of Trinidad's 300,000 inhabitants. As evidenced in the novel, dozens of East Indians lived in a single dwelling or squatted in ramshackle squatter's cabins erected illegally on others' property, as Mr. Biswas's mother and many aunts and uncles do in the novel. Ideally the East Indian household sheltered one nuclear family or one extended family (traditionally a mother, father, unmarried children, and married sons with their wives and children), with the family sharing "a common kitchen" and "family purse" (Klass, p. 44). But the complications of life in Trinidad, including the dearth of dwelling places, often interfered with realizing the ideal. The acute housing problem among East Indians helps explain why home ownership is an all-consuming passion for Mr. Biswas in the novel (as does Biswas's search for individual identity).

East Indian social life in Trinidad. East Indians at first voluntarily segregated themselves from other communities, in large part because of cultural tradition. They practiced Hindu or Muslim religions, which were not officially recognized by the colonial government, and married within their own religious group. As evidenced in the novel, interaction between cultural groups in Trinidad was very limited. Occasionally Mr. Biswas sneaks off to Chinese restaurants, but this is a clear act of defiance against his wife's family. In fact, friendships, business relationships, and formal marriages between Trinidad's various cultural groups were rare in Trinidad until the 1940s, when social and political change began to occur. In the novel, Mr. Biswas's uncle marries a Chinese woman, whom the family never formally recognizes. They acknowledge only Hindu marriages, ironically, since the British government only acknowledged Christian marriages at the time. Similarly children borne by Chinese or African women to East Indian men were not officially recognized by East Indian families; such "illegitimate" children could not inherit property and were otherwise ostracized.

While East Indians in Trinidad maintained Hindu (85 percent) and Muslim traditions by keeping the patriarchal family structure and to some extent the caste system alive, both traditions weakened over time. Most Hindus practiced daily *puja,* or worshipful offerings to gods; ate in accordance with religious teachings; and observed customary religious holidays and rites (though, like the Tulsis in the novel, many eventually adopted the celebration of Christmas). Women usually filled traditional roles as wife, mother, and homemaker, laboring also in agriculture or at home-based businesses, while men worked outside the home. The education of boys took priority over that of girls—a policy reinforced by the local school system in which just three in 200 girls advanced to secondary school (Williams, p. 22). As in India, women dressed modestly in *saris* or *salwar kameez*; men sported Eastern or Western attire. Dowries were required for Hindu girls to marry, and their marriages were arranged, ideally to someone above their family's station. In the novel, Mr. Biswas is paired with Shama, one of the Tulsi family daughters, because he is a Brahmin—the highest caste. Though he has no real occupation or property, his caste brings honor to the Tulsi family. Their daughter is "marrying up."

Unequal education. The educational system proved to be another dividing factor in Trinidad. Until World War II, the government had no universal system of primary education and spent little on the education it did provide. The majority of schools were private and secular, operated by Christian religious institutions that did not cater to Hindus or Muslims. The consequences of the government abdicating responsibility for public education were serious: racial and economic differences were accentuated. Poor, non-Christians were discriminated against, performance standards for teachers were nonexistent,

"DOWN BY LAW"

With no right to vote, little education, and no political representation until 1946, East Indians felt persecuted by the law and distrusted the official legal system in Trinidad, so they implemented their own system of justice: the law of the cutlass. "The Indian agricultural worker in Trinidad was a man with the cutlass [blade that cuts sugar cane], oppressed by the law which, instead of being his protector, was his principal enemy" (Williams, p. 20). In the novel, East Indians invoke the "law of the cutlass" to settle disputes among themselves, and maintain control over their households. The successful way to resolve conflicts in the Tulsi home is via physical force, not through the legal system. When considering the possibility of local law enforcement's getting involved in a dispute, Mr. Biswas has a "fleeting vision of black policemen, courthouses, gallows, graves, coffins" (*Biswas*, p. 135). Resorting to official law is clearly a frightening option. In fact, the police force was dominated by foreigners—90 percent from Barbados or other islands. Routinely the Tulsi women give their children "a dose of licks" as a sort of "ritual" to make them "big men"; and when Mr. Biswas is exasperated with his children he has "visions in which he cutlassed, poisoned, strangled, burned, Anand and Savi" (*Biswas*, pp. 197, 154, 273). The one time that Mr. Biswas decides to resolve a problem by hiring a lawyer, he is sued for slander and loses his case. British law, as demonstrated by this incident, favored the upper classes, not the commoner or the ethnic outsider.

and there was no uniformity of curriculum. As a result, just one in ten East Indian boys attended primary school, one in 14 East Indian girls. In contrast, the island average at the time was one in two boys, three in five girls.

An even worse situation existed at the secondary-school level. There were just four secondary schools in Trinidad, all very expensive and strictly urban. The only bridge for poor kids to secondary school was via government-sponsored exhibitions, whose winners received free tuition plus textbooks. A second exhibition or academic contest enabled winners to attend college abroad—usually Cambridge or Oxford in England—but the number of awards granted for each contest was extremely small. While just 800 students of about 47,000 advanced to secondary school in 1911, only four attended with exhibition scholarships, and only three advanced from secondary school to college abroad as exhibition winners. Of the lucky few, Mr. Biswas's son, Anand, and Naipaul himself won the secondary and college scholarships, as did Trinidad's first black prime minister, Eric Williams. For East Indians and Africans, the exhibitions were often the only opportunity for educational and socioeconomic advancement, and so were of paramount importance to families wishing to better themselves.

Ironically, though higher education enabled poor children to advance, it also became a social barrier separating students from family and friends, and dividing the generations. The main purpose of education in Trinidad was the Anglicization of the colony, and the secondary curriculum, according to Eric Williams, was indistinguishable from that of an English public school. Textbooks were written by J. O. Cutteridge, an aristocratic, non-Trinidadian British official who emphasized the classics and mathematics. There was no teaching of Creole, African, or East Indian culture and history, and the literary and scientific styles were "affected, pompous, high-flown and ponderous"—a far cry from colloquial speech or daily experience in the cane fields or Port of Spain (Williams, p. 23). Non-European students exposed to this type of education became far more "British" than their families, yet remained clearly *not* British in the eyes of mainstream society. Like Mr. Biswas, an avid reader, and his educated children, the students themselves often felt alienated from, even repelled by, their inherited traditions and questioned their cultural identity. Naipaul's characterization of the ethnic outsider seems to stem from his own experience as a product of this educational system, from his "rootlessness" as a colonial divided from his cultural heritage yet unable to share in that of Trinidad's imperial ruler (Chapman, p. 303).

"Picong"—a tradition of satire. In Trinidad, a unique tradition of political satire became a major force in society. By the mid-twentieth century there were no less than four daily newspapers and an abundance of weeklies for a population of one million, with each featuring humorous political attacks on local government, bureaucracy, and traditions. Called "picong," this unique form of "sniping satire," which originated in Calypso music, conveyed the popular "Trinidadian" attitude of refusing to take anyone or anything too seriously (Saft, p. 81). Most Trinidadians viewed the established order as unrepresentative and corrupt. Yet an inherent *joie de vivre* generally provided "a studied philosophy of life which rests upon a highly developed sense of humor" (Saft, p. 82). In the weeklies no topic was sacrosanct and "a major part of the attraction" was "their punching holes in public figures" (Saft, p. 82). The humor "level[ed] all hierarchies" and, as in the novel, poked fun at tradition and the status quo (Saft, p. 82).

Naipaul's novel is a masterpiece of "picong." A newspaper columnist, Mr. Biswas specializes in biting satire. He, like Naipaul's father, exposes the folly of society and finds his muse in his editor Mr. Burnett (for Naipaul's father, it was Mr. MacGowan), who openly encourages his outlandish stories. With nothing above reproach, Mr. Biswas constantly satirizes his own life and experiences, recording events in his mind: "Amazing scenes were witnessed in St. Vincent Street yesterday when Mohun Biswas, 31, unemployed, of no fixed address, assaulted a receptionist at the offices of TRINIDAD SENTINEL. People ducked behind desks as Biswas, father of four, walked into the building with guns blazing, shot the editor and four reporters dead, and then set fire to the building" (*Biswas,* p. 319). Of course, Mr. Biswas does none of these things—they are random thoughts passing through his mind that illustrate his sensational, black sense of humor. The general focus of the newspaper he writes for conveys the same black humor, an attribute appreciated in Trinidad: "The peasant was then reported as saying that he read the *Sentinel* every day, since no other paper presented the news so fully, so amusingly, and with such balance" (*Biswas,* p. 328). In deference to Trinidad's penchant for "picong," the *Sentinel* editor includes "amusingly" in his description, a quality outside newspapers often do not equate with fine reporting.

Big changes on a small island. A mix of variables characterized Trinidadian society. "Class, colour, caste and race combined to create an immensely complex pattern of human relationships" and made it extremely difficult for change to occur (Bridget Brereton in Rogozinski, p. 317). The elite Protestant British and Roman Catholic French-Creole classes agreed on nothing but money. As mentioned earlier, blacks and East Indians clashed. Oil and farm workers were pitted against middle-class white-collar workers. And even within the East Indian community, Hindus and Muslims divided along religious lines. Reinforced by the social and educational systems, the divisions helped isolate power in the hands of a privileged few. In 1934, however, when the Wages Advisory Board recommended that peoples' needs were less, wages fell below those paid in 1920, at which point the repressed classes finally banded together for change. East Indians in particular became more public in their demands for improved wages and working conditions, staging a hunger strike. They also staged demonstrations, with East Indian sugar workers marching from San Fernando to Port of Spain, inspiring workers in other industries to follow suit.

MILK AND PRUNES—BRAIN FOOD

Because it was a life-making or life-breaking event, the government-sponsored educational exhibitions were a family priority in Trinidad. Families poured their energy and resources into the education of a select child as preparation for the scholastic exams. He or she would be tutored at the family's expense and would receive certain privileges. In the novel, milk and prunes are the special diet East Indian families prescribed for educational brilliance. Both foods were not only precious commodities but were seen as possessing special intellectual qualities. As a rule, milk would not be purchased from European-operated diaries but acquired from family cows or bought from "a man six lots away who, oblivious of the aspirations of the district, kept cows and delivered milk in rum bottles stopped with brown paper"; prunes were believed to be "especially nourishing to people who exercised their brains" (*Biswas,* pp. 336-37). Mr. Biswas at first scoffs at Mrs. Tulsi for indulging Owad [her son] in these excesses. But soon Mr. Biswas not only sees the wisdom of her choice but hopes his own son will some day be worthy of the treatment. "He was watching and learning, with an eye on his own household and especially on Anand. Soon, he hoped, Anand would qualify to eat prunes and drink milk from the Dairies" (*Biswas,* p. 337).

About this time East Indian advocate Krishna Deonarine, came to the fore of local politics. The grandson of indentured servants, he changed his name to Adrian Cola Reinzi to pass as a more-privileged Spaniard. Reinzi organized the Oilfield Workers Trade Union and the All Trinidad Sugar Estates and Factory Workers Trade Union in 1937, inaugurating a major turning point in race relations on the island, as "oil and sugar, African and Indian . . . joined hands" (Saft, p. 45). By 1941, 12 unions had been established in Trinidad, with workers finally putting aside cultural differences to form coalitions and agitate for change.

A second important impetus for change occurred three years later with the arrival of American service personnel. In September 1940 the British leased its military bases in Trinidad to the United States. Inadvertently the presence of Americans helped erode color and class distinctions because, in contrast to the British, the Americans provided high-paying jobs to Trinidadians, regardless of their cultural heritage. Also, whereas the British had maintained a very separate and formal public relationship with the general population, Americans "labored bareback, got drunk and brawled, and white respectability crumbled" (Saft, p. 46). In other words, they worked and lived with the public, frequented Port of Spain nightclubs, and dated locals. Meanwhile, the standard of living rose, aided by World War II oil exports (which rose by 1/3), increased urbanization, and American dollars. With more financial resources, people gained status, servility decreased, and society radically changed. By the war's end, a nationalist movement had evolved that would produce a new, self-governing Trinidad.

Postwar Trinidad. The close of World War II signaled the end of British colonial rule in Trinidad (though it would not gain full independence until 1962). Universal suffrage was granted in 1945 and "rowdy" elections took place the following year (Saft, p. 48). Because of the island's lack of party affiliation outside the British Crown Colony, elections were wide open, with 141 candidates vying for 18 seats in parliament. Politicians appealed to the citizenry along race and class lines. East Indians candidates sought the Hindu and Muslim vote. Among them was Ajodha Singh, a popular candidate because of his reputation as a colorful campaigner and "mystic masseur," who massages a person's aura or karma (Saft, p. 48). Naipaul's father, Seepersad, a local journalist, covered the political developments when Naipaul was just a boy. Drawing on these memories, and on his father's stories, Naipaul satirized the events surrounding Trinidad's first elections in his novels *The Mystic Masseur* and *The Suffrage of Elvira*. He also incorporated some of the characters into his masterpiece, *A House for Mr. Biswas*, including a fictionalized version of Ajodha Singh.

The postwar years in Trinidad brought a nationalist surge and increased prosperity, with the economy benefitting greatly from higher oil prices through the 1950s. Testament to the independent spirit sweeping the island, Eric Williams was elected prime minister in 1956. A respected intellectual and skilled politician, Williams was instrumental in Trinidad's achieving total independence from Great Britain in 1962, after a brief membership in the West Indies Federation (1958-62). Williams helped unify Trinidadians, instilling a strong sense of community and national pride where neither had existed before. He called for "nationalism and democracy" and "a mobilisation of all the forces in the community, cutting across race and religion, class and colour" (Williams in Rogozinski, p. 318).

With wages up 10 to 20 times what they had been before World War II, prosperity continued to grow and to help erase class and color lines. As Mr. Biswas does in the novel, East Indians migrated to the cities where educational and white-collar job opportunities increased. Literacy rates rose to 90 percent. Children of all races mixed at school, as did their parents in the workplace. Caste and culture barriers eroded in the desegregated urban environment, and the standard of living rose across the board. "Since the Second World War, the sense of self and the sentiment of nationalism intensified throughout the Caribbean," and "Hindu and Muslim East Indians formed coalitions with black Trinidadians" (Knight, pp. 302, 303). For the first time, East Indians—through education—became part of the recognized middle class as barriers of all forms began to erode and a new national society formed.

The Novel in Focus

Plot summary. Tracing the life of Mohun Biswas, a humble East Indian born and raised in Trinidad, *A House for Mr. Biswas* begins at the end, in the house Mr. Biswas spends his life pursuing. It then flashes back to the onset of Mohun Biswas's troubles. Because of chronic illness, he is fired by the *Trinidad Sentinel*, his employer since he moved to Port of Spain. Mohun has a considerable mortgage, his children, on whom he may have depended, are abroad at school, and he is dying of stress and a bad heart. Yet he is content at the thought of going to his final resting place from his own home, "his own portion of the earth. That he should be responsible for this seemed to him, in these last months, stupendous," and it was (*Biswas,* p. 8).

Born to indentured servants in "a crumbling mud hut in the swamplands," Mohun Biswas seems doomed from the outset (*Biswas,* p. 15). He has six fingers and comes out feet first—bad omens in his community—and shortly thereafter is inadvertently the cause of his father's death. To increase his fortune in life, he is named Mohun, which means "the beloved," but for years the trick does not seem to fool the gods and bad luck hovers overhead like a rain cloud. His mother sells the family shack just before oil is discovered on the property. The sale leaves her destitute, his brothers with a life of hard labor in the cane fields, and Mohun without vocation or direction. He tries in vain to become a *pundit,* or holy man, because of his birth into the Brahmin caste, but questions Hindu teachings and has neither the horoscope nor, quite literally, the hands for it. He works in rum shops and at odd jobs, but succeeds at nothing. In fact, Mohun's only marketable skill is sign painting—a craft from which he can at best eke out a minor living. But he has dreams—and books. Mohun is a voracious reader, devouring all the books he can acquire. They enable his escape into the outside world and fuel his desire to make his own place in it. For many years Mohun remains directionless, working as a sign painter for various businesses around town. One day a job brings him into contact with a 16-year-old East Indian girl named Shama. He thinks little of marriage and his mother has all but given up on the prospect when Shama's family abruptly intervenes. The Tulsis are one of the most influential Hindu families in Trinidad. They own sugar plantations, stores, and cinemas, and wield considerable power in the community. When Mrs. Tulsi realizes Mohun's attraction to Shama, as well as his Brahmin caste status, she quickly arranges his marriage to her daughter. Before Mohun fully realizes what is happening, he is part of the Tulsi household and living in their home in Arwacas: Hanuman House, named for the monkey god.

Life for Mohun in Hanuman House becomes quite literally like life in a monkey house. All of Shama's siblings and their families live there together—some 30 or more—with Mrs. Tulsi and her son Seth reigning supreme. Mohun bristles at everything having to do with the living situation, feels he has nothing in common with the Tulsis, and continually causes disruptions and quarrels. Though he clearly does not fit into the family structure or show aptitude for working on their plantations like the other sons-in-law, the Tulsis find places for him to serve the family business and interests. He is sent to other properties—first to operate a small general store, then to supervise fieldworkers on their plantation. During these years his own family continues to grow with the birth of three daughters and a son, but he remains disconnected from them as well as from his in-laws. Shama's loyalty lies with the Tulsis, and Mohun feels a stranger around his own children.

With the dream of building a home always firmly in the back of his mind—ever more so since living in Hanuman House—Mohun makes two attempts to realize his goal: the first while working at the plantation at Green Vale and the second when the Tulsis move to the country in Shorthills. But ill fortune still dogs him. Both homes are destroyed by natural disaster, leaving Mohun more dispirited, yet more determined, than ever. He "yearned after the outside world;

ALLEGORICAL NAMES

A House for Mr. Biswas invokes allegorical names, drawing on East Indian history and Hindu legend. The protagonist's name, Mohun, meaning "beloved," was the title most often associated with Mohandas Gandhi (though he did not approve of it). In this way, Naipaul is illustrating his sympathy for this flawed character and indicating that his experience as a confused, fallible non-hero or "Everyman" is honorable. Appropriately Naipaul dedicates the Tulsi residence to Hanuman, monkey god and savior in the Hindu epic *Ramayana,* an intricate tale of good and evil about the creation of Hindustan (India). In doing so, he employs the double-entendre of Hanuman House as monkey house and of Hanuman's unifying role in the epic. In the epic, Hanuman rescues Sita (the hero Rama's beloved) by building a bridge across the water to another land, and in the novel the Tulsi home serves as the bridge from India to Trinidad.

he read novels that took him there" and, with the destruction of his houses, felt he had nothing to lose by finally going to explore it for himself (*Biswas*, p. 207).

Following the lead of a friend who has gone to Port of Spain to work in the world's first psychiatric hospital, Mohun moves to the city and lands a job as a reporter for the *Trinidad Sentinel*. He teams up with a bold, bawdy Hindu editor who capitalizes on Mohun's keen powers of observation and black sense of humor. Mohun begins writing sensational columns, such as the roving Scarlet Pimpernel, about a reporter who seeks out the common man and, if recognized, pays him or her a reward.

> With memories coming from he knew not where, he wrote:
>
> SCARLET PIMPERNEL SPENDS NIGHT IN A TREE
>
> Anguish of Six-Hour Vigil
> *Oink! Oink!*
>
> The report then described a sleepless night, encounters with snakes and bats, two cars that passed in the night, heedless of the Scarlet Pimpernel's cries, the rescue early in the morning by peasants who recognized the Scarlet Pimpernel and claimed their prize.
> (*Biswas*, p. 329)

Most of his subject matter is made up; Mohun converts his disillusionment with his life into fuel for his creativity: His stories are largely fictional and thoroughly outrageous, as when he pens "I am Trinidad's Most Evil Man." Suddenly Mohun is respected by society—even by his family! His audacity and bold humor is rewarded, and his fortune begins to change.

Though the newspaper is eventually bought out and his writing assignments become more mundane, Mohun is content with his career and begins to focus on his family. All the Tulsis move to Port of Spain and for the first time he bonds with his children—especially his son, Anand, to whom he transfers his ambitions. They share a passion and gift for reading and composition, and Mohun invests his time and energy preparing Anand for the secondary school exhibition. Anand eventually wins a scholarship and, that accomplished, Mohun turns his sights one final time to owning a home.

The price is too high, the structure unsound, the seller unscrupulous, but Mohun purchases a house on Sikkim Street and at long last moves his family into a home of his own. Everything he dreamed of comes true. His relationships with his wife and children radically transform: "Since they had moved to the house Shama had learned a new loyalty, to him and to their children . . . and to Mr. Biswas this was a triumph almost as big as the acquiring of his own house" (*Biswas*, p. 8). He is awestruck at the wonder of being in his own house each time he enters,

> to walk in through his own front gate, to bar entry to whoever he wished, to close his doors and windows every night, to hear no one's noise except those of his family, to wander freely from room to room and about his yard, instead of being condemned, the moment he got home to the crowded room in one or the other of Mrs. Tulsis houses, crowded with Shama's sisters, their husbands, their children. (*Biswas*, p. 8)

He is thrilled to find his place in the world and, though short-lived, his happiness and life are at last complete. He dies in his own home, and his daughter Savi returns to pay the mortgage and care for the family while her brother is away at college.

Hanuman House as a microcosm of East Indian society. In colonial Trinidad, where the population outnumbered that of single dwellings sixfold and the majority lived in cramped quarters, slept on floors, and often cooked and bathed outdoors, the home could be seen as a microcosm of life in the immigrant community. Hanuman House, where the Tulsi family resides, is a perfect example of the living conditions of East Indians in Trinidad: crowded, undemocratic, chaotic, and part of, yet far removed from, mainstream society.

Relationships within Hanuman House are complex. As in the local political and social structure, one must forge alliances to survive. Mr. Biswas realizes this the moment he moves in: "It was a strain living in a house full of people and talking to one person alone, and after some weeks Mr. Biswas decided to look around for alliances. Relationships at Hanuman House were complex and as yet he understood only a few, but he had noted that two friendly sisters made two friendly husbands, and two friendly husbands made two friendly sisters" (*Biswas*, p. 105). Biswas seeks to ally with like-minded family members to change some of the "house rules" but cannot even secure the allegiance of his own wife. Within the house, sheltered by her family, Shama's first loyalty is to the Tulsis and she does not alter her sentiments until much later when Biswas breaks free from the Tulsis and buys his own home.

Seated firmly atop the hierarchy like the British colonials who ruled Trinidad, Seth and

Mrs. Tulsi run the family enterprise—Seth the business, Mrs. Tulsi the household. Despite his bold assertions to Shama that he is "not at his beck and call, like everyone else in this house," Mr. Biswas must answer to Seth and follow his directives (*Biswas,* p. 107). Mrs. Tulsi, hearing that he is making fun of Seth's spoiled children and refusing to work for the family, reminds Biswas of his obligations. Like an indentured servant, he is indebted because they have taken him in, "penniless, a stranger" and given him their daughter, a home, food and shelter (*Biswas,* p. 109). Mr. Biswas declares that his motto is "paddle your own canoe" yet, as an East Indian without a trade he literally cannot (*Biswas,* p. 107). He acquiesces to the family because he has no choice. Like most East Indians in his situation, he must become part of the system and not forget his place in it: at the bottom.

In time—even in Hanuman House—the system evolves, though not necessarily harmoniously. Like the rest of the community, Hanuman House is comprised of old and new generations, with those seeking to modernize and those clinging to old world tradition inhabiting the same small space. Brothers-in-law Hari and Govind represent the old-world East Indian culture, with Hari practising *puja* for the family and performing Hindu rites, and Govind committing the *Ramayana* to memory and singing its verses at every opportunity. At the opposite extreme are Mr. Biswas and the brother-in-law he nicknames W. C. Tuttle. They are avid readers who both feel "that by marrying into the Tulsis they had fallen among the barbarians" (*Biswas,* p. 459). While Hari and Biswas maintain a quiet disdain for each other, Tuttle and Govind opt for duelling gramophones: Govind "*Ramayana*-grunting" and Tuttle blaring modern "music of celebration" at full volume simultaneously from adjacent rooms (*Biswas,* p. 461).

In this setting, East meets West head on and, as in general society, the mixture is disjunctive; it does not blend smoothly. Yet the blending continues nonetheless. Seth marries a Protestant woman, the children study in Christian schools (the older boys attend British universities) and the Hindu family starts celebrating the Christian holiday Christmas. They eat traditional curries and *roti* but sample store-bought ice cream and Coca-Cola as well. The children learn English and forget Hindi, which becomes a "secret" language spoken only among the elders, and little by little the household becomes increasingly confused, as society in general desegregates and modernizes.

In less than 50 years the Tulsis build a strong foundation in Trinidad, acquiring real estate, cinemas, and businesses throughout the island, but still never feel at home.

> Despite the solidity of their establishment the Tulsis had never considered themselves settled in the town of Arwacas or even Trinidad. It was no more than a stage in a journey that began when Pundit Tulsi left India . . . and ever since they had talked, though less often . . . of moving on, to India.
>
> (*Biswas,* p. 390)

But the Tulsis, now the third and fourth generations who know only Trinidad, would never return east. Like others of their community they become part of the island, even as they remain outsiders, maintaining East Indian identities and adapting to change, however reluctantly. The result is a permanently displaced people—colonial immigrants who do not wholly belong to the land and are slowly losing ties to their cultural roots.

Hanuman House mirrors mid-twentieth-century East Indian life in Trinidad: the social stratification, the complex politics and economics of the upper and lower classes, the growing generation gap, and the East-West culture clashes. Along with these realities, it illustrates the isolation of the colonial immigrant searching for a sense of self and belonging in a foreign and often hostile environment. In the context of this house, Mr. Biswas struggles in pursuit of his own identity, or a place of his own. "As a boy he had moved from one house of strangers to another; and since his marriage he felt he had lived nowhere but in the houses of the Tulsis" (*Biswas,* p. 8). His experience and pursuit parallels that of the East Indian immigrant community as a whole—indentured servants, moving to an unfamiliar land, living with strangers, obligated to those who provide food and shelter. Hanuman House symbolizes the community within a community—East Indians in the West Indies, double-edged in that it has been both protective and repressive. For most of the Tulsi sisters, Hanuman House is a place of refuge where the brutal and unfamiliar outside world evaporates, but for Biswas it is a prison from which he must free himself in order to take his place in society and forge his own identity.

Sources and literary context. Naipaul based *A House for Mr. Biswas* on his own experiences in Trinidad, patterning the characters of Mr. Biswas and his son, Anand, on his father and himself.

In his most recent book, *Between Father and Son: Family Letters* (2000), Naipaul reveals that the relationship between himself and his father was strikingly similar to that of the characters. Like his own father, Mr. Biswas dreams of literary success, transfers those dreams to his son, and dies financially burdened but gratified that he is leaving a better future for his children. Naipaul, like Anand, was "torn between self-absorption and familial concern, writing home out of duty, need and affection" (Kakutani). Showing his deep affection and a growing realization of the relevance of his father's experience as a universal struggle for identity, Naipaul records and embellishes upon the life and memories of the man he knew.

The novel draws on what Naipaul describes as ostracized peoples, estranged from societies to which they ostensibly belong, seeking ways to genuinely belong. He deliberately broadened out from his family experience to that of the West Indian community in Trinidad, as he describes in his book *Reading and Writing*: "One day . . . I began to see what my material might be: the city street from whose mixed life we had held aloof, and the country life before that, with the ways and manners of a remembered India" (Naipaul in Schmitt, p. 132). He specifically portrayed the reality of descendants of indentured servants, of which he was one, and in so doing, conveyed larger truths about the general colonial predicament in Trinidad.

ENGLISH INFLUENCES

When Naipaul arrived in Britain as a young student, the nation was rebuilding after the ravages of World War II. Colonies in Britain's once vast empire gained independence, and British ties shifted from the areas of Caribbean, Africa, and Southeast Asia to the areas of Europe and the United States. In spite of Britain's demise as a colonial power, national pride remained strong at the time, especially in its ancient aristocratic institutions. At Cambridge and Oxford Universities, though more students of the lower classes were being admitted, many in the privileged class still believed that they alone deserved their place in Britain's finer institutions. The Dean of Balliol College, Oxford, is described as having often spoken derogatorily of the lower-class students—of whom Naipaul would have been considered one. "The snobbery," said one former student, "was absolute—as if they felt now was the last chance to re-establish things as things ought to be and as life had been before the war" (J. MacNaughton in Williamson, p. 100). There were some who publicly decried the leveling of society in the postcolonial era, arguing that "a recognisable and secure upper class . . . represents far less danger than would-be elites in an egalitarian' society, whose privileges would be hidden and therefore uncontrolled" (Worthestone in Williamson, p. 101). Class distinctions remained prevalent in British society, and nostalgia for the old colonial past was "coupled with a suspicion of strangers and some resentment of the newcomers who were increasingly arriving" (Williamson, p. 105). It is in the context of this climate of conditional acceptance, on top of his own background as an immigrant outsider, that Naipaul creates such a convincing portrayal of the East Indian colonial experience in Trinidad.

Reviews. Most critics agree that *A House for Mr. Biswas* is Naipaul's literary masterpiece, but not all responses to the novel have been positive. Naipaul has been criticized for depicting Third World peoples as culturally inferior to Westerners, and his works have received a less-than-favorable initial reception in India and the West Indies. But at least one reviewer identified with the portrayal in *A House for Mr. Biswas*, saying that "for the first time, he is able to feel his own history not merely as a squalid farce, but as an adventure in sensibility" (Schmitt, p. 151). Another reviewer praised the metaphors embedded in the novel: "The book is powerfully symbolic, but it is never crudely or obtrusively so"; Biswas "represents all things because he is fully presented as a person whose every quirk and idiosyncrasy we know" (Rohlehr in Schmitt, p. 153). Others agreed, calling Biswas "an archetypal figure"—the "Third World Everyman," the wanderer-stranger searching for his role in the universe (Schmitt, pp. 153, 133). Still others celebrated the novel's engaging humor, and the comic dimension of its epic hero. "If," said Paul Theroux writing in the *New York Times Book Review*, "the silting up of the Thames coincided with a freak monsoon" causing him to be marooned in South London, the one book he would want with him would be *A House for Mr. Biswas* (Theroux in Chapman, p. 303).

—Diane Renée

For More Information

Chapman, Jeff, and Pamela S. Dear, eds. *Contemporary Authors, New Revision Series*, Vol. 51. Detroit: Gale, 1996.

Kakutani, Michiko. "Naipaul's Letters Reveal True Nature of Mr. Biswas and Son." *Seattle Post Intelligencer.* 16 Feb. 2000. http://www.seattlepi.nwsource.com/books/boox166.shtml (20 Jan. 2001).

Klass, Morton. *East Indians in Trinidad.* Prospect Heights, Ill.: Waveland Press, 1961.

Knight, Franklin W. *The Caribbean: The Genesis of a Fragmented Nationalism.* New York: Oxford University Press, 1990.

Naipaul, V. S. *A House for Mr. Biswas.* New York: Penguin, 1961.

———. *Between a Father and a Son.* New York: Alfred A. Knopf, 2000.

Rodman, Hyman. *Lower-Class Families.* New York: Oxford University Press, 1971.

Rogozinski, Jan. *A Brief History of the Caribbean.* New York: Facts on File, 1999.

Saft, Elizabeth, ed. *Trinidad & Tobago.* Boston: APA, 1993.

Schmitt, Deborah A., ed. *Contemporary Literary Criticism,* Vol. 105. Detroit: Gale Group, 1998.

Williams, Eric. *Inward Hunger: The Education of a Prime Minister.* Chicago: University of Chicago Press, 1969.

Williamson, Bill. *The Temper of the Times.* Oxford: Basil Blackwell, 1990.

Wolpert, Stanley. *A New History of India.* New York: Oxford University Press, 1997.

The House Gun

by
Nadine Gordimer

Nadine Gordimer, the 1991 Nobel laureate in literature, was born in a small mining town near Johannesburg, South Africa, in 1923. Her heritage makes her a minority within a minority on three counts: in a country sharply divided along racial and ethnic lines, she is white in a predominantly black land, of British heritage in a markedly Afrikaner white culture, and Jewish in a predominantly Christian population. Gordimer stands out politically as well. She has always been outspokenly liberal—even radical—in a white population that is profoundly conservative. Beginning with her first novel, *Lying Days* (1953), Gordimer has used her fiction to critique the racism of South African society, a racism epitomized by the official policy of apartheid (strict racial segregation). Her twelfth novel, in addition to as many short-story collections and several nonfiction works, *The House Gun* marks an important transition in Gordimer's writing, taking it into the realm of the new, post-apartheid South Africa.

THE LITERARY WORK

A novel set in Cape Town, South Africa, in 1995; published in 1998.

SYNOPSIS

A young man from an upper-middle-class family shoots and kills a housemate. As his case moves towards trial, his parents grapple with how this could have happened and with conflicting emotions towards him and each other.

Events in History at the Time the Novel Takes Place

The heritage of apartheid. In 1948 the National Party, dominated by the Afrikaners (whites of Dutch heritage, formerly called Boers), won control of South Africa's government—a position that the party would retain for the next 46 years. Almost immediately, the new government set about instituting a system known as *apartheid* ("apartness"), which was both a government policy and "a rigorous and totalizing ideology" of racial separation and privilege that would dominate South African life and thought for the better part of half a century (Beinhart and Dubow, p. 11).

Apartheid worked by officially classifying all South Africans according to race—black, white, Asian (mostly Indian), or colored (mixed race)—and regulating virtually every aspect of their lives so as to keep the races apart. Under a program of legislation enacted in the 1950s and 1960s, mixed-race marriages and sexual relationships were forbidden, mixed-race trade unions and political parties were outlawed, and employment was restricted on the basis of race. Most significantly, residential areas were divvied up by race: the Group Areas Act of 1950 dictated racial requirements for both land ownership and residency in every part of the country. To meet the requirements, families were resettled and whole communities were razed.

Nadine Gordimer

Apartheid not only separated people by race; it also guaranteed greater privilege to coloreds and Asians than to blacks and by far the greatest privilege of all to whites. The choicest living areas and farmland were reserved for whites, white schools and hospitals received infinitely better funding and equipment than nonwhite institutions, and whites could avail themselves of opportunities open only to them. In contrast, huge numbers of blacks were effectively stripped of all citizenship rights by being officially relocated to nominally independent "homelands" far from the country's urban centers. As most employment opportunities were centered in these white urban areas, families were often divided, with wage-earners forced to spend much of the year living far from home. Moreover, they were not allowed to live in the cities where their jobs existed. So the black urban workers were housed on the fringes of cities, in overcrowded townships—often no more than vast squatters' camps, with little in the way of infrastructure. Black workers then had to carry identification papers stamped by their white employers any time they entered a white area.

Many South Africans—some of them white—protested the government's actions, but it, in effect, outlawed dissent. Anti-apartheid newspapers were shut down, organizations banned, and individuals placed under restrictions ranging from house arrest to imprisonment without trial. By the mid-1960s, many anti-apartheid activists had gone into exile, had been killed, or were serving life in prison. Meanwhile, thanks to its policies, South Africa had become a pariah state, barred from international athletic competition, subject to trade embargoes, and cut off from much of the outside world. Consequently several generations of races in South Africa grew up knowing little else but apartheid.

The new South Africa. By the late 1980s, the South African system of apartheid had become untenable. Black protest movements, which had rebounded beginning in 1976, escalated throughout the following decade and the nation's government had few remaining friends abroad. Bowing to both internal and international pressure, Prime Minister P. W. Botha began power-sharing negotiations with leaders of the Coloured and Asian communities that resulted in a tri-cameral national parliament. Power still remained in white hands, however, and Africans were still denied any voice in government.

As with Mikhail Gorbachev's efforts to reform the Soviet system, the first concessions to be made in South Africa's system marked the beginning of the end of the apartheid. The result was a dramatic restructuring of the South African government, and the demise of the apartheid system. By 1990, Botha's successor, F. W. de Klerk, had freed the nation's most prominent political prisoners, and had begun to dismantle most of the structures of apartheid. Progress was not entirely smooth—almost four years of negotiations were still to come—but in April 1994, the nation held its first multiracial democratic elections. The African National Congress (the largest black political party) won 252 of 400 seats in the new National Assembly, and its president, Nelson Mandela—a prisoner under the old regime for 27 years—became president of a new South Africa.

Although South Africa's transition from a repressive, single-party government to a modern democracy—complete with one of the most liberal constitutions in the world—was remarkably swift and peaceable, many of the inequities engendered by the old system remained. By the late 1990s, at the time *The House Gun* takes place, most of the land and money in the nation still lay in the hands of whites. The new government had not been as adept at promoting an even economic and, for that matter, social playing field as it had been at achieving greater political equality among the races.

The South Africa in which *The House Gun* takes place, then, is a country still very much in the process of transformation. Everyday living conditions are basically stable, but high levels of uncertainty—coupled with hope about the future—prevail.

The constitution. A major part of the reshaping of South Africa in the early 1990s involved the creation and adoption of a new constitution. In 1993, an interim constitution, accepted by both government and opposition leaders, declared "a new order in which all South Africans will be entitled to a common South African citizenship in a sovereign and democratic constitutional state in which there is equality between men and women and people of all races so that all citizens shall be able to enjoy and exercise their fundamental rights and freedoms" (Preamble of *Act 200* in *Constitution, 1993*). Such language, and the ideas behind it, represented a radical shift from the nation's past.

After the 1994 elections, one of the first tasks of the freshly elected National Assembly was the drafting of a permanent constitution for the new South Africa. Anxious to reverse the apartheid-era model of government that disenfranchised the majority of the country's citizens, the new government strove to build bridges and confidence by encouraging wide participation in the making of the constitution. Called "the largest public participation programme ever carried out in South Africa," the writers sought input not only from elected representatives, but from other political and civic leaders and from ordinary citizens; the final document declares itself to "therefore represent the collective wisdom of the South African people and [to have] been arrived at by general agreement" ("Explanatory Memorandum" in *Constitution, 1996*). The constitution is thus a symbolic as well as practical centerpiece of post-apartheid South Africa's participatory democracy.

The finalized version of the constitution, adopted at the end of 1996, is a strikingly liberal document—not only in the context of the country's formerly authoritarian government, but by any international standards. Enshrined in it are a dazzlingly comprehensive list of rights: the right to equality before the law, to legislative protection from discrimination on virtually any grounds, to privacy, and to freedom of religion and expression. Also guaranteed are the rights—long denied the mass of South Africans—to choose one's place of residence, and to move about freely both within and outside the country's borders.

Most significantly for *The House Gun*, the Bill of Rights states that "everyone has the right to life" and that "everyone has the right to freedom and security of the person, which includes the right . . . not to be treated or punished in a cruel, inhuman or degrading way" (chap. 2, secs. 11 and 12 [1] in *Constitution, 1996*). These are provisions that the Constitutional Court drew upon in 1995 in debating the constitutionality of the death penalty (in *The State v. T. Makwanyane and M. Mchunu*)—a court case described in *The House Gun*, and upon which the fate of the novel's young murderer hangs.

SCARS OF APARTHEID

Several of *The House Gun*'s scenes take place during hearings of the South African Constitutional Court. Harald, the father of the novel's young murderer, describes the court's justices in some detail, focusing on "a swarthy man (Italian or Jew?) with a scarred grin, and eyes, one dark-brilliant, one blurred blind, from whom radiant vitality comes impudently since he is gesticulating with a stump in place of one arm" (Gordimer, *The House Gun*, p. 135). This portrait, like many of those in the novel, is unmistakably drawn from life: the justice described is Albie Sachs, who as a young lawyer in the 1950s was active in the anti-apartheid movement. Sach's legal work led to his twice being detained without trial by South Africa's Security Police—a not-uncommon fate for those of all races who were opposed to the government's policies. In 1988, while he was working as a law professor and government minister in neighboring Mozambique, Sachs was nearly killed by a car bomb planted by the South African Security forces. The physical deformity Gordimer ascribes to the justice in the novel resulted from this attack.

Guns and violence in South Africa. South Africa is a country with a long history of violence. During the apartheid era, many of the nation's resources, both public and private, were geared toward preparation for possible armed conflict. The South African Police force enforced apartheid through measures notable for their violence and the oppressive type of order they sought to establish. In response to routine police brutality (including mass shootings of unarmed protestors and the torture of suspects in custody), black victims mounted peaceful political opposition. When nonviolent opposition proved ineffective, however, protestors fought back by attacking police stations, staging riots, and so forth. In the vacuum left by the police force's lack of moral authority, black vigilante forces roamed the townships, engaging in a kind of gang warfare condoned—and occasionally directed—by the police. South Africans of all races grew to accept physical violence as a normal element of social unrest—or even interaction.

FROM "THE BILL OF RIGHTS"

Rights

7. (1) This Bill of Rights is a cornerstone of democracy in South Africa. It enshrines the rights of all people in our country and affirms the democratic values of human dignity, equality and freedom. . . .

Equality

9. (1) Everyone is equal before the law and has the right to equal protection and benefit of the law. . . . (3) The state may not unfairly discriminate directly or indirectly against anyone on one or more grounds, including race, gender, sex, pregnancy, marital status, ethnic or social origin, colour, sexual orientation, age, disability, religion, conscience, belief, culture, language and birth. . . .

Human dignity

10. Everyone has inherent dignity and the right to have their dignity respected and protected.

Life

11. Everyone has the right to life.

Freedom and security of the person

12. (1) Everyone has the right to freedom and security of the person, which includes the right:

a. not to be deprived of freedom arbitrarily or without just cause;
b. not to be detained without trial;
c. to be free from all forms of violence from either public or private sources;
d. not to be tortured in any way; and
e. not to be treated or punished in a cruel, inhuman or degrading way. . . .

Constitution of the Republic of South Africa 1966

In the immediate post-apartheid era, vast economic disparities, frustration with slow social progress, and fear of change pushed the already-existing culture of violence to unprecedented dimensions. Crimes such as carjackings and robbery became commonplace; and even if victims showed no resistance, they were not infrequently wounded or killed. By the mid-1990s, South Africa had one of the highest murder rates in the world—between 60-70 annual murders per 100,000 people. During the same period, a study showed the average in 80 nations to be 5.5 per 100,000 (Barbarin & Richter, p. 86).

Throughout the 1990s, about 40-50 percent of the nation's murders were committed with firearms, and this percentage rose annually. Gun ownership in South Africa is extremely high: in the year 1998, when the population was 40 million, the country's registered firearm count reached 4.2 million, plus anywhere from 500,000-4,000,000 more unregistered weapons in circulation. In 1995, in an attempt to stem the tide of violence, the South African Parliament enacted legislation that stiffened registration requirements, noting that "every person has the right to life and the right to security of the person . . . [and] the increased availability and use of firearms and ammunition has contributed significantly to the high levels of violent crime in our society" (Government Gazette, p. 7). South Africans' desire to protect themselves from threat, and their mixed methods of doing so, were marked by the fact that in the late 1990s, fledgling, albeit vocal, gun-control groups coexisted with a citizenry that applied for new firearm licenses at a rate of 175,000 per year.

Observers debate whether violent crime levels actually rose sharply in South Africa in the 1990s, or inadequate earlier statistics and changes in reporting methods help explain the apparently steep increase. Either way, public perception was of a nation in the grip of a violent crime wave. Suburban homes disappeared from view behind high stone walls topped with coils of barbed wire, private security firms burgeoned, and publications dispensed safety advice, suggesting that one could make a regular practice of running red lights to foil the carjackers, who dragged victims from their vehicles with startling frequency. At the turn of the new century, researchers noted that "few issues dominate the collective psyche of the South African people as fully or generate as much debate as crime and violence" (Barbarin and Richter, p. 65).

The Novel in Focus

The plot. *The House Gun* opens with a phrase that will become a repeated refrain throughout the novel: "Something terrible happened" (*The House Gun*, p. 3). Harald and Claudia Lindgard, as yet unnamed, are watching the television news, passively observing tragedy in an unidentified part of the world, when the doorbell rings. It is a friend of their 27-year-old son Duncan, come to tell them, "Someone's been shot. He's arrested. Duncan" (*The House Gun*, p. 4). From this moment forward, Harald and Claudia's lives change in ways they never imagined possible.

The Lindgards are white, upper-middle-class members of South African society. Claudia is a doctor; Harald, an executive director of an insurance firm. They have always lived at a distance from the strife of their homeland. Neither of them has any frame of reference with which to understand their son's arrest, other than to assume it is a horrible mistake. Over the following few days, however, as they attend Duncan's arraignment, visit him in prison, and interview Julian, the friend who came to tell them of Duncan's arrest, they begin to realize that Duncan may actually be guilty of the crime he stands accused of committing.

The facts seem simple. Duncan has been living with his girlfriend, Natalie, in a garden cottage on the grounds of a house rented by three friends: David, Khulu, and Carl. It is Carl who has been shot, killed with the "house gun" owned in common for protection against burglaries. The murder was committed on a Friday evening. On the night before, all the friends had eaten dinner together in the house, after which they sat talking though the evening. When Duncan went to bed, Natalie stayed to help Carl wash up. Duncan was not jealous of the friendship between Carl and Natalie. Carl was a homosexual, along with Khulu and David. In fact, Carl and David were lovers. So there was little cause for jealously. But several hours later, Duncan awoke to find Natalie still gone. He returned to the main house to check on her, only to discover that she and Carl were making love on the couch. Natalie immediately got into her car and drove away. Duncan returned to the cottage, and stayed there throughout the night and the following day. On Friday, David and Khulu came home from work in the evening to find Carl dead; the gardener said he had seen Duncan crossing the yard a few hours earlier, and watched him drop something in a clump of ferns. Searching the yard, the police recovered the house gun.

The revelation of a probable motive implicating Duncan in his friend's death is jarring to Harald and Claudia on multiple levels. A crime of passion is no more explicable to them than a carefully plotted assassination would be. At first, they cannot fathom Duncan's ever committing such a crime. "That kind of act isn't in the range of emotional control in which their son's character was formed, or the contemporary ethic that men don't own women. Therefore the act could not have been committed" (*The House Gun*, p. 31). Yet, to their shock, Duncan's lawyer—a black man named Hamilton Motsamai—says Duncan has professed his guilt.

As the novel unfolds, the Lindgards' lives come to revolve around a regular regimen of prison visits, meetings with Duncan's lawyer, and bouts of agonized soul searching. Alienated from their friends and colleagues, who treat them with polite but uncomprehending sympathy, they retreat into a closed sphere of self-doubt. They spend their time seeking to understand what their son has done, and also probing their own consciences and past behavior—for "someone must be to blame. If Duncan says he's guilty" (*The House Gun*, p. 66). Rather than coming together in this time of crisis, Harald and Claudia grow isolated from each other in their bewilderment. They are driven apart by guilt and confusion:

> I have the feeling you're in some way suspicious of me. You're trying to . . . get me to explain, because I'm his mother. I ought to know, I should know *why*.
>
> And I'm his father! I ought to know!
>
> (*The House Gun*, p. 51)

Harald and Claudia's union is damaged not just by their mutual self-recrimination and accusations, but also by their different approaches to the problem: Harald, a devout Catholic, seeks a religious answer; Claudia, a rationalist, looks to psychology. Unhappily, both approaches yield results. The more they examine the matter, the more Claudia and Harald find flaws in themselves and in each other.

In their rehearsal of critical moments from Duncan's childhood, moments that might furnish clues, both Lindgards remember the first time something terrible happened: Duncan wrote home to them from boarding school that one of his classmates had hung himself. Shocked then, as they are now, that such a thing could happen to a child from a "good" background, they made a pact with their son: they told him—and each other—to keep open the channels of communication. "Whatever happens to him, whatever he has done . . . he can come to us. *There's nothing you cannot tell us. . . . We're always there for you. Always*" (*The House Gun*, p. 69). This covenant, though, has not prepared any of the three for what has come to pass. Harald and Claudia, to their shock, feel "a malignant resentment" against their son, for making them the parents of a killer (*The House Gun*, p. 63). Meanwhile, Duncan has not been forthcoming: he "had not been able to tell them anything that was leading him towards that Friday night when something terrible happened to him" (*The House Gun*, p. 159).

At the same time that the Lindgards reassess Duncan's childhood, they discover increasingly more unsettling information about his adult life. Natalie, they learn, is a deeply troubled young woman—one who had just given up a child for adoption and had a nervous breakdown shortly before she and Duncan became lovers. Since moving in with him, she has had several affairs with other men—affairs he found out about. When questioned by the lawyer, Motsamai, with Harald present, she hints darkly at a life with his son wracked by unrest and power struggles. Natalie resents Duncan's interference in her affairs; she says he thinks he owns her.

Friends of Duncan corroborate and expand on the young woman's story. Natalie, it turns out, had not just had a breakdown, but had tried to kill herself. "Duncan found her and took her to hospital. He brought her back to life. Literally. She owes her life to Duncan; or she blames him" (*The House Gun*, p. 113). These bits of information—both the suicide attempt and the resentment—lend a grim reality to jottings in a notebook of Duncan's that Harald has found and secretly read. In the notebook is a quote from ***Crime and Punishment*** (also in *Literature and Its Times*) by Fyodor Dostoyevsky. The quote concerns a woman named Nastasya: "She would have drowned herself long ago if she had not met me. . . . She doesn't do that because, perhaps, I am more dreadful than the water" (Dostoyevsky in *The House Gun*, p. 47). Far from living with a woman he may not be serious about, the Lindgards' son appears to have been locked in an ongoing life-or-death psychodrama.

Motsamai's interview with the housemate Khulu yields even more surprises. Before Duncan took up with Natalie, apparently, he and Carl—the murdered man—were lovers. Duncan took the relationship more seriously than Carl, and was quite upset when Carl called it off. The scene on the sofa thus gains yet another layer of complexity: Duncan has been betrayed not just by his lover and a friend, but by two lovers. Harald and Claudia are accepting parents; their son's bisexuality in and of itself does not disturb them. However, the number and extent of the ways they do not know their son appears never-ending. Their search to understand him and his actions therefore seems hopeless: "Discovery is not an end. Only a new mystery" (*The House Gun*, p. 120).

Despite the rocky ground onto which their relationship is thrown by Duncan's actions, Harald and Claudia do find a cause that reunites them. Motsamai, who has become almost as much a friend as a lawyer, points out a possibility they have not yet considered—their son may face the death penalty. There has been a moratorium on executions since the scrapping of the old constitution, but the penalty is still on the books. The Constitutional Court is about to hear a challenge of the penalty's constitutionality—and Motsamai expresses confidence that executions will be outlawed, but the Lindgards realize that they are "two creatures caught in the headlights of catastrophe. Nothing between Duncan and the judge, passing sentence, but Motsamai and his confidence" (*The House Gun*, p. 128). As the first of *The House Gun*'s two parts draws to a close, Harald takes to haunting the sessions of the Constitutional Court in which it considers the death penalty, and both parents begin to work even more closely with Motsamai, with one goal in mind: to "get him off" (*The House Gun*, p. 144).

Part 2 of *The House Gun* opens with a voice we have not yet heard: Duncan's. The only living witness to the murder, he is no less tortured and confused than his parents as he tries to figure out exactly how all this has come to pass. We learn that when he reentered the main house on Friday night, he found Carl lying there on the sofa—the same sofa he had lain on the night before with Natalie. Carl smiled at him, shrugged, said "Oh dear, I'm sorry, *Bra* [brother]"; and Duncan remembers that "it was exactly the manner, the words, with which the man had announced the end of the months they had lived as lovers" (*The House Gun*, p. 155). He shot Carl, he thinks, simply to stop the sound of the other man's talking.

The second half of the novel focuses on Duncan's trial, which we see through the perspective of Harald and Claudia—although Duncan's thoughts intervene. Natalie is the first witness called, and her testimony is key to setting the tone of the trial. How the judges and the assembled throng feel about Natalie may, the Lindgards know, be a critical part of how they judge Duncan. The young woman begins her time on the stand in charge of the situation: beautiful, poised in front of an audience, she testifies to Duncan's jealousy, his controlling behavior, his barely suppressed violence towards her. She characterizes her sex with Carl as something natural and comforting, in stark contrast to her troubled relationship with Duncan. Under Motsamai's questioning, however, she admits both to being pregnant and to not knowing who the father is—Carl or Duncan. Moreover, she does not care to know: the child is hers, "nobody's business but mine" (*The House Gun*, p. 195). Motsamai parlays this testimony into a portrait of Natalie as self-centered and callous, totally indifferent to her erstwhile lover's feelings. Instead of being seen as victim, she becomes reimagined as villain.

Duncan's official plea is "not guilty." Motsamai will argue that the psychological trauma of Carl and Natalie's actions caused him to "blank-out" at the time of the murder, leaving him unable to assess the nature of his actions. Both the prosecution and the defense thus call to the stand psychiatrists who have examined Duncan. The psychiatrist for the prosecution testifies that Duncan is a man "in whom self-control has been strongly established since childhood," and that the evening of the murder was no exception (*The House Gun*, p. 200). He spent the day in his cottage, she says, plotting revenge—and then seized the opportunity to take it. The psychiatrist for the defense, in contrast, states that Duncan has had a long history of emotional stress, and that Carl's provocation of him was a tremendous emotional blow. "As forceful as any external blow to the head," it precipitated him "into a state of dissociation from reason and reality" (*The House Gun*, pp. 228, 202). Claudia and Harald, listening to these two very different versions of their son, "cannot distinguish which Duncan is being described in truth" (*The House Gun*, p. 205).

Khulu, the only member of the household who could be presumed to be somewhat impartial, turns out to be a bastion of support for the Lindgards, both on and off the stand. Throughout the trial, he sits with Harald and Claudia in the courtroom, sheltering them from crowds during breaks. As a witness, he testifies to Natalie's mood swings and Duncan's infinite patience with her. In counterpoint to Natalie's testimony, he tells the courtroom that "she tortured him [Duncan]. Really" (*The House Gun*, p. 224). Moreover, as a friend who knows Duncan well, he testifies that when Duncan reentered the house Friday evening, he could not have been planning to kill Carl: "It is not in his nature. Never. I swear on my own life" (*The House Gun*, p. 225).

Duncan himself, when called to the stand, testifies that all he can remember about seeing Carl and Natalie together is a feeling of "disgust, a disintegration of everything" (*The House Gun*, p. 211). He spent the day in the cottage, he says, just thinking—"trying to explain, so that I could put—things—together again, understand myself" (*The House Gun*, p. 211). He rehearses again his confrontation with Carl: Carl's friendly dismissal of the events of the night before, his offer of a drink; "I suddenly picked up the gun on the table. And then he was quiet" (*The House Gun*, p. 214).

Duncan's case has been heard by a single judge, assisted by two judicial assessors. After all the witnesses have testified and the attorneys have made their closing remarks, the sitting judge sums up the case at length and notes that his verdict depends on two points of interpretation: "Did premeditation of revenge occupy the accused during the day he spent alone in the cottage?" and "Whether or not harmful intention was premeditated, when the accused picked up the gun . . . was he in a state of automatism in which . . . there was total loss of control?" (*The House Gun*, pp. 264-65). On the first point, he finds that no, the murder was not premeditated. On the second, however, he finds that although the crime was committed under conditions of extreme stress, Duncan still must bear criminal responsibility for his act. The judge notes that the murder has been facilitated by the culture of violence in South Africa: such disputes might formerly have been settled with an argument or a punch, but now they end in tragedy because "the guns *happen to be there*" (*The House Gun*, p. 267). Duncan is guilty, with extenuating circumstances. He is sentenced to seven years in prison, the lightest sentence that could reasonably have been hoped for.

In the final pages of the novel, all three Lindgards take the first steps towards adjusting to the realities of their new lives. Harald and Claudia get used to having a son in prison, while Duncan still tries to make sense of it all and set things as right as possible. Pondering the seemingly endless cycle of violence—not only in his own country and time, but throughout history—he seeks to "break the repetition" (*The House Gun*, p. 294). Likewise, the Constitutional Court seeks to break South Africa's repetition of violence by finally declaring the death penalty unconstitutional. To this end, Duncan asks his parents to do what they can to help Natalie's child, a son. Whether the child is his or Carl's does not matter. No one else may understand, he realizes, but for him, this is the only way to "bring death and life together" (*The House Gun*, p. 294).

Guilt and responsibility. Much of Harald and Claudia's unease in *The House Gun* centers on their own sense of guilt. They are Duncan's parents. Therefore, if he has killed, then they are the progenitors of murder. Each of them is revulsed by the idea of murder: to Harald, it is the ultimate violation of his religious faith; to Claudia, it runs counter to every humanist ideal she holds dear as a doctor, "the purpose of [whose] life is to defend the body against the violence of pain" (*The House Gun*, p. 13). Are they responsible? they wonder. Have they failed Duncan by not keeping him away from damaging influences? Have they failed society by setting loose a killer in its midst? Long before Duncan's trial gets underway, the novel portrays another kind of criminal prosecution. As Harald and Claudia question themselves, and one another, "the townhouse [becomes] a court, a place where there are only accusers and accused" (*The House Gun*, p. 96).

Moreover, this sense of guilt grows. It spreads outward from the immediate situation of Duncan's action to encompass larger questions of personal responsibility. Duncan's crime catapults the Lindgards out of their safe, middle-class world into a community of suffering neither would ever have imagined themselves part of. Claudia's free-clinic patients, many of whom have sons or a brother in prison, suddenly share more of a bond with them than Harald's politely sympathetic colleagues at the insurance firm—"most of [whom] had sons and daughters of their own for whom such an act would be equally impossible" (*The House Gun*, p. 49). This violent rearrangement of Harald and Claudia's world forces them to face head-on their own previously unexamined lives of privilege. The linchpin for the Lindgards' self-reassessment is in many ways Hamilton Motsamai, Duncan's lawyer, "the stranger from the Other Side of the divided past" (*The House Gun*, p. 86). Subject to his professional authority, a circumstance that could never have pertained under the old dispensation, Harald and Claudia uneasily remind themselves that they are not racist, not prejudiced. Harald's faith tells him that all men are equal in God's eyes; Claudia treats black patients with the same compassion as white ones. In years past, they dutifully voted against the government, which they agreed was not doing its duty.

Yet, as Harald is forced to acknowledge, he has never challenged racism in others; Claudia "did not risk her own skin by contact, outside the intimate professional one, with the black men and women she treated" (*The House Gun*, p. 86). Neither ever joined a protest march, spoke out in defense of his or her convictions, or fought against apartheid in any visible or meaningful way:

> They thought of themselves as simply not that kind of person; as if it were a matter of immutable determination, such as one's blood group, and not failed courage.
>
> (*The House Gun*, p. 49)

Now, the familiar power dynamic of black and white inverted, the Lindgards are forced to ask themselves, should they have acted differently?

Up until now, Harald and Claudia have never been in a position to be hurt by their own liberal complacency. The suffering of many in their country was tragic, to be sure, but "none of it had anything to do with them" (*The House Gun*, p. 126). With Duncan's fate potentially hanging, though, on the question posed by the new Constitutional Court's first case—should capital punishment remain legal?—the Lindgards realize that being concerned about human rights "in the general way of civilized people" is not enough (*The House Gun*, p. 126). Their son's life depends on their nation's collective morality—and that collective morality, they begin to see, depends on the moral behavior of individuals, such as themselves. In *The House Gun*, Gordimer begins with the basic skeleton of a courtroom thriller, but transforms and enlarges the central "whodunnit" into something vastly more profound. Even before Harald and Claudia are willing to accept that Duncan "believes or knows he's guilty," they are pressed into a realization that "he is not innocent in the sense of the context of the awful event, the kind of milieu in which it could take place" (*The House Gun*, pp. 41, 30). Moreover, as they, and we, come to understand, they are equally guilty: perhaps not guilty of bad parenting, but guilty nonetheless—for all are ultimately responsible for, and to, the time and place in which they live.

Sources and literary context. Gordimer's work has always been political, and often loosely drawn from historical events and characters. The main character Rosa Burger, for example, in her novel *Burger's Daughter*, is based on Ilse Fisher, daughter of the real-life anti-apartheid activist Bram Fisher. In *The House Gun*, the capital case before the Constitutional Court—as well as the court members themselves—are quite real, though the core of the novel, says Gordimer, is apolitical: "It has to do with intimate human relationships and how we know one another" (Gordimer in Garner, p. 2).

This seeming contradiction—of intense historical and sociopolitical specificity, on the one hand, and of classical realist attention to the minutiae of ordinary middle-class life, on the other—is a thread that has run throughout Gordimer's career. More than being merely a polemicist or argumentative type of fiction, Gordimer's stories have always concerned themselves with tracing the complicated connections between the political and personal, the public and private. *The House Gun*, as many critics have noted, continues this pursuit in its exploration of the way the Lindgards' private conflicts are forced into the glare of public attention, their family dynamic becoming unexpectedly and inextricably linked to larger political concerns: violence, individual guilt and responsibility, and the legacy of apartheid.

Gordimer is often compared to Alan Paton and J. M Coetzee (white South African writers of her generation; see Paton's ***Cry, the Beloved Country,*** also in *Literature and Its Times*). In her attention to power, social justice, and inequality, she also shares much with postcolonial writers from other regions, such as Nigeria's Chinua Achebe and Egypt's Naghib Mahfouz (see Achebe's ***Anthills of the Savannah*** and ***Things Fall Apart,*** also in *Literature and Its Times*). It is still too early to predict how the changes in South African government will alter the country's literary landscape, but Gordimer's fiction at least promises to retain a political dimension. While "South African writers are wriggling free of the stranglehold of political angst," she seems committed to the notion that—try as one might to escape it—the political emerges as a critical aspect of any encounter (Bristowe, p. 21).

Reviews. South African critics have tended to assess *The House Gun* in relation to broad literary and cultural concerns. Looking at the style of Gordimer's writing, David Medalie points out the modernist tendency in much of Gordimer's later fiction, especially when it investigates the breakdown of common understanding of the world that underlies most pre-modernist, realist fiction. Herein lies *The House Gun*'s refusal to neatly sum up the questions of guilt and responsibility that preoccupy it. The novel presents post-apartheid South Africa "as a place of perplexing indeterminacy," where the relationship between one's identity and one's context is ultimately unclear (Medalie, p. 644).

In contrast to this very literary analysis, Ronald Suresh Roberts focuses on *The House Gun's* portrayal of a "racially scarred society," in which the elder Lindgards, while not literally imprisoned, "remain caged in post-apartheid whiteness" (Roberts, p. 22). Roberts praises the novel as "unprecedented in its nuances," in its exploration of racialized identity: in it, he says, Gordimer makes "her boldest move" yet towards "exposing, demystifying and demeaning the particular ideology of whiteness" (Roberts, p. 22).

THE TRUTH AND RECONCILIATION COMMISSION

South Africa's transition from old regime to new was not, as one might expect, without hurdles. The old government had not been overthrown. It had voluntarily relinquished power. Also the new government, although in practice dominated by the African National Congress party, was in theory and name a "Government of National Unity." Former political prisoners, people who had seen their friends and relatives killed, ordinary citizens who had never been able to achieve their dreams, were now expected to work hand in hand with the very people who had formerly oppressed them. These people, in turn, were expected to cooperate with a population they had been raised to think of as inferior and dangerous. At both the governmental and the larger societal level, deep wounds cried out to be healed, and power structures still had to be negotiated. A balance needed to be struck between moving forward in cooperation, and yet still acknowledging past wrongs, wrongs of all kinds, committed by all sorts of people.

The solution was the Truth and Reconciliation Commission, established in 1995 and operational until 1998. The commission was charged with the task of hearing testimony from anyone and everyone, from people on the street to former Prime Minister Botha himself, about their experiences and actions under apartheid. "Focusing not only on those violations committed by the former state, the [commission] chose instead to focus on violations committed by *all* parties to the conflict" ("Truth and Reconciliation Commission Final Report"). The commission, the Minister of Justice stated, was "a necessary exercise to enable South Africans to come to terms with their past on a morally accepted basis and to advance the cause of reconciliation" ("Truth and Reconciliation Commission"). The examination of actions and consciences as well as testimony and confession, and the admission and apportioning of guilt were central to the nation's process of self-healing.

The House Gun was hailed by many American reviewers as a powerful exploration of a political and social context at once highly particular and at the same time painfully familiar. As one critic noted, the novel's setting—a society highly concerned with crime, with decent people debating the role of guns and capital punishment in the culture of violence—would resonate forcefully with American readers thinking about their own country. Another reviewer compared the novel to Philip Roth's *American Pastoral*, also about parents whose child had committed murder, noting that "both masterful novelists create compelling portraits of unravelling middle-class lives" (Hartigan, p. 496). A few critics applauded *The House Gun*'s skillful portrayal of the psychological and emotional state of its characters, but were less impressed with the novel as social commentary. They found Gordimer's efforts to grapple with post-apartheid realities somewhat forced: "She . . . tries to shoehorn into her narrative political and social observations that ultimately have little to do with the story at hand" (Kakutani, sec. F, p. 1). But even such reviewers tended to forgive what they saw as the occasional lapse into didacticism, observing that nonetheless "the message of this powerful novel rings true" (*Publishers Weekly*, p. 52).

—Ruth Feingold

For More Information

Barbarin, Oscar, and Linda Richter. *Mandela's Children: Growing Up in Post-Apartheid South Africa*. London: Routledge, 2001.

Beinhart, William, and Saul Dubow, eds. *Segregation and Apartheid in Twentieth-Century South Africa*. London: Routledge, 1995.

Bristowe, Anthea. "Escaping the Intellectual Swamplands." *The Sunday Times* (Johannesburg), 21 April 1996, 21.

Constitution of the Republic of South Africa, 1993. 1993. http://www.polity.org.za/govdocs/legislation/1993/constit0.html (14 March 2002).

Constitution of the Republic of South Africa, 1996. 1996. http://www.polity.org.za/govdocs/constitution/saconst.html (12 March 2002).

Garner, Dwight. "The *Salon* Interview: Nadine Gordimer." 1998. http://www.salon.com/books/int/1998/03/cov_si_09int.html (11 March 2002).

Gordimer, Nadine. *The House Gun*. New York: Farrar, Straus and Giroux, 1998.

Government Gazette. *The Firearms Control Act 2000*. Cape Town, South Africa: Government Gazette, 2000.

Hartigan, Rosemary. Review of *The House Gun*, by Nadine Gordimer. *Antioch Review* 56, no.4 (fall 1998): 496.

Kakutani, Michiko. "*The House Gun:* A Fatal Triangle in the Long Shadow of Apartheid." The *New York Times*, 16 January 1998, sec. F, p. 1.

Medalie, David. "'The Context of the Awful Event': Nadine Gordimer's *The House Gun*." *Journal of Southern African Studies* 25, no. 4 (December 1999): 633-44.

Publishers Weekly. Review of *The House Gun*, by Nadine Gordimer. *Publishers Weekly* 244, no. 43 (20 October 1997): 52.

Roberts, Ronald Suresh. "An Intimacy of Menace." *Mail and Guardian*, 13-19 March 1998, 22.

Truth and Reconciliation Commission. "Truth and Reconciliation Commission Final Report." 1998. http://www.polity.org.za/govdocs/commissions/1998/trc (14 March 2002).

———. "Truth and Reconciliation Commission." 2002. http://www.doj.gov.za/trc (10 March 2002).

In the Time of the Butterflies

by
Julia Alvarez

Only ten years old in 1960 when her family escaped their homeland, Julia Alvarez fled the brutal "justice" of the Dominican dictator Rafael Leonidas Trujillo Molina. Her father had been active in an anti-Trujillo underground plot that was detected by the Dominican police. Before they could detain him, Alvarez's father fled with his family to New York and remained in the United States thereafter. Alvarez made her fictional debut with *How the García Girls Lost Their Accents,* which is set in the United States. Her second novel, *In the Time of the Butterflies,* takes place in the Dominican Republic and concerns the destiny of three actual anti-Trujillo female activists.

THE LITERARY WORK

A novel set in the Dominican Republic, mostly from 1938 to 1960 but also in 1994; published in English in 1994.

SYNOPSIS

Four sisters grow up to uncover a hoax—that the leader of their country, Rafael Leonidas Trujillo, is not the Great Benefactor he pretends to be. Three of them organize to unseat the viciously cruel dictator and together they suffer a brutal fate.

Events in History at the Time the Novel Takes Place

Dominican overview. An island sits between Puerto Rico and Cuba in the Caribbean Sea. Called Hispaniola or Española, the western third of this island is inhabited by Haiti. On its eastern two-thirds is the Dominican Republic, an area that was controlled mostly by Spain from 1493 to 1822, then by Haiti until 1844. A shaky independence followed, marred by civil strife, periods of U.S. intervention, and 31 years under Rafael Leonidas Trujillo Molina—an allegedly benevolent dictator who, in fact, resorted to torture and thinly disguised murder.

By 1960, the year of the novel's climax, the Republic's population exceeded 3 million (3,047,070). Its cities, primarily Santo Domingo in the south and Santiago in the north, were growing rapidly, although 65 percent of the people still lived in rural areas. The largely agricultural nation boasts a fertile, north-central valley, the *Cibao,* where the novel's Mirabal sisters lived. Farmers like their father often raised cacao in the Cibao. The nation's most profitable crop, sugarcane, grew in the north; cattle were reared in the south.

Poverty was widespread (average per capita income $200), as was illiteracy in 1960 (80 to 90 percent in rural areas). Almost everyone subscribed to the Roman Catholic faith, and people of mixed ancestry dominated the population. But in contrast to other Latin American nations, mulattos (of black and white ancestry) made up the most numerous ethnic group here. The mulattos, along with some mestizos (of Indian and white ancestry), comprised 70 percent of the population, greatly outnumbering a black minority

(20 percent) and an even smaller white minority (10 percent) in 1960 (Hanover, p. 66).

In control of government, the economy, education, and social life at the time was the dictator Trujillo, who prided himself on his whiteness (though his family history included some black blood) and kept an all-white corps of elite guards. Obsessed not only with skin color but also with all other aspects of his appearance, Trujillo would fly to New York to purchase whitening cremes, elevator shoes that made him taller, and rare bird feathers for his Napoleon-style bicorne hats. He had a passion for clothes, often outfitting himself in full military dress and draping a plethora of medals across his chest. In a nation that measured 260 miles from its eastern tip to its western border with Haiti, Trujillo owned 12 residences and kept a complete wardrobe in each of them. A mix of dissonant traits, he was charismatic, extremely hard-working, a deft organizer, and an administrator with a keen memory. Trujillo was also arrogant, aloof, a megalomaniac who fed on flattery, and a ruler who ultimately lost touch with reality.

Trujillo's rise. Trujillo's Napoleon-style hats conjure up an appropriate comparison. Certainly he ruled like an emperor, though he took pains to observe the letter if not the spirit of the democracy that his republic was supposed to be. Trujillo has been likened to Joseph Stalin, Adolf Hitler, and, by the novel's María Teresa Mirabal, to Benito Mussolini. The allusions are to Trujillo's political cruelty—his ability to call coldly for the murder of someone he suspected to be an enemy, then to stage a lavish public funeral for the same person without flinching. His dictatorship has been described as the most absolute in Latin America. For 31 years (1930–61), Trujillo ruled with an iron hand, keeping a tight rein on the populace either directly as president himself, or indirectly through a puppet president.

His country was in dire need of stable leadership—there is no doubt about that. It had seen 56 revolutions in the 70 years between 1846 and 1916. The location of the island nation made it strategically important to the United States, which aimed to keep the area stable and out of the clutches of powers from the Eastern Hemisphere. In 1916 the U.S. Navy moved in, occupying and—to the chagrin of the Dominican upper class—administering affairs in the small Caribbean nation. Many upper-class Dominicans were so resentful that they left the country during the U.S. occupation (1916–24), clearing the path for the rise of a Dominican middle class, whose members would, in time, assume the reins of national control.

The U.S. occupiers created the Republic's first modern professional armed forces. In 1919 Trujillo became a lieutenant in the nation's U.S.-created police force. Rumor has it that he rose unethically into position as police chief by leaking news about a rendezvous between his superior (the police chief) and the wife of another man. Forewarned about the rendezvous, the other man killed his wife and the police chief at their meeting place. While there is no evidence to confirm his role in the scandal, Trujillo was quick to take advantage of the vacancy it created. He stepped into office as chief of the police force, a body that he would soon transform into an army. Meanwhile, the population in general grew resentful of the U.S. troops. Their occupation benefited the nation in some ways—in addition to the creation of the first modern police, roads were built, education was expanded, and the nation's debt was reduced. But relations soured between the occupiers and the occupied, with a rash of violent incidents erupting in Santo Domingo and other cities. On one occasion, U.S. troops killed a Dominican who resisted arrest, then murdered an innocent woman and burned some houses in the vicinity. Such misconduct by U.S. servicemen continued, fueling ill-will in the citizenry until anti-American sentiment was nearly universal. Some patriots hid in the hills and fought the U.S. servicemen from there. In the novel, the Mirabals speak admiringly of these rebel patriots.

When the U.S. troops withdrew in 1924 the Dominican Republic reverted to a politically unstable independence. Six years later Trujillo won the presidency in a ruthless election. He ran for office unopposed, after beating, jailing, exiling, or killing his rivals. Both cunning and good fortune seemed to be on his side. Just 18 days after Trujillo took office, a hurricane blasted the island, prompting the Dominican Congress to bestow dictatorial powers on the new president. Trujillo quickly used these powers to eliminate the remaining opposition.

Trujillo's style. In 1931 Trujillo created the "Dominican Party" to replace all other political parties. Over the years, he would maintain the appearance of democracy in the virtually one-party state, rigging elections to produce the desired outcome and making citizens join his Party and attend its local meetings. Invariably the citizens were required to sing Trujillo's praises. He was to be called "Generalissimo Doctor Rafael Leonidas Trujillo Molina, Honorable president of

Rafael Leonidas Trujillo

the Republic, Benefactor of the Fatherland," a title bestowed upon him by the Republic's main university, though Trujillo probably never attended more than elementary school. Less formally, people fell into the habit of referring to him as *El Jefe* (The Boss)—the designation used in *In the Time of the Butterflies.*

As the years passed, Trujillo's honors mounted. January 11 became the Day of the Benefactor, an annual celebration in his honor. The highest peak in the central mountain range was dubbed "Pico Trujillo" (Trujillo Peak). In 1936 the capital city, Santo Domingo, was renamed "Ciudad Trujillo" (Trujillo City); and in 1937 the city celebrated the first anniversary of its renaming with a carnival whose queen was the ravishing Lina Lovatón, one of Trujillo's many mistresses. By then the seemingly insatiable sexual appetite of El Jefe, which would turn to younger and younger girls, had become legendary.

Encouraged by Trujillo himself, the adulation continued as the decades passed. Statues were sculpted in his image; 1955 was declared the Year of the Benefactor; neon signs blazoned *God and Trujillo* in the capital city and a mandatory portrait of El Jefe hung in every home, paying homage to a man who promoted himself as the savior, the hero, the father of his people. After a generation, citizens grew accustomed to praising Trujillo and to having his lackeys monitor their every action. Many Dominicans even accepted and believed in the mythical image of the man, as reflected in the initial regard for him held by the novel's Mirabal sisters. A young girl at the time, María Teresa takes a few moments in the privacy of her diary "to wish El Jefe Happy Benefactor's Day with all my heart. I feel so lucky that we have him for a president" (Alvarez, *In the Time of the Butterflies,* p. 37). Older and a bit wiser, the religious Patria admits that Trujillo is no saint, but reasons that "among the *Bandidos* that had been in the National Palace, this one at least was building churches and schools, paying off our debts" (*Butterflies,* p. 51).

Patria is right. Trujillo's regime did bring improvements—the building of schools, highways, and water systems; repayment of foreign debts; a balanced budget; the end of civil war; and better medical services. But the benefits didn't reach everyone, and there was tremendous graft. Trujillo amassed a personal fortune—about $800 million in a nation that meanwhile remained poverty-ridden. He ranked first among the country's storekeepers, industrialists, and agriculturists, holding 60 to 70 percent of the finest farming and grazing land. Trujillo took a 10 percent cut of everything the government bought or sold, even when it purchased goods from his own firms. He used his economic clout to bully uncooperative businessmen, getting banks to refuse them loans, officials to deny them export permits, gangs to destroy their property. And while such tactics were unethical, they paled beside Trujillo's treatment of citizens who turned against him. In the novel, at the tender age of 12, Minerva learns that Trujillo has murdered her friend Sinita's uncles, father, and brother because the uncles plotted against him. Incredulous, Minerva tries hard to swallow the news that El Jefe does "bad things": "it was as if I had just heard Jesus had slapped a baby" (*Butterflies,* p. 17).

External resistance. Sinita's uncles had planned to "do something to Trujillo"—that is, to oust him from power (*Butterflies,* p. 17). They were not the first, nor would they be the last, although Trujillo and his *calies* (informers) kept a tight rein on the citizenry, first through strong-arm tactics and later by a cloak-and-dagger system of recording devices and spies, along with the manhandling of dissidents in jail until, their spirits broken, they submitted to his regime. Inspiring terror and keeping close tabs on the populace was the *Servicio de Inteligencia Military* (SIM), a military intelligence service that became especially brutal from 1957 to 1960, when it was run by Johnny Abbés Garcia. The SIM made use of two interrogation and torture centers, *La Cuarenta* (in the novel "La 40"), on 40th Street in upper Ciudad Trujillo, and Kilometer Nine on a highway located nine kilometers east of the capital. Among the SIM's instruments were the electric chair, electric cattle prods, and the *pulpo* (which means "octopus"; it was an electric apparatus with tentacles to place on body parts and a cap to screw onto the head).

Outside the torture chambers, the general population lived under the constant surveillance of soldiers and secret policemen. Wherever people congregated, plainclothesmen were there to keep hawklike eyes on them. Mail was censored, phones were wiretapped, and it became prudent to suspect servants of spying for the regime (in the novel, the yardboy Pietro reports all he hears in the Mirabal household for a few pesos and a bottle of rum). It was not only forbidden for citizens to criticize Trujillo, but also to remain silent about him. Young and old, men and women, they all had to sing El Jefe's praises or suffer the consequences.

Of course, an alternative was to go, or to be sent, into exile. With the aid or knowledge of foreign powers, Dominican exiles attempted several times to topple Trujillo.

1947—Invasion of Cayo Confites: Exiles congregate on the deserted island Cayo Confites, near Cuba. Their arsenal consists of three ships, assorted weaponry, and light bombing planes purchased in the United States. The invaders never get outside Cuban waters—a Cuban fleet arrests them for a few hours, then lets them go.

1949—Invasion of Luperón: The invaders plan to leave Guatemala and land in several spots in the Dominican Republic, where they will be joined by dissidents in the country itself. Their only amphibious plane lands in the small port of Luperón, where a Trujillo guard foils their plans by cutting off electric power. In the darkness, the invaders shoot at one another before escaping to the mountains. Trujillo's army hunts them down and kills almost all of them, keeping only a few alive to profess communist support for the plot.

1959—June 14 Invasion: A rash of strongmen have recently been ousted from power in Argentina (Juan Perón), Colombia (Gustavo Rojas Pinilla), Venezuela (Marco Pérez Jiménez), and Cuba (Fulgencio Batista). Encouraged by these successes, Dominican exiles stage a third invasion, landing by boat in two places and by plane in the Constanza Mountain Valley. The invaders are chased by Trujillo's army until all but a few of them have been killed. It is at this point in the novel that Patria, the eldest Mirabal sister, on a religious retreat in the valley, commits herself to the rebel movement.

Internal resistance. Despite talk of human rights abuses, other nations tolerated Trujillo. In truth, U.S. leaders feared a communist takeover of the Dominican Republic more than they feared Trujillo. The ongoing Cold War—the competition between the United States and Soviet Union for world power—encouraged U.S. leaders to tolerate him for years. They finally took a position against him in 1960, having their Central Intelligence Agency (CIA) send over weapons to help oust him from power.

Trujillo's regime had fallen into worldwide disrepute by 1960, a problem El Jefe tried to remedy. In 1955–56 he staged an International Fair of Peace and Brotherhood, a $40 million project that turned out to be a financial disaster. Attracting far fewer than the anticipated 500,000 foreigners, it drew only 24,000, many of whom were flown in by Trujillo, all expenses paid, as part of the effort to repair his badly damaged image.

Some of the exiles (backed by Cuba's Fidel Castro and Venezuela's Rómulo Betancourt) went on to stage the unsuccessful June 14, 1959, invasion. By then, people inside the Republic had begun to form a rebel movement of their own—made up largely of young people, the children of landowners, businessmen, and professionals. Taking their name from the failed invasion, in tribute to its martyrs, the young rebels formed the *Catorce de Junio* (Fourteenth of June Movement). They divided into small groups, secretly building explosives, planning to assassinate Trujillo. It was a goal with which U.S. diplomat Henry Dearborn, who was stationed in the Dominican Republic, heartily concurred: "If I were a Dominican . . . I would favor destroying Trujillo as being the first necessary step in the salvation of my country and I would regard this, in fact, as my Christian duty" (Dearborn in Diederich, p. 47).

Minerva Mirabal's husband, Manolo Tavárez Justo, led this actual Fourteenth of June Movement, which Minerva and her sisters Patria and María Teresa joined. The three sisters would become an inspiration to the underground, which grew to include 30,000-40,000 Dominicans. In her lifetime, Minerva, alias Mariposa (or "Butterfly") #1, showed a defiance that made her their secret heroine. In death, María Teresa and Patria, known as Mariposas #2 and #3, were esteemed as heroines too.

Human rights abuses. The dissidents settled on the time and place to kill Trujillo—January 21, 1960, at a cattle fair. But led by Johnny Abbés, SIM agents cracked down on them before they could execute their plan. Hundreds of Fourteenth of June Movement members were arrested and dragged to the La Cuarenta torture chamber before they were thrown in La Victoria prison. Minerva Mirabal's husband, Manolo, was arrested on January 13, Minerva on the 20th, and María Teresa on the 21st. Patria escaped arrest, but her husband, Pedro, her son Nelson, and María Teresa's husband, Leandro, did not.

Historical accounts indicate that the men were separated from the women and taken to private cells after brutal interrogation. Manolo was tortured in an electric chair, and subjected to beatings and the extraction of his fingernails. Kept in jail by Trujillo, he and the other Mirabal husbands served unbroken prison sentences.

Minerva and María Teresa meanwhile endured two periods of arrest—January 20–21 to February 7, 1960, and May 18 to August 9, 1960. During their first arrest, the women were thrown into small mosquito-ridden rooms and denied adequate food. They received better treatment during the second arrest, by which time the Trujillo regime was feeling the brunt of worldwide pressure. On June 8 a committee of the international Organization of American States (OAS) released a report accusing the Dominican Republic of violating human rights and terrorizing its political prisoners. The regime then committed an international blunder that further soiled its reputation. On June 24, in Caracas, Venezuela, terrorists attempted to assassinate President Betancourt, who was an unremitting critic of Trujillo's rule. The assassins placed a dynamite bomb (whose triggering device was manufactured in the Dominican Republic) in a parked car on a parade route taken by Betancourt's vehicle. The bomb exploded at the proper time, killing a bystander and a presidential aide, and inflicting severe burns on President Betancourt himself. The outraged President blamed Trujillo, after which the OAS broke off diplomatic relations with the Dominican Republic and imposed economic sanctions. OAS nations suspended trade to the Dominican Republic, refusing to sell it weaponry, petroleum, trucks, or spare parts.

The pressure prompted Trujillo to treat his political prisoners better. Minerva and María Teresa were allowed to buy food and were given something to ward off the mosquitoes. Sharing their cell with prostitutes, killers, and other such prisoners, the two were let out to appear at their trial. The court sentenced them to 30 years each, then, on appeal, reduced the sentence to five years each. But, on August 9, 1960, the two were pardoned and released for good, thanks not only to international pressure but also to the Catholic Church.

THE CONSUMMATE SHOWMAN

Trujillo committed atrocities that outraged the world—for example, the massacre of 20,000 workers from Haiti in 1937. Yet he somehow managed to cultivate an image of himself as a proponent of democracy. In the post-World War II era, he shrewdly presented himself as a virulent anticommunist, a ruse that forced him to increase democracy at home in the 1940s, in order to substantiate his image. He even secretly helped found a communist faction in his country, then, in a perverse turnabout snuffed it out of existence during his 1946–47 wave of terror.

Church politics. The Church had long stayed out of politics, but the terror visited on Fourteenth of June Movement prisoners stirred its leaders. No longer willing to stand by and do nothing, the nation's six bishops signed the first of several pastoral letters, public proclamations stating that human rights did not exist in their land and that this was an offense against God. The first letter, read on January 25, 1960, to 624 churches in the Republic, asked Trujillo to halt the "excesses, dry the tears, heal the wounds," and return the human rights to which all Dominican citizens were entitled (Diederich, p. 37). Pastoral letters had preceded the downfall of dictators in Argentina, Venezuela, and Colombia, and the letters about Trujillo enraged him—but he released the female prisoners.

Meanwhile, U.S. emissaries tried persuading Trujillo to change his ways. Senator George Smathers of Florida pleaded with Trujillo, appealing to his vanity. Smathers prophesied, correctly, that all the statues and pictures of Trujillo would be ripped down if he did not transform his government from a dictatorship into a democracy. At the root of his concern was the U.S. fear that if such a transition did not occur, communists would gain the upper hand in the Dominican Republic.

In the end, this fear prompted U.S. agents to break with the Fourteenth of June Movement, whose rebels identified too much with Cuba (and communist notions) for U.S. tastes. Still interested in unseating Trujillo, the United States began making common cause with more conservative conspirators. Toward the end of *In the Time of the Butterflies,* Minerva informs her husband that the U.S. agents have switched their support from the Fourteenth of June Movement to other domestic rebels. The news distresses Manolo, who protests that the *gringos* will take over the revolution, which he is still committed to waging. And, in fact, a revolution of sorts is about to materialize, but not before the three so-called *mariposas,* or butterflies, are caught.

DEFIANT DRAMA

The novel's description of a skit performed by Minerva and her friends recalls an actual historical incident. The actors were older and did not write their own play; but, as in Minerva's case, it was performed for the 1944 centennial. The university's vice-president, Bonilla Atiles, directed some students to enact *La Viuda de Padilla,* a drama about rebels who defied the Spanish Emperor Charles V in the sixteenth century. As in the novel, Trujillo's minions did not detect the play's hidden meaning. Its student-actors went on to join the Democratic Youth and the communist movement, two factions that flourished briefly in 1945 before Trujillo's regime launched a campaign of terror in 1946–47.

The Novel in Focus

The plot. *In the Time of the Butterflies* is a family saga told from the viewpoints of four sisters—Patria, Minerva, María Teresa, and Dedé—all of whom come of age during the course of the novel. It moves from sister to sister, flashing backward and forward in time. The action opens in 1994 with the only surviving sister, Dedé, now a successful life-insurance salesperson. "Everyone wants to buy a policy from the woman who just missed being killed along with her three sisters" (*Butterflies,* p. 5). In the frame-story, Dedé is interviewed by a Dominican American, ostensibly the author herself.

Part 1 (1938–46) introduces the four sisters and their parents, characterizing the girls as sensible (Dedé), smart and rebellious (Minerva), preoccupied with religion (Patria), and naive and romantic (María Teresa). The family lives in rural Ojo de Agua, no place for a girl to get an education, although their father, Enrique, who shows genuine fondness for his daughters, doubts that they really need one, especially since it means sending them away to live at a Catholic school. But his wife convinces him that now that their farm and store are prospering, schooling is part of his family's success.

Away at school, 12-year-old Minerva befriends a waif named Sinita, who turns Minerva's world upside down. Her new friend shares with a horrified Minerva the details of how Trujillo murdered Sinita's uncles. One rude awakening follows another, as the girls watch a beautiful classmate, Lina Lovatón, being whisked off to the capital to become Trujillo's mistress. The school benefits from the affair when El Jefe constructs the Lina Lovatón gymnasium. In 1944, the centennial of the Republic's independence, Minerva and her friends perform a skit in this gym about how their nation gained its freedom from Spain. Written by the girls, their play is a subtle protest against Trujillo's regime, but this is clear only to them. They later perform the skit for Trujillo, and in a hair-raising scene, without warning anyone, Sinita makes the protest more overt. To dodge Trujillo's wrath, the quick-thinking Minerva improvises an ending that honors him. It is the first of many risky moments for her.

In Part 2 of the novel (1948–59), Dedé recalls a romantic rivalry between herself and Minerva over a radical named Virgilio Morales. To escape Trujillo's henchmen, Virgilio fled the country and lived in exile; he returned briefly to the Dominican Republic in the 1940s, when Trujillo made a show of increasing democracy in the country.

Dedé marries a cousin, Jaimito, who refrains from getting involved in politics or anything else that might cause trouble. Falling in step with her husband, she remains detached from the underground, though privately she agrees with her sisters that the regime must be brought down.

Minerva discovers that her father is having an adulterous relationship with a peasant, who has borne him four daughters, a mirror illegitimate family. First outraged, then resigned to the existence of this family, she demands an explanation. "'Cosas de los hombres,' he said. Things a man does" (*Butterflies,* p. 92). She herself falls victim to things that the man Trujillo does when her prosperous family attends a party at which he is the guest of honor. El Jefe picks Minerva as a dance partner. As they dance, she appeals to his vanity, hoping to win permission to attend law school, reasoning that her father will have to let her enroll if Trujillo prescribes it. Minerva reminds Trujillo that he gave women the right to vote, which he did in 1942 to appear democratic. But Trujillo discourages her from enrolling, then makes a vulgar pass at her, whereupon she slaps him. Fortunately, a rainstorm allows the family to escape the outdoor party and head for home. Minerva, however, forgets her purse, which contains incriminating anti-Trujillo letters from the exiled Virgilio. Her father suffers the punishment. He "disappears" (is arrested) and emerges from jail a broken man, proving that those who survive prison are often so ruined physically and mentally that Trujillo need not fear their release.

The novel progresses to the 1950s, a decade covered mostly by María Teresa's diary entries, which are illustrated with occasional diagrams. She enrolls in the university while Minerva is still there and becomes privy to her sister's secret passions—her love for the poetry of José Martí, for example. On vacation, 29-year-old Minerva meets a kindred spirit named Manolo, whom she marries. Still guiding her younger sister, Minerva helps María Teresa prepare a speech when she is elected Miss University, reminding her not to overdo it because the crowd will be restless after the "disappearance" of Galíndez, a former teacher of theirs. As María Teresa's diary explains, her peers are no longer taking such injustices lying down—a national underground is forming, and she has joined it. María Teresa builds grenades and helps run a supply center for the underground; in the process she meets her future husband, a fellow rebel in the underground named Leandro Guzmán Rodriguez.

The action flashes forward to the end of the decade. It is 1959 and the eldest sister, the religious Patria, has now been married to the landowner Pedrito González for 18 years. She stays out of the rebel movement at first, taking care of her son and daughter, but then gets "braver like a crab going sideways. I inched towards courage the best way I could, helping out with the little things" (*Butterflies*, p. 154). Patria goes on a religious retreat to the Constanza Valley, but an invasion of Dominican exiles, the "June 14 Invasion," shatters her peace; the sight of a bloody boy who is her own child's age converts her into a die-hard member of the underground, and her son and husband are also drawn into the movement. Their home becomes a motherhouse; Patria's set of church rebels meets there with Minerva's and Manolo's secular rebels to form the Fourteenth of June Movement, a fledgling group of 40 dissidents whose mission is to effect an internal revolution rather than wait for an outside rescue.

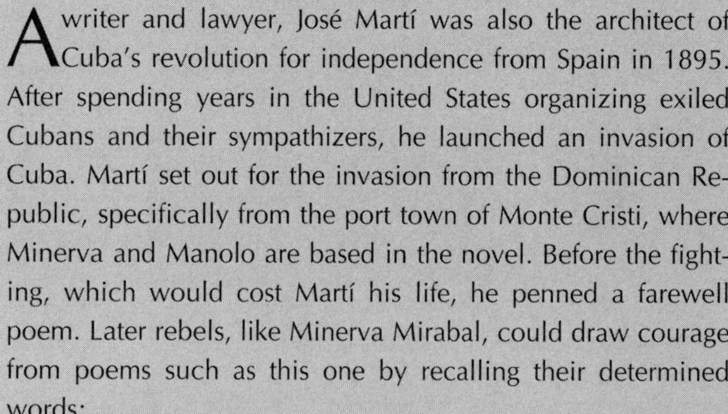

MARTÍ'S COURAGE

A writer and lawyer, José Martí was also the architect of Cuba's revolution for independence from Spain in 1895. After spending years in the United States organizing exiled Cubans and their sympathizers, he launched an invasion of Cuba. Martí set out for the invasion from the Dominican Republic, specifically from the port town of Monte Cristi, where Minerva and Manolo are based in the novel. Before the fighting, which would cost Martí his life, he penned a farewell poem. Later rebels, like Minerva Mirabal, could draw courage from poems such as this one by recalling their determined words:

And of me I must say
That following serenely,
Without fear of the lightning and thunder
I am working out the future.

(Martí in Foner, p. 14)

Part 3 of the novel, which focuses on the year 1960, begins with the roundup. Patria remembers how the SIM came to arrest her loved ones. It would be three months before she again saw her husband, her two sisters, or her son. In the meantime, her mentors, the church padres, draft pastoral letters to be read from every pulpit, condemning the regime and throwing in their lot with the people. Her father's other, illegitimate daughters help smuggle supplies to the prison-bound sisters. Minerva wants books, especially José Martí's poems. Even in prison, she shows defiance, forming a school, discussing Martí with her cellmates, singing the national anthem, and refusing to give up her crucifix when the regime retaliates against the Church by confiscating all prisoners' crucifixes. Minerva is punished a few times for her defiance—removed from the cell that she shares with others, and thrown into solitary confinement.

María Teresa, again through diary entries, shares her experience in jail, disclosing the worst of it only after her release from prison. The entry describes her being taken to the torture chamber, stripped to her underclothes, and tortured in front of her husband to make him divulge information.

THE INFLAMMATORY ANTHEM

These lines from the Dominican anthem show why the prisoners offended Trujillo and his guards by singing it:

No country deserves to be free
If it is an indolent and servile slave,
If the call does not grow loud within it,
Tempered by a virile heroism
But the brave and indomitable Quisqueya ["Mother of All Lands"]*
Will always hold its head high,
For if it were a thousand times enslaved,
It would a thousand times regain freedom.

*The Republic's original, Taino Indian, name

(Reed and Bristow, p. 160)

After seven months in prison, the Mirabal sisters are released and placed under house arrest at their mother's home. El Jefe attends a reception at which he speaks of having only two problems—the "damn church and the Mirabal sisters" (*Butterflies,* p. 281). His henchmen tackle the Mirabal problem, transferring Minerva's and María Teresa's husbands to a prison up north in Puerto Plata, reachable only by way of a mountainous road full of hairpin turns. Returning from a visit to the two husbands, Minerva, Patria, and María Teresa are ambushed and killed by Trujillo's henchmen. The husbands are afterwards transferred back to the jail down in the capital.

In the novel's Epilogue, Dedé explains how the truth finally came out in 1962, after Trujillo died, at the trial of the Mirabals' murderers. There were four killers, one each for the three women and their driver, Rufino de la Cruz. As in other cases, the killers made the grisly scene look like an accident, loading the four corpses back into the jeep and shoving it over some sugarcane fields into a ravine. The court sentenced the sisters' killers to 20 or 30 years. But shortly thereafter they were set free in the rash of revolutions that rocked the nation.

Reflecting history—a pivotal "disappearance." When preparing her Miss University acceptance speech, María Teresa is advised by her sister Minerva not to overdo it because the students are "going to be a hard crowd to address after this Galíndez thing" (*Butterflies,* p. 136). The kidnapping and murder of Jesús Galíndez has been described as the turning point in Trujillo's whole evil career. A student and teacher at Columbia University in New York, Galíndez was a Basque from Spain, not a Dominican. But he had lived in the Dominican Republic for six years, working in Trujillo's government and teaching at the main university. Now, at Columbia University, he wrote *The Era of Trujillo* to earn his doctorate. His thesis was a frank but fair disclosure of facts, full of no-nonsense revelations like: "The hard truth is that freedom of speech has not existed [in the Dominican Republic] since May, 1930" (Galíndez, p. 129).

On March 12, 1956, Galíndez suddenly disappeared. He had delivered a lecture at the university, then caught a ride from a student to the New York subway so he could take a train to his lower Fifth Avenue apartment. After walking down some subway stairs, Galíndez was never heard from or seen again. Investigators concluded that he was drugged, placed on a chartered plane, and flown by a 23-year-old American pilot named Gerald Murphy to Trujillo's side. According to one account, the dictator ordered the dazed Galíndez to eat his thesis. When Galíndez failed to respond, Trujillo stalked out, after which the young scholar "was stripped and handcuffed. Then a rope was tied to his feet and led through an overhead pulley. Inch by inch Galíndez was lowered into a vat of boiling water. Sometime later Galíndez's body was fed to the sharks" (Diederich, p. 9). Within a few months, the pilot Murphy was arrested by the SIM, and the next year he was found hanging in a Dominican prison, the victim of a so-called suicide. The U.S. Federal Bureau of Investigation tried to uncover the truth, and the affair grew into a worldwide scandal, badly blighting Trujillo's image.

Sources and literary context. Based heavily on fact, *In the Time of the Butterflies* blends the concerns of four girls growing into womanhood with the grimness of daily existence in a police state. The characters are the creation of the author's imagination, but she has aspired to make them true to the spirit of the real sisters. Alvarez did extensive research, athough she makes no pretense of trying to recreate the Mirabals' characters with exactitude. At times she took liberties with history too, "by changing dates, by reconstructing events, and by collapsing characters or incidents," but Alvarez likewise based the novel's plot on a solid foundation of research (*Butterflies*, p. 324).

The Mirabal sisters became national heroes—monuments and museums were erected, and poems written in their honor. *In the Time of the Butterflies* demythologizes them by portraying them as people rather than as icons. The novel belongs to a growing corpus of Hispanic Caribbean literature written in exile, which harks back to mid-to-late-nineteenth-century writings by Puerto Rican and Cuban exiles such as the already-cited José Martí.

Events in History at the Time the Novel Was Written

From the sisters' murders to the writing of the novel. As indicated, leadership of the conspiracy to unseat Trujillo eventually passed from the June Fourteenth Movement to a more conservative group, made up of military men, professionals, and business leaders. In the end, the United States withheld its support even from these conservatives, concerned that if Trujillo were assassinated there would be a breakdown in law and order and the leftist June Fourteenth Movement would seize power. The Dominican plotters decided to proceed anyhow. By this time, Dominicans were bent on ridding themselves of Trujillo, in part because of the Mirabal murders.

> The cowardly killing of three beautiful women in such a manner had greater effect on Dominicans than most of Trujillo's other crimes. It did something to their machismo. They could never forgive Trujillo this crime. More than Trujillo's fight with the Church or the United States, or the fact that he was being isolated by the world as a political leper, the Mirabals' murder tempered the resolution of the conspirators plotting his end.
>
> (Diederich, pp. 71–72)

The so-called *ajusticiamiento*—just assassination—of Trujillo took 15 minutes. He was on his way to his San Cristobál estate, southeast of the capital, to meet a lover, when two cars of assassins descended on him. They succeeded in killing Trujillo. The killers had planned to afterward seize control of the government, but no coup d'état followed. Instead, Trujillo's family took charge, hunting down and jailing most of the assassins. One of them, General José "Pupo" Roman, suffered barbaric tortures, including the stitching of his eyebrows to his eyelids so his eyes would never close.

THE MIRABAL MURDERS—THE FACTS UNCOVERED

Reports indicate that the Mirabal sisters arrived at Puerto Plata to visit their husbands about 2:00 P.M. on November 25, 1960, stopping at a friend's who was sending food to the jailed men. Manolo and Leandro were happy to see not only their wives but also Patria, whose husband had been left in the jail in the capital, and who had come solely to show her support. The sisters left the men to return home at 4:30 P.M. About three kilometers outside Puerto Plata, a car with SIM agents forced the jeep to a stop and the three women were transferred by the agents into their SIM car. Patria broke away momentarily and tried to alert a passing vehicle without success. Two other SIM agents hopped into the jeep with the Mirabals' driver and made him follow the SIM car. The vehicles took a main road toward a nearby estate of Trujillo's, then veered onto a side road. About 7:30 P.M., a neighbor heard the Mirabal's jeep crash into a ravine. It was later determined that the women died from trauma to the base of the brain and side of the neck. They were apparently strangled after losing consciousness. Multiple fractures indicated that they had also been severely beaten.

Altogether, six men were convicted of murdering Trujillo and sentenced to maximum prison terms, then whisked off and executed illegally by Trujillo's son Ramfis. The Trujillo family remained in power for several months, until a military coup ousted them. This was followed by the 1962 election to power of writer Juan Bosch, referred to in the novel as the "poet president." That same year it became a crime for citizens to praise the dead Trujillo in speech, writing, or art. Statues of him were torn down, as U.S. Senator Smathers had predicted. Turmoil followed. An army coup ousted Bosch within months. Then more coups interrupted presidential terms until there was civil war (April-August 1965) and the U.S. Marines intervened. New elections brought Joaquin Balaguer, president under Trujillo when he died,

The mural "A Song to Liberty," paying homage to the Mirabal sisters, is illuminated during an inauguration ceremony in Santo Domingo on March 6, 1997. The mural was painted on an obelisk that had been constructed by Trujillo.

into power again in 1966, and again in 1994, the year in which Dedé Mirabal ends her story. "I never dreamed that thirty-three years after the fall of Trujillo the Dominican people still wouldn't have a definite democracy" mused one citizen in 1994, the year that *In the Time of the Butterflies* was published (Cambeira, p. 202).

Reviews. Many, but not all, reviews of the novel have been positive. A critique in the *New York Times* argues that *In the Time of the Butterflies* focuses too much on the sisters' "rather naïve" development into womanhood and includes too many misfortunes (Gonzáles Echevarría, p. 28). On the other hand, a review in *World Literature Today* praises its "strong believable characters" and applauds the literary style as one that "seems to emerge from the core of woman's experience," as evidenced by such descriptions as "'Dedé's courage unraveled like a row of stitches not finished with a good sturdy knot'" (Pritchett, p. 789). Other reviews speak of the novel as a compelling read that manages to balance the personal with the political. More high praise comes from fellow Latino authors such as Rudolfo Anaya, who asserts that Alvarez's work "is destined to take its place on the shelf of great Latin American novels" (Anaya in Alvarez, p. iii).

—Joyce Moss

For More Information

Alvarez, Julia. *In the Time of the Butterflies.* New York: Plume, 1994.

Cambeira, Alan. *Quisqueya la Bella: The Dominican Republic in Historical and Cultural Perspective.* Armonk, N.Y.: M. E. Sharpe, 1997.

Diederich, Bernard. *Trujillo: The Death of the Goat.* Boston: Little, Brown, 1978.

Foner, Philip S., ed. *José Marti: Major Poems: A Bilingual Edition.* Trans. Elinor Randall. New York: Homes and Meier, 1982.

Galíndez, Jesús de. *The Era of Trujillo.* Tucson: University of Arizona Press, 1973.

Gonzáles Echevarría, Roberto. "Sisters in Death." *The New York Times,* December 18, 1994, sec. 7, p. 28.

Hanover, Francesca Miller. *Latin American Women and the Search for Social Justice.* Hanover, Mass.: University Press of New England, 1991.

Pritchett, Kay. Review of *In the Time of the Butterflies. World Literature Today* 69, no. 4 (Fall 1995): 789.

Reed, W. L., and M. J. Bristow. *National Anthems of the World.* 8th ed. London: Cassell, 1993.

Japan, the Ambiguous, and Myself

by
Kenzaburo Oe

> **THE LITERARY WORK**
>
> A collection of four lectures on Japanese literature and culture delivered in Scandinavia and the United States between 1986 and 1994; published in 1995.
>
> **SYNOPSIS**
>
> An eminent Japanese writer explores his country's uncertain place in the modern world.

Considered Japan's leading contemporary novelist, Kenzaburo Oe (pronounced OH-ay) was born in 1935 in a small village on the western Japanese island of Shikoku. In 1957 Oe graduated from Tokyo University with a degree in French literature, and the following year he won Japan's prestigious Akutagawa Prize for his short story *Shiiku* (1958; *The Catch*, 1958). Oe married Yukari Ikeuchi in 1960, and three years later had a son, Hikari, who was born suffering from severe brain damage. Much of Oe's subsequent writing reflects his experience as a father of a mentally disabled son. The motif appears not only in his best known novel, *Kojinteki na taiken* (1964; *A Personal Matter*, 1968), but also in later works such as *Pinchi ranna chosho* (1976; *The Pinch Runner Memorandum*, 1995) and *Shizuka na seikatsu* (1990; *A Quiet Life*, 1996). In general, Oe's fiction exhibits an elusive poetic style and a deep empathy for the dispossessed or downtrodden. These qualities were cited when, in 1994, Oe became the second Japanese author to receive the Nobel Prize for Literature. His acceptance speech for the Nobel Prize, "Japan, the Ambiguous, and Myself," is the title piece of the collection considered here. Like its three companion lectures, it offers probing criticisms of modern Japanese culture.

A note about names. In presenting personal names, Japanese usage (in contrast with English) puts the family name first and the given name second. Some recent scholars have begun following this practice when rendering Japanese names into English, for example writing Oe's name as Oe Kenzaburo. Traditionally, however, most commentators have conformed to English usage when writing Japanese names in English.

Events in History at the Time of the Lectures

Japan after the Meiji Restoration. Japan's entry into the modern age is commonly held to have begun with the so-called Meiji Restoration of 1868. Although some reforms were undertaken as early as the 1850s, the Restoration can be considered a rough starting point for the historical background of the cultural topics addressed in *Japan, the Ambiguous, and Myself*. For two and a half centuries before the Restoration era, Japan had remained a closed and essentially feudal society, ruled by a network of local aristocratic lords called *daimyo,* who were supported by a warrior class known as *samurai*. Most powerful among the lords was the Tokugawa dynasty (1603-1858), whose successive dynastic leaders monopolized the title *shogun* (general). Altogether some 260 daimyo ruled over about three-quarters of Japan's arable land. Most of the rest was under the direct control of the Tokugawa shoguns, who ruled from their political seat in the city of Edo, dominating a figurehead emperor and his ancient but politically enfeebled imperial house. Since coming to power in the early seventeenth century, the Tokugawa shoguns had assiduously warded off outsiders, preventing foreigners—especially Western Europeans—from penetrating Japanese society. During this long period of isolation, the feudal state attempted, with varying degrees of success, to head off any change in the country's feudal structure and its largely agrarian economy.

Beneath this static surface, however, pressures for change had been building since the early nineteenth century. In response to these pressures, a coalition of young samurai leaders overthrew the Tokugawa shogunate in late 1867. Early the following year, they proclaimed the restoration of the imperial house under the newly enthroned young emperor, Mutsuhito, otherwise known as the Meiji emperor. In reality, however, while revered more conspicuously than before, the emperor remained little more than a figurehead. For the next several decades, the actual power in Japan sat with the group of aging samurai who had overthrown the Tokugawa dynasty and curtailed the influence of the daimyo. Under the slogan *fukoku kyohei* ("enrich the nation, strengthen the army"), they set about overhauling Japan's political and economic system. Looking to Western models for inspiration, they reversed Japan's centuries-old policy of isolation while pursuing a strongly nationalistic agenda.

What emerged was a constitutional monarchy along British lines, with the emperor as head of state, and with political authority shared between a legislative assembly, the Diet, and a government of ministries, headed by a prime minister. Edo, the home city of shoguns, was renamed Tokyo (literally, "Eastern Capital"), and became the capital of the new Japan; the emperor's place of residence was changed from Kyoto to the new capital. The nation's leaders promoted economic activity, and an industrial revolution of sorts ensued, built on a preexisting foundation of textiles manufacturing. Important new companies included Kanegafuchi Spinning (1889; now Kanebo), Kawasaki Heavy Industries (1896), Yahata Steel Works (1901; now New Japan Steel), Hitachi (1896), and Toshiba (founded in 1939 from the merger of Shibaura Works [1875] and Tokyo Electric [1890]). Even more influential were the broad cartels called *zaibatsu*, of which the four largest were Mitsubishi, Mitsui, Sumitomo, and Yasuda (now Fuji Bank). Each of these powerful, family-controlled conglomerates consisted of a number of firms operating in various financial and industrial areas. For example, Mitsubishi's oldest companies spanned shipbuilding, coal mining, real estate, trade, and banking interests.

To work in the factories and manage the businesses, more and more Japanese began moving to cities, where the enterprises were located. By the 1930s, the six largest cities—Tokyo, Osaka, Kyoto, Nagoya, Kobe, and Yokohama—together accounted for about one-fourth of the population, up from perhaps one-tenth in 1890. New social groups emerged in the developing cities; conspicuous among these groups were the fashionable, well-educated, and affluent families centered around husbands with white-collar managerial

JAPAN'S EMPEROR SYSTEM

In addition to his given name, the emperor is also known by a "reign name"; the Meiji Restoration takes its name from Mutsuhito's reign name of Meiji. Mutsuhito and his successors are listed here, with their dates and reign names:

- Mutsuhito, reign name Meiji: 1867-1912
- Yoshihito, reign name Taisho: 1912-26
- Hirohito, reign name Showa: 1926-89
- Akihito, reign name Heisei: 1989-

Traditionally Japan's emperors were popularly thought to be descended from the people's indigenous gods. Under the Meiji Restoration, Japanese rulers laid new stress on the emperor's divinity, in order to instill reverence for the emperor and marshal popular support for his regime. Today divinity is no longer part of the imperial image. Yet in other ways, Oe suggests, "Japan's emperor system, which had apparently lost its social and political influence after the defeat in the Pacific War [World War II], is beginning to flex its muscles again, and in some respects it has already recouped much of its lost power" (Oe, *Japan, the Ambiguous, and Myself*, p. 35). Oe is one of a number of present-day Japanese intellectuals concerned about the possibility of a revival of state-centered nationalism in Japan.

jobs in growing companies. Education itself was an early priority of the modernizing Restoration-era leaders, who established a Ministry of Education in 1871, very soon after assuming power. Tokyo University, Japan's first such institution and still its most prestigious, was founded in 1877. By the 1930s, there were almost 50 colleges and universities in Japan, attended by some 200,000 students. Nearly all of the students were men, in keeping with the state's promotion of a version of Japanese tradition under which women were encouraged to remain domestic and submissive. Restoration leaders summarized and reinforced this expectation, beginning in the 1890s with a slogan derived from Confucius—*ryosai kenbo*, or "good wife and wise mother."

The Restoration leaders' aim of ending Japan's isolation included the desire to build a Japanese empire in Asia, one that would rival the world empires of European colonial powers such as Britain, France, and Germany. Proud that their nation was the only one in Asia to succeed in resisting European colonial encroachment, Japanese leaders believed that Japan ought to be an equal partner with the great European powers. This belief lay behind their exhortation to "enrich the nation, strengthen the army." The newly mechanized Japanese Army was itself an influential proponent of aggressive expansion. From the 1890s into the 1940s, Japan engaged in a series of military actions and territorial conquests aimed at expanding its power on the Asian continent.

- **1894-95** Japan defeats China in the first Sino-Japanese War, demanding control of the island of Taiwan and the Liaodong Peninsula in Manchuria. France, Germany, and Britain prevent Japan from occupying the peninsula, but Taiwan becomes Japan's first overseas colony.
- **1904-05** Japan defeats Russia in the Russo-Japanese War, resulting in Japanese colonial authority over Korea and control of northern Sakhalin Island. Japan also gains possession of the strategic South Manchurian Railway in Manchuria (northern China).
- **1915** Japan presents the so-called "Twenty-One Demands" to China, insisting on Japanese rights to China's territory, to its natural resources, and to influence over its domestic and foreign policy. China rejects most of the demands.
- **1918-22** The Japanese army attempts to conquer parts of Siberia.
- **1931** The Japanese army stages a bombing (the Mukden Incident) on the South Manchuria Railway, using it as a pretext for invading and occupying Manchuria. The so-called Fifteen Year War begins.
- **1937-39** Japan invades and conquers eastern China. In the city of Nanking in December 1938, General Iwane Matsui supervises the systematic murder of an estimated 100,000 to 300,000 Chinese civilians and prisoners of war, and the rape of tens of thousands of Chinese women, by Japanese soldiers. Called "the Rape of Nanking," this action becomes the most notorious Japanese war crime of the late 1930s and early 1940s. Matsui is later convicted and executed by an Allied war crimes tribunal.
- **1939-45** Japanese aggression in China and Southeast Asia merges into World War II, in which Japan sides with the Axis powers (Germany and Italy) against the Allies (led by Britain and, after 1941, the United States). In the early years of the war, Japan conquers most of Asia and the Pacific islands, including Singapore, the Philippines, and Indochina. Japanese soldiers perpetrate further systematic (and well-documented) war crimes on civilians and prisoners of war.

By the 1930s, Japan was completely under the sway of an alliance between the army and a group of nationalistic bureaucrats. Together they dominated the young emperor, Hirohito, who had ascended to the throne in 1926, and whose divine status they used to rally the people to support their aggressive policies. The militaristic government and the war against China thus enjoyed wide popularity among the Japanese people.

OE ON HIROSHIMA, NAGASAKI, AND HIS SON HIKARI

I have tried to define the meaning that the experience of these two cities has for people in Japan and elsewhere . . . but my fundamental perspective has always been that of the parent of a handicapped child. This is the experience that influences everything I write and everything I do. Thus, for example, my realization that life with a mentally handicapped child has the power to heal the wounds that family members inflict on one another led me to the more recent insight that the victims and survivors of the atomic bombs have the same sort of power to heal all of us who live in this nuclear age. This thought seems almost self-evident when one sees the survivors of Hiroshima and Nagasaki, by now frail and elderly, speaking up and taking an active part in the movement to abolish all nuclear weapons. They are, for me, the embodiment of a prayer for the healing of our society, indeed the planet as a whole.

(*Japan, the Ambiguous, and Myself*, pp. 34-35)

With the attack on the U.S. naval base at Pearl Harbor in 1941, which brought the United States into World War II, this alliance led the country into an equally popular war against the United States and the other Allies. The war resulted in a devastating and humiliating defeat for Japan, who surrendered after the United States dropped atomic bombs on two Japanese cities, Hiroshima and Nagasaki, in August 1945. Japan became the only nation to suffer the use of nuclear weapons in war, a special perspective that gave rise to a particularly strong anti-nuclear movement there in the postwar era. Oe has been very active not only in supporting the antinuclear movement, but also in advocating the cause of the survivors of the two atomic explosions.

After Japan's surrender, Allied forces under the United States occupied the country (1945-52). The forces set out with a new group of Japanese leaders to bring political, economic, and social reforms to the shattered island nation. A new constitution was written by American legal scholars, and after being examined by Japanese experts and leaders, it was adopted essentially unchanged—as the Occupation authorities demanded. Declaring that "the Japanese people forever renounce war as a sovereign right of the nation," the constitution permanently prohibits Japan from possessing an army (Allinson, p. 234). A major land reform enabled former tenant farmers to own the land they worked, and the zaibatsu—the industrial conglomerates that had profited immensely from decades of militarization—were dissolved. Hirohito was permitted to remain as emperor, but in a nationwide radio address, he renounced his divinity. In *Japan, the Ambiguous, and Myself* Oe recalls his deep shock and disillusionment when, as a ten-year-old boy, he heard this erstwhile omnipotent and cloistered figure speak in a human voice. Oe's reaction was shared even by many adult Japanese, who throughout decades of violence had trusted and answered the emperor's call to arms as being divinely inspired.

Japan's postwar rise to affluence. In 1954, two years after occupation ended, the Japanese government established an armed military unit known as the Self-Defense Force. By the 1990s the force, which stood at a relatively small 250,000 men, was ranked among the world's top ten armed forces in quality. While its legality under the constitution has survived repeated court tests, the existence of the Self-Defense Force has remained a highly controversial issue, one that reflects the ideological divisions that characterize contemporary Japan. Those on the left—who include Kenzaburo Oe—have continued to condemn it as unconstitutional, reflecting their pacifistic rejection of war and their support of the constitution. "Under the present constitution," Oe declares, "the so-called Self-Defense Force should not even exist, yet Japan's military buildup has been enormous" (*Japan, the Ambiguous, and Myself*, p. 36). Those on the right, such as noted author Yukio Mishima (who committed ritual suicide in 1970, in part over the issue), have maintained that Japan should reestablish a traditional army, and that the strict legal limitations restricting the use of force to national self-defense should be abandoned. With the postwar growth of Japan's economic might, the question of its rearmament has remained a continual and divisive irritant in the nation's public life.

Another early step the government took after occupation ended was to allow the components of many former zaibatsu to reconstitute themselves. The resulting network of financial alliances and business partnerships is known as the *keiretsu* system. As Japan's old companies reestablished themselves under the keiretsu system, they were joined by many new ones, of which the best known in the West is the electronics manufacturer Sony. Meanwhile, Japanese auto manufacturers such as Nissan and Toyota, established in the 1930s, brought in increasing revenues, especially after oil shortages in the 1970s allowed their more fuel-efficient models to outsell larger American cars and thus gain a permanent share of the U.S. market.

Although to some extent pitfalls such as the oil shortage hindered economic growth in Japan during the 1970s, the Japanese economy recovered and enjoyed an unprecedented boom during the 1980s. Auto companies and electronics manufacturers flourished, but the strongest performers were giant Japanese banks such as Sumitomo, Fuji, Sanwa, and Daiichi-Kangyo. However, the banks stumbled badly in the late 1980s, after making bad loans to finance overambitious real estate and stock market speculation. Furthermore, Japanese companies failed to make a strong showing in the emerging markets for the computers and software that were revolutionizing so many aspects of life in wealthy nations in the 1990s. So while the computer and internet revolutions fueled U.S. markets during the 1990s, Japan fell into a relative slump. Its effects were limited, however.

Overall most Japanese continued to enjoy a high standard of living, partaking of the same consumer comforts as their affluent American and European counterparts. By the 1990s, Japan's affluence had brought sweeping demographic changes. Most significantly, urbanization had accelerated sharply since the war, so that 80 percent of Japanese now lived in urban areas, 20 percent of them in cities of over one million people (Allinson, p. 103). One in five households consisted of a single person living alone, many of those being young urban professionals in their twenties or thirties who had postponed marrying and raising a family. Many of Japan's traditional lifestyle patterns have broken down, and its population has become more mobile and less cohesive. Style and fashion took a high priority among hip young urban Japanese, with new fads trumpeted in glossy magazines and electronic media. Commenting on the contemporary Japanese cultural scene in one of the lectures, Oe criticizes what he calls "Japan's grotesquely bloated consumer society," observing that the most popular writers among young Japanese readers are "the copywriters of commercial messages" (*Japan, the Ambiguous, and Myself*, p. 78).

Kenzaburo Oe

The Lectures in Focus

The contents. Spanning the period from 1986 to 1994, the four lectures collected in *Japan, the Ambiguous, and Myself* are presented in a different order from that in which Oe delivered them, except for the Nobel lecture, which is placed last and was delivered last. The other three appear to have been arranged thematically for the benefit of the reading audience. Likewise, an editor's note informs the reader that "with the approval of the author, some stylistic revisions have been made to the original English texts of these lectures" (*Japan, the Ambiguous, and Myself*, p. 4).

"Speaking on Japanese Culture before a Scandinavian Audience" (delivered in Scandinavia in 1992; translated by Kunioki Yanagishita). Oe introduces the first lecture by professing that it has been a dream of his since childhood to visit Scandinavia. His favorite children's book was *The Magical Adventures of Nils*, about a Scandinavian boy's fantastic journeys through Sweden. (Published in 1907, the book enjoyed global popularity and was translated into many languages; its author, Swedish novelist and 1909 Nobel laureate Selma Lagerlof, was the first woman to win the Nobel Prize for Literature). Oe considers several modern European authors whose careers are linked by the twin themes of wanderlust and Scandinavia: Karen Blixen (Danish; 1885-1962; pseudonym Isak Dinesen), Louis-Ferdinand Céline (French; 1894-1961), and Malcolm Lowry (British; 1909-57).

He then gets to the main subject of this first lecture, which he defines as "Japanese culture as seen through the filter of literature" (*Japan, the Ambiguous, and Myself*, p. 16). In the rest of the lecture, Oe approaches this topic by briefly examining the work of three Japanese writers:

JAPAN'S CONSUMER REVOLUTION

Figures indicate percentage of Japanese nonfarm households:

Commodity	1965	1990
Washing machines	72	100
Refrigerators	62	98
Cameras	58	88
Vacuum cleaners	41	99
Stereos	17	60
Automobiles	9	76
Color TVs	0	99
Air conditioners	2	66

(Adapted from Allinson, p. 250)

• **Shikibu Murasaki** (c. 978-c. 1076) Murasaki, a lady of the imperial court, wrote the founding masterpiece of Japanese prose literature, *The Tale of Genji* (also in *Literature and Its Times*). Considered by many critics to be the world's first novel, *The Tale of Genji* follows the amorous exploits of its princely hero, Genji; the part that Oe dwells on concerns Genji's plans for the education of his son, Prince Yugiri. Oe uses this part of the story as an example of how, since ancient times, education in pre-Meiji Japan meant "knowledge of Chinese literature" (*Japan, the Ambiguous, and Myself*, p. 17).

• **Soseki Natsume** (1867-1916) Soseki (known by his given name) was, in Oe's words, "Japan's greatest writer after the Meiji Restoration" (*Japan, the Ambiguous, and Myself*, p. 21). Oe quotes from Soseki's novel *And Then* (1909), in which Soseki characterizes Japanese modernization as a façade. In Soseki's view, Oe observes, the Japanese adopted the decadent appetites of Western culture without absorbing Western morality, that is, without the sense of responsibility that Soseki believed essential to individualism. Oe suggests that "this description applies equally well to the Japanese today," whose appetites, "manifested in every aspect of our greedy consumerism, all but dwarf those of Soseki's time" (*Japan, the Ambiguous, and Myself*, p. 24).

• **Kenzaburo Oe** (1935-) Finally Oe considers his own novels, *A Personal Matter* (1964; trans. 1968) and *The Silent Cry* (1967; trans. 1974). These works encompass the two subjects with which Oe has been most concerned. *A Personal Matter* represents Oe's attempts to find universal significance in his experience as the father of a brain-damaged son. *The Silent Cry*, set in a small village like the one Oe grew up in, reflects his desire to explore alternatives to Japan's "main, Tokyo-centered culture" by celebrating the smaller "peripheral cultures" like that of the novel's remote village (*Japan, the Ambiguous, and Myself*, p. 35).

"On Modern and Contemporary Japanese Literature" (delivered in San Francisco in 1990; no translation credit given). Oe traces the beginnings of modern Japanese literature to the Meiji Restoration, when Japanese intellectuals and writers began studying and adapting the literatures of Europe. Summarizing Japanese history since the beginnings of modernization in the Meiji era, he again discusses the career of Soseki Natsume, among others:

> Modernization had brought Japan into contact with the West, and, on its victory in the Russo-Japanese War, the people of Japan fell captive to a desire—stimulated by the outside world—for material gains. At the same time, moral urgencies declined. Soseki's criticism, however, was leveled not just at Japan's economic pursuit of the West; he criticizes the basic conditions of life as well (like the shabbiness of human dwellings), which had actually deteriorated in the process of modernization.
>
> (*Japan, the Ambiguous, and Myself*, p. 45)

Oe goes on to decry what he sees as the "chronic decline" of Japanese literary culture since the rise of Japan's postwar affluence and the attendant, accelerating consumerism (*Japan, the Ambiguous, and Myself*, p. 49). He dismisses the commercially successful novels of trendy young writers of the late 1980s and early 1990s, such as Haruki Murakami and Banana Yoshimoto: "Here we see Japan's economic boom making itself felt in the literary market" (*Japan, the Ambiguous, and Myself*, p. 50).

"Japan's Dual Identity: A Writer's Dilemma" (delivered in 1986 at a conference on the "Challenge of Third World Culture" at Duke University in the United States; translated by Kunioki Yanagishita). Oe argues that Japan is torn between two conflicting identities: on one hand, it is itself a third-world country (a term Oe uses somewhat ambiguously); on the other hand, in the modern period, it has been a wealthy oppressor of poorer third world countries. As an example of Japan's oppression, he points to its aggressive actions against its "fellow third world nations in Asia," Korea and China, during the period of modernization between the Meiji Restoration and World War II (*Japan, the Ambiguous, and Myself*, p. 59).

Oe again laments what he sees as the decline of Japanese culture and literature since the 1980s. He also criticizes the, in his view, sterile way that Japanese intellectuals have slavishly and successively embraced such Western intellectual fashions as structuralism and deconstruction (movements for analyzing literary texts and culture) without truly grasping their implications. Oe contrasts more recent Japanese writers with their predecessors in the immediate postwar period. He cites, with approval, such accomplished authors as Kobo Abe, Shohei Ooka, Taijun Takeda, and Yukio Mishma, whose major works spanned the period from the late 1940s (for example, Mishima's *Confessions of a Mask*, 1949) to the early 1970s (for example, Takeda's "Mount Fuji Sanitorium," 1971). "These were people," he suggests, "who had to endure silence while fascism prevailed prior to and during the war years. Their pent-up frustrations were released in a burst of activity that formed them as intellectuals" (*Japan, the Ambiguous, and Myself*, pp. 68-69).

"Japan, the Ambiguous, and Myself" (delivered in Stockholm, Sweden, in 1994; his acceptance of the Nobel Prize for Literature that year; translated by Hisaaki Yamanouchi). In the final lecture, Oe again returns briefly to the favorite books of his childhood, mentioning *The Magical Adventures of Nils* (mentioned previously) and adding to it another major influence, Mark Twain's ***The Adventures of Huckleberry Finn*** (1884; also in *Literature and Its Times*). His lecture's title, he explains, is taken from the Nobel acceptance speech of the only other Japanese author to win the prize for literature, Yasunari Kawabata. Kawabata, who won the prize in 1968, entitled his acceptance speech "Japan, the Beautiful, and Myself." According to Oe, Kawabata did so partly in order "to identify himself" with "the aesthetic sensibility pervading the classical literature of the Orient" (*Japan, the Ambiguous, and Myself*, p. 113).

Respectfully distancing himself from Kawabata, Oe by contrast identifies himself as more in sympathy with Western traditions. For example, he affirms a greater spiritual affinity with Irish poet William Butler Yeats (1865-1939), who won the same prize in 1923. On winning the prize, Yeats was praised by the Irish Senate for having brought Ireland into the ranks of civilized nations, and Oe aspires to perform a similar service for his country. Ultimately, in Oe's view, such an aspiration would amount to removing the ambiguity of the lecture's title:

> After a hundred and twenty years of modernization since the opening up of the country, contemporary Japan is split between two opposite poles of ambiguity. This ambiguity . . . is evident in various ways. The modernization of Japan was oriented towards the West, yet the country is situated in Asia and has firmly maintained its traditional culture. The ambiguous orientation of Japan drove the country into the position of an invader in Asia, and resulted in its isolation from other Asian nations not only politically but also socially and culturally. And even in the West, to which its culture was supposedly quite open, it has long remained inscrutable or only partially understood.
>
> (*Japan, the Ambiguous, and Myself*, p. 117)

Oe then reaffirms his conviction that the Japanese must uphold their current constitutional renunciation of war, by retaining "the principle of permanent peace as the moral basis for their rebirth" (*Japan, the Ambiguous, and Myself*, p. 119). "To remove the principle of permanent peace," he declares, "would be an act of betrayal toward the people of Asia and the victims of the bombs dropped on Hiroshima and Nagasaki" (*Japan, the Ambiguous, and Myself*, p. 120). In conclusion, he proposes that Japan's best hope for healing the wounds of the past lies in fully embracing the ideals embodied in the long-standing Western tradition of humanism, a movement that concerns itself with the individualistic and critical spirit, with secular rather than religious concerns, and with the revival of classical literature. He affirms his own allegiance, as a writer and thinker, to that tradition.

Japanese culture and the outside world. As Oe repeatedly stresses in the lectures that make up *Japan, the Ambiguous, and Myself*, the Meiji era represents a cultural as well as a historical divide for Japan. In the simplest terms, before about 1850, Japan had looked to the Chinese for cultural inspiration, while after 1850 it has looked increasingly to the West. Japanese literature especially exemplifies this progression, and accordingly in the first lecture Oe declares his intention of discussing "Japanese culture as seen through the filter of literature" (*Japan, the Ambiguous, and Myself*, p. 16). The other lectures share this approach, so that by the end of the book Oe has offered brief discussions of a remarkably large number of influential Japanese authors dating from the mid-nineteenth century, as well as major works from earlier periods. Before and after the Meiji Restoration, Oe suggests, writers exemplify how Japanese culture has both adopted outside influences and adapted them to its own society.

For example, says Oe, the eleventh-century ***The Tale of Genji*** (also in *Literature and Its Times.*) illustrates the central role that Chinese literature played in traditional Japanese education. Not spelled out by Oe are some basic details. From its earliest stages, Japanese literature was inspired by Chinese models and sources. The Japanese language had no written form until Japanese scribes adapted Chinese characters for writing it down in the first several centuries of the Common Era. The earliest surviving works of Japanese literature are two official court histories from the eighth century called the *Kojiki* ("Record of Ancient Matters") and the *Nihon-gi* ("Chronicle of Japan"). Modeled on similar Chinese works, they include parts in which Chinese characters spell out Japanese words phonetically, as well as sections written in Chinese. This adaptation and modification that has occurred in literature, finds parallels in other important aspects of culture. In religion, for example, Chinese forms of Buddhism and to a lesser extent Confucianism took root in Japan, existing alongside the native traditions that, in the nineteenth century, became known as Shinto.

As Oe remarks, after the Meiji Restoration, the literatures of Europe—especially of Russia, Germany, France, and England—became the sources from which Japanese writers drew their inspiration. Again, literature reflects broader cultural trends, from the founding of Western-style universities in Japan, to the rise of Japanese arms and industry in line with Western forms, to the rampant consumerism of which Oe complains. Over many centuries of development, Japan's use of Chinese forms resulted in one of the world's richest cultural traditions. In the years since 1868, that tradition has been further enriched through interaction with Western forms, although some fear at the same time that these more recent changes have undermined the cultural tradition.

"Yamato spirit" and "Yamato race." Central to understanding Oe's discussion of *The Tale of Genji* is an idea that first appears in that early novel, a concept known as "Yamato spirit." Oe refers to the novel to explain it:

> "Only after we have had enough book learning," Genji explains, "can we bring our Yamato spirit into full play"—Yamato being an old name for Japan. By "book learning" Genji means knowledge of Chinese literature; so he is arguing that it is only after establishing a solid foundation in the Chinese classics that intrinsically Japanese talents can be treated with due respect.
>
> (*Japan, the Ambiguous, and Myself*, p. 17)

During Japan's period of modernization, Oe observes, the expression "Yamato spirit with Chinese learning" was replaced by "Yamato spirit with Western learning" (*Japan, the Ambiguous, and Myself*, p. 20). However, "Yamato spirit," which Oe argues was used in the *The Tale of Genji* to denote a common Japanese sensibility, had by then come to signify a stronger, more nationalistic patriotism, one that was identified with Japan's restored emperor system and drive for empire. Thus, "Yamato spirit," Oe notes, was the Japanese Imperial Army's rallying cry throughout the World War II era.

Closely related to "Yamato spirit" (*yamato damashii*) has been the idea of "Yamato race" (*yamato minzoku*), which was also prevalent during the war years. Combining ideas of racial purity, ethnic homogeneity, and cultural conformity, Japanese authorities used such expressions to propagate a picture of the Japanese as a unified people set above the rest of humanity (even as the realities of empire, migration, and conquest made Japan an increasingly multicultural society in the 1930s and 1940s). During the war, this portrayal was contrasted with Western societies, especially the United States, whose individualism and ethnic plurality were seen as making it weak and inferior.

Writing in the mid-1990s, the historian John Dower saw echoes of such thinking in contemporary Japan:

> The truly virulent implications of the mystique of Japanese purity and homogeneity are exposed in Japanese attitudes toward the United States as a heterogeneous society. An unusually vivid expression of this appeared in the *Wall Street Journal* in 1982, when a Japanese official was quoted as stating that "the Japanese are a people that can manufacture a product of uniformity and superior quality because the Japanese are a race of completely pure blood, not a mongrelized race as in the United States." Since that time, Japanese disdain for ethnically pluralistic societies in general and peoples of color in particular has been exposed on numerous occasions.
>
> (Dower, p. 331)

In the four lectures comprising *Japan, the Ambiguous, and Myself*, Oe does not, however, explore such recent manifestations of the Japanese preoccupation with racial purity. He does, on the other hand, point to Japanese wartime propaganda based on "Yamato spirit," noting that as a child, he believed the wartime propaganda. "Like everyone else at that time, I was made to believe this mad conviction so alien to the [true] 'Yamato spirit,'" as originally propounded in *The Tale of Genji* (*Japan, the Ambiguous, and Myself*, p. 20).

Sources and literary context. As noted above, Oe's major sources of inspiration in general have included his son Hikari and the experiences of the Hiroshima and Nagasaki survivors. As should also be clear from the foregoing discussion, Oe has drawn on his wide reading in both Japanese and other world literatures, notably those of Western Europe, for the lectures collected in *Japan, the Ambiguous, and Myself*. A specific inspiration for Oe's thought becomes clear near the end of the title lecture, when he discusses the Western humanistic tradition in which he places such hope. Oe recalls his own academic studies of French literature under the tutelage of a Japanese professor of the French Renaissance, Kazuo Watanabe, who "dreamed of grafting the humanistic view of man onto the traditional Japanese sense of beauty and sensitivity to nature" (*Japan, the Ambiguous, and Myself*, p. 123). In particular, Watanabe introduced Oe to the Renaissance humanist François Rabelais (French; c. 1494-1553), whose satire *Gargantua and Pantagruel* Watanabe translated into Japanese during World War II. In addition to influencing Oe's fiction style, Watanabe's reverence for humanism deeply shaped Oe's thought, leading him to value ideals such as tolerance, individual freedom, and pacifism.

In discussing the direction of modern Japanese literature, Oe identifies himself with a tradition called *junbungaku*, "pure literature," or—as Oe chooses to translate it—"sincere literature," which began with Meiji-era novelists such as Soseki Natsume, Ogai Mori (1862-1922), and others. Oe defines the type as "serious literature" or "literature that has . . . cut itself off from the products published by the mass media; in other words, literature that is not 'popular' or 'mundane'" (*Japan, the Ambiguous, and Myself*, pp. 65-66). It is this serious tradition, carried on by postwar writers like Yukio Mishima and Kobo Abe, that Oe says began to decline in the early 1970s. In its place arose the literary reflection of superficial consumerism that, in Oe's eyes, is represented by popular contemporary authors such as Haruki Murakami and Banana Yoshimoto. Oe does see hope in some less widely read younger writers, however, citing Yoshikichi Furui, Kenji Nakagami, and Yuko Tsushima as among those addressing deeper social issues.

Reception. Oe's work, hitherto largely ignored in the West, was suddenly accorded wide publicity and attention when he won the Nobel Prize for Literature in 1994. His Nobel lecture, given after he accepted the prize on Wednesday, December 7, 1994, was broadly reported in the Western news media, including American newspapers such as the *New York Times* and the *Washington Post*. As his first publication since winning the prize (aside from new printings of older works), *Japan, the Ambiguous, and Myself* received several reviews in prominent British publications, including the *Economist* and the *Sunday Telegraph*. It received less notice in the American media, although the *Christian Science Monitor* ran a brief excerpt (in the May 10, 1995 issue). More detailed assessments could be found in Asian English-language newspapers. Writing in Japan's *Daily Yomiuri*, Ron Breines praised the book as "startlingly acute and uncompromising, filled with insight and passion. . . . Each sentence in this small but illuminating book reveals an intellect that is sharp, clear, brilliantly informed and humanistically endowed" (Breines, p. 17).

—Colin Wells

For More Information

Allinson, Gary D. *The Columbia Guide to Modern Japanese History*. New York: Columbia University Press, 1999.

Breines, Ron. "Oe Speaks with Unambiguous Voice," *Daily Yomiuri*, 2 April 1995, 17.

Dower, John W. *Japan in War and Peace: Selected Essays*. New York: Norton, 1993.

Giffard, Sydney. *Japan Among the Powers: 1890-1990*. New Haven: Yale University Press, 1994.

Keene, Donald. *Dawn to the West: Japanese Literature of the Modern Era*. New York: Holt, 1984.

Napier, Susan J. *Escape from the Wasteland: Romanticism and Realism in the Fiction of Mishima Yukio & Oe Kenzaburo*. Cambridge, Mass.: Council on East Asian Studies, Harvard University, 1995.

Oe, Kenzaburo. *Japan, the Ambiguous, and Myself: The Nobel Prize Speech and Other Lectures*. Tokyo: Kodansha, 1995.

Smith, Patrick. *Japan: A Reinterpretation*. New York: Pantheon, 1997.

Walker, Janet. *The Japanese Novel of the Meiji Period and the Ideal of Individualism*. Princeton: Princeton University Press, 1979.

Washburn, Dennis C. *The Dilemma of the Modern in Japanese Fiction*. New Haven: Yale University Press, 1995.

Waswo, Ann. *Modern Japanese Society*. Oxford: Oxford University Press, 1996.

Kindred

by
Octavia Butler

> **THE LITERARY WORK**
>
> A novel set in 1976 Los Angeles and early 1800s Maryland; published in 1979.
>
> **SYNOPSIS**
>
> Newly wed to a white husband, an African American woman starts traveling back and forth between her own post-Civil Rights-era West Coast and a pre-Civil War South inhabited by two of her ancestors: the heir of a white plantation owner and the black woman he enslaves and forces to become his concubine.

By the publication of *Kindred* in 1979, Octavia Estelle Butler had already established herself as the author of three successful and well-reviewed science-fiction novels, the first of which, *Patternmaster*, appeared when she was 29 years old. Butler was born in Pasadena, California, in 1947. Dyslexic and shy as a child, she began writing fiction very early, motivated in part—as she once confided in an interview—by a need to distance herself from the austere world of her mother and grandmother (O'Connor, p. 36). From these two women (her father died when she was still a baby), she received a strict Baptist upbringing and a vicarious memory of hard, ill-rewarded work: labor in Louisiana's cane fields in the case of her grandmother, and domestic work in the case of her mother. Butler's own adult experiences in the early 1970s closely resemble those of *Kindred's* Dana: temporary jobs obtained through an agency; hunger and anxiety while striving to become a published novelist; writing classes at the University of California at Los Angeles. Falling outside most definitions of science fiction, *Kindred* is Butler's most "mainstream" novel to date. Yet it still occupies a central place in her work, much of which concerns time travel, racial mixing, enslavement, and power relationships of all kinds.

Events in History at the Time of the Novel

The backward glance of 1976. While trying to explain to Rufus Weylin (the skeptical, though not unsympathetic plantation-owner's son who turns out to be Dana's ancestor) where and, more exactly, *when* they come from, Dana and Kevin show the boy a brand new bicentennial quarter stamped with two dates, 1776 and 1976. This detail conveys the sense of history that Americans were officially encouraged to preserve in commemoration of their nation's 200th birthday. While patriotic bumper stickers and T-shirts proclaiming "The Spirit of '76" celebrated the idea that a common spirit linked the America of the past with the America of the present, some saw the bicentennial as an occasion to reflect critically on how much the United States had progressed over two centuries, or—to put it in terms more directly relevant to the time-travels that occur in the novel—how much distance really separated America's present from its past.

Octavia E. Butler

This question had special importance for African Americans who, having achieved meaningful successes in the post-World War II struggle for racial equality, found themselves looking back on their role in American history with a new sense of accomplishment. In the late 1970s, many African Americans devoted careful study to the lives of their slave ancestors—if not from the "safe" perspective of a people no longer confronted with white oppression, then at least from the relatively confident perspective of a people who wished to size up their recent social and political gains and uncover the roots of their increasingly valued cultural identity. In fact, "roots" became a familiar byword after the 1976 publication of Alex Haley's *Roots*, an African American epic that combined fiction with family history. The phenomenal success of Haley's memoir—a bicentennial event in its own right—both reflected and inspired widespread black interest in family genealogies. Along with the airing of a landmark television adaptation of *Roots*, 1977 saw the publication of popular guides (like Charles Blockson's *Black Genealogy*) for people who wanted to trace family trees; it also marked the founding of the Afro-American Historical and Genealogical Society.

Many of the social changes that enabled African Americans to contemplate slavery with a new sense of detachment came about during the lifetime of *Kindred*'s Dana. Born in 1950, Dana could fairly be described as a child of the Civil Rights era, as could Butler herself. Children of this generation observed and participated in social transformations identified with the decade that Dana describes as "the militant nineteen-sixties" (Butler, *Kindred*, p. 145). Since the activism that became synonymous with the ´60s (see sidebar) lost its popular force only when the Vietnam War ended in 1975, 1976 was arguably the first year that offered a vantage from which the reforms and protests of the previous decade began to look more like historical events than current events. In *The Nation*'s August 14, 1976, issue, for example, Clayborne Carson opened an article entitled "Black Power after Ten Years" with this paragraph:

> In a single decade, an era of Afro-American politics came and went. A legacy remains, but its full meaning is still to be determined, even by blacks who came of age during the 1960s and were transformed by the events of those years. Now we must search our memories to recall the effect on our lives of the evolution from nonviolent desegregation sit-ins to massive marches and rallies to convulsive urban rebellions—the evolution from Martin Luther King to Malcolm X to Stokely Carmichael to Eldridge Cleaver. The 1963 march on Washington is separated from us by thirteen years and three Presidents and the rise and fall of a succession of movements, leaders and dreams.
>
> (Carson in Chafe and Sitkoff, pp. 147-48)

Carson describes the effect of a brief period of intense political action and aspiration as if history itself had somehow accelerated, confronting African Americans with a potentially disorienting accumulation of powerful memories, including victories such as the 1963 March on Washington in support of the Civil Rights Act (which indeed passed in 1964), and setbacks such as the Ku Klux Klan's 1964 killing of three members of the Student Non-Violent Coordinating Committee (SNCC) in Mississippi (James Chaney, Andrew Goodman, and Michael Schwerner). Dana's jarring back-and-forth time travel produces a comparably disorienting effect; one month of her life in 1976 compresses the events of nearly two decades at the Weylin plantation, spanning the period from her first appearance there in about 1812 to her last in 1831. And like Carson's catalogue of increasingly militant black leaders (from Martin Luther King, to Malcolm X, Stokely Carmichael, and Eldridge Cleaver), Dana's antebellum life leads from non-violent to violent resistance.

The "Storm" of 1831. In *Kindred* time seems to go by much more slowly in the past than it does in the present, but the past too has its transformative events. Even without the advantage of hindsight, 1831 could be seen as an ominous year for slavery in the southern United States. In January, William Lloyd Garrison released the first issue of his antislavery newspaper, *The Liberator*, which soon became the most influential organ of the movement for abolition, reaching some 2,000 subscribers before its final issue in 1865. In March, Garrison called upon his readers to mobilize against slavery and "scatter tracts like raindrops, over the land," a call that would be answered when Garrison succeeded in founding the New England Anti-Slavery Society one year later, and the American Anti-slavery society the year after that (Garrison in Mayer, p. 127). Abolitionists attacked slavery on several grounds, religious, philosophical, and moral. Slavery, they insisted, was not just a complex constellation of sins, but a violation of the fundamental republican principle of liberty. The moral arguments against slavery were advanced most compellingly by free blacks and fugitive slaves, many of whom gave personal accounts of the brutal punishments, the humiliating prejudices, the enforced ignorance, and the scant food and clothing that southern slaves lived with habitually. The most famous of those accounts (and a crucial source for Butler), the *Narrative of the Life of Frederick Douglass* (1845), supplies an example of the powerful shock that slave narrators delivered to their readers. Douglass describes in detail the traumatic childhood memory of a whipping suffered by his aunt at the hands of her master:

> Before he commenced whipping Aunt Hester, he took her into the kitchen, and stripped her from neck to waist, leaving her neck, shoulders, and back entirely naked. . . . Her arms were stretched up at their full length, so that she stood upon the ends of her toes. He then said to her, "Now, you d———d b—h, I'll learn you how to disobey my orders!" and after rolling up his sleeves, he commenced to lay on the heavy cowskin, and soon the warm, red blood (amid heart-rending shrieks from her, and horrid oaths from him) came dripping to the floor. I was so terrified and horror-stricken at the sight, that I hid myself in a closet and dared not venture out till long after the bloody transaction was over. (Douglass in Gates, p. 259)

The sexual overtones of this sadistic punishment suggest one of the likely reasons why women of the era—both white and black—stepped forward to argue with unique force against the cruelties of the slave system. The male-dominated culture of early nineteenth-century America tended to revere women as naturally gentle, near-angelic guardians of morality and family values. According to this popular view, women possessed their own specific moral authority (provided that no immodest or "unwomanly" behavior detracted from it). Among other vital services to their cause, abolitionist women made a point of exposing slavery's casual disrespect for the integrity of slave families, the sanctity of marriage, the education of children, and the physical and mental innocence of the numerous black women victimized by sexual assault or, in the case of concubines like *Kindred*'s Alice, sexual coercion.

If Garrison's activities troubled southern slaveholders in 1831, the news of Nat Turner's violent insurrection in August terrified them. Turner, a slave preacher from Southampton County, Virginia, was hunted down and executed in November along with many of his followers. But he had managed to lead an uprising that resulted in the deaths of 57 white men, women, and children. While this episode was by far the bloodiest instance of slave resistance in the antebellum period, documented cases of aggressive resistance against white authority (ranging from verbal threats to the killing of overseers and planters) occurred on plantations throughout the South during this period (Franklin and Schweninger, p. 7). Most confrontations of this kind occurred between individual slaves and masters or overseers; but slave conspiracies (like Denmark Vesey's, which was uncovered before it could be implemented, in 1822) were by no means unheard of before the Nat Turner uprising. Nevertheless, Turner's example galvanized southern anxieties about slave revolt in an unprecedented way.

In December, and into the following year, a sense of crisis animated the debates of the Virginia Legislature as a result of the uprising. A substantial minority of the delegates supported the abolition of slavery in Virginia, but the convention voted in the end to curtail the already minimal liberties accorded to Virginia's slaves and free blacks. As other slave states followed Virginia's example, patrols became more watchful, and permission to travel and hold meetings became harder for slaves to secure. Not surprisingly, in view of the increasing availability of abolitionist literature, as well as the fact that Turner had been taught to read, educated slaves would now face more mistrust in their dealings with whites.

Although Turner's liberationist interpretation of the Bible appears to have provided him with

OF THE PEOPLE, BY THE PEOPLE, FOR THE PEOPLE—
SOME POPULAR MOVEMENTS IN THE CIVIL RIGHTS AND POST-CIVIL RIGHTS ERAS

The late 1950s and the 1960s saw a surge in protest on behalf of civil rights across the nation. The frequently violent reaction to the protests provoked the emergence of more militant groups, and a determined push for greater equality in the North as well as the South. Meanwhile, the early civil rights groups provided a model for other disempowered minorities, most notably, for Kindred, that of women.

1955-56—Black activists stage Montgomery Boycott. Blacks in Montgomery, Alabama, boycott the city's bus system to protest the discrimination built into the system.

1957—Little Rock Crisis erupts. Whites in Little Rock, Arkansas, protest violently a court order mandating integration of Central High School; on September 25, the U.S. Army, called in by President Dwight D. Eisenhower, escorts nine black students to their first classes here.

1963—Birmingham Protest (May) turns violent. Anti-segregation demonstrators, including schoolchildren, are attacked by police and dogs in Birmingham, Alabama; televised images of the children being attacked galvanize national support for the civil rights movement.

March on Washington (August) achieves mass support. Black leaders head huge demonstration in nation's capital, advocating passage of the Civil Rights Act; Martin Luther King, Jr. delivers "I Have A Dream" speech to 250,000 people at Lincoln Memorial.

1964—Freedom Summer turns violent. Civil rights workers, including white volunteers, campaign in Deep South to register African American voters; many activists suffer brutal beatings by white mobs and police, and three are murdered in Mississippi, provoking national outrage.

1965—Selma marches attract more violence. Police beat black protestors who attempt to march from Selma to Montgomery, Alabama, to draw attention to struggle for black voting rights.

Watts riot erupts. Race riot sparked by police brutality against blacks; over five days 34 die and 1,000 are wounded; 35,000 African Americans take part.

1966—Feminists organize nationally. National Organization for Women (NOW) is founded to address sex discrimination against women.

Black Power movement begins. Stokely Carmichael launches the black power movement at a civil rights rally in Mississippi; militant Black Panthers Party forms in Oakland, California.

Black activists protest the Vietnam War. The Congress of Racial Equality and the Student Nonviolent Coordinating Committee issue antiwar statements.

1967—Race riots flare in urban areas. In one of the worst riots, in Detroit (July 23-30), 40 die, 2,000 are injured, and nearly 5,000 paratroopers from the Army's combat-tested 101st Airborne are sent in by order of President Lyndon B. Johnson.

Anti-Vietnam War protests spread. Spring Mobilization Committee sponsors massive antiwar protests in New York City, San Francisco and Washington, D.C.

1968—Political riot erupts. 10,000 protestors of the Vietnam war clash with police during the Democratic Convention in Chicago.

Martin Luther King Jr. is killed. Assassination occurs in Memphis, Tennessee.

Poor People's Campaign takes place. Some 50,000 demonstrators descend on Washington, D.C.

Race riots erupt. Riots hit New Orleans, Philadelphia, and other cities.

1972—Congress passes Equal Rights Amendment. It guarantees that equality of rights under the law will not be denied on account of sex. Amendement is sent to states for ratification; short of the needed number of states, it will be defeated in 1982.

1973—Black women organize nationally. National Black Feminist Organization is founded to combat racism and sexism, especially the idea that black women should defer their goals to attain those of black men.

1975—Court orders integration of schools in the North. National Association for the Advancement of Colored People (NAACP) wins fight to bus black children to white schools in Boston, Massachusetts; violence ensues.

all the justification he required for his actions, some defenders of slavery tried unconvincingly to accuse northern abolitionists like Garrison of planting seeds of unrest among slaves who would otherwise remain peaceful and loyal. Southern hostility to abolitionism mounted during the 1830s, leading ultimately to acts of mob violence—most notably the murder of antislavery newspaper editor Elijah Lovejoy in 1837. Like the violence that faced civil rights workers in the 1960s, this ugly crime tended to confirm the urgent need for reform in the minds of northern observers.

Segregation and education. Of the many forms of racial inequality that provoked significant protests and legal challenges during the 1950s and 1960s, the segregation of American schools and colleges proved to be one of the most inflammatory, prompting the lawsuit that gave activists the legal ammunition they needed to launch a nationwide civil rights movement. The landmark case in question was *Brown v. Board of Education of Topeka*, a class-action suit mounted by five groups of African American plaintiffs against segregated public school systems in Virginia, Delaware, South Carolina, Kansas, and the District of Columbia. The National Association for the Advancement of Colored People (NAACP) joined the plaintiffs in 1949, and the U.S. Supreme Court decided the case in 1954. Endorsing recent findings by psychologists and sociologists that segregation promoted lasting and damaging feelings of inferiority among black schoolchildren, the court ruled that "separate educational facilities are inherently unequal," and therefore unconstitutional under the Fourteenth Amendment. In several earlier cases, the NAACP had succeeded in proving that black students suffered due to underfunding and inferior facilities—sparse libraries, for example—as compared to their white counterparts; but before *Brown v. Board of Education*, there had been no successful challenge to the legitimacy of "separate but equal" schooling as established by the 1896 case of *Plessy v. Ferguson*.

The centrality of education as a civil rights issue provides a twentieth-century context for Butler's treatment of this issue in *Kindred*—more specifically, for Dana's secretly teaching two young slaves how to read. Although she regards this violation of plantation law as only mildly "subversive," its discovery occasions Dana's first violent beating at the hands of Rufus's father, Tom Weylin (*Kindred*, p. 101). The historian John Hope Franklin has observed that the laws against the teaching of slaves were often disregarded by white planters (Franklin and Moss, p. 155). Still slaveowners tried, in many cases, to monitor or discourage the spread of literacy among their slaves. The beating Dana receives for her "offense" thus qualifies as historically accurate. Moreover, it invites comparison with angry white responses to the desegregation of classrooms in the twentieth-century South. During the late 1950s, efforts to enroll black students at formerly all-white schools sparked violent reactions by white crowds in cities such as Little Rock, Arkansas and New Orleans, Louisiana; and Alabama's Governor George Wallace made national headlines in 1962 by appearing personally to obstruct the entry of newly admitted black students to the University of Alabama in Birmingham.

"Why you try to talk like white folks?" Before he asks Dana to teach him how to read, Nigel, one of the Weylin slaves, quizzes her about her accent and her education, both of which, to his ears, identify this black woman with "white folks" (*Kindred*, p. 74). In a bitter scene later in the novel, another character goes so far as to accuse Dana of being a "white nigger" (*Kindred*, p. 165). The question of whether literacy and the use of "standard" English implies a loss of identity for African Americans has relevance to both of the novel's time-frames.

Autobiographical slave narratives emerged during the antebellum period as one of America's more popular literary genres (besides being an effective means of advancing the cause of abolitionism and serving as a model for *Kindred's* narrative technique). Most of these narratives were told by eloquent black writers and public speakers. But often these speakers and writers had difficulty convincing a white audience that their stories were authentic, since this audience tended to assume that "real" slaves must be illiterate. White abolitionists therefore tried to discourage Frederick Douglass from using his most polished rhetorical abilities on the lecture platform and especially in the second version of his autobiography, *My Bondage and My Freedom* (1855). For the same reason, the articulate, well-crafted lectures and poetry of the black abolitionist Frances Ellen Watkins Harper seemed incredible to some audiences. They were convinced that she must be either a white woman made up in blackface, or a black man dressed as a woman.

A similar problem surfaced in the late twentieth century. African Americans whose accents and mannerisms did not reproduce more "typical" southern or urban-black speech patterns were sometimes seen as victims, willing or otherwise, of cultural assimilation. During the 1960s and 1970s, the Black Power movement's emphasis on the unique racial consciousness of African Americans made the fluent, uninhibited use of black vernacular speech an important sign of solidarity with the movement. Besides the fact that it preserves certain linguistic features of West African speech, the African American vernacular has always had its uses as a language of resistance, simply by virtue of its unfamiliarity to most white listeners. Although Carson notes that the preference for an "authentic" African American speech promoted divisive "blacker than thou" attitudes among some African Americans during the 1960s and ´70s, healthy debates about how to protect the distinctive features of African American culture from the homogenizing effects of standardized education and mass media changed the goals and approaches of many American educators and artists during this period. Butler is not closely identified with the self-consciously authentic, politically engaged vision of African American literature championed by the Black Arts Movement (widely regarded as the cultural extension of the Black Power Movement), but *Kindred* speaks directly to the issues that preoccupied that movement.

Interracial marriage. At the beginning of "The Fall" (the novel's third chapter, set in 1819), Rufus is shocked to learn that Dana and Kevin are married. Young as he is at this point in the novel, he knows enough to assert that black-white marriages are "against the law" (*Kindred*, p. 61). In 1664 Maryland became the first of Britain's North American colonies to enact laws against interracial marriage—later known as anti-miscegenation laws. The original motive behind these laws was economic: sex and marriage between the colony's free white laborers and its growing population of enslaved black laborers tended to erode the color-barrier that made free men and women distinguishable from slaves, and this distinction had to remain clear if the new slave economy was to stay stable. During the late seventeenth and early eighteenth centuries, other North American colonies adopted laws similar to Maryland's, and after the War of Independence, bans against mixed marriages remained in force throughout the new republic. Indeed, although Pennsylvania and Massachusetts would repeal their bans in 1780 and 1843, respectively, anti-miscegenation statutes remained on the books in most northern and southern states well into the twentieth century. When Dana replies to Rufus's objection by saying that her marriage to Kevin "isn't [illegal] where we come from," it should be kept in mind that the state of California officially legalized such marriages only in 1952, and that the U.S. Supreme Court recognized the freedom to choose a marriage partner regardless of race as a Constitutional right only in 1967 (*Kindred*, p. 61). Had they been married ten years earlier, Dana and Kevin would still have broken the law in 16 states.

The fact that Butler's protagonists must defend the legality of their marriage moments after having been summoned to the Weylin plantation from their own bedroom offers a parallel with *Loving v. Commonwealth of Virginia*, the case that led to the Supreme Court's 1967 ruling. After their 1958 wedding in Washington, D.C., Richard Loving (a white man) and Mildred Loving (née Jeter, a black woman) returned to their home state of Virginia, where they were actually dragged out of bed in the middle of the night and arrested. The trial judge suspended their sentence of one year in prison on the condition that they leave Virginia for 25 years and not return together. Beginning in 1963, the Lovings undertook a series of challenges to this decision, arguing that Virginia's anti-miscegenation statutes infringed their Fourteenth Amendment right to liberty and equal protection under the law; the Supreme Court of Appeals of Virginia upheld the statutes' constitutionality in 1966, but the Lovings appealed again, this time successfully. Chief Justice Earl Warren delivered the U.S. Supreme Court's decision that the Fourteenth Amendment "requires that the freedom of choice to marry not be restricted by invidious racial discriminations" (*Loving v. Virginia*, in Sollors p. 34). Though overshadowed by *Brown v. Board of Education* as the Warren Court's most famous decision, *Loving* stands as one of the major judicial breakthroughs of the civil rights era.

The Novel in Focus

The plot. Apart from the prologue and epilogue that frame the novel, each of Dana's journeys back to antebellum Maryland provides the subject for a different chapter. The prologue introduces Dana, the African American protagonist, as a hospital patient recovering from the loss of her left arm, concerning which the police have questioned both her and her husband, Kevin. Kevin has told them truthfully that he found Dana with her arm somehow "crushed into" the living room wall—but the details as to how this happened re-

Southern plantation similar to the one to which Dana is transported.

main unrevealed for the moment (*Kindred*, p. 11). Dana confides to the reader only that the arm was lost on her "last trip" (*Kindred*, p. 9).

Dana then relives the story, not of her last trip, but of her first. Unpacking books as she moves into a Los Angeles apartment with her newlywed (white) husband, Dana becomes dizzy and nauseous, and suddenly finds herself beside a river watching a young boy drown. While the child's mother looks on, helplessly, Dana rescues the redheaded boy (Rufus) and performs mouth-to-mouth resuscitation; an angry man then appears, and when he points a rifle at Dana, she abruptly finds herself back in her living room with Kevin, who insists that she has only disappeared for a few seconds. Her wet clothes, however, confirm her incredible story. It would grow more incredible.

A few hours later, Dana disappears again, and again she must rescue Rufus (now three years older) by putting out a fire that he has lit in his own bedroom to spite his physically abusive father. By questioning Rufus—especially after he refers to her casually as a "nigger"—Dana learns that she is on a slave plantation in 1815 Maryland and, recalling the name from an ancient family bible, she identifies Rufus Weylin as her "several times great grandfather" (*Kindred*, pp. 24-25, 28). (Interestingly, Rufus's use of the hateful term "nigger" is the first reference in the novel to Dana's racial identity—or to any racial identity.) Eager to leave the plantation, she gets Rufus to direct her to the house of Alice Greenwood—the free black girl whose destiny it will be to bear his daughter in 1831. Unfortunately she arrives at the house just as several patrollers assault and carry off Alice's slave father for visiting his free wife (Alice's mother) without permission. (In the slaveholding South, patrollers were members of local vigilance organizations charged with the surveillance of the slave and free black communities.) When one of the patrollers attempts to rape Dana, she knocks him unconscious—possibly dead—with a fallen branch and quickly loses consciousness herself; reviving in 1976, she mistakes her white husband momentarily for her attacker. As she and Kevin discuss her latest experiences, they realize that threats to Rufus's life seem to call her to his time, whereas threats to her life seem to call her back to her own time. Together, the couple tries to prepare for the next summons from the past.

This time however, they travel through time together. Dana begins to feel dizzy, Kevin throws his arms around her, and the two of them are carried to 1819; at the foot of a tree, they find Rufus, who has fallen and broken a leg. Although they reveal to him that they are husband and wife, they pose as master and slave when Rufus's father, Tom Weylin, arrives on the scene. Kevin later accepts Tom's offer of a job as Rufus's tutor, while Dana lives and works with the Weylins' slaves, sometimes nursing and reading stories to Rufus, and sometimes working for his temperamental mother, Margaret. At considerable risk, Dana also begins teaching two slave children to read; when Tom Weylin catches her doing this, he beats her severely, sending her back unwittingly to 1976 without Kevin.

After eight days at home, which she spends reading histories of slavery and recovering from her beating, Dana is again transported to Maryland, the year being 1824. Her first act is to intervene in a fight between Rufus, now full-grown, and a slave who turns out to be Alice's new husband, Isaac Greenwood; they are fighting over Alice. When Rufus loses consciousness, Dana persuades Isaac not to kill him, promising to buy time while Isaac and Alice attempt an escape to the northern states. While Dana nurses Rufus back to health, he explains that her husband, Kevin, has left the plantation for the North; she writes him a letter, which Rufus agrees to post for her. Dana's role as nurse continues when Isaac and Alice are captured and brutally punished. Rufus sells Isaac, but buys the badly injured Alice (her freedom having been revoked for "aiding a fugitive") and puts her in Dana's care. Once she recovers, however, Alice accuses Dana of acting as the Weylins' willing tool—an accusation that haunts Dana all the more when Rufus enlists her as his go-between with Alice. Seeking to make Alice his concubine, he asks Dana to "fix it so I don't have to beat her"; reluctantly Dana complies (*Kindred*, p. 164). Later, when she discovers that Rufus has not mailed her letters to Kevin, Dana attempts to escape the plantation, but is soon caught by Rufus and his father, who mocks her: "Educated nigger don't mean smart nigger, do it?" (*Kindred*, p. 175). Once again, she receives a beating, but the knowledge that she will survive prevents her from returning to her own time. Her much-desired return occurs later, after Kevin arrives at the plantation to take Dana back North; when Rufus tries to stop the couple at gunpoint, they disappear before he can pull the trigger.

Back home in Los Angeles, a disoriented, painfully distant Kevin gives his account of the five years he has spent stranded in the past. The next time Dana feels herself being pulled away from the present, she begs him to keep away; she arrives alone at the plantation in 1831, and finds Rufus dead drunk and face-down in a rain puddle. While she succeeds in saving Rufus from drowning, as well as from a dangerous fever he has contracted, she fails to save his father from a heart attack. Blaming her for his father's death, Rufus sends Dana to work in the cornfields, but he relents when she collapses from exhaustion and the beatings of the overseer. Dana then becomes the personal servant of Margaret Weylin, now a laudanum-addicted invalid. This work proves comparatively light, but Dana grows increasingly troubled as she witnesses Rufus's economic mismanagement of the plantation—specifically, his willingness to sell slaves away from their families to pay off his debts. Alice (who has had two sons by Rufus since 1824) also worries about this even though, thanks to Dana, Rufus has begun to take an interest in these sons. At last, in February, 1831, Alice gives birth to Hagar, the daughter through whom Alice and Rufus are related to Dana. Having waited anxiously for this event, on which her own existence ultimately depends, Dana begins to feel more independent in relation to Rufus: "I felt almost free, half-free if such a thing was possible, half-way home" (*Kindred*, p. 234). When he hits her in an argument about the sale of a slave, she cuts her own wrists, sending herself back home to the present.

Together again, Kevin and Dana discuss what to do next, as well as Rufus's increasingly possessive and sexually charged tendency to regard Alice and Dana as "two halves of the same woman" (*Kindred*, p. 229). Although the prospect disturbs her, Dana considers the possibility that she might have to kill Rufus. This is precisely what happens in the final chapter. On July 4, 1976, Dana returns to the Weylin plantation (still in 1831) and prevents Rufus from committing suicide. Sadly she arrives too late to do the same for Alice, who hangs herself when Rufus cruelly allows her to believe that he has sold their children. After Alice's funeral, Rufus reveals his intention to have Dana replace her as his concubine—at which point Dana stabs him. He dies grasping her arm, and she travels home for the final time, arriving to find that same arm painfully buried in, or fused with, the wall. In the novel's epilogue, she visits present-day Maryland with Kevin, researching her family history and hoping (without avail) to locate Rufus Weylin's grave.

Civil rights, women's rights. *Kindred* explores the complex balances and imbalances of power in gender relations as well as race relations, reflecting the close and longstanding association between the advocates of equality for women and the advocates of equality for African Americans.

Sara Evans observes that history has repeated itself in the course of this association:

> Twice in the history of the United States the struggle for racial equality has been a midwife to the feminist movement. In the abolition movement of the 1830s and 1840s, and again in the civil rights movement of the 1960s, women . . . gained experience in organizing and in collective action, an ideology that described and condemned oppression analogous to their own, and a belief in human "rights" that could justify them in claiming equality for themselves.
> (Evans, p. 24)

A recognition of the similarity between racial and sexual oppression proved equally crucial, in other words, for two very different generations of feminists. Although not all antebellum abolitionists acknowledged this similarity, many of the best-known ones—including Frederick Douglass, Sojourner Truth, William Lloyd Garrison, Wendell Philips, Sarah and Angelina Grimke, and Lucretia Mott—all propounded it, regarding antislavery and women's rights as inseparable causes. For those who shared this view, as Deborah Grey White argues, the sufferings of slave women like Truth had special significance since they combined the injustices faced by women and slaves. During and after the civil rights era, black women again occupied a unique position at the intersection of racial and sexual politics. In Dana's case, blackness and womanhood combine to erode her authority as the would-be custodian of Rufus's morality: "I was the worst possible guardian for him—a black to watch over him in a society that considered black subhuman, a woman to watch over him in a society that considered women perennial children" (*Kindred*, p. 68). From this perspective, Dana's chances of preserving Rufus's innocence from the corrupting influences of his environment look extremely slim.

In a more empowering light, antebellum feminists could and did point to the strenuous work and physical hardships endured by many female slaves as proof that women were not the delicate creatures that the stereotypes of a male-dominated culture made them out to be. Sometimes too nineteenth-century commentators on the strength and stamina of black women characterized these qualities (and the women who possessed them) simply as unfeminine. In her account of a visit to the antebellum South, the Swedish actress Frederika Bremer noted, for exmaple, that "black [women] are not considered to belong to the weaker sex" (Bremer in White, p. 120). The fact that Dana's twentieth-century habit of wearing pants causes Rufus (among others) to mistake her at first glance for a man suggests Butler's awareness of this characterization.

Rufus's mother, Margaret Weylin, has no real work to do, and so suffers the contempt of everyone on the plantation, including Rufus and Tom. Dana thus informs her husband Kevin that, in his assumed role as her "master," he must not allow her to be excused from ordinary slave duties, lest she earn the resentment of blacks and whites alike. Kevin frowns at her by way of reply: "You want to work?" (*Kindred*, p. 78). Certainly it can hardly please him to think of his wife engaged in slave labor. But his question also brings to mind the many late twentieth-century husbands who saw their wives' interest in work as an implicit threat to their traditional power as

LIFESAVER OR ICON OF URBAN CRIME?

On her second voyage to the past, Dana narrowly escapes being raped by a patroller. Back at home after this close call, Dana relates the incident to Kevin, who quickly supplies her with "the biggest switchblade knife [she has] ever seen" (*Kindred*, p. 45). His choice of weaponry is somewhat unusual, given that Congress had passed the Switchblade Knife Act in 1958, effectively prohibiting the sale and manufacture of all knives with blades that open automatically. Conceived ostensibly to prevent violent crime, the act proscribed knives that, though certainly deadly, were probably more threatening as symbols—especially from the perspective of America's white, suburban middle class—than as actual instruments of death. According to urban mythology, the criminals who typically favored switchblades were inner-city "hoods" and members of black or immigrant youth gangs. The lushly choreographed switchblade duel between the gang leaders Riff and Bernardo in the 1961 musical drama, *West Side Story* (also in *Literature and Its Times*), offers a fair illustration of the stereotype that Butler turns on its head in *Kindred.* Instead of an offensive weapon with which poor, non-Anglo criminals terrorize law-abiding citizens, the switchblade becomes a defensive weapon in the hands of a black woman who is herself terrorized by the antebellum plantation equivalent of police brutality. In the end, however, perhaps significantly, Dana kills Rufus, not with a switchblade, but with a pocketknife that she has the foresight to open in advance.

protectors, providers, and decision makers. In this later era, besides economic rewards, women sought the personal satisfaction and social recognition associated with the pursuit of a vocation. They gained ground on this issue when Congress modified the 1964 Civil Rights Act to include "sex" alongside the word "race" in Title VII, which guaranteed citizens the right to equal opportunity in employment.

Sympathetic as its overall characterization of Kevin is, the novel hints that male power over women in the twentieth century still bears some eerie resemblance to the master's power over the slave. At one point, Rufus asks Kevin if he owns Dana—to which Kevin replies "In a way . . . she's my wife" (*Kindred*, p. 60). Once again, an innocent response reveals the present-day specter of a relatively recent historical reality; while we have no concrete reason to conclude that Kevin is less sensitive and liberal than he seems, we do gather that these qualities are more recently acquired, and thus more fragile, than they might appear to be. Butler's novel is haunted at several intervals by intimations of what history has only narrowly saved Kevin from being. The most dramatic intimations of this kind may be seen in the way Dana's sister—and later the police—interpret the bruises and scars that Dana brings back to the present from her confrontations with slavery. The false suspicion of spousal abuse that falls on Kevin at these points reminds the reader that a violence indistinguishable from the violence of slavery still menaces women in the present, regardless of Kevin's innocence. Along with equality in the workplace and reproductive rights, American feminists made public awareness of sexual violence (including domestic violence) a top priority in the 1970s, emphasizing the statistical frequency of physical and sexual assault as well as the psychologically damaging fear of male aggression that women commonly experienced. Major feminist successes of this period include the building of a national consensus on this issue, and the significant proliferation of publicly and charitably funded women's shelters. Black women encounter both the threat and the reality of sexual violence throughout the time-travel sections of *Kindred*; in the aftermath of traumatic physical attacks, Alice and Dana survive by acting as nurses and brutally honest counselors to each other. "Her words touched something in me . . . started me crying," Dana relates bitterly after her failed escape attempt; "[w]e were both failures, she and I" (*Kindred*, p. 175). The novel dramatizes the persistence of this threat of sexual violence in the late twentieth century, representing it as one of slavery's most insidious legacies for black women and, by extension, all women. In this broad sense, the novel dramatizes the political implications of male sexual aggression, illustrating that it has functioned—as Kate Millet argued persuasively in *Sexual Politics* (1970)-"to provide [a dominant group with] a means of control over a subordinate group" (Millet in Ferree and Hess, p. 43).

Sources and literary context. During her apprenticeship as a fiction writer, Butler made the acquaintance (and gained the support) of more than one successful author while participating in a developmental program sponsored by the Writer's Guild of America. The most eminent of these mentors was Harlan Ellison, the prolific science fiction writer and futurist; Ellison offered constructive criticism in this formative phase of Butler's career, and he introduced Butler to several other reputable sci-fi authors at the Clarion Science Fiction Writer's Workshop in 1970—Joanna Russ, for example, whose feminist science fiction (e.g., *The Two of Them*, 1979) offers interesting thematic comparisons with Butler's fiction, including *Kindred*.

The feverish bout of historical home-study that Dana undertakes in Los Angeles (still smarting from the beating she gets for educating Nigel and Carrie) surely describes the author's reading, as well as the narrator's: "I read books about slavery, fiction and nonfiction. I read everything I had in the house that was even distantly related to the subject" (*Kindred*, p. 116). As for fiction, Alex Haley's multi-generation family saga, *Roots* (1976), stands out as the twentieth century's most successful literary treatment of slavery; the book itself sold 8.5 million copies, and the 1977 ABC miniseries based on it attracted an estimated 130 million viewers. Though less ambitious in its scope than *Roots*, *Kindred*, too, qualifies as a well-informed work of imaginative history in its own right, owing a visible debt to an approach to black history that was still new in the 1970s.

Academic interest in African American studies flourished during that decade, producing a good deal of new research by both black and white scholars, many of whom sought to place new emphasis on the slaves' own experience and understanding of slavery. Above all, the historians who participated in this change of focus in Black history stressed the resilience of African American culture and identity in spite of racist aggression and pressures to assimilate; accordingly, several of them focused on the prevalence of slave resistance, devoting careful study to the facts and attitudes disclosed in antebellum slave narratives. Of these narratives, Douglass's *Narrative of the Life of Frederick Douglass* (1845) proved most useful to Butler, who studied Douglass while attending Pasadena City College. Two of the nonfiction titles that Butler would have come across in her research for *Kindred* would include John Blassingame's *The Slave Community* (1972) and Eugene Genovese's *Roll, Jordan, Roll: The World the Slaves Made* (1974), both of which shed important light on the family lives and the inner lives that slaves tended to conceal from their masters. With respect to the related topics of punishment, resistance, and escape, Gerald Mullin's *Flight and Rebellion* (1972) and Benjamin Quarles' somewhat more traditional *Black Abolitionists* (1969) issued new challenges to the old but persistent myth of the docile, passive slave. Finally, there are passages in *Kindred* that compare the oppressive psychology of the plantation to that of Nazi concentration camps—"Like the Nazis, antebellum whites had known quite a bit about torture" (*Kindred*, p. 117). These passages point to extended reflections on this comparison in Stanley Elkins's controversial but widely read *Slavery: A Problem in American Institutional and Intellectual Life* (1959).

Reviews. The reviews that appeared immediately following *Kindred*'s publication were favorable, though not unmixed in their assessments. Joanna Russ found the novel "more polished" than [Butler's] previous work," praising its fast pace and realism despite objections to the indirect and slightly flat characterization of Dana's twentieth-century relatives and in-laws (Blaise, p. 70). *Kirkus Reviews* appreciated the "fresh, vivid" quality of *Kindred*'s attack on slavery—a "much-lamented" topic that could easily have yielded a more predictable tale (Blaise, p. 70). Writing for *Publishers Weekly*, Barbara A. Bannon was less impressed, judging the recurrent time-travel "obtrusive" and contrived (Blaise, p. 70).

Later responses to *Kindred* (several of which appeared after 1984, a year in which two prestigious awards—a Hugo and a Nebula—inaugurated a sharp rise in Butler's appeal) have gravitated into two camps. Sandra Govan inadvertently identifies the most probable cause of this polarization in her 1986 article in *MELUS*, noting accurately that *Kindred* does "something that is not generally asked of good historical fiction" by offering up an admirable historical novel to an "established science fiction readership which, taken as a whole, is more accustomed to future histories and alien spaces than it is to authentic African American landscapes" (Blaise, p. 50). For commentators who know and love Butler best for her science fiction, *Kindred* has sometimes seemed not just uncharacteristic, but unsatisfying. Burton Raffel, for example, judges *Kindred* to be "a comparative failure" in his otherwise enthusiastic 1995 survey of Butler's career to date (Blaise, p. 67). In Govan's view, on the other hand, *Kindred* is richly innovative in its blending of genres; it "define[s] the junction where the historical novel, the slave narrative, and science fiction meet" (Blaise, p. 43).

—M. Luke Bresky

For More Information

Blaise, Jennifer, ed. *Children's Literature Review: Excerpts from Reviews, Criticism, and Commentary on Books for Children and Young People*. Vol. 65. Detroit: Gale, 2001.

Butler, Octavia. *Kindred*. Boston: Beacon Press, 1979.

Chafe, William H., and Harvard Sitkoff, eds. *A History of Our Time: Readings on Postwar America*. New York: Oxford University Press, 1983.

Evans, Sara. *Personal Politics: The Roots of Women's Liberation in the Civil Rights Movement and the New Left*. New York: Vintage, 1979.

Ferree, Myra Marx, and Beth B. Hess. *Controversy and Coalition: The New Feminist Movement Across Four Decades of Change*. New York: Routlege, 2000.

Franklin, John Hope, and Alfred A. Moss, Jr. *From Slavery to Freedom: A History of African Americans*. Boston: McGraw-Hill, 2000.

Franklin, John Hope, and Loren Schweninger. *Runaway Slaves: Rebels on the Plantation*. New York: Oxford University Press, 1999.

Gates, Henry Louis, ed. *The Classic Slave Narratives*. New York: New American Library, 1987.

Lawson, Stephen F. *Running for Freedom: Civil Rights and Black Politics Since 1941*. New York: McGraw-Hill, 1996.

Mayer, Henry. *All On Fire: William Lloyd Garrison and the Abolition of Slavery*. New York: St. Martin's, 1998.

O'Connor, Margaret Anne. "Octavia E. Butler." In *Dictionary of Literary Biography*. Vol. 33. Ed. Thadious M. Davis and Trudier Harris. Detroit: Gale, 1984.

Sollors, Werner, ed. *Interracialism: Black-White Intermarriage in American History, Literature, and Law*. New York: Oxford University Press, 2000.

White, Deborah Gray. *Ar'n't I a Woman? Female Slaves in the Plantation South*. New York: Norton, 1985.

Krik? Krak!

by
Edwidge Danticat

> **THE LITERARY WORK**
>
> A collection of short stories set in both Haiti and New York from the 1930s to the 1980s; published in 1995.
>
> **SYNOPSIS**
>
> Haitians struggle with poverty and political persecution in their homeland and with cultural alienation and misunderstandings in their adopted country of America.

Edwidge Danticat was born in Haiti on January 19, 1969, and immigrated to the United States in 1981. Dandicat received her bachelor's degree in French literature from Barnard College and a master's degree in fine arts from Brown University. She began publishing short stories at the young age of 14, then produced her first novel, *Breath, Eyes, Memory* the following decade in 1995. Also that year she published *Krik? Krak!*—a finalist for the National Book Award in 1995. Its stories figure into Danticat's continuing effort to interject a degree of humanity into perceptions of a nation that is often publicly maligned because of its corrupt politicians and warring governmental factions. Amidst this turbulence, Danticat depicts the Haitians' struggles to survive in their own country and in their adopted country of the United States.

Events in History at the Time the Short Stories Take Place

The struggle for Haitian independence. While most of the stories in *Krik? Krak!* take place between the 1950s and 1980, some hearken back in spirit to seminal events in Haiti's history. Few moments were more pivotal than the revolution of 1804, which ultimately resulted in the country's obtaining its freedom from France. Since 1697 France had governed a third of the island as the colony of Sainte-Domingue; Spain governed the other two-thirds as the colony of Santo Domingo. The entire island was known as Hispaniola, the name given it by Christopher Columbus, who landed there in 1492. Within 50 years of his discovery, disease and mistreatment had virtually wiped out the island's indigenous population—approximately 10,000 Arawaks.

France governed its colony for close to a century before Haiti revolted. The seeds for a full-blown rebellion were sown as early as 1791, two years after the outbreak of the French Revolution in France. Inspired, even inflamed, by the slogan of "Liberty, Equality, and Fraternity" coined in France by the revolutionaries there, black slaves in Sainte-Domingue set about mounting their own revolution to wrest freedom from white slaveowners. On August 14, 1791, a rebel slave named Boukman organized a *vaudou* (often spelled *voodoo*) ceremony at the Turpin plantation, near Bois Cayman; among the attendees were Toussaint L'Ouverture, George Biassou, and Jean-François, all of whom would become leaders in the Haitian revolution that followed.

Edwidge Danticat

Shortly after the vaudou ceremony, the rebellion began in earnest. Slaves slaughtered whites and set fire to property, fields, and factories; in Cap-Français, whites responded by killing nonwhites at random, provoking further retaliation by blacks. Before the Cap-Français rebellion had been suppressed, 10,000 slaves and 1,000 whites were killed and 1,200 coffee estates and 200 sugar plantations destroyed (Metz, p. 268). Elsewhere in the French colony the fighting continued, and the whites found themselves unable to regain control of their former slaves. France's preoccupation with its own failing government and its ongoing war with Britain further helped the blacks' cause. There were, in short, two conflicts going on at once—the domestic strife of slave against slaveowner and the international strife of France against Spain for control of territory here. Slave leader Toussaint L'Ouverture emerged as a preeminent military strategist. Deeming it in the best interest of the slaves, he joined with the Spanish forces—led by two black generals, George Biassou and Jean-François—seeking to capture the northern part of Saint-Domingue. Then in 1794 the French National Assembly's promise to abolish slavery led Toussaint to throw in his lot with the French; a large portion of Biassou and Jean-François's now-disbanded forces joined him. Eventually achieving the rank of commander in chief over all the French forces on the island, Toussaint captured the port of Santo Domingo in 1801 and gained control over the entire island, nominally for the French but ultimately for himself and Haiti's black majority. Once in power, Toussaint abolished slavery in the region and appointed himself governor-general for life.

In 1802 Napoleon Bonaparte, first Consul of France, sent an army under the command of General Charles LeClerc to retake the island. After Toussaint's chief lieutenants Jean Jacques Dessalines and Henry Christophe went over to the side of the French, Toussaint himself was forced to surrender to LeClerc, who had the former leader imprisoned in France, where he died in 1803. On learning that Napoleon planned to restore slavery, Dessalines and Christophe, along with other soldiers of color, defected from the French army and became insurrectionists once more. Fierce fighting and yellow fever took their toll on French forces, who finally surrendered to the blacks in November 1803. On January 2, 1804, Dessalines announced the birth of a new nation, now called "Haiti" (the Arawak word for mountainous).

In *Krik? Krak!* the spirit of the revolution for independence is often evoked, especially in the story "A Wall of Fire Rising." As a young black couple tries to eke out a living in twentieth-century Haiti, their seven-year-old son wins the part of Boukman in a school play. The speeches the boy must learn—passionate calls for freedom and

HAITI'S TRUE RELIGION?

Vaudou, more commonly known as voodoo, is perhaps most accurately defined as a form of religion developed by Afro-Haitians, whose system of beliefs encompasses the natural and supernatural worlds. The concept of family spirits—often called *loua* or *mistè*—who are inherited through maternal or paternal lines is central to vaudou. These family spirits protect their descendants from misfortune and harm; in exchange, the families conduct rituals in which food, drink, and other gifts are offered to the spirits. Among foreigners, vaudou has acquired a sinister reputation over the centuries, becoming associated not only with service to the spirits but with witchcraft, sorcery, human sacrifice, and cannibalism. During the 1920s, however, radical Haitian intellectuals exalted vaudou as an example of their country's true culture and faith. Also the later national leader François "Papa Doc" Duvalier was a proponent of the practice of vaudou.

independence for blacks—form an ironic counterpoint to the day-to-day struggle for existence that his parents must face and that eventually claims his father's life.

The Duvaliers' regime. During the 1950s François Duvalier, a physician, writer, and patron of vaudou, rose to prominence in Haiti, capturing the allegiance of the army and winning a significant degree of popular support. Representing himself as a champion of Haitian blacks, "Papa Doc" Duvalier—so called because of his mild, fatherly demeanor—won a decisive majority in the presidential election of 1957; he was re-elected in 1961.

Within months of his victory, Duvalier set about establishing a totalitarian state. Dismissing the chief of staff, he seized direct control of the army, closed the nation's military academy, and founded several competing military bodies, headed by his own men. The most infamous of these was the Volunteers for National Security, more popularly known as the "tontons macoutes"—a reference from Haitian folklore to the bearded bogeymen who carried away badly behaved children during the night. Formed to keep the army in check, the macoutes spied upon, imprisoned, tortured, or killed any Haitians who might offer resistance to the Duvalier regime.

Meanwhile, Duvalier declared himself president for life in 1964, after bringing all national institutions—schools, churches, trade unions, the press, and the media—under his control. Censorship was widespread; even the Roman Catholic Church came under attack when Duvalier, in pursuit of unchallenged control, expelled its priests and closed its seminary. Hoping to escape Duvalier's oppressive regime, many Haitian journalists, writers, and intellectuals fled into exile; the predominantly black working classes and peasantry, however, remained behind, struggling against increasing poverty and political persecution. Several attempts were made to remove Duvalier from power, but these coups—usually undermanned and poorly executed—all resulted in failure and the execution of those responsible. Nonetheless, the threat of assassination or deposition was ever-present; Duvalier lived in constant fear for his life.

Shortly before his death in 1971, Duvalier changed the age requirement for the office of president from forty to eighteen years of age, enabling him to name his young son, Jean Claude Duvalier as his successor. Jean Claude "Baby Doc" Duvalier, whom many Haitians considered a playboy under the influence of his mother and sister, assumed the office of president at the age of nineteen. Initially, the younger Duvalier implemented some minor reforms: he released many political prisoners; declared an amnesty for all exiles who were not communists; and restored some degree of freedom to the press. "Baby Doc" did not, however, reform the voting process—election outcomes were rigged, as they had been in his father's time. Nor did he disband the tontons macoutes, who continued to thrive under the new regime. Meanwhile, Haiti itself continued to grow poorer; official corruption, population growth, natural disasters, and the decline of tourism all contributed to a severely depressed national economy. Matters between Duvalier and his subjects further deteriorated after his marriage to a woman who became notorious for her greed and extravagance. During the 1980s protests were mounted against political corruption and social injustice. The protests led by the Catholic clergy and other religious groups grew increasingly more frequent

DEATH AT THE DOMINICAN'S DOORSTEP

Danticat's fiction recalls another tragic event in Haitian history: the 1937 massacre of some 50,000 Haitian laborers by the army of the Dominican Republic. Relations between these two neighboring countries had long been strained and hostile. Formerly called Santo Domingo, the Dominican Republic, which occupies the eastern two-thirds of Hispaniola, only emerged as a separate, undominated part of the world after weathering a series of wars with Haiti and enduring a lengthy occupation by U.S. troops (1916-22). In 1922 the United States and Dominican leaders reached an agreement that led to the formation of a provisional government. The relatively peaceful, uneventful administration of Horacio Vásquez ended in 1930, when General Rafael Trujillo, a disciple of the American occupational forces, seized control of the government (see ***In the Time of the Butterflies,*** also in *Literature and Its Times*). Backed by the army, Trujillo ruled as a dictator until his assassination in 1961. During his regime, Trujillo encouraged anti-Haitian feeling, especially after Haitian sugarcane cutters migrated to the eastern side of the border between Haiti and the Dominican Republic in the 1930s. It was on Trujillo's orders that the cane cutters were slaughtered. In "Nineteen Thirty-Seven," the second story in *Krik? Krak!*, Danticat explores the ramifications of that massacre on the survivors and their descendants, who keep the memory of their dead alive.

A HISTORY OF POLITICAL INSTABILITY

Haiti has the distinction of being the first (and perhaps only) country to lead a successful slave revolt that resulted in the independence of black slaves, and it was the second nation to declare its independence in the western hemisphere. Consequently, Haiti has served as a symbol of liberation to many who have struggled against subjugation. However, despite its promising beginnings, the country has suffered much at the hands of violent dictators and powerful foreign influences. Jean Jacques Dessalines, who proclaimed himself emperor in 1804, was assassinated in 1806, setting an unfortunate precedent for the next century. A succession of strong-willed ambitious leaders seized power and resorted to repressive measures to maintain their position, only to be assassinated or overthrown, often by the person who replaced them in office. In 1915 the United States dispatched Marines to Haiti to protect American interests; for nearly 20 years, U.S. troops quashed native attempts at resistance against them, while the U.S. Government placed a series of puppet presidents in office. After U.S. troops left the country in 1934, Haiti continued to suffer political insurrections and was governed by military juntas during periods of instability until the presidency could be restored through election. This period of volatile rule in Haiti continued until the election of François Duvalier, who assured the stability of his presidency through an absolutist dictatorship and, upon his death, passed the reins of government to his son, Jean Claude. After three decades, however, Haitians rebelled against the Duvaliers, eventually driving Jean Claude and his family into exile. The fall of the dictatorship did not usher in a new age of order, stability, and democracy for the country. To this day, Haiti continues to be plagued by political unrest. Four of the six presidents who succeeded the Duvaliers were overthrown while still in office. Despite new political developments and new policies to improve the quality of life in Haiti, the country's image as a violent, unstable, poverty-stricken nation persists in mainstream societies. Edwidge Danticat's work attempts to combat the negative and often violent stereotypes associated with Haiti by emphasizing the humanity of its people and separating them from the politics of the land.

and clamorous. In 1986 the government collapsed, and Duvalier and his immediate family fled to France. Haiti's woes, however, did not end with the Duvaliers' fall; without a strong central government, the country experienced anarchy and confusion. Meanwhile, political and military institutions had been seriously discredited under the last two regimes. Strikes, protest marches, robberies, murders, and other abuses of power continued unabated, causing Haitians to describe their situation as "Duvalierism without Duvalier" (Metz, p. 295).

In "Children of the Sea," the opening story of *Krik? Krak!*, Danticat explores the effects of the Duvaliers' regime on two separated lovers—a politically active young man forced to flee into exile and his girlfriend, still in Haiti, who witnesses all the atrocities committed by the tontons macoutes. But the misdeeds of the Duvaliers' hated secret police reach past the country's borders, making themselves felt even in the boat on which the young man is traveling. One of his fellow passengers, a young girl named Célianne, has been gang-raped by the macoutes and is now pregnant as a result of their vicious attack.

The "boat people." Between the 1950s and 1980s, many Haitians fled the island to escape the Duvaliers' oppressive regime. In the 1950s and 1960s the majority of these refugees belonged to the urban middle and upper classes; by the 1970s poor Haitians, from both rural and urban areas, accounted for most of the refugees. Some of these Haitians migrated to the Dominican Republic, the Bahamas, Canada, France and

Sylvio Claude, leader of the Christian Democratic Party of Haiti and a leading opponent of the Duvalier regime.

sometimes Africa. The United States, however, was usually the primary destination, receiving an estimated 68 percent of all Haitian emigrants between 1950 and 1985 (Metz, p. 320). The cities of New York, Miami, Boston, Chicago, and Philadelphia reported sizable numbers of Haitian residents by the mid-1980s.

Escaping from Haiti was hardly a clandestine affair; the tonton macoutes sometimes helped would-be emigrants to boats that were waiting conspicuously in the harbor for them. In fact, Jean Claude Duvalier thought that the Haitian people's flight would help the country's economy, as those who fled would send money back to their relatives in Haiti. During the 1970s and 1980s these emigrants became known as the "boat people" because they often set off for foreign shores in small boats or rafts, without documentation. According to reports made by the U.S. Immigration and Naturalization Service, an estimated 55,000 "boat people" arrived in Florida between 1972 and 1981 (Metz, p. 327).

This Haitian diaspora, or dispersal of emigrants, created a host of new problems: adding to overpopulation in the countries who received this influx of refugees, leading to economic exploitation of emigrants because of their illegal status, and causing the deaths of many Haitians as they attempted to reach their destinations. The United States and various other Caribbean countries eventually called for Jean Claude Duvalier to forbid Haitians from leaving their country, a demand to which he finally acquiesced. In 1981 the United States formed an agreement with Haiti to intercept Haitian boats and return the passengers to their homeland; approximately 54,000 Haitians experienced such a return between 1981 and 1992 (Metz, p. 327).

In "Children of the Sea," Danticat depicts the plight of these "boat people," conveying everything from the physical discomfort they experience while crowded on a small craft, to the boredom they try to assuage by telling each other stories, to the growing sense of dread they experience as their boat begins to leak before land is sighted. The story ends on an ominous note as the young girl in Haiti reports that "last night on the radio, i heard that another boat sank off the coast of the Bahamas. i can't think about you being in there in the waves. my hair shivers" (*Krik? Krak!*, pp. 18-19).

Women in Haitian society. Theoretically, gender roles in Haiti follow traditional patterns. Among married couples, the husband is the breadwinner, the wife the housekeeper and caretaker of the children. Men have enjoyed higher legal standing in the courts; wives have been subject to greater sanctions against adultery than husbands, and only since 1983 have married women in Haiti been accorded adult rights.

Sexual stratification, however, blurs when one considers the realities of a disproportionately female society. Emigration and disease, among other causes, have resulted in there being far more women than men in Haiti; demographics show a shortage of men above the age of ten, especially in urban areas. Consequently women enter the labor force quite early: an estimated 10 percent of Haitian females begin working between the ages of five and nine, an estimated 33 percent between the ages of ten and fourteen (Metz, p. 336). Moreover, female heads of households have become increasingly common; an official survey in 1996 revealed that women headed 26 percent of rural households and 46 percent of urban households (Metz, p. 336).

In rural society, women play a pivotal role in Haiti's internal market system. They function as intermediaries between the peasant villages and the markets and towns, selling a villages' surplus produce and purchasing medicines and necessary household articles with the proceeds. Some women even amass sufficient capital to become full-time market traders and acquire economic independence from men. In urban society, women hold a variety of jobs, ranging from household servant to factory worker. In both rural and urban regions, Haitian women tend to be the mainstays of their families.

Krik? Krak! reflects the realities of life in Haiti's predominantly female society. Nearly all the stories are told from a women's point of view; moreover, most of the female protagonists are widows or single women who must support themselves or their families by their own efforts. Husbands and male lovers are usually absent (as in "Children of the Sea"), unreliable (as in "Between the Pool and the Gardenias"), or dead (as in "Caroline's Wedding"). Some men, unable to cope with the demoralizing realities of life below the poverty line, die in the course of the story (as in "A Wall of Fire Rising"). In the *Krik? Krak!* stories, the primary bond is not so much between husband and wife as between mother and child—specifically, mother and daughter. Time and again, an older generation of women attempts to impart its wisdom and experience to a younger generation, some of whom are more receptive to these teachings than others.

The Short Stories in Focus

The plot. Danticat's collection weaves together stories about various Haitians. Of the nine stories, seven take place in Haiti while the last two are set in New York. Many of the protagonists in the stories are linked through familial or communal ties.

The first story, "Children of the Sea," consists of letters written by two young lovers torn apart by politics. Branded as traitors because of their participation in a radical youth group, they are forced to flee, separately, from the wrath of the tonton macoutes, out to punish "enemies of the state." As the story begins, the male protagonist, with other refugees, has boarded a small boat bound for Miami; he decides to keep a journal, which he addresses to his sweetheart, even as he acknowledges that she may never see it. Meanwhile, his girlfriend is similarly occupied: writing an account of the days until she and her parents can escape the chaos of Port-au-Prince and find refuge in the small province, Ville Rose. The couple's parallel narratives reveal not only their undying love for each other—in letters that they will never be able to deliver—but the terrible atrocities they witness on their separate journeys.

The young man begins by expressing his anxiety over the thought of never seeing his lover again and the possibility that she will marry another, according to her father's wishes. The young woman's writings mirror his anxiety and sense of hopelessness, even as her concerns broaden to include her parents and the larger Haitian community, all of whom wonder when and if the country will ever be at peace. Disillusioned by the state of affairs in their country, the young woman's parents hide and destroy campaign paraphernalia that would link them to a departed president (to whom—it may be inferred—they had formerly pledged their allegiance).

The girlfriend's narrative further exposes the cruelty of the new regime as she relates the story of her next-door neighbor, Madam Roger, who was able to retrieve only her son's severed head after he was killed by the tonton macoutes. Meanwhile, the macoutes continue to harass Madam Roger about her son's political resistance, beating her to death after she excoriates the current regime and praises those, like her son, who had the courage to resist. While hiding in the outhouse, the girlfriend and her parents witness Madam Roger's murder but are too terrified to intervene. After the entire family flees to the countryside, the mother reveals that authorities had identified the young girl herself as a rebel and that the father had given all he possessed, including their house, to keep her from being arrested. While eternally grateful for her father's loyalty, the girlfriend still worries about the fate of her exiled lover.

Meanwhile, the male protagonist and his fellow refugees remain at sea, hoping to be picked up by the U.S. Coast Guard or to somehow reach the coast of Florida on their own. Needing something to sustain them through the risks and the boredom of their long voyage, the travelers comfort themselves by singing "Beloved Haiti" and telling each other "Krik? Krak!" stories: "Someone says, Krik? You answer, Krak! And they say, I have many stories I could tell you, and then they go on and tell these stories to you, but mostly to themselves" (*Krik? Krak!*, p. 14).

Over time, the young man hears some of his fellow passengers' stories, including that of Célianne, a 15-year-old girl who became pregnant after ten macoute officers invaded her home, forced her brother to sleep with his mother, and then raped Célianne while her family watched. Later, Célianne gives birth to a dead baby while aboard the vessel. Ominously, water begins to seep into the boat and the passengers are forced to throw their personal belongings overboard in order to stay afloat. Despite the urgings of her fellow travelers, Célianne refuses to throw her baby overboard. Eventually, she complies, but immediately takes a suicidal jump overboard after her child. Meanwhile, the boat continues to leak, and the male narrator is forced to throw his journal into the sea as well. The young man's narrative thus concludes as he tries to find some comfort in the thought of his possible death by drowning: "I go to them now as though it was always meant to be, as though the very day that my mother birthed me, she had chosen me to live life eternal, among the children of the deep blue sea, those who have escaped the chains of slavery to form a world beneath the heavens and the blood-drenched earth where you live" (*Krik? Krak!*, p. 27).

Back in Haiti, the young woman, ignorant of her lover's likely fate, beholds a black butterfly—a symbol of death—and reports hearing of another refugee-laden boat's sinking off the coast of the Bahamas. The possibility that her lover might have been on that boat fills her with fear, and she ends her own story with a poignant affirmation of her devotion to him: "Behind these mountains are more mountains and more black butterflies still and a sea that is endless like my love for you" (*Krik? Krak!*, p. 29).

Most of the subsequent stories in the collection explore Haitians' day-to-day struggles to survive in their troubled country, amid such obstacles as political persecution ("The Missing Peace"), ignorance and superstition ("Nineteen Thirty-Seven"), and the grinding realities of poverty ("A Wall of Fire Rising," "Night Women"). In the last two stories, however, the focus shifts to transplanted Haitians, now making their homes in New York. The final story, "Caroline's Wedding," depicts a Haitian-American family struggling to maintain connections with its homeland while forging a new sense of identity in the United States. "Caroline's Wedding" also brings the collection full-circle, in that the main plot of "Children of the Sea" resurfaces here as a subplot.

Featured in "Caroline's Wedding" are Mrs. Azile, a Haitian immigrant mother and her two daughters: Grace, who narrates the story, and Caroline, who is engaged to marry Eric, a Bahamian janitor. Mr. Azile, the father in the family, is dead but his memory lives on in the minds of his children who constantly think of him. His widow attempts to preserve Haitian traditions in the United States and adamantly opposes her younger daughter's wedding because Caroline's fiancé is not Haitian. The American-born Caroline, however, seems to have stronger ties to the United States than to Haiti; Caroline's missing left forearm, the result of being exposed before birth to a dangerous tranquilizer, comes to symbolize her limited involvement with her Haitian roots and her immediate family. Mother and daughter repeatedly clash over the importance of Haiti and Haitian culture in their present-day lives. By contrast, Caroline's older sister, Grace—who has just attained her American citizenship—embraces the traditions of both Haiti and the United States, while maintaining a neutral stance in the conflict between her mother and sister.

At one point, the mother asks both Grace and Caroline to attend a memorial mass for Haitian refugees who died while trying to flee their homeland. Caroline, who does not like to focus on the past, refuses, but Grace agrees to accompany her mother. During the service, the priest asks the congregation for special prayers on behalf of a young girl who gave birth on one of the boats bound for America, then jumped overboard with her dead baby. This reference to Célianne, whose history is recounted in "Children of the Sea," brings the story-cycle full-circle, emphasizing the Haitians' ongoing struggle to find refuge in a hostile world.

Meanwhile, on a more human, even comedic scale, the domestic disagreements between Mrs. Azile and Caroline continue. Caroline remains adamant about wedding Eric, while her mother continues to lament that her daughter is marrying a non-Haitian and worries as well about Eric's motivations. When Grace tries to reassure her mother about the couple's love for each other, Mrs. Azile retorts that love does not always last. Grace recalls that, in order to escape Haiti, her parents divorced and her father married another woman to gain American citizenship. Later, he divorced his second wife and sent for his first wife and daughters, but the Azile marriage never regained its earlier passion. Grace reflects soberly upon the price her family paid for the freedom they now enjoy as Haitian Americans.

Despite her anxieties, Mrs. Azile ultimately accepts Caroline's relationship with Eric and helps her daughter prepare for her wedding, a civil ceremony held in a judge's office. Grace and her mother serve as witnesses. Caroline leaves on her honeymoon, with thoughts of her mother. The newlywed sends her mother roses, which Mrs. Azile cherishes, despite feeling that the flowers are too expensive. Meanwhile, Grace continues to contemplate her own identity as a naturalized citizen, still bound to Haiti by memories and traditions. The story ends as mother and elder daughter bond over a Haitian game of questions and answers that Mr. Azile used to play with his children.

A tradition of orality. The importance of oral communication is a recurring theme in the stories comprising *Krik? Krak!* However different their experiences or situations, Danticat's characters are linked through various forms of shared speech. In "Nineteen Thirty-Seven," for example, the survivors of the 1937 Haitian massacre have developed a series of questions and answers by which one survivor recognizes another:

> "Who are you?" I asked her.
> "I am a child of that place," she answered. "I come from that long trail of blood."
> "Where are you going?"
> "I am walking into the dawn."
> "Who are you?"
> "I am the first daughter of the first star."
> (*Krik? Krak!*, p. 44)

In "Caroline's Wedding," sisters Grace and Caroline play a similar game with each other, learned from their mother. Grace recalls, "Ma too had learned this game when she was a girl. Her mother belonged to a secret women's society in Ville Rose, where the women had to question each other before entering one another's houses" (*Krik? Krak!*, p. 165). The game becomes a bridge between the generations, a ritual handed down from mother to daughter.

Other forms of speech take on a similar significance in Danticat's stories. In "A Wall of Fire Rising," the lines Little Guy must recite for his school play encompass Haiti's past and present woes, from political oppression to crushing poverty. Stories and songs also connect characters. In "Children of the Sea," the Haitian refugees attempting to reach Florida by boat sing the anthem "Beloved Haiti, there is no place like you" and enact the storytelling ritual of "Krik? Krak!" to make the long hours pass more quickly.

By using the catch-phrase "Krik? Krak!" as the title of her short-story collection, Danticat herself evokes a common form of storytelling in the Caribbean illustrated by the boat people. Although the ritual structure varies in different parts of the Caribbean, all varieties emphasize the call-and-response elements integral to this type of storytelling. In one common version, the storyteller asks "Krik?" at varying points in the narrative to see if her/his audience would like for her to continue. If they are willing, the audience replies "Krak!" and the tale continues. This type of storytelling has become a way of passing down the folklore and the history of the Haitian people to future generations. Oral communication may be even more vital among Haitians because of the country's high rate of illiteracy. The Haitian-American Danticat melds two traditions of storytelling—oral and written—in *Krik? Krak!*, quoting the following passage by Sal Scalora as an epigraph to her collection:

> Krik? Krak! Somewhere by the seacoast I feel a breath of warm sea air and hear the laughter of children.
> An old granny smokes her pipe,
> Surrounded by the village children . . .
> "We tell the stories so that the young ones will know what came before them.
> They ask Krik? We say Krak!
> Our stories are kept in our hearts."
> (Scalora in Danticat, *Krik? Krak!*, p. v)

Sources and literary context. Although Danticat has denied in interviews that any of her works are autobiographical, she nonetheless draws heavily upon her knowledge and experiences of Haiti. In an interview with National Public Radio, Danticat reveals that she "wanted to raise the voice of a lot of the people that [she] knew growing up, and this was, for the most part . . . poor people who had extraordinary dreams but also very amazing obstacles" (Danticat, Interview). Danticat also acknowledges a particular debt to the stories that she heard from the older women in her family when she was a young girl growing up in Haiti. In fact, she dedicates *Krik? Krak!* to two aunts who died the year that the work was published.

Danticat has been compared with other female authors from the Caribbean, especially Christina Garcia (*Dreaming in Cuban*) and Julia Alvarez (*In the Time of the Butterflies*). All three women choose to write in English as a way of expressing their situation of belonging to two places: the Caribbean and the United States. In another interview, Danticat further explains, "I came to English at a time when I was not adept enough at French to write creatively in French and did not know how to write in Creole because it had not been taught to me in school, so my writing in English was as much an act of personal translation as it was an act of creative collaboration with the new place I was in" ("A Conversation with Edwidge Danticat").

Events in History at the Time the Stories Were Written

Haitian New York. During the Haitian diaspora that took place between the 1950s and 1980s, many refugees entering the United States chose New York as their city of adoption. Indeed, New York is the home of more Haitians outside of Haiti than any other locale in the western hemisphere. In the 2000 census, estimates revealed that there were about 500,000 people in the New York Metropolitan Area who claimed Haitian ancestry. Of this number, approximately 200,000 Haitian Americans reside in Brooklyn, New York, including Edwidge Danticat herself.

Ties between the immigrants and their families still in Haiti remain strong. Nearly one-fourth of the income accumulated by the approximately 2.5 million Haitians living in the United States is sent back to help struggling relatives in Haiti. Meanwhile, many Haitian immigrants strive to hold onto their heritage, even as they try to make places for themselves in the United States, as illustrated in such stories as Danticat's "Caroline's Wedding."

Emigration in the 1990s. Tales about the "boat people" begin and end the story-cycle in *Krik? Krak!* At the time Danticat was writing and publishing these stories, U.S. policy towards Haitian refugees was undergoing a dramatic change. The influx of "boat people" slowed briefly during the early 1990s but resumed after the left-wing President Jean-Bertrand Aristide, a Roman Catholic priest, was ousted by a military coup in 1991. His successor, General Raoul Cedras, instituted a harsh military regime (1991-94), during which the army carried out "a savage and systematic repression of the slums and countryside," which resulted in thousands being killed (Dash, p. 24).

Once again, politically oppressed Haitians took to the seas on rafts and boats, attempting to reach safer shores. Many were picked up by the U.S. Coast Guard, which took them to an encampment at the U.S. naval base at Guantánama, Cuba. Using the terms of the old agreement with Jean Claude Duvalier, President George Bush ordered the Haitians returned to their homeland, a decision that elicited the condemnation of Democratic presidential candidate, William Clinton. Once Clinton himself took office, however, he did not immediately alter the existing policy regarding Haitian refugees. By 1994, strong criticism from the African American community had prompted Clinton to offer asylum to victims of political repression. But as the decade wore on, more Haitian boat people would be turned away than allowed into the United States. Clinton also denounced the Cedras regime for its violence and cruelty, and contemplated an invasion of Haiti to remove Cedras from power. Former U.S. president Jimmy Carter was dispatched to Haiti and managed to negotiate an agreement with the military; Clinton canceled the impending invasion but nonetheless deployed some 20,000 American troops to Haiti. In October 1994 President Aristide returned from exile in Venezuela and resumed his former office.

Reviews. Like Danticat's first novel (*Breath, Eyes, Memory*), *Krik? Krak!* was well received. Many reviewers hailed Danticat as a new and exciting talent who skillfully brought to life the customs and culture of her homeland. Reviewing the collection for the *Washington Post*, Joanne Omang wrote, "In Haitian-American Edwidge Danticat, modern Haiti may have found its voice . . . into these nine short stories she has woven the sad with the funny, the unspeakable with the glorious, the wild horror and deep love that is Haiti today" (Omang in Narins and Stanley, p. 93). Richard Eder, writing for *Newsday*, was similarly enthusiastic, declaring that "the best of [the stories in *Krik? Krak!*], using the island tradition of a semi-magical folk-tale, or the witty, between-two-worlds voices of modern urban immigrants, are pure beguiling transformation" (Eder in Narins and Stanley, p. 93). Some critics also noted—and were impressed by—the subtle interconnections that bound several stories together. Kimberly Hébert, writing for *Quarterly Black Review*, observed that "the awful-ness of the pain and the tragedy of Haitian poverty are not all Danticat has to tell. She weaves a rich web of remembered rituals and dream fragments that connects the first story to the last. As the stories progress from one to the next, we realize that Danticat is tracing a family lineage, a history of people related by circumstance" (Hébert in Narins and Stanley, p. 95). Summing up the strengths of the collection, Hébert concludes, "The stories that Edwidge Danticat has chosen to tell are deeply spiritual and ultimately disturbing. They are a powerful synthesis of the old with the new, the past with the present; a looking backward to go forward; a loud and powerful Krak! to her ancestors' spirit-giving Krik?" (Hébert in Narins and Stanley, p. 96).

—Pamela S. Loy and Keidra Morris

For More Information

Abbott, Elizabeth. *Haiti: The Duvaliers and Their Legacy*. New York: McGraw-Hill, 1988.

Casey, Ethan. "Remembering Haiti," in *Callaloo* 18, no. 2 (1995): 524-28.

"A Conversation with Edwidge Danticat," in *Behind the Books*. 2000. http://www.randomhouse.com/vintage/danticat.html (24 July 2002).

Danticat, Edwidge. *Krik? Krak!* New York: Soho Press, 1995.

———. Interview by Liane Hansen. NPR, 7 May 1995.

Dash, J. Michael. *Culture and Customs of Haiti*. Westport: Greenwood Press, 2001.

Davis, Rocio G. "Oral Narrative as Short Story Cycle: Forging Community in Edwidge Danticat's *Krik? Krak!*", in *MELUS* 26, no. 2 (summer 2001): 65-82.

Ferguson, James. *Papa Doc, Baby Doc: Haiti and the Duvaliers*. Oxford: Basil Blackwell, 1987.

Metz, Helen Chapin. *Dominican Republic and Haiti: Country Studies*. Washington, D.C.: Federal Research Division, 2001.

Narins, Brigham, and Deborah A. Stanley, eds. *Contemporary Literary Criticism*. Vol. 94. Detroit: Gale Research, 1997.

Rogozinski, Jan. *A Brief History of the Caribbean*. New York: Meridian, 1994.

Sherlock, Philip Manderson Sir. *The Iguana's Tail: Crick Crack Stories from the Caribbean*. New York: Crowell, 1969.

A Lesson Before Dying

by
Ernest J. Gaines

Born in Oscar, Louisiana in 1933, Ernest J. Gaines has won wide respect for his realistic, quietly powerful novels portraying African American life in a rural Louisiana plantation setting. Nearly all of his novels take place in the same mythologized locale around the fictional town of Bayonne, seat of St. Raphael Parish in rural Louisiana. Gaines, who left rural Louisiana with his family as a teenager, was educated at San Francisco State College and Stanford University in California, where he studied creative writing as a Wallace Stegner Fellow. Gaines published two novels (*Catherine Carmier* [1964] and *Of Love and Dust* [1967]) and a short-story collection (*Bloodline* [1968]) in the 1960s, but it was the following publication of ***The Autobiography of Miss Jane Pittman*** (1971; also in *Literature and Its Times)* that established Gaines as a leading contemporary black writer. Aired as a highly successful television movie in 1974, it remains Gaines's best known and most highly praised work. His subsequent novels *In My Father's House* (1978) and *A Gathering of Old Men* (1983) were also well received, and they consolidated Gaines's literary reputation. Like these earlier novels, *A Lesson Before Dying* focuses on the struggle of African American individuals to preserve their dignity in the face of the daily injustices and pervasive humiliation meted out by the Southern white social system.

THE LITERARY WORK

A novel set in and around the small Louisiana town of Bayonne in the late 1940s; published in 1993.

SYNOPSIS

A young schoolteacher is asked to instill human dignity in a semiliterate convict awaiting execution for murder.

Events in History at the Time the Novel Takes Place

Blacks in the American South after World War II. By the middle of the twentieth century, African Americans had made some significant gains in their ongoing effort to attain social and legal equality but much remained to be achieved. Many of the gains had been spurred by the two world wars that marked the first half of the century. As European immigration slowed during and after World War I (1914-18), blacks continued their mass exodus out of the South to seek jobs in northern industrial cities such as New York and Chicago, drawn in part by a demand for labor that had previously been filled by European immigrants. Called the Great Migration, this movement remains one of the most influential turning points in African American history after the abolition of slavery in 1865. It began in the 1890s and continued to about 1950, much of the migration occurring between the two world wars. Black soldiers played important roles in the defense of democracy in these wars, which lent new urgency to their hopes that the nation might now live up to its ideals of equality. Back home, in World War II (1939-45), black female

Ernest J. Gaines

workers contributed to the war effort too, laboring alongside white women to help manufacture weapons and equipment. Their efforts and sacrifices on behalf of their country in these conflicts made it seem all the more unreasonable that white society would expect African Americans to remain content with the burdens of legal inferiority, social subordination, and frequent humiliation that it imposed on them.

Those burdens lay especially heavily on the shoulders of the many blacks who remained in the South. While down from the 90 percent who had lived there before World War I, in 1950 nearly half of the nation's 15 million African Americans still lived in Southern states, most amid conditions of squalid rural poverty and hardship. Southern whites had long since successfully reversed the liberal reforms imposed on them by Northerners during Reconstruction (1865-77). Under the so-called Jim Crow system, a patchwork of often complex local and state laws mandated strict racial segregation in most public facilities. Barred from the ubiquitous public places bearing signs such as "Whites Only," Southern blacks were relegated to the uniformly shabby and second-rate hotels, waiting rooms, restrooms, theaters, shops, public transportation, and other facilities marked "Colored."

But the Jim Crow laws were only the most visible manifestation of a comprehensive and sustained campaign by which the Southern white establishment had sought—in large part successfully—to recover the power it once wielded during the days of slavery. This effort had been backed by a wave of white terrorism, as the Ku Klux Klan and other white supremacist groups (along with racist individuals acting in concert) lynched and otherwise murdered thousands of rural blacks with impunity in the closing decades of the nineteenth and early decades of the twentieth centuries. Violence and terror were familiar weapons from the slavery era, and Southern state governments generally either ignored or even supported such campaigns. Though the Fifteenth Amendment to the Constitution (passed during Reconstruction) extended the vote to blacks, Southern whites developed a number of ways to either weaken black voting power or eliminate it altogether. Most common was the simple threat of force. As historian John Hope Franklin observes:

> For many white Southerners . . . violence was still the surest means of keeping blacks politically impotent, and in countless communities they were not allowed, under penalties of severe reprisals, to show their faces in town on election day.
>
> (Franklin and Moss, p. 255)

Southern lawmakers also targeted black voters by making permanent disenfranchisement part of the penalty for certain crimes (such as petty theft) that blacks were thought more likely than whites to commit. Other methods included stuffing ballot boxes, moving polling places or blocking access to them, administering tests for voters designed to weed out blacks and putting job related pressure on the voters. As in the days of slavery, white plantation owners continued to use the black population as a ready pool of unskilled agricultural labor. Now that blacks were legally allowed to vote, plantation owners often simply rounded up their workers and took them to a polling place to vote as ordered. Though voting rights as such are not mentioned in *A Lesson Before Dying*, blacks' overall political subordination to the Southern white power structure looms as a constant and central element of the novel's background. Its Pichot sugar plantation is a place where such practices might credibly be imagined to occur alongside the events in the novel.

The novel's descriptions of the Pichot plantation—around which much of the action revolves—accurately reflect the general extension of antebellum attitudes into the twentieth-century South. For example, Grant Wiggins, the novel's black narrator, worked at the plantation as a boy. When he returns as an adult to call on

"NEW WANTS," NEW FRUSTRATIONS

In a review of *A Lesson Before Dying,* critic Carl Senna quotes the abolitionist preacher William Ellery Channing (1780-1842):

> There are seasons, in human affairs, of inward and outward revolution, when new depths seem to be broken up in the soul, when new wants are unfolded in multitudes, and a new and undefined good is thirsted for.
>
> (Channing in Senna, p. 21)

Senna observes that the 1940s were such a period of "new wants" for African Americans. Yet these years also brought new frustrations. For example, activist organizations such as the National Association for the Advancement of Colored People (NAACP), founded in 1908, had been pressing civil rights issues in court for decades, and yet segregation remained firmly entrenched in the South and in much of the North. Indeed, the rise of black activism contributed significantly to the stubborn grip that racist attitudes had on many Southern whites. At the same time, it also contributed to the racial pride that many blacks (like the novel's Grant Wiggins) began to feel. This newly enhanced sense of pride arose in opposition to—and contrasted sharply with—the subservience that Southern whites continued to demand from Southern blacks.

Also boosting blacks' pride were the accomplishments of athletes such as popular heavyweight boxing champion Joe Louis (1914-81) and baseball great Jackie Robinson (1919-72), both mentioned in the novel. Louis, nicknamed "the Brown Bomber," defeated German boxer Max Schmeling in 1938, avenging an earlier defeat by the German. In this famous second bout, Schmeling—touted by Nazi leaders as an example of white racial supremacy, went down to a knockout punch from Louis in the first round. The novel's Grant Wiggins still feels proud of Louis ten years later, accurately reflecting the resounding effect of Louis's victory. Robinson, who became the first black to break the color barrier in major league baseball when he joined the Brooklyn Dodgers in 1947, represents a more recent black hero for Grant and others in the novel. In one scene from the novel, an older man gleefully acts out to his friends some of Robinson's athletic exploits as they socialize in a bar room.

its owner, Henri Pichot, Grant is expected to enter through the back door and wait (with the black cook) in the kitchen. Such protocols represented a holdover from slavery and were still common throughout the South into and past the middle of the twentieth century. They were imposed not only on a plantation's black workers but also on all other black visitors to the "big house" (as a plantation owner's residence was usually called). White visitors, by contrast, were expected to use the main entrance and would be escorted to a waiting room while a black servant informed the owner of the visitor's presence. Like legal segregation, these and other practices echoed the values of the bygone slavery era. However, they rested not so much on the law as on a complex set of silent social assumptions understood by both blacks and whites alike.

Race and the criminal justice system. The main context in which *A Lesson Before Dying* depicts black political subordination to the Southern white establishment is that of the criminal justice system. Judges, juries, and lawyers in the segregated South were uniformly white and male, as the novel accurately reflects. But for blacks, the police officer—also virtually always a white male—embodied the most imposing projection of white power. In rural Southern areas, this usually meant the local sheriff and his deputies. A Southern police officer's unwritten responsibilities included not just law enforcement, but also the enforcement of the South's pervasive, racially discriminatory social practices, as Swedish sociologist Gunnar Myrdal concluded after visiting the South in the 1940s. Presenting his observations in his influential book *An American Dilemma: The Negro Problem and Modern Democracy* (1944), Myrdal observed that the Southern police officer "stands not only for civic order as defined in formal laws and regulations, but also for 'White Supremacy' and the whole set of social customs associated with this concept" (Myrdal, p. 535).

LOUISIANA SUGAR PLANTATIONS

While cotton was king in northern Louisiana, sugarcane ruled on plantations in the southern part of the state. The setup on sugar plantations in the 1940s remained essentially the same as during the era of slavery. The white owner occupied a mansion called "the big house," while the black workers lived in a row or a cluster of shacks called "the quarters." Larger plantations often featured a company store, where much of what was paid to the workers was recouped by the owner in the form of jacked-up prices. Many plantations, like the novel's Pichot plantation, also had their own school for the children of the black workers. As schoolteacher Grant Wiggins points out in the novel, black children in the South generally had a shortened school year in comparison with whites, so that they could work a long season in the cotton or cane fields. The novel's setting in time coincides with this shortened six-month school season, which extended from October to April.

In fact, Myrdal suggested, Southern police officers as a group exhibited more virulent racism than Southern society at large:

> Probably no group of whites in America have a lower opinion of the Negro people and are more fixed in their views than Southern policemen. To most of them . . . practically every Negro man is a potential criminal. They usually hold, in extreme form, all other derogatory beliefs about Negroes; and they are convinced that the traits are "racial."
>
> (Myrdal, p. 541)

Myrdal also noted that judges and other criminal justice officials routinely, if tacitly, acquiesced to measures taken by police officers to "keep law-abiding Southern blacks in their place," as the common expression went. Those measures, Myrdal continued, included illegal beatings, physical or verbal intimidation, and a range of other kinds of harassment. Confronted with the constant threat of such treatment, in the presence of policemen, black citizens had to behave with deference or risk an instant application of violence, followed by almost certain imprisonment. In *A Lesson Before Dying* Grant Wiggins repeatedly faces such choices as he deals with the sheriff and sheriff's deputies at the jailhouse in the novel's fictional town of Bayonne, near the Pichot sugar plantation.

All Southern jails segregated black from white prisoners, since integrated accommodations were viewed by many as an unfairly harsh punishment for even the most brutal of white criminals. Black prisoners not only suffered from markedly inferior conditions, they were also regularly leased out to local businesses as inexpensive laborers. Thus, as legal scholar Randall Kennedy writes, imprisonment in the South evolved into a partial replacement for slavery:

> After the abolition of slavery, incarceration became a "legal" way to subject blacks to servitude. To reduce public expenditures and aid private businesses, Southern officials leased convicts to private employers, who shouldered the burden of feeding, clothing, and confining prisoners in return for the authority to extract their labor.
>
> (Kennedy, p. 130)

Again, these practices are not part of the novel's explicit content. Yet as Grant Wiggins visits the hapless Jefferson, a black laborer awaiting execution for murder in the Bayonne jail, the novel's descriptions clearly evoke the racist milieu in which such historical practices did in fact take place.

The Novel in Focus

The plot. *A Lesson Before Dying* opens in early fall of 1948, as the narrator, a black schoolteacher named Grant Wiggins, recounts the recently concluded murder trial of Jefferson, a mildly retarded and semiliterate black field worker in his early twenties. Jefferson worked in the sugarcane fields of the Pichot plantation 13 miles from Bayonne. He claimed he had been walking to a nearby bar when two black acquaintances, Brother and Bear, offered him a ride. At an otherwise deserted country liquor store, Brother and Bear attempted to hold up the white owner, and a gunfight ensued in which the two would-be robbers and the owner were killed. Jefferson, the only one left alive, gathered up some bills from the cash register and confusedly began walking away when two white men entered. He was arrested a few minutes later.

At the trial Jefferson's white defense attorney argues that Jefferson was an innocent bystander and should be acquitted. Jefferson, the lawyer further claims, is not "a man" who can be held accountable for his actions, but "a thing to hold the handle of a plow, a thing to load your bales of cotton, a thing to dig your ditches, to chop your wood, to pull your corn" (*A Lesson Before Dying*, p. 8). Even if Jefferson were guilty, the lawyer concludes, he should not be executed, since he is no more responsible for his actions than an animal: "Why, I'd just as soon put a hog in the electric chair" (*A Lesson Before Dying*, p. 8). The jury, however, rapidly convicts Jefferson of first-degree murder, and soon afterward the judge sentences him to death by electrocution, on a date to be set by the governor.

Grant and Jefferson have very different existences. Grant worked at the Pichot plantation as a boy, but left the area to be educated as a teacher (essentially the only profession open to Southern blacks under segregation). Achieving this goal, he returned in order to live with his Tante (Aunt) Lou, who had raised him and sacrificed to pay for his education. Grant now teaches at the small school for the plantation's black workers, but dreams of moving away from the South with his light-skinned Creole girlfriend, Vivian. Jefferson, in contrast, can barely read and write and, before his arrest, seemed destined for a life of hard manual labor in the cane fields. Yet both men were raised by their aunts, and in fact Grant's Tante Lou and Jefferson's Aunt Emma are close friends. The two aunts now prevail upon the reluctant Grant to start visiting Jefferson in jail. "I didn't raise no hog," Aunt Emma explains, "and I don't want no hog to go set in that chair. I want a man to go set in that chair" (*A Lesson Before Dying*, p. 20). Grant's assignment during his visits will be to "make him know he's not a hog, he's a man" (*A Lesson Before Dying*, p . 21).

First, in a visit to the Pichot plantation that Grant finds humiliating, the aunts secure the help of Henri Pichot, who acknowledges that both women have done much for his family in the past. The influential plantation owner unenthusiastically agrees to talk to the sheriff in nearby Bayonne. After being kept waiting in the kitchen for nearly three hours during a second humiliating visit to Pichot, Grant personally asks the hostile Sheriff Guidry if he can visit the prisoner. Skeptical that any progress can be made with Jefferson, Guidry allows the visits but threatens to cut them off "at the first sign of aggravation" (*A Lesson Before Dying*, p. 50).

As Grant begins visiting Jefferson with Jefferson's Aunt Emma, at first the despondent prisoner is unresponsive and sullen. Moreover, the visits create a rift between Grant and Tante Lou, as Grant resents the constant humiliation of dealing with Pichot, Guidry, and their associates. "Everything you sent me to school for, you're stripping me of it," he tells his aunt (*A Lesson Before Dying*, p. 79). Shortly afterward Grant begins visiting Jefferson alone, and he slowly begins making progress in winning the prisoner's trust.

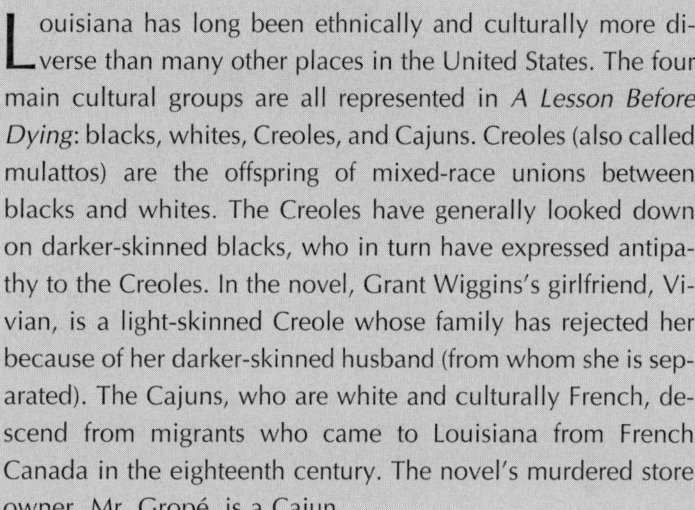

BLACKS, WHITES, CREOLES, AND CAJUNS

Louisiana has long been ethnically and culturally more diverse than many other places in the United States. The four main cultural groups are all represented in *A Lesson Before Dying*: blacks, whites, Creoles, and Cajuns. Creoles (also called mulattos) are the offspring of mixed-race unions between blacks and whites. The Creoles have generally looked down on darker-skinned blacks, who in turn have expressed antipathy to the Creoles. In the novel, Grant Wiggins's girlfriend, Vivian, is a light-skinned Creole whose family has rejected her because of her darker-skinned husband (from whom she is separated). The Cajuns, who are white and culturally French, descend from migrants who came to Louisiana from French Canada in the eighteenth century. The novel's murdered store owner, Mr. Gropé, is a Cajun.

As he struggles to persuade Jefferson to think of himself as a human being and not "a old hog they fattening up to kill," Grant comes into increasing conflict with Reverend Ambrose (*A Lesson Before Dying*, p. 83). A powerful force in the black community, the Baptist minister also takes an interest in the prisoner's spiritual state, viewing Grant's secular approach as a danger to Jefferson's immortal soul. At variance with the minister and openly quarreling with the aunt who raised him, Grant finds a haven in his relationship with Vivian, who offers support and advice. Though bored with his job as a teacher, as Christmas approaches, Grant also enjoys rehearsing the school's Christmas program with his students, one of whom, a girl, is Jefferson's cousin.

From Christmas the narrative jumps ahead in time to February, when the date is set for Jefferson's execution: Friday April 8, just a little more than a month away, between noon and 3:00 P.M. Soon afterward Grant brings Jefferson a radio, on which the prisoner avidly listens to music but which Reverend Ambrose condemns as a "sin box" (*A Lesson Before Dying*, p. 181). On his next visit Grant offers also to bring Jefferson a pencil and notebook, suggesting that Jefferson may wish to record his thoughts for the two of them to talk over. Grant brings the writing supplies, and on a later visit, he notices that both the pencil point and the eraser are worn down. This visit occurs about two weeks before the execution, on the day before Good Friday (which celebrates the suffering of Christ, who Christians believed to have been crucified on a Friday between noon and 3:00 P.M.). Jefferson asks Grant about Christ's death and also about Christ's Resurrection, which Christians believe occurred the following Sunday, when Christ arose from the grave. Jefferson now seems resolved to die with dignity, and Grant tells him, "You're more a man than I am, Jefferson" (*A Lesson Before Dying*, p. 225).

A short chapter entitled "Jefferson's Diary" interrupts Grant's first-person narrative at this point, as if Grant had later inserted into his text the thoughts Jefferson recorded while in prison. Presented without punctuation or spelling corrections, in a style that reflects the spoken language of uneducated Southern blacks, Jefferson's simple record takes the reader through the last two weeks of his life. The reader learns that Grant has brought the children of his class to visit Jefferson, and that other visitors have come from the quarter, the black workers' village on the plantation where Jefferson lived with his Aunt Emma. Sheriff Guidry has also come, concerned about what Jefferson is writing in his "tablet":

> . . . .he ax me what all i been ritin an i tol him jus things an he say aint he done tret me rite an i tol him yesir an he say aint his deptis done tret me fair an i tol him yesir an he say aint he done let peple vist me anytime an i say yesir an he say didn he let the chiren an all the peple from the quarter com an vist me jus two days ago an i say yesir an he say is you gon put that in yo tablet an i say yesir an he say good put that down in yo tablet i tret you good all the time you been yer. . . .
>
> (*A Lesson Before Dying*, p. 233)

As the hour of his execution draws near, Jefferson writes several brief entries, the last of which bids Grant farewell: "good by mr wigin tell them im strong tell them im a man" (*A Lesson Before Dying*, p. 234).

Returning to Grant's first-person perspective for the last two chapters, the narrative records the impressions of various townspeople as the truck arrives bearing the electric chair and the special generator that will power it. Grant cannot bring himself to visit Jefferson. Jefferson is instead comforted by Paul, a young white deputy who has shown growing compassion for him and who seems not to share the racist feelings of the others. Grant stays at the school during the execution itself. At noon he tells the children to bow down on their knees until permitted to rise, and he himself goes out into the schoolyard. Shortly afterward Paul arrives to inform Grant that the execution is over. Though "a little shaky" as he prepared himself for death, Paul says, Jefferson "was the strongest man there" (*A Lesson Before Dying*, p. 253). Grant quietly refuses credit for Jefferson's "transformation," but Paul insists that Grant is "one great teacher" and expresses the wish that they be friends (*A Lesson Before Dying*, p. 254). They clasp hands briefly before Grant returns to the classroom.

The unwritten rules of racial deference. Early in *A Lesson Before Dying*, Grant Wiggins visits the Pichot plantation to meet Henri Pichot and Sheriff Guidry. As he waits in the kitchen, he wonders how he should approach the white men:

> I tried to decide just how I should respond to them. Whether I should act like the teacher that I was, or like the nigger that I was supposed to be. . . . To show too much intelligence would have been an insult to them. To show a lack of intelligence would have been a greater insult to me. . . .
>
> "Been waiting long?" Sam Guidry asked me.
>
> "About two and a half hours, sir," I said. I was supposed to say, "Not long," and I was supposed to grin; but I didn't do either.
>
> (*A Lesson Before Dying*, p. 47)

Guidry reacts with a sharp look, and a few minutes later he tells Grant, "Maybe you're just a little too smart for your own good" (*A Lesson Before Dying*, p. 49). After that, Grant wisely remains silent: "I was quiet. I knew when to be quiet" (*A Lesson Before Dying*, p. 49).

Southern culture demanded strict etiquette from all ranks of society, but as in every area of life different rules applied to blacks and whites. A white committing a breach of etiquette might incur no more than a raised eyebrow or perhaps a mild verbal rebuke. Since Grant is a black man addressing a white law officer, a breach of etiquette on his part could easily carry more serious consequences. The unwritten rules for black

After the Emancipation Proclamation of 1863, Jim Crow laws legally enforced racial segregation until 1954.

behavior towards whites demanded constant deference, which reassured the whites that a black individual knew his or her "place." In return, upper-class whites offered deferential blacks a semblance of patronizing courtesy, as the novel's Henri Pichot does in acknowledging Tante Lou's and Aunt Emma's service to his family.

Legal historian Randall Kennedy points out the constant threat of imprisonment that lay behind white expectations of black deference in the era of the Jim Crow laws:

> During the age of segregation, authorities used the criminal law to impose a stigmatizing code of conduct upon Negroes, one that demanded exhibitions of servility and the open disavowal of any desire for equality.
>
> (Kennedy, p. 88)

Had a black man in Grant's position not backed down after a sheriff's warning that he was "too smart" for his own good (as Grant does in the novel by remaining silent), he might well have faced a harsh beating and a stretch in jail.

The passage from the novel quoted above also illustrates another important ingredient of racial deference: as part of the required servility, blacks were not supposed to display intelligence or learning in front of whites. Like so many elements of Southern race relations, the white injunction against black learning went back to the antebellum period, when slaves were generally forbidden to learn to read. This sort of hostility resurfaced in the violent era following Reconstruction, when white racists in the South killed thousands of blacks. As Randall Kennedy observes:

> Educated blacks were especially targeted for punishment. In Georgia, Ku Klux Klansmen killed Washington Eager because he could read. They also destroyed a teacher's library, declaring that they "just dare[d] any other nigger to have a book in his house."
>
> (Kennedy, p. 39)

Such historical events lend special aptness to Gaines's choice of a teacher to be the novel's narrator. Yet Grant is an unwilling teacher. As Gaines makes clear, Grant teaches only because teaching was essentially the only profession open to African Americans in the South in the Jim Crow era. Ironically (given Southern whites' antipathy toward educated blacks) segregated black schools themselves necessitated the education of black teachers. Moreover, as Gaines knew from his vantage point in the 1990s, just a few years after the novel takes place, schools would play a central role in the civil rights movement that finally ended legal segregation in the South.

Sources. *A Lesson Before Dying*'s setting of fictional Bayonne and St. Raphael Parish is based on rural

Pointe Coupee Parish, Louisiana, where Ernest Gaines was born and where he lived until the age of 15. There, on Riverlake plantation, his parents, Manuel and Adrienne Gaines, worked as sharecroppers in the same fields that their ancestors had worked in as slaves. Gaines, the oldest, and his younger brothers and sisters grew up at Riverlake in "the quarters," the rows of shacks where the black workers lived. Born when his mother was 16 years old, and deserted by a father who left when the boy was 8, Gaines was raised largely by his maternal aunt, Augusteen Jefferson. An important figure in his life, she inspired many of the strong female characters in his fiction, such as the two aunts in *A Lesson Before Dying*. These female characters often raise children who have been deserted by one or both parents, like both Grant and Jefferson in *A Lesson Before Dying*.

In researching the novel, Gaines spoke with men who had worked as lawyers and law enforcement officials in the South during the period in which *A Lesson Before Dying* is set, including a former sheriff and a former district attorney. The warden at Louisiana's Angola Prison, Gaines discloses in one interview, did not respond to Gaines's requests to be allowed to visit the prison.

Events in History at the Time the Novel Was Written

Education and civil rights. Starting immediately with the end of slavery in 1865, the issue of education has aroused keen interest among African Americans. Black leaders have consistently emphasized the importance of education in the struggle for civil rights. However, for the first half of the twentieth century they faced a major legal obstacle. In *Plessy v. Ferguson* (1896), the United States Supreme court had laid down its famous "separate but equal" doctrine, decreeing racial segregation in schools to be constitutional as long as the schools were equal in quality. In reality, however, black schools were far inferior and black children received fewer educational opportunities as compared with whites. Around the middle of the twentieth century, schools in the South spent less than a third as much on each black student than they spent on each white student; per pupil, Southern black school buildings and facilities were worth less than one-fifth of what white schools were worth (Franklin and Moss, p. 406). In *A Lesson Before Dying*, the school in which Grant Wiggins teaches is visited annually by an uninterested white school inspector, who ignores Grant's urgent requests for more books and other school supplies.

Grant's own education as a teacher, which would have taken place in the mid-1940s, would almost certainly have been at an all-black institution of higher learning, such as Howard University in Washington, D.C., or Fisk University in Nashville, Tennessee. There existed a number of other small black colleges and universities too, mostly in the South, generally funded by the federal government and by private donations.

In 1954, just a few years after the novel takes place, the Supreme Court overturned the doctrine of separate but equal with another landmark ruling in *Brown v. Board of Education of Topeka, Kansas*. Declaring that "separate educational facilities are inherently unequal," the court unanimously banned racial segregation in public schools (Franklin and Moss, p. 412). Historians have viewed this case as the starting gun for the black-led civil rights movement that would, by the mid-1960s, bring down the South's Jim Crow system of legal segregation. The civil rights movement can thus be said to have originated in issues to do with school segregation. In the years that followed *Brown v. Board of Education*, black students would often risk their own personal safety by attending white schools ordered to desegregate by the courts. Best known is James Meredith, who in 1962 was threatened by hostile white crowds at the University of Mississippi. Rioters "hurled rocks, bricks, lead pipes, and tear gas at [federal] marshals [sent in to protect Meredith] and finally even shot at them." (Kelley and Lewis, p. 503). After two deaths and some 350 injuries, President John F. Kennedy called out the National Guard to escort Meredith to class. Neither state nor school officials would take steps to assure his safety. The date was September 30, 1962.

By the 1990s—more than half a century after the novel's Grant Wiggins was educated at an all-black college—debates over race and education had focused on "affirmative action," an outgrowth of the earlier civil rights movement. Affirmative action refers to government policies designed to redress past discrimination and provide greater educational and employment opportunities to minorities. Though affirmative action efforts began during the mid-1960s, the Equal Opportunity Act of 1972 formulated affirmative action in terms of racial proportions or quotas, which have since become inextricably linked to the debate over affirmative action policies. Under the 1972 act, state and federally funded agencies and institutions—including universities and colleges—were required to take steps that would bring their racial proportions into line with those of the population at large. In practice, state and federally funded agencies recruited lower-income minority applicants rather than minority applicants with competitive SAT scores, and this led to the schools' accepting minority applicants who were less qualified than some white applicants. In the 1970s opponents of affirmative action began to label it as reverse discrimination, and during the presidency of Ronald Reagan (1980-88) the federal government took steps to begin dismantling it. Starting in 1989 and continuing into the 1990s, the Supreme Court began to issue rulings that seriously restricted many aspects of affirmative action.

Race and the death penalty. Like education, the issue of capital punishment has been closely linked to that of race in public debate in the United States. However, education has been a part of racial discussions since the slavery era. In contrast, widespread attention to the racial dimension of capital punishment is a relatively recent phenomenon, arising only since the 1960s. The main focus of this attention has been the consistent and striking racial disparity in the application of the death penalty in the United States. As numerous studies have demonstrated, when other factors are taken into account, blacks are significantly more likely to face the death penalty than whites. It is important to note that while this disparity has only recently become the focus of public attention, the disparity itself has existed since the end of slavery. Before that, under the so-called Black Codes, white slaveowners in most Southern states were legally able to execute black slaves essentially at will, and routinely did so for even the most trivial offenses.

Lynching, the execution of an alleged offender by an angry mob, became a primary means by which Southern whites intimidated blacks in the period after Reconstruction. Between 1882 and 1938, nearly 3,500 recorded lynchings occurred, usually in Southern states (though lynching was not confined to the South). The most common "offense" for lynching was the alleged rape of a white woman by a black man. Rape was also a crime for which disproportionately more blacks than whites were executed, until the suspension or temporary abolition of the death penalty in the United States in 1967. Capital punishment resumed in 1976, but the Supreme Court has disallowed capital punishment for the crime of rape. Since 1976 only those convicted of first-degree murder have been eligible for death sentences.

Capital Punishment in Black and White

- Around 1900, lynchings of black men for the alleged rape of white women were so common that newspapers simply reported a black man was hanged for "the usual crime."
- Currently, the U.S. population is about 12 percent black but the population of death row is 41 percent black.
- Since the reinstatement of the death penalty in 1976 . . . 86 percent of the executed have been convicted of killing whites, even though about half of all murder victims in the United States are black.
- Just before retiring in 1994, Justice Harry Blackmun who no longer supported capital punishment, concluded that "race continues to play a major role in determining who shall live and who shall die."
- More than any other factor, the race of the victim decides who faces the death penalty. One study of 700 homicides found that a white victim was more than twice as likely to result in a defendant's being charged with first-degree murder than a black victim.

(Adapted from Costanzo, pp. 79-81)

Of greater direct relevance to *A Lesson Before Dying* is another important issue touching on race and capital punishment, that of wrongful convictions. An influential study published in 1992 uncovered 416 cases between 1900 and 1991 in which the study's authors deemed it likely that wrongful convictions had been reached in cases potentially subject to the death penalty. Of that number, 188 involved black defendants. This study, writes scholar Randall Kennedy, makes it "clear that in a substantial number of cases, racial bias played a significant, sometimes decisive, role in convicting innocent black defendants" (Kennedy, p. 125). As the authors of the study themselves point out:

> Unknown hundreds of other cases have completely disappeared from sight; we will never know whether justice was done to the defendant. This is particularly true where the defendant was a member of a repressed minority—a Native American or Hispanic, a recent immigrant, a black.
>
> (Radelet et al., p. 19)

Reception. *A Lesson Before Dying* received uniformly strong praise from reviewers, winning the National Book Critics Circle Award for fiction in 1994, the year after its release. In June 1993, two months after publication, the novel had already also led to Gaines's winning the award commonly known as a "genius grant" from the MacArthur Foundation. These prestigious cash prizes cannot be applied for, but are offered only to those whom the foundation has sought out for exceptional contributions in a creative field of endeavor.

A number of critics declared *A Lesson Before Dying* to be Gaines's finest novel. Another common judgment was that previous to it Gaines's work had been woefully underrated. This observation was generally coupled with the hope that *A Lesson Before Dying* would bring its author a wider audience and more profound critical recognition. Critics also applauded the novel for its historical accuracy. Calling it "a moving and truthful work of fiction," Carl Senna in the *New York Times Book Review* praised the novel's accurate evocation of an era when black frustrations had just begun gathering the momentum that would soon result in the civil rights movement (Senna, p. 21). *Time Magazine*'s R. Z. Sheppard lauded Gaines's deft combination of painstaking realism with literary subtlety:

> There is an ominous courtesy between the races. The whites are soft-spoken and patronizing. The blacks reply with exaggerated deference and little eye-contact. Few writers have caught this routine indignity as well as Gaines. Fewer still have his dramatic instinct for conveying the malevolence of racism and injustice without the usual accompanying self-righteousness.
>
> (Sheppard, p. 66)

—Colin Wells

For More Information

Bedau, Hugo Adam. *The Death Penalty in America: Current Controversies*. New York: Oxford University Press, 1997.

Costanzo, Mark. *Just Revenge: Costs and Consequences of the Death Penalty*. New York: St. Martin's, 1997.

Franklin, John Hope and Alfred A. Moss, Jr. *From Slavery to Freedom: A History of African Americans*. New York: McGraw Hill, 1994.

Gaines, Ernest J. *A Lesson Before Dying*. New York: Knopf, 1993.

Kelley, Robin D. G., and Earl Lewis. *A History of African Americans*. Oxford: Oxford University Press, 2000.

Kennedy, Randall. *Race, Crime, and the Law*. New York: Pantheon, 1997.

Myrdal, Gunnar. *An American Dilemma: The Negro Problem and Modern Democracy*. New York: Harper and Brothers, 1944.

Radelet, Michael L., Hugo Adam Bedau, and Contance E. Putnam. *In Spite of Innocence: Erroneous Convictions in Capital Cases*. Boston: Northeastern University Press, 1992.

Rehder, John B. *Delta Sugar: Louisiana's Vanishing Plantation Landscape*. Baltimore: Johns Hopkins University Press, 1999.

Senna, Carl. Review of *A Lesson Before Dying*, by Ernest J. Gaines. *New York Times Book Review*, 8 August 1993, 21.

Sheppard, R. Z. Review of *A Lesson Before Dying*, by Ernest J. Gaines. *Time*, 29 March 1993, 66.

Let Us Now Praise Famous Men

by
James Agee and Walker Evans

James Agee (1909-55) was born in Knoxville, Tennessee, to Hugh and Laura Agee. His father died when Agee was 16, a traumatic event in the young man's life. From then on, Agee felt that he identified more intensely with his father's rural farming background than with his mother's more educated, bourgeois sensibility. His schooling with an Episcopalian order brought out a strong religious commitment in Agee. Afterward he attended Harvard University, where he gained experience in college journalism that led to employment with Henry R. Luce's new *Fortune* magazine in 1933. Agee married three times in ten years, engaging in the kind of dissolute lifestyle common to New York writers and journalists at that time, becoming over attached to drinking, smoking, and very late nights. Cultivating a distinct appearance, he commonly wore "factory-seconds sneakers and a sleazy cap" (Evans in Agee and Evans, p. vi). His independent publications began with the collection of poems *Permit Me Voyage* (1934). Agee published *Let Us Now Praise Famous Men* (1941) before going on to work for *Nation* magazine as a film critic, and collaborating on a number of screenplays. His novel about his father, ***A Death in the Family*** (also in *Literature and Its Times)* won him a posthumous Pulitzer Prize in 1958. Agee is also remembered for his nonfiction portrait of tenant farmers and their families in *Let Us Now Praise Famous Men*, a combination of his text and 64 photographs by Walker Evans.

Born in St. Louis, Missouri, Walker Evans (1903-75) went to Paris as a young man, where he was greatly influenced by the work of French photographer Eugène Atget, especially Atget's realistic street scenes of Parisian life. Returning to the United States at the end of the 1920s, Evans gained a reputation in photography that a decade later (in 1934) secured him a job at the Farm Security Administration, a federal agency charged with helping American farmers. His post here earmarked Evans as Agee's natural partner for an account that blends objectivity with intimacy to depict sharecropper life in Alabama.

THE LITERARY WORK

A quasi-documentary account of a visit to rural Alabama in the summer of 1936; first published in 1941.

SYNOPSIS

Interspersed with documentary material on three sharecropper families during the Great Depression is a series of meditations on hospitality, the job of a reporter, rights of privacy, and sexuality.

Events in History at the Time of the Account

The South and its past. The origin of southern sharecropping is rooted in the failure of the region's state governments to modernize the economy of the South after the Civil War. Cov-

James Agee

ering much of the territory from North Carolina to parts of eastern Texas, the crucially important "cotton belt" had been inextricably tied in with slavery until 1865, and afterwards the South found it difficult to transform itself into an economy based on free and mobile labor. Instead sharecropping and tenant farming became the order of the day. In exchange for seed, fertilizer, farm tools, and food and clothing for their families, sharecroppers grew what their landlord wanted and gave the landlord usually half of the harvest. Not exactly the same but similar to sharecropping, tenant farming required that tenants rent land, tools, and so forth from the local merchant and sell their crops to him. Also they had to buy goods on credit from his store. The whole arrangement cornered them into an unending cycle of debt. Although strictly speaking there is a distinction between *tenant farming* and *sharecropping*, the two terms have often been used interchangeably.

> Debt-slavery, or peonage, became the rule for most of the farmers in the South, white and black, as it was for the peasants of Latin America. It was made worse in bad years, when the price of the crop did not equal the outstanding debt . . . so the entire labouring class of the South fell into hopelessness, ill-clothed, ill fed.
>
> (Brogan, p. 377)

Resistance to reform was tied to another characteristic of the South: the fear that changes would upset the racial hierarchy of the region. There were many African American sharecroppers in the South, and reform proposals would have worked to their benefit also. The white farmer was often more concerned about remaining a step or two above his black neighbor on the racial ladder than about making broad-based improvements in the rural economy that would have benefitted them both.

On the other hand, many Southerners saw no alternative to sharecropping due to the fact that they had never experienced any other system, or heard anyone discuss one seriously. Practically speaking, the nature of sharecropping did not allow much time for meditating on new ideas; people felt pressed enough just focusing on their daily work and on their families. Planting and harvest seasons called for 12-hour working days, beginning at dawn, with children often being kept home from school to contribute labor. If crop prices were low, the rewards would be minimal, perhaps a total profit of $200 for the year, barely enough to survive in the 1930s.

This background points to an important comparative truth: while the Great Depression of the 1930s ravaged American economic life across the nation, in the rural South it was happening in a society that had, to a large extent, already been in structural recession for three generations or more. The benchmarks for poverty, degree of education, amount of health care, and so on were set much lower in Alabama than in, say, Illinois or Massachusetts. Agee's and Evans's book is a report from a region in which the expectations of the inhabitants are minimal, almost nonexistent. When it came to a varied diet, availability of basic utilities such as running water, or access to education for children, the norms within which the southern tenant farmer lived were far removed from those of Americans in other regions. To many Americans, the South seemed to be almost a separate nation. The experiences of the Great Depression sharpened this distinction in some ways. Coming to the fore in this decade were new kinds of communication, such as photojournalism, which made information move faster and introduced the public to revealing images of life in previously unfamiliar regions of the country.

America in the Great Depression. For almost a dozen years, from the stock-market crash in 1929 until 1942, the first full year of World War

II, the United States suffered the greatest economic slowdown in its history. The worst phase of this slowdown lasted from 1930 to 1934. Called the Great Depression, the slowdown arrived on the heels of the 1920s, a decade characterized by expanding consumer-purchasing potential, the meteoric rise of cinema and recorded music, and a feeling of distance from the problems of the rest of the world. Not expecting an economic collapse, the United States was ill-equipped to deal with it. The scale of the crisis proved to be overwhelming: out of a total working population of approximately 70 million, 4 million were already unemployed in 1930, and that figure would triple to 12 million within just two years. At its peak in 1933 the unemployment rate of nonagricultural workers approached 40 percent. Conditions improved somewhat by the release of *Let Us Now Praise Famous Men*, but still neared 25 percent (Nash, p. 819).

The depredation of unemployment and poverty affected not only industrial workers and their families, but also had a shocking impact on middle-class Americans, who often harbored the strongest belief in the American way of life. The shock waves began with the famous Wall Street Crash of 1929, when on Black Tuesday (October 29) over 16 million shares were sold frantically, resulting in a dizzying loss of $10 billion. As shares turned out to be not worth the paper they were printed on (that is, there were no real assets to back them up if their value was called in), the stock market disintegrated, driving many thousands of people, big investors and small, into financial ruin in a matter of hours.

The collapse of the stock market, which led to a series of crises in industry, had a devastating impact on agriculture as well. Mirroring industrial decline, agriculture suffered a drop in the demand for raw materials and produce, and prices fell. Many farmers found themselves unable to sell their crops at all or able to sell them but for less than it had cost to grow them. In the early years of the Great Depression, there was little recourse, for no federal assistance programs existed to rescue farmers and their families.

The collapse came to be widely perceived as the failure of the capitalist economic system in general, which opened the door to new alternatives. In both urban and rural areas, citizens of the 1930s became much more sympathetic to left-wing—even radical—politics and systems, including communism. This shift in attitude had an effect on the Democratic administrations of Franklin Delano Roosevelt (in office 1933-45), which dared to introduce major reform projects that made the federal government a more influential player in American life. Roosevelt's predecessor, Herbert Hoover, had been concerned about the economic crisis and unemployment, but his Republican administration (1929-33) had restricted itself to appealing to corporate leaders, asking that they voluntarily keep production and wages at reasonable levels, and refrain from firing workers as the demand for goods dropped, which went against the commercial instincts of corporate America. As far as directly relieving the needs of the jobless and their families was concerned, Hoover's administration saw this as the task of private charities and churches. It tried also to throw some of the burden back to state and local authorities

However, the ever-widening circle of poverty and social collapse meant that American private social services were incapable of handling the sheer scale of the Depression. At the beginning of the crisis, most charity workers, as well as the unemployed themselves, subscribed to the American belief that a man ought to depend upon his own initiative and enterprise for his material status. If an able-bodied man had no work and could not feed his family, the fault was to be found in him, not in the social and economic system. The Depression prompted a significant change in this attitude. It became clear to many that federal government intervention was indispensable to combat the effects of the Depression effectively. The realization would have far-reaching consequences. From this beginning, the concept of government as national caretaker would emerge. Later people would speak of this as the start of the welfare state, the juncture at which the government began to take responsibility for creating jobs, providing direct relief from economic hardship, and so forth.

Roosevelt put into operation a set of policies and ideas known as the New Deal, initiating one of the most significant moments of change in modern American history. Taking a groundbreaking step in peacetime, the Roosevelt administration began to promote specific job-creation measures for the unemployed in general and for specific groups, such as farmers. Going even further, it set up federal agencies with budgets to manage the job-creation measures for target groups. The Works Progress Administration (WPA) engaged in public works, repair, and construction; the Federal Theater Project tried to find positions for unemployed actors, stagehands, and musicians; the Federal Writers Project performed a similar service for authors. Reflecting Roosevelt's belief that the environment had something to do with the economy, the Civilian Conservation Corps (CCC) set people to work in forestry, flood control, and wildlife preservation—giving thousands of teenage boys from poverty-stricken families their first taste of life outside a city. The Tennessee Valley Authority (TVA), the largest publicly owned utility in the nation, also put people to work supplying electric power to even very isolated areas of the Upper South. Providing for the elderly, the Social Security Act introduced the concept of employment-based social insurance to the United States, establishing a minimal financial safety-net for retirees. Perhaps most pertinently to the subjects of *Let Us Now Praise Famous Men*, the Farm Security Administration (FSA) sought to roll back the wave of mortgage foreclosures and stem the proliferation of empty farmhouses afflicting rural America.

The New Deal and the South. One of the FSA projects that met with mixed success was the Agricultural Adjustment Act (AAA). Passed in 1933, this legislation aimed at stabilizing farm incomes by various methods, in particular by controlling overproduction of certain crops to keep prices high enough for farmers to survive. The objective was to limit the production of staple products like wheat, cotton, and tobacco by paying farmers to decrease the number of acres being cultivated. It was a policy that caused a storm of protest—the federal government had millions of pigs slaughtered and cotton acres destroyed while millions of Americans struggled to put clothes on their backs and food in their mouths.

In 1936 the Supreme Court declared the Agricultural Adjustment Act unconstitutional, but elements of the act survived, managing to somewhat alleviate the situation in which farmers found themselves. There was no wide-scale improvement, however, since many of the law's provisions failed to deal with the problems of the sharecropper system so pervasive in the South. In Alabama in 1935, 64 percent of all farmers in the state were tenant farmers and sharecroppers. Though they grappled with low, highly unpredictable income levels, the law regarded them as self-employed persons, which made them ineligible for assistance programs designed for unemployed wage earners. Further suffering resulted from another unintentionally harmful policy. To reduce a glut of cotton and other staples, the Agricultural Adjustment Act of 1933 paid farmers to take land out of production, and the land they withdrew was often that worked by sharecroppers, who were thus deprived of the little means they had to earn an income.

It was not just the Depression of the 1930s that put tenant farmers of the cotton belt in such dire straits, though. Their status even prior to the Depression was awfully grim. Also there had been a lack of economic development in the southern states over the 70 years since the Civil War. The infrastructure in the region was poor—it lacked schools, surfaced roads, and other key supports commonly found in American daily life, which could be explained by the very limited tax base in many of the counties across the South. The South adapted as best it could, hiring out forced convict labor to landowners at harvest time, for example, and putting convicts to work building roads. These strategies attracted criticism from outsiders, who saw them as a brutal sort of regionalism. But many Southerners regarded such arrangements as the only alternative to no public works at all.

Photojournalism. Thanks to photojournalism, at this precise moment, one part of the nation began to more clearly see another. Outside regions became better able to appreciate the plight of the rural South. The economic crisis of the 1930s led to the sudden growth of documentary reportage and photography. It was a trend fueled in part by the rise of new media (ambitious, popular photo magazines like *Life*), which had the resources to employ talented staff writers and

LUCE AND FORTUNE

Henry R. Luce was, after William Randolph Hearst, one of the most influential editors and publishers in American history. He founded *Time* magazine in 1923, whose flashy style and aggressive reporting would make it one of the leading news magazines in the world. To appeal to a different readership, the business community, Luce founded *Fortune* magazine in 1930. *Fortune* adopted an unusual editorial policy, hiring writers who had no background in industrial or economic reporting to research and write on business, thus bringing perspectives to its text that other business magazines could not offer. Writers for *Fortune* in the early days included poet Archibald MacLeish, critic and journalist Dwight MacDonald, and, of course, James Agee.

photographers. Like others in their day, the early media moguls recognized that America was a diverse, complex society, and that many people in the more prosperous regions knew little about life elsewhere—in the rural South, for example. As one historian puts it:

> [T]he literature of the Depression years turned from preoccupation with individual consciousness to reconsider men and women in their relation to society, and to rediscover the American continent.
>
> (Puckett, p. 2)

The growth in documentary reporting figured into the political debate in 1930s America. Photographs of the plight of tenant farmers were not just journalistic achievements; they were also the concrete evidence of real situations, plights that demanded action and amelioration. From photojournalism, for example, came visual evidence that pellagra, a disease caused by malnutrition, was rife among sharecroppers and their families. Such images and the texts that accompanied them drew national attention to forgotten or ignored segments of American society. Whether in Erskine Caldwell's and Margaret Bourke-White's study of southern farmers, *You Have Seen Their Faces*, or in Richard Wright's and Edward Rosskam's *12 Million Black Voices*, modern photojournalism both documented and took part in the dialogue of the era.

Floyd Burroughs, a cotton sharecropper from Hale County, Alabama. (Photo by Walker Evans.)

The Account in Focus

The contents. *Let Us Now Praise Famous Men* opens with a set of 64 photographs by Walker Evans (31 in the original 1941 edition). The photos, in black and white, include images of the houses and physical environment in which the families live, as well as snapshots of the three families themselves—sometimes of individual members, sometimes of a whole family. Both revealing and sympathetic, the photos reveal the grim conditions in which the people live, but highlight also their individuality and their defensive dignity.

Part One: A Country Letter. "A Country Letter" is divided into four subsections, each designated with a roman numeral followed by a colon (I:, II:, III:, and IV:); the colon takes on significance later in the chapter. The first subsection is a meditation on the family as the central economic unit of sharecropper life. The reporter thinks of the family as both a defense against loneliness, particularly the isolation of the deserted countryside, and a concentration of loneliness in itself. He imagines the family members, casting himself as a guardian on watch while they sleep: "I know almost the dreams they will not remember, and the soul and body of each of these seven, and all of them together in this room in sleep" (Agee, *Let Us Now Praise Famous Men*, p. 52).

The text then moves into its first real extended narrative, describing the departure of Emma, the 16-year-old daughter of Bud Woods, one of the three tenant farmers at the center of the story. The others are Fred Ricketts and George Gudger; Gudger's wife, Annie Mae, is a daughter of Bud Woods. Emma is married to an older man who has found work on a farm in another part of the state, and she is leaving to join him after a brief visit with her family. Obviously miserable about leaving, she seems to have had very little choice in the marriage; her husband is both tightfisted when it comes to money and suspicious of her every move. Clearly a warm-hearted young woman, Emma senses that there might be more to life than her marriage at sixteen to a mean-spirited, middle-aged man.

In subsection "I:" we also get the first dialogue between Agee the reporter and his subjects. Emma tells him how at ease they all feel with him and "Mr. Walker." The reporter is clearly surprised and deeply touched to realize that the Woods family likes having him around. Later that morning, the reporter accompanies some of the family as they drive to a meeting point where Emma has a ride arranged to take her to her husband. The final image is that of Emma in the car heading down the road, not looking back, sharing a traumatic sense of loss and torn emotional fabric with those she is leaving behind.

OUTSIDE THE MAIN NARRATIVE

Interwoven with the text of *Let Us Now Praise Famous Men* is a series of three short sections—one at the beginning, one in the middle and one at the end—called "On the Porch." These three "interchapters" echo the more documentary parts of the book in another way, often by imparting a poetic meditation on a theme that has already appeared in a different context. Other kinds of fragments are also interspersed in the main narrative of *Famous Men.* For example, "Intermission: Conversation in the Lobby," a seemingly unconnected text, reprints a questionnaire sent to a number of American writers by *Partisan Review* magazine in 1939. The questionnaire sought writers' ideas about politics, the upcoming world war, and the degree of political commitment in their work. Included are Agee's responses to the questionnaire, which clarify his feelings about the political dimension of *Let Us Now Praise Famous Men.* He sees himself as being sympathetic in a general way to communist ideas, and to Catholic concepts of both spirituality and social justice.

In subsection "II:" the reporter begins to describe the members of the three families. Often, during the course of *Let Us Now Praise Famous Men*, the family members and their looks, clothes, gestures and so on, become a spur for the reporter to consider both their individual fates and the social constraints surrounding them. Often, too, the reporter confronts the assumed middle-class sensibility of the reader with an alternative perception of the scene being described:

> The house a quarter-mile beyond, just on the right of the road, standing with shade trees, this is the Ricketts'. The bare dirt is more damp in the tempering shade; and damp, tender with rottenness, the ragged wood of the porch . . . the barn: shines on the perfect air; in the bare yard a twelve foot flowering bush . . . and within: naked, naked side by side those brothers and sisters, those most beautiful children; and the crazy, clownish, foxy father; and the mother; and the two old daughters; crammed on their stinking beds, are resting the night.
>
> (*Famous Men*, p. 68)

Assuming that the standard response to such a scene would be one of sympathy, perhaps even pity, the reporter invokes poetic language to complicate and upset any such reaction. The children's unselfconscious nudity becomes a moment of celebration and beauty, echoing the "bare dirt" and "bare yard," making bareness itself a quality to admire, rather than simply a report on the absence of covering. The reporter refuses to treat the Ricketts family as if they were nothing more than exotic welfare cases. His wording suggests that perhaps they even have some things in their lives that we, the readers, have lost. The chapter ends with a series of comments from neighbors. They dismiss the Ricketts family as "a bad lot" and make snide jokes about the Gudgers' hospitality: "And how do you like the food they give you? Yeah, aheh-heh-heh-heh, how do you like that fine home cookin'?" (*Famous Men*, p. 70)

In subsections "III:" and "IV:" the households awake at dawn, and the narrator describes how the silent intensity of eating breakfast so early is a result of everyone's feeling the pressure of the upcoming day's work. Especially during harvest time, much labor must be done before the sun gets too hot to bear. Now the narrative skips from family to family, as if it were a TV documentary in which a split-screen technique is showing various people doing different things at the same time.

In the final subsection—"Colon: Curtain Speech"—the reporter engages in an intense, philosophical meditation on the nature of human beings and if one can ever identify or describe the individual in a way that does not devalue him or her. Language that is too specific, describing by type or status (tenant farmer, poor rural working class, father, wife) causes the reader to objectify a person or group, but the refusal to specify, making the families a symbol of universal human desire or need, also betrays them. Agee the reporter sees dangers in both alternatives—sociological study and artistic portrayal. The image and use of the colon suggests a signal that something will follow, as an explanation or inventory follows a colon in standard English writing. In this case, the text and photos follow to bring the families alive in all their complexity.

Part Two: Some Findings and Comments. This chapter is the central documentary segment of *Let Us Now Praise Famous Men*. Devoted to "Money," "Shelter," "Clothing," "Education," and "Work," the reporter's approach changes to a more objective style, zooming in for a series of close-ups on the three families' lives. This approach, in contrast to that of the other sections, is almost coldly scientific. Pathetic details of the accommodations and possessions of the Gudgers, the Woods, and the Ricketts are laid bare for all to see, as in the case of the Ricketts' kitchen:

> The odor of the eating table, in the kitchen, is a thing in itself: for here the oilcloth is rotted away into scarcely more than a black net, and the cloth and the wood have stored up smoke and rancid grease and pork and corn and meat to a degree which extends a six-foot globe of almost uncombatable nausea thick and filming as sprayed oil.
>
> (*Famous Men*, p. 174)

This description abandons the celebratory tone found earlier in *Let Us Now Praise Famous Men*. No longer are the conditions of rural poverty poetically transformed into a sense of unembarrassed physical closeness, freedom from middle-class inhibitions, and the like. The account becomes a grim, almost nightmarish vision of economic deprivation and humiliation.

Inductions. The final section of the book draws back from the microscopic study of the families. The reporter becomes the more circumspect narrator once again, interacting with the people in social settings, delving more deeply into himself than anyone else in this part of the book. Returning to the earliest days of his visit, he describes how he gets to know the three families, and his concern that he, as a comparatively well-off, educated outsider, is intruding on them. The wives, in particular, seem to be hiding some feelings of anger and unhappiness at having their families' inner lives exposed to outsiders. The reporter describes the country graveyard nearby, and quotes the Lord's Prayer in such a way as to make it seem like a call to remember the forgotten dead. He remembers Mrs. Gudger with her smallest child, her son, on her lap and Ellen Woods asleep on the porch of her house. Reaching for words that do the women justice, he portrays them as vessels of strength and vitality that can withstand any force leveled against them—"a thing so strong, so valiant, so unvanquishable, it is without effort, without emotion, I know it shall at length outshine the sun" (*Famous Men*, p. 390). At the end of this last section is a passage from the Holy Book of Sirach, Chapter 44, the source of the reporter's title for his account: "Let us now praise famous men, and our fathers that begat us" (*Famous Men*, p. 393). The passage conjures the duty to remember those who live and die without public fame, who are born and do their work and have children and pass away. None of these lives is of interest to the outside world; yet none is worth any less than anyone else's life. These people deserve more, *Famous Men* says, much more, but this does not make what they are now despicable.

Conclusion. After a brief collection of random fragments compiled into "Notes and Appendices," the account ends with a meditation inspired by the sound of two unidentified creatures calling or singing to each other in the southern rural darkness. The sound is insistent, beautiful, but impossible to identify. Art, the reporter suggests, is like an attempt to represent such a sound, to understand its meaning. It must be undertaken even though success is not guaranteed. After the calling stops, the reporter and his friend, the photographer, drift off into silence, thinking of "matters of the present and of that immediate past which was a part of the present; and each of these matters had in that time the extreme clearness, and edge, and honor; which I shall now try to give you; until at length we too fell asleep" (*Famous Men*, p. 416).

A QUESTION OF COLOR?

That the three families profiled in *Let Us Now Praise Famous Men* are white seems to have much to do with the fact that the reporters themselves are white. At the opening of the book, a sequence of passages forms a kind of preface to *Part One*. One of these, "Late Sunday Morning," recounts the events of a day shortly after Agee's and Evans's arrival in northern Alabama. They meet a contact who shows them the nearby black neighborhoods. Agee and Evans feel uneasy, particularly when a landlord calls upon a few inhabitants to sing for them. Another brief section, "Near a Church," describes an African American religious service photographed by Evans and a misunderstanding with a young black couple whom Agee scares by chasing after them. All he wants is to talk. This he and Evans find they are more able to do with the white families who become the subject of their book.

Elements such as this questionnaire and the meditative "interchapters" are part of the totality of *Let Us Now Praise Famous Men*. The reporter brings together various external and internal registers of the day to completely portray the people and places he visits.

The observer and the observed. An account such as *Let Us Now Praise Famous Men* poses the problem of the reporter's impact on his subjects, something Agee struggles with in his book. First there is the question of how to get to know the subjects of study, whom in this case the reporter sees as innocents. Then there is the question of what to do with all the information unearthed about them. Is the reporter violating the trust of these families when he and Evans use that knowledge for their business advantage?

In the book's final section, Agee recalls meeting the Ricketts family for the first time. He remembers how Mrs. Ricketts felt angry and ashamed at her family being photographed by Evans, but did not want to say anything in front of her husband. Hurriedly she washed the children's faces for the photo. Her discomfort troubles Agee. After investigating the family's lives in painstaking detail, he struggles with thoughts of how open they were and how vulnerable they are to being exploited. Certainly Agee was not the only investigator facing this issue at the time.

The burgeoning interest in anthropology and folklore studies in the early twentieth century had led to many new studies of groups and societies both in America and overseas. The development of American anthropology began by devoting itself to the study of American Indian cultures. Meanwhile, folklore studies concentrated on the collection of stories and songs from Americans of European origin. Both these strands started to converge, particularly in the examination of African American culture and folklore. Zora Neale Hurston, a black writer and scholar who had studied at Columbia University under the leading anthropologist Franz Boas, would make a name for herself in the early 1900s with both her scholarly folklore researches and her fictional works based on this material. (See ***Their Eyes Were Watching God,*** and **"Spunk"** and **"Sweat,"** also in *Literature and Its Times.*)

A problem that presented itself to the ethnologist doing field work, however, was the difficulty of reporting on the life of, for example, a small village, without impacting that life just by being there. People might say and do things—or stop doing them—as a result of the presence of a visitor or guest. In her anthropological writings, Hurston seems to have functioned at times as an invisible presence, sometimes as a player in the situation. In *Let Us Now Praise Famous Men*, the reporter, Agee, functions as a visible presence to the people he is writing about. The issue is whether he has brought about responses or actions on the part of the families that would not have happened had he not been there, an eventuality that would interfere with gaining an impartial understanding of them. Agee seems to struggle with this issue, fluctuating between impartial and subjective reporting, incorporating both to do justice to his subjects.

Let Us Now Praise Famous Men is clearly haunted by the reporter's sense of loyalty to his subjects. "He had lived with these Alabama people and found that he loved them," observed one reviewer (Trilling, p. 395). Agee's desire to understand not only the physical and environmental details of these people's lives but also their inner experience makes him anxious about exposing them to an audience interested mainly in literary writing, or an audience that would look at them solely as "poor people"—social welfare cases to be pitied.

In one of the best examples of this anxiety, Agee's portrayal of Mrs. Ricketts when he first meets her and her family becomes a self-accusation pointing back at the reporter and photographer:

> [I]t was as if you and your children and your husband and those others were stood there naked in front of the cold absorption of the camera in all your shame and pitiableness to be pried into and laughed at; and your eyes were wild with fury and shame and fear, and the tendons of your little neck were tight, the whole time, and one hand continually twitched and tore in the rotted folds of your skirt like the hand of a little girl who must recite before adults, and there was not a thing you could do, nothing, not a word or remonstrance you could make.
>
> (*Famous Men*, p. 321)

Agee cannot escape the fact that his own presence must unavoidably affect the people he meets. They put him and Walker Evans up in their houses, talk to him, let Evans photograph them, share their food. How can he write about them and their poverty in such a way as to leave them some pride, some integrity as fellow Americans? The amalgam that is *Let Us Now Praise Famous Men*—the mix of objective reporting, impressionistic reaction, vivid photography—stands as his answer.

Sources and literary context. Commissioned in 1936 by *Fortune* magazine, *Let Us Now Praise Famous Men* was originally meant to be a series of articles on the conditions of the tenant farmers in the cotton belt of the South. As it turned out, what Agee wrote about his experiences in Alabama could not be shaped to fit the magazine's requirements. According to historian David Kennedy, *Fortune* found his text and Evans's photos of the suffering "too harrowing to publish," which led to their creating the book published four years later; Kennedy would deem it "one of the most sobering artistic achievements of the decade" (Kennedy, p. 208).

Inspiration to collect the material that became *Let Us Now Praise Famous Men* came from a new interest in two areas of study: in examining the real lives of Americans (particularly those outside the mainstream who had been previously ignored) and in exploring social behavior in general. Both scholarly and popular works in psychology, sociology, and anthropology were produced in the 1920s and 1930s to satisfy a wide readership: Dale Carnegie's 1936 self-help book *How to Win Friends and Influence People*, Margaret Mead's *Coming of Age in Samoa*, Robert and Helen Lynd's second study of Muncie, Indiana, *Middletown in Transition* (1937), and Ruth Benedict's *Patterns of Culture* (1934). The success of such books (often greater than many of the novels that would become classics of the era) testifies to a desire on the part of Americans of that time for a deeper understanding of themselves and their neighbors.

Let Us Now Praise Famous Men "represents," as Warren I. Susman has suggested, "much of what was characteristic of the thirties' finest contributions" (Susman, p. 217). The characteristic traits that Susman is talking about appeared in fiction as well as nonfiction. Two examples are forerunners to Agee and Evans's book: John Steinbeck's ***The Grapes of Wrath*** (1939; also in *Literature and Its Times*), about the migration of Oklahoma farming families from the dust-ridden Midwest to California, and Margaret Bourke-White's 1937 photographic study of migrant farmers (with text by the novelist Erskine Caldwell), *You Have Seen Their Faces*. Like Agee's and Evans's account, both of these works focus on the bottom rung of the U.S. economic ladder. In Agee's view, the lyrical, poetic, evocative qualities of these earlier works constitute a kind of betrayal of the humanity of the people portrayed; he wishes to avoid this trap with his fragmentary style and unpredictable shifts in perspective. So while *Let Us Now Praise Famous Men* falls into line with other 1930s documentary-style reporting, it takes a definitive step outside that tradition.

Reception. Although the initial critical response to *Let Us Now Praise Famous Men* was generally positive (or recognized the unique character of the book), the accolades did not translate into commercial success. Sales remained low for years, despite the fact that a wide range of reviewers praised the account when it first appeared: the *Nation* called the book extraordinary"; the *New Yorker* described it as "superior, highly original accurately poetic writing"; and the *New Republic* as "a rich, many-eyed book" (James and Brown, pp. 6-7). Yet the account languished on the shelves, almost dropping out of contemporary consciousness. The posthumous Pulitzer Prize for Agee drew attention to his other work, however, and in 1960 Houghton Mifflin republished *Let Us Now Praise Famous Men* with a new biographical sketch of Agee by Evans as well as 30 extra photos from Evans's files. In the 1960s, people suddenly wanted to find out about the Great Depression of the 1930s, possibly because it seemed to represent a forerunner of the attention paid to the dispossessed in this later, civil rights decade.

TRAVEL AND CURIOSITY

In many ways, the contemporary era of *Let's Go California, The Rough Guide to New York,* and dozens of similar publications began in the 1930s. People were not only interested in culture in an abstract sense, but they also became curious about the individual qualities and even eccentricities of different regions of the United States. As one of the smaller but more memorable New Deal programs, the Federal Writers Project (FWP) commissioned and funded the *States' Guides,* a series of informational and travel books on various states of the Union. The Alabama state guide appeared in 1941, the same year as Agee's account. These guides were very comprehensive, encompassing history, geology, local arts and cultures, and social and demographic data in an attempt to produce as accurate a picture of the region as possible. Many unemployed writers found work with the FWP, and although *Let Us Now Praise Famous Men* was not an FWP project, its passionate interest in the reality of life in one of the more remote parts of the United States makes it a part of this broad effort.

Reviewing the book in 1942 and then again in 1960, Lionel Trilling identified it as a major achievement both times. He stressed its greatness even more clearly in 1960, pinpointing a quality of the book that continues to impress readers today. Agee's vision of the tenant farming families is so pure, so unmarred by a perception of any flaws or bad traits, that the book seems more a declaration of love, or a prayer, than a work of documentary reporting. To its credit, the account delivers more than neutral reporting. It makes a broader statement about what kind of country America was in the 1930s, and what kind of country it ought to be. Perhaps most telling is Trilling's by now familiar phrase about the extraordinary account—"the most important moral effort of our American Generation" (Trilling, p. 379).

—Martin Griffin

For More Information

Agee, James, and Walker Evans. *Let Us Now Praise Famous Men: Three Tenant Families*. Boston: Houghton Mifflin, 2001.

Alabama: A Guide to Deep South. Comp. by the Writers' Program of the Work Projects Administration. New York: Richard R. Smith, 1941.

Brogan, Hugh. *The Penguin History of the United States of America*. Harmondsworth, Middlesex, England: Penguin, 1990.

James, Mertice M., and Dorothy Brown, eds. *Book Review Digest*. Vol. 37. New York: H. W. Wilson, 1942.

Kennedy, David M. *Freedom From Fear: The American People in Depression and War, 1929-1945*. New York: Oxford University Press, 1999.

McElvaine, Robert S. *The Great Depression: America, 1929-1941*. New York: Times Books, 1984.

Nash, Gary B., et al, eds. *The American People: Creating a Nation and a Society*. Vol. 2. New York: Harper and Row, 1990.

Puckett, John Rogers. *Five Photo-Textual Documentaries from The Great Depression*. Ann Arbor, Mich.: UMI Research Press, 1984.

Susman, Warren I. "The Thirties." In *The Development of an American Culture*. Ed. Stanley Coben and Lorman Ratner. Englewood Cliff, N.J.: Prentice-Hall, 1970.

Trilling, Lionel. "An American Classic." In *Speaking of Literature and Society*. Ed. Diana Trilling. New York: Harcourt Brace Jovanovich, 1980.

"Letter from Birmingham Jail"

by
Martin Luther King, Jr.

THE LITERARY WORK

A letter written in April 1963 in the city jail in Birmingham, Alabama; first published in pamphlet form in 1963.

SYNOPSIS

Arrested during demonstrations against racial segregation in Birmingham, King responds to a public statement by eight Birmingham clergymen challenging the demonstrations.

Martin Luther King, Jr. (1929-68) grew up in Atlanta, Georgia, where his father was pastor of the Ebenezer Baptist Church. As King was fond of pointing out, religion ran strongly in the family; his grandfather and great-grandfather had also been Baptist preachers. After studies at Crozer Theological Seminary and Boston University (where he earned a Ph.D.), Dr. King himself became a pastor at the Dexter Avenue Baptist Church in Montgomery, Alabama, in 1954. In the late 1950s and early 1960s King emerged as the moral voice of the growing civil rights movement to overturn racial segregation in the South. The year 1963 became pivotal for the movement. In widely televised demonstrations in Birmingham, Alabama, that spring, King was arrested with others; after his release, he would lead peaceful protesters in facing violent crackdowns by white police. That summer King would go on to help lead thousands of civil rights demonstrators in the March on Washington, the climax of which was his famous **"I Have a Dream"** speech (also in *Literature and Its Times*) from the steps of the Lincoln Memorial. In contrast to the stirring emotional appeal of that speech, the earlier "Letter from Birmingham Jail" offers a restrained and carefully reasoned defense of the technique of civil disobedience, or nonviolent confrontation, that King was about to invoke.

Events in History at the Time of the Letter

Historical background: the long reign of Jim Crow. For three-quarters of a century after the end of Reconstruction—that is, from about 1880 to about 1955—African Americans made little progress in their long struggle for equal treatment in American society. Throughout much of America, blacks faced daily discrimination and segregation in schools, housing, and employment. In the South, however, where most blacks lived until the 1930s and 1940s, racial segregation was even more pervasive. Varieties of segregation were enshrined in the so-called Jim Crow laws, state and local laws that forbade mixing in public places and restricted black train passengers to a single car (usually grimy and half-filled with cargo). These laws reversed the Reconstruction era's civil rights legislation and made official the South's traditional separation between the races. The laws rested on the Supreme Court's 1896 ruling in *Plessy v. Ferguson*, which upheld "separate but equal" facilities as constitutional. Under the Jim Crow system, blacks were legally denied service in many public facilities

Martin Luther King, Jr.

and businesses, which were designated as "White Only." Meanwhile, from public schools and transportation to restaurants and shops, blacks in southern states were expected to settle for services that were harder to find and far lower in quality than those offered to whites, despite the law's promise of "separate but equal."

For decades only one major national organization opposed the Jim Crow system and other discriminatory laws and practices in the United States. Founded by black leader W.E.B. Du Bois and others in 1909, the National Organization for the Advancement of Colored People (NAACP) emphasized legal action in promoting equality for blacks. After years of challenging discrimination in test cases throughout the United States, in 1954 the NAACP achieved a breakthrough victory in the Supreme Court. The NAACP's lawyers brought a lawsuit in support of Oliver Brown, whose daughter Linda had been denied entry into a white public school in Topeka, Kansas. In its 1954 ruling on *Brown v. Board of Education of Topeka*, the Supreme Court held that separate educational facilities were by their very nature unequal, and that school segregation violates the United States Constitution. Yet despite this landmark decision, which essentially overturned *Plessy v. Ferguson*, southern state and local governments continued to enforce Jim Crow laws, in schools and elsewhere. Southern blacks did not suffer this violation of their rights silently, however. Even earlier, signs of protest suggested that at least some blacks refused to sit back and endure what Martin Luther King, in his "Letter from Birmingham Jail," would call "the disease of segregation" (King, "Letter from Birmingham Jail," p. 83).

The civil rights movement. The first cracks in the wall of segregation came during and just after World War II (1939-45). Black leaders such as labor organizer A. Philip Randolph (1889-1979) had long pointed out the valuable contributions of black soldiers and workers in defending a nation that accorded them only the status of second-class citizens. Only at Randolph's repeated insistence did the federal government desegregate first the defense industries (1941) and then finally the armed forces (1948). Between these two victories came the founding of an organization whose philosophical approach would have a profound influence on future events. In 1942 an activist in Chicago, James Farmer, established the Congress of Racial Equality (CORE), which called on blacks and whites to use nonviolent direct action to resist all forms of racial discrimination. Based on techniques of civil disobedience developed by Indian leader Mahatma Gandhi and others, CORE's methods would play a major role in shaping the civil rights movement, which would emerge to combat segregation in the late 1950s and early 1960s.

The NAACP's 1954 victory in *Brown v. Board of Education* can be thought of as the event that gave the major impetus to the civil rights movement. With segregation's constitutionality called into question, blacks throughout the South were now emboldened to openly resist laws that both blacks and many liberal and moderate whites increasingly saw as unjust. Several sporadic protests occurred in southern cities in the early 1950s, but it was the historic act of one Montgomery, Alabama woman, Rosa Parks, that marked the beginning of effective opposition to segregation in 1955. A secretary at the local chapter of the NAACP, Rosa Parks boarded a Montgomery bus one day in December 1955 and sat in the so-called "neutral zone," between the white section in the front and black section in the rear. Blacks were allowed to sit in the neutral zone, but were obliged under law to give up their seats to white passengers if needed. Technically the zone was reserved for blacks unless the white section was filled. On this day, when the driver demanded she give her seat to a younger white man, Rosa Parks refused. Actually the driver told her whole row to stand so the white man could sit without having to keep company with any black person in the row. The whole row refused, then relented, except for Parks. She was arrested and jailed.

Montgomery's black leaders had already begun discussing ways of protesting segregation. This would make an ideal test case, they thought. When Rosa Parks was arrested, the community organized a one-day boycott of the bus company, the vast majority of whose riders were black. This temporary boycott was so successful that the organizers decided to extend it. Forming an organization they called the Montgomery Improvement Association (MIA), they chose as their leader and spokesman the energetic 25-year-old pastor of a prominent local church, Reverend Dr. Martin Luther King, Jr. King had arrived in Montgomery only about a year earlier, moving from Boston with his wife Coretta to take up his first job, as pastor at the Dexter Avenue Baptist Church. At the time of the boycott, his first child—a daughter, Yolanda—had just been born.

The Montgomery bus boycott lasted more than a year, nearly putting the bus company out of business. In late 1956, after King had been briefly jailed by city authorities and his house had been bombed by angry whites, the Supreme Court ruled that segregation on buses was unconstitutional. The Montgomery bus boycott had succeeded, and Martin Luther King Jr. had risen to national prominence as a civil rights leader. Building on its Montgomery success, in 1957 the organization changed its name to the Southern Christian Leadership Conference (SCLC), reflecting both a new expanded regional approach to civil rights activism as well as a strong religious component.

With King still at the helm, the SCLC started affiliates in cities throughout the South, each under the supervision of a local black church leader. King's approach, based on the tradition of civil disobedience already developed by Thoreau, Gandhi, and CORE, gained wide support, both among blacks and among liberal and moderate whites. In addition to targeting segregation, King and the SCLC turned their attention to voting rights, long denied to Southern blacks by white local and state governments. In the "Letter from Birmingham Jail" King refers to the "devious methods" used to stop Southern blacks from registering to vote ("Letter," p. 86). These included discriminatory literacy tests and poll taxes. White officials repeatedly arrested King as he led blacks to register.

By the late 1950s, King's strategy of nonviolent confrontation was attracting young people from around the country. In 1960 King's associate, Ella J. Baker, helped a group of black and white young people form the Student Nonviolent Coordinating Committee (SNCC). King encouraged SNCC to adopt the strategy of nonviolent tactics, and at first they obliged, coining a slogan borrowed from a speech he delivered to them—"jail not bail" (later many of them would abandon the nonviolent strategy). After students spontaneously began the "sit-in" movement to protest segregation in restaurants, this nonviolent method was taken up and expanded by SNCC. Purposefully remaining polite, the stu-

CIVIL DISOBEDIENCE

Civil disobedience has also been called "passive resistance," but King preferred the term "nonviolent confrontation," which stressed the idea of assertive action in opposing injustice. The tradition of civil disobedience has its roots in the thought of ancient writers such as Cicero (Roman, first century B.C.E.) and St. Augustine (Roman, fourth century C.E.), who distinguished between just and unjust laws. In the "Letter from Birmingham Jail" King quotes an idea of St. Augustine's, which, along with his other ideas, provided the basis of Western Christian theology: "an unjust law is no law at all" ("Letter," p. 84). The phrase itself comes from the influential essay **"Civil Disobedience"** (1849; also in *Literature and Its Times*) by the American writer Henry David Thoreau (American, 1817-62), who argued that people have a moral obligation to disobey unjust laws. Such civil disobedience should be practiced openly and nonviolently, in order to stir the conscience of lawmakers and force a change in the law. Those practicing civil disobedience should be prepared to accept punishment for breaking the unjust law. "Under a government that imprisons any unjustly," Thoreau wrote, "the true place for a just man is also a prison" (Thoreau in Oates, p. 86). While King does not quote Thoreau in the "Letter," he studied Thoreau's writings closely as a graduate student and found them deeply inspiring. He also found inspiration in the techniques of Indian leader Mohandas Gandhi (1869-1948), who developed nonviolent methods of civil disobedience in resisting British colonial rule in India. Gandhi, who was likewise influenced by Thoreau, also stressed the importance of being ready to go to jail for the cause of justice.

dents would sit at "white only" lunch counters and refuse to get up. Harassed and often beaten by angry whites, thousands were arrested throughout the South. Across the nation, sit-ins forced the desegregation not only of restaurants but also of department stores, shops, libraries, and other facilities. Another tactic, tried earlier (1947) by black activists in CORE was the "Freedom Ride," which entailed their sitting in any section of an interstate bus, a right confirmed by the Supreme Court (in *Morgan v. Virginia,* 1946). The year 1961 saw CORE begin a series of "Freedom Rides" that faced an even more violent backlash than the sit-ins had. Groups of blacks, who were joined later by sympathetic whites, sat where they wanted on interstate buses that traversed the South. When angry white mobs firebombed or attacked the buses, Southern police often stood by doing nothing or, in some cases, arrested the Freedom Riders. An estimated 70,000 Freedom Riders took part in these legal and peaceful demonstrations, and nearly 4,000 of them were arrested.

BLACK RELIGIOUS TRADITION AND THE CIVIL RIGHTS MOVEMENT

In its earliest days, Christianity exerted a powerful attraction to slaves of the ancient Greco-Roman world, who made up a significant part of the church's following in the days when Christians were a persecuted minority. Like their ancient counterparts, newly arrived African slaves in the Americas also found comfort in Christian beliefs (among them, the belief in a better world to come). Exposed to Christianity by their white masters, slaves in the American South developed their own distinctive church traditions, incorporating African elements into the service. The energetic music of the so-called "Negro spirituals" enlivened services, as did the black preachers' often impassioned sermons, featuring a type of call and response in which the audience would affirm "yes" or "amen" at key points (as audiences at King's speeches often did). A superb orator known for his powerful sermons, King fell strongly into step with the tradition of African American Christian worship. His generation of spiritual leaders differed from those before them, though. Whereas earlier generations had often comforted their audiences with the promise of justice in the next world, King's generation turned increasingly to the pursuit of justice in this world. It is this generation that formed the backbone of the Southern Christian Leadership Conference, which played such a leading role in the civil rights movement.

Birmingham. One of the cities in which Freedom Riders were arrested was Birmingham, Alabama, the state's largest city and leading industrial center. Located about 80 miles north of Montgomery, Birmingham was not just another segregated southern city. In King's words, it was "probably the most thoroughly segregated city in the country" ("Letter," p. 79). A die-hard segregationist, the city's Police Commissioner, Eugene "Bull" Connor, had vowed that "blood would run in the streets" before the city would desegregate (Connor in Oates, p. 212). Connor was the one who ordered his officers to arrest the Freedom Riders here. On the other side, doggedly pushing for desegregation was the colorful head of the SCLC's Birmingham affiliate, the Reverend Fred Shuttlesworth. In and out of jail since beginning demonstrations there in the late 1950s, harassed, beaten, his home bombed, and his wife stabbed during a street attack, Shuttlesworth doggedly tried to negotiate with city leaders. Though his efforts were repeatedly rebuffed, he was as determined to end segregation in Birmingham as Connor was to preserve it.

In early 1963 King and the SCLC were struggling to recover from a failed campaign the previous year to end segregation in Albany, Georgia. Responding to Shuttlesworth's requests for a Birmingham campaign, King and his aides decided that the very strength of segregation in that city could work in their favor. If they could break segregation in Birmingham, they reasoned, the rest of the South would surely follow. Furthermore, they thought they had learned two important lessons from Albany. First, they would focus their efforts not on Birmingham's political structure, but on its businesses, which relied heavily on black customers. Second, they realized that to be sure of results, they needed to provoke a reaction of such violence that federal intervention would be required to protect the demonstrators. Thus, they deliberately planned a campaign of provocation by breaking the city's segregation ordinances, such as the one against sitting at "whites only" lunch counters. By marching and demonstrating, they would induce the police to arrest them for violating ordinances like the one against parading without a permit. A nonviolent but provocative demonstrator, King reasoned, "would force his oppressor to commit his brutality openly—in the light of day—with the world looking on" through the lenses of media photographers and television cameras (King in Oates, p. 212). In their communications, the SCLC called the Birmingham campaign Project C, for Confrontation.

King announced the SCLC's Birmingham campaign in January 1963, and arrived with his staff in the city in February. The campaign itself was scheduled to begin in early March and to peak around Easter, normally the year's second-busiest shopping time. However, the city's mayoral election was to be held on March 5, with "Bull" Connor facing a more moderate candidate named Albert Boutwell. Fearing that the campaign would propel Connor to office, King delayed the start for several weeks. He was then forced to delay again when an indecisive election forced a run-off between Connor and Boutwell. Meanwhile, on March 28, Coretta King gave birth to a daughter, Bernice, the couple's fourth child.

On April 2 Boutwell won the run-off election by a wide margin, and the next day the SCLC kicked off its campaign. Issuing a "Birmingham Manifesto," King called for desegregation in some facilities downtown and demanded that a biracial committee be established to formulate a timetable for desegregating the city's remaining services. The statement informed local business that demonstrations and boycotts by black customers—up to 40 percent of the city's population—would go on until the city met the demands.

From the beginning, the campaign faced criticism, not just from segregationists but also from many who opposed segregation. Attorney General Robert Kennedy, brother of the President, summed up much liberal and moderate reaction nationwide: the campaign was badly timed, he declared, and the moderate Boutwell should be given a chance. Boutwell himself—who as King points out in the "Letter" was a committed segregationist—condemned the demonstrators and the SCLC staff as trouble-making outsiders, a commonly heard charge echoed even by some Birmingham blacks.

On April 11, the Birmingham sheriff served King with a court injunction prohibiting King and other SCLC officers from participating in any demonstrations. At a press conference the next day, Thursday, April 12, King announced his intention to disobey the injunction by leading a march the following day, April 13, Good Friday. That night, King was shaken to hear that, after weeks of sit-ins, the SCLC had run out of money to post bond for its jailed personnel. His aides argued that King was needed out of jail, in order to raise money. If King went to jail, they said,

King's efforts to peacefully end segregation resulted in his being arrested on several occasions. Here, he is welcomed home by his wife and children on his release from Georgia State Prison on bond.

the entire campaign would fail for lack of funds. After long thought, King resolved to march and go to jail, trusting God for the needed cash. The following day, Good Friday, King and about 50 other demonstrators were indeed arrested and

WHITE SOUTHERN REACTIONS TO CIVIL RIGHTS DEMONSTRATORS

As King was aware, media exposure of southern white hatred and violence towards blacks was capable of arousing strong disgust with the white behavior among northerners. White moderates and liberals in the North would not long tolerate such racism once the ugly picture of it was brought into their homes and offices. In the weeks after King's release from the Birmingham city jail, images of peaceful demonstrators being beaten, subjected to punishing jets of water from fire hoses, and mangled by police dogs assailed northern liberals in newspapers and on television, affecting viewers in ways that proved this hope to have been well founded. These powerful pictures of nonviolent protestors being savagely attacked helped turn the Birmingham campaign from a near failure to a resounding success.

taken downtown to the Birmingham City Jail. King was placed in solitary confinement, where he would remain for one week, until he was released on bail Saturday, April 20.

King went through bouts of loneliness and depression in jail, punctuated only by visits from his lawyers. The lawyers brought good news on Monday: black singer and actor Harry Belafonte had offered to guarantee any money needed for bonds. The following day, however, King was dismayed by the contents of a four-day-old Birmingham newspaper that his lawyers brought him to read. The paper contained an open letter against the demonstrations signed by eight white Alabama clergymen, Christian and Jewish, some of whom were on record as anti-segregationists. The letter made the same arguments King had heard already from many moderates. The demonstrations were badly timed, they were led by outsiders, and they incited violence, the clerics declared. In the name of racial harmony, they called for law and order, exhorting the city's blacks to be patient and to negotiate rather than resort to breaking the law. Nowhere did they chide southern racists for the recent beatings and bombings of demonstrators or the ongoing segregation that denied blacks their basic rights. Just two weeks later Birmingham police would unleash high-pressure fire hoses and police dogs on the demonstrators. Then came night bombings, the violence spiraling out of control, addressed on television by President John F. Kennedy, who sent 3,000 federal troops to the city. In his reply to the clerics, King sought to avert all this mayhem.

Scribbling feverishly on the newspaper's margins, on scraps of toilet paper, and finally on notepads that his lawyers were permitted to bring him, King composed his reply.

EXCERPTS FROM THE LETTER OF THE EIGHT WHITE CLERGYMEN

"We the undersigned clergymen are among those who, in January, issued "An Appeal for Law and Order and Common Sense," in dealing with racial problems in Alabama. We expressed understanding that honest convictions in racial matters could properly be pursued in the courts, but urged that decisions of those courts should in the meantime be peacefully obeyed. . . . In Birmingham, recent public events have given indication that we all have opportunity for a new constructive and realistic approach to racial problems. However, we are now confronted by a series of demonstrations by some of our Negro citizens, directed and led in part by outsiders. We recognize the natural impatience of people who feel that their hopes are slow in being realized. But we are convinced that these demonstrations are unwise and untimely. . . . Just as we formerly pointed out that "hatred and violence have no sanction in our religious and political traditions," we also point out that such actions as incite to hatred and violence, however technically peaceful actions may be [sic], have not contributed to the resolution of our local problems. We do not believe that these days of new hope are days when extreme measures are justified in Birmingham. . . . When rights are consistently denied, a cause should be pressed in the courts and in negotiations among local leaders, and not in the streets. We appeal to both our white and Negro citizenry to observe the principles of law and order and common sense."

Bishop C. C. J. Carpenter, Bishop Joseph A. Durick, Rabbi Hilton L. Grafman, Bishop Holan B. Harmon, Reverend George M. Murray, Reverend Edward V. Ramage, Reverend Earl Stallings (Garrow, vol. 1, p. 860).

The Letter in Focus

The contents. King begins his response to the eight clergymen in a tone of respect that he maintains throughout the work. Although he rarely answers "criticisms of my work and ideas," he writes, he is taking time to do so "while confined here in the Birmingham city jail" because "I feel that you are men of genuine good will and that your criticisms are sincerely set forth" ("Letter," p. 77).

The first criticism King addresses is the clergymen's characterization of him and the SCLC as outsiders. On a superficial level, he asserts, he has "organizational ties" to Birmingham through the local SCLC affiliate, at the invitation of which he has come to the city. On a deeper level, however, King argues, he is "in Birmingham because injustice is here" ("Letter," p. 78). Like St. Paul, who "carried the gospel of Jesus Christ to the far corners of the Greco-Roman world, so am I compelled to carry the gospel of freedom beyond my own home town" ("Letter," p. 78). Contending that "injustice anywhere is a threat to justice everywhere," King declares that "whatever affects one directly affects all indirectly" ("Letter," p. 79). Consequently, he concludes, no American can be considered an outsider anywhere within the nation's borders.

Responding to the clergymen's call for negotiation, King points out that earlier attempts by local black leaders to negotiate with the city were rebuffed. Negotiation with the city's merchants resulted only in broken promises, as "the stores' humiliating racial signs" remained in place despite the merchants' agreements to remove them ("Letter," p. 80). King agrees that good-faith negotiation is indeed desirable: "The purpose of our direct-action program is to create a situation so crisis-packed that it will inevitably open the door to negotiation" ("Letter," p. 82).

In a similar vein, King responds to the charge that the action is "untimely" by stating that he has never engaged in a campaign that whites thought was "well timed": "We know through painful experience that freedom is never voluntarily given by the oppressor; it must be demanded by the oppressed. . . . For years now I have heard the word 'Wait!' It rings in the ears of every Negro with piercing familiarity. This 'Wait' has almost always meant 'Never' " ("Letter," pp. 82-83).

King then catalogues racism's cruelties and inequities in a long paragraph marked by parallel constructions:

> When you have seen vicious mobs lynch your mothers and fathers at will and drown your sisters and brothers at whim; when you have seen hate-filled policemen curse, kick and even kill your black brothers and sisters; when you see the vast majority of your twenty million Negro brothers smothering in an airtight cage of poverty in the midst of an affluent society . . . then you will understand why we find if difficult to wait.
>
> ("Letter," p. 83)

He concludes this thundering litany with a mild and almost ironically polite request: "I hope, sirs, you can understand our legitimate and unavoidable impatience" ("Letter," p. 84).

Answering the objection that the demonstrators are breaking the law, King cites religious authorities such as St. Augustine and St. Thomas Aquinas in distinguishing between just and unjust laws. While we have an obligation to obey just laws, he argues, we have an equal obligation to disobey unjust ones. King sharply contrasts regular criminals who arbitrarily disobey just laws with demonstrators whose principles drive them to disobey unjust ones. As an example of just laws, he refers to the recent Supreme Court decisions overturning segregation:

> In no sense do I advocate evading or defying the law, as would the rabid segregationist. That would lead to anarchy. One who breaks an unjust law must do so openly, lovingly, and with a willingness to accept the penalty. I submit that an individual who breaks a law that conscience tells him is unjust, and who willingly accepts the penalty of imprisonment in order to arouse the conscience of the community over its injustice, is in reality expressing the highest respect for the law.
>
> ("Letter," p. 86)

King devotes much of the rest of the letter to voicing "two honest confessions" of disappointment ("Letter," p. 87). His first disappointment is with the white moderates, whom he says almost present more of an obstacle to progress in civil rights than the strongest racists. Preferring "order" to "justice," such moderates assume that "they can set the timetable for another man's freedom" ("Letter," p. 87). Order without justice merely gives the illusion of peace, King contends: the true source of Birmingham's tension is not the demonstrators, but segregation itself. The demonstrators "merely bring to the surface the hidden tension that is already alive" ("Letter," p. 88). To say that the demonstrators are causing the violence, King argues, is like "condemning a robbed man because his possession of money" led him to be robbed ("Letter," p. 88).

King's "other major disappointment" is with "the white church and its leadership" ("Letter," p. 93). Too often, King declares, the South's white religious leaders have either opposed the civil rights movement outright or else they have been "more cautious than courageous and remained silent" ("Letter," p. 94). He contrasts this behavior with the rigorous moral courage and fearless sacrifice of early Christians—who were themselves often condemned as "disturbers of the peace" and "outside agitators" ("Letter," p. 96). If the church remains a complacent "archdefender of the status quo," King warns, people will dismiss it "as an irrelevant social club with no meaning for the twentieth century" ("Letter," p. 96).

King expresses optimism about the civil rights movement's ultimate success, linking the movement with the same ideals of freedom that reside in America's most cherished traditions. In closing, King hails his fellow clergymen. He hopes that "the dark clouds of racial prejudice will soon pass away," leaving "the radiant stars of love and brotherhood" to "shine over our nation with all their scintillating beauty" ("Letter," p. 100).

King's middle road between passivity and anger. One aspect of the white clergymen's letter that

King particularly objects to is their characterization of the demonstrations as "extreme." Very much to the contrary, King defines his position and goals as centrist: "I stand in the middle of two opposing forces in the Negro community" ("Letter," p. 90). On one side are those "who, as a result of long years of oppression, are so drained of self-respect" that "they have adjusted to segregation," while on the other side are those consumed by "bitterness and hatred," who come "perilously close to advocating violence" ("Letter," p. 90). As an example of the latter, King cites black nationalist organizations such as the Nation of Islam:

> Nourished by the Negro's frustration over the continued existence of racial discrimination, this movement is made up of people who have lost faith in America, who have absolutely repudiated Christianity, and who have concluded that the white man is an incorrigible "devil."
> ("Letter," p. 90)

Without the constructive outlet for black resentment offered by nonviolent protest, King suggests, "by now many streets of the South would . . . be flowing with blood" ("Letter," p. 91). King furthermore foresees that if moderate whites continue to reject blacks' nonviolent efforts at reform, "millions of Negroes will, out of frustration and despair, seek solace and security in black-nationalist ideologies—a development that would inevitably lead to a frightening racial nightmare" ("Letter," p. 91). If blacks cannot win freedom through nonviolence, he warns, "they will seek expression through violence; this is not a threat, but a fact of history" ("Letter," p. 91).

By 1963 a potent rival to nonviolence had indeed emerged in growing militant movements, like the Nation of Islam, that sanctioned violent responses to white oppression. Disparaging the Birmingham campaign as "an exercise in futility," the Nation of Islam's fiery spokesman Malcolm X derided the goal of desegregation: "a chance to sit at a lunch counter and drink coffee with a cracker—that's success?" (Malcolm X in Oates, pp. 252-53). Arguing that nonviolence left blacks defenseless, Malcolm X called King "a traitor to the Negro people" (Malcolm X in Branch, *Pillar of Fire*, p. 13). After Birmingham, as King was in the middle of an otherwise triumphant tour across the country, Malcolm X's angry followers would pelt King's car with rotten eggs in Harlem, New York City's black ghetto. In such northern slums, racism and economic oppression were reflected in practice but not in law. Overturning entrenched practices in the North would prove far more complex than overturning local laws in the South. As the African American battle for social equality shifted north after the mid-1960s, nonviolence would face greater challenges than ever in winning their support.

Sources. While in jail, King had no access to books or any other literary material other than a few newspapers. However, in composing the "Letter from Birmingham Jail" he was able to draw on his extensive past reading. In the text he refers to both secular and religious writers, occasionally quoting from memory. He quotes secular writings by Thomas Jefferson, Abraham Lincoln, and T. S. Eliot, but the vast majority of his references are to religious works, either scriptural or theological. One of the white clergymen was a rabbi, and King refers to the Jewish theologian Martin Buber and incorporates quotations from Old Testament prophets such as Amos into his argument. The Christian writers on which he draws include St. Augustine (Roman, fourth century), St. Thomas Aquinas (Italian, thirteenth century), John Bunyan (English, seventeenth century), and Paul Tillich (American, twentieth century). Tillich, a leading modern Christian theologian, was a major influence on King's graduate studies (as were the ideas on civil disobedience of Thoreau, Gandhi, and others discussed above).

However, the first Christian writer King names is the one who stands out as the predominant inspiration for King's letter: St. Paul of Tarsus, known as the Apostle to the Gentiles. Paul's own letters are an important element of the New Testament, and King explicitly compares himself to Paul in being "compelled to carry the gospel of freedom beyond my home town" ("Letter," p. 78). As critic Malinda Snow has observed, King's choice of model was especially appropriate considering the audience he addresses himself to in the "Letter from Birmingham Jail." Paul did not write his New Testament letters to convert non-Christians, but to strengthen the faith of those already converted. Likewise, in the "Letter from Birmingham Jail" King aims not to change the minds of segregationists, but to instruct those, like the eight clergymen, who oppose segregation but lack the resolve or the vision to embrace the implications of that conviction.

Publication and impact. After King's lawyers smuggled out the motley scraps of paper that comprised the "Letter from Birmingham Jail," his aides typed it up at a nearby motel. Wyatt Walker, a leading SCLC official, gave it the title by which it is still known. Walker predicted, "This is going to be one of the historic documents of this movement" (Walker in Oates, p. 230). While Walker's expectation would eventually be borne out, the letter received little attention at first. Instead, the nation's attention was focused on events in Birmingham itself. Despite an air of discouragement as King entered jail, the demonstrations in Birmingham did, after his release, finally succeed in arousing the conscience of the nation. Now seen as a major turning point in the civil rights movement, the Birmingham campaign is credited with much of the success of the March on Washington later that year. It is also believed to have contributed to the passage of the landmark 1964 Civil Rights Act, as well as the 1965 Voting Rights Act.

First published as a pamphlet in 1963 by a Quaker organization, the "Letter from Birmingham Jail" also appeared that year in several religious and progressive journals. While it evoked no public response from the white clergymen it is addressed to, it did slowly find a growing readership in churches and among moderate politicians (such as Robert Kennedy) in Washington. It was largely ignored by the mainstream media until excerpts appeared in *Time* magazine in January 1964, whose own position had been far from neutral during the Birmingham demonstrations. Along with *The New York Times*, the magazine had echoed the white clergymen in condemning the Birmingham demonstrations as untimely and inflammatory.

That same year the "Letter from Birmingham Jail" was included as a separate chapter in King's book *Why We Can't Wait* (1964), and since then it has been widely acknowledged as the most concise and powerful statement of his ideas. Historian and King biographer Stephen Oates calls it "a classic in protest literature, the most eloquent and learned expression of the goals and philosophy of the nonviolent movement ever written" (Oates, p. 230). Looking back on events and their relation to the letter, historian Taylor Branch points out the irony of its early obscurity:

> In hindsight, it appeared that King had rescued the beleaguered Birmingham movement with his pen, but the reverse was true: unexpected miracles of the Birmingham movement later transformed King's letter from a silent cry of desperate hope to a famous pronouncement of moral triumph.
>
> (Branch, *Parting the Waters*, p. 744)

—Colin Wells

For More Information

Blumberg, Rhoda Lois. *Civil Rights: The 1960s Freedom Struggle*. Boston: Twayne, 1991.

Branch, Taylor. *Parting the Waters: America in the King Years 1954-63*. New York: Simon & Schuster, 1988.

———. *Pillar of Fire: America in the King Years 1963-65*. New York: Simon & Schuster, 1998.

Fairclough, Adam. *To Redeem the Soul of America: The Southern Christian Leadership Conference and Martin Luther King, Jr.* Athens: University of Georgia Press, 1987.

Findlay, James F., Jr. *Church People in the Struggle: The National Council of Churches and the Black Freedom Movement, 1950-70*. Oxford: Oxford University Press, 1993.

Garrow, David, ed. *Martin Luther King, Jr.: Civil Rights Leader, Theologian, Orator*. 3 vols. Brooklyn: Carlson, 1989.

King, Martin Luther, Jr. "Letter from Birmingham Jail," in *Why We Can't Wait*. New York: Harper & Row, 1964.

Oates, Stephen B. *Let the Trumpet Sound: A Life of Martin Luther King, Jr.* New York: HarperCollins, 1994.

Lolita

by
Vladimir Nabokov

Vladimir Nabokov, a novelist, poet, playwright, and translator, as well as a collector of butterflies and inventor of chess problems, was born in St. Petersburg, Russia, in 1899. His idyllic childhood and adolescence were abruptly ended by the 1917 Bolshevik Revolution, which forced his family to flee from Russia to Europe. From 1919 to 1922 Nabokov studied Slavic and Romance Languages at Cambridge University, then moved to Berlin, Germany, where he married his wife, Véra. In Berlin and later in Paris, he supported his family by giving lessons in tennis, boxing, and the English language as well as by publishing original works of literature in Russian. Because Nabokov's wife and son were Jewish, however, the family eventually had to escape from Europe to the United States to avoid Nazi persecution. *Lolita,* the third novel that Nabokov wrote after arriving in America, is narrated by a European émigré with a terrible secret: he is attracted to little girls. Nabokov's protagonist finds that in postwar America he can fulfill his darkest fantasies—with tragic consequences for himself as well as the child.

THE LITERARY WORK

A novel set in three fictional towns and on the road throughout the United States between 1947 and 1952; published in France in 1955, and in the United States in 1958.

SYNOPSIS

A man abducts and sexually abuses his twelve-year-old stepdaughter after her mother dies. Later, in prison awaiting trial for murder, he composes a memoir devoted to his stepdaughter, in which he tries to explain his actions.

Events in History at the Time the Novel Takes Place

European immigration. Millions of European citizens were displaced from their homes, their livelihoods, and their native countries by the Second World War. Many of these "displaced persons" were Jews, gypsies, homosexuals, and other outcast groups who were persecuted by the Nazis. During the war, and immediately after it, various displaced persons tried desperately to leave Europe for the United States. Nabokov's own family was a case in point. His younger brother Sergei, who was homosexual, died in a German concentration camp; Nabokov's wife and son, who were Jewish, were also in jeopardy. The family fled first from Berlin to Paris in the late 1930s, and then to the United States in May 1940, immediately before German tanks rolled into Paris.

After the war, the proportion of American immigrants who were political refugees increased dramatically. The Displaced Persons Act, which Congress passed in 1948 and renewed in 1950, allowed over 400,000 Europeans to become American citizens, relaxing the rigid quotas established after the First World War. As Ameri-

Vladimir Nabokov

cans grew anxious about international communism, however, the McCarran-Walter Act of 1952 returned to earlier quotas and barred entry to anyone who had ever belonged to an organization seeking to overthrow the United States government. The following year, the Refugee Relief Act set aside the quota in the case of individuals who had been persecuted by communist regimes.

Anticommunism. After Nabokov's family fled Russia, that country established a communist government and became known as the Union of Soviet Socialist Republics. By the time Nabokov wrote *Lolita*, the United States was engaged in a protracted "Cold War" with the Soviet Union, the only other dominant nation after the Second World War. Competing for world leadership, the two superpowers conducted their hostilities at a distance by supporting different sides in conflicts around the globe, engaging in espionage, and stockpiling nuclear weapons of mutual destruction. In 1948 the so-called Cold War heated up. The Soviet Union blockaded Berlin and took control of Czechoslovakia, while North Korea established a communist government. In 1949 China established a communist government and began a strategic alliance with the Soviets; in response, the United States joined forces with European countries to create the opposing North Atlantic Treaty Organization.

Seeing the rapid rise of international communism, Americans were afraid that this political philosophy might spread to the United States as well. In 1947 hundreds of workers in the motion picture industry were threatened with being "blacklisted"—included on a list of individuals barred from employment—unless they cooperated with the House Un-American Activities Committee by acknowledging their guilt and naming other suspects. In 1950 Alger Hiss, a prominent lawyer, was convicted of perjury for denying his involvement with Whittaker Chambers, an admitted communist. That same year, Joseph McCarthy, a new Republican senator from Wisconsin, became famous overnight after announcing that he could name 205 communists who had infiltrated the State Department. McCarthy later claimed that he could identify over 30,000 books by communists and communist sympathizers in American libraries. In 1953, Julius and Ethel Rosenberg were convicted of espionage—a judgment that is still controversial—and sentenced to death by electrocution. Before long, many Americans were swept up in the belief that the country was rife with communist spies and secret agents. Jews, homosexuals, artists, people who had not been born in the United States, and anyone who had ever belonged to the American Communist Party fell under suspicion. Meanwhile, American popular culture became dominated by anticommunist themes in comic books, detective stories, spy novels, and science-fiction films.

As an émigré who had left Russia over 30 years earlier, Nabokov disavowed both communism and the Soviet Union. In 1950 he even volunteered to write a series of articles on Soviet culture for the *New Yorker*, explaining that "I think I am the right man for it since I know exactly all the moves in the Soviet anti-American game" (Nabokov, *Selected Letters*, p. 108). At a time when most American academics protested government inquiries into a possible communist presence on campus, Nabokov, who was teaching at Cornell University, "befriended the FBI agent assigned to Cornell and declared he would be proud to have his son join the FBI in that role" (Boyd, p. 311). Themes of paranoia, detection, espionage, and political assassination dominate Nabokov's fiction from this period. In addition, many of his major characters—such as Humbert Humbert in *Lolita*—are political refugees, members of oppressed ethnic and religious groups, social misfits, or sexual deviants.

Child-molestation laws. *Lolita*, which features a protagonist who sexually abuses his stepdaughter, reflects trends in American popular culture as well as Nabokov's own writing during these years. Case studies and legislative changes suggest that at least some Americans at the time were concerned about child molestation. In a 1953 study of young adults, for example, 35 percent of female college students reported that they had been sexually molested in childhood. "The mean age at the time of the molestation was 11.7 years," which is the girl's approximate age in 1947 in *Lolita*, when she is first abused (Landis in de Young, p. 6). Recognizing the extent of the problem, some states passed laws to address it. Utah, for example, in 1953 made it "a felony to engage in sexual penetration or sexual contact with a person who is under eighteen where the offender is the victim's parent, stepparent, adoptive parent, or legal guardian, or occupies a position of special trust in relation to the victim" (de Young, p. 125). In *Lolita*, the main characters travel through a number of states with similar statutes. Indeed, the child's stepfather refers knowingly to various local and federal laws, especially those that forbid statutory rape and the transportation of minors across state lines for immoral purposes.

America at the wheel. Meanwhile, during the period of unprecedented economic growth that followed the Second World War, the United States consolidated its position as the richest country in the world. The gross national product rose from about $200,000 million in 1940, to $300,000 million in 1950, to over $500,000 million in 1960. As their earnings increased, more and more Americans joined the middle class. With the aid of the G.I. Bill, expanded credit, and federal housing loans, even young couples with little money could buy a house. Many bought low-cost homes in the surburbs. In 1947, William J. Levitt began to produce "Levittowns," enormous housing developments that contained thousands of similar homes laid out on identical plots in new residential streets. These houses were so popular that 14,000 were sold to individual families on a single day in 1949. In addition to owning their own homes, more Americans than ever before could now afford such luxuries as a college education, household appliances, and one or more automobiles.

Even as Americans were settling down in suburbia, they were also spending more time in cars. In the suburbs, after all, automobiles were necessary for husbands to commute to work and for wives to shop, run errands, and chauffeur children. Owning a new car became an important status symbol, and traveling by automobile a common leisure activity. More and more families chose—in the words of a popular advertisement of the time, sung by Dinah Shore—"to see the U.S.A. from [their] Chevrolet." Service stations, road maps, and tour books helped make such travel possible. At the same time, a host of other products and pastimes organized around the automobile sprang up: fast-food restaurants, diners, and drive-in restaurants; motels; roadside attractions; drive-in movie theatres; billboards and other highway advertisements. It was in 1949 that Richard and Maurice McDonald devised the cheap, quick hamburger sandwich that eventually dominated fast food franchises from coast to coast. In 1952, the first Holiday Inn opened in Memphis, Tennessee. Four years later, the federal government introduced the Interstate Highway System, which was constructed for national defense purposes but made long car trips easier and faster for everyone. Driving became a national pastime, celebrated in "road movies," chase scenes, and novels set on the American highway. During three weeks in the spring of 1951, Jack Kerouac wrote, on a scroll of paper 120 feet long, one lengthy, single-spaced paragraph about his travels across America, which was published six years later as the underground classic **On the Road** (also in *Literature and Its Times*).

ROADSIDE SIGNS

As the two main characters of Lolita cross the country by car, Humbert describes the advertisements and other sights that he and Dolores glimpse with the remark: "The Bearded Woman read our jingle and now she is no longer single" (Nabokov, *Lolita*, p. 158). This sentence parodies the over 7,000 red-and-white signs advertising Burma Shave shaving cream that were common on American highways at the time. The Burma Shave Company divided such ad lines into a series of six signs spaced along the road for a mile. In 1953, as he finished *Lolita*, Nabokov composed another such rhyme—"He passed two cars; then five; then seven; and then he beat them all to Heaven"—and ended it with the usual refrain, "Burma Shave." He offered to sell it to Burma Shave, but the company replied that it already had more jingles than it could use (Nabokov, *Selected Letters*, p. 137).

Nabokov knew firsthand many of the aspects of America's automotive culture that appear in *Lolita*. Every summer from 1949 to 1959, as soon as his teaching duties at Cornell University were over, he and his family would set off on butterfly-hunting expeditions that took them all over the United States. Indeed, Nabokov completed the manuscript of *Lolita* in various motels and assorted cars (his wife did all the driving) during such automotive tours in the summers of 1951, 1952, and 1953.

The Novel in Focus

The plot. *Lolita* takes the form of a two-part memoir written by Humbert Humbert, a child molester, to help his attorney defend him against a murder charge. As Part One opens, Humbert recalls his happy childhood on the French Riviera, where at 13 he met Annabel Leigh, a young girl his own age. They fell in love, but Annabel died a few months later. Humbert cites this tragic romance as the reason for his sexual attraction to little girls, whom he calls "nymphets."

Humbert struggles to both satisfy and control his urges over the next 25 years, at one point even marrying a woman who dresses and acts like a little girl. The marriage does not last, however, and as the Second World War begins Humbert leaves France for America. He ends up in Ramsdale, a small New England town, where he decides to rent a room from Charlotte Haze, a young widow, because her 12-year-old daughter Dolores—whom he calls "Lolita"—resembles Annabel.

Humbert seizes every opportunity to be alone with Dolores; meanwhile, the girl's mother tries to seduce him. Charlotte, a middle-class housewife bored with a life of gossip, shopping, and social clubs, used to dream about being "a career girl" before Humbert became her lodger (*Lolita*, p. 56). She now believes that marrying Humbert will make her happy. However, because she envies Dolores's youth and vaguely senses Humbert's interest in her, she sends the child to camp for the summer. After Dolores leaves, Humbert consents to marry Charlotte—who declares her love in a letter—because he thinks that he will have more access to the girl as her stepfather. He begins to collect sleeping pills in order to drug both his wife and his stepdaughter, so that he can fondle Dolores without anyone's knowing. Although Charlotte learns of Humbert's intentions, she dies in a car accident before she can do anything to stop him.

After the funeral, Humbert picks up Dolores at camp. Hiding the news of her mother's death, he takes her to the glamorous Enchanted Hunters Hotel, where he coaxes her to swallow some sleeping pills and then locks her in their room until they take effect. It turns out that the pills are placebos, and Humbert doesn't dare touch the girl in case she is not asleep. When Dolores wakes up the next morning, however, she herself suggests that they have sex—and Humbert agrees.

At the beginning of Part Two, Humbert recounts his year-long automobile trip with Dolores throughout America, during which he uses both promises and threats to force her to engage in various sexual acts several times a day. Most of his bribes involve the opportunity to visit a particular motel, diner, or tourist attraction—"a lighthouse in Virginia, a natural cave in Arkansas converted to a café, a collection of guns and violins somewhere in Oklahoma . . . anything whatsoever-anything, but it had to be there, in front of us, like a fixed star" (*Lolita*, pp. 151-52).

> We had been everywhere. We had really seen nothing. And I catch myself thinking today that our long journey had only defiled with a sinuous trail of slime the lovely, trustful, dreamy, enormous country that by then, in retrospect, was no more to us than a collection of dog-eared maps, ruined tour books, old tires, and her sobs in the night—every night, every night—the moment I feigned sleep.
>
> (*Lolita*, pp. 175-76)

After he runs out of money, Humbert takes Dolores back to New England, where he has a temporary teaching job at Beardsley, a women's college. There she attends school, makes friends, flirts with boys her own age, and even stars in the school play—which has the same name as the Enchanted Hunters Hotel because, as it turns out, the playwright Clare Quilty stayed there the night that Humbert and Dolores did.

At the end of the school year, Humbert discovers that Dolores has been skipping her piano lessons and lying about it. They have a bitter fight, during which he twists her arm, and she accuses him of both molesting her and murdering her mother. Afterwards, though, Dolores suddenly forgives him and suggests that they go on another cross-country trip, asking if this time she can plan the itinerary. During their journey, Humbert keeps thinking that they are being followed. Although the color, make, and license plate of the car changes, Humbert believes that the same mustachioed man is always at the wheel—and that he has managed to establish communication with Dolores. At any rate, this second trip ends abruptly after Dolores develops a fever and enters the hospital. When Humbert goes to pick her up, he learns that she checked out the day before, on Independence Day, in the care of a man claiming to be her uncle.

Over the next several months Humbert retraces their steps, looking for clues to the man's identity in the registration books at motels where they stayed. Although he finds many entries that seem suspicious, he can't figure out who the man is. Eventually he gives up. Three years pass, which Humbert spends pining for Dolores—until suddenly he receives a letter from her. She is now 17, married, and pregnant, and has written to ask for money so that she and her husband can move to another state where he can get a better job. When Humbert sees Dolores again, he notices how much she has grown. Now that she is no longer a child, he even decides that he loves her for herself instead of her appeal as a nymphet. He is still determined, however, to find the man who stole her from him. When Dolores reveals the man's name (Clare Quilty), Humbert realizes that he should have known it all along. Indeed, Humbert explains that he has scattered clues throughout his narrative so that readers, at this point, will enjoy the same feeling of sudden comprehension.

As Humbert prepares to track the man down and kill him, he recalls the entire saga of his relationship with Dolores, now acknowledging, for the first time, various incidents that demonstrated how unhappy she had been. And after Humbert murders Quilty—in a climactic scene that parallels the rape in the Enchanted Hunters Hotel at the end of Part One—he waits quietly to be arrested. Humbert concludes his memoir by stating that he feels guilty of committing rape, not murder. He now realizes that he and Dolores can never be together except in the pages of his memoir, which he wishes to be published only after her death.

Humbert's case. Except for a foreword by John Ray, Jr., the memoir's fictitious editor, the entire novel is told from Humbert's point of view. This device is crucial to the overall design and meaning of *Lolita*. Humbert is an exceptionally unreliable first-person narrator. He is biased, deceptive, manipulative, and mentally unstable, and his testimony relies on his poor recall of past events. Although he often cites evidence that supports his case—such as a photograph of himself and Annabel, a journal detailing his relationship with Dolores, and a love letter from Charlotte—he admits that these items exist only in his memory. In addition, Humbert's account of his early infatuation with Annabel Leigh, which he uses to explain his sexual attraction to little girls, is transparently modeled on Edgar Allan Poe's 1849 poem "Annabel Lee." Poe's speaker recalls how, even though "*I* was a child and *she* was a child, in this kingdom by the sea," he and Annabel enjoyed "a love that was more than love" until "the winged seraphs of Heaven" envied them and killed her (Poe, pp. 957-58). Humbert describes the childhood romance with his Annabel, which also began at the seaside and ended with her sudden death, in similar imagery. Such blatant allusions to "Annabel Lee" seem especially suspicious because it turns out that Humbert is a Poe scholar.

Despite his unreliability, however, Humbert is a witty, amusing, and charming narrator. The fact that readers know only his version of events makes it easy to accept them on his terms. Indeed, Nabokov has designed *Lolita* so that readers cannot help but identify with Humbert, even though he is a child molester. The novel achieves this effect by suppressing Dolores's own point of view almost completely. Only at the end of his memoir does Humbert acknowledge that he deliberately tried to conceal her utter misery. "In order to enjoy my phantasms in peace," he now admits, "I firmly decided to ignore what I could not help perceiving, the fact that I was to her not a boy friend, not a glamour man, not a pal, not even a person at all, but just two eyes and a foot of engorged brawn—to mention only mention-

DID VIVIAN DARKBLOOM REALLY WRITE *LOLITA*?

Although Nabokov considered *Lolita* his best novel, he was afraid that it could never appear in print because of its subject matter. At one point he even decided to burn the manuscript in the backyard, but his wife stopped him at the last minute. Nabokov thought that if *Lolita* were published, it would have to be anonymously or under a pseudonym. In order to encode his actual authorship within the text, therefore, he introduced a minor character whose name, "Vivian Darkbloom," is an anagram of "Vladimir Nabokov." After Alfred Appel's edition of *The Annotated Lolita* appeared, Nabokov playfully reused the anagram, publishing his own annotations to a later novel, *Ada* (1969), under the name "Vivian Darkbloom."

able matters" (*Lolita*, p. 283). At this point, readers who accepted Humbert's earlier portrait of Dolores as sexually experienced, spoiled, shallow, uncooperative, ungrateful, and faithless must confront the fact that they too were indifferent to her suffering. Nabokov's novel thus forces readers to acknowledge their own prurient curiosity and smug condemnation, in response to a case that evokes many sensational news stories about troubled teens and poor parents in the 1950s.

Humbert's skillful and deceptive presentation of his case suggests an acute awareness of his audience. In fact, he continually interrupts his memoir to address readers directly. He asks for their pity, remarks that they will be disappointed to learn of his psychological instability, and teases them by promising to describe various sexual encounters and then skipping over such scenes, explaining that he does not want to "bore [his] learned readers with a detailed account" (*Lolita*, p. 133). (Significantly, masturbation is the only sexual act that the novel does describe in detail.)

In addition, because his memoir outlines his legal defense, Humbert often invokes his readers as jurors—"ladies and gentleman of the jury"—who will decide his fate (*Lolita*, p. 3). At the end of the novel, Humbert's readers must indeed determine his guilt or innocence. At a time when the United States was obsessed with charges of espionage, subversion, sexual deviancy, "un-American activities," and other forms of suspicious behavior, it is significant that *Lolita* takes the form of a criminal trial. Nabokov carefully constructed the novel, however, so that readers cannot settle for the simple, easy distinctions between right and wrong that most Americans accepted at the time. Rather than merely identifying Humbert as a sexual pervert, readers must decide for themselves the exact nature of his crime, whether he has truly acknowledged, repented, and atoned for it, and whether he really did love Dolores Haze. Indeed, Nabokov's attempt to make his readers ponder the moral, psychological, social, therapeutic, and legal implications of Humbert's behavior parallels contemporaneous efforts to understand sexual crime better. In 1950, for example, the California state legislature gave the Department of Mental Hygiene $100,000 to plan and perform scientific research into the reasons and cures for sexual deviation, including deviation that led to sex crimes against children. According to a sociologist at the time, "passage of the California Sexual Deviation Research Act . . . was most significant in that it highlights a new era in our thinking about human sexuality" (Mangus, p. 177).

Sources and literary context. Vladimir Nabokov disliked approaches to literature that focus on an imagined narrative's relation to real events, and claimed that his own novels were works of fiction, rather than social history or autobiography. Nevertheless, there are suggestive parallels between Humbert's romance with Annabel Leigh and Nabokov's own childhood infatuation with a little girl he calls "Colette"—whom he met at a seaside resort on the French Riviera—which he describes in his memoir, *Speak, Memory*.

Otherwise, *Lolita* seems most indebted to an earlier novella, *The Enchanter*, which Nabokov wrote (in Russian) in 1939, but which was neither published nor translated into English until after his death in 1977. More generally, *Lolita* derives from an international tradition of avant-garde, experimental, often sexually shocking fiction—such as James Joyce's *Ulysses*—that depicts an artist's social alienation. In America in the late 1940s and 1950s, in particular, such works included plays like Tennessee Williams's *A Streetcar Named Desire* (1947), novels like J. D. Salinger's *Catcher in the Rye* (1951), and poems like Allen Ginsburg's revolutionary and sexually explicit "Howl"(1956). (At the same time that *Lolita* resembles such works, its exuberant wordplay, parody, and subversive humor also led the way for American literature of the 1960s and 1970s.) While there is no evidence that *Lolita* is based on any actual people, it does reflect Nabokov's fascination with and detailed observations of American popular culture and codes of behavior in the decade after the Second World War.

Events in History at the Time the Novel Was Written

Troubled teens. Although the 1950s are often considered a period of great social conformity, important changes were afoot. Two such changes were the burgeoning youth culture—exemplified by the musical, social, and sexual rebellion of rock and roll—and the concerns that it prompted about disobedient or criminal teenagers. According to one social historian, "the teenager [came to replace] the Communist as the appropriate target for public controversy and foreboding" (Friedenberg in Breines, p. 8). Between 1946 and 1960, the number of teens in the United States more than doubled, from 5.6 million to

11.8 million. And with the increase in adolescents came an increase in delinquency: between 1948 and 1953, the number of juveniles charged with crimes rose 45 percent. In 1955 Benjamin Fine chose *1,000,000 Delinquents* as his title for a book on this phenomenon, because he believed that there were already one million adolescent criminals in the United States and would be twice that number by the decade's end. Although male hoodlums and gang members caused the most concern, female delinquents were also a source of worry. By 1949, girls accounted for one out of four juvenile court cases. In 1958, the year that *Lolita* finally appeared in the United States, Americans were especially horrified by the case of 14-year-old Caril Ann Fugate. After Caril Ann's boyfriend, Charles Starkweather, killed her entire family, the young couple embarked on a crime spree that left a trail of bodies throughout the Midwest. Charles Starkweather was executed for murder; Caril Ann, who maintained her innocence, was sentenced to life in prison but eventually paroled.

Commentators proposed various explanations for juvenile crime. In 1955, the United States Senate even formed a committee to investigate whether aspects of popular culture marketed to children and adolescents, including rock and roll, television shows, movies, comic books, and pulp fiction, were responsible for the alarming increase in juvenile delinquency. Most Americans believed, however, that the problem stemmed from a lack of guidance and discipline in the home. Hollywood films like *The Wild One* (1953) or *Rebel Without a Cause* (1955) and the Broadway musical *West Side Story* (1957) expressed parents' fears that they could not understand or control their own children. (In retrospect, these fears anticipated the "generation gap" that would divide the United States in the 1960s.) Sociologists associated female juvenile delinquency, in particular, with a troubled father-daughter relationship, and urged men to acknowledge their daughters' sexual maturity so that the girls would learn to become appropriately feminine.

The feminine mystique. Most women in the 1950s sought fulfillment in marriage rather than a career. Once married, they kept house, raised children, and participated in civic organizations and social clubs while their husbands worked. Popular television shows, such as *I Love Lucy* and *Leave It to Beaver*, suggested that women were happier at home than in the workplace. In 1963, though, Betty Friedan published *The Feminine Mystique*, a book that analyzed the psychological cost of women's attempts to model themselves after a "mystique" of femininity that stressed passivity and consumption.

During the 15 years after the Second World War, according to Friedan, American culture taught women to find happiness through marriage, motherhood, and domesticity. By the end of the 1950s, she points out, the average age of American brides had dropped into the teens. The proportion of female college students sank from 47 percent in 1920 to 35 percent in 1958. Of those women who did attend college in the 1950s, 60 percent dropped out, either to marry or because they feared that too much education would make them undesirable. The pressure to marry early led girls to start "going steady" at 12 or 13 and become engaged a few years later. Girls' clothing became more seductive, and advertisements emphasized youthful attractiveness. Meanwhile, adult women began dieting in an attempt to look like thin, young models; department store buyers reported that the average American woman had become three or four dress sizes smaller since 1939.

Friedan singles out the suburban housewife, in particular, as that generation's feminine ideal:

> In the fifteen years after World War II, this mystique of feminine fulfillment became the cherished and self-perpetuating core of contemporary American culture. Millions of women lived their lives in the image of those pretty pictures of the American suburban housewife, kissing their husbands goodbye in front of the picture window, depositing their stationwagonsful of children at school, and smiling as they ran the new electric waxer over the spotless kitchen floor.
>
> (Friedan, p. 16)

NABOKOV CALLS *LOLITA* "TRAGEDY," NOT "PORNOGRAPHY"

I know that *Lolita* is my best book so far. I calmly lean on my conviction that it is a serious work of art, and that no court could prove it to be "lewd and libertine." All categories grade, of course, into one another: a comedy of manners written by a fine poet may have its "lewd" side; but *Lolita* is a tragedy. "Pornography" is not an image plucked out of context; pornography is an attitude and an intention. The tragic and the obscene exclude each other. (Nabokov, Selected Letters, p. 184)

Friedan rejects this notion of the happy homemaker, arguing instead that being a housewife can make a woman feel a sense of inner emptiness, which she calls "the problem that has no name" (Friedan, p. 18). *The Feminine Mystique* led the way for the second wave of feminism—"women's liberation"—which became powerful in the early 1970s. In *Lolita*, Nabokov anticipates Friedan's analysis by revealing Charlotte Haze's boredom, frustration, and despair, as well as by tracing various experiences that Charlotte has. Meeting older men who find her sexually appealing and attending a school that stresses "the four D's: Dramatics, Dance, Debating and Dating" lead Dolores to marry as soon as she can. Tellingly, for both mother and daughter in Nabokov's novel, marriage seems to lead to death; the fictional foreword to the book indicates that Lolita dies in childbirth.

Reception. Because of its controversial subject, Nabokov was initially unable to publish *Lolita* in the United States. When the novel first appeared in print in 1955, it was as two slim green volumes in the "Traveller's Companion" series of pornography and avant-garde literature published by the Olympia Press in Paris. *Lolita* was considered obscene and could not be legally purchased in England or America, although readers managed to smuggle in copies from France. Only after critics published an excerpt and essays on the novel in the *Anchor Review*, without facing obscenity charges, did publication in the United States seem possible. *Lolita* was brought out by Doubleday, an American press, in 1958, and became an immediate bestseller as well as a critical success. Although a few schools, libraries, and townships banned the book, most readers apparently agreed with critic Lionel Trilling, who remarked at the time that "*Lolita* is not about sex, but about love" (Trilling, p. 15).

Since its initial publication, *Lolita* has been recognized as a major work of American literature. It has inspired a Broadway musical, two film adaptations, and a host of imitations. The Modern Library recently named it one of the five best novels of the twentieth century. Although *Lolita* has become a classic, however, it remains controversial. Adrian Lyne's 1997 film adaptation was not distributed for two years because companies were wary of being charged with disseminating child pornography. The novel remains timely, too, as Americans continue to grapple with the nature and treatment of child abuse. By means of its subtle and intricate design, *Lolita* forces readers to confront lasting questions about crime, punishment, and redemption in all their moral complexity.

—Susan Elizabeth Sweeney

For More Information

Boyd, Brian. *Vladimir Nabokov: The American Years*. Princeton, New Jersey: Princeton University Press, 1991.

Breines, Wini. *Young, White, and Miserable: Growing up Female in the Fifties*. Boston: Beacon, 1992.

Devlin, Rachel. "Female Juvenile Delinquency and the Problem of Sexual Authority in America, 1945-1965," in *Delinquents and Debutantes: Twentieth Century Girls' Cultures*. Ed. Sherrie Inness. New York: New York University Press, 1998.

de Young, Mary, comp. *Child Molestation: An Annotated Bibliography*. Jefferson, N.C.: McFarland, 1987.

Fine, Benjamin. *1,000,000 Delinquents*. Cleveland, Ohio: World, 1955.

Friedan, Betty. *The Feminine Mystique*. New York: W. W. Norton, 1963.

Mangus, A. R. "Sexual Deviation Research in California," in *Sociology and Social Research* 37, no. 3 (Jan.-Feb. 1953): 175-81.

May, Elaine Tyler. *Homeward Bound: American Families in the Cold War Era*. New York: Basic Books, 1988.

Nabokov, Vladimir. *The Annotated Lolita*. Ed. Alfred Appel Jr. Rev. edition. New York: Vintage, 1991.

———. *Selected Letters 1940-1977*. ed. Dmitri Nabokov and Matthew J. Bruccoli. New York: Harcourt Brace Jovanovich, 1989.

———. *Speak, Memory: An Autobiography Revisited*. New York: Vintage, 1989.

Poe, Edgar Allan. "Annabel Lee," in *Complete Tales and Poems*. New York: Vintage, 1975.

Trilling, Lionel. "The Last Lover: Vladimir Nabokov's *Lolita*," in *Encounter* 11 (October 1958): 9-19.

The Lone Ranger and Tonto Fistfight in Heaven

by
Sherman Alexie

Sherman J. Alexie, Jr. is of Spokane Indian ancestry on his mother's side and Coeur d'Alene Indian descent on his father's. A novelist, short-story writer, poet, filmmaker, and stand-up comedian, Alexie was born one of six siblings on October 7, 1966, and grew up in Wellpinit, Washington, located on the Spokane Indian Reservation approximately 50 miles northwest of Spokane. The author was born hydrocephalic—with water on the brain—and underwent major brain surgery when he was six months old. He was not expected to survive and suffered seizures through childhood. After receiving the same textbook his mother used when she attended the reservation's school, a sign of the decrepit state of reservation education, Alexie transferred to a school off the reservation to complete his high-school years. Alexie attended Gonzaga University in Spokane on a scholarship in 1985, spending two years there before transferring to Washington State University in Pullman. Soon after graduating with a degree in American Studies, Alexie received a Washington State Arts Commission Poetry Fellowship (1991) and a National Endowment for the Arts Poetry Fellowship (1992). In the past decade, he has composed three novels, nine books of poetry, two collections of short stories, and two screenplays. Entwining traditional and modern Indian life on the reservation, the 22 related stories in *The Lone Ranger and Tonto Fistfight in Heaven* offer a glimpse into the complex and varied identities of modern American Indians.

THE LITERARY WORK

A collection of 22 interlocked short stories, all centered around Wellpinit, Washington, the heart of the Spokane Indian Reservation, between 1966 and 1990; published in 1993.

SYNOPSIS

Alexie's short stories examine modern life on the Spokane Indian Reservation, focusing loosely on three characters: Victor Joseph, a former reservation basketball star and an on-and-off-the-wagon alcoholic; Junior Polatkin, a quiet and sometimes misdirected reservation youth; and Thomas Builds-the-Fire, a present-day tribal visionary whose stories draw guffaws and dismissals.

Events in History at the Time of the Short Stories

The reservation system. On February 21, 1928, Lewis Meriam, a well-educated statistician, submitted *The Problem of Indian Administration* to Hubert Work, secretary of the interior to the United States. The report, begun in November 1926, investigated the state of Indian health, education, and economic welfare, as well as the federal government's administration of these services when compared to those provided to non-Indians by private or public agencies. The Meriam Report, as it is commonly known, stated, "An overwhelming majority of the Indians are poor, even

Sherman Alexie

extremely poor, and they are not adjusted to the economic and social system of the dominant white civilization. The poverty of the Indians and their lack of adjustment to the dominant economic and social systems produce the vicious circle ordinarily found among any people under such circumstances" (Price, *Problem of Indian Administration*, p. 3). High infant mortality, extreme rates of disease, malnutrition, deplorable educational opportunity, and general poverty plagued American Indian reservations across the country. In the end, the report, despite its grim findings, would do little to change these conditions. During the presidencies of Herbert Hoover and Franklin D. Roosevelt (1929-1945), however, change was seen through the formulation of the Indian New Deal, which allowed Indians more self-governing powers and the right to practice cultural ceremonies and events. Still, life on most reservations since the Meriam Report has not altered dramatically. While tribes are able to practice their distinct cultural lifestyles freely, various health and educational needs remain unmet by the federal government. The Meriam Report is considered an important piece of history because it documents that the services provided to Indians by the federal government fell far short of those offered to non-Indians in the public and private sectors. The idea of the reservation began with the English colonizers, who removed native peoples to restricted tracts of land to open up white settlement areas. As early as 1638, the Puritans established reservations for New England tribes, such as the Quinnipiac of the New Haven, Connecticut, area. In addition to opening up land for Anglo settlement, early reservations provided places for missionaries to teach American Indians, sometimes by force, Western European ways of life. After the American colonies won their independence and the United States came into being, its federal government continued the policy of often-forced removal of tribes to restricted tracts of land.

Treaties between tribes and the United States typically stated that American Indians would receive pieces of land (where they would be expected to reside) in exchange for surrendering claims on vast territories. The lands on which native peoples often found themselves were not conducive to the sedentary lifestyles they were forced to adopt. Very few reservations contain fertile soil and fewer offer the means to maintain traditional tribal subsistence activities, such as hunting or fishing.

Regardless of the condition of the soil, federal authorities enforced yeomanry, or farming, on the reservations; they also forced Christian education on the tribes. U.S. troops were often called in to squash native religious ceremonies and practices, and American Indian children had to attend government-controlled and missionary schools that taught Christian principles and frowned on tribal pride or distinction. The last 50 years have seen fewer uses of military force on reservations, and religious ceremonies have slowly been legalized. Despite these changes, however, reservations remain geographically isolated and poverty-stricken. Life on the reservation was, and is, filled with both material and spiritual obstacles. "It's hard to be optimistic on the reservation," Alexie writes. "When a glass sits on a table here, people don't wonder if it's half filled or half empty. They just hope it's good beer" (Alexie, *The Lone Ranger and Tonto Fistfight in Heaven*, p. 49). Alexie's black humor often speaks to the bleakness of the reservation. The question for many reservation peoples, Alexie argues, is not one of optimism, but one of escape—through alcohol, in this instance—from the tragedy that so often surrounds them.

Still, the reservation is home to many tribal members and remains a place apart from mainstream society, where an independent identity can be preserved. "Notwithstanding the oppression and land loss associated with their founding, reservations also represent a valiant struggle on the part of Indians for autonomy, self-sufficiency, religious freedom, and cultural identity" (Riding in, "Reservations," p. 546). While Indian Country (communities with a predominantly American Indian population) faces problems, it is a place where tribal traditions grow and change, a place where kinship and identity surmount poverty and isolation. As Alexie described in an interview, "Even my worst enemies will pick me up if my car breaks down on the reservation" (Alexie, "Screenwriter"). Moreover, conditions promise to improve to some degree in the future. With the development of gaming facilities on many reservations across the United States, including the Spokane Reservation where Sherman Alexie grew up, economic and cultural independence is on the rise.

The Spokane Reservation, created in 1881, consists of 155,000 acres and is home to approximately 1,500 people (roughly another 1,500 tribal members live off the reservation). By tradition, the Spokane Indians base their livelihood on fishing; many of their customs center on salmon. But the development of the Little Falls Dam in 1908 and the Grand Coulee Dam in 1935 stopped all salmon migration to the reservation. Today the reservation runs a fish hatchery, which stocks the Spokane River with salmon and trout.

The Spokane War. The Spokane first encountered Europeans when the Lewis and Clark Expedition passed among them in 1805. In 1846 and 1853, the tribe, along with other tribes on the Plateau, experienced two smallpox epidemics that may have wiped out as much as half the area's tribal population. Around this time, gold was discovered in California and along the West Coast, attracting missionaries and settlers to the region. The interactions among settlers, missionaries, and natives deteriorated through the 1850s, culminating in the Spokane War of 1858. On May 6, 1858, Lieutenant Colonel Edward J. Steptoe along with "two companies of infantry and three of dragoons," left Fort Walla Walla (located near present-day Walla Walla in southeast Washington, near the Oregon border). Heading for Colville, Steptoe intended to impress (and threaten) the area's Indians with the U.S. Army's might. "His force included 152 men, 5 officers, and a few civilian men," as well as a few howitzers (Ruby and Brown, p. 109). Near Spokane on May 16, the men were met by approximately 1,000 Indians of Spokane, Palouse, Yakima, and Coeur d'Alene descent ready to do battle. They had assembled to protest the Missouri-to-Columbia road, a government plan to cut through native lands and open the area to increased settlement. After being told to return home, Steptoe and his soldiers started heading back to the fort. At dawn the next day, the Indians ambushed Steptoe and his soldiers as punishment for their ill-intended trip, killing two officers and many others in the ten-hour battle. The remainder of the command escaped that night, returning to Fort Walla Walla. As Alexie's storyteller Thomas Builds-the-Fire explains in "The Trial of Thomas Builds-the-Fire,"

> They [Steptoe and his men] tried to negotiate a peace, but our war chiefs would not settle for anything short of blood. You must understand these were days of violence and continual lies from the white man. Steptoe said he wanted peace between whites and Indians, but he had cannons and had lied before, so we refused to believe him this time.
>
> (*Lone Ranger*, p. 100)

In retribution for this attack, Colonel George Wright and his Nez Perce allies began a vigorous campaign against these same tribes later that year. The Battle of the Four Lakes transpired on September 1 and took with it a large number of Indian casualties (as the Indians carried off their dead, it was difficult to ascertain an exact body count). A few days later, on September 5, the two sides fought the Battle of Spokane Plains, which left many more natives dead than whites. The Army had scored a second victory.

In ruthless pursuit of the resistant Plateau Indians, Wright chased the defiant warriors through the Spokane Valley, burning any belongings or foodstuffs he encountered along the way. On September 8 Wright and his men came across 800 to 900 horses belonging to members of the various tribes. While he left approximately 200 horses to officers, quartermasters, and the Nez Perce allies, Wright ordered the remaining animals killed outright, ignoring frontier laws that made horse slaughter a crime:

> [T]he soldiers built a log corral. One by one, they took the horses from the corral to a river bar. There the older ones were shot singly and the colts knocked in the head, causing the brood mares to neigh in the night. This process proving too slow, two companies lined up on the banks and fired volleys into the corral. Two more companies were later detailed to shoot the rest of the horses, until a gruesome total of about 690 horses had been killed.
>
> (Ruby and Brown, p. 137)

Evidence of the criminal execution would lay in plain sight. For years, piles of bleached bones could be viewed at the location, which settlers began referring to as Wright's Boneyard. Wright was never penalized for his crimes, as the United States deemed it his duty to rid the frontier of what the United States saw as a threat to their future settlement in the area.

The official end to the Spokane War came with the hanging of Qualchan, a Yakima warrior with a militant attitude toward whites, whom he thought of as thieves and liars. In late September, Wright called for a meeting of tribal leaders involved in the recent battles. Among the leaders who agreed to Wright's terms of surrender was Owhi, a Upper Yakima chief and father of Qualchan. Wright placed the elder in chains and sent word to his son that if Qualchan did not meet Wright at his camp, his father would be hanged. When Qualchan arrived on the morning of September 25 he, not his father, was immediately hanged. The creek along which the warrior was killed is still called Hangman's Creek.

In one of the short stories, the tribesman Thomas Builds-the-Fire takes on Qualchan's persona: "The City of Spokane is now building a golf course name after me, Qualchan, located in that valley where I was hanged" (*Lone Ranger,* p. 99). Indeed, The Creek at Qualchan Golf Course is the newest of the city's public courses and, as its promotional materials attest, the course sits alongside winding Hangman Creek.

HUMOR AND THE AMERICAN INDIAN

American Indians often reached for humor to lighten the oppressive forces of American history that they have built up a storehouse of choice sayings and observations:

Being Indian is . . .

. . . Watching John Wayne whip 50 of your kind with a single shot pistol and a rusty pocket knife on the late show.

. . . Having every third person you meet tell you about his great grand-mother who was a real Cherokee princess.

. . . "Graduating" from a reservation high school and not being able to read an 8th grade English book from your white urban friends' school.

. . . Never drinking alone.

. . . Meeting at least two dozen anthropologists before you're 21.

(Lincoln, pp. 315-19)

American Indian humor. Despite the atrocities of the soldiers such as Wright, or maybe because of them, American Indians have developed a distinct brand of humor that draws on details of Indian life. Sometimes the humor may be tribe-specific, such as when Alexie's Victor quips, "Ain't no salmon left in our river. Just a school bus and a few hundred basketballs." When asked to elaborate, Victor explains, "Our basketball team drives into the river and drowns every year. . . . It's tradition" (*Lone Ranger*, p. 39). In other words, instead of salmon, the customary Spokane staple, cultural nourishment now comes from basketball. Of course, the basketball players do not truly drown themselves each year, though they often sabotage their future by leaving the sport behind and falling prey to alcohol, teen angst, and depression. Apart from the tribe-specific humor, there is a general brand of comic relief, one that crosses tribal lines. Vine Deloria, Jr., a Standing Rock Sioux, jokes, "It is said that when Columbus landed, one Indian turned to another and said, 'Well, there goes the neighborhood'" (Deloria, p. 148).

Certainly Indian humor has helped tribal members better digest their oppressive history and continues to help them confront the challenges they now face. "When a people can laugh at themselves and laugh at others and hold all aspects of life together without letting anybody drive them to extremes, then it seems to me that that people can survive," observed Deloria (Deloria, p. 167).

In fact, native humor has a traditional tribal base. Kenneth Lincoln states in *Indi'n Humor* that Indians draw on "millennia-old traditions of the Trickster gods and holy fools, comic romance and epic boast" in order to revitalize themselves and survive current hardships (Lincoln, p. 22). Trickster figures, deceptive and contradictory spiritual beings, abound in American Indian mythology. Often a tribe's spiritual universe largely revolves around such a trickster figure. Of course, each trickster possesses features particular to the tribe, but certain features pertain to North American Indian tricksters across tribes.

Tricksters are frequently male animals. Some of the more common include the coyote, raven, rabbit, and turtle. Typically central to Native American religions, the trickster often creates the world through a series of lucky mishaps. As a religious liaison, tricksters are Merlins of sorts, messengers between the spirit and the human worlds. In addition, tricksters are teachers. American Indians have used trickster stories for centuries to teach morals and survival tips to children. For example, a trickster who disguises himself for some gain (to gain money or win a woman, for example) may be used to teach children the value of honesty, humility, and self-acceptance. A trickster's penchant for trouble and appetite for food, sex, and other indulgences give him attributes comparable to various types of human desires and blunders. The balance and humor that the trickster possesses lie at the core of many American Indian communities and religions. Just as many tribal societies were once organized to provide balance between men and women, between work and play, and between religion and the mundane, they often incorporated humor into beliefs that are quite serious and sacred. Trickster gives concrete shape to these ideas.

The Spokane's trickster is Coyote, a major creative force in the tribe's spiritual beliefs. Alexie mentions Coyote several times in the short stories that comprise *The Lone Ranger and Tonto Fistfight in Heaven* and a trickster spirit pervades his work. Thomas's grandfather Samuel Builds-the-Fire, the focus of "A Train Is an Order of Occurrence Designed to Lead to Some Result," spins stories that make the flat everyday world into something more interesting. He recites a Coyote story to himself:

> "Listen," Samuel said. "Coyote, who is the creator of all of us, was sitting on his cloud the day after he created the Indians. . . . *This is good*, he kept saying to himself. But he was bored . . . so he decided to clip his toenails. He clipped his right toenails and held the clippings in his right hand. Then he clipped his left toenails and added those clippings to the ones already in his right hand. He looked around and around his cloud for somewhere to throw away his clippings. . . . Then he accidentally dropped his toenail clipping over the side of the cloud and they fell to earth. The clippings burrowed into the ground like seeds and grew up to be the white man. Coyote, he looked down at his newest creation and said, *Oh, shit*."
>
> (*Lone Ranger*, pp. 134-35)

Like Samuel, Alexie uses humor in his short stories to lighten the harness of life. "Do you believe laughter can save us?" the unnamed narrator asks the reader in "Imagining the Reservation." "All I know is that I count coyotes to help me sleep" (*Lone Ranger*, p. 152).

Book cover from the 1993 edition of *The Lone Ranger and Tonto Fistfight in Heaven.*

The Short Stories in Focus

The plots. Sherman Alexie claims that all his characters are pieces and parts of him, making the 22 stories in *The Lone Ranger and Tonto Fistfight in Heaven* somewhat autobiographical. The characters who host most of the stories are Victor, a dried-up reservation basketball star and fair-weather alcoholic; Thomas, "a storyteller that nobody wanted to listen to"; and Junior, a kind man with alcoholic tendencies (*Lone Ranger*, p. 61).

An exploration of Victor's dysfunctional childhood, the story "Every Little Hurricane" studies the effects of alcoholism and poverty on children. Nine-year-old Victor's private hurricanes consist of drunken arguments, violent outbreaks, and uncomfortable solitude. "Victor had seen the news footage of cities after hurricanes had passed by. . . . Memories not destroyed, but forever changed and damaged. . . . Victor wanted to know if memories of his personal hurricanes would be better if he could change them" (*Lone Ranger*, p. 4). The most dramatic "hurricane" of Victor's traumatic childhood drops down during his parent's New Year's Eve party. Throughout most of the story, the child sits in his room, watching the party's action from his window. His fists clinch as he watches two Indians—his uncles—fall into a violent drunken brawl, an episode that affects everyone at the party: "But there was other pain. Victor knew that . . . One molar ached from cavity; his chest throbbed with absence" (*Lone Ranger*, p. 4). When Victor finds his alcoholic parents passed out in the bedroom during the party, he climbs between them, hoping their liquored-up sweat will put him to sleep.

Thomas, an unnoticed tribal visionary, rides through history and sees life the way no other character in the collection can. In the story "The Trial of Thomas Builds-the-Fire," he transforms into characters from the tribe's past, trying to escape the claws of the Bureau of Indian Affairs (BIA), which plans to have him shipped off to prison for "threaten[ing] to make significant changes to the tribal vision" (*Lone Ranger*, p. 93). In other words, tribal members might begin to listen to Thomas's stories, which describe Spokane history and a distinct Indian reality. This would empower them, making them a threat to the federal government, which, it is implied, tries to keep native peoples from gaining self-sufficiency. As the only witness to his crimes, he takes the stand and speaks of being a pony captured by Colonel Wright on September 8, 1858. While he is spared, he watches 600 of his brothers and sisters slaughtered by white gunfire. One rider after another tries to break the pony, but he bucks all of them off, until the men concede. "It was glorious. . . . They could not break me. Some may have wanted to kill me for my arrogance, but others respected my anger, my refusal to admit defeat. I lived that day, even escaped Colonel Wright, and galloped into other histories" (*Lone Ranger*, p. 98). Qualchan, a great Yakima warrior hanged by Colonel Wright, speaks through Thomas, then through Wild Coyote, a young Spokane fighting Colonel Steptoe's soldiers. As Thomas tells his stories, the courtroom fills with tribal members, who listen to his tales for the first and last time. The district judge ships Thomas to Walla Walla State Penitentiary the next day. What he is convicted of is never made clear in the story (the omission is no doubt a statement about the unfair treatment of native peoples). In any case, it is obvious that because of his powerful Indian storytelling, "There is no possibility of parole" (*Lone Ranger*, p. 102).

"Jesus Christ's Half-Brother Is Alive and Well on the Spokane Indian Reservation" is perhaps the most complex story in the collection. Junior, through a series of mishaps, adopts a newborn. The tribe calls the infant James; his real name is "unpronounceable in Indian and English, but it means: *He Who Crawls Silently Through the Grass with a Small Bow and One Bad Arrow Hunting for Enough Deer to Feed the Whole Tribe*" (*Lone Ranger*, p. 111). Written in a journal-like format, the story consists of separate entries, each representing an event in James's life and a step toward Junior's salvation. James remains mute for the first six years of his life, but Junior is convinced the problem will resolve itself: "I see in his eyes a voice, and I see in his eyes a whole new set of words" (*Lone Ranger*, p. 115). When James finally speaks on Christmas in 1973, he offers wisdom and guidance to Junior, whose recovery from alcoholism leaves him "shaking and quaking and needing just one more beer before I stop for good" (*Lone Ranger*, p. 128).

The complexity and importance of basketball, an incredibly popular sport on many Indian reservations, is not lost on Alexie, who mentions it in nearly every short story in *The Lone Ranger and Tonto Fistfight in Heaven*. In particular, "The Only Traffic Signal on the Reservation Doesn't Flash Red Anymore," which eavesdrops on Victor and his friend Adrian as they pass the day on the reservation, offers a glimpse into the sport's importance. Included in a group of Indian kids walking by ("I'd like to think there were ten of them. But there were actually only four or five," Victor relates) is Julius Windmaker, the best basketball player on the reservation. Julius, who has "those fingers like a goddamn medicine man," is drunk by the close of the story (*Lone Ranger*, p. 44). "A year later, Adrian and I sat on the same porch in the same chairs. . . . We sat there for a few minutes, hours, and then Julius Windmaker staggered down the road" (Lone *Ranger*, p. 50). Affected by the reservation's grim circumstances, Julius never makes pro. The story suggests that the poverty of reservation life defeats Julius at the outset—he begins drinking before the possibility of a pro-basketball career is even a fantasy.

BASKETBALL—RESERVATION STYLE

"Late summer night on the Spokane Indian Reservation. Ten Indians are playing basketball on a court barely illuminated by the streetlight above them. They will play until the brown, leather ball is invisible in the dark. They will play until an errant pass jams a finger, knocks a pair of glasses off a face, smashes a nose and draws blood. They will play until the ball bounces off the court and disappears into the shadows."

(Alexie, "The Unauthorized Biography of Me," p. 4)

Other characters speckle the collection, telling their stories and making the work a true tribal narrative, arising straight from the reservation. The multiple voices and many tales are connected so deeply that it is difficult to pull them apart. Alexie's ability to weave humor and tragedy among a large number of characters harkens back to tribal Coyote lore, which brings together the spiritual and the secular, the laughable and the serious. Certainly Alexie is employing such Spokane traditions in his modern storytelling.

The stories range in length and style. Journal entries, historical documents, dreams, newspaper clippings, and court transcripts offer a sometimes magical, sometimes horribly realistic depiction of Indian life at the turn of the twenty-first century. Each piece examines modern warriors paralyzed by years of colonization, corruption, drinking, and discrimination. The end result is a world in which cars drive only in reverse, basketball is a new religion, and hurricanes touch down in the interior of Washington State in the middle of winter without notice (as in "Every Little Hurricane").

Basketball and sport. "Indians kind of see ballplayers as saviors," Victor narrates. "I mean, if basketball would have been around, I'm sure Jesus would've been the best point guard in Nazareth" (*Lone Ranger*, p. 52). Indeed, basketball ranks first among other popular sports on Indian reservations in the United States. The court and ring offer an economic way to socialize and an opportunity to bring new heroes into the tribal fold.

Sporting activities have long played a central role in tribal identity, although there has been wide variation in the nature of the activities from tribe to tribe throughout history. Often the tribes tied ceremony to sports: "In many societies, months of physical training, along with dietary practices, took place prior to major races or ball games. . . . Among many tribes, the ritual and ceremony surrounding these contests appear to have been as important as the contest itself" (Oxendine, p. 11). Among these sports, ball games, such as lacrosse, invented by tribes along the East Coast, and shinny, an early form of hockey played across Native America, have probably been the most valued and widespread. And while one version of history claims basketball was invented by Scottish-American James Naismith in 1861, Alexie's Junior watches Indian kids shooting hoops and argues, "basketball was invented by an Indian long before that Naismith guy ever thought of it" (*Lone Ranger*, p. 127). The reference may be to a sixteenth-century game—ollamalitzl—played by the Aztec Indians of Mexico, the object being to shoot a solid rubber ball through a stone ring positioned on a side of a stadium. Even earlier the Olmec Indians played pok-to-pok, a tenth century game that called for dropping a round object though a stationary ring.

NOTABLE AMERICAN INDIAN ATHLETES

George Armstrong (b. 1930)
Ojibway
Professional hockey player for the Toronto Maple Leafs (21-year career 1949-1971)

Charles A. "Chief" Bender (1883-1954)
Chippewa
Pitcher for the Philadelphia Athletics (1903-1917)
Pitched a no-hitter in 1911

Hawk Chief (early 1850s-?)
Pawnee
First sub-four-minute runner in recorded history (unofficial)

Jack Jacobs (1919-1974)
Creek
Quarterback for the University of Oklahoma football team
Professional football player for the Washington Redskins and Green Bay Packers

William M. "Billy" Mills (b. 1938)
Oglala Sioux
Olympic Gold-Medallist in 10,000-meter run (1964)

Jessie B. Renick (b. 1917)
Choctaw
Forward for the Oklahoma A & M basketball team
Captain of the U.S. Olympic basketball team of 1948, which won the gold medal

Allie P. Reynolds (b. 1917)
Creek
Major League baseball player for the Cleveland Indians (1942-1946) and New York Yankees (1947-1954)

Jim Thorpe (1888-1953)
Sac and Fox
Olympic Gold-Medallist in Track and Field (1912)
Professional football and major league baseball player

Modern reservation basketball has garnered substantial attention over the past decade. *Sports Illustrated* devoted at least two articles to American Indian ballplayers in the early 1990s, a trend that would continue after Alexie's stories were published. Former Los Angeles Laker player Kareem Abdul-Jabar would spend the 1998-99 basketball season coaching the Alchesay High School Falcons of the White Mountain Apache Reservation. While a number of people are following the trend, no Indian has ever played on a National Basketball Association team. One of the *Sports Illustrated* articles describes a basketball frenzy among the Crow, mentioning a "Sean Fitzer, who averaged 29.8 points a game as a senior in 1989, shot 68% from the field and was valedictorian of his class at Plenty Coups High School [on the Crow Reservation in Montana], did not receive a letter of interest from a single university" (Smith, p. 65).

Playing basketball on the reservation—and off the reservation against area public schools—remains popular nevertheless. Adopting the sport, the Indians infuse certain rites into it that have made it their own.

> Some players tucked tiny medicine bundles . . . inside their socks or tied them to their jerseys, the way warriors once had tied them to their braids before entering battle. Some burned cedar and prayed before big games. The same drum cadence and honor songs used 200 years ago . . . now reverberated through gymnasiums and community halls at the capture of a basketball trophy.
>
> (Smith, pp. 64-65)

It is through basketball that a number of American Indians (men and women), battle to heal scars wrought by years of colonization, finding through the sport the status and recognition that have long been their due. Tribal teams face largely non-Indian public schools in the area and are able to show pride in their heritage and traditions. Tribal fame, not outside influence, commands the life of a reservation sports star. Reservation players are known to and admired by most reservation residents, heightened to an almost divine status.

Alexie brings basketball's importance into most of his stories, particularly "The Only Traffic Signal on the Reservation Doesn't Flash Red Anymore," discussed above. Julius, a flash-in-the-pan reservation hoop player, like those who came before him, leaves a mark on the reservation's new tribal stories, which now incorporate ballplayers. His playing raises him to rez-style superstar status. As Victor clarifies,

> In the outside world, a person can be a hero one second and a nobody the next. Think about it. Do white people remember the names of those guys who dove into that icy river to rescue passengers from that plane wreck a few years back? Hell, white people don't even remember the names of the dogs who save entire families from burning up in house fires by barking. And, to be honest, I don't remember none of those names either, but a reservation hero is remembered. A reservation hero is a hero forever. In fact, their status grows over the years as the stories are told and retold.
>
> (*Lone Ranger*, p. 48)

The stories about these players become part of American Indian oral tradition, a vibrant, expanding tradition, one that incorporates people of the moment into the reservation, one generation at a time.

American Indians and alcohol. The son of two alcoholics (one recovering), Sherman Alexie is a recovering alcoholic himself. He gave up alcohol at age 23 and has not had a drink since. While many Indian authors before him have dealt with the taboo issue, Alexie confronts it head on without regret or apology. *The Lone Ranger and Tonto Fistfight in Heaven* is soaked with characters whose relationship with alcohol is complicated and deeply felt.

"I was conceived during one of those drunken nights, half of me formed by my father's whiskey sperm, the other half formed by my mother's vodka egg," explains Victor in one of the short stories (*Lone Ranger*, p. 24). Certainly he is not alone. "[A]lcohol abuse and alcoholism combine to be the leading cause of mortality" among Indians (May, p. 229). The Indian Health Service, an agency within the U.S. Department of Health and Human Services, reports that between 1986 and 1988, 17 to 19 percent of all Indian deaths were probably alcohol-related, compared to the general U.S. average of 4.7 percent (May, p. 228). Similarly, Fetal Alcohol Syndrome, a serious health condition caused by alcohol use during pregnancy, is also of major concern on many Indian reservations. Children with Fetal Alcohol Syndrome often suffer mental problems, facial deformities, growth deficiency, and central nervous system dysfunction. A recent study indicates that, "The Centers for Disease Control and Prevention Birth Defects Monitoring Program reported an FAS rate, based on hospital diagnosis, among Indians that was 33 times the rate among Whites for the years 1981 to 1986" (Rhoades, p. 143). Thus, alcohol-related problems are indeed severe among American Indian peoples, but a multitude of misconceptions and stereotypes exist about the issue.

First and most basically, not all Indians abuse alcohol. While each of Alexie's characters has a relationship to alcohol, it is not always a dependent one. There are several characters who do not drink, or have switched from hard liquor to Pepsi:

> "I'm thirsty," Adrian said. "Give me a beer."
> "How many times do I have to tell you? We don't drink anymore."
> "Shit," Adrian said. "I keep forgetting. Give me a goddamn Pepsi."
> "That's a whole case for you today already."
> "Yeah, yeah, fuck these substitute addictions."
> (*Lone Ranger*, p. 50)

Secondly, evidence indicates that alcohol use varies from tribe to tribe. In some tribes, including the Navajo and Standing Rock Sioux, drinking prevalence is lower than it is for the general U.S. population. For other tribes on other reservations, such as the Southern Ute and Broken Head Ojibwa, adult drinking is more common than for the general American population (May, p. 231).

Probably one of the grossest misconceptions regarding Indians and liquor is that native peoples are genetically predisposed to alcoholism, or that they metabolize alcohol more slowly than other ethnic groups, which makes them more vulnerable to addiction. This myth is almost completely unsubstantiated: "Only one study ever reported that Indians metabolize alcohol more slowly than non-Indians, but it was criticized as highly flawed in its use of controls and other methods" (May, p. 229).

Such stereotypes have deeply affected the way American Indians have perceived themselves over the years. This effect surfaces in Alexie's stories, when James, Junior's adopted son, who has been silent for the first six years of his life, finally speaks to his dad: "He says he and I don't have the right to die for each other and that we should be living for each other instead. He says the world hurts. He says the first thing he wanted after he was born was a shot of whiskey" (*Lone Ranger*, p. 128). He refers to an impulse to drink in order to blot out the bleakness of modern Indian reality, a bleakness into which infants are born. Of course, the alcohol is debilitating. As depicted in these stories, it often robs the Indians of power and makes them pull each other into helpless voids of dependence and addiction.

Alexie's "A Train Is an Order of Occurrence Designed to Lead to Some Result" is a fictional study of alcoholism's development. Samuel Builds-the-Fire, Thomas's grandfather, loses his job as a hotel maid at Spokane's Third Avenue Motel on his birthday. While Samuel did not yet drink, he had "watched his brothers and sisters, most of his tribe fall into alcoholism and surrendered dreams" (*Lone Ranger*, p. 133). Years of dismal wages, discrimination, detached relatives, and dashed hopes, however, finally take him over. From Third Avenue Motel he takes himself to the Midway Tavern. Ordering his first beer, Samuel drinks deeply:

> *I understand everything*, Samuel thought. He knew all about how it begins; he knew he wanted to live this way now.
>
> With each glass of beer, Samuel gained a few ounces of wisdom, courage. But after a while, he began to understand too much about fear and failure, too. At the halfway point of any drunken night, there is a moment when an Indian realizes he cannot turn back toward tradition and that he has no map to guide him toward the future.
> (*Lone Ranger*, p. 134)

Sources. The Blackfeet/Gros Ventre writer James Welch, *The Brady Bunch*, and folksy countryman Hank Williams top Alexie's jumbled list of influences. Old Westerns and Western-influenced television have affected Alexie's writing (as evident from the title of his novel). Alexie mentions American popular culture as it fits into modern Indian life. In "Because My Father Always Said He Was the Only Indian Who Saw Jimi Hendrix Play 'The Star-Spangled Banner' at Woodstock," for example, Victor says,

> During the sixties, my father was the perfect hippie, since all the hippies were trying to be Indians. Because of that, how could anyone recognize that my father was trying to make a social statement?
> (*Lone Ranger*, p. 24)

The observation here is that hippies of the 1960s tried to be like Indians, an astute perception coming from the knowing vantage point of an Indian writer.

Alexie's literary influences include Stephen King, John Steinbeck, his mother, and his grandmother. He also recognizes native writers who broke literary ground before him. *The Lone Ranger and Tonto Fistfight in Heaven* is dedicated to four Indian authors "whose words and music have made mine possible": Adrian Louis (Paiute), Joy Harjo (Muskogee), Leslie Marmon Silko (Laguna Pueblo), and Simon Ortiz (Acoma Pueblo).

Certainly life on the Spokane Indian Reservation has played the most prominent role in shaping Alexie's art. One of the first Spokane writers to garner national recognition, he has drawn heavily from his experiences growing up on the reservation in Washington to do so. His work brings traditional Spokane storytelling into the present, even as it brings modern-day tales about the Spokane into the fold of native storytelling.

Reception. *The Lone Ranger and Tonto Fistfight in Heaven* won the PEN/Hemingway Award for Best First Book of Fiction, the Lila Wallace-Reader's Digest Writers' Award, and the Washington State Governor's Writers Award. Most critics greeted *The Lone Ranger and Tonto Fistfight in Heaven* with laudatory reviews. "Alexie blends an almost despairing social realism with jolting flashes of visionary fantasy and a quirky sense of gallows humor," Carl L. Bankston III wrote of the book in *The Bloomsbury Review* (Bankston, *Bloomsburg Review* p. 11). There were a number of mixed reviews, by critics like Reynolds Price, who wondered in *The New York Times Book Review*, "Has Sherman Alexie moved too fast for his present strength?" But in the same review, Price applauded the cumulative effect of the collection:

> Sherman Alexie has a striking lyric power to lament and praise that same crucial strain of modern American life—the oldest and most unendingly punished strain, the Native American, as it's been transformed for many Indians through a long five centuries of brutal reduction to powerlessness and its lethal companions: alcoholism, malnutrition, and suicidal self-loathing.
>
> (Price, "One Indian Doesn't Tell Another," p. 16)

—Amy M. Ware

For More Information

Alexie, Sherman. *The Lone Ranger and Tonto Fistfight in Heaven*. New York: HarperCollins, 1993.

———. "Screenwriter Identifies with Character in *Smoke Signals*," *Seattle Times*. 28 June 1998. http://www.seattletimes.com (3 July 2002).

———. "The Unauthorized Biography of Me." In *Here First: Autobiographical Essays by Native American* Writers. Ed. by Arnold Krupat, and Brian Swann. New York: The Modern Library, 2000.

Bankston III, Carl L. Review of *The Lone Ranger and Tonto Fistfight in Heaven*, *The Bloomsbury Review* 13, no. 5 (Sept.-Oct. 1993):11.

Deloria, Vine, Jr. *Custer Died for Your Sins: An Indian Manifesto*. New York: The Macmillan Company, 1969.

Lincoln, Kenneth. *Indi'n Humor: Bicultural Play in Native America*. New York: Oxford University Press, 1993.

May, Philip A. "The Epidemiology of Alcohol Abuse among American Indians: The Mythical and Real Properties." In *Contemporary Native American Cultural Issues*. Ed. Duane Champagne. Walnut Creek, Calif.: AltaMira Press, 1999.

Oxendine, Joseph B. *American Indian Sports Heritage*. Lincoln: University of Nebraska Press, 1995.

Price, Reynolds. "One Indian Doesn't Tell Another." in *The New York Times Book Review*, 17 October 1993, 15-16.

———. *The Problem of Indian Administration*. New York: Johnson Reprint Corporation, 1971.

Rhoades, Everett R., ed. *American Indian Health: Innovations in Health Care, Promotion, and Policy*. Baltimore: John Hopkins University Press, 2000.

Riding In, James. "Reservations." In *Encyclopedia of North American Indians*. Ed. Frederick E. Hoxie. New York: Houghton Mifflin, 1996.

Ruby, Robert H., and John A. Brown. *The Spokane Indians: Children of the Sun*. Norman: University of Oklahoma Press, 1970.

Smith, Gary. "Shadow of a Nation." *Sports Illustrated*, 18 February 1991, 60.

The Lord of the Rings

by

J. R. R. Tolkien

J. R. R. Tolkien's literary reputation rests almost entirely on a single work, his massive novel *The Lord of the Rings*. His novel ***The Hobbit*** (1937; also in *Literature and Its Times*), a short, equally popular novel intended mainly for children, is a prelude to the longer work. Born in 1892 in Bloemfontein, South Africa, but reared (from the age of 4) in Birmingham, England, Tolkien was a scholar of the Anglo-Saxon language by trade. His work on *The Lord of the Rings* took more than a decade, not least because of his time-consuming duties at Oxford University, where he was Professor of English Language and Literature. Although his fiction was influenced by the northern traditions of epic and saga, it was also profoundly shaped by twentieth-century events: World War I, in which he fought, and the rise, during the 1920s and 1930s, of Nazi Germany and Fascist Italy. Through the creation of Middle Earth, an imaginary world, Tolkien's *Lord of the Rings* meditates on a series of modern dilemmas: the evils of authoritarian power, the horrors of total war, and how necessary it is for good people to resist such evils and horrors. It was during a cataclysmic period in his own time that Tolkien gave rise to a fantasy preoccupied with these particular dilemmas.

THE LITERARY WORK

A fantasy novel set in the imaginary world of Middle Earth at a distant but unspecified time; written during World War II and published in three separate volumes in 1954-55.

SYNOPSIS

Amidst an epic confrontation between Good and Evil, two hobbits (short man-like creatures) attempt to destroy a ring of power and thereby avert world conquest by the satanic Sauron.

Events in History at the Time of the Novel

Tolkien's disclaimer. *The Lord of the Rings* is a work of fantasy, and Middle Earth is an imaginary world, belonging to no specific time or place. In addition, Tolkien, who despised allegory and "topical reference," was adamant that no direct connections be drawn between the events of his novel and those of recent European history. Thus he could claim that, though his novel was written during World War II, "the real war does not resemble the legendary war in its process or conclusion" (Tolkien, *The Lord of the Rings,* p. xvi). That having been said, *The Lord of the Rings* is emphatically a work of the twentieth century, and bears the scars of its major upheavals.

The war in the trenches. Germany declared war on Serbia on July 28, 1914. Russia, along with its ally France, quickly responded in Serbia's defense. Within a week, all of the major European powers were embroiled in World War I, England entering the fray on August 3. The immediate pretext for England's decision was a German in-

J. R. R. Tolkien

vasion of neutral Belgium, which in fact was part of a broader German attack on France. The deeper causes of conflict were a tangle of economic and political interests, formalized by treaties and alliances, that bound England to France and Russia against Germany, Austria-Hungary, and the Ottoman Empire. By the time it was over, four years later, World War I had claimed the lives of more than 750,000 British soldiers; more than 2 million had been wounded.

After a volatile start, with rapid German advances and equally rapid retreats, the war quickly reached a stalemate. Beginning with the winter of 1914, each army faced the other from a system of heavily fortified trenches, parallel lines—German on one side, British and French on the other—that extended south from the North Sea coast of Belgium to the border of neutral Switzerland. Paul Fussell estimates that, between them, the opponents constructed more than 25,000 miles of trenches. "Theoretically," Fussell comments, "it would have been possible to walk from Belgium to Switzerland entirely underground" (Fussell, p. 27). The zone between the enemy lines, at its narrowest no more than a few hundred yards, was "No Man's Land": a sodden landscape destroyed by artillery and littered with armaments and dead bodies. In his memoir of the war, the poet and novelist Robert Graves recalls patrolling this area:

> We planned our rushes from shell-hole to shell-hole, the opportunities being provided by artillery or machine-gun fire, which would distract the sentries. Many of the craters contained the corpses of men who had been wounded and crept in there to die. Some were skeletons, picked clean by the rats.
>
> (Graves, pp. 138-39)

The "Western Front," as it was called, did not move more than ten miles during four years of fighting. Instead, the armies engaged in a war of attrition, a slow wearing down of enemy forces, punctuated by bloody but largely unsuccessful attempts at advance.

The battle of the Somme earned a particular notoriety for futility and gore. On the morning of July 1, 1916, in broad daylight, British troops advanced across No Man's Land towards the German lines, walking forward from their trenches in even, orderly rows. A heavy bombardment of the German trenches had failed to dislodge the enemy troops, or even to break through the barbed wire that fronted those trenches.

So the advancing British faced an enemy at the ready, becoming easy fodder for German machine-gunners. On the first day of battle, 20,000 British were killed and another 40,000 wounded (Fussell, p. 13). Tolkien participated in the battle of the Somme. Though he was not in the first wave, he witnessed its horrible aftermath, as the dead and wounded were carried back to secure positions. Most of his friends were less lucky. Indeed, by 1918 Tolkien's prewar social circle had been decimated. As he wrote in his "Foreword to the Second Edition" of *The Lord of the Rings:*

> One has indeed to come under the shadow of war to feel fully its oppression; but as the years go by, it seems forgotten that to be caught in youth by 1914 was no less hideous an experience than to be involved in 1939 and the following years. By 1918 all but one of my close friends were dead.
>
> (*Lord of the Rings*, p. vii)

The images and emotions of World War I are easily recognizable throughout *Lord of the Rings*. As he admitted in a letter, the central friendship between Frodo Baggins and Sam Gamgee was inspired by the comradery he observed in battle between officers and men. The battle of Helm's Deep in Book 3 has strong echoes of trench warfare, and of the Somme specifically (curiously, the sides are reversed, with the enemy charging). The blasted landscape of Mordor, Sauron's kingdom, is an obvious echo of No Man's Land, as are the Dead Marshes that Tolkien's heroes cross in Book 4:

> The fens grew more wet, opening into wide stagnant meres, among which it grew more and more difficult to find the firmer places where feet could tread without sinking into gurgling mud. . . . Wrenching his hands out of the bog, [Sam] sprang back with a cry. "There are dead things, dead faces in the water," he said with horror. [Frodo answers:] "I saw them: grim faces and evil, and noble faces and sad. . . . But all foul, all rotting, all dead."
>
> (*Lord of the Rings* 4, p. 614)

Tolkien survived the war, but not unscathed. The British trenches were overrun by rats, and thousands of soldiers fell ill with "trench fever," a malady spread by lice. A particularly debilitating case struck Tolkien in late 1916, resulting finally in his discharge.

The rise of right-wing dictatorships. If *The Lord of the Rings* is marked by the experience of one world war, it was planned and begun during the late 1930s, as another global conflict grew ever more likely. Forced to accept a humiliating peace at Versailles, Germany in the 1920s was still an economic and political power. Dangerous because of its location at the center of Europe, it was doubly so for having a large, depressed, and disaffected population. The German Workers' Party, formed shortly after the armistice, was one of several violently nationalistic groups catering to this population. Renamed the National Socialist German Worker's Party (Nazis) and led by Adolf Hitler after 1920, it slowly grew in influence, attracting support mainly from Germany's lower middle class. The Nazis won a bare majority in the national elections of 1933. Yet, even without overwhelming support, once in office as chancellor, Hitler quickly moved to assume dictatorial powers, abolishing the trappings of democratic government.

The character Sauron in *The Lord of the Rings*, a figure of satanic evil whose literary and cultural antecedents stretch back to the Bible, is, among other things, a meditation on the new authoritarian leaders in Europe: not only Hitler after 1933, but also Benito Mussolini, whose Fascists had seized power in Italy 11 years earlier (1922). In both Germany and Italy, leadership rested on a combination of intense devotion and abject terror. As *Führer* and *Duce* respectively (both mean "leader"), Hitler and Mussolini were the objects of nearly religious personality cults, each with its own sacred images or totems. The Nazis had their own stiff-armed salute, distinctive way of marching (the goose-step), identifiable uniforms (the elite SS wore black), and particular symbols of power (the swastika, the eagle). In a similar way, the villain Sauron in Tolkien's fantasy is known among his people simply as "The Eye" and badges with that image adorn his soldiers' uniforms. In both Italy and Germany, power was bolstered by potent secret police forces. The German Gestapo, with concealed agents among the populace and in every branch of government, was a powerful tool to root out the regime's political (communist, democratic) and ethnic (Jewish, Gypsy) enemies, as well as keep the people in line. When Tolkien's two heroes, Frodo and Sam, enter Mordor, they too become dimly aware of an omnipresent, unseen vigilance. In a typical moment, Sam observes,

> I've met nothing alive, and I've seen nothing, but I'm not easy. I think this place is being watched. I can't explain it, but well: it feels to me as if one of [Sauron's agents] was about, up in the blackness where he can't be seen.
>
> (*Lord of the Rings* 6, p. 892)

In their rise to power, both the Nazi and Fascist regimes conceived of their country in Darwinist terms, that is, in terms based on Charles Darwin's theory about how forms of life evolved (see Darwin's ***On the Origin of Species,*** also in *Literature and Its Times*). As the Nazis and Fascists saw it, strength of will, in both the leader and his people, was best demonstrated through aggressive policies towards weaker neighboring countries. It

TOLKIEN AND TREES

"I am (obviously) much in love with plants and above all trees, and always have been; and I find human maltreatment of them as hard to bear as some find ill-treatment of animals" (Tolkien in Curry, p. 65). During his service as a signaling officer in the trenches, Tolkien watched the green landscapes of Belgium slowly reduced to muck by artillery bombardment. In *The Lord of the Rings,* he allows the trees their revenge. Book 3 introduces one of Tolkien's most original creations, the "ents," mighty "shepherds of the forest," who take care of (and closely resemble) trees. At the climax of the book, they exact a horrible retribution on the wizard Saruman (and the men who are in league with him), for the crimes of deforestation and environmental pollution. Although Tolkien's work predates current "ecological" writing, some commentators have begun to view him as foreshadowing these movements.

was the active pursuit of such policies that finally precipitated the Second World War.

Annexation and appeasement. In agreements reached at Versailles immediately after World War I, then later at Locarno (1925), the German army was limited to 100,000 men. Also, Germany's Rhineland, with its close proximity to France, Belgium, and the Netherlands, was demilitarized. Shortly after taking power, claiming that these arrangements had been imposed unfairly on Germany, Hitler began openly to flaunt them. In 1935 he reintroduced conscription, and began rebuilding a large and powerful military; then, one year later, German troops reoccupied and fortified the Rhine Valley. Britain and France, despite these blatant betrayals of Versailles, did nothing. This inaction, in turn, only encouraged the Nazis' imperial ambitions. As early as 1931, the new authoritarian governments (of Italy and Germany) had entered an alarming, expansionist phase. In that year, in a move that brought little response from the West, Japan invaded and annexed Chinese Manchuria. By 1935 things were hitting closer to home: Mussolini's troops attacked Abyssinia (present-day Ethiopia) in Africa, ostensibly in revenge for a defeat 40 years earlier. Again, the British, who could have responded by cutting off Mussolini's access to the Suez Canal (and thus to Abyssinia), were confused in their foreign policy. Still hoping that Mussolini might be an ally in the future against the more serious threat of Germany, the British and French tolerated his aggression. The result, again, was a predictable increase in that aggression. When civil war broke out in Spain between forces of the left (liberals and radicals) and the right (conservatives and reactionaries), the major European powers adopted an official position of neutrality. In fact, Germany and Italy sent thousands of troops to Spain to assist the rightist Nationalists ultimately led by General Francisco Franco, while the Soviets helped organize fighting for the leftist Second Republic. All three great powers correctly perceived Spain as a rehearsal for a larger European conflict ahead. Britain, though several of its citizens went to fight on their own accord (mostly for the Republic) remained truly neutral.

England's foreign policy in the late thirties has, understandably, come under considerable scrutiny. Some voices in the government, Winston Churchill among them, perceived the magnitude of Hitler's threat, and advocated a return to British policies of the late nineteenth century: the forging of strategic alliances, often with unsavory partners, in order to ensure that no power on the continent grow strong enough to threaten England. Neville Chamberlain, then prime minister, was unwilling to pursue such tactics. Britain's most likely partner against Germany, Soviet Russia, was viewed with considerable (and largely justified) suspicion; indeed, many elements in Britain trusted Hitler more than they did Russia's Joseph Stalin. The United States, meanwhile, was locked in an isolationist withdrawal from the European scene.

So Chamberlain pursued an alternate course, *appeasement;* that is, he granted concessions to his potential enemies to keep the peace. The hope behind appeasement was that, by selectively and strategically giving in to Hitler's demands, larger conflicts might be avoided. In retrospect, the hope that Hitler might listen to the voice of reason was either naive or willfully deluded: British appeasement policies, like Britain's refusal to intervene in either Abyssinia or Spain, were perceived by the Germans as signs of weakness, and only led to more aggressive demands. After Hitler invaded and annexed Austria in March 1938 (the

FROM FANTASY INTO REALITY

In a letter written to his son Christopher, who was fighting in the Royal Air Force, Tolkien characterized the war against Hitler as "attempting to conquer Sauron with the Ring [of Power]" (Tolkien, *Letters*, p. 78). Since, however, *The Lord of the Rings* was conceived largely before World War II began, the war between Sauron and the rest of Middle Earth does not closely resemble actual events. Nevertheless, certain passages surely capture the mood in England during the Blitz, the massive air war Hitler launched against London and other major cities. The Blitz itself was perceived as but a prelude to an eventual invasion of England by Germany's seemingly undefeatable army. In Tolkien's fantasy, Gondor, the kingdom closest to Sauron's Mordor, which resembles England in many ways, suffers a similar attack. The sentiments uttered by Gondor's leader—shortly before he kills himself—must capture something of the despair some Britons felt in 1940-41: "Against the Power that now arises there is no victory. . . . All the East is moving. . . . The West has failed. It is time for all to depart who would not be slaves" (*Lord of the Rings* 5, p. 835). On the other hand, despite a similar beginning, Tolkien's war ends in a way no European conflict ever could.

so-called *Anschluss*), Chamberlain still refused to forge alliances with Russia or France, despite urging from the Russians, and from elements in his own government. Shortly thereafter, Hitler began threatening to annex Sudetenland, a region of Czechoslovakia with a large ethnic German population. In September 1938, Chamberlain met with Hitler on three occasions, at Berchtesgaden, Godesberg, and Munich. At the Munich Conference (on September 29-30), without consulting the Czechs—he characterized Czechoslovakia as "a far-away country of which we know nothing"—Chamberlain acceded to most of Hitler's demands, including the seizure of Sudetenland (Chamberlain in Young, p. 123). In return, he received a letter promising an end to hostilities. His words upon returning to England were full of hope.

> For the second time in our history, a British Prime Minister has returned from Germany bringing peace with honor. I believe that it is peace for our time.
>
> (Address from 10 Downing Street, September 30, 1938; Chamberlain in Kaplan, p. 606)

Chamberlain's hope proved unjustified. A few months later, going back on his promise, Hitler seized Czechoslovakia in its entirety. The Russians, by now tired of waiting for an alliance from England, quickly reached a nonaggression pact with Germany. This was widely perceived as an invitation to subdivide Poland, and as an assurance that any European war begun by Germany would have only a single front, in the west. Hitler invaded Poland on September 1, 1939. Two days later, England finally declared war on Germany—for the second time in a quarter century.

The geopolitical situation in *The Lord of the Rings* is broadly comparable to that of Europe in the 1930s. The fictional villain Sauron, having suffered a defeat earlier, begins to re-arm, first covertly, and then openly (in Europe, Germany was ready to wage war again after only one generation; in *The Lord of the Rings*, Sauron is dormant for some 3,000 years). As his intentions towards the rest of Middle Earth grow more nakedly aggressive and imperial, his opponents consider the options open to them. One leader, the wizard Saruman, who later proves a formidable villain in his own right, counsels a Chamberlain-like course of appeasement, even cooperation with Sauron. Others urge a course of stoic resistance in the face of Sauron's overwhelming military superiority. The strongest echoes of the Munich agreement come towards the end. Just before launching a total war against the West, Sauron offers terms: in return for a fragile (and doubtless short-lived) peace, he demands large concessions of land and security.

> All lands east of the Anduin shall be Sauron's for ever, solely. West of the Anduin as far as the Misty Mountains and the Gap of Rohan shall be tributary to Mordor, and men there shall bear no weapons, but shall have leave to govern their own affairs.
>
> (*Lord of the Rings* 5, p. 872)

Here, in pointed contrast to Chamberlain, the offer is met with a rebuff, and so the inevitable war begins sooner than later.

The Novel in Focus

The plot. *The Lord of the Rings* was conceived as a novel in six books. Because, however, of its size (there are more than 50 major characters; it runs to more than 1000 pages), it was first published as three separate novels, with two books apiece. The three novels are, in order, *The Fellowship of the Ring, The Two Towers,* and *The Return of the King*. Preceding the whole series, and serving as a preface of sorts, is another novel ***The Hobbit*** (1937; also in *Literture and Its Times*). Intended mainly for children, this short novel sets up some important plot points for the longer work. As Book 1 of *The Fellowship of the Ring* begins, Bilbo Baggins, the hero of *The Hobbit,* is celebrating his 111th birthday with his neighbors, the other hobbit residents of a rural community called the Shire. At the end of a large party, Bilbo disappears, literally vanishing into thin air, and leaving the Shire forever. In fact, he has put on a magic ring, discovered on his earlier adventure, that makes its wearer invisible. Before he leaves for good, Bilbo bequeaths his home and possessions, including (with some reluctance) the ring, to his nephew Frodo.

Seventeen years pass. At the end of this period, Gandalf the Wizard, one of Bilbo's mysterious friends, visits Frodo with bad news. The ring is no mere trinket; it is, indeed, the most dangerous object in the world, the "One Ring" of power forged many thousands of years before by the evil Sauron. A wearer of sufficient will might use it to conquer and rule all of Middle Earth. After millennia of dormancy, Sauron has reawakened, and is now aware that the ring, long thought lost, has been found, and is in the Shire. Already, Sauron has sent his agents, nine black-robed riders called "Nazgul," to find it. Before leaving on his own pressing business, Gandalf urges Frodo to flee the Shire and head for Rivendell, the do-

LORD OF THE RINGS GLOSSARY

Heroes and Heroines

Gandalf A wizard, leader of the struggle against Sauron.

Ents Treelike creatures who live in the forest of Fangorn and help overthrow Saruman (see below); their leader is Treebeard.

The Free Peoples Four races opposed (mostly) to Sauron:

1) **Hobbits** A diminutive, manlike race. Rustic and unadventurous; thrust unwillingly onto the world stage. Principal hobbits:

Bilbo Baggins Hero of *The Hobbit,* finder of the ring.

Frodo Baggins His nephew; as Ring bearer (and Ring destroyer), he is the main character of the novel.

Sam Gamgee Frodo's gardener; later his closest companion on the quest.

Meriadoc Brandybuck ("Merry") Frodo's cousin, also a member of Frodo's company.

Peregrin Took ("Pippin") Frodo's cousin, also a member of Frodo's company.

Gollum (see below) was originally a hobbit.

2) **Men** Sauron's main opponents. Principal men:

Aragorn Early protector of Frodo; heir to the throne of Gondor (see below).

The Gondoreans Most powerful nation of men; live in Gondor, a kingdom in the south, near Mordor, the realm of the villains. Gondor's main city is Minas Tirith. Long without a king, the kingdom has been ruled by stewards. Their current steward is Denethor, and his two sons are Boromir (one of Frodo's companions) and Faramir.

The Rohirrim A nation of horse-riding warriors; they live in Rohan, near Isengard. Their king is Theoden; his niece is Eowyn, who kills the chief of the Nazgul (see below).

3) **Elves** An ancient immortal race; former opponents to Sauron, less active in the present struggle. Principal elves:

Elrond Lord of Rivendell (Frodo's refuge at the end of Book 1).

Arwen Elrond's daughter, eventually wife to Aragorn (see above).

Galadriel Queen of Lothlorien (a forest where Frodo briefly finds refuge in Book 2).

Legolas A member of Frodo's company.

4) **Dwarves** Smiths, craftsmen, who live in underground kingdoms. Now largely dispossessed. The largest of their realms, now abandoned, was Moria. One of Frodo's companions—Gimli—is the most important dwarf to appear in the novel.

Villains

Sauron Satanic figure with designs to conquer Middle Earth; his stronghold is the southern realm of Mordor. Forger and pursuer of the Ring.

Saruman A wizard; based at Isengard. Originally sent to Middle Earth to oppose Sauron, he was gradually corrupted. He too has designs to capture the ring and conquer Middle Earth.

The Nazgul Nine erstwhile men, once kings, seduced into the service of Sauron; his most powerful agents; also called Ringwraiths.

Shelob A giant spider who guards a mountain pass into Mordor. Shelob incapacitates Frodo at the end of Book 4.

The Balrog An ancient spirit of fire who defeats Gandalf (temporarily) at Moria.

Gollum A former possessor of the Ring; loses it to Bilbo Baggins in *The Hobbit;* a companion (and later a traitor) to Frodo Baggins.

Orcs, trolls Creatures in the service of Sauron and Saruman.

Map of Middle Earth as depicted in the 2001 film version of *The Lord of the Rings: The Fellowship of the Ring.*

main of the elf-lord Elrond. The remainder of Book 1 tracks Frodo's journey to Rivendell, pursued by the Nazgul and accompanied by three other hobbits: his gardener Sam Gamgee and two younger cousins, Merry and Pippin. After a few diversions, they meet a mysterious man who calls himself "Strider," and who conducts them safely to Rivendell, but not before Frodo has been seriously wounded by one of the Nazgul.

At Rivendell, where Book 2 begins, the larger geopolitical situation becomes clearer. Sauron has returned to Mordor, his ancient kingdom in the southeast, has rebuilt his armies, and will shortly be launching a war of conquest against the rest of Middle Earth. Against this threat, the "free peoples" of the world—hobbits, elves, dwarves and men—have little hope. Gondor, the chief realm of men, has been in long decline; ruled by stewards instead of kings, it now has too little power to withstand Sauron. The dwarves are disorganized, the elves quietistic. Already one seeming ally, the wizard Saruman, has revealed himself to be in league with Sauron. Only one course of action remains: the Ring, in which Sauron has invested much of his personal force, must be destroyed; with its destruction,

Sauron will also be consumed. Unfortunately, the Ring can only be undone in the place where it was forged: Mount Doom, a volcano in the heart of Mordor. Frodo, now healed, volunteers for this death mission, and is given eight companions to assist him: the three other hobbits, the wizard Gandalf, the dwarf Gimli, the elf Legolas, and two men. One of these men, Boromir, is the son of the current steward of Gondor; the other is "Strider," who turns out to really be Aragorn, heir to the ancient rulers of that land. This "fellowship" of nine heads south towards Mordor, passing through the old dwarf-kingdom of Moria (now inhabited by orcs, apelike monsters in the service of Sauron and Saruman), and Lorien, a forest ruled by the mysterious elf queen Galadriel. Slowly, but inevitably, the fellowship is dissolved: Gandalf falls into darkness in Moria fighting a Balrog (a demonic spirit), and Boromir is overcome by the temptation to seize the Ring for himself. After he attacks Frodo, Frodo and Sam resolve to complete the journey to Mordor alone.

In *The Two Towers,* the narrative therefore splits. Book 4 follows Sam and Frodo on their trek towards Mordor, while Book 3 deals with the rest of the company. At the very beginning of Book 3, Boromir is killed by orcs, and Merry and Pippin are abducted by them. Aragorn, Gimli, and Legolas follow the orcs in hot pursuit. It slowly becomes clear that the kidnappers are agents not of Sauron, but of the turncoat wizard Saruman, who wants the Ring for himself, to use in his own war of conquest, and who thinks that either Merry or Pippin possesses it. Before reaching Saruman's stronghold of Isengard, Merry and Pippin manage to escape their captors, and flee into the forest of Fangorn. There they encounter the ents, "shepherds of the forest," vast treelike creatures who have been observing their neighbor Saruman (and his habit of chopping down trees needlessly) with growing restiveness. Merry and Pippin urge the ents to strike against Saruman. Meanwhile, Aragorn and his companions, having lost track of Merry and Pippin, encounter Gandalf, mysteriously returned. Fearing a war on two fronts, against both Saruman and Sauron, Gandalf urges quick action against Saruman. Enlisting the aid of the Rohirrim, a nation of horse-riding men, Gandalf and Aragorn defeat Saruman's troops in battle, then arrive at Isengard to find it sacked by the ents. Saruman is thus overthrown, and Merry and Pippin reunited with their companions, just as Sauron is launching his own war.

As these events are taking place, Frodo and Sam are slowly approaching Mordor (Book 4). On this journey they are joined by Gollum, a former possessor of the Ring, who lusts to wear it again (it was his when Bilbo found it, and he still calls it his "precious"). A curious relation develops among the three, and finally the two hobbits enlist Gollum's unwilling aid as a guide into Sauron's kingdom. Along the way they briefly encounter Faramir, Boromir's brother, who, with a small expeditionary force of men from Gondor, is on the lookout for signs of war from Sauron. Gollum, wavering between an odd affection for Frodo and his lust for the Ring, finally betrays Frodo and Sam just as they are entering Mordor. The mountain pass is guarded by Shelob, a giant spider, and Gollum delivers the hobbits to her. Sam manages to fight off both Shelob and Gollum, but not before Frodo has been stung. Believing Frodo dead, Sam takes the Ring, only to discover a short while later that Frodo has only been paralyzed. By this time, however, Frodo has been captured by orcs. The book ends.

The Return of the King (Books 5 and 6) brings these several plots to a conclusion. In battle before the gates of Minas Tirith, the main city of Gondor, Gandalf and Aragorn deal Sauron a momentary setback: the chief of the Nazgul is killed (by Merry and Eowyn, a woman disguised as a man), but so are the steward of Gondor (by suicide) and the king of the Rohirrim (in battle). Realizing that Sauron possesses superior numbers, and that defeat in war is inevitable, Aragorn and Gandalf resolve to meet Sauron's armies in a final confrontation before the gates of Mordor. This tactic, they hope, will allow Frodo the necessary time to complete his quest. This indeed happens in Book 6, but under ironic circumstances. Having been saved by Sam from the orcs, Frodo finally reaches Mount Doom. At the very last moment, however, he succumbs to the Ring's temptations, and claims it for his own. Sauron instantly becomes aware of his presence, but before any harm can result, Gollum re-emerges to bite off Frodo's ring finger. Hardly has he regained his "precious," however, when he loses his balance and falls into the volcano. The ring is destroyed, and Sauron with it.

Celebrations ensue. Sam and Frodo are received as heroes in Minas Tirith, and Aragorn reclaims the kingship of Gondor. Upon returning to the Shire, however, Frodo and his friends receive a nasty surprise: their homeland has been turned into a petty dictatorship by an exiled and decrepit Saruman. Drawing on their experiences in the wide world, the four companions organize the other hobbits into armed resistance. After being overthrown (once again), Saruman is killed by one of his own lackeys. The Shire returns to normal, but after a year, Frodo, still in pain from the many injuries he has received, and suffering also from a deeper spiritual malaise, finds himself unable to tolerate life. Sam accompanies him to the far west coast of Middle Earth, where Frodo boards a ship, along with Bilbo, Gandalf, Elrond and Galadriel, for the "Undying Lands," a paradise across the sea. The novel ends with Sam's returning to his family.

Tolkien and race. *The Lord of the Rings* is notable for its ambivalence towards race theory, a mixture of science and pseudo-science that had considerable influence in the early twentieth century. As early as 1775, the German naturalist J. F. Blumenbach had categorized humanity into five separate races, based on such factors as comparative anatomy and skin color. By the mid-nineteenth century, in some quarters, race theory had given way to full-blown racism. In his *The Inequality of the Human Races* (1853), the French diplomat Joseph Arthur, the count of Gobineau (1816-82), urged the superiority of the Nordic race over the rest of humanity. In these opinions he was echoed by his friend the German composer Richard Wagner (1813-83). Houston Stewart Chamberlain (1855-1927), a cousin of England's prime minister Neville Chamberlain, and a life-long admirer of Wagner and Gobineau, added significantly to this tradition with his *The Foundations of the Nineteenth Century* (1899). His book depicts Western culture as a struggle of races, with the superior northern race (Germanic or "Aryan") constantly fending off dilution by inferior breeds, notably the Jews. This work and subsequent writings by Chamberlain were a formative influence on Hitler; when the two met in 1923, their admiration was mutual. Nazi policies towards the Jews and Gypsy peoples, first of exclusion, and then of extermination, had a long intellectual heritage.

The Lord of the Rings is also influenced by this tradition. Tolkien's academic training was in historical linguistics, the study of languages in their development over time. From the late eighteenth century, the study of races and the study of languages were closely allied. The insight that widely dispersed language groups (Germanic, Latin, Greek, Celtic, Indo-Iranian, etc.) in fact shared a common ancestry, had obvious implications for understanding racial groupings. Indeed, the word "Aryan" itself, before it was tarnished by association with the Nazis, was an accepted term in linguistics, used to describe this ancient common mother tongue. By Tolkien's own admission, all of his creative work was "fundamentally linguistic in inspiration" (Tolkien, *Letters*, p. 219). Even before World War I, as a boy, he was an enthusiastic inventor of languages and language families; only later did he begin to invent histories, stories about population migrations and ethnicities, to "explain" the connections between these made-up tongues. The invented languages that appear in *The Lord of the Rings* (several varieties of elvish, dwarvish, and so forth) are fully formed and usable. Actually they were made up long before the "fictional peoples" that speak them. *The Lord of the Rings*, drawing on the histories of these peoples, came last in a series of inventions. Tolkien explains in a letter.

> Languages and names are for me inextricable from the stories. They [i.e. the stories] are and were so to speak an attempt to give a background or a world in which my expressions of linguistic taste could have a function. The stories were comparatively late in coming.
>
> (Letter to W. H. Auden. 7 June, 1955—Tolkien, *Letters*, p. 214)

With such origins, it can hardly be a surprise that racial differences are noted in minute detail in *The Lord of the Rings*. In his war against the West, Sauron enlists the aid of neighboring, backward, human races. They are almost exclusively "peoples of color": some are black—"out of Far Harad black men like half-trolls with white eyes and red tongues"— others seemingly Mongoloid (*Lord of the Rings* 5, p. 828).

> They are fierce. They have black eyes, and long black hair, and gold rings in their ears; yes lots of beautiful gold. And some have red paint on their cheeks, and red cloaks. . . . Not nice; very cruel wicked Men they look.
>
> (*Lord of the Rings* 4, p. 632)

The Rohirrim, conversely are modeled on the Anglo-Saxons. They are blue-eyed, blond-haired, invested with a rude barbaric vigor, and given, like the Anglo-Saxons whose literature Tolkien made a career of studying, to improvising bursts of alliterative poetry. The men of Gondor, finally, belong to a particularly distinguished race, grey-eyed, black-haired and tall of stature, but plagued by a long decline. The culprit is a dilution through intermarriage. At the time of the novel, the chief features of the thoroughbred Gondorean are uncommon "save in some houses of purer blood" (*Lord of the Rings* 5, p. 842).

At such moments, Tolkien's novel sounds uncannily like H. S. Chamberlain's racist book.

Nonetheless, Tolkien was no admirer of the Nazis' ideology. He in fact took issue with Hitler, not because of Hitler's "admiration for Northern culture" but because of the racist conclusions he drew from that admiration. As he explained in a letter to his eldest son during World War II,

> I have spent most of my life . . . studying Germanic matters (in the general sense that includes England and Scandinavia). There is a great deal more force (and truth) than ignorant people imagine in the 'Germanic' ideal. I was much attracted by it as an undergraduate. . . . You have to understand the good in things, to detect the real evil. . . . Anyway, I have in this War a burning private grudge . . . against that ruddy little ignoramus Adolf Hitler. . . . Ruining, perverting, misapplying, and making for-ever accursed, that noble northern spirit, a supreme contribution to Europe, which I have ever loved, and tried to present in its true light.
>
> (Letter to Michael Tolkien, 9 June 1941—Tolkien, *Letters*, pp. 55-56)

ALTERNATIVE ENGLANDS

Tolkien was very careful in constructing the world of Middle Earth, preparing detailed maps and making sure distances and travel times were observed minutely in the narrative. Yet the geography of Middle Earth is less spatial than temporal. That is, the different cultures visited by Tolkien's characters resemble English culture at different stages of its development.

Rohan Abode of the Rohirrim, who are blond haired and blue eyed and have a strong oral tradition. They build burial mounds and compose a highly alliterative poetry. Their culture—and their names—closely resemble those of Anglo-Saxon England, c. 500-1066.

Gondor Principle kingdom of men, closely resembles England in the High Middle Ages.

Rivendell Kingdom of the elves, who withdraw from worldly engagement but produce exquisite works of art, are strongly reminiscent of the group of artists known as decadents and aesthetes (followers of the aesthetic movement) at the end of the nineteenth century.

The Shire Home of the hobbits (the wealthier ones), who resemble country gentlemen at the turn of the twentieth century, in the Edwardian period of English history.

Mordor Kingdom of the dark lord Sauron, envisioned as the military-industrial hell Tolkien, among others, feared England might become in the twentieth century.

Other letters express Tolkien's particular disgust with Hitler's anti-Semitic policies. Tolkien was especially disturbed by the eugenics or genetically engineered human improvement movements of the 1930s. In their quest to produce perfect Aryan types, the Nazis engaged in breeding experiments: "perfect" human specimens were encouraged to mate, while imperfect types, like the disabled or mentally handicapped, were murdered. Both Sauron and Saruman, the latter especially, are enthusiastic eugenicists—a source of exceptional horror.

Sources. As noted, *The Lord of the Rings* was inspired to a large degree by Tolkien's professional life. In addition to his work on language, Tolkien was a scholar of Anglo-Saxon literature. His most famous contribution to that field, for which he would still be known today had he never turned to fiction, is an essay on *Beowulf* called "Beowulf: The Monsters and the Critics." In this essay, he admires the Old English epic for its balance between the author's Christianity and the pagan outlook of its characters. *The Lord of the Rings* preserves this equilibrium: although the peoples of Middle Earth are not explicitly religious, the work is saturated with Tolkein's own deeply held Catholic beliefs. Frodo cannot complete his quest on his own; only an act of grace—Gollum's sudden appearance—makes this resolution possible. At moments of crisis, the elves call out to a female spirit strongly reminiscent of the Virgin Mary. Like priestly figures, the Ring-bearers Frodo and Bilbo never marry.

Besides *Beowulf,* Tolkien's literary sources are almost too numerous to mention, ranging from early medieval germanic epic and saga to the fairy stories of such nineteenth-century predecessors as George MacDonald and Andrew Lang. In the end, however, Tolkien's novel stands apart for its uniqueness and originality. With *The Lord of the Rings,* he practically invents the modern fantasy novel, using a made-up world as a distant mirror for his own time.

Reception. From the very start, most critical debate about *The Lord of the Rings* has focused on genre: whether a work of fantasy could be treated as serious literature at all. Fantasy writer C. S. Lewis, who had belonged to Tolkien's social circle at Oxford, and to whom Tolkien had read much of the novel in manuscript, gave it a particularly warm reception. Comparing it to "lightning from a clear sky," he predicted that the book would "soon take its place among the indispensables" (Lewis pp. 519, 525). The poet and playwright W. H. Auden, writing in the *New York Times Book Review* (October 31, 1954), similarly enthused that "no fiction I have read in the last five years has given me more pleasure than 'The Fellowship of the Ring,'" (Auden, p. 37). But other voices were dismissive. The English poet Edwin Muir and the American social critic Edmund Wilson both found the novel emotionally adolescent. Subsequent criticism has attempted to assess Tolkien's worth on other grounds. In the 1970s he bore the brunt of particularly hostile attacks (from Raymond Williams, Fred Inglis, and others on the British left) because of his perceived conservatism and sentimentality. His defenders have been drawn increasingly from academics (medievalists especially) and from fans of fantasy literature. These debates are not likely to cease any time soon, as even his staunchest defenders admit. As Auden put it in a second review he wrote for the *New York Times* (January 22, 1956),

> Nobody seems to have a moderate opinion; either, like myself, people find it a masterpiece of its genre, or they cannot abide it.
>
> (Auden, p. 5)

—David Rosen

For More Information

Auden, W. H. Review of *The Lord of the Rings,* by J. R. R. Tolkein. *New York Times Book Review,* 31 October 1954, 37.

———. Review of The Lord of the Rings. *New York Times Book Review,* 22 January 1956, 5.

Carpenter, Humphrey. *Tolkien: A Biography*. Boston: Houghton Mifflin, 1977.

Curry, Patrick. *Defending Middle Earth: Tolkien, Myth and Modernity*. New York: St. Martin's Press, 1997.

Fussell, Paul. *The Great War and Modern Memory*. New York: Oxford University Press, 1975.

Giddings, Robert, ed. *J. R. R. Tolkien: This Far Land*. London: Vision Press, 1983.

Graves, Robert. *Goodbye to All That*. New York: Anchor, 1998.

Kaplan, Justin, ed. *Bartlett's Familiar Quotations*. 16th ed. Boston: Little, Brown, 1992.

Lewis, C. S. *C. S. Lewis: Essay Collection and Other Short Pieces*. Ed. Lesley Walmsley. London: HarperCollins, 2000.

Shippey, T. A. *J. R. R. Tolkien: Author of the Century*. London: HarperCollins, 2000.

Tolkien, J. R. R. *The Letters of J. R. R. Tolkien*. Ed. Humphrey Carpenter. Boston: Houghton Mifflin, 1994.

———. *The Lord of the Rings*. 2nd ed. Boston: Houghton Mifflin, 1994.

Young, John W. *Britain and the World in the Twentieth Century*. London: Arnold, 1997.

The Martian Chronicles

by
Ray Bradbury

While Ray Bradbury (1920–) is best known as a science-fiction writer, no one genre adequately subsumes all of his work. Bradbury is at once deeply interested in technology and suspicious of its misuse. He has refused to drive a car or to ride in an airplane, yet has written lyrically about space travel, and his stories are full of speculations about the benefits and dangers of machines (Mogen, p. 22). He tends not to share the traditional interest of other science-fiction writers in speculating on how a new technology might physically operate. Instead, Bradbury's work is often very like a complex and intelligent fairy tale, in which machines, for good or ill, work the magic. While Bradbury's stories always have some element of the fantastic, this element may just as easily take the form of a pretty young girl as that of some more classically science-fictional creature, such as a Martian or a computer-run house. His second book of short stories (after *Dark Carnival*, 1947), *The Martian Chronicles,* was followed by novels, drama, poetry, and children's stories. Included in Bradbury's works (see ***Dandelion Wine*** and ***Fahrenheit 451***, also in *Literature and Its Times*) are poetic reveries on childhood and small-town life, meditations on love, and protests against censorship, along with tales about spacemen on rockets. All these elements appear in *The Martian Chronicles*, whose stories reflect an earth-threatening contest for world power in Bradbury's time.

THE LITERARY WORK

A series of short stories set on the planet Mars in the near future; published in 1950.

SYNOPSIS

Humans arrive on Mars in search of scientific knowledge and a better life, as well as in flight from rising nuclear tensions at home. As the humans encounter telepathic Martians, Earth's problems become at once more distant and more immediate.

Events in History at the Time of the Short Stories

The Cold War. The Second World War ended in Europe with Germany's surrender on May 7, 1945. At the Potsdam Conference, held from July 17 to August 2, 1945, the "Big Three"—the United States of America, the Union of Soviet Socialist Republics, and Britain—agreed to "demilitarize, de-Nazify and democratize Germany" (Graebner, p. 72). Germany was accordingly divided into Soviet, British, French, and American administrative zones, while the city of Berlin, which sat deep within the Soviet zone, was also placed under joint administration. In September 1946, the Western authorities merged the British, French, and American zones into one territory, that of West Germany; the Soviet zone became East Germany. These divisions would determine

Ray Bradbury

the map of Europe until the fall of the Berlin Wall in 1989.

The division of Europe between the Soviets and the West did not end with Germany. The Soviets maintained control of the Eastern European countries, from which they had driven the Germans, and nothing short of another war was going to drive them out. America and Western Europe began to fear that Soviet expansion would not stop with Eastern Europe. The Soviet prime minister, Joseph Stalin, made no secret of his desire to control the rest of Europe. The United States' first reaction to this threat was the Truman Doctrine, a "vague and indeterminate promise to support governments under Communist attack" (Graebner, p. 77). U.S. policy aimed to contain communism—that is, to prevent its spread. While the Truman Doctrine was general and highly ideological, the administration also adopted the specific, highly practical Marshall Plan, named after U.S. Secretary of State George C. Marshall. Under this plan, the United States offered the war-ravaged European countries financial aid to help rebuild their economies. Marshall explained that the policy was "directed not against country or doctrine, but against hunger, poverty, desperation, and chaos" (Graebner, p. 77). Marshall even offered to extend aid to the Soviets and their satellite nations, but the offer was refused. The Marshall Plan had its strategic as well as its humanitarian goals. Economically viable and militarily stable European nations made far better allies against Soviet expansion than unstable nations would and, again, the foremost U.S. goal was to stop the spread of communism. In 1949 the North Atlantic Treaty Organization (NATO), came into existence as an alliance against the Soviets, who responded by forming the Warsaw Pact in 1953. American precautions against Soviet aggression became more and more open, and the escalating hostility between the two nations gained a name. It became known as the "Cold War."

The Red Scare. In a reaction to the threat of Soviet expansion, anticommunist hysteria in America grew widespread. The House Committee on Un-American Activities (HUAC, founded in 1938 to root out both communists and fascists) tried to eradicate subversive communist agents who were thought to have infiltrated all levels of U.S. government and industry. In 1947, HUAC held much-publicized Hollywood hearings. These hearings, which were intended to clear the film industry of subversive agents, were based on Federal Bureau of Investigation (FBI) files and on denunciations by informers, among whom was the actor and future president Ronald Reagan. These hearings exposed "a handful of communists, mostly screenwriters"; ten men went to jail for contempt of court and "more than a dozen people committed suicide" (Rose, p. 35). In the aftermath of the hearings, studio officials refused to hire anyone who might be suspected of "un-American" leanings. Hundreds of actors, writers, producers, and technical workers were blacklisted as a result of the HUAC hearings; the committee's actions had a good measure of popular support. Across the country, people denounced, harassed, or refused to employ individuals suspected of being communist sympathizers. Bookstores stocked their shelves with anticommunist tracts. The major magazines printed anticommunist articles. The Catholic Church issued pamphlets with titles like Communism Means Slavery and The Enemy in Our Schools (Rose, p. 35).

While "hot" battles would be fought outside the United States and the Soviet Union, in Korea, Vietnam, and Afghanistan, the Cold War on home soil remained "a war of nerves, a war of images" (Von Bencke, p. 10). Two of the defining images of the Cold War are the mushroom cloud and the rocket. While the distinctive cloud raised by the detonation of an atom bomb remains the symbol of utter destruction, the rocket is more ambiguous: it is the delivery vehicle of both the bomb and the astronaut, symbolizing progress and adventure as well as the possibility of catastrophe.

The arms race. During the Second World War, scientists in the United States, the Soviet Union, and Germany researched the possibility of nuclear weapons. America was the first to succeed. On August 6, 1945, the American plane Enola Gay dropped an atom bomb on the Japanese city Hiroshima, and three days later the Americans dropped another bomb on Nagasaki. Each city was devastated. According to U.S. sources, 64,000 people were killed instantly (Japanese sources have the figure closer to 200,000) and thousands more died from radiation sickness. By 1950, when *The Martian Chronicles* was published, the long-term effects of radiation from nuclear bombs (increased cancer rates, thyroid disorders, birth defects) were becoming clear (Rose, pp. 81-82). Already some physicists were adamantly opposed to further research and testing in nuclear weapons.

After the war, research in atomic weapons continued in America at a slower pace, until the Soviet Union exploded its first atomic device (based on the American plans) in September 1949. This event was described in the *Bulletin of the Atomic Scientists* as a "new Pearl Harbor," and it led to intensified American research (Rose, p. 72). The first atom bombs were comparatively limited in scope, depending on a single fission reaction of uranium and plutonium. But subsequent bombs, developed in America in reaction to the Soviet atomic weapons, grew substantially more powerful and destructive. These so-called "super" bombs were hydrogen bombs. H-bombs depended upon fusion reactions that added hydrogen to the explosion of the rarer elements (uranium and plutonium) already in the A-bombs. A conventional A-bomb acted as a trigger mechanism for the significantly more powerful H-bomb, which was developed independently in each of the two countries this time. Its development led to years of nuclear escalation and stockpiling by both sides.

The nuclear threat was very present in daily life. Schools instituted "duck and cover drills," in which children would practice putting their heads between their knees and shielding their eyes, a maneuver that would supposedly help them to survive a nuclear attack. Instructional film strips offered similar advice, showing idyllic scenes of summer picnics whose picnickers (mother, father, son, and daughter) would protect themselves from the sudden dropping of the bomb by hiding under their picnic blankets. Homeowners—including John Wheeler, one of the designers of the A-bomb—erected private fallout shelters in which to survive the effects of a nuclear attack.

The space race. Modern rocketry was initially developed for military use at the time of the Second World War. The technology that would eventually send astronauts to the moon was first used to send explosives to their targets. While gunpowder-fuelled rockets had been around for centuries, mostly as fireworks or signal flares, the military had no use for these rockets since they flew only very short distances and could not carry heavy payloads. This problem was overcome in the 1920s, when scientists in Germany, America, and Russia began building liquid-fuelled rockets. Rocket-enthusiast engineers, encouraged by their childhood science-fiction reading and by military funding, began developing rockets capable of carrying large explosives. The German V-2 rocket was the first ballistic missile, launched from the ground and aimed at targets up to 190 miles away.

SCIENCE FICTION AND ROCKET DEVELOPMENT

The German mathematics teacher Hermann Oberth was one of the first to design a rocket using liquid fuel instead of gunpowder. Working in the 1920s, Oberth borrowed a number of ideas from the science-fiction writer Kurd Lasswitz, including his proposal for an orbiting space station, which among other things would have giant solar reflectors "to keep the shipping lane to Spitsbergen and the North Siberian ports ice-free by concentrated sunlight" (Heppenheimer, p. 6).

After the war, the Soviets and the Americans took what information they could from the Germans. The Soviets seized plans and prototypes of V-2 rockets, and the Americans hired many of the German scientists to form a team led by Werner von Braun, who had designed the V-2. The American and Soviet space programs both began from the same base, that of V-2 technology. For the next 40 years, rocket development remained a practical as well as a symbolic tool of Cold War aggression. Rocket science became a forum in which the Soviet Union and the United States vied to demonstrate their scientific—and, by implication, military—superiority.

Popular reactions. The growing importance of science fiction as a literary genre and a cultural indicator dates to the 1950s. In this, as in the previous decade, science fiction reflected the mood of uncertainty and paranoia in mid-twentieth-century America. One very clear example of how science fiction can highlight larger cultural concerns is the science-fiction movie *Them!* (1954), in which giant mutant ants threaten the American Southwest. The ants are mindless communist drones; the movie's heroes, acting on the instructions of a white-haired scientist, eradicate the ants by burning them out. As literary historian M. Keith Booker explains, the bomb is both the problem and the solution in this film: the ants have mutated after being exposed to radiation at a test site, but they are killed off by soldiers wielding flamethrowers. *Them!* dramatizes both a popular fear that highbrow scientists and short-sighted politicians were putting the American public in the way of unknown and unspeakable dangers, and the popular hope that those same scientists and politicians, employing American know-how and elbow grease, would be able to get out of whatever trouble came along. Similar hopes and fears are addressed with more psychological and artistic complexity in *The Martian Chronicles.*

The Series of Short Stories in Focus

The plot. *The Martian Chronicles* consists of a series of linked short stories and vignettes. While some characters appear more than once, the real focus of the book is not on a few individuals but on the American colonists of Mars as a group. Bradbury's frontier Mars is also a picture of America: not only the nineteenth-century American frontier, which Mars resembles, but also modern, militarized America with its rural and suburban areas that produce the colonists. It is to this modern America that the outer-space colonists will eventually return.

The first set of stories chronicles the initial attempts of the human beings to reach and colonize Mars. The book begins with "Rocket Summer," in which the heat generated by a rocket launch briefly melts the winter snow in a small Ohio town. The heat of the rocket is at once miraculous and unnatural: it causes housewives, taking off their coats, to "shed their bear disguises," and melts the snow to reveal "last summer's ancient green lawns" (Bradbury, *The Martian Chronicles*, p. 1). The everyday images of women in coats and snow over grass give way to a magical transformation: the melting snow and discarded coats reveal the women and the lawns behind the "disguise" of winter. But the transformation comes at the cost of a reddening sky and oven-level heat: clearly the rocket, as it is launched on the first page, is already a dangerous tool.

The first three expeditions to Mars fail because the astronauts are killed by the Martians. In each case, their deaths are connected to the Martians' telepathic powers. The two-man crew of the first rocket is killed by a jealous husband, whose wife has dreamed of the Earth men. The men on the second rocket encounter Martians who mistake them for lunatics. The hallucinations of these lunatics (including their rocket and their human bodies) are infectious because of telepathy, think the Martians, who kill the lunatics so the "contamination" will not spread (*Martian Chronicles*, p. 30). The larger crew on the third expedition, wary after the failure of the first two, lands in what appears to be an Ohio town populated by their dead relatives; they have been hypnotized by the Martians, who then catch the men off guard and kill them in the night. These stories combine speculation about the nature of reality with musings on hostility between rival powers. "What," wonders the captain of the third expedition, shortly before he is killed, "would the best weapon be that a Martian could use against Earth Men with atomic weapons?" The answer comes to him right away: "Telepathy, hypnosis, memory, and imagination" (*Martian Chronicles*, p. 46). The only way for the Martians to defend themselves against the brute force of nuclear weapons is to change the way the Earth Men think—to make the men on the third expedition believe they are in a kind of heaven.

The crew of the fourth rocket finds that the invaders, in their turn, have inadvertently killed off the Martians. They perish from chicken pox, which they apparently caught from earlier expeditions. There are a few survivors, but not enough to be a "native problem" (*Martian Chronicles*, p. 51). This begins the second phase of the book, in which American colonists arrive on Mars and modify the planet, planting trees and building American-style cities and towns. The colonization parallels stages of civilization in world history. The first colonists are sometimes crass and unpleasant. They smash the beautiful

Martian cities and dump beer bottles in the Martian canals. The havoc wreaked by later arrivals is more subtly damaging. They bring to Mars censorship, intolerance, greed, and violence, elements of American culture that Bradbury himself disdains (Mogen, p. 22).

In the third phase of the book, the long-expected nuclear war breaks out on Earth, and with a few lonely exceptions, the colonists rush home. The last stories show how the few remaining settlers on Mars deal with loneliness. One man stores freezers full of steaks and watches movie after movie; another, at once more human and more terrifying, builds robots to replace his dead wife and daughters. At the very end, after the war on Earth is over, Mars becomes the home of a fledgling human society, a new social order, whose members have a second chance. In the final story, "The Million-Year Picnic," the Thomas family arrives on Mars in a small private rocket. Mars has been evacuated at this point; all the colonists have gone home to Earth. The parents pretend at first that this is a fishing trip, and the children—three boys—are excited to see Martians. Slowly, however, the parents explain to their sons that they have come to Mars to stay. The Thomases blow up their rocket lest any unknown survivors from Earth use it to trace them, for their trip is actually illegal. With the exception of the Edwards family, who may be arriving in a similar small rocket, the Thomases do not want to be found. If the Edwards family make it to Mars with their four daughters (a number which Mrs. Thomas says will "cause trouble later," the two families will together begin a new society (*Martian Chronicles,* p. 179). The story ends with the boys seeing their long-anticipated Martians when they look at their own reflections in a Martian canal. No longer citizens of Earth, they are the new population of Mars. Their birth planet has been unequivocally left behind, memorialized only by the Earth birds and plants that now thrive on Martian soil.

Technology and humanity. Bradbury's ambivalence about technology is most evident in the second-to-last story of the collection, "There Will Come Soft Rains." One of the few stories set on Earth, it tells the fate of the only house left standing in the town of Allendale, California, after a nuclear war. The house is fully automated, containing computerized elements like a speaking clock, a stove that automatically cooks breakfast, and mouselike robot cleaners. The humans for whom these luxuries are designed, however, are absent. We learn about their habits and interests as the house cooks their breakfasts and reads them poetry, but all we see of the people themselves are their silhouettes burnt by an atomic blast into the paint on the side of the house. At the beginning of the story, the house's activities seem merely useful. When it becomes evident that the humans are gone, the house appears pathetic. By the end of the story, a fire had broken out and the house has gone insane, its different computerized elements frantically and uselessly

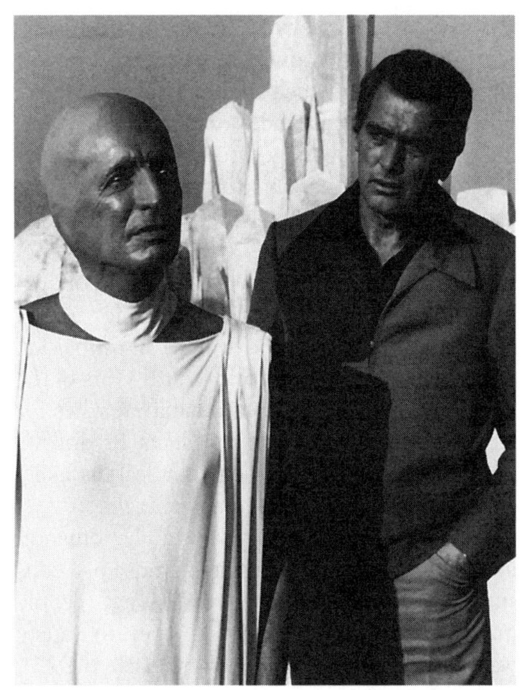

Terence Longdon (left) and Rock Hudson in the 1979 film version of *The Martian Chronicles.*

OUTER SPACE MEETS THE AMERICAN WEST

The critic David Mogen argues that *The Martian Chronicles* is about, among other things, the American frontier. "The Million-Year Picnic" is the last of Bradbury's frontier visions, in which the colonists finally cut their ties with their first homes. Mr. Thomas and his family leave Earth in order to escape the problems that the machines in "There Will Come Soft Rains" are powerless to solve: war, violence, cruelty, indifference. The small rocketships that the fathers in "The Million-Year Picnic" have carefully obtained resemble the fallout shelters real-life people were installing in their homes. They are small, private attempts to save a single family from a world-shattering event.

trying to save themselves. "There Will Come Soft Rains" is a double warning to its readers. First, it shows a world in which all the people have been killed. Secondly, in the destruction of the house, it suggests that the tragedy came about through a human failure: the robots in the house, like the absent people, have a tendency to pay too much attention to trivial details (cleaning the house, washing the dishes) and not enough to more urgent demands (preserving resources for a true emergency). Throughout *The Martian Chronicles*, as throughout the post World War II years of the late 1940s and the 1950s, humanity reaches for technology to solve human problems. Bradbury's stories suggest that technology is at least as likely to add to the problem as to solve it.

The story furthermore reflects a phenomenon in post World War II America—the rise of a consumer society. Economic growth gave people more "discretionary income—money to satisfy wants as well as need" than before (Nash, p. 923). At the same time consumer goods multiplied. Television sets found their way into more and more households while miniature electronic devices called transistors began to power computers, radios, and hearing aids now available to the average consumer. Using their discretionary income, families purchased electric gadgets for the home, from can openers, to toothbrushes and pencil sharpeners. Historians point to an "ominous technological trend" of the day, namely "the advent of automation" that made people expendable because a machine could do a task instead (Nash, p. 931).

Sources and literary context. The vision of small-town America in *The Martian Chronicles* is based on Bradbury's childhood in Waukegan, Illinois, disguised here as Green Bluff, Illinois, and elsewhere in his work as Green Town. Bradbury's vision of space owes a great deal to contemporary researchers and earlier science-fiction writers, two disparate groups that may actually have had a good deal in common. T. A. Heppenheimer argues that space-travel science fiction like Fritz Lang's movie *Frau im Mond (The Woman in the Moon)* and Hugo Gernsback's pulp magazine *Science Wonder Stories*, may have helped shape the science that followed both by inspiring real-life scientists and by helping create groups like the American Rocket Society, formed in 1930 by science-fiction writers who wanted to assess the feasibility of space travel (Heppenheimer, pp. 33-34).

Bradbury draws specifically on a long tradition of literature in which Mars and Earth invade each other. He furthermore filters those invasions through the lens of surrounding events in the late 1940s. His Martians are not Russians, but in their focus on cultural conflict and the uses of psychological warfare, his stories are heavily influenced by the tensions of the times.

The death of the Martians in *The Martian Chronicles* has both literary and historical sources. The Martians' extermination by chicken pox contracted from the early astronauts recalls the American Indians who perished by the thousands from diseases like smallpox, brought to America by colonists from Europe. Bradbury underscores the similarity of the fate of the Martians and the fate of the American Indians by placing a crew member named Cheroke (after the Cherokee Indians) aboard the fourth expedition. Cheroke is fairly sympathetic to the natives of the planet: "If there's a Martian around," he says, "I'm all for him" (*Martian Chronicles*, p. 59).

The literary source for the Martians' death is H. G. Wells's ***The War of the Worlds*** (1897; also in *Literature and Its Times*). In Wells's novel, Martians equipped with spaceships and death rays invade Earth. Humans have no weapons powerful enough to repel the invaders, and humankind survives only because the Martians unexpectedly die of Earth diseases.

The Martian Chronicles was written during the heyday of American science fiction. Hundreds of short stories were published in pulp magazines like *Science Wonder Stories* and *Amazing Science Fiction*. In the decade preceding the publication of *The Martian Chronicles*, George Orwell published ***Animal Farm*** (1945) and ***Nineteen Eighty-Four*** (1949), dystopian novels about corrupt communist dictatorships (both also in *Literature and Its Times*). Also E. E. "Doc" Smith

THE MYTH OF THE MARTIAN CANALS

In 1877, the Italian astronomer Giovanni Schiapparelli announced that he had observed that Mars's surface was covered with a large number of straight lines, which he called *canali*, a word that may mean either "channel" or "canal." English-speaking astronomers adopted the word with its English meaning, and imagined that the lines they saw on the planet (actually the result of an optical illusion [North, p. 578]) were built by intelligent Martians. This idea gave rise to the first Martian science fiction.

published his "space operas," interstellar adventure sagas. Robert A. Heinlein began a series of highly political novels, which were to include the well-known *Starship Troopers* (1959). And Isaac Asimov began publishing early versions of his *Foundation* trilogy, a series about scientific attempts to manipulate long-term political destiny, as well as *I, Robot* (1950), a novel that was to define the rules for later robot-specific science fiction (e.g., a robot must never hurt a person). Within this context, *The Martian Chronicles* is unusual for its poetic, meditative style and comparatively apolitical message and for the relative disinterest shown in a physically plausible scientific basis for the stories.

Publication and reception. The release of *The Martian Chronicles* brought Bradbury his first mainstream recognition, thanks to a review published by the important novelist and critic Christopher Isherwood in *Tomorrow* magazine in October 1950. For Isherwood, the quality of Bradbury's work suggested that science-fiction writing, generally ignored by critics, might have literary merit after all, but it also, paradoxically, removed Bradbury from the classification of science-fiction writer. Comparing Bradbury to Edgar Allan Poe (whose work Bradbury overtly refers to in *The Martian Chronicles* story "Usher II"), Isherwood points out that "his interest in machines seems to be limited to their symbolic and aesthetic aspects," a distinction that Isherwood believes separates Bradbury from the orthodox (and therefore inferior) genre writers of the day (Isherwood in Mogen, p. 16). Other critics followed Isherwood's lead. Bradbury garnered positive reviews from Aldous Huxley, J. B. Priestley, Angus Wilson, and Kingsley Amis.

While Bradbury's willingness to ignore the physical plausibility of his worlds pleased Isherwood, some science-fiction *aficionados* objected. Science-fiction ingredients, protested Donald A. Wolfheim, should be more central. Bradbury's "stories are stories of people—real and honest and true in their understanding of human nature—but for his purposes the trappings of science fiction are sufficient—mere stage settings" (Wolfheim, p. 99). Many fans and reviewers were delighted to see a science-fiction writer gaining critical respect, but others doubted that Bradbury's work really counted as science fiction at all.

The text of *The Martian Chronicles* has changed a little since its initial publication. "Way Up in the Middle of the Air," a story dealing with race relations in the rural South, was removed after the 1950 edition, and "The Fire Balloons," which features Episcopal priests who come to Mars, and "The Wilderness," in which two women prepare to join their men on Mars, were added. Since the collection is composed of linked short stories, individual additions and subtractions fit easily into the collection. Several different versions of it have appeared over the years, always with the same focus on humans' interactions with the world—or worlds—around them.

—Rachel Trousdale

For More Information

Booker, M. Keith. *Monsters, Mushroom Clouds, and the Cold War: American Science Fiction and the Roots of Postmodernism, 1946-1964*. Westport, Conn.: Greenwood Press, 2001.

Bradbury, Ray. *The Martian Chronicles*. New York: Bantam, 1979.

Graebner, Norman. *The Age of Global Power: The United States Since 1939*. New York: John Wiley and Sons, 1979.

Heppenheimer, T. A. *Countdown: A History of Space Flight*. New York: John Wiley and Sons, 1997.

Levine, Alan J. *The Missile and Space Race*. Westport, Conn.: Praeger, 1994.

Mogen, David. *Ray Bradbury*. Boston: Twayne, 1986.

Nash, Gary B., et al., eds. *The American People: Creating a Nation and a Society*. Vol. 2. New York: Harper & Row, 1990.

North, John. *The Fontana History of Astronomy and Cosmology*. New York: Fontana, 1994.

Rose, Lisle A. *The Cold War Comes to Main Street: America in 1950*. Lawrence: University Press of Kansas, 1999.

Von Bencke, Matthew J. *The Politics of Space: A History of U.S.-Soviet/Russian Competition and Cooperation in Space*. New York: Westview, 1997.

Wolfheim, Donald A. *The Universe Makers*. New York: Harper & Row, 1971.

Wulforst, Harry. *The Rocketmakers*. New York: Orion, 1990.

"MASTER HAROLD" . . . *and the boys*

by
Athol Fugard

> **THE LITERARY WORK**
> A play set in Port Elizabeth, South Africa, in 1950; published in 1982.
>
> **SYNOPSIS**
> Two black workers at a café and the white son of its owner come to grips with their relationship when the strains of the apartheid system become manifest.

Widely regarded as one of the most significant dramatists of the twentieth century, Athol Fugard (1932—) was born in Middleburg, South Africa, to white parents (of English and Afrikaner [Dutch] heritage). His childhood years in Port Elizabeth in the Cape Province would prove to be fertile soil for many of his dramatic responses to the apartheid regime, which dictated racial relations in his native land. Fugard's boyhood experiences filtered directly into a series commonly called "The Port Elizabeth Plays," which include the semiautobiographical *"MASTER HAROLD" . . . and the boys*, as well as *The Blood Knot* (1960), *Hello and Goodbye* (1965), and *Boesman and Lena* (1969). In Fugard's own words, *MASTER HAROLD* is a play to "exorcise [the] personal guilt" he felt for failing to challenge the inequalities of the oppressive system of apartheid as a youth (Fugard in Jacobus, p. 1464). The play centers on the comradery between a white teenager and black workers which suddenly explodes to reveal racism born of a lifetime under apartheid.

Events in History at the Time the Play Takes Place

Nationhood and the beginning of racial separation. Racial tension in South Africa is not just a twentieth- and twenty-first-century phenomenon. The roots of the divisions between blacks and whites stretch back to Dutch colonization in the mid-1600s, when the native blacks chafed at the increasingly stringent trade terms of the powerful Dutch East India Company and at their lands being seized from them by force. As white settlers (mostly of Dutch, French, and German descent) grew in number, so did the economic gulf between blacks and whites. Land ownership fell increasingly into the control of whites, who used black slave labor to work "their" land. The British exacerbated the situation in the nineteenth century by taking a growing colonial interest in the region—early in the century because it could serve as a buffer against the French leader Napoleon and later because of the discovery of diamonds and gold in the region. British involvement angered the Afrikaners (whites of Dutch descent, earlier called Boers), who felt their rights to the gold and diamond reserves were being usurped. It also angered the Africans (blacks), for they became subject to a wide range of discriminatory labor practices under the British. Tensions between whites of British and of Dutch descent came to a head,

Athol Fugard

erupting in the South African War in 1899, which ended in British victory in 1902. As one historian points out, "initially a war between Afrikaner and British, all South Africans were eventually pulled into it, White and Black" (Beck, p. 92). Ironically, before the war Britain had officially condemned Afrikaner discrimination against blacks. Yet afterwards the British victors allowed the country's provinces, including those dominated by Afrikaners, to decide separately on the contentious issue of voting rights for blacks. Not one province, as it turned out, would grant these rights. Alfred Milner, the British High Commissioner of South Africa who drafted the peace terms of the South African War, had earlier stated that blacks and whites would never be politically equal in the region. His prediction would be borne out in policy a few years later. In 1905, when a government committee met to decide on "native policy," as illustrated below, there was strong popular white sentiment in South Africa for permanent separation of the races.

> The *ultimate* end is a self-governing white Community, supported by *well-treated* and *justly-governed* black labour from Cape Town to Zambesi.
>
> —Alfred Milner,
> British High Commissioner for South Africa, 1899
> (Milner in Thompson, p. 144)

> We Afrikaners are not the work of man, but a creation of God. It is to us that millions of semi-barbarous blacks look for guidance, justice, and the Christian way of life.
>
> —D. F. Malan,
> South African Prime Minister, 1948
> (Malan in Pinchuck, p. 54)

> Do not allow yourselves to be talked out of the biblical truth that God subdivided humanity into peoples and that He set boundaries for them. . . . The erasure of ethnic identities . . . is not the true message of the Bible.
>
> —Andries Treurnicht,
> founder of the S.A. Conservative Party, 1989
> (Treurnicht in Thompson, p. 121)

Thereafter, Britain began to dissociate itself from South Africa, due largely to a sluggish economy and to an increasingly unruly white settler population. By 1910 the separation was complete. The country became the semi-independent Union of South Africa, ruled over by a united English-Afrikaner parliamentary government of whites, who were left to decide the race question.

Unsurprisingly, in light of popular white sentiment, the new government enacted a series of restrictive laws designed to ensure separation of the races and domination by the white minority over the black majority, especially in the workforce. The Native Labour Regulation Act (1911) made it a crime for blacks to break a labor contract. The Mines and Works Act (1911) effectively restricted blacks to semiskilled and unskilled jobs in the mines. Perhaps most divisive was the Natives Land Act (1913), which formally separated South Africa into areas in which the respective races could own land. Blacks were allotted just 7.5 percent of the entire landmass, even though they comprised nearly 70 percent of the population. Further legislation deepened the divide. The Native (Urban Areas) Land Act (1923) limited the right of blacks to enter white towns, and the Wage Act (1925) forced employers to show preference to white over black workers when hiring.

The World War II years (1939-45) created a boom in the South African economy. Although there was debate for a time over which side of the war to join—many Afrikaners wanted to side with Hitler's Germany—South Africa eventually aligned itself with the British and the Allies. Wartime mobilization created a huge demand for labor, particularly in the major cities, promoting a mass movement of blacks to urban areas (despite official ideology that they remain rural). So massive was the movement that by 1946 there were more blacks than whites in the cities (including Cape Town and Port Elizabeth). While most of the blacks worked in the city, they lived in squatter "villages," or townships, just outside the city limits.

The implementation of apartheid. Given the mass movement of blacks to cities, and a high number of black labor strikes, many whites feared being "overwhelmed" by the black majority, particularly the conservative Afrikaners. They registered this fear in the critical election of 1948, when they voted into Parliament a majority of candidates from the National Party (NP), which ran on the platform that only complete racial separation could inhibit this "overwhelming." The National Party wanted to make sure that blacks would receive no representation in Parliament and would essentially be restricted to "homelands." These homelands would be designated by ethnic (or tribal) classification as first suggested by the Natives Land Act of 1913. Strict quotas were to be instituted on black migration to towns, and there was to be no hope of blacks gaining social or political parity with whites. Almost immediately, the new Afrikaner-dominated government set about ensuring its continued domination of blacks by passing a host of laws under the label of *apartheid*, meaning "separation."

The first step was the banning of interracial relations. The Prohibition of Mixed Marriages Act (1949), which outlawed any marriage between a white and a nonwhite, was followed shortly by the infamous Immorality Act (1950), which banned sexual relations between the same. (Fugard was later to make the Immorality Act the subject of a 1972 play, aptly entitled Statements after an Arrest under the Immorality Act.) Advancing the case of inequality, 1950 also saw the passage of the Population Registration Act, which formally classified South Africans into four official racial categories—white, native (black), Asian (mostly Indian), and "coloured" (mixed race)—and mandated the issuing of identity cards. But perhaps most crucial to apartheid was the Group Areas Act (1950), which empowered the government to forcibly remove a person from an area not designated for him or her. Predictably, authorities used the law to remove nonwhites from the "white" areas, which again encompassed most of the South African landscape. From 1950 to 1976, a string of other laws designed to consolidate the apartheid system would be passed, but it was in the seminal year 1950 that the bedrock laws of the system were enacted. These laws relegated "natives" in the cities to semiskilled or unskilled jobs, in which they labored in the shadow of the ruling whites.

Black resistance and white dissent, 1910-50. From the outset, the racist laws met with resistance. In 1909 nonwhites objected to their absence from constitutional meetings in 1908-09 by holding the South African Native Convention. In 1912 discontented blacks founded the African National Congress (ANC); a group that would prove critical to the dissolution of apartheid, its initial aim was to, in moderate fashion, protest racial discrimination in South Africa. The ANC appealed to the British to intervene, but its complaints were largely left unanswered. The 1920s saw the rise and fall of the Industrial and Commercial Workers Union (ICU), a multiracial but black-dominated labor organization that attracted followers through the country's black churches. The ICU sought to eliminate discrimination in South African society in a more militant fashion than the ANC, by enacting work stoppages, stealing livestock, and destroying property to get the government's attention. Its efforts met with no concessions and the organization collapsed, but its strategy foreshadowed more militant opposition in the latter half of the twentieth century.

Organized resistance in the 1930s was light compared with the ICU actions of the 1920s. The ANC focused on education and self-improvement, distancing itself from direct confrontation with the government. Some members of the ANC disagreed with this strategy and splintered off into the All-African Convention (AAC), which took a more direct approach but avoided militarism. Then came World War II and the early 1940s, which saw the rise of more militant clashes of black labor groups with the government. An outbreak of strikes by newly formed black trade unions nearly crippled the economy. Notable was the strike of the African Mineworkers Union, beaten down by the police in 1946.

The election of 1948, which brought victory to the Afrikaner-dominated National Party (NP), also brought about the downfall of the United Party, which had ruled South Africa in one form or other since 1910. While United Party members were not for integration, they felt that complete separation of the races was impossible and that the labor situation needed to be stabilized in South Africa's cities. (The NP's victory, it turned out, was due largely to the rural vote.) As the NP became the dominant force in white politics, the mostly black African National Congress (ANC) took the lead in resistance to white minority rule. In 1949 it assumed more confrontational tactics when its younger members—among them Nelson Mandela—succeeded in adopting a policy of boycotts, work stoppages, and the like. The activities begun by ANC members in the 1950s and the government's defiant retaliations would largely define the turbulent struggle over apartheid in the second half of the twentieth century. Many outbursts would occur in major cities of the Cape Province, where Fugard sets his play.

The Play in Focus

The plot. *"MASTER HAROLD" . . . and the boys* is designed to be performed continuously, without intermission, primarily because there are no act or scene divisions but also because there are no logical breakpoints in the action. Almost the entire first half is devoted to defining the relationship among the three characters. The play opens with two black waiters, Sam and Willie, practicing for an upcoming ballroom-dance championship at their place of employment, the St. Georges Park Tea Room in Port Elizabeth. Sam, clearly the expert on the dance, attempts to convey to Willie the need to "make it smooth. . . . And give it more style" (Fugard, *"MASTER HAROLD" . . . and the boys*, p. 7). Willie, while enthusiastic about the competition, expresses frustration with Sam's directions. In doing so, he reveals that he is practicing without his partner, Hilda, because, Willie reluctantly admits, he "gave her a hiding [beating]" four days ago (*MASTER HAROLD*, p. 9).

During Sam and Willie's practice session, Hally, the 17-year-old (white) son of the tea room's owners, returns from a morning at school. His interchange with Sam and Willie indicate that they have been friends since Hally was a young boy. It furthermore becomes clear that their relationship flowers in the absence of Hally's parents; he gleefully but "conspiratorial[ly]" whispers to the waiters that they have the afternoon to spend together (*MASTER HAROLD*, p. 12). Hally's momentary worry about his hospitalized, crippled father—the worry is that he will come home prematurely, giving the audience the first sense of their strained relationship—is quickly dismissed. It fades into a pleasant passing of the afternoon. Much of the time revolves around Hally's homework, which bores Hally but interests Sam. Hally soon launches into a minilecture on "Social Reformers," which quickly escalates into a spirited debate on great reformers in society. Even though Sam has had little formal schooling, he can hold his own in the debate because he's been "educated" by Hally, or so Hally says (*MASTER HAROLD*, p. 26). Hally's mini-lecture segues into a recollection of their long friendship, ending with the time Sam constructed a kite for Hally to fly on an otherwise "useless, nothing-to-do afternoon" (*MASTER HAROLD*, p. 31). The incident makes him realize how significant Sam has been in his young life.

Just then, the phone rings and Hally speaks to his mother, who is at the hospital visiting his father. Learning that his father may indeed be coming home to resume his round of alcohol abuse agitates Hally, who convinces his mother to dissuade his father from leaving the hospital. After the phone conversation, Sam's attempts to be conciliatory are met with frustration and anger: "Life is a plain bloody mess, that's all. And people are fools" (*MASTER HAROLD*, p. 38). The topic turns to Hally's homework, which is to write a composition on a significant cultural or historical event, but his frustration persists. The men resume their dancing (while Hally does his homework), and a playful scuffle ensues, during

BALLROOM DANCING IN 1950S SOUTH AFRICA

The 1950s gave rise to a ballroom-dance craze that caught on in various parts of the world, including South Africa, largely because of its enduring British heritage. The ballroom dancing known to South Africans, blacks and whites, was in great part influenced by the so-called "English style," which included dances like the Quickstep and the Foxtrot. (Both are mentioned in the play.) Dance competitions, in vogue since the end of the Second World War, were extremely well-attended mass entertainments attracting South Africa's various racial groups in the urban centers. It was said that to be an audience member at such competitions was to witness "physical discipline" akin to "classical ballet" (Franks, p. 195). This resonates in the play when Sam, in recalling the careful precision of the dance competition, confidently states that in these events "accidents don't happen" (*MASTER HAROLD*, p. 50). By the early 1960s, South Africa had members sitting on the prestigious International Council of Ballroom Dancing, which helped regulate such competition.

A 1983 production of "Master Harold" . . . and the boys with (from left) Ramolao Makhene as Willie, Duart Sylwain as Hally, and John Kani as Sam.

which Sam's criticism of Willie stops abruptly, thanks to a slap with a ruler and a Hitler-like tirade from Hally on how he's been "too lenient with the two of [them]" (*MASTER HAROLD*, p. 42). Sam defuses the situation by persuading Hally that the dance competition is a significant cultural event, a worthy subject for his composition. Hally buys into this while Sam and Willie attempt to recreate the tension and other feelings generated at such a competition. In the process, Hally arrives at his thesis: the dance competition is a microcosm of global politics.

The phone rings again. Hally learns that his father has been discharged, which sends him into a fit of rage at his mother. She forces him to talk to his father on the phone, and in a strained conversation, Hally struggles to quell his fury. After the call, he lapses into a depression, and when Sam tries to cheer him up, Hally responds with another tirade—this time about the futility of life. It becomes clear as he rants that his father is at the center of his frustration: "the cripples are also out there tripping up everybody . . . and it's all called the All-Comers-How-To-Make-A-Fuckup-of-Life Championship" (*MASTER HAROLD*, p. 56). Sam, who can no longer stand Hally's mockery of his father, admonishes him for his behavior. Infuriated, Hally turns on Sam and invokes race to vent his anger, insinuating that even an alcoholic cripple is automatically superior to Sam if the cripple is white. In a heated exchange, Hally attempts to erase the familiar relationship he has with Sam, insisting that Sam call him "Master Harold" instead of Hally. This prospect leaves a bad taste in Sam's mouth: "If you make me say it once, I'll never call you anything else again" (*MASTER HAROLD*, p. 59). Hally's behavior grows still uglier as he gleefully recalls a racist joke his father often tells about the buttocks of a black man—to which Sam responds by showing his own backside in defiance. Hally, seemingly defeated, calls Sam over but spits in his face when he comes. This is the last straw for Sam, who now feels that the friendship has suffered an irrevocable blow, though he realizes the true target of Hally's gesture is his father, whom Hally has been afraid to face. In a tirade of his own, Sam recalls how, from a very young age, Hally was forced to deal with his father's shortcomings and that the kite episode was designed to help him feel better about himself: "You hadn't done anything wrong but you went around as if you owed the world an apology for being alive" (*MASTER HAROLD*, p. 64). Hally, completely flattened, begins to exit. Sam stops him and expresses the hope that they might "fly another kite" someday soon, but Hally leaves in a state of confusion (*MASTER HAROLD*, p. 65). The play ends with Sam and Willie once again trying to find joy and hope in the dance.

SOME SOUTH AFRICAN COLLOQUIALISMS IN FUGARD'S PLAY

Boet: "Brother." Afrikaans term of affection, e.g. "Boet Sam."

Boy: A pejorative term for a black male, regardless of age.

A cooldrink: A soft drink.

Haai: An expression of surprise, shock, or disbelief. A variation of it is **Haaikona**, which indicates more urgency.

Ja: Yes.

Struesgod: A mild oath a contraction of "As true as God."

A paternal system. Despite official attempts at the complete separation of blacks and whites, the wartime boom of the early 1940s brought thousands of "natives" (later officially called Bantu) to the cities of South Africa. This was especially true in the Cape Province, considered the most liberal of the four provinces that comprised the apartheid-era nation (the other three being Transvaal, Natal, and the Orange Free State). This may be because blacks "have had a longer period of contact with whites in the Cape than in [the other provinces] . . . especially . . . around Fugard's Port Elizabeth home" (Vandenbroucke, p. xv). The legislation that formed the apartheid system officially and practically limited blacks to semiskilled and unskilled jobs. Positions as servants in white households and small businesses were common. Sam and Willie's connection to Hally's family's business would have been usual for the day, particularly in the Cape. Also usual is the fact that any sense of stable employment could evaporate at a moment's notice, given any white person's power of discretion and the police's power of action. In the drama, Hally reacts to Sam and Willie's playful rough-housing by observing that if "a customer had walked in . . . or the Park Superintendent," their jobs would be finished (*MASTER HAROLD*, p. 42). The Group Areas Act would have allowed the police to "remove" Sam and Willie from the city and force them to relocate to one of the rural "homelands" designated for blacks. Even in the liberal Cape, though, blacks and whites did not live in close proximity to each other, despite their co-existence in the workplace. The reality for "native" city workers was residence in designated "townships" that might be far from the city in which they worked, or closer if there was an (illegal) squatter community outside the city limits. In the play, Willie makes a reference to the long bus ride from Port Elizabeth to his suburb (New Brighton), a considerable trek for anyone to walk. In a powerful moment, Willie chooses to forego his bus fare and walk home to make the play's final expression of brotherhood: a jukebox dance with Sam.

While racial attitudes in the Cape in the 1950s may have been more relaxed than in South Africa's other provinces, the supremacist ideologies among whites—particularly Afrikaners—still held sway when relationships were challenged. Hally echoes racist rhetoric in his tirades, and, in a gesture ostensibly designed to link him to history, Fugard instructs the actor playing Hally to "strut . . . around like a little Hitler" (*MASTER HAROLD*, p. 42). Despite the fact that it is ultimately dismissed by Willie as the act of a "little boy," the rhetoric is a product of what Fugard refers to as a "massive assault . . . on the soul": the ingraining of white supremacist attitudes from generation to generation (*MASTER HAROLD*, p. 62; Fugard, *Cousins*, p. 42). Hally's attempt to assert domination, from a 1950s South African standpoint, has sharp teeth to it: legally he had power over the fate of the "boys." The relationship among the three, despite its tender moments, constantly has an "unseen specter" of apartheid-inspired inequity—one that becomes visible when Hally, unable to vent his frustrations toward his father, uses Sam as a scapegoat. It is a paternalistic relationship—strikingly similar to master-slave ideology in the pre-Civil War American South—in which Hally (and, by extension, his parents) are in a position to either reward or punish the black men in their employ. The only real boy here, Hally is in a position of authority that conditions him to pervert the age relationship and call the black men "boys."

The audience sees an example of exactly how the "punishment" can be meted out when an early instance of horseplay is met with the boy Hally's "vicious whack on the bum [buttocks]" of the man, Sam, just as a parent would discipline a child (*MASTER HAROLD*, p. 42). The fact that Hally's parents are never seen in the play—only "heard" through Hally's conversations with them—reinforces the idea that there is a paternalistic "specter," the apartheid authority, hanging over Sam and Willie's heads. It is no small irony to note that over their years together Sam's relationship to Hally has been akin to that of father and son. Sam has provided Hally with the example the real father never furnished, showing Hally "the way a boy grows up to be a man" (*MASTER HAROLD*, p. 64).

Sources and literary context. Athol Fugard has unabashedly admitted that this play is the most autobiographical of his works. Hally is Fugard's partial projection of himself into the world of the play. (Fugard's parents even called him Hally, instead of Harold, his given name [his full name is in fact Harold Athol Lanigan Fugard]). Sam Semela and Willie Malopo, on whom the two other characters are based, were real men in Fugard's Port Elizabeth adolescence. Also there actually was a St. Georges Park Tea Room, which his parents owned and in which Sam and Willie worked. Of Sam, Fugard recalled that:

> There was an ambivalence in my relationship with him: a love-hate thing. And as a little white boy, ten or eleven years old, I had authority over this powerful mature man of about twenty-eight. [In the play, Sam is fifty.]
>
> (Vandenbroucke, p. 185)

This statement hints at the guilt Fugard has admitted to having injected into the play as a result of his tacit acceptance of apartheid relations in boyhood. He speaks here generally and more specifically of an incident he recalls in his relationship with Sam that mirrors the starting turn of events in the play. After a "rare quarrel" started by something that Fugard no longer remembers, Sam Semela began walking home. Infuriated, Fugard rode his bicycle to catch up with him. Then, as Fugard recalls,

> As I rode up behind him, I called his name, he turned in mid-stride to look back and, as I cycled past, I spat in his face. Don't suppose I will ever deal with the shame that overwhelmed me the second after I had done that.
>
> (Fugard, *Notebooks*, p. 26)

In addition to his pangs of guilt over the incident with Semela, Fugard draws on his sometimes stormy relationship with his father.

> I was dealing with the last unlaid ghost in my life, who was my father. Our relationship was as complex as Master Harold expresses it in the play. I had a resentment at his infirmity (Fugard's father was crippled due to a childhood injury—he fell down the gangway of a ship) and other weaknesses, but, as Master Harold says, "I love him so."
>
> (Fugard in Vandenbroucke, p. 190)

Among these "other weaknesses," Fugard goes on to explain, were his father's alcoholism and bigotry.

ATHOL FUGARD ON THE "REAL" SAM SEMELA

"I vaguely recall shyly 'haunting' the servants' quarters in the well of the [Jubilee] hotel—cold, cement-gray world—the pungent mystery of the dark little rooms—a world I didn't understand. . . . Sam, broad-faced, broader based—he smelled of woodsmoke. . . . Realize how he was the most significant—the only—friend of my boyhood years. On terrible windy days when no one came to swim or walk in the park, we would sit together and talk. Or I was reading—Introductions to Eastern Philosophy or Plato and Socrates—and when I had finished he would take the book back to New Brighton."

(Fugard, *Notebooks*, p. 25)

In addition to the relationships that inform the play, *MASTER HAROLD* is chock full of references to details in Fugard's own life. For example, the name of the dance band that Willie and Sam will dance to at the competition, the Orchestral Jazzonians, was the name of Fugard's father's dance band before Fugard was born. But some of the dramatic details differ from those in real life too, and Fugard is quick to point out the differences. In his memoir *Cousins*, he discusses the character Hally's professed distaste for the "boring" days at the Jubilee Boarding House, which his parents operated prior to their purchase of the St. Georges Park Tea Room. Fugard seemingly reprimands Hally for calling it that: "Hally is being a little unfair. Those years in the old Jubilee were not as bad as he makes out" (Fugard, *Cousins*, p. 64). Reviewing Fugard's memoirs and interviews, one senses that his *MASTER HAROLD* characters are more of a fanciful (yet genuinely remorseful) dialogue with the past than a realistic representation of it. Yet, ironically, it is a highly realistic play. It dares to "let life happen" and hold the conflict until quite late in the play, giving the audience the impression that an authentic life experience is occurring, in both its slow moments and its frenzy.

Events in History at the Time the Play Was Written

Apartheid revisited. Apartheid was still very much a fact of South African life in 1982, but the shape and strength of it had changed in response to many forces, both internal and external. Cracks in the apartheid hull began to appear as early as the 1950s, when a government commission determined that the so-called designated "homelands" for blacks—which were supposed to become self-sustaining—would never be so because of the poor land on which they sat. The previously weak African National Congress grew in membership and influence as blacks heeded its calls for nonviolent resistance to segregation. But resistance was met with increasingly hard-line enforcement of the system. A 1960 police massacre of 69 peacefully protesting blacks in the black township of Sharpeville was one of the many flashpoints in the crackdown. International censure of South Africa for the Sharpeville incident prompted the government to withdraw from the British Commonwealth and declare its total independence as The Republic of South Africa in 1961. The government also outlawed the ANC and its related organizations, and enforced more stringently the Group Areas Act, so that ANC members felt they had little choice but to turn to strategic acts of violence. This turn of events led, in 1963, to the capture and sentencing of Nelson Mandela to life imprisonment, as part of a ruthlessly efficient government counter-strategy to eliminate the insurgencies.

The tide against apartheid did not truly begin to turn until the 1970s, when a series of events began to signal the sharp decline of the system. In 1973, the United Nations declared apartheid to be a crime against humanity, and four years later it banned arms sales to the country. The year 1976 saw the worst of the flare ups of government responses to internal black resistance in Soweto (a township outside Johannesburg), when a protest of black high-school students was met with tear gas and bullets. At least two children were killed. Enraged Soweto residents rioted, igniting many government structures, sparking, in return, more police violence. Lasting for months, the cycle of violence ended, according to official records, in the deaths of 575 victims, many of them black teenagers. Meanwhile, labor unrest was on the rise, enfeebling the South African economy. The government reacted by emphasizing the "rural essence" of its black citizens, despite their having gone on strike as urban laborers. To reinforce this idea, it, one by one, declared the homelands "independent states."

Assistance to black resistance groups by newly independent (and anti-apartheid) neighboring African states, along with growing international opposition to apartheid, began to take a toll on the already stumbling South African economy. The early 1980s saw some white officials try to reform apartheid, but the prime ministership of P. W. Botha (1978-84) remained committed to white power. The government introduced some reforms that toned down "petty apartheid" policies (separate restroom facilities, etc.) in the 1980s, but it meanwhile made thousands of arrests of anti-apartheid activists. It would take an increasing divergence of viewpoints within government and mounting international pressure to bring down apartheid. The system finally collapsed in the decade following Fugard's play, paving the way for the election of Nelson Mandela as South Africa's first black president in 1994.

Reviews. Fugard felt that it would be problematic to premiere *"MASTER HAROLD" . . . and the boys* in South Africa for several reasons. Most notable were its intense connection to real figures in his life and the possibility that the local censors would ban it. So *"Master Harold" . . . and the boys* debuted at the Yale Repertory Theatre, New Haven, Connecticut, on March 12, 1982. This was the first time Fugard chose to debut one of his plays outside South Africa. Frank Rich of *The New York Times* echoed best the highly positive reception of the Yale premiere, noting that Fugard, in composing the play, "has journeyed so deep into the psychosis of racism that all national boundaries quickly fall away, that no one is left unimplicated by his vision" (Rich, p. 17). In South Africa, the play was, as expected, banned by the government at first. It took exactly a year for the drama to be staged in Johannesburg, and then it struck a powerful chord. The interracial audience was "visibly shaken and stunned. . . . Many, blacks and whites, were crying" (Lelyveld, p. 22). On the other hand, the play, and Fugard's work in general, has met with some sharp criticism. "Fugard, as a white man," say the critics, "cannot acceptably describe South African racism and its capitalistic exploitation of blacks." (Durbach in Wertheim, p. 136). Perhaps the strongest retort is the continuing popularity of *"MASTER HAROLD" . . . and the boys,* which, among all of Fugard's works, is often declared his masterpiece. Even now, in the post-apartheid era, the play resonates with audiences, compelling them to face the ugliness of inner, learned racial codes and ideologies.

—Christopher Mitchell

For More Information

Beck, Roger B. *The History of South Africa*. Westport, Conn.: Greenwood Press, 2000.

Franks, A. H. *Social Dance: A Short History*. London: Routledge and Kegan Paul, 1963.

Fugard, Athol. *Cousins: A Memoir*. New York: Theatre Communications Group, 1997.

———. *Notebooks 1960-1977*. New York: Knopf, 1983.

———. *"MASTER HAROLD" . . . and the boys*. New York: Samuel French, 1982.

Jacobus, Lee A. "Introduction to *'MASTER HAROLD' . . . and the boys*." In *The Bedford Introduction to Drama*. Boston: Bedford-St. Martin's, 2002.

Lelyveld, Joseph. "'Master Harold' stuns Johannesburg Audience." *New York Times*, 24 March 1983, 22.

Pinchuck, Tony. *Introducing Mandela*. Cambridge: Totem, 1994.

Rich, Frank. "Theater: World Premiere of Fugard's New Play." The *New York Times*, 17 March 1982, 17.

Thompson, Leonard. *A History of South Africa*. Rev. ed. New Haven, Conn.: Yale University Press, 1995.

Vandenbroucke, Russell. *Truths the Hand Can Touch: The Theatre of Athol Fugard*. New York: Theatre Communications Group, 1985.

Walder, Dennis. *Athol Fugard*. New York: Grove, 1985.

Wertheim, Albert. *The Dramatic Art of Athol Fugard: From South Africa to the World*. Bloomington: Indiana University Press, 2000.

Midnight's Children

by
Salman Rushdie

THE LITERARY WORK

A magical realist novel, set in India and Pakistan from 1915 to 1977; published in 1981.

SYNOPSIS

The fantastic life of a "child of midnight" allegorically embodies India's dream of independence, as well as the devastating effects of a colonial legacy and of partition on the goal of national unity.

On June 19, 1947, just two months before India's independence and partition, (Ahmed) Salman Rushdie was born in Bombay, India. Like his father, Rushdie was well educated—first at Cathedral school in Bombay, then at his father's alma mater, King's College, Cambridge, in Great Britain. He earned a Master of History degree in 1968, focusing on Arabic and Islamic civilization, but aspired to be a writer like his hero, Urdu poet Faiz Ahmad Faiz. Upon graduation Rushdie moved to Karachi, Pakistan, where his family had relocated in 1964, intending to pursue a career in television writing. In 1969 he returned to London, frustrated by censorship in Pakistan, and for the next ten years made his living as an advertising copywriter, while devoting his off-hours to fiction. In 1975 his first novel, *Grimus,* was published to less-than-critical acclaim but his subsequent novel, *Midnight's Children,* won the Booker Prize, launching Rushdie's career and introducing a new type of novel in Britain. The novel's scathing attacks on political dynasties, corruption, and the legacy of British colonialism are tempered with abundant humor and self-deprecating jokes, yet it gave offense. Foreshadowing the political turmoil that would embroil his later career (the 1989 religious edict from Iran condemning him to death for his *The Satanic Verses*), India's Prime Minister Indira Gandhi sued Rushdie and his publisher for libel, forcing them to make a public apology. But that did not deter Rushdie from tackling controversial subjects. Following the publication of *Midnight's Children* he appeared frequently on talk shows and wrote nonfiction pieces attacking the Thatcher government in Britain and the nostalgic 1980s film and television revivals of the old British Raj, or ruling colonial government, in India. Considered by many to be "the great Indian novel," *Midnight's Children* had a profound impact on British literature by giving voice to those affected most by colonialism and partition.

Events in History at the Time of the Novel

Toward independence. After nearly two centuries of colonial rule, in 1918 the British Raj passed reforms that granted the people of India "complete responsibility as conditions permit" and created a new "dyarchy" in which power would be shared between the British and elected

Salman Rushdie

Indian representatives (Wolpert, p. 297). Coinciding with the reforms, however, was the passage of the Rowlatt Acts (March 1919), which imposed wartime emergency measures to combat "seditious conspiracy" (Wolpert, p. 298). In real terms, the Rowlatt Acts, which extended the 1915 Defense of India Act, denied basic civil rights and due process and censored the press. Disparaged as the "Black Acts," they encountered universal opposition from Indian members of the Imperial Legislative Council and even prompted several members to resign, including Muhammad Ali Jinnah, a prominent Muslim politician and the future "Father of Pakistan." He lambasted the government as an "incompetent bureaucracy" and declared that "the fundamental principles of justice have been uprooted and the constitutional rights of the people have been violated" (Jinnah in Wolpert, p. 298). Mohandas Karamchand Gandhi, a pacifist grassroots leader of the independence movement, called the Acts symptoms of a "deep-seated disease in the governing body" and urged citizens to peacefully defy them (Gandhi in Wolpert, p. 298). He proclaimed a *hartal*, or national strike, to be "accompanied by fasting and prayer, which was normally associated with mourning a loved one (Chandra, p. 182). In the novel, Naseem, the protagonist's grandmother, wonders why there is a call for fasting and prayer when no one is dead, but her husband, Dr. Aziz, understands. He murmurs, "The British are wrong to turn back the clock. It was a mistake to pass the Rowlatt Act" (Rushdie, *Midnight's Children,* p. 34). Indeed, it proved to be a grave mistake, leading not only to death but to a tragedy of unimaginable proportions.

While Indians heeded Gandhi's call for a strike, paralyzing the railway system and business operations nationwide, Sikhs in particular, led by Drs. Kitchlu and Satyapal, organized meetings to discuss their response to Rowlatt. Fearing the potential action, British officials in Amritsar had Kitchlu and Satyapal arrested and deported on April 10. But instead of defusing the situation, the arrests outraged supporters and prompted them to march en masse to the British commissioner's camp. Raj troops opened fire on the crowd as they approached, killing several and turning the remainder into a terrorized mob that set fire to British banks and attacked English men and women in the streets. Order was restored when Brigadier-General R. E. H. Dyer arrived on the scene, but only temporarily. Three days later, on April 13, a crowd of 10,000 men, women, and children gathered in a park on a Sunday afternoon, not for political reasons but to celebrate a Hindu festival. Upon hearing that Sikhs had gathered at Jallianwala Bagh—in defiance of his order forbidding public assembly—Dyer's troops marched there, cornered the picnicking peasants, and, without warning, opened fire. "Dyer's troops fired for ten minutes, pouring 1,650 rounds of live ammunition into the unarmed mass of trapped humanity at point blank range. Some four hundred Indians were left dead, and twelve hundred wounded, when the brigadier and his force withdrew at sunset from the garden they had turned into a national graveyard" (Wolpert, p. 299). In the novel, Dr. Aziz is at the scene of the massacre. When he returns home covered in blood, Naseem cries out, "'But *where* have you *been,* my *God!*' 'Nowhere on earth,' he said, and began to shake in her arms" (*Midnight's Children*, p. 37).

News of the Jallianwala Bagh Massacre spread quickly and enraged not only Sikhs but Hindus and Muslims across India. The event turned even the staunchest loyalists of the British Raj into Indian nationalists, and calls for independence and the end of British rule echoed far and wide. The Raj, led by Viceroy Montagu, responded by relieving Dyer of his command (though he was given a hero's welcome in England, hailed as the "Saviour of the Punjab"). Montagu promised to implement immediate reforms, but Indian National Congress President Motilal Nehru (father/founder of the Nehru dynasty) called promises made by an "irresponsible executive and military" a "mockery," and leaders looked to their own means of achieving independence (Wolpert, p. 299).

Voices of division and unity. Though Indian leaders agreed on the urgent need for independence, they strongly disagreed on the form the new nation or government should take. Under Gandhi's influence, Congress had become an all-inclusive political entity dedicated to nationhood and Hindu-Muslim unity. But India was 70 percent Hindu, with the Hindu-dominated (though nominally secular) Congress as its primary mouthpiece; many Muslims therefore felt underrepresented and distrusted Hindu leaders to heed their concerns. Moreover, using "divide and conquer" tactics, the British system of government had instituted separate electorates for Hindus and Muslims, thereby splitting leadership along religious lines and enhancing divisions. Congress President Jawaharlal Nehru proposed abolishing this system in a new Indian constitution, but Muslim League President Muhammad Ali Jinnah wanted to maintain it in order to guarantee Muslims one-third of the seats in the legislature. Nehru, like Gandhi, was opposed to division along religious lines, and Congress put forward a proposal to redistribute provincial boundaries on a linguistic basis. But Jinnah strongly denounced the proposal and warned that unless a new constitution assured Muslims greater security, there would be "revolution and civil war" (Jinnah in Wolpert, p. 312).

During the next 20 years, negotiations between Congress and the Muslim League over the issue of representation deteriorated as the positions of the two groups became more polarized. In 1930 Jinnah began to speak of partition, arguing that Hindus and Muslims belong to "two different religious philosophies, social customs, and literatures . . . indeed, they belong to two different civilizations," and in 1939 he and Fazlul Huq of Bengal drafted the Lahore Resolution that first put forward the idea of Pakistan as a separate nation (Jinnah in Wolpert, p. 331). Gandhi called the Resolution the "vivisection of India" and tried to persuade both sides to compromise. But he could not convince either Congress or the League to make any significant concessions, and as World War II began, prospects of forging a consensus greatly diminished.

Independence and partition. By the end of World War II, the British had lost all desire to maintain rule in India. In February 1947, British

"EVENTS OF INDEPENDENCE"

1885 Indian National Congress founded to promote Indian self-rule.

1906 Muslim League founded.

1919 Rowlatt Acts; Jallianwala Bagh Massacre.

1920 *Satyagraha* campaign of "non-violent non-cooperation" and boycott of British goods and services, led by Mohandas Karamchand (M. K.) Gandhi.

1929 Constructive campaign of self-sufficiency, led by M. K. Gandhi, featuring "homespun" drive.

1930 Independence Day proclaimed by Jawaharlal Nehru (Jan. 26); Gandhi defies British salt tax.

1938 Sir Muhammad Iqbal murdered (April 21).

1939 Lahore Resolution—articulating demands that Pakistan become a separate nation comprised of the Muslim-majority provinces in eastern and northwestern India.

1942 Quit India movement, led by M. K. Gandhi, to oust the British Raj.

1946 Direct Action Day riots in Calcutta (Aug. 16); beginning of "civil war of secession"—5,000 dead, 100,000 homeless.

1947 Independence and partition (Aug. 15); 1-5 million die in communal violence; Congress leader Jawaharlal Nehru named first prime minister of independent India.

1948 M. K. Gandhi assassinated (Jan. 30); Muhammad Ali Jinnah dies (Sept. 1).

1951 Liaquat Ali Khan assassinated (Oct. 16).

1958 Pakistan military coup brings General Muhammad Ayub Khan to power.

1962 War with China over Himalayan border conflict; major military defeat for India.

1964 Jawaharlal Nehru dies of heart attack.

1965 India-Pakistan War over Kashmir—ends in stalemate in 22 days.

1971 Bangladesh War and independence (Dec. 16).

1975 State of Emergency declared by Indian Prime Minister Indira Gandhi.

1977 Emergency ends; Mrs. Gandhi defeated by Morarji Desai in national elections.

Prime Minster Clement Attlee announced that no later than June 1948, His Majesty's Government would transfer power to India and sent Lord Louis Mountbatten to serve as new Viceroy to oversee the operation. Mountbatten met with Jawaharlal Nehru and Liaquat Ali Khan (who represented the Muslim League and would become the first prime minister of Pakistan), and on April 20 Nehru agreed to the partition of the country.

On July 15, 1947—a year ahead of schedule—Mountbatten announced that independence and partition would take place in one month. Sheer pandemonium set in at his abrupt announcement. While government officials attempted to tally and divide India's assets and liabilities equally between two new nations in less than 30 days—82.5 percent for India, 17.5 percent for Pakistan—10 million Hindus and Muslims scrambled from their homes to find new ones, unsure of the exact borders they needed to cross or what they would encounter en route or at their final destinations. Tragically, what millions did encounter was a savage butchery perpetrated by all sides. From one to five million Indians—Muslim, Sikh, Jain, and Hindu—are estimated to have been killed in August 1947. Trainloads of slaughtered Muslims who arrived in Lahore, Pakistan, with the message "A present from India" written in blood across the car were answered with trainloads of murdered Hindus and Sikhs with the bloody message "A present from Pakistan" scrawled back (Mosley, p. 243). Muslims abducted, raped, and killed Hindu women; Hindus abducted, raped, and killed Muslim women; children caught in the wrong Hindu- or Muslim-controlled region were picked up by the feet, their heads dashed against the wall; neighbors turned guns on one another, buildings and farms were torched, land and life's work were lost, and families were torn apart forever. "There is no way of knowing how many parents were lost to their children in the sweep of this history, no way of knowing how many of them were lost by accident and how many by design" (Butalia, p. 41).

Whatever the final count, on all fronts the loss was catastrophic and the blame widespread. British haste and lack of adequate supervision during the transfer of power was grossly irresponsible, and the carnage and destruction perpetrated by Hindus and Muslims were indefensible. "Step by step, Delhi (Mountbatten) had been advised of the increasing gravity of the situation in the Punjab. The Viceroy had at least three chances to avert a massacre, and each time—from weariness, from lack of foresight, or from aversion to another clash with Jinnah—he looked the other way. The result was disastrous" (Mosley, p. 216). Independence had finally come, but it was, in the words of Urdu poet Faiz Ahmad Faiz, "a scarred daybreak, a night-bitten dawn" (Ahmad Faiz in Tully, p. 13). In *Midnight's Children* Saleem and Shiva are born at the moment of India's independence and partition. The offspring of a violent and difficult birth, both the characters and the countries came about "in the age of darkness; so that although we found it easy to be brilliant, we were always confused about being good" (*Midnight's Children*, pp. 196-97).

Democratic underdevelopment. Redeeming his nation's "tryst with destiny," Jawaharlal Nehru became India's first prime minister; he sought "life and freedom" for the country after two centuries of foreign domination (Nehru in Wolpert, p. 349). However, he inherited a nation beset with problems that could not be easily overcome. As historian Bipin Chandra notes, "All the euphoria of freedom in 1947 could not hide the ugly reality of the colonial legacy that India inherited—the misery, the mud and filth . . . the changes that had come had led only to the development of underdevelopment" (Chandra in Tully, p. 149).

The development that the British had undertaken had indeed led to underdevelopment of the masses, as well as to the creation of an elite ruling class. Teeming with natural resources and a vast potential market for British goods, India had been a business enterprise for the British Empire, and the actions it took were designed to further those interests. The railway system was built to facilitate industry, the educational system to groom civil servants, and, while the majority of Indians remained illiterate, an elite group was singled out for privilege. The British created a vast bureaucratic network—the Indian Civil Service—and staffed it with their chosen elite, which included the Nehru family. These Anglicized, upper-caste and predominantly urban Indians became ICS administrators and politicians and alone were granted the vote (they comprised 14.2 percent of the population). Within the confines of this framework, class divisions widened, preparing only a select few for independence and leaving the majority uneducated, ostracized, agrarian, and wholly unfamiliar with the democratic process. This resulted in the "chosen elite" becoming a virtual monarchy at independence and created a political dynasty of the Congress Party and Nehru family in particular, who en-

Hundreds of Muslim refugees crowd atop a train leaving New Delhi for Pakistan in September 1947, when India became independent of its British colonizers.

joyed an almost uninterrupted rule for the first 30 years.

1965 Indo-Pak War. In Pakistan the transition from independence to nationhood was not smooth, either. Jinnah died shortly after independence in 1948, Prime Minister Liaquat Ali Khan was assassinated in 1951, and a military coup in 1958 brought General Muhammad Ayub Khan to power. The territory of Kashmir had been disputed since partition, and at Nehru's death in 1964 tensions led to war. In the spring of 1965 the two nations began "sparring" in the Rann of Kutch, a desolate region both claimed, and the fighting escalated from there to Kashmir and the Punjab in August. Though Pakistan's Zulfikar Ali Bhutto officially denied that Pakistani soldiers were fighting in Kashmir, India's new Prime Minister Lal Bahadur Shastri declared that Pakistan's forces had invaded and vowed that "force and aggression against us will never be allowed to succeed" (Shastri in Wolpert, p. 375). Indian troops were sent to the Uri-Pooch "bulge" in Kashmir and also attacked Lahore in Pakistan. In the novel, Saleem insists the war was actually started by smugglers, working for the powerful Zulfikar family, whom Pakistani soldiers mistook for the Indian Army. "The story . . . is likely to be true as anything," Saleem says, "that is to say, except what we were officially told" (*Midnight's Children*, p. 324). Whatever the cause, fighting easily escalated with the aid of propaganda on both sides. With memories of the bloody partition still fresh and easily exploitable, the governments of India and Pakistan each bolstered support through wild exaggerations. "In the first five days of the war Voice of Pakistan announced the destruction of more aircraft than India had ever possessed; in eight days, All-India Radio massacred the Pakistan Army down to, and considerably beyond, the last man" (*Midnight's Children*, pp. 328-29). On September 23, 1965, a UN-sponsored cease-fire took effect—just three weeks after the war had begun. Both sides were low on ammunition, more than 2,000 were dead, and neither had made any significant gains (India conquered 500 square miles of Pakistan, Pakistan 340 square miles into Indian-controlled Kashmir). Pre-war borders were restored exactly as they had been before the conflict, and an icy peace again developed.

1971 Indo-Pak War. Six years later, the legacy of partition laid its claim to the present again. Pakistan, now under another military ruler, General Yahya Khan, held its first nationwide popular election in December 1970. Sheikh Mujibur Rahman—an East Pakistani lobbying for Bengali autonomy—swept the elections, which put him in line to become prime minister. Yahya Khan was vehemently opposed to Bengali leadership in West Pakistan and immediately canceled the meeting of the National Assembly that would officially vote in Sheikh Mujib (Mujibur Rahman). In March 1971 talks to resolve the conflict broke down, and Mujib proclaimed East Pakistan to be "Bangladesh," a free country. As national flags were unfurled in Dacca (now Dhaka), Yahya Khan sent his crack troops to East Pakistan, where they attacked the capital, arrested Mujib, and brought him back to Karachi. Fierce fighting broke out as the cry of "Jai Bangla!—Victory to Bengal!" filled the streets. But Bengalis were seriously outgunned, and, fearing slaughter, millions of terrified citizens poured across the border to India. India appealed to the United Nations to intervene and to United States President Richard Nixon to stop the flow of arms to West Pakistan. But Nixon refused (in fact, he was using Yahya Khan as a go-between to set up his summit with China) and, despite internal and international opposition, continued to supply weapons.

"NEHRU DYNASTY"

In Indian politics no family has been more influential than the so-called Nehru dynasty, which has ruled for more than 40 of the first 50 years of independence. Motilal inaugurated their life in government as the first president of the Indian National Congress. His son, Jawaharlal, followed his footsteps and became the first prime minister of India after independence in 1947. Two years after Jawaharlal's death in 1964, his daughter Indira Gandhi (no relation to M. K. Gandhi—she married a Parsi businessman, Firoze Gandhi, in 1952) became prime minister and served from 1966 to 1984, when she was assassinated (for three years, from 1977-80, she was out of office). Her sons, Sanjay and Rajiv, followed her into politics—Sanjay enthusiastically, Rajiv reluctantly. Sanjay, Mrs. Gandhi's close advisor who was being groomed to become prime minister, was killed in a plane crash in 1980, after *Midnight's Children* was written. Instead Rajiv became prime minister in 1984, then he too was assassinated in 1991. His widow, Sonia (an Italian), is currently head of the Congress party, serving in the Lok Sabha, or legislature, and has made several bids to become prime minister. Highly critical of this dynasty, Rushdie accuses Nehru and the Congress party of "clutching Time in their mummified fingers and refusing to let it move" (*Midnight's Children,* p. 317). He asserts that true democracy and progress will not take place in India until there is an end to this political legacy and a real changing of the guard.

Bengali refugees flooded the Indian border—the largest mass exodus in history. By September 1971, 8-10 million were living in refugee camps, costing India $200 million a month to feed. Prime Minister Indira Gandhi, who had just overwhelmingly won her second term in office, realized that India had to intervene militarily. In December she sent Indian troops to attack Yahya Khan's forces in East Pakistan and maintain a "holding action" to contain his forces in the West. With both air superiority and mass popular support, the Indian Army advanced easily in the east and closed in quickly on Yahya Khan's forces in Dacca. On December 15 Pakistan surrendered and Mrs. Gandhi proclaimed, "Dacca is now the free capital of a free country!" (Wolpert, p. 390). Mujib was released, returned to Dacca, and became the first prime minister of Bangladesh in January.

Neocolonial nepotism. The 1971 war victory was a major triumph for Mrs. Gandhi and greatly broadened her power base, enabling her to push a sweeping reform package through the Indian parliament. Included in her program was a vow to eliminate corruption and nepotism—two of India's "oldest traditions" (Wolpert, p. 394). However, the Gandhi-Nehru family was as guilty as anyone in these practices. In fact, as she announced the crackdown on nepotism, she had just appointed her son Sanjay to be one of her top government advisors and given him a plum management job at India's new automobile factory (Maruti). As Saleem laments in the novel, "O endless sequence of nefarious sons-of-the-great!" (*Midnight's Children*, p. 323). In Pakistan, Saleem is quick to point out, the corruption, lies, and nepotism were equally prevalent—they just took different forms. In Pakistan, "a country where truth is what it is instructed to be," he says, "reality quite literally ceases to exist, so that everything becomes possible except what we are told is the case" (*Midnight's Children*, p. 315).

Though certainly perpetuated by post-colonial society, the British colonial legacy greatly contributed to corruption and the practice of nepotism in India and Pakistan. By creating elite ruling classes, the Raj vested power in privileged families who continue to run the nations' businesses and governments. With the creation of the ICS (which became the Indian Administrative Service) the British virtually institutionalized bribery and favoritism in a red-tape-engulfed bureaucratic system that rulers and administrators perfected through years of practice. It is a system, known in India as the "Neta-Babu Raj" (Politician Bureaucrat Government), that has thwarted progress and has become, in the eyes of many, the "bane" of India's national situation (Tully, p. 104; Fernandez in Tully, p. 48). As Rushdie notes, midnight's children, or the citizens born at independence, became both the "masters and victims of their own times"—victimized by the colonial systems they inherited and learned to master (*Midnight's Children*, p. 443).

Indira Raj and the Emergency. Though her popularity soared after India's military victory in 1971, Mrs. Gandhi found herself in political turmoil just four years later. In June 1975, with social unrest brewing due to massive inflation, allegations of corruption, and widespread poverty, Mrs. Gandhi was found guilty of election fraud in the 1971 elections—a charge that carried with it a mandatory penalty of banishment from public office for six years. Her political opponents—chiefly Jaya Prakash (known as J. P.) Narayan and Morarji Desai of the *Janata Morcha* (People's Front)—called for her immediate ouster and declared a national strike. Like "the spring of a cornered tigress determined to survive and keep her grip on what she had," Mrs. Gandhi responded by dissolving the government, arresting agitators, and declaring a state of emergency (Fishlock, p. 87). Much like the Rowlatt Acts, the Emergency suspended civil rights, dispensed with due process, and censored the press.

By August more than 10,000 of her political opponents were in jail, and Mrs. Gandhi put into effect her Twenty-Point Program of radical reforms. Included in the Program were two very unpopular reforms, led by her son Sanjay: slum eradication and forced sterilization. "Forced sterilization spread terror among the poor and illiterate. Village men fled at the sound of a jeep. In population control, as in slum clearance, officials felt licensed to act as brutally as they wished, as if the end justified even the cruellest of means" (Fishlock, p. 88). Sanjay—India's "man of tomorrow"—led the nation's youth movement (the Sanjay Youth Central Committee), forcing sterilization on the lower-class masses. At the same time, as part of the civic beautification program, bulldozers rolled through the big cities, leveling urban slums and leaving tens of thousands homeless. In the novel, Mrs. Gandhi and her programs prove to be Saleem's chief enemy. His dwelling is flattened by her government-sponsored bulldozers, his wife killed in the process, and he is sterilized, leaving him, he feels, without any future. "Test- and hysterectomized, the children of midnight were denied the possibility of reproducing themselves . . . but they drained us of more than that: hope, too, was excised" (*Midnight's Children*, p. 423). For India's poor, the inability to procreate was a devastating blow economically as well as psychologically. Children meant workers, and workers meant income. Therefore the inability to reproduce robbed them of their livelihood as well as of their progeny. Rushdie, vehemently opposed to Mrs. Gandhi's suspension of democracy, says his children of midnight are "a metaphor of hope" whose purpose was ultimately "destroyed by Mrs. Gandhi" (Rushdie in Weatherby, p. 47).

In 1977 the Emergency ended and Mrs. Gandhi was ousted in national elections by Morarji Desai. But as Saleem notes in the novel, like most his is an "amnesiac nation," and just months later "the Emergency was rapidly being consigned to the oblivion of the past" (*Midnight's Children*, p. 428). Indeed, before publication Mrs. Gandhi and the Congress party were back in power.

The Novel in Focus

Plot summary. Sitting in a Bombay pickle factory near the end of his life, Saleem begins telling his fantastic life story to his fiancée, Padma. A "child of midnight" born at the exact moment of India's independence and partition, Saleem is bestowed with not only an incredible life but with extraordinary gifts. He discovers he has the power of telepathy at age 10, and when his sinuses are drained he gains an uncanny sense of smell. His life becomes "embroiled in Fate"—specifically the fate of post-independence India as seen through the eyes of an English-educated Muslim boy from Bombay: "I have been a swallower of lives; and to know me, just the one of me, you'll have to swallow the whole lot" (*Midnight's Children*, p. 11). With this pronouncement, Saleem begins the story of his grandfather, Aadam Aziz, a doctor educated in Germany who returns to practice in Kashmir. A Muslim with an orthodox clientele, Dr. Aziz is repeatedly called to treat a young woman who seems to suffer from every ailment. Religious mores dictate that he can only examine the virgin Naseem through a hole in a perforated sheet, and he falls in love with her three square inches at a time. They marry and move to Amritsar, where Dr. Aziz finds himself in the midst of the Jallianwala Bagh massacre and cheats death due to the opportune timing of a sneeze.

Dr. Aziz becomes a supporter of Mian Abdullah's Islamic movement, which brings him into contact with Nadir Khan, Abdullah's secretary. When Abdullah is murdered, Nadir Khan is forced to go into hiding in Dr. Aziz's basement. While there, he falls in love with the doctor's daughter Mumtaz (an ebony-skinned beauty), and the two live underground in a Taj Mahal of their own making. But their happiness is short-lived; Nadir Khan is forced to divorce Mumtaz when he fails to consummate their marriage.

Mumtaz then marries Ahmed Sinai, who had been courting her sister Alia, and renames herself Amina. They move to Old Delhi, which is in the grip of the Ravana gang (*Ravana* is also the name of the villain of the Hindu epic *Ramayana*). An anti-Muslim band, the Ravana gang extort money and destroy those who don't pay. The gang ultimately burns down Sinai's business, but he is left with enough insurance money to begin a new life. At this time, Amina is pregnant and troubled by a prophecy told by a local fortuneteller about the son in her womb. The soothsayer, Ramram Seth, says, among other things: "There will be two heads—but you shall only see one. . . . Newspapers praise him, two mothers raise him! Sisters will weep, cobra will creep . . . spittoons will brain him—doctors will drain him . . . soldiers will try him—tyrants will fry him" (*Midnight's Children*, p. 87). In short, everything the soothsayer predicts comes true, but it's all riddles to Amina and serves only to disturb her sleep.

It is the summer of 1947, and at the behest of friends who tell Ahmed that the price of land is "dirt cheap" in Bombay, he takes the insurance money and moves his family west. They move into a large villa atop a hill purchased from an exiting Englishman, William Methwold. Two months later, at the stroke of midnight, August 15, 1947, Saleem is born to the Sinais. Actually Shiva is born to the Sinais, and Saleem is born to a poor woman named Vanita as Mr. Methwold's illegitimate child. But ayah (nanny) Mary Pereira switches the babies at birth, performing her own revolutionary act—giving the illegitimate child a life of privilege and the rich-born child a life of poverty. Just as the soothsayer predicted, *The Times of India* hails Saleem as the first baby of independence and posts his picture on the front page. He and 1,000 other children of midnight will grow with the nations. A letter from Nehru predicts that Saleem's fate will "in a sense mirror the country's," and Saleem proceeds to fulfill that prophecy (*Midnight's Children*, p. 122).

Book Two brings us to Saleem's childhood in Bombay. He is greatly influenced by the cosmopolitan city in which he grows up, particularly by the glitz and escapism of Bombay's film industry, or "Bollywood." He keeps in touch with his fellow midnight children by organizing conferences he facilitates with the help of his mind—he can bring everyone together through the power of telepathy he gains on his tenth birthday. There are 581 in his "club" (which represents the number of seats in the Lok Sabha or lower house of the Indian parliament; the other 419 did not survive their first decade of life), and he "plunged whenever possible into the separate, and altogether brighter reality of the five hundred and eighty-one" (*Midnight's Children*, pp. 194-95). While the distance grows between his father and mother as his father falls deeper and deeper into alcoholism, and they ignore him and his sisters annoy him, Saleem escapes into his other world. Repeatedly he "turns inwards to my secret Children" where he finds companionship and kinship (*Midnight's Children*, p. 247).

Saleem becomes a teenager and the family moves to Pakistan. Far from his children of midnight now, his telepathic ability dwindles, but when his sinuses are drained he gains incredible olfactory powers instead. His new power of smell is uncanny, and he begins to perfect a "science of nasal ethics" (*Midnight's Children*, p. 308). He can smell the good and the bad in people and events and creates his own moral hierarchy of odors. The problem is, he prefers the baser odors to those morally superior and starts to question his own moral fiber.

Just after the move to Pakistan, war with India breaks out (the Indo-Pak War of 1965). Aunt Alia, who moved to Karachi in the wake of Amina's marriage to her "rightful" husband, finally gets revenge against her sister. Both she and the war literally destroy the Sinai family—all but Saleem and his sister Jamila Singer escape falling bombs. Saleem is hit on the head with that prophesied spittoon, however, and the blow, combined with the sudden death of his parents and the trauma of the war, devastates him. Over the next six years, he becomes extremely withdrawn and introspective; the narration dubs him "the Buddha."

When war again breaks out in 1971, Saleem puts his keen olfactory powers to work and becomes a "man-dog," a tracker for the West Pakistani Army. He is the one who sniffs out Mujib in Dacca, but the deed causes him to question his actions and loyalties. Luckily, at this point a fellow Midnight Child, Parvati the witch, finds him and smuggles him back to Delhi with a band of circus magicians. Saleem comes to live in the magicians' ghetto with Parvati and marries her when he discovers she is pregnant with Shiva's child. By this point, Shiva has become a war hero and local playboy. He is working for Sanjay Gandhi's slum eradication campaign, whose bulldozers one day clear the magician's ghetto, killing Parvati. But the baby and Saleem live, and along with his snake-charmer friend, Picture Singh, they return to Bombay, where, Saleem discovers, Mary has made a fortune manufacturing pickles (highly apropos, considering the pickle she made of his life). He goes to work for the only mother he has left and meets his fiancée, Padma, there. Certain that his death is imminent, he begins telling his life's story to Padma in order that "one day, perhaps, the world may taste the pickles of history" (*Midnight's Children*, p. 444). Saleem marries Padma once the "pickles" are preserved, that is, once his history has been recorded and, while winding through the crowd after the ceremony, at last comes into contact with his destiny. Saleem foresees that he will be trampled by the crowd, but he has already preserved his life, as well as insured the future—through his son who is not his son and his history preserved in pages and pickles that are "waiting to be unleashed upon the amnesiac nation" (*Midnight's Children*, p. 443). Like the other children of midnight, he is trampled underfoot, but he will never be silenced. "A thousand and one children have died, because it is the privilege and the curse of midnight's children to be both masters and victims of their times, to forsake privacy and be sucked into the annihilating whirlpool of the multitudes, and to be unable to live or die in peace" (*Midnight's Children*, p. 446).

Methwold's legacy. Linking the microcosm to the macrocosm, Salman Rushdie uses the clever analogy of William Methwold fathering Saleem and abandoning his responsibility to illustrate the devastating long-term effects of British colonialism on India. Methwold represents the British Raj, Saleem the Indian born to chaos at midnight when the nation gains independence. Methwold, anxious to leave, sells out cheap to Saleem's family and exits hastily, leaving behind influences and institutions intended and unintended, just as the British did in August 1947.

Intentionally Methwold leaves behind his mansions—his institutions—modeled after the best in Europe: Versailles, Buckingham, Escorial, Sans Souci. They are the palaces of Europe "sold on two conditions: that the houses be bought complete with every last thing in them, that the entire contents be retained by the new owners; and that the actual transfer should not take place until midnight on August 15, [1947]" (*Midnight's Children*, p. 95). Like the Raj, Methwold leaves his enormous Roman structures behind—an allegory of the vast bureaucratic and democratic frameworks that the British implemented and abruptly abandoned. They built their European monstrosities and filled them with their "things," which were of little or no use to the average Indians who inherited them. Amina has no use for portraits of "old Englishwomen" or Methwold's clothes in the cupboards (*Midnight's Children*, p. 96). In fact, there are so many British things cluttering the house, there is no place for any of her family's possessions or traditions. In Rushdie's analogy, Methwold's estate is the British government's colonial legacy—a vast entanglement of European institutions and systems that are preventing India from implementing its own democracy.

"I'm transferring power, too," Methwold tells Ahmed. "Got a sort of itch to do it at the same time the Raj does" (*Midnight's Children*, p. 96). But even he realizes that the British are pulling out too abruptly and leaving too much of a mess behind. "Bad show. Lost their stomachs for India. Overnight. . . . Seemed like they washed their hands—didn't want to take a scrap with them" (*Midnight's Children*, p. 96). As in Rushdie's allegory, after 200 years the British pulled up stakes and hurried back to England and like Methwold left more than just dirty laundry behind. They left a legacy; they left a people partly fathered by the British who now had to "live like those Britishers" and, as Amina says, clean up the stains that they left on the carpets (*Midnight's Children*, p. 96).

Like Mr. Methwold's conquest, the susceptible Vanita who bore his child, many Indians succumbed to British charms and seductive offers. When groomed for prime civil service positions, many eagerly accepted. In this way, as in the coupling of Vanita and Methwold, the Raj fathered a whole new class within India—the ICS bureaucracy and political dynasty that would linger long after the British pulled out. But, as with

Methwold's progeny, some offspring of this union were unintentional. The British seeds surely impregnated these "chosen elite," but, as in the case of Saleem, they also produced unplanned and illegitimate heirs. These "unintentional" children born at midnight represented the masses who were left to rebuild and to contend with the British institutions left behind. Like Saleem, these bastard children were impeded by the massive foreign structures that barred their entry, while others, like Indira Gandhi—part of the legitimate "chosen elite"—were born into those halls and held power so tightly that no others could wrest it away.

In this elaborate analogy, Rushdie also attributes the bloody communal violence at independence to Methwold's charms and powers of illusion. His hair—perfectly parted down the middle—is a gorgeous vision of India unified and equally divided. But, as Padma says, it is "too good to be true" and turns out to be a wig (*Midnight's Children*, p. 113). It is a hairpiece masking a barren landscape. It comes off as the lid comes off in India and communal rioting tears the nation apart. Methwold's hair is as slick as his talk and just as false. When the truth is revealed, he "distributes, with what looks like carelessness, the signed title—deeds to his palaces; and drives away" (*Midnight's Children*, p. 113). And Saleem, though he's never seen his father, finds him "impossible to forget," as does the rest of India, who are left with his colonial legacy (*Midnight's Children*, p. 113).

Using the allegory of Methwold, Rushdie mingles history and fantasy to show the lasting effects of colonialism on India. Like Saleem, the nation of India is the illegitimate offspring of the English. Saleem is both Ahmed and William's son-who-is-not-their-son and repeats the process with a son-who-is-not-his-son (but Shiva's son). In fact, all the children of Saleem's generation are born with this dual legacy and lineage. "All over the new India, the dream we all shared, children were being born who were only partially the offspring of their parents—the children of midnight were also the children of the time: fathered, you understand, by history" (*Midnight's Children*, p. 117). Through these relationships—these illegitimate children—Rushdie's novel shows that the neocolonial pattern will persist until there is real change in India. It seems to be arguing that until the European chains are broken and there is a substantive restructuring of the institutions and dynasties left behind, neocolonialism will continue to thwart Indian democracy and progress.

Sources and literary context. Though it is set at the independence of India, Pakistan, and Bangladesh and traces many related events, Rushdie himself hesitates to call *Midnight's Children* a "historical" novel. He describes it as a "political novel which transcends politics" (Rushdie in Weatherby p. 47). Clearly impacted by the Emergency of 1975 and the colonial legacy that contributed to it, Rushdie bases much of the novel and characters on actual people and events. But he is also quick to point out that the main characters are not based on himself or his family—in fact, the "most autobiographical things in the book are the places. Saleem's house is the house I grew up in . . . the school that he goes to is my school . . . those things are certainly based on my childhood" (Rushdie in May, p. 415). Rushdie cites the novel's literary influences, crediting, in addition to Gabriel García Márquez, Laurence Sterne, and Günter Grass, Nicolai Gogol, and Franz Kafka. He draws equally on Western and Eastern influences, consciously choosing the imagery of Saleem's family nose to invoke "The Nose" (Gogol), *Tristram Shandy* (Sterne), *Cyrano de Bergerac* (Edmond Rostand), and Ganesh (the elephant-headed god of good fortune, as well as the patron deity of literature in the Hindu pantheon). He also uses the Hindu gods Shiva and Parvati as characters and evokes Krishna often.

The structure of the novel draws from Indian epics like the *Mahabharata* and the *Ramayana* and is indebted to the traditions of oral cultures. Most obviously, the storyteller Saleem serves as a bard who relates his version of an epic tale, recording individual histories to convey a universal truth. Rushdie also blends the grandeur of epic with the melodrama of Bombay cinema. Not only does the novel's reproduction of memory imitate the long shots and close-ups of cinematic technique, but scenes in the novel conjure up the "Bombay talkies" of which Rushdie was enamored during his childhood. Children's classics and fairy tales, such as *The Arabian Nights,* clearly influence the content and structure of the novel as well. It is no coincidence that there are 1,001 children of midnight—the novel is at once a fantasy and a morality tale designed to entertain and enlighten its audience.

Reception. Upon publication, *Midnight's Children* was almost universally acclaimed. It won the 1981 Booker Prize for fiction, garnering praise as "comic, exuberant, ambitious, and stylistically brilliant" (May, p. 412). Anita Desai declared that Rushdie had painted a new portrait of India, and wrote, "*Midnight's Children* will surely be recognized as a great tour de force, a dazzling exhibition of the gifts of a new writer of courage, impressive strength, the power of both imagination and control and sheer stylistic brilliance" (Desai, p. 13). Writing for the *New York Times,* Clark Blaise said Rushdie's novel provided the ingredient Indian fiction had been missing: "a touch of Saul Bellow's Augie March brashness, Bombay rather than Chicago-born and going at things in its own special Bombay way" (Blaise, p. 18). Robert Towers in the *New York Review of Books* wrote that "no one should pick up *Midnight's Children* in the expectation of a rousing good story" and discredited its movement as "constantly impeded, dammed up, clogged." But despite that criticism, the review concluded by saying that Rushdie was one of the most important writers to come out of the English-speaking world in this generation (Towers, p. 30). The novel signified a bold new direction in British literature and was called the "great Indian Novel" (Weatherby, p. 41). It later won the Best of the Bookers award in 1993 as the best novel of the first 25 years of the prize's history.

—Diane Renée

For More Information

Blaise, Clark. Review of *Midnight's Children,* by Salman Rushdie. *New York Times Book Review,* 19 April 1981, 18.

Butalia, Urvashi. *The Other Side of Silence.* Durham, N.C.: Duke University Press, 2000.

Chandra, Bipan, Mridula Mukherjee, et al. *India's Struggle for Independence.* New Delhi: Penguin India, 1989.

Desai, Anita. Review of *Midnight's Children,* by Salman Rushdie. Book World, *Washington Post,* 15 March 1981, 13.

Fishlock, Trevor. *Gandhi's Children.* New York: Universe Books, 1983.

May, Hal, ed. *Contemporary Authors.* Vol. 111. Detroit: Gale Research, 1984.

Mosley, Leonard. *The Last Days of the British Raj.* New York: Harcourt Brace and World, 1961.

Reder, Michael R. ed. *Conversations with Salman Rushdie.* Jackson: University Press of Mississippi, 2000.

Rushdie, Salman. *Midnight's Children.* New York: Knopf, 1989.

Tharoor, Shashi. *India: From Midnight to the Millennium.* New York: Arcade, 1997.

Towers, Robert. Review of *Midnight's Children,* by Salman Rushdie. *New York Review of Books,* 24 September 1981, 30.

Tully, Mark. *India: 40 Years of Independence.* New York: George Braziller, 1988.

Weatherby, W. J. *Salman Rushdie: Sentenced to Death.* New York: Carroll & Graf, 1990.

Wolpert, Stanley. *A New History of India.* New York: Oxford University Press, 1997.

The Milagro Beanfield War

by
John Nichols

Born in Berkeley, California, in 1940, John Nichols was raised on Long Island and educated at Hamilton College in Clinton, New York. His first novel, *The Sterile Cuckoo* (1965), was generally well received, as was a second novel, *The Wizard of Loneliness* (1966). In 1969 Nichols moved from New York to New Mexico, and most of his subsequent writings, both fiction and nonfiction, deal with his adopted state. *The Milagro Beanfield War*, his third novel, is the first volume of Nichols's New Mexico Trilogy, which is continued in *The Magic Journey* (1978) and *The Nirvana Blues* (1981). Nichols's other novels include *American Blood* (1987), *An Elegy for September* (1992), and *The Voice of the Butterfly* (2001). A committed environmentalist, Nichols has also written several nonfiction volumes celebrating New Mexico's natural beauty, as well as the autobiographical *An American Child Supreme: The Education of a Liberation Ecologist* (2001). In *The Milagro Beanfield War* Nichols reveals an equal commitment to social justice, portraying New Mexico's traditional Hispanic subsistence farmers as under threat from encroaching white society.

THE LITERARY WORK

A novel set in a small fictional village in northern New Mexico's upper Rio Grande Valley c. 1970; first published in New York City in 1974.

SYNOPSIS

A clash between a wealthy white developer and a Hispanic farmer broadens into a larger conflict between New Mexico's dominant Anglo culture and that of the Hispanos who inhabited the area before the Anglos' arrival.

Events in History at the Time of the Novel

Historical background: Hispanos in New Mexico. Like the rest of the lands that are now the American Southwest, the upper Rio Grande Valley at the beginning of the nineteenth century lay in the far northern reaches of New Spain, the vast Spanish empire in the Americas. The high desert and mountains around the valley were inhabited by American Indians such as the Pueblo, Ute, and Apache, some of whom had been pushed out of the lower, more fertile areas along the Rio Grande by Spanish-speaking settlers starting in the sixteenth century. Essentially Spanish in culture, the settlers included both creoles (descendants of Spanish colonists) and mestizos (those of mixed Spanish and Indian descent). Most lived in small villages along the river valleys, farming communally and grazing sheep or (to a lesser extent) cattle on surrounding grassland.

In the 1820s Mexico won independence from Spain, and the area thus came under Mexican control. Contacts with Anglo-Americans also increased in the 1820s, as traders from Kansas and Missouri established the Santa Fe trail, linking Santa Fe—the Rio Grande Valley's major settle-

John Nichols

ment—with Independence, Missouri to the northeast and Chihuahua, Mexico to the south. Mexico's short-lived sovereignty over the region ended, however, with its defeat by the United States in the Mexican War (1846-48). Under the Treaty of Guadalupe Hidalgo (1848), Mexico ceded to the United States present-day California, Nevada, Utah, Arizona, New Mexico, and parts of Colorado, as well as recognizing U.S. claims over Texas. In return the United States paid Mexico $15 million, extended citizenship to Mexicans living in the ceded lands, and promised to recognize earlier land grants there. Such grants, originally given to individuals and villages by Spanish and then Mexican governors, comprised the framework on which legal rights to land had been based in both New Spain and, later, Mexico. The land grant system would come into conflict with the incoming Anglo-Americans' approach to land ownership, despite the treaty's promise to honor past grants. In real life, as in *The Milagro Beanfield War*, disputes over land would lie at the center of New Mexico's ethnic divisions and would arise when implementing the Treaty of Guadalupe Hidalgo. In the words of a character in the novel, "The war never ended in 1848" (Nichols, *Milagro Beanfield War*, p. 68).

Census figures for 1850 record over 80,000 Mexican Americans living in the American Southwest at that time, with nearly 55,000, by far the largest regional grouping, living in the New Mexico Territory (which then included Arizona). Smaller numbers lived in California (the so-called Californios) and Texas (the Tejanos). Of those in New Mexico, the densest population occupied the Rio Grande Valley from a point south of Albuquerque north through Santa Fe and the Taos Valley. They and their descendants have commonly referred to themselves as *Hispanos*, which is usually translated as "Spanish" (also they have used *Spanish Americans* to describe themselves in English).

Land, water, and economic culture. In contrast with Texas and California, New Mexico (which became a state only in 1912) did not immediately attract large numbers of Anglo-American immigrants. Only in the 1940s did Anglos begin to outnumber Hispanos in the state. However, the Hispanos' land began slipping out of their grasp long before the 1940s, and it became clear to them that numerical superiority did not guarantee political power or social equality under the Anglo-American system. For well over a century the complex issue of the land grants has been the major focus of controversy, but disputes about land have spilled over into other areas as well, which Nichols also dramatizes in the novel.

Land. Under the old system, land grants had been obtained by applying to the Spanish or Mexican governor; both individuals and villages could apply. Land was granted to successful Hispano applicants in three ways:

- Unconditional grants called *sitios* given to wealthy individuals for private ranches or *haciendas*. These were most common in the rolling grasslands of the Rio Abajo (lower river) area south of Sante Fe.
- Grants to powerful individuals called *patrones* who undertook to establish a village of at least 30 families.
- Communal grants to existing villages of at least 10 families. The community then distributed some lots for private use such as home-building and subsistence farming, holding the rest for common use such as grazing sheep or cattle. Communal grants were most common in the sheltered valleys of the Rio Arriba (upper river) area north of Santa Fe, where the novel's fictional village of Milagro is located; Milagro is portrayed as having received such a grant.

Problems arose for all three categories of land grant recipients and their heirs over the century following the Treaty of Guadalupe Hidalgo. Individuals were given deadlines to prove their grants under Anglo-American law, which often required time-consuming efforts to obtain documentation from Mexico City, where records were kept. Getting the records in time (or at all) frequently proved impossible for the commonly illiterate Hispanos. Even if the grant was accepted, U.S. authorities might reduce its scope by hundreds or even thousands of acres. Grants customarily did not spell out precise boundaries or areas, instead using landmarks like boulders or trees, for example, or the distance that a man can walk in a day. Such claims were easily challenged in court by the Anglo speculators who began arriving in New Mexico in the early twentieth century. As sociologist Carolyn Zeleny explains,

> The conflicts over land were turned over to a supposedly impersonal third party, the Court, which technically fulfilled the Anglo-American conception of "justice" but at the same time proceeded to fix the Spanish-American[s] in a position of subordination. . . . Enmeshed in a culture they little understood, in procedures and standards mysterious and technical, they were powerless to resist Anglo-American encroachment, but their sense of justice was outraged, and their hostility took the form of growing resentment against the usurpers of their country.
>
> (Zeleny, pp. 154-55)

The novel's Ladd Devine the Third, heir to an Anglo land dynasty in New Mexico, is the grandson of one such usurper. Devine's fictional fortune is based on the historical fact that, despite the Treaty of Guadalupe Hidalgo, Anglo-American authorities did not recognize communal land grants. All such communal lands were transferred over to the federal government, which then sold them to homesteaders, developers, and others, or else retained them as National Forest lands. Beginning in the 1880s, such lands became highly desirable as the railroads opened the west, and the prices of beef, cattle, and mutton rose sharply. The original Ladd Devine is depicted as having used political influence during this period to obtain, from the federal government, the lands once granted to Milagro. Such lost communal land grants make up a large proportion of the more than four million acres of land that Hispanos are estimated to have lost in the period between 1848 and 1970.

Water. Because the region receives little rainfall, farming there has always relied on irrigation, which has been practiced since before the Hispanos' arrival, when the Pueblo Indians farmed corn, beans, and squash in irrigated plots along the river. Traditional Hispano irrigation in the Rio Grande Valley relies on networks of river-fed main ditches called acequias, from which the farmer diverts water into smaller ditches in outlying fields using a shovel. Every year the farmers along each acequia elected a *mayordomo*, or mayor, to allocate the water and supervise the ditch's maintenance. This system was threatened as incoming Anglo-Americans developed their own ways of dealing with irrigation and other water-management issues such as flood control. The historical clash between the Hispanos' traditional use of acequias and the Anglos' reliance on large, expensive concrete dams plays a central role in the *Milagro Beanfield War.*

GRAZING RIGHTS AND THE U.S. FOREST SERVICE

By the late 1960s the federal government, and specifically the U.S. Forest Service, had become the focus of much of the Hispanos' growing resentment. The most contentious issue grew out of the Taylor Grazing Act of 1934, which was intended to address Hispanos' complaints about their decreasing pasture lands. The act provided for a permit system by which individuals would be able to purchase permits for grazing prescribed numbers of sheep, cattle, or horses on Forest Service lands. Already poor in cash, over the coming decades the Hispanos also faced rising permit fees, reductions in the number of permits available, a shortened grazing season, and a general lack of cultural understanding on the parts of Anglo federal employees. Many, like Joe Mondragón in The *Milagro Beanfield War,* found themselves with herds of sheep they were unable to graze on the lands that had once belonged to their communities. Throughout the 1960s Forest Service facilities in northern New Mexico were subjected to acts of vandalism such as arson and fence cutting. In the novel, Smokey the Bear symbolizes the federal role in depriving the villagers of their communal lands. The Forest Service mascot is a despised figure to the villagers.

Historian E. B. Fincher explains irrigation's legal background:

> An immense body of law dealing with community irrigation ditches (acequias) had developed in New Mexico between 1540 and 1847. Where water was so precious, where human organization was so utterly dependent upon a complex irrigation system, it was natural that water rights should seem almost sacrosanct. Among Ameri-

cans there was no appreciation of the attitude that land meant little without water, for until the acquisition of Texas and the Mexican Cession there had been no irrigated deserts in the United States.

(Fincher, p. 28)

While Anglo-American courts adopted many of the legal principles upon which the earlier laws were based, they did so within a framework that was alien for the Hispanos. As with the land itself, the Anglos' unfamiliar requirements and practices put the Hispanos at a disadvantage with respect to the water that they needed to irrigate the terrain. Their unfamiliarity with Anglo-American ways resulted in the erosion of their legal rights and access. The novel's plot hinges on the Hispano attitudes to irrigation that Fincher describes. Because of changes in the water laws, the small beanfield of a Hispano named Joe Mondragón no longer has legal irrigation rights, but he takes up a shovel and illegally irrigates it anyway, escalating the tensions already present between Anglos and Hispanos in the community.

Economic culture. As the above discussion suggests, disputes over land and water in New Mexico have a cultural dimension that reveals stark differences between Anglo and Hispano approaches to such issues. In economic terms, these differences can be summarized by observing that whereas Anglo culture stresses cash profits and land ownership, traditional Hispano culture emphasizes subsistence farming and land use. Accustomed to raising enough food and livestock to meet their own demands, Hispanos have viewed land not as a possession to capitalize for profit but as a life-sustaining resource. This attitude is reflected not only in the widespread phenomenon of communal lands but also in two other crucial facts. First, under Spanish and Mexican law, products were taxed, not the land itself; second, taxes were customarily paid in kind, such as crops and goods, not in cash.

Hispanos have traditionally put a low cultural value on cash, which is the very thing that Anglo-American culture has valued above all. American governments taxed land, not products, and those taxes had to be paid in cash, a reality for which the Hispanos were unprepared because of their different way of operating. Materially, the Hispanos' culture left them ill equipped to pay large amounts of land tax. In short, a leading reason for the Hispanos' loss of their lands—unpaid taxes—can be traced to the different economic cultures of the settled Hispanos and incoming Anglo-Americans.

Clashes over "conservancy districts." These cultural differences came to a head during the twentieth century, as Hispanos and Anglos clashed over the establishment of so-called "conservancy districts." The conservancy district essentially embodied the idea that in certain geographical areas, like river valleys, bonds should be sold and special taxes imposed in order to pay for expensive projects (such as dams, levees, and canals) that would, it was argued, benefit everyone. In 1925 the New Mexico Supreme Court upheld the constitutionality of the state's first such proposal, for the area of the Rio Grande near Albuquerque, and the Middle Rio Grande Conservancy District (M.R.G.C.D.) thereby passed into law.

Sixteen major floods had struck the Rio Grande between 1884 and 1925, causing numerous deaths and extensive property damage. Proponents of the M.R.G.C.D. argued that the project would control the floods and at the same time improve the region's irrigation. In their ranks were Anglo-American landowners, local business owners, and city officials, most of whom could afford to buy the bonds and pay the conservancy taxes, and many of whom also stood to benefit from the project. From the start, however, they were opposed by a mostly Hispano group of small farmers and others who believed that the project was unnecessary and who also knew that they could not afford to pay the conservancy taxes. Before the first decade was over, more than half the taxes assessed by the conservancy had become delinquent, and in 1937 a moratorium was declared on further construction taxes. But for many the moratorium came too late. Numerous Hispanos had already lost their lands because they could not pay the taxes. Some 10,000 Hispano residents of the valley were involved in protesting the M.R.G.C.D. by the time the movement finally collapsed in the late 1940s.

In 1971 another, much smaller, conservancy district was proposed in the area of the upper Rio Grande surrounding Taos. Called the Rancho Del Rio Conservancy District, this project included the construction of the proposed Indian Camp Dam, which would create a lake more than a mile long. By offering recreational opportunities such as fishing and sailing, proponents argued, the dam would benefit local businesses, as well as provide an additional supply of water to local farmers. At first the area's mostly Hispano farmers supported the proposal, but their support turned to opposition when they learned that landowners in the proposed district would be taxed to pay for part of the dam's construction and half of its maintenance costs. They feared that, like Hispanos in the M.R.G.C.D. to the south, they would be unable to pay the taxes and would lose their land. The Hispano farmers allied with Anglo-American environmentalists and with Chicano activists (see below) to form a grass-roots organization called the Tres Rios Association. The association fought the proposed conservancy district in the courts for five years before winning victory in 1975, when the measure was defeated.

Editorial by the Tres Rios Association
***Taos News*, April 26, 1972**

> We are . . . afraid of the wide powers of a conservancy district. Anyone familiar with recent articles in the *Albuquerque Journal* about the Middle Rio Grande Conservancy District understands by now that a district is a complicated and ever-expanding enterprise. . . . Also their district down there has come to be managed by the Bureau of Reclamation instead of the people of the Middle Rio Grande Valley. Members of the board [the district's governing body, with power to assess taxes] aren't even elected.
>
> (*Taos News* in Orona, forthcoming)

The public debate over the Del Rio Conservancy District in the early 1970s finds many parallels in the fictional saga that makes up the *Milagro Beanfield War* and its two sequels. For example, the Del Rio Conservancy District comprises a real-life model for *The Milagro Beanfield War*'s Milagro Valley Conservancy District, while the Indian Camp Dam is thinly fictionalized in the novel's Indian Creek Dam. Similarly, the novel's Milagro Land and Water Protection Association is loosely based on the Tres Rios Association. In the novel, however, environmentalists and Chicano activists are largely absent from the struggle, although Nichols does allude to Chicano activism as part of his story's background. In real life, democratic political activism actually played a major role in the struggle. A stereotype exists of Chicano or Hispano "'peasant' whose only recourse against government injustice and capitalist oppression is to engage in spontaneous acts of banditry and revolution," but in fact Hispano farmers resorted to peaceful, proper means of protest, quickly seeking "legal expertise from political leaders, lawyers, and business people," understanding "the rule of law and their place in it" (Orona, forthcoming).

The Chicano movement. As civil rights movements attracted increasing attention in American public life during the 1960s, some Mexican Americans became more militant in protesting their subordinate position in American society. The term *Chicano*, originally a pejorative label (short for *Mexicano*) for any unskilled Mexican worker, was adopted by the militants as a sign of unity against Anglo culture. At least part of the movement's origins can be traced to the Hispanos of New Mexico's Rio Grande Valley. Led by the charismatic preacher Reies Lopéz Tijerina, Hispano activists sought to reclaim land grants that they argued had been lost through fraud and legal trickery. They began confronting authorities in northern New Mexico in 1966, spurring a movement for greater political awareness and cultural pride that spread to other areas with large Mexican American populations such as California and Colorado.

Though Chicano activism plays no overt role in the novel, Nichols does refer to the movement several times in passing. Moreover, the violent atmosphere that occasionally surrounded movements such as Tijerina's (though Tijerina himself did not espouse violence) are reflected, perhaps

REIES TIJERINA AND THE TIERRA AMARILLA COURTHOUSE RAID

On June 5, 1967, three carloads of armed Chicano activists invaded the Rio Arriba County courthouse in the small, dusty village of Tierra Amarilla, the county seat. When the activists drove off into the mountains after two hours of gunfire and threats, two lawmen had been shot, and one of them lay close to death. A massive police manhunt ensued. The activists were members of Reies Tijerina's Alianza Federal de Mercedes (Federal Alliance of Land Grants), which had been agitating for the return of lost Hispano land grants since 1963. The widely publicized courthouse raid was part of an increasingly angry campaign to reclaim the lost Tierra Amarilla land grant of nearly 600,000 acres, given by the Mexican government to one Jose Manuel Martinez in 1832. Tijerina himself was arrested 5 days later, and eventually he was convicted on two charges stemming from the raid (accounts had varied as to whether he was actually present). *Newsweek* magazine estimated the Alianza's membership at about 14,000 people. One observer suggested that "While about 90 percent of those northern people think the land was really stolen from them, only about 20 percent think Reies can get it back." (Nabokov, p. 18)

Ruben Blades as Bernabé Montoya in the 1988 film version of *The Milagro Beanfield War.*

in exaggerated form, by the rambunctious, colorful, and often trigger-happy characters who populate Nichols's fictional story.

The Novel in Focus

The plot. *The Milagro Beanfield War* opens with a paragraph-long summary of the motives that various Milagro townspeople attribute to Joe Mondragón in illegally irrigating his tiny, dried-up beanfield. The brief passage introduces a few of the novel's major characters, as well as indirectly revealing much about the town's built-up tensions and the potentially incendiary nature of Joe's seemingly trivial action. Milagro's sheriff, Bernabé Montoya, thinks Joe simply has "a king-size chip on his shoulder." The owner of the Frontier Bar, Tranquilino Jeantete, thinks Joe wants to make a defiant gesture towards the Devine Company, which runs the small, half-deserted town. The town's storekeeper, Nick Rael, thinks Joe hopes to make trouble and "drive up ammo sales at the same time he put Nick out of business," thereby wriggling out of the $90 debt he owes to the store for items bought on credit. The Devine Company's owner, Ladd Devine the Third, thinks Joe intends "a personal assault on his empire"; and the old-timer Amarante Córdova thinks "Joe did it because God had ordered him to start the Revolution without any further delay." (All citations are from *Milgaro Beanfield War*, p. 3).

Joe Mondragón, 36 years old, and his wife Nancy have three children and live in Milagro, in a small hand-made adobe house "surrounded by junk" (*Milagro Beanfield War*, p. 25). A generally unemployed jack-of-all-trades who can fix anything, Joe has a tool shop full of "begged, borrowed, or stolen" tools (*Milagro Beanfield War*, p. 25). He drives a beat-up old pick-up truck, and usually has several small-time (and often shady) projects underway at a time. Joe shows little respect for the law. He is regularly in and out of the local jail for fighting, drunkenness, and stealing sheep owned by the Devine Company. And like many in Milagro, he feels resentful:

> He was tired, like most of his neighbors were tired, from trying to earn a living off the land in a country where the government systematically gathered up the souls of little ranchers and used them to light its cigars. . . . And he was damn fed up with having to buy a license to hunt deer on land that had belonged to Grandfather Mondragón and his cronies, but which now resided either in the pockets of Smokey the Bear, the state, or the local malevolent despot, Ladd Devine the Third.
>
> (*Milagro Beanfield War*, p. 26)

For over a century the company, founded by the first Ladd Devine in the nineteenth century, has controlled the town. Joe's family, like many Hispano families in Milagro, used to own a fine house and fields on the west side of town. But in a series of "complicated legal and political maneuverings" in 1935, much of the water from nearby Indian Creek was "reallocated to big-time farmers down in the southeast portion of the state or in Texas, leaving folks like Joe Mondragón high and much too dry" (*Milagro Beanfield War*, p. 28). Now the west side is barren and deserted. Though Joe and his family live elsewhere in town, he still owns his parents' old house and a small beanfield on the west side. Most of the others (except for the stubborn ninety-three-year old, Amarante Córdova) have sold their west side land to the Devine Company. Unbeknownst to the villagers, the company now stands to make a killing on the abandoned west side land, which will skyrocket in value when the planned Indian Creek Dam returns water to it. The townspeople are to pay for the dam, through legislation taxing them as part of a so-called conservancy district. Yet the company—which orchestrated the scheme, and which also plans an exclusive vacation resort along the shores of the resulting lake—will be the main beneficiary.

Joe's decision to irrigate his small west side beanfield threatens the company's plans, because it amounts to a direct challenge against the forces that have dominated the town's history:

> irrigating his field was an act as irrevocable as Hitler's invasion of Poland [which started World War II] . . . because it was certain to catalyze tensions which had been building for years, certain to precipitate a war.
>
> (*Milagro Beanfield War*, p. 28)

News of Joe's action quickly spreads, and two sides emerge in a struggle to determine what it will mean for the community. The two sides are not cleanly divided on ethnic lines, since the official establishment has enlisted Hispanos (such as Sheriff Montoya) in its structure just as its opponents enlist Anglos (such as the liberal lawyer Charley Bloom). Backed by wealth and political influence, Ladd Devine mobilizes the state engineer's office, the state police, and the U.S. Forest Service in his support. Hesitant to act for fear of arousing unfavorable publicity, Devine's allies make informal attempts to dissuade Joe from continuing to divert water into his field. Joe pugnaciously runs several of them off his land, including Eusebio Lavadie, "Milagro's only wealthy Chicano rancher," and Carl Abeyta, a Hispano Forest Service employee (*Milagro Beanfield War*, p. 36). An undercover state police operative named Kyril Montana cruises through the town to assess the situation—unaware that his every move is tracked by locals, who gossip over the phone. Outraged by this covert police reconnaissance and other incidents, a citizens' group opposed to Devine organizes under the leadership of the fiery and beautiful local businesswoman Ruby Archuleta, owner of Milagro's Body Shop and Pipe Queen (specializing in car repair and plumbing).

Claiming that he simply wants to grow some beans, Joe resists Ruby's attempt to politicize the issue, but she insists on its larger significance.

MAJOR CHARACTERS ON BOTH SIDES IN *THE MILAGRO BEANFIELD WAR*

Local Activists	The Devine Company's Supporters
Joe Mondragón a chronic troublemaker who illegally irrigates his field, touching off the war.	**Ladd Devine the Third** owner of the Devine Company.
Ruby Archuleta a beautiful widow who leads the community in rallying support for Joe and opposing the Devine Company.	**Eusebio Lavadie** a Hispano who has grown wealthy through association with the company.
Amarante Córdova an old man who symbolizes the resilience of Hispano culture. He guards Joe's beanfield with his ancient pistol.	**Bernabé Montoya** the Hispano sheriff who reluctantly does the company's bidding.
Nancy Mondragón Joe's wife.	**Horsethief Shorty Wilson** a former rodeo rider who is Ladd Devine's right hand man.
Charley Bloom a liberal lawyer from the East, married to a Hispano woman.	**Nick Rael** the Hispano owner of the town's general store, he generally cooperates with the company.
Onofre Martinez an old man who assists Amarante Córdova in harassing the company.	**Kyril Montana** an undercover agent for the state police.
Tranquilino Jeantete owner of the Frontier Bar.	**Carl Abeyta** a Hispano who works for the hated Forest Service.

"It's your beanfield," Ruby tells him, "but it represents all our beanfields. That dam is gonna hurt all of us, and we're all gonna pay the conservancy taxes, and there isn't anybody here who hasn't been screwed by Ladd Devine" (*Milagro Beanfield War*, p. 154). A period of "Waiting for the War to Start" ensues, as tensions escalate in series of incidents (*Milagro Beanfield War*, p. 373). Supporters from both sides are beaten or threatened, and a brawl erupts at a softball game pitting locals against company players. Events come to a head, however, when word gets out that Joe has shot a local man named Seferino Pacheco in a brawl over Pacheco's pig, which is famous in the town for causing trouble and which has gotten into Joe's beanfield. While Pacheco lies close to death in the hospital, a manhunt begins for Joe, who is thought to have escaped into the nearby mountains. Led by Kyril Montana, the posse fails to find the fugitive, and Montana himself is mysteriously attacked in the mountains by three gunmen (who turn out to be Ruby Archuleta, her son Eliu, and her lover, a man named Claudio Garcia). Joe's supposed flight is revealed as a ploy to distract the police, and at the right moment Joe—who never left Milagro—turns himself in. Pacheco recovers, and after it is established that Joe shot him in self-defense Joe is released.

In a meeting with the governor, who is alarmed at the prospect of bad publicity, Devine is forced to abandon his plan for the dam and the conservancy district. As the representative from the state engineer's office tells him, "We underestimated the people's ability to comprehend the complexities and to react against what none of them actually understands, other than instinctively, to this day" (*Milagro Beanfield War*, p. 613). As the novel ends, Joe Mondragón reflects uncomfortably that "his field, his bunch of crummy beans" may have made him into something he never wanted to be: a leader (*Milagro Beanfield War*, p. 616).

The collective, the individual, and the 1960s counterculture. Many critics have observed that the real protagonists in *The Milagro Beanfield War* are not any of the characters portrayed, but the two clashing cultures they represent, along with two sets of opposing cultural values. In Anglo-American culture a leading value is individualism, whose economic side is free enterprise capitalism, as represented in the novel by the aptly named Devine Company. In Hispano culture, by contrast, a chief value is collectivism, represented in the novel by Joe Mondragón's determination to reassert a traditionally shared communal right—and by the communal support with which he succeeds in doing so. Joe's old uncle, Juan Mondragón, reflects this collective spirit when he argues in favor of opposing the company: "In the old days people were more together," he says (*Milagro Beanfield War*, p. 153).

Individualism has always been at the heart of Anglo-American culture, but in the 1960s and 1970s many young Americans began increasingly to question it. This reaction against individualism played a central role in the rise of the connected movements known as the New Left and the so-called hippie counterculture. Hippie communes, for example, attempted to "get back to nature" by achieving (with varying degrees of success) a communal lifestyle based on collective work and shared participation. Indeed, one such fictional commune, located near Milagro, plays a peripheral role in the novel. And in real life, the northern New Mexico town of Taos—a bastion of the Hispano homeland—became a mecca for counterculture artists, writers, and others who sought an alternative lifestyle in the late 1960s and early 1970s.

One early Anglo-American immigrant was John Nichols, who moved to Taos in 1969, and who was very much a part of the counterculture. In addition Nichols is a self-professed socialist, and as such he exemplifies the counterculture's exaltation of communal or collective values as against individualism, and especially as against capitalism. In his portrayal of New Mexico's threatened Hispano culture, with its traditional emphasis on a communal life based on subsistence not profit, Nichols thus dramatizes some of the important social issues that preoccupied his own generation.

Sources and literary context. The violent events surrounding Reies Tijerina's 1967 courthouse raid provided the immediate inspiration for *The Milagro Beanfield War*'s confrontation between Hispano resentment and Anglo institutions, although Nichols had not yet moved to New Mexico in 1967. After moving to Taos, Nichols visited many of the smaller villages of the Taos Valley, near the western slopes of the beautiful Sangre de Christo Mountains. Along with their inhabitants, these villages—Arroyo Hondo, San Cristóbal, San Antonio, Arroyo Seco, as well as Taos itself—offered the basis for the novel's descriptions of Milagro. The novel's fictional Miracle Valley (in which Milagro is set; Milagro means "miracle" in Spanish) is a thinly disguised fictional version of the Taos Valley. The two subsequent novels in Nichols's New Mexico

Trilogy continue the story of encroaching real estate development in the Miracle Valley, which ends up (like the Taos Valley) with vacation resorts, condominiums, and middle-class housing projects.

The Milagro Beanfield War falls within a well established tradition of social protest writing in American literature. One clear literary model is John Steinbeck's novel *The Grapes of Wrath* (1939), which chronicles the Joad family's displacement from their land in Oklahoma and their subsequent mistreatment as migrant workers in California. Another leading example from this tradition is Frank Norris's novel *The Octopus* (1901), which condemns the rapacious land-grabbing methods by which the railroad industry expanded in the late nineteenth century. Like these classic American novels, *The Milagro Beanfield War* is based on historical events, and like them it celebrates common farmers while mourning their eviction by the forces of capitalist progress from land they have worked for generations.

Reception. *The Milagro Beanfield War* received generally positive reviews, with most critics finding its lively depiction of colliding cultures both humorous and powerful. Comparing Nichols with both Steinbeck and Norris, Motley Deakin writes in *Western American Literature* that its "basic seriousness" complements a colorful, "episodic" wit, recalling "the American humor of the frontier West" (Deakin, p. 250). Not all were charmed by Nichols's hyperbolic, often profane writing style, however. The *National Observer*'s Larry L. King, for example, finds the novel to be "a big, gassy, convoluted book that adds up to a disappointment—one somehow failing to equal the sum of its parts" (King, p. 27). Frederick Busch in the *New York Times Book Review* also belittles Nichols's informal prose, calling it "so slack as to be hastily composed, or so folksy as to be patronizing to the folk" (Busch, pp. 53-54). While praising parts of the novel as "gentle, funny, transcendent," Busch also faults its characterization as shallow and stereotypical.

However, John E. Loftis, responding to such criticisms at length in the *Rocky Mountain Review of Language and Literature*, defended the novel, suggesting that Busch "condemns it for . . . the wrong reasons" and arguing that Nichols's approach fits a novel in which cultures, not characters, are the main protagonists (Loftis, p. 210). "Nichols's concerns as a novelist are primarily social," Loftis writes, "and he has created an unusual kind of protagonist . . . to give artistic form to these concerns," one that has "reshaped the genre" of the social novel (Loftis, p. 213).

—Colin Wells

For More Information

Busch, Frederick. Review of *The Milagro Beanfield War*. *New York Times Book Review,* 27 October 1974, 53-54.

Deakin, Motley. Review of *The Milagro Beanfield War*. *Western American Literature* 10, no. 3 (November 1975): 249-50.

Fincher, E. B. *Spanish-Americans as a Political Factor in New Mexico, 1912-1950*. New York: Arno Press, 1974.

King, Larry L. "Few Shots in a 'Beanfield War.'" *The National Observer*, 16 November 1974, 27.

Loftis, John E. "Community as Protagonist in John Nichols' '*The Milagro Beanfield War*.'" *Rocky Mountain Review of Language and Literature* 38, no. 4 (1984): 201-13.

Nabokov, Peter. *Tijerina and the Courthouse Raid*. Albuquerque: University of New Mexico Press, 1970.

Nichols, John. *The Milagro Beanfield War*. New York: Ballantine, 1976.

Nostrand, Richard L. *The Hispano Homeland*. Norman, Okla.: University of Oklahoma Press, 1992.

Orona, Kenneth M. *Muddy Water: Power, Contest, and Identity in New Mexico's Middle Rio Grande Valley, 1848-1947*. Forthcoming.

Rosenbaum, Robert J. *Mexicano Resistance in the Southwest*. Austin: University of Texas Press, 1981.

Zeleny, Carolyn. *Relations Between the Spanish-Americans and Anglo-Americans in New Mexico*. New York: Arno Press, 1974.

Native Speaker

by
Chang-rae Lee

Chang-rae Lee was born in South Korea in 1965 and immigrated to the United States when he was three years old. He and his family lived in Pittsburgh, Pennsylvania, and New York City before moving to the suburb of Westchester, New York. Lee's father completed his medical training in the United States and became a psychiatrist after learning English. Lee himself attended Phillips Exeter Academy and then Yale University. After college, he worked as a financial analyst on Wall Street and then, in 1993, acquired a master of fine arts from the University of Oregon where he also taught creative writing. Lee went on to direct the creative writing program at Hunter College in New York and to launch his own set of novels before joining the creative writing faculty at Princeton University in 2002. His initial novel, *Native Speaker*, won widespread critical acclaim and distinction as one of the first Korean American novels to be released by a major American publisher. Fictionalizing a Korean American experience, *Native Speaker* portrays the diversity of and tensions between immigrant communities in late-twentieth-century New York.

THE LITERARY WORK

A novel set in New York City and its suburbs during the 1990s; published in 1995.

SYNOPSIS

A young man confronts past conflicts with his immigrant father and the frustrations of assimilating into American society as a second-generation Korean American.

Events in History at the Time the Novel Takes Place

Post-1965 immigration from Korea. Anti-Asian sentiment in the second half of the nineteenth century led to Congress's curtailing Asian immigration to the United States through the beginning of the twentieth century until the passage of the 1924 National Origins Act. Effective from 1929 to 1965, this act limited the number of immigrants from a country to 2 percent of their population already in the United States according to the census of 1890. Extending an earlier 1917 restriction, the Act almost entirely banned immigration from Asia. The measure that finally lifted this ban was the Hart-Cellar Act of 1965, which opened up immigration by allowing 20,000 newcomers from every country. In addition to the quota, immediate family members of U.S. citizens—specifically spouses, minor children, and parents— qualified for entry under the provision for family reunification. In the first 10 years of the act, preferences were given to skilled workers and professionals, such as doctors, nurses, and engineers. The impact of the act on Asian American immigration has been monumental. Since 1965, immigrants from Asia have comprised half of all newcomers to the United States. The Asian American population more than doubled from 1970 to 1980, increasing from 1.4 to 3.5 million people (Osajima, p. 168).

Chang-rae Lee

By the mid-1970s, Asian nations had replaced Western European nations as the top countries of origin for immigrants to America each year.

Before the twentieth century, there were fewer than 50 Korean immigrants in the United States (Park, *The Korean American Dream*, p. 9). The early- to mid-twentieth century saw a scant number of immigrants enter the United States from Korea in contrast to the totals from Japan, China, and the Philippines. One reason for the scant number lay in Korea's status as a colonial land under Japanese rule until the end of World War II (1905-45). Since Koreans were colonial subjects of the Japanese empire, the U.S. authorities considered them part of the Japanese population. Meanwhile, Japan imposed restrictions on its own populace; in 1907 it entered into a "Gentlemen's Agreement" with the United States: in exchange for fair treatment and protection of Japanese residents who were already in America, Japan would prevent the emigration of new laborers to the land. Hawaii was an exception; wives and families of Korean immigrants who had earlier settled there were allowed entry until 1924. In any case, the "Gentlemen's Agreement" affected Korea only minimally, since by 1905 Japan was already restricting emigration from Korea, to prevent the growth of Korean independence efforts abroad.

Some Korean war orphans, war brides, and scholarship students immigrated to the United States after the Korean War (1950-53), thanks to post-World War II legislation admitting entry to refugees and families of servicemen. But it was not until the previously mentioned Hart-Cellar Act of 1965 that a substantial increase occurred in the population of Korean immigrants. According to the United States census, the Korean American population grew astronomically from 70,598 in 1970 to 798,849 in 1990, an elevenfold increase (Park, *The Korean American Dream*, p. 17). With this post-1965 influx, highly visible and substantial Korean American communities emerged across the nation, especially in urban areas such as New York and Los Angeles. Los Angeles has the largest population of Korean immigrants; New York, the second largest: "As of 1994, approximately 100,000 Korean Americans lived in New York City proper, with an estimated 150,000 to 200,000 living in the entire New York-New Jersey metropolitan area" (Kim, p. 43).

This surge in population entailed the immigration of a certain strata of Korean newcomers. Because of occupational preferences in the 1965 Hart-Cellar Act, almost three-quarters of the post-1965 Korean immigrants were middle class and college educated. The emigration of this strata of Koreans has been attributed not only to American policy but also to the South Korean economy. Its focus on industrialization and modernization after the Korean War created an internal demand for lower-paid, unskilled labor and resulted in a scarcity of jobs for the college graduates, so many opted to seek their fortunes in the United States. By the early 1990s, however, emigration from South Korea had slowed because of a booming domestic economy.

Korean American entrepreneurs. By the mid-1980s journalists had begun to chronicle the proliferation of Korean-owned businesses in New York City and Los Angeles. Journalists focused attention on these small businesses to a degree not experienced by other facets of the Korean American population. Mainstream media such as the *New York Times* reported on the increasing success and dominance of Korean American enterprises, such as the greengroceries owned by Mr. Park in the novel. In the 1980s and 1990s, Korean Americans owned most of the greengroceries in a host of neighborhoods around New York City as well as other urban centers. Profitable in their own right, these Korean-owned small businesses also boosted the economies of their local areas.

The initial economic resources of Korean immigrants partially explains their tendency to become small business owners in the United States. Because a large majority of the post-1965 immigrants came from a middle-class background, some brought financial resources from Korea. Others pooled the savings they had earned in America with fellow immigrants or borrowed from relatives and friends. In *Native Speaker*, Henry's father is such an entrepreneur. The seed money for his first store comes from a *ggeh* (also spelled *kye*), a "Korean 'money club,'" described as an informal "rotating credit association" (Lee, *Native Speaker*, p. 50; Abelmann and Lie, p. 133). Like a bank, the *ggeh* collects savings from members, then doles out funds on a rotating basis, an arrangement that helps jump-start small businesses owned by Korean entrepreneurs. The strategy appears effective. More than twice as many Koreans work for themselves than whites in America, and with considerable success. In a 1989 survey, 40 percent of employed Korean American men owned their own businesses, and 44 percent had household incomes over $50,000 (Abelmann and Lie, p. 129). While other Americans may be impressed by this degree of financial success, it does not alleviate the many obstacles that Korean entrepreneurs must face: "crime, high commercial rents and taxes, unwieldy city regulations, and stiff business competition" (Kim, p. 169). Also many entrepreneurs are plagued with less visible social problems. Even in the success stories featured in the *New York Times*, many small business owners and their frequently unpaid family members report ten-hour workdays for six or seven days a week and, in certain cases, dangerous working conditions. Crimes or bankruptcies of these businesses are likely underreported and missing from popular statistics (Tabor, p. B1). In *Native Speaker*, Lee balances Mr. Park's apparent financial success and security with stories of other Korean shopowners who are robbed, beaten, killed, or forced to watch their stores burn to the ground.

The myth of the model minority. Early-twentieth-century America considered Jews the "model minority" in relation to mainstream society when it came to achieving economic and academic success (Bell, p. 28). In mid-to-late-twentieth century America, the media portrayed Asian immigrants as the new "model minority," whose members embodied the ethics of hard work, discipline, and duty to family and community stressed in their Asian homelands.

At the height of the civil rights movement during the 1960s, the economic and educational success of Asian Americans was compared to the lack of educational achievement or community infrastructure among other racial minorities. The mainstream press has portrayed Asian Americans as succeeding without the help of federal programs like welfare, in contrast to other minority groups. But recent critics note that this comparison masks underlying conditions that perpetuate poverty and other social ills in Asian American, African American and Latino communities. Journals of the mid-to-late twentieth century continued to portray Asian Americans as a model minority. Articles depicting Chinese Americans and Japanese Americans as such appeared in the *U.S. News & World Report* and *Newsweek* in 1966, citing above-average academic achievement and family income as some of the markers of Asian American success. In the 1980s, articles in journals like the *New Republic* reiterated these reasons for Asian American success and reestablished Asian Americans as the model minority for another generation. The articles showed them as surpassing whites in education and income: Asian American students appeared in substantial numbers in elite universities; they scored higher on the math Scholastic Aptitude Test (SAT) than whites; Asian immigrants were more likely to be college educated than white Americans; and the Asian American median family income had exceeded the white median by the 1980s. But scholars have countered such favorable look at these generalizations with often overlooked statistics: below-average

THE "KOREAN AMERICAN DREAM" FOR THE SECOND GENERATION

In recent interviews, Korean immigrants showed disappointment in their occupations as shopkeepers and small business owners and surprise at their entrepreneurial status, given the advanced academic degrees they acquired back in Korea or even in America. Although more than 70 percent of the men emigrate intending to own businesses in America, first-generation immigrants have expressed hope that their children will not face the same discrimination, economic uncertainty, and occupational isolation they have encountered as small urban business owners. The dream is for their children to become professionals and to thereby avoid this fate (Abelmann and Lie, p. 129).

per capita income; uncompensated overtime; and underemployment and poverty among the more recent immigrant groups, as well as the more established Asian American communities. A majority of Southeast Asian refugees, to take one example, live below the poverty line, and many do indeed depend on welfare because of unemployment, forced occupational changes and lack of English proficiency (Le, pp. 176-79). Economic success and above-average family income are balanced against the hours of uncompensated labor by family members in family-owned businesses and against the high number of family members who contribute to the overall household income. In the 1980s, the rate of Korean Americans working without pay in a family business was nearly three times that of any other ethnic group (Bell, p. 30).

The Novel in Focus

The plot. The novel unfolds from the first-person perspective of Henry Park, a second-generation Korean American. Henry contemplates the recent departure of his white American wife, Lelia. They are now separated, and their 10-year marriage is in danger of disintegration. He and Lelia have become increasingly estranged since the accidental death of their seven-year-old son, Mitt, a few years earlier. Lelia is unnerved by Henry's unemotional reaction to their son's death and his refusal to discuss it or their failing marriage; at one point she accuses him of being an "emotional alien" (*Native Speaker,* p. 5).

During their 10 years together, Lelia has provided the benchmark for what "American" means to Henry. His non-Korean wife seems to be Henry's foray into American society. In particular, Lelia provides for Henry a standard measure for the English language, for she is a freelance speech therapist for children learning English as a second language or struggling with speech impediments. Henry is continually fascinated by Lelia's seemingly effortless ability to speak the language and guilelessly express her emotions: "What I found was this: that she could really speak. At first I took her as being exceedingly proper, but I soon realized that she was simply executing the language. She went word by word. Every letter had a border. I watched her wide full mouth sweep through her sentences like a figure touring a dark house, flipping on spots and banks of perfectly drawn light" (*Native Speaker*, p. 11). During their first meeting, Lelia notices that Henry is fastidious regarding language, and her noticing this attracts him to her: "You look like someone listening to himself. You pay attention to what you're doing" (*Native Speaker*, p. 12).

As Henry attempts to adjust to life without his son, and now without his wife, he reflects on his troubled relationship with his father, pondering how his father's stoicism and silence toward him conditioned Henry to behave in much the same way as an adult. Much of Henry's childhood is spent apart from his father, who comes home exhausted and short-tempered from managing the greengroceries Mr. Park owns. When Henry's mother dies while Henry is young, Henry is further distanced from his father by the sudden unexplained arrival of a Korean housekeeper, who becomes his father's companion and presumably his mistress. Kept at a distance, Henry learns little of his parents' lives in Korea and in America.

Henry muses on his son's death and the loss of his dreams for Mitt's future. He sees his son, a biracial child, as having a claim on opportunities available to white Americans, opportunities that have been denied to Henry and his immigrant parents. Frustrated by his inability to assimilate fully into white American life and wanting his son to be free of this limitation, Henry treats Mitt accordingly. He encourages the boy to spend as much time with his mother as possible and to avoid contact with his father's racial heritage so that it will not "contaminate" Mitt's American future. But Henry recognizes the flaws in this approach. In privileging American culture over Mitt's Korean heritage, he seeks an entirely American identity for his son, "a singular sense of his world, a life univocal, which might have offered him the authority and confidence that his broad half-yellow face could not. Of course, this is assimilist [*sic*] sentiment," observes Henry, "part of my own ugly and half-blind romance with the land" (*Native Speaker*, p. 267). After his son's death, Henry finally recognizes that he attempted to abandon his own Korean heritage through his aspirations for Mitt.

Professionally, Henry is a spy for a private intelligence agency. His characteristic guardedness and secrecy serve him well in this capacity. Since graduating from a prestigious East Coast university, Henry has spied on individuals targeted by anonymous industrial and political concerns from all over the world. Before Mitt's death, Henry enjoyed the subversive nature of his occupation, reveling in his ability to gain the confidence of and information from his unwitting subjects. But after his son dies, Henry's failure to express his emotions compromises his ability not only to preserve his marriage but also to perform his job. In working as a spy, Henry attempts to avoid the trauma of his son's death and the responsibility of being Korean American: "I had always thought that I could be anyone, perhaps several anyones at once. . . . I found a sanction from our work, for I thought I had finally found my truest place in the culture" (*Native Speaker*, p. 127). He finds security in the different personas he takes on in his work as a spy; he assimilates to the point of invisibility.

At the beginning of the novel, Henry reveals that he has already failed in one assignment with a Filipino American psychiatrist. In order to reestablish his loyalty to the company and his dedication to the work, Henry takes on a new assignment to gather information on John Kwang, a city councilman from Flushing, New York, and a tremendously successful self-employed Korean immigrant. Although Henry is never told how the information will be used, he suspects that Kwang's political ambitions have made him an enemy of the current mayor. Against the ineffectual rhetoric and inaction of the Mayor De Roos, Kwang's charismatic leadership of the multiethnic communities of New York City places him in the forefront of the next mayoral race.

As Henry continues to work undercover as a volunteer in Kwang's political campaign, he finds himself gaining the friendship and confidences of the enigmatic politician himself. He keeps comparing Kwang to Henry's own father and also to himself as he attempts to fathom the true nature of the councilman. Kwang seems to be a quintessentially self-made man and a leader whose charisma can win over New York City's often fractious, multiethnic populations. As he continues to work with Kwang, Henry finds himself increasingly unable to forget about the past traumas of his life: his mother's sudden death, his father's emotional inaccessibility, his son's accidental death, and possible failure of his marriage.

After Kwang's campaign office is mysteriously fire bombed and two of the workers are killed, Kwang chooses Henry to manage a money fund not unlike the *ggeh*, the rotating credit association, that financed the first greengrocery opened by Henry's father. However, unlike his father's *ggeh*, Kwang's fund sets out to help all his constituents of various racial backgrounds, not just the Koreans. Kwang develops the idea of the *ggeh* from a fund to promote the financial success of family and friends into one that incorporates the larger network of his constituency. The aim is not only to promote their economic prosperity but also to mobilize them politically. A hostile media perverts the truth, though. The press portrays Kwang's interracial, interethnic *ggeh* as an unsavory operation, "a pyramidal laundering scheme, a people's lottery, an Asian numbers game" (*Native Speaker*, p. 301). Thanks to his enemies, vast records of contributors to his *ggeh*, including names and addresses of illegal immigrants, wind up in the hands of the Immigration and Naturalization Service. Soon after, Kwang is involved in a car accident with a young undocumented woman. The incident has immoral overtones for the general public, since the woman is not his wife and is in the country illegally. Publicly disgraced in all aspects of his life, the incident irrevocably ruins Kwang's political career.

A KOREAN AMERICAN CASUALTY IN THE LOS ANGELES UPRISING

In *Native Speaker* John Kwang refers to the death of Charles Lee in a store bombing of his family's business. The fictional death of Lee, a young Korean American, echoes the real-life shooting of eighteen-year-old Edward Lee during the 1992 Los Angeles Uprising. Of the 58 fatalities in the uprising, Lee was the only Korean American to die in the urban violence.

As he watches Kwang's downfall, Henry begins to reconsider his role in it and his more general undermining of other Asian Americans and of immigrant communities. He faces the fact that he has pursued his occupation at the expense of other Asian Americans and irrevocably destroyed the lives of immigrants who, like his father, like John Kwang, and even like himself, aspire to prosper in America. In the final scene, Henry has left his job and assists his wife in teaching English to immigrant children, adopting a final mask as a "Speech Monster" to entertain the students.

Interracial tensions. Set in New York City, *Native Speaker* takes place in a multiethnic, racially strained environment. Both Henry's father and John Kwang have roots as small business owners in communities that cater to a diverse nonwhite clientele. Kwang rises to citywide prominence because of his talent for forming multiracial political coalitions and developing broad support among immigrants and citizens. Often he is called upon to resolve misunderstandings between

Korean immigrant shop owners and their black customers. The strain reflects a real-life tension, which came to a head in two crises that shook Korean Americans in the 1990s: the 1990 to 1991 African American boycotts of Korean-owned stores in New York City and the 1992 Los Angeles uprising.

KOREAN AMERICANS IN POLITICS

The Los Angeles Uprising galvanized Korean American community leaders to meet and discuss unified political objectives in the wake of racial scapegoating (Park, "The Impact," p. 286). Forming Korean American Democrat and Republican organizations, the Korean American community helped elect Republican Jay Kim a United States Representative of California in November 1992. Kim would become the first Korean American to win election to federal office.

The 1990-91 boycott of Korean American stores in New York attracted national attention in the black and Korean American press. An earlier 1988 boycott in the Bronx had put so much pressure on a store after it fired a black employee that the store was forced to close down altogether. Now, in 1990, a second boycott began that would last for 16 months. It is alleged that on January 18, 1990, Bong Ok Jang, manager of the Family Red Apple store in Flatbush, Brooklyn, argued with and beat up a black female customer. An angry crowd gathered when an ambulance arrived and rumors circulated that the woman had slipped into a coma. The crowd began a protest that would become a boycott not only of the Family Red Apple store but also of another greengrocery across the street, which had protected an employee fleeing the crowd that gathered after the dispute began. The 16-month boycott, including picket lines outside the Family Red Apple and Church Fruits stores, was mostly organized by the December 12th Movement, a New York City coalition of black political organizations that had been protesting hate crimes and violence against African Americans since the late 1980s. The movement called for a "merchant apology, the conviction of the Korean merchant(s) involved in the alleged beating, and the closing of the two Korean-owned stores" (Kim, p. 43). Korean and black groups sought out newly elected Mayor David Dinkins, New York's first African American mayor, to mediate the dispute. Political inaction on his part as well as that of President George Bush after multiple appeals led to thousands of Korean Americans' gathering at City Hall on September 18, 1990, in the "largest rally of Korean Americans in New York City history" (Kim, p. 179). Still, the picket lines continued until finally the Family Red Apple store was sold on May 30, 1991.

In *Native Speaker*, over the course of Henry's relationship with Kwang, Korean-owned businesses endure store-burnings, demonstrations, vandalism and boycotts. Racial strife blights all of New York's boroughs, testing Kwang's leadership of his multiethnic constituency. In a pivotal speech that appears to clinch his mayoral candidacy, Kwang mentions the shooting death of Saranda Harlans, an African American mother of two. This anecdote echoes the real-life killing of African American teenager Latasha Harlins in South Central Los Angeles in 1991. A Korean storeowner, Soon Ja Du, shot Harlins in the back of the head after a physical struggle between the two women over a purchase. For her crime, Du received a light sentence of probation and community service, which outraged African American communities across the country. In Lee's fictional New York, the death of Saranda Harlans and the perceived injustice in the severity of the offender's legal punishment leads to arson, rioting and boycotts of Korean-owned stores that jeopardize Kwang's ability to lead the city.

Another incident highlighted the explosive relationship between the Los Angeles Police Department and African Americans. After a traffic stop in 1991, Rodney King, an African American, was displayed on a truncated snippet of video tape to have been beaten repeatedly by four white police officers. The final portion of the episode was recorded by a home video camera and sold to and broadcast over national media networks. On April 29, 1992, the four white police officers were acquitted of criminal charges in the King beating. The verdict sparked the Los Angeles Uprising of April 29-May 1, which took place in South Central Los Angeles and resulted in the deaths of 58 persons, injuries suffered by more than 2,400, and $717 million in property damage. Korean American businesses sustained the highest percentage of damage in this urban conflict (Abelmann and Lie, pp. 2, 8).

Sources and literary context. After immigrating to the United States at an early age, Lee examined his own struggle with assimilation into American society, a struggle that found its way into *Native Speaker*. "Did I so desperately want to belong so much that I did things—like refusing to translate for my mother, like going to Exeter, like dating white women—for that reason? . . . I wonder about the betrayals I had made—to myself, to my family" (Lee in Belluck, p. 1). More specifically, because Korean was his first language and he acquired English only in grade school, Lee has expressed in interviews an anxiety about the English language that troubles his protagonist Henry in *Native Speaker*.

Lee acknowledges diverse literary influences such as Walt Whitman and James Joyce, crediting especially Whitman's descriptions of Queens and Joyce's character Gabriel from "The Dead" (a short story in ***Dubliners,*** also in *Literature and Its Times*). Among other influences cited by Lee are the novelists Kazuo Ishiguro, John Cheever, and Yukio Mishima.

Novels by and about Asian Americans have historically been characterized by the strong presence of an ethnic community that not only provides the thematic conflict but also nurtures the main character as he or she struggles with the experience of assimilation into American society. The novel's protagonist Henry Park is distinctive because of his isolation from other Korean Americans and even his father, leading one reviewer to describe Lee's work as a "newer and rawer" portrayal of a contemporary immigrant experience than those that preceded it (Eder, p. 13). *Native Speaker* has also been described as an ethnic *bildungsroman,* or coming-of-age novel, in light of the self-knowledge and self-awareness attained over the course of the story by its protagonist.

Reception. *Native Speaker* was published to critical acclaim in mainstream newspapers and magazines. In 1996 the book won the Hemingway Foundation/PEN Award for a first novel. Most reviewers identify two dominant themes in *Native Speaker*, the spy thriller and the *bildungsroman* of ethnic assimilation into larger society. One reviewer for *The Independent* discusses Lee's development of the detective element "while adding in the question of immigrant identity as well" (Beckett p. 30). Some reviewers were disappointed by the spy plot in its implausibility, but these same reviewers showed enthusiasm for the poignant depiction of the immigrant family in contemporary American society. Although Richard Eder deemed Lee's story and writing choppy at times, he showered praised on "the figure of Henry's father, whose love is expressed in sacrifice, whose sacrifice is expressed in harshness and whose harshness distills into an odd hint of poetry," deeming the portrayal to be "a memorable one" (Eder, p. 13).

—Lynn Itagaki

For More Information

Abelmann, Nancy, and John Lie. *Blue Dreams: Korean Americans and the Los Angeles Riots*. Cambridge: Harvard University Press, 1995.

Beckett, Andy. "I Spy with My Little Eye." Review of *Native Speaker*. *The Independent*, 13 August 1995, 30.

Bell, David A. "The Triumph of Asian-Americans." *New Republic*, July 1985, 24-31.

Belluck, Pam. "Being of Two Cultures and Belonging to Neither: After an Acclaimed Novel, a Korean-American Writer Searches for His Roots." *New York Times*, 10 July 1995, B1.

Eder, Richard. "Stranger in a Strange Land: A Novel of a Newer, Rawer Immigrant Experience." *Los Angeles Times Book Review*, 19 March 1995, 3, 13.

Kim, Claire Jean. *Bitter Fruit: The Politics of Black-Korean Conflict in New York City*. New Haven: Yale University Press, 2000.

Le, Ngoan. "The Case of the Southeast Asian Refugees: Policy for a Community 'At Risk.'" *The State of Asian Pacific America: Policy Issues to the Year 2020*. Los Angeles: LEAP Asian Pacific Public Policy Institute and UCLA Asian American Studies Center, 1993.

Lee, Chang-rae. *Native Speaker*. New York: Riverhead, 1995.

Osajima, Keith. "Asian Americans as the Model Minority: An Analysis of the Popular Press Image in the 1960s and 1980s." In *Reflections on Shattered Windows: Promises and Prospects for Asian American Studies*. Eds. Gary Y. Okihiro et al. Pullman: Washington State University Press, 1988.

Park, Edward J. W. "The Impact of Mainstream Political Mobilization on Asian American Communities: The Case of Korean Americans in Los Angeles, 1992-1998." In *Asian Americans and Politics: Perspectives, Experiences, Prospects*. Stanford: Stanford University Press, 2001.

Park, Kyeyoung. *The Korean American Dream: Immigrants and Small Business in New York City*. Ithaca: Cornell University Press, 1997.

Song, Min. Review of *Native Speaker*. *Amerasia Journal* 23, no. 2 (fall 1997): 185-89.

Tabor, Mary B. W. "Unfulfilled Promises." *New York Times*, 26 October 1992, B1.

On the Road

by
Jack Kerouac

THE LITERARY WORK

A novel, set in various parts of the United States and in Mexico, in the late 1940s; first published in 1957.

SYNOPSIS

Sal Paradise and Dean Moriarty attempt to escape the dull conformity of American life in the late 1940s by crossing the country from coast to coast.

The son of French Canadian parents who had immigrated to the United States, Jack (Jean-Louis Lebris de) Kerouac was born in 1922 in Lowell, Massachusetts. He grew up in a French-speaking household, first learning English at the age of six, when he began to attend school. After America entered World War II, Kerouac enlisted in the Merchant Marine but was eventually dismissed on medical grounds due to his erratic and psychologically unbalanced behavior. He returned to New York's Columbia University, where he had a football scholarship. In the late 1940s Kerouac met a number of fringe bohemian characters such as Allen Ginsberg and William Burroughs, who were experimenting with new ways of artistic expression as well as with drugs. Kerouac also met at this time Neal Cassady, an uneducated drifter and a manic depressive with a magnetic personality. During the period 1947-49 the two traveled widely in the United States. *On the Road* fictionalizes Kerouac's years with Cassady (renamed Dean Moriarty in the story). Credited with inventing the term "beat generation," Kerouac became an unwilling media figure, whom the press identified with the new "beat" movement and its ideas. Much of his personal story and his qualities as a writer were essentially ignored. Kerouac remained a Catholic all his life, though in the course of his erratic life he made a serious commitment to Zen Buddhism. The religious duality points to a general split between order and chaos, powerful tradition and extreme novelty, which seems to have been one of the characteristics he hoped Buddhism could resolve. Kerouac's later books, including *The Dharma Bums* (1958), *Big Sur* (1962), and *Visions of Cody* (1972), were modestly successful, but none of them achieved the level of attention and popularity attained by *On the Road*. A slice-of-life novel, it captures a fringe variant of life in mid-twentieth-century America, given to wild and unpredictable experimentation with travel, sex, drugs, and friendship.

Events in History at the Time the Novel Takes Place

Victory and the suburb. In 1945 the United States emerged from World War II as the uncontested military and political power in the western world. The defeat of Germany and Japan would have been impossible without the Unites States, and for its pains it garnered much international credit as the leading power of the free

Jack Kerouac

world. The unleashing of the full potential of the American economy during the war had brought not only victory to the Allied countries, but also jobs to Americans (both men and women) at home, which in turn brought secure incomes and upward social mobility. The GI Bill gave servicemen job priority, education benefits, and low-interest loans for homes. The first large-scale federal higher education access law in U.S. history, the bill opened up the possibility of a college education for veterans (called GIs, for Government Issue), who otherwise could not have attended. Postwar life seemed dynamic and prosperous.

The clearest indicator of American economic progress was the growth of the suburbs. As general wealth and average family income increased through the late 1940s, people became less connected with the old ethnic neighborhoods of the cities, particularly in the East and in the industrial cities. The dream of buying one's own house, with a garden out back and a car in the driveway—elements of an unattainable middle-class lifestyle during the Depression—was now an achievable target, and millions of ordinary Americans worked toward reaching it. The car in the driveway meanwhile began to symbolize a new kind of travel: once a privilege reserved for the rich, driving as a leisure-time activity started becoming a given of ordinary American life. The end of wartime rationing and the solid prosperity of the postwar era made the automobile the norm rather than the exception for American families of almost any economic status. Prices of automobiles proved widely affordable. In 1950 a typical mid-price car, with an eight-cylinder, 100-horsepower engine and manual "stick-shift" transmission, cost about $1,800 new (Rae, p. 176).

It often appeared as if the promise of mobility in American culture, which seemed unmerited in the prewar Depression, was now completely redeemed in a very literal way by the automobile production lines in Detroit. Promoting this mobility was a growing network of roads across America. Along with expansion in automobile ownership came the rapid development of state and national roadways—from the ambitious 1,000-mile blacktops of the famous Route 66 between Chicago and Los Angeles (constructed from 1926-38), to the continent-spanning Interstate highways (introduced by the Eisenhower Administration in the early 1950s).

Despite traditional objections to "big government," the construction industry welcomed the major role the federal government was taking in promoting the construction branch. Setting the framework for new suburban development in the late 1940s, the Federal Housing Agency extended large credit lines to construction companies, which made possible the rapid building of standardized, single-family housing areas outside cities. As noted, the growth of these suburbs resulted from personal postwar ambition. It also fit with a social and political agenda on the part of the U.S. government at the time. As one of the principal developers of suburban housing on the East Coast, William J. Levitt, explained: "No man who owns his own house and lot can be a communist. He has too much to do" (Levitt in Homberger, p. 128).

From Levittowns to bebop music. For many people, particularly young parents with children, moving to a new suburb was an escape from the cramped tenement apartments of the early twentieth century. Another unspoken motive for the move had to do with a gradual identification of the city with the lower economic classes and with a non-white population. Leaving one's old inner-city neighborhood and taking a mortgage in an outlying area was a way of becoming 100 percent American. Formerly distinct ethnic identities (Italian, Irish, Jewish, Armenian, and so on) could be left behind with the parents and grandparents.

The price for becoming "American," however, was a certain amount of standardization. Although the suburbs were to become the most common American living environment by the 1960s, their low-density demographics and cookie-cutter middle-class lifestyle caused some critics to regard them as nothing but "machines for the nuclear family" (Homburger, p. 128). A popular folk song of the time by Malvina Reynolds zeroed in on their homogeneous character, "Little boxes on the hillside / And they're all made out of ticky-tacky / And they all look just the same." What could be read between the lines was the sense of safety in sameness. It was not just that houses and social attitudes were becoming standardized, but also that American culture was dividing into two camps: the norm and the deviant. The norm consisted of that which was white, suburban, and well-behaved; the deviant, that which was non-white, urban, and, according to the general presumption, criminal and unsafe.

In such a conformist atmosphere, the "unsafe" became attractive precisely because it seemed to offer excitement, risk, and escape. Some of these unsafe possibilities surfaced in music. Particularly in the late 1940s, as the challenging form of jazz known as bebop began to seep into people's consciousness, it became clear that there were new developments in music that involved an aggressive individuality and a belief in experiment. Bebop was the bending—and often the rejection—of traditional rules of harmony and syncopation that had made "Swing" jazz the most popular music form in the western world before the war. An intellectual and racially conscious variety of jazz, bebop was the badge of a new generation of African American musicians: "Charlie Parker, Dizzy Gillespie, his cheeks blown out like a football, and Miles Davis were the new names, Thelonius Monk the new pianist . . . . Bop was, above all, loud" (Jenkins, pp. 82-83). Often, the more avant-garde black jazz artists did not play in the established venues, and therefore the only places to see and hear them were the bars and apartments in black neighborhoods. There, in a part of town that white folks normally avoided, a nonconformist could hear jazz and possibly, if one wanted, buy marijuana (known as "tea" at that time) or even harder drugs. This image appears in the famous opening lines of Allen Ginsberg's 1956 poem "Howl," in which he sees:

> The best minds of my generation destroyed by madness,
> starving hysterical naked, dragging themselves through the negro streets at dawn looking for an angry fix.
>
> (Ginsberg, p. 126)

The experience of hearing the music and visiting such areas often left young white men feeling as if they had been deprived of something, a sense of freedom and vitality that other ethnic groups had. As Sal meditates in *On the Road*, wandering through the black and Mexican neighborhoods of Denver:

> All my life I'd had white ambitions, that was why I'd abandoned a good woman like Terry in the San Joaquin Valley. I passed the dark porches of Mexican and Negro homes. . . . I was only myself, Sal Paradise, sad, strolling in this violet dark, this unbearably sweet night, wishing I could exchange worlds with the happy, true-hearted, ecstatic Negroes of America.
>
> (Kerouac, *On the Road*, p. 180)

Sal's evocation of the mentality of the "white Negro," an almost obsessive identification with the marginalized elements of the nation, is a classic expression of alienation from the bouncy, consumerist culture that white America was embracing. Although many would later point to racist elements in its portrayal of African Americans and jazz culture, *On the Road* is an attempt to put into the style of a novel some of the energy and emotion that jazz could create.

The Novel in Focus

The plot. Sal Paradise, a young writer living in New York in the winter of 1947, meets Dean Moriarty and his wife Marylou. Dean is a larger-than-life figure, a tall, good-looking adventurer from Colorado who has served time in prison; true to his beginnings, he was born on the road as his parents were driving across the country to California in the 1920s. In New York, Sal introduces Dean to Carlo Marx (in real life, the poet Allen Ginsberg) and other writers and intellectuals on the New York fringe cultural scene. Sal sees something fresh in Dean Moriarty:

> His "criminality" was not something that skulked and sneered; it was a wild yea-saying overburst of American joy; it was Western, the west wind, an ode from the Plains, something new, long prophesied, long a-coming.
>
> (*On the Road*, pp. 7-8)

Dean's energy and dynamism make Sal increasingly dissatisfied with the empty philosophizing of his New York friends and increasingly aware of the fact that he too is looking for real adventure.

Later that year, in the summer, Sal travels to the West Coast, taking the bus to Chicago and hitching rides from there. At Des Moines, Iowa,

Sal realizes the distance he has traveled: "I was halfway across America, at the dividing line between the East of my youth and the West of my future" (*On the Road*, p. 15). The West fascinates Sal, who takes in its size and open horizons with the eyes of an Easterner adjusted to a smaller scale. On the road, he meets college students hitch-hiking around the country, itinerant farm boys moving from harvest to harvest for work, and old-timer hobos who have been traveling since the 1930s—all on the move back and forth across America.

In Denver, Sal encounters a number of former acquaintances including Carlo Marx and Dean Moriarty, now with a different woman called Camille. Dean, still married to Marylou, is having an affair with Camille and trying to deal with the logistical problems of managing his time, now that two women expect his undivided attention. Carlo and Dean have an odd relationship, marked by a mixture of mutual fascination and mutual dislike. Both Dean and Carlo, in Sal's estimation, are "rising from the underground, the sordid hipsters of America, a new beat generation" (*On the Road*, p. 54). Sal spends some time in Denver before moving on.

Finally arriving in San Francisco, Sal meets up with his old friend from the merchant navy, a Frenchman named Remy Boncoeur. Remy is married to a wife whom he fooled into thinking he was rich and who hates him for it. He is working as a security guard at an army transit barracks and gets Sal a job there also. Sal dislikes the work and the atmosphere at the barracks, as well as the tension in Remy's tiny house between Remy and his wife, Lee Ann. One morning, Sal sneaks off and boards a bus to Los Angeles. On the bus, he summons up courage to talk to a young woman, and they hit it off.

Terry (Teresa), a Latino woman, has been living near Fresno with an abusive husband and their child. To escape her husband for a while, she intends to live with her sister in Southern California. Terry and Sal are smitten with each other. They spend a couple of weeks together in the black and Mexican neighborhoods of Los Angeles, where the music makes an impression on Sal. He describes the wildly rhythmic Central Avenue, "with chickenshacks barely big enough to house a jukebox, and the jukebox blowing nothing but blues, bop, and jump" (*On the Road*, p. 88). Sal and Teresa plan to hitch cross country to New York, but end up in Teresa's home town, Sabinal, California, where they stay with her family. Sal savors the realistic, earthy atmosphere that prevails among the Mexican farmworkers and their families. Despite their mutual affection, Sal realizes it's time to go back East, and Terry makes the decision to stay behind.

Sal meets up with Dean again around Christmastime of 1948, while spending the holiday with Sal's relatives in Virginia. Dean is back with his first wife, Marylou, traveling with her and a man named Ed Dunkel. Ed has married a young woman named Galatea in San Francisco and invited her along on the trip, but he and the others, bored with her whining, give her the slip in a motel in Tucson. Sal, Dean, and the others head back to New York. They are staying in Sal's aunt's house in New Jersey when Old Bull Lee (in real life the novelist William S. Burroughs) calls from New Orleans to say that Galatea has shown up at his house looking for Ed and Dean.

The sexual dynamic among the group begins to alter. Marylou appears to develop an attraction for Sal, which does not appear to bother Dean. They all attend wild parties in Manhattan that last for hours and listen to jazz. One night Dean asks Sal to have sex with Marylou (which she has already agreed to). The plan is for the two of them to have sex with Dean looking on, but when they get to the apartment, Sal discovers that he cannot perform in Dean's presence. He also suspects that Marylou just sees the sexual experimentation as a way of keeping tabs on Dean, rather than her really being interested in Sal.

Sal, Dean, Marylou, and Ed Dunkel leave New York together, driving south to visit New Orleans, where Old Bull Lee lives with his family. Lee is a strange figure, a kind of grim anarchist with a taste for the macabre. A heroin addict, he single-handedly rejects modern America, hating the federal government, liberals, and big business alike. He carries individual grudges no less lightly. Sal describes an altercation that Lee has had with his Portuguese neighbor regarding their children:

> The old man rushed out and yelled something in Portuguese. Bull went in the house and came back with a shotgun, upon which he leaned demurely; the incredible simper on his face beneath the long hatbrim, his whole body writhing coyly and snakily as he waited, a grotesque, lank, lonely clown beneath the clouds. The sight of him the Portuguese must have thought something out of an old evil dream.
>
> (*On the Road*, p. 151)

Leaving Lee's house (without Ed Dunkel) and driving through the nighttime swamps of Louisiana, the car skids off the blacktop and sticks in the mud. Trying to free the wheels, Sal and Dean ruin their clothes and end up covered in mud. The two men and Marylou all remove their clothes in the car as the morning dawns and they enter Texas. Truck drivers swerve when they notice Marylou, "a golden beauty sitting naked" in the car (*On the Road*, p. 161). The trio decide to visit some Indian ruins they pass in the desert. Sal and Marylou put on long jackets but Dean walks around naked—shocking a small group of tourists at the site.

They finally arrive in San Francisco, and Dean leaves Marylou to call on Camille. The promised love affair between her and Sal does not materialize. Sal meditates in a dreamy, surreal way on the city, sensing it as a mixture of music, fog, and whiffs of food from the various districts, all combining into one poetic identity. He decides to leave almost immediately, and returns by bus to New York. A few months later, in spring 1949, he heads back West by way of Denver. Calling on Dean, who is very pleased to see him, he finds that Camille grows suddenly angry, believing that once Sal and Dean get together, Dean will disappear for months, leaving Camille and their little daughter, Amy, alone. Sal tries to conciliate Camille, but she doesn't trust him.

When Camille throws Dean out of the apartment, Sal realizes that he feels a certain responsibility for him. Previously, Sal has always been the one responding to Dean's energy, his spontaneous wild ideas, and so forth. Dean looks at him strangely in response to Sal's offer to help him out of his current fix. "I'd never committed myself before with regard to his burdensome existence," says Sal, "and that look was the look of a man weighing his chances at the last moment before the bet" (*On the Road*, p. 189).

On the way back to the East Coast, they stop to spend time in Denver with Frankie, a poor farm migrant from Oklahoma whom Sal knows from an earlier trip. Frankie's husband has left her to support herself and their four children, and they have a chaotic but friendly household that is regarded with disfavor by Lucille's respectable neighbors. Much drinking and partying takes place, with Dean unable to stay out of trouble. He bothers a neighbor's young daughter and steals a car that turns out to belong to a police detective, so he and Sal have to leave Frankie's at high speed. In Denver they have the good fortune of being offered a good deal: a wealthy man wants his expensive 1947 Cadillac driven to Chicago for him.

After they reach New York, Dean falls in love with a girl called Inez, but soon heads out west again. Sal plans to see him a little while later in Denver, but now Dean's presence, once invigorating, is more than a little intimidating. "It was like the imminent arrival of Gargantua; preparations had to be made to widen the gutters of Denver and foreshorten certain laws to fit his suffering bulk and bursting ecstasies" (*On the Road*, p. 259). Together with another traveler called Stan Shephard, Dean and Sal head south for Texas and Mexico. They drive through dry, red central Texas and on to the border town of Laredo. Dean is enchanted by Mexico when they cross the line southwards. He sees it as natural and earthy, light years away from the uptight snobbery of Middle America with its consumer obsessions, Protestant work ethic, and authoritarian law enforcement. Their experiences with drugs, brothels, and the police in Mexico are, from their point of view, satisfying. For Sal, Dean, and Stan, Mexico is a new world of sensuality and exotic locations, a place in which they no longer feel that they are fighting a whole society that looks down on them with contempt and hostility.

When they all get back to New York, Dean marries Inez (having received his divorce papers from Marylou) and immediately heads back to San Francisco to be with Camille and the new baby. Sal is left in New York, trying to make sense of the experience of the last couple of years. Sitting on a pier on the Hudson River, he imagines the enormous scale of the continent, the thousands of miles from coast to coast, the millions of people in the cities and on the remotest farms, and "think[s] of Dean Moriarty" (*On the Road*, p. 307).

The road from ethnicity. The treatment of ethnic and racial identities in Kerouac's novel highlights a curious and ambiguous aspect of American culture of the 1940s. *On the Road* contains a classic statement of the hunger shown by some whites for the presumed authenticity and grounded reality of the African Americans, Hispanic Americans, and others perceived as living outside the American mainstream: "I walked with every muscle aching among the lights of 27th and Welton in the Denver colored section, wishing I were a Negro" (*On the Road*, p. 179). Sal's romantic ideas of black people's lives in the United States exclude, of course, the painful reality of racism and poverty suffered by African Americans during this period. This and other passages caused black writer James Baldwin to comment that he wouldn't like to be in Kerouac's shoes if Kerouac were to read them aloud in a Harlem theater (Campbell, p. 209). Sal's notions suggest a lack of awareness of both the black experience of his day and works by its African American writers, such as Ralph Ellison's ***Invisible Man*** (also in *Literature and Its Times*). Nevertheless, the image of a writer hungry for something he cannot quantify describes a genuine condition for some people of the era.

WILL THE REAL NEAL CASSADY PLEASE STAND UP?

The real-life model for Dean Moriarty, Neal Cassady, became something of a mini-celebrity after Kerouac's novel was published, as Cassady's life seemed to offer much sensational material for the media. Son of an unemployed drifter and alcoholic, Cassady grew up in the worst neighborhoods in Denver. He claimed he had stolen 500 cars between the ages of 14 and 21. Equipped, luckily, with a natural intelligence, Cassady emerged from the juvenile penitentiary looking for something else in life.

Cassady was married to three women (two sequentially but one as a bigamist) and had relationships with many more. Altogether he conceived four children in various places. His sexuality, although decidedly focused on women in *On the Road,* seems in reality to have been flexible enough to have permitted at least one energetic homosexual encounter with Allen Ginsberg. Tall and good-looking, Cassady represented the ideal of the untrammeled male sexual ego. He seemed to do all the things that Kerouac, Ginsberg, and others were doing to one degree or another (or wanted to), without guilt and other emotional interference.

Cassady spent more time in prison between 1958 and 1960, then got a railway job, and lost it. In 1967, he teamed up with the writer Ken Kesey and his so-called Merry Pranksters, driving their Magic Bus around the country and experimenting with hallucinogenic drugs (recounted in Kesey's *The Electric Kool-Aid Acid Test*). Neal Cassady died in 1968 in Mexico, having suffered a heart attack while walking along a railroad track.

In Kerouac's case, the condition carries with it a curious twist. Jack Kerouac was the child of French-Canadian parents who emigrated to the United States. His mother tongue was the old-fashioned French of Quebec's rural Catholic communities, a resentful minority in anglophone Canada. In *On the Road* he not only does not make use of this background but also creates a narrator, Sal Paradise, who is clearly meant to be of Italian ethnic origin.

What the novel does not do, however, is create any sense of what distinguishes Sal from Dean Moriarty's white Protestant naiveté. As someone of Italian descent, Sal would generally be affiliated with the Catholic rather than the Protestant faith and with Mediterranean rather than Anglo tastes. No such differences come to the fore in the novel, though, an indication perhaps of the greater ease with which various European ethnic societies were melting into the American ethnic mix than Latinos or African Americans. In Sal's case, it is as if he wants to strip off his own East Coast ethnic background and be taken up into Dean's muscular, frontier Americanness despite the rebel streak manifested by his travels. As once-vital ethnic identities were jettisoned in post-war America, people who had earlier been Greek, Russian, and Irish had now become merely white Americans in the suburban melting pot. The more intractable ethnic and racial identities of African Americans and Latinos remained unassimilated—and therefore attractive.

Sources and literary context. The journeys back and forth across the U.S. made by Kerouac himself between 1947 and 1950 form the basis of *On the Road*, and real people of his era form the basis for characters. As noted, Neal Cassady inspired Dean Moriarty; Allen Ginsberg, Carlo Marx; and William S. Burroughs, Old Bull Lee. Kerouac's aim went beyond capturing the flavor of their experiences in print, however. Beyond the bare travel narrative lies the issue of the kind of novel he wanted to write. Kerouac, Ginsberg and others placed themselves in direct opposition to the reigning literary values of the day and the writers and critics who had created them. In particular, the fiction writer Ernest Hemingway became a target for the younger generation. Through novels such as ***The Sun Also Rises*** (also in *Literature and Its Times*), Hemingway had brought American prose to a high level of accomplishment, with a spare, no-frills style in which a superfluous word was a sign of an author's weakness.

In composing *On the Road* Kerouac aimed to do the opposite: to capture even subconscious moments of memory by writing in a flood of non-stop prose. As Ann Charters notes in her introduction to *On the Road*, Kerouac wrote the original draft in about one month (April 1951) on a single, 120-foot long sheet of paper that moved through his typewriter without a new page having to be inserted (Charters in *On the Road*, p. xix). Although the final published version of *On the Road* is more structured than Kerouac originally intended, the experiment was important as it suggested that new ways of writing could be as important as new novels themselves.

Allen Ginsberg, whose first collection *Howl and Other Poems* was published in 1956, a year before Kerouac's novel appeared, was trying to shape a new poetry in the same way that Kerouac was attempting to open up a new way of working with the traditional novel. Whereas Kerouac wanted to capture the flow of experience in prose before it dried out, Ginsberg wanted to foreground the performance of his poetry, to expose the poet's subjective experience to the audience as a key part of the whole work. Ginsberg's poetry, as well as Kerouac's fiction, took a deeply jazz-influenced approach. In Kerouac's case, the approach reflects the belief being that "the writer of spontaneous prose can work freely within this structure [of the novel], 'blowing' as deeply and as truly as Charlie Parker" (Bartlett, p. 121). In general, the beats deemed the established ideals of modern literature—irony, allusiveness, a taut and complex structure—to be only, fashions. These were not the only values that writers could aspire to, and it was possible to experiment with other approaches.

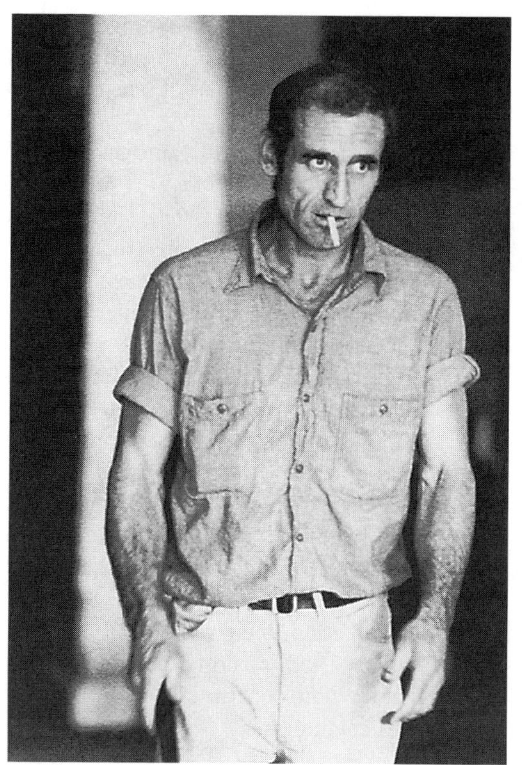

Beat generation drifter Neal Cassady. Cassady was the inspiration for Kerouac's character Dean Moriarty.

Events in History at the Time the Novel Was Written

Paranoia and timidity. Between 1949 and 1951 a major shift in the atmosphere of American political culture took place. As President Roosevelt's successor in the White House, Harry S Truman, once expressed it, Americans knew the world was a risky place, but they were prepared to stand behind his declaration of their responsibility as the leading western democracy: "It must be the policy of the United States to support free peoples who are resisting subjugation by armed minorities or by outside pressures" (Truman in Saunders, p. 25). In another way, however, Americans had become unsure of their world. Not only did the fact that the Russians, unexpectedly, had obtained the atomic bomb make them unsure. There were other unsettling developments too—the tense stand off during the Berlin Blockade of 1948-49 when Soviet occupation forces in Germany blocked access to the American and British sectors of the city; the unsatisfactory conclusion to the Korean War in 1953; and growing racial tensions in the southern United States all added to a sense of uncertainty about future days.

This uncertainty led to increasing suspicion of anything that appeared ideologically foreign or unwholesome. Before the war, during the Depression era of the 1930s, socialist and other left-wing solutions to America's problems had been part of the mainstream of political debate. This remained the case through World War II (during which the Soviet Union and the United States were allies) but began to change around 1948. The Alger Hiss trial that year, in which a former State Department officer was convicted of espionage for the Soviet Union, cast disfavor on the progressive and liberal political circles that had been become so influential in government, underpinning five Democratic presidential administrations since 1932. The Cold War, or competition between the Soviet Union and the United States for world leadership, did much to aggravate tensions.

The event that created the most vigorous national and international debate, and left a kind of cultural scar on American life, was the 1951 trial for espionage of husband and wife Julius and Ethel Rosenberg. The Jewish New York couple had been found guilty of spying for the Soviet Union. Julius Rosenberg was a key figure in a Soviet espionage network that sought to get hold of the secret research America had used to build the atomic bomb and the later hydrogen bomb. The trial and execution in 1953 of both husband and wife touched on a number of sensitive areas of American life

For many Americans, it became an issue of some importance that the couple were Jewish immigrants, a heritage that attracted a renewal of old anti-Semitic and nativist prejudices. More generally, the Rosenberg case threw a shaft of suspicion onto Americans from immigrant families with left-wing political traditions. The 1948 trial of Alger Hiss had had the same effect on upper-middle-class liberals with white Anglo-Saxon Protestant backgrounds. Both cases contributed to a rising tide of suspicion that proved unstoppable. The House Un-American Activities Committee began investigations of alleged subversive activities, and the Senate equivalent, chaired by Senator Joseph McCarthy, joined in. Together they created an atmosphere of national paranoia from 1950 to 1953, making unsubstantiated charges that the state department and army were riddled with communists.

"BEAT"

There has been some disagreement over the origin of the term. Kerouac uses the phrase "the new beat generation" early on in *On the Road,* but it had been around for some time before that. The first use of the term occurred in the title of an article by John Clellan Holmes in the *New York Times* in 1952: "This is the Beat Generation," a reference to the atmosphere and the New York social milieu that was home to Kerouac and others.

Kerouac claimed to have first heard the phrase even earlier, in New York in the mid-1940s, from a Herbert Huncke, a member of the criminal and bohemian circles in New York City. "Beat" meant a combination of two related ideas: the kind of empty exhaustion brought on by too many drinks, drugs, and partying, and a quasi-religious ecstasy that could be generated by such extreme experiences.

From *On the Road*'s publication in 1957, the phrase became the standard description for writers such as Kerouac, Ginsberg, and Burroughs, their milieu, and their ideas. The dismissive term "beatnik" came into vogue a little later, after the Soviet Union successfully put a satellite, Sputnik, into space before the United States. The addition of the Russian suffix "nik" became a way of implying that certain ideas or people were somehow un-American and disloyal.

Suspicion of unorthodox ideas was reflected in attitudes to literature. This was the period when works by American writers such as Langston Hughes, Ernest Hemingway, and Henry David Thoreau were removed from the shelves of American libraries overseas for being "pro-communist," and the poet William Carlos Williams was not appointed Poetry Consultant to the Library of Congress because his FBI file described his poetry as difficult and obscure (Saunders, pp. 193-95). The fact that Thoreau's "Civil Disobedience" had been written a hundred years earlier (in 1848) was simply ignored. Open expression of progressive views, particularly in respect to racial desegregation, was often enough for the FBI to open a file on an individual and label the person as subversive—even if the opinions held were well inside the normally accepted parameters of public debate in a democratic society.

The "beat generation." Increasing prosperity and the tendency to condemn unfamiliar ideas as communist-inspired made some people think twice, about what being an American really meant. The frontier spirit in which Americans were supposed to believe seemed to have disappeared behind a blind faith in technology and an ethic of social obedience. Moving to the suburbs, gaining some space and property, could be a legitimate individual decision, of course, but en masse it looked as if the process was creating a homogeneous society of people who acted and thought alike. People also appeared to be increasingly victimized by the consumption trap, as they buttressed their lives with ever more things (television sets, automobiles, freezers, and so forth) as if the accumulation of possessions would protect them from the vicissitudes of fate.

By around 1956 the cities of New York and San Francisco had become the East and West Coast poles of a cultural underground, a collection of writers, artists, and disaffected individuals who felt that they did not fit in well with the American mainstream. In their different ways, both places became a breeding-ground for the "beat generation," the name identified with a challenge to American values and suburban lifestyles mounted in the 1950s. In New York the fringe group that mounted the challenge was traditionally combative, intellectual, gloomy; in San Francisco the group was cultural, activist, with a more individualized, celebratory lifestyle. The beats of New York had ties to Columbia University; the San Francisco beats had links to the University of California at Berkeley. Although people moved about, New York would be identified with writers such as Jack Kerouac and Allen Ginsberg, and San Francisco with poets such as Gary Snyder and Lawrence Ferlinghetti, owner of the famous City Lights bookstore.

Despite the pressures and hostilities of American public discourse, the resistance to the homogenization of life and thought, whether in New York or in San Francisco, was largely nonpolitical during the 1950s. Jazz, drugs, Harley-Davidson motorcycles, and avant-garde theater represented the kind of lifestyle changes adopted by the beats to open up alternatives for themselves in the late 1940s and early 1950s. The Oakland, California, chapter of the Hell's Angels, would organize a large gathering, for example, attended by hundreds of motorcyclers riding there across the Southern Californian desert. The underground literary communities in New York and San Francisco would perform strange combinations of poetry and jazz. But in neither case would the new cultural opposition to the American norm show much interest in politics. The question instead was, how can one keep some spark of vitality alive in an America where going to work, mowing the lawn, and watching the new mass entertainment medium of television marked the limits of social acceptability? The answer might be elusive, but the important thing, as in *On the Road,* was to *do* something, to strike a blow for real freedom and authentic experience, not settle for it second-hand, through television or any other medium.

Publication, reception and impact. By the late 1950s, the politics of paranoia associated with the early years of the Cold War had begun to recede. America under President Dwight D. Eisenhower (1952-60) became a more relaxed society as the years of the anti-communist witch-hunt in Congress gave way to the era of Elvis Presley and the rise of a youth culture in America. But some of the sensitivities created by the paranoia would linger in ways that affected the publication of Kerouac's book. His publishers demanded many changes, particularly stylistic ones and themselves made a few without telling Kerouac (Charters in Kerouc, p. xxvii). Even so, the book remained a provocative work when it finally appeared in September 1957, more than ten years after Kerouac had made his first trip across the United States.

From the *New York Times*, the novel received a positive review—"*On the Road* is the second novel by Jack Kerouac, and its publication is a historic occasion . . . writing on jazz that has never been equalled" (Millstein in Campbell, pp. 203-04). But many reviewers objected to the plot's subject matter—illicit or unorthodox sexual relations, drugs, and subversion of middle-class American values. The headline of the review in the *San Francisco Chronicle*, as one critic notes, was a review in itself: "Sick Little Bums" (Campbell, p. 204).

The critical but balanced assessment of the book in *Nation* magazine is of particular interest, as it came from the writer Herbert Gold, who had had connections to the "beats" in previous years. Gold spotted what he considered a crucial weakness:

> *On the Road* asks us to judge the lives of its characters; it requires no real-life acquaintance with them to see that they are "true" projections—that is, the book represents Kerouac's attempt to do justice to his [real-life] friends. This is a very different matter from the artist's attempt to project meaningful people through the medium of his imagination onto the medium of the imagination of readers.
>
> (Gold, p. 353)

The flaw for this critic is that the novel does not succeed completely as a work of fiction, because the real people behind the pseudonyms are ultimately more interesting than the quasi-fictional characters they inspired.

On the Road nevertheless endured. In the late 1960s, the novel *On the Road* was taken up by the counterculture that emerged then—despite the fact that the events it depicted had occurred almost two decades earlier. The novel's vigorous style and emotional directness attracted young readers and may well have helped inspire a similar search by a new generation, for a less respectable and more authentic America.

—Martin Griffin

For More Information

Bartlett, Lee, ed. *The Beats: Essays in Criticism*. Jefferson, N.C.: McFarland, 1981.

Campbell, Joseph. *This Is the Beat Generation: New York-San Francisco-Paris*. London: Secker and Warburg, 1999.

Gold, Herbert. "Hip, Cool, Beat—and Frantic." Review of *On the Road,* by Jack Kerouac. *The Nation*, 16 November 1957, 349-55.

Ginsberg, Allen. *Collected Poems, 1947-1980*. New York: Harper & Row, 1984.

Homberger, Eric. *The Penguin Historical Atlas of North America*. Harmondsworth, England: Penguin, 1995.

Jenkins, Alan. *The Forties*. London: Heinemann, 1977.

Kerouac, Jack. *On the Road.* Intro. Ann Charters. Harmondsworth, England: Penguin, 1991.

Rae, John B. *The American Automobile: A Brief History.* Chicago: The University of Chicago Press, 1965.

Reynolds, Malvina. "Little Boxes." *Folk Classics: Roots of American Folk Music.* CBS Records CD 45026.

Saunders, Frances Stonor. *The Cultural Cold War: The CIA and the World of Arts and Letters.* New York: The New Press, 1999.

Tanenhaus, Sam. "A Family Affair." Review of *On the Road*, by Jack Kerouac. *The New York Review of Books*, 11 April 2002, 41-44.

Parrot in the Oven: Mi Vida

by
Victor Martinez

Victor Martinez, the fourth of 12 children, was born into poverty in 1954 and raised in Fresno, California. Like many Mexican Americans in Fresno, he worked in the fields. After graduating high school, he was able through an affirmative action program to attend California State University at Fresno, where he studied poetry with Philip Levine. Martinez also attended Stanford University, where he took graduate courses in creative writing. Over the years Martinez has also held various jobs: welder, truck driver, firefighter, teacher, and office clerk. Known before *Parrot in the Oven* as a short-story writer and poet, he is the author of *Caring for a House* (1992), a collection of poems, and a contributor to the *High Plains Literary Review* and *The Bloomsbury Review*. In *Parrot in the Oven*, Martinez broadens the scope of the coming-of-age novel, exploring the plight of poor Mexican Americans while vividly portraying Chicano life in the American West.

THE LITERARY WORK

A Chicano novel of development, set in Fresno County, California, during the early 1970s; published in 1996.

SYNOPSIS

The second son of poor Mexican American parents, Manny recounts his coming of age, focusing on familial strife and scenes of inclusion and exclusion that help him find his place in the world.

Events in History at the Time the Story Takes Place

Mexican American activism. *Parrot in the Oven*, though set during the early to mid 1970s, registers the sweeping effects of late 1960s activism, when Mexican Americans began to seek political rights commensurate with their status as U.S. citizens. While they looked in the first instance to the path taken by blacks in the civil rights struggles, Mexican Americans also agitated for rights specific to their particular historical condition in the United States. Much political activism was centered in the West and Southwest, particularly in California and Texas where the majority of Mexican Americans lived. The activists aimed mainly to attain their fair share of legal, political, and economic rights, but they concerned themselves too with matters of ethnic pride and cultural self-determination, agitating for the right to tell their own stories, to have their distinctive histories included in school curriculums, and to participate fully in the imaginative life of the nation.

Like other Mexican Americans, those who agitated for civil rights trace their history to peoples resident in the West and the Southwest who until 1848 were citizens of Mexico. When, as a result of its defeat in the Mexican War, Mexico lost the upper half of its territory to the United States, including California, political boundaries changed almost overnight. Mexicans suddenly became Americans of Mexican descent; they did

Victor Martinez

not cross a border as much as it crossed them. That their new American leaders acknowledged this fact was reflected in the promises of the Treaty of Guadalupe Hidalgo, signed at the conclusion of the war. As it turned out, these promises were made to little effect. Despite the treaty, the defeated Mexicans did not receive fair treatment under the law. U.S. law never delivered the land promised them. They faced rampant discrimination at election time, and suffered oppressive labor laws and conditions. Confronted with a population growth that outpaced the number of jobs in Mexico, many migrated to the United States in search of economic opportunity, freely crossing a border that was not actively policed until the 1920s, making their way over in any way they could. The rich agricultural economy of California's San Joaquin Valley (which includes Fresno County) was a principal draw, especially between 1910 and 1930, when many migrated north to provide seasonal labor in the fields.

As more acreage fell under the plow between 1930 and 1970, California's agricultural economy boomed. Americans across the country filled their grocery carts with grapes, lettuces, and other vegetables from the rich, alluvial soil of the Central and San Joaquin valleys. Fresno County alone accounted for 99 percent of California's raisins, soon becoming the richest agricultural county in the United States. Yet journalists were sounding the alarm about the plight of California farm workers, or more accurately re-sounding an alarm of the a mid-to-late nineteenth century. The plight had been recognized even then, in a period when America was experiencing a tremendous overall agricultural boom. An 1870s editorial in the *San Francisco Morning Chronicle* proclaimed that "The farm labor problem of California is undoubtedly the worst in the United States. . . . In many respects, it is even worse than old-time slavery" (*San Francisco Chronicle* in Haslam, p. 210). Power resided in the hands of owners, not workers, and a steady supply of cheap labor, coupled with the growing influence of agribusiness in the halls of government, meant that the complaints of farm workers fell on deaf ears. They fell on deaf ears, that is, until the 1960s, when César Chávez began organizing workers in the Central Valley.

Born in Arizona to a family of migrant farm workers from Mexico, Chávez attained only a seventh-grade education. But he had enormous energy and a gift for rallying people to his cause. In 1962, Chávez became head of the United Farm Workers Organizing Committee, which later became the UFW AFL-CIO. In 1965, he organized a grape strike, picketing growers in Delano, California, 80 miles south of Fresno, where the novel takes place. Thus began *La Huelga*, what turned out to be a five-year strike that for the first time brought the lives of farm workers to the attention of ordinary Americans. Chávez, a soft-spoken man who modeled his style of leadership after India's Mahatma Ghandi, practiced civil disobedience and espoused nonviolent protest. He marched, led rallies, and organized boycotts—all to focus attention on what he simply called *La Causa* (i.e., the cause). Over 17 million Americans joined in his grape boycott before the grape growers agreed to sign a contract granting a minimum wage to farm workers. It was the first of several boycotts Chávez would lead on behalf of farm laborers.

While some Mexican Americans rallied in the fields for workers' rights, others took to the streets—protesting, marching, and forming organizations to create ethnic pride and empowerment. Some embraced *el moviemiento*, the Chicano movement. Originally *Chicano* was a pejorative label (short for *Mexicanos*) used to describe any unskilled worker of Mexican descent; activists embraced the term, calling themselves

Chicano as a mark of difference, a sign of unity against white culture. Chicano student organizations were particularly active during the movement's heyday in the 1960s. Groups like UMA (the United Mexican Students) and MeCHA (*Moviemiento Estudiantil Chicano de Aztlán*) agitated for the formation of Chicano Studies programs on college campuses and led teach-ins about Mexican history. Chicano artists decorated city walls with colorful murals; Chicano writers and poets gained new prominence; political change fermented. An especially important group was the Brown Berets, to which one of the characters in *Parrot in the Oven* belongs. Modeled after the famous Black Berets, the Brown Berets formed chapters throughout the West and Southwest, thriving from 1967 to about 1972. Though nonviolent, they insisted on "the right to self-defense against aggression and for self-determination" (Gómez Quiñones, p. 120). They published a newspaper, *La Causa*, and established a successful health clinic. Their ten-point program "addressed issues of housing, culture, justice, employment, and education, and they held, at least as an ideal, a code of ethical conduct and required specific organizational discipline" (Gómez Quiñones, p. 120).

Mexican Americans recognized their historical significance to the nation, and they wanted to be included within it as equals. The gaining of labor rights was fundamental to this cause, but the movement was also concerned more broadly with matters of politics and culture. Groups such as the Brown Berets and MeCHA played an important role in galvanizing campus activism, raising consciousness, and pushing for the inclusion of Mexican American perspectives within the educational establishment.

The Mexican American family. Mexican American families, like American families in general, register the effects of broader economic, social, and political forces in U.S. culture. But Mexican American families also reflect the unique pressures of another culture and another place: Mexico. So while in many respects Mexican American families differ little from American families more broadly considered, there are also key differences to keep in mind, with identifiable origins.

Not all Mexican American families are comprised of new immigrants. Many Mexican Americans have roots in the United States dating back several decades; some trace their lineage back to the seventeenth and eighteenth centuries. Yet there is no mistaking Mexico's immense cultural influence in Mexican American life. While some of that influence has deep historical sources, much of it stems from Mexico's sheer proximity, as well as from the steady influx of new immigrants, who bring their culture and its problems to the United States when they arrive. It is easy to forget that the primary causes of immigration from Mexico, which grew apace after World War II, were conditions *in* Mexico itself, principally its growing population and low standard of living, both of which accelerated after the 1960s; its population grew by 30 million from the mid 1960s to the mid 1980s. As one writer puts it, the "Mexican economy finds it increasingly difficult to feed and clothe its population" (Juan Gonzalez, p. 97). By 1996, 80 percent of the Mexican population lived in poverty (Manuel Gonzalez, p. 225).

THE BRACERO PROGRAM

The word for "arm" in Spanish is *brazo;* a *bracero* is someone who works with his arms—a laborer. Hence the term for a program begun in 1942 to supply needed farm and industrial labor during World War II. Extending the program, the United States issued temporary work permits to over 4 million Mexican workers between 1945 and 1964, when the program was abolished. At its peak, some 25 percent of all farmworkers in the United States were *braceros.* Most *bracero* contracts lasted one year, but some workers came back year after year to work seasonally under the program.

Pushed northward by a worsening Mexican economy and by dreams of prosperity in the United States, Mexican immigrants frequently arrived impoverished, a state they had to overcome by taking the most menial jobs: dishwasher, busboy, maid, house cleaner, and, for the most unskilled, field worker. Although, like other immigrants, Mexican Americans enjoyed a rise in income in the second and third generations, stark inequalities remained. From 1950 to 1979, even "Mexican-American adults with native-born parents had from 15 to 20 percent less schooling than non-Hispanic whites," with a "similarly persistent gap in annual earnings . . . between third (plus)-generation Mexican Americans and non-Hispanic whites" (Skerry, p. 360). While the exact number of illegal immigrants is difficult to measure, the INS (Immigration and Naturalization Service) apprehended over one million Mexicans in the 1960s and over seven million in the '70s (Manuel Gonzalez, p. 225). It is not surprising, then, that some Mexican Americans began to have ambivalent feelings towards new immigrants; the newly arrived, willing to work at most jobs, threatened the livelihood of those already here.

Political leaders and sociologists have struggled to explain the inability of Mexican Americans to advance through the traditional channels of public education—a path to prosperity well worn by other immigrant groups in the United States. In 1986, a few years after the novel takes place, average SAT (Scholastic Aptitude Test) scores showed that those for Mexican Americans fell 126 points below the average for non-Hispanic whites (National Center for Education Statistics). Aside from poverty and poor access to education in Mexico, what cultural factors account for this failure? Students of Mexican culture point to a prevailing anti-intellectualism, born of respect for work but not book learning. The noted Mexican essayist Carlos Monsiváis observes: "It is not uncommon in Mexican homes to hear parents scolding their kids for reading when they could be doing something useful, like fixing the door," and Skerry suggests that recent immigrants may feel a general distrust of institutions outside the immediate family (Monsiváis in Manuel Gonzalez, p. 237; Skerry p. 344). These points are borne out in Richard Rodriguez's autobiography, ***Hunger of Memory*** (also in *Literature and Its Times*), which describes growing up in Sacramento during the 1960s and 1970s. He observes that his parents, who were immigrants from Mexico, did not understand the meaning and purpose of his graduate work at the University of California at Berkeley, nor his decision to abandon a career in academia for one as a writer; they expected him to get a "real" job like everybody else.

If tendencies of Mexican American family life influence educational achievement, they also have a more immediate impact on family members themselves, particularly women and children. Observers of Mexican culture point especially to corrosive and wide-ranging effects of *machismo*, a code of strong male behavior with roots in the Aztec ideal of the strong warrior. The Spanish Conquest, which reduced the native population to servitude, produced a corrupted model of masculinity, in which the principal virtue was to endure (*aguantar* in Spanish), silently, sullenly, sometimes with barely repressed rage: "the man who could no longer protect his wife took to beating her; the wish to be brave inspired the bully; the hero got drunk" (Shorris, p. 432). Some Chicano scholars have disputed the prevalence of this model, arguing that it represented the theory, not the actuality, of the Mexican American family, which was in fact held together by strong women (Manuel Gonzalez, p. 237). Still the effects of *machismo* should not be ignored. These range from domestic violence, marital infidelity, alcoholism, and unusually high crime rates, to a battered sense of self-worth for women, children, and the *macho* himself. Mexican American literature and culture is full of such depictions of *machismo*, from Sandra Cisneros's ***House on Mango Street*** and ***Woman Hollering Creek*** (both also in *Literature and Its Times*), to Helena Viramontes's *The Moths and Other* Stories, to Arturo Islas's *The Rain God*.

The Novel in Focus

The plot. Manny Hernandez, a 14–year-old, working-class Mexican American from Fresno, California, is both the narrator and central character of the novel. Manny lives in a housing project with his mother and father; his older brother, Bernardo (known as Nardo); his older sister, Magda; and Pedi, his little sister. Manny's father, whose drinking has cost him his job as a translator for the city, prowls about the house in a perpetual bad mood. Nardo, who is infatuated by his own reflection in the mirror, takes after his father in his distaste for work. Madga, on the other hand, contributes to the family income with money from her job in a laundry, and Manny's mother labors to keep the house clean and her family intact. Manny himself follows his mother's example; the beginning of the novel finds him thinking, "Without work, I was as empty as a Coke bottle" (Martinez, *Parrot in the Oven*, p. 7).

The opening of the novel describes Manny's desire for a new baseball glove, a longing so great that he decides to spend a day in the fields with Nardo picking chili peppers. When officers arrive from the INS—Immigration and Naturalization Service, or *la migra* in Spanish)—the migrant workers next to them run off, while Manny and Nardo cash in the sacks of peppers they leave behind. Manny's father, depicted as a classic *macho*, spends his hours at Rico's Pool Hall sullenly dreaming of "escaping back to Mexico" (*Parrot in the Oven*, p. 21). Embittered and shamed by his failure to provide for his family, Mr. Hernandez refuses to accept government handouts. His failed dreams for upward mobility are symbolized by a croquet set he had once purchased for his children; when the Garcia boys across the street throw one of the mallets into a tree, Mr. Hernandez vows "never again to favor [the] neighborhood with culture" (*Parrot in the Oven*, p. 23). Mrs. Hernandez escapes from her world by watching romantic movies on television in the afternoons. When she moons over a Tony Curtis film, the disgusted Mr. Hernandez, fifth of tequila in hand, storms over to a familiar place—the pool hall.

Mrs. Hernandez, however, proves to be the family's pillar and strength. She holds high ambitions for Manny, and tries to get him admitted to a better school across town, one that might graduate him into "places that would make her eyes gleam" (*Parrot in the Oven*, p. 38). When Manny goes to his own school to pick up his report card, he encounters one of his teachers, the well-meaning Mr. Hart, who gives him $20 for school supplies and a lift home back to the projects. Manny soon regrets accepting the offer, for on coming home he finds his father pruning shrubs in the front yard. The sight of Manny arriving with Mr. Hart fills Mr. Hernandez with rage—a rage born from contempt for do-gooders like Mr. Hart and from his own failure as a father. Mr. Hernandez, evincing the anti-intellectualism of the lower class Mexican immigrant, believes that Manny should give up school altogether, get a job as a dishwasher, and work his way up (*Parrot in the Oven*, p. 38). When Hart leaves, Mr. Hernandez rifles through Manny's pockets until he finds the money, which soon serves an unexpected purpose.

Mr. Hernandez fuels a two-day drinking binge at Rico's with the $20 he has taken from Manny. This next chapter's title, "The Bullet," refers to events narrated later, after Mrs. Hernandez goes to the bar to fetch her husband. Feeling embarrassed and emasculated, Mr. Hernandez comes home in a storm of anger, takes his rifle from a closet, and goes in search of his wife, who has left to a neighbor's house. Only the arrival of the police and the failure of his gun to load prevent him from shooting her. Mrs. Hernandez at first tries to protect her husband, claiming that no one owns a gun. But the officers find the weapon in a back room and then arrest Mr. Hernandez for owning a non-registered gun. Feeling the delayed impact of her husband's actions, Mrs. Hernandez now refuses to stand by him. "Go ahead, take him!" she says (*Parrot in the Oven*, p. 68). After they leave, she bends down to pick up a speck of dirt from the floor. "I don't even have a vacuum cleaner," she observes (*Parrot in the Oven*, p. 68). The comment registers her weary alienation from a world of middle-class comfort that she can imagine but never attain.

A few days later, Mr. Hernandez is released from jail. When he promises to stay out of further trouble, he and his wife reconcile. Anger is now directed at the two sons; on one of the hottest days of the year, Mr. Hernandez orders them to spend the day weeding the garden of Mrs. Hernandez's elderly mother. This job is particularly painful for Nardo, who has come home the night before stone drunk. Behind the action, it becomes evident that development is slowly lacing the community of Fresno—once a sleepy farm town—with a network of new roads. Manny's grandmother, who carefully tends her garden and her memories of Mexico, is one of the last holdouts against a planned freeway. Her death, narrated in the chapter, suggests the passing of the old lifestyle, or more exactly, the passing of a connection to the land signified by her garden and threatened by the scourge of spreading asphalt.

"THE PARROT IN THE OVEN"

The novel's title comes from a Mexican saying about a parrot that complains how hot it is in the shade, only to discover he is sitting in an oven. His father uses the saying, according to Manny, not to suggest that Manny is stupid, but because "I trusted everything too much, because I'd go right into the oven trusting people all the way—brains or no brains" (*Parrot in the Oven*, p. 52). As much as this describes a trait in Manny—his capacity for trust—it also says something about Mr. Hernandez, who is skeptical to a fault, even to the point of thinking the worst of Manny's teacher when he gives Manny money for school supplies and a ride home.

The title of the next chapter, "The Rifle," suggests a return to the subject of violence examined previously, but with a surprising twist. First there is one transgression; Magda asks Manny to watch Pedi while she sneaks out for a tryst with her teenaged lover. We then learn that Mr. Hernandez, who could not afford to buy his wife a $7 dress for her mother's funeral, has scraped together $150 to pay a lawyer to retrieve his rifle from the police—a rifle worth only one third as much (*Parrot in the Oven*, p. 94). Manny finds

César Chávez leads a grape strike in Delano, California in 1965.

the rifle in a closet and plays with it while watching Pedi. At first the loader remains jammed, but as he works it, the mechanism frees and a bullet enters the chamber, followed by a loud crack as the gun unexpectedly fires in Pedi's direction. Manny believes he has surely killed her and is overcome with relief when he learns she has not been struck but only frightened. Moments later, first Madga, then Mrs. Hernandez, returns, neither suspecting anything about the gun. But the sight of Magda's makeup and clothes causes Mrs. Hernandez to draw another upsetting conclusion. She lectures her daughter about "ruining [her] life" by getting pregnant, just as she [Mrs. Hernandez] had done when she was a teenager (*Parrot in the Oven*, p. 104). Defiant, Magda has a reply at the ready; she threatens to move out, leaving Mrs. Hernandez with no money.

From domestic entanglements, the thread of the story moves to the trials of manhood. Lencho, a powerfully built student at Manny's school, announces that he is fielding an unofficial boxing team to challenge the school's team, composed largely of African Americans. A member of the Brown Berets, Lencho dresses in the style favored by Chicano youth—"Big Ben pants, starched stiff as ironing boards, and a Pendleton shirt with the lap and tail out" (*Parrot in the Oven*, p. 111). He frames his boxing venture as a measure of ethnic pride, telling Manny how Chicanos were a "special people, how power slept in our fists and we could awaken it with a simple nod of our heroic will" (*Parrot in the Oven*, p. 122). On the day of the boxing matches, however, that power fails and the Chicanos lose all three matches, including Lencho's. For this, Lencho is kicked out of the Berets, who say he "brought embarrassment to them, and worse, caused a loss of unity between them and their black brothers" (*Parrot in the Oven*, pp. 138-39).

In "Family Affair," the following chapter, the novel focuses on Magda, heretofore a marginal figure in the story. She is taken to the hospital because she has lost her baby in a miscarriage. The novel here narrates events in reverse chronological order. We learn first of her miscarriage, not the pregnancy. The interest is not in the events leading to the miscarriage, but in its consequences. She becomes quite ill, and because of her ethnicity is treated shabbily at the hospital. Worse, she must come home prematurely because the family has neither money for a doctor nor health insurance. During these events, Mrs. Hernandez and Manny stand by Magda's side, and they keep Magda's pregnancy a secret from Mr. Hernandez. But at chapter's end, with Magda's fever worsening, he performs a saving and heroic act, rising from his bed, stiff and arthritic, to carry her to the bathtub, which he has ordered filled with cold water. The fever breaks, and Magda looks at Mr. Hernandez, "amazed" (*Parrot in the Oven*, p. 158).

Magda's recovery, which has the aura of a baptism or rebirth, spawns other recoveries. Mr. Hernandez finds a job, as does Nardo, who works as a delivery boy for a local pharmacist, Mr. Giddens. Manny helps from time to time, and on one occasion finds himself pressed by Mr. Giddens to attend a party being thrown in his absence by his daughter, Dorothy, who is about Manny's age. The offer paints Manny into a corner, who knows Dorothy does not want him to go but feels obliged to his brother's employer. Against the advice of Nardo and Magda, who fear Manny will be out of place among the well-to-do whites, Manny shows up for the party, only to be forced to leave when during a dance his leg accidentally slides between the legs of one of Dorothy's friends, embarrassing her and angering Dorothy.

In the novel's final two chapters, Manny moves from trying to belong to white society to an attempt to join a small group of neighborhood toughs, or *vatos firmes*, as they call themselves. The price of admission to this gang is suffering a beating at the hands of its members, and the payoff is being able to kiss one of the girls who fall in their orbit. Eddie, a member of the gang, recruits Manny to help him pull off a robbery. But Manny soon realizes that his desire for acceptance has again pulled him in a negative direction. The turning point comes just after Eddie brutally knocks a woman down, steals her money, and runs off. As Eddie rounds a corner, Manny recognizes him as Magda's secret boyfriend, whose face he had never seen before, and in that moment of recognition sees himself, understanding "who I really should be" (*Parrot in the Oven*, p. 210). On Manny's return to his house, he sees the living room, recognizing it as the place where his family builds and destroys its own life together—a place where he belongs after a "long journey of being away" (*Parrot in the Oven*, p. 215).

Forms of inclusion and exclusion. The novel deftly captures one of the most important realities about the Hispanic population in the United States: its sheer variety. There are many Hispanic populations, and they have as many differences as similarities. Even names are subjects of dispute. Some, especially on the East Coast, prefer to be called *Hispanics*. Others find it offensive, an ill-conceived term created by federal bureaucrats, and prefer Latinos. Still others, desiring more specificity or political charge, elect Chicano (for Mexican Americans) or Boricua (for Puerto Ricans). There are also important differences within Mexican and Mexican American populations themselves.

The novel's opening chapter deftly captures some of these differences. When Manny and Nardo decide to spend a day picking chili peppers, they arrive too late in the morning for the best rows, which hard-working migrant laborers have already taken. Manny and Nardo have *chosen* to work in the fields for spending money, while the migrants, as Nardo points out, "pick like their goddamned lives depended on it," which is, of course, true (*Parrot in the Oven*, p. 13). Manny's hands progress slowly through the plants; a nearby worker moves like a whirlwind, never tiring, filling sack after sack with dizzying speed. When officers from the INS show up, the migrants drop their sacks and run, while Manny and Nardo nonchalantly stand and watch, unconcerned because they are American citizens, not undocumented or "illegal" aliens who have broken U.S. law by coming across the border without official authorization. At chapter's end, Manny cinches the difference between the fieldworkers and himself, imagining how his new baseball glove will bring him status at school, where people would admire him in centerfield—"not these people picking chiles . . . but people I had yet to know" (*Parrot in the Oven*, p. 20). The baseball glove symbolizes his desired American-ness, his wish to melt into white America, but also his sense of superiority over newly arrived immigrants—a feeling not uncommon among more established Mexican Americans in the United States.

The novel also explores how generational differences produce conflict among Latinos. Manny's maternal grandfather carries stories of Mexico that "smoldered in his heart," including the memory of the "the desert he crossed to plant a foot in this country" (*Parrot in the Oven*, p. 81). Mr. Hernandez dreams of "escaping" from the United States and returning to Mexico. But the next generation—Manny, Nardo, Magda, and Pedi—regards Mexico only as the present looks back to the past: a distant, receding horizon. Their future will be in the United States, not in Mexico; their language English, not Spanish. Manny and Nardo dabble as field hands, but do not seem destined to earn their labor by the sweat of their brow.

Divisions within the same generation often spring from differences of politics and ideology. In the chapter entitled "The Boxing Match," Manny comments on the "ornery *vatos*," Chicanos who "just hung around and smoked and ditched class and acted like school was some kind of contaminated nuclear zone" (*Parrot in the Oven*, p. 117). He listens to Lencho, who is a Brown Beret, lecture on the "treasures buried deep inside our blood, hidden treasures we hardly knew existed" (*Parrot in the Oven*, p. 119). Yet however inspiring these "inspirational talks" may be, they do not transform Manny into a committed Chicano (*Parrot in the Oven*, p. 122). He remains estranged and detached, on the outside looking in, invested in his own dreams of success and too prone to ironic undercutting to accept these models of identity. Manny's dreams of assuming a place in white society, however, are also dashed. When he goes to Dorothy's party, he feels alienated from the young (white) men dressed in "ironed slacks, wool sweaters, and blazers" (*Parrot in the Oven*, p. 177). He senses their eyes looking him over, and is conscious of his ethnic difference, his otherness. When he makes his faux pas during the dance, he senses his "dream collapsing" and, catching a mirror image of himself in a sliding glass door, says, "I saw the reflection of a ridiculous boy, a clumsy boy. It was me, looking at myself, except that it wasn't me, but someone ghostly and strange" (*Parrot in the Oven*, pp. 179, 181). This moment of mirroring symbolizes his estrangement from the image of himself he has tried to project, a false image that belies the clumsy boy he really is. There is a flash of self-recognition in the moment that causes a psychological fragmentation—he does not recognize himself in the glass.

This moment prepares us for a related recognition, when he sees Eddie running down the street and finally recalls his identity. Eddie, he now realizes, is the boy who visited Magda the day the gun went off, the father of Magda's dead baby. These moments of desiring to belong ultimately lead to the reverse. Manny finds that he does not belong to that aspect of white society symbolized by Dorothy's party, nor to that aspect of Chicano society represented by the *vatos firmes*. He realizes that he harbors false ideals of belonging; only when Manny rejects these can he realize his true place of belonging with which the novel concludes.

Sources and literary context. *Parrot in the Oven* is based loosely on the author's experience of growing up in Fresno. Like Manny, Martinez encountered poverty and discrimination and lived with the threat of violence from the gang culture that surrounded him. Academic expectations for Hispanics were in his life also low. When Martinez went to see a guidance counselor, she told him his good grades and high test scores meant he could be a welder. But like his protagonist, Martinez cultivated a love for language, one that eventually led to the writing of this novel.

The work itself is composed of a series of short chapters, each with a strong narrative thrust. One can easily imagine any one of these pieces standing self-contained in a short-story anthology. The stories exemplify Martinez's mastery of the short narrative. On a small canvas, every word must count; the telling detail is paramount. The short story has a rich tradition among both Latinos in the United States and Latin Americans. Sandra Cisneros (1954-) is regarded as one of the contemporary masters of the form; like Martinez, her subject in, for example, ***The House on Mango Street***, (also in Literature and Its Times) is the trial of growing up Mexican American. Another important influence is the work of Hispanic writer Gary Soto, who, like Martinez was born in Fresno. Soto has published novels, like *Taking Sides* and *A Summer Life*, that also explore the inner lives of young Chicanos.

Martinez's plots, like the Russian writer Anton Chekhov's (1860-1904), contain no extraneous details (see **"Rothschild's Fiddle"** and **"The Lady with the Dog,"** also in *Literature and Its Times*). Chekhov had written that if a gun is seen on the mantelpiece in Act 1, it should go off in Act 3. This principle of inevitable causality is born out in *Parrot in the Oven* when the same gun

Mr. Hernandez uses to frighten his wife unexpectedly fires a few chapters later, this time towards his daughter. Martinez's character development is also highly economical, a result perhaps of the influence of Ernest Hemingway (1899-1961), particularly in regards to the oft-quoted iceberg theory, whereby the author reveals only a small fraction of what lies beneath the surface (see ***The Old Man and the Sea*** and ***The Sun Also Rises,*** also in *Literature and Its Times*). Mr. Hernandez, who says little, is one of the most powerful characters in Martinez's novel. Even more skillful is the portrayal of Mrs. Hernandez, whose sweeping and dusting capture her desire for order and control in a domestic world fraught by violence and emotional trauma.

Above all, Martinez's fiction stands out most in its use of figurative language. His prose is studded with figurative devices: a car engine "wound and gathered like a powerful animal"; in season, cherries "glowed ripe and flashed like Christmas balls"; a mother's voice is like "an accusing needle" (*Parrot in the Oven*, pp. 60, 77, 104). These figures of speech are not merely decorative. They point to the artistic consciousness of a narrator who sees the ordinary world through the eyes of a poet. Manny's sensitivity to the hidden beauty of everyday things is a sign of his capacity for transcendence. It also makes him into a figure for the author himself, whose special gift is the ability to present a world hidden from most readers in a rich and literary language. Indeed, one of the extraordinary facets of this novel is the frequent contrast between the sordidness of Manny's reality and the brilliance of the language used to describe it. Language literally transforms Manny's world.

Events in History at the Time the Novel Was Written

The Hispanic boom. Between 1980 and 1990, the Hispanic population in the United States rose from 14 to 22 million. During the same period California, which leads the nation in Hispanic inhabitants, saw their number rise from 4.5 million to 7.7 million (Hornor, p. 3). The 1990s experienced an even greater increase; the 2000 Census showed a jump in the U.S. Hispanic population to 32.8 million—66 percent were of Mexican descent (Therrien, p. 1). This means approximately one in eight persons in the United States is Hispanic. In California's San Joaquin Valley, the figure is closer to one in three persons, and in Fresno County nearly one in two. The faces of Hispanic politicians, entertainers, and athletes have become familiar; courses in Hispanic literature and culture are now commonplace at colleges and universities; presidential candidates woo Hispanic voters with speeches delivered in Spanish. In many ways, it seems, the activism of the 1960s and 1970s appeared to have yielded fruit.

The 1990s also witnessed a powerful political backlash against Hispanics, with stiffening of immigration laws and rollbacks of programs to accommodate the disadvantages suffered in history. Some of the resentment stemmed from the increasing number of immigrants arriving illegally: INS records reveal that apprehensions between 1980 and 1990 increased by two thirds nationally, with over one third of those occurring in the San Diego area, where most Mexicans cross over (Manuel Gonzalez, p. 225). The backlash is nowhere more evident than in California, a state with a long history of reactionary politics. In the 1990s, Californians passed the first of three ballot initiatives aimed directly at Hispanics. The first, called the "Save Our State Initiative" (Proposition 187), banned undocumented immigrants—who perform the majority of the state's menial labor—from receiving public education and other public benefits, such as welfare and health care, except in the case of emergency. The initiative passed in 1994 with 59 percent of the vote. Meanwhile, the anti-immigrant rhetoric led to still tighter enforcement of the border, though, it has often been noted, there were few penalties against employers who hired immigrants, a laxity supported by business leaders, especially in agriculture. In 1996, voters passed a related measure (Proposition 209) prohibiting the use of race, sex, color, ethnicity, or national origin as a criterion for granting preferential treatment to any individual or group in State employment, public education, or public contracting. Affirmative action programs, long a means of access to higher education for Hispanics, were particularly affected, with Hispanic enrollments plummeting across the University of California system. Victor Martinez, who himself had been a beneficiary of such a program, expressed his dismay at Proposition 209: "Just that little bit of help with affirmative action did so much for me. It was a great program, you put in a dollar, you get a million back" (Ganahl, sec. A, p. 1). The policy would continue through the time of his novel's publication. In 1998, Californians would vote on proposition 227, a measure severely restricting bilingual education in their public schools. Since the majority of bilingual students are Hispanic, the proposition was strongly opposed by Hispanic leaders. It nevertheless passed by 61 percent. These initiatives, and the demographic and political climate that brought them into law, illuminate the growing tensions faced by California's Latinos in the 1990s—when Martinez wrote *Parrot in the Oven*.

To make matters worse, the Hispanic population continues to suffer high rates of unemployment and poverty and poor rates of educational achievement, problems that are a central preoccupation of *Parrot in the Oven*, and which also contribute to a pronounced schism among Mexican Americans, many of whom resent the increasing numbers of immigrants coming to the United States. A 1992 poll conducted by a prominent Latino political scientist found that while 74 percent of non-Hispanic whites "felt that there were too many immigrants in the country," 75 percent of Mexicans with U.S. citizenship and 84 percent without it felt the same. Hispanics are more likely to live in poverty than non-Hispanic whites (22.7 percent Hispanics to 7.7 percent non-Hispanics) and twice as likely to be unemployed (6.8 percent Hispanics to 3.4 percent non-Hispanics). Only 20 percent can afford health insurance, and more than two in five have not graduated from high school (Manuel Gonzalez, p. 236; Therrien, pp. 4-6). As noted, Mexican American students have lagged behind in SAT scores; in 1992 their average scores reached only 797, while non-Hispanic whites averaged 933 (Manuel Gonzalez, p. 234). To examine predominantly Hispanic towns in Fresno County is to confront poverty unimaginable to most Americans. According to the 1990 census, "California's five towns with the lowest per-capita annual income were located in Fresno County: Orange Cove ($4,385), Parlier ($4,784), Mendota ($4,920), San Joaquin ($5,356), and Huron ($5,501). Two other south Valley towns also qualified for the bottom ten" (Johnson, p. 143). As before, these towns occupy a county that continues to produce more agricultural wealth than any other in the nation.

The stubborn economic immobility of Hispanics presents a stark contrast to their increased media visibility, as does their larger disempowerment at the level of political representation. Though the Hispanic population grew rapidly from 1980 to 2000, Hispanics have not yet achieved political clout commensurate with that growth. Five years after the publication of Martinez's novel, in 2001, Hispanics still held only 20 of the 435 seats in the House of Representatives, and none in the Senate. In other words some 50 percent of all the nation's Hispanics are represented by non-Hispanics.

Reception. *Parrot in the Oven: Mi Vida* appears not to have been widely noticed in the mainstream press upon its initial publication, perhaps because it was classified as youth literature and perhaps because the Hispanic subject matter did not immediately appeal to reviewers and editors. It received brief notices in several publications devoted to adolescent literature, where it was highly praised. Once it won the National Book Award, however, Martinez himself became the subject of many articles in major newspapers, including the *Los Angeles Times* and the *San Francisco Examiner*. These articles focused as much on the author's own rise out of poverty and literary obscurity as they did on the novel's merits. The *Fresno Bee* ran a series of articles on Martinez, focusing on his new celebrity as well as his contribution to the literature of the San Joaquin Valley. It also ran an editorial on him, noting wryly that "Fresno's sometimes arid cultural soil has thrust another artist into the light" ("*Victor Martinez's Triumph,*" sec. B, p. 6). Perhaps the best measure of the novel's reception is the rich array of honors it garnered, including a *Publishers Weekly* "Best Book of 1996" distinction, the National Book Award, the Americas Award, the Pura Belpre Award, given by the American Library Association for a work of young adult or children's literature that best portrays the Hispanic experience.

—Robert D. Aguirre

For More Information

Ganahl, Jane. "Former Farmworker Writes Himself into a Field of Dreams." The *San Francisco Examiner*, 10 November 1996, Sunday, 5th edition, sec. A, p. 1.

Gómez Quiñones, Juan. *Chicano Politics: Reality and Promise, 1940-1990*. Albuquerque: University of New Mexico Press, 1990.

Gonzalez, Juan. *Harvest of Empire: A History of Latinos in America.* New York: Viking, 2000.

Gonzales, Manuel G. *Mexicanos: A History of Mexicans in the United States*. Bloomington: Indiana University Press, 1999.

Haslam, Gerald. *The Other California: The Great Central Valley in Life and Letters*. Reno: University of Nevada Press, 1994.

Hornor, Louise L., ed. *Hispanic Americans: A Statistical Sourcebook*. Palo Alto, Calif.: Information Publications, 1996.

Johnson, Stephen, Gerald Haslam, and Robert Dawson. *The Great Central Valley: California's Heart-*

land. Berkeley: University of California Press, 1993.

Martinez, Victor. *Parrot in the Oven: Mi Vida*. New York: Harper Collins, 1996.

Mclellan, Dennis. "Books And Authors; How Did Award Affect His Career As A Writer? It Gave Him One." *Los Angeles Times*, 23 February 1997, Orange County edition, sec. E, p. 4.

National Center for Educational Statistics. "Table 134. Scholastic Assessment Test (SAT) Score averages, by race/ethnicity: 1986-87 to 2000-01." 2001. *National Center for Educational Statistics*. http://nces.ed.gov/pubs2002/digest2001/tables/dt134.asp (15 July 2002).

Shorris, Earl. *Latinos: A Biography of the People*. New York: Norton, 1992.

Skerry, Peter. *Mexican Americans: The Ambivalent Minority*. Cambridge: Harvard University Press, 1993.

Therrien, Melissa, and Roberto R. Ramirez. *The Hispanic Population in the United States*. 2000. http://www.census.gov/population/socdemo/hispanic/p20-535/p20-535.pdf (15 July 2002).

"Victor Martinez's Triumph; The Writer's Deep Valley Roots Produce a Well-deserved National Book Award." *The Fresno Bee,* 9 November 1996, Home edition, sec. B, p. 6.

The Piano Lesson

by
August Wilson

Frederick Kittel, later known as August Wilson, was born in 1945 in Pittsburgh, Pennsylvania, in the Hill District, where *The Piano Lesson* takes place. He learned to read at the age of four, but this early promise of educational success was dashed when he dropped out of high school, disgusted by the racism in both public and private schools. In 1968 Wilson founded Black Horizons on the Hill, a theater company; he did not begin writing plays until 1978, after moving to St. Paul, Minnesota. Success followed shortly thereafter. His first play to be produced, *Black Bar,* opened in 1981 in St. Paul. His first play to reach Broadway, *Ma Rainey's Black Bottom* (1984), won the New York Drama Critics' award in 1985. At this writing, Wilson has produced eight of the ten plays needed to complete a series. The series represents African-American history of the twentieth century, with each play set in a different decade: *Joe Turner's Dead and Gone* (1910s); *Ma Rainey's Black Bottom* (1920s); *The Piano Lesson* (1930s); *Seven Guitars* (1940s); ***Fences*** (1950s; also in *Literature and Its Times*); *Two Trains Running* (1960s); *Jitney* (1970s); and *King Hedley II* (1980s). Set in the 1930s, Wilson's *The Piano Lesson* features characters who engage in a struggle to develop a sense of black identity during this decade by wrestling with threads that reach back to the past.

THE LITERARY WORK

A play set in Pittsburgh, in 1936; first performed in 1988; first published in 1990.

SYNOPSIS

Boy Willie plans to sell an heirloom piano to buy land in Mississippi on which the family was once enslaved but encounters firm resistance at the home of his sister Berniece. The standoff leads to a supernatural struggle with ancestral spirits.

Events in History at the Time the Play Takes Place

Pittsburgh and the Great Migration. After Emancipation, ex-slaves began slowly to move, not only around the South, but out of it. The main migration at first was out of the rural areas and into the cities of the South; it was in the 1890s, when the first generation born into freedom reached maturity, that black Southerners began to migrate northward in large numbers. But what is called the Great Migration is usually dated from 1915, when, with the advent of World War I, job opportunities for African Americans opened up in Northern cities, especially in factories and steel mills. Black rural Southerners started to move to the Northern cities in large numbers, drawn by the prospect of work and of escaping the general poverty of the South, which would remain economically depressed throughout much of the twentieth century. They also fled the rampant racism in the South, whose segregation laws would not be repealed until the 1960s, three decades after Wilson's play takes place. Having already been displaced from Africa, blacks experienced a second displacement when

August Wilson

poverty and racism drove them out of the American South. This time they left behind an African American culture that their ancestors had been creating since the seventeenth century.

The force of the migration would not remain steady through the rest of the century—the flow was interrupted especially by the Great Depression of the 1930s, when job opportunities in the North became not much better than those in the South, as well as by a steady counter migration of Southerners returning home and then going back North. These were interruptions, though, in a continuing process, the height of which lasted from 1915-60, and it greatly transformed the distribution of African Americans in the United States. In 1865, at the end of the Civil War, 91 percent lived in the South (though they comprised just 36 percent of the total population; by 1960, only a hundred years later, only 51 percent of America's black population lived in the South. There was a shift in the rural-urban balance too. Whereas in the mid-nineteenth century, some 75 percent of African Americans lived on farms, by the mid-twentieth century, 75 percent lived in cities.

Especially in the first few decades of the twentieth century, cities of the North and West—New York, Chicago, Los Angeles—would become home to families whose ancestors had been moved from Africa to South Carolina and Virginia. The massive influx of blacks from the South greatly affected the business sector of Northern society. In Pittsburgh, the setting for *The Piano Lesson*, the number of black iron and steel workers increased by almost 500 percent between 1910 and 1920 alone. From 1916, when hiring quickened at the steel mills because of the war effort, most of the African American immigrants clustered in either the mill towns near Pittsburgh, settling close to the steel mills that employed them, or in Pittsburgh's Hill District. Though a concentrated black population lived in the Hill District prior to the Great Migration, during these earlier days, it had been populated by Eastern European and Italian immigrants as well. By the 1930s, the Hill District, now mostly African American, had given rise to such famous sites as Greenlee Field, home of the powerful Pittsburgh Crawfords of the Negro National League; the *Pittsburgh Courier*, the most widely circulated black-owned newspaper in the country; and the Crawford Grille, still an influential jazz club. Charles "Teenie" Harris, who photographed the Hill while working for the *Pittsburgh Post-Gazette* in the 1930s, would live there, as would August Wilson, whose mother had migrated from the South, more exactly, from North Carolina. Information about job openings and places to live in Pittsburgh, as well as ways to get there—most often by rail—had reached even the most remote areas of the South by the 1920s. At work was a complex network of information sources including personal contact with migrants (who wrote home, visited, and sometimes moved back); conversations with railway workers (a rich source of information); public relations campaigns in newspapers such as the *Pittsburgh Courier*; and responses from various public agencies, community organizations, and employers to letters of inquiry that had been sent north. Within the South itself, communities marshaled support for would-be migrants. Clubs and churches sometimes sponsored members who decided to migrate, for example, while parents and children would work and save to send one family member after another up north.

As noted, during the Great Depression (1929-40) migration northward slowed when job opportunities dried up. In *The Piano Lesson*, which is set in the late 1930s, three members of the Charles family—Doaker Charles, his niece Berniece, and her young daughter Maretha—live in Pittsburgh. All three migrated from Mississippi. Doaker, who works as a railway cook, travels a lot; Berniece, who cleans houses for a living, has no desire to move back—"This ain't a bad city once you get to know your way around," she says (Wilson, *The Piano Lesson*, p. 139). Avery, her fiancé, also from Mississippi, is a preacher and has a paid position as an elevator operator—the prestige may be no greater than the cotton picking he did down South, but the working conditions are more comfortable. As studies of the 1920s indicate, such an assortment of jobs was typical for Pennsylvania's black workers at the time. It becomes even more so if one adds the heavy number of black men employed in the coal mines and steel mills. As described in an issue of the *Monthly Labor Review* (June 22, 1926) during the era:

> It appears that in the larger mills which employ and retain men more on a basis of the workman's actual efficiency than the smaller mills, more negroes in proportion are found at work, which leads us to believe that negro steel workers have "made good," notwithstanding any reports to the contrary.
>
> (Foner and Lewis, p. 38)

The Piano Lesson's Boy Willie lives not in Pittsburgh but down south, where he is determined to stay and buy land from the Sutter family, who once owned his ancestors. "Ain't no mystery to life," he says, "If you got a piece of land you'll find everything else fall right into place. You can stand right up to the white man and talk about the price of cotton . . . the weather, and anything else you want to talk about" (*Piano Lesson*, p. 1314). *The Piano Lesson*'s Charleses comprise a representative black family of the decade. Some members have gone north, others have remained in the South; some live in the rural South, others have become urbanites.

That Boy Willie has the sudden opportunity to buy the Sutter land is also realistic for the era. Mississippi was in dire straits in the 1930s. A heavy cotton producer, the state had experienced trouble in the 1920s, which saw a steady fall in cotton prices. They would plummet in the 1930s, dropping from close to 17 cents a pound in 1929 to 5.5 cents a pound in 1931, causing farm income to plunge to new depths and banks to foreclose on farm after farm. "On a single day a quarter of the entire state of Mississippi went on sale at auction for nonpayment of taxes" (Holley, p. 55).

Railroads and the Great Migration. By 1925, the year the Brotherhood of Sleeping Car Porters began to organize black laborers into a union, they had constituted the vast majority of railway porters for nearly 60 years. Soon after the Civil War, George Pullman had begun to recruit ex-slaves for the position in the belief that his people's history of personal service meant they were well-trained for a job that demanded servility. In the pecking order, porters ranked below railway mechanics and conductors, who were always white. Still the position held prestige as one of the best jobs open to African American men; conferring middle-class status on its occupants, it had become especially prized by the 1910s. This would change with the opening of factory jobs to blacks during World War I, but the Brotherhood would grow stronger, becoming an important force for social progress, linking its agenda to that of the National Association for the Advancement of Colored People (NAACP).

AFRICAN AMERICAN WORKERS IN 1930s PITTSBURGH

Close to three quarters of all black workers in 1930s Pittsburgh labored in its industries, with the remainder working largely in domestic and personal services.

	Total Employees	Black Employees
Builders' supplies	645	75
Building construction	459	67
Domestic (hotels, etc.)	4,248	1,235
Education (janitors, *not* teachers)	1,216	74
Manufacturing	81,642	6,055
Mining	10,712	1,949
Printing, Publishing	2,397	24
Professional (hospitals, etc.)	929	130
Trade	17,445	806
Transportation	11,237	406
Total	130,930	10,821

(Adapted from Foner and Lewis, p. 126)

Pullman's hiring of porters ties the railways directly to the Great Migration, since he typically hired porters from the South and moved them up to the cities of the North, after which their families would follow. They, in turn, sent information back to the South about life and job opportunities in the North, becoming yet another link in the inter-regional chain of information flowing between black families in the North and in the South. Of course, the railways themselves played a key part in the Great Migration, since they transported both the migrants and information that drew them northward. Towards the end of the nineteenth century, the number of railways increased dramatically, serving as conduits of information to multiple destination points in the South. Conducting passengers along pathways that led out of known oppression into freedom and safety, they became a major symbol in the creative works about the Great Migration, in the collage art of Romare Bearden and the poetry of Langston Hughes, for example, as in the plays of August Wilson. "I pick up my life," writes Langston Hughes, "And take it with me, / And I put it down in . . . / Any place that is . . . not Dixie" (Hughes, p. 188).

RAILWAY COOKS

The Pullman porters are the most famous of the black railway workers of the first half of the twentieth century. But there were others too, notably the railway cooks. Before trains had dining cars, black cooks were commonly hired at depots and later they gained positions on dining cars, often as undercooks. It was possible even then to work one's way up from undercook to chef, learning from a head chef, who often came from Europe. Conditions for cooks were less comfortable than for porters, though both jobs were respectable. William Jackson, hired in 1946 as a cook on the Santa Fe Chief, describes the experience:

> Everything was first class. . . . The meals were all fresh. The chicken had to be plucked, the fish had to be scaled. Also the peas had to be shelled. It was quite an experience. Many of the movie stars rode with us, and we had to wait on them, and prepare food to their liking. The kitchen on these dining cars weren't equipped with air condition, so it was very hot. We used coal and wood burning stoves and a charcoal broiler for the steaks and chops, and to broil the fish. . . . We prepared the food to the letter—the way they wanted it.
>
> (Jackson in Paige, p. 108)

Featured in *The Piano Lesson* is a family patriarch, Doaker, who labors as a railway cook. The family's stories furthermore center around The Yellow Dog, a Mississippi railroad line. At the climax of the play, when Berniece raises the spirits of her ancestors, the sound of an approaching train is heard. A useful symbol, it not only propels people forward but also connects them back to the past and allows Doaker, on the job for 27 years now, to comment on how advisable it is to try to escape it: "They got so many trains out there they have a hard time keeping them from running into each other. Got trains going every whichaway. Got people on all of them. Somebody going where somebody just left. If everybody stay in one place I believe this would be a better world" (*Piano Lesson*, p. 1290).

The Play in Focus

The plot—Act 1. Early in the morning, Boy Willie Charles arrives at the Pittsburgh home of his uncle, Doaker, and his sister, Berniece, having driven a load of watermelons up from Mississippi. Boy Willie is accompanied by his friend Lymon Jackson. He brings news as well. Sutter, one of the descendants of the Sutter family who owned the Charles family as slaves before the Civil War, has died; he was pushed down a well, says Boy Willie, by the "Ghosts of the Yellow Dog," whose identity becomes clear later in the play. His brother, who lives in the North, is prepared to sell Boy Willie the last of the Sutter holdings in Mississippi—the choicest land, which Sutter had kept for himself, refraining from selling it, though he could have used the money. Boy Willie plans to sell his load of watermelons to help pay for the land, but he also wants Berniece to agree to sell a family heirloom, a piano she has in her possession. It should bring in a great deal of money from some white collector. When Berniece appears, it becomes clear that her relationship with her brother is not good—she blames him for the death of her husband three years earlier. Though she refuses to play the piano, she will not allow it to be sold either. At this point Sutter's ghost appears to her at the top of the stairs; the vision terrifies her.

Later (after Berniece is gone) we learn the story of her husband Crawley's death. He was hauling wood with Boy Willie and Lymon (they were keeping some for themselves) when a sheriff ambushed the three of them. Crawley shot back and was killed in the gunfight. Captured, Boy Willie and Lymon had to serve time in the infamous Parchman penitentiary (where Doaker has also been jailed). Shedding light on another mystery, Doaker tells Lymon the story of the piano. Sutter's grandfather, Robert Sutter, who owned the Charles family, bought a piano for Miss Ophelia, his wife, trading Mama Berniece and her son Walter for it. Mama Berniece's husband, Papa Boy Willie, was left behind to keep working the Sutter holdings. Though Miss Ophelia loved the piano, she missed Berniece and Walter, so her husband told Papa Boy Willie, a woodworker, to carve their pictures on the piano. To the annoyance of Robert Sutter, Papa Boy Willie went beyond his instructions, carving the entire history of his family up to that point on the piano. In 1911, during a Fourth of July picnic, Boy Charles, his grandson and the father of Berniece and Boy Willie, stole the piano from the Sutter home and hid it with relatives. He made his escape on the 3:57 Yellow Dog train, but his pursuers stopped the train. When they found him in a boxcar along with four hobos but failed to find the piano, they set the boxcar on fire. The ghosts of the dead men, now called the "Ghosts of the Yellow Dog," are held responsible for the later deaths of several white men involved in the incident, and of their descendants. Boy Willie agrees that the piano has enormous sentimental value, but thinks its monetary value is more important now; if they sell it, they can purchase land that the Charles family has worked for over 100 years, as slaves and then as tenant farmers. The piano ought, he argues, to help the living.

A 1990 playbill for *The Piano Lesson.*

Act 2. Lymon and Boy Willie go out to enjoy Pittsburgh night life on the Hill. Berniece is planning to take a bath when her beau, a preacher named Avery, stops by. We learn the reason she refuses to touch the piano: she believes the spirits of not only the ancestors carved on it, but also of her father, who died for it, and her mother, who spent her widowhood grieving over it, could be waked by her playing. She won't have their spirits walking around the house, she says. Later, Boy Willie brings a girl home and Berniece throws them out; Lymon comes home alone and gives her perfume. The next morning, Boy Willie enters with a rope and gets Lymon to help him with the piano, but it won't budge. Boy Willie goes off to find a plank and casters. Lymon brings a rope, and they start moving the piano. Avery, who has come by, attempts to exorcise the spirits haunting it, to no avail. Hearing Sutter's ghost upstairs, Boy Willie goes to fight him. The noise they make tells the others Boy Willie is clearly in a life-or-death struggle. Slowly Berniece moves to the piano and begins to play, calling out her ancestors' names, chanting, "I want you to help me" (*Piano Lesson,* p. 132). A train is heard approaching, and Sutter's ghost apparently gives up and leaves. Coming back downstairs, Boy Willie lets Bernice know she will keep the piano.

Boy Willie takes on Sutter's ghost; Berniece calls in the ancestors. The piano itself is the central player in this drama. The instrument takes up imposing space not only in the history of the Charles family, which it carries carved into it, but onstage, where it is the most visually riveting piece of furniture. Like Berniece and Doaker, the piano carries Southern history up North. Its carvings are a text belonging not only to the Charles family, but also to the family history of the Sutters. Though the Sutter family's history is not carved on it, the piano itself stands as an emblem of the bitter and vexed relationships between black and white Southerners, a condensation of the problem of "ownership" in the South. In the eyes of the ex-slave family, the instrument has been paid for three times over already: first through the backbreaking labor of their ancestors to enrich the whites; second by trading Mama Berniece and Walter for it; and last, through the blood of a family member.

At the play's climax, the sister and brother each confront their separate ghosts. For Berniece, who has moved up North, they are the ghosts of her ancestors, of her history, which she has carried with her quite literally, in the form of the piano, despite having fled the South. She confronts these ghosts when she dares to play the spirit-laden instrument and call out the names of her ancestors in search of support. In doing so, she allows the pain and the love embodied by her ancestors into her life, so that they can become, not merely a horror to be escaped, but a foundation for growth and stability. For Boy Willie, who has remained in the South, the American homeland of his ancestors, the struggle is different. His ghost is quite literally the ghost of the white man who owned the land upon which Boy Willie's family has lived. It is also symbolically the ghost of the white race that previously enslaved his family and continues to subjugate them, by passing and enforcing segregation laws and systemically treating them unfairly. Berniece's ghosts seem located in the past, Boy Willie's in the present. But the sister and brother are in fact engaged in a similar struggle to confront the past in the present, to move forward by facing history directly, be it national or familial history. The very ending in which Boy Willie gives up his claim to the piano—at least conditionally—was not part of the play for the first year and a half. The struggle with the ghosts was the original ending, until the director, Lloyd Richards, convinced August Wilson to give the play a resolution: "I said, do you know what we're doing? We're not dealing with the other rights to the piano. The Sutters have a right to the piano too. That ghost is here, his rights are being disregarded" (Richards in Pettengill, p. 201). Wilson finally agreed, but the matter was, essentially, irrelevant to him. For Wilson the crucial matter was the struggle itself, not who finally got the piano:

> We had about five different endings to the play. But it was always the same ending: I wanted Boy Willie to demonstrate a willingness to battle with Sutter's ghost, the ghost of the white man—that lingering idea of him as the master of slaves—which is still in black Americans' lives and needs to be exorcized. I wasn't so much concerned with who ended up with the piano as with Boy Willie's willingness to do battle.
>
> (Wilson, "How to Write a Play," sec. 2, p. 17)

Boy Willie wrestles with the ghost of slavery and Berniece with the ghosts of her beloved dead and their common history. According to August Wilson, it is Boy Willie's struggle that must take place, but Berniece's struggle that causes resolution. In discussing alternative methods of staging her struggle, Wilson has touched on the wideness of his image:

> At one point we had pictures lining up in the backdrop which were the ghosts of the yellow dog. I think we should have stuck with that idea, but with like 2000 pictures. So that it becomes every man. When Berniece is calling out the names of her ancestors, Papaboy Charles and Mama Ola, I always wanted people in the audience to toss out their grandmothers' names, somebody that *they* were calling on.
>
> (Wilson in Pettingill, p. 224)

There is no clear resolution in this climactic image of the double struggle with past ancestors and past owners. The dialogue suggests that what is crucial is not a final outcome, but a continual willingness to be engaged with one's heritage, both in its cultural and its personal forms. As Boy Willie tells Berniece when he relinquishes the piano, "if you and Maretha don't keep playing that piano . . . ain't no telling . . . me and Sutter both liable to be back" (*The Piano Lesson*, p. 1320).

Sources and literary context. The original idea for *The Piano Lesson*, explains August Wilson, sprang from a collage by the Harlem Renaissance artist Romare Bearden—the second of his plays to be so inspired, the first being *Joe Turner's Come and Gone*. Bearden was himself inspired by the Great Migration. Born in North Carolina in 1912, he migrated north to Harlem with his family in 1915, and much of his work reflects the themes and problems associated with that displacement. The collage, called *Homage to Mary Lou [The Piano Lesson]*, depicts a little girl at a piano, with her teacher beside her.

> So I got the idea from the painting that there would be a woman and a little girl in the play. And I thought that the woman would be a character who was trying to acquire a sense of self-worth by denying her past. And I felt that she couldn't do that. She had to confront the past, in the person of her brother, who was going to sweep through the house like a tornado coming from the South, bringing the past with him.
>
> (Wilson in Rothstein, p. 8)

Wilson's drama draws not only on Bearden's images, but also on his technique of collage—the creation of a single whole out of disparate fragments. One sees the technique at work in *The Piano Lesson*, with its disparate histories, understandings, and needs.

Part of a cycle of plays *The Piano Lesson* concerns the core problem of how to deal with inherited history. The scholar Alan Nadel explains that Wilson's method of writing history is to present various histories working "in consort and conflict"; of *The Piano Lesson*, Nadel says that Berniece "wants to hide from history and Boy Willie wants to get rid of it. Wilson, however, wants to rewrite it," that is, to write what happened anew, from an other-than-standard point of view (Nadel, p. 3).

Events in History at the Time the Play Was Written

Going home—reverse migration. The half century between the setting and the writing of *The Piano Lesson* gave rise to a curious phenomenon in the United States, the trend of reverse migration—of African Americans moving back to the South, reclaiming their home ground, so to speak. Some 5 million African Americans had relocated from the South to the North at the height of the Great Migration (1915-60). All the while there was a trickle of return migrants, who, disillusioned by life in the North—where racism, though not as overt as in the South, is nevertheless pervasive—moved back to the South. But from 1970 to 1990 this trickle turned into a healthy stream that brought one-half million returnees back to the South. Certainly they were not drawn by economic promise. The U.S. economy as a whole suffered a recession from the early 1970s to the mid 1980s, with unemployment rates mounting everywhere, but in the South conditions were even worse. In Mississippi, where the play's Boy Willie lives, 67 percent of Jefferson County, for example, lived below the poverty line. So why has the reverse migration been so persistent?

> The resolve to return home is not primarily an economic decision but rather a powerful blend of motives. . . . People feel an obligation to help their kin, or even a sense of mission to redeem a lost community. . . . The years have not changed conditions at home so much as they have changed the people who once left home so urgently. . . . They have . . . set about appropriating local time and memory and blood and symbols for intimate community purposes of their own.
>
> (Stack, p. xv)

Migration to the North is a recurring subject in August Wilson's plays, but *The Piano Lesson* is the first to tackle the phenomenon of reclaiming or going back to the South. The play does so through Boy Willie, who resolves not only to stay in the South, but also to buy the parcel of the land upon which his ancestors were enslaved. "Instead of migrating north to live as a third-class citizen on the outskirts of a resentful society, he wants to stay home and do the work that generations of his race have done before him—this time as an owner, not as a slave" (Pereira, pp. 97-98). To some extent the character reflects the views of Wilson himself:

> I think we should all go back. . . . We should go down there and register to vote, elect ourselves as representatives within the framework of the Constitution of the United States of America, and begin to provide do-for-self food, clothing, and shelter. I think if we did that, fifty years later we'd be in a much stronger position in society than we are today. If we continue to stay up in here in the cities and go along the path that we're going along now, I'm not sure we're going to be here fifty years from now.
>
> (Wilson in Pettengill, p. 218)

ROMARE BEARDEN

Romare Bearden's family moved north, to Harlem, New York, from Charlotte, North Carolina, when he was three years old. In New York, his father worked as an inspector for the city sanitation department, and his mother became a community activist, serving at one point as the national treasurer for the Council of Negro Women. Bearden knew the South from visits back home to his grandparents in his youth. He began to paint in 1935, and in 1950, studied at the Sorbonne in Paris, under the G.I. Bill. Later, turning to jazz, he founded the Bluebird Music company. Finally in 1964 Bearden focused on creating collages. The Museum of Modern Art produced a retrospective of his work in 1971, and he afterward remained influential in artistic and community circles until his death in 1988. Since the Great Migration is a major theme in Bearden's work, trains feature prominently in it, as in Wilson's drama. Wilson's view of the train resembles Bearden's; the playwright uses it as a symbol of white civilization and its encroachment on the lives of American blacks. His indebtedness to Bearden is something the Wilson himself has been quick to discuss:

> What I saw was black life presented on its own terms, on a grand and epic scale, with all its richness and fullness, in a language that was vibrant and which, made attendant to everyday life, ennobled it, affirmed its value, and exalted its presence.
>
> (Wilson in "August Wilson at Dartmouth")

Often people return with the idea of not just reclaiming the South, but remaking it. One such migrant says of his move back,

> You've heard people talk about a second Reconstruction. I guess it was the civil rights movement, when that idea came in. The first Reconstruction didn't take root, and so the thinking is, well, maybe that was partly our own fault, we hadn't laid the ground work. Maybe it wasn't only a matter of how they had the guns

and we didn't. But I'm not sure I go along with that theory. Because, really, what killed off Reconstruction? What did they call those folks? The Redeemers. The white people who felt like they were getting robbed—they were losing control. In Reconstruction, they'd been shoved off to the side, and they rose up and made a power play, right? They said they were "redeeming" their rightful place—taking back their land. And the way I see it, that's how we need to look at it today—not a second Reconstruction but a second Redemption. We're the ones now that have been shoved aside, we're the folk who've gotten everything robbed from us. And we just have to move in and say, "This is ours, it's rightfully ours. It's our land, too."

(Stack, p. 171)

Reviews. Acclaim for *The Piano Lesson* has not been universal. From the beginning, critics have objected to aspects of the play. Some complained too much didacticism; David Stearns, reviewing the play for *USA Today* when it first opened on Broadway, observed that "though [it is] easy to respect, it isn't always easy to enjoy" (Stearns, sec. D, p. 4). The most famous attack on the play—one that led to a public debate between the reviewer and Wilson—was by Robert Brustein, drama critic for *New Republic*, who said *The Piano Lesson* was "the most poorly composed of Wilson's four produced works," and went on to attack the entire cycle itself: "This single-minded documentation of American racism is a worthy if familiar social agenda, and no enlightened person would deny its premise, but as an ongoing artistic program, it's monotonous, limited, locked in a perception of victimization" (Brustein, p. 28). This was the minority view, though. Most critics did not agree with the former assessment of either the play or the larger project. In another contemporary review, Frank Rich, writing for the *New York Times*, applauded the play as a praiseworthy achievement: "That heavenly music belongs to the people who have lived it, and it has once again found miraculous voice" (Rich, sec. C, p. 15). An assortment of judges agreed, deeming the drama worthy of Best Play of the Year award from the New York Drama Critics' Circle, a Pulitzer prize, and a Drama Desk award, as well as a Tony nomination. At the time, Wilson himself called *The Piano Lesson* "my best play" (Wilson in Shannon, p. 163). More than a decade later many critics still agree with him.

—Anne Brannen

For More Information

"August Wilson at Dartmouth." 1998. http://www.dartmouth.edu/~awilson/Bearden/ (3 May 2002).

Brustein, Robert. "The Lesson of *The Piano Lesson*." *New Republic*, 21 May 1990, 28.

Foner, Phillip S., and Ronald L. Lewis, Eds. *The Era of Post-War Prosperity and the Great Depression, 1920-1936*. Vol. 6 of *The Black Worker*. Philadelphia: Temple University Press, 1981.

Holley, Donald. *The Second Great Emancipation: The Mechanical Cotton Picker, Black Migration, and How They Shaped the Modern South*. Fayetteville: The University of Arkansas Press, 2000.

Hughes, Langston. "One Way Ticket." *The Poems: 1941-1950*. Vol. 2 of *The Collected Works of Langston Hughes*. Ed. Arnold Rampersand. Columbia: University of Missouri Press, 2001.

Nadel, Alan, ed. *May All Your Fences Have Gates: Essays on the Drama of August Wilson*. Iowa City: University of Iowa Press, 1994.

Paige, Howard. *Aspects of Afro-American Cookery*. Southfield, Michigan: Aspects, 1987.

Pereira, Kim. *August Wilson and the African-American Odyssey*. Urbana: University of Illinois Press, 1995.

Pettengill, Richard. *August Wilson: A Casebook*. New York: Garland, 1994.

Rich, Frank. "A Family Confronts Its History in August Wilson's *Piano Lesson*." *New York Times*, 17 April 1990, sec. C, pp. 13, 15.

Rothstein, Mervyn. "Round Five for the Theatrical Heavyweight," *New York Times*, 19 April 1990, sec. 2, pp. 1, 8.

Shannon, Sandra G. *The Dramatic Vision of August Wilson*. Washington D.C.: Howard University Press, 1995.

Stack, Carol. *Call to Home: African Americans Reclaim the Rural South*. New York: Basic Books, 1996.

Stearns, David Patrick. "*The Piano Lesson*: Heavy on Drills," *USA Today*, 17 April 1990, sec. D, p. 4.

Wilson, August. "How to Write a Play Like August Wilson." *New York Times*, 10 March 1991, sec. 2, p. 17.

———. *The Piano Lesson*. In *Drama: Classical to Contemporary*. Ed. John C. Coldewey and W. R. Streiberger. Upper Saddle River, N.J.: Prentice Hall, 2001.

Praisesong for the Widow

by
Paule Marshall

Born in Stuyvesant Heights, New York in 1929, Paule Marshall was the daughter of immigrants from Barbados. She grew up in a largely immigrant community and, after graduating from Brooklyn College in 1953, worked as a journalist for *Our World*, a small black magazine. During her employment there, Marshall wrote her first novel *Brown Girl, Brownstones* (1959), which dealt with the issues of ethnic autonomy and assimilation. Later, she published a collection of short stories, *Clap Hands and Sing* (1961), and a second novel, *The Chosen Place, the Timeless People* (1969). While Marshall's works were well received, she did not become widely known as an author. Her third novel, *Praisesong for the Widow*, was not published until 1983, but then garnered critical praise for its unlikely heroine—a well-to-do African American widow—and her quest to rediscover her cultural identity.

THE LITERARY WORK

A novel set during the late 1970s in Grenada and Carriacou, with flashbacks to the 1940s-1960s New York and South Carolina; published in 1983.

SYNOPSIS

A middle-aged, middle-class African American widow undergoes a spiritual journey and comes to terms with her troubled past while vacationing in the Caribbean.

Events in History at the Time of the Novel

Grenada—an overview. In *Praisesong for the Widow*, the true journey of the African American protagonist begins on the remote West Indian island of Grenada. Discovered by Christopher Columbus in 1498, Grenada was originally named Concepcion and inhabited by fierce Carib Indians; the latter circumstance may have discouraged Spanish settlers from establishing a colony there. In 1652 the French became the first to colonize the island—known by then as Grenada—and in 1674, Grenada officially became French territory. By this time, the region had begun importing African slaves as laborers because the native populations had fallen victim to disease and harsh conditions resulting from their contact with the colonists.

On Grenada, French settlers planted indigo, tobacco, and, later, sugar. The colony prospered, attracting the attention of the British, who captured it in 1762, during the Seven Years' War. The French retook the island briefly in 1779 but it was returned to the British in 1783 and they governed it as a colony until 1958. Like the French, the British colonizers established sugar plantations and imported large numbers of African slaves to work those plantations. All this slave labor had far-reaching ramifications for the racial composition of Grenada; during the 1980s, approximately 91 percent of the island's population was black. East Indians and whites constituted only 9 percent (Meditz, p. 352).

Paule Marshall

In 1958 Grenada, along with nine other island territories, formed the West Indies Federation, but the union, plagued by differences between Jamaica and Trinidad—the two largest members—collapsed after only a few years. Subsequently, Britain granted independence to its West Indian colonies; Grenada became an independent country in 1974. Five years later, Maurice Bishop staged a military coup that attempted to establish a Marxist state, modeled on Cuba and the Soviet Union. Bishop himself was overthrown and killed by Vice Minister Bernard Coard in 1983, leading to joint military intervention by Caribbean and U.S. troops, which succeeded in restoring democratic government to Grenada.

Like the other West Indian islands, Grenada's economy was based largely on agriculture. Its major export crops included cocoa, nutmeg, bananas, mace, sugarcane, and cotton. Agriculture got competition during the 1980s from what became another major facet of the island's economy. Grenada experienced a boom in tourism, especially after the Marxist revolutionary government was overthrown. In 1985, the number of cruise-ship passengers who visited Grenada was about 90,000, nearly three times the number who had visited the previous year; receipts from tourism amounted to $23.8 million in U.S. currency (Meditz, p. 363). To accommodate the increased number of tourists, the island had to build more large hotels, some with as many as 500 to 600 rooms.

In *Praisesong for the Widow*, Avey experiences firsthand the beginning of the tourist boom in Grenada. After deciding to leave the Caribbean cruise, she disembarks upon the island and finds herself witnessing two aspects of its culture: the traditional, in the form of out-islanders (people who work in Grenada but were not born there) preparing to depart for an annual excursion to Carriacou, and the modern, in the form of increasing urban development. The taxi driver who rescues the disoriented widow reassures her that he will find accommodations befitting her position and means, "Plenty hotels, oui. That's all we got in Grenada now. And only the best . . . I gon' take you to one to suit" (Marshall, *Praisesong for the Widow*, p. 75).

Carriacou—culture and celebrations. The most significant step in Avey's journey is her decision to go on an excursion to the remote island of Carriacou. Included in the chain of West Indian islands known as the Grenadines, Carriacou lies between St. Vincent to the north and Grenada to the south; legally, Carriacou and Petite Martinique belong to the state of Grenada. Although Carriacou is considered one of the larger Grenadine islands, its proportions are still quite small: only 7.5 miles long and 2.5 miles wide.

The society of Carriacou is described as "neoteric," meaning that it developed from plantation societies composed of European masters and African slaves, with little input from an indigenous population. The blending of colonial administrations—both French and English—with African cultural traditions is one of Carriacou's most distinctive features. Anthropologist Donald R. Hill writes,

> Carriacou society is made up of two components, metropolitan and folk. . . . The organized political, economic, educational, and religious structure of the island is largely of French and British origin. This social structure is maintained by metropolitan institutions and modified by the folk society. The folk society has its origins in the traditional cultures brought to the island from West Africa, the Congo, Britain, and France. During the early colonial period, a single yet varied folk society emerged from these diverse sources. The folk society of present-day Carriacou is the result of continuous interplay between the traditional folk culture and the metropolitan culture.
>
> (Hill, pp. 196-97)

This interplay between folk and metropolitan cultures seems especially apparent during marriages, baptisms, and funerals, as well as during holidays like Christmas, New Year, Carnival, Easter, All Saints' Day, and All Souls' Day. Most Carriacouans are either Catholic or Anglican; however, their celebrations are marked not only by prayers and church services but by fetes—often known as "Big Drums" because drums are the main instruments—where traditional African songs and dances are performed. Especially popular are the Nation Dances, each of which is said to belong to a specific African tribe—for example, the Cromanti, Moko, Igbo (formerly spelled Ibo), or Chamba. Another Big Drum dance is the Beg Pardon, during which the dancers kneel and ask forgiveness from their ancestors for various transgressions.

Carriacouan rituals and dances play a pivotal role in *Praisesong for the Widow*. Suffering from some mysterious disorder of body and spirit, Avey Johnson only discovers the cause after encountering Lebert Joseph, an ancient Carriacouan of Chamba descent, who persuades her to accompany him on his annual excursion to the island. Witnessing and then participating in the African rituals faithfully preserved on Carriacou enables Avey to reclaim her heritage and to free herself of the materialism that has oppressed her for so many years.

Black history and genealogy. During the 1970s many African Americans became increasingly concerned with defining their culture and place in history. New works—both fictional and nonfictional—were published that addressed those very issues, including John Blassingame's *The Slave Community: Plantation Life in the Ante-Bellum South* (1972), Gerda Lerner's *Black Women in White America* (1973), and Ernest Gaines's *The Autobiography of Miss Jane Pittman* (1971).

Arguably, the most influential of these works was Alex Haley's Pulitzer Prize-winning *Roots* (1976), a fictionalized memoir tracing the author's family history from the capture and enslavement of a single man, Kunta Kinte, in eighteenth-century Africa to the time of Haley himself. An international bestseller, *Roots* was made into two highly rated television miniseries—airing in 1977 and 1978—which heightened African Americans' interest in family history and genealogy. In 1977 Charles Blockson's *Black Genealogy*, a popular guide for those who wanted to trace family trees, appeared in print; the Afro-American Historical and Genealogical Society was founded that same year.

Black women were no less enthusiastic than black men about rediscovering and excavating the past. In *In Search of Our Mother's Gardens* (1974), Alice Walker explored the rituals and art forms of black southern women, including quilting, gardening, and storytelling. Walker also revived interest in such authors as Phillis Wheatley, an eighteenth-century African American poet, and Zora Neale Hurston, a writer of the Harlem Renaissance. Meanwhile, the acclaimed novelist Toni Morrison helped facilitate the publication of *The Black Book* (1971), an African American scrapbook containing traditional recipes as well as accounts of historical events.

While many African American authors chose to focus on the era of slavery, some, such as Paule Marshall, delved into other aspects of black culture. As the offspring of immigrant parents from Barbados, Marshall brought a unique perspective to her writings, demonstrating that the effects of the African diaspora could be found not only in America but also in the Caribbean and newly liberated African nations as well. (Of the 10 to 15 million slaves imported to the so-called New World, some 2 million had been shunted to the Caribbean, a very considerable number whose experience formed a significant part of the whole.) In Marshall's *Praisesong for the Widow*, Avey Johnson discovers in the course of her travels to Grenada and Carriacou just how much of a stranger she has become to her own heritage and *roots*.

Emergence of a black middle class. In the 1900s, large numbers of African Americans migrated from the rural South to the urban North, with ramifications that would be felt throughout the century. While black migrant workers still faced racial discrimination, unemployment, poverty, and inadequate housing in northern cities, they nonetheless had more opportunities there than in the South. This was especially true in the decades surrounding the two world wars. Increased industrialization and enlistments of soldiers led to job openings and economic opportunities for black workers at home. Then, after the wars, black veterans, who had served their country with distinction, felt less inclined to accept second-class citizenship back home in America and did what they could to improve their status.

Between the 1940s and 1980s, an increasingly populous black middle class began to emerge, its members making advances in a wide spectrum of professions. The civil rights movement of the 1950s and 1960s opened the door even wider for African American advancement. The 1954 ruling of *Brown v. Board of Education* outlawed racial segregation in schools, while the Civil

THE IMPORTANCE OF NAMES

In *Praisesong for the Widow,* names as well as tribes also carry great significance. Avey's full first name is "Avatara," derived from the word "avatar"—an incarnation of a spirit on earth; moreover, Avey shares that name with her late grandmother, a woman many considered insane. Avey's great-aunt Cuney believed that this first Avatara was a visionary and insisted that Avey always give her full name when introducing herself to others. Other names—and their usage—also prove important in the novel. Avey's husband was named Jerome Johnson, but during the happy early years of their marriage, Avey calls him by the more casual "Jay." As Jay becomes increasingly driven to achieve middle-class status and security, Avey finds herself thinking of her husband as "Jerome" instead and mourns the loss of "Jay." Place names prove similarly significant: "North White Plains," the suburb to which the Johnsons eventually move, suggests their achievement of middle-class affluence and their increased estrangement from their black heritage. Similarly, the cruise ship from which Avey flees in confusion is named "Bianca Pride," "Bianca" being an Italian name meaning "white." The name of Lebert Joseph, who guides Avey on her spiritual journey, is also significant. His first name, Lebert, recalls the African trickster figure "Legba," while his Hebrew surname "Joseph" means "God will increase." However, Joseph's name is less important than his fully defined sense of self. He is as connected to his roots as Avey is alienated from hers; he recognizes his name's familial significance when he declares "I's a Joseph, oui! . . . From Ti Morne, Carriacou. The oldest one still living from that part of the island if you please" (*Praisesong for the Widow,* p. 163). He also knows his nation, announcing, "I's a Chamba! From my father's side of the family. They was all Chambas. My mother now was a Manding and when they dance her nation I does a turn or two out in the ring so she won't feel I'm slighting her. But I must salute the Chambas first" (*Praisesong for the Widow,* p. 166). Joseph's knowledge of and pride in his cultural identity ultimately inspire Avey to reclaim her own, starting with her remembering that her given name is "Avatara."

Rights Act of 1964 forbade discrimination based on a person's race, color, religion, national origin, or sex in public facilities. Such reforms paved the way for African American students to enroll in historically white universities such as Harvard, Cornell, and Princeton. Greater numbers of blacks also entered the white business world, where many scaled the corporate ladder to achieve executive status. Inevitably, however, the division between middle-class professional blacks and working-class blacks widened, especially as the former separated themselves physically by moving to more affluent communities and by attending different schools and churches.

In *Praisesong for the Widow*, the initially working-class Avey and Jay Johnson strive for upward mobility, like many of their contemporaries. A domestic quarrel brought on by economic hardships, overwork, and an unplanned pregnancy nearly wrecks the Johnsons' marriage, but then Jay pushes himself relentlessly to attain material success. After establishing his own accounting business, he can afford to move his family into a larger house in the suburbs of North White Plains, New York. Their success does not receive unqualified applause, however. The novel depicts the Johnsons' rise to the top ambivalently; even as Avey and Jay achieve social position and financial security, they forfeit something of equal or greater importance: their intimacy as a couple and their connection with their African heritage. Jay, in particular, becomes alienated from his roots in Harlem and his sense of himself as an African American. Ultimately even Avey can no longer recognize the man she loves in the remade Jerome Johnson who "viewed the world and his fellow man according to a harsh and joyless ethic" (*Praisesong for the Widow*, p. 131).

Arial view of part of the West Indies visited by Avey Johnson in *Praise Song for the Widow.*

The Novel in Focus

The plot. The novel begins as Avey Johnson, an affluent African American widow in her sixties, suddenly decides to leave a Caribbean cruise—her third in as many years—after only five days and return home. Avey's decision astounds her two traveling companions (also middle-aged black women), all the more so because Avey herself cannot explain it. During the last several days of the cruise, Avey has suffered from an odd sensation of bloating in her stomach; more disturbingly, she has begun to dream, which she has not done since 1963.

In her most recent dream, Avey encountered her great-aunt Cuney, who used to take the young Avey to a special place in Tatem, South Carolina, where slave ships carrying Ibos landed. According to Aunt Cuney, the Ibos turned around and walked all the way back across the sea to Africa without sinking or drowning, a story that fascinated Avey as a child. In the dream, however, the adult Avey, in mink stole and high heels, resists her aunt's attempts to take her to Ibo Landing. The two women come to blows; so violent and real does their struggle seem that Avey's wrists are sore when she awakens from the dream.

Disembarking from the cruise ship in Grenada, Avey goes ashore and becomes increasingly disoriented when she finds herself among a crowd of islanders who do not seem to speak English. A taxi driver comes to her aid and escorts her to a lavish hotel. On the drive, he explains that the people Avey saw on the wharf were "out-islanders" from Carriacou, preparing to go home on an annual excursion that lasts two or three days. The taxi driver, however, does not understand the appeal of the excursion, on which he has never gone, although he once dated a girl from Carriacou.

Arriving at the hotel, Avey has the clerk make reservations for her on a plane leaving for New York the next day, then checks into her room. Once alone, doubts assail her as to whether she made the right decision by cutting her trip short. She cannot even take refuge in imagining the comforts of her home in North White Plains, New York. Falling into an uneasy slumber, Avey dreams again—this time of her late husband, Jerome Johnson, who berates her for forfeiting $1,500 dollars by leaving the ship.

The second dream stirs up poignant memories of Avey's past life and the early years of her marriage. She and Jerome—then called Jay—had been a struggling young married couple, living in Brooklyn on Halsey Street. Avey was employed by the state motor vehicle department, while Jay had worked long hours at a department store as a warehouse clerk who also handled the shipping and receiving. Hardworking, efficient, and conscientious, Jay was a model employee, but he did not receive all the credit or money due him because he was black. Nonetheless, the Johnsons had a happy, affectionate marriage, complete with shared rituals like dancing to Jay's phonograph records at night, eating coffee cake together on Sunday mornings, and taking summer trips to Tatem to see Ibo Landing.

Everything changes after Avey unexpectedly becomes pregnant for the third time. Worried about finances and the burden of caring for another child, Avey tries without success to terminate her pregnancy. Jay becomes increasingly distant after hearing about the pregnancy and his wife's self-abortion attempts; he begins to work longer hours at the department store. Tensions escalate as Avey's pregnancy advances, coming to a head in the winter of 1945. Worn out by caring for two ailing daughters in a house that lacks sufficient heat, Avey lashes out at her husband one night on his return from work, accusing him of having affairs with the store's white shopgirls. During the ensuing quarrel, Jay shouts at his wife "Do you know who you sound like, who you even look like . . . ?" He alludes here to a shrewish neighbor who continually fights with a husband whom she must fetch home from bars every Friday night.

Jay's question ultimately haunts the Johnsons for the rest of their life together. From that point on, Jay becomes obsessed with achieving material success and escaping from Halsey Street. He takes a second job as a door-to-door salesman, enrolls in night school and correspondence courses, and eventually builds a small accounting business that enables the Johnsons to move to a house in the more upscale North White Plains. But the passion and joy has gone out of the Johnsons' marriage. They abandon the rituals they shared, almost becoming strangers to each other. Avey begins thinking of her husband as "Jerome" rather than "Jay," a sign that he is not quite the same person he was before. Remembering his funeral four years ago, Avey suddenly realizes she did not weep then because the husband she loved had disappeared long before Jerome Johnson's death. Now, in Grenada, she weeps for what she and Jay lost when they began their upward climb.

The next morning, after breakfasting and changing her clothes, Avey wanders aimlessly on the beach. Losing her bearings, she finds herself in a deserted part of the island, where the only building visible is a small bar, or rum shop. Ducking into the shop for a brief rest, a disoriented Avey meets the proprietor, an elderly, crippled man named Lebert Joseph. Although both are initially wary and testy, they begin a conversation. Avey learns that Joseph is an out-islander preparing to depart for the Carriacou excursion and very proud of his African heritage—its songs, prayers, dances, and history—which he wishes to impart to all his descendants, even those whom he has not yet seen. Avey, in turn, finds herself confiding all her troubles and misgivings, including her strange dreams, to the old man. On hearing her out, Lebert Joseph identifies her problem as being unable to identify her heritage: "[Grenada] have quite a few like you. People who can't call their nation. For one reason or another they just don't know. Is a hard thing. . . . You ask people in this place what nation they is and they look at you like you's a madman. No, you's not the only one" (*Praisesong for the Widow*, pp. 174-75). Joseph then invites Avey to accompany him on the excursion, suggesting that it might do her good. Ultimately Avey accepts the invitation, reschedules her flight to New York, and boards ship with the other out-islanders that afternoon.

During the passage, Avey's sense of malaise returns; in scenes reminiscent of a ritual purging, she suffers from vomiting and loose bowels. Her fellow passengers minister to her needs and escort her to the deckhouse midship so she can recover and rest in solitude. Lying alone in the darkness, Avey has the strange impression of "other bodies lying crowded in with her in the hot airless dark. . . . Their suffering—the depth of it, the weight of it in the cramped space—made hers of no consequence" (*Praisesong for the Widow*, p. 209).

Later, Avey awakens in the house of Rosalie Parvay, Lebert Joseph's daughter, on Carriacou. The kindness of Rosalie and the other female elders soothes away Avey's lingering embarrassment. Their touch also proves healing as they bathe, oil, and massage their reluctant guest. Now recovered from her difficult journey, Avey joins the islanders on their yearly rituals.

At night all the Carriacou pilgrims gather at a meetinghouse at the top of a hill, where they pray, sing, and finally perform the ritual dances from their individual African nations. Avey watches with interest but does not take part until the all-inclusive Carriacou Tramp begins. Recognizing the dance as the Ring Shout, which she saw performed in Tatem years before, Avey joins in, slowly at first, then with a growing confidence and sense of belonging. The other dancers bow to her, and one elderly woman takes Avey's hand and introduces herself. Avey returns the courtesy, remembering that Aunt Cuney had always instructed her to give her name as "Avey, short for Avatara" (*Praisesong for the Widow*, p. 251).

The following morning, Avey bids an affectionate farewell to Lebert Joseph and his daughter before flying back to Grenada. Healed in body and spirit, her cultural identity restored, Avey resolves to make major changes in her life once she returns to New York and to enlist the help of her youngest, most politically active daughter, Marion in carrying them out: she will sell the house in White Plains, rebuild Aunt Cuney's house in Tatem as a summer residence, and pass on to her grandchildren the stories, traditions, and history of their African heritage.

Ancestors and descendants. The need to reconnect with and embrace one's past is a major theme of *Praisesong for the Widow*. Even the surface of the novel illustrates that need, by portraying generational conflicts between ancestors and descendants. Throughout the first part of the novel, Avey is haunted by memories and dreams of her great-aunt Cuney, the domineering woman who named her and instructed her in all the family history and legends. In her most recent dream, the old woman tries to drag her back to the places they had gone when Avey was a child, while the adult Avey, clad in all the finery of a well-heeled suburban lifestyle, strenuously resists. The dream ends as the two women engage in a furious brawl, but in the morning, Avey can still feel "the pressure of the old woman's iron grip" on her wrist (*Praisesong for the Widow*, p. 47).

Although Avey herself tries to dismiss the dream, she is unable to do so, finally relating it to Lebert Joseph, the elderly Carriacouan proprietor of a rum shop in Grenada. Initially hostile towards this African American tourist, Joseph becomes "all-understanding, all-compassion" once he learns of her troubles (*Praisesong for the Widow*, p. 172). From that point on, he is also more determined than ever to persuade her to accompany him to Carriacou, possibly because he recognizes the source of her distress: her estrangement from her past, her heritage, and her ancestors.

Avey's dream visitation by her great-aunt has an established historical and cultural precedent. As noted, in the Caribbean and in certain parts of the United States, Africans' reverence for their ancestors survives in various rituals, both religious and secular. Many West Indians believe that to neglect those rituals—leaving food or other offerings for the deceased, for example—is to incur their ancestors' displeasure and risk misfortune, illness, and even death.

Dreams in which ancestors appeared to their descendants were also taken quite seriously, as the principal means by which the dead contacted the living. In his anthropological study of Carriacouan society, Donald R. Hill classified these "dream messages" from Old Parents (ancestors) to descendants as falling into five sometimes overlapping categories: 1) disturbances by a recently departed spouse or parent; 2) advice for personal, often health-related problems; 3) sooth-saying; 4) requests for a ceremony to be performed; 5) a response to a malevolent action that is to be taken or has already been taken. Avey's own dream-message from her great-aunt Cuney seems to be both a disturbance and a request, an attempt to jolt Avey from her complacent but stifling

THE MIDDLE PASSAGE

In *Praisesong for the Widow,* Avey Johnson becomes violently ill during the crossing from Grenada to Carriacou, an occurrence that recalls the sufferings of African slaves undergoing transport from Africa to the Americas on what became known as "the middle passage." Most slave ships sailed due west, nearing the Ascension Islands, then turning north towards the West Indies, Martinique, or Barbados. The passage could take from six weeks to half a year, depending on the severity and frequency of tropical storms near the equator. Regardless of the duration, the slaves suffered horribly; considered cargo rather than passengers, they were generally held in shackles below decks and packed together like sardines. Captains of slave ships stowed an average of 300 slaves in the cargo hold, allotting them only half the space afforded convicts, emigrants, and soldiers. In such close quarters, the spread of communicable diseases, including smallpox and measles, was inevitable, while anemic dysentery, scurvy, and malnutrition were ever-present threats. As many as 8 million Africans may have perished while undergoing the middle passage during the slavery era (Rogozinski, p. 128). In the novel, Avey, lying down in the deckhouse to recover from her illness, experiences what might be described as a psychic echo of her ancestors' sufferings on the middle passage: the cramped quarters, filth, and stench. The knowledge of what they endured makes her own discomfort easier to bear.

middle-class existence and an entreaty for Avey to reclaim the rituals she was taught as a child and take up her place as her great-aunt's spiritual heir. Initially resistant to the idea, Avey embraces her past and her mission after her pilgrimage to Carriacou, resolving to fulfill her duty to her people and her ancestors.

Sources and literary context. Marshall's earliest literary models included Charles Dickens, Thomas Mann, and Joseph Conrad, from whom she derived her sense of character development, especially in relation to culture and setting. Later, she read the works of African American writers Paul Laurence Dunbar, Richard Wright, Ralph Ellison, and James Baldwin. Like many of her female contemporaries, Marshall did not encounter the writings of other black women writers until the 1960s; among those, however, she admired Zora Neale Hurston, Dorothy West, and, especially, Gwendolyn Brooks, whom she cited as having a strong influence on her own work.

BLACK FEMINISM

Although African American women played key roles in the civil rights movement of the 1950s and 1960s, many felt that their own needs were being subordinated to those of black men. During the 1970s, however, black women came into their own, founding several organizations intended to address their particular issues and aspirations. The most important of these groups was the National Black Feminist Organization (NBFO), which was established in 1973. One of the NBFO's founders, Margaret Sloan, declared, as a rallying cry for new members, that "there can't be liberation for half a race" (Sloan in Franklin and Moss, p. 556). Paule Marshall's emphasis on black women in her novels corresponds to an increasingly vocal black feminism of the times.

Marshall also drew upon her personal experiences as a child growing up in an immigrant community and upon her professional experiences as a globetrotting journalist. Her travels to the Caribbean and South America fueled the plots of several of her works, including *Praisesong for the Widow*. Perhaps the most striking aspect of Marshall's work is her emphasis on the lives and experiences of black women. This focus, in her early writings, was considered ahead of its time, since most of the attention was long riveted on black urban males in relation to both cultural nationalism and African American literature. Marshall addressed what she felt to be a necessary and much-neglected perspective. In an interview, she explained that she wanted "to make women—especially black women—important characters in [my] stories. . . . To make up for the neglect, the disregard, the distortions, and untruths, [I] wanted them to be center-stage" (Marshall in Alexander, p. 196).

Reviews. *Praisesong for the Widow* received mostly positive reviews on its publication in 1983. Darryl Pinckney, writing for the *New York Review of Books*, complained that the novel lacked substance but conceded that "the attraction of [Marshall's] work lies in a deep saturation in the consciousness of her characters and the ability to evoke the urban or tropical settings in which they toil" (Pinckney in Stine, p. 315).

Other reviewers were more enthusiastic. In *Booklist*, William Bradley Hooper called *Praisesong for the Widow* "uncomplicated but resonant," adding "There is no limit to the kind of readership to which this novel will appeal; with deft exploration of character, Marshall speaks to anyone interested in thoughtful fiction" (Hooper in Stine, p. 314). Novelist Anne Tyler, writing for the *New York Times Book Review*, noted an improvement over Marshall's previous writings, calling *Praisesong for the Widow* "a firmer book, obviously the product of a more experienced writer. It lacks the soft spots of the earlier work. From the first paragraph, it moves purposefully and knowledgeably towards its final realization" (Tyler in Stine, p. 315). Tyler was especially taken with the protagonist's vivid memories of her past and evocations of her young husband. Avey's "wistful journey to her younger self," struck Tyler as both "universal" and "astonishingly moving" (Tyler in Stine, p. 315).

—Pamela S. Loy

For More Information

Alexander, Simone A. James. *Mother Imagery in the Novels of Afro-Caribbean Women*. Columbia: University of Missouri Press, 2001.

Crawford, Vicki L., Jacqueline Anne Rouse, and Barbara Woods, eds. *Women in the Civil Rights Movement: Trailblazers and Torchbearers, 1941-1965*. Bloomington, Indiana University Press, 1993.

DeLamotte, Eugenia C. *Places of Silence, Journeys of Freedom*. Philadelphia: University of Pennsylvania Press, 1998.

Franklin, John Hope, and Alfred A. Moss, Jr. *From*

Slavery to Freedom. New York: Alfred A. Knopf, 2000.

Gates, Henry Louis, Jr., and Nellie Y. McKay, eds. *The Norton Anthology of African American Literature*. New York: W. W. Norton, 1997.

Hill, Donald R. *The Impact of Migration on the Metropolitan and Folk Society of Carriacou, Grenada*. New York: American Museum of Natural History, 1977.

Marshall, Paule. *Praisesong for the Widow*. New York: Plume, 1983.

Meditz, Sandra W., and Dennis M. Hanratty, eds. *Islands of the Commonwealth Caribbean: A Regional Study*. Washington, D.C.: Federal Research Division, 1989.

Pettis, Joyce. *Toward Wholeness in Paule Marshall's Fiction*. Charlottesville: University Press of Virginia,1995.

Rogozinski, Jan. *A Brief History of the Caribbean*. New York: Meridian, 1994.

Stine, Jean C., ed. *Contemporary Literary Criticism*. Vol. 27. Detroit: Gale Research, 1984.

Rosencrantz and Guildenstern Are Dead

by
Tom Stoppard

Sir Tom Stoppard, born Tomas Straussler on July 3, 1937, in Zlin, Czechoslovakia, believed that he became "a playwright by historical accident," since plays were the dominant mode of literary expression in late 1950s and 1960s England (Gussow, p. 3). A former journalist and novelist, Stoppard experienced his first real success with *Rosencrantz and Guildenstern Are Dead*, which premiered in 1966 (as part of the Edinburgh fringe festival). Despite not being born English himself, or perhaps because of it, many of Stoppard's plays have focused on the canon of classic British and Irish literature: *The Real Inspector Hound* (1968) satirizes mystery writer Agatha Christie; *Travesties* (1974) features novelist James Joyce as a character; *Arcadia* (1993) focuses on the comings and goings of the poet Lord Byron; and *The Invention of Love* (1997) is about the poet A. E. Housman, with playwright Oscar Wilde in a prominent role. In *Rosencrantz and Guildenstern Are Dead* Stoppard rewrites Shakespeare's masterpiece *Hamlet* from the point of view of its most minor characters, and in doing so, makes the play newly relevant to 1960s British society.

THE LITERARY WORK

A play set within the world of Shakespeare's *Hamlet;* first performed in 1966.

SYNOPSIS

Two minor characters—Rosencrantz and Guildenstern—wander through and around Shakespeare's *Hamlet,* pondering the meaning of their existence and the roles they play in both theater and life.

Events in History at the Time the Play Takes Place

A note about the setting of Stoppard's play. One might think that since *Rosencrantz and Guildenstern Are Dead* takes place within the world of Shakespeare's *Hamlet*, the setting of the play must be identical to that of *Hamlet*, which is Denmark before 780 C.E. But *Rosencrantz and Guildenstern Are Dead* is not set within Shakespeare's fictional Denmark as much as it is within Shakespeare's classic tragedy itself. Stoppard tells us in the opening stage directions that Rosencrantz and Guildenstern are "two Elizabethans passing the time in a place without any visible character" (Stoppard, *Rosencrantz and Guildenstern Are Dead*, p. 11). The place without any visible character is the bare Shakespearean stage. Unlike the modern "realist" theater, Shakespeare's theater used no fixed sets and few props. This allowed Shakespeare to move his stories easily from place to place. A throne and a crown could indicate a castle; a skull established the scene as a graveyard; a few goblets suggested a banquet in progress. Because Shakespeare wasn't bound by a lot of heavy scenery, he could change his setting quickly from scene to scene, which gave his work a cinematic quality. Stoppard uses the Shakespearean stage to similar

Tom Stoppard

advantage, allowing his own characters to move fluidly from a road to a castle to a boat over the course of the play.

The identification of Rosencrantz and Guildenstern as "Elizabethans" reinforces what we already suspect from the play's title: that these two men are characters in Shakespeare's *Hamlet*, which was first performed in England about 1601 under the reign of Queen Elizabeth I. Rosencrantz and Guildenstern are not, in the strictest sense, "real people" at all—they are characters in an already famous play. So it is perfectly acceptable to announce their fate at the outset: as everyone who has read or seen *Hamlet* already knows, Rosencrantz and Guildenstern die at the end.

In Shakespeare's *Hamlet*, Prince Hamlet is visited by his recently deceased father's ghost, who informs Hamlet that his father was murdered by his brother Claudius (Hamlet's uncle). Claudius has since compounded his crime by taking the throne and marrying the murdered king's widow and Hamlet's mother, Queen Gertrude. After hearing the ghost out, Hamlet is not sure what to make of this horrible news. Can the ghost be believed? How does Hamlet know that the ghost has not been sent by demonic forces to tempt him to evil? Hamlet's suspicion of the ghost's origins and desire to do the right thing contributes to his famous indecision. For most of the play, he does not know how to *act*. Also he muses upon *acting* in a way that fully exploits both meanings of the word: acting as *doing* and acting as *pretending*, as in the theater.

In order to bide time, Hamlet pretends that he is mad, while he plans what actions to take regarding King Claudius. This pretend-madness distresses his love-interest, Ophelia, as well as the king and queen, who send Hamlet's friends Rosencrantz and Guildenstern to discover what is bothering him. Hamlet tests King Claudius by having some traveling actors perform a play about a man who murders a king and marries his wife. When Claudius reacts with horror, Hamlet is convinced of his guilt and rushes to kill him. He, however, finds Claudius praying and so decides not to kill him, since murdering a sinner while he is repenting would send him straight to heaven. Instead, Hamlet confronts his mother with the fact that she has married her husband's killer. During their conversation, Hamlet hears someone hiding behind a tapestry and stabs him, thinking he has killed Claudius; the person turns out to be Polonius, Ophelia's father and the king's advisor.

Thereafter, Claudius sends Hamlet, accompanied by Rosencrantz, Guildenstern, and a message in their care to England. The message is an ultimatum to the English to either kill Hamlet or else fight a war with Denmark. The King's plan founders, however. A brush with pirates allows Hamlet to escape the ship, and he returns to the Danish court to find that Ophelia, who went insane because of her father's sudden murder, has drowned herself. Her brother Laertes, egged on by Claudius, challenges Hamlet to a duel to avenge his father and his sister. Hamlet accepts, and Claudius tries to ensure Hamlet's defeat by poisoning both the tip of Laertes sword and the victory wine. Almost all the major characters are killed in the final act: Laertes and Hamlet each wound each other with the poisoned sword; Gertrude drinks the poisoned wine by accident, and Hamlet finally stabs Claudius. Dying, Hamlet asks his friend Horatio to tell his story to the world. This is the storyline with which Stoppard's play starts.

Since the storyline is a given, Stoppard's play does not concern what happens—we know what happens: we are familiar with *Hamlet* and how it unfolds. Rather, Stoppard's play is about what the events mean to the lives of the two minor characters. The question becomes, What does *Hamlet*, a story of kings and ghosts and revenge, look like from the perspective of two insignificant men? How does it feel to be a minor character in a play about someone more important than you?

The dramatic renaissance in the Elizabethan Age. The reign of Queen Elizabeth I (1558-1603) is widely considered to be one of England's golden ages. When Elizabeth ascended the throne at 25, England was not yet a major power, but the country gained great stature during her reign. In 1588 the English navy defeated the Spanish Armada, turning England into the dominant sea power in Europe. As a result, the English began a period of great overseas expansion and became a global force in maritime trade, which bolstered national confidence and brought widespread prosperity. The English at this time were better housed and better fed than most nations in Europe.

The arts flourished in this climate of wealth and international sophistication. Poets and playwrights such as Philip Sidney (*Astrophel and Stella*, 1591), Edmund Spenser (*The Faerie Queene*, 1596), and Christopher Marlowe (*Edward II*, 1594) contributed to the rapidly expanding English language. The most important writer of the day was William Shakespeare, who composed more than thirty-five plays, at least two-thirds of them, including *Hamlet*, during Elizabeth's reign. Shakespeare tended to adapt already existing plots from history or literature, transforming them into masterpieces through his language and characterization. The practice was not at all unusual in his day. Many writers then and since (Tom Stoppard included) have made a name for themselves by retelling classic tales in ways that make them fresh and unique.

It is worth noting that while the theater was hugely popular in Shakespeare's day, it was also controversial. Some were suspicious of its popularity, claiming that the theater lured people away from work; others objected to acting itself, calling it a form of idolatry; still others disliked the rowdy, often criminal atmosphere that flourished around theaters. Female prostitutes plied their services to theatergoers, and pubs and other drinking establishments clustered nearby. Actors were thought of as disreputable too. Not long after Shakespeare's day, the Puritans would close down the playhouses completely, but later Elizabethan drama would make a triumphant return to the stage.

"Words, words, words": the expansion of English. The English language that appeared in print grew rapidly during the Elizabethan Era for a number of reasons. First, literacy was on the rise, and newly literate readers wanted books in their own language. While Latin remained the language of scholars, Elizabethan intellectuals imported words like *catastrophe* (Greek) and *habitual* (Latin) into English from the classics. Meanwhile, the scientific revolution required new terms to describe the inventions and the phenomenon being studied—words like *atmosphere, pneumonia,* and *gravity*. England's seafaring explorers and traders contributed to the growth of the language too, bringing back to their native land "foreign" words (such as the French *détail* and the Spanish *desperado*), which became part of the English vocabulary (McCrum, pp. 93-95).

"YOU ARE QUOTING SHAKESPEARE"

"If you cannot understand my argument, and declare 'It's Greek to me', you are quoting Shakespeare; if you claim to be more sinned against than sinning, you are quoting Shakespeare; if you recall your salad days, you are quoting Shakespeare; if you act more in sorrow than in anger, if your wish is father to the thought, if your lost property has vanished into thin air, you are quoting Shakespeare; if you have ever refused to budge an inch or suffered from green-eyed jealousy, if you have played fast and loose, if you have been tongue-tied, a tower of strength, hoodwinked or in a pickle, if you have knitted your brows, made a virtue of necessity, insisted on fair play, slept not one wink, stood on ceremony, danced attendance (on your lord and master), laughed yourself into stitches, had short shrift, cold comfort, or too much of a good thing, if you have seen better days or lived in a fool's paradise . . . it is a foregone conclusion that you are (as good luck would have it) quoting Shakespeare . . . if you think I am an eyesore, a laughing stock, the devil incarnate, a stony-hearted villain, bloody-minded or a blinking idiot, then . . . but me no buts!—it is all one to me, for you are quoting Shakespeare."

(Levin in McCrum, pp. 99-100)

Shakespeare was particularly interested in new words—*assassination, obscene,* and *premeditated* are just a few that first appear in his writings (McCrum, p. 99). He also combined words to form new phrases, such as "hoisted by his own petard" and "the time is out of joint, both of which come from *Hamlet*. This penchant for word-coining strongly affected how Shakespeare shaped his characters. Its is Hamlet who observes, for example, that his murderous uncle is "a little more than kin and less than kind" (Shakespeare, *Hamlet*, 1.2.65) and later that Polonius is at supper, "Not where he eats, but where 'a is eaten," a reference to maggots feeding off his dead corpse (*Hamlet*, 4.3.19).

The struggle for succession. In the centuries before Shakespeare, England witnessed a series of bloody struggles over who would reign. Once the Wars of the Roses (1399-1485), a tussle for power between the Lancaster and York families, were resolved, the Tudor family would rule for more than a century (1485-1603). The throne of Elizabeth, the last Tudor monarch, was repeatedly challenged by Mary, Queen of Scots, a member of the Stuart family, until Elizabeth, at the behest of her advisors, had Mary put to death in 1587. But the Stuart line regained the throne after Elizabeth's death in 1603, when Mary's son was crowned as James I.

Shakespeare told the story of the Wars of the Roses in his history plays (*Richard II,* **Henry IV Part I** and *Part II, Henry V, Henry VI Part I, Part II*, and *Part III,* and **Richard III** [also in *Literature and Its Times*]). The plays illustrated a longstanding belief that once the rightful king was displaced, England would lose God's favor until things could be put to rights once again. Shakespeare examines this issue in *Hamlet* as well, but this time through a fictional lens. The tragedy is actually a cautionary tale against the dangers of regicide: what is "rotten in the state of Denmark" is that the rightful king, Hamlet's father, has been murdered and the crown has passed into the wrong hands, a message as relevant to Shakespeare's England as it is to Prince Hamlet's Denmark (*Hamlet*, 1.4.90). In Hamlet's Denmark, having a murderer on the throne poisons the entire state, from top to bottom, until Hamlet can restore things to rights once again.

The Play in Focus

The plot—Act 1. Two Elizabethans are sitting in a nondescript place, passing the time by flipping coins and betting on the results. Guildenstern's bag of coins is almost empty; Rosencrantz's almost full. Guildenstern, who is betting tails, loses seventy-six times in a row because each time the coin comes up heads. This, it should be noted, is statistically almost impossible, since a coin has a 50-50 chance of coming up heads or tails. Rosencrantz grows bored with the game when the coin keeps landing on heads, but Guildenstern, who understands just how impossible this result is, gets very upset. He tries to come up with a rational explanation for this impossible situation—perhaps time has stopped and they're watching the same coin come up heads over and over, or maybe God is responsible for this strange result. From a scientific point of view, something is seriously wrong with the laws of probability in this universe. But, of course, there is no room for scientific probability in this particular universe, since everything that will happen has already been scripted by Shakespeare in *Hamlet*. Everything is predetermined because of the script; Rosencrantz and Guildenstern have few, if any, choices and little free will. (Shakespeare, like other Elizabethans, believed events were guided by God's will, or Divine Providence.)

We soon learn that neither Rosencrantz nor Guildenstern can remember much beyond this very moment; the only thing they recall is that they were sent for by a messenger this morning. Guildenstern looks around the bare stage and concludes, somewhat doubtfully, that they must be traveling. At this point, they begin to hear the faint music of a band. A Player and his group of Tragedians—a traveling theater troupe—appear on the stage. The troupe pushes a cart containing theatrical props that opens to form a makeshift stage. The Player greets Rosencrantz and Guildenstern enthusiastically with the cry of "An audience!" Rosencrantz and Guildenstern introduce themselves—except at this point the audience realizes that they are not even sure themselves which of them is Rosencrantz and which is Guildenstern! (In *Hamlet*, Rosencrantz and Guildenstern are almost indistinguishable as characters, more like props than fully formed human beings.)

The troupe offers to perform. It becomes clear that they are not only actors but also prostitutes and that the performance can be a sexual one if Rosencrantz and Guildenstern would like. Guildenstern is disgusted, but Rosencrantz is interested and offers the Player one of his coins. When the coin falls to the floor, Guildenstern offers to bet the Player on whether it has landed heads or tails up. The Player bets heads—and of course, he wins. Rosencrantz and Guildenstern bet the Player several more times and in different ways. After losing one of these bets, the Player agrees to perform for them; they will see play number thirty-eight. The tragedians busy themselves with pulling props off their cart. Meanwhile, Rosencrantz bends to pick up a coin that he has dropped—for the first time, his coin has landed on tails, which indicates a radical shift in the play's reality.

A lighting change occurs and Ophelia runs on stage, followed by Hamlet. Hamlet, looking mad, pantomimes his state of mental anguish to Ophelia, and then they both flee the stage. Hamlet's mother, Gertrude, and his uncle, Claudius, then arrive with their attendants. The king and queen greet Rosencrantz and Guildenstern, and ask them to spend some time with Hamlet so they may discover what is bothering him and why he is acting so crazy[1] (see the box with the **Hamlet Key** to discover which lines from Shakespeare correspond to this part of Stoppard's play).

When the royal entourage has left the stage, a confused Rosencrantz turns to Guildenstern and says, plaintively, "I want to go home" (*Rosencrantz and Guildenstern*, p. 37). Neither man understands what is going on or what the two of them are supposed to be doing in this situation, as they have not been given enough information. Finally, Guildenstern decides that "it's a matter of asking the right questions and giving away as little as we can. It's a game" (*Rosencrantz and Guildenstern*, p. 40). Much of their conversation consists of word games and puns to pass the time while the two wait for something in *Hamlet* to happen.

To prepare for their upcoming meeting with Hamlet, Rosencrantz and Guildenstern decide to play a game of "Questions." The nature of this game is to answer a question with a question, rather than provide any answers: "What does it all add up to?" "Can't you guess?" "Were you addressing me?" "Is there anyone else?" (*Rosencrantz and Guildenstern*, pp. 42-43). The game is scored like a tennis match with phrases like "one-all," "two-love," "game point," and so forth. Once they have played a couple of matches against each other, they try a different version. In this new version, one of them pretends to be Hamlet and the other questions him about his madness. They have a little trouble getting started because Rosencrantz keeps forgetting which role he is playing. But eventually they act out a pretend interview with Hamlet, and afterwards evaluate the facts as they know them.

> ROS: To sum up: your father, whom you love, dies, you are his heir, you come back to find that hardly was the corpse cold before his young brother popped onto his throne and into his sheets, thereby offending both legal and natural practice. Now why exactly are you behaving in this extraordinary manner?
>
> GUIL: I can't imagine.
>
> (*Rosencrantz and Guildenstern*, p. 51)

(Their conversation in many ways sums up the essential problem of Shakespeare's *Hamlet*. On the one hand, Hamlet's situation is perfectly clear: he is the dispossessed son of a murdered monarch; on the other hand, critics have spent four centuries wondering why Hamlet behaves as he does, since his circumstances do not quite explain his unusual behavior.) The act ends with Rosencrantz and Guildenstern meeting Hamlet just as they do in Shakespeare's text[2].

Act 2. The second act begins with Rosencrantz and Guildenstern still talking to Hamlet[3]. They tell him that the Players are coming to perform at the castle. When Hamlet leaves, Rosencrantz and Guildenstern evaluate the conversation they have just had with him. They realize that Hamlet asked a lot more questions than he answered, so they still do not know why he is acting so strangely:

> GUIL: We got his symptoms, didn't we?
>
> ROS: Half of what he said meant something else, and the other half didn't mean anything at all.
>
> (Rosencrantz and Guildenstern, p. 57)

They then spend some time discussing Hamlet's last statement—"I am but mad north-north-west. When the wind is southerly, I know a hawk from a hand-saw"[4]. The two try to determine if the wind is, in fact, coming from the south. (Hilariously, Rosencrantz and Guildenstern have completely misunderstood the meaning of Hamlet's words—namely, that he is only pretending to be mad.) Polonius and Hamlet come back onstage with the Player and his troupe. Hamlet asks the Player to perform *The Murder of Gonzago*, hoping to provoke Claudius into confessing his murder of Hamlet's father[5]. When Hamlet leaves again, the Player yells at Rosencrantz and Guildenstern for abandoning his troupe on the road during their performance of play number 38; for actors, what makes life worth living is having an audience. Rosencrantz and Guildenstern apologize by implying that they are responsible for getting Hamlet to invite the players to perform, but the Player explains that this is not the first time he and his troupe have acted for Hamlet:

> PLAYER: I've been here before.
>
> GUIL: We're still finding our feet.
>
> PLAYER: I should concentrate on not losing your heads.
>
> GUIL: Do you speak from knowledge?
>
> PLAYER: Precedent.
>
> GUIL: You've been here before.
>
> PLAYER: And I know which way the wind is blowing.

GUIL: Operating on two levels, are we?! How clever! I expect it comes naturally to you, being in the business so to speak.
(*Rosencrantz and Guildenstern*, p. 66)

(The Player, being in the business of acting and knowing the stories of various plays, is perhaps the only one who knows they are all smack in the middle of Shakespeare's *Hamlet*. Both a character in this play and an actor who has read a number of other plays, this man of the theater can predict events. He knows that Rosencrantz and Guildenstern are going to lose their heads—there is literally no chance that they will not, as the title of Stoppard's play indicates.) The Player then gives the two men a few hints about the plot of *Hamlet* and goes off to learn more of his lines.

A PLAY WITHIN A PLAY WITHIN A PLAY

In Shakespeare's *Hamlet,* a troupe of actors performs before Claudius at Hamlet's request. The troupe first acts out a pantomime that tells the story of Hamlet: a king is murdered, and the murderer marries the dead king's wife. The players then perform *The Murder of Gonzago,* which tells the same story again: there is a murder by poison, after which the widow marries her husband's killer. So Shakespeare has already inserted a play within his play: the characters of *Hamlet* watch *The Murder of Gonzago.* Stoppard adds yet another level to the action: now *The Murder of Gonzago* is performed within *Hamlet,* which, in turn, is performed within *Rosencrantz and Guildenstern Are Dead.*

Rosencrantz and Guildenstern wait yet again for something to happen, and their thoughts turn to the subject of death. After all, Guildenstern notes, waiting is a kind of death, and after death comes eternity, which is yet another kind of waiting, one with no end. Rosencrantz suddenly gets tired of waiting for something to happen, and tries to assert control over his destiny by yelling, "Keep out, then! I forbid anyone to enter!" (*Rosencrantz and Guildenstern*, p. 72). At this point, a grand procession enters, including Claudius, Gertrude, Polonius, and Ophelia, who begin to act a scene from Shakespeare's *Hamlet*[6]. They discuss the performance of the tragedians who will be entertaining them, and soon the Player instructs his troupe to rehearse its performance of *The Murder of Gonzago*.

The troupe rehearses its performance while the Player narrates the story to Rosencrantz and Guildenstern, laying out the entire tale of *Hamlet* for our two confused heroes. This drama, a work of art, provides Rosencrantz and Guildenstern with all the answers they have been seeking. Here, finally, is the whole story: a king is murdered by his brother, who marries the dead king's wife.

The rehearsal is interrupted at this point by the "real" Hamlet, who bursts in with Ophelia. Hamlet tells her to "Get thee to a nunnery!"[7] and throws her to the floor. When Hamlet leaves, King Claudius enters and delivers a speech from Shakespeare's play consoling Ophelia and resolving to send Hamlet to England[8]. The *Hamlet* characters leave, and the Player calls for the rehearsal to continue. Guildenstern is surprised, having thought that the play was over. But the Player just laughs:

PLAYER: Do you call that an ending?—with practically everyone on his feet? My goodness no—over your dead body.
(*Rosencrantz and Guildenstern*, p. 79)

The standard expression, of course, is "over my dead body"—but the Player wryly twists it into "your body" because he knows the play will not end until all its main characters, including Rosencrantz and Guildenstern, are dead. Guildenstern, getting nervous, asks, "Who decides?" (*Rosencrantz and Guildenstern*, p. 80). "Decides?" the Player echoes. "It is written." He further explains, "We're tragedians, you see. We follow directions—there is no choice involved" (*Rosencrantz and Guildenstern*, p. 80).

The Player proceeds to narrate the rest of the play as the other players act it out. The prince is upset by his father's death and his mother's marriage, and begins to behave madly. The king, tormented by guilt, sends his nephew to England with two of his friends. Onto the Player's stage come actors in the roles of these friends (who are, of course, Shakespeare's Rosencrantz and Guildenstern in his play *Hamlet*). The two friends appear and take the nephew on a ship, but he escapes them and returns to Denmark while the two friends are put to death in England as spies.

Rosencrantz and Guildenstern stare at the two actors who are playing them in *The Murder Of Gonzago*. These two actors are dressed identically to Rosencrantz and Guildenstern themselves. But still they do not recognize their own situation, although Guildenstern is now very nerve-wracked indeed. He argues that the Player does not understand what death really is:

GUIL: No, no, no . . . you've got it all wrong . . . you can't act death. The fact of it is nothing to do with seeing it happen—it's not gasps and blood and falling about—that isn't what makes it death. It's just a man failing to reappear, that's all—now you see him, now you do not, that's the only thing that's real: here one minute and gone the next and never coming back—an exit, unobtrusive and unannounced, a disappearance gathering weight as it goes on, until, finally, it is heavy with death.

(*Rosencrantz and Guildenstern*, p. 84)

There is a blackout, during which there is a cry for "Lights, lights, lights!" lights!"[9] We are hearing, though not seeing, Claudius's reaction to the actual performance of *The Murder of Gonzago* in *Hamlet*.

When the lights come on again, it is morning, and the play within the play has ended. Claudius arrives to tell Rosencrantz and Guildenstern that Hamlet has killed Polonius and he needs their help to find him[10]. Rosencrantz and Guildenstern agree to look, but then cannot make up their mind whether to go separately or together, so they just stay put. Hamlet appears briefly, dragging Polonius's corpse onto the stage and then off again. When he returns, they confront him about where he has hidden the body[11]; Hamlet answers evasively, and Rosencrantz and Guildenstern deliver him to King Claudius at the king's request[12].

At this point, Rosencrantz and Guildenstern think that their role in the story of *Hamlet* is over: Hamlet is now in the custody of the king. Rosencrantz sighs, "For my part, I'm only glad that that's the last we've seen of him—" (*Rosencrantz and Guildenstern*, p. 92). But at that very moment he turns and sees Hamlet talking to a soldier[13, 14]. They are asked to escort Hamlet to England.

Act 3. The act opens in pitch darkness, and Rosencrantz and Guildenstern soon ascertain that they are alive, together, and on a boat. Guildenstern is quite happy to be on a boat because a person need not make any decisions on a voyage: the voyager just travels in whatever direction the boat is going. Hamlet is also there, on the boat, sleeping behind them under an umbrella. They are taking Hamlet to England. Rosencrantz is worried about what will happen when they actually get to England, but Guildenstern reassures him that they have a letter from King Claudius explaining everything. Still, Rosencrantz is not reassured, so, as before, they try to anticipate what will happen to them in England by acting out the scene. Rosencrantz plays the part of the English king, and Guildenstern speaks for them. As the English king, Rosencrantz questions Guildenstern, and Guildenstern explains that he bears a letter from the king of Denmark. Rosencrantz, caught up in his role as pretend-king, snatches the letter, opens it, and reads it. The letter contains an order for the English king to execute Hamlet.

Rosencrantz and Guildenstern feel terrible about this; "We're his friends," Rosencrantz says, agonized (*Rosencrantz and Guildenstern*, p. 110). But Guildenstern tries to rationalize the situation: "We are little men, we do not know the ins and outs of the matter, there are wheels within wheels, etcetera—it would be presumptuous of us to interfere with the designs of fate or even of kings" (*Rosencrantz and Guildenstern*, p. 110). Their minds eased a bit, they go to sleep—whereupon Hamlet sneaks downstage, steals the letter, and replaces it with another one.

When they wake up the next morning, Rosencrantz and Guildenstern discover that the players are on the ship. King Claudius, upset with their performance in *The Murder of Gonzago*, has banished them from the country. Soon afterwards, the ship is attacked by pirates, and Hamlet, the Player, and Rosencrantz and Guildenstern hide themselves in three barrels on the ship's deck. Hamlet jumps into the left barrel, the Player jumps into the right barrel, and Rosencrantz and Guildenstern jump into the one in the middle. At the end of the chaotic fighting, the middle barrel is missing. But Rosencrantz and Guildenstern appear in the Player's barrel, and the Player peeks out of Hamlet's barrel—Stoppard is here staging the theatrical equivalent of the old "shell game," where an object is put under one of three shells and the shells are moved rapidly around by a slight-of-hand artist to confuse the viewer. Inexplicably, Hamlet is missing—now you see him, now you do not. This, of course, is Guildenstern's definition of death.

GUIL: (rattled) He's not coming back?

PLAYER: Hardly.

ROS: He's dead then. He's dead as far as we're concerned.

PLAYER: Or we are as far as he is.

(*Rosencrantz and Guildenstern*, p. 119)

Hamlet has left them to go back to Denmark and finish his destined role in Shakespeare's *Hamlet*; they have now parted ways with him forever. At this point, Rosencrantz and Guildenstern are really worried about their fate in England: how will they ever explain themselves to the English king without Hamlet? Again they act out their hypothetical situation, this time with Guildenstern playing the English king. Rosencrantz explains that they have a letter—and Guildenstern, as the king, snatches it up and reads it. The letter now contains orders for Rosencrantz and Guildenstern to be put to death because Hamlet has switched letters. Rosencrantz and Guildenstern are stunned by this development:

> ROS: They had it in for us, didn't they? Right from the beginning. Who'd have thought that we were so important?
>
> GUIL: But why? Was it all for this? Who are we that so much should converge on our little deaths? (In anguish to the Player:) Who are we?
>
> PLAYER: You are Rosencrantz and Guildenstern. That's enough.
>
> GUIL: No—it is not enough. To be told so little—to such an end—and still, finally, to be denied an explanation—
>
> PLAYER: In our experience, most things end in death.
>
> (*Rosencrantz and Guildenstern*, pp. 122-123)

HAMLET KEY

Stoppard's play intersects with scenes from *Hamlet* (at junctures indicated in the plot summary by the superscript numbers1-15). At these junctures, Rosencrantz and Guildenstern snap into their Shakespearean roles and speak in Shakespeare's blank verse.

Act, Scene, and Lines from Hamlet in Stoppard's Play

1) *Hamlet* 2.2.1-49	**9)** *Hamlet* 3.2.255
2) *Hamlet* 2.2.201-23	**10)** *Hamlet* 4.1.33-39
3) *Hamlet* 2.2.356-82	**11)** *Hamlett* 4.2.4-29
4) *Hamlet* 2.2.367-68	**12)** *Hamlet* 4.3.11-15
5) *Hamlet* 2.2.517-28	**13)** *Hamlet* 4.4.9-14
6) *Hamlet* 3.1.10-31; 87-91	**14)** *Hamlet* 4.4.28-31
7) *Hamlet* 3.1.145-48	**15)** *Hamlet* 5.2.349-68
8) *Hamlet* 3.1.161-68	

Furious at the Player's answer, Guildenstern grabs the Player's knife off his belt and stabs him, determined to show him what death really looks like when it is not faked. The Player clutches at the wound, falls to his knees, and dies. But after a moment, the other Players start to applaud, and the Player gets up and takes a bow; the dagger is merely a prop with a retractable blade, and the Player has merely performed death yet again. The Player then declares that he sells death, romantic deaths, "deaths for all ages and occasions! Deaths by suspension, convulsion, consumption, incision, execution, asphyxiation and malnutrition! Climactic carnage, by poison and by steel! Double deaths by duel!" (*Rosencrantz and Guildenstern*, p. 124) Next, the other actors begin to mime all the death scenes in *Hamlet*: Ophelia drowns, Gertrude drinks from a poison cup; Hamlet stabs King Claudius; Hamlet gets stabbed by Laertes. But Guildenstern explains tiredly that their deaths will not be like that, and of course he is right: in *Hamlet*, Rosencrantz and Guildenstern are killed offstage—they just disappear and never come back. Here too they just vanish, with Guildenstern's last words being: "Now you see me, now you—" (*Rosencrantz and Guildenstern*, p. 126).

Shakespeare is given the play's final word; we close with the scene from *Hamlet* in which the English Ambassador arrives to report to the Danish Court "that Rosencrantz and Guildenstern are dead."[15]

To Be Or Not To Be? Shakespeare's *Hamlet* begins with a question—"Who's there?" (*Hamlet*, 1.1.1)—and the play has continued to raise questions for 400 years. How trustworthy is the ghost of King Hamlet? Why does Prince Hamlet wait so long to avenge his father's death? How much did Gertrude suspect about her husband's murder? Is Hamlet really losing his mind or just pretending? Was Hamlet romantically involved with Ophelia or not, and if so, how can he be so cruel to her? Is revenge morally justified for Hamlet or not? Scholars have been debating these and other puzzles almost since the play was first written. In fact, the dialogue of Shakespeare's play itself is full of questions. When Rosencrantz and Guildenstern first meet Hamlet, he asks them at least twenty-five questions: "Were you not sent for? Is it your own inclining? Is it a free visitation?" (*Hamlet*, 2.2.269-270). The rush of questions mirrors the quizzical, provocative nature of the Elizabethan era.

Shakespeare was writing at a time of new questions. It was the Age of Reason; philosophers and scientists were using observation and experimentation to make sense of the world, rather than tacitly accepting what people before them said. Copernicus (1473-1543) argued that the earth revolves around the sun and not the other way around. Galileo (1564-1642) made a name for himself as the first astronomer to use a telescope. The explorer Sir Francis Drake (1543-1596) became the first Englishman to sail around

A 1990 film version of *Rosencrantz and Guildenstern are Dead,* with (from left) Gary Oldman, Tim Roth and Richard Dreyfuss.

the world. From this flurry of activity, undertaken to answer questions, there arose a fresh stream of questions, pertaining to religion, philosophy, science, politics, society. If the earth was only one of a number of different planets, what was man's actual status in the universe? Was there a God at all? If the world was ordered by scientific principles and not by God's will, what became of the divine right of kings to rule? Was one still obligated to serve a bad ruler? Did life have any larger purpose, or was mankind simply alone on a satellite, orbiting the sun?

Three hundred sixty-five years later, when *Rosencrantz and Guildenstern* was first staged, not only were many of those questions still relevant, but the world was facing a host of new moral, ethical, and scientific questions in the wake of World War II. What does civilization mean when a sophisticated nation like Germany can produce a Nazi regime that perpetrates mass murder? How can people resist murderous leaders—not autocratic kings, but military dictators such as Germany's Adolph Hitler and Russia's Joseph Stalin? Many people in the postwar era shared Hamlet's opinion that madness was the only reasonable solution. How are people supposed to live in a world where life on earth can be obliterated by atomic weapons—to be or not to be, indeed! The question "To be or not to be?"—perhaps the most famous line in Shakespeare's *Hamlet*—was one that many people were asking themselves in Stoppard's war-shocked, newly nuclear age.

Hamlet's "To be or not to be?" soliloquy questions the very point of existence itself. During World War II and its aftermath, a number of philosophers and writers, including Søren Kierkegaard, Franz Kafka, Albert Camus, Samuel Beckett, and Jean-Paul Sartre asked very similar questions about the nature of being and the meaning of human existence. The name "existentialism" was coined to refer to these philosophical questions and ideas. Many of the various ideas attached to existentialism are perfectly illustrated in *Rosencrantz and Guildenstern Are Dead*: the fear of an inevitable death, a sense of boredom from the unending repetition of situations, the absurd position of human individuals caught between their limitless aspirations and their finite possibilities, the feeling that man is lost in an absurd universe in which any or all of his decisions inevitably lead toward death.

The philosophy of existentialism, as its name suggests, is deeply concerned with issues of being/existing and what it means to be—issues that preoccupy Shakespeare's Hamlet as well. Of course, Shakespeare lived long before the existentialists, but many of the issues that he raises in *Hamlet* were also central concerns among these twentieth-century existentialist philosophers.

Stoppard's play was influenced not only directly by existentialism but also by existentialist literary works, which are often grouped under the label, "theater of the absurd." The most important for Stoppard was undoubtedly Samuel Beckett's **Waiting For Godot** *(also in* Literature and Its Times*), in which two men, Didi and Gogo, wait passively on a bare stage for a meeting with Godot, who never does appear. Two other men in the play burst onto the stage at intervals and stumble past Didi and Gogo. Beckett's contrasting pairs of characters brutally illustrate the limited "choices" available in life: people can move about madly as if they are going somewhere, or they can stand around and wait for something to happen—it makes little difference in the end. In similar fashion, Stoppard's play contrasts the pathetic confusion of the minor characters Rosencrantz and Guildenstern with the larger revenge story of* Hamlet's *major characters—in the end, Rosencrantz and Guildenstern are dead, but so are Hamlet, Claudius, Polonius, Gertrude, Laertes, and Ophelia. Death comes to us all.*

Sources and literary context. The most obvious literary source for *Rosencrantz and Guildenstern Are Dead* is, of course, Shakespeare's *Hamlet*; without knowledge of its plot, Stoppard's play makes little sense. Early reviewers also noted Stoppard's debt to existential writers such as Albert Camus, who spoke of human existence as being both utterly free and ultimately pointless, and to more recent theater, such as Luigi Pirandello's *Six Characters in Search of an Author* (1921) and the already mentioned *Waiting For Godot*.

Stoppard was not the first playwright to stage a Shakespearean theatrical joke, nor was he even the first to show extended interest in Rosencrantz and Guildenstern. W. S. Gilbert (of the famous Gilbert and Sullivan team of light-opera writers) composed a comedy called *Rosencrantz and Guildenstern* in 1891. Many of Stoppard's contemporaries did serious or comic Shakespearean rewrites as well. For instance, *West Side Story* (music, Leonard Bernstein; lyrics, Stephen Sondheim), the musical reworking of *Romeo and Juliet*, appeared on the Broadway stage in 1957 and as a film in 1961. *MacBird* (by Barbara Garson) was a mid-1960s reinterpretation of Shakespeare's *Macbeth*, featuring American president Lyndon B. Johnson in the title role. Other reworkings of *Hamlet* include Heiner Muller's *Hamletmachine* (1979), Melissa Murray's *Ophelia* (1979) and Lee Blessing's *Fortinbras* (1991).

Events in History at the Time the Play Was Written

Elizabeth II and the second dramatic renaissance. Like her namesake Elizabeth I, Queen Elizabeth II ascended to the English throne at the youthful age of twenty-five. Both Elizabeths were also crowned during a time when the English nation was feeling depressed and powerless. In the years before Elizabeth II's coronation in 1952, England had been struggling to recover from the effects of the Second World War. Severely bombed during the war, the English had lost many soldiers and civilians, and now faced difficult financial times. The country was literally in the process of rebuilding. Many items—even staple foods—were so scarce they had to be rationed from the end of the war through 1951.

Problems plagued the arts too in wartime and postwar England: many literary journals, for instance, had suspended publication because of a shortage of paper. What theater existed came under harsh examination; critics felt the English theater had grown stale, that it said little of importance to the new, postwar world. Into this depressed climate, the crowning of the young, vibrant queen brought renewed hope. Her very name, Elizabeth, evoking the past glories of England under Elizabeth I, elicited the happy thought that England might soon pull through its current difficulties and rise into yet another golden Elizabethan Age.

In 1956, four years after Elizabeth II's coronation, John Osborne's play *Look Back In Anger* premiered at the Royal Court Theater. The play was successful, as well as controversial, because it featured an angry, working-class protagonist who complained loudly about the current state of England. Audiences and critics quickly embraced the drama, and the British theater seemed relevant once again. Into fashion came plays from young, working-class writers articulating the common person's point of view. The revitalized theater staged works by a host of new dramatists including Arnold Wesker, Ann Jellico, Harold Pinter, John Arden, N. F. Simpson, Joe Orton, Edward Bond, and Tom Stoppard. A bevy of talented writers, actors, and directors contributed to this rebirth in the 1950s and 1960s, producing what many call the second English dramatic renaissance.

Swinging London and the rise of the "new aristocracy." The post-1956 excitement in the theater world soon began to spread to other arts, particularly to the worlds of music and fashion.

As with the theater, the arts were revitalized by young people who came primarily from working-class backgrounds. This was a new and exciting state of affairs for England, which had historically been bound up in a very traditional class system. Previously people who were successful in public life or the arts were either highborn or soon took pains to appear as if they had been, often by losing regional or working-class accents and adopting "posher" tones. But in the 1950s and 1960s, a working-class background and accent were no longer a liability. In fact, swank London life in the 1960s was dominated by four young working-class men from Liverpool who not only kept their regional *scouse* (Liverpool) accents but showed them off with pride. John Lennon, George Harrison, Paul McCartney, and Ringo Starr—known collectively as The Beatles—became England's top trendsetters and greatest export, earning millions for the crown and receiving MBEs (Member of the Most Excellent Order of the British Empire) from a grateful Queen Elizabeth. The Beatles were only the most famous of a slew of artists, fashion designers, musicians, writers, photographers and actors who helped make London swing in the 1960s. Collectively, these talented trendsetters formed a new, classless aristocracy whose position in the world was based on merit rather than background or high birth. For maybe the first time in history, England's role models were commoners, not kings. In this context, it makes sense for Stoppard to present Shakespeare's *Hamlet* from the point of view of its least important characters. A reversal of the typical class hierarchy was a larger cultural characteristic of the 1960s.

Reviews. *Rosencrantz and Guildenstern Are Dead* was a huge hit both for Stoppard and for England's National Theater in 1967. In the London *Times*, theater critic Irving Wardle crowed that, "As a first stage play, it is an amazing piece of work" (for all reviews cited, see Elsom, pp. 186-91). Harold Hobson, writing in the Sunday *Times*, went so far as to call it, "the most important event in the British professional theater of the last nine years" because of the way in which it united present and past British theatrical achievements. Milton Shulman, writing in the *Evening Standard*, noted the "echoes of Sartre, Beckett and Kafka." There were very few dissenting opinions: W. A. Darlington, writing in the *Daily Telegraph* on April 12, 1967, thought that the play was "clever," but noted that "it happens to be the kind of play that I do not enjoy," and Robert Brustein in his book, *The Third Theater*, claims that while the play is ingenious, it is, in his opinion, "derivative and familiar." Most critics, then and since, however, have lauded the play for the clever way in which it re-imagines England's most famous tragedy for a new generation.

—Francesca Coppa

For More Information

Brustein, Robert. *The Third Theater*. Jonathan Cape: 1970.

Delaney, Paul, ed. *Tom Stoppard in Conversation*. Ann Arbor: University of Michigan Press, 1994.

Elsom, John. *Post-war British Theater Criticism*. London: Routledge, 1981.

Greenblatt, Stephen. Introduction in *The Norton Shakespeare*. Ed. Stephen Greenblatt. New York: W.W. Norton, 1997.

Gussow, Mel. *Conversations with Stoppard*. New York: Grove Press, 1996.

Jenkins, Anthony. *The Theater of Tom Stoppard*. Cambridge: Cambridge University Press, 1989.

Kelly, Katherine E., ed. *The Cambridge Companion to Tom Stoppard*. Cambridge: Cambridge University Press, 2001.

McCrum, Robert, et al. *The Story of English*. New York, Viking Press, 1986.

Shakespeare, William. *Hamlet*. Ed. Susanne L. Wofford. Boston: Bedford Books, 1994.

Stoppard, Tom. *Rosencrantz and Guildenstern Are Dead*. New York: Grove Press, 1967.

Shizuko's Daughter

by
Kyoko Mori

Kyoko Mori was born in 1957 in Kobe, Japan, a city that is the setting for much of the novel. When she was just 12, Mori was devastated by her mother's suicide. A year later her father remarried and the remarriage resulted in a less than happy home life for the author. Anxious to be away from home, Mori moved to the United States at the age of 16 to attend college. Some years later she received her Ph.D. from the University of Wisconsin at Milwaukee, going on to become a teacher as well as a writer. A series of short stories written in graduate school would later evolve into *Shizuko's Daughter*. Mori has also written *Fallout*, a collection of poetry (1994); *The Dream of Water* (1995), a well-received memoir about her travels to Kobe to visit family and bring closure to her mother's suicide; *O Bird* (1995), her second young adult novel; and *Polite Lies: On Being a Woman Caught Between Cultures* (1998), a collection of essays about being a Japanese American in the Midwest. Her most recent work, *Stone Field, True Arrow* (2000) is her first novel for adults; it concerns a middle-aged woman's reflections and transformation upon the death of her father in Japan, touching on preoccupations that are rife in Mori's writing, beginning with *Shizuko's Daughter*. In this, her first published work, Mori takes a critical look at Japanese culture from the perspective of a female adolescent who has undergone a traumatic loss.

THE LITERARY WORK

A young adult novel set in Japan, mainly in the cities of Kobe and Himeji on the island of Honshu, and in the city of Nagasaki on Kyushu, spanning the seven years from 1969 to 1976; published in 1993.

SYNOPSIS

The adolescent protagonist Yuki struggles to come to terms with the void left by her mother's suicide; bereft, she wrestles with an emotionally absent father, a cruel stepmother, and a culture that discourages independence of mind and spirit.

Events in History at the Time the Novel Takes Place

World War II and the Allied Occupation. Perhaps the most significant events in the history of modern Japan are its defeat in World War II and its occupation by the Allied forces beginning in 1945. The war was devastating to Japan in terms of the effects on its economy, the destruction of its cities, and the incredible loss of life (the Japanese suffered 668,000 civilian casualties from aerial bombings alone). The atomic bombs that were dropped on Hiroshima and Nagasaki wrought destruction of nightmarish proportions. In Hiroshima, 150,000 people either died upon impact or succumbed to deadly radiation sickness during

Kyoko Mori

the aftermath, and more than 60 percent of the city itself was levelled by the bomb. An additional 35,000 Japanese were killed at Nagasaki. In addition to these very concrete casualties, the war inflicted damage to the Japanese psyche. The Japanese were docile in the face of the occupying forces, most likely because of the "shattering impact of defeat on the values of the Japanese people. All of their pre-war and wartime indoctrination was proved wrong, their sense of national pride and mission destroyed, their leadership and institutions discredited" (Ward, p. 159).

In theory, eleven countries comprised the council of Allied forces that were to be in charge of Japan's military occupation, but since the United States had borne the brunt of the fighting in the Pacific Theater of the war, America took practical responsibility for Japan's occupation. General MacArthur was made the Supreme Commander of the Allied Powers, and his office was commonly referred to as SCAP. In addition to the radical demilitarization of Japan, which was expected and was similar to other postwar occupations, SCAP instituted a program of rapid democratization in the hope that this would prevent Japan from going to war in the future. The office set out to achieve nothing less than a reformation of Japanese society:

> There were few aspects of the culture that SCAP did not in some degree become involved with. . . . One is dealing here not so much with an episode in military history as with one of man's most ambitious attempts at social engineering. What was being attempted was no less than the redirection along democratic lines of an entire nation's socio-political values, behaviour, and institutions.
>
> (Ward, p. 162)

To this end, SCAP drafted a new constitution for Japan, and at General MacArthur's request the document had a very pronounced pacifist bent. Perhaps the most famous clause of the new constitution was Article 9, which renounced war as an alternative that Japan could invoke in the future and earned the document the label of "Peace Constitution." Japan's new constitution included a list of popular rights exceeding those enumerated in the American Bill of Rights, and its myriad of reforms included reorganizing the government along parliamentary lines, establishing an independent judicial branch, extending compulsory education by nine years, reorganizing the education system to reduce its hierarchical authority structure, and giving women the vote. SCAP also attempted to implement an almost socialist egalitarianism economically, in the hopes that this too would be a deterrent to future Japanese imperialism. The efforts aimed at economic reform included a redistribution of property to reduce the rate of tenant farmers, the encouragement of the formation of labor unions, the passing of pro-labor legislation, and the dissolution and reorganization of Japan's huge industrial conglomerates known as *zaibatsu* firms. Other measures along these lines were initiated and later abandoned (e.g., an attempt to confiscate and redistribute what little personal wealth remained after the war through the levying of a huge tax) out of fear that they would prove to sound the death knell of the Japanese economy.

Conformism. Key to an understanding of the Japanese people is their emphasis on group identity and membership. As one scholar notes, Japan's feudalism, which lasted from the twelfth century (beginning with the emergence of the samurai lords) until 1868 (the start of the Meiji rule), is an essential piece of Japan's past. The values of the samurai stressed obedience to one's ruler and to the samurai code, even at the expense of the individual. The code "made loyalty paramount and made no allowance for the inner voice. . . . Loyalty and filial piety together required obedience, even at the sacrifice of reason or conscience" (Smith, p. 51).

It was not only the samurai, however, who were taught to deny their individuality and selfhood in favor of the values of the group to which they belonged. Society in Tokugawa Japan (1600-1868) was highly regimented, and a strict class structure based on Confucian theory was rigidly enforced. Individuals in the society were divided into the classes of samurais, peasants, artisans, and merchants, each with its own set of values and responsibilities, and there was very little mobility among groups.

Emphasis on the importance of the group persisted beyond the feudal past. Even though the Meiji government (1868-1912) attempted to encourage more focus on the individual by eliminating class barriers and writing individual rights into the constitution, many Japanese still saw themselves not as individuals, but primarily as part of a collective. The Allied post-war reforms towards democracy and egalitarianism encouraged individualism too. When adopting such reforms, many Japanese intellectuals were forced to look to Europe, the Soviet Union, and even the United States for theoretical models upon which to base their campaigns for individuals to establish a modern sense of self, these kinds of models were simply lacking in Japanese culture.

Whether due to Japan's parochial history, its isolated geography, or other reasons, contemporary Japanese people still tend to identify themselves as members of a group, be it their profession, their corporation, their sports team, their village, their youth group, their school, or the PTA (Parent Teacher Association). When it comes to professions, for example, Americans tend to see themselves as individuals. The average American thinks of him or herself as possessing a certain talent or skill to market to the prospective employer who is willing to pay the most for the skill. The Japanese worker, on the other hand, sees his or her position as being with a particular company. To be a member of the Mitsubishi Organization, for instance, brings with it a sense of belonging, pride, and loyalty to the company: "There is little of the feeling, so common in the West, of being an insignificant and replaceable cog in a great machine. Both managers and workers suffer no loss of identity but rather gain pride through their company" (Reischauer, p. 133).

The group structure so prevalent in Japan is reflected in, and perhaps even reinforced by, one of the most essential Japanese social values—harmony. Employees are expected to avoid confrontation at all costs. Society greatly prizes skill in social interaction, called *haragei*, otherwise known as the art of the belly: "In Japan, speaking frankly is discourteous. Japan has developed techniques for communicating intentions through attitude and expression, what Japanese call 'gut-to-gut transmission' (Sakaiya, p. 175). The art lies in a person's knowing intuitively or instinctively how to avoid a conflict before it ever erupts into an open dispute. Thus, in Japan, voices are seldom raised. Mothers tend not to

SHIZUKO'S DAUGHTER AND POSTWAR REFORMS

Although *Shizuko's Daughter* takes place in the 1960s and '70s, the novel refers to various occupation reforms. In the past, schoolchildren, for example, were not even supposed to look at the emperor's picture, the belief being that to do so would result in blindness, since "he was so holy" (Mori, *Shizuko's Daughter,* p. 119). Shizuko once got into trouble because instead of bowing her head as she walked by his picture, she looked straight at it and said that he had a funny nose. She wanted to "prove the truth," that the "teachers were lying" to them about going blind (*Shizuko's Daughter,* p. 119). She was punished for this defiant act. After World War II, the emperor came on the radio to inform the nation that he was no longer to be worshipped, that he was only human like everyone else. Shizuko's classmate, Mr. Kimura said he thought of Shizuko and how she had been proven right.

Another real-life occupation policy referred to in the novel is the great land reform. In order to reduce tenancy rates, which stood at 45 percent, and redistribute agricultural property more equitably, SCAP banned absentee ownership of land and restricted the village landowners to keeping only a small parcel for themselves for subsistence farming. The remainder was sold at pre-war prices to the tenant framers "for next to nothing" (*Shizuko's Daughter,* p. 21). The result was a virtual confiscation of property from the landowners and a redistribution of the land to former tenant farmers, who suddenly found themselves property owners. Yuki's Aunt Aya admits to her that "maybe it was a good thing for many people, but it wasn't for us. We were suddenly very poor" (*Shizuko's Daughter,* p. 21). It is because of this sudden poverty that Shizuko's mother, Masa, arranges for Shizuko's marriage to the son of a wealthy family in an adjoining village. The match would make Shizuko the financial savior of her family, but, unable to marry a man she does not love, she walks all night to the next village to break off the engagement.

In *Shizuko's Daughter,* Claude Monet's painting *Gladioli* (1876) triggers Yuki's nostalgia for her deceased mother.

scold their children, and teenagers tend not to be loud-mouthed. Many Japanese have shown themselves to be highly averse to open displays of emotion of any kind. While Yuki too is generally quiet, she nurses a private defiance that sometimes surfaces in rebellious acts. Even Masa, Yuki's own grandmother with whom she has a good relationship, is often at a loss to explain Yuki's behavior. Time and again, Yuki refuses to behave as expected, refusing to cry on cue, for example, at her mother's funeral, following instead her own inclinations.

The Novel in Focus

The plot. The novel tells the story of a girl who must overcome an emotionally devastating event in her life: the loss of her mother to suicide. Shizuko kills herself when Yuki is only 12, by suffocating with gas in the kitchen. When she comes home from a music lesson, Yuki is the first one to discover her mother's body.

Yuki's life is forever changed. Not only has she lost her mother, with whom she had an extremely close and affectionate relationship, but she must also deal with her feelings of guilt and constant uncertainty about whether she might have done something different to prevent the suicide. Yuki recalls a conversation she had with her mother wherein Yuki had admitted a harsh truth: "if something happened to you, I would still go on. I would be very sad and I would never forget you. Still, I would go on. It wouldn't be true to say otherwise" (*Shizuko's Daughter*, p. 40). Shizuko reacted very emotionally to Yuki's statement, feeling both proud of her daughter and sad for herself. In her mind, Yuki constantly reflects on moments like these, rewriting the past. She has her own way of dealing with her grief. She feels sadness but is hesitant to share it with others or put it on display.

As a result of her mother's death, Yuki's life changes in dramatic ways. Yuki lives with her mother's sister for about a year after her mother's suicide, a fairly happy situation for her. When her father remarries, however, Yuki is told that she'll have to return to Kobe to live with him and his new bride because she is her father's "only child," and Shizuko's family members "have no claim" on her (*Shizuko's Daughter,* p. 23). Yuki, who has never gotten along well with her father, rails against the injustice of being forced to live with a father and stepmother for the sake of appearances:

> You know it's a lie. . . . It's all a lie, the whole thing. They know I want to stay in Tokyo with you, and they'd like it that way too. They don't care about me. They only came to see me twice the whole time I was with you. They'd as soon

> be by themselves. Only they won't do it because it would look bad. People would talk.
>
> (*Shizuko's Daughter*, p. 24)

Yuki proves to be right. In the years after her mother's death, she has very little to do with either her father or his wife. Some days they do not speak at all, except to exchange cursory greetings. Meanwhile, Yuki sorely misses her mother. She receives absolutely no love, support, or affection from either her father, Hideki, or his new wife, Hanae. In contrast to other parents, they do not show up to cheer for Yuki at student track meets or awards ceremonies. Even when she becomes class president and gets the highest marks in her class every year, Hideki and Hanae say nothing. It is up to strangers to congratulate Yuki, and they usually do so by saying "your mother would be so proud" (*Shizuko's Daughter,* p. 44).

Hanae is very jealous and resentful toward Yuki for several reasons. First, she is no longer able to have children of her own, and blames her childlessness on Hideki's refusal to set her up in her own household and allow her to start a family while he was still married to Shizuko, as many other husbands did. For eight years, while Shizuko had her own home and child, Hanae and Hideki had been carrying on an affair, and this arrangement, as Hanae bitterly sees it, left her barren. Hanae also resents Hideki's saying nothing to reproach Yuki when she ignores them or behaves less respectfully than she should. Yuki has told Hanae that she doesn't believe in "good manners," because "why should I pretend to be nice to people when they don't like me and I don't like them? It's not honest" (*Shizuko's Daughter*, p. 90). Hanae herself resents having to pretend to the world that she and Yuki have a good relationship. She is "sick of the compliments—compliments that implied that she was fortunate to have such an exceptional stepdaughter. Above all, she was sick of not being able to contradict them. She had to thank the admirers with a smile and never let on that she and Yuki hardly spoke to each other" (*Shizuko's Daughter*, pp. 94-95).

There is much that Yuki must endure just to be able to survive in such a household. She is not even able to enjoy simple pleasures like seeing her mother's family from time to time. Her father has forbidden any contact between Shizuko's family and Yuki, so even though Yuki writes them every month, she never receives an answer. She is not even allowed to visit them. The only time her father makes an exception is to allow her to attend her Aunt Aya's wedding, and he only does this because he feels he owes Aya a debt of gratitude for taking in Yuki after Shizuko's death. Yet again, appearances of propriety are more important to Hideki than Yuki's happiness.

Yuki deals with the harsh, at times almost sadistic, antics of her stepmother and father. Her stepmother tries to push her down the stairs, and throws out the beautiful clothes that Shizuko spent so much time lovingly hand sewing for her child. Her father burns all of the things that Shizuko was saving for Yuki in the attic. Consequently Yuki throws herself even more intensely into her athletic pursuits and her education, retreating more and more into an emotional cocoon, where she thinks she will not be hurt. Her mother has instilled in her a love of all things beautiful, and when Hanae throws away the beautiful clothes Shizuko made, Yuki decides to draw them from memory, in a sketchbook just like her mother used to do while she was alive (her sketchbook is the one thing of Shizuko's that Hideki does not burn). Not only does Yuki draw; she also pursues photography in order to capture the fleeting natural beauty of this world.

By the end of the novel, Yuki has reached adulthood. She escapes her father and his wife by attending a small college on the island of Nagasaki, where she can study art. She has no contact with her father and accepts no financial help from him. And since the college is far from Kobe, she does not have to keep up the pretense of going home for summer and holidays. Her situation allows her to rekindle a relationship with her aunt and grandparents, and for the most part Yuki feels satisfied with her adult life. A major obstacle to her happiness dissolves when she overcomes her doubts and insecurities about romance, and decides to let herself fall in love with Isamu, a fellow student who has become her best friend, and wants to move the relationship to a new level. Spirited, intelligent, and caring, Yuki has indeed grown up to be the "strong woman" her mother envisioned (*Shizuko's Daughter*, p. 6).

It also becomes clear that Yuki was never rebelling against tradition *per se*; rather she felt she was being strangled by everyone's expectations of her, unable to carve out some space for herself. At the novel's end, Yuki asks her grandmother for some of her old kimonos that she has stored away. Even though Masa does not say so, she is secretly pleased that Yuki wants her old things. Sometime later to her surprise, Masa receives a photo of Yuki wearing a quilted vest made from the kimonos. "What do you think?"

she asks her grandmother. "I hope you don't mind my cutting them up so much. I wanted to wear the same things you did, only in a different way" (*Shizuko's Daughter*, p. 199).

Changing attitudes in Japan. One of the recurring themes of the novel is the way in which Yuki's attitude differs from traditional attitudes in Japan, particularly when compared with those of her mother and grandmother. For example, *Shizuko's Daughter* reflects a generational gap in Japanese society in the mid-to-late twentieth century with respect to religious practices. The grandmother in the novel observes elaborate daily rituals at the "family altar," which is said to represent the spirit of the ancestors. Her daughter Shizuko is skeptical, but often engages in the rituals nonetheless. Masa's granddaughter Yuki shows very little reverence for the rituals, and refuses to engage in them at all.

The daughter and granddaughter's attitudes are fairly common in Japan today due to the highly secularized nature of its society. Japan's religious history is complex, and encompasses a variety of religious and philosophical systems of thought, primarily Shintoism, Buddhism, and Neo-Confuciansism. Additionally various new–age religions have become prominent in contemporary Japan. The existence of a mix of religions is in keeping with tradition. In the past, religions were often not mutually exclusive in Japan—there was a blending of various faiths. Pre-modern Japanese were "both Buddhists and Shintoists at the same time and often enough Confucianists as well" (Reischauer, p. 209).

> All in all, religion in Japan offers a confused and indistinct picture. Shinto shrines and Buddhist temples are found everywhere. The lives of most Japanese are intertwined with religious observances—shrine festivals, "god shelves" and Buddhist altars in the homes, and Shinto or Christian marriages. . . . Popular religious customs are derived mostly from traditional Shinto and Buddhism, in which few really believe.
>
> (Reischauer, p. 214)

Even for the grandmother's generation in *Shizuko's Daughter*, religious beliefs were relegated to the background of one's life. Yet rituals played an important role. The fact that the grandchild's generation finds little or no use for rituals that are quite significant for the older generation parallels a real-life situation that has elicited a general anxiety. The Japanese fear that the nation's youth are losing their sense of what is their "Japaneseness." The disregard for once venerated rituals bespeaks a larger countercultural element among the youth, which is not readily detectable. In Japan the restlessness and rebelliousness of the youth are often concealed by a veil of social conformity: "The university student may eat breakfast quietly with his parents before setting out with his comrades to destroy his university" (Reischauer, p. 160).

Another issue in the novel that Yuki considers in a nontraditional way is suicide, which in the past has often been viewed as an honorable way out of a no-win situation. The ritual form of suicide known as *seppuku* was part of the code prevalent among the military rulers of Japan. It involved making precise incisions in one's abdomen that would insure death but not damage any vital internal organs.

Although statistically suicide is no more prevalent in Japan than it is in the West, "even today suicide is looked on as an acceptable or even honorable way out of a hopeless dilemma" by the Japanese, and sepukku remains an integral theme in Japan's art, news, literature, and culture in general (Reischauer, p. 168). The perception of suicide in Japan notwithstanding, however, Yuki seems not to view her mother's suicide as honorable. In fact, when scolded by her grandmother for not showing proper respect to her mother's memory, Yuki asks "How can I respect someone who was cowardly enough to kill herself?" (*Shizuko's Daughter*, p. 77). She feels this way despite the fact that her mother's desperately unhappy situation might be viewed as hopeless.

Neglected and emotionally mistreated by her husband who has been having an affair with a co-worker for eight years, Shizuko finds herself locked into a wretched position. Divorce was not a conventional answer to her predicament at the time the novel was set or, for that matter, was written. Although legal reforms instituted during the Allied occupation made divorce an option for women, divorce rates in Japan are still far below those of the United States: For example, the divorce rate of 35 to 50 year olds in Japan is only 5 percent (Skov and Moeran, p. 41). Reasons for this include the practical difficulty of supporting oneself in the face of severe wage discrimination and the fact that under the Japanese legal system, a woman has almost no hope of obtaining custody or even visitation rights in the case of a male child or only child should she divorce. At one point in the novel, Yuki recalls a conversation with her mother about the plight of "a poor motherless classmate" of Yuki's whose parents were divorced. When Yuki asks why the girl couldn't have stayed with her mother, Shizuko explains that when there is a divorce, the children stay with the father (*Shizuko's Daughter*, p. 121). If there are several children, one might be allowed to stay with the mother, but:

> If there's only one child, the mother almost always winds up alone. The way her mother looked at Yuki, her face completely without a smile, Yuki knew what she meant. Like me, she thought but didn't say.
>
> (*Shizuko's Daughter*, p. 122)

The question of motherhood and feminist implications. One of the most artful aspects of *Shizuko's Daughter* is the way in which the story invokes certain feminist issues without overtly raising them. At issue in the novel is the proper role of family and motherhood in the lives of contemporary women in Japan.

The evolution of the concept of motherhood in Japanese society is the result of official governmental policies. Beginning with the Meiji government in 1898, the Confucian slogan of "rich country and strong army" was interpreted to place emphasis on the family, in particular, the mothers. The government shifted the responsibility of producing intelligent, able-bodied soldiers and workers from the state to the mothers, whose child-bearing and child-rearing capacities were said to be the key to enabling Japan to compete with the West. Mothers were to raise strong, well-nourished children who would grow up to, among other things, form a strong, competitive army. In the 1920s, during the Taisho period, the notion of motherhood and motherly love was sanctified, and the idea developed that "motherly love and devotion are the keys to a child's development and education" (Ohinata, p. 200). Evidence of this trend could be seen in public statements by politicians, scholars, and writers, as well as the appearance of magazines devoted to childcare, featuring articles like "Mother's Love How Great" and "Model Mothers" (Ohinata, p. 201). When war broke out with China in 1937, and then in the Pacific in 1941, the government's policy was "Have more Babies! Prosper!", and the Patriotic Women's Association exhorted mothers to "return to your homes" (Ohinata, p. 202). Later in the 1950s when economic growth and production was the government's overriding goal, mothers were again urged to be the center of the domestic sphere. Their duties included not only raising and giving birth to the future labor force but also providing a home where tired male workers could rest and recharge themselves for the next day's work. When Japan experienced an economic slowdown in the 1970s, the idea of motherhood was again lauded, this time as a solution to budgetary cutbacks. Instead of allocating money for child and elderly care, women were urged to strengthen the family by assuming these duties themselves. The image of ideal mother, who practices selfless devotion to her child, "comes close to that of a religious faith" in Japan (Ohinata, p. 205).

WOMEN'S QUIET REBELLION

Shizuko's Daughter is fairly brimming with examples of quiet or subtle rebellion on the part of the female protagonists. One of Yuki's more public acts of rebellion is to violently throw down the sake bowl that is being passed around as part of her father's marriage ceremony to his second wife. Shizuko tears up her suicide note to her husband right before she dies, knowing that to leave him no note would be a source of embarrassment to him. Even Yuki's grandmother, Masa, has issues with her husband:

> Masa suddenly remembered what he had written in his diary . . . on the day of Shizuko's death: We are thankful for the peacefulness of her face. It was such an obvious remark. Thankful for the peacefulness, Masa repeated to herself resentfully as she stepped into the kitchen—why did he say "we"?—it wasn't how she had felt at all; he had no business saying "we" without asking her.
>
> (*Shizuko's Daughter*, pp. 78-79)

The question of whether or not motherhood and family life are the path to fulfillment for Japanese women today is the subject of much debate. A Confucian adage referring to a woman's role in life as "good wife, wise mother" is still invoked in Japanese society, but whether it is still considered a valid way of describing the female ideal is contested. According to one source, women constituted 40.8 percent of the Japanese labor force in 1991; yet the attitudes and status of working women in Japan are still "complex and contradictory" (Kawashima, p. 271).

> Ambitious career women claim a place equal to men in the business world. On the other hand, some working women view their responsibility at home as their primary occupation and their work outside as secondary. Surveys of working women have shown that the majority of Japanese

Japanese school girls dressed in the traditional kimono, circa 1950.

> women do not desire a job with great responsibility and consider earning supplementary income for the household as a primary reason for working. Even among the younger generation many women still think that the primary caretakers of children are their mothers and, therefore, that women should stay home while children are small.
>
> (Kawashima, p. 271)

Certain tendencies in contemporary Japan have strengthened the expectation that women will identify primarily with their roles as mothers. The first is the sheer physical absence of the father in Japanese societies. Like Shizuko's husband in the novel, most Japanese males dedicate an incredible number of hours to their work and must add a long commute to the end of an already long day. And due to the tendency towards group immersion that already exists in Japan, professionals are expected to put in a good deal of time engaging in various social activities with their co-workers and clients. Japanese corporations cover the costs of dinners at restaurants, late-night drinking parties at bars and dance clubs, and frequent outings to sporting events on weekends, with attendance being mandatory. These job-related demands not only make a father unavailable to share the responsibilities of parenting, but they also limit the time he is able to spend on his relationship with his wife. It is perhaps due to his long absences from home that the novel's Hideki begins an affair with a co-worker at his company.

Another factor encouraging Japanese women to embrace their roles as mothers is the limited range of career options open to women. Although things are slowly changing in Japan, there are still primarily two ways of referring to women's roles: "OL for office lady, or *shufu* (housewife)" (Reingold, p. 125). Japanese companies generally have two training tracks: one is *ippanshou*, a clerical track; the other is *sogoshoku*, an "integrated" track, where training is offered for a variety of management positions. Women are overwhelmingly confined to the former track; only 1 percent of all female employees in Japan become managers (Ogasawara, p. 19). If a woman has little education, she is likely to work in production or manufacturing. Those with more education can aspire to become "office ladies" (a type of secretary), but they are still expected to perform tasks such as serving tea to all the men in the office. With limited career options and only minimal interaction with their spouses, it is not surprising that many Japanese women reinforce society's expectations of them and immerse themselves in the raising of their children.

Today's Japanese mothers are still expected to make incredible sacrifices for their children. Almost always their responsibilities entail taking charge of their children's education and helping them navigate the complex labyrinths of the Japanese educational system. Thousands of housewives hold after-school study sessions for their children and others in the neighborhood (most children attend formal after-school study systems in addition to these groups). Many mothers also participate in extra-curricular sessions such as music classes, at which their presence is required. So prevalent is the mother's presence in education that it has given rise to an ideal of its own, the *kyoiku mama*, or education mother—in short, a mother's involvement is critical to the child's future success.

Motherhood for Shizuko does seem to be a positive experience. Through Yuki's flashbacks, we learn of their close relationship, of the hours Shizuko spent teaching Yuki about the things she loved, such as painting, drawing, flower arrangement, and gardening. Shizuko attends Yuki's track meets and spelling bees, and the child becomes very successful academically. In fact, in her final hours, Shizuko's thoughts seem to be primarily focused on Yuki. She worries that she has the materials for Yuki's new dresses, but has not been able to finish sewing them for her yet. Ultimately, Shizuko sees her suicide as being in her daughter's best interest, to save her from following her example: "This is the best I can do for her, she thought, to leave her and save her from my unhappiness, from growing up to be like me" (*Shizuko's Daughter*, p. 6). Shizuko wants something better for her daughter, wants her to aspire to something more than fulfilling the "good wife, wise mother" role. She writes in her note: "When you grow up to be a strong woman, you will know that this was for the best. . . . You will no doubt get over this and be a brilliant woman. Don't let me stop you or delay you" (*Shizuko's Daughter*, p. 6).

Sources and literary context. Much of the novel is inspired by personal experience. Like her protagonist, Mori grew up in Kobe, Japan, she lost her mother to suicide when she was only 12, and looked for ways to escape her unhappy household after her father's remarriage. *Shizuko's Daughter* began as a collection of short stories about three women in reverse chronological order. Mori started with the grandmother's story, then wrote a few stories about the mother, then a few stories about the daughter. It was not until years later that Mori went back to these stories and turned the collection into a novel. Despite the similarities, Mori explains that there is no one-to-one correspondence between the stories and her life.

> My novels are more about what could, might, or even should have happened, not about what did happen in my real life. All the characters are reflections of some aspect of myself, but none of them are strictly myself.
>
> ("Kyoko Mori: A Personal Glimpse")

Kyoko Mori joins a rich tradition of young adult novelists who focus on descriptions of the relationship between mothers and their adolescent daughters in other cultures. Suzanne Fisher Staples's *Shabanu: Daughter of the Wind* and Sook Choi's *Echoes of the White Giraffe* are set in South Korea. Featured in these two novels are mothers who raise their daughters to live in their patriarchal culture, teaching them how "to fit into their proper place in family and society"; but the novels show how the women manage also to "resist or find space for themselves" within the limiting culture (Crew, p. 199). Kyoko Mori's works occupy a unique space in this rich literary tradition. Like Mori's other daughter heroines, Yuki defies a patriarchal society that requires her subordination as a female.

Events in History at the Time the Novel Was Written

Women's rights and roles. Many changes were occurring in Japan during the late 1980s and early '90s, which prompted the Japanese to once again re-evaluate many aspects of their society. In 1989 Emperor Hirohito died. His successor, Akhito, is the first emperor to have obtained an education outside the confines of the imperial palace, and the first to have married a "commoner." His son, crown prince Naruhito, married a Harvard-educated member of the Foreign Ministry who had had an impressive diplomatic career in her own right.

Meanwhile, conditions had improved for women in Japan. In 1986 Japan finally passed an Equal Opportunity Employment Law, with a special provision on sexual harassment policy. In 1989 a woman was elected as head of Japan's socialist party, and that same year the reigning prime minister, Takeshita Noburu, was forced to resign amid charges of womanizing (a "charge" traditionally not taken very seriously by Japanese males), along with other charges of large-scale political corruption. The liberal Democratic Party selected two female cabinet members in 1987 and appointed a woman to a major post in 1989.

Yet, despite all the seeming changes, the situation of women in Japan remained disadvantageous in many ways. By 1990 women held less than 3 percent of the corporate managerial slots, only 3 percent of lawyers were women, and only 3 percent of chemical engineers were women. Most of the positions held by women continued to be clerical or manufacturing posts, many of them part-time. Part-time workers receive no benefits and poor wages. "Women are encouraged to assume part-time work but discouraged from developing careers. It is a pin-money mentality" (Smith, p. 155). Even the crown prince's Harvard-educated wife quit her job upon their marriage, her wardrobe changing "from efficient professional to dowdy matron" (Smith, p. 158). This sudden change in appearance was most likely due to the fact that the Imperial Household Agency has to dictate "her hats and make-up," "how long her skirts would have to be," and "how many steps behind her husband she would walk" (Smith, p. 158). When it comes to sustained and meaningful change in Japan, not just for women, but for all citizens, one scholar described it quite aptly:

> The struggle toward the open expression of individuality is an old one. . . . It is impossible not to come away with a sense of great expectation: They seem always on the edge of some immense breakthrough. And yet, even amid change, nothing ever seems to move forward, or moves forward at a painful pace. [This scenario] makes the business of predictions a treacherous thing.
>
> (Smith, p. 3)

EQUAL EMPLOYMENT?

The much-touted and long-awaited EEOL (Equal Employment Opportunity Law) of 1986 did little more than call on businesses to try giving women equal opportunity in the job market with regards to hiring and promotion. The law only encouraged companies to make a "best-effort" at establishing equality and without a provision for penalizing violators, was easy for most companies to ignore. In 1999 a revised "Law Concerning Equality of Employment Opportunities and Benefits Between Genders" was finally adopted. The new law prohibits gender discrimination in employment and provides specific guidance as to what employers should or should not do. For example, after passage of the 1986 act, many employers continued to advertise jobs for "males only." The 1999 act specifically prohibits such discriminatory practices. Still, the only enforcement "teeth" this law has are that offending companies and officials risk having their names made public as violators and that wronged employees find it easier to begin a mediation process once they feel their rights have been violated. A controversial aspect of the law repeals practices regarding limits on the amount of overtime and night-shift hours women can work. Supporters of this measure feel that it will open up many more opportunities for women in Japan, since most production jobs (and even some white-collar ones) frequently require overnight or late-night hours. But women's rights advocates protest that it allows for women to be exploited in new ways and that such women will still have to bear the burden of domestic responsibilities. A report issued by the Prime Minister's office in the late 1990s showed that Japanese men spend less than half an hour a day on chores relating to the household and children, even when their wife works (Pollack, p. D1).

Reception. *Shizuko's Daughter* garnered fine reviews in the *New York Times Book Review*, the *Los Angeles Time Book Review*, and *Kirkus Reviews,* and *Horn Book Magazine*. The *Horn Book* review referred to it as a "stunning first novel" praising the novel's narrative style—Mori "paints beautiful pictures with words, creating visual images that can be as haunting and elliptical as poetry" (Vasiliakis, p. 603). Lauding the novel's honesty, *The New York Times Book Review* observed that Mori "doesn't pull any punches, doesn't soften the unfeeling father or terrible stepmother" and it too spoke of "a poetic quality to the prose" (Rosenberg, p. 19). *Shizuko's Daughter* garnered awards as well. The novel won distinction as an American Library Association's Best Book for Young Adults, and it was singled out as a *Publishers Weekly* Best Book of 1993.

—Despina Korovessis

For More Information

Crew, Hillary S. *Is It Really Mommie Dearest? Daughter-Mother Narrative in Young Adult Fiction*. Lanham, Md.: The Scarecrow Press, 2000.

Kawashima, Yoko. "Female Workers of Past and Current Trends," in *Japanese Women: New Feminist Perspectives on the Past, Present, and Future*. Ed. Kumiko Fujimura-Fanselow and Atsuko Kameda. New York: The Feminist Press, 1995.

"Kyoko Mori: A Personal Glimpse," in *Random House Author Profiles*. http://www.randomhouse.com/highschool/authors/mori.html (29 Aug. 2002).

Mori, Kyoko. *Shizuko's Daughter*. New York: Ballantine, 1993.

Ogaswara, Yuko. *Office Ladies and Salaried Men: Power, Gender, and Work in Japanese Companies*. Berkley: University of California Press, 1998.

Ohinata, Masami, "The Mystique of Motherhood: A Key to Understanding Social Change and Family Problems in Japan," in *Japanese Women: New Feminist Perspectives on the Past, Present, and Future*. Ed. Kumiko Fujimura-Fanselow and Atsuko Kameda. New York: The Feminist Press, 1995.

Ogasawara, Yuko. *Office Ladies and Salaried Men: Power, Gender, and Work in Japanese Companies*. Berkley: University of California Press, 1998.

Pollack, Andrew. "For Japan's Women, More Jobs and Longer and Odder Hours," in *New York Times*, 8 July 1997, D1.

Reingold, Edwin M. *Chrysanthemums and Thorns: The Untold Story of Modern Japan*. New York: St. Martin's Press, 1992.

Reischauer, Edwin O., and Marius B. Jansen. *The Japanese Today: Change and Continuity*. Cambridge: Harvard University Press, 1995.

Rosenberg, Liz. Review of *Shizuko's Daughter. The New York Times Book Review*, 22 August 1993, p. 19.

Sakaiya, Taichi. *What Is Japan? Contradictions and Transformations*. Trans. Steven Karpa. New York: Kodansha International, 1993.

Skov, Lisa, and Brian Moeran, eds. *Women Media and Consumption in Japan*. Honolulu: University of Hawaii Press, 1995.

Smith, Patrick. *Japan: A Reinterpretation*. New York: Pantheon Books, 1997.

Vasiliakis, Nancy. Review of *Shizuko's Daughter, The Horn Book Magazine* 69, no. 5 (September-October 1993): 603.

Ward, R. E. "Defeat and Occupation." in *Japan: Yesterday and Today*. Ed. Ray F. Downs. New York: Bantam, 1970.

Song of Solomon

by
Toni Morrison

Toni Morrison was born in Lorraine, Ohio, in 1931 as Chloe Anthony Wofford. An avid reader, Morrison studied literature, earning a bachelor's degree at Howard University followed by a master's degree in English at Cornell University in 1955. After earning her degrees she worked as an editor for Random House, becoming instrumental in the publication of autobiographies and fiction by African American women such as Angela Davis and Toni Cade Bambara. In 1970 Morrison published her own first novel, ***The Bluest Eye*** (also in *Literature and Its Times*). She followed it with the National Book Award-nominated *Sula* (1973), and a few years later with *Song of Solomon*. Using myths and folktales, *Song of Solomon* details the coming-of-age of a young black man, meanwhile tackling African American issues that emanate from the experience of slavery (displacement, naming, loss of ancestry and homelands). It was this novel, critics concur, that "established [Morrison] as a major American writer" (Draper, p. 216).

THE LITERARY WORK

A novel set in African American communities in Michigan, rural Virginia, and Pennsylvania between 1930 and the early 1960s; published in 1977.

SYNOPSIS

A young African American man searches for his identity and discovers his real and mythical family history.

Events in History at the Time the Novel Takes Place

A Promised Land? Repressive and oppressive conditions plagued the South following the post-Civil War Reconstruction era. In addition to dehumanizing laws that mandated segregation between the races and lynching campaigns that targeted blacks, widespread poverty plagued the region. A lack of job opportunities, coupled with agricultural setbacks (the boll weevil, flooding), made it difficult to climb out of that poverty if one remained in the region. So to improve their lot in life, nearly 5 million African Americans rode the rails, trekked, and otherwise made their ways north from 1890 to 1950, a movement otherwise known as the Great Migration. The North seemed to be a sort of Promised Land, offering jobs and hope for a more equitable life than in the South. Leaving behind the rural landscape and agrarian lifestyle that had been home for roughly three centuries since the first Africans had landed in Jamestown in 1619, most of these migrants stepped out of the southern countryside into sprawling metropolises and, far more often than before, out of rural work into industrial jobs. The transition was not a simple one, nor was it always even desirable.

The black press had done much to promote the North, "To die from the bite of frost is far more glorious than at the hands of a mob," advised the *Chicago Defender* in the 1910s

Toni Morrison

(Franklin and Moss, p. 376). And indeed conditions seemed promising at first. Especially during World War I (1914-18) blacks entered the industrial workforce in large numbers, finding jobs in the ammunition, iron, and steel manufacturing industries, in car and truck assembly, and in the production of electrical items. World War II (1939-45) likewise saw mass hiring of black workers in manufacturing, again largely in iron and steel works but also in the newer aircraft industry. But social change lagged behind occupational breakthroughs. Much to the chagrin of the hopeful migrants, the segregation of the South appeared in the North as well, only in a less direct manner:

> Black Southerners who moved north hoping to leave behind the color line and racial hostilities quickly learned a harsher reality. The rules were unwritten in the North, but they were rules nonetheless. These neighborhoods were off-limits; those restaurants "don't serve Negroes."
>
> (Kelley and Lewis, p. 396)

Arriving in northern cities, migrant families, like those featured in the novel, experienced housing and employment discrimination. Unwelcome in European-dominated neighborhoods or in the suburbs, the newcomers moved into the less desirable inner cities and established all-black communities in the early 1990s. As blacks continued to migrate, their numbers increased but the physical dimensions of their neighborhoods did not. "What segregation meant was that neither black newcomers nor established residents could move beyond the borders of the emerging ghettos" (Kelley and Lewis, p. 389). The result was severe overcrowding in black ghettos, putting a strain not only on the buildings themselves, which began to deteriorate, but on the people who inhabited them. There emerged a type of existence in the North, despite better jobs and educational conditions, that made the region far from the haven for a better life that some people had made it out to be. "No one had told [the migrants] 'about one of the most important aspects of the Promised Land: it was a slum ghetto. . . . There were too many people full of hate and bitterness crowded into a dirty, stinky, uncared-for closet-size section of a great city'" (Nash, p. 946).

By 1950, more than 7.5 million African Americans (52 percent of all blacks in the U.S.) lived in northern metropolitan areas, concentrated in these black ghettos. As blacks flowed into the cities, whites and jobs flowed out to the suburbs. "The factories that remained, if any, were updated into high-tech industries requiring special skills and fewer personnel, thus creating structural unemployment that would remain a critical problem for blacks and for many other Americans for the remainder of the century" (Franklin and Moss, p. 515). Combined with the ever-increasing inner city population, the factors of job and housing discrimination, postwar industrial restructuring, and relocation produced a steady rise in un- and under- employment in urban areas. Unemployment escalated to nearly 14 percent in 1957, directly affecting more than half of the black population in the U.S. With nearly one in six out of work, the local economy and tax revenues (including school levy and city budgets) were hard hit. While most of the nation was experiencing an economic boom, urban minorities were not. The ratio of unemployment of blacks to whites was 2:1, and for every one dollar a white man earned, a black man earned from 40 to 60 cents for performing the same job. This discrepancy helped contribute to a growing disparity of wealth and to rising tensions between blacks and whites. It also contributed to a widening rift between middle- and upper-class blacks and the struggling majority of lower-class blacks.

For black women, the picture was even more dismal—especially for young black women. Those aged 16-19 averaged nearly 35 percent unemployment annually (through 1988); those aged 20-24 averaged 22 percent (Ploski and Williams, p. 611). As shown in the novel, Corinthians Dead is a well-educated woman yet she has not been able to get a job befitting her education since she graduated Bryn Mawr in the 1940s. "After graduation she returned to a work world in which colored girls, regardless of their background, were in demand for one and only one kind of work" (Morrison, *Song of Solomon*, p. 189). That "one" kind of work was domestic service, which the majority of black women, regardless of education or skill level, undertook out of necessity.

Power in numbers. There were some positive aspects to the "ghettoization" or concentration of African Americans in America's northern inner cities. Residents of black communities found themselves relatively safe from racial attack in their own enclaves. It proved easier—especially in Harlem—for artists and other residents to express themselves culturally in the all-black neighborhoods. And the community gave rise to a black press, which detailed race crimes, political issues, and social ills that white papers would not report. Most of all, the concentration of African Americans in all-black communities created a political power base out of a formally powerless and dispersed ethnic minority in America.

> The movement to the cities resulted in conditions favorable to protest: the amassing of large numbers of people with similar grievances, a slight economic improvement over rural poverty so that folks could be less concerned with their daily bread, a nucleus of organizations through which communication and mobilization could occur, and a cultural support system for black pride and militancy.
>
> (Blumberg, p. 30)

This power base, primed for protest, emerged in the North just as the civil rights movement was gaining momentum in the South. From their relative position of strength and with the black press able to publicize events and concerns, northern blacks greatly aided the fledgling movement in the South. They added volume, organization, and fiery leadership, including the words of Malcom X who "seemed best able to capture the imaginations of urban blacks and verbalize their smoldering resentment" (Blumberg, p. 30).

Riots, rights, protest. As the decade of the 1960s began, the plight of blacks worsened. One million farm jobs were lost from 1950 to 1969. In most urban areas, unemployment levels and living conditions were becoming intolerable. In the community of Watts in Los Angeles, for example, the unemployed made up 30 percent of the 83,000 blacks who comprised the area's all-black population, which was cramped into an area four times as congested as the rest of the city (Franklin and Moss, p. 546). Because of housing discrimination "few blacks were able to secure housing elsewhere, even when they could afford it" (Franklin and Moss, p. 546).

Meanwhile in the South, violence against blacks reached new heights. The Ku Klux Klan and hard-line segregationists reacted against civil rights victories inside and outside the courts, which required Southerners to desegregate (schools, for example, [*Brown v. Board of Education,* 1954] and buses [Birmingham Boycott, 1956]). Refusing to accept defeat, the segregationists embarked on a campaign of terrorism. "City buses were fired upon, injuring some black passengers . . . a wave of bombings hit black churches and . . . homes" (Blumberg, p. 48). In Birmingham, Alabama, there were 17 unsolved bombings between 1957 and 1964, mostly of black churches, homes, and businesses. One of the bombings occurred at the 16th Street Baptist Church and killed four young black girls (Addie Mae Collins, Denise McNair, Carole Robertson, and Cynthia Wesley). In the novel, this incident spurs strong reaction from Guitar and his protest group, the Seven Days.

Despite the violence, bent on securing voting and civil rights for blacks once and for all, the civil rights movement continued to take direct action. The decade had started with a grassroots student protest by a group of four freshman from North Carolina Agricultural and Technical College, who on January 31, 1960, refused to budge from an all-white lunch counter at a Woolworth's drug store. Beginning here, students and others staged sit-ins and freedom rides across the country, held marches, and conducted protests and strikes to call attention to blacks being deprived of their rights and force the passage of new civil rights legislation.

The Tactic of Non-Violence. A mass civil rights movement unfolded in the 1960s, beginning early in the decade with nonviolent protest. The goal was securing passage of legislation to guarantee voting rights and civil liberties. Patterned after Gandhi's successful passive resistance campaign that won India freedom from Great Britain in 1949, Dr. Martin Luther King Jr. organized and became the national voice of nonviolent protest for black civil rights in the U.S. His organization, the Southern Christian Leadership

Conference, produced many great leaders whose main emphasis was getting legislation passed to end segregation and ensure the rights of minorities. Their efforts and those of the Student Nonviolent Coordinating Committee led to the passage of the Civil Rights (1964) and Voting Rights (1965) acts, which outlawed discrimination in places of public accommodation and permitted federal agents to register black voters when needed.

While the nonviolent approach did produce legal victories, many felt that their achievements had involved unprovoked violence against blacks that ought to be met with an in-kind response. The unmet needs of the urban majority, including economic relief, job and educational opportunity and reform, and black control over black communities, became paramount through the 1960s. In the process, the nonviolent, legislative-focused civil rights movement gave way to a more publicly combative, urban-focused movement that became known as Black Power. The Black Power movement, championed by leaders such as Stokely Carmichael, took the position that legislation alone would not solve the problems facing most African Americans. Well aware of the harsh realities of urban life, these leaders sought greater job opportunities for the majority of poor blacks, better housing, and an increased voice in and control over their future.

While King urged integration and nonviolent direct action, Black Power advocates touted black independence and said they should gain rights by "any means necessary," including armed rebellion. As a former SNCC leader who had tried the passive, integrationist approach, Carmichael was frustrated by the limited gains those tactics had produced. He was ready to lead a new type of protest movement, and others were clearly ready to follow. "The positive response of many young people to Carmichael's words seemed to prove that the civil rights revolution had shifted" (Blumberg, p. 118). Indeed, by 1966 race riots had erupted in many major cities, including Harlem (1964), Watts (1965), and Detroit (1967). Prominent leaders had been assassinated, including Medgar Evers (1963), John F. Kennedy (1963), and Malcolm X (1965), not to mention scores of lesser-known local civil rights workers and protesters. And grave problems remained. The passage of civil rights legislation had done little or nothing to alleviate unemployment, poverty, urban overcrowding, or racial tensions. By the end of the 1960s the death-by-assassination toll would include Martin Luther King Jr. and Robert F. Kennedy, and a staunch conservative, Richard Nixon, would be the president in the White House. For the black community the future did not look bright. As the 1960s came to a close, the civil rights movement ended and the Black Power movement began.

The Novel in Focus

The plot. *Song of Solomon* opens with flight, birth, and death—recurrent themes of the African American experience, as well as the novel. Combining seemingly random events, Morrison establishes at the outset the connection between the past, present, and future; how history shapes current events in both obvious and subliminal ways. As an insurance agent leaps from the Mercy hospital roof in an attempt to "fly away on my own wings," the mayhem this causes leads to a breach in protocol that allows a black mother to deliver her child inside the white hospital (*Solomon*, p. 3). Macon Dead III is born inside, the first black child to be birthed in the white-only hospital where his maternal grandfather worked as its first and only black doctor. Dead's birth inside Mercy occurs because of the insurance agent's action, illustrating from the outset how one action sparks another in this tale. The insurance agent's wish to "fly away on my own wings" will become central to the novel.

Called "Milkman" because his mother breastfeeds him longer than usual, Dead is born into a dysfunctional upper- middle-class black family in an all-black subsection of an unnamed Michigan city in 1931. Milkman's father, Macon Dead II, owns much of the real estate in the working-class community where they live and, because of his presumed arrogance and self-imposed class distinction, has no friends. Milkman's sisters (Magdalene, called Lena, and First Corinthians), raised to marry professionals of whom there are virtually none in this town, seem doomed to a life of unful-filled aspirations. Milkman's father does not speak to his sister, Pilate, even though they reside in the same town, and forbids his wife and children to have anything to do with that part of the family.

Babied by his mother, Ruth, and spoiled by his father, Milkman enters manhood still very much a boy. Drawn to the forbidden side of his family, he begins sleeping with his cousin, Hagar, while his aunt, Pilate, becomes the parent or guiding force he never had. Milkman's father has taught him to value things; in contrast, Pilate

AFRICAN FOLKLORE

Africans have long believed that the spirits of the dead are tied to the land they inhabited in life and must be properly interred there. Throughout Africa, funerals have traditionally been important, elaborate events, the belief being that the spirits of the dead play "an important part in the life of the kinship group" (Franklin and Moss, p. 26). Family history and ancestry are considered vital to contemporary life. In fact, traditionalists have long thought of death as the climax of life and extensive rituals as "sacred obligations of the survivors" (Franklin and Moss, p. 26). In the novel, Pilate shows her respect for this custom by carrying a sack of human bones with her for years until, with the help of Milkman, she manages to properly bury them.

Africans also generally believed that their ancestors' spirits dwelt on family land, in the ground, the trees, and rocks. In the novel, Milkman returns to his family's southern homeland and uncovers the mythology of their—and his—life story. It seems, as in many African folktales about slaves, that his great-grandfather, Solomon, escaped slavery by flying away. His spirit now lives in a double-headed rock that looks like a bird, and his wife's spirit lives in the gulch. When the wind blows, you can hear her crying, just as she did the day he flew away. As Milkman learns in the novel, these traditions and history are kept alive in African and African American culture orally. Always a key element of African societies, storytelling through words and music has been used to educate as well as entertain. "Handed down principally through the kinship group, the oral literature was composed of supernatural tales, moral tales, proverbs, epic poems, satires, love songs, funeral pieces, and comic tales" (Franklin and Moss, p. 28). In the novel, Milkman learns of his ancestry through the song the children sing in his southern home, the "Song of Solomon." In a larger sense, the "Song of Solomon" is an education and passing on of cultural heritage not only of a particular story but of the African American experience as a whole. Just as her ancestors have done, Morrison is carrying on the African tradition of storytelling in order to enlighten and keep culture and history alive.

teaches him strength of character through her own example. She is a bootlegger who has raised her daughter and granddaughter on her own, cares nothing for material possessions, and has a reputation as someone with supernatural powers. Pilate retains earthly ties to the natural world that have been all but lost by others who have moved to the northern cities.

Although Milkman works a little, collecting rent for his father, he spends the majority of his time roaming the streets and idly passing the time with his friend and alter ego, Guitar. Though the civil rights movement and racial violence dominate the news, Milkman remains oblivious and apathetic. Guitar, however, is becoming increasingly involved in the movement. Milkman soon learns that his friend is one of the Seven Days, a covert radical group that advocates violent retribution against whites whenever blacks are attacked.

As Milkman matures, he becomes more curious about his origins. His parents tell him conflicting stories, as does Pilate, which only makes him more inquisitive. One day his father informs him that the source of conflict between himself and Pilate is a bag of gold he thinks she has stolen. Simultaneously Milkman learns that his friend is in trouble; Guitar must get a great sum of money for the Seven Days or risk being killed. Milkman thinks that a bag of bones Pilate keeps in her house is the gold his father spoke of and steals it to help Guitar. When it turns out that it is indeed a bag of bones and not gold, Milkman unwittingly begins the most important chapter of his life.

Journeying to the South in search of the gold he now thinks is there, Milkman retraces his family's migration north and learns of his proud ancestry. Instead of finding gold, he finds riches he never imagined. In the town of Shalimar, he discovers what an amazing man his paternal grandfather was and that his great-grandfather is mythologized by the local population. Milkman slowly solves the riddle of the song he constantly hears the local children sing—the "Song of Solomon":

> Solomon done fly, Solomon done gone
> Solomon cut across the sky, Solomon gone home
>
> (*Solomon*, p. 303)

The song conveys the myth of Milkman's great-grandfather, a slave who freed himself by flying back to Africa.

When he realizes that he has a proud heritage, Milkman's entire outlook changes. In the short period of time he spends in the South, he matures more than in all of his previous years. He returns to Michigan to bring Pilate back to Shalimar so they can properly bury the bones he stole from her.

However, thinking that Milkman has found the gold and is keeping the news from him, Guitar tracks them down South. Just as Pilate predicts, she saves Milkman's life, taking a bullet intended for him from Guitar. Coming full circle from his family's and the novel's beginning, Milkman leaps from a cliff toward Guitar in an effort to free them both. It does not matter, says the novel, which one will "give up his ghost in the killing arms of his brother" (*Solomon*, p. 337). In a conclusion whose nuances are open to interpretation, Milkman at this point realizes he must embrace all facets of his history, his identity, and his fellow African Americans in order to procure any future. So like his great-grandfather, he surrenders to the air and it does not make a difference which of the two—Milkman or Guitar—lives or dies because in essence they both become free.

Reclaiming history. Through the character of Milkman, *Song of Solomon* illustrates the need for the black community to reclaim the history and traditions that have been lost or "whitewashed" in American society. The novel affirms a need in Morrison's day for African Americans to forge their own identity, not in terms of the white majority, but in terms of African and African American history and tradition.

The Great Migration north of nearly 5 million African Americans from 1890 to 1950 once again uprooted blacks and placed them in a foreign and often hostile environment, just as slavery had done. Forced through brutality and economic necessity to relocate, this by-and-large rural population moved to the inner cities and took industrial jobs. In contrast to the individual responsibility and comparative freedom of farming, industrial employment meant punching a time clock, working on assembly lines and performing repetitive tasks. The rural landscape most had known and loved was replaced by pavement and factories; gardens by tenements and housing projects. Extended families, part and parcel of rural life, became harder to maintain in the confines of the city. And old gathering spots, such as a country store or someone's porch, which had been sites of nightly storytelling and merrymaking, were gone.

Though the North offered greater opportunity and clear economic and educational advantages, this second loss of homeland had devastating social effects—especially to the maintenance of African and African American history and tradition. The nightly storytelling, or "lying sessions," as Zora Neale Hurston called them, had kept cultural heritage alive for centuries. Part of African oral tradition, storytelling was how family histories, folklore, and myths were passed on and preserved, how the individual, to a large degree, attained a sense of self. In the bustle of city life and dispersion of family and friends to various cities and jobs, these stories and hence, the sense of self in relation to one's past, and of pride in that past, often disappeared. First the ethnic group lost its home in Africa, then it suffered a second loss of the home it made for itself in the American South.

The novel illustrates what this second loss entails and how badly it can affect contemporary youth. Milkman knows nothing of his heritage because in the city it is lost. His parents have been caught up in the drive for assimilation. The lack of a sense of lineage contributes to his aimlessness and feeling of futility about life. He is amazed when he visits his southern homeland and hears the old men talk about his father and grandfather as "extraordinary men" (*Solomon*, p. 234). "The more the old men talked—the more he heard about the only farm in the county that grew peaches, real peaches like they had in Georgia, the feasts they had when hunting was over, the pork kills in winter and the work, the backbreaking work of a going farm—the more he missed something in his life" (*Solomon*, p. 234). For the first time Milkman takes pride in himself and acquires a sense of identity and purpose in life. "There was something he felt now—here in Shalimar, and earlier in Danville—that reminded him of how he felt in Pilate's house . . . he didn't have to get over, to turn on, or up, or even out" (*Solomon*, p. 293). He felt connected and alive, as if he finally belonged.

According to psychologist and art dealer George N'Namdi, "The anchor for any people, for any civilization, is its culture, is its art, is its history" (N'Namdi in Dent, p. 226). *Song of Solomon* shows how the black community has lost this "anchor" through forced migrations and stresses the importance of finding it again for the self-esteem and success of current and future generations. "If you're not the protector of your culture, someone else other than yourself controls your culture, and they really control you. . . . They end up defining you" (N'Namdi in Dent, p. 226). Making this very point, *Song of Solomon*, by affirming the value of the Southern heritage, itself drops anchor and reclaims control over black identity.

Sources and literary context. The issue of reconnecting with the Southern roots of black culture remained an important cultural and artistic concern for African American artists, poets, and novelists throughout the twentieth century. While novels of the 1920s (such as Jean Toomer's *Cane* [1923]), began to examine the Southern rural heritage, later works concentrated on the relocated Southerners and their struggles with the more subtle racism of northern cities. In the 1970s, black authors began to refocus their attention on the question of African American culture and the origins of a common black American experience during slavery, and on the African heritage that preceded it. Helping to touch off widespread interest in African American genealogy, Alex Haley released the memoir *Roots* (1976), which recounted seven generations in Haley's search for his slave forebears and their origins. Published the following year, *Song of Solomon* participates in and encourages this search of roots. The novel actually incorporates a successful finding of the author's own personal search. Morrison notes that the genealogical song Milkman learns in the novel is a version of a song from the Alabama wing of her family (Jones and Vinson in Taylor-Guthrie, pp. 173-74). The year 1977 also saw the release of international books like Charles L. Blockson's *Black Genealogy*. In the same year the Afro-American Historical and Genealogical Society was founded to promote scholarship of black history and genealogy.

Events in History at the Time the Novel Was Written

Disillusionment and backlash, 1970s. While great strides had been made to increase the rights and opportunities of African Americans through the 1960s, by the end of the decade there was growing disillusionment within the black community. The view surfaced—especially among black youth—that the civil rights movement had failed. Because leaders such as Dr. King and groups such as the NAACP pursued legal remedies to racial injustices, many urban social ills went unaddressed or worsened. "The masses of Negroes are now starkly aware that the recent civil rights victories benefited primarily a very small percentage of middle class Negroes while their predicament remained the same or worsened" (Kenneth Clark in Franklin and Moss, p. 554). By the end of the 1970s—despite desegregation of the schools and affirmative action programs—just 15 percent of blacks had jobs in the medical and other professions or held managerial positions. The vast majority—85 percent of those employed—held service, unskilled, or skilled labor positions. At the same time, the unemployment rate remained high, averaging 15 percent for black adults, compared to 6 percent for whites, and 36 percent for black youth (aged 16 to 19) compared to about 14 percent for white youth (Ploski and Williams, p. 634-35). By 1970 nearly one third of all blacks labored under the poverty line, earning less than $3,968 per year for a family of four.

Gains for the few, tensions for the many. Because of increased educational and professional opportunities, a rising number of African Americans entered the upper and middle classes, reaching 32 percent by 1970. However, the number of welfare recipients also increased during this time period, to nearly 3 million by 1972. Rather than producing substantive economic and professional opportunities, early civil rights legislation produced "massive tokenism"—that is, a few blacks were placed in high-profile, widely-publicized positions, while "more than 80 percent worked at the bottom of the economic ladder" (Franklin and Moss, p. 545). "Between 1949 and 1964 the relative participation of African Americans in the total economic life of the nation declined significantly" (Franklin and Moss, p. 545). Unemployment in 1963, for example, was more than twice that of whites.

For those who did land managerial, professional, or corporate jobs, race-based wage dis-

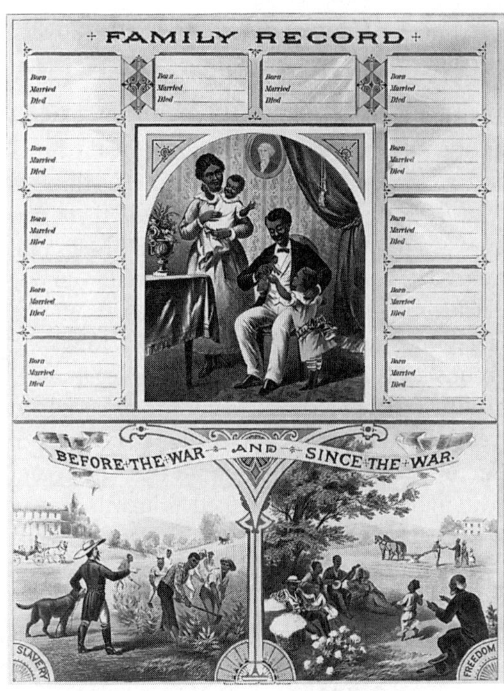

A portrayal of an African American family tree before and after the Civil War.

crimination quickly surfaced. For example, the average pay for a black person with eight years of education was $4,472 in 1969 as compared to $7,018 for a comparable white. As evidenced in the novel, disparity of wealth within the black community widened as unemployment increased, leading to rifts not only between blacks and whites but also between upper- and lower-class blacks. In the novel, the Deads are ostracized inside and outside their hometown. Outside, they face race prejudice, as when Macon Dead II cannot purchase certain tracts of land in white neighborhoods; inside, their social position prevents their daughters from finding husbands.

Black Power. As the economic plight worsened, racial tensions heightened. Riots again erupted. Disillusioned by the failure of legislation to improve living and working conditions and feeling under-represented in government, blacks again took to the streets—this time forcefully. The year of 1970 "was marked by violence, militant campaigns, racial tensions, and new movements demanding social justice" (Kelley and Lewis, p. 544). Riots erupted in major cities across the country as groups such as the Black Panther party, the Republik of New Africa, the National Committee to Combat Fascism, and the Black Liberation Front gained strength. These groups voiced the outrage and impatience of contemporary black youth, intent on challenging the white-dominated governments and institutions that seemed deaf to so many black concerns. In the novel, the Seven Days are an extreme example of the Black Power branch. When the four girls are killed in the 16th Street Baptist Church, Guitar indicates that his group, the Seven Days, will kill four whites, any four whites. An eye for an eye, says Guitar by way of explanation to Milkman, who is questioning how the group could justify randomly killing four whites:

> It doesn't matter who did it. Each and every one of them could do it. So you just get any one of them. There are no innocent white people, because every one of them is a potential nigger-killer, if not an actual one.
>
> (*Solomon*, p. 155)

Most African Americans did not advocate all-out or random violence such as this. Past leaders had advocated various, nonviolent paths to address the inequities of life for blacks. Booker T. Washington founded the Tuskegee Institute (1881) to train blacks with skills that would enable their full participation in American society. Led by W. E. B. Dubois, early-twentieth-century radicals began the Niagara Movement (1905) to mount aggressive (nonviolent) action to end discrimination and achieve other urgent goals. A third leader, Marcus Garvey, did much to transform the group's self-image, insisting that *black* stood not for "inferior," but for "beautiful and strong." Garvey bolstered the black sense of community, as well as pride, developing the Black Star Steamship Line (c. 1920) to promote commerce among peoples of African descent worldwide and to provide transportation for those who wanted to leave the United States. Four decades later Stokely Carmichael, a former SNCC leader, echoed some of these leaders' ideas and added others, calling on black people to "unite, to recognize their heritage, to build a sense of community" (Hamilton in Blumberg, p. 117). Along with Charles V. Hamilton, Carmichael wrote the manifesto of the Black Power movement (1967), outlining its ideas: blacks needed to practice self-defense, define their own goals, lead their own organizations, and support each other instead of depending on whites.

Black pride. But the new Black Power movement was not just militant; it had a socio-political agenda. It aimed to restore black pride and have blacks exert control "in all areas where black people are in the majority, and for a proportional share of key decision-making posts where they are in the minority" (Carmichael in McElroy, p. 48). Many participants in the movement rejected their slave names and adopted African names; they abandoned the racial designation of "Negro" and replaced it with "black" or "African American." As Carmichael wrote, "Black power is a black declaration of independence. It is a turn inward, a rallying cry for a people in the sudden labor of self-discovery, self naming, and self legitimisation" (Carmichael in McElroy, p. 48). A new sense of race pride permeated popular culture; "black is beautiful" became a catch phrase and both black and white youth donned traditional African dress and revived cultural art forms.

On the academic level, the new Black Power movement demanded control over community programs and schools—specifically calling for black studies programs to be implemented in public schools and universities. "As far as African Americans were concerned, the black pride that a reorganized curriculum could stimulate would compensate for the disillusionment and despair that years of frustration and embitterment had produced" (Franklin and Moss, p. 555). Written during the peak of this movement, *Song of Solomon* shows the clear correlation between the acknowledgment of a people's historical and cultural achievements and their success in garnering respect and pride. In the novel, Milkman's journey is an illustration of the process of self-discovery Carmichael talks about and shows that contemporary black youth—who are clearly in jeopardy in this era—can be liberated if respect is paid to their culture.

Fear and misunderstanding. Unfortunately, Black Power for many—especially conservative whites—inspired fear and misunderstanding. Black demands for "land, power, and freedom" frightened many whites, even those who had been involved in the civil rights movement (Kelley and Lewis, p. 519). The riots, such as the 1967 rebellion in Detroit—which resulted in 43 deaths, 2,000 wounded, and the destruction of 5,000 homes—worried not only the government but also many liberal citizens. They "saw chaos and feared true anarchy" (Kelley and Lewis, p. 532). The FBI and local police "declared war" on Black Power groups—especially the Black Panthers. Eight Black Panthers were killed by police in 1968; the infiltration and destruction of black organizations and wire tapping of leaders' phones became policy. "One of [Richard] Nixon's campaign promises was to get rid of 'troublemakers'" and his arch-conservative administration did its best to do so, as well as dismantle President Lyndon Johnson's War on Poverty social welfare programs. (Kelly and Lewis, p. 545). Nixon's re-election in 1972 signified an "anti-black backlash" and white middle-class resentment to government "handouts" to African Americans. Nixon supporters believed that, since civil rights legislation had been passed, racism no longer existed. Aversion to busing, the court-mandated solution for school desegregation, contributed heavily to the backlash as well. Again, even liberal whites opposed sending their kids to school outside their communities. It seemed that theoretical civil rights were easier to swallow than practical solutions.

Despite—or perhaps, in spite of—Nixon's election and the backlash against blacks, the Black Power movement evolved once again. The National Black Political Assembly held its first convention in 1972 and Shirley Chisholm became the first black person and woman to run for president (1972). Rather than be held back in the white-dominated business world or be represented by whites, blacks concentrated on forming their own businesses and on gaining seats in all areas of government. But the country experienced an economic decline and an energy crisis in the mid-1970s, felt intensely in the devastated, already-ailing inner cities. Changes in the world economy prompted massive unemployment, leading to "an expansion of poverty among African Americans not seen since the Great Depression of the 1930s" (Kelley and Lewis, p. 559). While all Americans suffered, the poor African American community felt the brunt of the recession. It is said, in fact, that the inner cities have never recovered from the recession of the 1970s and the troubles the novel alludes to for urban black youth have only worsened. Between 1975 and 1980 the number of unemployed blacks rose by 200,000 while it decreased by over 500,000 for whites, producing the widest unemployment gap between the races ever recorded.

Reception. Having achieved notable critical and popular success with *The Bluest Eye* and *Sula*, Morrison enjoyed a dramatic rise in reputation with the publication of *Song of Solomon*. Reviews generally credited the novel with elevating her literary standing. They concentrated particularly on Morrison's pre-eminence as a storyteller and on the connection between elements of her writing and Latin American "Magic Realism" (although Morrison herself has downplayed this connection). In the *New York Times Book Review*, Reynolds Price praised *Song of Solomon*'s largeness of scope and escape from realist limitations, calling it a "wise and spacious novel" (Price, p. 1). The *New Yorker*'s Susan Lardner focused on the oral elements in the novel, connecting its theme of flight with the soaring quality of its narrative style. In 1978 *Song of Solomon* received the National Book Critics Circle award. Morrison did not yet achieve with this novel the popular reach she would attain with the publication of *Beloved* (1987). But *Song of Solomon* established her as both a major American literary figure and an authority on African American culture and writing.

—Diane Renée

For More Information

Blumberg, Rhoda Lois. *Civil Rights: The 1960s Freedom Struggle*. Boston: Twayne, 1991.

Dent, David J. *In Search of Black America*. New York: Simon and Schuster, 2000.

Draper, James P., ed. *Contemporary Literary Criticism,* Vol. 81. Detroit: Gale Research, 1994.

Franklin, John Hope, and Alfred Moss Jr. *From Slavery to Freedom*. New York: Alfred A. Knopf, 2001.

Gwaltnet, John Langston. *Drylongso: A Self-Portrait of Black America*. New York: Random House, 1980.

Hamilton, Virginia. *The People Could Fly: American Black Folktales*. New York: Knopf, 1985.

Harrison, Alferdeen, ed. *Black Exodus: The Great Migration from the American South*. Jackson: University Press of Mississippi, 1991.

Kelley, Robin, and Earl Lewis, eds. *To Make Our World Anew: A History of African Americans*. New York: Oxford University Press, 1990.

McElroy, Dr. Njoki. *Black Journey*. North Vancouver: Gallerie, 1994.

Morrison, Toni. *Song of Solomon*. New York: Penguin, 1977.

Nash, Gary B., et al, eds. *The American People: Creating a Nation and a Society*, Vol. 2. New York: Harper & Row, 1990.

Ploski, Harry A., and James Williams, eds. *The Negro Almanac*. Detroit: Gale Research, 1989.

Price, Reynolds. Review of *Song of Solomon. New York Times Book Review,* 11 September 1977, 1.

Taylor-Guthrie, Danielle, ed. *Conversations with Toni Morrison*. Literary Conversations Series. Jackson: University of Mississippi Press, 1994.

Stones for Ibarra

by
Harriet Doerr

Born in Pasadena, California, in 1910, Harriet Doerr married and raised a family before graduating from Stanford University in 1977 with a degree in European History. She then enrolled in Stanford's graduate program in Creative Writing and shortly afterward published several short stories that later became individual chapters of her first novel, *Stones for Ibarra*. Its success inspired a second best-selling novel, *Consider This, Señora* (1993), also set in Mexico. Doerr produced two short-story collections as well, *Under an Aztec Sun* (1990) and *The Tiger in the Grass* (1995). Like much of her other writing, *Stones for Ibarra* illuminates the cultural differences that can impede communication between Mexicans and Americans, while also suggesting that each culture has valuable lessons to learn from the other.

THE LITERARY WORK

A novel set in Mexico c. 1960; first published in New York City in 1984.

SYNOPSIS

An American couple, Richard and Sara Everton, move to a remote Mexican village to reopen an old abandoned copper mine originally founded by Richard's grandfather. Soon after making the move, they learn that Richard has been stricken by a fatal disease and has only six years to live.

Events in History at the Time the Novel Takes Place

Historical background: the Díaz era and the Mexican Revolution. In the last quarter of the nineteenth century, Mexico emerged from fifty years of chaos into an era of relative calm. Political and social upheaval had followed Mexico's Wars of Independence from colonial Spain in 1810-1821, and subsequent events compounded the upheaval. Worsening the chaos were disasters such as the Mexican-American War of 1846-48, in which Mexico lost vast areas of its far north to the United States. (These lands, extending from California to Texas, subsequently became the American Southwest.) In 1861 Mexico's anarchic conditions had led to invasion and attempted conquest by France, but Mexican forces decisively defeated the French on May 5, 1862, a date that Mexicans celebrate as a major national holiday. The hero of the battle was a young Mexican general named Porfirio Díaz. The French were finally defeated in 1867, after which came continued political turbulence. Díaz seized power in 1876 and proceeded to quell the turbulence. Restoring stability and initiating a series of economic reforms, he retained control of Mexico until 1910, leaving his mark on his country's political system.

Encouraged by the newfound stability and by Díaz's modernizing reforms, by the late 1880s American and European investors were flocking to pour much-needed capital into the Mexican economy. Catching up on fifty years of industrial

Harriet Doerr

and technological development, the Díaz years ushered in the rapid expansion of railroads, telegraph lines, and roads. Industry too benefitted from the infusion of foreign capital, including oil and especially mining, which now revived after a long slump. Mexico's rich mineral resources featured large gold, silver, and copper deposits, and in 1884 the Díaz government enacted a new mining code that offered tax breaks and other incentives to mine owners. A few made their fortunes in the process, but on the whole the Mexican people would grow poorer during Díaz's regime, which turned into a dictatorship.

By the early 1900s more than 1,000 mining companies were operating in Mexico, with Americans owning about 85 percent of them. The mining companies varied from huge conglomerates such as the American Smelting and Refining Company, owned by the Guggenheim family (whose Mexican mining interests were valued at $12 million in 1902), to smaller independent operations. The best known independent operator was Colonel William Greene, the so-called "copper king of Sonora," who came to Mexico in 1898 with little money, but soon built his Cananea Mining Company into one of the world's largest copper producers. The company employed 3,500 men and operated eight large smelting furnaces. Like Greene's Cananea mines, the most abundant copper mines sat in the northern Mexican state of Sonora, near the United States border. In *Stones for Ibarra* Richard Everton's grandfather is said to have opened and operated a smaller independent copper mine farther south, at Ibarra, a fictional town in a fictional state somewhere in the central part of the country. Called the Malagueña mine, the novel's fictional mine dates from the Díaz era. For many Mexicans, such companies—like Greene's Cananea Consolidated Copper Company—came to symbolize the foreign domination of Mexico's natural resources and industry under the Díaz regime.

Díaz's government manipulated property laws to encourage the concentration of land in the hands of a few wealthy supporters. Land passed out of the control of peasants and Indians (both groups could rarely prove ownership of land that they had occupied for generations), increasing the already vast estates, or *haciendas*, of the wealthy. By 1910 only 2 percent of Mexicans legally owned land, while 3 percent of the property holders owned nearly 60 percent of the country (Foster, p. 148). More than two-thirds of Mexicans were landless farmers, most working as *peónes*, or agricultural laborers, for wealthy landowners (known as *hacendados)* in exchange for low wages and the right to farm a small plot. The system was one of debt-peonage; the *peones* were often forced into debt to the *hacendados* in order to survive, which in effect perpetuated their servitude. Hunger and poverty were widespread. As noted, most Mexicans were materially worse off in 1910 than they had been a century earlier.

In 1910 popular discontent with the Díaz regime finally spilled over into revolution. The Mexican Revolution of 1910 was long and complex, prompting historians to divide it into two major phases. The military phase extended from 1910 to 1920; as many as 2 million Mexicans—an eighth of the total population—may have died in its anarchic and complicated civil wars. The so-called constructive or reconstructive phase lasted from 1920 to 1940, as Mexicans slowly and painfully struggled to implement the ideals for which the revolutionaries had originally fought. As embodied in the Constitution of 1917, those ideals included anticlericalism (the desire to limit the influence of the traditionally predominant Roman Catholic Church), the redistribution of land, workers rights, and an end to foreign economic exploitation. (New fighting—the Cristero rebellion—broke out from 1926-29 in relation to limits placed on the Church.) The Revolution of 1910 is mentioned repeatedly in the novel in connection with these and other issues, forming a constant background presence. Indeed, although the novel's events take place half a century later, in the first paragraph the reader is introduced not only to Richard and Sara Everton, but also to "the copper mine that Richard's grandfather abandoned fifty years ago, during the Revolution of 1910" (Doerr, *Stones for Ibarra*, p. 1). It is the impulse to reopen this mine that brings the couple back to Mexico.

Postwar economic boom: the "Mexican miracle." By World War II (1939-45) Mexico's revolutionaries had managed to consolidate their gains and catapult one or another leader to power. The leader of the moment now gave greater weight to business and industrial interests, and less to the mix of agrarian reformers, workers rights advocates, and intellectuals who had made up much of the Revolution's original backing. Under the Constitution of 1917, presidential succession brought a series of men into office, each serving one six-year term without reelection. Control under this system rested in the tenacious hands of one party, the Mexican Revolutionary Party (P.R.M). In 1946, reflecting its status as the organ of the political establishment, the party changed its name to the Institutional Revolutionary Party (P.R.I.).

Mexico's industry had expanded during World War II, and under its first two postwar presidents, Miguel Alemán (1946-52) and Adolfo Ruiz Cortines (1952-58), the country embarked on three decades of unprecedented prosperity. Fueled partly by foreign investment, this phenomenon has been called the "Mexican miracle." However, as Ruiz Cortines suggested on leaving office, Mexicans still faced some daunting problems in the late 1950s. Chief among them was an alarming population explosion; in less than two and a half decades Mexico's population had more than doubled, from about 16 million in 1934 to over 32 million in 1958. Cities—in particular the rapidly growing capital, Mexico City—were hit by heavy migration from the countryside, causing Mexico's urban population to surpass its rural population for the first time in 1960. The country's riches continued to be concentrated in the hands of relatively few, poverty remained widespread, and many Mexicans lacked basic health care and educational opportunities. Though largely restricted to a rural context, the novel faithfully portrays these and other social problems, often from the Evertons' only partly comprehending point of view.

In 1958 the P.R.I. selected a young left-leaning liberal, Adolfo López Mateos, as its presidential candidate. Promising to renew the party's revolutionary social agenda, López Mateos won 90 percent of the vote (surprising some commentators, who had expected the conservative opposition party, the pro-Catholic P.A.N., to do better). The novel is set during this popular president's tenure (1958-64), as the government moved away from a business orientation back towards providing social programs and basic services such as water and electrical power for more of Mexico's people. *Stones for Ibarra* reflects these programs in its depiction of a fictional town, Loreto, whose newly installed water, electricity, and telephone lines contrast with the lack of such amenities in smaller, nearby Ibarra.

COPPER AND POLITICS: LABOR UNREST AT THE CANANEA MINES

In 1906, Mexican workers at the American-owned Cananea Consolidated Copper Company went on strike. Their grievances included lower pay than American workers performing similar jobs, and the fact that qualified Mexicans were routinely passed over for managerial or technical jobs in favor of Americans. Colonel William Greene, the company's American owner, refused to arbitrate, and when unarmed workers tried to force their way into the company lumberyard, they were met by rifle fire, and an estimated 20-40 were killed. When further demonstrations ensued, the Mexican governor of Sonora authorized 275 Arizona rangers to enter Mexico from the United States and patrol Cananea's streets; in the ensuing exchanges of rifle fire, several rangers and workers were killed. When the Mexican *rurales* (state police) arrived later, their commander oversaw the lynching of the workers' leaders. For many Mexicans, the Cananea strike not only symbolizes America's willingness to use force in pursuing its economic exploitation of Mexicans, but also represents the first time that Mexican workers organized to resist such exploitation.

The Novel in Focus

The plot. The novel opens as Richard and Sara Everton, "two North Americans, a man and a woman just over and just under forty," make their way by car through the countryside of central Mexico towards Ibarra, the "declining village of one thousand souls" where they plan to make their new home (*Stones for Ibarra*, p. 1). Nearby, Richard's grandfather had opened the Malagueña

A terraced copper mine.

copper mine in the late nineteenth century, then had to abandon it during the Revolution of 1910. Now the couple have come "to extend the family's Mexican history and to patch the present onto the past" by reopening the mine and fixing up the family's once lavish adobe house:

> They have experienced the terrible persuasion of a great-aunt's recollections and adopted them as their own. They have not considered that memories are like corks left out of bottles. They swell. They no longer fit.
>
> (*Stones for Ibarra*, p. 3)

The Evertons have mortgaged their home in San Francisco, taken out bank loans, and borrowed against their insurance in order to finance the project. Yet, as the reader is informed right away, their hopes for a long life together in Mexico are to be dashed the summer after they arrive, when Richard is diagnosed with leukemia and doctors tell them he has only about six years left to live.

Under the cloud of this impending tragedy, the Evertons persist with their plans, continuing to renovate the house, hiring local workers, and beginning mining operations. The village benefits from the mine's payroll, but at first the Evertons and the villagers coexist in a haze of mutual incomprehension. "They are not people," Sara tells herself, "but silhouettes sketched on a backdrop to deceive us into thinking the stage is crowded" (*Stones for Ibarra*, p. 11). For their part, the villagers are baffled by the Americans' strange behavior: for example, the Evertons carefully plant rows of maguey cactus not for the purpose of making *pulque* or *mescal*, the popular cactus-based alcoholic beverages, but simply because they admire the way the plants look. They read separate books, and even plan to vote for different candidates in the upcoming American presidential elections. "At last the village found a word that applied to the North Americans. It was a long word, *mediodesorientado*, meaning half-disoriented," like a blindfolded child trying to hit a *piñata*, the paper rooster stuffed with candy commonly featured at children's parties (*Stones for Ibarra*, p. 24).

Gradually, as she learns more and more Spanish, Sara begins to penetrate the villagers' world, but always incompletely, hearing of local incidents but embroidering them in her imagination to fill out parts she hasn't understood. In this unreliable way she (and through her, the reader) hears a number of tales, each of which is given a chapter in the novel. "The Life Sentence of José Reyes," for example, tells the story of a village drunk who kills two brothers with his machete when they refuse to lend him money, then is stoned to death by their friends and family. Another chapter, "Kid Muñoz," features a battered boxer who was blinded in the ring, and now sells lottery tickets on the street. Sara encounters Kid Muñoz on one of her weekly trips to Concepción, the (fictional) state capital 80 kilometers (50 miles) from Ibarra. Woven into these tales are brief notices that keep the reader up to date on Richard's ever-impending illness. She and Richard buy supplies in Concepción, and they also receive regular reports on the progress of his disease from the medical laboratory there.

Another chapter concerns Pablo, a nine-year-old boy with mental retardation. Pablo drowns in the mine's tailings dump (where the refuse from the smelting process is discarded). Sara hears—or concocts—an intricate plot suggesting that Pablo's older cousin Juan, burdened by having to look after the boy, may be at least partly to blame. In much the same way, other characters are introduced to the reader, including a whole succession of priests who arrive and, for various reasons, soon depart from the small town. One is a womanizer, and another—inexplicably chased by dogs wherever he goes—is savagely bitten while praying in church. In "The

Red Taxi," Chuy Santos—"not the sort of man who would kill his two best friends in order to own a car" (at least in Sara's imagination)—nevertheless does for a red Volkswagen beetle, which becomes Ibarra's only taxi (*Stones for Ibarra*, p. 68).

Sara weaves an especially melodramatic, romantic past around Madre (Mother) Petra, an aristocratic old nun who gives Sara lessons in Spanish grammar and vocabulary. The excesses of this fantasy finally lead Sara to abandon the game:

> And together with one fantasy, she renounced another. Until this moment, she had refused to consider the sort of future that included hospital rooms and nurses, that threatened emergencies and an ambulance. She had denied a whole vocabulary of words: radiation, transfusion, hemorrhage. Until today she had convinced herself that Richard might be spared them all.
>
> (*Stones for Ibarra*, p. 101)

Only now, during their third year in Ibarra, does Sara slowly begin to accept the fact that her husband is going to die.

Sara begins to notice the small charms—buttons, thorns, a length of thread—that María de Lourdes, a local woman who cleans for her, conceals in various places throughout the house. Although Sara has kept Richard's illness as secret as possible, the villagers believe he has a bad heart. When it seems especially serious, they notice, "the señora drives away by herself to place a long-distance call to the North American doctor" (*Stones for Ibarra*, p. 109). The villagers are skeptical of the couple's reliance on medical science, and baffled when they reject the help of local *brujos* and *curanderos*, the folk healers of popular tradition. Yet as Richard's illness becomes more debilitating, the local doctor, Dr. Vásquez, is called on to treat him, and Dr. Vásquez thinks to himself that "the sick man's wife believed doctors had supernatural powers. She believed this of the American specialist and of Dr. Vásquez himself" (*Stones for Ibarra*, p. 149).

Up to now Richard has played along with her denial of his illness, letting her pretend they have all the time in the world in front of them, but in the fifth year he confronts her: "You've got to stop making things up. Stop making each day up. See it," he tells her. She struggles to do so. When the village is visited by a Mexican family of converts to the American-style Baptist church, Sara plays in her mind with the idea of being born again:

> All we would want out of being born again is this place to live and die in, as we are living and dying in it now. Then she amended her words. As Richard is dying in it now, in spite of the hematologist's pills, in spite of me.
>
> (*Stones for Ibarra*, p. 182)

In November of the last year Sara panics when Richard is taken with a bad fever, and she endures a hair-raising trip in Chuy Santos's red taxi to fetch a doctor from Concepción. Though it is a false alarm, the reader is told now that Richard will in fact "die more than a year later in a San Francisco hospital" (*Stones for Ibarra*, p. 194).

ADVANCES IN TREATING LEUKEMIA

Leukemia, a cancer of the blood, takes its name from Greek words meaning "white" and "blood," and occurs when the body produces too many white blood cells and not enough red ones. Several different types of leukemia exist, and though author Harriet Doerr does not specify which type Richard Everton suffers from in *Stones for Ibarra*, her description fits chronic myelogenous leukemia, which most often strikes adults in their forties, as Richard Everton is in the novel. Symptoms include weight loss and weakness, so the novel appropriately describes Richard as thin and occasionally exhausted. His visits to the medical lab in Concepción are to learn the results of blood tests; fewer white cells in the blood means good news for leukemia sufferers. In the 1960s, radiation treatment, which Richard receives in the novel, was commonly used to kill the white blood cells. Doctors since then have relied more heavily on chemotherapy, the selective use of highly toxic drugs, to do so. The disease is still considered incurable. Like the novel's Richard, most victims can expect to live no more than five to ten years, though, in many cases, chemotherapy can extend the remaining life span by several years or more.

The narrative skips ahead to a month after Richard's death, as Sarah returns to Ibarra. Meeting with the Canadian geologist who has assisted Richard in the past, she learns that the mine is just "beginning to show what it's worth" (*Stones for Ibarra*, p. 203). But the reader never learns what becomes of the mine. Preparing to move back to San Francisco, Sara dismisses the villagers who have helped her with domestic chores and closes up the house. She sends her belongings north in a moving van that successfully negotiates the ancient gate to the house. By the gate

Sara notices a pile of stones, which a villager tells her have been left to commemorate a fatal accident on the road. As the novel closes, she sees two villagers passing by and feels an urge to call to them, "Stop for a minute. Look through these gates and see the lighted house. An accident has happened here. Remember the place. Bring stones" (*Stones for Ibarra*, p. 214).

RELIGION AND FOLK BELIEF

Next to Mexico's predominant Roman Catholic faith, which reflects its Spanish colonial heritage, are older folk beliefs from pre-Columbian times that exist side-by-side with Catholic practices and doctrines. *Stones for Ibarra* acknowledges this coexistence when a local priest leads the villagers in a rain dance, a procession that moves from the town's plaza to a chapel outside of town, where the priest "will conduct a service and pray for rain" (*Stones for Ibarra,* p. 109). Other folk beliefs reflected in the novel include the shamanistic practices of *curanderos* (healers) and *brujos* (sorcerors), who combine an often sophisticated knowledge of herbal and other traditional remedies with what many believe to be supernatural powers. *Curanderos* and *brujos* often ingest hallucinogens such as mescal and jimson weed (both grown as ornamental plants by the novel's Evertons) to enter a trancelike state that helps them determine how to treat an illness. Among Mexico's poor, the traditional treatments of *curanderos* and *brujos* are often all one can afford.

A literary reflection of cultural fatalism. While *Stones for Ibarra* presents a number of cultural contrasts between the villagers and the North Americans, the novel's central movement concerns Sara's slow awakening to the fatalism that rules the villagers' lives:

> Believing as they did in a relentless providence, the people of Ibarra, daily and without surprise, met their individual dooms. They accepted as inevitable the hail on the ripe corn, the vultures at the heart of the starved cow, the stillborn child.
>
> (*Stones for Ibarra*, p. 113)

As she gradually perceives the "relentless providence" that resigns the villagers to their often violent fates, Sara also learns to accept her own destiny, which is to suffer the bereavement of Richard's inevitable death.

In an influential book about his culture, *The Labyrinth of Solitude* (1950; in Spanish) Mexican author Octavio Paz distinguishes Mexican attitudes to death from those found elsewhere: "The word death is not pronounced in New York, in Paris, in London, because it burns the lips. The Mexican, in contrast, is familiar with death, jokes about it, caresses it, sleeps with it, celebrates it" (Paz, p. 57). A well-known example is the Mexican holiday called Día de los Muertos, the Day of the Dead, which coincides with the North American holiday Halloween. Whereas Halloween's associations with the dead have become almost entirely symbolic, the Mexican Day of the Dead continues to represent a meaningful chance for people to commune with dead family members and friends.

Paz traces Mexicans' special intimacy with death to the Aztec culture of pre-Columbian times, and to that culture's characteristic fatalism, its belief that fate predetermines all events and they cannot be changed. It is in fact this fatalism, say some, that resigned the Aztecs to the idea of conquest, and thus allowed the Spanish Conquistadors to overcome Aztec culture in the first place. Paz goes on to contrast the richly historic Mexican conception of death not only with other cultures, but with a modern "philosophy of progress" that he claims encourages a need to deny death's very existence:

> Everything in the modern world functions as if death did not exist. Nobody takes it into account, it is suppressed everywhere: in political pronouncements, commercial advertising, public morality, and popular customs; in the promise of cut-rate health and happiness offered to all of us by the hospitals, drug-stores and playing fields.
>
> (Paz, p. 57)

Sara, the modern North American, clings to precisely such a "promise of cut-rate health and happiness" before finally yielding to the villagers' traditional "relentless providence." In this sense, by accepting fate, Sara and Richard (whose outlook has always been more fatalistic than his wife's) do indeed fulfill their ultimate aim: "to extend the family's Mexican history and to patch the present onto the past" (*Stones for Ibarra*, p. 3).

Sources and literary context. While *Stones for Ibarra*'s plot is fictional, Harriet Doerr lived in Mexico for fifteen years with her husband, spending some of that time in a small village on which she modeled the village of Ibarra. Similarly, Doerr's observations of Mexican life in general provided the basis for the cultural contrasts that run

CULTURAL CONTRASTS BETWEEN MEXICANS AND NORTH AMERICANS THAT SURFACE IN *STONES FOR IBARRA*

Mexican Culture	North American Culture	Reflections of the Two Cultures
Shows strong sense of history, with a living past.	Less identification with the past than with the present.	Historical events such as the Revolution of 1910 are often mentioned as if they occurred just recently.
Often values emotions over reason; more readily turns to nonscientific.	Usually values reason over emotion; turns most often to scientific solutions	The Evertons appear overly rational and emotionally cold to the more intuitive and passionate villagers. Sara denies the effectiveness of charms, yet seems to find solace in them.
Stresses loyalty to family, relies on family first for help.	Stresses self-reliance; Americans use public institutions for help.	The Evertons get bank loans for their mine; villagers (e.g. Chuy Santos with auto) try family, friends, acquaintances for loans. While readers never hear about Richard's or Sara's families, they learn all about those of the villagers.
Tends to be Catholic and patriarchal.	Tends to be Protestant or secular and have a greater degree of gender equality.	The secular Evertons often appear next to priests in the story. Mexican women (who as Sara notes, just won the right to vote in 1954, a few years before the story takes place) vote as their husbands dictate; voting separately for different candidates (as the Evertons do) seems silly to the villagers.

through the novel. For the vanished world of the Díaz era's American expatriate community, Doerr could rely upon literary accounts such as Charles Flandrau's well known *Viva Mexico!* (1908), a portrait of Mexican life in the early 1900s from an American traveler's point of view. *Viva Mexico!* includes an amusing depiction of American expatriates, and in *Stones for Ibarra* Doerr mentions Flandrau's classic book as being on the Everton's shelves.

Doerr has been compared with other English-speaking writers who have written about Mexico, such as Katherine Anne Porter (American, 1890-1980) and Graham Greene (English, 1904-91), both of whom she includes among her major influences. Porter's writing career began after she traveled to Mexico in 1920, and her first published story, "María Concepción" (1923) is set there, as are several others. Greene visited Mexico in 1938 to report on the persecution of the Catholic Church. Out of his trip came the nonfiction account *The Lawless Roads* (1939) and a novel, *The Power and the Glory* (1940), which follows a drunken priest who is hunted down in the anticlerical atmosphere of revolutionary Mexico. Doerr's writing has also evoked comparisons with another writer whom she acknowledges as a strong influence, the Colombian novelist Gabriel García Márquez (1928-). García Márquez's novel ***One Hundred Years of Solitude*** (1967; also in *Literature and Its Times*), blends fact with magical events to describe life in a small, decaying, fictional Colombian village.

Events in History at the Time the Novel Was Written

Political and economic turbulence. The popular López Mateos's term as president expired in 1964, and the P.R.I. selected a relatively conservative government minister named Gustavo Díaz Ordaz as his successor. Historians have generally deemed it an unfortunate choice, for like many other nations, Mexico experienced student unrest during the turbulent 1960s, and Díaz Ordaz's harsh reactions only fanned the flames of the demonstrators' dissatisfaction. As Mexico City prepared to host the 1968 Summer Olympics, the city experienced a summer of escalating confrontations between students and police. On October 2, about 5,000 students were demonstrating peacefully in the Plaza of the Three Cultures in the district of Tlatelolco. Police arrived, armed with machine guns and backed by army tanks, and when the shooting ended—accounts disagree on whether police or demonstrators fired first—an estimated several hundred student demonstrators had been killed. The Tlatelolco massacre remains a leading national tragedy for Mexicans, one that for many marked the beginning of a growing distrust towards the P.R.I. and the government.

Under President José López Portillo (1976-82) Mexico developed vast oil reserves and enjoyed the economic benefits of the 1970s' high energy costs. Oil replaced mining as Mexico's largest revenue producer, but falling oil prices in the early 1980s brought the Mexican economy close to collapse. In 1982, when Miguel de la Madrid Hurtado assumed the presidency, Mexico faced high unemployment, mounting national debt, and staggering rates of inflation. American-dominated foreign financial institutions, such as the International Monetary Fund and the World Bank, assumed much of the responsibility for steering Mexico out of the crisis—but they demanded greater control of Mexico's domestic economic policies as well. By the mid-1980s—as during the Díaz era—many Mexicans once again felt that control over their future lay in the hands of others, and particularly in the hands of their powerful northern neighbors.

Reception. *Stones for Ibarra* was published to wide critical acclaim, winning the American Book Award for first fiction in 1984 and the National Book Award in 1985, as well as numerous other awards. Critics uniformly praised Doerr's depiction of the interactions between the Evertons and the villagers, as well as her spare and understated literary style. Calling the novel "intelligent, honest," and "a masterpiece," Ruth Doan MacDougall wrote in *The Christian Science Monitor* that despite its "terrible poignancy" *Stones for Ibarra* "never becomes sentimental. The writing is as shaded with nuance and as shining with clarity as the Ibarra landscape" (MacDougall, p. B6). Like Jonathan Yardley in the *Washington Post Book World*, many critics noted the first-time author's relatively advanced age, and agreed that *Stones for Ibarra* is "no mere novelty" and that "Harriet Doerr has mastered the art of fiction to a degree that would be remarkable in almost any writer of any age" (Yardley, p. 3).

In the *New York Times Book Review*, Leslie Marmon Silko praised Doerr's "distinctive vision" but found fault with the author for excluding the relationship between the Evertons from her field of focus: "We never see nor hear much more about the intimate life of Sara and Richard than the villagers manage to glean by standing outside the Evertons' windows . . . and herein lies the chief flaw in this novel" (Silko, p. 80). Ann Hulbert in *The New Republic*, however, found Doerr's unconventional treatment of the Evertons' relationship to be a strength, calling it "unexpectedly but effectively mysterious" and contrasting it with the "strange and violent sagas" of the villagers' lives, which "we hear in full" through "Sara's vivid extrapolations" (Hulbert, p. 40).

—Colin Wells

For More Information

Condon, John C. *Good Neighbors: Communicating with the Mexicans*. Yarmouth, Maine: Intercultural Press, 1985.

Doerr, Harriet. *Stones for Ibarra*. New York: Penguin, 1985.

Foster, Lynn V. *A Brief History of Mexico*. New York: Facts On File, 1997.

Flandrau, Charles Macomb. *Viva Mexico!* Urbana: University of Illinois Press, 1964.

Hall, Edward. *Beyond Culture*. Garden City, New York: Anchor, 1977.

Hulbert, Ann. "Visitations," in *The New Republic* 190, no. 4 (30 January 1984):40-41.

MacDougall, Ruth Doan. "For Richer, For Poorer . . . " in *The Christian Science Monitor*, 6 January 1984, B6.

Meyer, Michael C., and William L. Sherman. *The Course of Mexican History*. New York: Oxford University Press, 1987.

Paz, Octavio. *The Labyrinth of Solitude: Life and Thought in Mexico*. New York: Grove, 1961.

Silko, Leslie Marmon. "Pablo, Domingo, Richard and Sara," in *New York Times Book Review*, 8 January 1984, 8.

Yardley, Jonathan. "Mexican Escape: Patching the Present onto the Past," in *The Washington Post Book World*, 25 December 1983, 3.

The Stranger

by
Albert Camus

> **THE LITERARY WORK**
> A novel set in Algeria in the late 1930s; first published in French (as *L'Etranger*) in 1942, in English in 1946.
>
> **SYNOPSIS**
> A young man commits an inexplicable murder for which he is tried and sentenced to death.

Albert Camus (1913-60) was born and raised in French colonial Algeria. After publishing two books of essays on Algeria, *Betwixt and Between* (1937) and *Nuptials* (1938), he became a journalist for the newspaper *Alger-Républicain*. In 1940, the year after the onset of World War II, the writer moved to France, where he contributed to *Combat,* the leading newspaper of the French Resistance. In 1942 the success of *The Stranger* catapulted the 29-year-old Camus to immediate fame. That same year, he also published an influential philosophical essay, *The Myth of Sisyphus* (1942). Camus would go on to author two more novels, *The Plague* (1947) and *The Fall* (1956), as well as several plays and further philosophical works, including *The Rebel* (1951). In 1957 he won the Nobel Prize for Literature at the unusually early age of 44; less than three years later he met sudden and tragic death from a road accident in France. *The Stranger* remains Camus' most widely read work. The novel focuses on his lifelong concerns—individual freedom and the quest for meaning in the face of inevitable death. Though set in French colonial Algeria, the novel responds as well to the rise of fascism in 1930s Europe and to important developments in European philosophy.

Events in History at the Time of the Novel

Historical background: French colonial Algeria. The French colonial presence in Algeria dates from 1830, when France invaded the northern coastal part of the African land, which up to then had been part of the Ottoman Empire. First wresting Algiers, the largest city, from the Ottoman dey, or regent, the French then stamped out other Algerian resistance in a war of conquest that lasted until 1847. Over the next half century, the French extended their rule southward, and in 1902 French surveyors drew up the borders that still define the nation's territory today. Amidst vigorous nineteenth-century imperial expansion by European nations in continents around the globe, Algeria took a leading role as the heart of French West Africa. In fact, after 1848 Algeria was legally and politically regarded as not a colony at all, but an integral part of France.

This unusual arrangement arose from the large numbers of Europeans who began settling in Algeria almost immediately after the occupation of Algiers in 1830. These land-hungry working-class farmers and laborers came from poverty-stricken areas along the southern coasts

THE RISE OF THE ALGERIAN INDEPENDENCE MOVEMENT

The French made sporadic and generally unsuccessful efforts to integrate Muslims into the French educational system. In the end, the efforts backfired. By the early nineteenth century, an elite class of French-educated Muslims had emerged in Algeria, the *évolués* or "evolved ones." It was largely from this class that a group of Muslim leaders arose in Algeria by the 1920s and 1930s. Some of the early groups (for example, Young Algerians, formed in 1908) promoted the integration of Muslims into French society. But there was a contrary trend too. In 1926 the Muslim socialist Ahmed Messali Hadj formed the first group to call for Algerian independence. Called Star of North Africa, his group was outlawed by the French in 1929. The group operated underground until 1934. In 1937 Hadj organized a new group, the Party of the Algerian People, which attempted to combine socialist ideas with Islamic values. Rejecting such European influences as socialism, in 1931 the Muslim cleric Shaykh Abd al Hamid Ben Badis founded the Association of Algerian Muslim Ulama (religious teachers), which appealed more broadly to poor and working-class Muslims. While Algerian nationalism is not alluded to in *The Stranger,* it forms an important element of the novel's background, in which Arabs comprise a vague but sullen and threatening presence to the Europeans on whom the novel focuses. Tensions mounted during the years the novel was written, erupting the following decade. In 1954 the Algerian independence movement undertook a long and bloody war against French rule, finally winning independence in 1962. Today, fewer than 1 percent of Algerians are descended from *colons,* nearly all of whom fled to France before or during the war.

not just of France, but of Italy and Spain as well. Called *colons* (colonists) or more commonly *pieds noirs* (literally, black feet), they melded into a uniform group that was fundamentally French in language and culture. At the top of their society were the wealthy landowning or business families known as *grands colons* (great colonists), while those in the lower ranks were called *petits blancs* (little whites).

Like Meursault, the narrator of *The Stranger* (whose first name is never given), Albert Camus came from a working-class *petit blanc* family in Algiers, where the novel is set. As the administrative capital of French Algeria and the major city in French West Africa, Algiers in the 1930s was essentially French in look and feel as well as in population, including about 170,000 European residents and only 55,000 Arabs. By contrast, in the overall population outside of Algiers, Muslims (Arabs and the nomadic or seminomadic Berbers) heavily outnumbered Europeans by more than six to one (over 6 million Muslims against fewer than one million Europeans).

Despite greater numbers and theoretical equality under French law, Algeria's indigenous Muslim population in reality comprised a downtrodden underclass. Fewer than half a million Muslims had the right to vote. In the countryside, *colons* had seized much of the best agricultural land, evicting Muslim farmers. While Muslims made up more than 80 percent of the population, in the struggle to survive, they produced only 20 percent of the nation's income, and yet they paid well over half the taxes. The *colons*, who were exempt from many taxes, nevertheless controlled how the taxes were spent, so that *colon* communities enjoyed public facilities and good schools while Muslim areas had few or none. In politics within the home country of France, the *colons* made up a powerful political block. Their primary concern was to maintain their supremacy within French Algeria, and historians have characterized their now vanished society as reactionary and racist. In *The Stranger,* Meursault is put on trial for killing an Arab, but the novel's *colon* authorities appear to condemn him less for that act than for his refusal to conform to their social norms.

Responses to European fascism. Algerians became embroiled in a series of mounting economic and political crises in Europe as its nations drifted towards World War II. In 1931, after a period of seeming resilience, the French economy was sucked into the now two-year-old global depression. France had always suppressed industry in Algeria, viewing the land as a source of raw materials for French industry. Lacking an industrial base, Algerian colons already contended with a lower standard of living than people in mainland France, and the depression hit them even harder. Economic trouble affected Algeria's Arabs too, many of whom lost their farms. Flooding into Algiers and other cities, they formed a disenfranchised and increasingly angry constituency for the growing Arab protest movements.

At the time, the French faced an even more ominous scene in Europe. The rise of right-wing fascist dictatorships in Italy and Germany was leaving France diplomatically isolated and militarily threatened. In 1935 Italian dictator Benito Mussolini invaded Ethiopia, hoping to establish an Italian colony in Africa to rival those of France and Britain. The following year, Nazi Germany under Adolph Hitler invaded the Rhineland, a strategically important area along the Rhine river. Under the Treaty of Versailles, which had ended World War I in 1917, the Rhineland was supposed to act as a demilitarized buffer between France and Germany. Violating the treaty's terms in a way that posed a direct threat to France, Hitler remilitarized the Rhineland, converting factories to arms production, fortifying strategic points, and installing troops. That same year, 1936, the tensions between the conservative and liberal factions in Spain exploded into civil war, which would give rise to the fascist dictatorship of General Francisco Franco (1939-75).

Increasingly demoralized, many of the French struggled to confront the fascist threat—both abroad and at home. In February 1934 right-wing riots in Paris left 15 dead and hundreds injured. Shocked into momentary unity, French Communists and Socialists from the left joined with moderates in the center to form a coalition party called the Popular Front, which came to power under Prime Minister Léon Blum in 1936. Similar Popular Front coalitions had formed in other European countries, but only in Spain had another come to power. It was this Spanish Popular Front government that was now in the process of being defeated by Franco's fascist forces.

In Algeria, Blum's Popular Front government attempted to implement the Blum-Viollette Plan, which would have gradually extended greater political representation to the Arabs. Camus strongly supported the Popular Front. Like many young, left-wing intellectuals, he joined the French Communist Party in 1935. Camus left the party two years later, by which time the Blum-Viollette Plan had failed and the Popular Front had been voted from power in France. In 1938 Camus took an editorial job at a newspaper called *Alger-Républicain*, newly founded to promote the now imperiled ideals of the Popular Front. War with Nazi Germany seemed certain. At this bleak time in history, Camus began work on the novel that would become *The Stranger*.

The next year, 1939, brought further troubles. In March, Franco's fascists won the Spanish Civil War and Franco came to power. This was especially painful for Camus, not just because of his political ideals but also because his mother's family was Spanish. While his feelings for his mother were deeply ambivalent—as suggested by his treatment of motherhood in the novel—Camus valued his Spanish heritage. Other disturbing developments wracked Europe at the time too:

- **March 15, 1939** Germany occupies Czechoslovakia.
- **September 1, 1939** Germany invades Poland after signing a mutual nonaggression pact with the Soviet Union.
- **September 3, 1939** Bound by treaty obligations to Poland, Britain and France declare war on Germany, and World War II begins.
- **June 5, 1940** German forces invade mainland France, defeat the mighty French army with shocking ease, and occupy the country. To rule France and Algeria, the Germans install a puppet government, the Vichy regime, named after the French city that serves as its capital.

Existentialism. At about the time he began writing *The Stranger* in the fall of 1938, Camus reviewed a new novel entitled *Nausea* by a then unknown French author named Jean-Paul Sartre. Camus had read the novel the previous summer. In his review of *Nausea* for *Alger-Républicain*, Camus related fiction to the science of ideas: "A novel is only philosophy put into images, and in a good novel, all the philosophy goes into the images" (Camus in Todd, p. 84). Though he found much to praise in the work, one problem with *Nausea*, Camus decided, was that the images and the philosophy were not unified. "That bothers me," he had written earlier in a letter to a friend, "because I agree with the philosophy, and it pains me to see it lose its power as one reads" (Camus in Todd, p. 85).

THE STRANGER AND THE ABSURD

Central to Camus's thought is the concept of the absurd, which is associated with existentialism and which arose largely from the ideas of Søren Kierkegaard. For Camus, the absurd springs from the realization that human existence is ultimately pointless. Like the existentialists, he rejects the existence of any fixed source of meaning outside the individual. But for Camus, there is no source of meaning, even inside the individual. (Here he diverges from the existentialists, who believe every action and choice creates meaning, not only for the individual who makes it but also as a claim about universal value.) In Camus' view, the universe offers no *ultimate* meaning or value, just the *fleeting* fact of our existence. The traditional attempt to impose meaning from without (for example, by invoking the idea of God) gives the comforting illusion of ultimate meaning, but it is only that—an illusion. This idea is essential to understanding *The Stranger,* and it helps to explain what Camus means by the novel's title. In his philosophical work *The Myth of Sisyphus* (1942), often seen as complementary to *The Stranger,* Camus writes that grasping the absurd shatters our comforting illusion of outside meaning, creating a feeling of separation and alienation. Anyone who sees the true pointlessness of existence is potentially a "stranger":

> In a universe suddenly divested of illusions and lights, man feels an alien, a stranger. His exile is without remedy since he is deprived of the memory of a lost home or the hope of a promised land [outside meaning, founded on illusions]. This divorce between man and his life, the actor and his setting, is properly the feeling of absurdity.
>
> (Camus in Sprintzen, p. 32)

Yet the absurdity of human existence, the stripping away of one's illusions and the resulting sense of alienation, argues Camus, should not be viewed as a cause for despair. On the contrary, only by acknowledging the absurdity of life does one find true liberation and then happiness, even in the face of death, which is precisely Meursault's situation at the end of the novel.

Sartre would call his philosophy existentialism. The public has linked it not only with the name of Sartre, its founder, but also with that of Camus and especially with *The Stranger*, which has gone down in popular imagination as the classic existentialist novel. Camus would later object that he was not an existentialist. Indeed, in his reviews of both *Nausea* and Sartre's next book, *The Wall* (1939), Camus disagreed with much of the philosophy he found in them. Scholars have cautioned against simplistically labeling *The Stranger* an existentialist work. Nevertheless, while differing in some important ways, Sartre and Camus shared a common outlook, one based on developments in European philosophy during the late nineteenth and early twentieth centuries.

Both Camus and Sartre studied the European philosophers who are generally viewed as forerunners of existentialism—Søren Kierkegaard (Danish, 1813-55), Friedrich Nietzsche (German, 1844-1900), Edmund Husserl (German, 1859-1938), and Martin Heidegger (German, 1889-1976). These philosophers contributed to some of the ideas that surface in *The Stranger*:

- **Alienation.** The novel's Meursault fails to conform to society's expectations because he sees no meaning in those expectations (though often he feels embarrassed for diverging from them).
- **Existence as a concrete phenomenon.** Meursault's narrative focuses on his bodily sensations; it is not a spiritual or metaphysical phenomenon.

- **Lack of absolute moral values.** Meursault does not give any moral weight to the fact that he has killed a man; he regrets that it happened but feels no remorse for killing a human being.
- **Absence of external meaning.** In keeping with the idea that no meaning comes from outside the individual, Meursault angrily rejects a Catholic priest's attempts to absolve him; he denies the existence of God or of an afterlife.

In weighing these ideas, remember that Camus and Sartre studied philosophy while coming of age in the political environment of 1930s France, which is outlined above. They took up the ideas that shaped existentialism in the context of a larger, more general mood of pessimism that grew partly out of that discouraging political atmosphere. At its most extreme, this pessimism gave rise to nihilism, a philosophy according to which there is no value or meaning in human life. To many in the 1930s, the ominous atmosphere seemed to stretch endlessly; finally, in September 1939, it broke into open war. It is the sense of impending catastrophe that gives Meursault's narrative a quality critics have seen as resembling a snapshot—a frozen moment out of time, in the long decade before the French world was shattered by war.

The Novel in Focus

The plot. *The Stranger* is narrated by Meursault, a young French Algerian who works in a shipping office in Algiers. In two parts of equal length, Meursault tells his story in an emotionless, matter-of-fact style exemplified by *The Stranger*'s famous opening lines:

> Mother died today. Or, maybe, yesterday; I can't be sure. The telegram from the Home says: YOUR MOTHER PASSED AWAY. FUNERAL TOMORROW. DEEP SYMPATHY. Which leaves the matter doubtful; it could have been yesterday.
>
> (Camus, *The Stranger*, p. 1)

The old people's home where she lived is in Marengo, about 50 miles outside Algiers, where Meursault lives in the large apartment that he once shared with his mother. Taking two days off work, Meursault goes by an afternoon bus to Marengo. On the bus the glare from the hot sun and the gas fumes make him sleepy. At the home, he meets with the warden of the establishment, who has arranged for Meursault to spend the customary night's vigil by his mother's coffin (customary for Catholics, although Meursault's mother professed not to believe in God). His conversation with the warden makes Meursault feel embarrassed that he did not visit his mother more often, but it would have meant giving up part of his weekend and enduring the long, unpleasant bus journey.

The warden takes him to the mortuary, where he meets the mortuary keeper and the keeper's assistant, an Arab nurse whose face is bandaged as the result of a tumor that has eaten away part of her nose. Meursault declines to view his mother's body, though he again feels embarrassed at the keeper's reaction to this violation of custom. The keeper brings him coffee, and they smoke a cigarette together by the coffin. Waiting for his mother's friends from the home to join him for the vigil, Meursault dozes, waking as they begin to file into the room. After the night-long vigil, Meursault once again declines to view the body. During the long procession to the funeral the next day, the glare and heat from the sun seem oppressive. By the time he catches the bus back to Algiers, Meursault's head is throbbing and he feels dazed and exhausted. He goes straight to bed.

The next day is Saturday, and Meursault still feels exhausted, so he decides to go swimming. At the pool he meets Marie Cardona, a pretty former co-worker, and that night they go to a movie together, a comedy. They begin having an affair; Marie spends the night at Meursault's apartment. On Monday, after coming home from work, Meursault sees his neighbor Salamano, an old man who constantly beats his dog. He also runs into Raymond Sintès, who lives on Meursault's floor. A shady, uneducated character reputed to be a pimp, Raymond claims to work in a warehouse. He invites Meursault to dinner in his apartment, and tells Meursault about problems he is having with his girlfriend, an Arab. Believing that she has been unfaithful, Raymond beat her. He now asks Meursault to write a letter for him telling her off, and Meursault does so before going back to his own apartment.

The following Saturday, Meursault and Marie go swimming at a beach outside Algiers. The next day the police are called to his building after a fight between Raymond and his girlfriend disturbs the occupants. Later that week, Raymond tells Meursault that he has been "shadowed" by "some Arabs," one of whom is the brother of his girlfriend (*The Stranger*, p. 51). He thinks the Arabs want revenge on him for beating the girl. He also invites Meursault and Marie to spend the following Sunday with him and a friend, Masson, at Masson's beach house outside Algiers.

Shortly after that, Marie asks Meursault to marry her, and he casually agrees. She is bothered by his casualness, but he tells her that marriage means nothing, and if it would make her happy, he is willing. A while earlier, offered a promotion that involved more interesting work and a move out of Algiers to Paris, Meursault displayed a similarly nonchalant attitude, his lack of ambition surprising his boss. He seems to float along, not caring about things to which others attach value.

That weekend as they are leaving for the beach, they notice the Arabs following them. After lunch at the beach, a fight erupts in which one of the Arabs stabs Raymond in the arm. Masson and Meursault escort Raymond back to Masson's beach house, and Masson takes Raymond to the doctor. Afterward Raymond produces a revolver and insists on going after the Arabs. A tense confrontation ensues, in which Raymond hands the revolver to Meursault so as to be ready for a hand-to-hand fight. As the young men face each other, Meursault reports, "it crossed my mind that one might fire, or not fire—and it would come to absolutely the same thing" (*The Stranger*, p. 72).

The Arabs suddenly melt away, however, and the Europeans return to the beach house. Later, feeling overcome by the heat and blinding sunlight, Meursault decides to take a walk. When he comes to the spot where the confrontation occurred, he sees that one of the Arabs, the girl's brother, has returned. The Arab reaches into his pocket, and Meursault grips the revolver, which he realizes he is still carrying. As he stands in the sun, Meursault feels "just the same sort of heat as at my mother's funeral" and, unable to take the sun's stifling pressure, he steps forward (*The Stranger*, p. 75). The Arab draws his knife and holds it up in the glinting sun:

> A shaft of light shot upward from the steel, and I felt as if a long, thin blade transfixed my forehead . . . my eyes were blinded; I was conscious only of the cymbals of the sun clashing on my skull. . . . Then everything began to reel before my eyes, a fiery gust came from the sea, while the sky cracked in two, from end to end, and a great sheet of flame poured down through the rift. Every nerve in my body was a steel spring, and my grip closed on the revolver. The trigger gave, and the smooth underbelly of the butt jogged in my palm.
>
> (*The Stranger*, pp. 75-76)

Knowing that he has "shattered the balance of the day," Meursault fires "four more shots into the inert body," each of which constitutes "a loud, fateful rap on the door of my undoing" (*The Stranger*, p. 76). Exactly what has happened is murky. Certainly the gun has gone off in Meursault's hand, but little else is completely clear at this point.

Meursault's shooting of the Arab ends Part 1. Part 2 recounts his imprisonment, trial, and conviction for murder. In the days following the shooting, Meursault's interrogators gradually focus on his mother's funeral. They assert that he "showed great callousness" in not viewing the body, in drinking coffee and smoking casually with the keeper, and in not crying at the burial itself (*The Stranger*, p. 79). Meursault's state-appointed lawyer is dismayed when Meursault cannot bring himself to state that he felt grief at his mother's death. When the examining magistrate asks why Meursault fired the shots, Meursault cannot offer a single word of explanation. He further shocks the magistrate, who is a pious man,

THE JUDICIAL SYSTEM IN FRENCH ALGERIA

Algerian secular courts under French rule continued the court system in effect under the earlier Ottoman Empire, but with adaptations that incorporated French legal principles. French law ultimately goes back to Roman times, though it was modified by the Emperor Napoleon in the early nineteenth century. The most striking difference between Napoleonic law and the Anglo-Saxon tradition of British and American law is that the person on trial is presumed guilty until proven innocent, rather than the reverse. Camus, who covered a number of trials as a reporter for the newspaper *Alger-Républicain,* depicts the Algerian legal system with technical accuracy in *The Stranger.* For example, a prisoner tried on a capital offense would have waited outside the courtroom (as Meursault does in the novel) while the jury's verdict is read. Also Meursault's death sentence—he is ordered to be beheaded—reflects the historical reality that French executions were carried out by beheading with a guillotine. The guillotine came into use during the French Revolution (1789), and was thought to be more humane than hanging. On the other hand, the Irish critic Conor Cruise O'Brien has argued that a trial such as that depicted in *The Stranger* would never have occurred in the first place. Given the judicial bias in favor of the colons, says O'Brien, no colon would ever have been tried for killing a knife-wielding Arab, much less condemned to death.

by denying that he, Meursault, believes in God. Later, the magistrate's anger at Meursault's atheism wears off, and he jokingly calls Meursault "Mr. Antichrist" (*The Stranger*, p. 88). The expression conveys the magistrate's view of Meursault as a moral monster. (It is on this view that the prosecutor will build his case against Meursault more than on the crime itself.) Concluding his questioning, the magistrate sends Meursault to prison to await trial.

In prison Meursault finds that his fellow-prisoners are "mostly Arabs" (*The Stranger*, p. 89). When he tells them he is in prison for killing an Arab, they are silent for a while, but later one shows him how to use the thin mat provided for sleeping on the floor. Later he is moved to a cell by himself, where he occupies his days sleeping, exploring his memories, and weaving an imaginary tapestry around a story told in a scrap of newspaper that he finds in his mattress. Though Meursault spends more than six months in prison waiting for his trial, he "can't say that those months passed slowly" (*The Stranger*, p. 102).

The trial begins on a bright sunny day in June. As he is led into the hot, crowded courtroom, Meursault sees a row of people on the other side, staring hard at him. He guesses that they are the jury. Meursault also spots a reporter, who says that his newspaper has given extensive coverage to Meursault's case. The paper has also covered a more sensational case, one of parricide (the killing of one's father), which is due to come up right after Meursault's trial concludes.

The witnesses called to testify include not only Raymond, Masson, and Marie, but also several of Meursault's friends and acquaintances, as well as people from the home where Meursault's mother died. The crowd is especially indignant on hearing that Meursault had declined to view the body, had fallen asleep, and had then smoked cigarettes and drunk coffee. After Marie's testimony, the prosecutor further characterizes Meursault as a cold-hearted monster "for visiting the swimming pool, starting a liaison with a girl, and going to see a comic film" the day after his mother's funeral (*The Stranger*, p. 118). When Meursault's lawyer asks if Meursault is "on trial for having buried his mother, or for killing a man," the prosecutor responds that Meursault's behavior at his mother's funeral shows that "he was already a criminal at heart" (*The Stranger*, pp. 121-22). Meursault himself does not testify; as he puts it, "I had nothing to say" (*The Stranger*, p. 124). In his closing speech, the prosecutor stresses that Meursault has shown no remorse whatsoever, and Meursault has to agree that he is right. In fact, Meursault realizes he has never really regretted much of anything, and that he lives entirely in the present moment.

After a brief recess, Meursault remains outside the courtroom while the jury reads its verdict. As he is led back in for sentencing, he notices that the reporter no longer meets his eyes. He hears the presiding judge "pronouncing a rigmarole to the effect that 'in the name of the French people' I was to be decapitated in some public place" (*The Stranger*, p. 135). As he waits for the sentence to be carried out, Meursault remains calm until visited by the prison chaplain, who hopes to absolve him of his sins before he dies and passes into the afterlife. Denying the existence of any afterlife and rejecting the idea of sin, Meursault grows enraged at the priest's certainty. He shouts that all he can be certain of is his present life and his impending death. After the priest leaves, the tide of anger that washed over Meursault recedes, leaving him calm and serene. Empty of hope, he lays his "heart open to the benign indifference of the universe" (*The Stranger*, p. 154). He realizes that he is happy. He hopes only that "on the day of my execution there should be a huge crowd of spectators, and that they should greet me with howls of execration" (*The Stranger*, p. 153).

The Arabs as seen by the French. As Meursault, Marie, and Raymond are leaving for Masson's beach house on the Sunday of the murder, Meursault spots the Arabs outside his and Raymond's apartment building: "I saw some Arabs lounging against the tobacconist's window. They

THE SOURCE OF MEURSAULT'S HAPPINESS

By the end of *The Stranger*, Meursault recognizes his existence, all existence, as being absurd, and the recognition becomes the source of his happiness. Everyone dies, so why should he not die by execution and why not now? Will the crowd curse him at the execution? Well, as the world turns, they should. Caught up in the prevailing system of justice, they will just be playing their role in a public display, as will he. Meursault feels content to perform his part in the hand that life has dealt him, to see it through. After all, as he comes to understand life and death, neither one nor the other means anything anyway.

were staring at us silently, in the special way these people have—as if we were blocks of stone or dead trees" (*The Stranger*, p. 61). In the passage are some revealing aspects of the way *The Stranger* presents the Arabs. First, it leaves them nameless; no Arab in the novel is given a name. Second, they remain mute; no Arab in the novel is given dialogue either. Finally, the Arabs themselves are portrayed as seeing the French in the very way that the French see them, as anonymous, voiceless, dehumanized "blocks of stone." Just as Meursault is a stranger in his own society, so are Algeria's two societies—the colonizers and the colonized—strangers to each other in the world of the novel.

Critical responses to the novel's portrayal of Arabs have varied widely. Some have viewed it as betraying racist attitudes on the part of Camus, while others have regarded it as Camus' way of indirectly condemning colonialism and racism. In his other writings, Camus condemns racism, and his daughter Catherine has stated that her father was strict in rebuking his children if they made comments that might be construed as racist. While stopping short of supporting political independence for Algeria's Muslims, Camus was concerned with the plight of native peoples in Algeria. In fact, his most widely read work before *The Stranger* was a series of articles for *Alger-Républicain* exposing the harsh conditions endured by villagers in Algeria's mountainous Kabyle region.

Whatever Camus' own convictions, however, historical consensus suggests that *The Stranger* accurately if symbolically reflects the basic attitude of many French and French Algerians to the Arabs. In seeing a colonized people as voiceless, nameless, and faceless—the novel's deformed Arab nurse, for example, is literally so—the French were not alone. Europeans, it has often been observed, rarely attributed fully human status to the peoples they colonized around the globe. Colonized peoples were most frequently viewed as an undifferentiated mass, incapable or undeserving of individual self-expression. As a French Algerian, Camus belonged to a society shaped by the historical experience of colonialism. Much of his literary artistry lies in the way he uses the philosophical idea of existential alienation to portray this cultural and historical context.

Sources and literary context. A similar philosophical outlook to *The Stranger*'s had helped shape an earlier novel that Camus worked on and then abandoned in his twenties, *A Happy Death* (published posthumously in 1971). *A Happy Death* features a hero named Patrice Mersault who, like Meursault in *The Stranger*, commits a murder that resounds with echoes of the absurd. Though differing in plot details (the murder is committed for money and takes place in Prague), *A Happy Death* has been seen as a youthful experiment that led to *The Stranger*. An entry from August 1937 in Camus' notebooks records his earliest formulation of the themes he would elaborate in *The Stranger*: "A man who had sought life where most people find it (marriage, work, etc.) and who suddenly notices . . . how foreign he has been to his own life" (Camus, *Notebooks 1935-42*, p. 45). Like Patrice Mersault, Meursault was based partly on Camus himself. As Camus' notebooks reveal, he also based Meursault partly on Pascal Pia, the unconventional publisher of *Alger-Républicain*, and partly on Yvonne Ducailar, a philosophy student at Algiers University whom Camus met in 1939 and who became one of his lovers.

As noted, the novel's philosophical background can be traced to Camus' reading of thinkers such as Kierkegaard, Nietzche, and Heidegger. Other, literary influences can be found in the works of diverse writers whom Camus is known to have read and admired. A major idol for Camus—as for his entire literary generation—was the eminent French writer André Malraux (1901-76). Camus discusses Malraux's novel *Man's Fate* (1933) at length in *The Myth of Sisyphus*. Other influences range from Russian novelist Fyodor Dostoyevsky (1821-81) to the terse, spare style of the American writer Ernest Hemingway (1899-1961), who became popular among French readers in the 1930s (see Dostoyevsky's ***Crime and Punishment*** and Hemingway's ***The Old Man and the Sea*** and ***The Sun Also Rises***, also in *Literature and Its Times*.

Reception. With the help of Pascal Pia, Camus was able to have a manuscript of *The Stranger* read by his hero André Malraux. Finding the novel "obviously an important thing," Malraux praised its "power and simplicity" (Malraux in Todd, p. 130). He then recommended it for publication to Gallimard, the leading French publisher, which published it in May 1942. Early reviews were mixed, with many reviewers expressing outrage at the novel's apparent rejection of conventional morality. Nevertheless, the book enjoyed rapid sales and generated much heated discussion. In February 1943, Jean-Paul Sartre—by now a leading French literary figure—published a lengthy, detailed, and highly positive analysis of *The Stranger* for the influential journal *Cahiers du Sud*. Entitled "An Explication of *The*

Stranger," Sartre's 20-page article helped illuminate the puzzling Meursault. Describing Camus' hero as "neither good nor wicked, neither moral nor immoral," Sartre wrote that Camus "reveals a proud humility in . . . his refusal to recognize the limits of human thought," then characterized the novel as "a classical work . . . composed about the absurd and against the absurd" (Sartre in Todd, pp. 155-56). Sartre's review helped establish *The Stranger* as a fundamental examination of existential alienation. Striking a special chord with young adult readers, the novel has since achieved the status of essential reading for students around the world.

—Colin Wells

For More Information

Brée, Germaine, ed. *Camus: A Collection of Critical Essays*. Englewood Cliffs, N.J.: Prentice-Hall, 1962.

Brée, Germaine. *Camus*. New Brunswick, N.J.: Rutgers University Press, 1972.

Camus, Albert. *The Stranger*. Trans. Stuart Gilbert. New York: Vintage, 1946.

———. *Notebooks 1935-1942*. Trans. Philip Thody. New York: Knopf, 1969.

Champigny, Robert J. *A Pagan Hero: An Interpretation of Meursault in Camus'* The Stranger. Trans. Rowe Portis. Philadelphia: University of Pennsylvania Press, 1969.

Cruikshank, John. *Albert Camus and the Literature of Revolt*. Oxford: Oxford University Press, 1960.

Knapp, Bettina L. *Critical Essays on Albert Camus*. Boston: G. K. Hall, 1988.

Lottman, Herbert. *Albert Camus, A Biography*. New York: Doubleday, 1979.

McCarthy, Patrick. *Camus: The Stranger*. Cambridge: Cambridge University Press, 1988.

Sprintzen, David. *Camus: A Critical Interpretation*. Philadelphia: Temple University Press, 1988.

Todd, Olivier. *Albert Camus: A Life*. New York: Knopf, 1997.

The Things They Carried

by
Tim O'Brien

Born and raised in Minnesota, William Timothy O'Brien (1946-) grew up in a middle-class family in the town of Worthington, where his father was a life-insurance salesman and his mother a housewife. After graduating summa cum laude from Macalester College in St. Paul in 1968, O'Brien was drafted into the U.S. Army. From January 1969 to March 1970, he served in Vietnam, mostly as a combat infantry soldier. O'Brien subsequently pursued graduate studies in government at Harvard University. He also worked as a reporter and began writing about his war experiences, which have continued to inspire his literary output. His novels include *If I Die in a Combat Zone, Box Me Up and Ship Me Home* (1973), *Going after Cacciato* (1978), *In the Lake of the Woods* (1994), and *Tomcat in Love* (1998). O'Brien has won numerous prizes for his works, including a National Book Award (1979) for *Going After Cacciato*. Like that novel, *The Things They Carried* is heavily autobiographical, with more or less fictionalized characters and episodes closely based on O'Brien's own war-related memories. Unlike O'Brien's other books, however, *The Things They Carried* features a narrator named Tim O'Brien, whose life closely resembles—but is not identical to—that of the author himself. The novel takes on an intensely introspective approach to the author's mental anguish over the war, an approach that mirrors the larger cultural introspection in America after its traumatizing experience in Vietnam.

THE LITERARY WORK

A novel set largely in America in 1990 and in Vietnam from 1969 to 1970; first published in 1990.

SYNOPSIS

A middle-aged American writer tries to come to terms with his memories of combat during the Vietnam War.

Events in History at the Time of the Novel

The Cold War and Vietnam. Actual fighting by United States combat forces in Vietnam lasted from 1964 to 1973, but grew out of earlier events and produced effects that continue to be felt in the twenty-first century. In fact the war itself remained undeclared, and U.S. military involvement deepened only gradually over a long period, so that historians have difficulty in fixing a starting point for what Americans know as the Vietnam War (the Vietnamese have another name for it—the American War). The end date too does not parallel U.S. withdrawal. Although U.S. forces left in 1973, the fighting in Vietnam continued until 1975, when America's former Vietnamese allies were finally conquered by Soviet- and Chinese-backed Vietnamese communists. U.S. relations with communist Vietnam were not normalized until more than two decades later.

Tim O'Brien

America's involvement in Vietnam must thus be seen within the context of the larger struggle known as the Cold War, a global conflict that pitted the democratic United States against the communist superpowers of the Soviet Union and (to a lesser degree) China. The Cold War followed the end of World War II in 1945 and lasted until the collapse of Soviet communism in 1991, or roughly from Tim O'Brien's boyhood to the publication of *The Things They Carried.* Since the novel features Tim O'Brien's memories and thoughts ranging from childhood up to 1990, its setting in time can accurately be described as covering nearly the entire period of the Cold War.

While O'Brien was growing up in the comfort and security of 1950s America, events were unfolding in Vietnam that would shatter the sense of innocence and purpose that Americans enjoyed in the post-World War II era. Much of Vietnam had been under French colonial rule since the early nineteenth century, but like other European colonial powers, France lost effective control of its colonies during World War II. Resistance movements against the French had long been active in Vietnam and the World War years saw another power targeted as well. The communist Viet Minh movement, under its leader Ho Chi Minh, spearheaded Vietnamese resistance against Japanese occupation, declaring Vietnam independence at the war's end. The Viet Minh went on to lead the opposition to France's attempts to reassert colonial rule in the late 1940s and early 1950s. Meanwhile, in keeping with America's anti-communist policy in the Cold War, the United States supported France's fight against the Viet Minh with both money and arms. But in 1954 the Viet Minh inflicted a catastrophic defeat on the French at the battle of Dien Bien Phu and France withdrew. Vietnam was afterward divided into southern and northern halves. Ho and the Viet Minh ruled North Vietnam; the U.S.-backed Ngo Dinh Diem held sway in South Vietnam.

Not only was Diem's rule of South Vietnam corrupt; it was also unpopular. Elections were planned, after which Vietnam was to be united under a single government. Diem refused to hold the elections, and the United States supported his refusal, recognizing how likely it was that Ho and the communists would have won. The United States came to Diem's aid in another way too. By 1956 it had brought in some 700 military advisors to help his army destroy South Vietnam's communist remnants, former members of the Viet Minh left in the south who now became a guerrilla network known as the Viet Cong (also called the National Liberation Front, or N.L.F.). By the early 1960s, President John F. Kennedy had increased the number of U.S. military advisors to more than 16,000. Recognizing how ineffective Diem was, in 1963 the United States backed a coup that overthrew him. The coup proved useless. It did not bring to power any more stable leadership in the South, which saw a series of unpopular and shaky U.S. puppet rulers come to power. Meanwhile, from North Vietnam, Ho and the communists stepped up

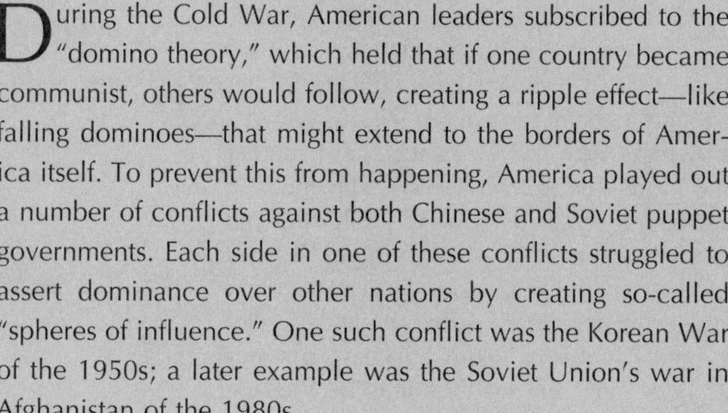

DOMINO THEORY

During the Cold War, American leaders subscribed to the "domino theory," which held that if one country became communist, others would follow, creating a ripple effect—like falling dominoes—that might extend to the borders of America itself. To prevent this from happening, America played out a number of conflicts against both Chinese and Soviet puppet governments. Each side in one of these conflicts struggled to assert dominance over other nations by creating so-called "spheres of influence." One such conflict was the Korean War of the 1950s; a later example was the Soviet Union's war in Afghanistan of the 1980s.

their efforts to take over the South, supporting the Viet Cong's guerrilla campaign by sending men and arms along the Vietnamese border of neighboring Laos. This famous network of routes through the Laotian rain forest became known as the Ho Chi Minh Trail.

America steps directly into the quagmire. A major turning point came in 1964, when North Vietnamese forces fired on a U.S. Navy intelligence-gathering ship in the international waters of the Tonkin Gulf, off the coast of North Vietnam. Although no damage was done, Congress rapidly passed the so-called Tonkin Gulf Resolution, giving President Lyndon Johnson broad powers to step up U.S. military involvement. Johnson and his advisors had already planned bombing raids on North Vietnam, which now began in earnest, and the following year the first U.S. ground troops—about 50,000 soldiers—entered the conflict.

By 1968 Johnson's policy of escalation had gradually but steadily brought the number of American soldiers fighting in Vietnam to nearly 500,000, yet little progress had been made and the war was stalemated. Another major turning point came early that year, when the Viet Cong targeted the South's major cities in a broad attack during celebrations for the lunar New Year or *Tet*. Called the Tet Offensive, this bloody, hard-fought series of battles in the South resulted in a technical victory for South Vietnamese and U.S. forces, but at a steep cost. In the end, an estimated 50,000 Viet Cong soldiers were killed; some 4,000 South Vietnamese and 2,000 American soldiers died. The Tet Offensive's unexpected strength and violence—the Viet Cong came very close to taking the U.S. embassy in the Southern capital, Saigon—dramatically revealed the shortcomings of U.S. strategy. The U.S. media portrayed the Tet Offensive as a disaster, because it was completely unforeseen and because of the early American casualties. Widely publicized in the United States, the Tet Offensive turned the tide of public opinion against the war, convincing many that it could not be won. A growing number, too, saw the war as simply wrong. Among that number was the young Tim O'Brien, who graduated from Macalester College in the spring of 1968, a few months after Tet, and who was drafted into the U.S. Army that same summer.

The U.S. soldiers' experience in Vietnam. U.S. soldiers in Vietnam served under conditions that differed significantly from those Americans had encountered in previous wars. Most importantly, where local people had earlier hailed American troops as liberators (as in World War II), the South Vietnamese government's unpopularity and corruption led many South Vietnamese to view the Americans as hated occupiers. Fighting tactics changed too. Soldiers who had trained for traditional frontline combat against a uniformed enemy found themselves fighting instead against guerrillas who attacked and then disappeared, blending into an often sympathetic surrounding population. On the surface, villagers might seem friendly, but their smiles could conceal deadly intent. Marine Captain E. J. Banks described the resulting uncertainty:

> You never knew who was the enemy and who was a friend. They all looked alike. They all dressed alike. They were all Vietnamese. Some of them were Vietcong. Here's a woman of twenty-two or twenty-three. She is pregnant, and she tells an interrogator that her husband

THE DRAFT AND THE ANTIWAR MOVEMENT

While conscription had existed in America since 1948, in 1965 President Johnson sharply accelerated the draft of young men into the armed forces in order to wage war in Vietnam. From the start, the draft was closely associated with the growing antiwar movement, which began among draft-age students. For example, the first large draft call of nearly 50,000 men was announced on October 14, 1965, and the first large antiwar demonstrations were held in American cities starting the next day. Both the draft and the antiwar demonstrations became increasingly familiar features of American life in the turbulent 1960s.

Equally familiar was the phenomenon of draft evasion. An estimated 570,000 young men avoided military service by illegal means, many by fleeing to Canada (as Tim O'Brien contemplates doing in the novel). A further 15 million men avoided the draft or were exempted by legal means such as student deferments. In all, of 30 million men who became draft age (18) from 1964 to 1973, some 9 million served in uniform and some 2.7 million saw combat in Vietnam. Draft exemptions and deferments commonly went to middle- or upper-class educated whites; minorities and the poor were exposed to the draft and to combat dangers in disproportionately high numbers. In 1965, for example, African Americans comprised 5 percent of the U.S. population, yet they accounted for one in four or 25 percent of all combat deaths in the war.

works in Danang [a South Vietnamese city] and isn't a Vietcong. But she watches your men walk down a trail and get killed or wounded by a booby trap. She knows the booby trap is there, but she doesn't warn them. Maybe she planted it herself. It wasn't like the San Francisco Forty-Niners on one side of the field and the Cincinnati Bengals on the other. The enemy was all around you.

(Banks in Karnow, p. 467)

This pervasive hostility meant that all soldiers found themselves under the constant threat of attack, even those who would otherwise have felt secure, such as office personnel or warehouse workers. Adding to the effects of such stress was the extreme youth of the draftees: the average age of a U.S. soldier in Vietnam was only 19 years old, as compared with 26 years old in World War II. Furthermore, the military's system of rotation called for each soldier to serve only a one-year tour of duty, which meant that at any one time a significant number were inexperienced. The story "The Ghost Soldiers" in *The Things They Carried* illustrates how such inexperience could multiply the risks the soldiers already faced. When Tim O'Brien is wounded, despite the wound's uncritical nature he still nearly dies from shock when a young medic who has just been rotated in freezes in the fear of the moment and fails to give him the simple care he needs.

Platoons like O'Brien's carried out so-called "search-and-destroy" missions, in which a unit would patrol a given area of countryside seeking to engage the Viet Cong or North Vietnamese enemy. Other missions might include "pacifying" or "sweeping" a village, which in practice could mean facing withering Viet Cong sniper and machine-gun fire for several days while struggling to approach a village. When they finally took the village, the soldiers would commonly find only old men and women there. The enemy would vanish into the jungle. Then the soldiers would leave, and the Viet Cong would return.

By the early 1970s, the stressful, frustrating conditions had caused severe morale and discipline problems. As the novel reflects in several places, drug abuse was common. In 1971 an official report estimated that one-third of U.S. soldiers serving in Vietnam were addicted to opium or heroin and suggested that virtually all of them smoked marijuana. Corruption and disobedience grew widespread. A number of overzealous officers were murdered by their own men, who rolled fragmentation grenades into the officers' tents while they slept (a practice called "fragging"). The killings were committed by men unwilling to perform dangerous duties, such as search-and-destroy missions, in hopes that the dead officers' replacements would be less zealous.

The war's impact on American culture. The novel skips over the two decades between the end of Tim O'Brien's tour of duty in 1970 and the setting in 1990 from which he looks back on his war experiences. During that time, the war in Vietnam etched itself deeply into the American psyche, becoming a symbol of national failure and disillusionment. The process took time, however; for several years after the withdrawal of American troops in 1973, Americans seemed inclined to forget about the war completely. Vietnam veterans complained of feeling shunned rather than welcomed home by the society that had sent them to war. In *The Things They Car-*

THE MY LAI MASSACRE

Combat tactics in Vietnam produced general fear and frustration, exacerbating tensions, leaving nerves very raw. On March 16, 1968, American soldiers massacred more than 300 unarmed Vietnamese civilians—mostly women, children, and old men—in the village of My Lai in South Vietnam's Quang Ngai province. The village was supposedly harboring 250 Viet Cong. As it turned out, there were no Viet Cong, and the Americans had encountered no hostile fire: they simply rounded up the villagers and shot them.

> We made them squat down. . . . The mothers was hugging their children. . . . Well, we kept right on firing. They was waving their arms and begging. . . . I still dream about it.
>
> (Private Paul Meadlo in Nash, p. 983)

The stubborn insistence of Vietnam veteran Richard Ridenhour forced the army to investigate the incident, with the result that charges were brought against several soldiers amid wide publicity in 1971. Only one soldier (Lieutenant William Calley) was convicted, however, and another simultaneous mass slaying at nearby My Khe was never investigated at all. Tim O'Brien's platoon served in the Quang Ngai province—O'Brien himself arrived in Vietnam less than a year after the massacre—and the village of My Khe appears several times in *The Things They Carried.* As for the massacre at My Lai, it has come to symbolize the horrible excesses of a war in which soldiers targeted innocent civilians.

ried, the story "Speaking of Courage" focuses on the difficulties faced by returning veterans. As historian Stanley Karnow suggested in 1983, it was "as if the nation has projected onto them its own sense of guilt or shame or humiliation for the war" (Karnow, p. 25). Only in the late 1970s did the war in Vietnam begin appearing as a subject in popular books and movies. Then, as later, soldiers in Vietnam were often portrayed as drug-crazed, brutalized killers, an image that also attached itself to popular portrayals of returned Vietnam veterans.

The war also had a profound impact on American politics. Noting the public's growing distrust of politicians since the Vietnam era, historians have attributed much of it to the fact that presidents Kennedy, Johnson, and Nixon regularly lied to the public in order to justify their conduct of the war. In addition, the war has overshadowed virtually every overseas American military involvement since. Both political and military leaders, as well as the general public, have commonly used the phrase "No more Vietnams" to invoke caution about committing U.S. armed forces on foreign soil. In the 1980s the U.S. military underwent far-reaching reforms as a result of the war, the most important of which was the end of the draft (1973) and the switch to an all-volunteer force. These reforms were tested the year after the novel's publication in the Persian Gulf War (1991). America's rapid victory allowed President George Bush to proclaim, "By God, we've kicked the Vietnam syndrome once and for all"—revealing more than anything else just how powerful a hold Vietnam still had on the public imagination (Neu, p. 31).

The Novel in Focus

Contents overview. Though usually referred to as a novel, *The Things They Carried* has also been called a collection of short stories. Its 22 stories are indeed unconnected by any overarching plot, but all are linked by reappearing characters from the narrator's platoon, Alpha Company, and most by the narrator's first-person voice. A few (including the initial story, "The Things They Carried," from which the collection takes its title) are told in the third-person. The stories range in length from just over one page to 30 pages.

In general, the pieces can be divided into two categories: narratives (which usually relate a particular episode or episodes) and essay-like commentaries. The five longest pieces are all narratives: "The Things They Carried," "On the Rainy River," "Sweetheart of the Song Tra Bong," "Speaking of Courage," and "The Ghost Soldiers." Shorter pieces include both narratives (such as "Spin," "Stockings," and "Enemies") and reflections (such as "How to Tell a True War Story,"

American soldiers during the Vietnam war, anxiously open mail that has arrived from home.

POST TRAUMATIC STRESS DISORDER

World War I veterans knew it as "shell shock," World War II veterans as "combat fatigue," but psychologists use the clinical label "Post Traumatic Stress Disorder" (P.T.S.D.) to describe the psychological condition suffered by many returning Vietnam veterans. After an initial trauma such as combat, the victim of P.T.S.D. usually experiences a period of numbness followed by irritability, depression, and often, intense feelings of guilt at having survived while others perished. Flashbacks, nightmares, and violent outbursts may also occur, especially if provoked by a sensory stimulus that recalls the circumstances of the initial trauma. A backfire, for example, may provoke physical symptoms of panic, as if the victim were being fired upon, causing the victim to relive the traumatic experience. Since the Vietnam era, psychologists have recognized P.T.S.D. as a possible outcome of any strong psychological trauma, from automobile accidents to hostage incidents.

"Notes," and the final piece, "Lives of the Dead"). While the narratives may include brief allusions to the narrator's later vantage point, they are generally set mostly during the war itself (two exceptions are "Speaking of Courage," set in 1975, and "Field Trip," set in 1990). Conversely, the essays generally look back in time from a later standpoint, and often qualify or comment on a preceding narrative.

Contents summary. The title story introduces some of the men of Alpha Company who are the novel's major reappearing characters: the platoon's commander, Lieutenant Jimmy Cross; the experienced medic Rat Kiley; the part-Native American called Kiowa, who is also a devout Baptist; and Norman Bowker, who is "otherwise a very gentle person," but who carries a desiccated human thumb "cut from a VC [Viet Cong] corpse" as a good-luck charm (O'Brien, *The Things They Carried*, p. 13). The story focuses on Jimmy Cross, who is preoccupied by thoughts of Martha, a girl at home, and who consequently blames himself for the death of a soldier named Ted Lavender. Cross's problems unfold in briefly related episodes interspersed with descriptions of the weapons, gear, and personal items that the soldiers carry—as well as the metaphorical burdens they also bear, such as Cross's feelings of guilt. A brief reflective essay called "Love" then comments on the story, relating how Jimmy Cross has visited the narrator "many years after the war" and revealed that he still loves Martha, whom he saw at a high school reunion in 1979 but who rejected his advances and became a missionary (*The Things They Carried*, p. 29).

The next two pieces, "Spin" and "On the Rainy River," combine episodic fragments from the past with the narrator's later reflections. The brief and fragmentary "Spin" is set during the war, while the longer "On the Rainy River" relates Tim O'Brien's reactions in the summer of 1968 after he learns that he has been drafted. Driving north to the Rainy River on the Canadian border, he stays for six days in a motel as he contemplates fleeing across the border. The motel's perceptive owner, an older man named Elroy Berdahl, asks no questions, but befriends him and takes him fishing on the river, as if aware of the boy's dilemma and need to make a choice. Although O'Brien's conscience tells him not to participate in a war he feels is wrong, in the end he decides not to cross the river: "I was a coward. I went to war," the story ends (*The Things They Carried*, p. 63). Two shorter linked pieces, "Enemies" and "Friends," describe how two soldiers fight over a trivial matter but then later become fast friends, until one has his leg blown off and dies.

In one piece, "How to Tell a True War Story," Tim O'Brien discusses storytelling and the nature of truth. He tells a story about the death of a soldier named Curt Lemon, assuring the reader "it's all exactly true" but then qualifying that statement by suggesting that truth is not equivalent to factuality: "Absolute occurrence is irrelevant. A thing may happen and be a total lie; another thing may not happen and be truer than the truth" (*The Things They Carried*, pp. 77, 89). Later, in the brief essay "Good Form," he calls mere factuality "happening-truth," which he distinguishes from the more deeply significant "story-truth" (*The Things They Carried*, p. 203).

In another narrative, "Sweetheart of the Song Tra Bong," Rat Kiley tells the platoon a tale he has heard, the story of Mary Anne Bell, the 17-year-old girlfriend of a soldier named Mark Fossie. Circumventing army regulations somehow, Fossie daringly arranges for his young high-school sweetheart to travel from America and join his combat unit, encamped on the Song Tra Bong River. Though timid at first, the pretty and athletic girl soon begins to enjoy the routine of army life. Gradually, however, Fossie realizes that she is spending time with a small detachment of six Special Forces men, Green Berets, who have a base nearby from which they conduct their secret missions into the jungle. Though at first he suspects she is having an affair with one of the Green Berets, in fact the girl has been seduced by jungle warfare. She eventually completes her transformation by donning a necklace of human tongues, and the story ends with her simply vanishing into the jungle, where she is thought to have merged with the shadows and darkness.

In two stories, "The Man I Killed" and "Ambush," Tim O'Brien recounts his feelings after killing a young Vietnamese man he has encountered on a trail. He cannot stop staring at the man's body:

> He lay at the center of the trail, his right leg bent beneath him, his one eye shut, his other eye a huge star-shaped hole. It was not a matter of live or die. There was no real peril. Almost certainly the young man would have passed by. And it will always be that way. Later, I remember, Kiowa tried to tell me that the man would've died anyway. He told me it was a good kill, that I was a soldier and this was a war, that I should shape up and stop staring. . . . Even now I haven't finished sorting it out. Sometimes I forgive myself, other times I don't.
>
> (*The Things They Carried*, p. 149)

"Speaking of Courage" tells the story of another member of Tim O'Brien's platoon, Norman Bowker, following his return to his hometown in Iowa. Bowker feels responsible for the death of Kiowa, who literally drowned in human excrement during a firefight when the platoon was encamped in what turned out to be a field of sewage. Frozen in panic, Bowker could not bring himself to move and pull the wounded Kiowa out of the stinking sewage. Now, back in Iowa, he simply drives in circles around town, feeling aimless and out of place. In "Notes," the essay that follows, Tim O'Brien states that he wrote the story in 1975, after getting a letter from Bowker, and that Bowker killed himself three years later. He ends the essay by declaring:

> In the interests of truth, however, I want to make it clear that Norman Bowker was in no way responsible for what happened to Kiowa. Norman did not experience a failure of nerve that night. He did not freeze up. . . . That part of the story is my own.
>
> (*The Things They Carried*, p. 182)

The next story, "In the Field," also features Kiowa's death, as does "Field Trip." This second story, set "a few months after completing 'In the Field,'" describes Tim O'Brien's return, 20 years later with his ten-year-old daughter Kathleen, to the place where Kiowa died (*The Things They Carried*, p. 207).

Another of the longer narratives, "The Ghost Soldiers," relates how Tim O'Brien was wounded and recounts his revenge on the inexperienced medic who replaced his friend Rat Kiley after the latter suffered a nervous breakdown. The fear-stricken youngster neglected to give Tim O'Brien basic treatment for shock after Tim O'Brien was shot in the buttock, with the result that Tim O'Brien nearly died from what should have been a minor wound. Tim O'Brien later takes revenge by terrifying the young medic while the man is on nighttime guard duty. The next narrative, "Night Life," tells the story of Rat Kiley's breakdown. A final essay, "The Lives of the Dead," relates Tim O'Brien's feelings of loss and guilt over the war to similar feelings he carries from childhood, when a little girl he loved died from a brain tumor. He begins the tale by declaring "this is true: stories can save us" and ends on a similar note, saying that now he is a middle-aged writer trying to save the life of the young boy he once was "with a story" (*The Things They Carried*, pp. 255, 273).

Credibility gaps. In interviews Tim O'Brien has maintained the disregard of factual truth that he proclaims in *The Things They Carried*. He at one moment, for example, asserts that a real person named Norman Bowker existed, then declares a moment later that "there was no Norman Bowker" (Naparsteck, p. 6). Indeed, the novel's copyright page features a disclaimer describing it as "a work of fiction" and stating that "except for a few details regarding the author's own life, all the incidents, names, and characters are imaginary" (*The Things They Carried*, copyright page). Facing that page, however, the reader finds that the book is "lovingly dedicated to the men of Alpha Company, and in particular Jimmy Cross, Norman Bowker, Rat Kiley, Mitchell Sanders, Henry Dobbins, and Kiowa," all of whom are named characters in the novel (*The Things They Carried*, dedication).

Of course, such contradictory statements may amount to no more than purposeful literary ambiguity, and have certainly occurred in other postmodern literary works that have nothing to do with America's war in Vietnam. Yet it is striking to note that historians have found a similar disregard of factual truth to be the defining feature of the attitude that allowed American politicians to prosecute the war. By 1968 this so-called "credibility gap"—that is, the gap between what the government said was happening in Vietnam and what was actually happening there—had become a major pillar of the growing antiwar movement. The Tonkin Gulf incident serves as an example. In the summer of 1964, U.S. naval destroyers suffered two attacks in the Gulf of Tonkin. Although they did no real damage and U.S. planes retaliated, the incident was used as a pretext to win approval for a massive bombing campaign against North Vietnam, one that had already been carefully planned by the Johnson administration.

The credibility gap has remained a central part of American public life ever since. As historian Brian Balogh puts it, the willingness of America's leaders to lie about Vietnam created a situation in which Americans "no longer trusted their public officials" (Balogh in Neu, p. 34).

Another historian, Christopher Lasch, observes that

> It was because prestige and credibility had become the only measure of effectiveness that American policy in Vietnam could be conducted without regard to . . . the political situation in that country. . . . The object of American policy in Vietnam was defined from the outset as the preservation of American credibility.
>
> (Lasch, p. 78)

More important than any actual success in the war was the appearance of success, Lasch argues, for the appearance was what maintained the government's credibility both at home and with its Cold War allies. Indeed, the appearance of success was equated with success itself: if America appeared to have succeeded, then it had succeeded.

Scarred by a war based on a political credibility gap, O'Brien created a novel with a literary credibility gap. This gap makes it impossible for the reader to take the novel's statements at face value. It also differs strikingly in purpose from the political credibility gap, which manipulated truth to justify the war in Vietnam to the public. O'Brien's gap, in contrast, dismisses "absolute occurrence" in the interest of exposing deeper truths that underlie the events of the war rather than focusing on the events themselves.

Sources and literary context. Without attempting to pierce Tim O'Brien's carefully constructed veil of authorial ambiguity, suffice it to say that his personal experiences in the war (and after) provide models and inspiration for characters and events in *The Things They Carried.* Two apparent exceptions are "Sweetheart of the Song Tra Bong" and "The Man I Killed." "Sweetheart of the Song Tra Bong" derives its ultimate inspiration from Joseph Conrad's novella ***Heart of Darkness*** (1902; also in *Literature and Its Times*), in which a European named Kurtz descends into moral decay in central Africa. "The Man I Killed," in which Tim O'Brien briefly imagines details from the life of a young Vietnamese man he kills with a hand grenade, recalls in both its title and subject matter Thomas Hardy's poem "The Man He Killed" (1909), about a soldier the speaker has killed in combat.

O'Brien is often compared with Philip Caputo and Ron Kovic, two Vietnam veterans who wrote well-known memoirs of their experiences: Caputo's is entitled *A Rumor of War* (1977); Kovic's, *Born on the Fourth of July* (1976). Both believed in the war at first, taking a stance against it only after having served. As O'Brien has pointed out, he differs from both in that he opposed the war when he was drafted, a fact he sees as increasing his own guilt for having participated.

Reception. *The Things They Carried* won the *Chicago Tribune*'s Heartland Prize in 1990, and was highly praised by a chorus of reviewers. Writing in the *New York Times Book Review*, Robert R. Harris places the novel not only on "the short list of essential fiction about [the American war in] Vietnam," but "high up on the list of best fiction about any war" (Harris, Robert, p. 8). Praising the "bleak immediacy" of the novel's interconnected stories, Julian Loose in the *Times* (of London) *Literary Supplement* writes that "O'Brien fully exploits the freedoms offered by the [story] sequence, a form which encourages variety and experimentation" (Loose, p. 705). A few critics have taken issue with O'Brien's deliberate blurring of fact and fiction, such as the *Wall Street Journal*'s Bruce Bawer, who calls it "disingenuous game playing" (Bawer, p. A13). Others have objected to the stories' introspective focus, characterizing O'Brien's treatment of, for example, female and Vietnamese perspectives as superficial or nonexistent. Most, however, would agree with Richard Eder, writing in the *Los Angeles Times*: "The fuller justification for *The Things They Carried* is the writing itself," which Eder praises as possessing "the sharp edge of a honed vision" (Eder, p. 3).

—Colin Wells

For More Information

Bawer, Bruce. "Confession or Fiction? Stories from Vietnam." *Wall Street Journal*, 23 March 1990, A13.

Eder, Richard. "Has He Forgotten Anything?" *Los Angeles Times Book Review*, 1 April 1990, 3, 11.

Harris, David. *Our War*. New York: Random House, 1996.

Harris, Robert R. "Too Embarrassed Not to Kill." *New York Times Book Review,* 11 March 1990, 8.

Herzog, Tobey C. *Tim O'Brien*. New York: Twayne, 1997.

Karnow, Stanley. *Vietnam: A History*. New York: Viking, 1983.

Lasch, Christopher. *The Culture of Narcissm*. New York: Norton, 1979.

Loose, Julian. "The Story That Never Ends." *Times Literary Supplement*, no. 4552 (29 June-5 July 1990): 705.

Naparsteck, Martin. "An Interview." *Contemporary Literature* 32, no. 1 (spring 1991): 1-11.

Nash, Gary B., et al. *The American People: Creating a Nation and a Society*. Vol 2. New York: Harper & Row, 1990.

Neu, Charles E., ed. *After Vietnam: Legacies of a Lost War*. Baltimore: Johns Hopkins, 2000.

O'Brien, Tim. *The Things They Carried*. New York: Penguin, 1990.

"Tuesday Siesta" and "One of These Days"

by
Gabriel García Márquez

Gabriel García Márquez, winner of the Nobel Prize for Literature in 1982, was born March 6, 1927, in Aracataca, a small town in the Caribbean coastal region of Colombia. His grandparents reared him and during this time he heard many of the stories from his grandmother that would later influence his writing. After abandoning law studies, García Márquez began to write articles for the newspaper *El Heraldo* and to publish short stories. "Tuesday Siesta" and "One of These Days" are among the first stories published in the collection, *Los funerales de la mamá grande* (*Big Mama's Funeral,* published as a set in *No One Writes to the Colonel and Other Stories,* 1968). They form part of the cycle of Macondo, a series of tales based in a fictional village modeled on Aracataca. Macondo serves as the setting not only for many of García Márquez's short stories, but also for many of his novels beginning with his first one, *Leafstorm* (1955), and lasting through the release of his masterpiece ***One Hundred Years of Solitude*** (1967; also in *Literature and Its Times*). The two short stories focused on here describe a couple of unrelated incidents in Macondo in ways that refer subtly to an undeclared civil war between Liberals and Conservatives in Colombia known as La Violencia.

THE LITERARY WORKS

Two short stories set in the fictional town of Macondo, Colombia, in the 1950s; published in Mexico (as "La siesta del martes" and "Un día de estos") in 1962, in English in 1968.

SYNOPSIS

In "Tuesday Siesta" a mother travels to a village cemetery where her son has been buried after breaking into a home and being killed by the homeowner. In "One of These Days" a dentist takes revenge when he extracts a tooth from his village's mayor.

Events in History at the Time the Short Stories Take Place

La Violencia—historical background. A dispute between two political parties (the Liberals and the Conservatives), the undeclared civil war known as La Violencia roughly spanned the decade 1948-58 in Colombia. Conflicts between the Liberal and Conservative parties in Colombian politics date back to the nineteenth century. Traditionally the Conservative Party has supported the Catholic Church and the landed aristocracy while the Liberal Party has been more influenced by the middle classes. Membership in one party or the other has sometimes depended more on birth than convictions; for this reason, some members "born into" one party may have political beliefs that resemble those of the other party. Speaking of the strength of the Catholic Church in Colombia, rather than aligning it with one side or the other García Márquez once wrote: "the only difference between conservatives and liberals in Colombia is that the conservatives go to mass earlier" (García Márquez in Williams and Guerrieri, p. 15).

Gabriel García Márquez

Earlier in the twentieth century, before the breakout of the civil war known as La Violencia, Colombia experienced rapid and self-conscious modernization and industrialization under a series of Liberal governments. A mildly reformist president, Enrique Olaya Herrera (1930-34) instituted the Progressive Modern State, a Liberal party project. Herrera, a mildly reformist president, governed the National Concentration, a coalition of Liberals and Conservatives, one of whose most important legacies was an insistence on the development of highways connecting Colombian towns. Historically the different regions of Colombia had been severely isolated from each other because of geographic phenomenon. Three Andean mountain ranges and two major rivers separate the regions—the Magdalena River, which flows to the Caribbean Sea, and the Cauca River, which empties into the Pacific Ocean. Its early network of highways distinguished Colombia from other Latin American countries, as did the extensive air transportation system that it built as early as the 1920s. These systems helped break down the regional isolation. The railroad system, however, was not extensively developed until much later and did not connect all the major centers. The two large cities Bogotá and Medellín remained unconnected from railway transportation until 1960.

During his leadership, Alfonso López Pumarejo (1934-38) created La Revolución en Marcha ("Revolution on the March"), which promoted land reform and modernization within Colombia. Under the succeeding Liberal government of Eduardo Santos (1938-42), there followed a period known as the "Great Pause," a name ascribed to his tenure because it was less progressive than earlier Liberal governments. Problems associated with World War II and corruption within the Liberal Party marred the next presidency, that of López Pumarejo (1942-45), which led to the Conservative Mariano Ospina Pérez's winning the election for president in 1946.

One of the reasons for the failure of López Pumarejo's second term is the drop in industrialists' support of his presidency: in his second term, they joined the landowners to resist the labor movements organizing among the lower classes. Ospina Pérez was able to take over power from the Liberals as the first Conservative Party president in 16 years because of the Liberal Party's internal divisions. The shift in power caused an increase in political violence, mainly in the rural regions. Although Ospina Pérez was a Conservative, the majority of the political officials in the rural areas were Liberals and the shift to a Conservative government provoked violence between the existing Liberal pockets and the incoming Conservatives. Many of the Conservatives were upper-class landowners with ties to the Catholic Church and they received favorable treatment from the new Conservative government. In contrast, the outgoing Liberals were tied to the rural masses and dedicated to social and economic reforms that would favor them. Conservative politicians in the rural areas, under the government's protection, resorted to violence in an attempt to stamp out Liberal strongholds. Rural guerrillas began to work independently, fighting against the local government and soldiers. Many villagers, with no recourse for justice, were caught between the rural guerrillas, the government soldiers, and the local political strongmen, or *caudillos*.

La Violencia—the death-filled decade. On April 9, 1948, Jorge Eliécer Gaitán, the populist candidate representing the Liberal Party, was assassinated in Bogotá, Colombia. Along with the following popular uprising, this event in Bogotá, known as the *Bogotazo*, marks what most sources identify as the beginning of a ten-year period known as La Violencia. During the Bogotazo riot, around 2,000 people were killed and much of downtown Bogotá was destroyed. (The duration is in some dispute—some historians date La Violencia from 1946, adding that the civil war did not die out entirely until the 1980s.) It is believed that roughly between 200,000 and 300,000 people died in La Violencia, during which most of the violence centered in the rural areas of the country.

Toward the end of López Pumarejo's Liberal government (1942-45) and at the beginning of Ospina Pérez's Conservative government (1946-50), rural violence escalated. Civilians, including the minority of rural Conservatives, had less and less say in the governing of the country and they lashed out by violently attacking Liberals across the countryside. Although the National Police supported the Liberal party, rural police officers took the Conservatives' side and aided in much of the violence committed against the Liberals—which extended to burning the houses of Liberal supporters. During Laureano Gómez's Conservative presidency (1950-53), the divisions and violence among rural sectors became more of an issue of support for or resistance against the president himself, mainly due to his increasing repression in an attempt to contain the violence.

Toward the end of La Violencia, the Conservative government of Laureano Gómez (1950-53) suffered a coup d'état by Gustavo Rojas Pinilla, who governed as dictator of Colombia from 1953 until his forced resignation in 1957. Although at first the Rojas Pinilla government did not appear to be dictatorial, it soon became evident that it was. (It was to be the only military dictatorship in Colombia in the twentieth century.) Though the dictator took steps to extinguish La Violencia, his government itself was riddled with brutality and corruption. One example of the increasing brutality of the dictator was the 'Bullring Massacre' of February 5, 1956, in which supporters of the dictator killed fans point blank simply because they failed to cheer for the president. In effect, the dictator had passed a law that made it illegal to speak negatively about him. As a result, during his dictatorship freedom of the press was hampered by government censorship. Its censorship extended as well to novelist and short story writers of the period, including García Márquez. Rojas Pinilla's top officials asked the dictator to surrender, after which they governed until peace agreements were signed and a new government took control in 1958. One of the major events that led to Rojas Pinilla's resignation and temporary time of exile in Spain was the growing discontent from both Liberals and Conservatives over the increased violence perpetuated by his government. When he ordered the arrest of Guillermo León Valencia, a Conservative leader who had been supporting the talks between Liberals and Conservatives attempting to establish what was later to be the National Front system, riots broke out. Eventually this led to the general disapproval of his dictatorship by the Church and the military. The new National Front government brought La Violencia to its unofficial end.

PRESIDENTS IN THE PRE-LA VIOLENCIA AND LA-VIOLENCIA ERAS

1934-38: Alfonso López Pumarejo (Liberal)
1938-42: Eduardo Santos (Liberal)
1942-45: Alfonso López Pumarejo (Liberal)
1945-46: Alberto Lleras Camargo (Liberal)
1946-50: Mariano Ospina Pérez (Conservative)
1950-53: Laureano Gómez (Conservative)
1953-57: Gustavo Rojas Pinilla (military dictatorship)

There followed a period of joint control, with the reins of government alternating between the Liberal and Conservative parties. This joint arrangement, provided for by the National Front agreements, would last until 1974, including the following successive governments:

- Liberal: Alberto Lleras Camargo (1958-62)
- Conservative: Guillermo León Valenica (1962-66)
- Liberal: Carlos Lleras Restrepo (1966-70)
- Conservative: Misael Pastrana Borrero (1970-74)

Economic situation in Columbia during La Violencia. In the years leading up to La Violencia, living conditions in Colombia reached an alarming low for well over half the population, who farmed barely enough to subsist. In 1938, 81 percent of the buildings in Colombia were without electricity, water, and plumbing (Bejarano Ávila, pp. 153-54). In the 1940s and '50s, well over half of the population was marginalized from the economy, living in poverty in isolated, rural regions, where villagers were very vulnerable to the ongoing violence of the period. They could not rely on local government to protect them since the local officials were often themselves tied to the violence. The plight of the lower classes persisted while the upper classes enjoyed a steady increase in their income. This highlights a situation in Colombia that is common in many Latin

American countries: the gap between the rich and the poor has historically been very wide, the upper classes sharing first-world conveniences at the same time that the remaining inhabitants live in third-world conditions. Colombia's lower classes, in dire need of social and economic changes, were ignored by many administrations, such as Rojas Pinilla's. Later, during the succession of Liberal and Conservative governments, those in control did not tend to the lower classes either. Much of the money was directed toward those who were already wealthy—top military officials, church leaders, local officials—rather than those who sorely needed it—the rural masses who were forced to subsist on what few resources they could gather.

Soul-searching aftereffects. Many scholars are still trying to define the events surrounding La Violencia in terms of their impact on Colombian government and society. Certainly La Violencia played a key role in shaping the national consciousness, comparable only to one other episode in Columbia's history—its earlier War of a Thousand Days (1899-1903). During this earlier war, tensions between the authoritarian state and a Liberal opposition mounted until the Liberals revolted against the rigid presidency of Manuel Antonio Sanclemente. Both La Violencia and the earlier War of a Thousand Days forced Colombians to contemplate the kind of government their country had traditionally implemented and the type of government they would have in the future.

Attempts to define La Violencia in the years following the civil war show that it left the nation with many questions about what exactly occurred and why. There was agreement about one facet of it, however—the final 1950s government of Rojas Pinilla ushered in, above all else, a period of political repression. Like the literary censorship, this political repression left a lasting impact on the generation of García Márquez.

Hand-in-hand with the repression came developments that bolstered the strength of the opposition. In 1949 Mario Laserna founded the Universidad de los Andes, an institution modeled after the American private university. This marked the turning point in the rejection of the colonial *ciudad letrada.* ("lettered city"), the old model in which writing and power intermixed to create a ruling aristocracy surrounded by an elite group of intellectuals (churchmen, educators, and professionals). Instead of espousing the conservative traditions of the old educational institutions, this new university began a tradition of more technologically friendly education geared toward modernization.

The period of the National Front that followed La Violencia further stimulated the growth of the opposition. The 1960s saw an upsurge of leftist guerrilla movements such as the FARC (Fuerzas Armadas Revolucionarias de Colombia [Revolutionary Armed Forces of Colombia]) and the ELN (Ejército de Liberación Nacional [National Liberation Army]). In the early 1970s, the first groups professing adherence to the communist tenets of Leon Trotsky began to attract attention. García Márquez, whose *One Hundred Years of Solitude* was a nationally celebrated event in 1967, selling copies as quickly as they were published, founded the leftist magazine *Alternative* in 1974. For this brief interlude in a mostly rigid history, the government tolerated dissent but the days of toleration were numbered. As the 1970s progressed, internal problems weakened the National Front, leading to increasingly authoritarian and exclusionary practices.

La Violencia affected García Márquez personally, forcing him to leave Bogotá, and the chaos that followed the assassination of Eliécer Gaitán (1948), to seek refuge in Cartagena, Colombia. Before returning to Bogotá, he moved to Barranquilla, which brought him into contact with a group of intellectuals and writers (the Barranquilla Group), who would influence his later work. García Márquez remained here for a time, studying and working as a reporter. He returned to Bogotá in 1954, traveled to Paris the following year as a correspondent for the newspaper *El Espectador,* then found himself unemployed when the Colombian government closed it down. During the ensuing three years, García Márquez remained in Paris and worked on the manuscripts for *In Evil Hour* and *No One Writes to the Colonel*. He also wrote many of the stories that would appear in *Big Mama's Funeral*. Although outside Colombia, he produced stories haunted by the social, historical, and political realities of his country. Unlike other writers who covered La Violencia in documentary-style narrative that meticulously described the brute violence and misery, García Márquez alluded to the civil war through understatement.

The novel of La Violencia. More than 100 Colombian novels can be considered products of La Violencia. They deal with assassinations, death, injustices, and other violent crimes in an explicit, direct style that conveys realistic descriptions of the violence of the Colombian civil war. One of the Liberal novels that describes the violence during this time period in a documentary style is Pedro Gómez Corena's *El 9 de abril* (1951; The 9th of April). It explicitly narrates the violent events following the 1948 assassination of Jorge Eliécer Gaitán, known as the Bogotazo. Many such blatantly violent, Liberal novels confused or held little appeal for readers who were either uninformed about the political events or uninterested in them. Moreover, the content of the Liberally slanted novels was not what the Conservative upper class wanted to read. They were generally ignored or censored by the Conservative establishment. Other novels of the period took distinctly Conservative positions. Also written in slanted documentary style, these novels served as a form of propaganda for the government. Alonso Hilarión Sánchez, for example, defends the Conservatives in *Las balas de la ley* (1953; The Bullets of the Law), which features a narrator-protagonist who describes the violence perpetrated by the Liberals during the 1930s and '40s. Actually, since the 1840s, when the first brief fictionalized political pamphlets were published as novels, aesthetic value in Colombia has largely been determined by the politics of those in power.

In contrast to the realism, as well as the propaganda, García Márquez's stories refer to La Violencia indirectly through various techniques, including symbolic allusions and understatement. His stories were the first though not the only ones to treat La Violencia in this subtle and indirect manner. Four other novels that tended to follow the same path of insinuation include: Manuel Zapata Olivella's *La calle 10* (1960; 10th Street), García Márquez's own *La mala hora* (1962; *In Evil Hour,* 1979), Mejía Vallejo's *El día señalado* (1963; The Assigned Day), and Álvarez Gardeazábal's *Cóndores no entierran todos los días* (1972; Condors Don't Bury Everyday). In *El día señalado,* for example, Mejía Vallejo stimulates reader involvement through the structure of his novel and its changes in point of view. The novel tells of a town overtaken by La Violencia as government soldiers pursue rural guerrillas and relates a personal story of violence; worthy of blame for the mayhem is not party politics but acts of human irrationality. The reader of *La mala hora* encounters virtually no physical violence; rather, the power in this novel is wielded by language. The town's secrets are revealed through written documents that are so powerful as to strike terror into the villagers.

Unlike much of the fiction of the period, the four novels named above work indirectly, inviting the reader to reflect upon and accept or reject the many interpretations of La Violencia. Censorship promoted this indirect approach to the issues raised by La Violencia. García Márquez's own *In Evil Hour* became subject to censorship, constituting an example of the handicaps under which writers labored. The novel was originally published in 1962 but a proofreader and an editor made two major changes that caused García Márquez to reject the edition and publish the novel in Mexico in 1966 as he had originally written it. The changes made, concerning the words "masturbate" and "condom," reflect the conservative atmosphere of Colombia in the 1960s as well as the level of censorship with which Colombian writers had to deal (McNerney, p. 120).

The Short Stories in Focus

The plot. In "Tuesday Siesta" a mother travels by train to a village where her son has been buried after breaking into a house and being killed by Rebecca, the house's owner. The woman travels with her daughter—whose name, like her own, is never revealed. We do learn, however, that the daughter is still a child and that the murdered son was named Carlos Centeno Ayala. Aside from Rebecca's and Carlos's names, the only other name given is the man's who owns the gun used by Rebecca to kill Carlos, Aureliano Buendía, a character who will reappear in *One Hundred Years of Solitude.*

The third-person narrative begins by describing the train ride, including the unbearable heat and humidity to which the mother and daughter are subjected. It is evident from the beginning that they are a family of modest means: "They were both in severe and poor mourning clothes" (García Márquez, "Tuesday Siesta," p. 65). There is an air of resignation and serenity about the mother. She instructs the daughter on the necessity of guarding her dignity. The mother asks the daughter to put on her shoes and comb her hair, then gives her some firm directions: "If you feel like doing anything, do it now," said the woman. "Later, don't take a drink anywhere even if you're dying of thirst. Above all, no crying" ("Tuesday Siesta," pp. 66-67).

Upon arriving at the village, the mother must go to the parish house to retrieve the key to enter the cemetery where her son is buried. When they arrive, the priest is napping but the mother insists on speaking with him. His sister awakens him and he finally greets the mother and daughter. He is evidently surprised and not a little intrigued when he finds that they are the family of Carlos Centeno Ayala, the boy killed the previous week. When the priest questions the mother about her upbringing of Carlos, she answers: "I told him never to steal anything that anyone needed to eat, and he minded me. On the other hand, before, when he used to box, he used to spend three days in bed, exhausted from being punched" ("Tuesday Siesta," p. 71). Although boxers did not make large amounts of money, the sport was one of the few avenues of upward mobility open to the lower classes in Colombia. Carlos would have boxed to earn what money he could to fight off his family's poverty. The mother's answers illustrate the set of morals that families such as this tended to live by, taking only from those who can afford it and never taking from those, like themselves, who must fight to survive. No such set of morals governs the actions of the rural power mongers. The mother defends her son's apparent choice to earn a living this way as more dignified than having to physically suffer and be humiliated. (The mother's words also highlight a pervasive aspect of Colombian society at the time of the collection's publication: much of the population lived in extreme poverty and saw themselves forced to break upper-class rules to be able to survive.) The last words of the story reinforce the self-sufficient attitude that the mother taught her son and that she practices herself; by this time a crowd, who knows her to be the mother of a thief, has formed around the parish house: "She took the girl by the hand and went into the street" ("Tuesday Siesta," p. 72). The personification of human dignity, the mother continues on to the cemetery despite the disapproving onlookers.

"One of These Days" features village dentist, Aurelio Escovar. The third person narrative describes Aurelio's morning routine, which is interrupted by the arrival of the mayor. Aurelio's son informs his father of the mayor's arrival, but the dentist refuses to see the mayor, telling his son to say that the dentist is not in. The son relays the mayor's answer: "He says if you don't take out his tooth, he'll shoot you" (García Márquez, "One of These Days," p. 74). At this, the dentist presents himself and agrees to extract the mayor's infected tooth, informing the patient that he will not be able to perform the procedure with anesthesia. As the wisdom tooth is being pulled, with the mayor on the verge of tears, the dentist says cryptically: "Now you'll pay for our twenty dead men" ("One of These Days," p. 75). After recovering from the extraction, the mayor exits as the dentist asks where to send the bill: "To you or the town?" to which the mayor replies "It's the same thing" ("One of These Days," p. 76).

Evidence of La Violencia in the short stories. The violence of the Colombian civil war was mostly carried out in the countryside. As suggested in "Tuesday Siesta," the inhabitants of the village were so victimized by violence that they stood ready at a moment's notice to retaliate. Rebecca reacts swiftly to the sound of an intruder. When Carlos attempts to enter her house, she retrieves a revolver—referring to it as Colonel Aureliano Buendía's—and shoots in the direction of the door. "Then she heard a little metallic bump on the cement porch, and a very low voice, pleasant but terribly exhausted: 'Ah, Mother.' The man they found dead in front of the house in the morning, his nose blown to bits" ("Tuesday Siesta," p. 70). From the larger context of La Violencia comes Rebecca's quick uses of the revolver, and the vivid description of the victim's body brings to mind other such killings of the era. Other consequences of La Violencia are apparent in the short story: the locked door of the village parish house and the reluctance of the priest's sister to open the door to strangers; the emptiness of the car on the train that must travel through rural areas that were particularly dangerous during the time period; and the differences between the conservative priest as representative of the Catholic Church and the upper classes and the woman and child as representative of the lower class, which, at times, had to profess allegiance to one party or another to survive.

In "One of These Days" the traces of La Violencia are less evident but still fundamental to the short story. Just as the woman and her child in "Tuesday Siesta" represent the working classes, Aurelio Escovar, the village dentist, represents the common people in this story. The mayor, like the priest in the former story, represents the upper class. He is the type of official who benefited from the favoritism practiced by governments such as that of Rojas Pinilla, which condoned violence and corruption among Conservative politicians. Such a mayor would have been appointed by Rojas's government instead of being elected to office. One of the most revealing yet subtle lines of the story is: "Now you'll pay for our twenty dead men" ("One of These Days," p. 75). Certainly the line makes sense in light of the fact that the majority of the violent acts of the civil war occurred in the rural areas of Colombia under authoritarian governments like the one controlled by the mayor. The pain inflicted by the tooth extraction performed without anesthesia and the sight of the mayor humbled in the dentist's chair are the only small revenges that the dentist can effect against a violence that has victimized his fellow villagers. The corruption of the ruling classes is also evident in the mayor's final response to the dentist that the bill can be mailed to him or the town because they are one and the same. The mayor controls the town; its money is his money. One other subtle reference to the political situation lies in the observation that "While the dentist washed his hands, he saw the crumbling ceiling and a dusty spider web with spider's eggs and dead insects" ("One of These Days," p. 75). The decay of his home is juxtaposed with the mayor's flaunting of the town's money. The allusion to the home's decay illustrates the wide gap between rich and poor in Colombia during La Violencia. The mayor, of the upper class, assumes a devil-may-care attitude with the town's money, which he is quite ready to spend freely, while the dentist labors to maintain his poor working conditions.

Sources and literary context. The historical inspiration for the two short stories, "Tuesday Siesta" and "One of These Days" is La Violencia. The characters are not based on real-life people but are representative of the conflict between the working and upper classes in Colombia in the 1950s. Growing up in his grandparents' home, García Márquez heard tall tales that influenced the atmosphere he would create in his Macondo cycle, his novels involving Macondo—a fictional town based on his birthplace Aracataca. The cycle culminates with *One Hundred Years of Solitude*. Some of the characters sketched in "Tuesday Siesta" and "One of These Days" are ones that he would further develop in the cycle.

As noted, García Márquez's fiction stands out for the subtlety of its references to La Violencia in a time when other Colombian writers treated the civil war more explicitly. Again García Márquez belonged to the Group of Barranquilla (named after the coastal town where it was formed) in the 1940s and 1950s. Among other goals, the group aimed to modernize Colombian culture and to this end paid rapt attention to works by modernist European and American writers such as Franz Kafka and William Faulkner (both of whom are also covered in *Literature and Its Times*).

García Márquez's writing style was greatly influenced by his readings of Ernest Hemingway (see, for example, ***The Sun Also Rises,*** also in *Literature and Its Times*), as well as his involvement in journalism. Other literary influences include the Argentine writer Jorge Luis Borges, the Spanish writer Miguel de Cervantes, and certain classic Greek writers. García Márquez's fictional world of Macondo can be compared to William Faulkner's Yoknapatawpha County.

García Márquez's stories belong to the literary era known as the "Boom"—the 1960s, during which the Latin American novel won international recognition. Other members of the Boom include the Peruvian writer Mario Vargas Llosa and the Mexican writer Carlos Fuentes (both of whom are also covered in *Literature and Its Times*).

"Tuesday Siesta" and "One of These Days" helped initiate the second phase of García Márquez's writing. The first phase, pre-magic realism (1947-54), includes early short stories that were not published in a volume. The second phase, characterized by the cycle of Macondo and (in some of the other stories) magic realism (1955-67), begins with *Leafstorm* (1955), continues with stories such as those in *Big Mama's Funeral* (1962), and ends with *One Hundred Years of Solitude* (1967). The last phase, considered post-Macondo and post magic realism (1968-present), consists of later novels and short stories that have left the magical realist strategy behind.

Reception. In Colombia, García Márquez's first short stories were virtually ignored until the extremely successful publication of his most important novel, *One Hundred Years of Solitude* in 1967. In Mexico, Carlos Fuentes recognized his talent from reading the short stories before *One Hundred Years of Solitude* was published. Likewise, Imanuel Carballo refers to García Márquez before the publication of this novel. Later Seymour Menton, one of the most important Latin American short-story critics, would declare that the early collection of stories was worthy of the future Nobel Prize that García Márquez would win (Menton, p. 559).

Similarly his popularity in the English-speaking world grew immensely after the 1970 translation of *One Hundred Years of Solitude*. García Márquez's *No One Writes to the Colonel* generated mixed reviews. Some critics were disappointed by the lack of action: "a reader of fiction is not desirous of a vivid documentary on the lives of faceless little people. He wants something to happen, and not merely more of the same, going on and on" (Dooley, p. 550). Other reviewers disagreed. They applauded the subtlety of prose, singling this out as one of the collection's most endearing qualities. That this subtlety of prose achieved its desired effect is evident in the following summation of the work: "There are no spare parts in *No One Writes to the Colonel*. Everything is done with 'a minimum of words.' . . . Clarity, precision, understatement, a deceptive simplicity, seduce where rhetoric never could" (Harss and Dohmann, pp. 320, 322-24).

—Traci Roberts

For More Information

Bejarano Avila, Jesús Antonio. "La economía colombiana entre 1946 y 1958." *Nueva Historia de Colombia: Economía, Café, Industria*. Vol. 5. Bogotá: Planeta, 1989.

Dooley, E. A. *Best Sell* 28, no. 284 (15 October 1968): 550.

Fiddian, Robin, ed. *García Márquez*. New York: Longman, 1995.

García Márquez, Gabriel. "Tuesday Siesta." *No One Writes to the Colonel and Other Stories*. Trans. J. S. Bernstein. New York: Harper & Row, 1968.

———. "One of These Days." *No One Writes to the Colonel and Other Stories*. Trans. J. S. Bernstein. New York: Harper & Row, 1968.

Harss, Luis, and Barbara Dohmann. *Into the Mainstream*. New York: Harper & Row, 1967.

McNerney, Kathleen. *Understanding Gabriel García Márquez*. Columbia, S.C.: University of South Carolina Press, 1989.

Menton, Seymour. *El cuento hispanoamericano*. Mexico: Fondo de Cultura Económica, 1991.

Oberhelman, Harley D., ed. *Gabriel García Márquez: A Study of the Short Fiction*. Boston: Twayne, 1991.

Williams, Raymond L. *The Colombian Novel: 1844-1987*. Austin: University of Texas Press, 1991.

———. *Gabriel García Márquez*. Boston: Twayne, 1984.

Williams, Raymond L., and Kevin G. Guerrieri. *Culture and Customs of Colombia*. Westport, Conn.: Greenwood Press, 1999.

Waiting for Godot

by
Samuel Beckett

Samuel Barclay Beckett was born in Foxrock, Dublin, in 1906. Though his early interests were athletic—he played on the cricket and rugby teams at the Portora Royal School in Northern Enniskillen—he studied and excelled in French and Italian at Trinity College in Dublin. In 1928 Beckett began a two-year-exchange fellowship at *l'Ecole Normale Supérieure* in Paris, where he befriended the Irish writer James Joyce and became a member of his intellectual and social circle. A decade later, in 1937, after teaching in Dublin and traveling through Europe, he decided to take up permanent residence in Paris. With the outbreak of World War II in September 1939, Beckett became a member of the French Resistance Movement, whose objective was subversive and sabotage activity against the Nazis to assist the advance of the Allied armed forces. Afterwards he was awarded the *croix de guerre* and other citations for his work in the French underground. For approximately two years in the post-war era, Beckett concentrated on writing fiction, most notably novels such as *Mercier & Camier, Murphy, Molloy, and Malone Dies.* He acquired the habit of writing first in French, then translating his works into English, believing that in this way he avoided verbal superfluity. Without any experience in theatrical production, Beckett ventured into composing drama as a respite from his flurry of fiction writing. From 1952 to 1956, *En Attendant Godot* and its English translation, *Waiting for Godot,* catapulted Beckett to international prominence. In 1969 Beckett received the Nobel Prize for literature, and before his death in 1989, he composed close to 30 works of fiction and more than 30 plays, poems, translations, and critical commentaries. *Waiting for Godot* portrays the major issues that preoccupied Beckett in his lifetime: the instability of one's own existence, the failure to communicate with others, and both the loneliness and camaraderie of the human condition. The play grows out of, and casts these concerns in, Beckett's experience of Europe in the years surrounding World War II.

THE LITERARY WORK

A play set on a country road in an unspecified era; written in 1948-49; published in French (as *En Attendant Godot*) in 1952, in English in 1954.

SYNOPSIS

Two men pass the time by a tree near a roadway as they await the arrival of Godot, who does not appear. Through a boy messenger, Godot sends word that he will appear the next day. This recurs in the second act, leaving the two men in a state somewhere between hope and despair.

Events in History at the Time the Play Takes Place

The French underground. France capitulated to World War II's Nazi aggressors in June 1940. Just days before the conquest, Samuel Beckett fled

Samuel Beckett

south for a few months, then returned to Paris. After the arrest of Paul Léon, a Jewish friend, who was ultimately tortured to death, Beckett joined the Resistance. More exactly, he joined a circuit of the British secret service, or Special Operations Executive (SOE). The mission of the SOE was to coordinate and promote clandestine sabotage against the Nazis, which it did through various sections—one supplied clothing, another forged documents, a third conducted passengers along escape routes out of France, and the so-called F section, the main body of British agents organizing subversion in France, destroyed telephone switchboards, transformers that powered factories, and railroad yards that transported German supplies. Almost 100 independent circuits of the F section operated on French soil, each as a network of subversive agents, of whom Beckett himself was one. Together they armed thousands of resisters at perilous risk to life and limb; some 100 of the 400 or so F agents sent to France never returned, among them Beckett's colleague, Alfred Péron. Arrested after one of the circuit's members was tortured into confession, Péron was sent to Mauthausen concentration camp, where he endured hard labor and malnourishment as long as possible, so poignantly reciting poetry in the midst of the nightmare that a capo, a Nazi commandant, came to him in search of a poem for his wife on their anniversary. As a member of the circuit, Beckett collected information on German troop movements, which he would decode and type to prepare for its being smuggled out to London. Once the secrecy of the circuit was compromised, he fled south to the small inconspicuous rural community of Rouissillon, where Beckett engaged in more subversion, aiding and abetting the *maquis,* the guerrilla units formed by young men, who, instead of reporting for service as forced laborers for the Nazis, took to the hills to combat them. (*Maquis* is a Corsican word, designating the thick local brushwood.)

In Rouissillon, as elsewhere, there was a paramount need for secrecy in the Resistance, so dire a need that no one used real names, and two agents on the same mission manipulated circumstances so as not to see each other. That way, if they were caught and subjected to torture, they would have nothing to confess. When an agent guided an escapee to a prearranged drop-off spot, a park bench, for example, the agent would disappear and the escapee would wait maybe 15 minutes before being collected by a second agent, who never laid eyes on the first. Similarly, messengers carried information between agents in coded language the messenger did not understand, again so that nothing could be divulged to the enemy.

Days were filled with waiting and nights with clandestine activity and writing for Beckett. (He is said to have begun his plan for *Waiting for Godot* during his two and a half years in Roussillon [1942-45]). Afterwards, film footage made public the horror of the concentrations camps of Bergen-Belsen, Dachau, and Auschwitz, while Georges Loustaunau-Cacau wrote books about life in Mauthausen, where Beckett's friend Péron perished, after carrying coal and reciting poetry in the midst of hellish camp life. "These are the kinds of human issues that inform the varied relationships between the characters in [Beckett's] play," which features not only two tramps committed to each other but also another pair of men, a master wielding a whip over a menial, who dances, sings, recites, and carries, recalling, among others, the abused, poetry-reciting, coal-carrying Péron (Knowlson, p. 345).

In the midst of World War II's human degradation and cruelty were the sacrifice and nobility of the Resistance.

> By D day, 30,000 Resistance and maquis had been executed; another 30,000 had been killed

> in battles with the enemy. Of the 115,000 deported to the Buchenwald, Ravensbruck, Dachau, and Mauthausen camps, and countless others deported for forced labor only 35,000 returned.
>
> (Gordon, p. 167)

Meanwhile, in France, many more abided the German oppressor, taking "the easier road of *attentisme* . . . of 'rolling with the punch' or waiting for outside salvation," even as the two tramps await salvation in *Waiting for Godot* (Wright, p. 402).

From tragedy to comedy—the music hall. Characters in *Waiting for Godot* wear bowlers, play musical hats, fall down, and try to help each other up, only to all fall down in slapstick fashion, reminiscent of variety theater in Beckett's day. In fact, before becoming an expatriate in Paris in 1928, Beckett regularly attended variety in Dublin. Its antecedent was the music hall, which gave way to "variety" after World War I, though the two terms have often been used interchangeably. An amalgamation of acts, music hall harked back to 1852, the opening of Canterbury Hall, a type that would soon become widespread. By the end of the century, music hall featured animal acts, dancers, serious singers of stirring patriotic tunes and ballads, and the most popular act of all, the comics. There were solo comics who appeared as character types—an egg salesman, for example, the humor stemming not from jokes but from the character sketch. Strong social satire in the early days of music hall gave way to performers who seemed to "preach ironic acceptance of a hard life" during the decline of this form of entertainment (1913-23) and the rise of variety (Wilmut, p. 14). Variety would endure for roughly 40 years (1919-60), enduring difficult times for much of the 1930s, during the economic depression, but rallying at the end of the decade. In revue-like style, variety featured a series of unconnected routines whose performers composed a momentary ensemble, only to afterwards part company and move on to other locations, where they would appear with totally new sets of performers. Variety saw the rise of the double act: two comedians teamed up, one delivering the funny lines, the other acting as his stooge, the dialogue between the straight man and funny man becoming known as "cross talk." The two "often indulged in 'turns,' borrowing each other's hats, boots and even trousers, or doing slapstick with ladders and chairs" (Cronin, p. 57). They engaged in a rhythmic type of patter with each other: the straight man would question what the comic said by repeating it and then the comic would repeat it again. There is dialogue in Beckett's play that echoes this sort of patter, just as the relationship between the two main characters echoes the distinctive comedy of the double act.

From *Waiting for Godot*

> Estragon [speaking about Lucky, a carrier]: Why doesn't he put down his bags?
>
> . . .
>
> Vladimir: Damn it haven't you already told us?
> Pozzo: I've already told you?
> Estragon: He's already told us?
>
> (Beckett, *Waiting for Godot,* p. 43)

ECHOES OF THE RESISTANCE

In writing the play, Beckett at first gave one of the tramps a Jewish name, Lévy, evoking the persecution of World War II, but then made their two names Vladimir and Estragon. The tramps have other appellations—Didi and Gogo, respectively, which could be cryptic ways of mutual recognition by members of the French underground. Each name has four letters, or two syllables, the latter repeating the former, an apt way of generating a sign and the countersign. In addition, the setting of the play—a country road with a solitary tree—typifies a landmark for a clandestine location; at such a site members of a circuit could conduct their rendezvous safely and apart from outside surveillance. Also the meeting of Vladimir and Estragon may reenact a rendezvous of two members of a circuit at a location from which they anticipate departure under the direction of a guide—Godot, perhaps also a code name. When Godot does not arrive, Vladimir and Estragon separate for the night, then return to the same setting on the following eve to wait. This activity mimics procedures that would compartmentalize members of a circuit, reducing their knowledge of one another's whereabouts, and minimizing the damage to the circuit as a whole from the capture of a single member.

Most renowned in the interwar period was the double act of Bud Flannagan and Chesney Allen. Their act entailed a complicated sort of word play that called into question communication, something Beckett's characters struggle with less comically; in the dialogue above, there is a sharp undertone of seriousness associated with the seemingly vain attempt to exchange information. On the variety stage, the attempt is equally vain, but the dialogue remains slapstick, going no deeper than the surface:

From Flannagan and Allen's Double Act

FLANNAGAN: I went down to the docks.
ALLEN: Oh, you saw the ships?
FLANNAGAN: Yes, I saw all the ships coming into whisky.
ALLEN: Coming into port.
FLANNAGAN: Coming into port—oh, a marvellous sight. . . . See all the labradors at work.
ALLEN: The what?
FLANNAGAN: The labradors.
ALLEN: The labradors—the salvadors!
FLANNAGAN: The stevedores, you fool—oi!
(Adapted from Wilmut, p. 61)

TRAGICOMIC SONG, TRAGICOMIC DANCE

Integrated into *Waiting for Godot* is both song and dance. Opening Act 2, the song "A dog came in" tragically recounts how a dog, having stolen a crust of bread, is beaten to death by a ladle-wielding cook. Tending to their own, other dogs assemble to dig a grave for the victim: Then all the dogs came running / And dug the dog a tomb— / And dug the dog a tomb (Godot, p. 64). Likewise, dance assumes tragic overtones in the play, when one character entertains the others with his less-than-fancy footwork:

POZZO: He used to dance the farandole, the fling, the brawl, the jig, the fandango, and even the hornpipe. He capered. For joy. Now that's the best he can do. Do you know what he calls it?
ESTRAGON: The Scapegoat's Agony.
VLADIMIR: The hard stool.
POZZO: The Net. He thinks he's entangled in a net.
(*Godot,* p. 42)

From their initial performance in 1931 until they retired in 1945, Flannagan and Allen remained the most popular double act in the business. What distinguished them from other comedians was the bond of affection they conveyed on stage.

Usually the straight man in such acts showed complete irritation with the antics of the funny man, but no matter how irritating Flannagan's antics were, Allen still emoted a tenderness for the man. Similarly, Vladimir and Estragon show deep-seated affection for each other in Beckett's play. "I'll never walk again," complains Estragon, rather comically after trying to comfort the weeping passerby Lucky, who promptly kicks his would-be benefactor; "I'll carry you," volunteers Vladimir "(*tenderly*)," then pauses and adds a comical "if necessary" (*Waiting for Godot,* p. 32).

Beckett and philosophy. An avid reader of philosophy, Beckett declared that he himself was no philosopher, yet his literature resounds with ideas peculiar to his time. Various related philosophies flourished during the World War II era, particularly in France, where they manifested themselves in such works as Albert Camus's novel *L'Étranger* (1942; *The Stranger*) and his essay *Le Mythe de Sisyphe* (1942; *The Myth of Sisyphus*). Camus saw humanity as confronting a universe that is unintelligible. In his view, the universe provides no answers to profound questions about where one comes from or where one is going, a situation he considered absurd.

Drama too gave expression to philosophies of the era, with Jean-Paul Sartre's *Huis clos* (1945; *In Camera,* also titled *No Exit*) featuring existential philosophy. Coined by French journalists in the World War II era, *existentialism* became a popular term for a family of philosophies of despair, though much in existential writing did not fit this definition. The philosophies aimed to interpret human existence. A human being has no God-given or nature-given essence, taught the existentialists; instead each being makes himself or herself to be what he or she is through his or her choices and actions. Building on prior philosophers (such as Søren Kierkegaard and Martin Heidegger), the existentialists became preoccupied with ideas like 1) nothing truly exists, 2) even if something does exist, it cannot truly be known, and 3) even if it can be known, it cannot be truly communicated to others. Taken together, these ideas comprise the skeptical extreme known as "nihilism." Existentialism became preoccupied too with death and suicide. One must face death, taught Heidegger, to enter into "authentic" being. Sartre addressed the subject of a person's social responsibility. Human consciousness, he taught (in *Existentialism and Humanism,* 1946), gives rise to the freedom of the individual, and freedom, to social responsibility. The individual, said the existentialists, is not a detached observer in this world but a participant—again, humans define themselves by the choices they make, the way they act. Actually the existentialists were philosophers of creation. One can better take their full measure by distinguishing between their diagnosis of humanity's current condition and the possibilities for an ethical life that their diagnosis opened up. As shown, Sartre's view does not ultimately lead to despair but to engagement, pointing to the responsibility of the individual to make life worth living.

Beckett did not identify himself with any of these thinkers per se; in fact, he "distanced himself from existentialism" (Kern, p. 170). Yet Beckett's literature addresses many of these same subjects, as well as those posed by other philosophers, such as Arthur Schopenhauer (1788-1860), whom Beckett avidly read and whose teachings support his view that suffering is the norm for humanity. Beckett did not, however, prefer one philosopher to the exclusion of others or develop a system of philosophy separate from his drama and fiction. He nevertheless has been regarded as a philosophical writer, and his works mined for ideas of modern life, perhaps because of his overall intent. Beckett aimed, he said, "to imitate the universal mess. . . . To find a form that accommodates the mess, that is the task of the artist now" (Beckett in Cormier and Pallister, p. 118). In the process, he evokes "existential" and other ideas about existence—the condition of irremediable solitude, the experience of cosmic absurdity, the failure to communicate.

Of course, historical events as well as philosophy impinged on Beckett's outlook. His, it should be remembered, was a lifetime that before the brutalities of World War II had witnessed the bloody carnage of the First World War and of the Irish Civil War, whose "cumulatory effect . . . was a general cynicism and disbelief in either virtue or decency, in goodness or uprightness or honesty" (Gordon, p. 20). However, Beckett's personal theater, or field of battle, was neither the Irish Civil War nor the First World War but rather the civilian underground in World War II France, and it did *not* present him with unrelieved human depravity. There were the activists in the Resistance—everyday teachers, farmers, and parents—who risked life and limb to combat the Nazis. Also, to the south of Beckett's rural refuge, Roussillon, was another village, Le Chambon, a Protestant town whose ordinary citizens took bold yet unobtrusive action, sneaking into the protective folds of their homes hundreds of Jewish children and raising them as their own. Such valiance paled beside the butchery of millions in the Nazi gas chambers, or the torture of Resistance agents captured by the Nazis, or the passive attitudes toward Nazi evils adopted by many other citizens. Still, it existed, validating the idea of "suffering redeemed through camaraderie" that "would resound throughout [Beckett's] work and life," and that would surface in the not unrelieved despair of *Waiting for Godot* (Gordon, p. 17).

The Play in Focus

Plot summary. A drama in two acts, *Waiting for Godot* spans two days. The first act begins in the evening and ends with the onset of nightfall, and the second act occurs during the same time the next day. Onstage the action takes place only at the darkening stages of twilight. The setting consists of a country road and a tree; nearby are a mound and a ditch, a type of area one might find in rural France. In the first act, the tree has no leaves, but in the interval between the first and second acts, it sprouts four to five leaves. Near the tree, the two major characters of the play, Vladimir and Estragon, wait for the coming of Godot, whom they have never met and about whom they know nothing, except his name. As they wait, they become very time-conscious and experience nervous agitation, which they strive to alleviate by conversation. Seemingly inconsequential chatter, at moments their conversation verges on profound deliberation. But they never wish to face the implications of what they say.

At the beginning of Act I Vladimir wakens Estragon, who complains "Why will you never let me sleep?" to which Vladimir replies "I felt lonely" (*Godot,* p. 10). Estragon rather comically struggles to pull off his boots, which are too small. They contemplate hanging themselves, but decide they cannot, for Vladimir is too heavy for the hanging to work, and, without Estragon, he would be left alone. "Well?" asks Vladimir, "What do we do?" to which Estragon replies "Nothing," because doing nothing is safer (*Godot,* p. 13).

Interrupting them as they wait for Godot are Pozzo, owner of the land on which they wait, and Lucky, whom Pozzo leads on a rope like a dog and who carries his bag, basket, and stool. "He carries," complains Pozzo, "like a pig. It's not his job" (*Godot,* p. 30). Clearly Lucky has come down in the world; he can sing, dance, and think, less effectively than he once did but better than any of the others there. Lucky dances, feebly, and he thinks for them, also feebly.

Pozzo treats Lucky abusively, and speaks of plans to sell him, whereupon Lucky weeps and Estragon attempts to comfort him, but gets kicked violently by Lucky for his pains. The conversation wanders. All four men wear bowler hats and Vladimir observes sarcastically what a

Peter Woodthorpe, Paul Daneman, and Peter Bull in a 1955 production of *Waiting for Godot* at London's Arts Theatre.

charming evening they are having; worse, he says than "the music-hall" (*Godot,* p. 35). Estragon introduces himself to Pozzo as Adam, the world's first man; later he compares himself to Christ and still later, in a comical interchange, equates Pozzo with Abel. At the time, Pozzo is lying in a helpless heap on the ground.

> VLADIMIR: I tell you his name is Pozzo.
> ESTRAGON: We'll soon see. (He reflects.) Abel! Abel!
> POZZO: Help!
> ESTRAGON: Got it in one!
>
> (*Godot,* p. 95)

The names conjure the image of universal human being that other action in the play promotes. Pozzo and Lucky take their leave, and a Boy enters, a messenger who reports that Godot is not coming; he will be there tomorrow. Asked if he is unhappy, the Boy, who minds goats, says he does not know. "You're as bad as myself," ventures Vladimir, continuing to equate one instance of humanity with another (*Godot,* p. 56). The Boy, it turns out, has a brother, who minds the sheep and suffers beatings, as does Estragon, who is beaten during the day. As night falls and Act I ends, Estragon and Vladimir contemplate hanging themselves again, discuss Estragon's attempted suicide in former days when they harvested grapes by the Rhone, and recall how long they have been together—50 years maybe. "I sometimes wonder if we wouldn't have been better off alone," muses Estragon, "each one for himself" (*Godot,* p. 58).

Act 2 opens as Vladimir and Estragon reunite on the same ground, again at twilight. Vladimir wants to embrace Estragon, but Estragon protests, for he has been beaten, but he wants Vladimir to stay with him. "I wouldn't have let them beat you," volunteers Vladimir protectively, saying he would have stopped Estragon from doing whatever angered them; but, protests Estragon, "I wasn't doing anything" (*Godot,* p. 65).

The two converse again, so they won't have to hear "all the dead voices" or think about "all these corpses," "these skeletons," references perhaps to World War II, as well as to a more general dance of death (*Godot,* p. 71). They notice that the tree has sprouted leaves and marvel that this happened in a single night. Was it only yesterday that they were there? "Yes," says Estragon, "now I remember, yesterday evening we spent blathering about nothing in particular. That's been going on now for half a century" (*Godot,* p. 73). Comically again, Estragon staggers around trying on a pair of boots he finds by the roadside. Lucky left his hat there yesterday, so they engage in a game of musical bowlers—exchanging one hat for another and then another. They play too at being Pozzo and Lucky. Estragon leaves momentarily, returns, and falls into Vladimir's arms.

> ESTRAGON: There you are again at last! . . .
> VLADIMIR: Where were you? I thought you were gone for ever.
>
> (*Godot*, p. 82)

They rejoice at the sound of someone approaching, thinking Godot has finally arrived, but it is only Pozzo, now blind, and Lucky, now dumb. Lucky and Pozzo fall down, and Estragon and Vladimir consider whether to help them up gladly or subordinate their good offices to certain conditions for some tangible reward. Vladimir grows decisive, energetic:

> Let us not waste our time in idle discourse! (Pause. Vehemently.) Let us do something, while we have the chance. It is not every day that we are needed. Not indeed that we personally are needed. Others would meet the case equally well, if not better. To all mankind they were addressed those cries for help still ringing in our ears! But at this place, at this moment of time, all mankind is us, whether we like it or not. Let us make the most of it, before it is too late! Let us represent worthily for once the foul brood to which a cruel fate consigned us!
>
> (*Godot*, p. 90)

Comically and tragically, Vladimir tries to pull Pozzo up and stumbles down himself, then Estragon pulls Vladimir and stumbles and falls as well. Estragon observes that Pozzo, who again cries "help," is all humanity. Vladimir and Estragon get up and help Pozzo up, who does not recall meeting them yesterday. Pozzo explains that Lucky cannot sing or recite or even groan for them: "one day he went dumb, one day I went blind, one day we'll go deaf, one day we were born, one day we shall die, the same day, the same second, is that not enough for you?" (*Godot*, p. 103). Pozzo and Lucky leave.

Vladimir and Estragon continue to wait for Godot. Exasperated, Estragon cannot sleep because again Vladmir wakes him to stave off loneliness. Vladimir refuses to hear about Estragon's dream, and the two wonder if Pozzo could have been Godot. Struggling with his boots again, Estragon cries "help me!" whereupon Vladimir has a fit of remorse;

> Was I sleeping, while the others suffered? Am I sleeping now? To-morrow, when I wake, or think I do, what shall I say of to-day? That with Estragon my friend, at this place until the fall of night, I waited for Godot? . . . But in all that what truth will there be?
>
> (*Godot*, p. 104)

Vladimir muses about how habit deadens the cries for help that are everywhere in the air.

The Boy messenger arrives again to say Mr. Godot will not keep the appointment today but will come tomorrow. "Tell him that you saw me," says Vladimir, somewhat frantically, as if questioning his own existence (justifiably, in light of Pozzo's not having remembered him). ". . . You're sure you saw me, you won't come and tell me to-morrow that you never saw me!" (*Godot*, p. 106). The Boy leaves, and Vladimir and Estragon contemplate suicide again. Will they hang themselves tomorrow, or will Godot come, in which case they would be saved, or would they be? As the curtain falls, the two characters are immobile, and the audience is left wondering.

A brave new world—or not? "Let us not then speak ill of our generation," philosophizes Pozzo in the play. "It is not any unhappier than its predecessors. (Pause.) Let us not speak well of it either. Let us not speak of it at all," he adds, unwilling to dwell on the subject (*Godot*, p. 32).

Written in the 1940s, the play speaks to a World War II and postwar generation that spanned extremes, ranging from grim wartime horrors to high postwar hopes for a greatly improved society. These hopes surfaced in both Britain and Beckett's adopted home, France. In England, earlier than most, George Orwell expressed an idealistic vision in his 1941 essay "The Lion and the Unicorn," which anticipated an entirely new social order, one that did away with the class system and inaugurated a practical type of socialism in Britain. The war, it was thought, had fortified the commitment to general human decency and justice for all. People had sacrificed together to combat Nazism, and to protect British independence in a way that excited hopes for a more equitable postwar Europe. Beckett himself referred to such hopes in a 1946 BBC radio broadcast. After the war, he labored with the Irish Red Cross to build a hospital in a ravaged French community. In just one night, explained Beckett, Saint-Lô had been bombed to pieces.

> [People] continue two years after the liberation, to clear away the debris, literally by hand. . . . [S]ome of those who were in Saint-Lô [to build the hospital] will come home realising that they

> got at least as good as they gave, that they got indeed what they could hardly give, a vision and sense of a time-honoured conception of humanity in ruins, and perhaps even an inkling of the terms in which our condition is to be thought again.
>
> (Beckett, "Capital of the Ruins," pp. 75-76)

Would there be a fundamentally new order in postwar Britain? Political developments were encouraging at first. By a wide margin, the people elected into power the Labour Party under Clement Attlee on a platform of sweeping reforms: the Labour Party would provide decent housing for all, effect full employment, and initiate the welfare state. Labour's government, which endured from 1945 to 1951 (Beckett was in France during these years, writing *Waiting for Godot*), did indeed establish the modern-day British welfare state. The government passed the National Health Service Act (1946), which provided free health care to all, constructed council housing for the homeless, and achieved full employment of the workforce. There was a failure, however, to change underlying structures in a revolutionary way that would lead to a more equitable society. "The Labour Party was in the end unable to use the institutions of the state to bring about the social transformation many of its supporters had hoped for. . . . 'The welfare measures . . . did not of themselves produce a more egalitarian or open society'" (Williamson, pp. 84, 85). Discussion of social revolution filled the air, yet postwar society remained class-riven and class-conscious. By the early 1950s, British leaders stopped envisioning a government that would take collective responsibility for the welfare of everyone by providing services and benefits to all.

People blamed the Cold War for the failure. A competition for world leadership between the Soviet Union and the United States and their respective allies, the Cold War "destroyed any socialist vision, dragooned people into flocks of Atlanticist sheep or pro-Soviet goats, and blocked off any 'third way'" (Thompson in Williamson, p. 61). The global competition dashed hopes for a socialist Europe, instead holding the continent hostage to the specter of one superpower's threatening another with nuclear death. Britain linked itself to the United States after World War II, securing U.S. loans. If, thought its leaders, we do not ally with America, then Europe will remain under the threat of Soviet domination. So the Cold War took precedence over any fundamental reorganization of society in Britain. Postwar France went through a similar experience: "It is true enough that much of the wartime idealism soon curdled; that resistance dreams of a wholly new era . . . were quickly shattered; that the Fourth Republic as a political system turned out to be not very much different from the Third" (Wright, p. 401). Neither Britain nor France experienced pivotal institutional change; nor was there much fundamental change in human interaction.

Racist and abusive behavior blights some of the human relations in *Waiting for Godot.* As noted, Pozzo abuses Lucky in a way reminiscent of the Nazi capo's abuse of Jews in World War II's extermination camps. There was little bald anti-Semitism in Britain after the war, but controversy over Palestine led to attacks on Jewish shops and to individual remarks such as one editor's in the press that "The Jews, indeed, are a plague on Britain" (Caunt in Williamson, p. 52). British law prosecuted the editor, but the instance illustrated that racism persisted. And with post World War II immigration from the far reaches of the dwindling empire—India, Pakistan, the Caribbean, and Hong Kong—racism flared. A 1948 survey showed that schoolbooks in Britain promoted misguided stereotypes of these immigrants, a "sophisticated" example of the failure to communicate that plagues characters in *Waiting for Godot.*

At the same time, there were improvements in postwar British society. Welfare legislation eased poverty, concluded a 1950 study of York, and also expanded everyone's rights (Williamson, p. 77). The 1944 Education Act, to cite a specific example, guaranteed free secondary education to all. With good cause, then, one might echo Pozzo's lines in the play: let us not speak ill of postwar humanity; let us not speak well of it. As in the wartime era, humanity afterwards had some successes, and it had some profound failures.

Sources and literary context. Beckett's sources for *Waiting for Godot* are multiple and various, ranging from his own real-life experience in World War II and as a fan of the music hall (described above) to paintings and readings. According to Beckett himself, the visual setting of the play stemmed from a painting he saw by Caspar David Friedrich. At the end of each act in the play, Vladimir and Estragon stand by the tree as the moon rises, forming silhouettes against the evening sky. The image resembles two paintings by Friedrich—*Two Men Contemplating the Moon* (1819) and *Man and Woman Observing the Moon* (1824). Exactly which one inspired Beckett re-

INFECTIOUS CINEMA

Along with the music hall, Beckett drew on his experience as a purveyor of early cinema. In the 1920s, film was the newest medium of entertainment. Influenced by music-hall entertainment, early cinema was often humorous. Beckett, a young man in his late teens and early twenties at the time, regularly frequented the cinema in Dublin. There he saw the films of Charlie Chaplin, Laurel and Hardy, and Harold Lloyd, all of whom began their careers as vaudevillians. When the Marx Brothers began to make films, he saw them too. Among the hallmarks of these films were physical humor—slapstick, pratfalls, cross-talk, and the like. Also, ill-fitting clothes, hats, and shoes or boots were integrated into the humor. Charlie Chaplin, for instance, wore a tight jacket but baggy trousers. Beyond the physical and verbal humor, the deadpan demeanor of the performers was crucial to the success of early cinema. Chaplin, Buster Keaton, and Laurel and Hardy—the so-called stoic comedians—perfected the deadpan demeanor in cinema. In effect, the stoic comedians maintained straight faces despite the laughter that they evoked from their audiences. (Later cinema would feature Keaton in Beckett's one venture into moviemaking—the 1964 production *Film*.)

Like the stoic comedians of early cinema, the protagonists in *Waiting for Godot* have a complementary relationship. The first to appear in the play is Estragon, typically played by a short, fat man. Vladimir is taller and leaner, if not gaunt. In stage productions, both men wear hats like the bowlers of early cinema as well as variety theater. Humor derives from Vladimir's reaction to his hat, just as it does from Estragon's annoyance with his boots. As Vladimir removes his hat, knocks on the crown, and seems intent on dislodging a foreign object, Estragon removes one of his boots, turns it upside down, and shakes it. Their actions mix humor into the tragedy, another resemblance between *Waiting for Godot* and early cinema. Melodrama informed some of the comedians' theatrics with tragedy until a reversal in fortune resulted in their happiness. The audience's response would shift from one extreme to the other—from fear and anxiety, on the one hand, to joy, on the other. But ultimately the tragic threat gave way to a comic resolution, and here the resemblance ends, as this is not the case at the end of *Waiting for Godot*.

mains unclear. In the first, two men in cloaks, viewed from behind, gaze at a full moon pictured against the dark branches of a great leafless tree.

Literary influences include philosophers such as René Descartes, Martin Heidegger and Albert Camus, as well as Arthur Schopenhauer, mentioned above. When asked what dramatist influenced his own playwrighting the most, Beckett named John Millington Synge, whose mingling of tragedy and comedy Beckett particularly admired. The French playwright Racine also influenced Beckett greatly. Racine aimed for the classic unity of action, place, and time, a dramaturgic device ultimately derived from the doctrine of Aristotle. Certainly *Waiting for Godot* observes a unity of place and action. As for time, "Racine and French classical criticism had extended the allowable period to twenty-four hours," the extent of Beckett's play (Cronin, p. 60). A familiar complaint about Racine's plays was that nothing much happened, except that pairs of characters went on chattering to each other, an influence on Beckett that needs no elaboration. Also, in the manner of French classical drama, which taught that the setting should not be specific, Beckett's is nondescript—"A country road. A tree. Evening" (*Godot,* p. 1). Other possible sources include Christian writings, specifically the *Confessions* of St. Augustine, which may have inspired the "fifty-fifty chance of salvation that runs through [Beckett's] play" (Knowlson, p. 343).

Beckett's storyline—waiting for a person to arrive or an event to occur that might change a situation—resounds in drama he knew. John Millington Synge's *The Playboy of the Western World* (1907), whose heroine seizes on a young man to deliver her from a tedious future is one example; W. B. Yeats's *At the Hawk's Well* (1916), whose characters must wait for the dry bed of a well to fill before they can drink its waters of youth and immortality, is another.

That other drama of the day addressed philosophical concerns has already been noted in the case of Jean-Paul Sartre's *No Exit* (1944), which focuses on three characters who have recently died and are trapped in the eternal damnation of the hold they have on each other. Other contemporary drama includes Eugène Ionesco's *The Bald Soprano* (1950), which features meaningless dialogue between two couples that degenerates into babbling. Ionesco's play was part of the theater of the absurd, a new genre that reduced setting and action to the minimum, strove to generalize characters, sometimes to the point of not naming them, and incorporated elements from the circus, like the marionette or the clown, as well as from the music hall. In contrast to others, Beckett did not see himself as part of the new genre; in fact "public association with Ionesco . . . and the 'theatre of the absurd' would always annoy him" (Cronin, p. 525).

Reception. *Waiting for Godot* opened in France at the Théâtre de Babylone 5 January, 1953. The curtain fell, reported Sylvain Zegel in *Libération,* before a confused audience that nevertheless realized they had just seen an important play. Preeminent French playwright Jean Anouilh cemented its success with his review in *Arts-Spectacle*. "*Godot,*" he said is "a masterpiece that will cause despair for men in general and for playwrights in particular" (Anouilh in Cronin, p. 421). Dazzled by the reviews, crowds stormed into the playhouse for every performance but often left after the first act, confused by it and, many of them, bored. Yet the praise from critics continued; a month after the play's opening Alain Robbe-Grillet observed that though "made out of nothingness," *Waiting for Godot* flowed forward seamlessly "without an empty space" (Robbe-Grillet in Cronin, p. 423).

Outside France, *Waiting for Godot* was a resounding success. The audience in Ireland appears to have been more steadfast about staying for the duration. In *The Irish Times* (February 18, 1956), Vivian Mercier contended that Beckett has "achieved a theoretical impossibility—a play in which nothing happens, that yet keeps audiences glued to their seats" (Mercier in Andonian, p. 95). In England's *The Spectator* (August 12, 1955), Anthony Hartley described *Waiting for Godot* as "a play of great power and skill (the dialogue is masterly)" (Hartley in Andonian, p. 92). Brooks Atkinson, who reviewed the American production on Broadway for the *New York Times,* sensed "an illusion of faith flickering around the edges of the drama. It is as though Mr. Beckett sees very little reason for clutching at faith, but is unable to relinquish it entirely" (Atkinson, p. 21). The play prompted not only such comments but also a flurry of interpretation. All the interpretation distressed Beckett, who thought it reflected a fundamental misunderstanding of the intent of *Waiting for Godot.* "'The end,' Beckett said, 'is to give artistic expression to something hitherto almost ignored—the irrational state of unknowingness where we exist . . . which is beyond reason'" (Beckett in Cronin, p. 457).

—Albert Labriola and Joyce Moss

For More Information

Andonian, Cathleen Culotta. *The Critical Response to Samuel Beckett.* Westport, Conn.: Greenwood, 1998.

Atkinson, Brooks. Review of *Waiting for Godot. New York Times,* 20 April 1956, 21.

Beckett, Samuel. "The Capital of the Ruins." In *As No Other Dare Fail.* London: John Calder, 1986.

———. *Waiting for Godot: A Tragicomedy in Two Acts.* Trans. Samuel Beckett. New York: Grove, 1954.

Cormier, Ramona, and Janis L. Pallister. *Waiting for Death: The Philosophical Significance of Beckett's* En Attendant Godot. University, Ala.: University of Alabama Press, 1979.

Cronin, Anthony. *Samuel Beckett: The Last Modernist.* New York: HarperCollins, 1997.

Foot, M. R. D. *SOE in France: An Account of the Work of the British Special Operations Executive in France 1940-1944.* London: Her Majesty's Stationery Office, 1966.

Gordon, Lois. *The World of Samuel Beckett.* New Haven, Conn.: Yale University Press, 1996.

Kern, Edith. *Existential Thought and Fictional Technique.* New Haven: Yale University Press, 1970.

Knowlson, James. *Damned to Fame: The Life of Samuel Beckett.* New York: Simon & Schuster, 1996.

Williamson, Bill. *The Temper of the Times: British Society since World War II.* Oxford: Basil Blackwell, 1990.

Wilmut, Roger. *Kindly Leave the Stage! The Story of Variety 1919-1960.* London: Methuen, 1985.

Wright, Gordon. *France in Modern Times.* Stanford: Norton, 1987.

The Way to Rainy Mountain

by
N. Scott Momaday

Born February 27, 1934, in Lawton, Oklahoma, Navarre Scott Momaday was reared in New Mexico and Arizona as well as Oklahoma. He is of mixed Kiowa, Euro-American, and Cherokee descent. Momaday studied at the University of New Mexico, where he earned his bachelor's degree in political science in 1958, and at Stanford University, where he received his master's degree in 1960 and his Ph.D. in 1963. *The Way to Rainy Mountain* was published the same year that Momaday's ***House Made of Dawn*** (also in *Literature and Its Times*) won the Pulitzer Prize for literature. Weaving together three distinct voices—Kiowa tribal stories, history, and personal narrative—*The Way to Rainy Mountain* is largely an exploration of American Indian identity. The book represents the author's attempt to uncover and preserve the stories and history of the Kiowas and to determine his place among them. After the 1965 death of his paternal grandmother, Aho, Momaday retraces the travels of the Kiowas across what would become the United States. With the help of the three distinct voices specified above, the memoir shows how myth, history, and individual experience intersect to create a person's, indeed a people's, identity.

THE LITERARY WORK

A memoir set along the migratory route of the Kiowa tribe (Montana, Wyoming, Colorado, and Oklahoma) in 1965, including stories reaching back to 1700; published in 1969.

SYNOPSIS

Momaday recounts the movement of his tribe, the Kiowas, from the source of the Yellowstone River in Montana to Rainy Mountain Cemetery in Oklahoma, where his grandmother is buried.

Events in History at the Time of the Memoir

American Indian identity. For more than 300 years, British and American colonial powers attempted to wipe out those cultural markers of language, religion, and livelihood that distinguish American Indian tribal identities. Then came a reversal in this pattern. The 1960s, in particular, witnessed the reversal, and a corresponding rise in Indian self-awareness and self-determination. The result was that more tribes, or Indian nations, reclaimed their status as distinct peoples (or groups) within the United States. Today there are more than 500 tribes in the United States, each maintaining a particular belief system.

The civil rights movement of the 1960s and 1970s incorporated a diverse group of U.S. citizens. African Americans, women, Latinos, Asian Americans, homosexuals, and American Indians all worked to push their political and social agendas to the fore of national awareness. In relation to the Indians, debates centered on such issues as land loss, adverse legal decisions, and ineffective educational policies—all of which left many

N. Scott Momaday

Indians without a clear vision of themselves. There was, meanwhile, a social side to the civil rights movement that amounted to a cultural unearthing for many native peoples. American Indians began to question their identity, asking themselves what exactly distinguished them from other groups in the nation. More pointedly, they began to ask, What (and Who) is an American Indian? a question Momaday has answered: "An Indian is an idea which a given man has of himself. And it is a moral idea, for it accounts for the way in which he reacts to other men and to the world in general" (Momaday in Hobson, p. 162). A Native American, in other words, is more than a racially distinct person, more than a person of minimum blood quantum, as the federal government has defined it. (*The Indian Reorganization Act of 1934* had qualified as Indian those of Indian descent who belonged to a tribe under federal jurisdiction, as well as their descendants and anyone with at least one-half Indian blood.) A native lives life in a manner separate from non-native peoples.

This kind of cultural introspection had become a crucial aspect of native life precisely because for 400 years American Indians were denied the public practice and celebration of traditions that marked them as unique. Broken treaties, mass slaughters, geographic removal and isolation, harsh government-run boarding schools (teachers beat children and put them in solitary confinement when they spoke their own language), and urban relocation ensued from contact between whites and native nations. Centuries of attempted cultural genocide left many native peoples without a publicly recognized cultural identity. Along with attempts to erase Indian uniqueness had gone other attempts to force a sham cultural identity on native nations, through such falsified popular images as Longfellow's Hiawatha (in the 1855 poem of that name), Twain's sinister Injun Joe (in the 1876 novel *The Adventures of Tom Sawyer*), and twentieth-century sports mascots. The civil unrest of the 1960s and early 1970s began to reverse these trends, offering native nations a new chance to pronounce their distinct tribal voices and talk back to an erstwhile colonizer that had silenced them for too long. The talking back took various forms, from the development of a new American Indian literary movement (inaugurated by Momaday's 1968 *House Made of Dawn*) to massive protests and demonstrations. The year *The Way to Rainy Mountain* was published, to take one example, a group calling itself Indians of All Tribes seized Alcatraz Island, the site of a defunct maximum-security prison near San Francisco. The group occupied the island for 19 months, claiming it as soil belonging to the tribal nations. Hundreds of native peoples from various tribes came together to demand cultural and political recognition from the American mainstream. Their insurgency gave rise to both the Red Power Movement and the American Indian Movement (AIM). The two would take dramatic action against the federal government over the next ten years, effecting, among other incidents, the takeover of the Bureau of Indian Affairs building in 1972.

Anthropology and American Indians. At the time of publication, *The Way to Rainy Mountain* was distinct from other works on American Indians in that it presented Indian tradition and life as an ongoing process, one that has been evolving, incorporating new stories and visions along the way. One of the memoir's many lessons is that, although fragile, native traditions have not been lost but continue to survive despite years of suffering.

Until the late 1960s, when new and sometimes radical thought regarding American Indians emerged, native peoples were publicly represented in large part by anthropologists who specialize in the study of human beings, their environment, and their culture. Anthropological

Activists at a 1977 rally of the American Indian Movement (AIM), in San Francisco, California.

work in the 1960s (and before) often misrepresented native peoples as static or extinct in its attempts to piece together American Indian cultures before white contact. While valuable in many ways, as evidenced by the anthropological data in *The Way to Rainy Mountain*, anthropologists' observations and interpretations were often misguided and limited. Their status as outsiders made it difficult for the anthropologists to accurately portray American Indian lifestyles, which entail a more diversified view of the world. Acknowledging this more diversified view, *The Way to Rainy Mountain* begins a dialogue with the anthropologists and challenges the limited tone of their work. It adds a modern tribal voice to the mix of anthropological data acquired over time. Conversational phrases dot the narrative, reminding readers that tradition is still alive, still being passed down orally from one generation to the next. Momaday, unlike mainstream anthropologists, offers up information in Kiowa storytelling style, from the start—"You know, everything had to begin"—through the middle—"The Kiowa language is hard to understand, but, you know, the storm spirit understands it"—to the end—"This is how it was . . . " (Momaday, *Rainy Mountain*, pp. 16, 48, 80). His text represents Kiowa history from a tribal perspective, providing a new, authentic view of Native American life, as a rather indulgent corrective. "They're a mischievous bunch," observed Momaday about the anthropologists, "out to put literature in its place, . . . My feeling is that the anthros need only to be converted, not destroyed" (Momaday in Lincoln, p. 108).

Momaday was not the only native writer of the time questioning academic anthropology. Vine Deloria, Jr., whose *Custer Died for Your Sins: An Indian Manifesto* was published the same year as *The Way to Rainy Mountain*, also challenged contemporary anthropology. For example, Deloria discussed a 1968 book by anthropologist Peter Farb (*Man's Rise to Civilization as Shown by the Indians of North America from Primeval Times to the Coming of the Industrial State*): "Sometimes Farb's anthropological references to the Plains Indians are irrelevant and ridden with historical mythologies. . . . The Mandans, for example, are found to be extinct—which they will be happy to know about. Plains Indians in general are declared to be as make-believe as a movie set—which will make them welcome Farb warmly when he next appears on the plains" (Deloria, p. 99). Once American Indians began to talk back to these scholars, anthropologists worked to change their approaches and methods, consulting more closely with tribes and incorporating tribal ideologies into their studies.

CHRONOLOGY OF *THE WAY TO RAINY MOUNTAIN* AND THE KIOWAS' MIGRATORY MOVEMENT

1700 Approximate emigration of the Kiowas from the Yellowstone region of Montana.
1740 Golden era of the Kiowas commences.
1770 Approximate date of expulsion of the Kiowas from the Black Hills of Wyoming.
1790 Peace and alliance established with the Comanches.
1833 Osages massacre Kiowas; Tai-me, the tribe's sacred Sun Dance doll, is stolen by the Osage; Leonid meteor storm (November 13).
1834 Kau-au-ointy, Momaday's great-great grandfather, is born; official contact between the Kiowas and the United States Government begins.
1837 Kiowas sign first treaty with the U.S. Government at Fort Gibson.
1839 Smallpox epidemic.
1849 Cholera epidemic.
1867 Medicine Lodge Treaty, in which Kiowas agree to move to a reservation.
1868 Battle of Washita; Utes steal Tai-me.
1869 Kiowas move to reservation in southwest Oklahoma.
1874-75 Kiowas confront US troops at Palo Duro Canyon in Texas; Kiowas surrender; their golden era ends.
1880 Aho, Momaday's grandmother, and Mammedaty, his grandfather, are born.
1887 Kiowas hold their last Sun Dance north of Rainy Mountain Creek.
1890 U.S. federal agent ends the Kiowa Sun Dance.
1913 Mayme Natachee Scott (Momaday's mother) is born; Alfed Morris Mammedaty (Momaday's father) is born.
1934 Navarre Scott Momaday is born.
1963 Momaday, along with his father and Aho, visits the Tai-me bundle.
1965 Aho dies; Momaday traces the migration of the Kiowas and, with the assistance of his father, collects stories from Kiowa elders.

(Adapted from Roemer, pp. 156-157)

Kiowa Sun Dance. In *The Way to Rainy Mountain*, Momaday describes the coming of Tai-me (the tribe's sacred medicine doll) to the Kiowas. During a period of starvation, sometime in the mid-eighteenth century, a Kiowa man left camp to search for food. After four days, the man arrived at a canyon.

> Suddenly there was thunder and lightning. A voice spoke to him and said, "Why are you following me? What do you want?" The man was afraid. The thing standing before him had the feet of a deer, and its body was covered with feathers. The man answered that the Kiowas were hungry. "Take me with you," the voice said, "and I will give you whatever you want." From that day Tai-me has belonged to the Kiowas.
>
> (*Rainy Mountain*, p. 36)

Accompanying this tribal story is a historical description of the Tai-me doll. The figure is "less than 2 feet in length" and is "preserved in a rawhide box in charge of the hereditary keeper, and is never under any circumstances exposed to view except at the annual Sun Dance" (*Rainy Mountain*, p. 37). Thus, with the arrival of Tai-me came the Sun Dance, a ceremony of great religious import. Held just once a year, the ceremony's spirituality remained with the tribe throughout the year, reaffirming Kiowa traditions until the performance of the next Sun Dance. The importance of the ceremony can be seen in events recorded on Kiowa calendars, which reference time according to the Sun Dances.

The Sun Dance itself, called Skaw-tow in the Kiowa language, was held during early summer, when all six bands of the tribe reunited after a year of traveling separately to hunt and raid. When the six bands came together for the Sun Dance, they camped in a circle in a particular order, according to their roles in the ceremony. The Tai-me keeper, a priest of sorts, decided the exact place and time for the ceremony and sent messengers out to inform the other Kiowa bands of the tribal meeting. Often the site was near a river close to cottonwood trees, used in the ceremony. "The Kiowa Sun Dance usually included about ten days of tribal activity, including four to six 'getting ready days' and four dancing days" (Boyd, p. 38). On the first day of preparation, the Tai-me keeper carried the figure around the camp and encouraged people to act respectfully toward each other. Two men searched for the sacred tree to be used as the central pole of the Sun Dance lodge. The search began with their purification, after which they discovered the tree and notified the Tai-me keeper. Then, the tribe relocated around the tree.

The second day was spent honoring the buffalo through a ceremonial kill. Buffalo provided all the material possessions the tribe needed to survive—tipis, hides, bedding, food, clothing. Because the animal was central to their lives, its head and skin would be placed on the y-shaped pole that held up the Sun Dance lodge. Kiowa warriors performed a mock battle on the third day, entering the ceremonial circle from the east and surrounding foot soldiers and a makeshift fort around the sacred tree. After circling the fort four times, the mounted warriors had "won" the tree, and it was cut down to become the Y-shaped center pole of the Sun Dance or medicine lodge. The next two days were reserved for building the medicine lodge, from cottonwood logs around the sacred pole. More wooden poles from the top of the central forked pole to the surrounding logs formed a circular bower that would be filled in with branches. In the end, the lodge was enclosed completely, save for a small door. The sixth day of preparation was marked by humor, as the mud heads, mud-covered clowns, ran through the encampment tricking people. The same day, a buffalo-hunting ceremony featured tribal members disguised under buffalo skins. Hidden under the hides were the four greatest warriors; revealed in the finale, they were cheered and honored for their brave deeds. The day ended with the presentation of Tai-me, which was decorated and placed on an altar inside the lodge.

The Sun Dance itself lasted four days, with dancing that began at sunrise and ended at midnight. Dancers wore white buckskin shirts and blue breechcloths, and they danced facing Tai-me. While spectators could leave the lodge at midnight, dancers were required to stay, and could have no food or water for the entire four days. On the last day, dancing concluded at sunset and offerings were made to Tai-me to insure a good year ahead. Tai-me was then packed away and a social dance was held for the remainder of the night. Camp broke the next morning. Unlike the ceremony as practiced by other plains tribes, the Kiowa Sun Dance did not include body piercing of the dancers as a purification rite.

The U.S. Government took great pains to stop the Sun Dance. In fact, from the end of the Civil War until the mid twentieth century, the government tried to stop all native religious practices. In 1921, an Office of Indian Affairs circular stated:

> The sun-dance, and all other similar dances and so-called religious ceremonies are considered "Indian Offenses" under existing regulations, and corrective penalties are provided. I regard such restriction as applicable to any [religious] dance which involves . . . the reckless giving away of property . . . frequent or prolonged periods of celebration . . . in fact any orderly or plainly excessive performance that promotes superstitious cruelty, licentiousness, idleness, danger to health, and shiftless indifference to family welfare.
>
> (Indian Affairs circular in Cohen, p. 175 n. 347)

The repression did not erase the importance of the ceremony. Although the Kiowas have not held a complete Sun Dance since 1887, many of their beliefs are still strongly affected by it. As Momaday describes in *The Way to Rainy Mountain*, Tai-me brought ten medicine bundles, sources of great power that are still with the tribe. The Kiowas honor these bundles and consider them infused with spiritual healing energy. Held at a sacred site, the bundles remain under the protection of a tribal member. Momaday's text describes a visit to a Tai-me bundle:

> It was suspended by means of a strip of ticking from the fork of a small ceremonial tree. I made an offering of bright red cloth, and my grandmother prayed aloud. It seemed a long time that we were there. I had never come into the presence of Tai-me before—nor have I since. There was a great holiness all about the room, as if an old person had died there or a child had been born.
>
> (*Rainy Mountain*, p. 37)

Other plains tribes—the Sioux, Ute, Crow, Cheyenne, and Shoshone—revitalized the Sun Dance. This revival began around the time *The Way to Rainy Mountain* was published, when tribes started to reclaim their right to religious freedom and cultural independence.

The Memoir in Focus

The contents. *The Way to Rainy Mountain* is framed by two of Momaday's best-known poems, "Headwaters" and "Rainy Mountain Cemetery," which mark the book's physical and spiritual movement through Momaday's life as well as his understanding of the Kiowas' historic progress. "Headwaters" describes "A log, hollow and weather-stained," from which the Kiowas emerged into this world (*Rainy Mountain*, p. 2). This is the foundational moment—much like the biblical instant God created Adam—in which Momaday begins his exploration. Confronted, as the memoir progresses, with tribal stories, historic accounts, and personal anecdote, readers come to understand the importance of this introductory poem: just as headwaters merge to form a larger, much stronger river, so the tribal, historical, and personal voices distinguished in *The Way to Rainy Mountain* flow into Momaday's identity and define the Kiowas' place in the world.

DIVERGENT PERSPECTIVES

"An examination of the [Kiowa] calendars affords a good idea of the comparative importance attached by the Indian and the white man to the same event. From the white man's point of view many of the things recorded in these aboriginal histories would seem to be of the most trivial consequence while many events which we [white men] regard as marking eras in the history of the plains tribes are entirely omitted."

(Mooney, p. 145)

The book begins in 1965, the year Momaday sets out for the Kiowa landmark, Rainy Mountain, where his grandmother, Aho, who has died the same year, is buried. Aho was born in 1880, at the close of the Kiowas' golden age, when their religious practice of the Sun Dance was forbidden and their migratory lifestyle stymied by the U.S. Cavalry. Momaday realizes that Aho's death may mark the loss of something great: the memory, first, of his tribal family; and second, because he himself is a part of Aho's tribal reminiscences, the chance for a broader and deeper understanding of himself. "I wanted to see in reality what she had seen in her mind's eye, and traveled fifteen hundred miles to begin my pilgrimage" (*Rainy Mountain*, p. 7). With this, Momaday embarks on his attempt to piece together his people's past.

Starting in Yellowstone, in western Montana and northern Wyoming, Momaday follows the historical route of his people east over the Rocky Mountains to the Devil's Tower region of eastern Wyoming. From there, the Kiowa author travels south through Colorado and southeast into the Kiowas' present-day homeland, the Wichita Mountains of southwestern Oklahoma. His journey is graced with a mix of the tribe's official history and his family's personal narratives about life in the past and in the present, explaining how the tribe and the author himself came to be.

In addition to the poetic frame, a prologue, introduction, and conclusion encase the prose in yet another layer of reflective musings. The prose itself is separated into three sections—"The Setting Out," "The Going On," and "The Closing In," and subdivided more finely into 24 story groups, or triads. A triad consists of three varieties of story—the tribal, historical, and personal—each typeset in a different font. Line drawings created by Al Momaday, the author's father, illuminate the tribal retellings, pointing to the importance of the visual in this narrative strand.

The book's first section, "The Setting Out," recounts stories of long ago, beginning with the Kiowas' emergence into this world: "You know, everything had to begin, and this is how it was: the Kiowas came one by one into the world through a hollow log" (*Rainy Mountain*, p. 16). Mythic retellings of the sun's child and his development and of the coming of Tai-me (the sacred Sun Dance doll) offer insight into the tribe's subsistence and survival methods. Such Kiowa tales "constitute a kind of literary chronicle. In a sense they are the milestones of that old migration in which the Kiowas journeyed from the Yellowstone to the Wichita" (Momaday in Hobson," pp. 170-71). They recount Kiowa history and remind tribal members how they came to their present state, spiritually, historically, and physically. The stories act as cultural signposts, directing Kiowa people through their past and into their future.

Throughout the text, the second voice, that of official history, helps flesh out the ancient tribal stories, offering a factual account of the Kiowas. This factual account occasionally provides dates and draws on the findings of anthropologists and historical scholars. Finally, the personal voice, which assumes a poetic rhythm and a deeply reflective tone, describes the author's reactions to the land he sees and recounts personal and familial stories he recalls as he makes his way through tribal history.

The second section, "The Going On," offers an account of the Kiowas' golden age, from approximately 1740 to 1875, when the Kiowas become dominant on the southern plains and develop warrior skills and social systems conducive to the harsh environment. Like the rest of the book, "The Going On" is divided into three sections and explores how arrows are made, the complex relationships between men and women, the harsh weather of the plains, and the Kiowas' relationship to the buffalo.

Throughout the third section, "The Closing In," the three voices begin to mingle with one another. The mythic or tribal passages, for example, include discussions of Aho and Mommedaty, Momaday's paternal grandmother and grandfather, whose lives and stories have become a part of Momaday's individual, as well as his tribal, identity. When Momaday discusses the Tai-me bundles, or the sacred medicine bundles, central to ancient Kiowa religion, he pulls his grandmother Aho into the tribal section, making her a part of the tribe's collective history:

> Aho remembered something, a strange thing. This is how it was: You know, the Tai-me bundle is not very big, but it is full of power. Once Aho went to see the Tai-me keeper's wife. The two of them were sitting together . . . when they heard an awful noise, as if a tree or some very heavy object had fallen down. It frightened them, and they went to see what on earth it was. It was Tai-me—Tai-me had fallen to the floor. No one knows how it was that Tai-me fell; nothing caused it, as far as anyone could see.
>
> (*Rainy Mountain*, p. 80)

The personal stories Momaday told of his grandmother in the first part of the book become tribal stories as Momaday moves toward the Kiowa present. Similarly the historical voice becomes more entwined with the personal and tribal accounts, this time in connection with his grandfather: "For a time, Mommedaty wore one of the grandmother bundles . . . on a string tied around his neck [personal and tribal] . . . If anyone who wore a medicine bundle failed to show it the proper respect, it grew extremely heavy around his neck [historical]" (*Rainy Mountain*, p. 81). The tribal, historical, and personal sketches, which complement each other in the beginning of the text, meld together toward its close, showing Momaday's integrated idea of himself as an American Indian.

FROM MOONEY'S CALENDAR HISTORY OF THE KIOWA INDIANS

"Sett'an stated that he had been fourteen years drawing it [the calendar]; i.e., that he had begun work on it fourteen years before, noting the events of the first six years from the statements of older men, and the rest from his own recollection. . . . This will be understood when it is explained that it is customary for the owners of such Indian heirlooms to bring them out at frequent intervals during the long nights in the winter camp, to be exhibited and discussed in the circle of warriors about the tipi fire. . . . At these gatherings the pipe is filled and passed around, and each man in turn recites some mythic or historic tradition, or some noted deed on the warpath, which is then discussed by the circle. Thus this history of the tribe is formulated and handed down."

(Mooney, pp. 144-45)

The last personal narrative sums up the journey Momaday (and his readers) have just taken: "Once in his life a man ought to concentrate his mind upon the remembered earth, I believe. He ought to give himself up to a particular landscape in his experience, to look at it from as many angles as he can, to wonder about it, to dwell upon it" (*Rainy Mountain*, p. 83). By knowing the earth from whence his people came and recounting their perceptions of the world, Momaday has come to understand himself.

The Kiowa calendars. *The Way to Rainy Mountain* relies heavily on tribal history and stories, the cruxes of native identity. In addition to tribal stories, which were passed through the generations verbally, pictographically designed calendars also perserved Kiowa history. Prior to the reservation period, when the Kiowa people were forced onto a specific territory, these tribal calendars, which were created by specialists in the tribe, highlighted important events in the Kiowas'

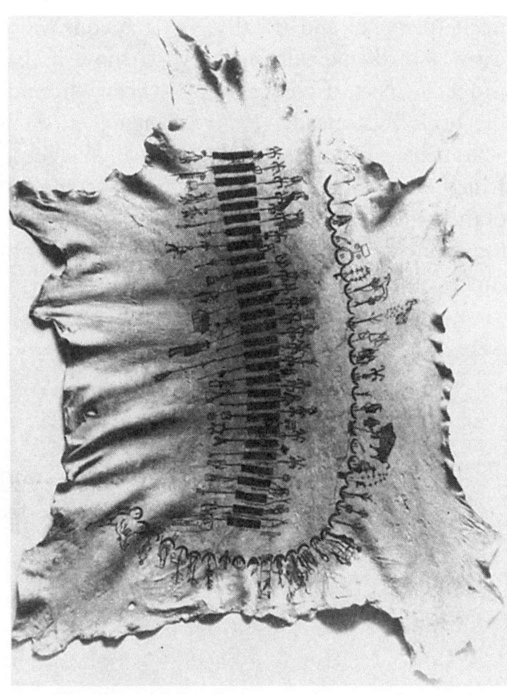

The Kiowa Pictorial Calendar encapsulates Kiowa history through its drawings.

past. Present-day historians do not know how many calendars existed. Many of them may have been buried with their keepers or otherwise lost through history. Thankfully James Mooney, an ethnologist of the nineteenth century, acquired three of these tribal timepieces. Mooney describes them in his 1898 Smithsonian Institution Bureau of American Ethnology report, *Calendar History of the Kiowa Indians*, which Momaday consulted in writing *The Way to Rainy Mountain*.

These calendars reflect the tribe's closeness to the land, their ideas about themselves, and the events that changed them. The pictographs, or ancient drawings, which depict the major events of each winter and summer, are arranged in a continuous spiral starting in one corner of the page or animal hide (various materials were used) and moving inward as the years marched on. A black upright bar, symbolizing the lack of vegetation, marks each winter, while summers are usually indicated by a medicine lodge, the central object of the Sun Dance.

The three calendars Mooney describes in his work are named after their creators. There are the 1) Sett'an, or Set-tan, yearly calendar (covering the years 1833 to 1893); 2) the Anko yearly calendar (1864-1893); and 3) the Anko monthly calendar, which accounts for 37 months of Kiowa life. The specialists drew the two yearly calendars with colored pencil on heavy manila paper; for the monthly account, they first used black pencil in a small ledger notebook, then redrew it with colored pencil on hide.

Recorded on the calendars are momentous tribal incidents, happenings that were of immediate importance to the Kiowa. Many of the deeds depicted on the Sett'an calendar are mentioned in *The Way to Rainy Mountain*, including the "fine heraldic tipi [that] was accidentally destroyed by fire" in the winter of 1872 and 1873, the Kiowa man who stabbed his wife during the 1843 Sun Dance, and the Horse-eating Sun Dance of 1879 (*Rainy Mountain*, p. 45). The memoir includes a description of the Leonid meteor shower of November 13, 1833. Marking the end of the Kiowas' golden era, the event found its way into Sett'an's winter description of that year, which shows a child with stars above his head. This is one of the calendar's earliest entries. Such an event, Mooney writes, is often considered the start of an era by tribal peoples. Momaday himself declares that the calendar's pictograph "marks the beginning as it were of the historical period of the tribal mind. . . . The falling stars seemed to image the sudden and violent disintegration of an old order" (*Rainy Mountain*, p. 85).

Another image, Sett'an's pictographic description of the final, unfinished Sun Dance of 1890 shows the medicine pole left standing outside the completed lodge. As Mooney tells it:

> The Kiowa had decided to celebrate their usual annual sun dance at the *Piho* or bend in the Washita, where they had already held it twice before, when the agent determined to prevent it. The news [that troops were coming to stop the dance] was brought to Stumbling-bear . . . by Quanah, chief of the Comanche, who advised him to send word to the Kiowa to stop, as the soldiers would kill them and their horses if they persisted.
>
> (Mooney, p. 359)

Their survival threatened, the Kiowas dispersed on hearing the news, going to their respective dwellings, leaving the unfinished medicine pole and lodge standing. This was the tribe's last attempt to practice the Sun Dance.

American Indian oral tradition. The Kiowas have a verbal tradition to be mined, says Momaday, a task *The Way to Rainy Mountain* begins to take up and that its epilogue calls vital:

> The [Kiowa] culture would persist for a while in decline, until about 1875, but then it would be gone, and there would be very little material evidence that it had ever been. Yet it is within

> the reach of memory still, though tenuously now, and moreover it is even defined in a remarkably rich and living verbal tradition which demands to be preserved for its own sake.
>
> (*Rainy Mountain*, pp. 114-15)

Oral tradition is always one generation away from extinction, Momaday notes, making its future precarious and its telling cherished. In his words, this tradition is the process by which the lore of a people is "formulated, communicated, and preserved in language by word of mouth, as opposed to writing" (Momaday in Hobson p. 167). Momaday insists on factoring it into his portrayal of the past. His memoir's combination of tribal, official historical, and personal stories suggests a new way of understanding, or imagining, past events. The suggestion is that the people's oral tradition must be taken into account when recalling years past. Because official history is often ethnocentric and incomplete, oral traditions complement and add depth to this more familiar type of documentation.

In traditional Kiowa life, verbal stories were used to address various tribal needs. Sometimes such accounts taught appropriate behaviors; other times the accounts offered serious insight into sacred religious beliefs. In either case, the art of storytelling was exceptionally refined and difficult to master.

Stories, such as the Kiowa tale describing Devil's Tower—which became America's first national monument in 1906—and the Big Dipper, explain how parts of the world came to be. "Two centuries ago, because they could not do otherwise, the Kiowas made a legend at the base of the rock," says the text (*Rainy Mountain*, p. 8). In the legend, a boy becomes a bear and chases his seven sisters to the stump of a tree. At the tree's command, the girls climb its trunk, whereupon they are lifted into the air and carried into the sky to become the stars of the Big Dipper. This tale is of particular importance to Momaday, for it is the source of his first Kiowa name, Tsoai-talee, or Rock-Tree Boy.

Tales such as these connect the Kiowas to the world, giving them a sense of place, helping to specify how the tribe relates to its environmental surroundings. "From that moment, and so long as the legend lives," Momaday writes, "the Kiowas have kinsmen in the night sky" (*Rainy Mountain*, p. 8). As long as the oral tradition is passed from one generation to the next, the Kiowas, like other native peoples, will be able to define themselves in their own voices, using their distinct world views.

Sources. N. Scott Momaday sees all his work as connected, all part of one tribal, literary, and artistic opus. In an interview with Joseph Bruchac, Momaday states:

> I think that my work proceeds from the American Indian oral tradition, and I think it sustains that tradition and carries it along. . . . I've written several books, but to me they are all parts of the same story. . . . My purpose is to carry out what was begun a long time ago; there's no end to it that I can see.
>
> (Momaday in Bruchac, p. 187)

The Way to Rainy Mountain draws in particular on Kiowa oral tradition and storytelling. In the acknowledgments preceding the memoir, Momaday thanks "those of my kinsman who willingly recounted to me the tribal history and literature which informs this book." Indeed, after the 1965 death of his grandmother, Momaday, aided by his father's knowledge of the Kiowa language, collected tribal stories from the tribe's elders. These tellers have been a primary source for all of Momaday's work, particularly *The Way to Rainy Mountain*. The memoir draws on them for its personal and tribal narratives; for the latter, as noted, it draws also on James Mooney's 1898 *Calendar History of the Kiowa Indians*.

Beyond tribal sources, it is difficult to pinpoint exactly where Momaday acquired his historical knowledge. What is certain is that there were several academics—anthropologists and historians—whose work contributed to the historical portions of the book. Other probable influences include Ann Marriott's *The Ten Grandmothers* (1945), Mildred P. Mayhall's *The Kiowas* (1962), Elsie Clews Parsons's *Kiowa Tales* (1929), and William Sturtevant Nye's *Bad Medicine and Good: Tales of the Kiowa* (1962). Since Momaday is himself an academic, these types of sources were numerous and varied.

While attending Stanford University, Momaday worked closely with poet and literary critic Yvor Winters and was no doubt influenced by him. Winters supervised Momaday's doctoral dissertation and critiqued Momaday's later creative output, including *The Journey of Tai-me* (1967), a limited-edition writing Momaday has identified as the model for *The Way to Rainy Mountain*.

Reception. Because of its refusal to fall neatly into an existing genre, *The Way to Rainy Mountain* was difficult to publish. Social scientists questioned the work, while literature lovers lauded its artful sketches of Kiowa life. When the manuscript was sent out to anthropologists for review in 1968, it was, by and large, rejected: "It isn't the kind of book that I would go for," one academic reviewer wrote. "The book would certainly not be of any interest to anthros or folklorists," another crooned (Lincoln, p. 106). Thankfully, Momaday's editor sent the work to literary types as well. Edward Abbey encouraged its publication, saying "Scott Momaday conjures the spirit of a place" (Abbey in Lincoln, p. 110). Wallace Stegner too lauded the memoir, saying the writer's "recreation of Kiowa myth and history, that is something no white man could ever have given us" (Stegner in Lincoln, p. 110). A few months later, *The Way to Rainy Mountain* was in press.

The book received brief mention in a variety of major publications, including the *New York Times*, the *Atlantic Monthly*, and the *New Yorker*, typically without being featured in many. Those who reviewed the memoir tended to praise it for its pious, stately language and captivating dignity. In *The Southern Review*, Kenneth Fields lauded the text as "far and away his [Momaday's] best book" (Fields, p. 196). Despite its quiet appearance, the book would become staple reading in American Indian studies courses across the country. Ten years after its publication, the late Michael A. Dorris, then chair of Dartmouth College's Native American Studies Department, named *The Way to Rainy Mountain* one of the finest books available on Native Americans (Dorris, p. 48).

—Amy M. Ware

For More Information

Boyd, Maurice. *Kiowa Voices: Ceremonial Dance, Ritual, and Songs.* Vol. 2. Fort Worth: Texas Christian University Press, 1981.

Bruchac, Joseph, ed. *Survival This Way: Interview with American Indian Poets.* Tucson: University of Arizona Press, 1987.

Cohen, Felix S. *Felix S. Cohen's Handbook of Federal Indian Law.* Albuquerque: University of New Mexico Press, 1971.

Deloria, Vine, Jr. *Custer Died for Your Sins: An Indian Manifesto.* New York: The Macmillan Company, 1969.

Dorris, Michael A. "The Best Books on Native Americans." In *The American West*, 16 (May 1979): 48.

Fields, Kenneth. "More Than Language Means: A Review of N. Scott Momaday's *The Way to Rainy Mountain.*" *The Southern Review* (winter 1970): 196-204.

Hobson, Geary, ed. *The Remembered Earth: An Anthology of Contemporary Native American Literature.* Albuquerque: University of New Mexico Press, 1979.

Irwin, Lee. "Freedom, Law, and Prophecy: A Brief History of Native American Religious Resistance." In *Native American Spirituality: A Critical Reader.* Ed. Lee Irwin. Lincoln: University of Nebraska Press, 2000.

Lincoln, Kenneth. "Tai-me to Rainy Mountain: The Makings of American Indian Literature." In *American Indian Quarterly* 10, no. 2 (spring 1986): 101-117.

Momaday, N. Scott. *The Way to Rainy Mountain.* Albuquerque: University of New Mexico Press, 1969.

Mooney, James. *Calendar History of the Kiowa Indians.* Bureau of American Ethnology, 17th Annual Report. Washington, D.C.: Government Printing Office, 1898.

Roemer, Kenneth M., ed. *Approaches to Teaching The Way to Rainy Mountain.* New York: Modern Language Association of America, 1988.

West with the Night

by
Beryl Markham

> **THE LITERARY WORK**
>
> A memoir set mainly in British East Africa from the 1900s to 1936; published in 1942.
>
> **SYNOPSIS**
>
> After coming of age in British East Africa, a young Englishwoman breaks new ground as a pilot, distinguishing herself as the first person leaving from England, to cross the North Atlantic from a westerly direction.

Born in Leicestershire, England, in 1902, Beryl Clutterbuck (later Markham) moved to Kenya with her family when she was three years old. Her father started a farm at Njoro, but discovered his true talent was in breeding and training horses for racetracks in Kenya's capital city, Nairobi. Beryl spent most of her childhood on what turned into a horse farm, receiving little formal schooling but learning to speak several African dialects, such as Nandi, from the families employed by her father. As a playmate of Nandi children, Beryl also accompanied the Nandi on their hunts, learning to hunt wild game with a spear. Later, following in her father's footsteps, Beryl established herself as a successful horse trainer in Nairobi; she married twice during that period—unsuccessfully to Jock Purves and Mansfield Markham, whose name she kept after they separated. In her late twenties, Markham learned to fly a plane, becoming the first woman in Kenya to receive a professional pilot's license. She worked for several years as a bush pilot, transporting goods, mail, and people to the more remote regions of Africa, and also flew to locate big game for safaris. During the 1930s, Markham returned to England. In 1936 she took up the challenge to fly solo from London to New York, a risky enterprise that involved flying against prevailing winds. Although Markham came down somewhat short of the mark, crash-landing her plane into a peat bog in Nova Scotia, she survived the flight and became an instant celebrity. After the death of a close friend and fellow pilot, Markham lost interest in flying but she wrote about her achievement and her Kenyan childhood in *West with the Night* (1942). The memoir has been celebrated as both a lyrical depiction of her life in Kenya and an exciting account of her experience breaking new ground as an aviatrix.

Events in History at the Time of the Memoir

Settling British East Africa. During the late nineteenth century, Britain, along with France, Portugal, Germany, and Italy, engaged in a scramble for control of Africa. Spurred on by tiny Belgium's establishment of the Congo Free State in 1879, Britain sent troops and missionaries into West Africa, subduing indigenous peoples by military force and religious conversion. In the 1880s, Britain explored and laid claim to territories in the East African interior as well. Germany had already made formidable inroads in

Beryl Markham

the region; in 1885, after negotiating a deal with the sultan of Zanzibar, the nominal ruler over most of the East African coast, Germany established the German East Africa Company, which conducted trade and exploration through what is now Tanzania. Shortly thereafter, Britain's dealings with the sultan bore fruit too; in 1887 the sultan leased the lands of what would become present-day Kenya to the Imperial British East Africa Company. True colonization, however, did not occur until 1895, when British East Africa became a protectorate under the direct control of the British government.

Between 1895 and 1914, a series of British military expeditions quelled the resistance of African peoples to colonial rule. The British government also constructed a railroad from Mombasa to Lake Victoria to connect the parts of present-day Kenya and increase their political control over the region; dubbed the "Lunatic Express" by detractors, the railroad, which was completed in 1901, cost British taxpayers almost 6 million pounds. To offset some of the expense, Charles Eliot, the governor of the Protectorate, recruited European settlers to develop the region and make the railroad economically viable. As an inducement, the British Foreign Office offered thousands of virgin acres to wealthy, socially prominent Europeans, such as Hugh Cholmondley, third Baron Delamere, hoping that others of similar birth and fortune would follow suit.

Markham's own family was among those early settlers. Her father, Charles Clutterbuck, a former army officer of good family but little financial means, emigrated from England to South Africa in 1904, hoping to make a fortune as a farmer. Not long after arriving in South Africa, Clutterbuck learned of the opportunities to be found in British East Africa; so he headed for Nairobi, then only a settlement of tin-roofed shanties surrounding the railway station, where he met Lord Delamere and was hired as manager for Delamere's farm in the Kenyan highlands. Delamere also offered Clutterbuck suggestions about several parcels of land for which he could apply. Clutterbuck eventually purchased 1,000 acres of land in the highlands at three rupees an acre, and, with the help of African laborers, started a farm that he called Green Hills. In late 1905, Clutterbuck's wife, Clara, and their children, Richard and Beryl, joined him.

Upper-class settlers in East Africa gradually began to establish a comfortable lifestyle in the African bush. The town of Nairobi underwent a period of rapid development; hotels and private bungalows sprang up as more and more Europeans immigrated to East Africa. The rigors of the African climate and the isolation of the wilderness, however, took its toll on some settlers. Clutterbuck's wife and son failed to adapt successfully to life in East Africa, returning to England in 1906. Beryl, however, remained with Clutterbuck in Africa and flourished. Paying tribute to her father and other early settlers who succeeded in carving a living out of Kenya, Markham later wrote, "The farm at Njoro [in the Kenyan highlands] was endless, but it was no farm at all until my father made it. He made it out of nothing and out of everything—the things of which all farms are made. . . . He made it out of labour and out of patience. He was no farmer. He bought the land because it was cheap and fertile, and because East Africa was new and you could feel the future of it under your feet" (Markham, *West with the Night*, p. 67).

The Kalenjin. Although Markham mentions several indigenous peoples of East Africa in her memoir, she writes most frequently of the Kipsigis and Nandi, with whom she had the most contact during her childhood years. Both peoples belong to what has become known, since the 1940s, as the Kalenjin ("I tell you"), a group living in the western highlands of Kenya in the Rift Valley Province. Mainly farmers and herders, the Kalenjin consists of not only the Kipsigis and Nandi but also the Tugen, the Pokot, the Elgeyo, and the Marakwet. Kalenjin culture, though comprised of all these subgroups, is notable for having two branches of ancient customs and values, one for each sex after initiation (circumcision). Men hunted, fought, and became "Morani" (warriors); women tended their homes and families. As the daughter of a British settler, Markham faced fewer restrictions than the Africans. They seemed to her to observe strict gender distinctions: "If the men of the Nandi were like unto stone, their women were like unto leaves of grass. They were shy and they were feminine and they did the things that women are meant to do, and they never hunted" (*West with the Night*, p. 77)

As a child, Markham played with Kibii, a Kalenjin boy, and participated in Morani hunts; her participation was probably permitted because she was white and British, the daughter of a sahib (European master). Whatever the reason, the Morani nicknamed her "Lakweit" (little girl), taught her how to use a spear and how to familiarize herself with the different ways of the game being hunted. The hunting incidents described in *West with the Night* provide much of the memoir's excitement; however, the memoir is guilty of some inaccuracies. Markham's two closest African friends, Kibii—later called Arap Ruta—and his father Arap Maina were actually Kipsigis, though Markham identifies them in the memoir as Nandi. While Kipsigis and Nandi both belong to the Kalenjin, some critics have speculated that Markham may have designated her friends as Nandi because of the Nandi's more colorful reputation as warriors (Kipsigis were allied to the Nandi but theirs was a more pastoral lifestyle). During the 1890s the Nandi strongly resisted the imposition of British rule. They were forced to capitulate, however, after a series of British military expeditions in 1896, 1897, and 1905 resulted in major casualties among the Nandi.

Safaris. Other dramatic episodes of *West with the Night* deal with Markham's participation in safaris, or hunting expeditions; its vast supply of wild game remained one of East Africa's key attractions for foreign visitors. After railroads came to Africa and major cities such as Nairobi appeared, wealthy hunters poured into Africa to participate in safaris. Conducting safaris became a very lucrative business; the wealthy hunters hired white guides to show them the region and often employed as many as 30 African porters to convey their food and equipment. Often the wealthiest hunters also brought cooks, gun-bearers, and other servants to provide them with "home comforts" in the African bush. The duration of safaris varied, with some of the longest lasting up to several months.

The success of a safari often depended on a skillful guide—one who knew the terrain intimately, spoke Swahili and perhaps other African dialects fluently, understood the habits of wild game, and knew how to interact smoothly with his clients as well as the indigenous peoples. One such guide was Denys Finch-Hatton, an English earl's son, who had moved to British East Africa in 1912 and established a successful trading business. An avid sportsman, Finch-Hatton soon acquired worldwide fame as a professional leader of safaris, an enterprise he had started during the 1920s.

In *West with the Night*, Beryl Markham's life intersects dramatically with that of Finch-Hatton. The two had known each other for several years and shared common interests, including hunting and flying. After learning to pilot a plane, Finch-Hatton became interested in using it in safaris. Markham writes, "Denys said he wanted to try something that had never been done before . . . to see if elephant could be scouted by plane; if they could, he thought, hunters would be willing to pay very well for the service" (*West with the Night*, p. 193). Markham, herself a pilot-in-training at the time, saw the possibilities in Finch-Hatton's scheme and agreed to go with him on a trip to the town of Voi. The warning of another good friend, Tom Campbell Black, however, persuaded Markham to delay joining Finch-Hatton, who departed for Voi without her. Although Finch-Hatton's elephant-scouting mission was successful, his plane crashed on the way back to Nairobi, killing Finch-Hatton and the African servant who had accompanied him. Remembering her deceased friend, Markham credits him with "a charm of intellect and strength, of quick intuition" and humor like that of the French writer Voltaire. Denys, she says, "would have greeted doomsday with a wink—and I think he did" (*West with the Night*, p. 192). After his death, Markham herself scouted game by plane, often in the company of Bror von Blixen, a Swedish baron, formerly married to writer Isak Dinesen, and a notable sportsman and organizer of safaris himself (see **Out of Africa**, also in *Literature and Its Times*).

Aviation and record-setting flights. Labored on over the centuries by inventors of various nations and patented in the early 1900s by American brothers Wilbur and Orville Wright, airplanes surely represented one of the foremost techno-

THE LOVE OF HER LIFE?

Although Markham married three times and had several romantic involvements in her long life, her closest relationship may have been with Tom Campbell Black, the man who taught her to fly and with whom she remained close friends for the rest of their lives. Born in Brighton, England in 1898, Tom was educated at Brighton College and at the Royal Naval College, Greenwich. During his schooldays, he acquired an interest in aviation and, after the First World War broke out, he immediately joined the Royal Naval Air Service, adding a year to his age to be accepted. Tom later transferred to the Royal Flying Corps; towards the end of the war, he led the first British squadron in the attack on Cologne, Germany. During the 1920s, Tom studied law for a time, then moved out to Kenya, where he and his brother started a coffee-farm at Rongai. But, flying being Tom's passion, he eventually turned the farm over to a full-time manager and attained his commercial license as a pilot, going on to do freelance flying work. While opening air routes for mail deliveries in East Africa, Tom conceived of establishing a commercial air service there. With the backing of a wealthy widow, Florence Kerr Wilson, he founded Wilson Airways in 1929, for which he acted as managing director. Markham, who had known Tom on and off through the 1920s, became his pupil in 1931. For a time, the two were romantically involved, though they separated in 1933, after Tom took a new job in England. While abroad, he participated in and won an air race from London, England, to Melborne, Australia; he also fell in love with an English actress, Florence Desmond, whom he married in 1935. Markham was sufficiently distressed by the news of the upcoming nuptials in the press to send a cable to Tom with the following message: "DARLING IS IT TRUE YOU ARE TO MARRY FLORENCE DESMOND? PLEASE ANSWER STOP HEARTBROKEN BERYL" (Markham in Lovell, p. 147). It is not known how this potentially volatile situation was resolved but Markham's friendship with Tom apparently remained intact. The following year, shortly after Markham's record-breaking flight from England to North America, Tom was killed when his plane, taxiing to a take-off position on the Liverpool Aerodrome, was struck by another incoming plane. Markham was devastated to learn of his death; over the years, she often told close friends that Tom had been the love of her life.

logical advances of the twentieth century. In 1903, the Wrights became the first to achieve flight in an aircraft of their own design, making four short flights in one day. The Wrights' achievement sparked renewed interest among European inventors, who introduced further modifications and innovations to their own models of flying machines. Following the Wright brothers' example, European aviators made their own daring trial flights. In 1907 the French-born Henri Farman became the first person to remain in the air for as long as the Wright brothers; the following year, Farman also became the first to complete a circular flight of one kilometer in Europe. In 1909 Frenchman Louis Bleriot made the first flight—37 minutes long—across the English Channel in the Bleriot XI, a monoplane of his own design. That same year the first great flying meet was held at Reims, France. In England, Alliot Verdon Roe built and tested a Wright-type model in 1908, then went on to design his own line of biplanes, including the often-used Avro 504 in 1913.

By 1913 the British War Office and the British Admiralty acknowledged the advanced state of the airplane and accepted it as "a potential weapon of significance" (Tangye, p. 24). The use of airplanes by both sides during the First World War, often as reconnaissance planes to scout out enemy positions, led to the rapid development of superior machines. Technological advancement of the airplane continued through the next two decades. This period is considered the golden age of aviation. With the backing of government-subsidized research and development programs, military and civilian aircraft increased in speed, range, altitude, and carrying capacity.

This period from 1919 to 1939 also marked the advent of record-setting long-distance flights. In 1919 the U.S. Navy Curtiss flying boat NC-4 made the first Atlantic crossing; John Alcock and Arthur Whitten-Brown, the first nonstop Atlantic crossing; and the British airship R.34, the first round-trip Atlantic crossing. That same year Ross Smith made the first flight from London to Australia. More astonishing efforts followed in the 1920s and 1930s, including Charles A. Lindbergh's solo flight from New York to Paris in 1927. The American aviatrix Amelia Earhart, meanwhile, became the first woman to fly solo across the Atlantic in 1932 and the first ever to fly west to east from Honolulu to California in 1935. British aviatrix Amy Johnson flew from England to Australia in 1930; her husband Jim Mollison became the first to fly east to west across the Atlantic Ocean, soaring from Ireland to eastern Canada in 1932. Few pilots chose to cross the Atlantic east to west because it meant flying against the prevailing winds. In *West with the Night*, Markham describes how she decided to accept this challenge, with the backing of wealthy acquaintance John Carberry. "A number of pilots have flown the North Atlantic, west to east" he informs her. "Only Jim Mollison has done it alone the other way—from Ireland. Nobody has done it alone from England—man or woman. I'd be interested in that but nothing else. . . . I'll furnish the plane and you fly the Atlantic—but, gee, I wouldn't tackle it for a million. Think of all that black water! Think how cold it is!" (*West with the Night*, p. 279).

The Memoir in Focus

The contents. Beryl Markham's memoir weaves back and forth in time, relating incidents from her earliest childhood in what is now Kenya to her adult experiences as a horse trainer and bush pilot. The structure of the work is episodic—a series of vividly rendered memories loosely strung together. Markham asks at the outset: "How is it possible to bring order out of memory? I should like to begin at the beginning, patiently, like a weaver at his loom. I should like to say, 'This is the place to start; there can be no other.' But there are a hundred places to start" (*West with the Night*, p. 3).

The first incident Markham chooses to relate takes place in 1935, when she is a freelance bush pilot, working in Nairobi, Kenya. Markham's mission is to fly a canister of oxygen to a sick miner in the village of Nungwe; arriving at her destination, she delivers the canister and spends some time talking with another patient, a German or Dutchman, who is dying of a disease known as blackwater. She is distracted, however, by the knowledge that a colleague and fellow pilot, named Wood, has been lost somewhere on the Serengetti Plains for the last two days. As soon as she can get away, Markham heads out to look for Wood herself, finally locating him—alive—after a long search by air. While Markham is settling Wood into her own plane, she encounters an African who used to work on her father's farm. The two exchange greetings and reminiscences, remembering the time that Markham, as a child, was attacked by a lion. After their safe return, Markham and Wood discuss why they put up with all the dangers, hardships, and in-

MARKHAM ON THE ESSENCE OF AFRICA

Woven through Markham's memoir are observations tinged with a reverence for Africa and its people that flew in the face of contrary images, which held it to be a less developed and therefore less worthy environment than any in Europe.

> White men's wars are fought on the edges of Africa. . . . Competitors in conquest have overlooked the vital soul of Africa herself. . . . Racial purity, true aristocracy, devolve . . . from the preservation of kinship with the elemental forces and purposes of life whose understanding is not farther beyond the mind of a Native shepherd than beyond the cultured fumblings of a mortar-board intelligence.
>
> The soul of Africa, its integrity, the slow inexorable pulse of its life, is its own and of such singular rhythm that no outsider, unless steeped from childhood in its endless, even beat, can ever hope to experience it, except only as a bystander might experience a Masai war dance knowing nothing of its music nor the meanings of its steps.
>
> The Serengetti plain . . . the great sanctuary of the Masai People . . . harbour more wild game than any similar territory in all of East Africa. . . . They are endless and they are empty, but they are as warm with life as the waters of a tropic sea.
>
> (*West with the Night*, pp. 7, 13, 33)

conveniences of flying, and finally agree that life without flying "would all be so dull" (*West with the Night*, p. 53).

The autobiography then relates stories of Markham's childhood. Having left England for British East Africa, Markham's father builds a farm in the highlands at Njoro and then a mill; he also gains repute as a breeder and trainer of racehorses. The young Beryl spends her days roaming the valleys and forests, usually in the company of the Nandi Murani people; one of her closest friends is Kibii, a Nandi boy. Young Beryl experiences many adventures, including the previously mentioned attack by a neighbor's pet lion, who has been allowed to roam free. Only the owner's quick intervention prevents Beryl from being killed; the lion is subsequently caged for the remainder of his life. When Beryl is slightly older, she often joins the Nandi men on their hunts, a privilege denied the Nandi women. During one eventful hunt, the prey—a fierce warthog—attacks and badly mauls Beryl's dog, Buller. Beryl kills the warthog with a spear. Afterwards, Arap Maina, a Morani hunter who is Beryl's friend and Kibii's father, comforts the child and helps her bring the dog home, where it eventually recovers. (The memoir misspells the name *Arap Maina* as *Arab Maina*.)

Beryl's life changes with the coming of the First World War. In Africa, as in Europe, the men—English and native—leave to fight the Germans on the colonial frontier; Arap Maina is among those killed in the war. Beryl and Kibii grow slowly towards adulthood. As a teen, Beryl becomes more involved with her father's horse-training business. In 1917 she helps a mare give birth and her father rewards her by allowing her to keep the foal, which Beryl names Pegasus. After the war, Beryl's life undergoes further changes. Her father ends up selling his farm, house, stables, and horses to fulfill a mill contract with the government during a period of savage drought. He decides to leave Africa and start over again as a horse trainer in Peru, inviting 17-year-old Beryl to join him. Beryl opts instead to remain in Africa and try to become a horse trainer herself. Her father advises her to go north to Molo and work hard but not expect too much. Beryl sets out for Molo with only her horse, Pegasus, and two saddlebags of personal belongings.

Some time later, after acquiring her license as a trainer and setting up her own stable, Beryl is reunited with her childhood friend Kibii, now grown to manhood and called Arap Ruta. Several Africans who worked on the Njoro farm have already followed Beryl to Molo; Arap Ruta also wishes to offer his services. Beryl readily employs him and the two begin a successful working relationship. One day, while out riding, Beryl has a chance encounter with Tom Black, a motorist whose car has broken down by the roadside. The two strike up a conversation; Beryl learns that Tom, a pilot during the war, aspires to purchase an airplane. She listens to Tom's vivid descriptions of flight but does not at that time recognize the door of opportunity that has been opened for her.

Meanwhile, Beryl's reputation as a horse trainer grows. A filly trained by her stable wins a prestigious race in Nairobi, beating a colt Beryl had formerly trained but whose owner had moved him to another stable. Fate brings about another meeting with Tom Black, who has acquired a new airplane, with which he has carried out a daring rescue. Two men on safari had badly wounded a lion, then tried to photograph him; the wounded lion attacked, killing one man and mauling another, before being killed itself. Tom rescued the injured man, flying him and the cremated ashes of his dead companion back to Nairobi; Tom had lit the funeral pyre with a match, then stored the ashes in a biscuit tin to carry them back. Over coffee, Tom relays the adventure to Beryl. "Just remember," he concludes, "never to fly without a match or a biscuit tin. And of course you're going to fly. I've always known it. I could see it in the stars" (*West with the Night*, pp. 181-82). After some thought, Beryl behaves accordingly. She leaves her career as a horse-trainer and learns to fly. Arap Ruta supports the decision: "If it is to be that we must fly, Memsahib, then we will fly. At what hour of the morning do we begin?" (*West with the Night*, p. 182).

Tom Black undertakes Beryl's flying lessons himself and proves to be an excellent teacher who hones her flyer's instincts and recognizes her right to make mistakes. After 18 months, Beryl gains her pilot's license and embarks upon her new career in Nairobi. Some time later, as a free-lance pilot, she becomes involved with the safari set, including the famous English guide and hunter Denys Finch-Hatton. Beryl and Finch-Hatton become interested in the possibility of scouting elephant by plane; he invites her to fly down to Voi with him and explore the possibilities. On hearing of Finch-Hatton's invitation, Tom Black advises Beryl to wait a day before accompanying the guide. Beryl reluctantly agrees, then receives the startling news that Finch-Hatton was killed in a plane crash on the way to Voi.

Beryl Markham's plane after her crash in Nova Scotia.

More changes occur. Tom leaves Africa for a job in England, Beryl's father returns from Peru, Beryl purchases a farm of her own and continues her career as a freelance pilot, transporting mail and passengers. The profit to be made in scouting big game—especially elephant—by plane continues to attract Beryl. She soon acquires a companion in this often risky enterprise, a man she regards as the Great White Hunter, Baron Bror von Blixen ("Blix"). The pair have several adventures while locating elephant for safaris led by Winston Guest, a wealthy American client. At one point, Beryl and Blix are nearly attacked by an aggressive bull elephant, which backs off at the last minute. On another venture, Beryl and her plane rescue Blix and Winston who, along with their hunting party, are stranded on the Yatta Plateau when the rivers flood. Soon after this second incident, Beryl becomes restless and begins to wonder if she should introduce more changes in her life, "A life has to move or it stagnates. Even this life, I think" (*West with the Night*, p. 238). She proposes a scheme of flying to England from Africa, inviting Blix to join her.

After bidding farewell to her father and Arap Ruta, Beryl—with Blix—sets off on her flight in March 1936. In the course of their journey, during which they cross the Sudan, Egypt, Libya, and the Mediterranean Sea, they experience more adventures and some bureaucratic difficulties that delay their departure from North Africa. Reaching Bengazi, Libya, the travelers find all the accommodations occupied by the military. They are forced to spend the night in a filthy, vermin-ridden brothel. Touched by the sad life story of its procuress—she was kidnapped as a child and sold into prostitution—Blix leaves her some money. The journey resumes. While traveling from Cagliari, Italy, to Cannes, France, Beryl flies into a storm but ultimately lands safely at their destination. Beryl and Blix spend the night in Paris, France, and reach London, England, the next afternoon.

After several months in England, Beryl accepts another challenge. Record flights have been made over the North Atlantic Ocean, but always from west to east. According to John Carberry, one of Beryl's wealthy acquaintances, "Only Jim Mollison has done it alone the other way—from Ireland. Nobody has done it alone from England—man or woman" (*West with the Night*, p. 279). With Carberry's financial backing and a new plane—a Vega Gull—built especially for the occasion, Beryl undertakes the journey, leaving on September 4, 1936. Although many of Beryl's friends and associates anticipate the worst possible outcome, she succeeds in crossing the North Atlantic from a westerly direction, despite strong headwinds and adverse weather conditions. During the last stage of the flight, a chunk of ice

"THE FLYING TOMBSTONE?"

In *West with the Night,* Markham mentions several models of airplane that she flew in Kenya and England. One of the most frequently used British models was the De Havilland Moth, a light plane designed by the De Havilland company for sale to the British public. Introduced in 1925, the D.H. 60—nicknamed the Moth—was powered by a four-cylinder engine and boasted 60 horsepower. Three years later, the De Havilland Company developed an engine with more horsepower (100 hp)—the Gypsy—and installed it in a D.H. 60, thereafter known as the Gypsy Moth. This popular two-seater plane, often used for touring and sports, also became a favorite with long-distance pilots. Markham herself learned to fly in a Gypsy Moth. The model was much in demand; most planes purchased in England during the 1930s were in fact Moths produced by De Havilland. Another De Havilland model, the larger, three-seater Leopard Moth could carry two-passengers side-by-side behind the pilot. It was a high-wing monoplane with a cruising speed of 120 miles per hour, which Markham would fly as well. But, despite their popularity in other areas, Moths were not the planes best suited to bush work; according to Markham's instructor, the Avro Avian was. So Markham purchased a blue-and-silver Avro Avian IV, a two-seater with a 120 horsepower (De Havilland Gypsy II) engine, which served her well for years. For her transatlantic flight, however, she used neither an Avian nor a Moth. Instead she flew a Vega Gull, a two-passenger plane with a 200 horsepower (De Havilland Gypsy VI) engine and a cruising speed of 163 miles per hour. The Gull had six fuel tanks—two in the wings, two in the center section of the plane, and two in the cabin—and no radio. Before Markham's flight, Tom Black joked about the plane's name. Knowing that her backer for the flight lived on a farm called "Place of Death" and that the Gull was being built at a place called "Gravesend," he suggested that she call the plane "The Flying Tombstone." Instead Markham christened it "The Messenger."

lodges in the plane's petrol tank, choking off the fuel to the carburetor. Beryl makes a forced landing in a Newfoundland bog but survives with minor injuries—bruises and a gashed forehead. Found by a local fisherman, Beryl alerts the airport in Nova Scotia to her safe arrival, 21 hours and 25 minutes after her departure from England. Flying from Ireland to New Brunswick, Canada, had taken Jim Mollison over 31 hours.

Arriving at Floyd Bennett Field in New York, which was her original destination, Beryl receives a hero's welcome from the press, but her triumph is overshadowed by terrible news from London: her friend and teacher Tom Black has been killed in an airfield accident. The memoir ends some months later, as Beryl travels by ship to visit her father, now living in South Africa. Unlike a plane, the freighter on which Beryl sails hardly seems to move: "She was old and weather-weary, and she had learned to let the world come round to her" (*West with the Night*, p. 294).

Women in aviation. In *West with the Night*, Markham frequently contends with the engrained prejudices against women that were characteristic of British and African culture at the time. Even in the African bush, the ideal woman was still passive and domestic, leaving the income earning to the men. During childhood, a Nandi girl expresses astonishment that the young Beryl dares to hunt with the men, remarking, "Your body is like mine . . . it is the same and is no stronger" (*West with the Night*, p. 78). On the hunt, Beryl must prove to be as strong and capable as any Nandi warrior. Later, as a female horse-trainer, she must again prove herself. Early in this career, she loses a prize colt because the owner decides that a young girl is incapable of providing the necessary finishing touches to make the horse a racing champion.

Six weeks before a major race in Nairobi, the newly licensed Markham reflects,

> Winners. Losers. Money changing hands. Trainers big-chested, trainers flat-chested, explaining how it might have happened, 'except just for this.' All of them men. All of them older than my eighteen years, full of being men, confident, cocksure, perhaps offhand. They have a right to be. They know what they know—some of which I have still to learn, but not much, I think. Not much, I hope. We shall see, we shall see.
>
> (*West with the Night*, p. 144)

By contrast, Markham's transition from horse-trainer to airplane pilot does not appear to have been similarly problematic, perhaps because by the time Markham learned to fly—at age 28—she had already proven herself in a man's world. She may have benefited too from the fact that flying was still a comparatively new profession, whose opportunities were being taken by both men and women.

Although the first pilots and inventors had been men, it was not long before women followed them into the air. In 1910, a French baroness Raymonde de Laroche, who had taken flying lessons from French aviator Charles Voisin, became the first woman ever to gain a pilot's license. Laroche is on record as saying that she did not see why women should not fly as well as men, arguing, "It does not rely so much on strength as on physical and mental coordination" (Laroche in Lomax, p. 24). The following year, the American Harriet Quimby became one of a few more women to acquire their licenses. Unfortunately Quimby also became one of the first women killed, in an air accident in 1912. Her death and the ghoulish crowd expectations of similar tragedies whenever women took to the air discouraged several promising aviatrixes from pursuing flying as a career. But others persevered. Bessica Raiche was honored as the first American woman aviator after making a short solo flight in a fragile aircraft—constructed of bamboo, silk, and wire—that she had designed herself. Another American, Ruth Law, also enjoyed a successful career, becoming the first woman to fly at night—a 20-minute moonlit flight around Staten Island in November 1913—and to perform a loop-the-loop in the air.

While women were not permitted to fly planes in the First World War, they returned to the airfields soon after peace was declared. During the 1920s and 1930s, several British women, most of them titled and wealthy, took up flying. Although two of them perished with their pilots in ill-fated attempts to cross the Atlantic Ocean, others survived to advance the cause of women's rights in aviation. The feminist Lady Heath actively campaigned for advances in civil aviation and equality for women in the air, writing a letter of protest to the International Commission for Air Navigation, which—in 1924—had excluded women from "any employment in the operating crew of aircraft engaged in public transport" (Lomax, p. 38). Summoned before the commission to prove her competence as a pilot, Lady Heath—then Sophie Elliott-Lynn—demonstrated her skill to the satisfaction of witnesses and qualified for her B license, which allowed her to pursue a career as a professional pilot. The B license stipulated that all applicants had to be between 19 and 45, physically fit, and have flown solo for at least 100 hours. Applicants also had to possess sufficient technical knowledge of mechanical theory, meteorology, and navigation. In 1926 the commission's ban on passenger-carrying women pilots was reversed, though women had to undergo medical re-examination every three months, whereas their male counterparts were re-examined every six months.

By the time Markham received her own B license in the 1930s, the presence of women pilots was, for the most part, grudgingly accepted. Some aviatrixes had even achieved fame and been hailed as conquering heroines after flying new routes or setting records on long-distance flights. Among these women were America's Amelia Earhart and Britain's Amy Johnson, both of whom were Markham's immediate contemporaries. Ironically, Earhart and Johnson's fates were eerily similar; both went mysteriously missing on their last recorded flights—Earhart vanishing over the South Pacific in 1937, Johnson over the Thames River estuary in 1941. Their bodies were never recovered. Musing about how hazardous early flying was, one historian sums up the accomplishments of these first women pilots:

> The pioneers of aviation needed courage and determination, qualities shown by the women who, although in a minority, followed the men into the air, where their presence was often resented. Their successes made them instant heroines, their failures were used to prove that women were physically and psychologically unfit to fly, and their survival as proof of the safety of aviation.
>
> (Lomax, p. 1)

Sources and literary context. Markham drew primarily from her own experiences—her childhood in Kenya, her years as a horse trainer and professional pilot, her daring trans-Atlantic flight—for *West with the Night*. The people who appear in the memoir were taken from life as well—Beryl's trusted African servant, Arap Ruta; pilot and instructor Tom Campbell Black; safari guide Denys Finch-Hatton; and Great White Hunter Bror von Blixen. Perhaps out of a desire to focus on the more successful aspects of her life or to avoid giving offense, Markham also omitted several people and incidents from her memoir, which may be as remarkable as what she chose to include.

In *West with the Night*, little mention is made of Markham's mother, Clara, or her brother Richard, both of whom left Africa in 1906. Richard, who was sickly as a child, fared poorly in the Kenyan climate, while Clara could not adapt to the settlers' life. After returning to England, Clara divorced Charles Clutterbuck and remarried. Beryl, who remained in Africa with her father, was an adult before she saw her mother and brother again. Also omitted are Markham's two youthful marriages, to rugby player Jock Purves in 1919 and to Mansfield Markham in 1927; both ended in divorce. Likewise, Markham does not mention her only son, Gervaise, born in 1929, whom she handed over to her mother-in-law to raise before returning to Kenya alone in 1930. Neither does Markham allude to her love affairs—with Prince Henry of England (this affair contributed to the failure of her second marriage); with Denys Finch-Hatton, who had also been romantically involved with Isak Dinesen; with Bror Blixen, who accompanied Markham on several adventures, and with Tom Campbell Black, who first taught her to fly a plane.

Markham was not the only woman to compose a memoir about her life as a British settler in Kenya. Isak Dinesen published ***Out of Africa*** (1937) and Elspeth Huxley, *The Flame Trees of Thika* (1959) not too long before and after Markham (Dinesen's memoir is also in *Literature and Its Times*). Nor was she the only woman to write about her experiences as a pilot during the 1920s and 1930s. Amelia Earhart (*20 hrs. 40 min.*, 1929) and Anne Morrow Lindbergh (*North to the Orient*, 1935) also wrote of their adventures in the air. It is unclear whether the writings of Markham's fellow aviatrixes influenced her own contribution to the literature of flight. However, one definite influence upon Markham's writing was Raoul Schumacher, an American ghost writer and editor, who became her third husband and made various recommendations about the manuscript of *West with the Night*, such as which incidents to include and to leave out of the finished book. Schumacher may also have been the person to suggest Markham choose a loose, episodic structure for her memoir. Another subtler influence on Markham's writing may have been the French aviator and writer, Antoine de Saint-Exupery, whom she first met in 1932. Markham's biographer Mary S. Lovell notes similarities of tone and style in samples by both authors and theorizes that Saint-Exupery may have helped Markham find her literary voice (see Saint-Exupery's ***The Little Prince,*** also in *Literature and Its Times*).

Reviews. *West with the Night* was well-received from the start, garnering mostly positive reviews. Critics praised Markham's vivid depictions of her life in Africa and her experiences as a flyer. E. M. of the *Boston Globe* wrote that "Markham has made a real contribution to the literature of flight" (E. M. in James and Brown, p. 512). Likewise, Clifton Fadiman, writing for the *New Yorker*, observed, "The chapters on flying over Africa are unusually fresh and even thrilling. . . . Her descriptions of the strange country over which she travelled are sensitive, not unworthy of comparison with the books of Anne Morrow, and a lit-

A QUESTION OF AUTHORSHIP

In recent years, some doubt has been cast upon whether Beryl Markham truly wrote West with the Night, or whether the actual author was Raoul Schumacher, a writer and journalist who later became Markham's third husband. Those who hold to the latter view, including biographer Errol Trzebinski, argue that Markham had little formal education, did not like to read, and began writing only after she met Schumacher. Moreover, much of the comments on the typewritten manuscript of West with the Night were in Schumacher's handwriting and contained inaccuracies with regard to African terminology (the name "Arab" instead of "Arap") and to flying that Markham would not have made. Mary S. Lovell, another of Markham's biographers, argues that on the contrary Schumacher's manuscript comments prove only that he edited, not that he authored the book, and that "the Americanization of Beryl's anglicized spelling" may have resulted in the errors in African terms. Lovell also claims that Markham had already started her manuscript before meeting Schumacher in late 1941, citing as evidence letters that passed between Markham and the publishing house Houghton Mifflin. In sum, Schumacher was clearly involved in creating the memoir; biographers disagree only over to what extent.

tle rapturous about the 'feel' of Africa" (Fadiman in James and Brown, p. 513). J. S. Southron of the *New York Times* was also impressed, calling *West with the Night* "[a] book quite unlike anything that has been written by any other woman or about Africa, its natives, its hunting and its future by anybody. . . . And it is written with exceptional, simple beauty in a style that, without aiming at distinction, achieves it unquestionably" (Southron in James and Brown, p. 513). Rose Feld, writing for *Books*, similarly declared, "When a book like Beryl Markham's 'West With the Night' comes along it leaves a reviewer very humble. . . . For 'West With the Night' is more than autobiography; it is a poet's feeling for her land; an adventurer's response to life; a philosopher's evaluation of human beings and human destinies" (Feld in James and Brown, p. 512).

—Pamela S. Loy

For More Information.

Gunston, Bill, ed. *Aviation*. London: Octopus Books, 1978.

James, Metrice M., and Dorothy Brown, Eds. *Book Review Digest*. New York: H. W. Wilson, 1943.

Lomax, Judy. *Women of the Air*. London: John Murray, 1986.

Lovell, Mary S. *Straight On Till Morning*. New York: St. Martin's Press, 1987.

Markham, Beryl. *West with the Night*. San Francisco: North Point Press, 1983.

Ogot, Bethwell A. *Historical Dictionary of Kenya*. Metuchen: Scarecrow Press, 1981.

Tangye, Nigel. *Britain in the Air*. London: William Collins, 1944.

Trzebinski, Errol. *Kenya Pioneers*. New York: W. W. Norton, 1986.

———. *The Lives of Beryl Markham*. New York: W. W. Norton, 1993.

Woman Hollering Creek and Other Stories

by
Sandra Cisneros

Sandra Cisneros was born in Chicago in 1954 to a Mexican father and a Mexican American mother, the only daughter among seven children. Her upbringing was marked by the constraining influence of her brothers—because they insisted that she play a traditional female role, she often felt like she had "seven fathers" (Cisneros in Matuz, p. 150). She also contended with the displacement caused by her family's frequent moves between the United States and Mexico. So, from an early age Cisneros confronted the questions about her identity as a female and a Mexican American that would become central to her writing as an adult. Cisneros has dealt with many of these questions in books of poetry and in her widely acclaimed collection of vignettes, *The House on Mango Street* (1985). In *Woman Hollering Creek,* written mainly while Cisneros was living in San Antonio, Texas, she focuses on the varied experiences of girls and women with a Mexican heritage—characters who are distinguished by their different levels of income, education, independence, and Americanization, but united by similar histories, needs, and desires.

THE LITERARY WORK

A collection of 22 short stories and vignettes set in Mexico and the southwestern United States between the early 1900s and the late 1980s; published in English in 1991.

SYNOPSIS

A series of mostly female Mexican and Mexican American narrators share snapshots of their lives and reflect on their identities, cultures, and relationships.

Events in History at the Time of the Short Stories

Some of the events included in this section take place before the action of the stories, but the effects of these events have proved long-lasting. They play a significant role in twentieth-century Mexican and Mexican American culture, and their impact resonates in the lives of Cisneros's characters.

Guadalupe and Mexican Catholicism. When Hernán Cortés conquered the Aztec Empire in 1521, he brought with him the religion of his native Spain, Catholicism. Spanish missionaries came to Mexico during and after the Conquest, eager to Christianize—and, in their view, civilize—the natives. However, before Cortés's arrival the Aztecs and other cultures in Mexico had long practiced their own religions. Therefore, many of these natives, although forced to convert, initially resisted the teachings of Catholicism. Just the same, the missionaries were ultimately quite successful at gaining converts.

Part of the missionaries' success was due to a reported miracle that allowed the Aztecs to conceive of Catholicism as linked to their own native religion. In December 1531 the Virgin Mary is said to have appeared outside Mexico City, at the hill of Tepeyac—a site that was a shrine to Tonantzín, the Aztec mother goddess. The Virgin Mary sup-

Painting of the Virgin of Guadalupe by Juan de Villegas.

posedly spoke here to a native convert to Catholicism named Juan Diego, asking him to tell the bishop of Mexico of her wish that a church be built here in her honor. When the bishop rebuffed him, demanding some proof that this request had come from the Virgin Mary, Juan Diego returned to the hill. This time the Virgin told him to pick some flowers, which grew nearby in a place where flowers normally did not grow and were out of season. He was to place them in his cloak, and open it in front of the bishop. When Juan Diego opened his cloak for the bishop, the flowers fell to the floor and imprinted on the cloak was a picture of the Virgin as she had appeared, with brown skin and dark hair. Juan Diego afterward returned home to find that his uncle had also been visited by the Virgin, who told him that the church was to be dedicated to "the ever Virgin Saint Mary of Guadalupe," afterwards known simply as the Virgin of Guadalupe (Laso de la Vega in Poole, p. 28).

After hearing of the Virgin of Guadalupe's appearance, thousands of Indians agreed to be converted. Indians and Spanish colonists alike embraced her as a source of comfort and a symbol of a uniquely Mexican religion and identity—a Catholicized Tonantzín. She came to represent the blending of European and Indian societies, the rebirth of the native goddess Tonatzín as the Virgin of Guadalupe. The cult of Guadalupe is still a powerful force in Mexican and Mexican American life, as Cisneros's stories "Tepeyac," "Anguiano Religious Articles . . . ," and "Little Miracles, Kept Promises" indicate. The Virgin is regarded by many not just as a symbol of Mexican heritage, but as a source of strength, a confidante, and a granter of miracles. In fact, the Mexican poet Octavio Paz (see ***The Labyrinth of Solitude,*** also covered in *Latin American Literature and Its Times*) once observed, "The Mexican people, after more than two centuries of experiments and defeats, have faith only in the Virgin of Guadalupe and the National Lottery" (Paz in Lafaye, p. xi). Demonstrating this faith, millions of pilgrims every December visit the site where the Virgin of Guadalupe is said to have appeared.

The Chicano in America. In 1848 a war between Mexico and the United States ended with the signing of the Treaty of Guadalupe Hidalgo, in which Mexico was forced to sell the present-day states of Arizona, California, New Mexico, Utah, Nevada, and parts of Colorado to the United States for $15 million. Texas, also a former Mexican territory, had been annexed by the United States in 1845, a move that helped ignite the war. In the course of just a few years, Mexico had lost about one-half of its land.

Although Mexico no longer owned the territory that became the southwestern United States, many Mexicans (between 86,000 and 116,000) remained on the land after the war. The U.S. government allowed these original Mexican Americans—Chicanos—to choose the citizenship they preferred, and promised to protect their political, land, and property rights. It failed, however, to honor their property claims, tolerating flagrant wrongdoing by newcomers from more established parts of the United States. Many Chicanos found that their unfamiliarity with American language, culture, and laws made it easy for them to be exploited by the growing numbers of Anglo Americans that were settling among them, and also by a few wealthy and powerful members of the Chicano elite.

The California gold rush of 1849 and the promise of work building railroad lines in the 1860s brought more Mexicans to the United States. At the end of these events, some returned home, but many settled in California, Texas, and other formerly Mexican lands. Immigration continued from the 1860s into the twentieth century, when political turmoil and economic trouble in Mexico—as well as recruitment efforts by U.S. agriculture interests—heightened the appeal of crossing the border. By 1990 Chicanos in the United States, including recent immigrants and those whose ancestors lived in the Southwest when it had been Mexico, numbered 14.5 million.

Emiliano Zapata and the Mexican Revolution. In Mexico the three decades following the Treaty of Guadalupe Hidalgo were marked by instability, including a series of internal conflicts and a brief period of rule by the French-installed Emperor Maximilian (1864-66). Staging a coup d'état in 1876, Porfirio Díaz began a 34-year pres-

ZAPATA'S LOOK

Emiliano Zapata, bandit-hero of the Revolution, was a peasant. Nonetheless, he cut an impressive figure, as described by one historian:

> In tight black pants with giant silver buttons along the outer seam of each leg, an embroidered leather or cotton jacket, a silk handkerchief tied loosely around his neck, silver spurs, a pistol at his waist and, to top it off, a wide felt sombrero with a flowered border, Zapata was impressive and clearly more than a little vain. Somewhat taller than the average villager and of a normal build, he had a long, thick moustache that curled up slightly at the ends, dark skin, dark eyes, and a penetrating gaze. . . . He wasted little time with talk; when he did speak[,] his words—emerging in "rushes and sparks"—betrayed the nervous energy he had had since childhood.
>
> (Brunk, p. 23)

Emiliano Zapata

idency (1876-80 and 1884-1911) that ended this instability, though at a great cost. Before he came to power, Díaz had aligned himself with the Liberal Party of Mexico, a group that sought to lessen some of the country's economic inequalities. The party drafted a constitution that limited the special privileges of the wealthy Catholic Church and the military, and provided a bill of rights similar to that of the United States. Once his presidency began, however, Díaz left many of his liberal principles behind and became a dictator.

One of Díaz's early supporters was José Zapata, a farmer and soldier from the town of Anenecuilco in the southern state of Morelos. Zapata's support for Díaz hinged on a promise Díaz had made before he came to power: he would see to it that the people of Anenecuilco, whose land had been seized illegally by *hacendados*—hacienda owners, many of whom descended from 16th-century Spanish colonists—would have their land titles honored by the new government. This promise was one of many that Díaz did not keep, but Zapata's family did not forget it.

In 1910 Porfirio Díaz was still in power, and frustration with his dictatorship was widespread. Mexicans across the country wanted reform and were willing to fight for it. Some called for protective labor laws, some for an improved public education system, others for a curtailment of Church power; ironically, many of these grievances had been rallying points decades earlier for the Liberals whom Díaz ostensibly supported. When Francisco Madero, a liberal-minded hacendado, called for a national uprising on November 20, 1910, Mexicans across the country slowly began to respond.

In Morelos the battle cry was for land redistribution. Not only did the peasants of Morelos seek to regain the land José Zapata had spoken of—the land that was seized illegally by hacendados—they now had even greater losses to contend with. In an attempt to weaken the economic power of the Catholic Church, the Liberals had banned corporate landholding in their 1857 constitution. Incidentally, this ban also affected land that was held communally by groups of peasants. Putting the ban into practice, the government auctioned off, usually to the highest hacendado bidder, any land that was still communally held in Morelos in the mid-nineteenth century.

By the spring of 1911 a horse trader, farmer, and village council president named Emiliano Zapata had decided that his people's legal and political attempts to regain their land had been exhausted. It was time to enter the Revolution in quest of justice. Zapata was to become a hero to the peasants of Morelos and neighboring states and a bandit to hacienda owners and a succession of Mexican presidents. For almost nine years, Zapata led the fight for "Land and Liberty"—the goal of his ancestor, José Zapata, and of generations of Morelos's inhabitants.

The Revolution was long, devastating, and complicated. Presidential power shifted often, as did alliances among rebel groups. It was difficult for those involved to know whom to support and whom to trust. This was especially true for Emiliano Zapata, who counted many former allies among his enemies as the war progressed. Although Zapata and his rebels fought first against President Díaz's federal troops, or *federales,* their opponents later included the liberal hacendado Francisco Madero, who had failed to deliver on a promise of land reform after winning the presidency; General Victoriano Huerta, who ousted Madero and terrorized rebel strongholds like Morelos; and Venustiano Carranza, whom Zapata denounced as a corrupt politician after he won the presidency, though they had fought against a common enemy only a month before. Zapata trusted almost no one outside of Morelos during the war, and trusted outsiders even less when they gained the power of the presidency. "Revolutions will come and revolutions will go," he said in 1914, "but I will continue with mine" (Zapata in Womack, pp. 197-98).

Zapata's revolution was about land. His "Plan of Ayala," written in November 1911, called for the immediate return of land to the citizens and villages that held title to it, and for the seizure of remaining hacienda properties held by those who opposed his movement; these lands were to be donated to needy peasants who had no legitimate claims to land.

Zapata never saw the Plan of Ayala enacted, although the peasants of Morelos did have a portion of their land returned to them in the 1920s. He continued to fight stubbornly, however, even after suffering a major defeat at the hands of the *Carrancistas* (Carranza's forces) in 1915. In the years following this defeat, his troops and the people of Morelos suffered from food shortages and a plague of deadly diseases. In 1918, in fact, the population of Morelos dropped an astounding 25 percent. Still, Zapata continued to lead the fight until April 1919, when the rebel who trusted no one was deceived by a federal colonel whose soldiers shot him dead at point-blank range.

In "Eyes of Zapata," Inés speaks of "the hard man's work I do clearing the field with the hoe and the machete, dirty work that leaves the clothes filthy, work no woman would do before the war" (Cisneros, *Woman Hollering Creek and Other Stories,* p. 86). Throughout the Revolution, women were forced to take on many roles formerly relegated to men. Some, like Inés, worked the fields because their husbands were away fighting. Others, *soldaderas,* traveled with bands of soldiers, and in addition to cooking and cleaning for them, took charge of medicine, munitions, mail, and train dispatches, and often spied behind enemy lines. *Soldadas* (female soldiers) actually fought alongside the men. Although most women returned to traditional ways of life after the Revolution, the roles they played during this period helped pave the way for an improvement of the Mexican woman's position in the late twentieth century.

THE DESTRUCTION OF MORELOS

Only three years into the war, Zapata's home state of Morelos had already been burned and looted almost beyond recognition by Huerta's soldiers. The balladeer Marciano Silva, who traveled with Zapata's forces during this time, describes its appearance:

> Our pueblos only plains
> White ashes, pictures of horror
> Sad deserts, isolated places
> Where only sorrow stirs. . . .
> (Silva in Brunk, p. 148)

"Mericans" or Mexicans? One of the issues raised repeatedly in *Woman Hollering Creek* is the clash between Mexican and American culture in the Chicano communities of the United States. In "Mericans," for example, a young girl tells of her "awful grandmother" who prays in a church for "the grandchildren born in that barbaric country [the United States] with its barbarian ways" while the girl and her brothers play "B-Fifty-two bomber" and "Flash Gordon" outside (*Woman Hollering Creek,* pp. 18-19). The contrast between the grandmother's traditional, religious lifestyle and the carefree, Americanized lifestyle of the children illustrates a larger trend in Chicano society during the 1940s and 1950s.

The World War II era was a period of great change in Mexican American history. With a large number of Americans (including some 400,000 Chicanos) fighting overseas, many Mexican American men and women were able to fill vacant jobs at home. Often these jobs—especially the ones producing weapons and equipment for the war—paid higher salaries than previous jobs, allowing Mexican American workers to improve their position in society. As their social positions improved, they began to move out of the barrios and rural areas they had shared with other Mexican Americans and into more diverse urban areas, often leaving behind much of their Mexican culture in the process.

At the same time that World War II was improving the lot of Mexican Americans, Mexican immigration to the United States was dropping significantly. Whereas 44 percent of Mexican Americans in 1930 had been born in Mexico, only 17 percent were Mexican-born in 1950. This change also contributed to the increasing Americanization of Mexican American society, since those born in the United States tended to identify more strongly with American culture than with Mexican culture.

FAR FROM HIS FATHER'S FOOTSTEPS

Although Zapata never veered from his fight for "Land and Liberty," he did not display the same steadfastness in his relationships with women. In fact, at the time of his death Zapata had fathered at least eight children by a number of different women; his first two children, Nicolás and María Elena, were the children of Inés Aguilar, the inspiration for the narrator in Cisneros's "Eyes of Zapata." As a sad final chapter to Zapata's story, his son Nicolás would gain considerable power in Morelian politics in the 1930s and 1940s because of his father's name, only to abuse it by seizing land from the people of Anenecuilco for himself and his cronies. Ironically, Nicolás's actions made his father's famous words about politicians, spoken about 25 years before, ring true: "They're all a bunch of bastards!" (Zapata in Womack, pp. 205-06).

Of course, a large number of Mexican Americans—regardless of their birthplace—remained ambivalent about their cultural identities and loyalties. Furthermore, ill treatment by members of white society continued, no matter whether one identified more strongly with American or Mexican culture. Like African Americans, Mexican Americans were forced to confront segregation in schools, restaurants, hotels, and movie theaters in the 1940s and 1950s; whether or not they felt American, they knew that signs reading "No Dogs or Mexicans Allowed" applied to them (Gutiérrez, p. 131).

Chicanos vs. *vendidos*. The 1960s were a time of profound social change in the United States, and the Mexican American community contributed to this change. In the 1950s most Mexican American political leaders sought to integrate their community peacefully into mainstream American society, but, by the early 1960s, many young Mexican Americans were frustrated by the lack of cultural pride and political power in their community. They identified themselves proudly as "Chicanos"—a formerly disparaging term for rural Mexican immigrants—and spoke of the unity of all people of Mexican origin, glorifying Mexican historical figures and embracing Mexicans and Mexican Americans of all classes in a struggle to build a political platform and inspire a cultural renaissance.

Although the Chicano movement had a good deal of support among young people and students, many Mexican Americans thought it was a mistake, preferring the gradual process of reform to the cultural revolution that was being proposed. In 1969 Mexican American activist José Angel Gutiérrez and San Antonio congressman Henry B. González debated the validity of the movement in a famous discussion. González, who had gained esteem for his legislative work on civil rights issues, prided himself as a representative of all groups in his district, not just Mexican Americans. He labeled Gutiérrez and other Chicano activists as "professional Mexicans" who were trying "to stir up the people by appeals to emotion [and] prejudice in order to become leader[s] and achieve selfish ends." He claimed that their movement was based on "a new racism [that] demands an allegiance to race above all else" (González in Gutiérrez, p. 186).

Gutiérrez, on the other hand, accused González of behaving like a *gringo*, a white American, and claimed that González and any other Mexican Americans whose goal was assimilation into mainstream culture were *vendidos*, or sellouts, who were contributing to the oppression of their people. According to Gutiérrez, what the Chicano people needed was "social change that will enable La Raza [literally, "The Mexican Race"] to become masters of their destiny, owners of their resources, both human and natural, and a culturally separate people from the gringo" (Gutiérrez in Gutiérrez, p. 187).

Although the Chicano movement did revitalize Mexican identity and culture within the United States in the 1960s and early 1970s, its goal of creating a "culturally separate people" within American society was not realized. In fact, despite the attempts by its leaders to gloss over their group's class differences, the fact remains that the lives of working class and impoverished Mexican Americans were largely unaffected by the movement. Nonetheless, it did leave a permanent mark on American society. Many students, artists, and intellectuals continued to embrace the themes of the Chicano movement well into the 1990s, although it never regained the broad appeal it had enjoyed earlier. As the 1980s approached, most Mexican American members of the middle and working classes seemed more interested in finding a permanent place in the mainstream workforce than in exploring their cultural identities.

Chicanas break with tradition. While male activists and politicians debated the best way to increase the Chicano community's political power, many Mexican American women struggled to gain power in their personal lives. Traditionally, Mexican women were expected to be passive, subordinate homemakers, faithful to their husbands but accepting of their husbands' infidelity, much like Cleófilas at the beginning of the short story "Woman Hollering Creek."

One way in which Chicanas, or female Mexican Americans, were able to step beyond the confines of this traditional role was by working outside the home. Between 1960 and 1970 the number of employed Mexican American wives aged 14 to 54 rose from 24 to 35 percent. By 1980 the percentage of Chicanas in the labor force almost equalled that of white women. Although a number of these Chicanas took jobs out of economic necessity, many gained a sense of freedom and independence from their role as breadwinner and claimed greater authority at home over how money was spent.

Not all Mexican American women found work outside the home liberating, however. For many, the competing demands of home and work were a major source of stress and anxiety. While some working Chicanas found that their spouses were willing to share household chores, a large number had to contend with husbands resentful of their wives' role as breadwinner and therefore even more insistent that they fulfill all of their traditional marital responsibilities. The tension and conflict that arose out of such situations helped contribute to a growing divorce rate among Mexican Americans and to an increase in Chicana-headed households.

By the 1980s more and more Chicana women—like the narrator of "Never Marry a Mexican"—had rejected the traditional Mexican-style marriage in search of a lifestyle that balanced family responsibilities with personal fulfillment. In Mexico itself in recent years, the status and lifestyles of women have changed in similar, though less extreme, ways. Although traditional ideas of womanhood still weigh heavily on their lives, many Mexican women have begun to work outside the home and to question the dominant influence men have had over their public and private lives.

CÓMO SE LLAMA? (WHAT'S YOUR NAME?)

Since their first incarnation as a group in 1848, Mexican Americans have called themselves by a number of different names, all charged with special significance. First-generation immigrants often identify themselves as *Mexicanos,* while the terms "Spanish" and "Hispanic" have been associated with those seeking to assimilate into white culture or downplay their Mexican heritage. Cisneros writes in "La Fabulosa": "She likes to say she's 'Spanish,' but she's from Laredo like the rest of us" (*Woman Hollering Creek,* p. 61). In 1983 the *Los Angeles Times* surveyed the Mexican American population of Los Angeles and found that most Mexican Americans born in the United States preferred the term "Mexican American." "Latino," a term referring to the entire Spanish-speaking community, was the second choice, and "Hispanic" was third, though especially popular among the middle class. Only four percent of those surveyed identified themselves as "Chicano."

The Short Stories in Focus

Plot summary. The 22 stories in *Woman Hollering Creek* are broken into three sections. The first section deals with childhood on both sides of the Mexican-United States border and includes the stories "My Lucy Friend Who Smells Like Corn," "Eleven," "Salvador Late or Early," "Mexican Movies," "Barbie-Q," "Mericans," and "Tepeyac." The young narrators of these stories describe moments of happiness, sadness, shame, and confusion, while raising issues to which Cisneros returns throughout the collection. In "Eleven," for example, 11-year-old Rachel tells of the embarrassment she feels when her teacher, Mrs. Price, forces her to wear an ugly sweater that was left behind in the classroom. Although Rachel tells the teacher that the sweater is not hers, Mrs. Price insists, and it is not until "stupid" Phyllis Lopez remembers that she owns the sweater that Rachel is allowed to take it off (*Woman Hollering Creek,* p. 9). This is the first of many times that one of Cisneros's female characters struggles against another character's controlling influence to assert her own desires.

The second section consists only of two stories, "One Holy Night" and "My *Tocaya,*" both of which deal with love, deception, and the confusion of adolescence. In "One Holy Night," an eighth-grade girl in a Southwestern town falls in love with a Mexican man, Chaq Uxmal Paloquín, or "Baby Boy," who enchants her with stories about his royal Mayan ancestry. After she is "initiated" as his Queen, the girl is not ashamed but excited to finally find out how sex feels, and is even tickled that "it wasn't a big deal" (*Woman Hollering Creek,* p. 30). When the girl's grandmother learns what has happened, she goes searching for the man responsible, only to find that he has left town. A few weeks later, the girl discovers that she is pregnant. While she spends the last months of her pregnancy living with relatives in Mexico, her family contacts Baby Boy's sister, who reveals that his words to the girl have been lies. His name is Chato, meaning "fat-face," and he has no Mayan blood. This revelation—and the newspaper clippings his sister sends that suggest he has been involved in rape or murder—does not change the girl's feelings, however. She stares at the face in the clippings and muses about the children she will have and the man she loves.

The third section of stories deals primarily with grown women, all of Mexican heritage but from very different walks of life. "Little Miracles, Kept Promises" is a collection of letters requesting help from above or giving thanks for help granted. In one letter, college-educated Barbara Ybañez of San Antonio asks San Antonio de Padua for "a man who isn't a pain in the *nalgas.* . . . Someone please who never calls himself 'Hispanic' unless he's applying for a grant from Washington, D.C." (*Woman Hollering Creek,* p. 117). After a fire has destroyed her home, Adelfa Vásquez from Escobas, Texas, asks San Martín de Porres to send "clothes, furniture, shoes, dishes . . . anything that don't eat" and to convince her daughter to quit school so she can stay home and help her parents (*Woman Hollering Creek,* p. 117). Leocadia Dimas of San Marcos, Texas, writes to thank Don Pedrito Jaramillo, the Healer of Los Olmos, for "THE GOOD DOCTORS THAT DID THEIR JOB WELL" while operating on the cancer in her granddaughter (*Woman Hollering Creek,* p. 119). Finally, Rosario De Leon, who has just cut off her hair to give to the Virgin of Guadalupe, sorts through the web of emotions that led her, after years of resistance, to embrace Guadalupe and what she represents:

> I don't know how it all fell into place. How I finally understood who you are. No longer Mary the mild, but our mother Tonantzín. . . . That you could have the power to rally a people when a country was born, and again during civil war, and during a farmworkers' strike in California made me think maybe there is power in my mother's patience, strength in my grandmother's endurance.
>
> (*Woman Hollering Creek,* p. 128)

Rosario's struggle to accept the nurturing aspects of her culture while rejecting its oppressive elements is a struggle faced by other characters in *Woman Hollering Creek,* though some face more extreme oppression than others. In the title story, a young Mexican woman, Cleófilas, marries a Mexican man and moves with him across the border to the United States, where she discovers desolation in traditional married life. Beaten by her husband and isolated from society except for her widowed neighbors, Dolores (meaning "pain") and Soledad (meaning "solitude"), Cleófilas withdraws into a fantasy world of *telenovelas* (soap operas) and romance novels. Meanwhile, while watching her infant son laugh, she muses about what the name of the creek near her house—La Gritona, or "Screaming Woman"—might signify. She concludes that it may be a reference to "La Llorona," the "weeping woman" of Mexican folklore who kills her own child. When Cleófilas subsequently breaks down in a doctor's exam room, a sympathetic woman there arranges for a friend to drive Cleófilas to a bus station so she can escape from her husband and return to Mexico. Felice, the Chicana woman driving her to freedom (whose name means "happiness"), is a revelation to Cleófilas. She is brash, independent, irreverent, and single, and when she drives over La Gritona Creek, she lets out a "holler like Tarzan" in honor of its name (*Woman Hollering Creek,* p. 55). Amazed at Felice's behavior and at her own realization that the name of the creek might represent a woman hooting in joy instead of howling in pain, Cleófilas discovers that she herself is laughing, released for a moment from her pain by this woman hollering next to her.

The remaining pieces in the third section of *Woman Hollering Creek* share some issues with the pieces above and also introduce new subjects. They include stories of personal discovery, conflicting cultural loyalties, broken hearts, and gossip, and are told by a number of different voices, including an artist who has an affair with her white teacher and, later, his son ("Never Marry a Mexican"); a common-law wife of Zapata who transforms herself into a bird so she can transcend the limits of space and time to relive the moments spent with him ("Eyes of Zapata"); a working-class Chicana incensed at the "crab ass" owner of a religious store ("Anguiano Religious Articles Rosaries Statues Medals Incense Candles Talismans Perfumes Oils Herbs"); and an artist who falls in love with her exterminator, a poet who looks like an Aztec god, only to be left by him after he reveals that he is married and has four children ("Bien Pretty").

Redefining Guadalupe and La Malinche. At the end of the title story of *Woman Hollering Creek,* two women meet. Cleófilas, a Mexican, is the wounded product of an oppressive marriage. Felice, a Chicana, is a free-spirited, independent woman. Discussing the creek they're driving over, which is called "La Gritona," or "Screaming Woman," the Chicana says to the Mexicana "Did you ever notice . . . how nothing around here is named after a woman? Really. Unless she's the Virgin. I guess you're only famous if you're a virgin" (*Woman Hollering Creek,* p. 55).

In another story in this collection, "Little Miracles, Kept Promises," a young woman explains to the Virgin of Guadalupe how the woman was treated when she rejected the Virgin because of the "self-sacrifice" and "silent suffering" she represented:

> Don't think it was easy going without you. Don't think I didn't get my share of it from everyone. Heretic. Atheist. *Malinchista. Hocicona.* But I wouldn't shut my yap. My mouth always getting me in trouble. Is that what they teach you at the university? *Miss High-and-Mighty. Miss Thinks-She's-Too-Good-for-Us.* Acting like a bolilla, a white girl. Malinche.
>
> (*Woman Hollering Creek,* pp. 127-28)

These two excerpts refer to two central paradigms by which women in Mexican and Mexican American society have been judged. The Virgin of Guadalupe represents purity, unselfish sacrifice, motherhood, and, to many, passivity verging on martyrdom, characteristics echoed darkly by the broken life of Cleófilas. La Malinche, on the other hand, is the incarnation of cultural betrayal: the Indian woman who, with the Spaniard Cortés, is credited with creating the first *mestizo* child—and may have killed him. Felice attests to the ubiquity of the Virgin in Mexican and Mexican American culture. She is, as Felice explains, the only woman things are named for in her part of Texas. The name of Malinche likewise surfaces quite often in Mexican and Mexican American culture, but only when insults are being hurled, as Rosario of "Little Miracles, Kept Promises" can attest.

LA MALINCHE/LA LLORONA

Cortés may have brought Catholicism to Mexico, but he is probably better known in Mexico for being the first to mix Indian blood with European. The legend relates that his Indian mistress, Malinche (also called Doña Marina), was a willing perpetrator of what some have described as a crime of cultural betrayal. She is said to have given birth to the first mestizo child, the mixed European-Amerindian issue of her union with Cortés. In fact, Malinche served as a translator and go-between for the Indians and Spaniards, a border figure who linked the two cultures in other ways besides having a mestizo child. Legend, however, overpowers history in the matter of this original birth. In some versions of the legend, La Malinche rejects her role as a mother, stabbing her child to protest Cortés's decision to return to Spain and then becoming a "weeping woman" ("La Llorona") who forever laments what she has done. However, Chicana writers tend to separate the figures of La Malinche and La Llorona. They associate La Llorona with creating as well as destroying life, connecting her particularly to changeable nature, especially to water, death by drowning, and forces cloaked by night. Her weeping they associate with a mourning for their lost selves, lost because of the discrimination and violence pressing in on them, and because of the assimilation of their children into the overpowering mainstream American culture. In other words, La Llorona has become associated with a search for one's self, taking on a positive dimension. In this way, Sandra Cisneros, in *Woman Hollering Creek,* "can play on the folklore surrounding La Llorona and turn her into an active heroine" (Rebolledo and Rivero, p. 194).

These two paradigms for womanhood appear repeatedly in *Woman Hollering Creek*. They are part of the cultural heritage with which Cisneros's characters must wrestle. Rather than accept Guadalupe as the paragon of womanhood and Malinche as the embodiment of evil, however, these characters tell stories that help to redefine the significance of each figure. In the process, Cisneros's women help to redefine themselves.

When Rosario decides to accept the Virgin of Guadalupe into her life, she does so strictly on her own terms. To her, Guadalupe now represents the birth of Mexican culture, a tie to her Indian heritage, the power and unity of her people, and the strength of her mother and grandmother. Similarly, when Cleófilas joins Felice in laughter, she is choosing to put a positive spin on an ambiguous figure. La Gritona may be "La Llorona/La Malinche," crying because she has betrayed her society by rejecting the traditional role of motherhood, but she could also be a hollering woman, like the cheerful, liberated Chicana at Cleófilas's side. Rosario and Cleófilas—two women from different countries (the United States and Mexico, respectively) and radically different circumstances—have both learned to start shaping for themselves the models of womanhood that Mexican culture has bequeathed to them.

The story's reinterpretation of traditional role models is part of a larger literary trend. Other Chicana writers have modified their estimation of the Virgin of Guadalupe, acknowledging her goodness but viewing her tendency to accept and endure as a negative rather than a positive quality, and condemning what they deem to be her failure to act on her own behalf. Similarly, while the reaction of Chicano writers to the traditionally traitorous La Malinche is "varied and complex," many think of her as a survivor, "a woman who, with a clairvoyant sense, cast her lot with the Spaniards in order to ensure survival of her race. . . . It was often because of Malinche's diplomacy and intelligence that a more total annihilation of the Indian tribes of Mexico did not occur" (Rebolledo and Rivero, pp. 192-93).

Literary context. Sandra Cisneros is one of the three or four best known Latina writers in the United States and probably the best known Chicana writer. Set in Chicago, her first major success, *The House on Mango Street* (1985), has been translated into a number of languages and is used widely in American classrooms from middle school to graduate school. Such far-reaching acclaim for an American Latina writer would have been unheard of before the early 1980s. Although some magazines and journals that grew out of the Chicano movement printed Latina literature in the 1970s, it was not until 1983 that established Latina writers began to emerge. Cisneros has explained that she began writing because of what was missing in the literature around her. "She couldn't see herself in the novels and stories she was reading" (Stavans, p. 74). In essence, her stories or "verbal photographs" in *Woman Hollering Creek* help fill the vacuum by bringing to life recognizable females, ones that defy old stereotypes. "Cisneros's intention isn't only to explain a trauma or to re-create a certain flavor of childhood, but to offer a persuasive portrait of Chicanas as aggressive and independent" (Stavans, p. 74). According to at least one scholar, she has "inherited the mantle of Tomás Rivera." She did not speak in Spanish, however; she was the next generation; she had an authentic Mexican American voice (Shorris, p. 390).

Reviews. *Woman Hollering Creek* was received by Mexican American and mainstream critics as a huge success. It won a number of awards and was praised for its emotional power, its range of characters, and the originality of its style, which was described as "poetic descriptions" into which Cisneros "breathes narrative life" (Prescott and Springen in Mooney, p. 348).

Chicano scholar Ilan Stavans spoke of Cisneros's "breathtaking prose" and described *Woman Hollering Creek and Other Stories* as a "candid, engaging" work. "Cisneros's major contribution to Latino letters," this critic declared, "can be found in her strength of approaching the Hispanic experience north of Rio Grande in a non-apologetic, authentic fashion" (Stavans, pp. 16, 74). Similarly, the scholar Earl Shorris applauded *Woman Hollering Creek and Other Stories* as a superior work. Shorris preferred it to Cisneros's *House on Mango Street*; in his estimation, "the style and tone often wobbled, but the book contained some beautifully realized stories, characters that the reader married and remarried at the end of the paragraph" (Shorris, p. 390).

—Allison Weisz

For More Information

Brunk, Samuel. *Emiliano Zapata: Revolution and Betrayal in Mexico*. Albuquerque: University of New Mexico Press, 1995.

Cisneros, Sandra. *Woman Hollering Creek and Other Stories*. New York: Vintage Books, 1991.

Gutiérrez, David G. *Walls and Mirrors: Mexican Americans, Mexican Immigrants, and the Politics of Ethnicity*. Berkeley: University of California Press, 1995.

Lafaye, Jacques. *Quetzalcoatl and Guadalupe: The Formation of Mexican National Consciousness, 1531-1813*. Trans. Benjamin Keen. Chicago: University of Chicago Press, 1974.

Matuz, Roger, ed. *Contemporary Literary Criticism*. Vol. 69. Detroit: Gale Research, 1992.

Mooney, Martha T., ed. *The Book Review Digest, 1991*. New York: H. W. Wilson, 1992.

Poole, Stafford, C. M. *Our Lady of Guadalupe: The Origins and Sources of a Mexican National Symbol, 1531-1797*. Tucson: The University of Arizona Press, 1995.

Rebolledo, Tey Diana, and Eliana S. Rivero, eds. *Infinite Divisions: An Anthology of Chicana Literature*. Tuscon: The University of Arizonia Press, 1993.

Shorris, Earl. *Latinos: A Biography of Power*. New York: W. W. Norton, 1992.

Stavans, Ilan. *The Hispanic Condition: Reflections on Culture and Identity in America*. New York: HarperCollins, 1995.

Womack, John Jr. *Zapata and the Mexican Revolution*. New York: Knopf, 1969.

Index

Note: Bold print indicates the volume number. For example, **4**:145, 148 indicates Volume 4, pages 145 and 148. **S1.1** represents *Supplement 1, Part 1*. **S1.2** represents *Supplement 1, Part 2*.

A

Index

Index

Index

B

Index

C

Index

D

Index

E

F

G

H

I

Index

J

K

L

M

N

O

P

Index

Q

R

Index

V

Index

X

Y

Z